TO:

_____

FROM:

_____

THE

PASSION

TRANSLATION

THE
NEW TESTAMENT

WITH PSALMS, PROVERBS, AND SONG OF SONGS

BroadStreet
PUBLISHING

The Passion Translation® New Testament with Psalms, Proverbs, and Song of Songs

Translated from Hebrew, Greek, and Aramaic texts by Dr. Brian Simmons

Published by BroadStreet Publishing® Group, LLC
BroadStreetPublishing.com
thePassionTranslation.com

The Passion Translation and TPT are registered trademarks of Stairway Ministries.

For information about bulk sales or customized editions of The Passion Translation, please contact tpt@broadstreetpublishing.com.

The publisher and TPT team have worked diligently and prayerfully to present this version of The Passion Translation Bible with excellence and accuracy. However, all translations of the Bible are subject to human limitations and imperfections. If you find a mistake in the Bible text or footnotes, please contact the publisher at tpt@broadstreetpublishing.com.

ISBN: 978-1-4245-5529-1 (black faux leather)   ISBN: 978-1-4245-5564-2 (hardcover ivory)
ISBN: 978-1-4245-5530-7 (brown faux leather)   ISBN: 978-1-4245-5585-7 (hardcover floral)
ISBN: 978-1-4245-5532-1 (pink faux leather)   ISBN: 978-1-4245-5586-4 (hardcover slate)
ISBN: 978-1-4245-5531-4 (purple faux leather)   ISBN: 978-1-4245-5533-8 (e-book)
ISBN: 978-1-4245-5569-7 (red faux leather)

Printed in China
17 18 19 20 5 4 3 2 1

CONTENTS

ABOUT THE PASSION TRANSLATION

The message of God's story is timeless; the Word of God doesn't change. But the methods by which that story is communicated should be timely; the vessels that steward God's Word can and should change. One of those timely methods is Bible translation. Bible translations are both a gift and a problem. They give us the words God spoke through his servants, but words can be poor containers for revelation because they leak! The meanings of words change from one generation to the next. Meaning is influenced by culture, background, and many other details. Just imagine how differently the Hebrew authors of the Old Testament saw the world three thousand years ago from the way we see it today!

There is no such thing as a truly literal translation of the Bible, for there is not an equivalent language that perfectly conveys the meaning of the biblical text. It must be understood in its original cultural and linguistic settings. This problem is best addressed when we seek to transfer meaning, not merely words, from the original text to the receptor language.

The purpose of the Passion Translation is to reintroduce the passion and fire of the Bible to the English reader. It doesn't merely convey the literal meaning of words. It expresses God's passion for people and his world by translating the original, life-changing message of God's Word for modern readers.

You will notice at times we've italicized certain words or phrases. These highlighted portions are not in the original Hebrew, Greek, or Aramaic manuscripts but are implied from the context. We've made these implications explicit for the sake of narrative clarity and to better convey the meaning of God's Word. This is a common practice by mainstream translations.

We've also chosen to translate certain names in their original Hebrew or Greek form to better convey their cultural meaning and significance. For instance, some translations of the Bible have substituted Jacob with James and Judah with Jude. Both Greek and Aramaic leave these Hebrew names in their original form. Therefore, this translation uses those cultural names.

God longs to have his Word expressed in every language in a way that would unlock the passion of his heart. Our goal is to trigger inside every English-speaking reader an overwhelming response to the truth of the Bible. This is a heart-level translation, from the passion of God's heart to the passion of your heart.

We pray this version of God's Word will kindle in you a burning desire for him and his heart, while impacting the church for years to come.

Please visit **thePassionTranslation.com** for more information about the Passion Translation.

PSALMS,
PROVERBS,
AND
SONG OF SONGS

PSALMS

Introduction

AT A GLANCE

Author: Multiple authors, including David, Solomon, the Asaphites, the Kohrites, and Moses

Audience: Originally Israel, but Psalms speak to humanity in general

Date: From the Monarchy to Postexilic eras

Type of Literature: Poems, which reflect several types: wisdom, lament, prayer, praise, blessings, liturgy, and prophetic oracles

Major Themes: Prayer, praise, wisdom, prophecy, lamentation, and Jesus Christ

Outline: The Psalms are really five books in one. Moses gave us the five books of the Law called the Pentateuch; David gives us the five books of the Psalms. Each division ends with a doxology that includes the words "Amen and Amen." The last division ends with Ps. 150 as the doxology, forming an appropriate conclusion to this "Pentateuch of David." These five divisions have been compared to the first five books of the Bible:

Psalms 1–41 (Genesis) — Psalms of man and creation
Psalms 42–72 (Exodus) — Psalms of suffering and redemption
Psalms 73–89 (Leviticus) — Psalms of worship and God's house
Psalms 90–106 (Numbers) — Psalms of our pilgrimage on earth
Psalms 107–150 (Deuteronomy) — Psalms of praise and the Word

ABOUT PSALMS

I have loved the Psalms for over forty years. They have been my comfort and joy, leading me to the place where worship flows. When discouraged or downcast, I have never failed to take new strength from reading the Psalms. They charge my batteries and fill my sails. In fact, they seem to grow even more powerful as I grow older. Their thunder stirs me; their sweet melodies move me into the sacred emotions of a heart on fire. The dark rain clouds of grief turn to bright rainbows of hope just from meditating on David's soul-subduing songs.

The Psalms find the words that express our deepest and strongest emotions, no matter what the circumstances. Every emotion of our hearts is reflected in the Psalms. Reading the Psalms will turn sighing into singing and trouble into triumph. The word *praise* is found 189 times in this book. There is simply nothing that touches my heart like the Psalms. Thousands of years ago my deepest feelings were put to music—this is what we all delightfully discover when reading the Psalms!

A contemporary name for the book of Psalms could be *Poetry on Fire!* These 150 poetic masterpieces give us an expression of faith and worship. They become a mirror to the heart of God's people in our quest to experience God's presence. Much of Christianity has become so intellectualized that our emotions and artistic creativity are often set aside as unimportant in the worship of God. The Psalms free us to become emotional, passionate, sincere worshipers. It is time to sing the Psalms!

PURPOSE

The Psalms are clearly poetic. They are praises placed inside of poetry. Everyone who reads the Psalms realizes how filled with emotion they are! You will never be bored in reading the poetry that spills out of a fiery, passionate heart. These verses contain both poetry and music that touch the heart deeply, enabling you to encounter the heart of God through your emotional and creative senses.

AUTHOR AND AUDIENCE

Most of these poetic masterpieces come to us from David, King of Israel. He wrote them during specific periods of his life: when he was on the run from Saul, grateful for the Lord's protection and provision, scared for his future, mournful over his sin, and praising God with uplifted hands. Other authors include David's son Solomon, Moses, the Asaphite temple singers, and Korahite priests.

While they were written during specific periods in the history of Israel—from the monarchy to the postexilic eras—they connect to our own time as much as they reflect their time. So in many ways these poems are written to you and me. The original audience was the children of Israel, but the Psalms reflect the hopes and dreams, fears and failures of humanity in general.

MAJOR THEMES

Poetry of Praise. The Psalms are pure praise, inspired by the breath of God. Praise is a matter of life and breath. As long as we have breath we are told to praise the Lord. The Psalms release a flood of God-inspired insights that will lift heaviness off the human heart. The Psalms are meant to do to you what they did to David: they will bring you from your cave of despair into the glad presence of the King who likes and enjoys you.

Poetry of Prayer. Mixed with intercession, the Psalms become the fuel for our devotional life. Each psalm is a prayer. The early church recited and sang the Psalms regularly. Many contemporary worship songs have been inspired by this book of prayer-poetry!

Poetry of Wisdom. The Psalms unlock mysteries and parables, for in the purest praise is the cryptic language of a wise messenger. The wisdom of God is contained in these 150 keys; you have a key chain with master keys to unlock God's storehouse of wisdom and revelation. It is the "harp" (anointed worship) that releases divine secrets. Read carefully Ps. 49:4: "I will break open mysteries with my music, and my song will release riddles solved."

Poetry of Prophecy. Prophetic insights rest upon the Psalms. David's harp brings revelation and understanding to the people. Singers who tap into the insights of the Psalms will bring forth truths in their songs, which will break the hearts of people and release divine understanding to the church. The prophets must become musicians and the musicians must become prophets for the key of David to be given to the church.

Poetry of Christ. As with every part of the Old Testament, we are called to read the Psalms in two ways: (1) as the original audience heard them in their ancient Hebrew world; and (2) as the fulfillment of messianic prophesies, submitting by faith that these poems point to Jesus Christ. Therefore, at one level, these poems are all about him. There are 150 Psalms and each of them reveals a special and unique aspect of the God-Man, Christ Jesus. We could say every Psalm is messianic in that they find their fulfillment in Christ. Looking backward in light of Christ's revelation, we see they all point to our Lord Jesus, whom God has chosen as King over all.

Since these songs are all about Jesus, one of the keys to understanding the Psalms is to look for Jesus within its pages. Luke 24:44 says: "I told you that everything written about me would be fulfilled, including all the prophecies from the law of Moses through the Psalms and the writings of the prophets— that they would all find their fulfillment." There are many secrets about Jesus waiting to be discovered here!

PSALMS

Poetry on Fire

BOOK 1

THE GENESIS PSALMS

Psalms of man and creation

1 THE TREE OF LIFE *a*

¹ What delight comes to those *b* who follow God's ways! *c*
They won't walk in step with the wicked,
nor share the sinner's way,
nor be found sitting in the scorner's seat.

² Their pleasure and passion is remaining true to the Word of "I Am,"
meditating day and night in his true revelation of light. *d*

³ They will be standing firm like a flourishing tree
planted by God's design, *e*
deeply rooted by the brooks of bliss,
bearing fruit in every season of their lives.
They are never dry, never fainting,
ever blessed, ever prosperous. *f*

⁴ But how different are the wicked.
All they are is dust in the wind—
driven away to destruction!

---

a Although we cannot be sure, it is possible that Ezra compiled the Psalms and wrote Ps. 1 as an "introduction" to the Psalter. Others believe it was written by David or Jeremiah.

b 1:1 The Hebrew text is actually "that One" and refers prophetically to the Lord Jesus Christ, our Tree of Life. Every one of us who belongs to "that One" can also walk in the light of this psalm.

c 1:1 Ps. 1 is the contrast of those who follow God's ways and those who choose their own path. Read through this psalm with the purpose of learning how to live with God in first place.

d 1:2 Or "Torah."

e 1:3 Or "transplanted." That is, God planted our lives from where we were into a place of blessing. See Ps. 92:13–14.

f 1:3 The metaphors found in this verse can be paraphrased as "No matter what he sets out to do, he brings it to a successful conclusion."

[5] The wicked will not endure the day of judgment,
  for God will not defend them.
  Nothing they do will succeed or endure for long,
  for they have no part with those who walk in truth.
[6] But how different it is for the righteous!
  The Lord embraces their paths as they move forward
  while the way of the wicked lead only to doom.

2 THE CORONATION OF THE KING

Act I – The Nations Speak

[1] How dare the nations plan a rebellion.
  Their foolish plots are futile![a]
[2] Look at how the power brokers of the world
  rise up to hold their summit
  as the rulers scheme and confer together
  against Yahweh and his Anointed King, saying:
[3] "Let's come together and break away from the Creator.
  Once and for all let's cast off these controlling chains
  of God and his Christ!" [b]

Act II – God Speaks

[4] God-Enthroned[c] merely laughs at them;
  the Sovereign One mocks their madness!
[5] Then with the fierceness of his fiery anger
  he settles the issue[d] and terrifies them to death[e] with these words:
[6] "I myself have poured out my King on Zion,[f] my holy mountain. [g]

Act III – The Son Speaks

[7] "I will reveal the eternal purpose of God.
  For he has decreed over me, 'You are my favored Son.
  And as your Father I have crowned you as my King Eternal.
  Today I became your Father.

---

a 2:1 Or "Why are they devising emptiness?"
b 2:3 The word found here for "Christ" is the Hebrew word for "Messiah" or "Anointed One."
c 2:4 The Aramaic is *Maryah*, the Aramaic form of YHWH or Lord Jehovah.
d 2:5 Or "In good time he drives them away."
e 2:5 Or "snorts with anger." The Hebrew word *'aph* (fiery anger) is a homonym that also means "nose."
f 2:6 The word *Zion* is found 157 times in the Bible and 38 times in the Psalms.
g 2:6 For the believer today, Zion is not only a place but also a realm where Christ is enthroned. Jesus was "poured out" as a consecrated offering.

[8] Ask me[a] to give you the nations and I will do it,
 and they shall become your legacy.
 Your domain will stretch to the ends of the earth.
[9] And you will shepherd them[b] with unlimited authority,
 crushing their rebellion as an iron rod smashes jars of clay!'"

Act IV – The Holy Spirit Speaks

[10] Listen to me, all you rebel-kings
 and all you upstart judges of the earth.
 Learn your lesson[c] *while there's still time.*
[11] Serve and worship the awe-inspiring God.
 Recognize his greatness and bow before him,
 trembling with reverence in his presence.[d]
[12] Fall facedown before him and kiss the Son[e]
 before his anger is roused against you.
 Remember that his wrath can be quickly kindled!
 But many blessings are waiting for all
 who turn aside to hide themselves in him!

3 COVERED BY THE GLORY

King David's song when he was forced to flee from Absalom, his own son

The Humbling of a King

[1] Lord, I have so many enemies, so many who are against me.
[2] Listen to how they whisper their slander against me, saying:
 "Look! He's hopeless! Even God can't save him from this!"

Pause in his presence[f]

The Help of God

[3] But *in the depths of my heart I truly know*
 that you, Yahweh, have become my Shield;

---

a 2:8 Or in the Masoretic text, "Ask wealth of me."

b 2:9 As translated from the Septuagint.

c 2:10 Or "Do what is wise."

d 2:11 Or "Rejoice with trembling." The Hebrew word for "rejoice" means "to spin around with excited emotions" or "to twirl."

e 2:12 Or "be ruled by the Son." The Hebrew word for "kiss" is *nashaq* and can also mean "to be ruled by" or "be in subjection to" (the Son). Yet another possible translation of this difficult verse is "be armed with purity."

f 3:2 This is the Hebrew word *Selah*, a puzzling word to translate. Most scholars believe it is a musical term for pause or rest. It is used seventy-one times in the Psalms as an instruction to the music leader to pause and ponder in God's presence. An almost identical word, *Sela*, means "a massive rock cliff." It is said that when *Selah* is spoken, the words are carved in stone in the throne room of the heavens.

You take me and surround me with yourself. *a*
Your glory covers me continually. *b*
You lift high my head when I bow low in shame.
⁴I have cried out to you, Yahweh, from your holy presence. *c*
You send me a Father's help.

Pause in his presence

The Song of Safety
⁵So now I'll lie down and sleep like a baby—
then I'll awake in safety, for you surround me with your glory.
⁶Even though dark powers prowl *d* around me,
I won't be afraid.

The Secret of Strength
⁷*I simply cry out to you:*
"Rise up and help me, Lord! Come and save me!"
And you will slap them in the face,
breaking the power of their words to harm me. *e*
⁸*My true hero comes to my rescue,*
for the Lord alone is my Savior. *f*
What a feast of favor and bliss he gives his people!

Pause in his presence

4 AN EVENING PRAYER FOR HELP

For the Pure and Shining One *g*
For the end, *h* *a melody by King David*
¹God, you are my righteousness, my champion defender.
Answer me when I cry for help!

---

a 3:3 Many translations render this "You are a shield around me." The ancient Hebrew can be translated "You, O Lord, are my taker" (Augustine). The implication is that God shields us by taking us into himself. Jesus Christ is the taker of humanity, the one who was made flesh. He not only took our nature, he also took our sins that he might take us into glory.

b 3:3 Or "my glory."

c 3:4 Or "from your holy hill."

d 3:6 Or "military troops."

e 3:7 Or "You broke the teeth of the wicked."

f 3:8 The Hebrew word used sixty times in the Psalms for deliverance is *Yeshuah,* a variant form of the name for Jesus. This is pointing us to where our salvation is found.

g The Hebrew word used here, found in the inscription of fifty-four Psalms, is usually rendered as "choirmaster" or "chief director of music." It is taken from the root word for "shining" or "brilliant" (i.e., purity, holiness). Another way to translate "choirmaster" is "the shining one" or "the one who glitters from afar." Jesus Christ is the chief musician of all eternity who sings in the midst of his people (Heb. 12:2).

h As translated from the Septuagint. The Hebrew is "stringed instruments" or "smiting."

Whenever I was in distress, you enlarged me. [a]
I'm being squeezed again—I need your kindness right away!
Grant me your grace, hear my prayer, and set me free!

[2] Listen to me, you elite among men:
How long will you defame my honor [b]
and drag it down into shame?
Will you ever stop insulting me?
How long will you set your heart on shadows,
chasing your lies and delusions?

Pause in his presence

[3] May we never forget that the Lord works wonders [c]
for every one of his devoted lovers.
And this is how I know that he will answer my every prayer.

[4] Tremble in awe before the Lord, and do not sin against him.
Be still upon your bed and search your heart before him. [d]

Pause in his presence

[5] Bring to Yahweh the sacrifice of righteousness and put your trust in him.
[6] Lord, prove them wrong when they say, "God can't help you!"
Let the light of your radiant face
break through and shine upon us!
[7] The intense pleasure you give me
surpasses the gladness of harvest time,
even more than when the harvesters
gaze upon their ripened grain
and when their new wine overflows.
[8] Now, because of you, Lord, I will lie down in peace and sleep comes at once,
for no matter what happens, I will live unafraid!

---

a   4:1 Or "You created room for me."
b   4:2 Or "my glorious one."
c   4:3 There is considerable variation in possible translations from different manuscripts. Some
     manuscripts read "The Lord sets apart a faithful one for himself." Another possible transla-
     tion is "The Lord has revealed to me his marvelous love."
d   4:4 Or "Meditate on your bed and repent [lament]." It is always wise at the end of every day
     to cleanse our hearts in God's grace and mercy.

5 SONG OF THE CLOUDED DAWN

For the Pure and Shining One
For her who receives the inheritance, [a] *by King David*

Morning Watch

[1] Listen, Yahweh, to my passionate prayer! [b]
 Can't you hear my groaning?
[2] Don't you hear how I'm crying out to you?
 My King and my God, consider my every word,
 for I am calling out to you.
[3] At each and every sunrise you will hear my voice
 as I prepare my *sacrifice of* prayer to you. [c]
 Every morning I lay out the pieces of my life on the altar
 and wait *for your fire to fall upon my heart.* [d]

Making It Right

[4] I know that you, God, are never pleased with lawlessness,
 and evil ones will never be invited as guests in your house.
[5] Boasters collapse, unable to survive your scrutiny,
 for your hatred of evildoers is clear.
[6] You will make an end of all those who lie.
 How you hate their hypocrisy and despise all who love violence!

Multitude of Mercy

[7] But I know that you will welcome me into your house,
 for I am covered by your covenant of mercy and love.
 So I come to your sanctuary [e] with deepest awe
 to bow in worship and adore you.

---

a The Hebrew word used here is *neliloth* or flutes. It can also be translated "inheritances." The early church father Augustine translated this: "For her who receives the inheritance," meaning the church of Jesus Christ. The Father told the Son in Ps. 2 to ask for his inheritance; here we see it is the church that receives what Jesus asks for. We receive our inheritance of eternal life through the death and resurrection of the Son of God. The Septuagint reads "For the end," also found in numerous inscriptions of the Psalms.

b 5:1 Or "My words—give them a hearing, Lord!"

c 5:3 The Hebrew word for "prepare" is *'arak*, a priestly term for lighting the altar fire, preparing a sacrifice, and laying it out in order upon the altar to be consumed.

d 5:3 Implied in the concept of preparing the morning sacrifice. The Aramaic text states, "At dawn I shall be ready and shall appear before you." The Hebrew can also be translated "I'll be on the watchtower (for the answer to come)." See Pss. 59:16; 88:13; Hab. 2:1.

e 5:7 Or "I come to the temple of your holiness."

[8] Yahweh, lead me in the pathways of your pleasure
just like you promised me you would,
or else my enemies will conquer me.
Smooth out your road in front of me,
straight and level so that I will know where to walk.

Multitude of Sins

[9] For you can't trust anything they say.
Their hearts are nothing but deep pits of destruction,
drawing people into their darkness with their speeches. [a]
They are smooth-tongued deceivers who flatter with their words.
[10] Declare them guilty, O God!
Let their own schemes be their downfall!
Let the guilt of their sins collapse on top of them,
for they rebel against you.

Multitude of Blessings

[11] But let them all be glad,
those who turn aside to hide themselves in you.
May they keep shouting for joy forever!
Overshadow them in your presence as they sing and rejoice.
Then every lover of your name will burst forth with endless joy.
[12] Lord, how wonderfully you bless the righteous.
Your favor wraps around each one and covers them
under your canopy of kindness and joy.

6 A Cry for Healing [b]

For the Pure and Shining One
A song for the end, sung for the new day by King David
[1] No, Lord! Don't condemn me.
Don't punish me in your fiery anger.
[2] Please deal gently with me;
show me mercy, for I'm sick and frail.
I'm fading away with weakness.
Heal me, for I'm falling apart.
[3] How long until you take away this pain in my body and in my soul?
Lord, I'm trembling in fear!
[4] Turn to me and deliver my life
because I know you love and desire
to have me as your very own.

---

a 5:9 Or "Their throat is an open grave."
b Ps. 6 is a part of the daily prayer ritual of religious Jews.

⁵ How can I be any good to you dead?
    For those who are in the graveyards sing no songs.
    In the darkness of death who remembers you?
    How could I bring you praise if I'm buried in a tomb?
⁶ I'm exhausted and worn-out with my weeping.
    I endure weary, sleepless nights filled with moaning,
    soaking my pillow with my tears.
⁷ My eyes of faith won't focus anymore, for sorrow fills my heart.
    There are so many enemies who come against me!
⁸ Go away! Leave me, all you workers of wickedness!
    For the Lord has turned to listen to my thunderous cry.
⁹ Yes! The Lord *my healer* has heard all my pleading
    and has taken hold of my prayers and answered them all.
¹⁰ Now it's my enemies who have been shamed.
    Terror-stricken, they will turn back again,
    knowing the bitterness of sudden disgrace!

7 SONG FOR THE SLANDERED SOUL

A passionate song to the Lord
To the tune of "Breaking the Curse of Cush, the Benjamite," by King David

¹ O Lord my God, I turn aside to hide my soul in you.
    I trust you to save me from all those
    who pursue and persecute me.
² Don't leave me helpless!
    Don't let my foes fall upon me like fierce lions with teeth bared.
    Can't you see how they want to rip me to shreds,
    dragging me away to tear my soul to pieces?
³ Lord, if I were doing evil things, that would be different,
    for then I would be guilty, deserving all of this.
⁴ If I have wronged someone at peace with me,
    if I have betrayed a friend, repaying evil for good,
    or if I have unjustly harmed my enemy,
⁵ Then it would be right for you
    to let my enemy pursue and overtake me.
    In fact, let them grind me into the ground.
    Let them take my life from me and drag my dignity in the dust!

Pause in his presence

⁶ Now, Lord, let your anger arise against the anger of my enemies.
    Awaken your fury and stand up for me!
    Decree that justice be done against my foes.
⁷ Gather all the people around you.
    Return to your place on high to preside over them
    and once more occupy the throne of judgment.

[8] You are the Exalted One who judges the people,
   so vindicate me publicly and restore my honor and integrity.
   Before all the people declare me innocent.
[9] Once and for all, end the evil tactics of the wicked!
   Reward and prosper the cause of the righteous,
   for you are the righteous God, the soul searcher,
   who looks deep into every heart
   to examine the thoughts and motives.
[10] God, your wrap-around presence
   is my protection and my defense.
   You bring victory to all who reach out for you.
[11] Righteousness is revealed every time you judge.
   Because of the strength of your forgiveness,[a]
   your anger does not break out every day,
   even though you are a righteous judge.
[12-13] Yet if the wicked do not repent,
   you will not relent with your wrath,
   slaying them with your shining sword.
   You are the conqueror with an arsenal of lethal weapons
   that you've prepared for them.
   You have bent and strung your bow,
   making your judgment-arrows shafts of burning fire.
[14-15] Look how the wicked conceive their evil schemes.
   They go into labor with their lies and give birth to trouble.
   They dig a pit for others to fall into,
   not knowing that they will be the very ones
   who will fall into their own pit of failure.
[16] For you, God, will see to it that every pit-digger
   who works to trap and harm others
   will be trapped and harmed by his own treachery.
[17] But I will give all my thanks to you, Lord,
   for you make everything right in the end.
   I will sing my highest praise to the God of the Highest Place![b]

8 GOD'S SPLENDOR

For the Pure and Shining One
Set to the melody of "For the Feast of Harvest,"[c] by King David

[1] Lord, your name is so great and powerful!
   People everywhere see your splendor.

---

a 7:11 As translated from the Septuagint.
b 7:17 Or "to Adonai Elyon."
c This inscription in the Septuagint is "To the director over the wine vats."

Your glorious majesty streams from the heavens,
  filling the earth with the fame of your name!
² You have built a stronghold by the songs of babies.
  Strength rises up with the chorus of singing children.
  This kind of praise has the power to shut Satan's mouth.
  Childlike worship will silence *a*
  the madness of those who oppose you.
³ Look at the splendor of your skies,
  your creative genius glowing in the heavens.
  When I gaze at your moon and your stars,
  mounted like jewels in their settings,
  I know you are the fascinating artist who fashioned it all!
  But when I look up and see
  such wonder and workmanship above,
  I have to ask you this question:
⁴ *Compared to all this cosmic glory,* *b*
  why would you bother with puny, mortal man
  or be infatuated with Adam's sons?
⁵ Yet what honor you have given to men,
  created only a little lower than Elohim, *c*
  crowned like kings and queens *d* with glory and magnificence.
⁶ You have delegated to them
  mastery over all you have made,
  making everything subservient to their authority,
  placing earth itself under the feet of your image-bearers. *e*
⁷⁻⁸ All the created order and every living thing
  of the earth, sky, and sea—
  the wildest beasts and all the sea creatures—
  everything is in submission *to Adam's sons.*
⁹ Lord, your name is so great and powerful.
  People everywhere see your majesty!

---

a 8:2 There may be a vast difference between the glory of the heavens and the little mouths of children and babies, yet by both the majestic name of the Lord is revealed. It is amazing that perfected praises do not rise to God from the cherubim or seraphim, but from children and babies, the weakest of humanity.
b 8:4 David looked away from the darkness of earth and saw the divine order of the universe. This psalm is meant to join the earth to the heavens and to bring the heavenly glory into the earth, making the heavens and the earth one.
c 8:5 This is the same Hebrew word used for the Creator-God in Gen. 1:1.
d 8:5 The concept of kings and queens is implied in the text by the word *crowned.*
e 8:6 The Septuagint translation of 8:5–7 is quoted in Heb. 2:6–8. Today, all things are not yet under our feet. Even mosquitoes still come to defeat us. But there will be a time of restoration because of Christ's redemption, when everything will rest beneath our authority. See Isa. 11:6–9; 65:25; Matt. 19:28; Rev. 20:4–6.

What glory streams from the heavens,
   filling the earth with the fame of your name!

9 TRIUMPHANT THANKS

For the Pure and Shining One
To the tune of "The Secrets of the Son,"[a] by King David

¹ Lord, I will worship you with extended hands
   as my whole heart explodes with praise!
   I will tell everyone everywhere about your wonderful works
   and how your marvelous miracles exceed expectations!
² I will jump for joy and shout in triumph
   as I sing your song and make music for the Most High God.
³ For when you appear, I worship
   while all of my enemies run in retreat.
   They stumble and perish before your presence.
⁴ For you have stood up for my cause
   and vindicated me when I needed you the most.
   From your righteous throne you have given me justice.
⁵ With a blast of your rebuke nations are destroyed.
   You obliterated their names forever and ever.
⁶ The Lord thundered and our enemies have been cut off,
   vanished in everlasting ruins.
   All their cities have been destroyed—
   even the memory of them has been erased.
⁷ But the Lord of eternity, our mighty God, lives and reigns forever!
   He sits enthroned as King ready to render his verdicts
   and judge all with righteousness.
⁸ He will issue his decrees of judgment,
   deciding what is right for the entire world,
   dispensing justice to all.
⁹ All who are oppressed may come to you as a
   shelter in the time of trouble, a perfect hiding place.
¹⁰ May everyone who knows your mercy
   keep putting their trust in you,
   for they can count on you for help no matter what.
   O Lord, you will never, no never, neglect those
   who come to you.
¹¹ Listen, everyone! Sing out your praises to the God
   who lives and rules within Zion!
   Tell the world about all the miracles he has done!

---

a   As translated by Augustine, an early church father. The Hebrew is "to the death of the Son."

[12] He tracks down killers and avenges bloodshed,
   but he will never forget the ones forgotten by others,
   hearing every one of their cries for justice.
[13] So now, O Lord, don't forget me.
   Have mercy on me.
   Take note of how I've been humiliated
   at the hands of those who hate me.
   Bring me back again from the brink, from the very gates of death.
[14] Save me! Bring me to the spiritual gates of Zion [a]
   so I can bring you the shout of praise you deserve.
[15] For the godless nations get trapped
   in the very snares they set for others.
The hidden trap they set for the weak
   has snapped shut upon themselves—guilty!
[16] The Lord is famous for this: his justice will punish the wicked.
   While they are digging a pit for others,
   they are actually setting the terms for their own judgment.
   They will fall into their own pit.

Consider the truth of this and pause in his presence [b]

[17] Don't forget this: all the wicked will one day
   fall into the darkness of death's domain and remain there,
   including the nations that forget God and reject his ways.
[18] He will not ignore forever all the needs of the poor,
   for those in need shall not always be crushed.
   Their hopes shall be fulfilled, *for God sees it all!*
[19] Lord, won't you now arise to judge and
   punish the nations who defy you?
   Aren't you fed up with their rebellion?
[20] Make them tremble in fear before your presence.
   Place a lawgiver over them.
   Make them know that they are only puny, frail humans
   who must give account to you!

Pause in his presence

10 THE CRY OF THE OPPRESSED [c]

[1] Lord, you seem so far away when evil is near!
   Why do you stand so far off as though you don't care?
   Why have you hidden yourself when I need you the most?

---

a 9:14 Or "Daughter Gates of Zion."
b 9:16 The Hebrew word *higayon* means "to consider the truth of the matter."
c It is likely that Pss. 9 and 10 were originally one psalm. Eight Hebrew manuscripts unite
   them as well as the Aramaic, Septuagint, and the Latin Vulgate. The Catholic Bible is based
   on the Latin Vulgate and therefore has a different numbering for the Psalms.

²The arrogant in their elitist pride persecute the poor and helpless.
May you pour out upon them
the very evil they've planned against others!
³How they brag and boast of their cravings, exalting the greedy.
They congratulate themselves as they despise you.
⁴These arrogant ones, so smug and secure!
In their delusion the wicked boast, saying,
"God doesn't care about what we do.
There's nothing to worry about!
Our wealth will last a lifetime."
⁵So seemingly successful are they in their schemes,
prosperous in all their plans and scoffing at any restraint.
⁶They boast that neither God nor men will bring them down.
They sneer at all their enemies, saying in their hearts,
"We'll have success in all we do
and never have to face trouble"—
never realizing that they are speaking this in vain.
⁷Their mouths spout out cursing, lies, and threats.
Only trouble and turmoil come from all their plans.
⁸⁻⁹Like beasts lurking in the shadows of the city
they crouch silently in ambush for the people to pass by.
Pouncing on the poor, they catch them in their snare
to murder their prey in secret
as they plunder their helpless victims.
¹⁰They crush the lowly as they fall beneath their brutal blows,
watching their victims collapse in defeat!
¹¹Then they say to themselves,
"The Lofty One is not watching while we do this.
He doesn't even care! We can get away with it!"
¹²Now is the time to arise, Lord! Crush them once and for all!
Don't forget the forgotten and the helpless.
¹³How dare the wicked think they'll escape judgment,
believing that you would not
call them to account for all their ways.
Don't let the wicked get away with their contempt of you!
¹⁴Lord, I know you see all that they're doing,
noting their each and every deed.
You know the trouble and turmoil they've caused.
Now punish them thoroughly for all that they've done!
The poor and helpless ones trust in you, Lord,
for you are famous for being the helper of the fatherless.
I know you won't let them down.

[15] Break the power of the wicked and all their strong-arm tactics.
Search them out and destroy them
for the evil things they've done.
[16] You, Lord, are King forever and ever!
You will see to it that all the nations perish from your land.
[17] Lord, you know and understand all the hopes of the humble
and will hear their cries and comfort their hearts,
helping them all!
[18] The orphans and the oppressed will be terrified no longer,
for you will bring them justice, and no one will trouble them.

11 SONG OF THE STEADFAST

For the Pure and Shining One, by King David

[1-2] Lord, *don't you hear*
what my well-meaning friends keep saying to me:
"Run away while you can!
Fly away like a bird to hide in the mountains for safety.
For your enemies have prepared a trap for you!
They plan to destroy you with their slander and deceitful lies.
Can't you see them hiding
in their place of darkness and shadows?
They're set against you and all those who live upright lives."
But don't they know, Lord,
that I have made you my only hiding place?
Don't they know that I always trust in you?
[3] What can the righteous accomplish
when truth's pillars are destroyed and law and order collapse?
[4] *Yet the Eternal One is never shaken—*[a]
he is still found in his temple of holiness,
reigning as Lord and King over all.
He is closely watching everything that happens.
And with a glance, his eyes examine every heart.[b]
For his heavenly rule will prevail over all.
[5] He will test both the righteous *and the wicked,*
exposing each heart.
God's very soul detests those who love to resort to violence.
[6] He will rain down upon them judgment for their sins.
A scorching wind will be their portion and lot in life.

---

a 11:4 This is an implied contrast made explicit from the text. This psalm shows the contrast between what can be shaken and what is unshakable.

b 11:4 The actual Hebrew is "his eyelids." Some see the "eyelid" as the lid of the ark of covenant, which was the mercy seat.

⁷ But remember this: the Righteous Lord loves
    what is right and just, and every godly one
    will come into his presence and gaze upon his face!

12 Song for the New Day

For the Pure and Shining One
A song of smiting, sung for the new day by King David[a]

¹ Help, Lord! Save us! For godly ones are swiftly disappearing.
    Where are the dependable, principled ones?
    They're a vanishing breed!

² Everyone lies, everyone flatters, and everyone deceives.
    Nothing but empty talk, smooth talk, and double-talk.
    Where are the truthful?

³⁻⁴ I know the Lord will not deal gently with people like that!
    You will destroy every proud liar who says, "We lie all we want.
    Our words are our weapons, and we won't be held accountable.
    Who can stop us?"
    May the Lord cut off their twisted tongues
    and seal their lying lips.
    May they all be silenced—those who boast and brag with their
    high-minded talk about doing whatever they want.

⁵ But the Lord says, "Now I will arise!
    I will defend the poor,
    those who were plundered, the oppressed,
    and the needy who groan for help.
    I will arise to rescue and protect them!"

⁶ For every word God speaks is sure and every promise pure.
    His truth is tested, found to be flawless, and ever faithful.
    It's as pure as silver refined seven times in a crucible of clay.[b]

⁷⁻⁸ Lord, you will keep us forever safe,
    out of the reach of the wicked.
    Even though they strut and prowl,
    tolerating and celebrating what is worthless and vile,
    you will still lift up those who are yours!

---

a   The events surrounding this psalm could be the killing of the priests by Saul in 1 Sam.
    22:17–19. Saul ordered the death of "eighty-five men who wore the linen ephod." The kill-
    ing rampage continued until an entire community of priests had been slaughtered with their
    women and children. This great evil marked David from that day forward. The inscription
    found in the Septuagint is "The Eighth Psalm of David."

b   12:6 The clay furnace is the heart of man. We are the earthen vessels inside which God
    has placed his flawless words. His words test us, they try us, and they refine us, seven times
    over, until they are purified and assimilated into our spirits. The fire of testing purifies us
    as vessels to carry the Word within our hearts.

13 PRAYER TURNS DEPRESSION INTO DELIGHT [a]

For the Pure and Shining One, by King David

¹ I'm hurting, Lord—will you forget me forever? [b]
How much longer, Lord?
Will you look the other way when I'm in need? [c]
² How much longer must I cling to this constant grief?
I've endured this shaking of my soul.
So how much longer will my enemy have the upper hand?
It's been long enough!
³ Take a good look at me, God, and answer me!
Breathe your life into my spirit.
Bring light to my eyes in this pitch-black darkness
or I will sleep the sleep of death.
⁴ Don't let my enemy proclaim, "I've prevailed over him."
For all my adversaries will celebrate when I fall.
⁵ Lord, I have always trusted in your kindness, *so answer me.*
I will yet celebrate with passion and joy
when your salvation [d] lifts me up.
⁶ I will sing my song of joy to you, the Most High,
for in all of this you have strengthened my soul.
My enemies say that I have no Savior,
but I know that I have one in you!

14 GOD LOOKS DOWN FROM HEAVEN [e]

For the Pure and Shining One, by King David

¹ Only the withering soul [f] would say to himself,
"There is no God."

---

a Some believe David composed this shortly after being anointed to be the king of Israel. David knew greatness was his destiny, but he struggled with the persecution and challenges that came before his exaltation. In the wilderness David trusts and prays his way out.

b 13:1 This is the psalm that describes the journey from self to God, from despair to delight, from feeling abandoned to feeling affirmed. It begins with pain and ends with praise. Moaning gives way to music. We each can take comfort in what David experienced.

c 13:1 David feels as though God is hiding his face from his cries. David is left alone to wrestle with his doubts, feeling as though his patience can hold on no longer. Have you ever been there?

d 13:5 The term for "salvation" is *yeshu'sh*, which is nearly identical to *Jesus, our Salvation.* Our Savior plans blessings and hope for each of us as we trust in him.

e With few differences, Ps. 14 and Ps. 53 are nearly identical. Ps. 14 is practical; Ps. 53 is prophetic. Ps. 14 deals with the past, Ps. 53 with the future.

f 14:1 Or "fool." The word for "fool" comes from a Hebrew word meaning "withering." If we make no room for God, we have withered hearts, our moral sense of righteousness is put to sleep, and the noble aspirations of the heart shrivel up and die.

Anyone who thinks like this is corrupt and callous,
depraved and detestable, devoid of what is good.
² The Lord looks down in love,
bending over heaven's balcony,
looking over all of Adam's sons and daughters.
He's looking to see if there is anyone who acts wisely,
any who are searching for God and wanting to please him.
³ But no, everyone has wandered astray,
walking stubbornly toward evil.
Not one is good; he can't even find one.
⁴ Look how they live in luxury while exploiting my people!
Won't these workers of wickedness ever learn?
They don't ever even think of praying to God.
⁵ But just look at them now, in panic, trembling with terror.
For the Lord is on the side of the generation of loyal lovers.
⁶ The Lord is always the safest place for the poor
when the workers of wickedness oppress them.
⁷ How I wish that Israel's rescue
would arise from the midst of Zion!
When his people are restored,
Jacob's joy will break forth
and Israel will be glad!

15 LIVING IN THE SHINING PLACE ª

A poetic song, by King David

¹ Lord, who dares to dwell with you?
Who presumes the privilege of being close to you,
living next to you in your shining place of glory?ᵇ
Who are those who daily dwell in the life of the Holy Spirit?ᶜ
² They are passionate and wholehearted,
always sincere and always speaking the truth—
for their hearts are trustworthy.
³ They refuse to slanderᵈ or insult others;

---

a Perhaps David's prophetic minstrels sang this song of instruction as they laid the ark to rest in David's tent. It is a song that reveals who will dwell in God's holy presence and who will live with him in heaven's glory. It actually is a description of Zion's perfect Man, Christ Jesus, and all those who are transformed into his image (Rom. 8:29).

b 15:1 The Hebrew word for "sanctuary" is taken from a root word for "shining place."

c 15:1 This psalm gives us David's Sermon on the Mount. If we will dwell in the Holy Place, there must first be a holy place in our spirits where God dwells. God's guests must submit to the holiness that lives there. There is etiquette for God's house revealed in this psalm.

d 15:3 The Hebrew word for "slander," *ragal*, means to spy on someone and look for evil to use against him.

they'll never listen to gossip or rumors,
nor would they ever harm another with their words.

⁴ They will speak out passionately against evil and evil workers
while commending the faithful ones who follow after the truth.
They make firm commitments and follow through,
even at great cost.

⁵ They never crush others with exploitation or abuse
and they would never be bought with a bribe
against the innocent.
They will never be shaken; they will stand firm forever.

16 THE GOLDEN SECRET

A precious song, engraved in gold, by King David ᵃ

¹ Keep me safe, O mighty God.
I run for dear life to you, my safe place.

² So I said to the Lord God,
"You are my Maker, my Mediator, and my Master.
Any good thing you find in me has come from you." ᵇ

³ *And he said to me,* "My holy lovers are wonderful,
my majestic ones, my glorious ones,
fulfilling all my desires."

⁴ Yet there are those who yield to their weakness, ᶜ
and they will have troubles and sorrows unending.
I never gather with such ones, ᵈ
nor give them honor in any way.

⁵ Lord, I have chosen you alone as my inheritance.
You are my prize, my pleasure, and my portion.
I leave my destiny *and its timing* in your hands. ᵉ

⁶ Your pleasant path leads me to pleasant places.
I'm overwhelmed by the privileges
that come with following you,
for you have given me the best!

ᵃ The Hebrew word used in the inscription is *michtam.* There are many variations of
translation for this word. Here are the major ones: *golden, graven, a permanent writing,
precious, hidden,* or *jewel.* The Septuagint renders this "a sculptured writing of gold";
other translations call it a "golden poem." Perhaps the most accepted translation of
michtam is "engraved in gold." This speaks of the divine nature engraved into our hearts
by the Word. A new humanity is now stamped with God-life, engraved in his golden
glory.

ᵇ 16:2 The Aramaic text states, "My goodness is found in your presence."

ᶜ 16:4 As translated from the Septuagint.

ᵈ 16:4 As translated from the Septuagint.

ᵉ 16:5 Implied in the text. The Aramaic reads "You are restoring my inheritance to me."

⁷ The way you counsel and correct me makes me praise you more,
  for your whispers in the night give me wisdom,
  showing me what to do next.
⁸ Because you are close to me and always available,
  my confidence will never be shaken,
  for I experience your wrap-around presence every moment.
⁹ My heart and soul explode with joy—full of glory!
  Even my body will rest confident and secure.
¹⁰ For you will not abandon me to the realm of death,
  nor will you allow your Holy One to experience corruption. ᵃ
¹¹ For you bring me a continual revelation of resurrection life,
  the path to the bliss that brings me face-to-face with you. ᵇ

17 A CRY FOR JUSTICE

A priestly prayer, by King David

¹ Listen to me, Lord.
  Hear the passionate prayer of this honest man.
  It's my piercing cry for justice!
  My cause is just and my need is real.
  I've done what's right and my lips speak truth.
² Lord, I always live my life before your face,
  so examine and exonerate me.
  Vindicate me and show the world I'm innocent.
³ For in a visitation of the night
  you inspected my heart and refined my soul in fire
  until nothing vile was found in me.
  I've wanted my words and my ways to always agree.
⁴ Following your word has kept me from wrong.
  Your ways have molded my footsteps, keeping me
  from going down the forbidden paths of the destroyer.
⁵ My steps follow in the tracks of your chariot wheels,
  always staying in their path,
  never straying from your way.
⁶ You will answer me, God; I know you always will,
  like you always do as you listen with love to my every prayer.
⁷ Magnify the marvels of your mercy to all who seek you. ᶜ
  Make your Pure One wonderful to me, ᵈ

ᵃ 16:10 Or "the pit." This is likely a metaphor for Sheol.
ᵇ 16:11 There is no Hebrew word for "presence." When the Psalmist wanted to speak of
  God's presence, he used the Hebrew word for "face."
ᶜ 17:7 As translated from the Septuagint.
ᵈ 17:7 As translated from the Aramaic.

like you do for all those who turn aside
to hide themselves in you.
[8] Protect me from harm;
keep an eye on me like you would a child [a]
reflected in the twinkling of your eye.
Yes, hide me within the shelter of your embrace,
under your outstretched wings. [b]
[9] Protect me there from all my foes.
For there are many who surround my soul
to completely destroy me.
[10] They are pitiless, heartless—hard as nails,
swollen with pride and filled with arrogance!
[11] See how they close in on me,
waiting for the chance to throw me to the ground. [c]
[12] They're like lions eager to tear me apart,
like young and fearless lions lurking in secret,
so ferocious and cruel—ready to rip me to shreds.
[13] Arise, God, and confront them!
Challenge them with your might! [d]
Free me from their clutches and rescue me from their rage.
[14] Throw them down to the ground,
those who live for only this life on earth.
Thrust them out of their prosperity
and into their portion in eternity,
leaving their wealth and wickedness behind!
[15] As for me, because I am innocent I will see [e] your face
until I see you for who you really are.
Then I will awaken with your form and be fully satisfied, [f]
fulfilled in the revelation of your glory in me!

---

a 17:8 Or "daughter."
b 17:8 This could also be a reference to the mercy seat, where sacred blood was sprinkled in
   the Holy of Holies. There the golden cherubim overshadowed all who entered the divine
   chamber (Ex. 25:18–20).
c 17:11 This is also what the soldiers did to Jesus. They threw him to the ground and nailed
   him to the cross.
d 17:13 The word used here is *sword*. An alternative translation would be "Rescue my soul
   from the wicked one, who is your sword." The wicked are sometimes God's tools to execute
   his judgments (Isa. 10:5; Jer. 51:20).
e 17:15 The Hebrew word for "gaze," *chaza*, means "to see a vision."
f 17:15 The Aramaic can be translated "I will be satisfied when your faith is awakened."

18 I LOVE YOU, LORD

Praises sung to the Pure and Shining One, by King David,
his servant,ᵃ composed when the Lord rescued David from all
his many enemies, including from the brutality of Saulᵇ

¹ Lord, I passionately love you and I'm bonded to you!ᶜ
   I want to embrace you,ᵈ for now you've become my power!

² You're as real to me as bedrock beneath my feet,
   like a castle on a cliff, my forever firm fortress,
   my mountain of hiding, my pathway of escape,
   my tower of rescue where none can reach me.
   My secret strength and shield around me,
   you are salvation's ray of brightness shining on the hillside,ᵉ
   always the champion of my cause.

³ All I need to do is to call to you,
   singing to you, the praiseworthy God.
   When I do, I'm safe and sound in you.

⁴⁻⁵ For when the ropes of death wrapped around me
   and terrifying torrents of destruction overwhelmed me,ᶠ
   taking me to death's door, to doom's domain,

⁶ I cried out to you in my distress, the delivering God,
   and from your temple-throne you heard my troubled cry.
   My sobs came right into your heart
   and you turned your face to rescue me.ᵍ

---

a This magnificent poem is so important to the Holy Spirit that it appears twice in the Bible. You will find it again in 2 Sam. 22.

b Or "the paw of Saul." He was like a beast that chased David until his death.

c 18:1 David doesn't employ the common Hebrew word for "love," *'ahav*, but instead uses the Hebrew word for "pity" or "mercy." How could David have mercy for God? The word he uses, *raham*, is the word used for a mother who loves and pities her child so much it manifests with a deep love and emotional bond. This concept, although difficult to convey in English, is brought forth as David is saying, "I love you passionately and my life is forever bonded to you!"

d 18:1 The Hebrew word used here for "love" is not the usual word to describe love. It is a fervent and passionate word that carries the thought of embrace and touch. It could actually be translated "Lord, I want to hug you!" Haven't you ever felt like that?

e 18:2 The Hebrew word for "horn" (i.e., horn of my salvation) comes from a root word meaning "ray of brightness" or "hillside." The translator has chosen to include both concepts in the translation.

f 18:4–5 Or "waves of Sheol [death] engulfed me." See 2 Sam. 22:5.

g 18:6 This scene is not only a poetic portrayal of how God answered David's prayer, but also a picture of the sufferings of a greater Son of David, Jesus, who hung on the cross with cries of agony. God heard him and shook the planet as thick clouds covered the sun.

⁷ The earth itself shivered and shook.
It reeled and rocked before him.
As the mountains trembled, they melted away!
For his anger was kindled, burning on my behalf.
⁸ Fierce flames leapt from his mouth,
erupting with blazing, burning coals as smoke
and fire encircled him.
⁹⁻¹⁰ He stretched heaven's curtain open and came to my defense.
Swiftly he rode to earth as the stormy sky was lowered.
He rode a chariot of thunderclouds amidst thick darkness,
a cherub his steed as he swooped down,
soaring on the wings of Spirit-wind.
¹¹ Wrapped and hidden in the thick-cloud darkness,
his thunder-tabernacle surrounded him.
He hid himself in mystery-darkness;
the dense rain clouds were his garments.
¹² Suddenly the brilliance of his presence broke through
with lightning bolts and with a mighty storm from heaven—
like a tempest dropping coals of fire.
¹³ The Lord thundered, the great God above every god
spoke with his thunder-voice from the skies.
What fearsome hailstones and flashes of fire were before him!
¹⁴ He released his lightning-arrows, and routed my foes.
See how they ran and scattered in fear!
¹⁵ Then with his mighty roar he laid bare the foundations of the earth,
uncovering the secret source of the sea.
The hidden depths of land and sea were exposed
by the hurricane-blast of his hot breath.
¹⁶ He then reached down from heaven,
all the way from the sky to the sea.
He reached down into my darkness to rescue me!
He took me out of my calamity and chaos
and drew me to himself,
taking me from the depths of my despair!
¹⁷ Even though I was helpless in the hands
of my hateful, strong enemy, ᵃ
you were good to deliver me.
¹⁸ When I was at my weakest, my enemies attacked—
but the Lord held on to me.
¹⁹ His love broke open the way

---

a 18:17 Death is our strong enemy. Only through Christ are we delivered from its grip.

and he brought me into a beautiful broad place. *a*

He rescued me—because his delight is in me! *b*

²⁰ He rewarded me for doing what's right and staying pure.

²¹ I will follow his commands and never stop.

I'll not sin by ceasing to follow him, no matter what.

²² For I've kept my eyes focused on his righteous words

and I've obeyed everything that he's told me to do.

²³ I've done my best to be blameless and to follow all his ways,

keeping my heart pure.

²⁴ I've kept my integrity by surrendering to him.

And so the Lord has rewarded me with his blessing.

This is the treasure I discovered

when I kept my heart clean before his eyes.

²⁵ Lord, it is clear to me now that how we live

will dictate how you deal with us. *c*

Good people will taste your goodness, Lord.

And to those who are loyal to you,

you love to prove that you are loyal and true.

²⁶ And for those who are purified, they find you always pure.

But you'll outwit the crooked and cunning with your craftiness.

²⁷ To the humble you bring heaven's deliverance.

But the proud and haughty you disregard.

²⁸ God, all at once you turned on a floodlight for me!

You are the revelation-light in my darkness,

and in your brightness I can see the path ahead.

²⁹ With you as my strength I can crush an enemy horde,

advancing through every stronghold that stands in front of me.

³⁰ What a God you are! Your path for me has been perfect!

All your promises have proven true.

What a secure shelter for all those

who turn to hide themselves in you!

You are the wrap-around God giving grace to me. *d*

³¹ Could there be any other god like you?

You are the only God to be worshiped,

for there is not a more secure foundation

to build my life upon than you.

---

a 18:19 This could be the throne room of heaven.

b 18:19 Here in verses 16–19 you can see the glorious resurrection of Christ as the Father reached down and kissed the Son with life and love. Read it again and think of Christ in the tomb being raised by the Father.

c 18:25 This is a summary of the passage, implied in the text.

d 18:30 The Hebrew word used here for "shield" means "to wrap around in protection." God himself is our shield of grace.

³² You have wrapped me in power,
and now you've shared with me your perfection.
³³ Through you I ascend to the highest peaks of your glory
to stand in the heavenly places, strong and secure in you.
³⁴ You've trained me with the weapons of warfare-worship;
now I'll descend into battle with power
to chase and conquer my foes.
³⁵ You empower me for victory with your wrap-around presence.
Your power within makes me strong to subdue,
and by stooping down in gentleness
you strengthened me and made me great!
³⁶ You've set me free from captivity
and now I'm standing complete, ready to fight some more!
³⁷ I caught up with my enemies and conquered them,
and didn't turn back until the war was won!
³⁸ I pinned them to the ground and broke them to pieces.
I finished them once and for all; they're as good as dead.
³⁹ You've placed your armor upon me
and defeated my enemies, making them bow low at my feet.
⁴⁰ You've made them all turn tail and run,
for through you I've destroyed them all!
Forever silenced, they'll never taunt me again.
⁴¹ They shouted for help but not one dared to rescue them.
They shouted to God but he refused to answer them.
⁴² So I pulverized them to powder and cast them to the wind.
I swept them away like dirt on the floor.
⁴³ You gave me victory on every side,
for look how the nations come to serve me.
Even those I've never heard of come and bow at my feet.
⁴⁴ As soon as they heard of me they submitted to me.
Even the rebel foreigners obey my every word.
⁴⁵ Their rebellion fades away as they come near;
trembling in their strongholds,
they come crawling out of their hideouts.
Cringing in fear before me, their courage is gone.
⁴⁶ The Almighty is alive and conquers all!
Praise is lifted high to the unshakable God!
Towering over all, my Savior-God is worthy to be praised!
⁴⁷ Look how he pays back harm to all who harm me,
subduing all the people who come against me.
⁴⁸ He rescues me from my enemies;
he lifts me up high and keeps me out of reach,
far from the grasp of my violent foe.

⁴⁹ This is why I thank God with high praises!
  I will sing my song to the highest God,
    so all among the nations will hear me.
⁵⁰ You have appointed me king and rescued me
  time and time again with your magnificent miracles.
  You've been merciful and kind to me, your anointed one.
  This favor will be forever seen upon your loving servant, David,
  and to all my descendants!

19 GOD'S WITNESSES

For the Pure and Shining One
A poem of praise by King David, his loving servant

God's Story in the Skies

¹ God's splendor is a tale that is told;
  his testament is written in the stars. *ᵃ*
  Space itself speaks his story every day
  through the marvels of the heavens.
  His truth is on tour in the starry vault of the sky,
  showing his skill in creation's craftsmanship.
² Each day gushes out its message *ᵇ* to the next,
  night with night whispering its knowledge to all.
³ Without a sound, without a word, without a voice being heard,
⁴ Yet all the world can see its story.
  Everywhere its gospel *ᶜ* is clearly read so all may know.
⁵ What a heavenly home God has set for the sun,
  shining in the superdome of the sky!
  See how he leaves his celestial chamber each morning,
  radiant as a bridegroom ready for his wedding,
  like a day-breaking champion eager to run his course.
⁶ He rises on one horizon, completing his circuit on the other,
  warming lives and lands with his heat.

God's Story in the Scriptures

⁷ God's Word is perfect in every way;
  how it revives our souls!
  His laws lead us to truth,
  and his ways change the simple into wise.
⁸ His teachings make us joyful and radiate his light;

---

a 19:1 Or "The heavens are continually rehearsing the glory of God."
b 19:2 Or "speaks its prophecy."
c 19:4 Literal translation from the Aramaic. There are many who believe that constellations
   (Heb. *mazzarot*) of the sky bring us the revelation of the gospel of Jesus Christ. A message
   is being given without words, sound, or a voice. See Job 38:31–33.

his precepts are so pure!
His commands, how they challenge us to keep close to his heart!
The revelation-light of his word makes my spirit shine radiant.
⁹ Every one of the Lord's commands is right;
following them brings cheer. *a*
Nothing he says ever needs to be changed.
¹⁰ The rarest treasures of life are found in his truth.
That's why I prize God's word like others prize the finest gold.
Nothing brings the soul such sweetness
as seeking his living words.
¹¹ For they warn us, his servants,
and keep us from following the wicked way,
giving a lifetime guarantee:
great success to every obedient soul!
¹² *Without this revelation-light,*
how would I ever detect the waywardness of my heart? *b*
Lord, forgive my hidden flaws whenever you find them.
¹³ Keep cleansing me, God,
and keep me from my secret, selfish sins;
may they never rule over me!
For only then will I be free from fault
and remain innocent of rebellion.
¹⁴ So may the words of my mouth, my meditation-thoughts,
and every movement of my heart be always pure and pleasing,
acceptable before your eyes,
my only Redeemer, my Protector-God. *c*

20 A SONG OF TRUST

For the Pure and Shining One
For the end times, by King David *d*

¹ In your day of danger may the Lord answer and deliver you.
May the name of the God of Jacob *e* set you safely on high!
² May supernatural help be sent from his sanctuary.
May he support you from Zion's fortress!
³ May he remember every gift you have given him
and celebrate every sacrifice of love you have shown him.

Pause in his presence

---

a 19:9 As translated from the Septuagint. The Hebrew is "The fear of the Lord is clean."
b 19:12 The word *waywardness* is taken from the Hebrew word for "errors."
c 19:14 Or "my rock (of protection)."
d The inscription for Ps. 20–22 is "For the End Times," as translated from the Septuagint.
e 20:1 Jacob was one transformed by God's grace, changed from a schemer who took from others into Israel, God's prince.

⁴May God give you every desire of your heart
and carry out your every plan *as you go to battle.*
⁵When you succeed, we will celebrate and shout for joy.
Flags will fly when victory is yours!
Yes, God will answer your prayers and we will praise him!
⁶I know God gives me all that I ask for
and brings victory to his anointed king.
My deliverance cry will be heard in his holy heaven.
By his mighty hand miracles will manifest
through his saving strength.
⁷Some find their strength in their weapons and wisdom,
but my miracle deliverance can never be won by men.
Our boast is in the Lord our God,
who makes us strong and gives us victory!
⁸Our enemies will not prevail; they will only collapse and
perish in defeat while we will rise up, full of courage.
⁹Give victory to our king, O God!
The day we call on you, give us your answer!

21 THROUGH YOUR STRENGTH

For the end time, to the Pure and Shining One
King David's poem of praise

¹Lord, because of your strength the king is strong.
Look how he rejoices in you! *ᵃ*
He bursts out with a joyful song because of your victory!
²For you have given him his heart's desire,
anything and everything he asks for.
You haven't withheld a thing from your betrothed one.

Pause in his presence

³Rich blessings overflow with every encounter with you,
and you placed a royal crown of gold upon his head.
⁴He wanted resurrection—you have given it to him and more!
The days of his blessing stretch on one after another, forever!
⁵You have honored him and made him famous.
Glory garments are upon him,
and you surround him with splendor and majesty.
⁶Your victory heaps blessing after blessing upon him.
What joy and bliss he tastes, rejoicing before your face!
⁷For the king trusts endlessly in you,
and he will never stumble, never fall.
Your forever-love never fails and holds him firm.

---

a 21:1 Think of this song as a praise song to Jesus, our true King.

⁸ Your almighty hands have captured your foes.
You uncovered all who hate you and you seized them.
^{9–10} When you appear before them,
unveiling the radiance of your face,
they will be consumed by the fierce fire of your presence.
Flames will swallow them up.
They and their descendants
will be destroyed by an unrelenting fire.
¹¹ We will watch them fail,
for these are ones who plan their evil schemes against the Lord.
¹² They will turn and run at the sight of your judgment-arrow
aimed straight at their hearts.
¹³ Rise up and put your might on display!
By your strength we will sing and praise your glorious power!

22 A PROPHETIC PORTRAIT OF THE CROSS ^a

For the Pure and Shining One
King David's song of anguish
To the tune of "The Deer at the Dawning of the Day"^b

¹ God, my God!
Why would you abandon me now?^c
² Why do you remain distant,
refusing to answer^d my tearful cries in the day
and my desperate cries for your help in the night?
I can't stop sobbing.
Where are you, my God?
³ Yet I know that you are most holy; it's indisputable.
You are God-Enthroned, surrounded with songs,
living among the shouts of praise of your princely people.
⁴ Our fathers' faith was in you—
through the generations they trusted and believed in you
and you came through.
⁵ Every time they cried out to you in their despair,
you were faithful to deliver them;
you didn't disappoint them.

---

a Thirty-three prophecies from this psalm were fulfilled when Jesus was on the cross.
b This could be an amazing picture of Christ giving birth at the cross to a generation of his seed. They are like children of God born in the dawning of that resurrection morning.
c 22:1 When Jesus quoted these words while dying on the cross, he was identifying himself as the one David wrote about in this psalm. It is a breathtaking portrayal of what Jesus endured through his suffering for us. The psalm ends with another quotation of Jesus on the cross: "It is finished!"
d 22:2 David uses poetic nuance here, for the word *answer* ('anah) is also a Hebrew homonym for "affliction."

⁶But look at me now; I am like a woeful worm,
  crushed, and I'm bleeding crimson. *ᵃ*
  I don't even look like a man anymore.
  I've been abused, despised, and scorned by everyone!
⁷Mocked by their jeers, despised with their sneers,
  as all the people poke fun at me, spitting their insults,
⁸saying, "Is this the one who trusted in God?
  Is this the one who claims God is pleased with him?
  Now let's see if your God will come to your rescue!
  We'll just see how much he delights in you!"
⁹Lord, you delivered me safely from my mother's womb.
  You are the one who cared for me ever since I was a baby.
¹⁰Since the day I was born, I've been placed in your custody.
  You've cradled me throughout my days.
  I've trusted in you and you've always been my God.
¹¹So don't leave me now; stay close to me!
  For trouble is all around me and there's no one else to help me.
¹²I'm surrounded by many violent foes;
  mighty forces of evil are swirling around me
  who want to break me to bits and destroy me. *ᵇ*
¹³Curses pour from their mouths!
  They're like ravenous, roaring lions tearing their prey.
¹⁴Now I'm completely exhausted; I'm spent.
  Every joint of my body has been pulled apart.
  My courage has vanished and
  my inward parts have melted away.
¹⁵I'm so thirsty and parched—dry as a bone.
  My tongue sticks to the roof of my mouth.
  And now you've left me in the dust for dead.
¹⁶They have pierced my hands and my feet.
  Like a pack of wild dogs they tear at me,
  swirling around me with their hatred.
  They gather around me like lions to pin *ᶜ* my hands and feet.
¹⁷All my bones stick out.
  Look at how they all gloat over me and stare!

---

a 22:6 The Hebrew word for "worm" is *tola*, which is also the word for "crimson" or "scarlet." *Tola* was a certain worm in the Middle East that, when crushed, bled a crimson color so strong it was used as a dye for garments. Jesus was not saying he was a despised worm, but that he will bleed as he is crushed for our sins.

b 22:12 Many translations have here "strong bulls of Bashan." The root word for "bull" means "to break or destroy." The word *Bashan*, although known as a fertile land northeast of the Sea of Galilee, is also a word for "serpent." These represent the many demonic spirits who came against the Son of God as he was being crucified.

c 22:16 Or "to maul" or "to pierce."

[18] With a toss of the dice they divide my clothes among themselves,
    gambling for my garments!
[19] Lord, my God, please don't stay far away.
    For you are my only might and strength.
    Won't you come quickly to my rescue?
[20] Give me back my life.
    Save me from this violent death.
    Save my precious one and only[a]
    from the power of these demons![b]
[21] Save me from all the power of the enemy,
    from this roaring lion raging against me
    and the power of his dark horde.
[22] I will praise your name before all my brothers;
    as my people gather I will praise you in their midst.[c]
[23] Lovers of Yahweh, praise him!
    Let all the true seed of Jacob glorify him with your praises.
    Stand in awe of him, all you princely people,
    the offspring of Israel!
[24] For he has not despised my cries of deep despair.
    He's my first responder to my sufferings,
    and he didn't look the other way when I was in pain.
    He was there all the time, listening to the song of the afflicted.
[25] You're the reason for my praise; it comes from you and goes to you.
    I will keep my promise to praise you before all who fear you
    among the congregation of your people.
[26] I will invite the poor and broken,
    and they will come and eat until satisfied.
    Bring Yahweh praise and you will find him.
    Your hearts will overflow with life forever!
[27] From the four corners of the earth,
    the peoples of the world will remember and return to the Lord.
    Every nation will come and worship him.
[28] For the Lord is King of all, who takes charge of all the nations.

---

a 22:20 Or "unique" or "darling." Each of us is that *one and only* child and "unique darling" mentioned here in this psalm. See also Song 6:9. On the cross, Jesus—like a deer giving birth at the dawning light (see inscription of Ps. 22)—cared less that his body was being torn apart and more about our protection and salvation. He prayed for us as he faced the death of the cross.

b 22:20 The Hebrew text uses the word *dogs,* which implies evil spirits who were bent on destroying Jesus on the cross. The Hebrew word for "dog" is taken from a root word meaning "to attack."

c 22:22 Between verse 21 and verse 22 the glorious resurrection of Jesus takes place. The music is elevated to a higher key as victory is sounded forth. "My people gather" is a reference to the church that was birthed through his resurrection glory. (See also v. 25.)

[29] There they are! They're worshiping!
  The wealthy of this world will feast in fellowship with him
    right alongside the humble of heart,
  bowing down to the dust, forsaking their own souls.
  They will all come and worship this worthy King!
[30] His *spiritual* seed [a] shall serve him.
  Future generations will hear from us
    about the wonders of the Sovereign Lord.
[31] His generation yet to be born will glorify him.
  And they will all declare, "It is finished!"

23 THE GOOD SHEPHERD

David's poetic praise to God [b]

[1] The Lord is my best friend and my shepherd. [c]
  I always have more than enough.
[2] He offers a resting place for me in his luxurious love. [d]
  His tracks take me to an oasis of peace, the quiet brook of bliss.
[3] That's where he restores and revives my life. [e]
  He opens before me pathways to God's pleasure
    and leads me along in his footsteps of righteousness [f]
  so that I can bring honor to his name.
[4] Lord, even when your path takes me through
    the valley of deepest darkness,
  fear will never conquer me, for you already have!
  You remain close to me and lead me through it all the way.

---

a   22:30 Jesus, our crucified Savior, had no natural offspring. These are the sons and daughters who were birthed by the work of the cross.

b   Most scholars conclude that Ps. 23 was written by David when he was a young shepherd serving his father, Jesse, while he was keeping watch over sheep near Bethlehem. He was most likely sixteen or seventeen years old. The other psalm that he wrote when but a young lad was Ps. 19. Those are two good psalms to memorize and meditate upon if you want to have the heart of the giant killer.

c   23:1 The word most commonly used for "shepherd" is *ra'ah,* which is also the Hebrew word for "best friend." The translation includes both meanings.

d   23:2 The Greek word for "love" is *agape,* which is a merging of two words and two concepts. *Ago* means "to lead like a shepherd," and *pao* is a verb that means "to rest." Love is our Shepherd leading us to the place of true rest in his heart.

e   23:3 Or "He causes my life [or soul, Heb. *nephesh*] to return." So often life drains out of us through our many activities, but David found that God restores our well-being by pursuing what pleases God and resting in him.

f   23:3 Or "circular paths of righteousness." It is a common trait for sheep on the hillsides of Israel to circle their way up higher. They eventually form a path that keeps leading them higher. This is what David is referring to here. Each step we take following our Shepherd will lead us higher, even though it may seem we are going in circles.

Your authority is my strength and my peace. [a]
The comfort of your love takes away my fear.
I'll never be lonely, for you are near.
⁵ You become my delicious feast
even when my enemies dare to fight.
You anoint me with the fragrance of your Holy Spirit; [b]
you give me all I can drink of you until my heart overflows.
⁶ So why would I fear the future?
For your goodness and love pursue me all the days of my life.
Then afterward, when my life is through,
I'll return to your glorious presence to be forever with you!

24 THE GLORIOUS KING

David's poetic praise to God [c]

¹ God claims the world as his.
Everything and everyone belongs to him!
² He's the one who pushed back oceans
to let the dry ground appear,
planting firm foundations for the earth.
³ Who, then, ascends into the presence of the Lord? [d]
And who has the privilege of entering into God's Holy Place?
⁴ Those who are clean—whose works and ways are pure,
whose hearts are true and sealed by the truth,
those who never deceive, whose words are sure.
⁵ They will receive the Lord's blessing
and righteousness given by the Savior-God.
⁶ They will stand before God,
for they seek the pleasure of God's face, [e] the God of Jacob.

Pause in his presence

⁷ So wake up, you living gateways!
Lift up your heads, you ageless doors of destiny!
Welcome the King of Glory,
for he is about to come through you.
⁸ You ask, "Who is this Glory-King?"
The Lord, armed and ready for battle,
the Mighty One, invincible in every way!

---

a 23:4 Or "Your rod and your staff, they comfort me."
b 23:5 The word *oil* becomes a symbol of the Holy Spirit.
c The Septuagint adds "for the Sabbath."
d 24:3 Or "hill of the Lord."
e 24:6 The Hebrew is plural ("faces").

[9] So wake up, you living gateways, and rejoice![a]
    Fling wide, you ageless doors of destiny!
    Here he comes; the King of Glory is ready to come in.
[10] You ask, "Who is this King of Glory?"
    He is the Lord of Victory, armed and ready for battle,
    the Mighty One, the invincible commander of heaven's hosts!
    Yes, he is the King of Glory!

Pause in his presence

25 DON'T FAIL ME, GOD![b]

King David's poetic praise to God

[1] Forever I will lift up my soul into your presence, Lord.
[2] Be there for me, God, for I keep trusting in you.
    Don't allow my foes to gloat over me or
    the shame of defeat to overtake me.
[3] For how could anyone be disgraced
    when he has entwined his heart with you?
    But they will all be defeated and ashamed
    when they harm the innocent.
[4] Lord, direct me throughout my journey
    so I can experience your plans for my life.
    Reveal the life-paths that are pleasing to you.
[5] Escort me along the way; take me by the hand and teach me.
    For you are the God of my increasing salvation;
    I have wrapped my heart into yours![c]
[6-7] Forgive my failures as a young man,
    and overlook the sins of my immaturity.
    Give me grace, Lord! Always look at me
    through your eyes of love—
    your forgiving eyes of mercy and compassion.
    When you think of me, see me as one you love and care for.
    How good you are to me!
[8] When people turn to you,
    they discover how easy you are to please—so faithful and true!

---

a   24:9 The Hebrew text says, "Lift up your heads," which is a figure of speech for rejoicing. We are the living gateways who rejoice as the Lord draws near to us from his temple.

b   Ps. 25–39 are fifteen poetic songs about bringing pure worship before God. Ps. 25–29 speak of our confidence to worship God. Ps. 30–34 point us to receiving life eternal from our Hero-God. The last five, Pss. 35–39, bring us to the importance of personal purity and holiness before God as we worship him in truth.

c   25:5 The Hebrew word most commonly translated as "wait" (wait upon the Lord) is *qavah*, which also means "to tie together by twisting" or "to entwine" or "to wrap tightly." This is a beautiful concept of waiting upon God, not as something passive, but entwining our hearts with him and his purposes.

Joyfully you teach them the proper path,
 even when they go astray.
⁹ Keep showing the humble your path,
 and lead them into the best decision.
 Bring revelation-light that trains them in the truth.
¹⁰ All the ways of the Lord are loving and faithful for those who follow the
  ways of his covenant.
¹¹ For the honor of your name, Lord,
 never count my sins, and forgive them all—
 lift their burden off of my life! ᵃ
¹² But still one question remains:
 How do I live in the holy fear of God?
 Show me the right path to take.
¹³ Then prosperity and favor will be my portion,
 and my descendants will inherit all that is good.
¹⁴ There's a private place reserved for the lovers of God,
 where they sit near him and receive
 the revelation-secrets of his promises. ᵇ
¹⁵ Rescue me, Lord, for you're my only hero.
¹⁶ Sorrows fill my heart as I feel helpless, mistreated—
 I'm all alone and in misery!
 Come closer to me now, Lord, for I need your mercy.
¹⁷ Turn to me, for my problems seem to be going from bad to worse.
 Only you can free me from all these troubles!
¹⁸ Until you lift this burden, the burden of all my sins,
 my troubles and trials will be more than I can handle.
 Can't you feel my pain?
¹⁹ Vicious enemies hate me.
 There are so many, Lord. Can't you see?
²⁰ Will you protect me from their power against me?
 Let it never be said that I trusted you
 and you didn't come to my rescue.
²¹ Your perfection and faithfulness are my bodyguards,
 for you are my hope and I trust in you as my only protection.
²² Zealously, God, we ask you
 to come save Israel from all her troubles,
 for you provide the ransom price for your people! ᶜ

---

a 25:11 The Hebrew word used here for "forgive" or "pardon" is a rare word used only twice
 in the Old Testament and comes from a root word meaning "to lift off a burden."
b 25:14 Or "covenant."
c 25:22 Ps. 25 is an acrostic psalm; that is, in the Hebrew text every verse begins with a progressive
 letter of the alphabet. It is considered a poetic device of Hebrew literature. Go back through

26 DECLARE ME INNOCENT

King David's poetic praise to God

[1] You be my judge and declare me innocent!
  Clear my name, for I have tried my best to keep your laws
    and to trust you without wavering.
[2] Lord, you can scrutinize me.
  Refine my heart and probe my every thought.
  Put me to the test and you'll find it's true.
[3] I will never lose sight of your love for me.
  Your faithfulness has steadied my steps.
[4] I won't keep company with tricky, two-faced men,
  nor will I go the way of those who defraud with hidden motives.
[5] I despise the sinner's hangouts, refusing to even enter them.
  You won't find me walking among the wicked.
[6-7] When I come before you, I'll come clean, [a]
  approaching your altar with songs of thanksgiving,
  singing the songs of your mighty miracles.
[8] Lord, I love your home, this place of dazzling glory,
  bathed in the splendor and light of your presence!
[9] Don't treat me as one of these scheming sinners
  who plot violence against the innocent.
[10] Look how they devise their wicked plans,
  holding the innocent hostage for ransom.
[11] I'm not like them, Lord—not at all.
  Save me, redeem me with your mercy,
  for I have chosen to walk only in what is right.
[12] I will proclaim it publicly in every congregation,
  and because of you, Lord,
  I will take my stand on righteousness alone!

27 FEARLESS FAITH

David's poetic praise to God before he was anointed king [b]

[1] The Lord is my revelation-light to guide me along the way; [c]
  he's the source of my salvation to defend me every day.
  I fear no one!
  I'll never turn back and run from you, Lord;
  surround and protect me.

---

the psalm and notice how almost every verse begins with the next letter of our English
alphabet. See if you can find them. (X was not included.)

a 26:6–7 Or "I wash my hands in innocence."
b Inscription from the Septuagint.
c 27:1 See also John 1:5, 9; 1 John 1:5.

² When evil ones come to destroy me,
   they will be the ones who turn back.
³ My heart will not be afraid even if an army rises to attack.
   I know that you are there for me, so I will not be shaken.
⁴ Here's the one thing I crave from God,
   the one thing I seek above all else:
   I want the privilege of living with him every moment in his house, [a]
   finding the sweet loveliness of his face,
   filled with awe, delighting in his glory and grace.
   I want to live my life so close to him
   that he takes pleasure in my every prayer.
^{5–6} In his shelter in the day of trouble, that's where you'll find me,
   for he hides me there in his holiness.
   He has smuggled me into his secret place,
   where I'm kept safe and secure—
   out of reach from all my enemies.
   Triumphant now, I'll bring him my offerings of praise,
   singing and shouting with ecstatic joy!
   Yes, listen and you can hear
   the fanfare of my shouts of praise to the Lord!
⁷ God, hear my cry. Show me your grace.
   Show me mercy, and send the help I need!
⁸ Lord, when you said to me, "Seek my face,"
   my inner being responded,
   "I'm seeking your face with all my heart."
⁹ So don't hide yourself, Lord, when I come to find you. [b]
   You're the God of my salvation;
   how can you reject your servant in anger?
   You've been my only hope,
   so don't forsake me now when I need you!
¹⁰ My father and mother abandoned me. I'm like an orphan!
   But you took me in and made me yours. [c]
¹¹ Now teach me all about your ways and tell me what to do.
   Make it clear for me to understand,
   for I am surrounded by waiting enemies.
¹² Don't let them defeat me, Lord.
   You can't let me fall into their clutches!

---

a 27:4 A temple had not yet been built when David wrote this psalm. He is saying that he longs to be surrounded with God's presence, enclosed and encircled with holiness.

b 27:9 The Septuagint is "Don't overlook me."

c 27:10 Every child needs four things: acceptance, focused attention, guidance, and protection. All four of these emotional needs are met by God (vv. 7–14).

They keep accusing me of things I've never done
while they plot evil against me.
¹³ Yet I totally trust you to rescue me one more time,
so that I can see once again how good you are while I'm still alive!
¹⁴ Here's what I've learned through it all:
Don't give up; don't be impatient;
be entwined as one with the Lord. *ᵃ*
Be brave and courageous, and never lose hope.
Yes, keep on waiting—for he will never disappoint you!

28 MY STRENGTH AND SHIELD

David's poetic praise to God

¹ I'm pleading with you, Lord, help me! *ᵇ*
Don't close your ears to my cry, for you're my defender.
If you continue to remain aloof and refuse to answer me,
I might as well give up and die.
² Can't you see me turning toward your mercy seat
as I lift my hands in surrendered prayer?
Now, Lord, please listen to my cry.
³ Don't allow me to be punished along with the wicked—
these hypocrites who speak sweetly to their neighbors' faces
while holding evil against them in their hearts.
⁴ Go ahead and punish them as they deserve.
Let them be paid back for all their evil plans
in proportion to their wickedness.
⁵ Since they don't care anything about you,
or about the great things you've done,
take them down like an old building being demolished,
never again to be rebuilt.
⁶ But may your name be blessed and built up!
For you have answered my passionate cry for mercy.
⁷ You are my strength and my shield from every danger.
When I fully trust in you, help is on the way.
I jump for joy and burst forth with ecstatic, passionate praise!
I will sing songs of what you mean to me!
⁸ You will be the inner strength of all your people,
the mighty protector of all,
the saving strength for all your anointed ones.
⁹ Keep protecting and cherishing your chosen ones;

---

a 27:14 Or "wait upon the Lord." See Ps. 25:5 footnote.

b 28:1 This psalm was likely written when David was exiled because of the rebellion of his son Absalom. He was not longing and looking for his throne but for God's throne (v. 2).

in you they will never fall.
Like a shepherd going before us, keep leading us forward,
forever carrying us in your arms!

29 THE GLORY-GOD THUNDERS

King David's poetic praise to God for the last days
The Feast of Tabernacles[a]

[1] Proclaim his majesty, all you mighty champions,
   you sons of Almighty God,
   giving all the glory and strength back to him!
[2] Be in awe before his majesty.
   Be in awe before such power and might!
   Come worship wonderful Yahweh, arrayed in all his splendor,
   bowing in worship as he appears in all his holy beauty.
   Give him the honor due his name.
   Worship him wearing the glory-garments
   of your holy, priestly calling!
[3-4] The voice of the Lord echoes through the skies and seas.
   The Glory-God reigns as he thunders in the clouds.
   So powerful is his voice, so brilliant and bright,
   how majestic as he thunders over the great waters![b]
[5] His tympanic thunder topples the strongest of trees.[c]
   His symphonic sound splinters the mighty forests.
[6] Now he moves Zion's[d] mountains by the might of his voice,[e]
   shaking the snowy peaks with his earsplitting sound!
[7] The lightning-fire flashes, striking as he speaks.
[8] God reveals himself when he makes the fault lines quake,
   shaking deserts, speaking his voice.
[9] God's mighty voice makes the deer to give birth.[f]
   His thunderbolt voice lays the forest bare.
   In his temple all fall before him with each one shouting,
   "Glory, glory, the God of glory!"[g]

---

a The additional words of the inscription are found in the Septuagint. Ps. 29 is one of the loveliest poems ever written. It is pure and unrestrained praise. The name Yahweh (Jehovah) is found eighteen times in eleven verses. David was a prophetic seer, and this psalm can properly be interpreted to speak of God's majesty revealed in the last days.
b 29:3–4 The sea (great waters) is a term often used in the Bible to symbolize the "sea of humanity." See Isa. 57:20; Rev. 17:15.
c 29:5 Trees in the Bible are symbols used for men. The strongest of men are toppled and bowed down when the Glory-God speaks.
d 29:6 Or "Sirion" (Mount Hermon), an ancient term for Mount Zion. See Ps. 133.
e 29:6 The "voice of the Lord" is used seven times (the seven thunders) in this psalm.
f 29:9 Or "God's mighty voice makes the oaks to whirl."
g 29:9 The Septuagint reads "Those who give him glory he carries to his house."

¹⁰ Above the furious flood, *ᵃ* the Enthroned One reigns,
   the King-God rules with eternity at his side.
¹¹ This is the one who gives his strength and might to his people.
   This is the Lord giving us his kiss of peace. *ᵇ*

30 He Healed Me

King David's poetic praise to God
A song for the Feast of Dedication of the dwelling place

¹ Lord, I will exalt you and lift you high,
   for you have lifted me up on high!
   Over all my boasting, gloating enemies,
   you made me to triumph.
² O Lord, my healing God,
   I cried out for a miracle and you healed me!
³ You brought me back from the brink of death,
   from the depths below.
   Now here I am, alive and well, fully restored!
⁴ O sing and make melody, you steadfast lovers of God.
   Give thanks to him every time you reflect on his holiness!
⁵ I've learned that his anger lasts for a moment,
   but his loving favor lasts a lifetime! *ᶜ*
   We may weep through the night,
   but at daybreak it will turn into shouts of ecstatic joy.
⁶⁻⁷ I remember boasting, "I've got it made!
   Nothing can stop me now!
   I'm God's favored one; he's made me steady as a mountain!"
   But then suddenly, you hid your face from me.
   I was panic-stricken and became depressed.
⁸ Still I cried out to you, Lord God. I shouted out for mercy, saying,
⁹ "What would you gain in my death,
   if I were to go down to the depths of darkness?
   Will a grave sing your song?
   How could death's dust declare your faithfulness?"
¹⁰ So hear me now, Lord; show me your famous mercy.
   O God, be my Savior and rescue me!

---

a 29:10 The Hebrew word for "flood" is found thirteen times in the Bible and is always used in connection to man's rebellion and turning away from God. Thirteen is the biblical number signifying apostasy. Sitting as king, he rules even over the dark flood of evil to make it end.

b 29:11 In Jewish synagogues this psalm is read on the first day of the feast of Pentecost. The Christian church was born on Pentecost two thousand years ago when the mighty "storm" of the Spirit came into the upper room. See Acts 2. The last word of this psalm is *peace*. It begins with a storm, but God brings his people peace even in the midst of storms.

c 30:5 The Septuagint says, "There is wrath in his anger but life in his will [promise]."

11 Then he broke through and transformed all my wailing
   into a whirling dance of ecstatic praise!
   He has torn the veil and lifted from me
   the sad heaviness of mourning.
   He wrapped me in the glory garments of gladness.
12 How could I be silent when it's time to praise you?
   Now my heart sings out loud, bursting with joy—
   a bliss inside that keeps me singing,
   "I can never thank you enough!"

31 How Great Is Your Goodness

For the Pure and Shining One
A song of poetic praise, by King David

1 I trust you, Lord, to be my hiding place.
   Don't let me down.
   Don't let my enemies bring me to shame.
   Come and rescue me, for you are the only God
   who always does what is right.
2 Rescue me quickly when I cry out to you.
   At the sound of my prayer may your ear be turned to me.
   Be my strong shelter and hiding place on high.
   Pull me into victory and breakthrough.
3-4 For you are my high fortress, where I'm kept safe.
   You are to me a stronghold of salvation.
   When you deliver me out of this peril,
   it will bring glory to your name.
   As you guide me forth I'll be kept safe
   from the hidden snares of the enemy—
   the secret traps that lie before me—
   for you have become my rock of strength.
5 Into your hands I now entrust my spirit. *a*
   O Lord, the God of faithfulness,
   you have rescued and redeemed me.
6 I despise these deceptive illusions,
   all this pretense and nonsense,
   for I worship only you.
7 In mercy you have seen my troubles and you have cared for me;
   even during this crisis in my soul I will be radiant with joy,
   filled with praise for your love and mercy.
8 You have kept me from being conquered by my enemy;

---

a 31:5 This was quoted by Jesus as he was dying on the cross. See Matt. 27:50.

you broke open the way to bring me to freedom,[a]
into a beautiful, broad place.[b]

[9] O Lord, help me again! Keep showing me such mercy.
For I am in anguish, always in tears,
and I'm worn-out with weeping.
I'm becoming old because of grief; my health is broken.

[10] I'm exhausted! My life is spent with sorrow,
my years with sighing and sadness.
Because of all these troubles, I have no more strength.
My inner being[c] is so weak and frail.

[11] My enemies say, "You are nothing!"
Even my friends and neighbors hold me in contempt!
They dread seeing me
and they look the other way when I pass by.

[12] I am totally forgotten, buried away like a dead man,
discarded like a broken dish thrown in the trash.

[13] I overheard their whispered threats, the slander of my enemies.
I'm terrified as they plot and scheme to take my life.

[14] I'm desperate, Lord! I throw myself upon you,
for you alone are my God!

[15] My life, my every moment, my destiny—it's all in your hands.
So I know you can deliver me
from those who persecute me relentlessly.

[16] Let your shining face shine on me.
Let your undying love and glorious grace
save me from all this gloom.

[17] As I call upon you, let my shame and disgrace
be replaced by your favor once again.
But let shame and disgrace fall instead upon the wicked—
those going to their own doom,
drifting down in silence to the dust of death.

[18] At last their lying lips will be muted in their graves.
For they are arrogant, filled with contempt and conceit
as they speak against the godly.

[19] Lord, how wonderful you are!
You have stored up so many good things for us,
like a treasure chest heaped up and spilling over with blessings—
all for those who honor and worship you!

---

a 31:8 This is a picture of the stone rolled away from the tomb of Jesus.
b 31:8 This could be the throne room where Jesus ascended after his death.
c 31:10 The Hebrew text says, "My bones grow weak." Bones in the Bible are symbols of our inner being.

Everybody knows what you can do
for those who turn and hide themselves in you.
[20] So hide all your beloved ones
in the sheltered, secret place before your face.
Overshadow them by your glory-presence.
Keep them from these accusations, the brutal insults of evil men.
Tuck them safely away in the tabernacle where you dwell.
[21] The name of the Lord is blessed and lifted high!
For his marvelous miracle of mercy protected me
when I was overwhelmed by my enemies.
[22] I spoke hastily when I said, "The Lord has deserted me."
For in truth, you did hear my prayer and came to rescue me.
[23] Listen to me, all you godly ones: Love the Lord with passion!
The Lord protects and preserves all those who are loyal to him.
But he pays back in full all those who reject him in their pride.
[24] So cheer up! Take courage all you who love him.
Wait for him to break through for you, all who trust in him!

32 FORGIVEN

A poem of insight and instruction, by King David. [a]

[1] How happy and fulfilled are those
whose rebellion has been forgiven, [b]
those whose sins are covered *by blood.*
[2] How blessed and relieved are those
who have confessed their corruption [c] to God!
For he wipes their slates clean
and removes hypocrisy from their hearts.
[3] Before I confessed my sins, I kept it all inside;
my dishonesty devastated my inner life,
causing my life to be filled with frustration,
irrepressible anguish, and misery.
[4] The pain never let up, for your hand of conviction
was heavy on my heart.

---

a   David wrote this psalm after he seduced the wife of his most loyal soldier, then had him
killed to try to keep her pregnancy a secret. This sin with Bathsheba brought great disgrace
to David, yet he finds complete forgiveness in God's mercy. The apostle Paul chose the first
two verses of Ps. 32 to support the important doctrine of salvation by grace through faith.
See Rom. 4:5–8. This was Saint Augustine's favorite psalm. He had it written on the wall
near his bed before he died so he could meditate upon it.

b   32:1 The Hebrew word for "forgiven" means "lifted off." Sin's guilt is a burden that must be
lifted off our souls. The Septuagint says, "because they have not hidden their sins."

c   32:2 David uses three Hebrew words to describe sin in these first two verses: *rebellion, sins*
(failures, falling short), and *corruption* (crookedness, the twisting of right standards).

My strength was sapped, my inner life dried up
like a spiritual drought within my soul.

Pause in his presence

⁵ Then I finally admitted to you all my sins,
refusing to hide them any longer.
I said, "My life-giving God,
I will openly acknowledge my evil actions."
And you forgave me!
All at once the guilt of my sin washed away
and all my pain disappeared!

Pause in his presence

⁶ This is what I've learned through it all:
All believers should confess their sins to God;
do it every time God has uncovered you
in the time of exposing.
For if you do this, when sudden storms of life overwhelm,
you'll be kept safe. ᵃ
⁷ Lord, you are my secret hiding place,
protecting me from these troubles,
surrounding me with songs of gladness!
Your joyous shouts of rescue release my breakthrough.

Pause in his presence

⁸⁻⁹ I hear the Lord saying, "I will stay close to you,
instructing and guiding you along the pathway for your life.
I will advise you along the way
and lead you forth with my eyes as your guide.
So don't make it difficult; don't be stubborn
when I take you where you've not been before.
Don't make me tug you and pull you along.
Just come with me!"
¹⁰ So my conclusion is this:
Many are the sorrows and frustrations
of those who don't come clean with God.
But when you trust in the Lord for forgiveness,
his wrap-around love will surround you.
¹¹ So celebrate the goodness of God!
He shows this kindness to everyone who is his.
Go ahead—shout for joy,
all you upright ones who want to please him!

ᵃ 32:6 Prov. 2:13 is a good commentary on this verse.

33 A SONG OF PRAISE

Poetic praise, by King David[a]

¹ It's time to sing and shout for joy!

Go ahead, all you redeemed ones, do it!

Praise him with all you have,

for praise looks lovely on the lips of God's lovers.

² Play the guitar as you lift your praises loaded with thanksgiving.

Sing and make joyous music with all you've got inside.

³ Compose new melodies[b] that release new praises to the Lord.

Play his praises on instruments

with the anointing and skill he gives you.

Sing and shout with passion; make a spectacular sound of joy—

⁴ For God's Word is something to sing about!

He is true to his promises, his word can be trusted,

and everything he does is reliable and right.

⁵ The Lord loves seeing justice on the earth.

Anywhere and everywhere you can find his faithful, unfailing love!

⁶ All he had to do was speak by his Spirit-wind command,

and God created the heavenlies.

Filled with galaxies and stars,

the vast cosmos he wonderfully made.

⁷ His voice scooped out the seas.

The ocean depths he poured into vast reservoirs.

⁸ Now, with breathtaking wonder,

let everyone worship Yahweh, this awe-inspiring Creator.

⁹ Words he breathed and worlds were birthed.

"Let there be," and there it was—

Springing forth the moment he spoke.

No sooner said than done!

¹⁰ With his breath he scatters the schemes of nations who oppose him;

they will never succeed.

¹¹ His destiny-plan for the earth stands sure.

His forever-plan remains in place and will never fail.

¹² Blessed and prosperous is that nation who has God as their Lord!

They will be the people he has chosen for his own.

¹³⁻¹⁵ The Lord looks over us from where he rules in heaven.

Gazing into every heart from his lofty dwelling place,

---

a Most manuscripts have no inscription for this psalm. However, ancient Qumran evidence suggests this is the original inscription that was later omitted.

b 33:3 There are seven new songs mentioned in the Bible. Six are in the Psalms (33:3; 40:3; 96:1; 98:1; 144:9; 149:1) and one in Isaiah (42:10).

he observes all the peoples of the earth.
The Creator of our hearts considers and examines everything we do.
[16] Even if a king has the best-equipped army,
it would never be enough to save him.
Even if the best warrior went to battle,
he could not be saved simply by his strength alone.
[17] Human strength and the weapons of man
are false hopes for victory;
they may seem mighty but they will always disappoint.
[18] The eyes of the Lord are upon
even the weakest worshipers who love him—
those who wait in hope and expectation
for the strong, steady love of God.
[19] God will deliver them from death,
even the certain death of famine, with no one to help.
[20] The Lord alone is our radiant hope
and we trust in him with all our hearts.
His wrap-around presence will strengthen us.
[21] As we trust, we rejoice with an uncontained joy
flowing from Yahweh!
[22] Let your love and steadfast kindness overshadow us
continually, for we trust and we wait upon you!

34 GOD'S GOODNESS

A song by King David composed after his escape from
the king when he pretended to be insane

[1] Lord! I'm bursting with joy over what you've done for me!
My lips are full of perpetual praise.
[2] I'm boasting of you and all your works,
so let all who are discouraged take heart.
[3] Join me, everyone! Let's praise the Lord together.
Let's make him famous!
Let's make his name glorious to all.
[4] Listen to my testimony: I cried to God in my distress
and he answered me. He freed me from all my fears!
[5] Gaze upon him, join your life with his, and joy will come.
Your faces will glisten with glory.
You'll never wear that shame-face again.
[6] When I had nothing, desperate and defeated,
I cried out to the Lord and he heard me,
bringing his miracle-deliverance when I needed it most. [a]

---

a 34:6 David wrote this psalm at perhaps the lowest point in his life. He was alone. He had to

⁷The angel of the Lord stooped down to listen as I prayed,
  encircling me, empowering me, and showing me how to escape.
  He will do this for everyone who fears God.
⁸Drink deeply of the pleasures of this God. ᵃ
  Experience for yourself the joyous mercies he gives
  to all who turn to hide themselves in him.
⁹Worship in awe and wonder, all you who've been made holy!
  For all who fear him will feast with plenty.
¹⁰Even the strong and the wealthy ᵇ grow weak and hungry,
  but those who passionately pursue the Lord
  will never lack any good thing.
¹¹Come, children of God, and listen to me.
  I'll share the lesson I've learned of fearing the Lord. ᶜ
¹²⁻¹³Do you want to live a long, good life,
  enjoying the beauty that fills each day?
  Then never speak a lie or allow wicked words
  to come from your mouth.
¹⁴Keep turning your back on every sin,
  and make "peace" your life motto.
  Practice being at peace with everyone. ᵈ
¹⁵The Lord sees all we do;
  he watches over his friends day and night.
  His godly ones receive the answers they seek
  whenever they cry out to him.
¹⁶But the Lord has made up his mind to oppose evildoers
  and to wipe out even the memory of them
  from the face of the earth.

---

part from Jonathan, his dearest friend. He was being chased by Saul and his paid assassins. He had run to hide in the cave of Adullam (meaning "their prey"). Yet the beautiful sounds of praise were heard echoing in his cavern. This is a lesson for all of us: we praise our way out of our difficulties into his light.

ᵃ 34:8 Many translations read "Taste and see." The Hebrew root word for "see" is taken from a word that means "to drink deeply."

ᵇ 34:10 Following the ancient versions (Septuagint, Syriac, and Vulgate), this phrase is translated "rich ones." Modern translations read "young lions."

ᶜ 34:11 See 1 Peter 3:10–12.

ᵈ 34:14 Twice the Hebrew uses the word shalom. This word means much more than peace. It means wholeness, wellness, well-being, safe, happy, friendly, favor, completeness, to make peace, peace offering, secure, to prosper, to be victorious, to be content, tranquil, quiet, and restful. The pictographic symbols for the word shalom (shin, lamed, vav, mem) read "Destroy the authority that binds to chaos." The noun shalom is derived from the verbal root shalam, which means "to restore," in the sense of replacing or providing what is needed in order to make someone or something whole and complete. So shalom is used to describe those of us who have been provided all that is needed to be whole and complete and break off all authority that would attempt to bind us to chaos.

¹⁷ Yet when holy lovers of God cry out
  to him with all their hearts,
  the Lord will hear them and come to rescue them
  from all their troubles.
¹⁸ The Lord is close to all whose hearts are crushed by pain,
  and he is always ready to restore the repentant one.
¹⁹ Even when bad things happen to the good and godly ones,
  the Lord will save them and not let them be defeated
  by what they face.
²⁰ God will be your bodyguard to protect you
  when trouble is near.
  Not one bone will be broken.
²¹ But the wicked commit slow suicide.
  For they hate and persecute the lovers of God.
  Make no mistake about it,
  God will hold them guilty and punish them;
  they will pay the penalty!
²² But the Lord has paid for the freedom of his servants,
  and he will freely pardon those who love him.
  He will declare them free and innocent
  when they turn to hide themselves in him.

35 RESCUE ME

A poetic song, by King David^a

Part One – David, a Warrior

¹ O Lord, fight for me! Harass the hecklers, accuse my accusers.
  Fight those who fight against me.
^{2–3} Put on your armor, Lord; take up your shield and protect me.
  Rise up, mighty God! Grab your weapons of war
  and block the way of the wicked who come to fight me.
  Stand for me when they stand against me!
  Speak over my soul: "I am your strong Savior!"^b
⁴ Humiliate those who seek my harm. Defeat them all!
  Frustrate their plans to defeat me and drive them back.
  Disgrace them all as they have devised their plans to disgrace me.

_a This is the first of seven Psalms in which David cried out for vengeance upon his enemies
  (Pss. 52, 58, 59, 69, 109, and 137).
_b 35:2–3 The Aramaic word used here is found thirty-three times in the Psalms and is clearly
  Savior. Although a New Testament concept, David had a deep understanding almost one
  thousand years before the Savior was born that God would become his Savior. The Hebrew
  word for "Savior," *Yasha*, is very similar to the name Jesus, Yeshua.

⁵ Blow them away like dust in the wind,
   with the Angel of Almighty God driving them back!
⁶ Make the road in front of them nothing but slippery darkness,
   with the Angel of the Lord behind them, chasing them away!
⁷ For though I did nothing wrong to them, they set a trap for me,
   wanting me to fall and fail.
⁸ Surprise them with your ambush, Lord,
   and catch them in the very trap they set for me.
   Let them be the ones to fail and fall into destruction!
⁹ Then my fears will dissolve into limitless joy;
   my whole being will overflow with gladness
   because of your mighty deliverance.
¹⁰ Everything inside of me will shout it out:
"There's no one like you, Lord!"
   For look at how you protect the weak and helpless
   from the strong and heartless who oppress them.

Part Two – David, a Witness

¹¹ They are malicious men, hostile witnesses of wrong.
   They rise up against me, accusers appearing out of nowhere.
¹² When I show them mercy, they bring me misery.
   I'm forsaken and forlorn, like a motherless child.
¹³ I even prayed over them when they were sick.
   I was burdened and bowed low with fasting
   and interceded for their healing,
   and I didn't stop praying.
¹⁴ I grieved for them, heavyhearted,
   as though they were my dearest family members
   or my good friends who were sick,
   nearing death, needing prayer.
¹⁵ But when I was the one who tripped up and stumbled,
   they came together to slander me,
   rejoicing in my time of trouble, tearing me to shreds
   with their lies and betrayal.
¹⁶ These nameless ruffians,
   mocking me like godless fools at a feast—
   how they delight in throwing mud on my name.
¹⁷ God, how long can you just stand there doing nothing?
   Now is the time to act.
   Rescue me from these brutal men,
   for I am being torn to shreds by these beasts
   who are out to get me.
   Save me from their rage, their cruel grasp.

[18] Then I will praise you wherever I go. [a]
    And when everyone gathers for worship,
    I will lift up your praise with a shout
    in front of the largest crowd I can find!

Part Three – David, a Worshiper

[19] Don't let those who fight me for no reason be victorious.
    Don't let them succeed, these heartless haters
    who come against me with their gloating sneers.
[20] They are the ones who would never seek peace as friends,
    for they are ever devising deceit against the innocent ones
    who mind their own business.
[21] They open their mouths with ugly grins,
    gloating with glee over my every fault.
    "Look," they say, "we caught him red-handed!
    We saw him fall with our own eyes!"
[22] But my caring God, you have been there all along.
    You have seen their hypocrisy.
    God, don't let them get away with this.
    Don't walk away without doing something.
[23] Now is the time to awake! Rise up, Lord!
    Vindicate me, my Lord and my God!
[24] You have every right to judge me, Lord,
    according to your righteousness,
    but don't let them rejoice over me when I stumble.
[25-26] Let them all be ashamed of themselves,
    humiliated when they rejoice over my every blunder.
    Shame them, Lord, when they say, "We saw what he did.
    Now we have him right where we want him.
    Let's get him while he's down!"
    Make them look ridiculous when they exalt themselves over me.
    May they all be disgraced and dishonored!
[27] But let all my true friends shout for joy,
    all those who know and love what I do for you.
    Let them all say, "The Lord is great,
    and he delights in the prosperity of his servant."
[28] Then I won't be able to hold it in—
    everyone will hear my joyous praises all day long!
    Your righteousness will be the theme of my glory-song of praise!

---

a 35:18 The Septuagint says, "My only child, I will save you from the lions."

36 THE BLESSING OF THE WISE

A poetic song, by King David, the servant of the Lord

¹ The rebellion of sin speaks as an oracle of God,
    speaking deeply to the conscience of wicked men. *a*
  Yet they are still eager to sin,
    for the fear of God is not before their eyes.
² See how they flatter themselves,
    unable to detect and detest their sins.
  They are crooked and conceited,
    convinced they can get away with anything.
³ Their wicked words are nothing but lies.
    Wisdom is far from them.
  Goodness is both forgotten and forsaken.
⁴ They lie awake at night to hatch their evil plots,
    always planning their schemes of darkness,
    and never once do they consider the evil of their ways.
⁵ But you, O Lord, your mercy-seat love is limitless,
    reaching higher than the highest heavens.
  Your great faithfulness is infinite,
    stretching over the whole earth.
⁶ Your righteousness is unmovable,
    just like the mighty mountains.
  Your judgments are as full of wisdom
    as the oceans are full of water.
  Your tender care and kindness leave no one forgotten,
    not a man nor even a mouse.
⁷ O God, how extravagant is your cherishing love!
  All mankind can find a hiding place *b*
    under the shadow of your wings.
⁸ All may drink of the anointing *c* from the abundance of your house.
  All may drink their fill from the delightful springs of Eden. *d*
⁹ To know you is to experience a flowing fountain,
    drinking in your life, springing up to satisfy.
  In the light of your holiness we receive the light of revelation. *e*

---

a 36:1 Or "The heart of the wicked is rebellious to the core."
b 36:7 Or "They will be satisfied [or watered] in the abundance of your house."
c 36:8 The Hebrew word for "abundance" is actually *butterfat* or *oil*. It is a symbol of the anointing of the Holy Spirit.
d 36:8 Or "Eden's rivers of pleasure." The garden of Eden had flowing rivers of delight. Eden means "pleasure." The Hebrew word used here is the plural form of Eden, *Edens*.
e 36:9 See John 1:4.

¹⁰ Lord, keep pouring out your unfailing love
  on those who are near you.
  Release more of your blessings to those who are loyal to you.
¹¹ Don't let these proud boasters trample me down;
  don't let them push me around
  by the sheer strength of their wickedness.
¹² There they lie in the dirt, these evil ones,
  thrown down to the ground, never to arise again!

37 A Song of Wisdom

Poetic praise, by King David^a

¹ Don't follow after the wicked ones or be jealous of their wealth.
  Don't think for a moment they're better off than you.
² They *and their short-lived success*
  will soon shrivel up and quickly fade away
  like grass clippings in the hot sun.
³ Keep trusting in the Lord and do what is right in his eyes.
  Fix your heart on the promises of God and you will be secure,
  feasting on his faithfulness.
⁴ Make God the utmost delight and pleasure of your life,^b
  and he will provide for you what you desire the most.
⁵ Give God the right to direct your life,^c
  and as you trust him along the way
  you'll find he pulled it off perfectly!
⁶ He will appear as your righteousness,^d
  as sure as the dawning of a new day.
  He will manifest as your justice,
  as sure and strong as the noonday sun.
⁷ Quiet your heart in his presence and pray;
  keep hope alive as you long for God to come through for you.
  And don't think for a moment that the wicked in their prosperity
  are better off than you.
⁸ Stay away from anger and revenge.
  Keep envy far from you, for it only leads you into lies.
⁹ For one day the wicked will be destroyed,
  but those who trust in the Lord
  will live safe and sound with blessings overflowing.

---

a Ps. 37 is an acrostic psalm, with every other verse beginning with a successive letter of the Hebrew alphabet.
b 37:4 The word *delight* means "to be soft or tender."
c 37:5 The Hebrew uses the word *commit*, which means "to roll over your burdens on the Lord."
d 37:6 The Hebrew verb found here is also used for giving birth. Perhaps this is a reference to the birth of Christ, our righteousness.

¹⁰ Just a little while longer and the ungodly will vanish;
    you will look for them in vain.
¹¹ But the humble of heart will inherit every promise *a*
    and enjoy abundant peace.
¹² Let the wicked keep plotting against the godly
    with all their sneers and arrogant jeers.
¹³ God doesn't lose any sleep over them
    and he knows their day is coming!
¹⁴ Evil ones take aim on the poor and helpless;
    they are ready to slaughter those who do right.
¹⁵ But the Lord will
    turn all their weapons of wickedness back on themselves,
    piercing their pride-filled hearts until they are the helpless.
¹⁶ It is much better to have little
    combined with much of God
    than to have the fabulous wealth of the wicked and nothing else.
¹⁷ For the Lord takes care of all his forgiven ones
    while the strength of the evil will surely slip away.
¹⁸ Day by day the Lord watches the good deeds of the godly
    and he prepares for them his forever-reward.
¹⁹ Even in a time of disaster he will watch over them,
    and they will always have more than enough
    no matter what happens.
²⁰ All the enemies of God will perish.
    For the wicked have only a momentary value, a fading glory.
    Then one day they vanish! Here today, gone tomorrow.
²¹ They break their promises, borrowing money
    but never paying it back.
    The good man returns what he owes with some extra besides.
²² The Lord's blessed ones receive it all in the end,
    but the cursed ones will be cut off
    with nothing to show for themselves.
²³ The steps of the God-pursuing ones
    follow firmly in the footsteps of the Lord,
    and God delights in every step they take to follow him.
²⁴ If they stumble badly they will still survive,
    for the Lord lifts them up with his hands.
²⁵ I was once young, but now I'm old.
    Not once have I found a lover of God forsaken by him,
    nor have any of their children gone hungry.

---

a 37:11 Jesus said it this way: "The meek will inherit the earth." See Matt. 5:5.

²⁶ Instead, I've found the godly ones
 to be the generous ones who give freely to others.
 Their children are blessed and become a blessing.
²⁷ If you truly want to dwell forever in God's presence,
 forsake evil and do what is right in his eyes.
²⁸ The Lord loves it when he sees us walking in his justice.
 He will never desert his devoted lovers;
 they will be kept forever in his faithful care.
 But the descendants of the wicked will be banished.
²⁹ The faithful lovers of God will inherit the earth
 and enjoy every promise of God's care,
 dwelling in peace forever.
³⁰ God-lovers make the best counselors.
 Their words possess wisdom and are right and trustworthy.
³¹ The ways of God are in their hearts
 and they won't swerve from the paths of steadfast righteousness.
³² Evil ones spy on the godly ones, stalking them
 to find something they could use to accuse them.
 They're out for the kill!
³³ But God will foil all their plots.
 The godly will not stand condemned when brought to trial.
³⁴ So don't be impatient for the Lord to act;
 keep moving forward steadily in his ways,
 and he will exalt you *at the right time.*
 And when he does, you will possess every promise,
 including your full inheritance.
 You'll watch with your own eyes
 and see the wicked lose everything.
³⁵ I've already seen this happen.
 Once I saw a wicked and violent man
 overpower all who were around him,
 a domineering tyrant with his pride and oppressive ways.
³⁶ Then he died and was forgotten.
 Now no one cares that he is gone forever.
³⁷ But you can tell who are the blameless and spiritually mature.
 What a different story with them!
 The godly ones will have a peaceful, prosperous future
 with a happy ending.
³⁸ Every evil sinner will be destroyed, obliterated.
 They'll be utter failures with no future!
³⁹ But the Lord will be the Savior of all who love him.
 Even in their time of trouble God will live in them as strength.

[40] Because of their faith in him, their daily portion will be
   a Father's help and deliverance from evil.
   This is true for all who turn to hide themselves in him!

38 A GROAN BEFORE THE THRONE

A poetic lament to remember, by King David[a]

[1] O Lord, don't punish me angrily for what I've done.
   Don't let my sin inflame your wrath against me.
[2] For the arrows of your conviction have pierced me deeply.
   Your blows have struck my soul and crushed me.
[3] Now my body is sick.
   My health is totally broken because of your anger,
   and it's all due to my sins!
[4] I'm overwhelmed, swamped, and submerged
   beneath the heavy burden of my guilt.
   It clings to me and won't let me go.
[5] My rotting wounds are a witness against me.
   They are severe and getting worse,
   reminding me of my failure and folly.
[6] I am completely broken because of what I've done.
   Gloom is all around me.
   My sins have bent me over to the ground.
[7-8] My inner being is shriveled up;
   my self-confidence crushed.
   Sick with fever, I'm left exhausted.
   Now I'm cold as a corpse and nothing is left inside me
   but great groaning filled with anguish.
[9] Lord, you know all my desires and deepest longings.
   My tears are liquid words and you can read them all.
[10-11] My heart beats wildly, my strength is sapped,
   and the light of my eyes is going out.
   My friends stay far away from me, avoiding me like the plague.
   Even my family wants nothing to do with me.
[12] Meanwhile my enemies are out to kill me,
   plotting my ruin, speaking of my doom
   as they spend every waking moment
   planning how to finish me off.
[13-14] I'm like a deaf man who no longer hears.
   I can't even speak up, and words fail me;
   I have no argument to counter their threats.

---

a The Septuagint has in the inscription "To be remembered on the Sabbath."

¹⁵ Lord, the only thing I can do is wait and put my hope in you.
   I wait for your help, my God.
¹⁶ So hear my cry and put an end to their strutting in pride,
   who gloat when I stumble in pain.
¹⁷ I'm slipping away and on the verge of a breakdown,
   with nothing but sorrow and sighing. *ᵃ*
¹⁸ I confess all my sin to you; I can't hold it in any longer.
   My agonizing thoughts punish me for my wrongdoing;
   I feel condemned as I consider all I've done.
¹⁹ My enemies are many.
   They hate me and persecute me,
   though I've done nothing against them to deserve it.
²⁰ I show goodness to them and get repaid evil in return.
   And they hate me even more when I stand for what is right.
²¹ So don't forsake me now, Lord!
   Don't leave me in this condition.
²² God, hurry to help me, run to my rescue!
   For you're my Savior and my only hope!

39 A CRY FOR HELP

For the Pure and Shining One
A song of praising, by King David ᵇ

¹⁻² Here's my life motto, the truth I live by:
   I will guard my ways for all my days.
   I will speak only what is right, guarding what I speak.
   Like a watchman guards against an attack of the enemy,
   I'll guard and muzzle my mouth
   when the wicked are around me.
   I will remain silent and will not grumble
   or speak out of my disappointment.
   But the longer I'm silent the more my pain grows worse!
³⁻⁴ My heart burned with a fire within me,
   and my thoughts eventually boiled over
   until they finally came rolling out of my mouth.
   "Lord, help me to know how fleeting my time on earth is.
   Help me to know how limited is my life
   and that I'm only here but for a moment more.
⁵ What a brief time you've given me to live! ᶜ

---

a 38:17 The Septuagint reads "I am prepared for all of their whips—prepared to suffer."
b The Hebrew inscription includes the name Jeduthun, which can be translated "praising."
c 39:5 Interestingly, the Hebrew word for "short" in this verse is "a handbreadth," or the span
   of a man's hand. Our life's duration is compared to a mere six-inch span!

Compared to you my lifetime is nothing at all!
Nothing more than a puff of air, I'm gone so swiftly.
So too are the grandest of men;
they are nothing but a fleeting shadow!"

Pause in his presence

⁶ We live our lives like those living in shadows. *ᵃ*
All our activities and energies are spent for things that pass away.
We gather, we hoard, we cling to our things,
only to leave them all behind for who knows who.
⁷ And now, God, *ᵇ* I'm left with one conclusion:
my only hope is to hope in you alone!
⁸ Save me from being overpowered by my sin;
don't make me a disgrace before the degenerate.
⁹ Lord, I'm left speechless and I have no excuse,
so I'll not complain any longer.
Now I know you're the one who is behind it all.
¹⁰ But I can't take it much longer.
Spare me these blows from your discipline-rod.
For if you are against me, I will waste away to nothing.
¹¹ No one endures when you rebuke and discipline us for our sins.
Like a cobweb is swept away with a wave of the hand,
you sweep away all that we once called dear.
How fleeting and frail our lives!
We're nothing more than a puff of air.

Pause in his presence

¹² Lord, listen to all my tender cries.
Read my every tear, like liquid words that plead for your help.
I feel all alone at times, like a stranger to you,
passing through this life just like all those before me.
¹³ Don't let me die without restoring
joy and gladness to my soul.
May your frown over my failure
become a smile over my success.

40 A JOYFUL SALVATION

For the Pure and Shining One
A song of poetic praise, by King David
¹ I waited and waited and waited some more,
patiently, knowing God would come through for me.
Then, at last, he bent down and listened to my cry.

---

a 39:6 Or "like phantoms going to and fro."
b 39:7 The Aramaic is Maryah, the Aramaic form of YHWH or Lord Jehovah.

² He stooped down to lift me out of danger
  from the desolate pit I was in,
  out of the muddy mess I had fallen into.
  Now he's lifted me up into a firm, secure place
  and steadied me while I walk along his ascending path.
³ A new song for a new day rises up in me
  every time I think about how he breaks through for me!
  Ecstatic praise pours out of my mouth until
  everyone hears how God has set me free.
  Many will see his miracles;
  they'll stand in awe of God and fall in love with him!
⁴ Blessing after blessing comes to those who love and trust the Lord.
  They will not fall away,
  for they refuse to listen to the lies of the proud.
⁵ O Lord, our God, no one can compare with you.
  Such wonderful works and miracles are all found with you!
  And you think of us all the time
  with your countless expressions of love—
  far exceeding our expectations!
⁶ It's not sacrifices that really move your heart.
  Burnt offerings, sin offerings—that's not what brings you joy.
  But when you open my ears and speak deeply to me,
  I become your willing servant, your prisoner of love for life. ᵃ
⁷ So I said, "Here I am! I'm coming *to you as a sacrifice,* ᵇ
  for in the prophetic scrolls of your book
  you have written about me.
⁸ I delight to fulfill your will, my God,
  for your living words are written upon the pages of my heart."
⁹ I tell everyone everywhere the truth of your righteousness.
  And you know I haven't held back in telling the message to all.
¹⁰ I don't keep it a secret or hide the truth.
  I preach of your faithfulness and kindness,
  proclaiming your extravagant love to the largest crowd I can find!
¹¹ So Lord, don't hold back your love or withhold
  your tender mercies from me.
  Keep me in your truth and let your compassion overflow to me
  no matter what I face.
¹² Evil surrounds me; problems greater than I can solve

---

a 40:6 The Septuagint is "a body you have prepared for me." The Hebrew says, "You have pierced my ear." This is a Hebraic reference to being a bond servant whose ear has been pierced by his master to signify a desire to serve for life. See Ex. 21:1–6; Isa. 50:5; Heb. 10:5.

b 40:7 Implied in the context. See Heb. 10:5–7.

come one after another.
Without you, I know I can't make it.
My sins are so many!
I'm so ashamed to lift my face to you.
For my guilt grabs me and stings my soul
until I am weakened and spent.
[13] Please, Lord! Come quickly and rescue me!
Take pleasure in showing me your favor and restore me.
[14] Let all who seek my life be humiliated!
Let them be confused and ashamed, God.
Scatter those who wish me evil; they just want me dead.
[15] Scoff at every scoffer and cause them all to be utter failures.
Let them be ashamed and horrified by their complete defeat.
[16] But let all who passionately seek you
erupt with excitement and joy over what you've done!
Let all your lovers rejoice continually in the Savior,[a] saying,
"How great and glorious is our God!"
[17] Lord, in my place of weakness and need, I ask again:
Will you come and help me?
I know I'm always in your thoughts.
You are my true Savior and hero,
so don't delay to deliver me now, for you are my God.

41 I NEED YOU, LORD

King David's poetic song for the Pure and Shining One

[1] God always blesses those who are kind to the poor and helpless.
They're the first ones God helps
when they find themselves in any trouble.
[2] The Lord will preserve and protect them.
They'll be honored and esteemed[b]
while their enemies are defeated.
[3] When they are sick, God will restore them,
lying upon their bed of suffering.
He will raise them up again and restore them back to health.
[4] So *in my sickness* I say to you,
"Lord, be my kind healer.
Heal my body and soul; heal me, God!
For I have confessed my sins to you."[c]
[5] But those who hate me wish the worst for me, saying,

---

a 40:16 This verse contains the root word for Yeshua in Hebrew.
b 41:2 Or "They will be blessed in the land."
c 41:4 Or "For I have sinned against you."

"When will he die and be forgotten?"

6 And when these "friends" come to visit me
   with their pious sympathy and their hollow words
   and with hypocrisy hidden in their hearts,
   I can see right through it all.
   For they come merely to gather gossip about me,
   using all they find to mock me with malicious hearts of slander.

7 They are wicked whisperers who imagine the worst for me,
   repeating their rumors, saying,

8 "He got what he deserved; it's over for him!
   The spirit of infirmity[a] is upon him and
   he'll never get over this illness."

9 Even my ally, my friend, has turned against me.
   He was one I totally trusted with my life,
   sharing supper with him,[b]
   and now he shows me nothing but betrayal and treachery.
   He has sold me as an enemy.[c]

10 So Lord, please don't desert me when I need you!
   Give me grace and get me back on my feet
   so I can triumph over them all.

11 Then I'll know you're pleased with me
   when you allow me to taste of victory over all my foes.

12 Now stand up for me and don't let me fall,
   for I've walked with integrity.
   Keep me before your face forever.

13 Everyone praise the Lord God of Israel, always and forever!
   For he is from eternity past
   and will remain for the eternity to come.
   That's the way it will be forever.
   Faithful is our King! Amen![d]

---

a 41:8 Or "a thing of Belial" or "an affliction from the abandoned one."

b 41:9 In the culture of that day, sharing a meal together was a sign of covenant friendship.

c 41:9 The Hebrew literally reads "He lifted up his heel against me." This is a powerful figure of speech meaning he was sold as an enemy and was treated treacherously. This verse was quoted, in part, by Jesus at the Last Supper (John 13:18).

d 41:13 Some scholars believe this last verse was added as a "doxology of praise," marking the end of the first book of Psalms. The word *amen* means "Faithful is our King!"

BOOK 2

THE EXODUS PSALMS
Psalms of suffering and redemption

42 A Cry for Revival [a]

For the Pure and Shining One
A contemplative poem for instruction,
by the prophetic singers of Korah's clan [b]

[1] I long to drink of you, O God,
   drinking deeply from the streams of pleasure
   flowing from your presence.
   My longings overwhelm me for more of you! [c]
[2] My soul thirsts, pants, and longs for the living God.
   I want to come and see the face of God.
[3] Day and night my tears keep falling
   and my heart keeps crying for your help
   while my enemies mock me over and over, saying,
   "Where is this God of yours? *Why doesn't he help you?*"
[4] So I speak over my heartbroken soul,
   "Take courage. Remember when you used to be
   right out front leading the procession of praise
   when the great crowd of worshipers
   gathered to go into the presence of the Lord?
   You shouted with joy as the sound of passionate celebration
   filled the air and the joyous multitude of lovers
   honored the festival of the Lord!"
[5] So then, my soul, why would you be depressed?
   Why would you sink into despair?
   Just keep hoping and waiting on God, your Savior.
   For no matter what, I will still sing with praise,
   for living before his face is my saving grace!
[6] Here I am depressed and downcast.
   Yet I will still remember you as I ponder the place

---

a   Ps. 42 and 43 were originally composed as one psalm and later made into two.
b   Korah was the great-grandson of Levi. The sons of Korah were a family of Levitical
     singers. David chose them to preside over the music of the tabernacle-tent on Mount
     Zion.
c   42:1 The literal Hebrew is "as the deer pants for the riverbank [water's edge]." The trans-
     lation takes the metaphor of a hunted deer and puts it into terms that transfer the mean-
     ing into today's context. David is describing the passion and longing he has that is yet
     unfulfilled.

where your glory streams down from the mighty mountaintops, lofty and
   majestic—*the mountains of your awesome presence.* [a]
[7] My deep need calls out to the deep kindness of your love.
   Your waterfall of weeping sent waves of sorrow
   over my soul, carrying me away,
   cascading over me like a thundering cataract.
[8] Yet all day long God's promises of love pour over me.
   Through the night I sing his songs,
   for my prayer to God has become my life.
[9] I will say to God, "You are my mountain of strength;
   how could you forget me?
   Why must I suffer this vile oppression of my enemies—
   these heartless tormentors who are out to kill me?"
[10] Their wounding words pierce my heart
   over and over while they say,
   "Where is this God of yours?"
[11] So I say to my soul,
"Don't be discouraged. Don't be disturbed.
   For I know my God will break through for me."
   Then I'll have plenty of reasons to praise him all over again.
   Yes, living before his face is my saving grace!

43 LIGHT AND TRUTH

For the Pure and Shining One, by the prophetic singers of Korah's clan [b]
A contemplative poem for instruction
[1] God, clear my name.
   Plead my case against the unjust charges
   of these ungodly workers of wickedness.
   Deliver me from these lying degenerates.
[2] For you are where my strength comes from [c] and my protector,
   so why would you leave me now?
   Must I be covered with gloom
   while the enemy comes after me, gloating with glee?
[3] Pour into me the brightness of your daybreak!
   Pour into me your rays of revelation-truth!
   Let them comfort and gently lead me onto the shining path,
   showing the way into your burning presence,
   into your many sanctuaries of holiness.

---

a 42:6 The Hebrew text contains *Mount Hermon* and *Mount Mizar*, considered to be sacred
   mountains in the Hebrew culture. *Hermon* means lofty and majestic. *Mizar* means littleness.
b Although there is no inscription for this psalm, it was originally part of Ps. 42.
c 43:2 Or "God of my strength."

4 Then I will come closer to your very altar
    until I come before you, the God of my ecstatic joy!
    I will praise you with the harp that plays in my heart,
    to you, my God, my magnificent God!
5 Then I will say to my soul,
    "Don't be discouraged; don't be disturbed,
    for I fully expect my Savior-God to break through for me.
    Then I'll have plenty of reasons to praise him all over again."
    Yes, living before his face is my saving grace!

44 WAKE UP, LORD, WE'RE IN TROUBLE

For the Pure and Shining One, by the prophetic singers of Korah's clan
A contemplative poem for instruction

The Past

1-2 God, we've heard about all the glorious miracles
    you've done for our ancestors in days gone by.
    They told us about the ancient times, how by your power
    you drove out the ungodly nations from this land,
    crushing all their strongholds and giving the land to us.
    Now the people of Israel cover the land
    from one end to the other,
    all because of your grace and power!
3 Our forefathers didn't win these battles by their own strength
    or their own skill or strategy.
    But it was through the shining forth of your radiantpresence
    and the display of your mighty power.
    You loved to give them victory,
    for you took great delight in them.
4 You are my God, my King!
    It's now time to decree majesties for Jacob!
5 Through your glorious name and your awesome power
    we can push through to any victory and defeat every enemy.
6 For I will not trust in the weapons of the world;[a]
    I know they will never save me.
7 Only you will be our Savior from all our enemies.
    All those who hate us you have brought to shame.
8 So now I constantly boast in you.
    I can never thank you enough!

Pause in his presence

---

a 44:6 Or "bow and sword."

The Present

⁹ But you have turned your back on us; you walked off and left us!
> You've rejected us, tossing us aside in humiliating shame.
> You don't go before us anymore in our battles.

¹⁰ We retreat before our enemies in defeat,
> for you are no longer helping us.
> Those who hate us have invaded our land
> and plundered our people.

¹¹ You have treated us like sheep in the slaughter pen,
> ready to be butchered.
> You've scattered us to the four winds.

¹² You have sold us as slaves for nothing!
> You have counted us, your precious ones, as worthless.

¹³ You have caused our neighbors to despise and scorn us.
> All that are around us mock and curse us.

¹⁴ You have made us the butt of their jokes.
> Disliked by all, we are the laughingstock of the people.

¹⁵⁻¹⁶ There's no escape from this constant curse, this humiliation!
> We are despised, jeered, overwhelmed by shame,
> and overcome at every turn
> by our hateful and heartless enemies.

¹⁷ Despite all of this, we have not forgotten you;
> we have not broken covenant with you.

¹⁸ We have not betrayed you; our hearts are still yours.
> Our steps have not strayed from your path.

¹⁹ Yet you have crushed us,
> leaving us in this wilderness place *of misery and desperation.*[a]
> With nowhere else to turn,
> death's dark door seems to be the only way out.

²⁰⁻²¹ If we had forsaken your holy name, wouldn't you know it?
> You'd be right in leaving us.
> If we had worshiped before other gods,
> no one would blame you for punishing us.
> God, you know our every heart secret.
> *You know we still want you!*

²² Because of you we face death threats every day.
> Like martyrs we are dying daily.
> We are seen as lambs lined up to be slaughtered as sacrifices.

---

a 44:19 Or "in this place of jackals."

The Future

²³ So wake up, Lord God!
   Why would you sleep when we're in trouble?
   Are you forsaking us forever?

²⁴ You can't hide your face any longer from us!
   How could you forget our agonizing sorrow?

²⁵ Now we lay facedown, sinking into the dust of death,
   the quicksand of the grave.

²⁶ Arise, awake, and come to help us, O Lord.
   Let your unfailing love save us from this sorrow!

45 THE WEDDING SONG

For the Pure and Shining One, by the prophetic singers of Korah's clan
A contemplative song of instruction for the Loved One
To the melody of "Lilies"[a]

¹ My heart is on fire, boiling over with passion.
   Bubbling up within me are these beautiful lyrics
   as a lovely poem to be sung for the King.
   Like a river bursting its banks, I'm overflowing with words,
   spilling out into this sacred story.[b]

His Royal Majesty

² Beautiful! Beautiful! Beyond the sons of men![c]
   Elegant grace pours out through every word you speak.[d]
   Truly God has anointed you, his favored one, for eternity!

³ Now strap your lightning-sword of judgment upon your side,
   O mighty warrior, so majestic!
   You are full of beauty and splendor as you go out to war!

⁴ In your glory and grandeur go forth in victory!
   Through your faithfulness and meekness
   the cause of truth and justice will stand.
   Awe-inspiring miracles are accomplished by your power,
   leaving everyone dazed and astonished!

⁵ Your wounding leaves men's hearts defeated
   as they fall before you broken.

---

a   Lilies in the Bible are metaphors of God's precious people. See Song 2:1–2; Hos. 14:5;
    Luke 12:27–28. Many believe this was the wedding song composed for Solomon as he married
    the princess of Egypt. But the language is so lofty and glorious that we see one greater than
    Solomon in its verses. This is a song of the wedding of Jesus and his Bride, the church.

b   45:1 The Hebrew is literally "My tongue is the pen of a skillful [inspired] scribe."

c   45:2 Or "You are the most wonderful and winsome of all men."

d   45:2 See John 6:68 and 7:46.

⁶ Your glory-kingdom, O God, endures forever,
    for you are enthroned to rule with a justice-scepter in your hand!
⁷ You are passionate for righteousness and you hate lawlessness.
    This is why God, your God,
    crowns you with bliss above your fellow kings.
    He has anointed you, more than any other,
    with his oil of fervent joy,
    the very fragrance of heaven's gladness.
⁸ Your royal robes release the scent of suffering love for your bride;ᵃ
    the odor of aromatic incense is upon you.ᵇ
    From the pure and shining place,ᶜ lovely music
    that makes you glad is played for your pleasure.

Her Royal Majesty

⁹ The daughters of kings, women of honor,
    are maidens in your courts.
    And standing beside you,
    glistening in your pure and golden glory,
    is the beautiful bride-to-be!ᵈ
¹⁰ Now listen, daughter, pay attention, and forget about your past.
    Put behind you every attachment to the familiar,
    even those who once were close to you!
¹¹ For your royal Bridegroom is ravished by your beautiful brightness.
    Bow in reverence before him, for he is your Lord!
¹² Wedding presents pour in from those of great wealth.ᵉ
    The royal friends of the Bridegroom shower you with gifts.
¹³ As the princess bride enters the palace,
    how glorious she appears within the holy chamber,
    robed with a wedding dress embroidered with pure gold!
¹⁴ Lovely and stunning she leads the procession with all her bridesmaidsᶠ
    as they come before you, her Bridegroom King.
¹⁵ What a grand, majestic entrance!
    A joyful, glad procession as they enter the palace gates!

---

a 45:8 The Hebrew word *myrrh* is taken from a root word that means "suffering." Jewish rabbis refer to myrrh as "tears from a tree," a symbol of suffering love.

b 45:8 The text reads "aloes and cassia." Both are equated with the anointing spice, the incense burned in the Holy Place.

c 45:8 Or "from the ivory palaces." This is an obvious reference to the Holy Place, as our High Priest comes from the chamber of glory to be with us. The word *ivory* is taken from a Hebrew word for "white and glistening."

d 45:9 Or "queen."

e 45:12 The Hebrew text is literally "the daughter of Tyre." This was symbolic of the merchants of the earth, those possessing great wealth.

f 45:14 Or "virgins." See Rev. 14:1–4 and 2 Cor. 11:2.

[16] Your many sons will one day be kings, just like their Father.
   They will sit on royal thrones all around the world.
[17] I will make sure the fame of your name
   is honored in every generation as all the people praise you,
   giving you thanks forever and ever!

46 GOD ON OUR SIDE

For the Pure and Shining One, by the prophetic singers of Korah's clan
A poetic song to the melody of "Hidden Things"[a]

[1] God, you're such a safe and powerful place to find refuge!
   You're a proven help in time of trouble—
   more than enough and always available whenever I need you.
[2] So we will never fear
   even if every structure of support[b] were to crumble away.
   We will not fear even when the earth quakes and shakes,
   moving mountains and casting them into the sea.
[3] For the raging roar of stormy winds and crashing waves
   cannot erode our faith in you.

Pause in his presence

[4] God has a constantly flowing river whose sparkling streams
   bring joy and delight to his people.
   His river flows right through the city of God Most High,
   into his holy dwelling places.[c]
[5] God is in the midst of his city,[d] secure and never shaken.
   At daybreak his help will be seen with the appearing of the dawn.
[6] When the nations are in uproar with their tottering kingdoms,
   God simply raises his voice
   and the earth begins to disintegrate before him.
[7] *Here he comes!*
   The Commander!
   The mighty Lord of Angel Armies is on our side.
   The God of Jacob fights for us!

Pause in his presence

---

a As translated in the Septuagint. Other versions read "for the maidens." Ps. 46 is known as
   one of the Songs of Zion. The others are Psalms 48, 76, 84, 87, and 122. These are psalms
   that praise Jerusalem as God's dwelling place.

b 46:2 Or "earth itself."

c 46:4 The plural "dwelling places" points to believers today. Each believer is now the holy
   dwelling place of God. God's river flows into us and through us.

d 46:5 This is a reference to Jerusalem, but today God calls his church a "city" on a hill.

⁸⁻⁹ Everyone look!
    Come and see the breathtaking wonders of our God.
    For he brings *both* ruin *and* revival.
    He's the one who makes conflicts end
    throughout the earth,
    breaking and burning every weapon of war.
¹⁰ Surrender your anxiety! [a]
    Be silent and stop your striving and you will see that I am God.
    I am the God above all the nations,
    and I will be exalted throughout the whole earth.
¹¹ Here he stands!
    The Commander!
    The mighty Lord of Angel Armies is on our side!
    The God of Jacob fights for us!

Pause in his presence

47 THE KING OF ALL THE EARTH

For the Pure and Shining One, by the prophetic singers of Korah's clan
A poetic song

¹ Go ahead and celebrate!
    Come on and clap your hands, everyone!
    Shout to God with the raucous sounds of joy!
² The Lord God Most High is astonishing, awesome beyond words!
    He's the formidable and powerful King over all the earth.
³ He's the one who conquered the nations before us
    and placed them all under our feet.
⁴ He's marked out our inheritance ahead of time,
    putting us in the front of the line, honoring Jacob, the one he loves. [b]

Pause in his presence

⁵ God arises with the earsplitting shout of his people!
    God goes up with a trumpet blast!
⁶ Sing and celebrate! Sing some more, celebrate some more!
    Sing your highest song of praise to our King!
⁷ For God is the triumphant King; the powers of earth are all his.
    So sing your celebration songs of highest praise
    to the glorious Enlightened One!
⁸ Our God reigns over every nation.
    He reigns on his holy throne over all.
⁹ All the nobles and princes,

---

a   46:10 The Septuagint reads "relax."
b   47:4 Or "the pride of Jacob." The Septuagint says, "the beauty of Jacob."

the loving servants of the God of Abraham,
they all gather to worship.
Every warrior's shield is now lowered
as surrendered trophies before this King.
He has taken his throne, high and lofty, exalted over all!

48 BEAUTIFUL ZION

A poetic song, for the prophetic singers of Korah's clan

[1] There are so many reasons to describe God as wonderful!
So many reasons to praise him with unlimited praise! [a]

[2] Zion-City is his home; he lives on his holy mountain—
high and glorious, joy filled and favored.
Zion-Mountain looms in the farthest reaches of the north, [b]
the city of our incomparable King!

[3] This is his divine abode, an impenetrable citadel,
for he is known to dwell in the highest place.

[4-6] See how the mighty kings united to come against Zion,
yet when they saw God manifest in front of their eyes,
they were stunned.
Trembling, they all fled away, gripped with fear. [c]
Seized with panic, they doubled up in frightful anguish
like a woman in the labor pains of childbirth.

[7] Like a hurricane blowing and breaking the invading ships, [d]
God blows upon them and breaks them to pieces.

[8] We have heard about these wonders,
and then we saw them with our own eyes.
For this is the city of the Commander of Angel Armies,
the city of our God, safe and secure forever!

Pause in his presence

[9] Lord, as we worship you in your temple,
we recall over and over your kindness to us
and your unending love.

[10] The fame of your name echoes throughout the entire world,
accompanied with praises.
Your right hand is full of victory.

---

a   48:1 This psalm was written to commemorate the defeat of the Assyrian army in the days of King Hezekiah.

b   48:2 Or "the sides of the north," a metaphor to describe God's heavenly home. See also Isa. 14:13.

c   48:4–6 This no doubt refers to the night the angel of the Lord descended into the ranks of the Assyrians and killed 185,000 men. See Isa. 37:36.

d   48:7 Or "ships of Tarshish."

¹¹ So let the people of Zion rejoice with gladness;
     let the daughters of praise leap for joy!*ᵃ*
     For God will see to it that you are judged fairly.
¹²⁻¹³ Circle Zion; count her towers.
     Consider her walls, climb her palaces,
     and then go and tell the coming generation
     of the care and compassion of our God.
¹⁴ Yes, this is our God, our great God forever.
     He will lead us onward until the end,
     through all time, beyond death,
     and into eternity!

49 WISDOM BETTER THAN WEALTH

For the Pure and Shining One
A poetic song, by the prophetic singers of Korah's clan

¹⁻² Listen, one and all!
     Both rich and poor together, all over the world—
     everyone listen to what I have to say!
³ For wisdom will come from my mouth;
     words of insight and understanding will be heard
     from the musings of my heart.
⁴ I will break open mysteries with my music,
     and my song will release riddles solved.
⁵ There's no reason to fear when troubling times come,
     even when you're surrounded with problems
     and persecutors who chase at your heels. *ᵇ*
⁶⁻⁷ They trust in their treasures and boast in their riches,
     yet not one of them, though rich as a king,
     could rescue his own brother from the guilt of his sins.
     Not one could give God the ransom price
     for the soul of another, let alone for himself.
⁸⁻⁹ A soul's redemption is too costly and precious
     for anyone to pay with earthly wealth.
     The price to pay is never enough
     to purchase eternal life for even one, to keep them out of hell.
¹⁰⁻¹¹ The brightest and best, along with the foolish and senseless,
     God sees that they all will die one day,
     leaving their houses and wealth to others.
     Even though they name streets and lands after themselves, *ᶜ*

---

a 48:11 Or "the daughters of Judah."
b 49:5 This phrase contains a variant form of the name Jacob, which means "heel grabber."
c 49:10–11 Or "They read their names in the ground."

hoping to have their memory endure beyond the grave,
    legends in their own minds,
    their home address is now the cemetery!
[12] The honor of man is short-lived and fleeting.
    There's little difference between man and beast,
    for both will one day perish.
[13] Such is the path of foolish men
    and those who quote everything they say,
    for they are here today and gone tomorrow!

Pause in his presence

[14] A shepherd called "Death" herds them,
    leading them like mindless sheep straight to hell.
    Yet at daybreak you will find the righteous ruling in their place.
    Every trace of them will be gone forever,
    with all their "glory" lost in the darkness of their doom.
[15] But I know the loving God will redeem my soul,
    raising me up from the dark power of death,
    taking me as his bridal partner.[a]

Pause in his presence

[16] So don't be disturbed when you see the rich
    surround you with the "glory" of their wealth on full display.
[17] For when they die they will carry nothing with them,
    and their riches will not follow them beyond the grave.
[18-19] Though they have the greatest rewards of this world
    and all applaud them for their accomplishments,
    they will follow those who have gone before them
    and go straight into the realm of darkness,
    where they never ever see the light again.
[20] So this is the way of mortal man—
    honored for a moment, yet without eternal insight,
    like a beast that will one day perish.

50 GOD HAS SPOKEN

A poetic song of Asaph, the gatherer[b]
[1] The God of gods, the mighty Lord himself, has spoken!
    He shouts out over all the people of the earth
    in every brilliant sunrise and every beautiful sunset,
    saying, "Listen to me!"

---

a 49:15 Or "He will offer his hand to me in marriage."
b Asaph's name means "gatherer." Like David, Asaph was anointed with the spirit of proph-
    ecy and wrote twelve psalms (Pss. 50 and 73–83).

[2] God's glory-light shines out of the Zion-realm [a]
   with the radiance of perfect beauty.
[3] With the rumble of thunder he approaches;
   he will not be silent, for he comes with an earsplitting sound!
   All around him are furious flames of fire,
   and preceding him is the dazzling blaze of his glory.
[4] Here he comes to judge his people!
   He summons his court with heaven and earth as his jury, saying,
[5] "Gather all my lovers,
   my godly ones whose hearts are one with me—
   those who have entered into my holy covenant
   by sacrifices upon the altar."
[6] And the heavens declare his justice:
"God himself will be their judge,
   and he will judge them with righteousness!"

Pause in his presence

[7] "Listen to me, O my people! Listen well, for I am your God!
   I am bringing you to trial and here are my charges. [b]
[8] I do not rebuke you for your sacrifices,
   which you continually bring to my altar.
[9] Do I need your young bull or goats from your fields
   as if I were hungry?
[10-11] Every animal of field and forest belongs to me, the Creator.
   I know every movement of the birds in the sky,
   and every animal of the field is in my thoughts.
   The entire world and everything it contains is mine.
[12-13] If I were hungry, do you think I would tell you?
   For all that I have created, the fullness of the earth, is mine.
   Am I fed by your sacrifices? Of course not!
[14] Why don't you bring me the sacrifices I desire?
   Bring me your true and sincere thanks,
   and show your gratitude by keeping your promises to me,
   the Most High.
[15] Honor me by trusting in me in your day of trouble.
   Cry aloud to me, and I will be there to rescue you.
[16] And now I speak to the wicked. Listen to what I have to say to you!
   What right do you have to presume to speak for me
   and claim my covenant promises as yours?

---

a 50:2 The Aramaic text can be translated "Out of Zion God has shown a glorious crown."

b 50:7 This summons to judgment is not against the heathen nations but against God's people. See 1 Peter 4:17.

¹⁷ For you have hated my instruction and disregarded my words,
　　throwing them away as worthless!
¹⁸ You forget to condemn the thief or adulterer.
　　You are their friend, running alongside them into darkness.
^{19–20} The sins of your mouth multiply evil.
　　You have a lifestyle of lies,
　　　devoted to deceit as you speak against others,
　　　even slandering those of your own household!
²¹ All this you have done and I kept silent,
　　so you thought that I was just like you, sanctioning evil.
　　But now I will bring you to my courtroom
　　and spell out clearly my charges before you.
²² This is your last chance, my final warning. Your time is up!
　　Turn away from all this evil, or *the next time you hear from me*
　　will be when I am coming to pass sentence upon you.
　　I will snatch you away and no one will be there
　　to help you escape my judgment.
²³ The life that pleases me is a life lived in the gratitude of grace,
　　always choosing to walk with me in what is right.
　　This is the sacrifice I desire from you.
　　If you do this, more of my salvation will unfold for you."

51　PARDON AND PURITY

For the Pure and Shining One

A prayer of confession when the prophet Nathan exposed King David's adultery
with Bathsheba ^a

David's Confession

^{1–2} God, give me mercy from your fountain of forgiveness!
　　I know your abundant love is enough to wash away my guilt.
　　Because your compassion is so great,
　　take away this shameful guilt of sin.
　　Forgive the full extent of my rebellious ways,
　　and erase this deep stain on my conscience. ^b
^{3–4} For I'm so ashamed.
　　I feel such pain and anguish within me.

---

a　This psalm is based on the incident that is recorded in 2 Sam. 12–13. This is a psalm of
　confession that has been sung for ages. Imagine composing a song about your failure and
　making it public for all time. David was not so much concerned about what the people
　thought but what God thought. He wanted to be clean before God.

b　51:1–2 Or "Wash me." David uses the Hebrew word *kabas*, which is used for washing
　clothes, not bathing. David is asking for his royal robes to be cleansed from the stains of his
　actions and publicly restored.

I can't get away from the sting of my sin against you, Lord!
Everything I did, I did right in front of you, for you saw it all.
Against you, and you above all, have I sinned.
Everything you say to me is infallibly true
and your judgment conquers me.
⁵ Lord, I have been a sinner from birth,
from the moment my mother conceived me.
⁶ I know that you delight to set your truth deep in my spirit.ᵃ
So come into the hidden places of my heart
and teach me wisdom.

David's Cleansing

⁷ Purify my conscience! Make this leper clean again!ᵇ
Wash me in your love until I am pure in heart.ᶜ
⁸ Satisfy me in your sweetness, and my song of joy will return.
The places within me you have crushed
will rejoice in your healing touch.ᵈ
⁹ Hide my sins from your face;ᵉ
erase all my guilt by your saving grace.
¹⁰ Create a new, clean heart within me.ᶠ
Fill me with pure thoughts and holy desires, ready to please you.ᵍ
¹¹ May you never reject me!
May you never take from me your sacred Spirit!

David's Consecration

¹² Let my passion for life be restored,
tasting joyʰ in every breakthrough you bring to me.
Hold me close to you with a willing spirit

---

a 51:6 The Hebrew word *bat-ṭuhôt*, although difficult to translate, can mean "something that is covered over, hidden, or concealed." You could paraphrase this as "You desire light in my darkness" or "You want truth to expose my secrets."

b 51:7 The Hebrew text contains the word *hyssop*. This was a bushy plant used for sprinkling blood on a healed leper to ceremonially cleanse him for the worship of God. See Lev. 14:3–7 and Num. 19.

c 51:7 Or "Wash me with the snow from above so I can be whitened."

d 51:8 In this beautiful verse, the "broken places" are literally "broken bones." Our bones speak allegorically of our inner being, our emotional strength.

e 51:9 David was not just ashamed of what others would think but that he had been seen by God. True remorse has no thought about reputation but righteousness.

f 51:10 The word used for "create" takes us back to Gen. 1, and it means to create from nothing. David knew he had no goodness without God placing it within him. David wanted a new creation heart, not just the old one changed.

g 51:10 Or "renew a reliable spirit in my inner being."

h 51:12 The Hebrew word for "joy" comes from two Hebrew roots: one means "bright" and

that obeys whatever you say.

[13] Then I can show to other guilty ones
    how loving and merciful you are.
    They will find their way back home to you,
    knowing that you will forgive them.

[14] O God, my saving God,
    deliver me fully from every sin,
    even the sin that brought bloodguilt. [a]
    Then my heart will once again be thrilled to sing
    the passionate songs of joy and deliverance!

[15] Lord God, unlock my heart, unlock my lips,
    and I will overcome with my joyous praise!

[16] For the source of your pleasure is not in my performance
    or the sacrifices I might offer to you.

[17] The fountain of your pleasure is found
    in the sacrifice of my shattered heart before you.
    You will not despise my tenderness
    as I humbly bow down at your feet.

[18] Because you favor Zion, do what is good for her.
    Be the protecting wall around Jerusalem.

[19] And when we are fully restored,
    you will rejoice and take delight
    in every offering of our lives
    as we bring our sacrifices of righteousness before you in love! [b]

52 THE FATE OF CYNICS

For the Pure and Shining One

*A song of instruction by King David composed when Doeg, the Edomite, betrayed
David to Saul, saying, "David has come to the house of Ahimilech!"* [c]

[1] You call yourself a mighty man, a big shot?
    Why do you boast in the evil you have done?
    Yet God's loyal love will protect me and carry the day!

---

the other means "lily [whiteness]." David wanted to taste a joy that was bright, pure, and
as beautiful as a lily.

a 51:14 Or simply "blood." David could be asking God to spare his life from death (lit. "blood";
  that is, deliverance from death because of his sin).

b 51:19 Or "Then they will offer up bulls on your altar."

c For this episode in David's life, see 1 Sam. 21:1–9; 22:9–23. The Edomites, although close
  relatives to the Hebrews, were bitter enemies to God's people. In spite of Doeg's lineage,
  he became a high-ranking official in Saul's kingdom. Herod the Great, who slaughtered the
  babes of Bethlehem, was an Edomite. At the time David wrote this psalm, Saul had already
  attempted to kill him sixteen times. Ahimilech, the caretaker of the sword of Goliath, was
  a descendant of Eli.

[2] Listen, O deceiver, trickster of others:
Your words are wicked, harming and hurting all who hear them.
[3] You love evil and hate what is good and right.
You would rather lie than tell the truth.

Pause in his presence

[4] You love to distort, devour, and deceive,
using your sly tongue to spin the truth.
[5] But the Almighty will strike you down forever!
He will pull you up by your roots
and drag you away to the darkness of death.

Pause in his presence

[6] The godly will see all this and will be awestruck.
Then they will laugh at the wicked, saying,
[7] "See what happens to those great in their own eyes
who don't trust in the Most High to save them!
Look how they trusted only in their wealth
and made their living from wickedness." [a]
[8] But I am like a flourishing olive tree, *anointed* in the house of God. [b]
I trust in the unending love of God;
his passion toward me is forever and ever.
[9] Because it is finished [c]
I will be praising you forever and giving you thanks.
Before all your godly lovers I will proclaim your beautiful name!

53 THE WICKEDNESS OF THE WORLD

For the Pure and Shining One
A contemplative song of instruction to the tune of "The Dancings of Mourning" [d]

[1] Only the withering soul would say to himself, [e]
"There's no God for me!"
Anyone who thinks like that is corrupt and callous;
depraved and detestable, they are devoid of what is good.

---

a 52:7 Or "and was strong in his destruction."
b 52:8 The olive tree was the source of the sacred anointing oil.
c 52:9 Or "You have acted [finished it]." The words "It is finished" were the last words of Jesus on the cross.
d Or "The Dance of Mourning." This could have been a footnote to Ps. 52 instead of an inscription for Ps. 53. If so, read Ps. 52 and imagine the dancing that broke loose when David and his mighty men knew that Doeg had been judged by God for his murderous betrayal.
e 53:1 The word for "fool" comes from a Hebrew word meaning "withering." If we make no room for God, we have withered hearts, our moral sense of righteousness is put to sleep, and the noble aspirations of the heart shrivel up and die. Ps. 53 clearly speaks of the downfall of those who oppose Israel. Ps. 14 and Ps. 53 are nearly similar psalms. Ps. 14 deals with God's verdict, while Ps. 53 speaks of God's vengeance. If God says it once, it is to be believed. If he says it twice, it demands our utmost attention!

[2] The Lord looks down in love, bending over heaven's balcony.
    God looks over all of Adam's sons and daughters,
    looking to see if there are any who are wise with insight—
    any who search for him, wanting to please him.
[3] But no, all have wandered astray, walking stubbornly toward evil.
    Not one is good; he can't even find one!
[4] Look how they live in luxury while exploiting my people.
    Won't these workers of wickedness ever learn!
    They never even think of praying to God.
[5] Soon, unheard-of terror will seize them while in their sins.
    God himself will one day scatter the bones
    of those who rose up against you. [a]
    Doomed and rejected, they will be put to shame,
    for God has despised them.
[6] Oh, I wish our time of rescue were already here.
    Oh, that God would come forth now— [b]
    arising from the midst of his Zion-people
    to save and restore his very own.
    When God fully restores his people,
    Jacob will rejoice and Israel will be filled with gladness!

54 DEFEND ME

For the Pure and Shining One, David's contemplative song of instruction
A song of derision [c] when the Ziphites betrayed David to Saul, saying, "David is hiding among us; come and get him!"

[1] God, deliver me by your mighty name!
    Come with your glorious power and save me!
[2] Listen to my prayer; turn your ears to my cry!
[3] These violent men have risen up against me;
    heartless, ruthless men [d] who care nothing about God
    seek to take my life.

Pause in his presence

[4] But the Lord God has become my divine helper.
    He leans into my heart and lays his hands upon me! [e]

---

a 53:5 This could refer to the scattering of the armies of Sennacherib in the days of Hezekiah. See 2 Kings 18–19.

b 53:6 This is considered to be an ecphonesis, a rhetorical literary device that amplifies the emotion of the text. It is equivalent to an emotional outburst. Clearly, this is a passionate psalm.

c The Hebrew word used here and translated in some versions as "stringed instrument" can also be rendered "a song of mocking." This is a psalm for anyone who feels betrayed, rejected, and in a difficult situation with no one at his side.

d 54:3 Or "foreigners."

e 54:4 The word used here is *uphold* or *sustain*. It comes from a root word that means "to lean upon or to lay hands upon." The translation uses both concepts in this verse.

⁵ God will see to it that those who sow evil will reap evil.
So Lord, in your great faithfulness, destroy them once and for all!
⁶ Lord, I will offer myself freely, and everything I am I give to you.
I will worship and praise your name, O Lord,
for it is precious to me.
⁷ Through you I'm saved—rescued from every trouble.
I've seen with my eyes the defeat of my enemies.
I've triumphed over them all!

55 BETRAYED

To the Pure and Shining One
King David's song of derision, for instruction

¹ God, listen to my prayer!
Don't hide your heart from me when I cry out to you!
²⁻³ Come close to me and give me your answer.
Here I am, moaning and restless.
I'm preoccupied with the threats of my enemies
and crushed by the pressure of their opposition.
They surround me with trouble and terror.
In their fury they rise up against me in an angry uproar.
⁴ My heart is trembling inside my chest
as the terror of death seizes me.
⁵ Fear and dread overwhelm me. I shudder before the horror I face.
⁶ I say to myself, "If only I could fly away from all of this!
If only I could run away to the place of rest and peace.
⁷ I would run far away where no one could find me,
escaping to a wilderness retreat."

Pause in his presence

⁸ I will hurry off to hide in the higher place,
into my shelter, safe from this raging storm and tempest."
⁹ God, confuse them until they quarrel with themselves.
Destroy them with their own violent strife and slander.
They have divided the city with their discord.
¹⁰ Though they patrol the walls night and day against invaders,
the real danger is within the city.
It's the misery and strife in the hearts of its people.
¹¹ Murder is in their midst.
Wherever you turn you find trouble and ruin.
¹² It wasn't an enemy who taunted me.
If it was my enemy, filled with pride and hatred,
then I could have endured it. I would have just run away.
¹³ But it was you, my intimate friend—one like a brother to me.

It was you, my advisor,[a] the companion
I walked with and worked with!

[14] We once had sweet fellowship with each other.
We worshiped in unity as one,
celebrating together with God's people.[b]

[15] Now desolation and darkness has come upon you.
May you and all those like you descend into the pit of destruction!
Since evil has been your home, may evil now bury you alive!

[16] But as for me, I will call upon the Lord to save me, and I know he will!

[17] Every evening I will explain my need to him.
Every morning I will move my soul toward him.
Every waking hour I will worship only him,
and he will hear and respond to my cry.

[18] Though many wish to fight and the tide of battle turns against me,
by your power I will be safe and secure;
peace will be my portion.

[19] God himself will hear me!
God-Enthroned through everlasting ages,
the God of unchanging faithfulness—
he will put them in their place,
all those who refuse to love and revere him!

Pause in his presence

[20] I was betrayed by my friend, though I lived in peace with him.
While he was stretching out his hand of friendship,
he was secretly breaking every promise he had ever made to me!

[21] His words were smooth and charming.
Yet his heart was disloyal and full of hatred—
his words soft as silk while all the time scheming my demise.

[22] So here's what I've learned through it all:
Leave all your cares and anxieties at the feet of the Lord,
and measureless grace will strengthen you.

[23] He will watch over his lovers,
never letting them slip or be overthrown.
He will send all my enemies to the pit of destruction.
Murderers, liars, and betrayers will face an untimely death.
My life's hope and trust is in you, and you'll never fail to rescue me!

---

a   55:13 The Greek word in the Septuagint can be translated as "a seer [prophet]."

b   55:14 David is speaking of Ahithophel, who had once been his friend and advisor, only to
betray him. This is foreshadowing of what happened between Jesus and Judas.

56 Trusting in God

For the Pure and Shining One

King David's golden song of instruction composed when the Philistines captured him in Gath, to the tune of "The Oppression of the Princes to Come". [a]

1 Lord, show me your kindness and mercy,
   for these men oppose and oppress me all day long.

2 Not a day goes by but that somebody harasses me.
   So many in their pride trample me under their feet. [b]

3 But in the day that I'm afraid, I lay all my fears before you
   and trust in you with all my heart.

4 What harm could a man bring to me?
   With God on my side I will not be afraid of what comes.
   The roaring praises of God fill my heart,
   and I will always triumph as I trust his promises.

5 Day after day cruel critics distort my words;
   constantly they plot my collapse.

6 Lurking in the dark, waiting, spying on my movements in secret
   to take me by surprise, ready to take my life.

7 They don't deserve to get away with this!
   Look at their wickedness, their injustice, Lord.
   In your fierce anger cast them down to defeat.

8 You've kept track of all my wandering and my weeping.
   You've stored my many tears in your bottle—not one will be lost.
   For they are all recorded in your book of remembrance. [c]

9 The very moment I call to you for a father's help
   the tide of battle turns and my enemies flee.
   This one thing I know: God is on my side!

10 I trust in the Lord. And I praise him!
    I trust in the Word of God. And I praise him!

11 What harm could man do to me?
    With God on my side I will not be afraid of what comes.
    My heart overflows with praise to God and for his promises.
    I will always trust in him.

12 So I'm thanking you with all my heart,
    with gratitude for all you've done.
    I will do everything I've promised you, Lord.

13 For you have saved my soul from death
    and my feet from stumbling

---

a Or "the distant dove of silence."
b 56:2 The Septuagint says, "They war with me in the high places."
c 56:8 See also Mal. 3:16.

so that I can walk before the Lord
bathed in his life-giving light.

57 TRIUMPHANT FAITH

To the Pure and Shining One
King David's golden song of instruction composed
when he hid from Saul in a cave [a]
To the tune of "Do Not Destroy"

[1] Please, God, show me mercy!
Open your grace-fountain for me,
for you are my soul's true shelter.
I will hide beneath the shadow of your embrace,
under the wings of your cherubim,
until this terrible trouble is past.
[2] I will cry out to you, the God of the highest heaven,
the mighty God, who performs all these wonders for me.
[3] From heaven he will *send a father's help to* save me.
He will trample down those who trample me.

Pause in his presence

He will always show me love
by his gracious and constant care.
[4] I am surrounded by these fierce and brutal men.
They are like lions just wanting to tear me to shreds.
Why must I continue to live among these seething terrorists,
breathing out their angry threats and insults against me?
[5] Lord God, be exalted as you soar throughout the heavens.
May your shining glory be seen in the skies!
Let it be seen high above over all the earth!
[6] For they have set a trap [b] for me.
Frantic fear has me overwhelmed.
But look! The very trap they set for me
has sprung shut upon themselves instead of me!

Pause in his presence

[7] My heart, O God, is quiet and confident.
Now I can sing with passion your wonderful praises!
[8] Awake, O my soul, with the music of his splendor-song!
Arise, my soul, and sing his praises!
My worship will awaken the dawn,
greeting the daybreak with my songs *of light*!

---

a This incident is recorded in 1 Sam. 24.
b 57:6 The Septuagint says, "They have dug a cesspool in front of me."

[9] Wherever I go I will thank you, my God.
  Among all the nations they will hear my praise songs to you.
[10] Your love is so extravagant it reaches to the heavens,
  Your faithfulness so astonishing it stretches to the sky!
[11] Lord God, be exalted as you soar throughout the heavens.
  May your shining glory be shown in the skies!
  Let it be seen high above all the earth!

58 JUDGE OF THE JUDGES

For the Pure and Shining One
King David's golden song of instruction
To the tune of "Do Not Destroy"

[1-2] God's justice? You high and mighty politicians
  know nothing about it!
  Which one of you has walked in justice toward others?
  Which one of you has treated everyone right and fair?
  Not one! You only give "justice" in exchange for a bribe.
  For the right price you let others get away with murder.
[3-4] Wicked wanderers even from the womb, that's who you are!
  Lying with your words, your teaching is poison. [a]
[5] Like cobras closing their ears to the most expert of the charmers,
  you strike out against all who are near.
[6] O God, break their fangs;
  shatter the teeth of these ravenous lions!
[7] Let them disappear like water falling on thirsty ground.
  Let all their weapons be useless.
[8] Let them be like snails dissolving into the slime.
  Let them be cut off, never seeing the light of day!
[9] God will sweep them away so fast
  that they'll never know what hit them. [b]
[10] The godly will celebrate in the triumph of good over evil.
  And the lovers of God will trample
  the wickedness of the wicked under their feet!
[11] Then everyone will say, "There is a God who judges the judges"
  and "There is a great reward in loving God!"

---

a 58:3–4 The Hebrew says, "venom of a serpent," which is a clear metaphor for wrong teaching.
b 58:9 The Hebrew here is recognized by nearly every scholar to be one of the most difficult verses in the Psalms to translate.

59 Protect Me

For the Pure and Shining One

King David's song of instruction composed when Saul set an ambush for him at his home [a]

To the tune of "Do Not Destroy"

¹ My God, protect me!

Keep me safe from all my enemies, for they're coming to kill me.

Put me in a high place out of their reach—

a place so high that these assassins will never find me.

² Save me from these murdering men, these bloodthirsty killers.

³ See how they set an ambush for my life.

They're fierce men ready to launch their attack against me.

O Lord, I'm innocent; *protect me!*

⁴ I've done nothing to deserve this,

yet they are already plotting together to kill me.

Arise, Lord, see what they're scheming, and come and meet with me.

⁵ Awaken, O God of Israel!

Commander of Angel Armies,

arise to punish these treacherous people who oppose you!

Don't go soft on these hardcase killers!

Pause in his presence

⁶ After dark they came to spy, sneaking around the city,

snarling, prowling like a pack of stray dogs in the night—

⁷ boiling over with rage, shouting out their curses,

convinced that they'll never get caught.

⁸ But you, Lord, break out laughing at their plans,

amused by their arrogance, scoffing at their sinful ways.

⁹ My strength is found when I wait upon you.

Watch over me, God, for you are my mountain fortress;

you set me on high!

¹⁰ The God of passionate love will meet with me.

My God will empower me to rise in triumph over my foes.

¹¹ Don't kill them; stagger them all with a vivid display of power.

And scatter them with your armies of angels,

O mighty God, our protector!

Use your awesome power to make them wanderers and vagabonds

and then bring them down.

¹² They are nothing but proud, cursing liars.

They sin in every word they speak, boasting in their blasphemies!

---

a This incident is recorded in 1 Sam. 19:11–18.

¹³ May your wrath be kindled to destroy them; finish them off!
   Make an end of them and their deeds until they are no more!
   Let them all know and learn
   that God is the ruler over Jacob,
   the God-King over all the earth!

Pause in his presence

¹⁴ Here they come again—
   prowling, growling like a pack of stray dogs in the city.
¹⁵ Drifting, devouring, and coming in for the kill,
   they refuse to sleep until they've eaten their fill.
¹⁶ But as for me, your strength shall be my song of joy.
   At each and every sunrise, my lyrics of your love will fill the air!
   For you have been my glory-fortress,
   a stronghold in my day of distress.
¹⁷ O my strength, I sing with joy your praises.
   O my stronghold, I sing with joy your song!
   O my Savior, I sing with joy the lyrics of your faithful love for me!

60 HAS GOD FORGOTTEN US?

To the Pure and Shining One
King David's poem for instruction ᵃ *composed when he fought against the*
Syrians with the outcome still uncertain and Joab turned back to kill 12,000
descendants of Esau in the Valley of Salt
To the tune of "Lily of the Covenant"

¹ God, it seems like you walked off and left us!
   Why have you turned against us?
   You have been angry with us.
   O Lord, we plead, come back and help us *as a father.*
² The earth quivers and quakes before you,
   splitting open and breaking apart.
   Now come and heal it, for it is shaken to its depths.
³ You have taught us hard lessons
   and made us drink the wine of bewilderment.
⁴ You have given miraculous signs to those who love you.
   As we follow you we fly the flag of truth,
   and all who love the truth will rally to it.

Pause in his presence

⁵ Come to your beloved ones and gently draw us out.
   For Lord, you save those whom you love.

---

a Or "According to Shushan Eduth. A Mikhtam of David, to teach." There is no scholarly
  consensus about what Shushan Eduth means. Some have concluded it refers to a specific
  tune or possibly an instrument, but it remains a mystery.

Come with your might and strength!

6-7 Then I heard the Lord speak in his holy splendor.
From his sanctuary I heard the Lord promise:
"In my triumph I will be the one to measure out
the portion of my inheritance to my people,
and I will secure the land as I promised you.
Shechem, Succoth, Gilead, Manasseh,
they are all still mine!" he says.
"Judah will continue to produce kings and lawgivers,
and Ephraim will produce great warriors.

8 Moab will become my lowly servant.
Edom will likewise serve my purposes.
I will lift up a shout of victory over the land of Philistia!

9 But who will bring my triumph into the strong city?
Who will lead me into Edom's fortresses?" [a]

10 Have you really rejected us, refusing to fight our battles?

11 Give us a father's help when we face our enemies.
For to trust in any man is an empty hope.

12 With God's help we will fight like heroes
and he will trample down our every foe!

61 PRAYER FOR PROTECTION

To the Pure and Shining One
A song for the guitar by King David

1 O God, hear my prayer. Listen to my heart's cry.

2 For no matter where I am, even when I'm far from home,
I will cry out to you for a father's help.
When I'm feeble and overwhelmed by life,
guide me into your glory, where I am safe and sheltered.

3 Lord, you are a paradise of protection to me.
You lift me high above the fray.
None of my foes can touch me
when I'm held firmly in your wrap-around presence!

4 Keep me in this glory.
Let me live continually under your splendor-shadow,
hiding my life in you forever.

Pause in his presence

5 You have heard my sweet resolutions
to love and serve you, for I am your beloved.
And you have given me an inheritance of rich treasures,

---

a 60:9 Edom is a variant form of the name Adam.

which you give to all your lovers.

⁶ You treat me like a king, giving me a full and abundant life,
   years and years of reigning, [a]
   like many generations rolled into one.

⁷ I will live enthroned with you forever!
   Guard me, God, with your unending, unfailing love.
   Let me live my days walking in grace and truth before you.

⁸ And my praises will fill the heavens forever,
   fulfilling my vow to make every day a love gift to you!

62 UNSHAKABLE FAITH

To the Pure and Shining One
King David's melody of love's celebration [b]

¹ I stand silently to listen for the one I love,
   waiting as long as it takes for the Lord to rescue me.
   For God alone has become my Savior.

² He alone is my safe place;
   his wrap-around presence always protects me.
   For he is my champion defender;
   there's no risk of failure with God.
   So why would I let worry paralyze me,
   even when troubles multiply around me?

³ But look at these who want me dead,
   shouting their vicious threats at me!
   The moment they discover my weakness
   they all begin plotting to take me down.

⁴ Liars, hypocrites, with nothing good to say.
   All of their energies are spent
   on moving me from this exalted place.

Pause in his presence

⁵ I am standing in absolute stillness, silent before the one I love,
   waiting as long as it takes for him to rescue me.
   Only God is my Savior, and he will not fail me.

⁶ For he alone is my safe place.
   His wrap-around presence always protects me
   as my champion defender.
   There's no risk of failure with God!
   So why would I let worry paralyze me,
   even when troubles multiply around me?

---

a 61:6 Or "add to the days of the king."
b The inscription includes the name Jeduthun, which means "one who praises."

⁷ God's glory is all around me!
  His wrap-around presence is all I need,
  for the Lord is my Savior, my hero, and my life-giving strength.
⁸ Join me, everyone! Trust only in God every moment!
  Tell him all your troubles and pour out your heart-longings to him.
  Believe me when I tell you—he will help you!

Pause in his presence

⁹ Before God all the people of the earth, high or low,
  are like smoke that disappears,
  like a vapor that quickly vanishes away.
  Compared to God they're nothing but vanity, nothing at all!
¹⁰ The wealth of the world is nothing to God.
  So if your wealth increases, don't be boastful or
  put your trust in your money.
  And don't you think for a moment that
  you can get away with stealing by overcharging others
  just to get more for yourself!
¹¹ God said to me once and for all,
  "All the strength and power you need flows from me!"
  And again I heard it clearly said,
¹² "All the love you need is found in me!"
  And it's true that you repay people for what they do.

63 THIRSTING FOR GOD

For the Pure and Shining One
King David's song when he was exiled in the Judean wilderness

¹ O God of my life, I'm lovesick for you in this weary wilderness.
  I thirst with the deepest longings to love you more,
  with cravings in my heart that can't be described.
  Such yearning grips my soul for you, my God!
² I'm energized every time I enter
  your heavenly sanctuary to seek more of your power
  and drink in more of your glory.
³ For your tender mercies mean more to me than life itself.
  How I love and praise you, God!
⁴ Daily I will worship you passionately and with all my heart.
  My arms will wave to you like banners of praise.
⁵ I overflow with praise when I come before you,
  for the anointing of your presence satisfies me like nothing else.
  You are such a rich banquet of pleasure to my soul.
⁶⁻⁷ I lie awake each night thinking of you
  and reflecting on how you help me like a father.

I sing through the night under your splendor-shadow,
offering up to you my songs of delight and joy!
[8] With passion I pursue and cling to you.
Because I feel your grip on my life,
I keep my soul close to your heart.
[9] Those who plot to destroy me shall descend into the darkness of hell.
[10] They will be consumed by their own evil
and become nothing more than dust under our feet.[a]
[11] These liars will be silenced forever!
But with the anointing of a king I will dance and rejoice
along with all his lovers who trust in him.

64 THE DESTROYER DESTROYED

For the Pure and Shining One
King David's song

[1-2] Lord, can't you hear my cry, my bitter complaint?
Keep me safe from this band of criminals and
from the conspiracy of these wicked men.
They gather in their secret counsel to destroy me.
[3-4] Can't you hear their slander, their lies?
Their words are like poison-tipped arrows
shot from the shadows.
They are unafraid and have no fear of consequences.
[5] They set their traps against us in secret;
they strengthen one another, saying,
"No one can see us. Who can stop us?"
They're nothing more than unruly mobs
joined in their unholy alliance,
[6] searching out new opportunities to pervert justice—
deceivers scheming together their ill-conceived plot
as they plan the "perfect crime."
How unsearchable is their endless evil,
trying desperately to hide the deep darkness of their hearts.
[7] But all the while God has his own fire-tipped arrows!
Suddenly, without warning,
they will be pierced and struck down.
[8] Staggering backward they will be destroyed
by the very ones they spoke against.
All who see this will view them with scorn.
[9] Then all will stand awestruck over what God has done,

---

a 63:10 Or "food for foxes."

seeing how he vindicated the victims of these crimes.
[10] The lovers of God will be glad, rejoicing in the Lord.
They will be found in his glorious wrap-around presence,
singing songs of praise to God!

65 What a Savior

For the Pure and Shining One
King David's poetic song

[1-2] O God in Zion, to you even silence is praise!
You are the God who answers prayer; [a]
all of humanity comes before you with their requests.
[3] Though we are overcome by our many sins,
your sacrifice covers over them all.
[4] And your priestly lovers, those you've chosen,
will be greatly favored to be brought close to you.
What inexpressible joys are theirs!
What feasts of mercy fill them in your heavenly sanctuary!
How satisfied we will be just to be near you!
[5] You answer our prayers with amazing wonders
and with awe-inspiring displays of power.
You are the righteous God who helps us like a father.
Everyone everywhere looks to you,
for you are the confidence of all the earth,
even to the farthest islands of the sea.
[6] What jaw-dropping, astounding power is yours!
You are the mountain maker who sets them all in place.
[7] You muzzle the roar of the mighty seas
and the rage of mobs with their noisy riots.
[8] O God, to the farthest corners of the planet
people will stand in awe,
startled and stunned by your signs and wonders.
Sunrise brilliance and sunset beauty
both take turns singing their songs of joy to you.
[9] Your visitations of glory bless the earth; [b]
the rivers of God overflow and enrich it.
You paint the wheat fields golden as you provide rich harvests.
[10] Every field is watered with the abundance of rain—
showers soaking the earth and softening its clods,
causing seeds to sprout throughout the land.
[11] You crown the earth with its yearly harvest,

---

a 65:1–2 The Aramaic could be translated "To you a vow is paid."
b 65:9 The Septuagint says, "You've made the earth drunk with your visitations."

the fruits of your goodness.
Wherever you go the tracks of your chariot wheels drip with oil.
[12] Luxuriant green pastures boast of your bounty
  as you make every hillside blossom with joy.
[13] The grazing meadows are covered with flocks,
  and the fertile valleys are clothed with grain,
  each one dancing and shouting for joy, creation's celebration!
  And they're all singing their songs of praise to you!

66 THANK YOU, LORD

For the Pure and Shining One
A song of awakening [a]

[1] Everyone everywhere, lift up your joyful shout to God!
[2] Sing your songs tuned to his glory!
  Tell the world how wonderful he is.
[3] For he's the awe-inspiring God, great and glorious in power!
  We've never seen anything like him!
  Mighty in miracles, you cause your enemies to tremble.
  No wonder they all surrender and bow before you!
[4] All the earth will bow down to worship;
  all the earth will sing your glories forever!

Pause in his presence

[5] Everyone will say, "Come and see the incredible things God has done;
  it will take your breath away!
  He multiplies miracles for his people!" [b]
[6] He made a highway going right through the Red Sea
  as the Hebrews passed through on dry ground,
  exploding with joyous excitement over the miracles of God.
[7] In his great and mighty power he rules forever,
  watching over every movement of every nation.
  So beware, rebel lands; he knows how to humble you!

Pause in his presence

[8] Praise God, all you peoples.
  Praise him everywhere and let everyone know you love him!
[9] There's no doubt about it; God holds our lives safely in his hands.
  He's the one who keeps us faithfully following him.
[10] O Lord, we have passed through your fire;
  like precious metal made pure,
  you've proved us, perfected us, and made us holy.

---

a As translated from the inscription found in the Septuagint.
b 66:5 The Septuagint says, "His works are more to be feared than the decisions of men."

¹¹ You've captured us, ensnared us in your net.
  Then, like prisoners, you *placed chains around our necks.* ᵃ
¹² You've allowed our enemies to prevail against us.
  We've passed through fire and flood,
    yet in the end you always bring us out better than we were before,
    saturated with your goodness. ᵇ
¹³ I come before your presence with my sacrifice.
  I'll give you all that I've promised, everything I have.
¹⁴ When I was overcome in my anguish,
  I promised to give you my sacrifice.
  Here it is! All that I said I would offer you is yours.
¹⁵ The best I have to bring, I'll throw it all into the fire
  as the fragrance of my sacrifice ascends unto you. ᶜ

                                          Pause in his presence

¹⁶ All you lovers of God who want to please him,
  come and listen, and I'll tell you what he did for me.
¹⁷ I cried aloud to him with all my heart and he answered me!
  Now my mouth overflows with the highest praise.
¹⁸ Yet if I had closed my eyes to my sin,
  the Lord God would have closed his ears to my prayer.
¹⁹ But praises rise to God,
  for he paid attention to my prayer and answered my cry to him!
²⁰ I will forever praise this God who didn't close his heart when I prayed
  and never said no when I asked him for help.
  He never once refused to show me his tender love.

67 It's Time to Praise Him

For the Pure and Shining One
A poetic song of praise for guitar
¹ God, keep us near your grace-fountain and bless us!
And when you look down on us, may your face beam with joy!

                                          Pause in his presence

² Send us out all over the world so that everyone everywhere
  will discover your ways and know who you are
  and see your power to save.
³ Let all the nations burst forth with praise;
  let everyone everywhere love and enjoy you!
⁴ Then how glad the nations will be when you are their King.

---

a 66:11 Or "You attached suffering to our hips."
b 66:12 Or "You brought us out into a wide-open space [a place of rest]."
c 66:15 The literal Hebrew describes the sacrifice as "burnt offerings of fat beasts and the
   smoke of rams, bulls, and male goats."

They will sing, they will shout, for you give true justice to the people.
Yes! You, Lord, are the shepherd of the nations!

Pause in his presence

⁵ No wonder the peoples praise you!
Let all the people praise you more! [a]
⁶ The harvest of the earth is here!
God, the very God we worship,
keeps us satisfied at his banquet of blessings.
⁷ And the blessings keep coming!
Then all the ends of the earth will give him
the honor he deserves and be in awe of him!

68 A SONG OF TRIUMPH

For the Pure and Shining One
David's poetic song of praise

¹ God! Arise with awesome power,
and every one of your enemies will scatter in fear!
² Chase them away—all these God-haters.
Blow them away as a puff of smoke.
Melt them away like wax in the fire.
One good look at you and the wicked vanish.
³ But let all your godly lovers be glad!
Yes, let them all rejoice in your presence
and be carried away with gladness. [b]
Let them laugh and be radiant with joy!
⁴ Let them sing their celebration-songs
for the coming of the cloud rider whose name is Yah! [c]
⁵⁻⁶ To the fatherless he is a father.
To the widow he is a champion friend.
To the lonely he gives a family.
To the prisoners [d] he leads into prosperity until they sing for joy.
This is our Holy God in his Holy Place!
But for the rebels there is heartache and despair. [e]
⁷ O Lord, it was you who marched in front of your people,
leading them through the wasteland.

Pause in his presence

---

a 67:5 The Septuagint says, "Let all the people come to know you."
b 68:3 As translated from the Septuagint. The Aramaic is "They rejoice in his sweetness."
c 68:4 More than an abbreviation, the name Yah is associated with the God of heaven, the God of highest glory and power.
d 68:5–6 The Septuagint says, "the bitter ones."
e 68:6 The Aramaic says, "The rebels will dwell among the tombs."

[8] The earth shook beneath your feet; the heavens filled with clouds
  before the presence of the God of Sinai.
  The sacred mountain shook at the sight of the face of Israel's God.
[9] You, O God, sent the reviving rain upon your weary inheritance,
  showers of blessing to refresh it.
[10] So there your people settled.
  And in your kindness you provided the poor with abundance.
[11] God Almighty declares the word of the gospel with power,[a]
  and the warring women of Zion deliver its message:[b]
[12] "The conquering legions have themselves been conquered.
  Look at them flee!"
  Now Zion's women are left to gather the spoils.
[13] When you sleep between sharpened stakes,[c]
  I see you sparkling like silver and glistening like gold,
  covered by the beautiful wings of a dove![d]
[14] When the Almighty found a king for himself,
  it became white as snow in his shade.[e]
[15–16] O huge, magnificent mountain,
  you are the mighty kingdom of God![f]
  All the other peaks, though impressive and imposing,
  look with envy on you, Mount Zion!
  For Zion is the mountain where God has chosen to live forever.
[17] Look! The mighty chariots of God!
  Ten thousands upon ten thousands,
  more than anyone could ever number.
  God is at the front,
  leading them all from Mount Sinai into his sanctuary
  with the radiance of holiness upon him.[g]
[18] He ascends into the heavenly heights,
  taking his many captured ones with him,
  leading them in triumphal procession.

---

a 68:11 As translated from the Aramaic.
b 68:11 As translated from the Masoretic text.
c 68:13 The Aramaic word *shaphya* can be translated "sharpened stakes or thorns," an obvious prophecy of the cross and our union with Christ as he was crucified.
d 68:13 As translated from the Aramaic text, this verse contains prophetic hints of Calvary, where Jesus "slept" the sleep of death between the "sharpened stakes" of the cross. The word *you* is plural and points us to our co-crucifixion with Christ.
e 68:14 Every scholar consulted concludes that this verse is difficult, if not impossible, to interpret properly and translate accurately. The last words are literally "Snow fell in Zalmon." Zalmon (or Salmon) was a wooded area and means "shady."
f 68:15 The Septuagint reads "mountain of provision."
g 68:17 The Septuagint says, "The Lord sends his provisions from his Holy Place on Mount Sinai."

And gifts were given to men, even the once rebellious,
so that they may dwell with Yah.
¹⁹ What a glorious God!^a
He gives us salvation over and over,^b
then daily he carries our burdens!^c

Pause in his presence

²⁰ Our God is a mighty God who saves us over and over!
For the Lord, Yahweh, rescues us
from the ways of death many times.
²¹ But he will crush every enemy, shattering their strength.
He will make heads roll
for they refuse to repent of their stubborn, sinful ways.
²² I hear the Lord God saying to all the enemies of his people,
"You'd better come out of your hiding places,
all of you who are doing your best to stay far away from me.^d
Don't you know there's no place to hide?
²³ For my people will be the conquerors;
they will soon have you under their feet.
They will crush you until there is nothing left!"^e
²⁴ O God, my King, your triumphal processions
keep moving onward in holiness;
you're moving onward toward the Holy Place!
²⁵ Leaders in front,^f then musicians,
with young maidens in between, striking their tambourines.
²⁶ And they sing, "Let all God's princely people rejoice!
Let all the congregations bring their blessing to God, saying,
'The Lord of the fountain! The Lord of the fountain of life!
The Lord of the fountain of Israel!'"
²⁷ Astonishingly, it's the favored youth leading the way:^g
princes of praise in their royal robes,
and exalted princes are among them,
along with princes who have wrestled with God.

---

a 68:19 The Aramaic is Maryah, the Aramaic form of YHWH or Lord Jehovah.
b 68:19 Salvation is in the plural form in the text (*salvations*).
c 68:19 Or "daily loads us with benefits."
d 68:22 The Hebrew text makes reference to Bashan (a high mountain) and to the depths of the sea. In other words, there's no place to hide.
e 68:23 The Hebrew text is literally "Your enemies will be food for the dogs."
f 68:25 As translated from the Septuagint. The Hebrew is "singers in front."
g 68:27 The Hebrew includes the names of four sons of Jacob, representing four tribes. Benjamin, the youngest son, means "son of my right hand" or "the favored one." Judah means "praise." Zebulon's name is the word for "exalted." Naphtali means "obtained by wrestling." Each name speaks of a princely group and is used here poetically not only for Israel but for all of God's "princely people" in this holy procession of worship.

²⁸⁻²⁹ Display your strength, God, and we'll be strong!ᵃ
For your miracles have made us who we are.
Lord, do it again,
and parade from your temple your mighty power.
By your command even kings will bring gifts to you.
³⁰ God, rebuke the beast-life that hides within us!ᵇ
Rebuke those who claim to be "strong ones,"ᶜ
who lurk within the congregation
and abuse the people out of their love for money.
God scatters the people who are spoiling for a fight.
³¹ Africa will send her noble envoys to you, O God.
They will come running, stretching out their hands in love to you.
³² Let all the nations of the earth sing songs of praise to almighty God!
Go ahead, all you nations—sing your praise to the Lord!

Pause in his presence

³³ Make music for the one who strides the ancient skies.
Listen to his thunderous voice of might split open the heavens.
³⁴ Give it up for God, for he alone has all the strength and power!
Proclaim his majesty! For his glory shines down on Israel.
His mighty strength soars in the clouds of glory.
³⁵ God, we are consumed with awe, trembling before you
as your glory streams from your Holy Place.
The God of power shares his mighty strength with Israel
and with all his people.
God, we give our highest praise to you!

69 A Cry of Distress ᵈ

To the Pure and Shining One
David's poetic song of praise to the tune of "Lilies"

¹⁻² God, my God, come and save me!
These floods of trouble have risen higher and higher.
The water is up to my neck!ᵉ
I'm sinking into the mud with no place to stand,
and I'm about to drown in this storm.

---

a 68:28–29 The Great Bible translated by Miles Coverdale (1488–1569) translates this "Your God has sent forth strength for you."

b 68:30 Literal Hebrew: "Rebuke the beasts in the reeds."

c 68:30 This verse has puzzled scholars, and many conclude that the Hebrew text is nearly incomprehensible, with tremendous variations in the translation.

d Ps. 69 is considered one of the most outstanding messianic psalms, with obvious prophetic references to the sufferings and cross of Jesus Christ. Next to Ps. 22 it is the psalm most often quoted in the New Testament.

e 69:1–2 Or "throat."

³ I'm weary, exhausted with weeping.
    My throat is dry, my voice is gone, my eyes are swollen with sorrow,
    and I'm waiting for you, God, *to come through for me.*
⁴ I can't even count all those who hate me for no reason.
    Many influential men want me silenced,
    yet I've done nothing against them.
    Must I restore what I never took away?
⁵ God, my life is an open book to you.
    You know every sin I've ever done.
    For nothing within me is hidden from your sight!
⁶ Lord Yahweh of Angel Armies,
    keep me from ever being a stumbling block to others,
    to those who love you.
    Lord God of Israel, don't let what happens to me
    be the source of confusion to those who are passionate for you.
⁷ Because of my love for you, Lord,
    I have been mocked, cursed, and disgraced.
⁸ Even my own brothers, those of my family,
    act as though they don't want anything to do with me.
⁹ My love for you has my heart on fire!
    My passion consumes me for your house!
    Nothing will turn me away,
    even though I endure all the insults of those who insult you.
¹⁰ When they see me seeking for more of you with weeping*ᵃ* and fasting,
    they all just scoff and scorn at my passion.
¹¹ When I humble myself with sorrow over my sin,
    it gives them a reason to mock me even more.
¹² The leaders, the influential ones—how they scorn my passion for you!
    I've become the talk of the town, the theme of drunkards' songs.
¹³ But I keep calling out to you, Yahweh!
    I know you will bend down to listen to me,
    for now is the season of favor.
    Because of your faithful love for me,
    your answer to my prayer will be my sure salvation.
¹⁴ Pull me out of this mess! Don't let me sink!
    Rescue me from those who hate me and from all this trouble I'm in!
¹⁵ Don't let this flood drown me.
    Save me from these deep waters
    or I'll go down to the pit of destruction.
¹⁶⁻¹⁷ Oh, Lord God, answer my prayers!
    I need to see your tender kindness, your grace,

---

a 69:10 Or "When I pour out my soul" or "When I weep soul-tears."

your compassion, and your constant love.
Just let me see your face, and turn your heart toward me.
Come running quickly to your servant.
In this deep distress, come and answer my prayer.

¹⁸ Come closer as a friend and redeem me.
Set me free so my enemies cannot say that you are powerless.

¹⁹ See how they dishonor me in shame and disgrace?
You know, Lord, what I'm going through, and you see it all.

²⁰ I'm heartsick and heartbroken by it all.
Their contempt has crushed my soul.
I looked for sympathy and compassion
but found only empty stares.

²¹ I was hungry and they gave me bitter food.
I was thirsty and they offered me vinegar. ᵃ

²² Let their "feasts" turn to ashes.
Let their "peace and security" become their downfall.

²³ Make them blind as bats, groping in the dark.
Let them be feeble, trembling continually.

²⁴⁻²⁵ Pour out your fury on them all!
Consume them with the fire of your anger!
Burn down the walled palace where they live!
Leave them homeless and desolate!

²⁶ For they come against the one you yourself have struck,
and they scorn the pain of those you've pierced.

²⁷ Pile on them the guilt of their sins.
Don't let them ever go free.

²⁸ Leave them out of your list of the living!
Blot them out of your book of life!
Never name them as your own!

²⁹ I am burdened and broken by this pain.
When your miracle rescue comes to me,
it will lift me to the highest place.

³⁰ Then my song will be a burst of praise to you.
My glory-shouts will make your fame even more glorious
to all who hear my praises!

³¹ For I know, Yahweh, that my praises mean more to you
than all my gifts and sacrifices.

³² All who seek you will see God do this for them,
and they'll overflow with gladness.
Let this revive your hearts, all you lovers of God!

---

a 69:21 This was fulfilled with Jesus being offered vinegar on the cross. See Luke 23:36.

³³ For Yahweh does listen to the poor and needy
and will not abandon his prisoners of love. ^a
³⁴ Let all the universe praise him!
The high heavens and everyone on earth, praise him!
Let the oceans deep, with everything in them, keep it up!
³⁵ God will come to save his Zion-people.
God will build up his cities of Judah,
for there his people will live in peace.
³⁶ All their children will inherit the land,
and the lovers of his name will live there safe and secure.

70 A Cry for Help

To the Pure and Shining One
David's poetic lament to always remember

¹ Please, Lord! Come quickly and rescue me!
God, show me your favor and restore me.
² Let all who seek my life be humiliated, confused, and ashamed.
God, send them sprawling, all who wish me evil;
they just want me dead.
³ Scoff at every scoffer and cause them all to be utter failures!
Let them be ashamed and horrified over their complete defeat.
⁴ But let all who passionately seek you erupt with excitement and joy
over what you've done!
Let all your lovers, who continually rejoice in the Savior, ^b
say aloud, "How great and glorious is our God!"
⁵ Lord, in my place of weakness and need,
won't you turn your heart toward me and hurry to help me?
For you are my Savior and I'm always in your thoughts.
So don't delay to deliver me now, for you are my God.

71 The Psalm of Old Age

¹ Lord, you are my secure shelter. Don't ever let me down!
² Let your justice be my breakthrough.
Bend low to my whispered cry
and save me from all my enemies!
³ You're the only place of protection for me.
I keep coming back to hide myself in you,
for you are like a mountain-cliff fortress where I'm kept safe.
⁴ Let me escape from these cruel and wicked men,
and save me from the hands of the evil one.

---

a 69:33 Or "those wearing shackles."
b 70:4 This verse contains the Hebrew root word for Yeshua.

⁵ For you are my only hope, Lord!
I've hung on to you, trusting in you all my life.
⁶⁻⁷ It was you who supported me from the day I was born,
loving me, helping me through my life's journey.
You've made me into a miracle;
no wonder I trust you and praise you forever!
Many marvel at my success,
but I know it is all because of you, my mighty protector!
⁸ I'm overflowing with your praise for all you've done,
and your splendor thrills me all day long.
⁹ Now that I'm old, don't set me aside.
Don't let go of me when my strength is spent.
¹⁰⁻¹¹ For all my enemies whisper behind my back.
They're waiting for me to fall so they can finish me off.
They're convinced you've left me
and that you'll never come to my rescue.
They're saying, "Let's get him now! He has no savior!"
¹² O God, stay close to me!
Don't just watch from a distance! Hurry to help me, my God!
¹³ Cover these accusers of mine with shame and failure!
Destroy them all, for they only want to kill me!
¹⁴ No matter what, I'll trust in you to help me.
Nothing will stop me from praising you to magnify your glory!
¹⁵ I couldn't begin to count the times you've been there for me.
With the skill of a poet I'll never run out of things to say
of how you faithfully kept me from danger.
¹⁶ I will come forth in your mighty strength, O my Lord God. ᵃ
I'll tell everyone that you alone are the perfect one.
¹⁷ From my childhood you've been my teacher,
and I'm still telling everyone of your miracle-wonders!
¹⁸ God, now that I'm old and gray, don't walk away.
Give me grace to demonstrate to the next generation
all your mighty miracles and your excitement,
to show them your magnificent power!
¹⁹ For your glorious righteousness reaches up to the high heavens.
No one could ever be compared to you!
Who is your equal, O God of marvels and wonders?
²⁰ Even though you've let us sink down with trials and troubles,
I know you will revive us again,
lifting us up from the dust of death.

---

a 71:16 Or "I will enter into the manliness of Lord Jehovah."

²¹ Give us even more greatness than before.
　Turn and comfort us once again.
²² My loving God, the harp in my heart will praise you.
　Your faithful heart toward us will be the theme of my song.
　Melodies and music will rise to you, the Holy One of Israel.
²³ I will shout and sing your praises for all you are to me—
　Savior, lover of my soul!
²⁴ I'll never stop telling others how perfect you are
　while all those who seek my harm slink away ashamed and
　　defeated!

72 THE RIGHTEOUS KING

Solomon's psalm [a]

¹ O God, make the king a godly judge like you
　and give the king's son the gift of justice too.
² Help him to give true justice to your people,
　honorably and equally to all.
³ Then the mountains of influence will be fruitful,
　and from your righteousness
　prosperity and peace will flow to all the people.
⁴ May the poor and humble have an advocate with the king.
　May he consider the children of the poor
　and crush the cruel oppressor.
⁵ The sun and moon will stop shining
　before your lovers will stop worshiping;
　for ages upon ages the people will love and adore you!
⁶ Your favor will fall like rain upon our surrendered lives, [b]
　like showers reviving the earth.
⁷ In the days of his reign the righteous will spring forth
　with the abundance of peace and prosperity forevermore.
⁸ May he subdue and take dominion from sea to sea;
　may he rule from the river to the rim.
⁹ Desert nomads are bowing at his feet,
　every enemy falling facedown, biting the dust!
¹⁰ Distant kings will surrender and come with their gifts
　from every continent and coastland;
　they will offer their tribute to you. [c]

---

a　The Septuagint indicates this could be a psalm written by David for his son Solomon. This
　royal psalm is a prayer for the king. Read through it as though it is referring to King Jesus—
　one who is greater than Solomon.
b　72:6 Or "like rain on mown grass."
c　72:10 Included in the Hebrew text are kings of Tarshish (Spain) and kings of Sheba and Seba
　(Ethiopia).

¹¹ O King of kings, they will all bow before you.
  O King of kings, every nation will one day serve you.
¹²⁻¹³ He will care for the needy and neglected
  when they cry to him for help.
  The humble and helpless will know his kindness,
  for with a father's compassion he will save their souls.
¹⁴ They will be rescued from tyranny and torture,
  for their lifeblood is precious in his eyes.
¹⁵ Long live this King!
  May the wealth of the world be laid before him. ᵃ
  May there be ceaseless praise and prayer to him.
  May all the blessing be brought to him.
¹⁶ Bless us with a bountiful harvest,
  with golden grain swaying on the mountain fields!
  May the cities be full of praising people, fruitful and filled—
¹⁷ So that his name may be honored forever!
  May the fame of his name spring forth!
  May it shine on, like the sunshine!
  In him all will be blessed to bless others,
  and may all the people bless the One who blessed them.
¹⁸ Praise forever Jehovah-God, the God of Israel!
  He is the one and only God of wonders,
  surpassing every expectation.
¹⁹ The blazing glory of his name will be praised forever!
  May all the earth overflow with his glory!
  Faithful is our King! Amen!
²⁰ This concludes the poetry sung by David, Jesse's son.

BOOK 3
THE LEVITICUS PSALMS
Psalms of worship and God's house

73 GOD'S JUSTICE

Asaph's psalm

¹ No one can deny it—God is really good to Israel
  and to all those with pure hearts.
  But I nearly missed seeing it for myself.
² Here's my story: I came so close to missing the way.
³ I was stumbling over what I saw with the wicked.

---

a 72:15 Or "the gold of Sheba."

For when I saw the boasters with such wealth and prosperity,
I became jealous over their smug security.

⁴⁻⁵ Indulging in whatever they wanted, going where they wanted,
doing what they wanted, and with no care in the world.
No pain, no problems, they seemed to have it made.
They lived as though life would never end.

⁶ They didn't even try to hide their pride and opulence.
Cruelty and violence is part of their lifestyle.

⁷ Pampered and pompous, vice oozes from their souls;
they overflow with vanity.

⁸ They're such snobs—looking down their noses.
They even scoff at God!
They are nothing but bullies threatening God's people.

⁹ Loudmouths with no fear of God, pretending to know it all.
Windbags full of hot air, impressing only themselves.

¹⁰ Yet the people keep coming back to listen
to more of their nonsense.

¹¹ They tell their cohorts, "God will never know.
See, he has no clue of what we're doing."

¹² These are the wicked ones I'm talking about!
They never have to lift a finger,
living a life of ease while their riches multiply.

¹³ Have I been foolish to play by the rules and keep my life pure?

¹⁴ Here I am suffering under your discipline day after day.
I feel like I'm being punished all day long.

¹⁵ If I had given in to my pain and spoken of what I was really feeling,
it would have sounded like unfaithfulness to the next generation.

¹⁶ When I tried to understand it all, I just couldn't.
It was too puzzling—too much of a riddle to me.

¹⁷ But then one day I was brought into the sanctuaries of God,
and in the light of glory, my distorted perspective vanished.
Then I understood that the destiny of the wicked was near!

¹⁸ They're the ones who are on the slippery path,
and God will suddenly let them slide off into destruction
to be consumed with terrors forever!

¹⁹ It will be an instant end to all their life of ease;
a blink of the eye and they're swept away by sudden calamity!
They're all nothing more than momentary monarchs—

²⁰ soon to disappear like a dream when one awakes.
When the rooster crows,
Lord God, you'll despise their life of fantasies. ᵃ

---

a 73:20 Or "shadows."

²¹ When I saw all of this, what turmoil filled my heart,
  piercing my opinions with your truth.
²² I was so stupid. I was senseless and ignorant,
  acting like a brute beast before you, Lord.
²³ Yet, in spite of all this, you comfort me by your counsel;
  you draw me closer to you.
²⁴ You lead me with your secret wisdom.
  And following you brings me into your brightness and glory!
²⁵ Whom have I in heaven but you? You're all I want!
  No one on earth means as much to me as you.
²⁶ Lord, so many times I fail; I fall into disgrace.
  But when I trust in you, I have a strong and glorious presence
  protecting and anointing me. Forever you're all I need!
²⁷ Those who abandon the worship of God will perish.
  The false and unfaithful will be silenced, never heard from again.
²⁸ But I'll keep coming closer and closer to you, Lord Yahweh,
  for your name is good to me. I'll keep telling the world of
  your awesome works, my faithful and glorious God!

74 WE NEED YOU NOW

Asaph's poem of instruction

¹ Are you really going to leave us, God?
  Would you turn your back on us, rejecting your people?
  We are yours, your very own. ^a
  Will your anger smolder against us forever?
² Don't forget that we are your beloved ones.
  Wrap us back into your heart again, for you chose us.
  You brought us out of our slavery and bondage
  and made us your favored ones, your Zion-people,
  your home on earth.
³ Turn your steps toward this devastation.
  Come running to bring your restoring grace to these ruins, ^b
  to what the enemy has done to devastate your Holy Place.
⁴ They have come into the very midst of your dwelling place,
  roaring like beasts, setting up their banners to flaunt their conquest.
⁵ Now everything is in shambles! They've totally destroyed it.
  Like a forest chopped down to the ground,
  there's nothing's left.
⁶ All of the beauty of the craftsmanship

---

a 74:1 Or "the sheep of your pasture."
b 74:3 This verse reads differently in the Aramaic: "Lift up your servants with your might
  above those who take them captive, for those who oppress us are enemies to your holiness."

of the inner place has been ruined,

    smashed, broken, and shattered. *a*

⁷ They've burned it all to the ground.

    They've violated your sanctuary,

    the very dwelling place of your glory and your name.

⁸ They boasted, "Let's completely crush them!

    Let's wipe out every trace of this God.

    Let's burn up every sacred place where they worship this God."

⁹ We don't see any miraculous signs anymore.

    There's no longer a prophet among us

    who can tell us how long this devastation will continue.

¹⁰ God, how much longer will you let this go on

    and allow these barbarians to blaspheme your name?

    Will you stand back and watch them get away with this forever?

¹¹ Why don't you do something?

    You have the power to break in,

    so why would you hide your great power from us?

    Don't hold back! Unleash your might and give them a final blow.

¹² You have always been, and always will be, my King.

    You are the mighty conqueror, working wonders all over the world.

¹³ It was you who split the sea in two by your glorious strength.

    You smashed the power of Tannin, the sea god. *b*

¹⁴ You crushed the might of Leviathan, *c* the great dragon,

    then you took the crumbs and fed them to the sharks. *d*

¹⁵ With your glory you opened up springs and fountains,

    then you spoke and the ever-flowing springs of Jordan

    dried up so we could cross over.

¹⁶ You own the day and the night.

    Sunlight and starlight call you Creator.

¹⁷ The four corners of the earth were formed by your hands,

    and every changing season owes its beauty to you.

¹⁸ O Jehovah, don't ever forget how these arrogant enemies,

    like fools, have mocked your name.

¹⁹ Lord, aren't we your beloved dove that praises you? *e*

---

a 74:6 This psalm also describes what the enemy of our souls has done spiritually to mar the image of God in the "inner place" of man's spirit. God will fully restore all things, including his image within us, as our hearts become his "Holy Place" on the earth.

b 74:13 As translated literally from the Hebrew. The Septuagint says, "You've crushed the heads of the dragons in the water [water spirits]."

c 74:14 Leviathan is mentioned six times in Job 41. Leviathan means "twisted or coiled" and is considered to be a sea monster. See Gen. 1:21.

d 74:14 The Septuagint says, "You fed them to the black peoples."

e 74:19 As translated from the Septuagint, Syriac, and one Hebrew manuscript.

Protect us from these wild beasts who want to harm us.
Don't leave us as lambs among wolves!
You can't abandon us after all we've been through!
²⁰ Remember your promises to us,
for darkness covers the land,
giving the violent ones a hiding place.
²¹ Don't let these insults continue.
Can't you see that we are your downtrodden
and oppressed people?
Make the poor and needy into a choir of praise to you!
²² Don't ignore these ignorant words, this continual mocking.
Rise up, God; it's time to defend yourself from all of this.
²³ Never forget what your adversaries are saying.
For their rage and uproar rise continually against you.
It's time to stand up to them!

75 A Cup in God's Hand

To the Pure and Shining One
Asaph's poetic song to the tune of "Do Not Destroy"

¹ God, our hearts spill over with praise to you!
We overflow with thanks, for your name is the "Near One."
All we want to talk about is your wonderful works!
And we hear your reply:
² "When the time is ripe I will arise,
and I will judge the world with perfect righteousness.
³ Though I have set the earth firmly on its pillars,
I will shake it until it totters and everyone's hearts will tremble."

Pause in his presence

⁴ God warns the proud, "Stop your arrogant boasting!"
And he warns the wicked,
"Don't think for a moment you can resist me!
⁵ Why would you speak with such stubborn pride?
Don't you dare raise your fist against me!"
⁶⁻⁷ This I know:
the favor that brings promotion and power
doesn't come from anywhere on earth,
for no one exalts a person but God, the true judge of all.
He alone determines where favor rests.
He anoints one for greatness
and brings another down to his knees.
⁸ A foaming cup filled with judgment mixed with fury
is in the hands of the Lord Jehovah,
full to the brim and ready to run over.

He filled it up for the wicked and they will drink it
down to the very last drop!
[9] But I will proclaim the victory of the God of Jacob.
My melodies of praise will make him known.
[10] My praises will break the powers of wickedness
while the righteous will be promoted and become powerful!

76 AWE-INSPIRING POWER

To the Pure and Shining One
Asaph's poetic tune, a song of smiting

[1] God is well known in the land of Judah.
He is famous throughout Israel,
[2] making his home in Jerusalem, living here on Mount Zion.
[3] That's where he smashes every weapon of war
that comes against him.
That's where he uses the broken arrows
as kindling for his mighty bonfire.

Pause in his presence

[4] God, you are so resplendent and radiant![a]
Your majesty shines from your everlasting mountain.
Nothing could be compared to you in glory!
[5] Even the mightiest of men have been paralyzed by your presence.
They were so stunned and lifeless,
not even the strongest one could lift a hand.
[6] When Jacob's God roared his rebuke,
soldiers and their steeds all fell to the ground,
stunned and lying still.
[7] No wonder you are greatly feared! You are the awe-inspiring God!
For who could ever stand before your face
when your fierce anger burns and live to tell about it.
[8] As the earth itself holds its breath in awe before you,
judgment is decreed from heaven.
[9] You arise to punish evil and defend the gentle upon the earth.

Pause in his presence

[10] You have power to transform man's futile anger into praise.[b]
The fury of your enemies only causes your fame to increase.[c]
[11] So you'd better keep every promise you've ever made
to the Awesome One, Jehovah-God!
Let all people bring their extravagant gifts to him alone.

---

a   76:4 The Hebrew-Aramaic word used here is *anointed*.
b   76:10 Or "The counsel of men will praise you."
c   76:10 The Septuagint reads "Survivors of your wrath keep your festivals."

¹² He is famous for breaking the spirit of the powers that be.
    And the kings of the earth will know him as the Fearsome One!

77 GOD OF COMFORT

To the Pure and Shining One
Asaph's poetic song of love's celebration

¹ I poured out my complaint to you, God.
    I lifted up my voice, shouting out for your help.
² When I was in deep distress, in my day of trouble,
    I reached out for you with hands stretched out to heaven.
    Over and over I kept looking for you, God,
    but your comforting grace was nowhere to be found.
³ As I thought of you I moaned, "God, where are you?" [a]
    I'm overwhelmed with despair as I wait for your help to arrive.

Pause in his presence

⁴ I can't get a wink of sleep until you come and comfort me.
    Now I'm too burdened to even pray!
⁵ My mind wandered, thinking of days gone by—
    the years long since passed.
⁶ Then I remembered the worship songs I used to sing
    in the night seasons,
    and my heart began to fill again with thoughts of you.
    So my spirit went out once more in search of you.
⁷ Would you really walk off and leave me forever, my Lord God?
    Won't you show me your kind favor, delighting in me again?
⁸ Has your well of sweet mercy dried up?
    Will your promises never come true?
⁹ Have you somehow forgotten to show me love?
    Are you so angry that you've closed
    your heart of compassion toward me?

Pause in his presence

¹⁰ Lord, what wounds me most is that it's somehow my fault that
    you've changed your heart toward me
    and I no longer see the years of the Mighty One
    and your right hand of power. [b]
¹¹ Yet I could never forget all your miracles, my God,
    as I remember all your wonders of old.
¹² I ponder all you've done, Lord, musing on all your miracles.

---

a 77:3 Or "When I am in heaviness [depressed], I will think upon God."

b 77:10 This difficult verse has a number of alternate translations, including "Your right hand
has changed [or withered]." The implication is that God's power and protection are no
longer being seen.

¹³ It's here in your presence, in your sanctuary,
     where I learn more of your ways.^a
     For holiness is revealed in everything you do.
     Lord, you're the one and only, the great and glorious God!
¹⁴ Your display of wonders, miracles, and power
     makes the nations acknowledge you.
¹⁵ By your glory-bursts you've rescued us over and over.
     Just ask the sons of Jacob or
     the sons of Joseph and they will tell you!
     And all of us, your beloved ones, know that it's true!

Pause in his presence

¹⁶ When the many waters of the Red Sea took one look at you,^b
     they were afraid and ran away to hide—
     trembling to its depths!
¹⁷ Storm clouds filled with water high in the skies;
     cloudbursts and thunderclaps announced your approach.
     Lightning-flashes lit up the landscape.
¹⁸ Rolling whirlwinds exploded with sonic booms of thunder,
     rumbling as the skies shouted out your story
     with light and sound and wind.
     Everything on earth shook and trembled as you drew near.
¹⁹ Your steps formed a highway through the seas
     with footprints on a pathway no one even knew was there.^c
²⁰ You led your people forward by your loving hand,
     blessed by the leadership of Moses and Aaron.

78 LESSONS FROM HISTORY

Asaph's poetic song of instruction

¹ Beloved ones, listen to this instruction.
     Open your heart to the revelation
     of this mystery that I share with you.
² A parable and a proverb are hidden in what I say—
     an intriguing riddle from the past.
³⁻⁴ We've heard true stories from our fathers about our rich heritage.
     We will continue to tell our children
     and not hide from the rising generation
     the great marvels of our God—
     his miracles and power that have brought us all this far.
⁵ The story of Israel is a lesson in God's ways.

---

a 77:13 This is an alternative translation.
b 77:16 Although the Red Sea is not mentioned in the verse, it is implied in the context.
c 77:19 This could be a prophecy of Jesus one day walking on water.

He established decrees for Jacob and established the law in Israel,
and he commanded our forefathers to teach them to their children.
⁶ For perpetuity God's ways will be passed down
from one generation to the next, even to those not yet born.
⁷ In this way, every generation will have a living faith in the laws of life
and will never forget the faithful ways of God.
⁸ By following his ways they will break the past bondage
of their fickle fathers, who were a stubborn, rebellious generation
and whose spirits strayed from the eternal God.
They refused to love him with all their hearts.
⁹ Take, for example, the sons of Ephraim.
Though they were all equipped warriors, each with weapons,
when the battle began they retreated and ran away in fear.
¹⁰ They didn't really believe the promises of God;
they refused to trust him and move forward in faith.
¹¹ They forgot his wonderful works and the miracles of the past,
¹² even their exodus from Egypt, the epic miracle of his might.
They forgot the glories of his power at the place of passing over. *ᵃ*
¹³ God split the sea wide open, and
the waters stood at attention on either side
as the people passed on through!
¹⁴ By day the moving glory-cloud led them forward.
And all through the night the fire-cloud stood as a sentry of light.
¹⁵⁻¹⁶ In the days of desert dryness he split open the mighty rock,
and the waters flowed like a river before their very eyes.
He gave them all they wanted to drink from his living springs.
¹⁷ Yet they kept their rebellion alive against God Most High,
and their sins against God continued to be counted.
¹⁸ In their hearts they tested God just to get what they wanted,
asking for the food their hearts craved.
¹⁹⁻²⁰ Like spoiled children they grumbled against God,
demanding he prove his love by saying,
"Can't God provide for us in this barren wilderness?
Will he give us food, or will he only give us water?
Where's our meal?"
²¹ Then God heard all their complaining and was furious!
His anger flared up against his people.
²² For they turned away from faith and walked away in fear;
they failed to trust in his power to help them when he was near.

---

a 78:12 Or "the fields of Zoan." *Zoan* means "crossing place" or "place of departure." See also
v. 43.

²³⁻²⁴ Still he spoke on their behalf and the skies opened up;
the windows of heaven poured out food,
the mercy bread-manna.
The grain of grace fell from the clouds.

²⁵ Humans ate angels' food—the meal of the mighty ones.
His grace gave them more than enough!

²⁶⁻²⁷ The heavenly winds of miracle power blew in their favor
and food rained down upon them;
succulent quail quieted their hunger as they ate all they wanted.

²⁸ Food fell from the skies, thick as clouds;
their provision floated down right in front of their eyes!

²⁹ He gave them all they desired, and they ate to their fill.

³⁰⁻³¹ But before they had even finished,
even with their food still in their mouths,
God's fiery anger arose against them,
killing the finest of their mighty men.

³² Yet in spite of all this, they kept right on sinning.
Even when they saw God's marvels,
they refused to believe God could care for them.

³³ So God cut their lives short with sudden disaster,
with nothing to show for their lives but fear and failure.

³⁴ *When he cared for them they ignored him,*
but when he began to kill them, ending their lives in a moment,
they came running back to God, pleading for mercy.

³⁵ They remembered that God, the Mighty One,
was their strong protector,
the Hero-God who would come to their rescue.

³⁶⁻³⁷ But their repentance lasted only as long as they were in danger;
they lied through their teeth to the true God of Covenant.
So quickly they wandered away from his promises,
following God with their words and not their hearts!
Their worship was only flattery.

³⁸ But amazingly, God—so full of compassion—still forgave them.
He covered over their sins with his love,
refusing to destroy them all.
Over and over he held back his anger,
restraining wrath to show them mercy.

³⁹ He knew that they were made from mere dust—
frail, fragile, and short-lived, here today and gone tomorrow.

⁴⁰ How many times they rebelled in their desert days!
How they grieved him with their grumblings.

⁴¹ Again and again they limited God, preventing him from blessing them.

Continually they turned back from him
and provoked *a* the Holy One of Israel!
[42] They forgot his great love, how he took them by his hand,
and *with redemption's kiss* he delivered them from their enemies.
[43] They disregarded all the epic signs and marvels they saw
when they escaped from Egypt's bondage.
They forgot the judgment of the plagues that set them free.
[44] God turned their rivers into blood, leaving the people thirsty.
[45] He sent them vast swarms of filthy flies that sucked their blood.
He sent hordes of frogs, ruining their lives.
[46] Grasshoppers consumed all their crops.
[47] Every garden and every orchard
was flattened with blasts of hailstones,
their fruit trees ruined by a killing frost.
[48] Even their cattle fell prey, pounded by the falling hail;
their livestock were struck with bolts of lightning.
[49] Finally, he unleashed upon them the fierceness of his anger.
Such fury!
He sent them sorrow and devastating trouble
by his mighty band of destroying angels;
messengers of death were dispatched against them.
[50-51] He lifted his mercy and let loose his fearful anger
and did not spare their lives.
He released the judgment-plagues to rage through their land.
God struck down in death all the firstborn sons of Egypt—
the pride and joy of each family.
[52] Then, like a shepherd leading his sheep, God led his people
out of tyranny, guiding them through the wilderness like a flock.
[53] Safely and carefully God led them out, with nothing to fear.
But their enemies he led into the sea.
He took care of them there once and for all!
[54] Eventually God brought his people to the Holy Land,
to a land of hills that he had prepared for them. *b*
[55] He drove out and scattered all the peoples occupying the land,
staking out an inheritance, a portion for each of Israel's tribes.
[56] Yet for all of this, they still rebelled and refused to follow his ways,
provoking to anger the God Most High.
[57-58] Like traitors turning back, they forsook him.

---

a 78:41 The Hebrew verb for "provoked" is *a hapax legomenon* and comes from a root word
for "marked." It is as though Israel's behavior wounded the heart of God.
b 78:54 The Aramaic reads "He brought them to the border of his holiness, the mountain
possessed by his right hand."

They were even worse than their fathers!
They became treacherous deceivers, crooked and corrupt,
and worshiped false gods in the high places,
bringing low the name of God with every idol they erected.
No wonder he was filled with jealousy and furious with anger!

⁵⁹ Enraged with anger, God turned his wrath on them,
and he rejected his people with disgust.

⁶⁰ God walked away from them and left his dwelling place at Shiloh,
abandoning the place where he had lived among them,

⁶¹ allowing his emblem of strength, his glory-ark to be captured. ᵃ
Enemies stole the very source of Israel's power.

⁶² God vented his rage, allowing his people to be butchered
when they went out to battle,
for his anger was intense against his very own.

⁶³ Their young men fell on the battlefield and never came back.
Their daughters never heard their wedding songs
since there was no one left to marry!

⁶⁴ Their priests were slaughtered and their widows were killed
before they had time to weep.

⁶⁵ Then all at once the Almighty awakened
as though he had been asleep.
Like a mighty man he arose, roaring into action!

⁶⁶ He blasted into battle, driving back every foe,
defeating them in disgrace for time and eternity.

⁶⁷ He rejected Joseph's family, the tribe of Ephraim. ᵇ

⁶⁸ He chose instead the tribe of Judah
and Mount Zion, which he loves.

⁶⁹ There he built his towering temple,
strong and enduring as the earth itself.

⁷⁰ God also chose his beloved one, David.
He promoted him from caring for sheep
and made him his prophetic servant.

⁷¹⁻⁷² God prepared David and took this gentle shepherd-king
and presented him before the people
as the one who would love and care for them
with integrity, a pure heart, and the anointing
to lead Israel, his holy inheritance.

---

a 78:61 Although the ark is not directly mentioned in this text, the obvious implication is that God allowed his "strength" to be stolen as a sign of his judgment.

b 78:67 The place of God's dwelling was moved from the land of Ephraim (Shiloh) to the land of Judah (Jerusalem).

79 PRAYER IN A TIME OF NATIONAL DISASTER

Asaph's poetic song

¹ God, won't you do something?
  Barbarians have invaded your inheritance.
  Your temple of holiness has been violated,
  and Jerusalem has been left in ruins.
² The corpses of your loving people are lying in the open—
  food for the beasts and the birds.
³ The shed blood of your servants has soaked the city,
  with no one left to bury the dead.
⁴ Now the nearby nations heap their scorn upon us,
  scoffing, mocking us incessantly.
⁵ How much longer, O Jehovah-God, must we endure this?
  Does your anger have no end?
  Will your jealousy burn like a raging fire?
⁶ If you're going to pour out your anger,
  pour it out on all these nations around us, not on us!
  They're the ones who do not love you like we do!
⁷ See how they've attacked us, consuming the land,
  leaving it desolate.
⁸ Please, God, don't hold the sins of our fathers against us.
  Don't make us pay for their sins.
  Hurry to our side, and let your tenderhearted mercy
  meet us in our need, for we are devastated beyond belief.
⁹ Our hero, come and rescue us!
  O God of the breakthrough, for the glory of your name,
  come and help us!
  Forgive and restore us; heal us and cover us in your love.
¹⁰ Why should all the nations sneer at us, saying,
"Where is this God of yours?"
  Now is the time, Lord.
  Show your people and all the world that
  you will avenge this slaughter and bloodshed once and for all!
¹¹ Listen, Lord! Hear the sighing of all the prisoners of war,
  all those doomed to die. Demonstrate your glory-power,
  and come and rescue your condemned children!
¹² Lord God, take what these mocking masses have done to us
  and pay it all back to them seven times over.
¹³ Then we, your lovers, will forever thank you,
  praising your name from generation to generation!

80 RESCUE AND RESTORE

For the Pure and Shining One

Asaph's poetic song, set to the tune of "Your Decrees Are Like Lilies"

[1] God-Enthroned, be revealed in splendor
   as you ride upon the cherubim!
   How perfectly you lead us, a people set free. [a]
   Loving shepherd of Israel—listen to our hearts' cry!
   Shine forth from your throne of dazzling light.

[2] In the sight of Benjamin, Ephraim, and Manasseh,
   stir up your mighty power in full display before our eyes. [b]
   Break through and reveal yourself by coming to our rescue.

[3] Revive us, O God! Let your beaming face shine upon us
   with the sunrise rays of glory;
   then nothing will be able to stop us.

[4] O God, the mighty Commander of Angel Armies,
   how much longer will you smolder in anger?
   How much longer will you be disgusted with your people
   even when they pray?

[5] You have fed us with sorrow and grief
   and made us drink our tears by the bowlful.

[6] You've made us a thorn in the side of all the neighboring lands,
   and now they just laugh at us with their mocking scorn.

[7] Come back, come back, O God, and restore us!
   You are the Pure Commander of Angel Armies.
   Let your beaming face shine upon us with the sunrise rays of glory,
   and then nothing will be able to stop us!

[8–9] Remember how you transplanted us here
   like a tender vine from Egypt.
   You cleared the land for your vineyard,
   evicting the nations from your land and planting us here.
   The roots of your vineyard went deep into the soil
   and filled the land with fruit.

[10–11] Because of your favor on your vineyard,
   blessing extended to every mountain of influence.

---

a   80:1 Or "You lead Joseph like a flock." Joseph, as a metaphor, becomes a picture of the saga
    of God's people once imprisoned and now set free to rule and reign.

b   80:2 The Hebrew text includes the names Ephraim ("doubly fruitful"), Benjamin ("son
    of my right hand"), and Manassah ("you made me forget"). These three sons of Rachel
    marched together behind the ark of glory (Num. 2:17–24) and became representatives of
    all who follow the glory of God. They will be "doubly fruitful," "sons of his right hand,"
    and those who have "forgotten" their lives in Adam.

Through this flourishing vineyard mighty ones were raised up.
The nations were blessed by your fruitful vineyard of Israel,[a]
all the way from the Mediterranean to the Euphrates.
[12–13] So Lord, why have you broken down
your fence of favor around us?
Trespassers can steal the fruit from off our vines,
and now every wild beast comes
breaking through our wall to ravage us.
You've left us without protection!
[14] Come back, come back, O God to restore us!
You are the Commander of Angel Armies.
Look down from heaven and see our crisis.
Come down and care for your lovely vineyard once again.
[15] Nurture our root and our fruit with your loving care.
Raise up the Branch-Man, the Son whom you've made strong.
[16] Enemies chopped down our vine and set it on fire;
now show them your anger and let them perish by your frown.
[17] Strengthen this Branch-Man, the Son of your love,
the Son of Man who dwells at your right hand.
[18] Then we will never turn back from you.
Revive us again, that we may trust in you.
[19] O God, the mighty Commander of Angel Armies,
come back and rescue us!
Let your beaming face shine upon us
with the sunrise rays of glory.
Then nothing will ever stop us again!

81 FOR THE FEAST OF TABERNACLES

For the Pure and Shining One
Asaph's poetic song, set to the melody of "For the Feast of Harvest"
[1] Lord, just singing about you makes me strong!
So I'll keep shouting for joy to Jacob's God, my champion.
[2] Let the celebration begin!
I will sing with drum accompaniment and with the sweet sound
of the harp and guitar strumming.
[3] Go ahead! Blow the jubilee trumpet to begin the feast!
Blow it before every joyous celebration and festival.[b]

---

a   80:10–11 In this passage the translator has chosen to make explicit the symbols in the
text. The vineyard is Israel, the mountains are the high places of influence in culture, the
cedars are the mighty and powerful of men, and the sea speaks of the nations ("sea of
humanity").
b   81:3 Or "on the day of the new moon and the day of the full moon."

⁴ For God has given us these seasons of joy,
  days that the God of Jacob decreed for us to celebrate and rejoice.
⁵ He has given these feasts to remind us of his triumph over Egypt,
  when he went out to wage war against them.
  I heard the message in an unknown tongue as he said to me,
⁶ "I have removed your backbreaking burdens
  and have freed your hands from the hard labor and toil. ᵃ
⁷ You called out to me in your time of trouble and I rescued you.
  I came down from the realm of the secret place of thunder,
  where mysteries hide.
  I came down to save you.
  I tested your hearts at the place where there was no water to drink,
  the place of your bitter argument with me." ᵇ

Pause in his presence

⁸ "Listen to me, my dear people.
  For I'm warning you, and you'd better listen well!
  For I hold something against you.
⁹ Don't ever be guilty of worshiping any other god but me.
¹⁰ I am your only God, the living God.
  Wasn't I the one who broke the strongholds over you
  and raised you up out of bondage?
  Open your mouth with a mighty decree;
  I will fulfill it now, you'll see!
  The words that you speak, so shall it be!
¹¹ But my people still wouldn't listen;
  my princely people would not yield to me.
¹² So I lifted my grace from off of their lives and I surrendered them
  to the stubbornness of their hearts.
  For they were living according to their own selfish fantasies.
¹³ O that my people would once and for all listen to me
  and walk faithfully in my footsteps, following my ways.
¹⁴ Then and only then will I conquer your every foe
  and tell every one of them, 'You must go!'
¹⁵ Those who hate my ways will cringe before me
  and their punishment will be eternal.
¹⁶ But I will feed you with my spiritual bread.
  You will feast and be satisfied with me,
  feeding on my revelation-truth like honey
  dripping from the cliffs of the high place."

---

a 81:6 Or "from holding the baskets," which alludes to the Hebrews carrying basket loads of
   burdens for their Egyptian masters.
b 81:7 The Hebrew includes the word *Meribah*, which means "the place of strife and contention."

82 TRUE JUSTICE

Asaph's poetic song

¹ All rise! For God now comes to judge
as he convenes heaven's courtroom. *ᵃ*
He judges every judge and rules over every ruler, saying,
² "How long will you judges refuse to listen
to the voice of true justice and continue to corrupt what is right
by judging in favor of the wrong?"

Pause in his presence

³ "Defend the defenseless, the fatherless and the forgotten,
the disenfranchised and the destitute.
⁴ Your duty is to deliver the poor and the powerless;
liberate them from the grasp of the wicked.
⁵ But you continue in your darkness and ignorance
while the foundations of society are shaken to the core!
⁶ Didn't I commission you as judges, saying,
'You are all like gods, since you judge on my behalf.
You are all like sons of the Most High, my representatives.'
⁷ Nevertheless, in death you are nothing but mere men!
You will be laid in the ground like any prince and you will die."
⁸ All rise! For God now takes his place as judge of all the earth.
Don't you know that everything and everyone belongs to him?
The nations will be sifted in his hands!

83 GOD, DON'T BE SILENT *ᵇ*

Asaph's poetic song

¹ God, you have to do something! *ᶜ* Don't be silent and just sit idly by.
²⁻³ Can't you see what they're doing?
All your enemies are stirred up in an uproar!
They despise you, Lord.
In their defiant arrogance they rise up
to host their secret council against your people.
They conspire together to come and harm
your cherished ones—your hidden ones.
⁴ Our enemies keep saying,
"Now is the time to wipe Israel off the map.
We'll destroy even the memory of her existence!"

---

a 82:1 Or "the council of El." The Aramaic says, "God now stands in the assembly of the
angels, and he will judge in their midst."
b The historical background to this psalm may be found in 2 Chron. 20:14–36.
c 83:1 Both the Aramaic and the Septuagint add a line in verse 1: "God, who is like you?"

⁵ They've made their pact, consulting and conspiring,
  aligning together in their covenant against God.
⁶⁻⁸ All the sons of Ishmael, the desert sheiks and the nomadic tribes,
    Amalekites, Canaanites, Moabites,
  and all the nations that surround us,
  Philistines, Phoenicians, Gadarenes,ᵃ and Samaritans;
  allied together they're ready to attack!

Pause in his presence

⁹ Do to them all what you did to the Midianites
  who were defeated by Gideon.
  Or what you did to Sisera and Jabin
  when Deborah and Barak defeated them by the Kishon River.
¹⁰ Do to your enemies what you did at Endor,
  whose rotting corpses fertilized the land.
¹¹⁻¹² Repeat history, God! Make all their "noble ones"
  die like Oreb, Zebah, and Zalmunna, who said in their pride,
  "We will seize God's people along with all their pleasant lands!"
¹³ Blow them away, God, like straw in the wind,
  like a tumbleweed in the wilderness!
¹⁴ Burn them up like a raging fire roaring down the mountainside;
  consume them all until only charred sticks remain!
¹⁵ Chase them away like before a mighty storm and terrifying tempest.
¹⁶ O Lord, disgrace them until their faces fill with shame,
  and make them acknowledge the glory of your name.
¹⁷ Make them utter failures in everything they do
  until they perish in total disgrace and humiliation
¹⁸ so they will know that you, and you alone,
  are Yahweh, the only Most High God exalted over all the earth!

---

a 83:6–8 As translated from the Aramaic. The Greek is "It includes the tents of Edom and Ishmael (Palestinians and those of southern Jordan), Moab (Palestinians and those of central Jordan) and Hagrites (Egyptians or possibly northern Jordanians), Gebal (Byblos and northern Lebanon), Ammon (Palestinians and northern Jordanians) and Amalek (Arabs of the Sinai Peninsula), Philistia (Gaza), and the inhabitants of Tyre (southern Lebanese). Even Assyria (Syrians and northern Iraqis) has become their ally as an arm [military might] for the sons of Lot." This comprises virtually every neighbor surrounding Israel.

84 LONGING FOR GOD

For the Pure and Shining One

A prophetic song written by the sons of Korah

Set to the melody of "For the Feast of Harvest"ᵃ

¹ God of Heaven's Armies, you find so much beauty in your people!
  They're like lovely sanctuaries of your presence. *ᵇ*

² Deep within me are these lovesick longings,
  desires and daydreams of living in union with you.
  When I'm near you my heart and my soul
  will sing and worship with my joyful songs of you,
  my true source and spring of life!

³ O Lord of Heaven's Armies, my King and my God,
  even the sparrows and swallows are welcome to build a nest
  among your altars for the birds to raise their young.

⁴ What pleasure fills those who live every day in your temple,
  enjoying you as they worship in your presence!

Pause in his presence

⁵ How enriched are they who find their strength in the Lord; *ᶜ*
  within their hearts are the highways of holiness! *ᵈ*

⁶ Even when their paths wind through the dark valley of tears,
  they dig deep to find a pleasant pool *where others find only pain.*
  He gives to them a brook of blessing
  filled from the rain of an outpouring.

⁷ They grow stronger and stronger with every step forward,
  and the God of all gods will appear before them in Zion.

⁸ Hear my cry, O God of Heaven's Armies!
  God of Jacob, listen to my loving prayer.

Pause in his presence

⁹ God, your wrap-around presence is our defense.
  In your kindness look upon the faces of your anointed ones. *ᵉ*

¹⁰ For just one day of intimacy with you*ᶠ* is like
  a thousand days of joy rolled into one!
  I'd rather stand at the threshold in front of the Gate Beautiful,

---

a   The Septuagint says, "For the wine vats."

b   84:1 The Hebrew word for "lovely" used here can also mean "beloved." The translator has
    chosen to use both of these concepts in this verse.

c   84:5 The Aramaic says, "How blessed is the Son of Man with you as his helper."

d   84:5 The Hebrew is literally "Roads are in their hearts." By implication it is the ways [roads]
    that lead us to God's holy presence.

e   84:9 Or "the face of your Anointed [Christ]."

f   84:10 Or "in your [temple] courts."

ready to go in and worship my God,
than to live my life without you
in the most beautiful palace of the wicked.
[11] For the Lord God is brighter than the brilliance of a sunrise!
Wrapping himself around me like a shield,
he is so generous with his gifts of grace and glory.
Those who walk along his paths with integrity
will never lack one thing they need, for he provides it all!
[12] O Lord of Heaven's Armies,
what euphoria fills those who forever trust in you!

85 MERCY AND TRUTH

For the Pure and Shining One
A prophetic song, composed by the sons of Korah

[1] Lord, your love has poured out
so many amazing blessings on our land!
You've restored Jacob's destiny from captivity.
[2] You've forgiven our many sins and covered
every one of them in your love.

Pause in his presence

[3] So now it's obvious that your blazing anger has ended and
the furious fire of wrath has been extinguished *by your mercy.*
[4] So bring us back to loving you, God our Savior.
Restore our hearts so that we'll never again
feel your anger rise against us.
[5] Will you forever hold a grudge?
Will your anger endure for all time?
[6] Revive us again, O God! I know you will! Give us a fresh start!
Then all your people will taste your joy and gladness.
[7] Pour out even more of your love on us!
Reveal more of your kindness and restore us back to you!
[8] Now I'll listen carefully for your voice
and wait to hear whatever you say.
Let me hear your promise of peace—
the message every one of your godly lovers longs to hear.
Don't let us in our ignorance turn back from following you.
[9] For I know your power and presence shines on all your lovers.
Your glory always hovers over all who bow low before you.
[10] Your mercy and your truth have married each other.
Your righteousness and peace have kissed.
[11] Flowers of your faithfulness are blooming on the earth.
Righteousness shines down from the sky.

¹² Yes, the Lord keeps raining down blessing after blessing,
  and prosperity will drench the land with a bountiful harvest.
¹³ For deliverance and peace are his forerunners,
  preparing a path for his steps.

86 A Prayer of Faith

King David's prayer

¹ Lord, bend down to listen to my prayer.
  I am in deep trouble. I'm broken and humbled,
  and I desperately need your help.
² Guard my life, for I'm your faithful friend, your loyal servant for life.
  I turn to you in faith, my God, my hero; come and rescue me!
³ Lord God, hear my constant cry for help;
  show me your favor and bring me to your fountain of grace!
⁴ Restore joy to your loving servant once again,
  for all I am is yours, O God.
⁵ Lord, you are so good to me, so kind in every way *a*
  and ready to forgive,
  for your grace-fountain keeps overflowing,
  drenching all your lovers who pray to you.
⁶ God, won't you pay attention to this urgent cry?
  Lord, bend down to listen to my prayer.
⁷ Whenever trouble strikes, I will keep crying out to you,
  for I know your help is on the way.
⁸ God, there's no one like you;
  there's no other god as famous as you.
  You outshine all others and your miracles make it easy to know you.
⁹ Lord Almighty, you are the one who created all the nations;
  Look at them—they're all on their way!
  Yes, the day will come when they all will worship you
  and put your glory on display.
¹⁰ You are the one and only God.
  What miracles! What wonders! What greatness belongs to you!
¹¹ Teach me more about you, how you work and how you move,
  so that I can walk onward in your truth
  until everything within me brings honor to your name.
¹² With all my heart and passion I will thank you, my God!
  I will give glory to your name, always and forever!
¹³ You love me so much and you placed your greatness upon me. *b*

---

a 86:5 The Septuagint says, "You're my provider."
b 86:13 As translated from the Aramaic.

You rescued me from the deepest place of darkness,
and you have delivered me from a certain death.

¹⁴ God, look at how these arrogant ones have defied me.
Like a vicious band of violent men they have tried to kill me.
They wouldn't worry for a moment that they were sinning against you!

¹⁵ But Lord, your nurturing love is tender and gentle.
You are slow to get angry yet so swift to show your faithful love.
You are full of abounding grace and truth. ᵃ

¹⁶ Bring me to your grace-fountain
so that your strength becomes mine.
Be my hero and come rescue your servant once again!

¹⁷ Send me a miraculous sign to show me how much you love me,
so that those who hate me will see it and be ashamed.
Don't they know that you, Lord, are my comforter,
the one who comes to help me?

87 FOUNTAINS OF JOY

A prophetic song, composed by the sons of Korah

¹ High upon his hills of holiness stands God's city. ᵇ
² How God loves the gates of Zion, his favorite place on earth. ᶜ
³ So many glorious things have been proclaimed
over Zion, God's holy city!

Pause in his presence

⁴ For the Lord says, "Here are the nations
who will acknowledge me as God: ᵈ
Egypt, ᵉ Iraq, ᶠ Palestine, ᵍ and the Mediterranean people, ʰ
even distant Ethiopia.
They will all boast, 'I was born in Zion!'"

⁵ But over Zion it will be said,
"The mighty Man was born there and he will establish it." ⁱ
For the God Most High will truly bless Jerusalem.

⁶ And when he counts her citizens, recording them in his registry,

---

a 86:15 As translated from the Aramaic and the Septuagint.
b 87:1 The Aramaic reads "His foundations are in his holy mountains."
c 87:2 Or "The Lord loves Zion's gates more than all the dwelling places of Jacob."
d 87:4 This is in anticipation of the nations of the earth coming to know Christ as the eternal King. See also Ps. 86:9.
e 87:4 Or "the proud one," which is a title given to Egypt. See Isa. 30:7.
f 87:4 Or "Babylon," which means "gate of God."
g 87:4 Or "Philistia," which means "land of sojourners."
h 87:4 Or "Tyre," which means "a rock."
i 87:5 As translated from the Aramaic. The Hebrew reads "Each one is born in Zion, and the Most High makes her secure."

he will write by their name: "This one was born again here!"

Pause in his presence

[7] And the princes of God's feasts will sing and dance, [a] singing,
"Every fountain of delight springs up from your life within me!"

88 SAVE ME FROM THIS SORROW [b]

To the Pure and Shining One
A prophetic song for the sons of Korah
To the tune of "Pierced," for instruction by Heman the Ezrahite

[1] Yahweh is the God who continually saves me.
  I weep before you night and day.
[2] Please bend down and listen to my sobbing,
  for my life is riddled with troubles
  and death is just around the corner!
[3] Everyone sees my life ebbing out.
  They consider me a hopeless case and see me as a dead man.
[4] They've all left me here to die, helpless,
  like one who is doomed for death.
[5] They're convinced you've forsaken me,
  certain that you've forgotten me completely—
  abandoned, pierced, with nothing to look forward to but death.
[6] They [c] have discarded me and thrown me down
  into the deepest darkness as into a bottomless pit.
[7] I feel your wrath and it's a heavy weight upon me,
  drowning me beneath a sea of sorrow.

Pause in his presence

[8] Why did you turn all my friends against me?
  You've made me like a cursed man in their eyes.
  No one wants to be with me now.
  You've caught me in a trap with no way out.
[9] Every day I beg for your help. Can't you see my tears?
  My eyes are swollen with weeping.
  My arms are wide, longing for mercy, [d]
  but you're nowhere to be found.
[10] How can those who are cut off from your care
  even know that you are there?

---

a 87:7 As translated from the Aramaic.
b This psalm has traditionally been used by Christians for reading on Good Friday. Many insights can be found here of the crucifixion of Jesus Christ.
c 88:6 As translated from the Septuagint. The Hebrew reads "You have discarded me."
d 88:9 As translated from the Septuagint. The Greek reads "My hands are stretched out to you."

How can I rise up to praise you if I'm dead and gone?

Pause in his presence

¹¹ Who can give thanks for your love in the graveyard?
Who preaches your faithfulness in the place of destruction?
¹² Does death's darkness declare your miracles?
How can anyone who's in the grave, where all is forgotten,
remember how you keep your promises?
¹³ Lord, you know my prayer before I even whisper it. [a]
At each and every sunrise you will
continue to hear my cry until you answer.
¹⁴ O Lord, why have you thrown my life away?
Will you keep turning the other way every time I call out to you?
¹⁵ I've had to live in poverty and trouble all my life. [b]
Now I'm humiliated, broken, and helpless before your terrors
and I can't take it anymore.
¹⁶ I'm overwhelmed by your burning anger.
I've taken the worst you could give me
and I'm speechless before you.
¹⁷ I'm drowning beneath the waves of this sorrow,
cut off with no one to help.
¹⁸ All my loved ones and friends keep far away from me,
leaving me all alone with only darkness as my friend.

89 WILL YOU REJECT US FOREVER?

Poems by Ethan the Ezrahite for instruction [c]

First Poem — God's Promises to David

¹ This forever-song I sing of the gentle love of God!
Young and old alike will hear about
your faithful, steadfast love—never failing!
² Here's my chorus: "Your mercy grows through the ages. [d]
Your faithfulness is firm, rising up to the skies."
³ I heard the Lord say, "My covenant has been made
and I'm committed forever to my chosen one, David.
⁴ I have made my oath that there will be sons of David forever,
sons that are kings through every generation."

Pause in his presence

⁵⁻⁶ Can you hear it? Heaven is filled with your praises, O Lord!

---

a 88:13 As translated from the Septuagint.
b 88:15 As translated from the Septuagint. The Greek reads "close to death all my life."
c Many scholars believe Ps. 89 contains four poems or stanzas. The translator has chosen to signify each poem with an inscription.
d 89:2 As translated from the Septuagint.

All the holy ones are praising you for your miracles.
The sons of God are all praising you for your mighty wonders.
We could search the skies forever and never find one like you.
All the mighty angels could not be compared to you.

[7] You are a God who is greatly to be feared
as you preside over the council of holy ones.
You are surrounded by trembling ones
who are overwhelmed with fear and dread,
stunned as they stand in awe of you!

[8] So awesome are you, O Yahweh, Lord God of Angel Armies!
Where could we find anyone as glorious as you?
Your faithfulness shines all around you!

[9] You rule over oceans and the swelling seas.
When their stormy waves rise, you speak, and they lie still. [a]

[10] You crushed the strongholds of Egypt
and all your enemies were scattered
at the mighty display of your glory-power.

[11] All the heavens and everything on earth belong to you,
for you are the Creator of all that is seen and unseen.

[12] The four corners of the earth were put in place by you.
You made the majestic mountains
that are still shouting their praises to your name.

[13] Breathtaking and awesome is your power!
Astounding and unbelievable
is your might and strength when it goes on display!

[14] Your glorious throne rests on a foundation
of righteousness and just verdicts.
Grace and truth are the attendants who go before you.

[15] O Lord, how blessed are the people
who experience the shout of worship,
for they walk in the radiance of your presence.

[16] We can do nothing but leap for joy all day long,
for we know who you are and what you do,
and you've exalted us on high.

[17] The glory of your splendor is our strength,
and your marvelous favor makes us even stronger,
lifting us even higher!

[18] You are our King, the holiest one of all;
your wrap-around presence is our protection.

---

a   89:9 This is a prophecy of Jesus, who would one day calm the stormy seas. See Matt.
8:23–27.

Second Poem — God Keeps His Promises

¹⁹⁻²⁰ You spoke to your prophets in visions, saying,
   "I have found a mighty hero for my people.
   I have chosen David as my loving servant and exalted him.
   I have anointed him as king with the oil of my holiness.
²¹ I will be strength to him and I will give him
   my grace to sustain him no matter what comes.
²² None of his enemies will get the best of him,
   nor will the wicked one overpower him.
²³ For I will crush his every adversary
   and do away with all who hate him.
²⁴ Because I love him and treasure him,
   my faithfulness will always protect him.
   I will place my great favor upon him,
   and I will cause his power and fame to increase.
²⁵ I will set his hand over the sea
   and his right hand over the rivers.
²⁶ And he will come before me, saying,
   'You truly are my Father, my only God, and my strong deliverer!'
²⁷ I am setting him apart, favoring him as my firstborn son.
   I will make him the most high king in all the earth!
²⁸ I will love him forever and always show him kindness.
   My covenant with him will never be broken.
²⁹ For I have decreed that he will always have an heir—
   a dynasty that will release the days of heaven on earth.
³⁰⁻³² But if his children turn from me and forsake my words,
   refusing to walk in my truth, renouncing and violating my laws,
   then I will surely punish them for their sins
   with my stern discipline until they regret it.
³³ But I will never, no never, lift my faithful love from off their lives.
   My kindness will prevail and I will never disown them.
³⁴⁻³⁵ How could I revoke my covenant of love that I promised David?
   For I have given him my word, my holy, irrevocable word.
   How could I lie to my loving servant David?
³⁶⁻³⁷ Sons of David will continue to reign on his throne,
   and their kingdom will endure as long as the sun is in the sky.
   This covenant will be an unbreakable promise that
   I have established for all time."

Pause in his presence

Third Poem — Why Has Our King Been Defeated?

³⁸ Why have you rejected me, the one you anointed?

Why would you cast me away?

Why would you lose your temper with me?

[39] You have torn up the contract you made with me, your servant.

You have stripped away my crown and thrown it to the ground. [a]

[40] You have torn down all my walls of defense

and have made my every hiding place into ruins.

[41] All the passersby attack and rob me while my neighbors mock!

[42] Instead of fighting for me, you took the side of my enemies,

even giving them strength to subdue me,

and then watched them celebrate their victory!

[43] You are no longer helping me in battle.

You've forsaken me to the swords of those

who would strike me down.

[44] You've made my regal splendor to decrease

and allowed my rule to be overthrown.

[45] Because of you, I've become old before my time and

I'm publicly disgraced!

Pause in his presence

Fourth Poem — Save Me, God

[46] How long will you hide your love from me?

Have you left me for good?

How long will your anger continue to burn against me?

[47] Remember, Lord, I am nothing but dust,

here today and so soon blown away.

Is this all you've created us for? For nothing but this?

[48] Which one of us will live forever?

We are all mortal, terminal, for we will all one day die.

Which one of us would ever escape our appointment with death

and dodge our own funeral?

Pause in his presence

[49] So God, where is all this love and kindness you promised us?

What happened to your covenant with David?

[50] Have you forgotten how your own servants are being slandered?

Lord God, it seems like I'm carrying in my heart

all the pain and abuse of many people.

[51] They have relentlessly insulted and persecuted us,

your anointed ones.

[52] Nevertheless, blessed be our God forever and ever.

Amen. Faithful is our King!

---

a   89:39 In place of the word *crown*, some translations render it "my dignity."

BOOK 4
THE NUMBERS PSALMS
Psalms of our pilgrimage on earth

90 GOD, THE ETERNAL

A prayer of Moses, God's prophet

[1] Lord, you have always been our eternal home,
   our hiding place from generation to generation.

[2] Long before you gave birth to the earth
   and before the mountains were born,
   you have been from everlasting to everlasting,[a]
   the one and only true God.

[3] When you speak the words "Life, return to me!"
   man turns back to dust.

[4] One thousand years pass before your eyes
   like yesterday that quickly faded away,
   like a night's sleep soon forgotten.[b]

[5-6] One day we will each be swept away into the sleep of death.
   We glide along through the tides of time—
   so quickly gone, like a dream that fades at dawn.[c]
   Like glistening grass that springs up one day
   and is dry and withered the next, ready to be cut down!

[7] Terrified by your anger, confined beneath the curse,
   we live our lives knowing your wrath.[d]

[8] For all of our faults and flaws are in full view to you.[e]
   Everything we want to hide, you search out
   and expose by the radiance of your face.

[9] We are banished to live in the shadow of your anger.
   Our days soon become years until our lifetime comes to an end,
   finished with nothing but a sigh.[f]

[10] You've limited our life span to a mere seventy years,
   yet some you give grace to live still longer.[g]
   But even the best of years are marred by tears and toils,

---

a 90:2 The Hebrew word for "eternity" is actually "horizon"—from one horizon to the other.

b 90:4 Or "like divisions [watches] of the night."

c 90:5–6 A poetic description of what is implied in the context.

d 90:7 Or "worn-out by your rage." Jesus has come and broken the curse and lifted the unbearable burden of our sins.

e 90:8 The Septuagint reads "The laws we have broken all stand before you."

f 90:9 The Septuagint reads "All our days have been filled with failures."

g 90:10 Or "if in strength eighty years."

and in the end with nothing more than a gravestone in a graveyard![a]
We're gone so quickly, so swiftly;
we pass away and simply disappear.

[11] Lord, who fully knows the power of your passion
and the intensity of your emotions?[b]

[12] Help us to remember that our days are numbered,
and help us to interpret our lives correctly.
Set your wisdom deeply in our hearts
so that we may accept your correction.[c]

[13] Return to us again, O God!
How much longer will it take until you show us
your abundant compassion?

[14] Let the sunrise of your love end our dark night.
Break through our clouded dawn again!
Only you can satisfy our hearts,
filling us with songs of joy to the end of our days.

[15] We've been overwhelmed with grief;
come now and overwhelm us with gladness.
Replace our years of trouble with decades of delight.

[16] Let us see your miracles again, and let the rising generation
see the glorious wonders you're famous for.

[17] O Lord our God, let your sweet beauty rest upon us
and give us favor.
Come work with us, and then our works will endure,
and give us success in all we do.

91 SAFE AND SECURE

[1] When you sit enthroned[d] under the shadow of Shaddai,[e]
you are hidden[f] in the strength of God Most High.

[2] He's the hope that holds me and the Stronghold to shelter me,

---

a 90:10 A poetic description of what is implied in the context. The Septuagint has the phrase "until we mellow and accept your correction."

b 90:11 As translated from the Aramaic. The Hebrew can be translated "Who could experience the strength of your anger? Who could endure the fear your fury can bring, and who truly comprehends the fear of God?"

c 90:12 As translated from the Septuagint.

d 91:1 Or "O, you who sits enthroned." The Hebrew word *yashab* is often associated with one seated as royalty. It is translated in Ezek. 27:8 as "leaders or rulers."

e 91:1 Shaddai (*šadday*) is taken from a Hebrew root word with many expressive meanings. It can mean "God of the Mountain, God the Destroyer of Enemies, God the Self-Sufficient One, God the Nurturer of Babies, God the Almighty."

f 91:1 Or "I endure through the night." See Job 39:28, where the same Hebrew word is used for an eagle passing the night on the high cliffs.

the only God for me, and my great confidence.

³ He will rescue you from every hidden trap of the enemy, *a*
and he will protect you from false accusation
and any deadly curse. *b*

⁴ His massive arms *c* are wrapped around you, protecting you.
You can run under his covering of majesty and hide.
His arms of faithfulness are a shield keeping you from harm.

⁵ You will never worry about an attack of demonic forces at night
nor have to fear a spirit of darkness coming against you.

⁶ Don't fear a thing!
Whether by night or by day, demonic danger will not trouble you, *d*
nor will the powers of evil launched against you.

⁷ Even in a time of disaster, with thousands and thousands being killed,
you will remain unscathed and unharmed.

⁸ you will be a spectator as the wicked perish in judgment,
for they will be paid back for what they have done!

⁹⁻¹⁰ When we live our lives within the shadow of God Most High,
our secret hiding place, we will always be shielded from harm.
How then could evil prevail against us or disease infect us?

¹¹ God sends angels with special orders to protect you wherever you go,
defending you from all harm.

¹² If you walk into a trap, they'll be there for you
and keep you from stumbling.

¹³ You'll even walk unharmed among the fiercest powers of darkness, *e*
trampling every one of them beneath your feet!

¹⁴ For here is what the Lord has spoken to me:
"Because you have delighted in me as my great lover,
I will greatly protect you.
I will set you in a high place, safe and secure before my face.

¹⁵ I will answer your cry for help every time you pray,

---

a 91:3 Or "hunter."

b 91:3 As translated from the most ancient Hebrew manuscripts and the Septuagint. The Hebrew word can mean "poisoned arrows."

c 91:4 Or "wings." Also found in the next sentence, "under his wings," which speaks not of God having wings, but of the wings of the cherubim resting on the mercy seat. The implication is that we can always come to the mercy seat and rest without fear.

d 91:6 Verses 5–6 are seen by many Jewish scholars as a reference not merely to pestilence and natural dangers but to the realm of spiritual darkness that would come against God's servants. These spirits are equated to "arrows that fly in daytime" or "a pestilence that walks" in the darkness. God's sheltered ones are kept from the harm that could come from natural sources or supernatural sources. What a wonderful place to hide and be secure!

e 91:13 The Hebrew includes the words for "lions," "snakes," and "dragons" (Heb. *basilisk*) as the three great symbols of satanic power.

and you will find and feel my presence
even in your time of pressure and trouble.
I will be your glorious hero and give you a feast.
¹⁶ You will be satisfied with a full life and with all that I do for you.
For you will enjoy the fullness of my salvation!"

92 A Sunday Morning Song of Praise

A poetic praise song for the day of worship^a

¹ It's so enjoyable to come before you
with uncontainable praises spilling from our hearts!
How we love to sing our praises over and over to you,
to the matchless God, high and exalted over all!
² At each and every sunrise we will be thanking you
for your kindness and your love.
As the sun sets and all through the night,
we will keep proclaiming, "You are so faithful!"
³ Melodies of praise will fill the air as every musical instrument,^b
joined with every heart, overflows with worship.
⁴ No wonder I'm so glad; I can't keep it in!
Lord, I'm shouting with glee over all you've done,
for all you've done for me!
⁵ What mighty miracles and your power at work, just to name a few.
Depths of purpose and layers of meaning
saturate everything you do.
⁶ Such amazing mysteries found within every miracle
that nearly everyone seems to miss.
Those with no discernment can never really discover
the deep and glorious secrets hidden in your ways.
⁷ It's true the wicked flourish, but only for a moment,
foolishly forgetting their destiny with death,
that they will all one day be destroyed forevermore.
⁸ But you, O Lord, are exalted forever
in the highest place of endless glory,
⁹ while all your opponents, the workers of wickedness,
will all perish, forever separated from you.
¹⁰ Your anointing has made me strong and mighty.
You've empowered my life for triumph^c
by pouring fresh oil over me.

---

a Ancient Jewish tradition holds that Adam composed this psalm on the first Sabbath of creation, and it was to be sung by the Levites on the Sabbath in the temple.
b 92:3 Or "a ten-stringed harp and lyre."
c 92:10 The Septuagint reads "I will raise my horn high like a rhinoceros [Hebrew translated to *wild ox*], and in my old age I will still have plenty of oil [anointing]."

[11]You've said that those lying in wait to pounce on me
   would be defeated,
      and now it's happened right in front of my eyes
      and I've heard their cries of surrender!
[12]Yes! Look how you've made all your lovers
   to flourish like palm trees,
      each one growing in victory, standing with strength![a]
[13]You've transplanted them into your heavenly courtyard,
   where they are thriving before you.
[14]For in your presence they will still overflow and be anointed.
   Even in their old age they will stay fresh,
      bearing luscious fruit and abiding faithfully.
[15]Listen to them! With pleasure they still proclaim:
"You're so good! You're my beautiful strength!
   You've never made a mistake with me."[b]

93 THE MAJESTY OF GOD

A Friday song, composed by King David after being resettled in the land [c]
[1]Look! Yahweh now reigns as King!
   He has covered himself with majesty and strength,
      wearing them as his splendor-garments.
   Regal power surrounds him as he sits securely on his throne.
   He's in charge of it all, the entire world,
      and he knows what he's doing!
[2]Lord, you have reigned as King from the very beginning of time.
   Eternity is your home.
[3-4]Chaos once challenged you.
   The raging waves lifted themselves over and over,
      high above the ocean's depths, letting out their mighty roar!
   Yet at the sound of your voice they were all stilled by your might.
   What a majestic King, filled with power!
[5]Nothing could ever change your royal decrees;
   they will last forever!
   Holiness is the beauty that fills your house;[d]
      you are the one who abides forevermore!

---

a 92:12 Or "growing high like a cedar in Lebanon." God makes us immortal and immovable.
b 92:15 Or "You are just and never unfair."
c This inscription is found in the Septuagint. Jews called this psalm "The Friday psalm." The Talmud indicates that this psalm was sung every Friday in the temple by the Levites.
d 93:5 Believers are now God's house, made holy by the blood of Jesus. See 1 Cor. 3:16 and Heb. 3:6.

94 GOD OF VENGEANCE

A Wednesday song, composed by King David [a]

1 Lord God Almighty, you are the God
  who takes vengeance on your enemies.
  It's time for you to punish evil!
  Let your rays of revelation-light shine from your people and
  pierce the conscience of the wicked and punish them.

2 It's time to arise as judge of all the earth;
  arise to punish the proud with the penalty they deserve!

3 How much longer will you sit back and watch the wicked
  triumph in their evil, boasting in all that is wrong?

4-5 Listen to them bragging among themselves,
  big in their own eyes, all because of the crimes
  they've committed against your people!
  See how they're crushing those who love you, God,
  cruelly oppressing those who belong to you. [b]

6 Heartlessly they murder the widows, the foreigners,
  and even the orphaned children.

7 They say to themselves, "The Lord God doesn't see this.
  Their God, the God of Jacob, he doesn't even care!"

8 But you'd better watch out, you stupid fools!
  You'd better wise up! Why would you act like God doesn't exist?
  Do you really think that God can't hear their cries?

9 God isn't hard of hearing; he'll hear all their cries.
  God isn't blind. He who made the eye has superb vision
  and he's watching all you do.

10 Won't the God who knows all things know what you've done?
  The God who punishes nations will surely punish you!

11 The Lord has fully examined every thought of man
  and found them all to be empty and futile.

12 Lord Yah, there's such a blessing that comes
  when you teach us your word and your ways. [c]
  Even the sting of your correction can be sweet.

13 It rescues us from our days of trouble
  until you are ready to punish the wicked. [d]

---

a This inscription is taken from the Septuagint. The Mishnah states that this psalm was sung
   by the Levites on the fourth day of the week, each Wednesday, in the temple.

b 94:4–5 Or "[the people of] his inheritance." See also v. 14.

c 94:12 Or "from your Torah."

d 94:13 Or "until a pit is dug for the wicked."

¹⁴ For the Lord will never walk away from his cherished ones,
nor would he forsake his chosen ones who belong to him. ^a
¹⁵ Whenever you pronounce judgments, they reveal righteousness. ^b
All your lovers will be pleased. ^c
¹⁶ Lord, who will protect me from these wicked ones?
If you don't stand to defend me, who will? I have no one but you!
¹⁷ I would have been killed so many times
if you had not been there for me.
¹⁸ When I screamed out, "Lord, I'm doomed!"
your fiery love was stirred and you raced to my rescue.
¹⁹ Whenever my busy thoughts were out of control,
the soothing comfort of your presence
calmed me down and overwhelmed me with delight.
²⁰ It's obvious to all; you will have nothing to do
with corrupt rulers who pass laws that empower evil
and defeat what is right.
²¹ For they gang up against the lovers of righteousness
and condemn the innocent to death.
²²⁻²³ But I know that all their evil plans will boomerang back onto them.
Every plot they hatch will simply seal their own doom.
For you, my God, you will destroy them,
giving them what they deserve.
For you are my true tower of strength,
my safe place, my hideout, and my true shelter.

95 It's Time to Sing

¹ Come on, everyone! Let's sing for joy to the Lord!
Let's shout our loudest praises to our God who saved us!
² Everyone come meet his face with a thankful heart.
Don't hold back your praises;
make him great by your shouts of joy!
³ For the Lord is the greatest of all,
King-God over all other gods!
⁴ In one hand he holds the mysteries of the earth
and in the other he holds the highest mountain peaks.
⁵ He's the owner of every ocean,
the engineer and sculptor of earth itself!
⁶ Come and kneel before this Creator-God;
come and bow before the mighty God, our majestic maker!

---

a 94:14 Or "[the people of] his inheritance."
b 94:15 Or "justice will prevail."
c 94:15 The Hebrew reads "and after it [judgment] are the pure in heart."

[7-9] For we are the lovers he cares for and he is the God we worship.
So drop everything else and listen to his voice!
For this is what he's saying:
"Today, when I speak,
don't even think about turning a deaf ear to me
like they did when they tested me at Meribah and Massah, [a]
the place where they argued with me, their Creator.
Your ancestors challenged me over and over with their complaining,
even though I had convinced them of my power and love.
They still doubted my care for them.
[10] So for forty long years I was grieved and disgusted by them.
I described them as wicked wanderers
whose hearts would not follow my ways or keep my words.
[11] So I made a vow in my anger and declared,
'They will never enter the resting place I've planned for them!'
So don't you ever be hard-hearted or stubborn like they were!"

96 KING OF THE WORLD

[1] Go ahead—sing your new song to the Lord!
Let everyone in every language sing him a new song. [b]
[2-3] Don't stop! Keep on singing! Make his name famous!
Tell everyone every day how wonderful he is.
Give them the good news of our great Savior.
Take the message of his glory and miracles to every nation.
Tell them about all the amazing things he has done.
[4] For the Lord's greatness is beyond description
and he deserves all the praise that comes to him.
He is our King-God and it's right to be in holy awe of him.
[5] Other gods are absolutely worthless. [c]
For the Lord God is Creator-God,
who spread the splendor of the skies!
[6] Breathtaking brilliance and awe-inspiring majesty
radiate from his shining presence.
His stunning beauty overwhelms all who come before him. [d]
[7] Surrender to the Lord Yahweh, all you nations and peoples.
Surrender to him all your pride and strength.
[8] Confess that Jehovah alone deserves all the glory and honor.
Bring an offering and come celebrate in his courts.

---

a 95:7–9 *Meribah* means strife, argument. *Massah* means testing.
b 96:1 Every new thing God does requires a new song to make it known.
c 96:5 The Septuagint reads "demons."
d 96:6 Or "Strength and beauty are in his sanctuary."

⁹ Come worship the Lord God wearing the splendor of holiness.
  Let everyone wait in wonder as they tremble in awe before him.
¹⁰ Tell the nations plainly that Yahweh rules over all!
  He is doing a great job, and nothing will disrupt him,
  for he treats everyone fair and square.
¹¹⁻¹² Let the skies sing for joy! Let the earth join in the chorus.
  Let oceans thunder and fields echo this ecstatic praise
  until every swaying tree of every forest joins in,
  lifting up their songs of joyous praise to him!
¹³ For here he comes, the Lord God,
  and he's ready to judge the world.
  He will do what's right and can be trusted
  to always do what's fair.

97 GOD RULES OVER ALL

A psalm of David when his kingdom was established[a]

¹ Yahweh now reigns as King! Let everyone rejoice!
  His rule extends everywhere, even to distant lands,
  and the islands of the sea, let them all be glad.
² Clouds both dark and mysterious now surround him.[b]
  His throne of glory rests upon
  a foundation of righteousness and justice.
³ All around him burns a blazing glory-fire consuming all his foes.
⁴ When his lightning strikes, it lights up the world.
  People are wide-eyed as they tremble and shake.
⁵ Mountains melt away like wax in a fire
  when the Lord of all the earth draws near.
⁶ Heaven's messengers preach righteousness and
  people everywhere see his glory in the sky!
⁷ Shame covers all who boast in other gods, for they worship idols.
  For all the supernatural powers once worshiped
  the true and living God.
⁸ But God's Zion-people are content,
  for they know and hear the truth.
  The people of praise rejoice over all your judgments, O Lord!
⁹ For you are King-God, the Most High God over all the earth.
  You are exalted above every supernatural power!
¹⁰ Listen, you lovers of God! Hate evil,
  for God can keep you from wrong
  and protect you from the power of wickedness.

---

a This inscription is from the Septuagint.
b 97:2 See also Deut. 4:11 and 5:22.

[11] For he sows seeds of light within his lovers,
and seeds of joy burst forth for the lovers of God!
[12] So be glad and continue to give him thanks,
for God's holiness is seen in everything he does.

98 SING A NEW SONG

David's poetic praise [a]

[1] Go ahead—sing your brand-new song to the Lord!
He is famous for his miracles and marvels,
for he is victorious through his mighty power and holy strength.
[2] Everyone knows how God has saved us,
for he has displayed his justice throughout history.
[3] He never forgets to show us his love and faithfulness.
How kind he has been to Israel!
All the nations know how he stands behind his people
and how he saves his own.
[4] So go ahead, everyone, and shout out your praises with joy!
Break out of the box and let loose
with the most joyous sound of praise!
[5] Sing your melody of praise to the Lord
and make music like never before! [b]
[6] Blow those trumpets and shofars!
Shout with joyous triumph before King Yahweh!
[7] Let the ocean's waves join in the chorus with their roaring praise
until everyone everywhere shouts out in unison,
"Glory to the Lord!"
[8] Let the rivers and streams clap with applause
as the mountains rise in a standing ovation
to join the mighty choir of exaltation.
[9] Look! Here he comes! The Lord and judge of all the earth!
He's coming to make things right and to do it fair and square.
And everyone will see that he does all things well!

99 GOD OF HOLINESS

[1] Yahweh is King over all! Everyone trembles in awe before him.
He rules enthroned between the wings of the cherubim.
So let the earth shake and quake in wonder before him!
[2] For Yahweh is great and glorious in the midst of his Zion-people.
He is exalted above all!

---

a   The Septuagint has David as the author. The Hebrew says simply, "A psalm."
b   98:5 Or "accompanied by a harp and the sound of music."

[3] Let everyone praise this breathtaking God, for he is holy.
[4] A lover of justice is our mighty King; he is right in all his ways.
   He insists on being fair to all,
      promoting true justice and righteousness in Jacob.
[5] So everyone, exalt the Lord our God
      facedown before his glory-throne, for he is great and holy.
[6] *God has his praying priests,*
      like Moses, Aaron, and Samuel, who all interceded,
      asking God for help.
      God heard their cries and came to their rescue.
[7] He spoke to them from the pillar of clouds
      and they followed his instructions,
      doing everything he told them.
[8] God, the great forgiver, answered their prayers.
      Yet he would punish them when they went astray.
[9] Keep exalting the Lord our God
      facedown before his glory-throne, for he is great and holy!

100 PRAISE GOD

A poetic song for thanksgiving

[1] Lift up a great shout of joy to the Lord!
      Go ahead and do it—everyone, everywhere!
[2] As you serve him, be glad and worship him.
      Sing your way into his presence with joy!
[3] And realize what this really means—
      we have the privilege of worshiping the Lord our God.
      For he is our Creator and we belong to him.
      We are the people of his pleasure. [a]
[4] You can pass through his open gates with the password of praise.
      Come right into his presence with thanksgiving.
      Come bring your thank offering to him
      and affectionately bless his beautiful name!
[5] For the Lord is always good and ready to receive you.
      He's so loving that it will amaze you—
      so kind that it will astound you!
      And he is famous for his faithfulness toward all.
      Everyone knows our God can be trusted,
      for he keeps his promises to every generation!

---

a 100:3 Or "the sheep of his pasture."

101 Integrity

David's poetic praise

¹ Lord, I will sing about your faithful love for me.
  My song of praise will have your justice as its theme.
² I'm trying my best to walk in the way of integrity,
  especially in my own home.
  But I need your help!
  I'm wondering, Lord, when will you appear?
³ I refuse to gaze on that which is vulgar.
  I despise what is evil
  and anything that moves my heart away from you.
  I will not let evil hold me in its grip.
⁴ Every perverse and crooked way I have put away from my heart,
  for I will have nothing to do with the deeds of darkness. *a*
⁵ I will silence those who secretly want to slander my friends,
  and I will not tolerate the proud and arrogant.
⁶ My innermost circle will only be those
  whom I know are pure and godly.
  They will be the only ones I allow to minister to me.
⁷ There's no room in my home for hypocrites,
  for I can't stand chronic liars who flatter and deceive.
⁸ At each and every sunrise I will awake to do what's right
  and put to silence those who love wickedness,
  freeing God's people *b* from their evil grip.
  I will do all of this because of my great love for you! c

102 From Tears to Praise

*A prayer for those who are overwhelmed and for all the discouraged who come
to pour out their hearts before the Lord d*

¹ Lord, listen to my prayer! Listen to my cry for help!
² You can't hide your face from me in the day of my distress.
  Stoop down to hear my prayer and answer me quickly, Lord!
³⁻⁴ For my days of happiness have gone up in smoke.
  My body is raging with fever, my heart is sick,
  and I'm consumed by this illness—
  withered like a dead leaf. I can't even eat.

---

a 101:4 Or "evil people."
b 101:8 Or "the city of Yahweh."
c 101:8 This phrase, implied in the Hebrew text, brings conclusion to the psalm.
d As translated from the Septuagint.

⁵ I'm nothing but skin and bones.
   Nothing's left of me but whispered groans.
⁶ I'm depressed, lonely, forgotten, and abandoned. ᵃ
⁷ I'm sleepless, shivering in the cold, forlorn and friendless,
   like a lonely bird on the rooftop.
⁸ My every enemy mocks and insults me incessantly.
   They even use my name as a curse to speak over others!
⁹⁻¹⁰ Because of your great and furious anger against me
   all I do is suffer with sorrow,
   with nothing to eat but a meal of mourning. ᵇ
   My crying fills my cup with salty tears!
   In your wrath you have rejected me,
   sweeping me away like dirt on the floor.
¹¹ My days are marked by the lengthening shadows of death.
   I'm withering away and there's nothing left of me.
¹² But then I remember that you, O Lord,
   still sit enthroned as King over all!
   The fame of your name will be revealed to every generation.
¹³ I know you are about to arise and show your tender love to Zion.
   Now is the time, Lord,
   for your compassion and mercy to be poured out—
   the appointed time has come
   for your prophetic promises to be fulfilled!
¹⁴ For your servants weep in sympathy over Zion's ruins
   and feel love for her every stone.
¹⁵ When you arise to intervene,
   all the nations and kings will be stunned
   and will fear your awesome name, trembling before your glory!
¹⁶ Yes, you will reveal yourself to Zion
   and appear in the brightness of your glory
   to restore her and give her children.
¹⁷ He responds to the prayer of the poor and broken
   and will not despise the cry of the homeless.
¹⁸ Write all this down for the coming generation,
   so re-created people ᶜ will read it and praise the Lord!
¹⁹ Tell them how Yah ᵈ looked down from his high and holy place,
   gazing from his glory to survey the earth.

---

a 102:6 The Hebrew makes reference to a "pelican" or "vulture" in the wilderness and "an owl in desolate ruins." The translator has chosen to use the obvious meanings of the metaphors.

b 102:9–10 Or "I eat ashes as if they were bread." Ashes speak of mourning, for mourners would often throw dust and ashes over their heads.

c 102:18 Or "those born anew [re-created]."

d 102:19 Taken from *Yah*weh. Yah is often used as the name of the God of Power.

²⁰ He listened to all the groaning of his people longing to be free,
and he set loose the sons of death to experience life.
²¹ Multitudes will stream to Jerusalem to
praise the Lord and declare his name in Zion!
²² Peoples from every land, their kings and kingdoms,
will gather together to worship the Lord.
²³ But God has brought me to my knees, shortening my life.
²⁴ So I cry out to you, my God, Father of eternity,
please don't let me die!
I know my life is not yet finished.
²⁵ With your hands you once formed the foundations of the earth
and handcrafted the heavens above.
²⁶⁻²⁷ They will all fade away one day like worn-out clothing,
ready to be discarded, but you'll still be here.
You will replace it all!
Your first creation will be changed,
but you alone will endure, the God of all eternity!
²⁸ Generation after generation our descendants will live securely,
for you are the one protecting us, keeping us for yourself.

103 OUR FATHER'S LOVE

King David's song of praise

¹ With my whole heart, with my whole life,
and with my innermost being,
I bow in wonder and love before you, the holy God!
² Yahweh, you are my soul's celebration.
How could I ever forget the miracles of kindness
you've done for me?
³ You kissed my heart with forgiveness, in spite of all I've done. *ᵃ*
You've healed me inside and out from every disease.
⁴ You've rescued me from hell *ᵇ* and saved my life.
You've crowned me with love and mercy.
⁵ You satisfy my every desire with good things. *ᶜ*
You've supercharged my life so that I soar again *ᵈ*
like a flying eagle in the sky!

---

a 103:3 Starting from this verse and through the rest of the psalm, the writer shifts to the second person (you). The translator has chosen to leave the psalm in the first person to enhance the poetic nuance for the English reader.

b 103:4 Or "redeemed me from the pit," a term often used for Sheol or hell.

c 103:5 The Hebrew text is somewhat difficult to understand. It is literally "who satisfies with good ornaments."

d 103:5 Or "your youth [implying both strength and beauty] he restores."

⁶You're a God who makes things right,
    giving justice to the defenseless.
⁷You unveiled to Moses your plans
    and showed Israel's sons what you could do.
⁸Lord, you're so kind and tenderhearted
    to those who don't deserve it *a*
    and so patient with people who fail you!
    Your love is like a flooding river
    overflowing its banks with kindness. *b*
⁹You don't look at us only to find our faults, *c*
    just so that you can hold a grudge against us.
¹⁰You may discipline us for our many sins,
    but never as much as we really deserve.
    Nor do you get even with us for what we've done.
¹¹Higher than the highest heavens—
    that's how high your tender mercy extends!
    Greater than the grandeur of heaven above
    is the greatness of your loyal love, towering over all
    who fear you and bow down before you!
¹²Farther than from a sunrise to a sunset—
    that's how far you've removed our guilt from us.
¹³The same way a loving father feels toward his children—
    that's but a sample of your tender feelings toward us, *d*
    your beloved children, who live in awe of you.
¹⁴You know all about us, inside and out. *e*
    You are mindful that we're made from dust.
¹⁵Our days are so few, and our momentary beauty *f*
    so swiftly fades away!

---

a 103:8 Or "Lord, you're so compassionate and merciful." The Hebrew word for "compassion" is a homonym for "womb." The Lord carries his people like a mother carries a child in her womb.

b 103:8 See Ex. 34:6.

c 103:9 Or "You [he] will not always fight with us [like fighting with enemies]."

d 103:13 Or "like a father has deep compassion on his children." The Hebrew word for "tender feelings" is *raham*, which is a homonym and can also be translated "womb." Our Father carries you in his womb. What a beautiful word play that our Father has a mother's nurturing love for his children.

e 103:14 The Hebrew word *yatsar* is a homonym and can be translated "form" or "frame." God knows our frame. But *yatsar* also means "to be in distress" or "to be frustrated." So this sentence could be translated "You know all about our frustrations and distress." These thoughts combined would mean that God hasn't forgotten that he formed us from dust and we'll experience frustrations as human beings. God is sympathetic to our difficulties.

f 103:15 The Hebrew word translated "beauty" actually means "shining."

[16] Then all of a sudden we're gone,
  like grass clippings blown away in a gust of wind,
  taken away to our appointment with death,
  leaving nothing to show that we were here.
[17] But Lord, your endless love stretches
  from one eternity to the other,
  unbroken and unrelenting toward those who fear you
  and those who bow facedown in awe before you.
  Your faithfulness to keep every gracious promise you've made
  passes from parents, to children, to grandchildren, and beyond.
[18] You are faithful to all those who follow your ways
  and keep your word.
[19] God's heavenly throne is eternal, secure, and strong,
  and his sovereignty rules the entire universe.
[20] So bless the Lord, all his messengers of power,
  for you are his mighty heroes who listen intently
  to the voice of his word to do it.
[21] Bless and praise the Lord, you mighty warriors,
  ministers who serve him well and fulfill his desires.
[22] I will bless and praise the Lord with my whole heart!
  Let all his works throughout the earth,
  wherever his dominion stretches,
  let everything bless the Lord!

104 OUR CREATOR'S COMPASSION [a]

[1] Everything I am will praise and bless the Lord!
  O Lord, my God, your greatness takes my breath away,
  overwhelming me by your majesty, beauty, and splendor! [b]
[2] You wrap yourself with a shimmering, glistening light.
  You wear sunshine like a garment of glory.
  You stretch out the starry skies like a tapestry.
[3] You build your balconies with light beams
  and ride as King in a chariot you made from clouds.
  You fly upon the wings of the wind.

---

a This psalm, attributed to David in the Septuagint, can be seen as an exposition of the days
  of creation:
  1st day: vv. 1–2
  2nd day: vv. 3–4
  3rd day: vv. 5–17
  4th day: vv. 18–23
  5th day: vv. 24–26
  6th day: vv. 21–30
b 104:1 See Job 40:10.

⁴ You make your messengers into winds of the Spirit
  and all your ministers become flames of fire.
⁵ You, our Creator, formed the earth,
  and you hold it all together so it will never fall apart.
⁶ You poured the ocean depths over the planet,
  submerging mountains beneath.
⁷ Yet at the sound of your thunder-shout
  the waters all fled away, filling the deep with seas.
⁸ The mountains rose and valleys sank
  to the levels you decreed for them.
⁹ Then you set a boundary line for the seas
  and commanded them not to trespass.
¹⁰ You sent springs cascading through the valleys,
  flowing freely between the mountains and hills.
¹¹ You provide drink for every living thing;
  men and beasts *a* have their thirst quenched because of you.
¹² The birds build nests near the tranquil streams,
  chirping their joyous songs from the branches above.
¹³ From your kindness you send the rain to water the mountains
  from the upper rooms of your palace.
  Your goodness *b* brings forth fruit for all to enjoy.
¹⁴ Your compassion brings the earth's harvest, feeding the hungry.
  You cause the grass to grow for livestock,
  along with the fruit, grains, and vegetables to feed mankind.
¹⁵ You provide sweet wine to gladden hearts.
  You give us daily bread to sustain life,
  giving us glowing health for our bodies. *c*
¹⁶ The trees of the Lord drink until they're satisfied.
  Lebanon's lofty trees stand tall right where you planted them.
¹⁷ Within their branches you provide for birds
  a place to build their nests;
  even herons find a home in the cypress trees.
¹⁸ You make the high mountains a home for wild goats
  and the rocky crag where the rock badgers burrow.
¹⁹ You made the moon to mark the months
  and the sun to measure the days.
²⁰ You turn off the light and it becomes night,
  and all the beasts of the forest come out to prowl.
²¹ The mighty lions roar for their dinner,
  but it's you, God, who feeds them all.

---

a 104:11 Or "wild donkeys."
b 104:13 Or "your works."
c 104:15 Or "oil for our faces to shine."

²² At sunrise they slink back to their dens
   to crouch down in the shadows.
²³ Then man goes out to his labor and toil,
   working from dawn to dusk.
²⁴ O Lord, what an amazing variety of all you have created!
   Wild and wonderful is this world you have made,
   while wisdom was there at your side.
   This world is full of so many creatures, yet each belongs to you!
²⁵ And then there is the sea! So vast! So wide and deep—
   swarming with countless forms of sea life, both small and great.
²⁶ Trading ships glide through the high seas.
   And look! There are the massive whales
   bounding upon the waves.
²⁷ All the creatures wait expectantly for you
   to give them their food as you determine.
²⁸ You come near and they all gather around,
   feasting from your open hands,
   and each is satisfied from your abundant supply.
²⁹ But if you were to withhold from them and turn away,
   they all would panic.
   And when you choose to take away their breath,
   each one dies and returns to the dust.
³⁰ When you release your Spirit-wind, life is created,
   ready to replenish life upon the earth.
³¹ May God's glorious splendor endure forever!
   May the Lord take joy and pleasure in all that he has made.
³² For the earth's overseer has the power to make it tremble;
   just a touch of his finger and volcanoes erupt
   as the earth shakes and melts.
³³ I will sing my song to the Lord as long as I live!
   Every day I will sing my praises to God.
³⁴ May you be pleased with every sweet thought I have about you,
   for you are the source of my joy and gladness.
³⁵ Now, let all the sinners be swept from the earth.
   But I will keep on praising you, my Lord, with all that is within me.
   My joyous, blissful shouts of "Hallelujah" are all because of you!

105 GOD'S WONDERFUL WORKS [a]

¹ Go ahead and give God thanks
   for all the glorious things he has done!
   Go ahead and worship him!
   Tell everyone about his wonders!
² Let's sing his praises! Sing, and put all of his miracles to music!
³ Shine and make your joyful boast in him, you lovers of God.
   Let's be happy and keep rejoicing no matter what.
⁴ Seek more of his strength! Seek more of him!
   Let's always be seeking the light of his face.
⁵ Don't you ever forget his miracles and marvels.
   Hold to your heart every judgment he has decreed.
⁶ For you are his servants, the true seed of Abraham,
   and you are the chosen ones, Jacob's sons.
⁷ For he is the Lord our God,
   and his wise authority [b] can be seen in all he does.
⁸⁻⁹ For though a thousand generations may pass away,
   he is still true to his word.
   He has kept every promise [c] he made to Abraham and to Isaac.
¹⁰ His promises have become an everlasting covenant to Jacob,
   as a decree to Jacob.
¹¹ He said to them, "I will give you all the land of Canaan
   as your inheritance."
¹² They were very few in number
   when God gave them that promise,
   and they were all foreigners to that land.
¹³ They were wandering from one land to another
   and from one kingdom to another. [d]
¹⁴ Yet God would not permit anyone to touch them,
   punishing even kings who came against them.
¹⁵ He said to them, "Don't you dare lay a hand on my anointed ones,
   and don't do a thing to hurt my prophets!"
¹⁶ So God decreed a famine upon Canaan land,
   cutting off their food supply.
¹⁷ But he had already sent a man ahead of his people to Egypt;
   it was Joseph, who was sold as a slave.

---

a   The first fifteen verses of this psalm were sung as the ark of glory was brought up to Jerusalem. See 2 Sam. 6 and 1 Chron. 13–16.
b   105:7 Or "judgments."
c   105:8–9 Or "promise of the covenant [pact]."
d   105:13 Or "from a kingdom to another nation."

¹⁸ His feet were bruised by strong shackles
  and his soul was held by iron.
¹⁹ God's promise to Joseph purged his character
  until it was time for his dreams to come true.
²⁰ Eventually, the king of Egypt sent for him, setting him free at last.
²¹ Then Joseph was put in charge of everything under the king;
  he became the master of the palace
  over all of the royal possessions.
²² Pharoah gave him authority over all the princes of the land,
  and Joseph became the teacher of wisdom to the king's advisors.
²³ Then Jacob, with all of Joseph's family,
  came from Canaan to Egypt and settled in Goshen. ^a
²⁴ God made them very fruitful, and they multiplied incredibly
  until they were greater in number than those who ruled them.
²⁵ God turned their hearts to hate his people
  and to deal treacherously with his servants.
²⁶ But he sent them his faithful servant, Moses, the deliverer,
  and chose Aaron to accompany him.
²⁷ Their command brought down signs and wonders,
  working miracles in Egypt.
²⁸ By God's direction, they spoke and released a plague
  of thick darkness over the land.
²⁹ God turned their rivers to blood, causing every fish to die.
³⁰ And the judgment-plague of frogs came in enormous numbers,
  swarming everywhere, even into Pharaoh's bedroom!
³¹ God spoke and another plague was released—
  massive swarms of flies, vast clouds of insects, covered the land.
³² God rained down hail and flaming fire upon Egypt.
³³ Their gardens and vines were all destroyed,
  shattering trees into splinters throughout the territory.
³⁴ God spoke, and devouring hordes of locusts swept over the land,
³⁵ picking the ground clean of vegetation and crops.
³⁶ Then God struck down their firstborn sons,
  the pride and joy ^b of every Egyptian family.
³⁷ At last, God freed all the Hebrews from their slavery
  and sent them away laden with the silver and gold of Egypt.
  And not even one was feeble ^c on their way out!
³⁸ Egypt was relieved at their exodus, ready to see them go,
  for the terror of the Lord of the Hebrews had fallen upon them!

---

a 105:23 Or "lived as a foreigner in the land of Ham [Egypt]." Ham was a son of Noah.
b 105:36 Or "the beginning of all their strength."
c 105:37 Or "Not one of his tribes was a pauper" or "Not one stumbled."

³⁹ God spread out a cloud as shade as they moved ahead
    and a cloud of fire to light up their night.
⁴⁰ Moses prayed and God brought them quail to eat.
    He satisfied them with heaven's bread falling from the sky.
⁴¹ He broke open the boulder
    and the waters poured out like a river in the desert.
⁴² For God could never forget
    his holy promise to his servant Abraham.
⁴³ So God brought out his chosen ones with singing;
    with a joyful shout they were set free!
⁴⁴ He gave them lands and nations, just like he promised.
    Fruitful lands of crops they had never planted were now theirs.
⁴⁵ All this was done for them so that they would be faithful
    to keep the ways of God, obeying his laws and following his truths.
    Hallelujah! Praise the Lord!

106 GOD IS GOOD

¹ Hallelujah! Praise the Lord!
    Everyone thank God, for he is good and easy to please.
    Your tender love for us, Lord, continues on forever.
² Who could ever fully describe your glorious miracles?
    Yahweh, who could ever praise you enough?
³ The happiest one on earth is the one who keeps your word
    and clings to righteousness every moment.
⁴ So remember me, Lord, as you take joy in your people.
    And when you come to bring the blessings of salvation,
    don't forget me!
⁵ Let me share in the wealth and beauty of all your lovers,
    rejoice with your nation in all their joys,
    and let me share in the glory you give to your chosen ones.
⁶ We have all sinned so much, just like our fathers.
    "Guilty" is written over our lives.
⁷ Our fathers who were delivered from Egypt
    didn't fully understand your wonders,
    and they took you for granted.
    Over and over you showed them such tender love and mercy!
    Yet they were barely beyond the Red Sea
    when they rebelled against you.
⁸ Nonetheless, you saved them more than once
    so they would know how powerful you are,
    showing them the honor of your name.
⁹ You roared over the waters of the Red Sea,
    making a dry path for your people to cross through.

¹⁰ You freed them from the strong power
  of those who oppressed them
  and rescued them from bondage.
¹¹ Then the waters rushed over their enemies and drowned them all—
  not one survived.
¹² Seeing this, the people believed your words,
  and they all broke out with songs of praise!
¹³ Yet how quickly they forgot your miracles of power.
  They wouldn't wait for you to act when they were hungry,
¹⁴ but demanded you satisfy their cravings and give them food!
  They tested you to the breaking point.
¹⁵ So you gave them what they wanted to eat,
  but their souls starved away to nothing.
¹⁶ They became envious of Moses and Aaron, your holy ones.
¹⁷ You split open the earth and it swallowed up
  Dathan and Abiram along with their followers.
¹⁸ Fire fell from heaven and burnt up all the band of rebels,
  turning them to ashes.
¹⁹ They made an idol of a calf at Sinai
  and bowed to worship their man-made statue.
²⁰ They preferred the image of a grass-eating ox
  to the presence of the glory-filled God.
²¹⁻²² They totally forgot it was you who saved them
  by the wonders and awesome miracles you worked in Egypt.
²³ So you were fed up and decided to destroy them.
  But Moses, your chosen leader,
  stood in the gap between you and the people
  and made intercession on their behalf
  to turn away your wrath from killing them all.
²⁴ Yet they still didn't believe your words
  and they despised the land of delight you gave to them.
²⁵ They grumbled and found fault with everything
  and closed their hearts to your voice.
²⁶ So you gave up and swore to them
  that they would all die in the desert.
²⁷ And you scattered their children to distant lands to die as exiles.
²⁸ Then our fathers joined the worshipers
  of the false god named "Lord of the Pit."
  They even ate the sacrifices offered to the dead!
²⁹ All they did made you burn with anger.
  It made you so angry that a plague broke out among them!

[30] It continued until Phineas intervened and executed
the guilty for causing judgment to fall upon them. [a]
[31] Because of this deed of righteousness
Phineas will be remembered forever.
[32] Your people also provoked you to wrath
at the stream called Strife. [b]
This is where Moses got into serious trouble!
[33] Because the people were rebellious against you,
Moses exploded in anger and spoke to them out of his bitterness.
[34] Neither did our fathers destroy the enemies in the land,
as you had commanded them.
[35] But they mingled themselves with their enemies
and learned to copy their works of darkness.
[36] They began to serve their gods and bow before their idols.
All of this led them away from you
and brought about their downfall.
[37] They even sacrificed their little children to the demon spirits,
[38-39] shedding the innocent blood of their sons and daughters.
These dark practices greatly defiled the land and their own souls,
through the murder and bloodshed of their own babies!
Their sins made them spiritual adulterers before you.
[40] This is why you were furious.
As your anger burned hot against them,
you couldn't even stand to look
at your very own people any longer!
[41] So you turned them over to the crushing hands of other nations,
and those who hated them became tyrants over them.
[42] Oppressive enemies subdued them,
ruling over them with their tyranny.
[43] Many times you would have come to rescue them,
but they continued in their rebellious ways,
choosing to ignore your warnings.
Then they sank lower and lower, destroyed by their depravity.
[44-45] Yet even so, you waited and waited,
watching to see if they would turn
and cry out to you for a father's help.
And then, when you heard their cry,
you relented and you remembered your covenant
and you turned your heart toward them again,
according to your abundant, overflowing, and limitless love.

a 106:30 This is implicit information found in the story of Phineas (Num. 25:7-9).
b 106:32 The word used here is Meribah, the Hebrew word for "strife" (Num. 20:1-13).

⁴⁶ Then you caused even their oppressors
  to pity them and show them compassion.
⁴⁷ Do it again, Lord! Save us, O Lord, our God!
  Gather us from our exile and unite us together
  so that we will give our great and joyous thanks to you again
  and bring you glory by our praises.
⁴⁸ Blessed be our Lord God forever and ever.
  And let everyone everywhere say, "Hallelujah!"
  Amen! Faithful is our King!

BOOK 5
THE DEUTERONOMY PSALMS
Psalms of praise and the Word

107 GOD'S CONSTANT LOVE

¹ Let everyone give all their praise and thanks to the Lord!
  Here's why—he's better than anyone could ever imagine.
  Yes, he's always loving and kind, and his faithful love never ends.
²⁻³ So, go ahead—let everyone know it!
  Tell the world how he broke through
  and delivered you from the power of darkness and
  has gathered us together from all over the world.
  He has set us free to be his very own!
⁴ Some of us once wandered in the wilderness like desert nomads,
  with no true direction or dwelling place.
⁵ Starving, thirsting, staggering,
  we became desperate and filled with despair.
⁶ Then we cried out, "Lord, help us! Rescue us!" And he did!
⁷ He led us right into a place of safety and abundance,
  a suitable city to dwell in.
⁸ So lift your hands and thank God for his marvelous kindness
  and for all his miracles of mercy for those he loves.
⁹ How he satisfies the souls of thirsty ones
  and fills the hungry with all that is good!
¹⁰ Some of us once sat in darkness,
  living in the dark shadows of death.
  We were prisoners to our pain, chained to our regrets.
¹¹ For we rebelled against God's word
  and rejected the wise counsel of God Most High.
¹² So he humbled us through our circumstances,

watching us as we stumbled, with no one there to pick us back up.
Our own pain became our punishment.

¹³ Then we cried out, "Lord, help us! Rescue us!" And he did!

¹⁴ His light broke through the darkness and
he led us out in freedom from death's dark shadow
and snapped every one of our chains.

¹⁵ So lift your hands and give thanks to God for his marvelous kindness
and for his miracles of mercy for those he loves!

¹⁶ For he smashed through heavy prison doors and
shattered the steel bars that held us back, just to set us free!

¹⁷ Some of us were such fools, bringing on ourselves
sorrow and suffering all because of our sins.

¹⁸ Sick and feeble, unable to stand the sight of food,
we drew near to the gates of death.

¹⁹ Then we cried out, "Lord, help us! Rescue us!" And he did!

²⁰ God spoke the words "Be healed," and we were healed,
delivered from death's door!

²¹ So lift your hands and give thanks to God for his marvelous kindness
and for his miracles of mercy for those he loves!

²² Bring your praise as an offering and your thanks as a sacrifice
as you sing your story of miracles with a joyful song.

²³ Some of us set sail upon the sea to faraway ports,
transporting our goods from ship to shore.

²⁴ We were witnesses of God's power out in the ocean deep;
we saw breathtaking wonders upon the high seas.

²⁵ When God spoke he stirred up a storm,
lifting high the waves with hurricane winds.

^{26–27} Ships were tossed by swelling sea, rising to the sky,
then dropping down to the depths,
reeling like drunkards, spinning like tops,
everyone at their wits' end until even sailors despaired of life,
cringing in terror.

²⁸ Then we cried out, "Lord, help us! Rescue us!" And he did!

²⁹ God stilled the storm, calmed the waves,
and he hushed the hurricane winds to only a whisper.

³⁰ We were so relieved, so glad as he guided us
safely to harbor in a quiet haven.

³¹ So lift your hands and give thanks to God for his marvelous kindness
and for his miracles of mercy for those he loves!

³² Let's exalt him on high and lift up our praises in public;
let all the people and the leaders of the nation know
how great and wonderful is Yahweh, our God!

[33] Whenever he chooses he can dry up a river
and turn the land into a desert.
[34] Or he can take a fruitful land and make it into a saltwater swamp,
all because of the wickedness of those who dwell there.
[35] But he also can turn a barren wilderness into an oasis with water!
He can make springs flow into desert lands
[36] and turn them into fertile valleys so that cities spring up,
and he gives it all to those who are hungry.
[37] They can plant their fields and vineyards there
and reap a bumper crop and gather a fruitful harvest.
[38] God will bless them and cause them to multiply and prosper.
[39] But others will become poor,
humbled because of their oppression, tyranny, and sorrows.
[40] For God pours contempt upon their arrogant abuse of power,
heaping scorn upon their princes,
and makes them wander among ruins.
[41] But he raises up the poor and lowly with his favor,
giving them a safe place to live where no one can touch them.
God will grant them a large family and bless them!
[42] The lovers of God will rejoice when they see this.
Good men are glad when the evil ones are silenced.
[43] If you are truly wise, you'll learn from what I've told you.
It's time for you to consider these profound lessons
of God's great love and mercy!

108 A PRAYER FOR GOD'S HELP

A poetic psalm, by King David

[1] My heart, O God, is quiet and confident, all because of you.
Now I can sing my song with passionate praises!
[2] Awake, O my soul, with the music of his splendor.
Arise, my soul, and sing his praises!
I will awaken the dawn with my worship,
greeting the daybreak with my songs *of light*.
[3] Wherever I go I will thank you.
All the nations will hear my praise songs to you.
[4] Your love is so extravagant, it reaches higher than the heavens!
Your faithfulness is so astonishing, it stretches to the skies!
[5] Lord God, be exalted as you soar throughout the heavens.
May your shining glory be seen high above all the earth!
[6] Come to your beloved ones and gently draw us out.
Answer our prayer for your saving help.
Come with your might and strength, *for we need you, Lord*!

⁷⁻⁹ Then I heard the Lord speak in his holy splendor,
and from his sanctuary I heard the Lord promise:
"In my triumph I will be the one to measure out
the portion of my inheritance to my people,
and I will secure the land as I promised you.
Shechem, Succoth, Gilead, Manasseh; ^a
they are all mine!" he says.
"Judah will continue to produce kings and lawgivers,
and Ephraim will produce great warriors.
Moab will become my lowly servant.
Edom will likewise serve my purposes.
I will lift up a shout of victory over the land of Philistia!
¹⁰ But who will bring my triumph into Edom's fortresses?" ^b
¹¹ Lord, have you really rejected us, refusing to fight our battles?
¹² Give us a Father's help when we face our enemies.
For to trust in any man is an empty hope.
¹³ With God's help we will prevail with might and power.
And with God's help we'll trample down our every foe!

109 GOD, IT'S TIME FOR VENGEANCE

To the Pure and Shining One
A poetic song by King David

¹ God of all my praise, don't stand silently by, aloof to my pain,
² while the wicked slander me with their lies.
Even right in front of my face they lie through their teeth.
³ I've done nothing to them, but they still surround me
with their venomous words of hatred and vitriol.
⁴ Though I love them, they stand accusing me like Satan
for what I've never done.
I will pray until I become prayer itself. ^c
⁵ They continually repay me with evil when I show them good.
They give me hatred when I show them love.
⁶⁻⁷ Show him how it feels! Let accusing liars be raised up against him,
like Satan himself standing right next to him.
And let him be declared guilty by a wicked judge.
May even his prayers be seen as sinful!

---

a   108:7–9 The Hebrew includes two geographical places in the text: Shechem and Succoth.
Shechem is where Jacob (Israel) first bought title to the land, paying one hundred pieces
of silver for the place where he camped. Succoth is another place where Jacob temporarily
camped in the Land of Promise. These two places speak of God being the one who brought
them in and portioned out the land for his people.

b   108:10 *Edom* is a variant form of the word *Adam.*

c   109:4 In the face of accusation and slander, David says literally in Hebrew, "I am prayer!"

⁸ Shorten his life and let another replace him!

⁹ Make his wife a widow and his children orphans!

¹⁰ Let them wander as beggars in the street,
    like homeless vagabonds, evicted from their ruins!

¹¹ Let the creditors seize his entire estate,
    and strangers, like vultures, take all that's left!

¹² Let no one be kind to him by showing pity to his fatherless children!

¹³ May all his posterity die with him! Cut down his family tree!

¹⁴⁻¹⁵ And may all the sins of his ancestors be recorded,
    remembered before you, forever!
    Cut off even the memory of his family from the face of the earth

¹⁶ because he never once showed love or kindness to others,
    but persecuted the poor, the brokenhearted, and afflicted ones,
    even putting them to death!

¹⁷ Since he enjoyed cursing them,
    may all his curses now come raining back on him
    until it all overwhelms him with misfortune!
    Since he refused to bless others,
    God, withhold every single blessing from him!

¹⁸ Bitterness, such vile vindictiveness, was upon everything he did.
    Cursing was his lifestyle.

¹⁹⁻²⁰ So smother him now with his own curses as his just reward.
    This will be the Lord's punishment upon him and
    all my lying accusers who speak evil against me.

²¹ But now, O Yahweh-God, make yourself real to me
    like you promised me you would. ᵃ
    Because of your constant love and your heart-melting kindness, come be
        my hero and deliver me!

²² I'm so broken, needy and hurting.
    My heart is pierced through and I'm so wounded.

²³ I'm slipping down a dark slope, shaken to the core, and helpless.

²⁴ All my fasting has left me so weak I can hardly stand.
    Now I'm shriveled up, nothing but skin and bones.

²⁵ I'm the example of failure and shame to all who see me.
    They just walk by me, shaking their heads.

²⁶ You have to help me, O Lord God!
    My true hero, come to my rescue and save me,
    for you are loving and kind.

²⁷ Then everyone will know that you have won my victory,
    and they will all say to the Lord, "You have finished it!"

---

a 109:21 The Hebrew text states, "for your name's sake."

²⁸ So let them curse me if they want,
  but I know you will bless me!
  All their efforts to destroy me will fail,
  but I will succeed and be glad.
²⁹ So let my Satan-like accusers fail!
  Make them look ridiculous if they try to come against me.
  Clothe them with a robe of guilty shame from this day on!
³⁰ But I will give my thanks to you over and over
  and everyone will hear my lavish praises.
³¹ For you stand right next to the broken ones
  as their saving hero to rescue them from all their accusers!

110 MESSIAH, KING, AND PRIEST [a]

King David's psalm

¹ Yahweh said to my Lord, the Messiah:
  "Sit with me as enthroned ruler [b]
  while I subdue your every enemy.
  They will bow low before you
  as I make them a footstool for your feet." [c]
² Messiah, I know God himself will establish your kingdom
  as you reign in Zion-glory.
  For he says to you, "Rule in the midst of your enemies!"
³ Your people will be your love offerings,
  like living sacrifices spilled out before you!
  In the day of your mighty power you will be exalted,
  and in the brightness of your holy ones you will shine
  as an army arising from the womb of the dawn,
  anointed with the dew of your youth!
⁴ Yahweh has taken a solemn oath
  and will never back away from it, saying,
  "You are a priest for eternity, my King of righteousness!" [d]
⁵ The Lord stands in full authority [e] to shatter to pieces
  the kings who stand against you
  on the day he displays his terrible wrath.

---

a This psalm is applied to Christ in the New Testament, where it is quoted more often than any other Old Testament passage.

b 110:1 Or "at my right hand." The right hand is the position of authority and honor.

c 110:1 A footstool symbolizes what is subdued. It is taken from the root word "to subdue."

d 110:4 The Hebrew text includes the word *Melchizedek*, the name of a Canaanite king and priest over the Jebusite kingdom that later became Jerusalem. The name Melchizedek means "my king of righteousness."

e 110:5 The Hebrew word used here for "Lord" is *Adonai* or *Adonay*. It is the plural form of *Adhon*. Jesus is called Lord of lords, and we are the lords that he is Lord over. We are seated at his right hand (Benjamin) to rule with him.

⁶ He will judge every rebellious nation,
  filling their battlefield with corpses,
  and will shatter the strongholds of ruling powers.
⁷ Yet he himself will drink from his inheritance
  as from a flowing brook;
  refreshed by love he will stand victorious!

111 CELEBRATE GOD'S GREATNESS

¹ Shout hallelujah to Yahweh!
  May every one of his lovers hear my passionate praise to him,
  even among the council of the holy ones.
² For God's mighty miracles astound me!
  His wonders are so delightfully mysterious
  that they leave all who seek them astonished.
³ Everything he does is full of splendor and beauty!
  Each miracle demonstrates his eternal perfection.
⁴ His unforgettable works of surpassing wonder
  reveal his grace and tender mercy.
⁵ He satisfies all who love and trust him,
  and he keeps every promise he makes.
⁶ He reveals mighty power and marvels to his people
  by handing them nations as a gift.
⁷ All God accomplishes is flawless, faithful, and fair,
  and his every word proves trustworthy and true.
⁸ They are steadfast forever and ever,
  formed from truth and righteousness.
⁹ His forever-love paid a full ransom for his people
  so that now we're free to come before Jehovah
  to worship his holy and awesome name!
¹⁰ Where can wisdom be found? It is born in the fear of God.
  Everyone who follows his ways
  will never lack his living-understanding.
  And the adoration of God will abide throughout eternity!

112 THE TRIUMPH OF FAITH

¹ Shout in celebration of praise to the Lord!
  Everyone who loves the Lord and delights in him
  will cherish his words and be blessed beyond expectation.
² Their descendants will be prosperous and influential.
  Every generation of his godly lovers will experience his favor.
³ Great blessing and wealth fills the house *of the wise*,
  for their integrity endures forever.

[4] Even if darkness overtakes them,
  sunrise-brilliance will come bursting through
  because they are gracious to others, so tender and true.
[5] Life is good for the one who is generous and charitable,
  conducting affairs with honesty and truth.
[6] Their circumstances will never shake them
  and others will never forget their example.
[7] They will not live in fear or dread of what may come,
  for their hearts are firm, ever secure in their faith.
[8] Steady and strong, they will not be afraid,
  but will calmly face their every foe
  until they all go down in defeat.
[9] Never stingy and always generous to those in need,
  their lives of influence and honor will never be forgotten,
  for they were full of good deeds.
[10] But the wicked take one look at a life lived like this
  and they grit their teeth in anger, not understanding their bliss.
  The wicked slink away speechless in the darkness that falls,
  where hope dies and all their dreams fade away to nothing,
  nothing at all!

113 GOD IS KIND

[1] Hallelujah! Praise the Lord! [a]
  Go ahead, praise the Lord, all you loving servants of God!
  Keep it up! Praise him some more!
[2] For the glorious name of the Lord is blessed forever and ever.
[3] From sunrise brilliance to sunset beauty,
  lift up his praise from dawn to dusk!
[4] For he rules on high over the nations
  with a glory that outshines even the heavens.
[5] No one can be compared to God, enthroned on high!
[6] He stoops down to look upon the sky and the earth.
[7] He promotes the poor, picking them up from the dirt,
  and rescues the needy from the garbage dump.
[8] He turns paupers into princes and seats them
  on their royal thrones of honor.
[9] God's grace provides for the barren ones a joyful home with children
  so that even childless couples find a family.
  He makes them happy parents surrounded by their pride and joy.
  That's the God we praise, so give it all to him!

---

a 113:1 Ps. 113–114 were sung before the meal, during the Jewish family's celebration of
  Passover, while Ps. 115–118 were sung after the meal (see Mark 14:26).

114 A SONG FOR PASSOVER

[1] Many years ago the Jewish people escaped Egypt's tyranny,
[2] so that Israel, God's people of praise, [a]
   would become his holy sanctuary,
   his kingdom on the earth.
[3] The Red Sea waters saw them coming and ran the other way!
   Then later, the Jordan River too
   moved aside so that they could all pass through.
[4] The land shuddered with fear.
   Mountains and hills shook with dread. [b]
[5] O sea, what happened to you to make you flee?
   O Jordan, what was it that made you turn and run?
[6] O mountains, what frightened you so?
   And you hills, what made you shiver?
[7] Tremble, O earth, for you are in the presence of the Lord,
   the God of Jacob.
[8] He splits open boulders and brings up bubbling water.
   Gushing streams burst forth *when he is near!*

115 THE ONE TRUE GOD

[1] God, glorify your name!
   Yes, your name alone be glorified, not ours.
   For you are the one who loves us passionately,
   and you are faithful and true.
[2] Why should the unbelievers mock us, saying,
   "Where is this God of yours?"
[3] But we know our God rules from the heavens
   and he takes delight in all that he does.
[4] The unbelievers worship what they make—
   their wealth and their work.
[5-8] They idolize what they own
   and what they make with their hands,
   but their things can't talk to them or answer their prayers.
   Their possessions will never satisfy.
   Their futile faith in dead idols and dead works
   can never bring life or meaning to their souls.
   Blind men can only create blind things.
   Those deaf to God can only make a deaf image.

---

a   114:2 Or *Judah,* which means "praise."
b   114:4 The literal Hebrew states, "Mountains skipped like rams, the hills like lambs." This
    does not mean they skipped with joy, but shook with fear, as the context reveals.

Dead men can only create dead idols.
And everyone who trusts in these powerless, dead things
will be just like what they worship—powerless and dead. [a]

⁹ So trust in the Lord, all his people.
For he is the only true hero,
the wrap-around God who is our shield!

¹⁰ You, his priests, trust in the Lord.
For he is the only true hero,
God-wrapped-around-us as our shield.

¹¹ Yes, all his lovers who bow before him, trust in the Lord.
For he is our only true hero,
God-wrapped-around-us as our shield.

¹² The Lord will never forget us in our need; he will bless us indeed!
He will bless the house of Israel;
he will bless the house of Aaron, his priest.

¹³ Yes! He will bless his lovers who bow before him,
no matter who they are.

¹⁴⁻¹⁵ God himself will fill you with more.
Blessings upon blessings will be heaped upon you
and upon your children from the maker of heaven and earth,
the very God who made you!

¹⁶ The heavens belong to our God; they are his alone,
but he has given us [b] the earth and put us in charge.

¹⁷⁻¹⁸ Dead people cannot praise the Lord, but we can!
Those who sink to the silence of the grave
can no longer give glory to God, but we can!
So let's praise the Lord!
Let's begin now and let it go on until eternity is done.
Hallelujah, and praise the Lord!

116 I'm Saved

¹ I am passionately in love with God because he listens to me.
He hears my prayers and answers them.

² As long as I live I'll keep praying to him,
for he stoops down to listen to my heart's cry.

³ Death once stared me in the face,
and I was close to slipping into its dark shadows.
I was terrified and overcome with sorrow.

---

a   115:5–8 Referring to the idols, the literal Hebrew could be translated "With mouths, but they
cannot speak; with eyes, but they cannot see; with ears, but they cannot hear; with noses, but
they cannot smell; with hands, but they cannot feel; with feet, but they cannot walk. Those
who make them will become like them and everyone who trusts in them."

b   115:16 Or "Adam's sons."

⁴ I cried out to the Lord, "God, come and save me!"
⁵ He was so kind, so gracious to me.
  Because of his passion toward me,
  he made everything right and he restored me.
⁶ So I've learned from my experience
  that God protects the childlike and humble ones.
  For I was broken and brought low,
  but he answered me and came to my rescue!
⁷ Now I can say to myself and to all,
  "Relax and rest, be confident and serene,
  for the Lord rewards fully those who simply trust in him."
⁸ God has rescued my soul from death's fear
  and dried my eyes of many tears.
  He's kept my feet firmly on his path
⁹ and strengthened me so that I may please him *ᵃ*
  and live my life before him in his life-giving light.
¹⁰⁻¹¹ Even when it seems I'm surrounded
  by many liars and my own fears,
  and though I'm hurting in my suffering and trauma,
  I still stay faithful to God and speak words of faith.
¹² So now, what can I ever give back to God
  to repay him for the blessings he's poured out on me?
¹³ I will lift up his cup of salvation and praise him extravagantly
  for all that he's done for me.
¹⁴ I will fulfill the promise I made to God
  in the presence of his gathered people.
¹⁵ When one of God's holy lovers dies,
  it is costly to the Lord, touching his heart.
¹⁶ Lord, because I am your loving servant,
  you have broken open my life and freed me from my chains.
¹⁷ Now I'll worship you passionately and bring to you
  my sacrifice of praise, drenched with thanksgiving!
¹⁸ I'll keep my promise to you, God,
  in the presence of your gathered people, just like I said I would.
¹⁹ I will worship you here in your living presence,
  in the temple in Jerusalem.
  I will worship and sing hallelujah, for I praise you, Lord!

---

a 116:9 As translated from the Septuagint.

117 GLORIOUS PRAISE

A praise psalm

¹ Let everyone everywhere shine with praise to Yahweh! [a]
  Let it all out! Go ahead and praise him!
² For he has conquered us with his great love
  and his kindness has melted our hearts.
  His faithfulness lasts forever and he will never fail you.
  So go ahead, let it all out!
  Praise Yah!
  O Yah! [b]

118 GLORIOUS THANKSGIVING

A praise psalm [c]

¹ Keep on giving your thanks to God, for he is so good!
  His constant, tender love lasts forever!
² Let all his princely people sing,
  "His constant, tender love lasts forever!"
³ Let all his holy priests sing,
  "His constant, tender love lasts forever!"
⁴ Let all his lovers who bow low before him sing,
  "His constant, tender love lasts forever!"
⁵ Out of my deep anguish and pain I prayed,
  and God, you helped me as a father.
  You came to my rescue and broke open the way
  into a beautiful and broad place.
⁶ Now I know, Lord, that you are for me,
  and I will never fear what man can do to me.
⁷ For you stand beside me as my hero who rescues me.
  I've seen with my own eyes the defeat of my enemies.
  I've triumphed over them all!
⁸ Lord, it is so much better to trust in you to save me
  than to put my confidence in someone else.
⁹ Yes, it is so much better to trust in the Lord to save me
  than to put my confidence in celebrities.
¹⁰ Once I was hemmed in and surrounded by those
  who don't love you.
  But by Yahweh's supernatural power I overcame them all!

---

a 117:1 The word for "praise" is taken from the word *shine*.

b 117:2 The name Yah is not an abbreviated form of Yahweh; it is the name of God as he displays his power. Yahweh is found 6,830 times in the Hebrew text, and Yah is found 49 times.

c This is the psalm or hymn that Jesus likely sang after the Passover supper with his disciples, before making his way to Gethsemane and Calvary.

¹¹⁻¹² Yes, they surrounded me,
  like a swarm of killer bees swirling around me.
  I was trapped like one trapped by a raging fire;
  I was surrounded with no way out and at the point of collapse.
  But by Yahweh's supernatural power, I overcame them all!
¹³ They pushed me right up to the edge, and I was ready to fall,
  but you helped me to triumph, and together we overcame them all.
¹⁴ Lord, you are my true strength and my glory-song,
  my champion, my Savior!
¹⁵ The joyful songs I now sing will be sung again
  in the hearts and homes of all your lovers.
  My loud shouts of victory will echo throughout the land. ᵃ
  For Yahweh's right hand conquers valiantly!
¹⁶ The right hand of Yahweh exalts!
  The right hand of Yahweh will never fail.
¹⁷ You will not let them kill me,
  but I will live to tell the world what the Lord has done for me.
¹⁸ Yes, the Lord punished me as I deserved,
  but he'll never give me over to death.
¹⁹ Swing wide, you gates of righteousness, and let me pass through,
  and I will enter into your presence to worship only you.
²⁰ I have found the gateway to God,
  the pathway to his presence for all his lovers.
²¹ I will offer all my loving praise to you,
  and I thank you so much for answering my prayer
  and bringing me salvation!
²² The very stone the masons rejected as flawed
  has turned out to be the most important capstone of the arch, ᵇ
  holding up the very house of God.
²³ The Lord himself is the one who has done this,
  and it's so amazing, so marvelous to see!
²⁴ This is the very day of the Lord that brings
  gladness and joy, filling our hearts with glee.
²⁵ O God, please come and save us again;
  bring us your breakthrough-victory!
²⁶ Blessed is this one who comes to us, the sent one of the Lord.
  And from within the temple we cry, "We bless you!"
²⁷⁻²⁸ For the Lord our God has brought us his glory-light.
  I offer him my life in joyous sacrifice.
  Tied tightly to your altar I will bring you praise.

---

a 118:15 Or "in the tents of the righteous."
b 118:22 The words "capstone of the arch" can also be translated "the head of the corner."

For you are the God of my life and I lift you high,
exalting you to the highest place.
²⁹ So let's keep on giving our thanks to God, for he is so good!
His constant, tender love lasts forever!

119 THE WORDS OF GOD ᵃ

The Way to Happiness

¹ You're only truly happy when you walk in total integrity, ᵇ
walking in the light of God's word.
² What joy overwhelms everyone who keeps the ways of God,
those who seek him as their heart's passion!
³ They'll never do what's wrong
but will always choose the paths of the Lord.
⁴ God has prescribed the right way to live:
obeying his laws with all our hearts.
⁵ How I long for my life to bring you glory
as I follow each and every one of your holy precepts!
⁶ Then I'll never be ashamed,
for I take strength from all your commandments.
⁷ I will give my thanks to you from a heart of love and truth.
And every time I learn more of your righteous judgments,
⁸ I will be faithful to all that your word reveals—
so don't ever give up on me!

True Joy

⁹ How can a young man stay pure?
Only by living in the word of God and walking in its truth.
¹⁰ I have longed for you with the passion of my heart;
don't let me stray from your directions!
¹¹ I consider your prophecies ᶜ to be my greatest treasure,
and I memorize them and write them on my heart
to keep me from committing sin's treason against you.

---

a This psalm is an acrostic poem, a mathematical masterpiece. It consists of twenty-two stanzas of eight lines each. Each stanza begins with the same Hebrew letter at the beginning of every one of its eight lines, going in succession, by strophes, from *alef*—the first letter of the Hebrew alphabet, as the first letter of each line in the first strophe—to *taw*—the last letter of the Hebrew alphabet, as the first letter of each line in the last strophe. Like the eight lines of each stanza, there are eight Hebrew words, all synonyms, used to refer to the word of God. Although many believe Ezra wrote Ps. 119, the acrostic poetic style is unique to King David within the book of Psalms, which points to his authorship of this psalm.

b 119:1 Or "perfection." The Hebrew reads "utterances."

c 119:11 As translated from the Septuagint.

¹² My wonderful God, you are to be praised above all;
  teach me the power of your decrees!
¹³ I speak continually of your laws
  as I recite out loud your counsel to me.
¹⁴ I find more joy in following what you tell me to do
  than in chasing after all the wealth of the world.
¹⁵ I set my heart on your precepts
  and pay close attention to all your ways.
¹⁶ My delight is found in all your laws,
  and I won't forget to walk in your words.

The Abundant Life

¹⁷ Let me, your servant, walk in abundance of life
  that I may always live to obey your truth.
¹⁸ Open my eyes to see the miracle-wonders hidden in your word.
¹⁹ My life on earth is so brief, so tutor me in the ways of your wisdom.
²⁰ I am continually consumed by these irresistible longings,
  these cravings to obey your every commandment!
²¹ Your displeasure rests with those who are arrogant,
  who think they know everything;
  you rebuke the rebellious who refuse your laws.
²² Don't let them mock and scorn me for obeying you.
²³ For even if the princes and my leaders choose to criticize me,
  I will continue to serve you and walk in your plans for my life.
²⁴ Your commandments are my counselors;
  your word is my light and delight!

Revived by the Word

²⁵ Lord, I'm fading away. I'm discouraged and lying in the dust;
  revive me by your word, just like you promised you would.
²⁶ I've poured out my life before you,
  and you've always been there for me.
  So now I ask: teach me more of your holy decrees.
²⁷ Open up my understanding to the ways of your wisdom
  and I will meditate deeply on your splendor and your wonders.
²⁸ My life's strength melts away with grief and sadness;
  come strengthen me and encourage me with your words.
²⁹ Keep me far away from what is false;
  give me grace to stay true to your laws.
³⁰ I've chosen to obey your truth
  and walk in the splendor-light of all that you teach me.
³¹ Lord, don't allow me to make a mess of my life,
  for I cling to your commands and follow them as closely as I can.

³² I will run after you with delight in my heart,
    for you will make me obedient to your instructions.

Understanding God's Ways

³³ Give me revelation about the meaning of your ways
    so I can enjoy the reward of following them fully.
³⁴ Give me an understanding heart so that I can
    passionately know and obey your truth.
³⁵ Guide me into the paths that please you,
    for I take delight in all that you say.
³⁶ Cause my heart to bow before your words of wisdom
    and not to the wealth of this world.
³⁷ Help me turn my eyes away from illusions
    so that I pursue only that which is true;
    drench my soul with life as I walk in your paths. ᵃ
³⁸ Reassure me of your promises, for I am your beloved,
    your servant who bows before you.
³⁹ Defend me from the criticism I face
    for keeping your beautiful words.
⁴⁰ See how I long with cravings for more of your ways?
    Let your righteousness revive my spirit!

Trust in the Lord

⁴¹ May your tender love overwhelm me, O Lord,
    for you are my Savior and you keep your promises.
⁴² I'll always have an answer for those who mock me
    because I trust in your word.
⁴³ May I never forget your truth, for I rely upon your precepts.
⁴⁴ I will observe your laws every moment of the day
    and will never forget the words you say.
⁴⁵ I will walk with you in complete freedom,
    for I seek to follow your every command.
⁴⁶ When I stand before kings, I will tell them the truth
    and will never be ashamed.
⁴⁷ My passion and delight is in your word,
    for I love what you say to me!
⁴⁸ I long for more revelation of your truth,
    for I love the light of your word as I meditate on your decrees.

---

a 119:37 Two Masoretic manuscripts and the Dead Sea Scrolls read "Preserve my life according to your word."

My Comfort

⁴⁹ Lord, never forget the promises you've made to me,
    for they are my hope and confidence.
⁵⁰ In all of my affliction I find great comfort in your promises,
    for they have kept me alive!
⁵¹ No matter how bitterly the proud mockers speak against me,
    I refuse to budge from your precepts.
⁵² Your revelation-light is eternal;
    I'm encouraged every time I think about your truth!
⁵³ Whenever I see the wicked breaking your laws, I feel horrible.
⁵⁴ As I journey through life, I put all your statutes to music;
    they become the theme of my joyous songs.
⁵⁵ Throughout the night I think of you, dear God;
    I treasure your every word to me.
⁵⁶ All this joy is mine as I follow your ways!

My Heart Is Devoted to You

⁵⁷ You are my satisfaction, Lord, and all that I need,
    so I'm determined to do everything you say.
⁵⁸ With all my heart I seek your favor;
    pour out your grace on me as you promised!
⁵⁹ When I realize that I'm going astray,
    I turn back to obey your instructions.
⁶⁰ I give my all to follow your revelation-light; I will not delay to obey.
⁶¹ Even when temptations encircle me with evil,
    I won't forget for a moment to follow your commands.
⁶² In the middle of the night I awake to give thanks to you
    because of all your revelation-light; so right and true!
⁶³ Anyone who loves you and bows in obedience to your words
    will be my friend.
⁶⁴ Give me more revelation of your ways,
    for I see your love and tender care everywhere.

My True Treasure

⁶⁵ Your extravagant kindness to me
    makes me want to follow your words even more!
⁶⁶ Teach me how to make good decisions,
    and give me revelation-light, for I believe in your commands.
⁶⁷ Before I was humbled I used to always wander astray,
    but now I see the wisdom of your words.
⁶⁸ Everything you do is beautiful, flowing from your goodness;
    teach me the power of your wonderful words!

⁶⁹ Proud boasters make up lies about me
   because I am passionate to follow all that you say.
⁷⁰ Their hearts are dull and void of feelings,
   but I find my true treasure in your truth.
⁷¹ The punishment you brought me through was the best thing
   that could have happened to me, for it taught me your ways.
⁷² The words you speak to me are worth more
   than all the riches and wealth in the whole world!

Growth through the Word

⁷³ Your very hands have held me and made me who I am;
   give me more revelation-light so I may learn to please you more.
⁷⁴ May all your lovers see how you treat me and be glad,
   for your words are entwined within my heart.
⁷⁵ Lord, I know that your judgments are always right.
   Even when it's me you judge, you're still faithful and true.
⁷⁶ Send your kind mercy-kiss to comfort me, your servant,
   just like you promised you would.
⁷⁷ Love me tenderly so I can go on,
   for I delight in your life-giving truth.
⁷⁸ Shame upon the proud liars! See how they oppress me,
   all because of my passion for your precepts!
⁷⁹ May all your lovers follow me
   as I follow the path of your instruction.
⁸⁰ Make me passionate and wholehearted to fulfill your every wish,
   so that I'll never have to be ashamed of myself.

Deliver Me

⁸¹ I'm lovesick with yearnings for more of your salvation,
   for my heart is entwined with your word.
⁸² I'm consumed with longings for your promises,
   so I ask, "When will they all come true?"
⁸³ My soul feels dry and shriveled, useless and forgotten,
   but I will never forget your living truth.
⁸⁴ How much longer must I wait until you punish my persecutors?
   For I am your loving servant.
⁸⁵ Arrogant men who hate your truth and never obey your laws
   have laid a trap for my life.
⁸⁶ They don't know that everything you say is true,
   so they harass me with their lies. Help me, Lord!
⁸⁷ They've nearly destroyed my life, but I refuse to yield;
   I still live according to your word.

[88] Revive me with your tender love and
spare my life by your kindness, and I will continue to obey you.

Faith in the Word of God
[89] Standing firm in the heavens and fastened to eternity
is the word of God.
[90] Your faithfulness flows from one generation to the next;
all that you created sits firmly in place to testify of you.
[91] By your decree everything stands at attention,
for all that you have made serves you.
[92] Because your words are my deepest delight,
I didn't give up when all else was lost.
[93] I can never forget the profound revelations you've taught me,
for they have kept me alive more than once.
[94] Lord, I'm all yours, and you are my Savior;
I have sought to live my life pleasing to you.
[95] Even though evil men wait in ambush to kill me,
I will set my heart before you to understand more of your ways.
[96] I've learned that there is nothing perfect
in this imperfect world except your words,
for they bring such fantastic freedom into my life!

I Love the Word of God
[97] O how I love and treasure the revelation of your word;
throughout the day I fill my heart with its light!
[98] By considering your commands I have an edge over my enemies,
for I take seriously everything you say.
[99] You have given me more understanding than those who teach me,
for I've absorbed your eye-opening revelation.
[100] You have graced me with more insight than the old sages
because I have not failed to walk in the light of your ways.
[101] I refused to bend my morals when temptation was before me
so that I could become obedient to your word.
[102] I refuse to turn away from difficult truths,
for you yourself have taught me to love your words.
[103] How sweet are your living promises to me;
sweeter than honey is your revelation-light.
[104] For your truth is the source of my understanding,
not the falsehoods of those who don't know you, which I despise.

Truth's Shining Light
[105] Truth's shining light guides me in my choices and decisions;
the revelation of your word makes my pathway clear.

[106] To live my life by your righteous rules
    has been my holy and lifelong commitment.
[107] I'm bruised and broken, overwhelmed by it all;
    breathe life into me again by your living word.
[108] Lord, receive my grateful thanks
    and teach me more of how to please you.
[109] Even though my life hangs in the balance,
    I'll keep following what you've taught me, no matter what.
[110] The ungodly have done their best to throw me off track,
    but I'll not deviate from what you've told me to do.
[111] Everything you speak to me is like joyous treasure,
    filling my life with gladness.
[112] I have determined in my heart to obey whatever you say,
    fully and forever!

Trust and Obey

[113] I despise those who can't keep commitments,
    for I passionately love your revelation-light!
[114] You're my place of quiet retreat, and your wrap-around presence
    becomes my shield as I wrap myself in your word!
[115] Go away! Leave me, all you workers of wickedness,
    for you can't stop me from following every command of my God.
[116] Lord, strengthen my inner being by the promises of your word
    so that I may live faithful and unashamed for you.
[117] Lift me up and I will be safe.
    Empower me to live every moment in the light of your ways.
[118] Lord, you reject those who reject your laws,
    for they fool no one but themselves!
[119] The wicked are thrown away, discarded and valueless.
    That's why I will keep loving all of your laws!
[120] My body trembles in holy awe of you, leaving me speechless,
    for I'm frightened of your righteous judgments.

I Will Follow Your Ways

[121] Don't leave me to the mercies of those who hate me,
    for I live to do what is just and fair.
[122] Let me hear your promise of blessing over my life,
    breaking me free from the proud oppressors.
[123] As a lovesick lover, I yearn for more of your salvation
    and for your virtuous promises.
[124] Let me feel your tender love, for I am yours.
    Give me more understanding of your wonderful ways.

¹²⁵ I need more revelation from your word
to know more about you, for I'm in love with you!
¹²⁶ Lord, the time has come for you to break through,
for evil men keep breaking your laws.
¹²⁷ Truly, your message of truth means more to me
than a vault filled with the purest gold.
¹²⁸ Every word you speak, every truth revealed, is always right
and beautiful to me, for I hate what is phony or false.

I Long to Obey You

¹²⁹ Your marvelous words are living miracles;
no wonder I long to obey everything you say.
¹³⁰ Break open your word within me until revelation-light shines out!
Those with open hearts are given insight into your plans.
¹³¹ I open my mouth and inhale the word of God
because I crave the revelation of your commands.
¹³² Turn your heart to me, Lord, and show me your grace
like you do to every one of your godly lovers.
¹³³ Prepare before me a path filled with your promises,
and don't allow even one sin to have dominion over me.
¹³⁴ Rescue me from the oppression of ungodly men
so that I can keep all your precepts.
¹³⁵ Let your shining face shine brightly on me, your loving servant.
Instruct me on what is right in your eyes.
¹³⁶ When I witness the rebellious breaking your laws,
it makes me weep uncontrollably!

His Word Is True

¹³⁷ Lord, your judgments reveal your righteousness,
and your verdicts are always fair.
¹³⁸ The motive behind your every word is pure,
and your teachings are remarkably faithful and true.
¹³⁹ I've been consumed with a furious passion to do what's right,
all because of the way my enemies disrespect your laws.
¹⁴⁰ All your promises glow with fire; ^a
that's why I'm a lover of your word.
¹⁴¹ Even though I'm considered insignificant and despised
by the world, I'll never abandon your ways.
¹⁴² Your righteousness has no end; it is everlasting,
and your rules are perfectly fair.

---

a 119:140 As translated from the Septuagint and implied in the Hebrew.

¹⁴³ Even though my troubles overwhelm me with anguish,
  I still delight and cherish every message you speak to me.
¹⁴⁴ Give me more revelation so that I can live for you,
  for nothing is more pure and eternal than your truth.

Save Me, God

¹⁴⁵ Answer my passionate prayer, O Lord,
  and I'll obey everything you say.
¹⁴⁶ Save me, God, and I'll follow your every instruction.
¹⁴⁷ Before the day dawns, I'll be crying out for help
  and wrapping your words into my life.
¹⁴⁸ I lie awake every night pondering your promises to me.
¹⁴⁹ Lord, listen to my heart's cry, for I know your love is real for me;
  breathe life into me again by the revelation of your justice.
¹⁵⁰ Here they come—these lawless rebels are coming near,
  but they are all so far away from your laws.
¹⁵¹ God, you are near me always, so close to me;
  every one of your commands reveals truth.
¹⁵² I've known all along how true and unchanging
  is every word you speak, established forever!

Breathe Life into Me Again

¹⁵³ Look upon all my misery and come be my hero to rescue me,
  for I will never forget what you've revealed to me.
¹⁵⁴ Take my side and defend me in these sufferings;
  redeem me and revive me, just like you promised you would.
¹⁵⁵ The wicked are so far from salvation,
  for they could not care less about your message of truth.
¹⁵⁶ Your tender mercies are what I need, O God;
  give me back my life again
  through the revelation of your judgments.
¹⁵⁷ I have so many enemies who persecute me,
  yet I won't swerve from following your ways.
¹⁵⁸ I grieve when I see how the faithless ones live,
  for they just walk away from your promises.
¹⁵⁹ Lord, see how much I truly love your instructions.
  So in your tender kindness, breathe life into me again.
¹⁶⁰ The sum total of all your words adds up to absolute truth,
  and every one of your righteous decrees is everlasting.

Devoted to God's Word

¹⁶¹ The powerful elite have persecuted me without a cause,
  but my heart trembles in awe because of your miracle-words.
¹⁶² Your promises are the source of my bubbling joy;
  the revelation of your word thrills me
  like one who has discovered hidden treasure.
¹⁶³ I despise every lie and hate every falsehood,
  for I am passionate about keeping your precepts.
¹⁶⁴ I stop to praise you seven times a day,
  all because your ways are perfect!
¹⁶⁵ There is such a great peace and well-being that comes
  to the lovers of your word, and they will never be offended.
¹⁶⁶ Lord, I'm longing for more of your salvation,
  for I want to do what pleases you.
¹⁶⁷ My love for your ways is indescribable;
  in my innermost being I want to follow them perfectly!
¹⁶⁸ I will keep your instructions and follow your counsel;
  all my ways are an open book before you.

I Want to Follow You

¹⁶⁹ Lord, listen to my prayer. It's like a sacrifice I bring to you;
  I must have more revelation of your word!
¹⁷⁰ Take my words to heart when I ask you, Lord;
  rescue me, just like you promised!
¹⁷¹ I offer you my joyous praise for all that you've taught me.
¹⁷² Your wonderful words will become my song of worship,
  for everything you've commanded is perfect and true.
¹⁷³ Place your hands of strength and favor upon me,
  for I've made my choice to follow your ways.
¹⁷⁴ I wait for your deliverance, O Lord,
  for your words thrill me like nothing else!
¹⁷⁵ Invigorate my life so that I can praise you even more,
  and may your truth be my strength!
¹⁷⁶ I'll never forget what you've taught me, Lord,
  but when I wander off and lose my way,
  come after me, for I am your beloved!

120 GOD HELPED ME

A song of the stairway[a]

[1] I was desperate for you to help me in my struggles, and you did!
[2] So come and deliver me now
   from this treachery and false accusation.
[3] O lying deceivers, don't you know what is your fate?
[4] You will be pierced through with condemnation
   and consumed with burning coals of fire!
[5] Why am I doomed to live as an alien,
   scattered among these cruel savages?[b]
   Am I destined to dwell in the darkened tents of desert nomads?[c]
[6] For too long I've had to live among those who hate peace.
[7] I speak words of peace while they speak words of war,
   but they refuse to listen.

121 GOD PROTECTS US

A song of the stairway

[1-2] I look up to the mountains and hills, longing for God's help.
   But then I realize that our true help and protection
   come only from the Lord,
   our Creator who made the heavens and the earth.
[3] He will guard and guide me, never letting me stumble or fall.
   God is my keeper; he will never forget nor ignore me.
[4] He will never slumber nor sleep;
   he is the Guardian-God for his people, Israel.
[5] Jehovah himself will watch over you;
   he's always at your side to shelter you safely in his presence.
[6] He's protecting you from all danger both day and night.
[7] He will keep you from every form of evil or calamity
   as he continually watches over you.
[8] You will be guarded by God himself.
   You will be safe when you leave your home

---

a Ps. 120–134 all begin with the words "A song to take you higher" or "A song of ascent" or "A song of the stairway." It is likely these fifteen songs were sung on the fifteen steps that would take the worshiper into the temple. On each step they would stop to worship and sing the corresponding psalm as they went up higher into the worship of God. Others believe they were the songs sung as David brought up the ark of glory to Jerusalem. They are also known as Songs of Degrees or Songs of Ascent. One Hebrew manuscript titles them "Songs of the Homeward Marches."

b 120:5 The Hebrew text includes the word *Meshech*, which is a foreign land. The meaning of the word *Meshech* is "to scatter" and may refer to ancient Persia.

c 120:5 The Hebrew text includes the word *Kedar*, who was one of Ishmael's sons, whose descendants became a wandering group of nomads. *Kedar* means a dark place. See Song 1:5.

and safely you will return.
He will protect you now,
and he'll protect you forevermore!

122 JERUSALEM

A song of the stairway, by King David[a]

[1] I was overjoyed when they said,
"Let's go up to the house of the Lord."
[2] And now at last we stand here, inside the very gates of Jerusalem!
[3] O Jerusalem, you were built as a city of praise,
where God and man mingle together.[b]
[4] This is where all the people of Israel are required
to come and worship Jehovah-God.
[5] This is where the thrones of kings have been established
to rule in righteousness;
even King David ruled from here.
[6] Pray and seek for Jerusalem's peace,
for all who love her will prosper!
[7] O Jerusalem, may there be peace for those
who dwell inside your walls
and prosperity in your every palace.
[8] I intercede for the sake of my family and friends
who dwell there, that they may all live in peace.
[9] For the sake of your house, our God,
I will seek the welfare and prosperity of Jerusalem.

123 A PRAYER FOR MERCY

A song of the stairway

[1] O God-Enthroned in heaven, I worship and adore you!
[2] The way I love you
is like the way a servant wants to please his master,
the way a maid waits for the orders of her mistress.
We look to you, our God, with passionate longing
to please you and discover more of your mercy and grace.
[3-4] For we've had more than our fill of this scoffing and scorn—
this mistreatment by the wealthy elite.
Lord, show us your mercy!
Lord, show us your grace!

---

a David wrote this song for the people to sing for the feasts. It was sung when the worshipers
entered the gates of the city Jerusalem.
b 122:3 The Hebrew phrase "a city bound together" is taken from a root word that means
"joined, united, coupled." By inference in the context, it is the city where God dwells and
man worships.

124 Victory

A song of the stairway, by King David

¹ What if God had not been on our side? Let all Israel admit this!

²⁻³ What if God had not been there for us?
Our enemies, in their violent anger,
would have swallowed us up alive!

⁴⁻⁵ The nations, with their flood of rage, would have swept us away
and we would have drowned,
perished beneath their torrent of terror!

⁶ We can praise God over and over that he never left us!
God wouldn't allow the terror of our enemies to defeat us.

⁷ We are free from the hunter's trap;
their snare is broken and we have escaped!

⁸ For the same God who made everything,
our Creator and our mighty maker,
he himself is our helper and defender!

125 God's Surrounding Presence

A song of the stairway

¹ Those who trust in the Lord are as unshakeable,
as unmovable as mighty Mount Zion!

² Just as the mountains surround Jerusalem,
so the Lord's *wrap-around* presence
surrounds his people, protecting them now and forever.

³ The wicked will not always rule over the godly,
provoking them to do what is evil.

⁴ God, let your goodness be given away to your good people,
to all your godly lovers!

⁵ But those who turn away from truth,
you will turn them away from you, to follow their crooked ways.
You will give them just what they deserve.
May Israel experience peace and prosperity!

126 Restored

A song of the stairway

¹ It was like a dream come true
when you freed us from our bondage and brought us back to Zion!

² We laughed and laughed and overflowed with gladness.
We were left shouting for joy and singing your praise.
All the nations saw it and joined in, saying,
"The Lord has done great miracles for them!"

³ Yes, he did mighty miracles and we are overjoyed!
⁴ Now, Lord, do it again! Restore us to our former glory!
   May streams of your refreshing flow over us
   until our dry hearts are drenched again.
⁵ Those who sow their tears as seeds ᵃ
   will reap a harvest with joyful shouts of glee.
⁶ They may weep as they go out carrying their seed to sow,
   but they will return with joyful laughter and shouting with gladness
   as they bring back armloads of blessing and a harvest overflowing!

127   GOD AND HIS GIFTS

A song of the stairway, by King Solomon
¹ If God's grace doesn't help the builders,
   they will labor in vain to build a house.
   If God's mercy doesn't protect the city,
   all the sentries will circle it in vain.
² It really is senseless to work so hard
   from early morning till late at night,
   toiling to make a living for fear of not having enough.
   God can provide for his lovers even while they sleep!
³ Children are God's love-gift; they are heaven's generous reward.
⁴ Children born to a young couple will one day rise to protect
   and provide for their parents. ᵇ
⁵ Happy will be the couple who has many of them!
   A household full of children will not bring shame on your name
   but victory when you face your enemies,
   for your offspring will have influence and honor ᶜ
   to prevail on your behalf!

128   THE BLESSINGS OF THE LORD

A song of the stairway
¹ How joyous are those who love the Lord and bow low before God,
   ready to obey him!
² Your reward will be prosperity, happiness, and well-being.
³ Your wife will bless your heart and home.
   Your children will bring you joy as they gather around your table.

ᵃ 126:5 Or "sow their seeds with tears." A sower weeps when he sows his precious seed while his children are hungry. This is a picture of sacrificing what little we have for the harvest to come.
ᵇ 127:4 The Hebrew text refers to children as "arrows in the hands of a warrior." Our children will be our future protection and provision. So the more the merrier!
ᶜ 127:5 The Hebrew includes a reference to "speaking with your enemies at the gate." This is in the context of children being God's way of blessing parents in their old age.

⁴ Yes, this is God's generous reward for those who love him.
⁵ May the Lord bless you out of his Zion-glory!
May you see the prosperity of Jerusalem
throughout your lifetime.
⁶ And may you be surrounded by your grandchildren.
Happiness to you! And happiness to Israel!

129 PERSECUTED BUT NOT DEFEATED

A song of the stairway

¹ Let all Israel admit it.
From our very beginning we have been persecuted by the nations.
² And from our very beginning
we have faced never-ending discrimination.
Nevertheless, our enemies have not defeated us. We're still here!
³ They have hurt us more than can be expressed,
ripping us to shreds, cutting deeply into our souls.
⁴ But no matter what, the Lord is good to us.
He is a righteous God who stood to defend us,
breaking the chains of the evil ones that bound us.
⁵ May all who hate the Jews
fall back in disgrace to a shameful defeat!
⁶ Let them be like grass planted in shallow soil
that soon withers with no sustenance.
⁷ Let them be like weeds ignored by the reaper
and worthless to the harvester.
⁸ Let no one who sees them say,
"May the blessings of Jehovah be upon your life.
May the Lord bless you." *ᵃ*

130 OUT OF THE DEPTHS

A song of the stairway

¹ Lord, I cry out to you out of the depths of my despair!
² Hear my voice, O God!
Answer this prayer and hear my plea for mercy.
³ Lord, if you measured us and marked us with our sins,
who would ever have their prayers answered?
⁴ But your forgiving love is what makes you so wonderful.
No wonder you are loved and worshiped!
⁵ This is why I wait upon you, expecting your breakthrough,
for your word brings me hope.

---

a 129:8 In the Jewish culture, if you passed by one who was harvesting his crops, you would
shout out, "The Lord bless you!"

⁶ I long for you more than any watchman
  would long for the morning light.
I will watch and wait for you, O God,
  throughout the night.
⁷ O Israel, keep hoping, keep trusting,
  and keep waiting on the Lord,
  for he is tenderhearted, kind, and forgiving.
  He has a thousand ways to set you free!
⁸ He himself will redeem you;
  he will ransom you from the cruel slavery of your sins!

131 MY HEART IS MEEK

A song of the stairway, by King David

¹ Lord, my heart is meek before you.
  I don't consider myself better than others.
  I'm content to not pursue matters that are over my head—
  such as your complex mysteries and wonders—
  that I'm not yet ready to understand.
² I am humbled and quieted in your presence.
  Like a contented child who rests on its mother's lap,ᵃ
  I'm your resting child and my soul is content in you.
³ O people of God,ᵇ your time has come to quietly trust,
  waiting upon the Lord now and forever.

132 DAVID'S DYNASTY

A song of the stairway

¹ Lord, please don't forget all the hardships
  David had to pass through.
² And how he promised you, Jacob's mighty God, saying,
³ "I will not cross the threshold of my own home
  to sleep in my own bed.
⁴ I will not sleep or slumber,
  nor even take time to close my eyes in rest,
⁵ until I find a place for you to dwell, O mighty God of Jacob.
  I devote myself to finding a resting place for you!"ᶜ
⁶ First we heard that the ark was at Bethlehem.ᵈ
  Then we found it in the forest of Kiriath-Jearim.

---

a 131:2 "Like a contented child" is literally "like a weaned child."
b 131:3 Or "O Israel."
c 132:5 Historically, this refers to David wanting to bring the ark of glory back to Jerusalem.
d 132:6 Although the Hebrew text does not have the word *ark* but simply *it*, the translator supplies the word *ark* from its reference in verse 8. For the sake of understanding the text, the translator has substituted *Ephrathah* for *Bethlehem* (Ephrathah was the ancient name for

[7] Let's go into God's dwelling place
   and bow down and worship before him.
[8] Arise, O Lord, and enter your resting place,
   both you and the ark of your glorious strength!
[9] May your priests wear the robes of righteousness,
   and let all your godly lovers sing for joy!
[10] Don't forsake your anointed king now,
   but honor your servant David.
[11] For you gave your word and promised David
   in an unbreakable oath that one of his sons
   would be sitting on the throne to succeed him as king.
[12] You also promised that if David's sons
   would be faithful to keep their promise to follow you,
   obeying the words you spoke to them,
   then David's dynasty would never end.
[13] Lord, you have chosen Zion as your dwelling place,
   for your pleasure is fulfilled in making it your home.
[14] I hear you say, "I will make this place my eternal dwelling,
   for I have loved and desired it as my very own!
[15] I will make Zion prosper and
   satisfy her poor with my provision.
[16] I will cover my priests with salvation's power,
   and all my godly lovers will shout for joy!
[17] I will increase the anointing that was upon David,
   and my glistening glory will rest upon my chosen ones.
[18] But David's enemies will be covered with shame,
   while on them I will make holiness bloom!" [a]

133 Unity

A song to bring you higher, by King David

[1] How truly wonderful and delightful
   to see brothers and sisters living together in sweet unity!
[2] It's as precious as the sacred scented oil
   flowing from the head of the high priest Aaron,
   dripping down upon his beard and running all the way down
   to the hem of his priestly robes. [b]
[3] This heavenly harmony can be compared to the dew

Bethlehem) and *Jaar* for *Kiriath-Jearim* ("the fields of Jaar" was a variant form for Kiriath-Jearim, which means "the city of forests").

a 132:18 As translated from the Septuagint. The Hebrew reads "His crown will sparkle and gleam."

b 133:2 Or "running down the collar of his robe."

dripping down from the skies upon Mount Hermon,
refreshing the mountain slopes of Israel.
For from this realm of sweet harmony
God will release his eternal blessing, the promise of life forever!

134 THE NIGHT WATCH

A song to bring you higher

¹ All his loving priests who serve and sing,
come and sing your song of blessing to God.
Come and stand before him in the house of God
throughout the night watch,
² lifting up your hands in holy worship; come and bless the Lord!
³ May the Lord, whom you worship,
the mighty maker of heaven and earth,
bless you from Zion's glory!

135 HIS WONDERFUL WORKS

A song to bring you higher

¹ Shout hallelujah and praise the greatness of God!
All his godly lovers, praise him!
² All you worshiping priests on duty in the temple,
³ praise him, for he is beautiful!
Sing loving praises to his lovely name.
⁴ For Yahweh has chosen Jacob for his own purpose,
and Israel is his special treasure.
⁵ Next to every other god the greatness of our God is unequaled.
For our God is incomparable!
⁶ He does what he pleases, with unlimited power and authority,
extending his greatness throughout the entire universe!
⁷ He forms the misty clouds and creates thunder and lightning,
bringing the wind and rain out of his heavenly storehouse.
⁸ He struck down the eldest child in each Egyptian home;
both men and beast perished that night.
⁹ He did great miracles—mighty signs and wonders throughout
the land
before Pharaoh and all his subjects.
¹⁰ He conquered many nations and killed their mighty kings,
¹¹ like Sihon, king of the Amorites, and Og, king of Bashan,
and kings from every kingdom in Canaan.
¹² He gave their land to Israel as an inheritance for his people.
¹³ O Jehovah, your name endures forever!
Your fame is known in every generation.

[14] For you will vindicate your persecuted people,
  showing your tender love to all your servants.
[15] The unbelieving nations worship what they make.
  They worship their wealth and their work.
  They idolize what they own and what they do.
[16-18] Their possessions will never satisfy.
  Their lifeless and futile works cannot bring life to them!
  Their things can't talk to them or answer their prayers.
  Blind men can only create blind things.
  Those deaf to God can only make a deaf image.
  Dead men can only create dead idols.
  And everyone who trusts in these powerless, dead things
  will be just like what they worship—powerless and dead! [a]
[19] Praise Lord-Yahweh, all the families of Israel!
  Praise Lord-Yahweh, you family of Aaron! [b]
[20] Let all the priests [c] bless Lord-Yahweh!
  Let all his lovers [d] who bow low before him
  praise the Lord-Yahweh!
[21] So bless the Lord-Yahweh who lives in Jerusalem
  and dwells in Zion's glory!
  Hallelujah and praise the Lord!

136 HIS SAVING LOVE

[1] Let everyone thank God, for he is good, and he is easy to please!
  His tender love for us continues on forever!
[2] Give thanks to God, our King over all gods!
  His tender love for us continues on forever!
[3] Give thanks to the Lord over all lords!
  His tender love for us continues on forever!
[4] Give thanks to the only miracle working God!
  His tender love for us continues on forever!
[5] Give thanks to the Creator who made the heavens with wisdom! [e]
  His tender love for us continues on forever!
[6] To him who formed dry ground, raising it up from the sea!
  His tender love for us continues on forever!
[7] Praise the one who created every heavenly light!
  His tender love for us continues on forever!

---

a   135:16–18 Referring to the idols, the Hebrew could be translated "with mouths, but they cannot speak; with eyes, but they cannot see; with ears, but they cannot hear."
a   135:19 The name Aaron means "light-bringer" or "light-bearer."
c   135:20 Or "all the family of Levi." Levi represents the holy priesthood.
d   135:20 Or "those who fear him."
e   136:5 See Ps. 104:24 and Prov. 8:27–31.

⁸ He set the sun in the sky to rule over day!

His tender love for us continues on forever!

⁹ Praise him who set in place the moon and stars to rule over the night!

His tender love for us continues on forever!

¹⁰ Give thanks to God, who struck down the firstborn in Egypt!

His tender love for us continues on forever!

¹¹ He brought his people out of Egypt with miracles!

His tender love for us continues on forever!

¹² With his mighty power he brought them out!

His tender love for us continues on forever!

¹³ He split open the Red Sea for them!

His tender love for us continues on forever!

¹⁴ And led his people right through the middle!

His tender love for us continues on forever!

¹⁵ He vanquished Pharaoh's armies, drowning them all!

His tender love for us continues on forever!

¹⁶ He led his people through the wilderness!

His tender love for us continues on forever!

¹⁷ He's the one who smashed mighty kingdoms!

His tender love for us continues on forever!

¹⁸ He triumphed over powerful kings who stood in his way!

His tender love for us continues on forever!

¹⁹ He conquered Sihon, king of the Amorites!

His tender love for us continues on forever!

²⁰ He conquered the giant named Og, king of Bashan! ᵃ

His tender love for us continues on forever!

²¹ Then he gave away their lands as an inheritance!

His tender love for us continues on forever!

²² For he handed it all over to Israel, his beloved!

His tender love for us continues on forever!

²³ He's the God who chose us when we were nothing!

His tender love for us continues on forever!

²⁴ He has rescued us from the power of our enemies!

His tender love for us continues on forever!

²⁵ He provides food for hungry men and animals!

His tender love for us continues on forever!

²⁶ Give thanks to the great God of the heavens!

His tender love for us continues on forever!

---

a 136:20 The name Og means giant.

137 The Song of Our Captivity

¹ Along the banks of Babylon's rivers
   we sat as exiles, mourning our captivity,
   and wept with great love for Zion.
² *Our music and mirth were no longer heard, only sadness.*
   We hung up our harps on the willow trees.
³ Our captors tormented us, saying, "Make music for us and
   sing one of your happy Zion-songs!"
⁴ But how could we sing the song of the Lord
   in this foreign wilderness?
⁵ May my hands never make music again
   if I ever forget you, O Jerusalem.
⁶ May I never be able to sing again if I fail to honor Jerusalem supremely!
⁷ And Lord, may you never forget
   what the sons of Edom did to us, saying,
   "Let's raze the city of Jerusalem and burn it to the ground!"[a]
⁸ Listen, O Babylon, you evil destroyer!
   The one who destroys you will be rewarded above all others.
   You will be repaid for what you've done to us.
⁹ Great honor will come to those who destroy you and your future,
   by smashing your infants against the rubble of your own destruction.

138 The Divine Presence

By King David

¹ I thank you, Lord, and with all the passion of my heart
   I worship you in the presence of angels![b]
   Heaven's mighty ones will hear my voice
   as I sing my loving praise to you.
² I bow down before your divine presence
   and bring you my deepest worship
   as I experience your tender love and your living truth.
   For the promises of your word and the fame of your name
   have been magnified above all else!
³ At the very moment I called out to you, you answered me!
   You strengthened me deep within my soul
   and breathed fresh courage into me.
⁴ One day all the kings of the earth
   will rise to give you thanks when they hear the living words

---

a 137:7 The Hebrew text reads "Strip her [Jerusalem] naked!'"
b 138:1 Or "gods." The Hebrew *elohim* is literally "mighty ones" and can refer to either angels or the gods of the heathen.

that I have heard you speak.
⁵ They too will sing of your wonderful ways,
for your ineffable glory is great!
⁶ For though you are lofty and exalted,
you stoop to embrace the lowly.
Yet you keep your distance from those filled with pride.
⁷ By your mighty power I can walk through any devastation
and you will keep me alive, reviving me.
Your power set me free from the hatred of my enemies.
⁸ You keep every promise you've ever made to me!
Since your love for me is constant and endless,
I ask you, Lord, to finish every good thing that you've begun in me!

139 YOU KNOW ALL ABOUT ME

For the Pure and Shining One
King David's poetic song

¹ Lord, you know everything there is to know about me.
² You perceive every movement of my heart and soul,
and you understand my every thought before it even enters my mind.
³⁻⁴ You are so intimately aware of me, Lord.
You read my heart like an open book
and you know all the words I'm about to speak
before I even start a sentence!
You know every step I will take before my journey even begins.
⁵ You've gone into my future to prepare the way,
and in kindness you follow behind me
to spare me from the harm of my past.ᵃ
With your hand of love upon my life,
you impart a blessing to me.
⁶ This is just too wonderful, deep, and incomprehensible!
Your understanding of me brings me wonder and strength.ᵇ
⁷ Where could I go from your Spirit?
Where could I run and hide from your face?
⁸ If I go up to heaven, you're there!
If I go down to the realm of the dead, you're there too!
⁹ If I fly with wings into the shining dawn, you're there!
If I fly into the radiant sunset, you're there waiting!ᶜ

---

a 139:5 Or "You hem me in [lit., "beseige me"] before and behind." The implication is that
God protects him from what may come in the future and what has happened in the past.
b 139:6 As translated from the Septuagint. The Hebrew reads "too high to understand."
c 139:9 Implied in the Hebrew, which states, "the remote parts of the sea" or "beyond the
horizon to the west." The sea is west of Israel.

¹⁰ Wherever I go, your hand will guide me;
your strength will empower me.
¹¹ It's impossible to disappear from you
or to ask the darkness to hide me,
for your presence is everywhere, bringing light into my night.
¹² There is no such thing as darkness with you.
The night, to you, is as bright as the day;
there's no difference between the two.
¹³ You formed my innermost being, shaping my delicate inside
and my intricate outside,
and wove them all together in my mother's womb. *a*
¹⁴ I thank you, God, for making me so mysteriously complex!
Everything you do is marvelously breathtaking.
It simply amazes me to think about it!
How thoroughly you know me, Lord!
¹⁵ You even formed every bone in my body
when you created me in the secret place, *b*
carefully, skillfully shaping me *c* from nothing to something.
¹⁶ You saw who you created me to be before I became me! *d*
Before I'd ever seen the light of day,
the number of days you planned for me
were already recorded in your book. *e*
¹⁷⁻¹⁸ Every single moment you are thinking of me!
How precious and wonderful to consider
that you cherish me constantly in your every thought!
O God, your desires toward me are more
than the grains of sand on every shore!
When I awake each morning, you're still with me.
¹⁹ O God, come and slay these bloodthirsty, murderous men!
For I cry out, "Depart from me, you wicked ones!"
²⁰ See how they blaspheme your sacred name
and lift up themselves against you, but all in vain!
²¹ Lord, can't you see how I despise those who despise you?
For I grieve when I see them rise up against you.
²² I have nothing but complete hatred and disgust for them.
Your enemies shall be my enemies!

---

a 139:13 The Hebrew word for "knit" or "wove" can also be translated "to cover" or "to defend." God places an eternal spirit inside the conceived child within the womb of a mother and covers that life, sends the child a guardian angel, and watches over him or her.
b 139:15 The Hebrew text is literally "the depths of the earth."
c 139:15 Or "embroidered me."
d 139:16 The Hebrew could be translated "as an embryo."
e 139:16 See Ps. 69:28.

23 God, I invite your searching gaze into my heart.
    Examine me through and through;
      find out everything that may be hidden within me.
    Put me to the test and sift through all my anxious cares.
24 See if there is any path of pain I'm walking on,
    and lead me back to your glorious, everlasting ways—
    the path that brings me back to you.

140 A PRAYER FOR PROTECTION

For the Pure and Shining One
King David's poetic song

1 Lord, protect me from this evil one!
    Rescue me from these violent schemes!
2 He concocts his secret strategy to divide and harm others,
    stirring up trouble one against another.
3 They are known for their sharp rhetoric
    of poisonous, hateful words.

Pause in his presence

4 Keep me safe, Lord, out of reach from these wicked and violent men,
    and guard me, God, for they have plotted an evil scheme
    to ruin me and bring me down.
5 They are proud and insolent; they've set an ambush for me in secret.
    They are determined to snare me in their net like captured prey.

Pause in his presence

6–7 O Lord, you are my God and my saving strength!
    My Hero-God, you wrap yourself around me to protect me.
    For I'm surrounded by your presence in my day of battle.
    Lord Yahweh, hear my cry.
    May my voice move your heart to show me mercy.
8 Don't let the wicked triumph over me,
    but bring down their every strategy to subdue me
    or they will become even more arrogant!

Pause in his presence

9 Those who surround me are nothing but proud troublemakers.
    May they drink the poison of their own poisonous words.
10–11 May their slanderous lives never prosper!
    Let evil itself hunt them down and pursue them relentlessly
    until they are thrown into fiery pits
    from which they will never get out!
    Let burning coals of hellfire fall upon their heads!
12 For I know, Lord, that you will be the hero
    of all those they persecute,
    and you will secure justice for the poor.

¹³ Your godly lovers will thank you no matter what happens.
  For they choose and cherish your presence
  above everything else!

141 An Evening Prayer

King David's poetic song

¹ Please, Lord, come close and come quickly to help me!
  Listen to my prayer as I call out to you.
² Let my prayer be as the evening sacrifice
  that burns like fragrant incense, rising as my offering to you
  as I lift up my hands in surrendered worship!
³ God, give me grace to guard my lips [a]
  from speaking what is wrong.
⁴ Guide me away from temptation and doing evil.
  Save me from sinful habits and from keeping company
  with those who are experts in evil.
  Help me not to share in their sin in any way!
⁵ When one of your godly lovers corrects me
  or one of your faithful ones rebukes me,
  I will accept it like an honor I cannot refuse.
  It will be as healing medicine that I swallow
  without an offended heart.
  Even if they are mistaken, I will continue to pray. [b]
⁶ When the leaders and judges are condemned,
  falling upon the rocks of justice, [c]
  then they'll know my words to them were true!
⁷ Like an earthquake splits open the earth,
  so the world of hell will open its mouth
  to swallow their scattered bones.
⁸ But you are my Lord and my God; I only have eyes for you!
  I hide myself in you, so don't leave me defenseless.
⁹ Protect me! Keep me from the traps of wickedness they set for me.
¹⁰ Let them all stumble into their own traps
  while I escape without a scratch!

---

a 141:3 The Septuagint reads "Set a fortress door before my lips."
b 141:5 This is one of most difficult verses to translate, with scholars divided over the meaning of the Hebrew text. Another translation could be "Don't let the oil of the wicked anoint my head, for I pray continually against their wickedness."
c 141:6 See 2 Chron. 25:12.

142 MY ONLY HOPE

King David's poetic song of instruction
A prayer when he was confined in a cave

¹ God, I'm crying out to you!
I lift up my voice boldly to beg for your mercy.
² I spill out my heart to you and tell you all my troubles.
³ For when I was desperate, overwhelmed, and about to give up,
you were the only one there to help.
You gave me a way of escape
from the hidden traps of my enemies.
⁴ I look to my left and right to see if there is anyone who will help,
but there's no one who takes notice of me.
I have no hope of escape, and no one cares whether I live or die.
⁵ So I cried out to you, Lord, my only hiding place.
You're all I have, my only hope in this life,
my last chance for help.
⁶ Please listen to my heart's cry,
for I am low and in desperate need of you!
Rescue me from all those who persecute me,
for I am no match for them.
⁷ Bring me out of this dungeon so I can declare your praise!
And all your godly lovers will celebrate
all the wonderful things you've done for me!

143 MY HUMBLE PRAYER

King David's poetic song when he was chased by Absalom[a]

¹ Lord, you must hear my prayer,
for you are faithful to your promises.
Answer my cry, O righteous God!
² Don't bring me into your courtroom for judgment,
for there is no one who is righteous before you.
³ My enemies have chased and caught me
and crushed my life into dust.
Now I'm living in the darkness of death's shadow.
⁴ My inner being is in depression
and my heart is heavy, dazed with despair.
⁵ I remember the glorious miracles of days gone by,
and I often think of all the wonders of old.

---

a As translated from the Septuagint.

⁶ Now I'm reaching out to you, thirsting for you
  like the dry, cracked ground thirsts for rain.

Pause in his presence

⁷ Lord, come quickly and answer me,
  for my depression deepens and I'm about to give up.
  Don't leave me now or I'll die!
⁸ Let the dawning day bring me revelation
  of your tender, unfailing love.
  Give me light for my path and teach me, for I trust in you.
⁹ Save me from all my enemies, for I hide myself in you.
¹⁰ I just want to obey all you ask of me.
  So teach me, Lord, for you are my God.
  Your gracious Spirit is all I need, so lead me on good paths
  that are pleasing to you, my one and only God!
¹¹ Lord, if you rescue me, it will bring you more glory,
  for you are true to your promises.
  Bring me out of these troubles!
¹² Since I am your loving servant, destroy all those
  who are trying to harm me.
  And because you are so loving and kind to me,
  silence all of my enemies!

144 RESCUE ME

King David's poetic song as he stood before Goliath ᵃ

¹ There is only one strong, safe, and secure place for me;
  it's in God alone and I love him!
  He's the one who gives me strength and skill for the battle.
² He's my shelter of love and my fortress of faith,
  who wraps himself around me as a secure shield.
  I hide myself in this one who subdues enemies before me.
³ Lord, what is it about us that you would even notice us?
  Why do you even bother with us?
⁴ For man is nothing but a faint whisper, a mere breath.
  We spend our days like nothing more than a passing shadow.
⁵ Step down from heaven, Lord, and come down!
  Make the mountains melt at your touch.
⁶ Loose your fiery lightning flashes and scatter your enemies.
  Overthrow them with your terrifying judgments.
⁷ Reach down from your heavens

ᵃ As translated from the Septuagint. Put yourself in David's place as he faced a giant named
  Goliath. Imagine how he felt as you read through this psalm.

and rescue me from this hell,
and deliver me from these dark powers.
⁸ They speak nothing but lies; their words are pure deceit.
Nothing they say can ever be trusted.
⁹ My God, I will sing you a brand-new song!
The harp inside my heart will make music to you!
¹⁰ I will sing of you, the one who gives victory to kings—
the one who rescues David, your loving servant,
from the fatal sword.
¹¹ Deliver me and save me from these dark powers
who speak nothing but lies.
Their words are pure deceit
and you can't trust anything they say.
¹² Deliver us! Then our homes will be happy.
Our sons will grow up as strong, sturdy men
and our daughters with graceful beauty,
royally fashioned as for a palace.
¹³⁻¹⁴ Our barns will be filled to the brim,
overflowing with the fruits of our harvest.
Our fields will be full of sheep and cattle,
too many to count,
and our livestock will not miscarry their young.
Our enemies will not invade our land,
and there'll be no breach in our walls.
¹⁵ What bliss we experience when these blessings fall!
The people who love and serve our God will be happy indeed!

145 GOD'S GREATNESS

King David's poetic song of praise

¹ My heart explodes with praise to you!
Now and forever my heart bows in worship to you,
my King and my God!
² Every day I will lift up my praise to your name
with praises that will last throughout eternity.
³ Lord, you are great and worthy of the highest praise!
For there is no end to the discovery
of the greatness that surrounds you.
⁴ Generation after generation will declare more of your greatness
and declare more of your glory.
⁵ Your magnificent splendor and the miracles of your majesty
are my constant meditation.
⁶ Your awe-inspiring acts of power have everyone talking!

I'm telling people everywhere about your excellent greatness!

[7] Our hearts bubble over as we celebrate the fame
of your marvelous beauty, *bringing bliss to our hearts.*
We shout with ecstatic joy over your breakthrough for us.

[8] You're kind and tenderhearted to those who don't deserve it
and very patient with people who fail you.
Your love is like a flooding river overflowing its banks with kindness.

[9] God, everyone sees your goodness,
for your tender love is blended into everything you do.

[10] Everything you have made will praise you, fulfilling its purpose.
And all your godly lovers will be found bowing before you.

[11] They will tell the world of the lavish splendor of your kingdom
and preach about your limitless power.

[12] They will demonstrate for all to see your miracles of might
and reveal the glorious majesty of your kingdom.

[13] You are the Lord who reigns over your never-ending kingdom through all
the ages of time and eternity!
You are faithful to fulfill every promise you've made.
You manifest yourself as kindness in all you do. *a*

[14] Weak and feeble ones you will sustain.
Those bent over with burdens of shame you will lift up.

[15] You have captured our attention
and the eyes of all look to you.
You give what they hunger for at just the right time.

[16] When you open your generous hand, it's full of blessings,
satisfying the longings of every living thing.

[17] You are fair and righteous in everything you do,
and your love is wrapped into all your works.

[18] You draw near to those who call out to you,
listening closely, especially when their hearts are true.

[19] Every one of your godly lovers receives
even more than what they ask for.
For you hear what their hearts really long for
and you bring them your saving strength.

[20] God, you watch carefully over all your lovers like a bodyguard,
but you will destroy the ungodly.

[21] I will praise you, Lord!
Let everyone everywhere join me in praising
the beautiful Lord of holiness from now through eternity!

---

a 145:13 The last two lines of this verse are only found in one reliable Hebrew manuscript
and in the Septuagint. It could also be translated "All your works are very holy."

146 Our True Help

A poetic psalm, by Haggai and Zechariah[a]

¹ Hallelujah! Praise the Lord!
   My innermost being will praise you, Lord!
² I will spend my life praising you and
   singing high praises to you, my God, every day of my life!
³⁻⁴ We can never look to men for help;
   no matter who they are, they can't save us,
   for even our great leaders fail and fall.
   They too are just mortals who will one day die.
   At death the spirits of all depart and their bodies return to dust.
   In the day of their death all their projects and plans are over.
⁵ But those who hope in the Lord will be happy and pleased!
   Our help comes from the God of Jacob!
⁶ You keep all your promises.
   You are the Creator of heaven's glory,
   earth's grandeur, and ocean's greatness.
⁷ The oppressed get justice with you.
   The hungry are satisfied with you.
   Prisoners find their freedom with you.
⁸ You open the eyes of the blind
   and you fully restore those bent over with shame.
   You love those who love and honor you.
⁹ You watch over strangers and immigrants
   and support the fatherless and widows.
   But you subvert the plans of the ungodly.
¹⁰ Lord, you will reign forever!
   Zion's God will rule throughout time and eternity!
   Hallelujah! Praise the Lord!

147 Our Amazing God

¹ Hallelujah! Praise the Lord!
   How beautiful it is when we sing our praises to the beautiful God,
   for praise makes you lovely before him
   and brings him great delight!
² The Lord builds up Jerusalem;
   he gathers up the outcasts and brings them home.
³ He heals the wounds of every shattered heart.

---

a As translated from the Septuagint. Pss. 146–150 are called "Hallelujah Psalms" because they all begin in Hebrew with the words "Hallelujah, praise the Lord."

⁴ He sets his stars in place, calling them all by their names.
⁵ How great is our God!
    There's absolutely nothing his power cannot accomplish,
    and he has infinite understanding of everything.
⁶ God supports and strengthens the humble,
    but the ungodly will be brought down to the dust.
⁷ Sing out with songs of thanksgiving to the Lord!
    Let's sing our praises with melodies overflowing!
⁸ He fills the sky with clouds, sending showers to water the earth
    so that the grass springs up on the mountain fields
    and the earth produces food for man. ᵃ
⁹ All the birds and beasts who cry with hunger to him
    are fed from his hands.
¹⁰ His people don't find security in strong horses,
    for horsepower is nothing to him.
    Man power is even less impressive!
¹¹ The Lord shows favor to those who fear him,
    to his godly lovers who wait for his tender embrace.
¹² Jerusalem, praise the Lord! Zion, worship your God!
¹³ For he has strengthened the authority of your gates.
    He even blesses you with more children.
¹⁴ He's the one who brings peace to your borders, ᵇ
    feeding you the most excellent of fare.
¹⁵ He sends out his orders throughout the world;
    his words run as swift messengers, bringing them to pass.
¹⁶ He blankets the earth with glistening snow,
    painting the landscape with frost.
¹⁷ Sleet and hail fall from the sky,
    causing waters to freeze before winter's icy blast.
¹⁸ Then he speaks his word and it all melts away;
    as the warm spring winds blow, the streams begin to flow.
¹⁹ In the same way, he speaks his word to Jacob,
    and to Israel he brings his life-giving instruction.
²⁰ He has dealt with Israel differently than with any other people,
    for they have received his laws.
    Hallelujah! Praise the Lord!

148 THE COSMIC CHORUS OF PRAISE

¹ Hallelujah! Praise the Lord! Let the skies be filled with praise
    and the highest heavens with the shouts of glory!

ᵃ 147:8 As translated from the Septuagint.
ᵇ 147:14 Or "He makes peace your borders" (LXX).

² Go ahead—praise him, all you his messengers!
  Praise him some more, all you heavenly hosts!
³ Keep it up, sun and moon!
  Don't stop now, all you twinkling stars of light!
⁴ Take it up even higher—up to the highest heavens,
  until the cosmic chorus thunders his praise! *ᵃ*
⁵ Let the entire universe erupt with praise to God.
  From nothing to something he spoke and created it all.
⁶ He established the cosmos to last forever,
  and he stands behind his commands
  so his orders will never be revoked.
⁷ Let the earth join in with this parade of praise!
  You mighty creatures of the ocean's depths,
  echo in exaltation!
⁸ Lightning, hail, snow, and clouds,
  and the stormy winds that fulfill his word.
⁹ Bring your melody, O mountains and hills;
  trees of the forest and field, harmonize your praise!
¹⁰⁻¹² Praise him, all beasts and birds, mice and men,
  kings, queens, princes, and princesses,
  young men and maidens, children and babes,
  old and young alike, everyone everywhere!
¹³ Let them all join in with this orchestra of praise.
  For the name of the Lord is the only name we raise!
  His stunning splendor ascends higher than the heavens.
¹⁴ He anoints his people with strength and authority,
  showing his great favor to all his godly lovers,
  even to his princely people, Israel,
  who are so close to his heart.
  Hallelujah! Praise the Lord!

149 Triumphant Praise

¹ Hallelujah! Praise the Lord!
  It's time to sing to God a brand-new song *ᵇ*
  so that all his holy people will hear how wonderful he is!
² May Israel be enthused with joy because of him,
  and may the sons of Zion pour out
  their joyful praises to their King.
³ Break forth with dancing!
  Make music and sing God's praises with the rhythm of drums!

---

a 148:4 Poetic implication in the text. The literal Hebrew reads "the waters above the sky."
b 149:1 Or "a spontaneous song."

[4] For he enjoys his faithful lovers.
   He adorns the humble with his beauty
   and he loves to give them the victory.
[5] His godly lovers triumph in the glory of God,
   and their joyful praises will rise even while others sleep.
[6] God's high and holy praises fill their mouths,
   for their shouted praises are their weapons of war!
[7] These warring weapons will bring vengeance
   on every opposing force and every resistant power—
[8] to bind kings with chains and rulers with iron shackles.
[9] Praise-filled warriors will enforce
   the judgment-doom decreed against their enemies.
   This is the glorious honor he gives to all his godly lovers.
   Hallelujah! Praise the Lord!

150 The Hallelujah Chorus

[1] Hallelujah! Praise the Lord! Praise God in his holy sanctuary!
   Praise him in his stronghold in the sky!
[2] Praise him for his miracles of might!
   Praise him for his magnificent greatness!
[3] Praise him with the trumpets blasting!
   Praise him with piano and guitar!
[4-5] Praise him with drums and dancing!
   Praise him with the loud, resounding clash of cymbals!
   Praise him with every instrument you can find!
[6] Let everyone everywhere join in the crescendo
   of ecstatic praise to Yahweh!
   Hallelujah! Praise the Lord!

PROVERBS

Introduction

AT A GLANCE

Author: Mostly Solomon, king of Israel, but other contributors too

Audience: Originally Israel, but these words of wisdom are for everyone—they are written to you

Date: Preexile (chs. 10–29) and Postexile (chs. 1–9, 30–31), the tenth to fifth centuries BC

Type of Literature: Poetry and wisdom literature

Major Themes: The fear of the Lord; God's transcendence and immanence; godly wisdom and human foolishness; the righteous and wicked wealth and poverty; men and women; husbands and wives; Jesus and wisdom

Outline:

Collection I: 1:1–9:18 — Introduction to Wisdom
Collection II: 10:1–22:16 — Sayings of Solomon, Part 1
Collection III: 22:17–24:22 — Sayings of the Wise
Collection IV: 24:23–34 — More Sayings of the Wise
Collection V: 25:1–29:27 — Sayings of Solomon, Part 2
Collection VI: 30:1–31:31 — Sayings of Agur and Lemuel

ABOUT PROVERBS

The Bible is a book of poetry, not simply starched, stiff doctrines devoid of passion. The Bible, including Proverbs, is full of poetic beauty and subtle nuances ripe with meaning. The ancient wisdom of God fills its pages!

Proverbs is a book of wisdom from above tucked inside metaphors, symbols, and poetic imagery. God could properly be described as the divine poet and master artisan who crafted the cosmos to portray his glory and has given us his written Word to reveal his wisdom. Inspired from eternity, the sixty-six books of our Bible convey the full counsel and wisdom of God. Do you need wisdom? God has a verse for that!

Five books of divine poetry show us the reality of knowing God through experience, not just through history or doctrines. Job points us to the end of our self-life to discover the greatest revelation of the Lord, which is his tender love and wisdom. Psalms reveals the new life we enter into with God, expressed through praise and prayer. Next is Proverbs, where we enroll in the divine seminary of wisdom and revelation to learn the ways of God. Ecclesiastes teaches us to set our hearts not on the things of this life but on those values that endure eternally. And finally, in Song of Songs, the sweetest lyrics ever composed lead us into divine romance where we are immersed in Jesus' love for his bride.

The nature of Hebrew poetry is quite different from that of English poetry. There is a pleasure found in Hebrew poetry that transcends rhyme and meter. The Hebrew verses come in a poetic package, a form of meaning that imparts an understanding that is deeper than mere logic. True revelation unfolds an encounter—an experience of knowing God as he is revealed through the mysterious vocabulary of riddle, proverb, and parable.

For example, the Hebrew word for "proverb," *mashal*, has two meanings. The first is "parable, byword, metaphor, a pithy saying that expresses wisdom." But the second meaning is overlooked by many. The homonym *mashal* can also mean "to rule, to take dominion" or "to reign with power."

What you have before you now is a dynamic translation of the ancient book of Proverbs. These powerful words will bring you revelation from the throne room—the wisdom you need to guide your steps and direct your life. What you learn from these verses will change your life and launch you into your destiny.

PURPOSE

Within this divinely anointed compilation of Proverbs there is a deep well of wisdom to reign in life and to succeed in our destiny. The wisdom that God has designed for us to receive will cause us to excel—to rise up as rulers-to-be on earth for his glory. The kingdom of God is brought into the earth as we implement the godly wisdom of Proverbs.

Although the Proverbs can be interpreted in their most literal and practical sense, the wisdom contained herein is not unlocked by a casual surface reading. The Spirit of revelation has breathed upon every verse to embed a deeper meaning of practical insight to guide our steps into the lives God meant for us to live.

AUTHOR AND AUDIENCE

You're about to read the greatest book of wisdom ever written, mostly penned by the wisest man to ever live. God gave his servant Solomon this wisdom to pass along to us, his servants, who continue the ministry of Jesus, the embodiment of wisdom, until he returns in full glory. While Solomon penned most of these words of wisdom, it is believed others had a hand too, including advisers to King Hezekiah and the unknown men Agur and Lemuel—which could be pseudonyms for Solomon. Regardless, the one who edited the final version of Proverbs brought together the wisest teachings from the the wisest person to ever live to write a book containing some of the deepest revelation in the Bible. When Solomon pens a proverb, there is more than meets the eye!

Who are these proverbs written to? This compilation of wisdom's words is written to you! Throughout the book we find words like "Listen, my sons. Listen, my daughters." The book of Proverbs is written to us as sons and daughters of the living God. The teaching we receive is not from a distant god who tells us we'd better live right or else. These are personal words of love and tenderness from our wise Father, the Father of eternity, who speaks right into our hearts with healing, radiant words. Receive deeply the words of the kind Father of heaven as though he were speaking directly to you.

MAJOR THEMES

The wisdom found in Proverbs is about the art of successful living. The appeal of these insights is that they touch on universal problems and issues that affect human behavior in us all. Several major themes are present in these godly sayings of God's servant Solomon:

Lady Wisdom, Revelation-Knowledge, Living-Understanding. Throughout Proverbs wisdom is personified with the metaphor of Lady Wisdom, who dispenses revelation-knowledge and living-understanding. Lady Wisdom is a figure of speech for God and his divine wisdom, who invites us to receive the best way to live, the excellent and noble way of life. She is personified as a guide (6:22), a beloved sister or bride (7:4), and a hostess who generously invites people to "come and dine at my table and drink of my wine" (9:1–6). In Proverbs, wisdom is inseparable from knowledge and understanding, which is not received independent of God's revelation. We are invited to "come to the one who has living-understanding" (9:10) in order to receive what Lady Wisdom has to offer. For God promises that revelation-knowledge will flow to the one who hungers for her gift of understanding (14:6).

The Fear of the Lord. From the beginning, in 1:7, Proverbs makes it clear that we gain "the essence of wisdom" and cross "the threshold of true knowledge" only when we fear the Lord—or, as the Passion Translation translates it, we live "in complete awe and adoration of God." Living in a way that our entire being worships and adores God is a constant theme throughout Proverbs.

God's Transcendence and Immanence. Proverbs teaches that God is both the author of (transcendent) and actor within (immanent) our human story. First, God is above and outside the world: as Creator "he broke open the hidden fountains of the deep, bringing secret springs to the surface" (3:20); "God sees everything you do and his eyes are wide open as he observes every single habit you have" (5:21); he is sovereign and steers "a king's heart for his purposes as it is for him to direct the course of a stream" (21:1).

Second, God is a part of and involved with the world: "The rich and the poor have one thing in common: the Lord God created each one" (22:2); "The Lord champions the widow's cause" (15:25); he "will rise to plead [the poor's] case" (22:23).

Proverbs teaches that God is all-powerful and transcendent while also taking part in our human story as our defender and protector.

Wise and Fool, Righteous and Wicked. Solomon believed there are basically two kinds of people in the world: the wise righteous and the wicked fools. The wise person possesses God's revelation-knowledge and living-understanding. Therefore, he is prudent, shrewd, insightful, and does what is right because he is righteous, a God-lover. This lover of God is just, peaceful, upright, blameless, good, trustworthy, and kind.

The wicked fool is different. He is greedy, violent, deceitful, cruel, and speaks perversely. It's no wonder "the Lord detests the lifestyle of the wicked!" (15:9). As a foolish person, he is described as being gullible, an idiot, self-sufficient, a mocker, lazy, senseless, and he rejects revelation-knowledge and living-understanding.

Many of Solomon's wise sayings relate to these two kinds of people, teaching us how to avoid being a wicked fool and instead live as God intends us to live, as his wise, righteous lovers.

Wealth and Poverty. As with many of Solomon's wise sayings, we cannot take one thought on wealth and poverty and apply it to every situation. Instead, Solomon teaches us seven major things about having wealth and being poor, and how wisdom and foolishness affect them both: the righteous are blessed with wealth by God himself; foolishness leads to poverty; fools who have wealth will soon lose it; poverty results from injustice and oppression; the wealthy are called to be generous with their wealth; gaining wisdom is far better than gaining wealth; and the value of wealth is limited.

Jesus and the Church. As with the rest of the Old Testament, we are called to read Proverbs in light of Jesus and his ministry. Throughout the gospels Jesus associates himself with wisdom. For instance, in Matt. 11:18–19 Jesus claims his actions represent Lady Wisdom herself. Where he is identified with Lady Wisdom in the New Testament, it is a powerful way of saying that Jesus is the full, entire embodiment of wisdom. In many ways Col. 1:15–17 mirrors Prov. 8. Likewise, the preface to John's gospel resonates with this same chapter when Jesus is associated with the Word, another personification of wisdom.

Jesus stands at the center of Scripture; he can be found throughout Scripture, not just in the New Testament. So as you read these important words of wisdom, consider how they point to the one who perfectly embodied and is our wisdom.

PROVERBS

Wisdom from Above

THE PROLOGUE

1 Here are kingdom revelations, words to live by,
    and words of wisdom given to empower you to reign in life, [a]
    written as proverbs by Israel's King Solomon, [b] David's son.
2 Within these sayings will be found the revelation of wisdom [c]
    and the impartation of spiritual understanding.
    Use them as keys to unlock the treasures of true knowledge.
3 Those who cling to these words will receive discipline
    to demonstrate wisdom in every relationship [d]
    and to choose what is right and just and fair.
4 These proverbs will give you great skill
    to teach the immature and make them wise,
    to give youth the understanding of their design and destiny.
5 For the wise, these proverbs will make you even wiser,
    and for those with discernment,
    you will be able to acquire brilliant strategies for leadership.
6 These kingdom revelations will break open your understanding
    to unveil the deeper meaning of parables,
    poetic riddles, and epigrams,
    and to unravel the words and enigmas of the wise.
7 How then does a man gain the essence of wisdom?

---

a 1:1 As stated in the introduction, the Hebrew word for "proverbs" means more than just a
    wise saying. It can also mean "to rule, to reign in power, to take dominion."
b 1:1 The name Solomon means "peaceable." There is a greater one than Solomon who gives
    peace to all of his followers. His name is Jesus. Solomon was the seed of David; we are the
    seed of Jesus Christ. Solomon had an encounter with God after asking for a discerning heart
    (1 Kings 3:5–14). This pleased God, so he gave Solomon wisdom, riches, and power. God is
    ready to impart these same things today to those who ask him. See James 1:5–8.
c 1:2 There are six Hebrew words translated "wisdom" in the book of Proverbs. Some of
    them require an entire phrase in English to convey the meaning. The word used here is
    chokmah, and it is used in Proverbs forty-two times. Forty-two is the number of months
    Jesus ministered and the number of generations from Abraham to Christ listed in Matt. 1.
d 1:3 The Hebrew word translated "wisdom" here also means "righteousness."

We cross the threshold of true knowledge
when we live in obedient devotion to God. *a*
Stubborn know-it-alls *b* will never stop to do this,
for they scorn true wisdom and knowledge.

The Wisdom of a Father

⁸ Pay close attention, my child, to your father's wise words
and never forget your mother's instructions. *c*
⁹ For their insight will bring you success,
adorning you with grace-filled thoughts
and giving you reins to guide your decisions. *d*
¹⁰ When peer pressure compels you to go with the crowd
and sinners invite you to join in,
you must simply say, "No!"
¹¹ When the gang says—
"We're going to steal and kill and get away with it.
¹² We'll take down the rich and rob them.
We'll swallow them up alive
and take what we want from whomever we want.
¹³ Then we'll take their treasures and fill our homes with loot.
¹⁴ So come on and join us.
Take your chance with us.
We'll divide up all we get;
we'll each end up with big bags of cash!"—
¹⁵ my son, refuse to go with them and stay far away from them.
¹⁶ For crime is their way of life and bloodshed their specialty.
¹⁷ To be aware of their snare is the best way of escape.

---

a 1:7 Many translations render this "the fear of the Lord." This is much more than the English
concept of fear. It also implies submission, awe, worship, and reverence. The Hebrew word
used here is found fourteen times in Proverbs. The number fourteen represents spiritual
perfection. The number fourteen is mentioned three times in the genealogy of Jesus (Matt.
1:1–17). It is also the number for Passover. You will pass from darkness to wisdom's light by
the "fear" of the Lord.

b 1:7 Or "foolish ones." There are three Hebrew words translated "fool" in Proverbs and
another six that are related to a fool or foolish acts. A fool is described in Proverbs as one
who hates true wisdom and correction, with no desire to acquire revelation knowledge.

c 1:8 Many expositors see this verse as the words of David to Solomon, yet we all must give
heed to this. The words of our father (God) and our mother (the church, the freewoman)
will bring us wisdom. See Gal. 4:21–31.

d 1:9 The Hebrew text here is literally translated "adornment for your head, chains for your
neck." The head is a metaphor for our thoughts, the neck a symbol for willing obedience
that guides our decisions, in contrast to being stiff-necked or proud. See Phil. 2:5.

¹⁸ They'll resort to murder to steal their victim's assets,
   but eventually it will be their own lives that are ambushed.
¹⁹ In their ungodly disrespect for God
   they bring destruction on their own lives.

Wisdom's Warning

²⁰ Wisdom's praises are sung in the streets
   and celebrated far and wide.
²¹ Yet wisdom's song is not always heard in the halls of higher learning.
   But in the hustle and bustle of everyday life
   its lyrics can always be heard above the din of the crowd. ᵃ
   You will hear wisdom's warning as she preaches courageously
   to those who stop to listen:
²² "Foolish ones, how much longer will you cling to your deception? ᵇ
   How much longer will you mock wisdom,
   cynical scorners who fight the facts?
²³ Come back to your senses and be restored to reality.
   Don't even think about refusing my rebuke!
   Don't you know that I'm ready
   to pour out my spirit of wisdom upon you
   and bring to you the revelation of my words
   that will make your heart wise?
²⁴ I've called to you over and over;
   still you refuse to come to me.
   I've pleaded with you again and again,
   yet you've turned a deaf ear to my voice.
²⁵ Because you have laughed at my counsel
   and have insisted on continuing in your stubbornness,
²⁶ I will laugh when your calamity comes
   and will turn away from you at the time of your disaster.
   Make a joke of my advice, will you?
   Then I'll make a joke out of you!
²⁷ When the storm clouds of terror gather over your head,
   when dread and distress consume you
   and your catastrophe comes like a hurricane,
²⁸ you will cry out to me, but I won't answer.
   Then it will be too late to expect my help.
   When desperation drives you to search for me,
   I will be nowhere to be found.

ᵃ 1:21 Literally translated, this verse reads "Wisdom sings out in the streets and speaks her
   voice in the squares, crying out at the head of noisy crowds and at the entrance of the city
   gates." This is a parabolic statement of wisdom being heard everywhere and in every place.
ᵇ 1:22 Or "Childish ones, how long will you love your childishness?"

²⁹ Because you have turned up your nose at me
  and closed your eyes to the facts
  and refused to worship me in awe— ᵃ
³⁰ because you scoffed at my wise counsel
  and laughed at my correction—
³¹ now you will eat the bitter fruit of your own ways.
  You've made your own bed; now lie in it!
  So how do you like that?
³² Like an idiot you've turned away from me
  and chosen destruction instead.
  Your self-satisfied smugness ᵇ will kill you.
³³ But the one who always listens to me
  will live undisturbed in a heavenly peace.
  Free from fear, confident and courageous,
  you will rest unafraid and sheltered from the storms of life.

SEARCHING FOR WISDOM

2 My child, will you treasure my wisdom?
  Then, and only then, will you acquire it.
  And only if you accept my advice
  and hide it within will you succeed.
² So train your heart to listen when I speak
  and open your spirit wide to expand your discernment—
  then pass it on to your sons and daughters. ᶜ
³ Yes, cry out for comprehension and intercede for insight.
⁴ For if you keep seeking it like a man would seek for sterling silver,
  searching in hidden places for cherished treasure,
⁵ then you will discover the fear of the Lord
  and find the true knowledge of God.
⁶ Wisdom is a gift from a generous God,
  and every word he speaks is full of revelation
  and becomes a fountain of understanding within you. ᵈ
⁷⁻⁸ For the Lord has a hidden storehouse of wisdom
  made accessible to his godly lovers. ᵉ
  He becomes your personal bodyguard as you follow his ways,
  protecting and guarding you as you choose what is right.

---

a   1:29 The Hebrew word used here can be translated "fear, dread, awe, and worship." Nearly every translation uses the word *fear* or *reverence* while ignoring the other aspects of the Aramaic word, *dekhlatha*. The New Testament is clear that there is no fear in love. See 1 John 4:18.
b   1:32 Or "your abundant prosperity."
c   2:2 As translated from the Septuagint.
d   2:6 The Septuagint adds "found in his presence."
e   2:7–8 Or "the righteous."

⁹ Then you will discover all that is just, proper, and fair,
and be empowered to make the right decisions
as you walk into your destiny.
¹⁰ When wisdom wins your heart and revelation breaks in,
true pleasure enters your soul.
¹¹ If you choose to follow good counsel,
divine design will watch over you
and understanding will protect you
from making poor choices.
¹² It will rescue you from evil in disguise
and from those who speak duplicities.
¹³ For they have left the highway of holiness
and walk in the ways of darkness.
¹⁴ They take pleasure when evil prospers
and thoroughly enjoy a lifestyle of sin.
¹⁵ But they're walking on a path to nowhere,
wandering away into deeper deception.

Wisdom, the Way of the Pure

¹⁶ Only wisdom can save you from the flattery
of the promiscuous woman—
she's such a smooth-talking seductress!
¹⁷ She left her husband and has forgotten her wedding vows. *ᵃ*
¹⁸ You'll find her house on the road to hell,
¹⁹ and all the men who go through her doors
will never come back to the place they were—
they will find nothing but desolation and despair.
²⁰ Follow those who follow wisdom and stay on the right path.
²¹ For all my godly lovers will enjoy life to the fullest
and will inherit their destinies. *ᵇ*
²² But the treacherous ones who love darkness
will not only lose all they could have had,
they will lose even their own souls!

---

a 2:17 Clearly this is a warning to those who would commit adultery, but there is a deeper
meaning within this text. Proverbs tells us of two women: the adulteress and the virtuous
woman of Prov. 31. Both women speak a parable of two systems in the church. One is religious and alluring, tempting the young anointed ones to come to her "bed" of compromise
(Mark 7:13). The other is the holy bride, virtuous and pure, keeping her first love ("wedding
vows") for Christ alone. Her "house" is the house of the Lord. One system brings shame
and despair; the other brings favor, honor, and glory. It is wisdom that protects us from one
and unites us to the other. See Jer. 50–52 and Rev. 17–18.
b 2:21 Literally "shall dwell in the land."

The Rewards of Wisdom

3 [1-2]My child, if you truly want a long and satisfying life,
never forget the things that I've taught you.
Follow closely every truth that I've given you.
Then you will have a full, rewarding life.
[3]Hold on to loyal love and don't let go,
and be faithful to all that you've been taught.
Let your life be shaped by integrity,[a]
with truth written upon your heart.
[4]That's how you will find favor and understanding
with both God and men—
you will gain the reputation of living life well.

Wisdom's Guidance

[5]Trust in the Lord completely,
and do not rely on your own opinions.
With all your heart rely on him to guide you,
and he will lead you in every decision you make.
[6]Become intimate with him in whatever you do,
and he will lead you wherever you go.[b]
Don't think for a moment that you know it all,[c]
[7]for wisdom comes when you adore him with undivided devotion
and avoid everything that's wrong.
[8]Then you will find the healing refreshment
your body and spirit long for.[d]
[9]Glorify God with all your wealth,
honoring him with your very best,[e]
with every increase that comes to you.
[10]Then every dimension of your life will overflow with blessings
from an uncontainable source of inner joy!

Wisdom's Correction

[11]My child, when the Lord God speaks to you,
never take his words lightly,
and never be upset when he corrects you.

---

a 3:3 Or "Tie them around your neck." The neck is a symbol of our will and conscience.
b 3:6 Or "He will cut a straight path before you."
c 3:6 We should always be willing to listen to correction and instruction.
d 3:8 Literally "healing to your navel and moistening to your bones." The blood supply for a baby in the womb comes through the navel. New cells are made in the marrow of our bones. As the navel and bones picture the life flow of our bodies, so the navel and bones are a picture of our inner being. See John 7:37–39.
e 3:9 Or "the firstfruits."

¹² For the Father's discipline comes only
    from his passionate love and pleasure for you.
    Even when it seems like his correction is harsh,
    it's still better than any father on earth gives to his child.
¹³ Those who find true wisdom obtain the tools for understanding,
    the proper way to live, *a*
    for they will have a fountain of blessing pouring into their lives.
    To gain the riches of wisdom is far greater
    than gaining the wealth of the world.
¹⁴ As wisdom increases, a great treasure is imparted,
    greater than many bars of refined gold.
¹⁵ It is a more valuable commodity than gold and gemstones, *b*
    for there is nothing you desire that could compare to her.
¹⁶ Wisdom extends to you long life in one hand
    and wealth and promotion *c* in the other.
    Out of her mouth flows righteousness,
    and her words release both law and mercy. *d*
¹⁷ The ways of wisdom are sweet,
    always drawing you into the place of wholeness. *e*
¹⁸ Seeking for her brings the discovery of untold blessings,
    for she is the healing tree of life to those who taste her fruits. *f*

Wisdom's Blueprints

¹⁹ The Lord laid the earth's foundations with wisdom's blueprints.
    By his living-understanding all the universe came into being. *g*
²⁰ By his divine revelation he broke open
    the hidden fountains of the deep,
    bringing secret springs to the surface
    as the mist of the night dripped down from heaven. *h*

Wisdom, Our Hiding Place

²¹ My child, never drift off course from these two goals for your life:

---

a 3:13 The Hebrew-Aramaic text here implies that wisdom gives the ability to take raw facts and draw right conclusions and meaning from them.
b 3:15 The Hebrew word translated as "gemstones" here can also refer to rubies, coral, or pearls.
c 3:16 Or "honor."
d 3:16 The Septuagint adds this last sentence, which is not found in the Hebrew.
e 3:17 The Hebrew word translated as "wholeness" here can also mean "peace" or "prosperity."
f 3:18 Verses 17 and 18 are recited in contemporary Torah services as the Torah scroll is returned to the ark, where it is kept.
g 3:19 When compared with Col. 1:16, we can see that Wisdom is used as a title in Proverbs for the Living Wisdom, Jesus Christ. See also 1 Cor. 1:30.
h 3:20 The dew is a metaphor for the Holy Spirit, who comes from the heavens and drenches us with God's presence. See Gen. 27:28; Deut. 32:2; Ps. 133:3; Judg. 6:37–40.

to walk in wisdom and to discover discernment. [a]
Don't ever forget how they empower you.
22 For they strengthen you inside and out
and inspire you to do what's right; [b]
you will be energized and refreshed by the healing they bring.
23 They give you living hope to guide you,
and not one of life's tests will cause you to stumble.
24 You will sleep like a baby, safe and sound—
your rest will be sweet and secure.
25 You will not be subject to terror, for it will not terrify you.
Nor will the disrespectful be able to push you aside, [c]
26 because God is your confidence in times of crisis,
keeping your heart at rest in every situation. [d]

Wisdom in Relationships

27 Why would you withhold payment on your debt [e]
when you have the ability to pay? Just do it! [f]
28 When your friend comes to ask you for a favor,
why would you say, "Perhaps tomorrow,"
when you have the money right there in your pocket?
Help him today!
29 Why would you hold a grudge [g] in your heart
toward your neighbor who lives right next door?
30 And why would you quarrel with those
who have done nothing wrong to you?
Is that a chip on your shoulder? [h]
31 Don't act like those bullies or learn their ways.
32 Every violent thug is despised by the Lord,
but every tender lover finds friendship with God
and will hear his intimate secrets. [i]
33 The wicked walk under God's constant curse,
but godly lovers walk under a stream of his blessing,
for they seek to do what is right.

---

a 3:21 Like many Hebrew words, there are various possible translations. The word translated as "discernment" here can also mean "discretion, counsel, meditation, and purpose."
b 3:22 Or "Adorn your neck." The neck is a picture of our will and conscience.
c 3:25 As translated from the Septuagint.
d 3:26 Or "keeping your foot from being caught."
e 3:27 The Septuagint is "Why would withhold from the poor [those who need it]?"
f 3:27 The Hebrew text here literally means "Do not withhold wealth from its owners." See Rom. 13:7.
g 3:29 Or "plot evil."
h 3:30 See Rom. 12:18.
i 3:32 See Ps. 25:14.

³⁴ If you walk with the mockers you will learn to mock,
  but God's grace and favor flow to the meek. *ᵃ*
³⁵ Stubborn fools fill their lives with disgrace,
  but glory and honor rest upon the wise.

A Father's Instruction

4 Listen to my correction, my sons,
  for I speak to you as your father. *ᵇ*
Let discernment enter your heart
  and you will grow wise with the understanding I impart.
² My revelation-truth *ᶜ* is a gift to you,
  so remain faithful to my instruction.
³ For I, too, was once the delight of my father *ᵈ*
  and cherished by my mother, their beloved child. *ᵉ*
⁴ Then my father taught me, saying,
  "Never forget my words.
  If you do everything that I teach you, you will reign in life." *ᶠ*
⁵ So make wisdom your quest—
  search for the revelation of life's meaning.
  Don't let what I say go in one ear and out the other.
⁶ Stick with wisdom and she will stick to you,
  protecting you throughout your days.
  She will rescue all those who passionately listen to her voice. *ᵍ*
⁷ Wisdom is the most valuable commodity—so buy it!
  Revelation knowledge is what you need—so invest in it!
⁸ Wisdom will exalt you when you exalt her truth. *ʰ*
  She will lead you to honor and favor
  when you live your life by her insights.
⁹ You will be adorned with beauty and grace, *ⁱ*
  and wisdom's glory will wrap itself around you, *ʲ*
  making you victorious in the race.

---

a 3:34 See James 4:6 and 1 Peter 5:5.
b 4:1 Read and study this entire chapter as though it were Jesus Christ speaking to you. He is the everlasting Father and we are called his sons. See Isa. 9:6–7 and Rev. 21:6–7.
c 4:2 Literally "Torah."
d 4:3 See Matt. 17:5 and John 3:35.
e 4:3 Or "unique." See Luke 1–2.
f 4:4 The lessons of wisdom are meant to be passed on from parents to children.
g 4:6 It is not enough to acquire wisdom; we must love her and listen wholeheartedly to her instruction.
h 4:8 The Septuagint says, "Build a fort for wisdom and she will lift you high."
i 4:9 Literally "She will place a garland of grace on your head and a crown of beauty upon you." A garland and a crown are metaphors for what is awarded a victor in a race. See 1 Cor. 9:24.
j 4:9 Or "wisdom's laurel of glory shielding you."

Two Pathways

[10] My son, if you will take the time to stop and listen to me
and embrace what I say,
you will live a long and happy life
full of understanding in every way.

[11] I have taken you by the hand in wisdom's ways,
pointing you to the path of integrity.

[12] Your progress will have no limits when you come along with me,
and you will never stumble as you walk along the way.

[13] So receive my correction[a] no matter how hard it is to swallow,
for wisdom will snap you back into place—
her words will be invigorating life to you.

[14] Do not detour into darkness or even set foot on that path.

[15] Stay away from it; don't even go there!

[16] For troublemakers are restless if they are not involved in evil.
They are not satisfied until they have brought someone harm.

[17] They feed on darkness and drink
until they're drunk on the wine of wickedness.[b]

[18] But the lovers of God walk on the highway of light,[c]
and their way shines brighter and brighter
until they bring forth the perfect day.

[19] But the wicked walk in thick darkness,
like those who travel in fog,
and yet don't have a clue why they keep stumbling!

Healing Words

[20] Listen carefully, my dear child, to everything that I teach you,
and pay attention to all that I have to say.

[21] Fill your thoughts with my words
until they penetrate deep into your spirit.[d]

[22] Then, as you unwrap my words,[e]
they will impart true life and radiant health
into the very core of your being.

[23] So above all, guard the affections of your heart,[f]
for they affect all that you are.

---

a 4:13 Wisdom will correct us and adjust our hearts to discipline. We must embrace the corrections of wisdom in order to mature spiritually.

b 4:17 Or "violence."

c 4:18 Or "the glow of sunlight."

d 4:21 See Col. 3:16.

e 4:22 Or "Discover my words."

f 4:23 The Hebrew word levav is the most common word for "heart." It includes our thoughts, our will, our discernment, and our affections.

Pay attention to the welfare of your innermost being,
for from there flows the wellspring of life.
24 Avoid dishonest speech and pretentious words.
Be free from using perverse words no matter what!

Watch Where You're Going

25 Set your gaze on the path before you.
With fixed purpose, looking straight ahead,
ignore life's distractions. [a]
26 Watch where you're going!
Stick to the path of truth,
and the road will be safe and smooth before you.
27 Don't allow yourself to be sidetracked for even a moment
or take the detour that leads to darkness.

Avoid Promiscuity

5 Listen to me, my son,
for I know what I'm talking about.
Listen carefully to my advice
2 so that wisdom and discernment will enter your heart,
and then the words you speak will express what you've learned.
3 Remember this:
The lips of a seductress seem sweet like honey,
and her smooth words are like music in your ears. [b]
4 But I promise you this:
In the end all you'll be left with is a bitter conscience. [c]
For the sting of your sin will pierce your soul like a sword.
5 She will ruin your life, drag you down to death,
and lead you straight to hell. [d]
6 She has prevented many from considering the paths of life.
Yes, she will take you with her where you don't want to go,
sliding down a slippery road
and not even realizing where the two of you will end up!
7 Listen to me, young men,

---

a 4:25 Implied in the text. See also Heb. 12:1–2.
b 5:3 Some Jewish expositors view this "promiscuous woman" as a metaphor for heresy. She
seduces, deceives, and drags to hell. For the believer, the promiscuous woman can be a
picture of the false anointing of the religious spirit that attempts to seduce us, weaken our
message, and rob the anointing of God from our ministries. Of course, there is also a clear
and dire warning for all to stay sexually pure or face the consequences.
c 5:4 Or "bitter as wormwood." See Rev. 8:10–11.
d 5:5 Or "Sheol." This is the Aramaic and Hebrew word for the place of the dead. The Greeks
call it Hades. Sheol is not eternal; it will be destroyed. See Hos. 13:14 and Rev. 20:4.

and don't forget this one thing I'm telling you—
run away from her as fast as you can!
[8] Don't even go near the door of her house
unless you want to fall into her seduction.
[9] In disgrace you will relinquish your honor to another,
and all your remaining years will be squandered—
given over to the cruel one. [a]
[10] Why would you let strangers take away your strength [b]
while the labors of your house go to someone else?
[11] For when you grow old you will groan in anguish and shame [c]
as sexually transmitted diseases consume your body. [d]
[12] And then finally you'll admit that you were wrong and say,
"If only I had listened to wisdom's voice
and not stubbornly demanded my own way,
because my heart hated to be told what to do!
[13] Why didn't I take seriously the warning of my wise counselors?
Why was I so stupid to think that I could get away with it?
[14] Now I'm totally disgraced and my life is ruined!
I'm paying the price—
for the people of the congregation are now my judges." [e]

Sex Reserved for Marriage

[15] My son, share your love with your wife alone.
Drink from her well of pleasure and from no other.
[16] Why would you have sex with a stranger
or with anyone other than her?
[17] Reserve this pleasure for you and her alone and not with another. [f]
[18] Your sex life will be blessed [g]
as you take joy and pleasure in the wife of your youth.

---

a 5:9 This would be the Devil, who torments the conscience as the result of this sin.
b 5:10 Or "wealth." This could also refer to spiritual strength and wealth.
c 5:11 The Hebrew word translated as "groan" here is also used for the roar of a lion or the ocean's roar.
d 5:11 Implied in the context of the topic of sexual promiscuity. The Hebrew word here means "diseases."
e 5:14 See John 8:1–11.
f 5:17 Because of the sudden change in the Hebrew text to the masculine gender ("stranger" or "another"), there is an inference that men having sex with men is forbidden, as well as sex with a woman who is not your wife.
g 5:18 The Hebrew phrase used here includes the word *fountain*, which is an obvious metaphor for the sex act. The root word for *fountain* can also refer to the eyes. It may be a poetic subtlety that the eyes should only be on your wife, not on the nakedness of another. See v. 19.

¹⁹ Let her breasts be your satisfaction, *ᵃ*
   and let her embrace *ᵇ* intoxicate you at all times.
   Be continually delighted and ravished with her love!
²⁰ My son, why would you be exhilarated by an adulteress—
   by embracing a woman *ᶜ* who is not yours?
²¹ For God sees everything you do and his eyes are wide open
   as he observes every single habit you have.
²² Beware that your sins don't overtake you
   and the scars of your own conscience
   become the ropes that tie you up.
²³ Those who choose wickedness die for lack of self-control,
   for their foolish ways lead them astray,
   carrying them away as hostages—
   kidnapped captives robbed of destiny.

Words of Wisdom

6 My son, if you cosign a loan for an acquaintance
   and guarantee his debt,
   you'll be sorry that you ever did it!
² You'll be trapped by your promise
   and legally bound by the agreement.
   So listen carefully to my advice:
³ Quickly get out of it if you possibly can!
   Swallow your pride, get over your embarrassment,
   and go tell your "friend" you want your name *ᵈ* off that contract.
⁴ Don't put it off, and don't rest until you get it done.
⁵ Rescue yourself from future pain *ᵉ*
   and be free from it once and for all.
   You'll be so relieved that you did! ᶠ

Life Lessons

⁶ When you're feeling lazy,
   come and learn a lesson from this tale of the tiny ant.

---

a 5:19 The Hebrew includes a picturesque metaphor of the wife being like a "friendly deer
   and a favored filly."
b 5:19 The Septuagint reads "Let her share conversation with you."
c 5:20 Or "breasts."
d 6:3 There is an implication in the Hebrew that the one whose loan was cosigned for is no
   longer a friend. The Hebrew word can also be translated "apostate."
e 6:5 The Hebrew word means "trap."
f 6:5 The life lesson to learn is that even when considering something that seems to be
   good, there may be unexpected consequences that should be considered before obligating
   yourself.

Yes, all you lazybones, come learn
from the example of the ant and enter into wisdom.
[7] The ants have no chief, no boss, no manager—
no one has to tell them what to do.
[8] You'll see them working and toiling all summer long,
stockpiling their food in preparation for winter.
[9] So wake up, sleepyhead. How long will you lie there?
When will you wake up and get out of bed?
[10] If you keep nodding off and thinking, "I'll do it later,"
or say to yourself, "I'll just sit back awhile and take it easy,"
just watch how the future unfolds!
[11] By making excuses you'll learn what it means to go without.
Poverty will pounce on you like a bandit [a]
and move in as your roommate for life. [b]
[12-13] Here's another life lesson to learn
from observing the wayward and wicked man. [c]
You can tell they are lawless.
They're constant liars, proud deceivers,
full of clever ploys and convincing plots. [d]
[14] Their twisted thoughts are perverse,
always with a scheme to stir up trouble,
and sowing strife with every step they take.
[15] But when calamity comes knocking on their door,
suddenly and without warning they're undone—
broken to bits, shattered, with no hope of healing. [e]

Seven Things God Hates
[16] There are six evils God truly hates
and a seventh[f] that is an abomination to him:

---

a 6:11 Or "vagabond." The Hebrew phrase here is literally translated "one who walks (away)."
b 6:11 The life lesson from Solomon's parable is this: the ant only lives six months yet stores more food than it will ever consume. We should learn the wisdom of preparing for the future and learn frugality in the present. Don't put off for the future the preparations you should make today. Now is always better than later. Today is the day to choose what's right and serve the Lord.
c 6:12–13 The Hebrew word translated "wayward and lawless" is actually "a man of Belial." This is a metaphor for a worthless man who worships other gods. The name Belial is found in numerous Dead Sea scrolls as a term for Satan.
d 6:12–13 The Hebrew gives a picture of those who "wink their eyes, shuffle their feet, and point their fingers." This is a figure of speech for the devious ways of the wicked.
e 6:15 The life lesson here is this: the clever and devious may look like they're getting ahead in life, but their path guarantees destruction, with no one to help them out of it.
f 6:16 The number seven is the number of fullness and completion. The poetic form here is stating that evil in its fullness is an abomination to God. The seven things are a description of the sin of man that stands in the temple of our bodies attempting to usurp God.

¹⁷ Putting others down while considering yourself superior,
    spreading lies and rumors,
    spilling the blood of the innocent,
¹⁸ plotting evil in your heart toward another,
    gloating over doing what's plainly wrong,
¹⁹ spouting lies in false testimony,
    and stirring up strife *between friends.*^a
    These are entirely despicable to God!
²⁰ My son, obey your father's godly instruction
    and follow your mother's life-giving teaching.^b
²¹ Fill your heart with their advice
    and let your life be shaped by what they've taught you.^c
²² Their wisdom will guide you wherever you go
    and keep you from bringing harm to yourself.
Their instruction will whisper to you at every sunrise
    and direct you through a brand-new day.
²³ For truth^d is a bright beam of light
    shining into every area of your life,
instructing and correcting you to discover the ways to godly living.

Truth or Consequences

^{24–25} Truth will protect you from immorality
    and from the promiscuity of another man's wife.
    Your heart won't be enticed by her flatteries^e
    or lust over her beauty—
    nor will her suggestive ways conquer you.
²⁶ Prostitutes reduce a man to poverty,^f
    and the adulteress steals your soul—
    she may even cost you your life!^g
²⁷ For how can a man light his pants on fire and not be burned?
²⁸ Can he walk over hot coals of fire^h and not blister his feet?
²⁹ What makes you think that you can sleep with another man's wife
    and not get caught?
    Do you really think you'll get away with it?

---

a 6:19 The Aramaic is "deception among brothers."
b 6:20 For the New Testament believer, our mother is the church, who nurtures us and feeds us life-giving words. See Gal. 4:21–31.
c 6:21 Or "Bind their words on your heart and tie them around your neck."
d 6:23 Or "Torah."
e 6:24–25 Or "Don't let her captivate you with her fluttering eyelids."
f 6:26 Or "Beg for a loaf of bread."
g 6:26 The Hebrew phrase here is literally translated "She hunts for your precious soul."
h 6:28 A picture of the lusts of the flesh.

Don't you know it will ruin your life?
[30] You can almost excuse a thief if he steals to feed his own family.
[31] But if he's caught, he still has to pay back what he stole sevenfold;
his punishment and fine will cost him greatly.
[32] Don't be so stupid as to think
you can get away with your adultery.
It will destroy your life, [a] and you'll pay the price
for the rest of your days.
[33] You'll discover what humiliation, shame,
and disgrace are all about,
for no one will ever let you forget what you've done.
[34] A husband's jealousy makes a man furious;
he won't spare you when he comes to take revenge.
[35] Try all you want to talk your way out of it—
offer him a bribe and see if you can manipulate him
with your money.
Nothing will turn him aside
when he comes to you with vengeance in his eyes!

Wisdom, Your True Love

7 Stick close to my instruction, my son,
and follow all my advice.
[2] If you do what I say you will live well.
Guard your life with my revelation-truth,
for my teaching is as precious as your eyesight. [b]
[3] Treasure my instructions, and cherish them within your heart. [c]
[4] Say to wisdom, "I love you,"
and to understanding, "You're my sweetheart."
[5] "May the two of you protect me, and may we never be apart!"
For they will keep you from the adulteress,
with her smooth words meant to seduce your heart.
[6] Looking out the window of my house one day
[7] I noticed among the mindless crowd
a simple, naïve young man who was about to go astray.
[8] There he was, walking down the street.
Then he turned the corner,
going on his way as he hurried on to the house of the harlot—
the woman he had planned to meet.

---

a 6:32 Or "The destroyer of his soul will do this."
b 7:2 Or "like you would the pupil of your eye." Literally "the little man of the eye," which is a figure of speech for your most prized possession.
c 7:3 Or "Write them upon the tablets of your heart."

⁹ There he was in the twilight as darkness fell,
  convinced no one was watching
  as he entered the black shadows of hell. *ᵃ*
¹⁰ That's when their rendezvous began.
  A woman of the night appeared,
  dressed to kill the strength of any man.
  She was decked out as a harlot, pursuing her amorous plan.
¹¹ Her voice was seductive, rebellious, and boisterous
  as she wandered far from what's right.
¹² Her type can be found soliciting on street corners
  on just about any night. *ᵇ*
¹³ She wrapped her arms around the senseless young man
  and held him tight—
  she enticed him with kisses that seemed so right.
  Then, with insolence, she whispered in his ear,
¹⁴ "Come with me. It'll be all right.
  I've got everything we need for a feast.
  I'll cook you a wonderful dinner. *ᶜ*
  So here I am—I'm all yours!
¹⁵ You're the very one I've looked for,
  the one I knew I wanted from the moment I saw you.
  That's why I've come out here tonight,
  so I could meet a man just like you. *ᵈ*
¹⁶ I've spread my canopy bed with coverings,
  lovely multicolored Egyptian linens spread
  and ready for you to lie down on.

---

a 7:9 Implied from verse 27.

b 7:12 This parable not only warns against the obvious evils of adultery and immorality, but also serves as a warning to the anointed young men in ministry not to be seduced by the religious system. Wisdom looks from the window (revelation and insight—Ezek. 8) of her house (the true church of Jesus) and sees a young man (not fully mature—1 John 2:12–14) who has placed himself in the path of sin. This made him vulnerable to the seduction of the "harlot" system of a works-based religion that enticed him into her bed (partnership, covering, and ordination with her and her system—Rev. 17–18) covered with Egyptian linens (Egypt is a picture of the world system that holds people in bondage). She is loud and stubborn (the old self-life never dealt with) and will not remain in her house (the true church of Jesus). She lives in the darkness of compromise and her ways are the ways of death. She doesn't remain faithful to her husband (the Bridegroom-God). The two women of Proverbs are the harlot mentioned here and the virtuous woman found in chapter 31, who speak of two systems of worship. One is true and virtuous; the other is false and seductive.

c 7:14 Or "offered peace offerings and paid my vows [in the temple]." This is a way of saying, "I have lots of meat left over from the sacrifices I've offered, enough for a great meal."

d 7:15 Compared to Song 3:1–4, this seems to be a parodic reversal of the Shulamite who goes out into the city to seek a man, and when she finds him, embraces him. This account of the harlot seems to be the converse of the theme of Song of Songs.

¹⁷ I've sprinkled the sheets with intoxicating perfume
  made from myrrh, aloes, and sweet cinnamon. ^a
¹⁸ Come, let's get comfortable and take pleasure in each other
  and make love all night!
¹⁹ There's no one home, for my husband's away on business.
²⁰ He left home loaded with money to spend,
  so don't worry.
  He won't be back until another month ends." ^b
^{21–22} He was swayed by her sophistication,
  enticed by her longing embrace.
  She led him down the wayward path right into sin and disgrace.
  Quickly he went astray, with no clue
  where he was truly headed,
  taken like a dumb ox alongside of the butcher.
  She was like a venomous snake coiled to strike,
  so she set her fangs into him!^c
²³ He 's like a man about to be executed with an arrow
  right through his heart—
  like a bird that flies into the net,
  unaware of what's about to happen.
²⁴ So listen to me, you young men.
  You'd better take my words seriously!
²⁵ Control your sexual urges and guard your hearts from lust.
  Don't let your passions get out of hand
  and don't lock your eyes onto a beautiful woman.
  Why would you want to even get close
  to temptation and seduction,
  to have an affair with her?
²⁶ She has pierced the souls of multitudes of men—
  many mighty ones have fallen
  and have been brought down by her. ^d
²⁷ If you're looking for the road to hell,
  just go looking for her house!

---

^a 7:17 Although these spices are found in the sacred anointing oil, the adulteress (religious system) has only a false anointing, with no true power.
^b 7:20 Or "He left with a bag of money and won't be back until the new moon."
^c 7:21–22 This last sentence is arguably a difficult verse to translate, with many variant options. The Aramaic is "taken like a dog to captivity." The Hebrew can be translated "bounding like a stag to a trap." Other ancient Jewish commentaries refer to this portion as "rushing like a venomous snake to discipline the foolish one," meaning that with the swiftness of a snake striking its prey, a fool lunges into his own destruction.
^d 7:26 The Aramaic is even more descriptive: "She has slain a multitude of mighty ones; they've all been killed by her."

Wisdom Calling

8 [1-3]Can't you hear the voice of Wisdom?[a]
From the top of the mountains of influence
she speaks into the gateways of the glorious city.[b]
At the place where pathways merge,
at the entrance of every portal,
there she stands, ready to impart understanding,
shouting aloud to all who enter,
preaching her sermon to those who will listen.[c]
[4]"I'm calling to you, sons of Adam,
yes, and to you daughters as well.
[5]Listen to me and you will be prudent and wise.
For even the foolish and feeble can receive an understanding heart
that will change their inner being.
[6]The meaning of my words will release within you revelation
for you to reign in life.[d]
My lyrics will empower you to live by what is right.
[7]For everything I say is unquestionably true,
and I refuse to endure the lies of lawlessness—
my words will never lead you astray.
[8]All the declarations of my mouth can be trusted;
they contain no twisted logic or perversion of the truth.
[9]All my words are clear and straightforward to everyone
who possesses spiritual understanding.
If you have an open mind, you will receive revelation-knowledge.
[10]My wise correction is more valuable than silver or gold.
The finest gold is nothing compared to the revelation-knowledge
I can impart."
[11]Wisdom is so priceless that it exceeds the value of any jewel.[e]
Nothing you could wish for can equal her.

---

a 8:1–3 Wisdom is personified throughout the book of Proverbs. Lady Wisdom is a figure of speech for God himself, who invites us to receive the best way to live, the excellent and noble way of life found in Jesus Christ. Jesus is wisdom personified, for he was anointed with the Spirit of wisdom. See 1 Cor. 1:30; Col. 2:3; Isa. 11:1–2.

b 8:1–3 As translated from the Aramaic. The church is also a gateway, the house of God, the portal to heaven, that Jesus calls a "city set on a hill." Christ is the head of the church, where the wisdom of God is revealed. See 1 Cor. 1 and Eph. 3:10–12.

c 8:1–3 In chapter 7 it was the harlot calling out to the simple; here it is Lady Wisdom. True wisdom is easy to find—we only have to listen to her voice. Though it comes from above, it is found on street level. Creation and conscience are two voices that speak to our hearts. To discover wisdom we don't need a brilliant intellect but a tender, attentive heart.

d 8:6 The Hebrew word is literally translated as "princely" or "noble" things. The implication is that these words of wisdom are for ruling and reigning in life.

e 8:11 Literally "corals" or "pearls."

[12] "For I am Wisdom, and I am shrewd and intelligent.
I have at my disposal living-understanding
to devise a plan for your life. [a]
[13] Wisdom pours into you
when you begin to hate every form of evil in your life,
for that's what worship and fearing God is all about.
Then you will discover
that your pompous pride and perverse speech
are the very ways of wickedness that I hate!"

The Power of Wisdom

[14] "You will find true success when you find me,
for I have insight into wise plans that are designed just for you.
I hold in my hands living-understanding, courage, and strength.
They're all ready and waiting for you.
[15] I empower kings to reign [b] and rulers to make laws that are just.
[16] I empower princes to rise and take dominion,
and generous ones to govern the earth. [c]
[17] I will show my love to those who passionately love me. [d]
For they will search and search continually until they find me.
[18] Unending wealth and glory
come to those who discover where I dwell.
The riches of righteousness and a long, satisfying life
will be given to them. [e]
[19] What I impart has greater worth than gold and treasure,
and the increase I bring benefits more than a windfall of income.
[20] I lead you into the ways of righteousness
to discover the paths of true justice.
[21] Those who love me gain great wealth [f] and a glorious inheritance,
and I will fill their lives with treasures.

Wisdom in the Beginning

[22] "In the beginning I was there,
for God possessed me [g] even before he created the universe.

---

a 8:12 Or "to discover clever inventions."

b 8:15 We have been made kings and priestly rulers by the grace of redemption.

c 8:16 As translated from many Hebrew manuscripts and the Septuagint. Other Hebrew manuscripts have "and all nobles who govern justly." The word *nobles* can also be translated "generous ones."

d 8:17 Wisdom is not found by the halfhearted. One must love wisdom to gain it. A superficial desire will yield only a superficial knowledge.

e 8:18 Or "riches and righteousness." The phrase "a long, satisfying life" is from the Aramaic.

f 8:21 The Aramaic is "I will leave great hope as an inheritance to my friends."

g 8:22 The Aramaic and the Septuagint read "The Lord created me at the beginning." The

²³ From eternity past I was set in place,
    before the world began.
    I was anointed from the beginning. ^a
²⁴ Before the oceans depths were poured out,
    and before there were any glorious fountains
    overflowing with water, ^b
    I was there, dancing! ^c
²⁵ Even before one mountain had been sculpted
    or one hill raised up,
    I was already there, dancing!
²⁶ When he created the earth, the fields,
    even the first atom of dust,
    I was already there.
²⁷ When he hung the tapestry of the heavens
    and stretched out the horizon of the earth,
²⁸ when the clouds and skies were set in place
    and the subterranean fountains began to flow strong,
    I was already there.
²⁹ when he set in place the pillars of the earth
    and spoke the decrees of the seas,
    commanding the waves
    so that they wouldn't overstep their boundaries,
³⁰ I was there, close to the Creator's side ^d as his master artist. ^e
    Daily he was filled with delight in me
    as I playfully rejoiced before him. ^f
³¹ I laughed and played,
    so happy with what he had made,
    while finding my delight in the children of men. ^g

Hebrew verb translated here as "possessed" has two basic meanings. One is "acquired," the other is "created." Poetically, it is a statement that the existence of Wisdom (Christ) was not independent of God at creation but was manifested and possessed by God as he created all things. Otherwise, it would sound like God was without wisdom before he created them.

a   8:23 The Hebrew word translated "anointed" here literally means "poured out" and is often used to describe the anointing oil poured out over a king.

b   8:24 The Hebrew uses the word *kabad*, which means "glory," in describing the fountains. It could also be translated "fountains of glory" or "glorious fountains."

c   8:24 Many translation have "I was born [or brought forth]." The Hebrew word for "born" is taken from a word that means "to kick and twirl" or "to dance."

d   8:30 See John 1:1.

e   8:30 Or "architect."

f   8:30 The Hebrew word translated here as "rejoicing" can also be translated as "joyfully playing" or "laughing."

g   8:31 What a beautiful picture we find here of Wisdom (Christ), who finds his fulfillment in us. See also Pss. 8:4–9; 16:3; Eph. 2:10; 19–22.

Wisdom Worth Waiting For

[32] "So listen, my sons and daughters, to everything I tell you,
for nothing will bring you more joy than following my ways.
[33] Listen to my counsel,
for my instruction will enlighten you.
You'll be wise not to ignore it.
[34] If you wait at wisdom's doorway, [a]
longing to hear a word for every day,
joy will break forth within you as you listen for what I'll say.
[35] For the fountain of life pours into you every time that you find me,
and this is the secret of growing in the delight
and the favor of the Lord.
[36] But those who stumble and miss me will be sorry they did!
For ignoring what I have to say will bring harm to your own soul.
Those who hate me are simply flirting with death!" [b]

Wisdom's Feast

9 Wisdom [c] has built herself a palace [d]
upon seven pillars to keep it secure. [e]
[2] She has made ready a banquet feast
and the sacrifice has been killed. [f]
She has mingled her wine, and the table's all set. [g]
[3] She has sent out her maidens,
crying out from the high place,
inviting everyone to come
and eat until they're full.

---

a 8:34 Or "Guard the door of my entrances."
b 8:36 To hate wisdom is not only a sign of stupidity, it is a mark of depravity.
c 9:1 Lady Wisdom is a poetic personification representing Christ, the Wisdom of God (1 Cor. 1:30). This is a classic form of a synecdoche. The Hebrew word *Chokmah* ("wisdom") can also mean "sacred sense." It is the understanding and insight given only by God.
d 9:1 There is a fascinating word play in the Hebrew text. The verb meaning "to build" and the word translated "son" come from the same root. "Build" is *banah* and "son" is *ben*. The house Wisdom is building is a son. You and I are sons of God who are being built into a spiritual house. There is also a verb in the Hebrew for "hewn" (as in stones). We are living stones raised up to be God's temple. See Ps. 127:1, Heb. 3:5–6; Matt. 7:24–27; 16:18.
e 9:1 The seven pillars of wisdom (plural, "wisdoms") point us to the seven days of creation, the seven spirits of God, and the seven components of heavenly wisdom given in James 3:17–18.
f 9:2 As translated from the Aramaic. The sacrifice points us to Calvary. Wisdom's pillar is a cross. The Hebrew phrase here literally means "She has prepared her meat."
g 9:2 Wisdom's feast will teach us the ways of God. We feed our hearts on revelation-truth that transforms us; then we implement with wise strategies the understanding we have learned at the feasting table.

[4] "Whoever wants to know me and receive my wisdom,
[5] come and dine at my table and drink of my wine.
[6] Lay aside your simple thoughts and leave your paths behind.
    Agree with my ways, live in my truth,
    and righteousness you will find."
[7] If you try to correct an arrogant cynic,
    expect an angry insult in return.
    And if you try to confront an evil man,
    don't be surprised if all you get is a slap in the face!
[8] So don't even bother to correct a mocker,
    for he'll only hate you for it.
    But go ahead and correct the wise;
    they'll love you even more. [a]
[9] Teach a wise man what is right
    and he'll grow even wiser.
    Instruct the lovers of God
    and they'll learn even more.
[10] The starting point for acquiring wisdom
    is to be consumed with awe as you worship Jehovah-God.
    To receive the revelation of the Holy One, [b]
    you must come to the one who has living-understanding.
[11] Wisdom will extend your life,
    making every year more fruitful than the one before.
[12] So it is to your advantage to be wise.
    But to ignore the counsel of wisdom
    is to invite trouble into your life. [c]

A Spirit Named Foolish

[13] There is a spirit named Foolish,
    who is boisterous and brash;
    she's seductive and restless.
[14] And there she sits at the gateway to the high places,
    on her throne overlooking the city.
[15] She preaches to all who walk by her
    who are clueless as to what is happening: [d]

---

a 9:8 See Ps. 141:5.
b 9:10 Literally "holy ones."
c 9:12 The Aramaic adds here "The liar feeds on the wind and chases fantasies, for he has
   forsaken what is true to travel in a barren wilderness; forgetting the right paths, he leaves
   his own vineyard to walk with thirst and gather nothing." The Septuagint adds here "If you
   forsake folly you will reign forever. Seek discretion and your understanding will bring you
   knowledge."
d 9:15 Or "who are walking straight ahead on their paths."

[16] "Come home with me."
     She invites those who are easily led astray, saying,
[17] "Illicit sex is the best sex of all.
     Our secret affair will be sweeter than all others." [a]
[18] Little do they know when they answer her call
     that she dwells among the spirits of the dead,
     and all her guests soon become citizens of hell! [b]

10

The wisdom of Solomon: [c]
When wisdom comes to a son,
joy comes to a father.
When a son turns from wisdom,
a mother grieves.
[2] Gaining wealth through dishonesty [d] is no gain at all.
    But honesty brings you a lasting happiness. [e]
[3] The Lord satisfies the longings of all his lovers, [f]
    but he withholds from the wicked what their souls crave. [g]
[4] Slackers will know what it means to be poor,
    while the hard worker becomes wealthy.
[5] Know the importance of the season you're in
    and a wise son you will be.
    But what a waste when an incompetent son
    sleeps through his day of opportunity! [h]
[6] The lover of God is enriched beyond belief,
    but the evil man only curses his luck. [i]
[7] The reputation of the righteous

---

a   9:17 The Hebrew phrase here literally means "Stolen waters are sweet, and bread eaten in secret is pleasant." This is an obvious metaphor of finding sexual pleasure with someone other than your spouse and trying to get away with it. Finding pleasure in your relationship with your spouse is like drinking from a pure, clean fountain. But stolen water from someone else's fountain is yielding to foolishness. Adultery is always sin.

b   9:18 Older Aramaic and Septuagint manuscripts add a verse here not found in the Hebrew: "But turn away; linger not in the place or even look at her. Don't drink from a strange fountain. Abstain and drink not from an alien fountain, so that you will enjoy a long life."

c   10:1 The title of this section starting with Prov. 10 indicates a different form. Solomon's four hundred sayings of wisdom fill this section, going through 22:16. This compilation is an assorted collection of proverbs that is not easily outlined but is profound in its scope.

d   10:2 Or "the treasures of wickedness."

e   10:2 Or "Righteousness [honesty] delivers you from death."

f   10:3 Or "satisfies the souls of the righteous."

g   10:3 The Aramaic is "The property of the evil he demolishes."

h   10:5 Or "To gather in the summer is to be a wise son, but to sleep through the harvest is a disgrace."

i   10:6 The Hebrew is ambiguous and is literally translated "The mouth of the wicked covers violence."

becomes a sweet memorial to him,
while the wicked life only leaves a rotten stench. *a*

⁸ The heart of the wise will easily accept instruction.
But those who do all the talking
are too busy to listen and learn.
They'll just keep stumbling ahead
into the mess they created.

⁹ The one who walks in integrity *b*
will experience a fearless confidence in life,
but the one who is devious
will eventually be exposed.

¹⁰ The troublemaker always has a clever plan
and won't look you in the eye,
but the one who speaks correction honestly
can be trusted to make peace. *c*

¹¹ The teachings of the lovers of God are like
living truth flowing from the fountain of life,
but the words of the wicked
hide an ulterior motive. *d*

¹² Hatred keeps old quarrels alive, *e*
but love draws a veil over every insult *f*
and finds a way to make sin disappear.

¹³ Words of wisdom flow from the one with true discernment.
But to the heartless, words of wisdom
become like rods beating their backside.

¹⁴ Wise men don't divulge all that they know, *g*
but chattering fools blurt out words
that bring them to the brink of ruin.

¹⁵ A rich man's wealth becomes like a citadel of strength, *h*
but the poverty of the poor leaves their security in shambles.

¹⁶ The lovers of God earn their wages for a life of righteousness,
but the wages of the wicked are squandered on a life of sin. *i*

¹⁷ If you readily receive correction,

---

a 10:7 Some Hebrew manuscripts and the Aramaic read "The name of the wicked will be extinguished."
b 10:9 Or "innocence." The Aramaic is "He who walks in perfection walks in hope."
c 10:10 As translated from the Septuagint. The Hebrew is "The babbling fool comes to ruin."
d 10:11 Or "hide violence."
e 10:12 The Aramaic is "Hatred stirs up judgment."
f 10:12 Love will cover up offenses against us, but never our own offenses.
g 10:14 Or "Those who are wise store up knowledge (like treasure)."
h 10:15 Or "his fortified city."
i 10:16 Or "their harvest of wickedness."

you are walking on the path to life.
But if you reject rebuke,
you're guaranteed to go astray. [a]

¹⁸ The one who hides his hatred while pretending to be your friend
is nothing but a liar.
But the one who slanders you behind your back
proves that he's a fool, never to be trusted.

¹⁹ If you keep talking, it won't be long
before you're saying something really wrong.
Prove you're wise from the very start—
just bite your tongue and be strong!

²⁰ The teachings of the godly ones are like pure silver,
bringing words of redemption to others, [b]
but the heart of the wicked is corrupt.

²¹ The lovers of God feed many with their teachings, [c]
but the foolish ones starve themselves
for lack of an understanding heart.

²² True enrichment comes from the blessing of the Lord,
with rest and contentment [d] in knowing
that it all comes from him.

²³ The fool finds his fun in doing wrong, [e]
but the wise delight in having discernment.

²⁴ The lawless are haunted by their fears
and what they dread will come upon them, [f]
but the longings of the lovers of God will all be fulfilled.

²⁵ The wicked are blown away by every stormy wind.
But when a catastrophe comes,
the lovers of God have a secure anchor.

²⁶ To trust a lazy person to get a job done
will be as irritating as smoke in your eyes—
as enjoyable as a toothache!

²⁷ Living in the worship and awe of God
will bring you many years of contented living.
So how could the wicked ever expect to have a long, happy life?

²⁸ Lovers of God have a joyful feast of gladness,
but the ungodly see their hopes vanish right before their eyes.

---

a 10:17 The Aramaic is even more blunt: "Reject rebuke and you're a moron!"
b 10:20 Or "The tongue of the just is like choice silver." Silver is a metaphor for redemption.
c 10:21 The Aramaic is "The lips of the righteous multiply mercy."
d 10:22 Or "with no labor or sorrow attached."
e 10:23 The word translated "fool" means "moron" in the Aramaic.
f 10:24 This speaks of the consequences of sin. There is a judge who sees all that we do and will call us to account one day.

²⁹ The beautiful ways of God are a safe resting place ᵃ
  for those who have integrity.
  But to those who work wickedness
  the ways of God spell doom.
³⁰ God's lover can never be greatly shaken.
  But the wicked will never inherit
  the covenant blessings. ᵇ
³¹ The teachings of the righteous are loaded with wisdom,
  but the words of the evil are crooked and perverse.
³² Words that bring delight pour from the lips of the godly,
  but the words of the wicked are duplicitous.

Living in Righteousness

11 To set high standards for someone else, ᶜ
  and then not live up to them yourself,
is something that God truly hates.
But it pleases him when we apply the right standards
of measurement. ᵈ
² When you act with presumption,
  convinced that you're right,
  don't be surprised if you fall flat on your face!
  But walking in humility helps you to make wise decisions.
³ Integrity will lead you to success and happiness,
  but treachery will destroy your dreams.
⁴ When Judgment Day comes,
  all the wealth of the world won't help you one bit.
  So you'd better be rich in righteousness,
  for that's the only thing that can save you in death.
⁵ Those with good character walk on a smooth path,
  with no detour or deviation.
  But the wicked keep falling because of their own wickedness.
⁶ Integrity will keep a good man from falling.
  But the unbeliever is trapped,
  held captive to his sinful desires.
⁷ When an evil man dies, all hope is lost,
  for his misplaced confidence goes in the coffin
  and gets buried along with him.

---

a 10:29 The Aramaic is "The way of Jehovah is power to the perfect."
b 10:30 Or "land." This is metaphor for all of the covenantal blessings.
c 11:1 The Hebrew phrase here literally means "scales of deception [false balances]."
d 11:1 The Hebrew phrase here literally means "a perfect stone." Stones were used as the legitimate weights of balance. Jesus is the perfect stone. See Rev. 2:17.

⁸ Lovers of God are snatched away from trouble,
    and the wicked show up in their place. *a*

⁹ The teachings of hypocrites can destroy you,
    but revelation knowledge will rescue the righteous. *b*

¹⁰ The blessing that rests on the righteous
    releases strength and favor to the entire city, *c*
    but shouts of joy will be heard when the wicked one dies.

¹¹ The blessing of favor resting upon the righteous
    influences a city to lift it higher, *d*
    but wicked leaders tear it apart by their words.

¹² To quarrel with a neighbor is senseless. *e*
    Bite your tongue; be wise and keep quiet!

¹³ You can't trust gossipers with a secret;
    they'll just go blab it all.
    Put your confidence instead in a trusted friend,
    for he will be faithful to keep it in confidence.

¹⁴ People lose their way without wise leadership,
    but a nation succeeds and stands in victory
    when it has many good counselors to guide it.

¹⁵ The evil man will do harm when confronted by a righteous man,
    because he hates those who await good news. *f*

¹⁶ A gracious, generous woman
    will be honored with a splendid *g* reputation,
    but the woman who hates the truth
    lives surrounded with disgrace *h* and by men
    who are cutthroats, only greedy for money. *i*

¹⁷ A man of kindness attracts favor,
    while a cruel man attracts nothing but trouble. *j*

¹⁸ Evil people may get a short-term gain, *k*

---

a 11:8 Haman is a classic example of this principle. See Est. 7:10; 9:24–25.

b 11:9 Or "The righteous will be strengthened."

c 11:10 As translated from the Aramaic and the Septuagint.

d 11:11 Jesus describes the church as a city. See Matt. 5:14.

e 11:12 Or "To disparage your neighbor is being heartless."

f 11:15 As translated from the Aramaic and the Septuagint. There is a vast difference between this and the Hebrew text, which reads "You'll be ruined if you cosign for a stranger, and a hater of handshakes will be safe."

g 11:16, Or "glorious."

h 11:16 As translated from the older Aramaic and Septuagint texts, but is not included in newer Hebrew manuscripts. There is an additional line added by the Aramaic and the Septuagint: "The lazy will lack, but the diligent support themselves financially."

i 11:16 The Septuagint is "The diligent obtain wealth."

j 11:17 The Hebrew text indicates this trouble could be physical, related to one's health.

k 11:18 Or "wages of deception."

but to sow seeds of righteousness
will bring a true and lasting reward.

[19] A son of righteousness[a] experiences the abundant life,
but the one who pursues evil hurries to his own death.

[20] The Lord can't stand the stubborn heart bent toward evil,
but he treasures those whose ways are pure.[b]

[21] Assault your neighbor and you will certainly be punished,[c]
but God will rescue the children of the godly.

[22] A beautiful woman who abandons good morals
is like a fine gold ring dangling from a pig's snout.

[23] True lovers of God are filled with longings
for what is pleasing and good,
but the wicked can only expect doom.

[24] Generosity brings prosperity,
but withholding from charity brings poverty.

[25] Those who live to bless others[d]
will have blessings heaped upon them,
and the one who pours out his life to pour out blessings
will be saturated with favor.

[26] People will curse the businessman with no ethics,
but the one with a social conscience receives praise from all.[e]

[27] Living your life seeking what is good for others brings untold favor,
but those who wish evil for others will find it coming back on them.

[28] Keep trusting in your riches and down you'll go!
But the lovers of God rise up like flowers in the spring.

[29] The fool who brings trouble to his own family
will be cut out of the will,
and the family servant will do better than he.

[30] But a life lived loving God bears lasting fruit,
for the one who is truly wise wins souls.[f]

[31] If the righteous are barely saved,
what's in store for all the wicked?[g]

---

a 11:19 As translated from one Hebrew manuscript, the Aramaic, and the Septuagint. Most Hebrew manuscripts have "the one who pursues righteousness."

b 11:20 Or "wholehearted."

c 11:21 As translated from the Aramaic and the Targum (Hebrew-Aramaic commentary).

d 11:25 The Hebrew phrase here literally means "The soul of blessing will grow fat."

e 11:26 The Hebrew phrase here literally means "The one who withholds produce will be cursed, but blessing will be on the head of the one who sells it."

f 11:30 As translated from the Hebrew. The Aramaic and the Septuagint read "The souls of violent ones will be removed."

g 11:31 As translated from the Septuagint. See also 1 Peter 4:18.

It's Right to Live for God

12 To learn the truth you must long to be teachable,[a]
or you can despise correction and remain ignorant.

[2] If your heart is right, favor flows from the Lord,
but a devious heart invites his condemnation.

[3] You can't expect success by doing what's wrong.
But the lives of his lovers are deeply rooted and firmly planted.

[4] The integrity and strength of a virtuous wife[b]
transforms her husband into an honored king.[c]
But the wife who disgraces her husband
weakens the strength of his identity.[d]

[5] The lovers of God are filled with good ideas
that are noble and pure,
but the schemes of the sinner
are crammed with nothing but lies.

[6] The wicked use their words to ambush and accuse,[e]
but the lovers of God speak to defend and protect.

[7] The wicked are taken out, gone for good,
but the godly families shall live on.

[8] Everyone admires a man of principles,
but the one with a corrupt heart is despised.

[9] Just be who you are and work hard for a living,
for that's better than pretending to be important
and starving to death.

[10] A good man takes care of the needs of his pets,
while even the kindest acts of a wicked man are still cruel.

[11] Work hard at your job and you'll have what you need.
Following a get-rich-quick scheme is nothing but a fantasy.

[12] The cravings of the wicked are only for what is evil,[f]
but righteousness is the core motivation for the lovers of God,
and it keeps them content and flourishing.[g]

---

a 12:1 There are times when even the wise need correction, but they will appreciate its value.

b 12:4 There is an amazing Hebrew word used here. It is more commonly used to describe warriors, champions, and mighty ones. Many translations read "an excellent wife." But the meaning of the Hebrew word *chayil* is better translated "an army that is wealthy, strong, mighty, powerful, with substance, valiant, virtuous, or worthy."

c 12:4 Or "An excellent wife is the crown of her husband." By implication, her dignity makes him a king.

d 12:4 Or "She is like cancer in his bones." Bones are a metaphor for inner strength, our inner being or identity.

e 12:6 Or "lie in wait for blood." This is a figure of speech for accusation.

f 12:12 As translated from the Septuagint. The Hebrew is "Thieves crave the loot of other thieves."

g 12:12 The meaning of the Hebrew text of verse 12 is uncertain.

Wisdom Means Being Teachable

[13] The wicked will get trapped by their words
  of gossip, slander, and lies. [a]
  But for the righteous, honesty is its own defense.
[14] For there is great satisfaction in speaking the truth,
  and hard work brings blessings back to you.
[15] A fool is in love with his own opinion,
  but wisdom means being teachable.

Learning to Speak Wisely

[16] If you shrug off an insult and refuse to take offense,
  you demonstrate discretion indeed. [b]
  But the fool has a short fuse
  and will immediately let you know when he's offended.
[17] Truthfulness marks the righteous,
  but the habitual liar can never be trusted.
[18] Reckless words are like the thrusts of a sword,
  cutting remarks meant to stab and to hurt.
  But the words of the wise soothe and heal.
[19] Truthful words will stand the test of time,
  but one day every lie will be seen for what it is.
[20] Deception fills the hearts of those who plot harm,
  but those who plan for peace [c] are filled with joy.
[21] Calamity is not allowed to overwhelm the righteous,
  but there's nothing but trouble waiting for the wicked.
[22] Live in the truth and keep your promises,
  and the Lord will keep delighting in you,
  but he detests a liar.
[23] Those who possess wisdom don't feel the need
  to impress others with what they know,
  but foolish ones make sure their ignorance is on display.
[24] If you want to reign in life, [d]
  don't sit on your hands.
  Instead work hard at doing what's right,
  for the slacker will end up working to make someone else succeed.
[25] Anxious fear brings depression,

---

a 12:13 The Hebrew is simply "sinful words," which implies gossip, slander, and lies.
b 12:16 Or "A shrewd man conceals his shame."
c 12:20 Or "counselors of peace."
d 12:24 The Hebrew word for "reign" (mashal) is the title of the book: Proverbs. See introduction and the footnote on 1:1.

but a life-giving word of encouragement
can do wonders to restore joy to the heart. [a]

²⁶ Lovers of God give good advice to their friends, [b]
but the counsel of the wicked will lead them astray.

²⁷ A passive person won't even complete a project, [c]
but a passionate person makes good use
of his time, wealth, and energy.

²⁸ Abundant life is discovered by walking in righteousness,
but holding on to your anger leads to death. [d]

Living Wisely

13 A wise son or daughter desires a father's discipline,
but the know-it-all never listens to correction.

² The words of the wise are kind and easy to swallow,
but the unbeliever just wants to pick a fight and argue.

³ Guard your words and you'll guard your life,
but if you don't control your tongue,
it will ruin everything.

⁴ The slacker wants it all and ends up with nothing,
but the hard worker ends up with all that he longed for.

⁵ Lovers of God hate what is phony and false,
but the wicked are full of shame and behave shamefully. [e]

⁶ Righteousness is like a shield of protection,
guarding those who keep their integrity,
but sin is the downfall of the wicked.

⁷ One pretends to be rich but is poor.
Another pretends to be poor but is quite rich. [f]

⁸ The self-assurance of the rich is their money, [g]
but people don't kidnap and extort the poor!

---

a 12:25 This insightful proverb can also be translated "Stop worrying! Think instead of what brings you gladness." Our focus must never be on what we can't change but on the everlasting joy we have in Christ. Sometimes we have to find the life-giving word of encouragement rising up in our own hearts. This is the secret of finding perpetual encouragement by the Word that lives in us.

b 12:26 As translated from older Aramaic manuscripts. The Hebrew is uncertain.

c 12:27 Implied in the text, paraphrased from an uncertain Hebrew phrase. An alternate translation would be "A lazy person won't get to roast the game he caught, but the wealth of a diligent person is precious."

d 12:28 As translated from the Septuagint and the Aramaic. The Hebrew is uncertain.

e 13:5 The Hebrew word used here literally means "to cause a stink" or "to emit an odor." This is a figure of speech for what is shameful.

f 13:7 It is never godly to be a phony. It's always better to be who you are and avoid pretense.

g 13:8 The Aramaic is "The salvation of the soul is a man's true wealth."

⁹ The virtues of God's lovers shine brightly in the darkness,
   but the flickering lamp of the ungodly will be extinguished.
¹⁰ Wisdom opens your heart to receive wise counsel,
   but pride closes your ears to advice
   and gives birth to only quarrels and strife.
¹¹ Wealth quickly gained is quickly wasted—ᵃ
   easy come, easy go!
   But if you gradually gain wealth,
   you will watch it grow.
¹² When hope's dream seems to drag on and on,
   the delay can be depressing.
   But when at last your dream comes true,
   life's sweetness will satisfy your soul. ᵇ
¹³ Despise the word, will you?
   Then you'll pay the price and it won't be pretty!
   But the one who honors the Father's holy instructions
   will be rewarded.
¹⁴ When the lovers of God teach you truth,
   a fountain of life opens up within you,
   and their wise instruction will deliver you from the ways of death.
¹⁵ Everyone admires a wise, sensible person,
   but the treacherous walk on the path of ruin. ᶜ
¹⁶ Everything a wise and shrewd man does
   comes from a source of revelation-knowledge, ᵈ
   but the behavior of a fool puts foolishness on parade! ᵉ
¹⁷ An undependable messenger causes a lot of trouble,
   but the trustworthy and wise messengers
   release healing wherever they go. ᶠ
¹⁸ Poverty and disgrace come to the one
   who refuses to hear criticism. ᵍ
   But the one who is easy to correct is on the path of honor.
¹⁹ When God fulfills your longings,
   sweetness fills your soul.
   But the wicked refuse to turn from darkness
   to see their desires come to pass. ʰ

---

a 13:11 Or "Wealth gained by fraud will dwindle."
b 13:12 Or "It is a tree of life."
c 13:15 As translated from the Aramaic and the Septuagint. The Hebrew is uncertain.
d 13:16 Or "A wise person thinks ahead."
e 13:16 The implication is that the fool is unable to finish anything he begins.
f 13:17 God's sons and daughters are peacemakers, healers, and faithful deliverers for others.
g 13:18 As translated from the Hebrew. The Septuagint is "Instruction removes poverty and disgrace."
h 13:19 Implied by the Hebrew parallelism of the text.

²⁰ If you want to grow in wisdom,
    spend time with the wise.
    Walk with the wicked
    and you'll eventually become just like them.
²¹ Calamity chases the sin-chaser,
    but prosperity pursues the God-lover.
²² The benevolent man leaves an inheritance
    that endures to his children's children,
    but the wealth of the wicked is treasured up for the righteous.
²³ The lovers of God will live a long life and get to enjoy their wealth,
    but the ungodly will suddenly perish. [a]
²⁴ If you withhold correction and punishment [b] from your children,
    you demonstrate a lack of true love.
    So prove your love and be prompt to punish them. [c]
²⁵ The lovers of God will have more than enough,
    but the wicked will always lack what they crave.

The House of Wisdom

14 Every wise woman encourages and builds up her family,
    but a foolish woman over time will tear it down by her own actions.
² Lovers of truth follow the right path
    because of their wonderment and worship of God.
    But the devious display their disdain for him.
³ The words of a proud fool will all come back to haunt him.
    But the words of the wise
    will become a shield of protection around them.
⁴ The only clean stable is an empty stable.
    So if you want the work of an ox and to enjoy an abundant harvest,
    you'll have a mess or two to clean up!
⁵ An honest witness will never lie,
    but a deceitful witness lies with every breath.
⁶ The intellectually arrogant seek for wisdom,
    but they never seem to discover
    what they claim they're looking for.
    For revelation-knowledge flows to the one
    who hungers for understanding.

---

a 13:23 As translated from the Septuagint. The Hebrew is "In the fallow ground of the poor there is abundance of food, but injustice sweeps it away." The Aramaic is "Those who don't find the way of life destroy many years of wealth and some are utterly destroyed." There is a vast difference in the three translations. The translator has chosen to follow the Septuagint.
b 13:24 Or "sparing the rod." Corporal punishment was common in premodern societies.
c 13:24 Or "The one who spares the rod hates his child."

⁷ The words of the wise are like weapons of knowledge. *ᵃ*
  If you need wise counsel, stay away from the fool.
⁸ For the wisdom of the wise will keep life on the right track,
  while the fool only deceives himself
  and refuses to face reality.
⁹ Fools mock the need for repentance, *ᵇ*
  while the favor of God rests upon all his lovers.
¹⁰ Don't expect anyone else to fully understand
  both the bitterness and the joys
  of all you experience in your life.
¹¹ The household of the wicked is soon torn apart,
  while the family of the righteous flourishes.
¹² You can rationalize it all you want
  and justify the path of error you have chosen,
  but you'll find out in the end that you took the road to destruction.
¹³ Superficial laughter can hide a heavy heart,
  but when the laughter ends, the pain resurfaces.
¹⁴ Those who turn from the truth get what they deserve,
  but a good person receives a sweet reward. *ᶜ*
¹⁵ A gullible person will believe anything,
  but a sensible person will confirm the facts.
¹⁶ A wise person is careful in all things and turns quickly from evil,
  while the impetuous fool moves ahead with overconfidence.
¹⁷ An impulsive person has a short fuse and can ruin everything,
  but the wise show self-control. *ᵈ*
¹⁸ The naïve demonstrate a lack of wisdom,
  but the lovers of wisdom are crowned with revelation-knowledge.
¹⁹ Evil ones will pay tribute to good people
  and eventually come to be servants of the godly. *ᵉ*
²⁰ The poor are disliked even by their neighbors,
  but everyone wants to get close to the wealthy.
²¹ It's a sin to despise one who is less fortunate than you, *ᶠ*

---

a 14:7 As translated from the Aramaic.
b 14:9 Or "Fools mock guilt [or guilt offering]." The Septuagint is "The house of the trans-
  gressor owes purification."
c 14:14 As translated from Hebrew manuscripts. The Aramaic is "A good man will be filled
  from the awe of his soul."
d 14:17 As translated from the Aramaic. The Hebrew is "And a crafty schemer is hated." The
  Greek Septuagint is "A sensible man bears up under many things."
e 14:19 The Hebrew phrase literally means "They will come [or bow] at the gates of the
  righteous."
f 14:21 Implied in the Hebrew parallelism. The Hebrew phrase here literally means "your
  neighbor."

but when you are kind to the poor,
  you will prosper and be blessed.
[22] Haven't you noticed how evil schemers always wander astray?
  But kindness and truth come to those
  who make plans to be pure in all their ways. [a]
[23] If you work hard at what you do,
  great abundance will come to you.
  But merely talking about getting rich
  while living to only pursue your pleasures [b]
  brings you face-to-face with poverty. [c]
[24] The true net worth of the wise [d] is the wealth that wisdom imparts.
  But the way of life for the fool is his foolishness. [e]
[25] Speak the truth and you'll save souls,
  but in the spreading of lies treachery thrives.
[26] Confidence and strength flood the hearts
  of the lovers of God who live in awe of him,
  and their devotion provides their children
  with a place of shelter and security. [f]
[27] To worship God in wonder and awe
  opens a fountain of life within you,
  empowering you to escape death's domain. [g]
[28] A king glories in the number of his loyal followers,
  but a dwindling population spells ruin for any leader.
[29] When your heart overflows with understanding
  you'll be very slow to get angry.
  But if you have a quick temper,
  your impatience will be quickly seen by all.
[30] A tender, tranquil heart will make you healthy, [h]
  but jealousy can make you sick.
[31] Insult your Creator, will you?
  That's exactly what you do

---

a 14:22 Both the Aramaic and the Septuagint insert a verse here that is not found in the Hebrew: "The followers of evil don't understand mercy and faith, but you'll find kindness and
  faith with those who do good."
b 14:23 As translated from the Septuagint.
c 14:23 There is an additional verse found here in the Aramaic that is missing from the Hebrew text: "The Lord Jehovah heals every sickness, but evil speaking makes you sick [harms
  you]."
d 14:24 Or "the crown of the wise."
e 14:24 The Aramaic word translated here as "foolishness" can also mean "insanity."
f 14:26 To live as a passionate lover of God will bring benefit even to your children.
g 14:27 Or "empowering you to turn from the deadly snares."
h 14:30 Or "A heart of healing is the life of the flesh."

every time that you oppress the powerless![a]

Showing kindness to the poor is equal to honoring your maker.

[32] The wicked are crushed by every calamity,

but the lovers of God find a strong hope

even in the time of death.[b]

[33] Wisdom soothes the heart of the one with living-understanding,

but the heart of the fool just stockpiles stupidity.

[34] A nation is exalted by the righteousness of its people,

but sin heaps disgrace upon the land.

[35] A wise and faithful servant receives promotion from the king,

but the one who acts disgracefully

gets to taste the anger of the king.[c]

Wisdom Far Better than Wickedness

15 Respond gently when you are confronted
and you'll defuse the rage of another.

Responding with sharp, cutting words[d] will only make it worse.

Don't you know that being angry

can ruin the testimony of even the wisest of men?[e]

[2] When wisdom speaks, understanding becomes attractive.

But the words of the fool make their ignorance look laughable.[f]

[3] The eyes of the Lord are everywhere[g]

and he takes note of everything that happens.

He watches over his lovers,

and he also sees the wickedness of the wicked.

[4] When you speak healing words,

you offer others fruit from the tree of life.

But unhealthy, negative words do nothing but crush their hopes.[h]

[5] You're stupid to mock the instruction of a father,

but welcoming correction will make you brilliant.[i]

---

a 14:31 Or "slander the poor." Every human being is made in God's image, including the poor.

b 14:32 Our strong hope is that our lives will continue in the presence of God in the resurrection glory. Both the Septuagint and the Aramaic read quite differently: "But the one who trusts in his integrity is righteous."

c 14:35 As translated from the Hebrew. The Septuagint reads "And by his good behavior shame is removed."

d 15:1 Or "painful words."

e 15:1 This is found only in the Septuagint.

f 15:2 The Aramaic reads "The mouths of fools vomit a curse."

g 15:3 The eyes of the Lord can also be a metaphor for his prophets.

h 15:4 Or "Perverse words are the crushing of the spirit."

i 15:5 The Septuagint adds a verse that is not found in the Hebrew: "In great righteousness there is great strength. But the ungodly will one day perish from the earth."

⁶ There is power in the house of the righteous, ^a
   but the house of the wicked is filled with trouble,
   no matter how much money they have.
⁷ When wisdom speaks, revelation-knowledge is released, ^b
   but finding true wisdom in the word of a fool is futile.
⁸ It is despicable to the Lord
   when people use the worship of the Almighty
   as a cloak for their sin, ^c
   but every prayer of his godly lovers is pleasing to his heart.
⁹ The Lord detests the lifestyle of the wicked,
   but he loves those who pursue purity. ^d
¹⁰ Severe punishment awaits the one
   who turns away from the truth,
   and those who rebel against correction will die.
¹¹ Even hell itself holds no secrets from the Lord God,
   for all is exposed before his eyes,
   and so much more the heart of every human being.
¹² The know-it-all never esteems the one who tries to correct him.
   He refuses to seek good advice from the wise. ^e

Living an Ascended Life

¹³ A cheerful heart puts a smile on your face,
   but a broken heart leads to depression.
¹⁴ Lovers of God ^f hunger after truth,
   but those without understanding
   feast on foolishness and don't even realize it.
¹⁵ Everything seems to go wrong
   when you feel weak and depressed.
   But when you choose to be cheerful,
   every day will bring you more and more joy and fullness. ^g
¹⁶ It's much better to live simply,
   surrounded in holy awe and worship of God,
   than to have great wealth with a home full of trouble.
¹⁷ It's much better to have a kind, loving family, even with little,

---

a 15:6 As translated from the Septuagint and the Aramaic. The Hebrew changes the concept of power to prosperity. Both concepts are valid.

b 15:7 Or "is scattered like seed."

c 15:8 Or "the sacrifice of the wicked"; that is, worshiping God with a wicked heart, only to hide sin. Our yielded hearts must be the sacrifice we offer to God.

d 15:9 The Aramaic reads "He shows mercy to the one who practices righteousness."

e 15:12 Another way to say this is "The one who hates authority has no love for being taught."

f 15:14 Or "the upright" (Aramaic).

g 15:15 The Septuagint reads quite differently: "And the good (heart) is always calm."

than to have great wealth
  with nothing but hatred and strife all around you. *a*

¹⁸ A touchy, hot-tempered man picks a fight,
  but the calm, patient man knows how to silence strife.

¹⁹ Nothing seems to work right *b* for the lazy man,
  but life seems smooth and easy when your heart is virtuous.

²⁰ When a son learns wisdom,
  a father's heart is glad.
  But the man who shames *c* his mother is a foolish son.

²¹ The senseless fool treats life like a joke,
  but the one with living-understanding makes good choices.

²² Your plans will fall apart right in front of you
  if you fail to get good advice.
  But if you first seek out multiple counselors,
  you'll watch your plans succeed.

²³ Everyone enjoys giving great advice.
  But how delightful it is to say the right thing at the right time!

²⁴ The life path of the prudent lifts them progressively heavenward,
  delivering them from the death spiral
  that keeps tugging them downward.

²⁵ The Lord champions the widow's cause, *d*
  but watch him as he smashes down the houses of the haughty!

²⁶ The Lord detests wicked ways of thinking, *e*
  but he enjoys lovely and delightful words.

²⁷ The one who puts earning money above his family
  will have trouble at home,
  but those who refuse to exploit others
  will live *in peace.*

²⁸ Lovers of God think before they speak,
  but the careless blurt out wicked words meant to cause harm.

²⁹ The Lord doesn't respond to the wicked,
  but he's moved to answer the prayers of his godly lovers.

³⁰ Eyes that focus on what is beautiful *f* bring joy to the heart,
  and hearing a good report
  refreshes and strengthens the inner being. *g*

---

a 15:17 Or "Better to have a meal of vegetables surrounded with love and grace than a fattened ox where there is hatred."

b 15:19 Or "The way is blocked with thorns."

c 15:20 Or "despises."

d 15:25 Or "The Lord maintains the boundaries of the widow."

e 15:26 Or "the thoughts of the wicked."

f 15:30 As translated from the Septuagint. The Hebrew is "The light of the eyes brings joy."

g 15:30 The Hebrew here literally means "makes fat your bones." Bones picture our inner being.

[31] Accepting constructive criticism
    opens your heart to the path of life,
    making you right at home among the wise.
[32] Refusing constructive criticism shows
    you have no interest in improving your life,
    for revelation-insight only comes as you accept correction
    and the wisdom that it brings.
[33] The source of revelation-knowledge is found
    as you fall down in surrender before the Lord.
    Don't expect to see Shekinah glory [a]
    until the Lord sees your sincere humility.

Wisdom Exalts God

16 Go ahead and make all the plans you want,
    but it's the Lord who will ultimately direct your steps. [b]
[2] We are all in love with our own opinions,
    convinced they're correct.
    But the Lord is in the midst of us, [c]
    testing and probing our every motive.
[3] Before you do anything,
    put your trust totally in God and not in yourself. [d]
    Then every plan you make will succeed.
[4] The Lord works everything together to accomplish his purpose. [e]
    Even the wicked are included in his plans—
    he sets them aside for the day of disaster.
[5] Exalting yourself is disgusting to the Lord,
    for pride attracts his punishment—
    and you can count on that!
[6] You can avoid evil through surrendered worship
    and the fear of God,
    for the power of his faithful love
    removes sin's guilt and grip over you.
[7] When the Lord is pleased with the decisions you've made,
    he activates grace to turn enemies into friends.

---

a 15:33 Or "Before honor is humility." The Hebrew uses the word *kabod*, which is translated
    as "glory" 156 times in the Old Testament..
b 16:1 As translated from the Septuagint. The Hebrew and Aramaic read "The Lord gives the
    right reply."
c 16:2 Or "in the midst of spirits."
d 16:3 Or "Commit your business to God."
e 16:4 Or "for its answer."

[8] It is better to have little with a heart that loves justice
 than to be rich and not have God on your side.
[9] Within your heart you can make plans for your future,
 but the Lord chooses the steps you take to get there.

Living like a King

[10] A king speaks the revelation of truth,
 so he must be extraordinarily careful in the decrees that he makes.
[11] The Lord expects you to be fair in every business deal,
 for he is the one who sets the standards for righteousness. [a]
[12] Kings and leaders despise wrongdoing,
 for the true authority to rule and reign
 is built on a foundation of righteousness.
[13] Kings and leaders love to hear godly counsel,
 and they love those who tell them the truth.
[14] The anger of a king releases the messenger of death, [b]
 but a wise person will know how to pacify his wrath.
[15] Life-giving light streams from the presence of a king, [c]
 and his favor is showered upon those who please him.
[16] Everyone wants gold, but wisdom's worth [d] is far greater.
 Silver is sought after,
 but a heart of understanding yields a greater return.
[17] Repenting from evil places you on the highway of holiness.
 Protect purity and you protect your life. [e]
[18] Your boast becomes a prophecy of a future failure.
 The higher you lift up yourself in pride, [f]
 the harder you'll fall in disgrace.
[19] It's better to be meek and lowly and live among the poor
 than to live high and mighty among the rich and famous.
[20] One skilled in business discovers prosperity,
 but the one who trusts in God is blessed beyond belief!

---

a 16:11 Or "Honesty with scales and balances is the way of the Lord, for all the stones in the bag are established by him."

b 16:14 See 1 Kings 2:25, 29–34, 46.

c 16:15 The Septuagint reads "The king's son is in the light of life."

d 16:16 The Septuagint is "nests of wisdom."

e 16:17 There are two proverbs inserted here in the Septuagint that are not found in the Hebrew or Aramaic: "Receive instruction and you'll be prosperous; he who listens to correction shall be made wise." "He who guards his ways preserves his own soul; he who loves his life will watch his words."

f 16:18 Or "overconfidence."

Walking with Wisdom

²¹ The one with a wise heart is called "discerning,"
  and speaking sweetly to others
  makes your teaching even more convincing.
²² Wisdom is a deep well of understanding
  opened up within you as a fountain of life for others,
  but it's senseless to try to instruct a fool.
²³ Winsome words pour from a heart of wisdom,
  adding value to all you teach.
²⁴ Nothing is more appealing
  than speaking beautiful, life-giving words.
  For they release sweetness to our souls
  and inner healing to our spirits. ª
²⁵ Before every person there is a path
  that seems like the right one to take,
  but it leads straight to hell! ᵇ
²⁶ Life motivation comes from the deep longings of the heart,
  and the passion to see them fulfilled urges you onward. ᶜ
²⁷ A wicked scoundrel wants to dig up dirt on others,
  only to spread slander and shred their reputation.
²⁸ A twisted person spreads rumors;
  a whispering gossip ruins good friendships.
²⁹ A vicious criminal can be persuasive,
  enticing others to join him as partners in crime,
  but he leads them all down a despicable path.
³⁰ It's easy to tell when a wicked man
  is hatching some crooked scheme—
  it's written all over his face.
  His looks betray him as he gives birth to his sin.
³¹ Old age with wisdom will crown you with dignity and honor,
  for it takes a lifetime of righteousness to acquire it. ᵈ
³² Do you want to be a mighty warrior?
  It's better to be known as one who is patient and slow to anger. ᵉ
  Do you want to conquer a city?
  Rule over your temper before you attempt to rule a city.

ª 16:24 Or "healing to the bones." Bones are a metaphor for our inner being.
ᵇ 16:25 As translated from the Septuagint. The Hebrew is "the ways of death."
ᶜ 16:26 The meaning of the Hebrew in this verse is uncertain.
ᵈ 16:31 Or "Gray hair is a crown of splendor." In the Hebrew culture the old were honored
  above all, especially if they acquired wisdom. See Lev. 19:32.
ᵉ 16:32 The Septuagint is "It's better to be forgiving than strong."

³³ We may toss the coin and roll the dice,
   but God's will is greater than luck. ^a

Wisdom's Virtues

17 A simple, humble life with peace and quiet
   is far better than an opulent lifestyle with nothing
   but quarrels and strife at home.

² A wise, intelligent servant will be honored above a shameful son.
   He'll even end up having a portion left to him in his master's will.

³ In the same way that gold and silver are refined by fire,
   the Lord purifies your heart by the tests and trials of life.

⁴ Those eager to embrace evil listen to slander,
   for a liar loves to listen to lies.

⁵ Mock the poor, will you?
   You insult your Creator every time you do!
   If you make fun of others' misfortune,
   you'd better watch out—your punishment is on its way.

⁶ Grandparents have the crowning glory of life:
   grandchildren!
   And it's only proper for children to take pride in their parents. ^b

⁷ It is not proper for a leader to lie and deceive,
   and don't expect excellent words to be spoken by a fool. ^c

⁸ Wise instruction is like a costly gem.
   It turns the impossible into success. ^d

⁹ Love overlooks the mistakes of others,
   but dwelling on the failures of others devastates friendships.

¹⁰ One word of correction breaks open a teachable heart,
   but a fool can be corrected a hundred times
   and still not know what hit him.

¹¹ Rebellion thrives in an evil man,
   so a messenger of vengeance ^e will be sent to punish him. ^f

¹² It's safer to meet a grizzly bear robbed of her cubs
   than to confront a reckless fool.

¹³ The one who returns evil for good
   can expect to be treated the same way for the rest of his life. ^g

---

a   16:33 Or "Into the center the lot is cast and from Jehovah is all its judgment." The casting
    of lots was a common form of divination in the premodern societies.

b   17:6 Or "fathers." There is an additional verse inserted here that is found in the Septuagint:
    "A whole world of riches belongs to the faithful, but the unfaithful don't get even a cent."

c   17:7 Two absurd things are: to find a fool in leadership and to have a leader in foolishness.

d   17:8 "Instruction" is taken from the Aramaic and the Septuagint. The Hebrew reads "bribe."

e   17:11 Or "merciless angels."

f   17:11 This could mean an evil spirit, or calamities and sorrows.

g   17:13 Or "Evil will haunt his house."

¹⁴ Don't be one who is quick to quarrel,
    for an argument is hard to stop,
    and you never know how it will end,
    so don't even start down that road!ᵃ
¹⁵ There is nothing God hates more
    than condemning the one who is innocent
    and acquitting the one who is guilty.
¹⁶ Why pay tuition to educate a fool?
    For he has no intention of acquiring true wisdom.
¹⁷ A dear friend will love you no matter what,
    and a family sticks together through all kinds of trouble.
¹⁸ It's stupid to run up bills you'll never be able to pay
    or to cosign for the loan of your friend.
    Save yourself the trouble and don't do either one.
¹⁹ If you love to argue,
    then you must be in love with sin.
    For the one who loves to boastᵇ is only asking for trouble.
²⁰ The one with a perverse heart never has anything good to say,ᶜ
    and the chronic liar tumbles into constant trouble.
²¹ Parents of a numskull will have many sorrows,
    for there's nothing about his lifestyle that will make them proud.
²² A joyful, cheerful heart brings healing to both body and soul.
    But the one whose heart is crushed
    struggles with sickness and depression.
²³ When you take a secret bribe,
    your actions reveal your true character,
    for you pervert the ways of justice.
²⁴ Even the face of a wise man shows his intelligence.
    But the wandering eyes of a fool will look for wisdom everywhere
    except right in front of his nose.
²⁵ A father grieves over the foolishness of his child,
    and bitter sorrow fills his mother.
²⁶ It's horrible to persecute a holy lover of God
    or to strike an honorable man for his integrity!
²⁷ Can you bridle your tongue when your heart is under pressure?
    That's how you show that you are wise.
    An understanding heart keeps you cool, calm, and collected,
    no matter what you're facing.

---

a 17:14 The Aramaic for this verse reads "To shed blood provokes the judgment of a ruler."
b 17:19 Or "he who builds a high gate." The gate becomes a picture of the mouth. This is a figure of speech for proud boasting.
c 17:20 Or "can expect calamity."

²⁸ When even a fool bites his tongue ᵃ
he's considered wise.
So shut your mouth when you are provoked—
it will make you look smart.

Wisdom Gives Life

18 An unfriendly person isolates himself
and seems to care only about his own issues.
For his contempt of sound judgment makes him a recluse. ᵇ
² Senseless people find no pleasure in acquiring true wisdom,
for all they want to do is impress you with what they know.
³ An ungodly man is always cloaked with disgrace,
as dishonor and shame are his companions.
⁴ Words of wisdom ᶜ are like a fresh, flowing brook—
like deep waters that spring forth from within,
bubbling up inside the one with understanding.
⁵ It is atrocious when judges show favor to the guilty
and deprive the innocent of justice.
⁶ A senseless man jumps headfirst into an argument;
he's just asking for a beating for his reckless words. ᵈ
⁷ A fool has a big mouth that only gets him into trouble,
and he'll pay the price for what he says.
⁸ The words of a gossip merely reveal the wounds of his own soul, ᵉ
and his slander penetrates into the innermost being.
⁹ The one who is too lazy to look for work
is the same one who wastes his life away.
¹⁰ The character of God is a tower of strength, ᶠ
for the lovers of God delight to run into his heart
and be exalted on high.
¹¹ The rich, in their conceit, imagine that their wealth
is enough to protect them.
It becomes their confidence in a day of trouble. ᵍ

ᵃ 17:28 The Septuagint is "when an unthinking man asks a question."
ᵇ 18:1 There are alternate possible translations of this verse in the Hebrew-Aramaic; for example, "An idle man meditates on his lusts and mocks wise instruction."
ᶜ 18:4 Or "words that touch the heart."
ᵈ 18:6 The Aramaic is "His rash words call for death."
ᵉ 18:8 Scholars are somewhat uncertain about an exact translation of this phrase. The Aramaic is "The words of a lazy man lead him to fear and evil."
ᶠ 18:10 The Hebrew word *migdal*, translated as "tower of strength," is a homonym that can also be translated "bed of flowers."
ᵍ 18:11 The Aramaic is "The wealth of the rich is a strong city, and its glory casts a broad shadow."

¹² A man's heart is the proudest when his downfall is nearest,
for he won't see glory until the Lord sees humility.

¹³ Listen before you speak,
for to speak before you've heard the facts will bring humiliation.

¹⁴ The will to live sustains you when you're sick, [a]
but depression crushes courage and leaves you unable to cope.

¹⁵ The spiritually hungry are always ready to learn more,
for their hearts are eager to discover new truths.

¹⁶ Would you like to meet a very important person?
Take a generous gift.
It will do wonders to gain entrance into his presence.

¹⁷ There are two sides to every story.
The first one to speak sounds true until you hear the other side
and they set the record straight. [b]

¹⁸ A coin toss [c] resolves a dispute
and can put an argument to rest
between formidable opponents.

¹⁹ It is easier to conquer a strong city
than to win back a friend whom you've offended.
Their walls go up, making it nearly impossible to win them back. [d]

²⁰ Sharing words of wisdom is satisfying to your inner being.
It encourages you to know
that you've changed someone else's life. [e]

²¹ Your words are so powerful
that they will kill or give life,
and the talkative person will reap the consequences.

²² When a man finds a wife,
he has found a treasure!
For she is the gift of God to bring him joy and pleasure.
But the one who divorces a good woman
loses what is good from his house. [f]
To choose an adulteress is both stupid and ungodly. [g]

---

a 18:14 The Septuagint is "A wise servant can calm a man's anger."
b 18:17 The text implies that a legal testimony in a courtroom may seem to be correct until cross-examination begins.
c 18:18 The Hebrew is "casting lots."
d 18:19 Or "A brother supported by a brother is like a high, strong city. They hold each other up like the bars of a fortress."
e 18:20 Or "A man's belly is filled with the fruits of his mouth, and by the harvest of his lips he will be satisfied."
f 18:22 The reference to divorce is not found in the Hebrew text but is included in both the Aramaic and the Septuagint.
g 18:22 This is not included in the Hebrew or Aramaic but is found in the Septuagint.

²³ The poor plead for help from the rich,
    but all they get in return is a harsh response.
²⁴ Some friendships don't last for long, *ᵃ*
    but there is one loving friend who is joined to your heart *ᵇ*
    closer than any other!

Wisdom Exalted

19 It's better to be honest, even if it leads to poverty,
    than to live as a dishonest fool.
² The best way to live is with revelation-knowledge,
    for without it, you'll grow impatient and run right into error. *ᶜ*
³ There are some people who ruin their own lives
    and then blame it all on God.
⁴ Being wealthy means having lots of "friends,"
    but the poor can't keep the ones they have.
⁵ Perjury won't go unpunished,
    and liars will get all that they deserve.
⁶ Everyone wants to be close to the rich and famous,
    but a generous person has all the friends he wants!
⁷ When a man is poor, even his family has no use for him.
    How much more will his "friends" avoid him—
    for though he begs for help, they won't respond. *ᵈ*
⁸ Do yourself a favor and love wisdom.
    Learn all you can,
    then watch your life flourish and prosper!
⁹ Tell lies and you're going to get caught,
    and the habitual liar is doomed.
¹⁰ It doesn't seem right when you see a fool
    living in the lap of luxury
    or a prideful servant ruling over princes.
¹¹ A wise person demonstrates patience,
    for mercy *ᵉ* means holding your tongue.
    When you are insulted,
    be quick to forgive and forget it,
    for you are virtuous when you overlook an offense.

---

a 18:24 Or "A man with too many friends may be broken to pieces."
b 18:24 The Hebrew word used here can be translated "joined together," "stick close," "to cleave," "to pursue," or "to overtake."
c 19:2 Or "sin."
d 19:7 The Aramaic and the Septuagint add a sentence not found in the Hebrew: "The one who is malicious with his words is not to be trusted."
e 19:11 The word translated "mercy" (merciful) here is found only in the Septuagint.

¹² The rage of a king is like the roar of a lion,
  but his sweet favor is like a gentle, refreshing rain.
¹³ A rebellious son breaks a father's heart,
  and a nagging wife can drive you crazy!
¹⁴ You can inherit houses and land from your parents,
  but a good*ᵃ* wife only comes as a gracious gift from God!
¹⁵ Go ahead—be lazy and passive.
  But you'll go hungry if you live that way.
¹⁶ Honor God's holy instructions
  and life will go well for you.
  But if you despise his ways and choose your own plans,
  you will die.
¹⁷ Every time you give to the poor you make a loan to the Lord.
  Don't worry—you'll be repaid in full for all the good you've done.
¹⁸ Don't be afraid to discipline your children
  while they're still young enough to learn.
  Don't indulge your children or be swayed by their protests.
¹⁹ A hot-tempered man has to pay the price for his anger.*ᵇ*
  If you bail him out once,
  you'll do it a dozen times.
²⁰ Listen well to wise counsel
  and be willing to learn from correction
  so that by the end of your life
  you'll be known for your wisdom.
²¹ A person may have many ideas concerning God's plan for his life,
  but only the designs of his purpose will succeed in the end.
²² A man is charming when he displays tender mercies to others.
  And a lover of God who is poor and promises nothing
  is better than a rich liar who never keeps his promises.
²³ When you live a life of abandoned love,
  surrendered before the awe of God,
  here's what you'll experience:
  Abundant life. Continual protection.*ᶜ*
  And complete satisfaction!
²⁴ There are some people who pretend they're hurt—
  deadbeats who won't even work to feed themselves.*ᵈ*

---

a 19:14 Literally "prudent" or "understanding" wife.
b 19:19 There is an implication in the Hebrew that he will get into legal trouble. An alternate translation of this verse could be "An evil-minded man will be injured; if you rescue him, his anger will only intensify."
c 19:23 Or "You will not be remembered for evil."
d 19:24 Or "The lazy man buries his fork in his plate and won't even lift it to his mouth."

²⁵ If you punish the insolent who don't know any better,
 they will learn not to mock.
 But if you correct a wise man,
 he will grow even wiser.
²⁶ Children who mistreat their parents
 are an embarrassment to their family and a public disgrace.
²⁷ So listen, my child.
 Don't reject correction
 or you will certainly wander from the ways of truth. *ᵃ*
²⁸ A corrupt witness makes a mockery of justice,
 for the wicked never play by the rules. *ᵇ*
²⁹ Judgment is waiting for those who mock the truth,
 and foolish living invites a beating.

Are You Living Wisely?

20 A drunkard is obnoxious, loud, and argumentative;
 you're a fool to get intoxicated with strong drink.
² The rage of a king is like the roar of a lion.
 Do you really want to go and make him angry?
³ A person of honor *ᶜ* will put an argument to rest.
 Only the stupid want to pick a fight.
⁴ If you're too lazy to plant seed,
 it's too bad when you have no harvest on which to feed. *ᵈ*
⁵ A man of deep understanding will give good advice,
 drawing it out from the well within.
⁶ Many will tell you they're your loyal friends,
 but who can find one who is truly trustworthy? *ᵉ*
⁷ The lovers of God will walk in integrity,
 and their children are fortunate
 to have godly parents as their examples.
⁸ A righteous king sits on his judgment seat.
 He scatters evil away from his kingdom
 by his wise discernment.
⁹ Which one of us can truly say,
"I am free from sin in my life,
 for my heart is clean and pure"? *ᶠ*

---

a 19:27 Or "Stop listening to instruction that contradicts what you know is truth."
b 19:28 Or "The heart of the wicked feeds on evil."
c 20:3 Or "It is the glory of a man." It's better to keep a friend than to win a fight.
d 20:4 The Aramaic and the Septuagint read "Rebuke a lazy man and he still has no shame, yet watch him go beg at harvest time."
e 20:6 Or "A compassionate man is hard to find, but it's even harder to find one who is faithful."
f 20:9 The Hebrew word translated "clean" can also mean "perfect" or "holy." The word

[10] Mark it down:
   God hates it when you demonstrate a double standard—
   one for "them" and one for "you."
[11] All children show what they're really like by how they act.
   You can discern their character,
   whether they are pure or perverse.
[12] Lovers of God have been given eyes to see
   with spiritual discernment
   and ears to hear from God.
[13] If you spend all your time sleeping, you'll grow poor. [a]
   So wake up, sleepyhead! Don't sleep on the job.
   And then there will be plenty of food on your table.
[14] The buyer says, as he haggles over the price,
"That's junk. It's worthless!"
   Then he goes out and brags,
   "Look at the great bargain I got!"
[15] You may have an abundance of wealth,
   piles of gold and jewels,
   but there is something of far greater worth:
   speaking revelation words of knowledge.
[16] Anyone stupid enough to guarantee a loan for a stranger [b]
   deserves to have his property held as security.
[17] What you obtain dishonestly may seem sweet at first,
   but sooner or later you'll live to regret it. [c]
[18] If you solicit good advice, then your plans will succeed.
   So don't charge into battle without wisdom,
   for wars are won by skillful strategy.
[19] A blabbermouth will reveal your secrets,
   so stay away from people who can't keep their mouths shut. [d]
[20] If you despise your father or mother,
   your life will flicker out like a lamp,
   extinguished into the deepest darkness.
[21] If an inheritance is gained too early in life,
   it will not be blessed in the end.
[22] Don't ever say, "I'm going to get even with them
   if it's the last thing I do!"

---

translated "pure" can also mean "clear, bright, shining, unmixed." Through God's grace,
by the blood of Jesus, believers have been purified, made holy, and set free from our sins.
a   20:13 The Septuagint reads "Don't love speaking evil."
b   20:16 Some manuscripts have "a promiscuous woman."
c   20:17 Or "The bread of falsehood may taste sweet at first, but afterward you'll have a mouth
full of gravel."
d   20:19 The Aramaic adds a line: "One who is faithful in spirit hides a matter."

Wrap God's grace around your heart
and he will be the one to vindicate you.
²³ The Lord hates double standards—
that's hypocrisy at its worst! *a*
²⁴ It is the Lord who directs your life,
for each step you take is ordained by God
to bring you closer to your destiny.
So much of your life, then, remains a mystery! *b*
²⁵ Be careful in making a rash promise before God,
or you may be trapped by your vow and live to regret it.
²⁶ A wise king is able to discern corruption
and remove wickedness from his kingdom. *c*
²⁷ The spirit God breathed into man *d* is like a living lamp,
a shining light
searching into the innermost chamber of our being.
²⁸ Good leadership *e* is built on love and truth,
for kindness and integrity
are what keep leaders in their position of trust.
²⁹ We admire the young for their strength and beauty,
but the dignity of the old is their wisdom. *f*
³⁰ When you are punished severely, you learn your lesson well—
for painful experiences do wonders to change your life.

God Is the Source of Wisdom

21 It's as easy for God to steer a king's heart *g* for his purposes
as it is for him to direct the course of a stream. *h*
² You may think you're right all the time,
but God thoroughly examines our motives.
³ It pleases God more when we demonstrate godliness and justice
than when we merely offer him a sacrifice.
⁴ Arrogance, superiority, and pride are the fruits of wickedness *i*
and the true definition of sin.

---

a 20:23 Or "The Lord hates differing weights, and dishonest scales are wicked."
b 20:24 The Aramaic reads "So what man is capable of ordering his way?"
c 20:26 Or "A wise king winnows the wicked and turns his chariot wheel over them."
d 20:27 Implied by the Hebrew word *nishmat*, used in Gen. 2:7.
e 20:28 Or "a king's throne."
f 20:29 Or "their gray hair."
g 21:1 Don't forget, we have been made kings and priests by the blood of the Lamb. See 1 Peter 2:9; Rev. 1:6; 5:10.
h 21:1 Because a leader's decisions affect so many people, God will intervene and steer them as a farmer steers the course of a stream to irrigate his fields.
i 21:4 Or "the tillage of the wicked." The Aramaic and the Septuagint has "the lamp of the wicked."

⁵ Brilliant ideas pay off and bring you prosperity,
  but making hasty, impatient decisions
  will only lead to financial loss. ᵃ
⁶ You can make a fortune dishonestly,
  but your crime will hold you in the snares of death! ᵇ
⁷ Violent rebels don't have a chance,
  for their rejection of truth and their love of evil
  will drag them deeper into darkness.
⁸ You can discern that a person is guilty by his devious actions
  and the innocence of a person by his honest, sincere ways.
⁹ It's better to live all alone in a rickety shack
  than to share a castle with a crabby spouse! ᶜ
¹⁰ The wicked always crave what is evil;
  they'll show no mercy and get no mercy. ᵈ
¹¹ Senseless people learn their lessons the hard way,
  but the wise are teachable.
¹² A godly, righteous person ᵉ has the ability
  to bring the light of instruction to the wicked
  even though he despises what the wicked do. ᶠ
¹³ If you close your heart to the cries of the poor,
  then I'll close my ears when you cry out to me!
¹⁴ Try giving a secret gift to the one who is angry with you
  and watch his anger disappear.
  A kind, generous gift goes a long way
  to soothe the anger of one who is livid. ᵍ
¹⁵ When justice is served,
  the lovers of God celebrate and rejoice,
  but the wicked begin to panic.
¹⁶ When you forsake the ways of wisdom,
  you will wander into the realm of dark spirits. ʰ

---

a 21:5 The Aramaic is "The thoughts of the chosen one are trusting, but those of the evil one lead to poverty." This verse is missing from the Septuagint.
b 21:6 As translated from the Aramaic and the Septuagint. The Hebrew is "The money will vanish into thin air."
c 21:9 The Septuagint reads "It's better to live in the corner of an attic than in a large home plastered with unrighteousness."
d 21:10 The Hebrew is "They show no mercy," while the Septuagint reads "They'll receive no mercy." The translator has chosen to merge both concepts.
e 21:12 The Hebrew is "a righteous one," which can also speak of God, "the Righteous One."
f 21:12 As translated from the Septuagint. There are many examples of this in the Bible: Daniel in Babylon, Joseph in Egypt, and the follower of Jesus today who is living among unbelievers.
g 21:14 The Aramaic and Septuagint translate this "He who withholds a gift arouses anger."
h 21:16 Or "the congregation of the Rephaim." The Rephaim were a pagan tribe of giants and have been equated with spirits of darkness. See Gen. 14:5 and Deut. 2:11.

¹⁷ To love pleasure for pleasure's sake
 will introduce you to poverty.
 Indulging in a life of luxury *a*
 will never make you wealthy.
¹⁸ The wicked bring on themselves
 the very suffering they planned for others,
 for their treachery comes back to haunt them. *b*
¹⁹ It's better to live in a hut in the wilderness
 than with a crabby, scolding spouse!
²⁰ In wisdom's house you'll find delightful treasures
 and the oil of the Holy Spirit. *c*
 But the stupid *d* squander what they've been given.
²¹ The lovers of God who chase after righteousness
 will find all their dreams come true:
 an abundant life drenched with favor
 and a fountain that overflows with satisfaction. *e*
²² A warrior filled with wisdom ascends into the high place
 and releases regional breakthrough,
 bringing down the strongholds of the mighty. *f*
²³ Watch your words and be careful what you say,
 and you'll be surprised how few troubles you'll have.
²⁴ An arrogant man is inflated with pride—
 nothing but a snooty scoffer in love with his own opinion.
 Mr. Mocker is his name! *g*
²⁵⁻²⁶ Taking the easy way out is the habit of a lazy man,
 and it will be his downfall.
 All day long he thinks about all the things that he craves,
 for he hasn't learned the secret that the generous man has learned:
 extravagant giving never leads to poverty. *h*
²⁷ To bring an offering to God with an ulterior motive is detestable,
 for it amounts to nothing but hypocrisy.
²⁸ No one believes a notorious liar,
 but the guarded words of an honest man stand the test of time.

---

a 21:17 Or "the lover of wine and oil."
b 21:18 Or "The evil become the ransom payment for the righteous and the faithless for the upright."
c 21:20 The Hebrew word for "oil" is an emblem of the Holy Spirit.
d 21:20 Or "a fool of a man."
e 21:21 Or "righteousness."
f 21:22 Or "demolishing their strength of confidence."
g 21:24 The Septuagint adds a line: "He who holds a grudge is a sinner."
h 21:25–26 This is implied in the context and is necessary to complete the meaning of the proverb. The last line of this verse reads in the Septuagint "The righteous lavish on others mercy and compassion."

²⁹ The wicked are shameless and stubborn,
    but the lovers of God have a holy confidence.
³⁰ All your brilliant wisdom and clever insight
    will be of no help at all if the Lord is against you.
³¹ You can do your best to prepare for the battle, *ᵃ*
    but ultimate victory comes from the Lord God.

How to Live a Life of Wisdom

22 A beautiful reputation *ᵇ* is more to be desired than great riches,
    and to be esteemed by others is more honorable
    than to own immense investments. *ᶜ*
² The rich and the poor have one thing in common:
    the Lord God created each one.
³ A prudent person with insight foresees danger coming
    and prepares himself for it. *ᵈ*
    But the senseless rush blindly forward
    and suffer the consequences.
⁴ Laying your life down in tender surrender before the Lord
    will bring life, prosperity, and honor as your reward.
⁵ Twisted and perverse lives are surrounded by demonic influence. *ᵉ*
    If you value your soul, stay far away from them.
⁶ Dedicate your children to God
    and point them in the way that they should go, *ᶠ*
    and the values they've learned from you will be with them for life.
⁷ If you borrow money with interest,
    you'll end up serving the interests of your creditors, *ᵍ*
    for the rich rule over the poor.
⁸ Sin is a seed that brings a harvest;
    you'll reap a heap of trouble with every seed you plant.
    For your investment in sins pays a full return—
    the full punishment you deserve! *ʰ*

---

a   21:31 Or "The horse is prepared for the battle."
b   22:1 The Hebrew is simply "name preferred to wealth." The Aramaic indicates it could be "the name [of God]."
c   22:1 Or "silver and gold." Remember, it is Solomon, one of the richest men to ever live, who penned these words.
d   22:3 Wise people solve problems before they happen.
e   22:5 Or "thorns and snares." This becomes a metaphor of demonic curses and troubles. Thorns are associated with the fall of Adam. Jesus wore a crown of thorns and took away our curse. The snares picture the temptations of evil that the Devil places in our path.
f   22:6 Or "Train them in the direction they are best suited to go." Some Jewish scholars teach this means understanding your children's talents and then seeing that they go into that field.
g   22:7 The Septuagint reads "The servant will lend to his own master."
h   22:8 As translated from the Septuagint.

⁹ When you are generous ᵃ to the poor,
    you are enriched with blessings in return.
¹⁰ Say goodbye to a troublemaker and you'll say goodbye
    to quarrels, strife, tension, and arguments,
    for a troublemaker traffics in shame. ᵇ
¹¹ The Lord loves those whose hearts are holy,
    and he is the friend of those whose ways are pure. ᶜ
¹² God passionately watches ᵈ over
    his deep reservoir ᵉ of revelation-knowledge,
    but he subverts the lies of those who pervert the truth.
¹³ A slacker always has an excuse for not working—
    like "I can't go to work. There's a lion outside!
    And murderers too!" ᶠ
¹⁴ Sex with an adulteress is like falling into the abyss.
    Those under God's curse jump right in to their own destruction.
¹⁵ Although rebellion is woven into a young man's heart, ᵍ
    tough discipline can make him into a man.
¹⁶ There are two kinds of people headed toward poverty:
    those who exploit the poor
    and those who bribe the rich. ʰ

Sayings of the Wise Sages

¹⁷ Listen carefully and open your heart. ⁱ
    Drink in the wise revelation that I impart.
¹⁸ You'll become winsome and wise
    when you treasure the beauty of my words.
    And always be prepared to share them at the appropriate time.
¹⁹ For I'm releasing these words to you this day,

ᵃ 22:9 The Hebrew word translated as "generous" here actually means "to have a bountiful eye." It is a figure of speech for generosity, a life of helping others.

ᵇ 22:10 As translated from the Aramaic.

ᶜ 22:11 As translated from the Septuagint. Followers of Jesus enjoy a relationship with our holy King as we live in the light and love to please him.

ᵈ 22:12 Or "the eyes of the Lord." In the church today, prophets become eyes in the body of Christ. They see and reveal God's heart for his people.

ᵉ 22:12 Although the concept of a reservoir is not found in the Hebrew, it is added by the translator for poetic nuance.

ᶠ 22:13 This humorous verse uses both satire and a metaphor. There's always an excuse for not working hard. The Aramaic text adds "and a murderer too!"

ᵍ 22:15 The Aramaic word used here means "senseless."

ʰ 22:16 The Hebrew is literally "Oppressing the poor is gain; giving to the rich is loss. Both end up only in poverty."

ⁱ 22:17 From this verse to 24:22 we have a collection of proverbs that lead to virtue. They are especially designed for the young person about to enter a career and start a family.

yes, even to you, so that your living hope
will be found in God alone,
for he is the only one who is always true.

^{20–21} Pay attention to these excellent sayings of three-fold things. ^a
For within my words you will discover true and reliable revelation.
They will give you serenity ^b so that you can reveal
the truth of the word of the one who sends you.

²² Never oppress the poor
or pass laws with the motive of crushing the weak.

²³ For the Lord will rise to plead their case
and humiliate the one who humiliates the poor. ^c

^{24–25} Walk away from an angry man
or you'll embrace a snare in your soul ^d
by becoming bad-tempered just like him.

²⁶ Why would you ever guarantee a loan for someone else
or promise to be responsible for his debts?

²⁷ For if you fail to pay you could lose your shirt! ^e

²⁸ The previous generation has set boundaries in place.
Don't you dare move them just to benefit yourself. ^f

²⁹ If you are uniquely gifted in your work,
you will rise and be promoted.
You won't be held back—
you'll stand before kings!

Wisdom Will Protect You

23 When you've been invited to dine with a very important leader,
consider your manners and keep in mind who you're with.

---

a 22:20–21 As translated from the Aramaic. Most translators find this verse difficult to convey. The Hebrew can be "I have written excellent things," "I have written three times," "I write thirty sayings [proverbs]," "I have written you previously," or "I have written you generals." The Septuagint reads "You should copy these things three times." If the Proverbs contain keys to understanding riddles and mysteries (Prov. 1:2–6), then we have one of those keys given to us here. God speaks in threes, for he is a triune God. We have a body, soul, and spirit. God lived in a three-room house (outer court, holy place, and the chamber of the Holy of Holies). These three-fold dimensions are throughout the Bible.

b 22:20–21 *Serenity* is only found in the Aramaic.

c 22:23 As translated from the Aramaic. The Hebrew is "He will rob the soul of the one who robs the poor."

d 22:24–25 As translated from the Aramaic.

e 22:27 Or "bed."

f 22:28 This refers to moving property lines of your neighbors to take more land, or it could mean moving landmarks and memorials placed there by ancestors. It also speaks to the moral boundaries that the previous generation modeled—they are to be upheld.

² Be careful to curb your appetite and catch yourself
   before you fall into the trap of wanting all you see.ᵃ
³ Don't crave their delicacies,
   for they may have another motive in having you sit at their table.
⁴ Don't compare yourself to the rich.ᵇ
   Surrender your selfish ambition and evaluate them properly.
⁵ For no sooner do you start counting your wealth
   than it sprouts wings and flies away like an eagle in the sky—
   here today, gone tomorrow!
⁶ Be sensible when you dine with a stingy manᶜ
   and don't eat more than you should.ᵈ
⁷ For as he thinks within himself, so is he.ᵉ
   He will grudgingly say, "Go ahead and eat all you want,"
   but in his heart he resents the fact that he has to pay for your meal.
⁸ You'll be sorry you ate anything at all,ᶠ
   and all your compliments will be wasted.
⁹ A rebellious fool will despise your wise advice,
   so don't even waste your time—save your breath!
¹⁰ Never move a long-standing boundary line
   or attempt to take land that belongs to the fatherless.
¹¹ For they have a mighty protector,
   a loving redeemer,ᵍ who watches over them,
   and he will stand up for their cause.
¹² Pay close attention to the teaching that corrects you,
   and open your heart to every word of instruction.
¹³ Don't withhold appropriate discipline from your child.
   Go ahead and punish him when he needs it.ʰ
   Don't worry—it won't kill him!
¹⁴ A good spanking could be the very thing
   that teaches him a lifelong lesson!ⁱ

ᵃ 23:2 Or "put a knife to your throat." When you spend time with an important person, think about his needs, not your own, and favor will come on your life.

ᵇ 23:4 As translated from the Septuagint.

ᶜ 23:6 The Hebrew here literally means "an evil eye," which is a metaphor for a stingy man.

ᵈ 23:6 Or "Don't crave his delicacies."

ᵉ 23:7 The Aramaic, the Septuagint, and a few Hebrew manuscripts read "Eating with him is like eating with someone with a hair in his throat—his mind is not with you!"

ᶠ 23:8 Or "You'll vomit up the little you've eaten."

ᵍ 23:11 The Hebrew word here is goel, which means "kinsman-redeemer." The Aramaic word means "Savior." This shows powerfully how God will take up the grievances of the oppressed.

ʰ 23:13 The Hebrew is "strike them with the rod."

ⁱ 23:14 Or "rescues him from death." The Hebrew word is Sheol.

¹⁵ My beloved child, when your heart is full of wisdom,
　my heart is full of gladness.
¹⁶ And when you speak anointed words,ᵃ
　we are speaking mouth to mouth!ᵇ
¹⁷ Don't allow the actions of evil men
　to cause you to burn with anger.ᶜ
　Instead, burn with unrelenting passion
　as you worship God in holy awe.
¹⁸ Your future is bright and filled with a living hope
　that will never fade away.
¹⁹ As you listen to me, my beloved child,
　you will grow in wisdom and your heart
　will be drawn into understanding,
　which will empower you to make right decisions.ᵈ
²⁰ Don't live in the excesses of drunkenness or gluttony,
　or waste your life away by partying all the time,ᵉ
²¹ because drunkards and gluttons sleep their lives away
　and end up broke!
²² Give respect to your father and mother,
　for without them you wouldn't even be here.
　And don't neglect them when they grow old.
²³ Embrace the truthᶠ and hold it close.
　Don't let go of wisdom, instruction, and life-giving understanding.
²⁴ When a father observes his child living in godliness,
　he is ecstatic with joy—nothing makes him prouder!
²⁵ So may your father's heart burst with joy
　and your mother's soul be filled with gladness because of you.
²⁶ My son, give me your heart
　and embrace fully what I'm about to tell you.
²⁷ Stay far away from prostitutes
　and you'll stay far away from the pit of destruction.

ᵃ 23:16 Or "speak what is right."
ᵇ 23:16 This is taken from the Septuagint, and it literally means "Your lips shall speak with my lips." The Hebrew is "My kidneys [soul] will rejoice." See Num. 12:6–8, which reveals that God spoke with Moses mouth to mouth (literal Hebrew).
ᶜ 23:17 The Hebrew word used here describes an emotion of intense passion. Many translate it "envy" ("Do not envy the sinner"), but that does not describe it fully. Another possible translation would be "zeal."
ᵈ 23:19 The Aramaic is "Set up my doctrines in your heart."
ᵉ 23:20 Translated from the Aramaic and the Septuagint.
ᶠ 23:23 The Hebrew word here literally means "create the truth" or "give birth to truth" or "possess the truth." This Hebrew word is also used for God as the Creator. See Gen. 14:19 and 22.

For sleeping with a promiscuous woman is like falling into a trap
that you'll never be able to escape!
28 Like a robber hiding in the shadows
    she's waiting to claim another victim—
    another husband unfaithful to his wife.
29 Who has anguish? Who has bitter sorrow?
    Who constantly complains and argues?
    Who stumbles and falls and hurts himself?
    Who's the one with bloodshot eyes?
30 It's the one who drinks too much
    and is always looking for a brew.
    Make sure it's never you!
31 And don't be drunk with wine *a*
    but be known as one who enjoys the company
    of the lovers of God, *b*
32 For drunkenness brings the sting of a serpent,
    like the fangs of a viper *c* spreading poison into your soul.
33 It will make you hallucinate, mumble,
    and speak words that are perverse.
34 You'll be like a seasick sailor being tossed to and fro,
    dizzy and out of your mind.
35 You'll awake only to say, "What hit me?
    I feel like I've been run over by a truck!"
    Yet off you'll go, looking for another drink!

Wisdom's Warning

24 Don't envy the wealth of the wicked or crave their company.
    2 For they're obsessed with causing trouble
    and their conversations are corrupt.
3 Wise people are builders— *d*
    they build families, businesses, communities.
    And through intelligence and insight
    their enterprises are established and endure.
4 Because of their skilled leadership

---

a 23:31 As translated from the Septuagint.
b 23:31 As translated from the Septuagint and a marginal reading of the Hebrew. The Aramaic
   is "Meditate on righteousness." The Septuagint adds a line not found in Hebrew or Aramaic
   that describes the unflattering life of a drunk: "You will walk around naked as a pestle!"
c 23:32 Or "horned serpent" or "dragon." This is the Hebrew word *basilisk*, which comes
   from a root word meaning "little king." It becomes an emblem of the poison of demonic
   power that can cause addictions and rule over the soul like a "little king."
d 24:3 Or "A house is built by wisdom." The house is more than a structure with roof and a
   floor. It becomes a metaphor for families, churches, businesses, and enterprises.

the hearts [a] of people are filled with the treasures of wisdom
and the pleasures of spiritual wealth.

⁵ Wisdom can make anyone into a mighty warrior, [b]
and revelation-knowledge increases strength.

⁶ Wise strategy is necessary to wage war,
and with many astute advisers
you'll see the path to victory more clearly.

⁷ Wisdom is a treasure too lofty [c] for a quarreling fool—
he'll have nothing to say when leaders gather together.

⁸ There is one who makes plans to do evil—
Master Schemer is his name.

⁹ If you plan to do evil, it's as wrong as doing it.
And everyone detests a troublemaker.

¹⁰ If you faint when under pressure,
you have need of courage. [d]

¹¹ Go and rescue the perishing! Be their savior!
Why would you stand back and watch them stagger to their death?

¹² And why would you say, "But it's none of my business"?
The one who knows you completely and judges your every motive
is also the keeper of souls—and not just yours!
He sees through your excuses and holds you responsible
for failing to help those whose lives are threatened.

¹³ Revelation-knowledge is a delicacy,
sweet like flowing honey that melts in your mouth.
Eat as much of it as you can, my friend!

¹⁴ For then you will perceive what is true wisdom,
your future will be bright, [e]
and this hope living within will never disappoint you.

¹⁵ Listen up, you wicked, irreverent ones—
don't harass the lovers of God [f]
and don't invade their resting place.

¹⁶ For the lovers of God may suffer adversity

---

a 24:4 Or "inner chambers."

b 24:5 Or "Wisdom makes anyone into a hero." The Aramaic and the Septuagint read "It's better to be wise than to be strong."

c 24:7 The Hebrew is actually "Wisdom is coral to a fool." That is, it is unattainable, deep and hidden.

d 24:10 Or "Your strength is limited." Our weakness often becomes an excuse to quit, but strength and courage come as the result of faithfulness under pressure. Some interpret this to mean "If you fail to help others in their time of need, you will grow too weak to help yourself."

e 24:14 The Septuagint is "Your death will be good."

f 24:15 Or "the righteous."

and stumble seven times,
      but they will continue to rise over and over again.
    But the unrighteous are brought down by just one calamity
      and will never be able to rise again. [a]
[17] Never gloat when your enemy meets disaster
      and don't be quick to rejoice if he falls.
[18] For the Lord, who sees your heart,
      will be displeased with you and will pity your foe.
[19] Don't be angrily offended over evildoers or be agitated by them. [b]
[20] For the wicked have no life and no future—
      their light of life will die out. [c]
[21] My child, stand in awe of the Lord Jehovah!
      Give counsel to others,
      but don't mingle with those who are rebellious.
[22] For sudden destruction will fall upon them
      and their lives will be ruined in a moment.
      And who knows what retribution they will face! [d]

Revelation from the Wise

[23] Those enlightened with wisdom have spoken these proverbs:
      Judgment must be impartial,
      for it is always wrong to be swayed by a person's status.
[24] If you say to the guilty, "You are innocent,"
      the nation will curse you and the people will revile you.
[25] But when you convict the guilty,
      the people will thank you and reward you with favor.
[26] Speaking honestly is a sign of true friendship. [e]
[27] Go ahead, build your career and give yourself to your work.
      But if you put me first, you'll see your family built up! [f]
[28] Why would you be a false accuser and slander with your words?
[29] Don't ever spitefully say, "I'll get even with him!
      I'll do to him what he did to me!"
[30-31] One day I passed by the field of a lazy man
      and I noticed the vineyards of a slacker.
      I observed nothing but thorns, weeds, and broken-down walls.

---

a 24:16 Implied in the text as it completes the parallelism.
b 24:19 The Septuagint is "Don't rejoice with those who do evil or be jealous of them."
c 24:20 Not only will they die out, but the implication is they will have no posterity.
d 24:22 Verses 21 and 22 are translated from the Aramaic.
e 24:26 The Hebrew is literally "An honest answer is like a kiss on the lips." In the culture of the day, kissing was a sign of authentic friendship and a mark of relationship, which was often expressed in public among friends.
f 24:27 As translated from the Septuagint.

³² So I considered their lack of wisdom,
and I pondered the lessons I could learn from this:
^{33–34} Professional work habits prevent poverty from becoming
your permanent business partner. And:
If you put off until tomorrow the work you could do today,
tomorrow never seems to come.

25

Solomon's proverbs, published by the scribes of King Hezekiah:
² God conceals the revelation of his word [a]
in the hiding place of his glory. [b]
But the honor of kings [c] is revealed
by how they thoroughly search out
the deeper meaning of all that God says.
³ The heart of a king is full of understanding,
like the heavens are high and the ocean is deep.
⁴ If you burn away the impurities from silver,
a sterling vessel will emerge from the fire.
⁵ And if you purge corruption from the kingdom,
a king's reign will be established in righteousness.
⁶ Don't boast in the presence of a king
or promote yourself by taking a seat at the head table
and pretend that you're someone important.
⁷ For it is better for the king to say to you,
"Come, you should sit at the head table,"
than for him to say in front of everyone,
"Please get up and move—
you're sitting in the place of the prince."
⁸ Don't be hasty to file a lawsuit.
By starting something you wish you hadn't,
you could be humiliated when you lose your case.
⁹ Don't reveal another person's secret
just to prove a point in an argument,
or you could be accused of being a gossip
¹⁰ and gain a reputation for being one
who betrays the confidence of a friend.
¹¹ Winsome words spoken at just the right time [d]

---

a 25:2 Many translate this "a matter," whereas the Hebrew is *dabar*, which is translated more than eight hundred times in the Old Testament as "word."

b 25:2 There is beautiful poetry in the Hebrew text. The word for "hide" is *cathar* and the word for "word" is *dabar*. The Hebrew is actually "*Kabod* (glory) *cathar* (hidden) *dabar* (word)."

c 25:2 We have been made kings and priests, royal lovers of God, because of God's grace and Christ's redeeming blood. See 1 Peter 2:9 and Rev. 5:8–10.

d 25:11 The Aramaic reads "The one who speaks the word is an apple of gold in a setting of

are as appealing as apples gilded in gold
and surrounded with silver. *a*

[12] To humbly receive wise correction
adorns your life with beauty *b*
and makes you a better person.

[13] A reliable, trustworthy messenger
refreshes the heart of his master, *c*
like a gentle breeze blowing at harvest time—
cooling the sweat from his brow.

[14] Clouds that carry no water
and a wind that brings no refreshing rain— *d*
that's what you're like when you boast
of a gift that you don't have. *e*

Wisdom Practices Self-Control

[15] Use patience and kindness when you want to persuade leaders
and watch them change their minds right in front of you.
For your gentle wisdom will quell the strongest resistance. *f*

[16] When you discover something sweet,
don't overindulge and eat more than you need,
for excess in anything can make you sick of even a good thing.

[17] Don't wear out your welcome
by staying too long at the home of your friends,
or they may get fed up with always having you there
and wish you hadn't come.

[18] Lying about and slandering people
are as bad as hitting them with a club,
or wounding them with an arrow,
or stabbing them with a sword.

---

silver." The Septuagint is "A wise word is like a golden apple in a pendant of rubies."

a 25:11 Each one of God's promises are like apples gilded in gold. When we are full of his Spirit we can speak and prophesy words of encouragement that are spoken at the right time for the blessing of others.

b 25:12 Or "an earring of gold, an ornament of fine gold." An earring pierces the ear and is an emblem of a listening heart.

c 25:13 Or "employer."

d 25:14 The symbols of clouds, wind, and rain are significant. Clouds are often a metaphor for the people of God filled with glory (Heb. 12:1; Rev. 1:7). Wind is an emblem of the Holy Spirit bringing new life (John 3:6–8). Rain often points to teaching the revelation-truths that refresh and water the seeds of spiritual growth (Isa. 55:8–11). God's anointed people are to be clouds carried by the wind of the Holy Spirit that bring refreshing truths to his people. When we are empty and false, we are clouds without rain. See 2 Peter 2:17 and Jude 1:12.

e 25:14 Or "boast of a promised gift you never intend to give." The Hebrew is literally "to make yourself shine in a gift of falsehood."

f 25:15 Or "Soft words break bones."

¹⁹ You can't depend on an unreliable person
   when you really need help.
   It can be compared to biting down on an abscessed tooth
   or walking with a sprained ankle.
²⁰ When you sing a song of joy to someone suffering
   in the deepest grief and heartache,
   it can be compared to disrobing in the middle of a blizzard
   or rubbing salt in a wound.
²¹ Is your enemy hungry? Buy him lunch.
   Win him over with your kindness. *a*
²² Your surprising generosity will awaken his conscience *b*
   and God will reward you with favor.
²³ As the north wind brings a storm,
   saying things you shouldn't *c* brings a storm to any relationship.
²⁴ It's better to live all alone in a rundown shack
   than to share a castle with a crabby spouse! *d*
²⁵ Like a drink of cool water to a weary, thirsty soul,
   so hearing good news revives the spirit.
²⁶ When a lover of God gives in and compromises with wickedness,
   it can be compared to contaminating a stream with sewage
   or polluting a fountain.
²⁷ It's good to eat sweet things,
   but you can take too much.
   It's good to be honored,
   but to seek words of praise *e* is not honor at all.
²⁸ If you live without restraint
   and are unable to control your temper,
   you're as helpless as a city with broken-down defenses,
   open to attack.

---

a 25:21 Or "Is he thirsty? Give him a drink."

b 25:22 Or "You will heap coals of fire on his head." His heart will be moved and his shame
   exposed.

c 25:23 Or "words of gossip."

d 25:24 With the exception of one Hebrew letter, this verse is identical to 21:9. See footnote.
   The Aramaic reads "than to live with a contentious woman in a house of divisions."

e 25:27 This line is translated from the Aramaic.

Don't Be a Fool

26 It is totally out of place to promote and honor a fool,
just like it's out of place to have snow in the summer
and rain at harvest time. [a]

2 An undeserved curse will be powerless to harm you.
It may flutter over you like a bird,
but it will find no place to land. [b]

3 Guide a horse with a whip,
direct a donkey with a bridle,
and lead a rebellious fool with a beating on his backside!

4 Don't respond to the words of a fool with more foolish words,
or you will become as foolish as he is!

5 Instead, if you're asked a silly question,
answer it with words of wisdom [c]
so the fool doesn't think he's so clever.

6 If you choose a fool to represent you,
you're asking for trouble.
It will be as bad for you as cutting off your own feet!

7 You can never trust the words of a fool,
just like a crippled man can't trust his legs to support him. [d]

8 Give honor to a fool and watch it backfire—
like a stone tied to a slingshot.

9 The statements of a fool will hurt others [e]
like a thorn bush brandished by a drunk.

10 Like a reckless archer shooting arrows at random
is the impatient employer
who hires just any fool who comes along—
someone's going to get hurt! [f]

11 Fools are famous for repeating their errors,
like dogs are known to return to their vomit.

12 There's only one thing worse than a fool,

---

a 26:1 Both snow and rain are good in their proper season but harmful in the wrong season. So is it harmful to the fool if you affirm him and honor him prematurely.

b 26:2 There is an implication in some Hebrew manuscripts that the curse will go back and land on the one who wrongly spoke it, like a bird going back to its nest.

c 26:5 As translated from the Aramaic.

d 26:7 As translated from the Aramaic.

e 26:9 As translated from the Aramaic.

f 26:10 Implied in the context. This is a difficult verse to translate and it reads quite differently in the Aramaic and the Septuagint. The Aramaic is "A fool suffers much like a drunkard crossing the sea." The Septuagint reads "Every fool endures much hardship and his fury comes to nothing."

and that's the smug, conceited man
always in love with his own opinions.

Don't Be Lazy

¹³ The lazy loafer says,
    "I can't go out and look for a job—
    there may be a lion out there roaming wild in the streets!"
¹⁴ As a door is hinged to the wall,
    so the lazy man keeps turning over, hinged to his bed!
¹⁵ There are some people so lazy
    they won't even work to feed themselves.
¹⁶ A self-righteous person ^a is convinced he's smarter
    than seven wise counselors who tell him the truth.
¹⁷ It's better to grab a mad dog by its ears
    than to meddle and interfere in a quarrel ^b
    that's none of your business.

Watch Your Words

^{18–19} The one who is caught lying to his friend
    and says, "I didn't mean it, I was only joking,"
    can be compared to a madman
    randomly shooting off deadly weapons.
²⁰ It takes fuel to have a fire—
    a fire dies down when you run out of fuel.
    So quarrels disappear when the gossip ends.
²¹ Add fuel to the fire and the blaze goes on.
    So add an argumentative man to the mix
    and you'll keep strife alive.
²² Gossip is so delicious, and how we love to swallow it!
    For slander ^c is easily absorbed into our innermost being.
²³ Smooth talk ^d can hide a corrupt heart
    just like a pretty glaze covers a cheap clay pot.
²⁴ Kind words can be a cover to conceal hatred of others,
    for hypocrisy loves to hide behind flattery.
²⁵ So don't be drawn in by the hypocrite,
    for his gracious speech is a charade,
    nothing but a masquerade covering his hatred and evil on parade. ^e

---

a 26:16 Or "sluggard." This speaks of a person who lives in fantasy and not reality.
b 26:17 Or "to become furious because of a quarrel that's not yours."
c 26:22 Or "complaining."
d 26:23 As translated from the Septuagint. The Hebrew is "burning words."
e 26:25 The Hebrew is "Seven abominations hide in his heart." This is a figure of speech for
   the fullness of evil, a heart filled to the brim with darkness.

²⁶ Don't worry—he can't keep the mask on for long.
  One day his hypocrisy will be exposed before all the world.
²⁷ Go ahead, set a trap for others—
  and then watch as it snaps back on you!
  Start a landslide and you'll be the one who gets crushed.
²⁸ Hatred is the root of slander[a]
  and insecurity the root of flattery.[b]

Heed Wisdom's Warnings

27 Never brag about the plans you have for tomorrow,
  for you don't have a clue what tomorrow may bring to you.
² Let someone else honor you for your accomplishments,
  for self-praise is never appropriate.
³ It's easier to carry a heavy boulder and a ton of sand
  than to be provoked by a fool and have to carry that burden!
⁴ The rage and anger of others can be overwhelming,
  but it's nothing compared to jealousy's fire.
⁵ It's better to be corrected openly
  if it stems from hidden love.
⁶ You can trust a friend who wounds you with his honesty,[c]
  but your enemy's pretended flattery[d] comes from insincerity.
⁷ When your soul is full, you turn down even the sweetest honey.
  But when your soul is starving,
  every bitter thing becomes sweet.[e]
⁸ Like a bird that has fallen from its nest
  is the one who is dislodged from his home.[f]
⁹ Sweet friendships[g] refresh the soul and awaken our hearts with joy,
  for good friends are like the anointing oil
  that yields the fragrant incense of God's presence.[h]
¹⁰ So never give up on a friend or abandon a friend of your father—
  for in the day of your brokenness[i]

---

a 26:28 Or "A slanderer hates his victims."
b 26:28 Implied in the text. The Aramaic is "Malicious words work trouble."
c 27:6 Or "Wounds by a loved one are long lasting [effective and faithful]."
d 27:6 Or "kisses."
e 27:7 When we are full of many things and many opinions, the sweet word of God, like revelation honey, is spurned. Instead, we eat and fill our souls with things that can never satisfy.
f 27:8 Or "banished from his place." As translated from the Aramaic.
g 27:9 Or "counsel."
h 27:9 The Hebrew text refers to the sacred anointing oil and the incense that burns in the Holy Place.
i 27:10 As translated from the Aramaic.

you won't have to run to a relative for help.
A friend nearby is better than a relative far away.
¹¹ My son, when you walk in wisdom,
my heart is filled with gladness,
for the way you live is proof
that I've not taught you in vain. ^a
¹² A wise, shrewd person discerns the danger ahead
and prepares himself,
but the naïve simpleton never looks ahead
and suffers the consequences.
¹³ Cosign for one you barely know and you will pay a great price!
Anyone stupid enough to guarantee the loan of another
deserves to have his property seized in payment.
¹⁴ Do you think you're blessing your neighbors
when you sing at the top of your lungs early in the morning?
Don't be fooled—
they'll curse you for doing it!^b
¹⁵ An endless drip, drip, drip, from a leaky faucet^c
and the words of a cranky, nagging wife have the same effect.
¹⁶ Can you stop the north wind from blowing
or grasp a handful of oil?
That's easier than to stop her from complaining.
¹⁷ It takes a grinding wheel to sharpen a blade,
and so a friendly argument can sharpen a man. ^d
¹⁸ Tend an orchard and you'll have fruit to eat.
Serve the Master's interests
and you'll receive honor that's sweet.
¹⁹ Just as no two faces are exactly alike,
so every heart is different. ^e
²⁰ Hell and destruction are never filled,
and the desires of men's hearts are insatiable.
²¹ Fire is the way to test the purity of silver and gold,
but the character of a man is tested
by giving him a measure of fame.^f

---

a 27:11 Or "that I may answer those who reproach me."
b 27:14 Or "He who sings in a loud voice early in the morning, thinking he's blessing his neighbor, is no different from he who pronounces a curse."
c 27:15 Or "a constant drip on a rainy day."
d 27:17 Or "a man's face."
e 27:19 As translated from the Aramaic and the Septuagint.
f 27:21 Or "by the things he praises."

²² You can beat a fool half to death
and still never beat the foolishness out of him. *a*

²³ A shepherd should pay close attention to the faces of his flock
and hold close to his heart the condition of those he cares for.

²⁴ A man's strength, power, and riches *b* will one day fade away;
not even nations *c* endure forever.

²⁵⁻²⁷ Take care of your responsibilities
and be diligent in your business
and you will have more than enough—
an abundance of food, clothing, and plenty for your household. *d*

Lovers of God

28 Guilty criminals experience paranoia
even though no one threatens them.
But the innocent lovers of God,
because of righteousness,
will have the boldness *e* of a young, ferocious lion!

² A rebellious nation is thrown into chaos, *f*
but leaders anointed with wisdom will restore law and order.

³ When a pauper *g* oppresses the destitute,
it's like a flash flood that sweeps away their last hope.

⁴ Those who turn their backs on what they know is right *h*
will no longer be able to tell right from wrong.
But those who love the truth strengthen their souls. *i*

⁵ Justice never makes sense to men devoted to darkness,
but those tenderly devoted to the Lord
can understand justice perfectly.

---

a 27:22 Or "If you pound a fool in a mortar like dried grain with a pestle, still his foolishness will not depart from him."

b 27:24 The Hebrew says merely "riches," while the Aramaic adds "power [dominion]" and the Septuagint adds "strength." The translator has chosen to combine them.

c 27:24 Or "a crown [dominion]."

d 27:25–27 An agricultural analogy is used in the Hebrew and Aramaic. The analogy of a farming enterprise has been changed to business here in order to transfer meaning. It is literally "Gather the hay of the field and hills, and new grass will appear. Lambs will provide clothing, goats will pay for the price of the field, and there will be enough goat's milk for you, your family, and your servant girls."

e 28:1 Or "confidence."

f 28:2 Or "A rebellious nation will have one leader after another."

g 28:3 This pauper can also be one who is spiritually poor. Some Jewish expositors believe it refers to corrupt judges.

h 28:4 The Hebrew word is "the Torah." See also vv. 7 and 9.

i 28:4 As translated from the Aramaic. The Septuagint is "build a wall to protect themselves."

[6] It's more respectable to be poor and pure than rich and perverse.

[7] To be obedient to what you've been taught[a]
proves you're an honorable child,
but to socialize with the lawless brings shame to your parents.

[8] Go ahead and get rich on the backs of the poor,
but all the wealth you gather will one day be given
to those who are kind to the needy.

[9] If you close your heart and refuse to listen to God's instruction,[b]
even your prayer will be despised.

[10] Those who tempt the lovers of God with an evil scheme
will fall into their own trap.
But the innocent who resist temptation will experience reward.

[11] The wealthy in their conceit presume to be wise,
but a poor person with discernment can see right through them.

[12] The triumphant joy of God's lovers releases great glory.[c]
But when the wicked rise to power, everyone goes into hiding.[d]

[13] If you cover up your sin you'll never do well.
But if you confess your sins and forsake them,
you will be kissed by mercy.

[14] Overjoyed is the one who with tender heart trembles before God,
but the stubborn, unyielding heart will experience even greater evil.

[15] Ruthless rulers can only be compared
to raging lions and roaming bears.[e]

[16] Abusive leaders fail to employ wisdom,
but leaders who despise corruption[f]
will enjoy a long and full life.[g]

[17] A murderer's conscience will torment him—
a fugitive haunted by guilt all the way to the grave
with no one to support him.

[18] The pure will be rescued from failure,
but the perverse will suddenly fall into ruin.

[19] Work hard and you'll have all you desire,
but chase a fantasy[h] and you could end up with nothing.

---

a 28:7 Or "the Torah."

b 28:9 Or "the Torah."

c 28:12 As translated from the Aramaic.

d 28:12 Or "People become victims."

e 28:15 David, before he killed Goliath, went after the lion and the bear. See 1 Sam. 17:34–37.
These beasts represented demonic forces of evil over the land. Daniel also mentions the
world's ruthless leaders as lions and bears. See Dan. 7:1–8

f 28:16 Or "injustice."

g 28:16 Or "enjoy a long reign."

h 28:19, Or "an empty dream." The Septuagint is "the one who pursues leisure,"

²⁰ Life's blessings drench the honest and faithful person,
    but punishment rains down upon the greedy and dishonest.
²¹ Giving favoritism to the rich and powerful is disgusting,
    and this is the type of judge who would betray a man for a bribe. *a*
²² A greedy man *b* is in a race to get rich,
    but he forgets that he could lose what's most important
    and end up with nothing. *c*
²³ If you correct someone with constructive criticism,
    in the end he will appreciate it more than flattery.
²⁴ A person who would reject *d* his own parents and say,
"What's wrong with that?" is as bad as a murderer.
²⁵ To make rash, hasty decisions
    shows that you are not trusting the Lord.
    But when you rely totally on God,
    you will still act carefully and prudently. *e*
²⁶ Self-confident *f* know-it-alls will prove to be fools.
    But when you lean on the wisdom from above,
    you will have a way to escape the troubles of your own making.
²⁷ You will never go without if you give to the poor.
    But if you're heartless, stingy, and selfish, *g*
    you invite curses upon yourself.
²⁸ When wicked leaders rise to power,
    good people go into hiding.
    But when they fall from power,
    the godly take their place.

Don't Be Stubborn

29 Stubborn people who repeatedly refuse to accept correction
    will suddenly be broken and never recover.
² Everyone rejoices when the lovers of God flourish,
    but the people groan when the wicked rise to power.
³ When you love wisdom, your father is overjoyed.

---

a 28:21 As translated from the Aramaic.
b 28:22 Both the Aramaic and Hebrew have "the man with an evil eye." This is a figure of speech for a stingy or greedy man. A person who shuts his heart to the poor is said to have an evil eye. A person with a good eye is someone who looks on the poor with generosity.
c 28:22 As translated from the Aramaic. The Aramaic text sounds very similar to what Jesus says about gaining the world but losing our souls. See Mark 8:36.
d 28:24 As translated from the Septuagint. The Hebrew is "the one who steals from his own parents."
e 28:25 As translated from the Septuagint. The Hebrew is "The greedy person stirs up trouble, but the one who trusts in the Lord will prosper."
f 28:26 Or "those who trust their instincts."
g 28:27 Or "he who hides his eyes from the poor."

But when you associate with prostitutes,
you waste your wealth in exchange for disgrace. [a]

[4] A godly leader who values justice
is a great strength and example to the people.
But the one who sells his influence for money [b]
tears down what is right.

[5] Flattery can often be used as a trap to hide ulterior motives
and take advantage of you.

[6] The wicked always have a trap laid for others,
but the lovers of God escape as they sing and shout
in joyous triumph!

[7] God's righteous people will pour themselves out for the poor, [c]
but the ungodly make no attempt to understand or help the needy.

You Can't Argue with a Fool

[8] Arrogant cynics love to pick fights,
but the humble and wise love to pursue peace.

[9] There's no use arguing with a fool, [d]
for his ranting and raving prevent you from making a case
and settling the argument in a calm way.

[10] Violent men hate those with integrity,
but the lovers of God esteem those who are holy. [e]

[11] You can recognize fools by the way
they give full vent to their rage
and let their words fly!
But the wise bite their tongue and hold back all they could say.

[12] When leaders listen to false accusations,
their associates become scoundrels.

[13] Poor people and their oppressors
have only one thing in common—
God made them both. [f]

[14] The best insurance for a leader's longevity
is to demonstrate justice for the poor.

[15] Experiencing many corrections and rebukes will make you wise.
But if left to your own ways, you'll bring disgrace to your parents. [g]

---

a 29:3 See Luke 15:11–24.
b 29:4 See 1 Tim. 6:10.
c 29:7 The Hebrew text implies standing up for the legal rights of the poor.
d 29:9 The Hebrew implies an argument in a court of law.
e 29:10 As translated from the Septuagint.
f 29:13 A figure of speech in Hebrew that can literally be translated "God gave them both the gift of eyesight." The Septuagint is "The contracts between lenders and debtors is observed by the Lord."
g 29:15 As translated from the Septuagint. The Hebrew is "your mother."

¹⁶ When the wicked are in power, lawlessness abounds.
  But the patient lovers of God will one day watch in triumph
  as their stronghold topples!
¹⁷ Correct your child and one day you'll find he has changed
  and will bring you great delight.
¹⁸ When there is no clear prophetic vision, ᵃ
  people quickly wander astray. ᵇ
  But when you follow the revelation of the word,
  heaven's bliss fills your soul.
¹⁹ A stubborn servant can't be corrected by words alone.
  For even if he understands, he pays no attention to you.
²⁰ There's only one kind of person who is worse than a fool:
  the impetuous one who speaks without thinking first.
²¹ If you pamper your servants,
  don't be surprised when they expect to be treated as sons. ᶜ
²² The source of strife is found in an angry heart,
  for sin surrounds the life of a furious man. ᵈ
²³ Lift yourself up with pride and you will soon be brought low, ᵉ
  but a meek and humble spirit will add to your honor.
²⁴ You are your own worst enemy when you partner with a thief,
  for a curse of guilt will come upon you
  when you fail to report a crime. ᶠ
²⁵ Fear and intimidation is a trap that holds you back.
  But when you place your confidence in the Lord,
  you will be seated in the high place.
²⁶ Everyone curries favor with leaders.
  But God is the judge, and justice comes from him.
²⁷ The wicked hate those who live a godly life,
  but the righteous hate injustice wherever it's found.

---

a 29:18 The Hebrew word used here can refer to "vision of the night," "dream," "oracle," or
  "revelation." The Septuagint reads "where there is no prophetic seer [or interpreter]."
b 29:18 Or "let loose, stripped, or made naked." The Septuagint reads "The people become
  lawless."
c 29:21 Or "If you pamper your servant when he is young, he'll become a weakling in the
  end." The Septuagint reads "If you live in luxury as a child, you'll become a domestic [ser-
  vant] and at last will be grieved with yourself." The Aramaic states, "You'll be uprooted in
  the end."
d 29:22 The Hebrew word translated as "a furious man" can also mean "lord of fury" or "Baal
  of wrath."
e 29:23 Or "to depression."
f 29:24 Or "when under oath to testify but you do not talk."

The Mysterious Sayings of Agur

30 These are the collected sayings of the prophet Agur, Jakeh's son—[a] the amazing revelation[b] he imparted to Ithiel and Ukal.[c]

[2] God, I'm so weary and worn-out,
 I feel more like a beast than a man.
 I was made in your image,[d]
 but I lack understanding.
[3] I've yet to learn the wisdom
 that comes from the full and intimate knowledge of you,
 the Holy One.

Six Questions

[4] Who is it that travels back and forth
 from the heavenly realm to the earth?[e]
 Who controls the wind as it blows[f] and holds it in his fists?
 Who tucks the rain into the cloak of his clouds?
 Who stretches out the skyline from one vista to the other?
 What is his name?
 And what is the name of his Son?
 Who can tell me?

A Pure Heart Is Filled with God's Word

[5] Every promise from the faithful God
 is pure and proves to be true.

---

a 30:1 This section of Proverbs is attributed to Agur, who gave these oracles to his protégés Ithiel and Ukal. Agur means "to gather a harvest." He was the son of Jakeh, which means "blameless" or "obedient." Jakeh could be another name for David, Solomon's father. Many Jewish expositors believe that Agur was a pseudonym for Solomon. Nothing more is mentioned about Agur in the Bible than what we have here, which is typical for other prophets mentioned in the Scriptures. Some believe he could be the "master of the collection of sayings" referred to in Eccl. 12:11. Agur (taken from Agar) means "collector."

b 30:1 Or "mighty prophecy."

c 30:1 The name Ithiel can mean "God is with me" or "God has arrived." This was fulfilled by Christ, for his birth was the advent, the arrival of God to the earth in human form. Ukal means "I am able" or "I am strong and mighty." When placed together, the meaning of these Hebrew names could read "Gather a harvest of sons who are blameless and obedient. They will have God with them, and they will be strong and mighty." This chapter contains some of the most mystical and mysterious sayings found in Proverbs, with hints of revelation from the book of Job.

d 30:2 Implied in the text, which is extraordinarily difficult to translate with certainty.

e 30:4 Jesus solves this riddle in John 3:13. Only Jesus Christ is the master of heavenly knowledge and wisdom. See also Eph. 4:7–10.

f 30:4 The Hebrew word ruach (wind) is also the term used for the Holy Spirit.

He is a wrap-around shield of protection for all his lovers
  who run to hide in him.
⁶ Never add to his words,
  or he will have to rebuke you and prove that you're a liar.
⁷ God, there are two things I'm asking you for before I die, only two:
⁸ Empty out of my heart everything that is false—
  every lie, and every crooked thing.
  And give me neither undue poverty nor undue wealth—
  but rather, feed my soul with the measure of prosperity
  that pleases you.
⁹ May my satisfaction be found in you.
  Don't let me be so rich that I don't need you
  or so poor that I have to resort to dishonesty
  just to make ends meet.
  Then my life will never detract from bringing glory to your name.
¹⁰ Never defame a servant before his master,
  for you will be the guilty one
  and a curse will come upon you.
¹¹ There is a generation rising that curses their fathers
  and speaks evil of their mothers.
¹² There is a generation rising that considers themselves
  to be pure in their own eyes, ᵃ
  yet they are morally filthy, ᵇ unwashed, and unclean.
¹³ There is a generation rising that is so filled with pride
  they think they are superior and look down on others.
¹⁴ There is a generation rising that uses their words like swords
  to cut and slash those who are different.
  They would devour the poor, the needy, and the afflicted
  from off the face of the earth!
¹⁵ There are three words to describe the greedy:
  "Give me more!"
  There are some things that are never satisfied.
  Forever craving more, they're unable to say, "That's enough!"
  Here are four:
¹⁶ The grave, yawning for another victim,
  the barren womb, ever wanting a child,
  thirsty soil, ever longing for rain,
  and a raging fire, devouring its fuel.
  They're all insatiable.

ᵃ 30:12 See Judg. 21:25.
ᵇ 30:12 The Hebrew uses the word *excrement*.

¹⁷ The eye that mocks his father and dishonors his elderly mother *a*
 deserves to be plucked out by the ravens of the valley
 and fed to the young vultures! *b*

Four Mysteries

¹⁸ There are four marvelous mysteries
 that are *c* too amazing to unravel—
 who could fully explain them? *d*
¹⁹ The way an eagle flies in the sky, *e*
 the way a snake glides on a boulder, *f*
 the path of a ship as it passes through the sea, *g*
 and the way a bridegroom falls in love with his bride. *h*
²⁰ Here is the deceptive way of the adulterous woman: *i*
 she takes what she wants and then says,
 "I've done nothing wrong."

Four Intolerable Things

²¹ There are four intolerable events
 that *j* are simply unbearable to observe:

---

a 30:17 As translated from the Septuagint.

b 30:17 This is a figure of speech for demonic powers that will remove their vision. Ravens and vultures are unclean birds associated with demonic powers in Hebrew poetry.

c 30:18 The Hebrew uses a poetic style of saying there are three mysteries, then saying there are four in order to emphasize their great importance. There could be within this poetic device a pointing to the fourth as the key, or the most important.

d 30:18 Notice that each of these four examples have to do with movement and mystery.

e 30:19 This is a picture of the overcoming life that soars above our problems and limitations with the wings of an eagle. It could also be a hint of the prophetic revelation that comes to God's servants mysteriously and supernaturally. See Isa. 40:31 and 1 Cor. 2:9–13.

f 30:19 The serpent becomes a picture of our sin that was placed on the Rock, Jesus Christ. See Num. 21:6–9; John 3:14–15; 2 Cor. 5:21.

g 30:19 This is a picture of the way our lives, like a ship, sail on the high seas of mystery until we reach our destiny. Our lives contain mysteries, such as where God decided that we were to be born, how we were raised, and the companions who join us until we reach our desired haven. See Ps. 107:23–30.

h 30:19 The Hebrew word translated "bride" can also mean "virgin," pointing to a wedding, thus implying the use of "bridegroom" instead of "man." (Consider Ruth and Boaz.) More important, this is a beautiful metaphor for the mystery of the love of our heavenly Bridegroom (Jesus), who romances his bride and sweeps us off our feet. Love is a mystery. See also 2 Cor. 11:2 and Eph. 5:32.

i 30:20 The adulterous woman of Proverbs is a metaphor for the corrupt religious system. See Rev. 17–18.

j 30:21 See footnote for 30:18. These four events each depict a promotion undeserved, a displacing of one who is virtuous with one who is corrupt. Each promotion indicates that they will carry their corruption with them. The unfaithful servant will likely become a tyrant. The fool who becomes wealthy will squander his wealth. The unfaithful woman

²² when an unfaithful servant becomes a ruler,
  when a scoundrel comes into great wealth,
²³ when an unfaithful woman marries a good man,
  and when a mistress replaces a faithful wife.

Four Creatures Small and Wise

²⁴ The earth has four creatures that are very small but very wise:[a]
²⁵ The feeble ant has little strength,
  yet look how it diligently gathers its food in the summer
  to last throughout the winter.[b]
²⁶ The delicate rock-badger isn't all that strong,
  yet look how it makes a secure home, nestled in the rocks.[c]
²⁷ The locusts have no king to lead them,
  yet they cooperate as they move forward by bands.[d]
²⁸ And the small lizard[e] is easy to catch
  as it clings to the walls with its hands,
  yet it can be found inside a king's palace.[f]

Four Stately Things

²⁹ There are four stately monarchs[g]
  who are impressive to watch as they go forth:
³⁰ the lion, the king of the jungle, who is afraid of no one,
³¹ the rooster strutting boldly among the hens,[h]
  the male goat out in front leading the herd,
  and a king leading his regal procession.[i]
³² If you've acted foolishly by drawing attention to yourself,
  or if you've thought about saying something stupid,
  you'd better shut your mouth.

(or "hated woman") will continue her immorality even after she's married. The girlfriend who replaced the faithful wife will likely find another man one day.
a 30:24 Or "They are the epitome of wisdom."
b 30:25 To prepare for the future is a mark of true wisdom.
c 30:26 This becomes a picture of the believer. Though feeling weakness at times, we can make our home in the high place, inside the cleft of the Rock. See John 14:1-3.
d 30:27 The locust army points us to Joel 1 and 2. There is an awakening army coming to devour the works of the Enemy. Their King, though invisible, guides them from on high as one army.
e 30:28 Or "spider."
f 30:28 Though we may see ourselves as insignificant (like the small lizard), God can place us in significant places where we can be used for him.
g 30:29 See footnote on 30:18.
h 30:31 As translated from the Septuagint.
i 30:31 Or "a king surrounded by his band of soldiers." The Hebrew text is abstruse.

³³ For such stupidity may give you a bloody nose![a]
   Stirring up an argument only leads to an angry confrontation.

31

King Lemuel's[b] royal words of wisdom:
   These are the inspired words my mother taught me.[c]

² Listen, my dear son, son of my womb.
   You are the answer to my prayers, my son.
³ So keep yourself sexually pure
   from the promiscuous, wayward woman.
   Don't waste the strength of your anointing
   on those who ruin kings—
   you'll live to regret it![d]
⁴ For you are a king, Lemuel,
   and it's never fitting for a king to be drunk on wine
   or for rulers to crave alcohol.
⁵ For when they drink they forget justice
   and ignore the rights of those in need,
   those who depend on you for leadership.
⁶⁻⁷ Strong drink is given to the terminally ill,
   who are suffering at the brink of death.
   Wine is for those in depression
   in order to drown their sorrows.
   Let them drink and forget their poverty and misery.
⁸ But you are to be a king who speaks up on behalf
   of the disenfranchised
   and pleads for the legal rights of the defenseless
   and those who are dying.
⁹ Be a righteous king, judging on behalf of the poor
   and interceding for those most in need.[e]

---

a 30:33 Or "Churning milk makes butter, and punching the nose brings blood, so stirring up anger produces quarrels." The Hebrew contains a word play with the word *anger*, which is almost identical to the word for "nose."

b 31:1 Jewish legend is that King Lemuel was a pseudonym for Solomon, which would make his mother mentioned here to be Bathsheba. There is no other mention of Lemuel in the Scriptures. The Hebrew word translated "inspired words" is *massa*, which some have surmised was a place, meaning "Lemuel, King of Massa."

c 31:1 The Septuagint is "These are words spoken by God, and through a king came an answer divine."

d 31:3 As translated from the Septuagint.

e 31:9 See James 1:27.

PROVERBS 31 ⟨ 283

The Radiant Bride

[10] Who could ever find a wife like this one—[a]
  she is a woman of strength and mighty valor![b]
  She's full of wealth and wisdom.
  The price paid for her was greater[c] than many jewels.
[11] Her husband has entrusted his heart to her,[d]
  for she brings him the rich spoils of victory.
[12] All throughout her life she brings him what is good and not evil.[e]
[13] She searches out continually to possess
  that which is pure and righteous.[f]
  She delights in the work of her hands.[g]
[14] She gives out revelation-truth[h] to feed others.

---

a   31:10 Starting with verse 10 through the end of the book, we have a Hebrew acrostic poem. It is alphabetical in structure, with each of the twenty-two verses beginning with a consecutive Hebrew letter of the alphabet. The implication is that the perfections of this woman would exhaust the entire language. The subject is the perfect bride, the virtuous woman. This woman is both a picture of a virtuous wife and an incredible allegory of the end-time victorious bride of Jesus Christ, full of virtue and grace.

b   31:10 The Hebrew word used to describe this virtuous wife is *khayil*. The meaning of this word cannot be contained by one English equivalent word. It is often used in connection with military prowess. This is a warring wife. *Khayil* can be translated "mighty; wealthy; excellent; morally righteous; full of substance, integrity, abilities, and strength; mighty like an army." The wife is a metaphor for the last-days church, the virtuous, overcoming bride of Jesus Christ. The word *khayil* is most often used to describe valiant men. See Ex. 18:21, where it is used for the mighty ones Moses was to commission as elders and leaders among the people. Because many of the cultural terms and metaphors used in this passage are not understood or even used in today's English-speaking world, the translator has chosen to make them explicit.

c   31:10 Or "her worth." The price paid for her was the sacred blood of the Lamb of God, her Bridegroom.

d   31:11 Or "has great confidence in her."

e   31:12 The virtuous bride will not bring disgrace to his name. Jesus will not be ashamed to display her to the world.

f   31:13 Or "wool and linen [flax]." Wool is a metaphor often used as a symbol of what is pure. See Isa. 1:18; Dan. 7:9; Rev. 1:14. Linen was made from flax and always speaks of righteousness. The priests of the Old Testament wore linen garments as they went before God's presence to offer sacrifices. The curtains of the tabernacle were likewise made of linen, signifying God's righteousness. See Ex. 28:39–43 and Rev. 19:8. The virtuous bride of Christ in the last days will be seeking for only what is pure and righteous in the eyes of her Bridegroom.

g   31:13 Or "eagerly works with her hands." The hands, with their five fingers, speak of the five ministries of the present work of Christ on the earth: apostles, prophets, evangelists, pastors, and teachers. These are often referred to as the five-fold ministries. Her delight is to equip others and help those in need.

h   31:14 Or "bread." This is a consistent emblem of spiritual food.

She is like a trading ship bringing divine supplies[a]
from the merchant.[b]

[15] Even in the night season[c] she arises[d] and sets food on the table
for hungry ones in her house and for others.[e]

[16] She sets her heart upon a nation[f] and takes it as her own,
carrying it within her.
She labors there to plant the living vines.[g]

[17] She wraps herself in strength,[h] might, and power in all her works.

[18] She tastes and experiences a better substance,[i]
and her shining light will not be extinguished,
no matter how dark the night.[j]

[19] She stretches out her hands to help the needy[k]
and she lays hold of the wheels of government.[l]

[20] She is known by her extravagant generosity to the poor,
for she always reaches out her hands[m] to those in need.

[21] She is not afraid of tribulation,[n]

---

a 31:14 Or "supplies from far away." The implication is from another realm. She is bringing heavenly manna for those she feeds.

b 31:14 Or "like merchant ships bringing goods." Like a ship loaded with cargo, the bride of Christ brings heavenly treasures to others. The use of the term *merchant* points to Jesus Christ. He is described as a merchant in Matt. 13:45 in the parable of the costly pearl. The "pearl" is the church or the believer, which cost all that Jesus had (his blood) to purchase us.

c 31:15 She is interceding in the night, laboring in a night season to help others.

d 31:15 The Hebrew word translated "arise" can also mean "to rise up in power." We are told to "arise and shine, for our light has come." See Isa. 60:1, which uses the same Hebrew word for "arise." The bride of Christ will arise with anointing to feed and bless the people of God.

e 31:15 Or "female servants." The servants are a metaphor for other churches and ministries.

f 31:16 Or "a land, a country."

g 31:16 Or "By the fruit of her hands she plants a vineyard." (The Septuagint is "possession.") For the hands, see 31:13 footnote. This vineyard becomes a metaphor for the local church. We are the branches of the vine (Christ). See John 15. She is passionate about bringing forth fruit. She becomes a missionary to the nations, planting churches and bringing new life.

h 31:17 Or "She girds her loins with strength and makes her shoulders strong." This is a figure of speech for being anointed with power to do the works of Jesus. See John 14:12.

i 31:18 Or "good merchandise."

j 31:18 Her prayer life (lamp) overcomes her circumstances, even in a culture where darkness prevails.

k 31:19 As translated from the Septuagint. The Hebrew uses a term for "distaff" (a weaver's staff), which is taken from a root word for "prosperity." The poetic nuance of this phrase is that she uses her prosperity to bless the needy.

l 31:19 Or "Her hands grasp the spindle." The word translated as "spindle" can also mean "governmental circuits" or "wheels." There is a hint here of the wheels mentioned in Ezek. 1. The throne of God's government sits on flaming wheels. See Dan. 7:9.

m 31:20 Notice the mention of her hands. See footnote on 31:13.

n 31:21 Or "snow." This is a figure of speech for the fear of a cold winter season.

for all her household is covered in the dual garments[a]
of righteousness and grace.
[22] Her clothing is beautifully knit together—[b]
a purple gown of exquisite linen.
[23] Her husband is famous and admired by all,
sitting as the venerable judge of his people.[c]
[24] Even her works of righteousness[d]
she does[e] for the benefit of her enemies.[f]
[25] Bold power and glorious majesty[g] are wrapped around her
as she laughs with joy over the latter days.[h]
[26] Her teachings are filled with wisdom and kindness
as loving instruction pours from her lips.[i]
[27] She watches over the ways of her household[j]
and meets every need they have.
[28] Her sons and daughters arise[k] in one accord to extol her virtues,[l]
and her husband arises to speak of her in glowing terms.[m]
[29] "There are many valiant and noble ones,[n]
but you have ascended above them all!"[o]
[30] Charm can be misleading,

---

a 31:21 As translated from the Septuagint. The Hebrew is "Everyone is covered in scarlet [blood]." Grace has brought righteousness to those in her house (under her ministry).

b 31:22 This garment speaks of the ministries of the body of Christ, woven and knit together by the Holy Spirit. See Eph. 4:15–16 and Col. 2:2.

c 31:23 Or "sitting at the city gates among the elders of the land." Judgment was rendered at the gates of a city in that day. It was their courtroom. Our heavenly King is also the judge. So famous, so glorious, yet he is our Bridegroom.

d 31:24 Or "linen." See footnote for 31:13 regarding linen as a symbol for righteousness.

e 31:24 Or "sells them." The root word for "sell" can also mean "surrender."

f 31:24 Or "aprons or belts for the Canaanites." The Canaanites were the traditional enemies of the Hebrews.

g 31:25 Or "beauty, honor, and excellence."

h 31:25 The virtuous and victorious bride has no fear for the days to come. She contemplates eternity and her forever union with the Bridegroom.

i 31:26 The Septuagint is "She opens her mouth carefully and lawfully."

j 31:27 Or "She is a watchman over her house [family]."

k 31:28 The Hebrew word translated "arise" can also mean "to rise up with power." The Septuagint is "She raises her children so they will grow rich."

l 31:28 Or "Hooray, hooray for our mother!"

m 31:28 For more of how the heavenly Bridegroom loves his bride, read the Song of Songs.

n 31:29 Or "Many daughters have obtained wealth because of her." These valiant and noble ones (daughters) represent the church of previous generations who remained faithful in their pursuit of Jesus. But this final generation will be the bridal company of the lovers of God who do mighty exploits and miracles on the earth.

o 31:29 Or "You are first in his eyes." See Song 6:8–9.

and beauty is vain and so quickly fades,
but this virtuous woman lives in the wonder, awe,
and fear of the Lord.
She will be praised *throughout eternity*.

³¹ So go ahead and give her the credit that is due,
for she has become a radiant woman,
and all her loving works of righteousness deserve to be admired[a]
at the gateways of every city!

SONG OF SONGS

Introduction

AT A GLANCE

Author: King Solomon, king of Israel

Audience: Every passionate lover of God

Date: The reign of King Solomon, 970–931 BC

Type of Literature: Love poetry and wisdom literature

Major Themes: Christ's passion for his bride, divine relationship, the Christian life, and Christian devotion

Outline:

ABOUT SONG OF SONGS

The first book translated in the Passion Translation was the Song of Songs (also known as the Song of Solomon), my favorite book in the Bible. I have fallen in love with this sweetest song of all the ages. We see the Shulamite's breathtaking journey unveiled in this amazing allegory. It is the path every passionate lover will choose. But this divine parable penned by Solomon also describes the journey that every longing lover of Jesus will find as his or her very own.

By translating this portion of the Word of God, the Song of Songs, I have attempted to translate not only from a scholarly or linguistic perspective, but also from the passion of a heart on fire. Love will always find a language to express itself. Fiery love for Jesus pushes our thoughts out of hiding and puts them into words of adoration. This articulation, out of the deepest places of our hearts, moves God and inspires each of us to a greater devotion. Everyone deserves to hear and feel the passion of our Bridegroom for his radiant and soon-to-be-perfected bride.

The inspired Song of Songs is a work of art. It is a melody sung from the heart of Jesus Christ for his longing bride. It is full of symbols, subtle art forms, poetry, and nuances that the translator must convey in order to bring it forth adequately to the English reader. This is what I have attempted to do with this project.

Some of the cultural symbols that conveyed rich texture of meaning to the Hebrew speaker nearly three thousand years ago have become almost impossible to leave in their literal form, since the English speaker of today has little or no connection to those symbols. This requires that much of the hidden meanings locked into the Hebrew text be made explicit. That is why I have chosen to make this a dynamic equivalent translation—transferring the *meaning*, not just the *words*, into a form that many will find refreshing.

So be prepared to see yourself in this journey and hear the Lord's lyrics of love sung over you. Invest the time to read this through in one sitting. Then go back and read slowly and carefully, pondering each verse and praying through each love principle revealed in this translation. I think you may be shocked to read some of the things spoken over your life, considering them almost too good to be true.

May heaven's glorious Bridegroom, the beloved of your soul, come and manifest himself to you in a wonderful fashion as you read Song of Songs in the Passion Translation. My prayer is that you will be as thrilled with what you read as I have been in translating it.

PURPOSE

In reading this Shulamite's journey, the storyline's purpose is often missed or overlooked. I believe the Holy Spirit has hidden within the Song of Songs an amazing story—a story of how Jesus makes his bride beautiful and holy by casting out her fear with perfect love. This sent-from-heaven revelation is waiting to be received with all its intensity and power to unlock the deepest places of our hearts.

Most of the earliest church fathers—including Origen, Gregory of Nyssa, Augustine, and Jerome—viewed the Song of Songs as a clear representation of Christ and his bride, presented in deeply symbolic and allegorical teaching.

Along with many other early church fathers, they wrote commentaries to reveal the beautiful secrets given to us in Solomon's masterpiece.

Unfortunately for some, the Song of Songs has become merely a book expressing sexuality, with hidden meanings and symbols of sensuality. Many modern expositors teach from the Song of Songs the sexual relationship appropriate to a husband and wife. They find it difficult when others see the symbols and apply them to the spiritual journey every believer must take as we move further into the passionate heart of our heavenly Bridegroom. Their fear is that we "over-spiritualize" the Song of Songs. How hard that would be! How wonderfully spiritual and holy is this song of all songs!

AUTHOR AND AUDIENCE

The author of this love poem is made clear at the first stanza: "The most amazing song of all, by King Solomon." We can be thankful and grateful this wise, stately king gave us such a passionate, symbolic picture of the love of God—first for his people and then for Christ's church! His poetic insights deepen our understanding of the love of God in the same way they did for his people from generations past!

MAJOR THEMES

Interpreting Song of Songs. This divine song of romance is one of the most difficult books to interpret. Over the centuries there have been no fewer than six dominant ways people have understood Song of Songs, including: typical, dramatic, mythological-cultic, dream, literal, and allegorical.

This translation reveals each symbol that the reader encounters in this song as a form of "virtual reality," which, when properly interpreted, helps us in our pursuit of Jesus Christ. Truly, if this is the song of all songs, its theme goes beyond and reaches higher than merely literal human sexuality. It extends to our union with the living God.

Christ's Divine Love for His Bride. From the second verse in this poem of divine romance, the love of God shines and springs forth! It opens by testifying to the Spirit's kiss of God's divine word breathing upon us the revelation of this love, equipping us as his warriors and intoxicating us with his love.

Throughout this most amazing song, it speaks of God's saving love, keeping love, forgiving love, and embracing love. Even the allegory itself of the bride and Bridegroom-King speaks of the passionate pursuit of our loving God! Sitting with this poem of divine romance will transform your understanding of God's love like never before!

The dominant voice in this divine love poem is the Shulamite. This word (Shulamite) and the word for Solomon are taken from the same Hebrew root word—one masculine, the other feminine. We are one spirit with our King, united with him. He longs for his bride to be his love prisoner, in the prison cell of his eternal love! Through our union with Christ we enjoy a joint possession of all things. You have become the Shulamite, and you will ultimately dwell in holy union with Jesus Christ.

Divine Christian Romance. The poem embedded in this romantic book tells the story of our journey of divine romance as bride of the Bridegroom-King, Jesus Christ. It speaks of the journey every longing lover of Jesus will find as his or her very own. The bride sees her beloved as a shepherd, a representation of the relationship between you and your Beloved. The suffering love of Jesus will be over our hearts for the rest of our days—the revelation of our Beloved tied onto the cross like a bundle of myrrh, a picture of the suffering love of Christ dripping down from Calvary's tree for every lover of God.

The symbol of the bride (Christians) pursuing and being given to the Bridegroom-King (Jesus) also represents the *community* of brides, the church. For the beautiful bride overflowing with her Lover's life is to be given to others, even as Jesus was given to us by the Father. She has become a feast for the nations, wine to cheer the hearts of others. In this poem of divine romance the "city" is a picture of the local church, a place with government, order, and overseers. And the king's "vineyard" is a picture of the church, the called-out multitude of those who follow Jesus.

Passionate Christian Devotion. Throughout this love song of divine romance, various symbols are used to speak of our passionate, emotional devotion to our Bridegroom-King-Lover: *lilies* are symbols of our pure devotion in the "temple" of our inner being to Christ; *foxes* are the compromises hidden deep in our hearts that keep the fruit of passionate devotion to Christ from growing within us; *hair* is a symbol of our devotion to Christ; *pomegranates* are equated to human passion and emotions, for when opened they speak powerfully of our hearts of passion opened to our Lover.

SONG OF SONGS

Divine Romance

1 The most amazing song of all, by King Solomon.

The Shulamite [a]
[2] Let him [b] smother me with kisses—his Spirit-kiss divine. [c]
  So kind are your caresses, [d]
  I drink them in like the sweetest wine! [e]
[3] Your presence releases a fragrance so pleasing—
  over and over poured out.
  For your lovely name is "Flowing Oil." [f]
  No wonder the brides-to-be adore you. [g]
[4] Draw me into your heart.
  We will run away together into the king's cloud-filled chamber. [h]

---

a 1:2 The word for *Shulamite* and the word for *Solomon* are taken from the same Hebrew root word; one is masculine, the other feminine. The name Solomon occurs seven times in this book, which points us to the perfect King, Jesus Christ. We are one spirit with our King, united with him. You have become the Shulamite.

b 1:2 To enter the doorway of Jesus' heart we must begin by saying, "Let him." We only bring him a yielded heart and must "let him" do the rest. God's loving grace means that he will be enough for us. We can "let him" be everything to us. We don't begin by doing but by yielding.

c 1:2 This Spirit kiss is what made Adam, the man of clay, into a living expression of God. Dust and deity met when the Maker kissed his Spirit wind into Adam. The Word of God is the kiss from the mouth of our Beloved, breathing upon us the revelation of his love.

d 1:2 Or "your breasts" or "your loves." This speaks of his saving love, keeping love, forgiving love, and embracing love. The love of Jesus cannot be singular; it is so infinite it must be described in the plural.

e 1:2 There is a wordplay in the Hebrew, similar to a pun. The word for "kisses" and the word for "take a drink [wine]" is nearly the same. The implication, as seen by ancient expositors, is that God's lovers will be drunk with love, the intoxicating kisses of his mouth. The Hebrew word for "kiss" is *nashaq*, which can also mean "to equip" or "to arm (for battle)." We need his kisses to become equipped warriors for him.

f 1:3 The Hebrew contains a wordplay with the words "name" (*shem*) and "oil" (*shemen*).

g 1:3 Because of the order of the consonants, some Jewish sources translate this "The maidens love you unto death." See Goldin, Song, 116; J. Sason, "On Pope's Song," 191.

h 1:4 The Hebrew text literally means "the king's chamber inside of a chamber." This points us to the Holy of Holies inside the temple chamber.

The Chorus of Friends
We will remember your love, rejoicing and delighting in you, [a]
    celebrating your every kiss as better than wine.
    No wonder righteousness adores you!

The Shulamite
[5] Jerusalem maidens, in this twilight darkness [b]
    I know I am so unworthy—so in need.

The Shepherd-King
Yet you are so lovely!

The Shulamite
I feel as dark and dry as the desert tents
    of the wandering nomads. [c]

The Shepherd-King
Yet you are so lovely—
    like the fine linen tapestry hanging in the Holy Place.

The Shulamite to Her Friends
[6] Please don't stare in scorn
    because of my dark and sinful ways. [d]
    My angry brothers quarreled with me
    and appointed me guardian of their ministry vineyards,
    yet I've not tended my vineyard within.
[7] Won't you tell me, lover of my soul,
    where do you feed your flock?
    Where do you lead your beloved ones [e]
    to rest in the heat of the day?
    For I wish to be wrapped all around you

---

a   1:4 The Hebrew word for "love" (*'ahab*) is found seven times in the Song of Songs (1:3, 4, 7; 3:1, 2, 3, 4). The Hebrew root word for "rejoice" (*gyl*) is a homonym for "spinning in a circle or dance." The implication is that we dance for joy when we remember his love.

b   1:5 Or "black." The Hebrew root word used here for "black" or "dark" means "twilight darkness" or "morning gray."

c   1:5 Literally "dark as the tent curtains of Kedar." There is a wordplay in the Hebrew, as the word *Kedar* means "a dark one" or "a dark place." This was the name of one of the sons of Ishmael and represents our old Adam life. See Ps. 120:5.

d   1:6 Or "Many morning suns have darkened (stared) at me."

e   1:7 She sees her beloved as a shepherd. This is a metaphor of the role he takes in her eyes. We need not develop a literal storyline of a lover and a shepherd, but a representation of the relationship between you and your Beloved, which cannot be described by one symbol or role.

as I wander among the flocks of your shepherds.
It is you I long for, with no veil between us! [a]

The Shepherd-King

[8] Listen, my radiant one—
  if you ever lose sight of me,
  just follow in my footsteps where I lead my lovers.
  Come with your burdens and cares.
  Come to the place near the sanctuary of my shepherds. [b]
[9] My dearest one, [c]
  let me tell you how I see you—
  you are so thrilling to me.
  To gaze upon you is like looking
  at one of Pharaoh's finest horses—
  a strong, regal steed pulling his royal chariot. [d]
[10] Your tender cheeks are aglow—
  your earrings and gem-laden necklaces
  set them ablaze.
[11] We will enhance your beauty, [e]
  encircling you with our golden reins of love.
  You will be marked with our redeeming grace. [f]

The Shulamite

[12] As the king surrounded me at his table, [g]
  the sweet fragrance of my praise perfume [h]
  awakened the night.
[13] A sachet of myrrh is my lover,
  like a tied-up bundle of myrrh [i] resting over my heart.

---

a 1:7 The Hebrew uses the verb 'atah, which means "to wrap [cloak/veil]." The Aramaic and Latin Vulgate use the verb for "to wander." This translation has included both concepts.
b 1:8 Or "graze your goats by the shepherds' tents." This is a metaphor that speaks of her responsibilities and labors.
c 1:9 Or "darling." The Hebrew word r'yh is found ten times in the Bible and nine of them are in the Song of Songs. The Hebrew wordplay is seen in that "tend the flock" and "darling" are homonyms.
d 1:9 The finest horses in Solomon's stables were imported from Egypt. See 2 Chron. 1:14–17.
e 1:11 This is the Trinity ("we"), which will be involved in making every Shulamite holy and radiant.
f 1:11 Or "with studs of silver." The concept of silver in the Bible always points to redemption, the price paid to set us free. The cross is a "stud of silver" planted into Calvary's hill that opened the grace fountain for all world to drink from.
g 1:12 This points to our enjoyment of the Lord as we have communion at the Lord's table.
h 1:12 Or "spikenard." See Mark 14:1–11 and John 12:1–11.
i 1:13 This bundle of tied-up myrrh is an incredible picture of the cross. Myrrh, known as an

[14] He is like a bouquet of henna blossoms—
henna plucked near the vines at the fountain of the Lamb. [a]
I will hold him and never let him part.

The Shepherd-King
[15] Look at you, my dearest darling,
you are so lovely!
You are beauty itself to me. [b]
Your passionate eyes are like gentle doves. [c]

The Shulamite
[16] My beloved one, [d]
both handsome and winsome,
you are pleasing beyond words.
Our resting place [e] is anointed and flourishing,
like a green forest meadow bathed in light.
[17] Rafters of cedar branches are over our heads
and balconies of pleasant-smelling pines. [f]

2 I am truly his rose,
the very theme of his song. [g]
I'm overshadowed by his love,
growing in the valley!

The Shepherd-King
[2] Yes, you are my darling companion.

---

embalming spice, is always associated with suffering. The suffering love of Jesus will be over her heart for the rest of her days—the revelation of our Beloved tied onto the cross like a bundle of myrrh.

a 1:14 Or "at Engedi." *Engedi* means "fountain of the Lamb." The Hebrew word for "henna" is a homonym that can mean "atonement" or "redeeming grace."

b 1:15 The Hebrew word for "beautiful," *yāpāh*, is used five times to describe the Shulamite, and three times she is called *hayyāpāh bannāšîm* (the most beautiful of women). Eight times her beauty is extolled. Eight is the number for new creation life.

c 1:15 The Hebrew text literally means "Your eyes are doves." Some see this as a hypocorism, but the dove points us to the Holy Spirit. She is commended for seeing him with spiritual revelation as she perceives the glory of the cross with its "myrrh."

d 1:16 The Hebrew word *dôḏî*, usually translated "beloved," is taken from a root word that means "to boil." The implication is that the beloved causes her heart to boil over with passion.

e 1:16 Or "canopied bed" or "luxuriant couch."

f 1:17 Or "cypress." Cedars and cypress were the two most common woods used in the construction of Solomon's temple.

g 2:1 The Hebrew text says, "a rose of Sharon." The word *Sharon* can be translated "his song." She now sees herself as the one he sings over. The root word for "rose" (Hebrew *habab*) can mean "overshadowed."

You stand out from all the rest.
For though the curse of sin surrounds you, [a]
still you remain as pure as a lily, [b]
even more than all others.

The Shulamite

[3] My beloved is to me
the most fragrant apple tree—
he stands above the sons of men. [c]
Sitting under his grace-shadow,
I blossom in his shade,
enjoying the sweet taste of his pleasant, delicious fruit,
resting with delight where his glory never fades.
[4] Suddenly, he transported me into his house of wine—
he looked upon me with his unrelenting love divine. [d]
[5] Revive me with your raisin cakes. [e]
Refresh me again with your apples. [f]
Help me and hold me, for I am lovesick! [g]
I am longing for more—
yet how could I take more?
[6] His left hand [h] cradles my head
while his right hand holds me close. [i]
I am at rest in this love.

The Shepherd-King

[7] Promise me, brides-to-be,

---

a 2:2 This is a thorn bush, which speaks of the curse of sin. See Gen. 3:18; John 19:5; Gal. 3:13.
On the cross, Jesus wore a crown of thorns, for he took away the curse of sin.

b 2:2 The emblem of a lily was engraved on the upper part of the pillars of Solomon's temple.
Lilies are symbols of purity in the "temple" of our inner being.

c 2:3 Or "trees of the forest." Trees in the Bible are often metaphors for humanity.

d 2:4 Or "His (tribal) banner covering me was love." There are two Hebrew words for banner:
nes is the military banner, and the one used here is *degel*, the tribal banner, one for each of
the twelve tribes of Israel. The bride lives under the banner of the tribe of love.

e 2:5 Or "goblet of wine." King David gave raisin cakes to the entire nations of Israel in
celebration of the Ark of Glory, God's presence, coming into Jerusalem (2 Sam. 6:19). Additionally, the Hebrew word for "with raisin cakes," *ba'ashishot*, is a homonym that can also
mean "fires." The fires of passion and love are overwhelming.

f 2:5 Or "apricots." These are the sweet promises of grace that sustain us.

g 2:5 Or "wounded by love."

h 2:6 The Hebrew word for "left" is *smowl*, which can also mean "dark." The left hand of the
Lord speaks of the mysteries of his ways—the unseen activities of grace, which are so little
understood.

i 2:6 For more on the right hand and left hand, see Prov. 3:16.

by the gentle gazelles[a] and delicate deer,
that you'll not disturb my love until she is ready to arise.

The Shulamite

[8] Listen! I hear my lover's voice.
   I know it's him coming to me—
   leaping with joy over mountains,
   skipping in love over the hills *that separate us,*[b]
   to come to me.

[9] Let me describe him:
   he is graceful as a gazelle,
   swift as a wild stag.
   Now he comes closer,
   even to the places where I hide.[c]
   He gazes into my soul,
   peering through the portal
   as he blossoms within my heart.

[10] The one I love calls to me:

The Bridegroom-King

Arise, my dearest. Hurry, my darling.
   Come away with me!
   I have come as you have asked
   to draw you to my heart and lead you out.
   For now is the time, my beautiful one.

[11] The season has changed,
   the bondage of your barren winter has ended,
   and the season of hiding is over and gone.
   The rains have soaked the earth[d]
[12] and left it bright with blossoming flowers.
   The season for singing and pruning the vines has arrived.[e]
   I hear the cooing of doves in our land,[f]

---

a 2:7 In the poetic imagery of the Song of Songs, deer and gazelle are symbols of the joys of
   love. The Septuagint says, "By all the powers and strengths of the field."

b 2:8 Implied in the context of 2:17.

c 2:9 Or "There he stands behind our wall." Fear and religious duty will always have a wall
   to hide behind. The contrast is striking. He is free and leaping over mountains, but the
   Shulamite was enclosed and restricted behind a wall.

d 2:11 The rains speak of the outpouring of the Holy Spirit. She is refreshed and prepared to
   move out with him.

e 2:12 Or "The season of singing has arrived." The Hebrew word for "pruning" is a homonym
   that can also mean "singing."

f 2:12 This is the turtledove, which is heard only at the time of harvest. The turtledove is also

filling the air with songs to awaken you
and guide you forth.
[13] Can you not discern this new day of destiny
breaking forth around you?
The early signs of my purposes and plans
are bursting forth. [a]
The budding vines of new life
are now blooming everywhere.
The fragrance of their flowers whispers,
"There is change in the air."
Arise, my love, my beautiful companion,
and run with me to the higher place.
For now is the time to arise and come away with me.
[14] For you are my dove, hidden in the split-open rock. [b]
It was I who took you and hid you up high
in the secret stairway of the sky.
Let me see your radiant face and hear your sweet voice. [c]
How beautiful your eyes of worship
and lovely your voice in prayer.
[15] You must catch the troubling foxes,
those sly little foxes that hinder our relationship. [d]
For they raid our budding vineyard of love
to ruin what I've planted within you.
Will you catch them and remove them for me?
We will do it together.

The Shulamite
[16] I know my lover is mine and I have everything in you,
for we delight ourselves in each other. [e]
[17] But until the day springs to life

---

an acceptable sacrifice of cleansing in place of a lamb. The words "our land" show the joint
possession of all things that we enjoy through our union with Christ.

a 2:13 This text is literally translated "The fig tree has sweetened and puts forth its early figs."
In the language of allegory, the fig tree is a picture of destiny and purpose. The sign of a fig
tree blooming is the sign of an early spring, a new season.

b 2:14 This speaks of the wounded side of Jesus, our Rock where we hide and rest. When
Moses asked God to see his glory, God hid Moses in the cleft of the rock. See Ex. 33:22.

c 2:14 The Hebrew text literally means "Your voice is delicious."

d 2:15 These "foxes" are the compromises that are hidden deep in our hearts. These are areas
of our lives where we have not yet allowed the victory of Christ to shine into. The foxes keep
the fruit of his Spirit from growing within us.

e 2:16 The Hebrew wording includes the phrase "He browses among the lilies." The Hebrew
word for "browse" can also mean "to take delight in" or "to be as a special friend." The same
Hebrew word, ra'ah, is used in Ps. 23:1, "The Lord is my Shepherd [Best Friend]."

and the shifting shadows of fear disappear,
turn around, my lover, and ascend
to the holy mountains of separation without me. [a]
Until the new day fully dawns,
run on ahead like the graceful gazelle
and skip like the young stag
over the mountains of separation.
Go on ahead to the mountain of spices—
I'll *come away another time.*

3 Night after night I'm tossing and turning on my bed of travail.
Why did I let him go from me?
How my heart now aches for him,
but he is nowhere to be found!
[2] So I must rise in search of him,
looking throughout the city, [b]
seeking until I find him.
Even if I have to roam through every street,
nothing will keep me from my search.
Where is he—my soul's true love?
He is nowhere to be found.
[3] Then I encountered the overseers as they encircled the city.
So I asked them, "Have you found him—
my heart's true love?"
[4] Just as I moved past them, I encountered him.
I found the one I adore!
I caught him and fastened myself to him,
refusing to be feeble in my heart again.
Now I'll bring him back to the temple within
where I was given new birth—
into my innermost parts, the place of my conceiving.

The Bridegroom-King
[5] Promise me, O Jerusalem maidens,
by the gentle gazelles and delicate deer,
that you'll not disturb my love until she is ready to arise.

---

a 2:17 This text literally means "mountains of Bether," the Hebrew word for "separation" or "gap." This could be the realm of holiness, being separated to God. Some scholars say Bether was a spiritual representation of a mountain of fragrant spices; i.e., the realm of holiness.

b 3:2 The city is a picture of the local church, a place with government, order, and overseers. She goes from church to church, looking for the one she loves.

The Voice of the Lord

⁶ Who is this one ascending from the wilderness
   in the pillar of the glory cloud?
   He is fragrant with the anointing oils
   of myrrh and frankincense—ᵃ
   more fragrant than all the spices of the merchant.
⁷ Look! It is the king's marriage carriage.
   The love seat surrounded by sixty champions,
      the mightiest of Israel's host,
   are like pillars of protection.
⁸ They are angelic warriors standing ready with swords
   to defend the king and his fiancée
   from every terror of the night.
⁹ The king made this mercy seat for himself
   out of the finest wood that will not decay.
¹⁰ Pillars of smoke, like silver mist—
a canopy of golden glory dwells above it.
   The place where they sit together
   is sprinkled with crimson.
   Love and mercy cover this carriage,
   blanketing his tabernacle throne.
   The king himself has made it
   for those who will become his bride.
¹¹ Rise up, Zion maidens, brides-to-be!
   Come and feast your eyes on this king
   as he passes in procession on his way to his wedding.
   This is the day filled with overwhelming joy—
   the day of his great gladness.

The Bridegroom-King

4 Listen, my dearest darling,
   you are so beautiful—you are beauty itself to me!
   Your eyes glisten with love,
   like gentle doves behind your veil.
   What devotion I see each time I gaze upon you.
   You are like a sacrifice ready to be offered.ᵇ

---

a 3:6 These spices are found in the Bible as ingredients of the sacred anointing oil. Myrrh points to the suffering and death of Christ, while frankincense reveals the fragrance of his perfect life and ministry.

b 4:1 The Hebrew text literally means "Your hair is like a flock of goats streaming down Mount Gilead." There is great symbolism in this verse. Hair is a symbol of our devotion to Christ. Mount Gilead ("hill of testimony") is where the sacrificial animals were kept in preparation for temple sacrifices. So a goat coming down Mount Gilead was a sacrifice ready to be offered.

[2] When I look at you,
  I see how you have taken my fruit and tasted my word.
  Your life has become clean and pure,
  like a lamb washed and newly shorn.
  You now show grace and balance with truth on display.
[3] Your lips are as lovely as Rahab's scarlet ribbon, [a]
  speaking mercy, speaking grace.
  The words of your mouth are as refreshing as an oasis.
  What pleasure you bring to me!
  I see your blushing cheeks
  opened like the halves of a pomegranate, [b]
  showing through your veil of tender meekness.
[4] When I look at you,
  I see your inner strength, so stately and strong.
  You are as secure as David's fortress.
  Your virtues and grace cause a thousand famous soldiers
  to surrender to your beauty.
[5] Your pure faith and love rest over your heart
  as you nurture those who are yet infants.

The Shulamite
[6] I've made up my mind.
  Until the darkness disappears and the dawn has fully come,
  in spite of shadows and fears,
  I will go to the mountaintop with you—
  the mountain of suffering love [c]
  and the hill of burning incense.
  Yes, I will be your bride. [d]

---

a 4:3 The "scarlet ribbon" in the text is a comparison to the ribbon Rahab placed at her dwelling to show the place where mercy would spare her life. The color scarlet points us to the blood of mercy, Christ's sacrifice that has spared us. See Josh. 2.

b 4:3 Pomegranates were engraved on the tops of the pillars of Solomon's temple and were also sewn into the hem of the robes of the high priest. They speak of our open hearts of love, filled with passion for him. The Hebrew word for "pomegranate" is *ramam*, a homonym that means "to rise up." Pomegranates were also placed on the hem of the robe of the high priest, interspersed with golden bells.

c 4:6 Literally "the mountain of myrrh"—the emblem of suffering love. To become the bride, she must experience Calvary, as did her Lord. We must be his co-crucified partner who will embrace the fellowship of his sufferings. See Gal. 2:20 and Phil. 3:10.

d 4:6 Implied in the context, affirmed by the bridegroom in v. 8. This is the first mention of the Shulamite as the bride.

The Bridegroom-King

[7] Every part of you is so beautiful, my darling.
Perfect is your beauty, without flaw within.
[8] Now you are ready, my bride,
to come with me as we climb the highest peaks together.
Come with me through the archway of trust. [a]
We will look down [b]
from the crest of the glistening mounts
and from the summit of our sublime sanctuary.
Together we will wage war
in the lion's den and the leopard's lair
as they watch nightly for their prey.
[9] For you reach into my heart.
With one flash of your eyes I am undone by your love,
my beloved, my equal, my bride.
You leave me breathless—
I am overcome
by merely a glance from your worshiping eyes,
for you have stolen my heart. [c]
I am held hostage by your love
and by the graces of righteousness shining upon you. [d]
[10] How satisfying to me, my equal, my bride.
Your love is my finest wine—intoxicating and thrilling.
And your sweet, perfumed praises—so exotic, so pleasing.
[11] Your loving words are like the honeycomb to me;
your tongue releases milk and honey,

---

a 4:8 Translated from the Septuagint. The Hebrew is "the crest of Amana." Amana comes from a Hebrew root word from which we get the English word *amen.* This is also one of the Hebrew words for "faith." The crest of Amana is the realm where all God's promises are kept and realized. Amana can also be translated "a place of settled security." *Dictionary of Scripture Proper Names* by J. B. Jackson.

b 4:8 The word for "look" is "survey, inspect, look all around, observe." The bride of Christ is seated on high with Jesus and is encouraged to survey all the blessings heaven contains in our co-exaltation with Christ.

c 4:9 Or "You have ravished my heart." This is the Hebrew word *libabthini,* which is taken from a Semitic root word that means "to tear bark off of a tree." He is saying that your loving eyes of worship have uncovered his heart and laid it bare, making him vulnerable to you. What a description of what happens to Jesus when he looks into your eyes. Your worship brings to him such an ecstasy and delight that it becomes hard to even imagine. Yet God has placed inside of you the ability to ravish the heart of your King—not someday in heaven, but now, even when you feel incomplete and weak.

d 4:9 Or "the jewels of your neck [necklace]." These divine jewels are the beautifying graces that the Holy Spirit gives to us. They are the graces of righteousness given to the redeemed bride of Christ.

for I find the Promised Land flowing within you. [a]

The fragrance of your worshiping love
surrounds you with scented robes of white. [b]

[12] My darling bride, my private paradise,
fastened to my heart.

A secret spring are you that no one else can have—
my bubbling fountain hidden from public view.

What a perfect partner to me now that I have you.

[13–14] Your inward life is now sprouting, bringing forth fruit.

What a beautiful paradise unfolds within you. [c]

When I'm near you, I smell aromas of the finest spice,
for many clusters of my exquisite fruit
now grow within your inner garden.

Here are the nine:

pomegranates of passion, [d]

henna from heaven, [e]

spikenard so sweet, [f]

saffron shining, [g]

fragrant calamus from the cross, [h]

sacred cinnamon, [i]

branches of scented woods, [j]

myrrh, like tears from a tree, [k]

and aloe as eagles ascending. [l]

---

a   4:11 Both the Promised Land and your heart flow with milk and honey. You have become the Promised Land of Jesus Christ.

b   4:11 Or "like the scent of Lebanon."

c   4:13–14 Or "Your shoots are a paradise of pomegranates."

d   4:13–14 "Pomegranate" is taken from a word that means "exalted." The temple pillars were adorned with pomegranates.

e   4:13–14 "Henna" comes from a root word for "ransom price" or "redemption." The fruit of mercy is seen in his maturing bride.

f   4:13–14 The Hebrew root word for "spikenard" means "light." She is walking in the light as he is the Light.

g   4:13–14 Saffron is the crocus, the lover's perfume, costly and fragrant.

h   4:13–14 Calamus is taken from a marsh plant known as "sweet flag," which produces fragrant oil. The Hebrew word for this spice means "purchased" or "redeemed."

i   4:13–14 Cinnamon emits a fragrance that is representative of an odor of holiness to the Lord. It was used in the sacred anointing oil of the priests and the tabernacle.

j   4:13–14 This is the incense that would be burned on the golden altar in the Holy Place.

k   4:13–14 Known as "tears from a tree," myrrh was a resin spice formed by cutting a tree. It is a picture of the suffering love of Christ dripping down from Calvary's tree.

l   4:13–14 Aloe is considered by many as a healing balm. The presence of the Lord within her is released as a healing balm to those she touches. Jesus' robes smelled of aloe (Ps. 45:8). One of the names used by some for aloe is "eagle wood." Like eagles, we fly above our wounds, free from the past as we walk in intimacy with him.

¹⁵ Your life flows into mine, pure as a garden spring.
   A well of living water springs up from within you,
   like a mountain brook flowing into my heart! ᵃ

The Shulamite Bride

⁴:¹⁶⁻⁵:¹ Then may your awakening breath
   blow upon my life until I am fully yours.
   Breathe upon me with your Spirit wind.
   Stir up the sweet spice of your life within me.
   Spare nothing as you make me your fruitful garden.
   Hold nothing back until I release your fragrance.
   Come walk with me as you walked
   with Adam in your paradise garden. ᵇ
   Come taste the fruits of your life in me.

The Bridegroom-King

I have come to you, my darling bride,
   for you are my paradise garden!

The Shulamite Bride

Come walk with me until I am fully yours.
   Come taste the fruits of your life in me.

The Bridegroom-King

5 I have gathered from your heart,
  my equal, my bride,
   I have gathered from my garden
   all my sacred spices—even my myrrh.
   I have tasted and enjoyed my wine within you.
   I have tasted with pleasure my pure milk, my honeycomb,
   which you yield to me.
   I delight in gathering my sacred spice,
   all the fruits of my life I have
   gathered from within you, my paradise garden.
   Come, all my friends—
   feast upon my bride, all you revelers of my palace.
   Feast on her, my lovers!
   Drink and drink, and drink again,

---

a 4:15 Or "like the flowing streams of Lebanon."

b 4:16–5:1 The scene of a garden and the breath of God point us back to Eden. Now this paradise is found in his bride. This is the reason the reference of Adam is given: to help the reader connect with the mystery of this scene. See also Jer. 31:12 and John 15:1–2.

until you can take no more.
Drink the wine of her love.
Take all you desire, you priests.
My life within her will become your feast. [a]

The Shulamite Bride

[2] After this I let my devotion slumber,
but my heart for him stayed awake.
I had a dream.
I dreamed of my beloved—
he was coming to me in the darkness of night.
The melody of the man I love awakened me.
I heard his knock at my heart's door
as he pleaded with me:

The Bridegroom-King

Arise, my love.
Open your heart, my darling, deeper still to me.
Will you receive me this dark night?
There is no one else but you, my friend, my equal.
I need you this night to arise and come be with me.
You are my pure, loyal dove, a perfect partner for me.
My flawless one, will you arise?
For my heaviness and tears are more than I can bear.
I have spent myself for you throughout the dark night. [b]

The Sleeping Bride

[3] I have already laid aside my own garments for you.
How could I take them up again
since I've yielded my righteousness to yours? [c]
You have cleansed my life and taken me so far.
Isn't that enough?

---

a 4:16–5:1 The beautiful bride overflowing with his life is to be given to others, even as Jesus
was given to us by the Father. She has become a feast for the nations, wine to cheer the
hearts of others.

b 5:2 The Hebrew text literally means "My head is filled with dew and my hair with the drops of
the night." This is clearly a picture of Jesus as the Gethsemane Man, the one who prayed all night
for us (John 17). This translation takes the liberty of taking the implicit and making it explicit in
order to express the dynamic equivalent and aid the reader in understanding the scene.

c 5:3 Garments in the Bible are frequently used as a picture of righteousness. Filthy garments
are a symbol of unrighteousness or self-righteousness. Clean white garments are a picture
of the righteousness of Christ. Laying aside her garments is a symbolic picture of what
happens when we come to know Jesus as Savior—we lay aside our self-righteousness and
take up his garments of true righteousness.

⁴ My beloved reached into me to unlock my heart.
　The core of my very being trembled at his touch.
　How my soul melted when he spoke to me!
⁵ My spirit arose to open for more of his touch.
　As I surrendered to him, I began to sense his fragrance—
　the fragrance of his suffering love!
　It was the sense of myrrh flowing all through me!
⁶ I opened my soul to my beloved, but suddenly he was gone!
　And my heart was torn out in longing for him.
　I sought his presence, his fragrance,
　but could not find him anywhere.
　I called out for him, yet he did not answer me.
　I will arise and search for him until I find him.
⁷ As I walked throughout the city in search of him,
　the overseers stopped me as they made their rounds.
　They beat me and bruised me until I could take no more.
　They wounded me deeply
　and removed their covering from me.
⁸ Nevertheless, make me this promise, you brides-to-be:
　if you find my beloved one,
　please tell him I endured all travails for him.
　I've been pierced through by love, ^a
　and I will not be turned aside!

Jerusalem Maidens, Brides-to-Be
⁹ *What love is this?*
　How could you continue to care so deeply for him?
　Isn't there another who could steal away your heart?
　We see now your beauty, more beautiful than all the others.
　What makes your beloved better than any other?
　What is it about him
　that makes you ask us to promise you this?

The Shulamite Bride
¹⁰ He alone is my beloved.
　He shines in dazzling splendor yet is still so approachable—
　without equal as he stands above all others,
　outstanding among ten thousand! ^b
¹¹ The way he leads me is divine.
　His leadership—so pure and dignified

---

a 5:8 As translated from the Septuagint.
b 5:10 Or "waving his banner to myriads." Jesus stands above all others.

as he wears his crown of gold.
Upon this crown are letters of black written
on a background of glory. [a]

[12] He sees everything with pure understanding.
How beautiful his insights—without distortion.
His eyes rest upon the fullness of the river of revelation,
flowing so clean and pure.

[13] Looking at his gentle face I see such fullness of emotion.
Like a lovely garden where fragrant spices grow— [b]
what a man!
No one speaks words so anointed as this one— [c]
words that both pierce and heal,
words like lilies dripping with myrrh.

[14] See how his hands hold unlimited power!
But he never uses it in anger,
for he is always holy, displaying his glory.
His innermost place is a work of art—
so beautiful and bright.
How magnificent and noble is this one—
covered in majesty!

[15] He's steadfast in all he does.
His ways are the ways of righteousness,
based on truth and holiness.
None can rival him,
but all will be amazed by him. [d]

[16] Most sweet are his kisses, even his whispers of love.
He is delightful in every way
and perfect from every viewpoint.
If you ask me why I love him so, O brides-to-be,
it's because there is none like him to me.
Everything about him fills me with holy desire!
And now he is my beloved—my friend forever.

---

a 5:11 Many Jewish interpreters have seen the phrase "His locks are wavy (like a palm branch) and black as a raven" as pointing us to the letters of the law written in heaven. Jewish rabbis teach that the precepts of the Word of God (Torah) are written in the heavenly realm, with black letters on top of white flames of glory fire. (Hebrew letters can appear as locks of hair.)
b 5:13 The Hebrew text is literally "like a tower of fragrance." These beds of spices would picture a garden of emotion and sweetness coming forth from her beloved.
c 5: 13 See Ps. 45:2, a psalm with an inscription stating it was written to the "tune of lilies."
d 5:15 Or "He looks like Lebanon, choice as its cedars." The Hebrew word for "choice" (bahur) is a homonym that also means "young man."

Brides-to-Be

6 O rarest of beauty,
where then has your lover gone?
We long to see him too.
Where may we find him?
We will follow you as you seek after him.

The Shulamite Bride

² My lover has gone down
into his garden of delight,
the place where his spices grow,
to feast with those pure in heart.
I know we shall find him there.
³ He is within me—I am his garden of delight.
I have him fully and now he fully has me!

The Bridegroom-King

⁴ O my beloved, you are lovely.
When I see you in your beauty,
I see a radiant city where we will dwell as one. *ᵃ*
More pleasing than any pleasure,
more delightful than any delight,
you have ravished my heart,
stealing away my strength to resist you.
Even hosts of angels stand in awe of you. *ᵇ*
⁵ Turn your eyes from me; I can't take it anymore!
I can't resist the passion of these eyes that I adore.
Overpowered by a glance, my ravished heart—undone.
Held captive by your love, I am truly overcome! *ᶜ*
For your undying devotion to me
is the most yielded sacrifice. *ᵈ*

ᵃ 6:4 The text includes a reference to Jerusalem. For the Jew, it is the city where God and man lived together. For the believer, it points to the New Jerusalem, where God and man dwell in holy union.

ᵇ 6:4 This is how various Hebrew scholars have interpreted the phrase: "awe inspiring, as an army with banners."

ᶜ 6:5 The Hebrew word for "overcome" is *Rahab*. Like the harlot who was chosen, favored, saved from Jericho's destruction, and included in the genealogy of Jesus, so you have "overcome" his heart. No one would have thought Rahab would be so honored, and many have said that about you. You have overcome many things, but to overcome him is love's delight.

ᵈ 6:5 Literally "Your hair is like a wave of goats streaming down Mount Gilead." We see hair as a picture of our devotion to Christ. See also Song 4:1.

⁶ The shining of your spirit *a*
   shows how you have taken my truth
   to become balanced and complete.
⁷ Your beautiful blushing cheeks
   reveal how real your passion is for me,
   even hidden behind your veil of humility.
⁸ I could have chosen any from among the vast multitude
   of royal ones who follow me. *b*
⁹ But one is my beloved dove—unrivaled in beauty,
   without equal, beyond compare,
   the perfect one, the favorite one.
   Others see your beauty and sing of your joy.
   Brides and queens chant your praise:
   "How blessed is she!"
¹⁰ Look at you now—
   arising as the dayspring of the dawn,
   fair as the shining moon.
   Bright and brilliant as the sun in all its strength.
   Astonishing to behold as a majestic army
   waving banners of victory.

The Shulamite Bride
¹¹ I decided to go down to the valley streams
   where the orchards of the king grow and mature.
   I longed to know if hearts were opening.
   Are the budding vines blooming with new growth?
   Has their springtime of passionate love arrived?
¹² Then suddenly my longings transported me.
   My divine desire brought me next to my beloved prince,
   sitting with him in his royal chariot.
   We were lifted up together! *c*

Zion Maidens, Brides-to-Be
¹³ *Come back! Return to us, O maiden of his majesty.*
   Dance for us as we gaze upon your beauty.

---

a 6:6 The word used in most translations is *teeth*, which is taken from a Hebrew root word
   that some believe means "white" or "shining." With our teeth we chew the Word of God
   and process its truths.
b 6:8 The Hebrew text literally means "sixty queens, eighty brides, and endless numbers of
   women."
c 6:12 Considered to be the most difficult verse to translate in the Song of Songs, the meaning
   of the Hebrew is uncertain.

The Shulamite Bride
Why would you seek a mere Shulamite like me?
    Why would you want to see my dance of love?

The Bridegroom-King
Because you dance so gracefully,
    as though you danced with angels! [a]

7 How beautiful on the mountains
    are the sandaled feet of this one bringing such good news.
    You are truly royalty!
    The way you walk so gracefully in my ways
    displays such dignity.
    You are truly the poetry of God—his very handiwork.
2-3 Out of your innermost being
    is flowing the fullness of my Spirit—
    never failing to satisfy.
    Within your womb there is a birthing of harvest wheat;
    they are the sons and daughters
    nurtured by the purity you impart.
    How gracious you have become!
4 Your life stands tall as a tower, like a shining light on a hill.
    Your revelation eyes are pure, like pools of refreshing— [b]
    sparkling light for a multitude.
    Such discernment surrounds you,
    protecting you from the enemy's advance.
5 Redeeming love crowns you as royalty.
    Your thoughts are full of life, wisdom, and virtue.
    Even a king is held captive by your beauty.
6 How delicious is your fair beauty;
    it cannot be described
    as I count the delights you bring to me.
    Love has become the greatest.
7 You stand in victory above the rest,
    stately and secure as you share with me
    your vineyard of love.
8 Now I decree, I will ascend and arise.
    I will take hold of you with my power,

---

a 6:13 This is literally "the dance of Mahanaim" or "the dance of two armies." When Jacob
    (Israel) returned to the Promised Land, he entered at Mahanaim, the place where two
    camps of angels gathered. See Gen. 32:1–2.
b 7:4 Or "the pools of Hesbon," which means "fertile thoughts."

possessing every part of my fruitful bride.
Your love I will drink as wine,
and your words will be mine.
[9] For your kisses of love are exhilarating,
more than any delight I've known before.
Your kisses of love awaken even the lips of sleeping ones.

The Shulamite Bride

[10] Now I know that I am filled with my beloved
and all his desires are fulfilled in me.
[11] Come away, my lover.
Come with me to the faraway fields.
We will run away together to the forgotten places
and show them redeeming love.
[12] Let us arise and run to the vineyards of your people[a]
and see if the budding vines of love are now in full bloom.
We will discover if their passion is awakened.[b]
There I will display my love for you.
[13] The love apples are in bloom,
sending forth their fragrance of spring.
The rarest of fruits are found at our doors—
the new as well as the old.
I have stored them for you, my lover-friend!

8 If only I could show everyone
this passionate desire I have for you.
If only I could express it fully,
no matter who was watching me,
without shame or embarrassment.
[2] I long to bring you to my innermost chamber—
this holy sanctuary you have formed within me.
O that I might carry you within me.
I would give you the spiced wine of my love,
this full cup of bliss that we share.
We would drink our fill until . . .
[3] His left hand cradles my head
while his right hand holds me close.
We are at rest in this love.

---

a 7:12 Or "villages." The Hebrew word *kefarim* has a homonym that means "atonement" and another that means "henna." Combined, the three words are "the henna villages of atonement."

b 7:12 Pomegranates are equated to human passion and emotions. When opened, they are a blushing fruit and speak powerfully of our hearts of passion opened to our Lover.

⁴Promise me, brides-to-be,
  by the gentle gazelles and delicate deer,
  that you'll not disturb my love until he is ready to arise.

The Bridegroom-King
⁵Who is this one? Look at her now!
  She arises out of her desert, clinging to her beloved.
  When I awakened you under the apple tree,
  as you were feasting upon me,
  I awakened your innermost being with the travail of birth
  as you longed for more of me.
⁶Fasten me upon your heart as a seal of fire forevermore.
  This living, consuming flame
  will seal you as my prisoner of love. ᵃ
  My passion ᵇ is stronger
  than the chains of death and the grave,
  all consuming as the very flashes of fire
  from the burning heart of God. ᶜ
  Place this fierce, unrelenting fire over your entire being.
⁷Rivers of pain and persecution
  will never extinguish this flame.
  Endless floods will be unable
  to quench this raging fire that burns within you.
  Everything will be consumed.
  It will stop at nothing
  as you yield everything to this furious fire
  until it won't even seem to you like a sacrifice anymore.

The Shulamite Bride
⁸⁻¹⁰My brothers said to me when I was young,
  "Our sister is so immature.
  What will we do to guard her for her wedding day?"

The Bridegroom-King
We will build a tower of redemption to protect her.

---

a 8:6 The ancient Hebrew word for "seal" can also be translated "prison cell." He longs for his bride to be his love prisoner, in the prison cell of his eternal love.
b 8:6 Or "jealousy."
c 8:6 The phrase in Hebrew is "a most vehement flame" and is actually two Hebrew words. The first is "a mighty flash of fire," and the second is "Yah," which is the sacred name of God himself. The Hebrew *shalhebet-yah* could be translated "The Mighty Flame of the Lord Most Passionate!"

Since she is vulnerable,
we will enclose her with a wall of cedar boards.

The Shulamite Bride
But now I have grown and become a bride,
and my love for him has made me
a tower of passion and contentment for my beloved.
I am now a firm wall of protection for others,
guarding them from harm.
This is how he sees me—I am the one who brings him bliss,
finding favor in his eyes.

[11] My bridegroom-king has a vineyard of love
made from a multitude of followers. [a]
His caretakers of this vineyard
have given my beloved their best.

[12] But as for my own vineyard of love,
I give it all to you forever.
And I will give double honor
to those who serve my beloved
and have watched over my soul.

[13] My beloved, one with me in my garden,
how marvelous that my friends, the brides-to-be,
now hear your voice and song.
Let me now hear it again.

The Bridegroom and the Bride in Divine Duet
[14] Arise, my darling!
Come quickly, my beloved.
Come and be the graceful gazelle with me.
Come be like a dancing deer with me.
We will dance in the high place of the sky,
yes, on the mountains of fragrant spice.
Forever we shall be united as one!

---

a 8:11 The Hebrew text literally means "Solomon had a vineyard at Baal-Hamon." The king's
vineyard is a picture of the church, the called-out multitude of those who follow Jesus. Baal-
Hamon can be translated "lord of a multitude," "lord of an uproar," or "lord of wealth."

THE
NEW TESTAMENT

The
New Testament

MATTHEW

Introduction

AT A GLANCE

Author: Matthew, the former Jewish tax collector and disciple of Jesus
Audience: Originally, the Jewish Christian church and the Jewish people
Date: AD 55–80
Type of Literature: Ancient historical biography
Major Themes: Gospel-telling, Old Testament fulfillment, heaven's kingdom realm, kingdom-realm living
Outline:
    Jesus' Birth and Ministry Preparation — 1:1–4:11
    Jesus Teaches His Kingdom Realm — 4:12–7:29
    Jesus Demonstrates His Kingdom Realm — 8:1–11:1
    Jesus Is Opposed — 11:2–13:53
    Jesus Disciples His Disciples — 13:54–18:35
    Jesus Marches to the Cross — 19:1–25:46
    Jesus Dies, Rises, and Sends — 26:1–28:20

ABOUT MATTHEW

Four centuries of silence. Where was the promised Messiah? The Jewish people were waiting for the word of the prophets to come true, for they had prophesied that he would come. Then suddenly, the angel Gabriel made an appearance to a teenage girl to announce his birth. Shepherds saw a brilliant angelic light show on the hillside.

    Wise men went out in search of him.
    The light of the star shone over his manger.
    Insecure Herod wanted to kill him.
    Satan cruelly tested him.
    The prophet John presented him to Israel.
    God anointed him with the power of the Holy Spirit.

    Then one day the King came into the synagogue and announced: "I'm here! I've come to set you free and to wash away sins, and liberate those who love and follow me."

We can thank God for Matthew, for in his Gospel he presents our eternal King. Matthew means "gift of Yahweh," and he lives up to his name. Thank you, Matthew, for the gift of your life and for what you have left for us in your Gospel!

PURPOSE

Matthew is a natural bridge between the Old Testament and the New because it has the most Jewish character. From the first verse to the last, Matthew establishes Jesus as a direct descendant of King David, preserving and fulfilling his royal line as the rightful heir as well as a descendant of Abraham, the father of Israel.

Furthermore, Matthew portrays Jesus as the new and greater Moses, who not only upholds the Jewish Torah but intensifies it—not in a legalistic way, but in a spiritual way, because following his teachings is the way into his heavenly kingdom realm.

It would be a mistake, however, to say there is only one purpose for this book. While one primary purpose is to communicate the Jesus story to the Jewish people, Matthew also means to communicate Jesus' story to us. One particular aspect of the Jesus story that Matthew wants to share is that Jesus is King of a heavenly kingdom realm. Mark and Luke also speak of God's kingdom realm, but Matthew focuses on how people behave as citizens of that realm, with Jesus as their loving King.

AUTHOR AND AUDIENCE

It is believed that Matthew may have been the first apostle to write a gospel, and he possibly wrote it in Hebrew (Aramaic). Though some maintain that Matthew wrote his Gospel after the destruction of the temple in AD 70, it's possible he wrote it anywhere from AD 55 to the mid-60s. He was a wealthy tax collector who profited greatly from his duty of representing Rome. And then one day, the Man from Galilee stood in front of him and said, "Come, follow me."

There continues to be debate over the original language of Matthew's account. In AD 170 Eusebius quoted Irenaeus as saying, "Matthew published his gospel among the Hebrews in their own language, while Peter and Paul in Rome were preaching and founding the church" (Eusebius, *Historia Ecclesiastica* III. 24.5–6 and V. 8, 2.) This, along with numerous other quotations from church fathers (Origen, Jerome, Augustine) would mean that the original manuscript of Matthew's Gospel was written in Hebrew. Regardless, it is without dispute that Matthew was a Jewish man who presents a Jewish King who now sits on the throne of glory for all people.

Perhaps an unbiased look at the Hebrew and Aramaic manuscripts would yield further nuances of our Jewish heritage as believers in *Yeshua*

(Jesus) and would strengthen our understanding of the inspired Scriptures. You will find ample footnotes throughout this translation to assist you in your study.

MAJOR THEMES

Gospel-Telling. The word *gospel* doesn't simply mean "good news." It is derived from the Greek verb *euangelizomai*, which means "to preach the good news." In other words, Matthew is writing to tell us heaven's truths embedded in the earthly events of the Man Jesus. Matthew isn't giving us dry theology, but sharing stories and teachings designed in such a way as to unfold the majestic, magisterial person of Jesus, who embodies all of our theologies!

Old Testament. As the first book of the New Testament, Matthew connects the past with the present and with the future. He quotes sixty times from the Old Testament, showing us that the New was enfolded in the Old, while the New Testament is the Old Testament unfolded and explained. The Old Testament is more central in Matthew than in any other Gospel, both in frequency and in emphasis. If the Jewish story is always pointing forward, Matthew's Gospel is its final act. It brings resolution to the Old Testament by presenting King Jesus and his kingdom realm and community as fulfilling their prophetic expectations.

Parables. There are unique components to Matthew's Gospel. For example, he records extensively the allegorical teachings of Jesus known as parables. Twelve are detailed by Matthew, and nine of them are unique to this account. He gives us two miracles of Jesus that are found nowhere else: the healing of two blind men and the miracle coin found in the fish's mouth. It is through these simple stories that the nature of both our King and his kingdom really come to life!

Heavenly Kingdom Realm. Matthew brings us the realm of the heavenly kingdom and sets its virtue and reality before us. The phrase "kingdom realm" is used nearly forty times as Jesus offers it to you and me. And Jesus is described as the King fourteen times. This is the Gospel of the King and his kingdom, but a different kingdom than even his followers expected. For the kingdom realm that Jesus ushered in would not liberate the Jewish people from oppression from the Roman government as they expected—we can define neither the King nor his kingdom ourselves. Instead, he offers not only Jews but every person access to an eternal, heavenly realm free from the consequences of sin and an oasis to refresh our lives!

Kingdom-Realm Living. Matthew's Gospel isn't only about our loving King and his kingdom, it's also about his subjects who act and live within that kingdom. The church is the community of Christ's heavenly kingdom realm, and Jesus' sermon on the hillside is the final Torah of the kingdom realm. For

Matthew, a godly lover (the "righteous") is someone who has chosen to submit to Jesus as King and whose life is lived in accordance with his ethics. The Gospel of Matthew will bring before your eyes the power and majesty of our loving King. Encounter the wonder of Jesus as you read this book!

MATTHEW

Our Loving King

From Abraham to Christ

1 This is the scroll of the lineage and birth[a] of Jesus,[b] the Anointed One, the son of David and descendant of Abraham.

2 Abraham had a son named Isaac, who had a son named Jacob, who had a son named Judah *(he and his brothers became the tribes of Israel)*.

3 Judah and Tamar[c] had twin sons, Perez and Zerah. Perez had a son named Hezron, who had a son named Ram, 4 who had a son named Amminadab, who had a son named Nashon, 5 who had a son named Salmon, who, along with Rahab, had a son named Boaz. Boaz and Ruth had a son named Obed, who was the father of Jesse, 6 and Jesse had a son named David, *who became the king.*

7 Then David and Bathsheba[d] had a son named Solomon, who had a son named Rehoboam, who had a son named Abijah, who had a son named Asa, 8 who had a son named Jehoshaphat, who had a son named Joram, who had a son named Uzziah, 9 who had a son named Jotham, who had a son named Ahaz, who had a son named Hezekiah, 10 who had a son named Manasseh, who had a son named Amos,[e] who had a son named Josiah, 11 who was the father of Jeconiah.[f]

It was during the days of Jeconiah and his brothers that Israel was taken

---

a 1:1 Or "the book of the origin (genesis) of Jesus Christ." The Greek text has no definite article ("This is the") and is most likely to be considered as a caption or title. The Son of God is eternal and had no beginning (John 1:1; 1 John 1:1). The entire book of Matthew presents the beginning of the glorious story of Jesus, God's Anointed One. The genealogy given by Matthew presents the legal claim of Jesus to be King through the lineage of David from Joseph all the way back to the promises given to Abraham. Some believe Luke's account gives the genealogy of Jesus from Mary's lineage through David all the way back to Adam.

b 1:1 The Hebrew name for Jesus is *Yeshua* and means "Yahweh is salvation."

c 1:3 Matthew includes four women in this genealogy: Tamar, Rahab, Ruth, and Bathsheba.

d 1:7 Or "the wife of Uriah."

e 1:10 Or "Amon."

f 1:11 In Jer. 22:24–30 God pronounced a curse on Jeconiah's family line, declaring that they were ineligible to sit on the throne as kings. However, Luke's genealogy goes through David to Mary via Nathan, not Solomon, thus bypassing the curse of Jeconiah's lineage. Matthew's genealogy is meant to establish the legal right of Jesus Christ to be king. So Joseph, as Jesus' *adoptive* father, passes the right of David's throne legally to Jesus and avoids the curse of Jeconiah through Mary's ancestry. Jesus is the Son of God paternally, and the Son of David

captive and deported to Babylon. [12] About the time of their captivity in Babylon, Jeconiah had a son named Shealtiel, who had a son named Zerubbabel, [13] who had a son named Abiud, who had a son named Eliakim, [14] who had a son named Azor, who had a son named Zadok, who had a son named Achim, who had a son named Eliud, [15] who had a son named Eleazar, who had a son named Matthan, who had a son named Jacob, [16] who was the father of Joseph, the husband[a] of Mary the mother of Jesus, who is called "the Anointed One."

[17] So from Abraham to David were fourteen generations, and from David to the Babylonian captivity, fourteen generation, and from the Babylonian captivity to Christ, fourteen generations. [b]

An Angel Comes to Joseph

[18] This was how Jesus, God's Anointed One, was born.

His mother, Mary, had promised Joseph to be his wife,[c] *but while she was still a virgin*[d] she became pregnant through the power[e] of the Holy Spirit.[f] [19] Her fiancé,[g] Joseph, was a righteous man full of integrity and he didn't want to disgrace her, but when he learned of her pregnancy he secretly planned to break the engagement. [h] [20] While he was still debating with himself about what to do,[i]

---

maternally through Heli, Mary's father. See footnote at Luke 3:23–38. From the beginning God said that the coming Savior would be the "seed of the woman." See Gen. 3:15; Gal. 4:4.

a 1:16 Notice that Joseph is named the husband of Mary, not the father of Jesus.

b 1:17 This would make a total of forty-two generations from Abraham to Christ. However, when the names are counted, there are only forty-one. There is a missing generation. What could this mean? Jesus gave birth to the forty-second generation when he died on the cross, for out of his side blood and water flowed. Blood and water come forth at birth. The first Adam "birthed" his wife out of his side, and so Jesus gave birth to his bride from his wounded side. Jesus wants to reproduce himself in us. His last name is not Christ. Christ is the title that explains who he is. He is the Anointed One. "Christ" is also now a corporate body, the body of Christ. We, as the body of Christ, are also anointed ones (Christians). See 1 Cor. 12:12.

c 1:18 In the Jewish culture the engagement was a prenuptial contract (*ketubah*), which was entered into before witnesses, that gave legal rights over the girl to the bridegroom. This agreement could only be nullified by going through the formal divorce process. Since the girl still lived with her family, sexual relations were prohibited until after the second event of the public marriage ceremony. This engagement period was usually entered into when the girl turned thirteen. Mary was just a teenager when she gave birth to Jesus.

d 1:18 Or "without them being united (sexually)."

e 1:18 Implied in the text. Although it is the genitive of source, not agency, "the power of the Holy Spirit" is supplied for clarity. See Deut. 20:7.

f 1:18 The "Holy Spirit" can also be translated "the Sacred Breath (Spirit-wind)" or "the Spirit of Holiness."

g 1:19 Or "Her husband." The Hebrew culture makes no distinction between a fiancé and a husband. The engagement period was a vital part of the marriage custom. See Deut. 22:23–28.

h 1:19 Or "divorce her." The Jewish custom of breaking off an engagement was tantamount to a divorce.

i 1:20 Or "during his inward passion about these things."

he fell asleep and had a supernatural dream. An angel from the Lord appeared to him in clear light and said, "Joseph, descendant of David, don't hesitate to take Mary into your home as your wife,[a] because the power of the Holy Spirit has conceived a child in her womb. [21] She will give birth to a son and you are to name him 'Savior,'[b] for he is destined to give his life[c] to save his people from their sins."

[22] This happened so that what the Lord spoke through his prophet would come true:

[23] Listen! A virgin[d] will be pregnant,
    she will give birth to a Son,
    and he will be known as "Emmanuel,"
    which means in Hebrew,
    "God became one of us."[e]

[24] When Joseph awoke from his dream, he did all that the angel of the Lord instructed him to do. He took Mary to be his wife, [25] but they refrained from having sex until she gave birth to her son, whom they named "Jesus."

The Wise Men Visit

2 Jesus was born in Bethlehem[f] near Jerusalem[g] during the reign of King Herod.[h] After Jesus' birth a group of spiritual priests[i] from the East came

---

a 1:20 Or "take Miriam your wife." Once again, the Jewish culture considered the betrothal period as part of the marriage custom.

b 1:21 Or "Jesus." The Hebrew name for Jesus is *Yeshua* (or *Y'hoshua*) and means "Yahweh is salvation, restoration, and deliverance." Implied in the text is that Hebrew (Aramaic) speakers would obviously understand how the name *Yeshua* and *salvation* were linked, reinforcing the theory that Matthew was originally written in Hebrew. This is lost in the Greek word *Iesous* (Jesus).

c 1:21 As translated from the Aramaic.

d 1:23 See also v. 25, which clarifies that Mary was indeed a virgin.

e 1:23 Or "God with us" or "God among us"; that is, God incarnated. See Isa. 7:14; 8:8, 10 (LXX).

f 2:1 *Bethlehem*, or *Byt-lehem*, means "house of bread," the prophesied birthplace of Messiah. However, the Hebrew word *lehem* can also mean "fighters." Jesus was born in "the House of Fighters!" This is the city of David, one of the greatest fighters in the entire Bible. Perhaps this is why the people of Jesus' day expected him to fight the Romans and free their land from foreign occupation. Jesus fulfilled both aspects of the meaning of Bethlehem in Gethsemane and on the cross, where he fought the "Goliath" of our souls and won, becoming Bread for the world. God controls all events, proven by the prophecy that Jesus would be born in Bethlehem even though his parents were living in Nazareth. See Mic. 5:2; Luke 2:1–19.

g 2:1 Or "in the land of Judea." The Hebrew Gospel of Matthew is "the land of Judah."

h 2:1 Herod died in 4 BC, which helps in dating the birth of Christ.

i 2:1 Or "astrologers," known as dream interpreters. These wealthy priests would have traveled with an entourage for protection as officials from the East. The Greek word *magos* is taken from the Mede language and means "spiritual advisors" or simply "priests." They were appointed by Darius over the state religion as priests of Persia, which is modern-day Iran, and served as official advisors to the king. By the time of Jesus' birth, Persia had been

to Jerusalem [2] and inquired of the people, "Where is the child who is born king of the Jewish people? We observed his star rising in the sky [a] and we've come to bow before him in worship."

[3] King Herod was shaken to the core when he heard this, and not only him, but all of Jerusalem was disturbed when they heard this news. [b] [4] So he called a meeting of the Jewish ruling priests and religious scholars, demanding that they tell him where the promised Messiah was prophesied to be born.

[5] "He will be born in Bethlehem, in the land of Judah," they told him. "Because the prophecy states:

[6] And you, little Bethlehem,
    are not insignificant among the clans of Judah,
    for out of you will emerge
    the Shepherd-King [c] of my people Israel!" [d]

[7] Then Herod secretly summoned the spiritual priests from the East to ascertain the exact time the star first appeared. [8] And he told them, "Now go to Bethlehem and carefully look there for the child, and when you've found him, report to me so that I can go and bow down and worship him too."

[9] And so they left, and on their way to Bethlehem, suddenly the same star they had seen in the East reappeared! Amazed, they watched as it went ahead of them and stopped directly over the place where the child was. [10] And when they saw the star, they were so ecstatic that they shouted and celebrated with unrestrained joy. [e] [11] When they came into the house and saw the young child with Mary, his mother, they were overcome. Falling to the ground at his feet they worshiped him. [f] Then

---

conquered and was being governed by successors to Alexander the Great. It is possible these *Magos* came from the Mesopotamian region of Seleucia. See also Dan. 2 and 5:11, where the prophet Daniel is given the title of "Chief of the *Magio*." It is probable that these *Magos* were descendants of those who had been taught by Daniel, and because of his prophecy of the Messiah being "cut off," they may have been able to decipher the date of his birth along with the interpretation of his star rising.

a 2:2 Or "his star in the east" or "shooting star" or possibly "comet." Note that it is also called "his star," not the star of Bethlehem.

b 2:3 Although we are not told how many "wise men" came to visit Bethlehem, it was likely quite a large entourage. It is doubtful that three men from Persia would cause such an uproar and commotion in the city. There were possibly over one hundred who traveled in the caravan from the East arriving in Jerusalem.

c 2:6 As translated from the Aramaic. The Greek is "the Leader who will shepherd my people Israel."

d 2:6 See Mic. 5:2. Both the Septuagint and the *Shem-Tob* (Hebrew Matthew) have "out of you will come to me a Ruler who will be King of Israel." The Septuagint adds, "He will shepherd my people in the strength of the Lord."

e 2:10 The Greek is hard to translate since it contains so many redundant words for joy in this one verse. It is literally "They rejoiced with a great joy exceedingly." They were ecstatic!

f 2:11 Turning their backs on human wisdom, these "wise men" bowed low before the true Wisdom of God. See 1 Cor. 1:24.

they opened their treasure boxes[a] full of gifts and presented him with gold, frankincense, and myrrh. [12] Afterward they returned to their own country by another route because God had warned them in a dream not to go back to Herod.

They Escape to Egypt

[13] After they had gone, Joseph had another dream. An angel of the Lord appeared to him and said, "Get up now and flee to Egypt. Take Mary and the little child and stay there until I tell you to leave, for Herod intends to search for the child to kill him."

[14] So that very night he got up and took Jesus and his mother and made their escape to Egypt [15] and remained there until Herod died. All of this fulfilled what the Lord had spoken through his prophet:

I summon my Son out of Egypt.[b]

[16] When Herod realized that he had been tricked by the wise men, he was infuriated. So he sent soldiers with orders to slaughter every baby boy two years old and younger in Bethlehem and throughout the surrounding countryside, based on the time frame he was given from interrogating the wise men. [17] This fulfilled the words of the prophet Jeremiah:

[18] I hear the screams of anguish,
weeping, and wailing in Ramah.
Rachel is weeping uncontrollably for her children.[c]
And she refuses to be comforted,
because they are dead and gone.[d]

They Return to Nazareth

[19] After Herod died, the angel of the Lord appeared again to Joseph in a dream while he was still in Egypt, [20] saying, "Go back to the land of Israel and take the child and his mother with you, for those who sought to kill the child are dead."

[21] So he awoke and took Jesus and Mary and returned to the land of Israel. [22] But when he heard that Archelaus, Herod's son, had succeeded him as ruler

---

a 2:11 These "wise men" were extremely wealthy. They presented gifts that totaled a great sum of money—not tiny presents wrapped with bows, but treasure chests full of financial wealth. Although we are not given the monetary value of each type of gift, we know that frankincense and myrrh were extremely costly. These gifts would have financed Joseph and Mary and Jesus' exodus to Egypt and supplied their living expenses for a number of years, even after returning to Israel. Gold is an often-used symbol of the deity of Christ. Frankincense points to his perfect life of holiness, excellence, and devotion. Myrrh, an embalming spice, speaks to us of the suffering love that would lead him to the death on the cross.

b 2:15 See Hos. 11:1. Both Jesus and the nation of Israel came up out of Egypt.

c 2:18 As translated from the Septuagint. *Rachel* becomes a metaphor for all of Israel.

d 2:18 See Jer. 31:14–15.

over all of the territory of Judah, he was afraid to go back. Then he had another dream from God, warning him to avoid that region and instructing him instead to go to the province of Galilee. [23] So he settled his family in the village of Nazareth, fulfilling the prophecy that he would be known as the "Branch." [a]

John the Baptizer

3 It was at this time that John the Baptizer [b] began to preach in the desert of Judah. [c] His message was this: [2] "The realm of heaven's kingdom [d] is about to appear—so you'd better keep turning away from evil and turn back to God!" [e]

[3] Isaiah was referring to John when he prophesied:

> A thunderous voice! One will be crying out in the wilderness,
> "Prepare yourself for the Lord's coming
> and level a straight path inside your hearts for him." [f]

[4] Now, John wore clothing made from camel's hair, tied at his waist with a leather strap, and his food consisted of dried locusts [g] and wild honey. [5] A steady stream of people from Jerusalem, all the surrounding countryside, [h] and the region near the Jordan came out to the wilderness to be baptized by him. [6] And

---

a 2:23 Or "a Nazarene." The Hebrew Scriptures give us a wonderful truth about the Branch (Sprout) of the Lord that would come and establish righteousness. The word for "branch" or sprout is *netzer*, the root word from which Nazareth, Nazarene, and Nazarite come. The teaching of the Branch of the Lord is a concept taught throughout the Bible, from the Tree of Life, to the seven branches of the Lampstand, to Jesus the Vine calling us his branches. Jesus is a Scion, a Branch that can be transplanted and grafted into a human life. Another variant form of this amazing word *netzer* can be translated "keeper, watchman, one who keeps secrets, guardian, one who keeps watch." All of these words are true of Jesus, the Branch who was raised in the village of the Branch (Nazareth). Additionally, the Aramaic word for Nazareth means "heir of a powerful family" or "victorious one." So it is entirely possible to translate this "he will be called the Victorious Branch (of Nazareth)." See Dan. 11:7; Isa. 11:1; 60:21. See also Isa. 4:2; Jer. 23:5; Zech. 6:12, which uses a Hebrew synonym for Branch, *tsemach*.

b 3:1 Or "John the Immerser." The name John means "Yahweh has graced him."

c 3:1 This was the desert region west of the Dead Sea including the lower Jordan. The prophet John was of a priestly family and possibly a member of the Qumran community of the Essenes.

d 3:2 Or "the kingdom realm of heaven." The word *heaven* is found 238 times in the New Testament and *hell* 23 times.

e 3:2 Or "repent." John was preaching in Aramaic, the language of the day. The word for "repent" in both Hebrew and Aramaic means "to return to God [and leave your sins behind]." This is much more than simply changing your mind; it is a powerful term for turning your life around and coming back to the holy God.

f 3:3 See Isa. 40:3, which is quoted in all four Gospels. The Aramaic has in place of Lord, "Lord Yahweh," an obvious implication of the deity of Christ. Isaiah's prophecy is more than a road-construction project. He uses the metaphor of clearing a path as a parable of cleansing our hearts and being prepared in our hearts to receive the Christ.

g 3:4 See Lev. 11:22; 2 Kings 1:8; Joel 1:4; Zech. 13:4; Mal. 4:5–6; Matt. 11:14.

h 3:5 Or "Judea."

while they were publicly confessing their sins, he would immerse them in the Jordan River.

⁷ But when he saw many coming from among the wealthy elite of Jewish society *a* and many of the religious leaders known as Pharisees *b* coming to witness the baptism, he began to denounce them, saying, "You offspring of vipers! Who warned you *to slither away like snakes from the fire of God's judgment?* *c* ⁸ You must prove your repentance by a changed life. ⁹ And don't presume you can get away with merely saying to yourselves, 'But we're Abraham's descendants!' For I tell you, God can awaken these stones to become sons of Abraham! *d* ¹⁰ The axe *e* is now ready to cut down the trees at their very roots. Every fruitless, rotten tree will be chopped down and thrown into the fire. ¹¹ Those who repent I baptize with water, but there is coming a Man after me who is more powerful than I am. In fact, I'm not even worthy enough to pick up his sandals. He will submerge you into union with the Spirit of Holiness and with a raging fire! *f* ¹² He comes with a winnowing fork *g* in his hands and comes to his threshing floor to sift what is worthless from what is pure. And he is ready to sweep out his threshing floor and gather his wheat into his granary, *h* but the straw he will burn up with a fire that can't be extinguished!"

¹³ Then Jesus left Galilee to come to the Jordan to be baptized by John. ¹⁴ But when he waded into the water, John resisted him, saying, "Why are you doing this? I'm the one who needs to be baptized by you, and yet you come to be baptized by me?"

¹⁵ Jesus replied, "It is only right to do all that God requires." *i* Then John

---

a 3:7 Or "the Sadducees."

b 3:7 Or "separated ones." The Pharisees and Sadducees were two of the sects of Judaism of that day.

c 3:7 John is telling them they can't escape the fire of judgment just by getting wet.

d 3:9 There is an interesting word-play in the Hebrew and Aramaic that is lost in an English translation. The Hebrew word for sons (běnayyā) and stones ('abnayyā) are similar. God builds his house with sons, not stones. John baptized the people at the place of the crossing of the Jordan during the time of Joshua. After their miracle crossing of the Jordan they were instructed to set up twelve stones, representing the twelve sons of Israel, as a memorial. Perhaps John the Baptizer was referencing those very stones from which God could raise up sons.

e 3:10 The "axe" becomes a metaphor of the word of truth that judges hearts and nations.

f 3:11 The text is somewhat ambiguous as to what fire is spoken of. Some see it as the fire of judgment, yet Jesus sent us the Holy Spirit, who baptized his church in fire at Pentecost. This last clause is a hendiadys and could be translated "He will baptize you in the raging fire of the Holy Spirit!"

g 3:12 This winnowing fork was like a pitchfork that would thresh grain by throwing it into the air so the wind could blow away the chaff.

h 3:12 See Isa. 41:15–16.

i 3:15 Or "fulfill all righteousness [complete every righteous requirement]." This was the presentation of the Lamb of God as the sacrifice for sins. It was important that John publicly wash the Lamb of God and fulfill the requirements of the law, proving to Israel that the Lamb that was soon to be offered was spotless and without blemish. There are

baptized Jesus. *[a]* [16] And as *[b]* Jesus rose up out of the water, the heavenly realm opened up over him *[c]* and he saw the Holy Spirit descend out of the heavens and rest upon him in the form of a dove. *[d]* [17] Then suddenly the voice of the Father shouted from the sky, saying, "This is the Son I love, and my greatest delight is in him." *[e]*

Jesus Tempted by the Devil

4 Afterward, the Holy Spirit led Jesus into the lonely wilderness in order to reveal his strength against the accuser *[f]* by going through the ordeal of testing. *[g]* [2] And after fasting for forty days, *[h]* Jesus was extremely weak and famished. [3] Then the tempter came to entice him to provide food by doing a miracle. So he said to Jesus, "How can you possibly be the Son of God and go hungry? Just order these stones to be turned into loaves of bread."

[4] He answered, "The Scriptures say:

---

four baptisms in this chapter: (1) John baptizing with water, (2) Father God baptizing Jesus with the power of heaven, (3) Jesus will baptize believers with the same Holy Spirit, (4) the baptism of fire.

a 3:15 Jesus would have been about thirty years old, the age when Levitical priests were ordained and qualified to serve. This was his ordination as the High Priest over the household of faith. Jesus' baptism was a form of dedication. Like Solomon, who dedicated the temple, John now dedicates the temple of Jesus' body, the dwelling place of God. In a sense, John was the true high priest who was ordaining his replacement. Jesus was not repenting, but offering himself as God's sinless Lamb.

b 3:16 There are Latin manuscripts and external evidence dating to Jerome indicating that the Hebrew Matthew included this sentence: "A great light flashed from the water, so that all who had gathered there were afraid." (Diatessaron and Romanos Melodos, *First Hymn on the Epiphany*, XVI.14.7–10.)

c 3:16 See also Acts 7:56.

d 3:16 The dove is a symbol for both meekness and purity. Two gentle animals are pictured at the baptism of Jesus, a dove resting upon a lamb. If you want the presence of the Dove you need to have the nature of the Lamb. The implication is that the Holy Spirit came upon Jesus and never left him.

e 3:17 Or "In him I find my delight." See also Ps. 2:7; Isa. 42:1. The church historian Jerome affirms that additional words were spoken by the Father: "My Son, in all the prophets I was waiting for you, that you might come and I might rest in you. For you are my rest and my firstborn Son, who reigns forever!" (*The Gospel of Matthew for the Hebrews* and *Commentary on Isaiah Chapter 4*. Throckmorton: 14 fn. Nicholson: 43. OMG II: 156 et seq.)

f 4:1 Or "devil." The Aramaic word for "devil" means "accuser." The Greek word is "slanderer."

g 4:1 Or "tribulation." God also tested Israel for forty years in the wilderness. See Deut. 8:2.

h 4:2 Moses and Elijah both fasted forty days. See Ex. 34:28; 1 Kings 19:8. The number forty usually signifies passing a test or enduring a time of trial. It rained for forty days in the time of Noah, and Jonah warned Nineveh for forty days. God told Ezekiel to lay on his right side for forty days (Ezek. 4:6).

Bread alone will not satisfy, [a]
but true life is found in every word,
which constantly goes forth from God's mouth." [b]

[5] Then the accuser transported Jesus to the holy city of Jerusalem and perched him at the highest point [c] of the temple [6] and said to him, "If you're really God's Son, jump, and the angels will catch you. For it is written in the Scriptures:

He will command his angels to protect you
and they will lift you up
so that you won't even bruise your foot on a rock." [d]

[7] Once again Jesus said to him, "**The Scriptures say:**

You must never put the Lord your God to a test," [e]

[8] And the third time the accuser lifted Jesus up into a very high mountain range and showed him all the kingdoms of the world and all the splendor that goes with it.

[9] "All of these kingdoms I will give to you," the accuser said, "if only you will kneel down before me and worship me."

[10] But Jesus said, "Go away, enemy! [f] For the Scriptures say:

Kneel before the Lord your God
and worship only him." [g]

[11] At once the accuser left him, and angels suddenly gathered around Jesus to minister to his needs.

---

a 4:4 Or "Man will not live by bread alone." The Aramaic is *Bar-nasha* and can be translated "The Son of Man will not live by bread alone."

b 4:4 See Deut. 8:3. God had not given Jesus permission to turn stones into bread, and Jesus would not be pushed into prematurely demonstrating his power. He was content with the timing of his Father. He refused to turn stones into bread to feed himself, but he multiplied bread for his hungry followers. Today he is still turning hearts of stone into living bread that will feed the nations with truth.

c 4:5 Or "wing." See Ps. 91:4.

d 4:6 See Ps. 91:11–12; Matt. 26:53. This was a temptation to capitalize on being the Son of God and to force God to protect him as he jumped. Jesus was being tested over restraining his power as the Anointed One and waiting until the timing of his Father in publicly releasing him to work miracles and display his power. He was not sent to throw himself down from the temple, but to throw down the temple and establish a new order of worship—as a true relationship with God is internal with every believer now becoming the temple of God. See 1 Cor. 3:16; 6:19.

e 4:7 See Deut. 6:16.

f 4:10 Or "Satan."

g 4:10 See Deut. 6:13–14.

Jesus Preaches in Galilee

[12] When Jesus heard that John the Baptizer had been thrown into prison, he went back into Galilee. [13] Jesus moved from Nazareth to make his home in Capernaum,[a] which is by Lake Galilee in the land of Zebulun and Naphtali. [14] He did this to make the prophecy of Isaiah come true:

[15] Listen, you who live in the land of Zebulun
  and the land of Naphtali,
  along the road to the sea
  and on the other side of the Jordan,
  and Galilee—the land of non-Jewish peoples!
[16] You who spend your days shrouded in darkness
  can now say, "We have seen a brilliant Light."[b]
  And those who live in the dark shadow land of death
  can now say, "The Dawning Light arises on us."

[17] From that time on Jesus began to proclaim his message with these words: **"Keep turning away from your sins and come back to God, for heaven's kingdom realm is now accessible."**[c]

Jesus Calls His Disciples

[18] As he was walking by the shore of Lake Galilee, Jesus noticed two fishermen who were brothers. One was nicknamed Keefa[d] (later called Peter), and the other was Andrew, his brother. Watching as they were casting their nets into the water, [19] Jesus called out to them and said, **"Come and follow me, and I will transform you into men who catch people for God."**[e] [20] Immediately they dropped their nets and left everything behind to follow Jesus.

[21] Leaving there, Jesus found three other men sitting in a boat, mending their nets. Two were brothers, Jacob[f] and John, and they were with their father,

---

a 4:13 Capernaum means "the village of Nahum." It was a fishing village on the northwestern shore of Lake Galilee. Nahum means "comforted." Jesus did many miracles and based his Galilean ministry in the "village of the comforted."

b 4:16 Light is a common name for the Messiah in rabbinical literature. It speaks of both Christ and the revelatory teaching he brings. See Isa. 9:1–2. The Aramaic word for Galilee (*Galeela*) means "revelation of God." Jesus was raised and ministered in the land of the "revelation of God."

c 4:17 Or "heaven's kingdom realm is close enough to touch!"

d 4:18 Or "Simon." The Aramaic is *Keefa*, which means "the rock" or "pebble." Peter (*Petros*) is his Greek name.

e 4:19 Or "fishers of men." The Aramaic word can mean either "fishers" or "hunters." See Ezek. 47:1–10.

f 4:21 Or "James." Most translations of the Bible have substituted Jacob with James. Both Greek and Aramaic leave the Hebrew name as it is, Jacob. This translation will use the correct name, Jacob, throughout.

Zebedee.[a] Jesus called Jacob and John to his side *and said to them,* "**Come and follow Me.**" [22] And at once they left their boat and their father, and began to follow Jesus.

Jesus' Ministry of Healing

[23] Jesus ministered from place to place throughout all of the province of Galilee. He taught[b] in the synagogues, preaching the hope of the kingdom realm[c] and healing every kind of sickness and disease among the people. [24] His fame spread everywhere![d] Many people who were in pain and suffering with every kind of illness were brought to Jesus for their healing—epileptics,[e] paralytics, and those tormented by demonic powers were all set free. Everyone who was brought to Jesus was healed!

[25] This resulted in massive crowds of people following him, including people from Galilee, Jerusalem, the land of Judah, the region of the Ten Cities known as the Decapolis, and beyond the Jordan River.[f]

Jesus' Sermon on the Hillside

5 One day Jesus saw a vast crowd of people gathering to hear him, so he went up the slope of a hill and sat down. With his followers and disciples spread over the hillside, [2] Jesus began to teach them:[g]

---

a 4:21 Zebedee's name means "my gift." The gift he gave to Jesus was his two sons. All parents have the privilege of giving their children back to God.

b 4:23 The Greek word *didasko* is a word often used for providing skilled training.

c 4:23 As translated from the Aramaic. The Hebrew Matthew is "the good gift of the kingdom of the heavens." The Greek is "the good news of heaven's reign."

d 4:24 As translated from the Hebrew Matthew. The Greek is "into Syria."

e 4:24 Or "the mentally ill."

f 4:25 This was the first encounter the non-Jewish peoples of the Middle East had with Jesus. He was proclaiming his universal kingdom and inviting all to enter into it.

g 5:2 It should be noted that Matt. 5–7, commonly known as the Sermon on the Mount, is the messianic Torah (law or teaching) and the Constitution of the kingdom of heaven. Jesus begins with giving his followers a superior way to live than the Ten Commandments of Moses. It is a superior version of all that God expects and provides for those who yield to him. Jesus gives us more than laws; he gives us promises of power to fulfill all that he asks of us. The emphasis is not on outward duty but on the inward transformation of our hearts by grace. God's kingdom is offered to those who will learn the ways of Christ and offer themselves to him in full surrender.

³ "What wealth is offered to you[a] when you feel your spiritual poverty![b] For there is no charge to enter the realm of heaven's kingdom.

⁴ "What delight comes to you when you wait upon the Lord![c] For you will find what you long for.[d]

⁵ "What blessing comes to you when gentleness[e] lives in you! For you will inherit the earth.[f]

⁶ "How enriched you are when you crave righteousness![g] For you will be surrounded with fruitfulness.[h]

⁷ "How satisfied you are when you demonstrate tender mercy![i] For tender mercy will be demonstrated to you.

⁸ "What bliss you experience when your heart is pure![j] For then your eyes will open to see more and more of God.[k]

⁹ "How blessed you are when you make peace! For then you will be recognized as a true child of God.[l]

---

a 5:3 Or, "Blessed are they." The Aramaic word *toowayhon* means "enriched, happy, fortunate, delighted, blissful, content, blessed." Our English word *blessed* can indeed fit here, but *toowayhon* implies more—great happiness, prosperity, abundant goodness, and delight! The word *bliss* captures all of this meaning. *Toowayhon* means to have the capacity to enjoy union and communion with God. Because the meaning of the word goes beyond merely being "blessed," the translation uses different phrases for each of the Beatitudes. Verses 3–10 are presented with third-person pronouns; however, it is not abstract truth, but spoken directly to Jesus' disciples. This is why the translation is in the second person. The implication of this verse is that the poor in spirit have only one remedy, and that is trusting in God. This total reliance upon God is the doorway into the kingdom realm. Notice the obvious parallel between Isa. 61:1–2 and these "beatitudes."

b 5:3 Or, "humble in spirit," or, "poor in spirit," which means to be humble and totally dependent upon God for everything. It is synonymous with "pious" or "saintly," not just in the sense of those who possess nothing. It could be translated "Delighted are those who have surrendered completely to God and trust only in him." See also Isa. 41:17; 57:15; 66:2.

c 5:4 As translated from the Hebrew Matthew. (See also Ps. 27:14.) The Greek is "mourn (grieve)." The Hebrew word for "wait" and for "mourn" is almost identical.

d 5:4 As translated from the Aramaic word for comfort, *nethbayoon*, which can mean "to see the face of what (or who) you long for." The Greek is "They shall be comforted."

e 5:5 Or "meekness." Jesus is saying that when you claim nothing as yours, everything will be given to you. The Aramaic word, *makeekheh*, implies being both gentle and flexible.

f 5:5 See Pss. 37:11; 149:4.

g 5:6 Or "goodness" or "justice."

h 5:6 As translated from the Aramaic word, *nesbhoon*, which is associated with planting and fruitfulness. The Greek is "They shall be satisfied." See Ps. 11:3–7; Zeph. 2:3.

i 5:7 Or "merciful to forgive." The Hebraic and Aramaic concept of mercy is that it comes from our innermost being. The root word for "mercy" is the root word for "womb." See 2 Sam. 22:26; Ps. 18:25; Prov. 14:21; James 2:13.

j 5:8 Or "when your heart is full of innocence." See Pss. 15:1–2; 24:4; 51:10.

k 5:8 The Aramaic word used for "see" is *nahzon* and can be translated either in the present tense ("They see God") or the future tense ("They will see God"). The Greek is "They will progressively see God." See also Ps. 17:15.

l 5:9 See Pss. 72:3–7; 122:8–9; Isa. 26:12.

¹⁰ "How enriched you are when you bear the wounds of being perse-cuted[a] for doing what is right![b] For that is when you experience the realm of heaven's kingdom.

¹¹ "How ecstatic you can be when people insult[c] and persecute you and speak all kinds of cruel lies about you because of your love for me![d] ¹² So leap for joy—since your heavenly reward is great. For you are being rejected the same way the prophets were before you.

¹³ "Your lives are like salt among the people. But if you, like salt, become bland, how can your 'saltiness' be restored? Flavorless salt is good for noth-ing[e] and will be thrown out and trampled on by others.

¹⁴ "Your lives light up the world. Let others see your light from a distance, for how can you hide a city that stands on a hilltop?[f] ¹⁵ And who would light a lamp and then hide it in an obscure place?[g] Instead, it's placed where ev-eryone in the house can benefit from its light. ¹⁶ So don't hide your light![h] Let it shine brightly before others, so that the commendable things you do will shine as light upon them, and then they will give their praise to your Father in heaven."

Fulfillment of the Law

¹⁷ "If you think I've come to set aside the law of Moses or the writings of the prophets, you're mistaken. I have come to fulfill and bring to perfection all that has been written. ¹⁸ Indeed, I assure you, as long as heaven and earth endure, not even the smallest detail[i] of the Law will be done away with until

---

a 5:10 The Aramaic is "being rejected."

b 5:10 See Ps. 38:20; Isa. 66:5; Acts 5:41; 1 Peter 3:14. The Hebrew Matthew is "for the Righ-teous One."

c 5:11 The Aramaic is "criticize you" (1 Peter 3:14; Acts 5:41). The Hebrew Matthew is "for the Righteous One."

d 5:11 See Ps. 119:85–87. We are to live in such a way that people have to lie when they speak evil of a believer in Christ.

e 5:13 Or "Salt that has lost its flavor is *foolish*." Both Greek and Aramaic use a word that can mean either "good for nothing" or "foolish." If salt that has lost its flavor is foolish, then salt that keeps its flavor is wise. Rabbinical literature equates salt with wisdom. After speaking of salt, Jesus speaks of lighting a lamp. It was a common practice in the time of Jesus to put salt on the wick of a lamp to increase its brightness. The "salt" of wisdom will make our lights shine even brighter. (Eduard Schweizer, *The Good News According to Matthew,* Atlanta: John Knox Press, 1975. W. A. Elwell and P. W. Comfort, *Tyndale Bible Dictionary,* Wheaton, Ill.: Tyndale House, Tyndale reference library, 2001, Lamp, Lampstand. 797–8.)

f 5:14 See Isa. 49:6.

g 5:15 Or "under a basket."

h 5:16 The Aramaic word for "light" (*noohra*) is often used as a metaphor for teachings that bring enlightenment and revelation into the hearts of men. Light can also represent the presence of God ("the light of his countenance"). Jesus is the light of God within us.

i 5:18 Or "not even one letter or even a part of the letter of the law."

its purpose is complete. [a] [19] So whoever violates [b] even the least important of the commandments, [c] and teaches others to do so, will be the least esteemed in the realm of heaven's kingdom. But whoever obeys them and teaches their truths to others will be greatly esteemed in the realm of heaven's kingdom. [20] For I tell you, unless your lives are more pure and full of integrity [d] than the religious scholars [e] and the Pharisees you will never experience the realm of heaven's kingdom."

Anger

[21] "You're familiar with the commandment that the older generation was taught, 'Do not murder or you will be judged.' [f] [22] But I'm telling you, if you hold anger in your heart [g] toward a fellow believer, you are subject to judgment. [h] And whoever demeans and insults [i] a fellow believer is answerable to the congregation. [j] And whoever calls down curses upon a fellow believer [k] is in danger of being sent to a fiery hell. [l]

[23] "So then, if you are presenting a gift before the altar in the temple and suddenly you remember a quarrel you have with a fellow believer, [24] leave your gift there in front of the altar and go at once to apologize with the one who is offended. Then, after you have reconciled, [m] come to the altar and present your gift. [25] It is always better to come to terms with the one who wants to sue you before you go to trial, or you may be found guilty by the judge, and he will hand you over to the officers, who will throw you into prison. [26] Believe me, you won't get out of prison until you have paid the full amount!"

---

a 5:18 Or "All its teachings come true."

b 5:19 Or "whoever loosens" (diminishes).

c 5:19 Or "these implanted goals."

d 5:20 Or "your deeds of righteousness."

e 5:20 Or "scribes," who were considered to be the expert theologians of the Scriptures.

f 5:21 See Ex. 20:13; Deut. 5:17.

g 5:22 Some manuscripts add, "without a cause." See 1 John 3:15. Both Aramaic and Hebrew Matthew read "if you provoke a fellow believer to anger," or "if you cause offense to the spirit of your brother."

h 5:22 The implication is that you would be judged as a murderer. Anger and murder are equally odious in God's eyes. Angry words kill.

i 5:22 The Aramaic is *raca* and can mean "spittle" or "lunatic." It is a word that could imply calling a fellow believer demon-possessed. The Greek is "worthless fool, imbecile."

j 5:22 Or "council" (Sanhedrin).

k 5:22 Or "whoever calls him a worthless fool." It is a word that could imply calling a fellow believer demon-possessed.

l 5:22 Or "the Gehenna of fire." Gehenna, which was an actual place where garbage was burned outside of Jerusalem, became a figure of speech for hell in the days of Jesus. It used to be the site of child sacrifice to the god Molech. See 2 Chron. 33:6.

m 5:24 A true heart of repentance means attempting to heal severed relationships, not just empty words.

Adultery

[27] "Your ancestors have been taught, 'Never commit adultery.'[a] [28] However, I say to you, if you look with lust in your eyes at the body of a woman who is not your wife, you've already committed adultery in your heart.[b] [29] If your right eye seduces you to fall into sin,[c] then go blind in your right eye![d] For you're better off losing sight in one eye than to have your whole body thrown into hell. [30] And if your right hand entices you to sin, let it go limp and useless![e] For you're better off losing a part of your body than to have it all thrown into hell.[f]

[31] "It has been said, 'Whoever divorces[g] his wife must give her legal divorce papers.'[h] [32] However, I say to you, if anyone divorces his wife for any reason, except for infidelity, he causes her to commit adultery, and whoever marries a divorced[i] woman commits adultery."

Making Oaths

[33] "Again, your ancestors were taught, 'Never swear an oath that you don't intend to keep,[j] but keep your vows to the Lord God.'[k] [34] However, I say to you, don't bind yourself by taking an oath at all. Don't swear by heaven, for heaven is where God's throne is placed.[l] [35] Don't swear an oath by the earth, because it is the rug under God's feet,[m] and not by Jerusalem, because it is

---

a 5:27 See Ex. 20:14.

b 5:28 The Aramaic is speaking of more than adultery with a married woman; it uses the word for any sex act outside of marriage. Jesus elevates the standard of righteousness. He is holy, and when he comes to live within the believer, his holiness is the fulfillment of what God requires of us.

c 5:29 The Greek word *skandalizo* means to "entice to sin," "offend," or "set a trap."

d 5:29 Or "pluck out your eye and throw it away."

e 5:30 Or "cut it off and throw it away." Verses 29 and 30 use obvious hyperbole to help us understand how intent we must be to guard our lives from sin.

f 5:30 Jesus is using an obvious figure of speech when he instructs us to "pluck out" our eyes or "cut off" our hands. The metaphor is clear: we are to end every evil habit that will lead us to destruction.

g 5:31 In this verse and in v. 32 the Greek word for divorce (*apolyo*) can also mean "to loose," "to dismiss," "to send away."

h 5:31 See Deut. 24:1. By serving her divorce papers, a husband was required to return his wife's dowry. The divorced woman would then leave his house and receive back her dowry.

i 5:32 The Aramaic can be translated "whoever marries a woman who is separated and not divorced."

j 5:33 That is, don't perjure yourself.

k 5:33 See Lev. 19:12; Isa. 66:1.

l 5:34 In the days of Jesus and in the Middle Eastern cultural setting of Israel, taking oaths and swearing by something greater than oneself was a common practice. Jesus' words trump culture and our bondage to doing things according to the expected norms of society. He instructs us to be faithful and true with our words.

m 5:35 As translated from the Aramaic. The Greek is "his footstool."

the city of the Great King. [a] [36] And why would you swear by your own head, because it's not in your power to turn a single hair white or black? *But just let your words ring true.* [b] [37] A simple 'Yes' or 'No' will suffice. Anything beyond this springs from a deceiver. [c]

[38] "Your ancestors have also been taught, 'Take an eye in exchange for an eye and a tooth in exchange for a tooth.' [d] [39] However, I say to you, don't repay an evil act with another evil act. [e] But whoever insults you by slapping you on the right cheek, turn the other to him as well. [f] [40] If someone is determined to sue you for your coat, give him the shirt off your back as a gift in return. [41] And should people in authority take advantage of you, do more than what they demand. [g] [42] Learn to generously share what you have with those who ask for help, and don't close your heart to the one who comes to borrow from you." [h]

Love Your Enemies

[43] "Your ancestors have also been taught 'Love your neighbors [i] and hate the one who hates you.' [44] However, I say to you, love your enemy, bless the one who curses you, do something wonderful for the one who hates you, [j] and respond to the very ones who persecute you by praying for them. [45] For that will reveal your identity as children of your heavenly Father. He is kind to all by bringing the sunrise to warm and rainfall to refresh whether a person does what is good or evil. [46] What reward do you deserve if you only love the

---

a 5:35 See Ps. 48:2.

b 5:36 Our words must be fulfilled by actions. All four things Jesus mentioned were considered sacred to the Jewish people—heaven, earth, Jerusalem, and a person's head. But Jesus teaches us that words of truth make our lives sacred. See James 5:12.

c 5:37 As translated from the Aramaic. See Eccl. 5:4–7.

d 5:38 See Ex. 21:24.

e 5:39 As translated from Hebrew Matthew. The Greek is "Do not resist evil (or evil doer)."

f 5:39 That is, simply stand and take it without responding in return with violence. In the cultural setting of the days of Jesus, to slap someone was the greatest insulting physical blow you could give a person. It is better to respond with kindness. This robs the oppressor of his ability to humiliate. See Prov. 15:1; 24:29; Isa. 50:6; Lam. 3:30.

g 5:41 "If someone forces you to go a mile with him, go two." This is in reference to the Roman authorities, who often compelled the Jewish men to carry their heavy items for them. In v. 40 we are challenged to give up our rights, in v. 41 to surrender our freedom, and in v. 42 to surrender our prosperity.

h 5:42 The Aramaic can be "If someone wants to benefit from you, do not stop him." In the agrapha sayings of Jesus, as quoted by early church fathers, an additional line is found here that reads, "It is more blessed to give than to receive." See also Acts 20:35.

i 5:43 The Aramaic is "your relatives." This phrase is found in the Torah; the following phrase is from oral tradition. See Lev. 19:18.

j 5:44 As translated from the Aramaic. The previous two clauses are not found in some reliable Greek manuscripts.

loveable? Don't even the tax collectors*a* do that? ⁴⁷How are you any different from others if you limit your kindness*b* only to your friends? Don't even the ungodly*c* do that? ⁴⁸Since you are children of a perfect Father in heaven, you are to be perfect*d* like him."

Giving with Pure Motives

6 "Examine your motives to make sure you're not showing off when you do your good deeds, only to be admired by others; otherwise, you will lose the reward of your heavenly Father. ²So when you give to the poor, don't announce it and make a show of it just to be seen by people,*e* like the hypocrites*f* in the streets and in the marketplace.*g* They've already received their reward! ³But when you demonstrate generosity, do it with pure motives and without drawing attention to yourself.*h* ⁴Give secretly and your Father, who sees all you do, will reward you openly."*i*

Prayer

⁵"Whenever you pray, be sincere and not like the pretenders who love the attention they receive while praying before others in the meetings and on street corners. Believe me, they've already received in full their reward. ⁶But whenever you pray, go into your innermost chamber and be alone with Father God,*j* praying to him in secret. And your Father, who sees all you do, will reward you openly. ⁷When you pray, there is no need to repeat empty phrases, praying like those who don't know God,*k* for they expect God to hear them because of their many words. ⁸There is no need to imitate them, since your Father already knows what you need before you ask him. ⁹Pray like this:

'Our Father, dwelling in the heavenly realms,
may the glory of your name

---

a 5:46 The Hebrew Matthew is "transgressors."

b 5:47 Or "ask for the peace of your brothers" (Hebrew Matthew and Aramaic).

c 5:47 Or "gentiles" (who worship other gods).

d 5:48 The Greek and Aramaic words for "perfect" can also mean "whole, complete, fully mature, lacking nothing, all-inclusive, well rounded."

e 6:2 Or "blow your own horn."

f 6:2 The Greek word *hupokrites* is not only used for people with double standards, it actually means "overcritical," "nitpicking," "splitting hairs over religious issues."

g 6:2 As translated from Aramaic and Hebrew Matthew. The Greek is "synagogues."

h 6:3 Or "Don't let your left hand know what your right hand is doing." This is a figure of speech for giving with pure motives, not to be seen and applauded by others.

i 6:4 As translated from the Aramaic and Hebrew Matthew. Most Greek manuscripts do not include the word *openly*.

j 6:6 Or "Go into your inner room [storehouse], close the door, and pray." This "inner room" can also be a metaphor for praying from the heart, from our innermost being, our storehouse.

k 6:7 Or "gentiles."

be the center on which our lives turn. [a]

¹⁰ Manifest your kingdom realm, [b]
and cause your every purpose to be fulfilled on earth,
just as it is fulfilled in heaven.
¹¹ We acknowledge you as our Provider
of all we need each day. [c]
¹² Forgive us the wrongs we have done [d] as we ourselves
release forgiveness to those who have wronged us.
¹³ Rescue us every time we face tribulation [e]
and set us free from evil. [f]
For you are the King who rules
with power and glory forever. Amen.' [g]

¹⁴ "*And when you pray*, make sure you forgive the faults of others so that your Father in heaven will also forgive you. ¹⁵ But if you withhold forgiveness from others, your Father withholds forgiveness from you."

Fasting

¹⁶ "When you fast, don't look like those who pretend to be spiritual. They want everyone to know they're fasting, so they appear in public looking miserable, gloomy, and disheveled. [h] Believe me, they've already received their reward in full. ¹⁷⁻¹⁸ When you fast, don't let it be obvious, but instead, wash your face [i] and groom yourself and realize that your Father in the secret place is the one who is watching all that you do in secret and will continue to reward you openly."

---

a 6:9 An alternate reading of the Aramaic text. The Aramaic word for "name" is *shema* (the Hebrew word, *shem*), a word with multiple meanings. It can also be translated "light," "sound," or "atmosphere." Placing a light, like a lantern, in an enclosed space magnifies that light. This is the meaning here of God's name being made sacred and magnified as we focus our lives on him. The Greek is "treated as holy."

b 6:10 Or "Come and begin your kingdom reign."

c 6:11 Or "Give us bread [or life] today for the coming day." Bread becomes a metaphor of our needs (physically, spiritually, and emotionally). Jesus is teaching us to acknowledge Father God as our Provider of all we need each day. Both the Greek and Hebrew Matthew can be translated "Give us this day our bread for tomorrow" (or "our continual bread").

d 6:12 Or "Send away the results of our debts (shortcomings)," used as a metaphor for our sins. The Aramaic can be translated "Give us serenity as we also allow others serenity."

e 6:13 Or "Do not let us be put into the ordeal of testing." God never tempts man. See James 1:13–14.

f 6:13 Or "the Evil One."

g 6:13 As translated from the Aramaic, Hebrew Matthew, and most Greek manuscripts. The Aramaic word for "forever" means "until the end of all the universes."

h 6:16 Or "disfigure their faces." Some of them would put saffron on their faces to make them appear a sickly yellow color in order to be seen as though they had been fasting.

i 6:17–18 Or "put oil on your head."

Treasures in Heaven

[19] "Don't keep hoarding for yourselves earthly treasures that can be stolen by thieves. Material wealth eventually rusts, decays, and loses its value.[a] [20] Instead, stockpile heavenly treasures[b] for yourselves that cannot be stolen and will never rust, decay, or lose their value. [21] For your heart will always pursue what you value as your treasure.[c]

[22] "The eyes of your spirit allow revelation-light[d] to enter into your being. If your heart is unclouded, the light floods in! [23] *But if your eyes are focused on money,*[e] the light cannot penetrate and darkness takes its place.[f] How profound will be the darkness within you[g] if the light of truth cannot enter!

[24] "How could you worship two gods at the same time? You will have to hate one and love the other, or be devoted to one and despise the other. You can't worship the true God while enslaved to the god of money!"[h]

Don't Worry

[25] "This is why I tell you to never be worried about your life, for all that you need will be provided, such as food, water, clothing—everything your body needs. Isn't there more to your life than a meal? Isn't your body more than clothing?

[26] "Look at all the birds—do you think they worry about their existence? They don't plant or reap or store up food, yet your heavenly Father provides them each with food. Aren't you much more valuable to your Father than they? [27] So, which one of you by worrying could add anything to your life?[i]

[28] "And why would you worry about your clothing? Look at all the

---

a 6:19 Or "where rust and moth destroy."

b 6:20 Heavenly treasures are eternal realities, such as loving others and doing good, revealing truth, and bringing Christ's light to the lost. None of these "treasures" can be stolen or ever lose their value.

c 6:21 Or "For your thoughts [heart] will always be focused on your treasure."

d 6:22 The teachings of Jesus are the "revelation-light" referred to here. Some scholars see "healthy eyes" as a Semitic figure of speech for generosity, due to the context of giving and money in the verses before and after. Or "Your eye is like a lamp for your body."

e 6:23 An "evil" eye can also be associated with being stingy and greedy.

f 6:23 Or "If your eye is healthy [focused], your whole body is full of light; but if it is sick (evil), your body is full of darkness." The "eye" becomes a metaphor for spiritual perception. The "body" is our spirit. The "light" is Jesus' teachings. The "darkness" is formed by the lies and opinions that blind us. These obvious metaphors have been made explicit in the translation.

g 6:23 Hebrew Matthew is "All your ways are dark."

h 6:24 Or "God and mammon." Mammon is an Aramaic term for money. See 1 Tim. 6:6–10. There is found after v. 24 a part of the agrapha that reads, "If you do not fast from the world, you will never discover the kingdom of God" (*Oxyrhyncus Papyrus 655*, pOxy 1:4–11).

i 6:27 The Aramaic and Hebrew Matthew is "add a cubit to your height." The Greek is "add one hour to your lifespan."

beautiful flowers of the field. They don't work or toil, [29] and yet not even Solomon in all his splendor was robed in beauty more than one of these! [30] So if God has clothed the meadow with hay, which is here for such a short time and then dried up and burned, won't he provide for you the clothes you need—even though you live with such little faith?

[31] "So then, forsake your worries! Why would you say, 'What will we eat?' or 'What will we drink?' or 'What will we wear?' [32] For that is what the unbelievers chase after. Doesn't your heavenly Father already know the things your bodies require? [a]

[33] "So above all, constantly chase after the realm of God's kingdom [b] and the righteousness that proceeds from him. Then all these less important things will be given to you abundantly. [c] [34] Refuse to worry about tomorrow, but deal with each challenge that comes your way, one day at a time. [d] Tomorrow will take care of itself."

Do Not Judge

7 "Refuse to be a critic full of bias toward others, and judgment [e] will not be passed on you. [2] For you'll be judged by the same standard that you've used to judge others. The measurement you use on them will be used on you. [f] [3] Why would you focus on the flaw in someone else's life and yet fail to notice the glaring flaws of your own? [g] [4] How could you say to your friend, 'Let me show you where you're wrong,' when you're guilty of even more? [5] You're being hypercritical and a hypocrite! First acknowledge your own 'blind spots' and deal with them, and then you'll be capable of dealing with the 'blind spot' of your friend. [h]

[6] "Who would hang earrings on a dog's ear or throw pearls [i] in front of

---

a 6:32 There is a part of the agrapha inserted here, which is confirmed by a number of church fathers who had access to more ancient manuscripts, that reads "So if you ask for the great things, God will add to you the little things." This is most likely from a variation of the Hebrew Matthew. (Clement of Alexandria, *Stromateis* 1.24.158; Origen, *Commentary on the Pss.* 4.4; *De Oratione* 2.2; 14.1; Eusebius, *Commentary on the Pss.* 16.2. See also Craig A. Evans, *Fabricating Jesus: How Modern Scholars Distort the Gospels* [IVP Press, 2006], 236–238.)

b 6:33 The Hebrew Matthew is "Above all, pray for the kingdom realm of God."

c 6:33 As translated from the Aramaic.

d 6:34 Or "One day's trouble is enough for one day."

e 7:1 It is God's judgment that is being implied by the passive verbs.

f 7:2 See Rom. 2:1.

g 7:3 Or "Why do you see a speck in your brother's eye but fail to see the beam of wood sticking out of your own eye?"

h 7:5 Or "You hypocrite, why don't you first remove the beam sticking out of your own eye? Then you can see clearly to remove the small speck out of your brother's eye." Jesus is clearly teaching that our blind spots prevent us from accurately evaluating the needs of others.

i 7:6 As translated from the Aramaic. The Greek is "Don't let the dogs have consecrated [holy] wild pigs? They'll only trample them under their feet and then turn around and tear you to pieces!

⁷ "Ask, and the gift is yours. Seek, and you'll discover. Knock, and the door will be opened for you. ⁸ For every persistent one will get what he asks for. Every persistent seeker will discover what he longs for. And everyone who knocks persistently will one day find an open door. ᵃ

⁹ "Do you know of any parent who would give his hungry child, who asked for food, a plate of rocks instead? ¹⁰ Or when asked for a piece of fish, what parent would offer his child a snake instead? ¹¹ If you, imperfect as you are, ᵇ know how to lovingly take care of your children and give them what's best, how much more ready is your heavenly Father to give wonderful gifts ᶜ to those who ask him?"

The Golden Rule

¹² "In everything you do, be careful to treat others in the same way you'd want them to treat you, for that is the essence of all the teachings of the Law and the Prophets."

The Narrow Gate

¹³ "Come to God through the narrow gate, because the wide gate and broad path is the way that leads to destruction—nearly everyone chooses that crowded road! ¹⁴ The narrow gate and the difficult way leads to eternal life—so few even find it!"

False Prophets

¹⁵ "Constantly be on your guard against phony prophets. They come disguised as lambs, appearing to be genuine, but on the inside they are like wild, ravenous wolves! ᵈ ¹⁶ You can spot them by their actions, for the fruits of their character will be obvious. You won't find sweet grapes hanging on

---

meat." The Aramaic word for "earrings" is almost identical to the word for "holy." Earrings and pearls are symbols of spiritual truths given to us by God. They give us beautiful "ears" to hear his voice and impart lovely pearls of wisdom, which are not to be regarded lightly or shared with those who have their hearts closed. The Aramaic word for "throw" is almost identical to the word for "to instruct" or "to teach." The value of wisdom is not appreciated by those who have no ears to hear it.

a 7:8 Clement of Alexandria attributes an additional saying to Jesus and states that it is from the Hebrew Matthew: "The one who seeks should not cease until he finds, and in finding he shall marvel, and having marveled he shall reign, and having reigned he shall rest." *Miscellanies* 2.9 (de Santos 3; Lagrange 9) and *Miscellanies* 5.14 (de Santos 4; Lagrange 10).

b 7:11 Or "although you are evil."

c 7:11 Hebrew Matthew is "give his good Spirit," a reference to asking for the Holy Spirit. See also Luke 11:13.

d 7:15 Hebrew Matthew adds a phrase, "They are full of deceit as wild, ravenous wolves." There is at least a hint here of the Benjamite prophecy found in Gen. 49:27.

a thorn bush, and you'll never pick good fruit from a tumbleweed. [17-19] So if the tree is good, it will produce good fruit; but if the tree is bad, it will bear only rotten fruit and it deserves to be cut down and burned. [20] Look at the obvious fruit of their lives and ministries, *and then you'll know whether they are true or false.*"

Jesus Warns of Pretenders

[21] "Not everyone who says to me, 'Lord, Lord,' will enter into the realm of heaven's kingdom. It is only those who persist in doing the will of my heavenly Father. [22] On the day of judgment many will say to me, 'Lord, Lord, don't you remember us? Didn't we prophesy[a] in your name? Didn't we cast out demons and do many miracles for the sake of your name?' [23] But I will have to say to them, 'Go away from me, you lawless rebels! I've never been joined to you!'[b]

[24] "Everyone who hears my teaching and applies it to his life can be compared to a wise man who built his house on an unshakable foundation. [25] When the rains fell and the flood[c] came, with fierce winds beating upon his house, it stood firm because of its strong foundation.

[26] "But everyone who hears my teaching and does not apply it to his life can be compared to a foolish man who built his house on sand. [27] When it rained and rained and the flood came, with wind and waves beating upon his house, it collapsed and was swept away."[d]

[28] By the time Jesus finished speaking, the crowds were dazed and overwhelmed[e] by his teaching, [29] because his words carried such great authority, quite unlike their religious scholars.[f]

Jesus Heals a Leper

8 After he came down from teaching on the hillside, massive crowds began following him.[g] [2] Suddenly, a leper walked up to Jesus and threw himself

---

a 7:22 Or "preach in your name."

b 7:23 The Aramaic can be translated "From everlasting I have not known you."

c 7:25 Or "rivers." See also Song. 8:7.

d 7:27 Or "and great was its fall!"

e 7:28 The Greek word used here, *ekplesso*, is a strong verb that means "awestruck, filled with amazement, astonished, panic stricken, something that takes your breath away (being hit with a blow), to be shocked, to expel, to drive out." Clearly, Jesus spoke with such glory and power emanating from him that his words were like thunderbolts in their hearts. May we hear his words in the same way today.

f 7:29 Or "scribes" (experts of the Law). Jesus taught from an inner knowledge of God and his Word, for his teaching emphasized obedience to God from the heart, not just outwardly keeping laws.

g 8:1 It is best to view this verse as an extension of 7:29. Chapter and verse breaks are not part of the inspired text but were added centuries later to aid in our study of God's Word.

down before him in worship[a] and said, "Lord, you have the power to heal me . . . if you really want to."

[3] Jesus reached out his hand and touched the leper and said, "Of course I want to heal you—be healed!" And instantly, all signs of leprosy[b] disappeared! [4] Then Jesus said to him, "Don't speak to anyone, but go at once and find a priest and show him what has happened to you. Make sure to take the offering Moses commanded so they can certify your healing."[c]

Jesus Heals the Son of a Roman Officer

[5] When Jesus entered the village of Capernaum, a captain[d] in the Roman army approached him, asking for a miracle.[e] [6] "Lord," he said, "I have a son[f] who is lying in my home, paralyzed and suffering terribly."

[7] Jesus responded, "I will go with you and heal him."

[8-9] But the Roman officer interjected, "Lord, who am I to have you come into my house? *I understand your authority,* for I too am a man who walks under authority and have authority over soldiers who serve under me. I can tell one to go and he'll go, and another to come and he'll come. I order my servants and they'll do whatever I ask. So I know that all you need to do is to stand here and command healing over my son and he will be instantly healed."

[10] Jesus was astonished when he heard this and said to those who were following him, "He has greater faith than anyone I've encountered in Israel! [11] Listen to what I am about to tell you. Multitudes of non-Jewish people will stream from the east and the west, to enter into the banqueting feast with Abraham, Isaac, and Jacob in the heavenly kingdom. [12] But many Israelites, born to be heirs of the kingdom, will be turned away and banished into the darkness where there will be bitter weeping and unbearable anguish."[g]

[13] Then Jesus turned to the Roman officer and said, "Go home. All that you have believed for will be done for you!" And his son was healed at that very moment.

Jesus Heals Everyone in Capernaum

[14] Then Jesus went into Peter's home and found Peter's mother-in-law bedridden,

---

a 8:2 As translated from the Aramaic and Hebrew Matthew, and implied in the Greek.

b 8:3 The word *leprosy* was used for various skin disorders. For Jesus to touch a leper was to render him ceremonially unclean, but Jesus wasn't defiled by touching the leper—the leper was healed!

c 8:4 Or "as a testimony to them." See Lev. 13–14 for the prescribed ritual for the cleansing of a leper.

d 8:5 Or "centurion."

e 8:5 Implied in the narrative.

f 8:6 As translated from the Aramaic and Hebrew Matthew. The Greek is "servant."

g 8:12 Or "gnashing of teeth." See also Job 16:9; Pss. 35:16; 37:12; 112:10; Jer. 9:9–14.

severely ill with a fever. [15] The moment Jesus touched her hand she was healed! Immediately she got up and began to make dinner for them.

[16] That evening the people brought to him many who were demonized. And by Jesus only speaking a word of healing over them, they were totally set free from their torment, [a] and everyone who was sick received their healing! [17] In doing this, Jesus fulfilled the prophecy of Isaiah:

> He put upon himself our weaknesses, [b]
> and he carried away our diseases and made us well.

[18] At the sight of large crowds gathering around him, Jesus gave orders to his disciples to get ready to sail back over to the other side of the lake. [c] [19] Just then, a religious scholar [d] approached him and said, "Teacher, I'll follow you wherever you go!"

[20] Jesus replied, **"Foxes have dens, birds have nests, but the Son of Man [e] has no true home in this world." [f]**

[21] Then another man spoke up and said, "Lord, I'll follow you, but first I must take care of my aged father and bury him when he dies." [g]

[22] But Jesus said to him, **"Now is the time to follow me, and let those who are dead bury their own dead." [h]**

Jesus Calms a Storm

[23] They all got into a boat and began to cross over to the other side of the lake. *And Jesus, exhausted, fell asleep.* [24] Suddenly a violent storm [i] developed, with waves so high the boat was about to be swamped. Yet Jesus continued

---

a 8:16 Matthew gives us five instances of setting the demonized free: here; 9:32–34; 12:22; 15:22–28; 17:18.

b 8:17 The Aramaic "wounds" or "sores." See Isa. 53:4.

c 8:18 This was the eastern bank of Lake Galilee, located on the Syrian side.

d 8:19 Or "expert of the Law" (scribe). These were the top religious scholars among the Pharisees, whose occupation was the systematic study of the law of Moses.

e 8:20 Or "this True Man." See Dan. 7:13–14.

f 8:20 Or "no place to lay my head" (homeless).

g 8:21 Or "but first let me go bury my father." This is a figure of speech for saying, "I can't follow you, but I will after my father dies."

h 8:22 Jesus requires that following him supersede any cultural or religious duty. Jewish culture in the time of Jesus gave the family the responsibility of a re-interment of the bones of the deceased into an ossuary one year after death. It is possible that this man's father had passed away but the year had not yet completed. He was saying, "I'll follow you after this year is completed." Jesus is not telling him to dishonor his father by not doing a burial, but that the custom of waiting a year (tradition) must never trump following him. He is telling the man that the spiritually dead are capable of burying the dead, so nothing should keep anyone from following him.

i 8:24 Or "earthquake." This could have been a temblor that caused tidal waves that swamped their boat. Most expositors equate this instead to the shaking of a violent storm.

to sleep soundly. [25] The disciples woke him up, saying, "Save us, Lord! We're going to die!" [a]

[26] But Jesus reprimanded them. "Why are you gripped with fear? [b] Where is your faith?" Then he stood up and rebuked [c] the storm and said, "Be still!" And instantly it became perfectly calm. [d]

[27] The disciples were astonished by this miracle and said to one another, "Who is this Man? Even the wind and waves obey his Word."

Jesus Sets Free Two Demonized Men

[28] When they arrived on the other side of the lake, in the region of the Gadarenes, [e] two demonized men confronted Jesus. They lived among the tombs of a cemetery and were considered so extremely violent that no one felt safe passing through that area. [29] The demons screamed at Jesus, shouting, "Son of God, what do you want with us? [f] Leave us alone! Have you come to torment us before the appointed time?"

[30] There was a large herd of pigs feeding nearby, [31] so the demons pleaded, "If you cast us out, send us into that herd of pigs." [32] Jesus commanded, "Then go!" And at once the demons came out of the men and went into the pigs. [g] Then the entire herd of crazed pigs stampeded down the steep slope and fell into the water and drowned.

[33] The men who were herding the pigs fled to the nearby town and informed the people of all that had happened to the demonized men. [34] Then everyone from the town went out to confront Jesus and urged him to go away and leave them alone. [h]

---

a 8:25 See Ps. 44:23.
b 8:26 Or "Why are you so cowardly, you of such little faith?" Jesus is implying that if they had faith, they could have commanded the storm to be stilled and it would happen.
c 8:26 This is the same Greek word that is used when Jesus rebuked demons.
d 8:26 See Pss. 89:9; 107:23–30.
e 8:28 There are three possible locations for the region of the Gadarenes. (1) It could be only a few miles from the city of Gadara (modern-day Um Qeis). Gadara means "thorn hedge." (2) The du Tillet translation of Hebrew Matthew has "the region of the Girgashites." (3) Other scholars have concluded that it is the region near the town of Gergesa.
f 8:29 The demons immediately sensed the true identity of Jesus and knew a day of judgment was coming for them. Sadly, many people today have yet to realize who Jesus is and that there is a coming day of judgment for them.
g 8:32 How amazing that Jesus answered the request of the demons. How much more will he answer your prayers. This mass exorcism is an astonishing miracle demonstrating the authority and power of Jesus. It is also amazing that the people of the town didn't ask Jesus to remain with them. The one who can deliver two men from demonic power can also deliver a city.
h 8:34 It is possible that the people of this region worshiped the sow goddess, called "Nut" in Egypt. In Rome she was called "Maia," from which we get the month of May. The swine herders were possibly soothsayers and shamans. The mass suicide of these pigs proved that

Forgiveness and Healing

9 Jesus got into the boat and returned to what was considered his hometown, *Capernaum.*[a] [2] Just then some people brought a paraplegic man to him, lying on a sleeping mat. When Jesus perceived the strong faith within their hearts, he said to the paralyzed man, **"My son, be encouraged, for your sins have been forgiven."**[b]

[3] These words prompted some of the religious scholars who were present to think, "Why, that's nothing but blasphemy!"

[4] Jesus supernaturally perceived their thoughts, and said to them, **"Why do you carry such evil in your hearts? [5] Which is easier to say, 'Your sins are forgiven,' or, 'Stand up and walk!'?**[c] **[6] But now, to convince you that the Son of Man has been given authority to forgive sins, I say to this man, 'Stand up, pick up your mat, and walk home.'"** [7] Immediately the man sprang to his feet and left for home.

[8] When the crowds witnessed this miracle, they were awestruck.[d] They shouted praises to God because he had given such authority to human beings.

Jesus Calls Matthew to Follow Him

[9] As Jesus left Capernaum he came upon a tax-collecting station, where a traitorous Jew was busy at his work,[e] collecting taxes for the Romans. His name was Matthew. **"Come, follow me,"** Jesus said to him. Immediately Matthew jumped up and began to follow Jesus.

[10] Later, Jesus went to Matthew's home to share a meal with him. Many other tax collectors and outcasts of society were invited to eat with Jesus and his disciples.

[11] When those known as the Pharisees saw what was happening, they were indignant, and they kept asking Jesus' disciples, "Why would your Master dine with such lowlifes?"

[12] When Jesus overheard this, he spoke up and said, **"Healthy people don't**

---

the Son of God had authority over the principality of that region that confronted him the moment he came into their region.

a 9:1 Jesus had moved from Nazareth to Capernaum. See Matt. 4:13.

b 9:2 The Hebrew Matthew reads, "By the faith of the Mighty One your sins are forgiven." See also Ps. 103:3.

c 9:5 It is easy for anyone to say, "Your sins are forgiven," for that cannot be proven. But if someone were to tell a paralyzed man to stand up, and he didn't stand up, that would prove the person is a fraud. Jesus didn't do the "easy thing" without accomplishing the hard thing, the miracle of healing. Forgiveness and healing both flow from Jesus Christ.

d 9:8 The Aramaic word used here can mean either "awestruck/marveled," or "seized with fear." This may explain the variation within Greek manuscripts.

e 9:9 Or "sitting at his tax-collecting booth." Matthew means "gift of God." He was also known as Levi, which means "joined." It is possible that he took the name Matthew after becoming a believer.

need to see a doctor, but the sick[a] will go for treatment." [13]Then he added, "Now you should go and study the meaning of the verse:

I want you to show mercy, not just offer me a sacrifice.[b]

For I have come to invite the outcasts of society and sinners, not those who think they are already on the right path."[c]

Jesus Brings a New Reality

[14]The disciples of John the Baptizer approached Jesus with this question: "Why is it that we and the Pharisees fast regularly, but not your disciples?"

[15]Jesus replied, "How can the sons of the bridal chamber[d] grieve when the Bridegroom is next to them? But the days of fasting will come when the Bridegroom is taken away from them. [16]And who would mend worn-out clothing with new fabric? When the new cloth shrinks it will rip, making the hole worse than before. [17]And who would pour fresh, new wine into an old wineskin? Eventually the wine will ferment and make the wineskin burst, losing everything—the wine is spilled and the wineskin ruined. Instead, new wine is always poured into a new wineskin so that both are preserved."[e]

Jesus Heals and Raises the Dead

[18]While Jesus was still speaking, an influential Jewish leader[f] approached and knelt before him, saying, "Help me! My daughter has just died. Please come

---

a 9:12 The Hebrew word for "sick" can also mean "evil."

b 9:13 See Hos. 6:6. To "offer a sacrifice" would be a metaphor for placing strict obedience to the law over the triumph of mercy's kiss in our dealings with others. Sadly, many religious people today read this as "I desire religious exactness, not mercy." Transforming ministry shows unmerited mercy to the "sick."

c 9:13 The obvious implication Jesus is making is that all are sinners who need to come to him for salvation.

d 9:15 See Song. 1:4. These sons of the bridal chamber are "Shulamites," lovers of God.

e 9:17 The teaching of Jesus is the new wine and the new cloth. What Jesus taught cannot patch up the old religious system, nor can it be contained in a wineskin of worn-out traditions. It is new, exhilarating, and powerful. It must be poured into a heart made new. The new and the old are not meant to be together. Jesus makes all things new. He didn't come to reform Judaism, but to form a twice-born company of people.

f 9:18 This was Jairus, who was the leader of the Jewish synagogue and possibly even a member of the Sanhedrin. See Mark 5:21–23; Luke 8:40–42. The interwoven miracles of the daughter being raised from the dead and the woman being healed symbolize Israel and the church. Israel is the "dead daughter" that Jesus will soon raise to new life. On his way to raise her from the dead, he encountered a woman and healed her. The church is the healed woman. The girl, according to Jesus, was only "sleeping." He will come back to Israel, but on his way, he will heal the woman who touched him by faith. Jesus touched the girl, and the woman touched Jesus. The girl lived twelve years, then died. The woman had been dying twelve years, and then she lived.

and place your hand upon her so that she will live again." [19] So Jesus and his disciples got up and went with him.

[20] Suddenly, a woman came from behind Jesus and touched the tassel of his prayer shawl *for healing.* [a] She had been suffering from continual bleeding for twelve years, *but had faith that Jesus could heal her.* [21] For she kept saying to herself, "If I could only touch his prayer shawl I would be healed."

[22] Just then Jesus turned around and looked at her and said, "My daughter, be encouraged. Your faith has healed you." [b] And instantly she was healed!

[23] When Jesus finally entered the home of the Jewish leader, he saw a noisy crowd of mourners, wailing and playing a funeral dirge on their flutes. [24] He told them, "You must leave, for the little girl is not dead; she's only asleep." Then everyone began to ridicule him.

[25] After he made the crowd go outside, he went into the girl's room and gently took hold of her hand. She immediately stood to her feet! [26] And the news of this incredible miracle spread everywhere.

Jesus Opens Blind Eyes

[27] As Jesus left the house, two blind men began following him, shouting out over and over, "Son of David, [c] show us mercy and heal us!" [28] And they followed him right into the house where Jesus was staying. [d] So Jesus asked them, "Do you believe that I have the power to restore sight to your eyes?"

They replied, "Yes Lord, we believe!"

[29] Then Jesus put his hands over their eyes and said, "You will have what your faith expects!" [30] And instantly their eyes opened—they could see! Then Jesus warned them sternly, "Make sure that you tell no one what just happened!" [31] But unable to contain themselves, they went out and spread the news everywhere!

Jesus Heals the Mute

[32] While they were leaving, some people brought before Jesus a man with a demon spirit who couldn't speak. [33] Jesus cast the demon out of him, and immediately the man began to speak *plainly.* The crowds marveled in astonishment,

---

a 9:20 Or "for salvation." The blue tassel on the corner of the prayer shawl was said to symbolize all commandments and promises of God. See Num. 15:38–40. The Hebrew word for "fringe" or "border" (of a garment) can also mean "wing." Some have interpreted Mal. 4:2 ("healing in his wings") as a reference to the tassels of the prayer shawl.

b 9:22 Or "saved you."

c 9:27 This phrase is an obvious messianic term. The blind men are hoping that Jesus is the Messiah who will come and restore sight to the blind. See Isa. 29:18; 35:5–6; 42:7. Other than the wise men at Jesus' birth, these two blind men were the first to recognize Jesus as King.

d 9:28 This was most likely in Capernaum.

saying, "We've never seen miracles like this in Israel!"[a] [34] But the Pharisees kept saying, "The chief of demons is helping him drive out demons."

Workers for the Harvest

[35] Jesus walked throughout the region[b] with the joyful message of God's kingdom realm. He taught in their meeting houses, and wherever he went he demonstrated God's power by healing every kind of disease and illness.

[36] When he saw the vast crowds of people, Jesus' heart was deeply moved with compassion, because they seemed weary and helpless, like wandering sheep without a shepherd. [37] He turned to his disciples and said, "**The harvest is huge and ripe! But there are not enough harvesters to bring it all in.** [38] **As you go, plead with the Owner of the Harvest to thrust out**[c] **many more reapers to harvest his grain!**"

Jesus Sends Out His Twelve Apostles

10 Jesus gathered his twelve[d] disciples and imparted to them authority to cast out demons and to heal every sickness[e] and every disease.

[2] Now, these are the names of the first twelve apostles: first, Simon, who is nicknamed Peter, and Andrew, his brother. And then Jacob[f] and John, sons of Zebedee. [3] Next were Phillip and Bartholomew;[g] then Thomas and Matthew, the tax collector; Jacob the son of Alphaeus; Thaddeus;[h] [4] Simon, the former member of the Zealot party,[i] and Judas the locksmith, who eventually betrayed Jesus.[j]

---

a 9:33 Matt. 8 and 9 give us ten miracles that Jesus performed as signs to prove that he is the Messiah. Five are found in each chapter. In ch. 8 we find the leper healed, the military captain's son healed, Simon's mother-in-law healed, the raging storm stilled, and two demon-possessed men set free. In ch. 9 we find the paraplegic man healed, the woman with constant bleeding healed, Jairus' daughter raised from the dead, and two blind men given sight. These signs demonstrated Jesus' authority and power over sickness, storms, Satan, and death.

b 9:35 Or "in all the towns and villages."

c 9:38 The Greek word *ekballo* is used many times in the Gospels for driving out or casting out demons. The Lord of the Harvest must cast the laborers out into the harvest fields.

d 10:1 The number twelve speaks of governmental authority. Israel had twelve tribes, and Jesus chose twelve disciples. Only after Jesus gave them this authority were they called apostles. The authority Jesus gave them is what he had demonstrated over the previous five chapters of Matthew. After Christ's resurrection he reminded them, as he sent them again to the nations, that "all authority has already been given to you." Here Jesus makes these twelve men the answer to their own prayers for the Lord of the Harvest to send out more reapers.

e 10:1 The Aramaic word is "ailment" or "affliction."

f 10:2 Or "James." Translations of the Bible have substituted Jacob with James. Both Greek and Aramaic leave the Hebrew name as it is, Jacob. This translation will use Jacob throughout.

g 10:3 Bartholomew is likely another name for Nathaniel. See John 1:45.

h 10:3 Or "Lebbaeus."

i 10:4 Or "the patriot." The Zealot party was also known as the Daggar party. Some manuscripts read "Simon the Canaanite."

j 10:4 The name Judas is actually Judah. Iscariot is not his last name, but could be taken from

[5] Jesus commissioned these twelve to go out *into the ripened harvest fields* with these instructions: "Don't go into any non-Jewish or Samaritan territory.[a] [6] Go instead and find the lost sheep[b] among the people of Israel. [7] And as you go, preach this message: 'Heaven's kingdom realm is accessible, close enough to touch.'[c] [8] You must continually bring healing to lepers and to those who are sick,[d] and make it your habit to break off the demonic presence from people,[e] and raise the dead back to life. Freely[f] you have received *the power of the kingdom*, so freely release it to others. [9] You won't need a lot of money.[g] [10] Travel light,[h] and don't even pack an extra change of clothes in your backpack. Trust God for everything, because the one who works for him deserves to be provided for.

[11] "Whatever village or town you enter, search for a godly[i] man who will let you into his home until you leave for the next town. [12] Once you enter a house, speak to the family there and say, 'God's blessing of peace be upon this house!' [13] And if those living there welcome you, let your peace come upon the house. But if you are rejected, that blessing of peace will come back upon you. [14] And if anyone doesn't listen to you and rejects your message, when you leave that house or town, shake the dust off your feet *as a prophetic act that you will not take their defilement with you.*[j] [15] Mark my

---

the name of the town, Kerioth, twelve miles south of Hebron. But more plausibly, Iscariot is taken from a Hebrew word meaning "lock," Judah being a locksmith. He likely was the one chosen to lock the collection bag, which means he had the key and could pilfer the fund at will. It is his sad history that he wanted to lock up Jesus and control him for his own ends.

a 10:5 Or "Don't go on the paths of the non-Jewish people."

b 10:6 The Hebrew Matthew is "the sheep who have strayed from the house of Israel."

c 10:7 The Hebrew Matthew and a few Greek manuscripts add the call to repentance with the word "Repent (turn from sin and turn to God), for the kingdom of heaven approaches."

d 10:8 Or "the weak."

e 10:8 The Aramaic is "cure the insane."

f 10:8 That is, don't charge for preaching the gospel.

g 10:9 Or "Don't take gold, silver, or copper." The Hebrew Matthew is "Don't heap up silver and gold in your money belts." The Aramaic has the nuance of more than not taking money, but of not going after the accumulation of money by using God's anointing.

h 10:10 Or "Don't take sandals or a staff," which is likely a figure of speech for "Travel light." The reason Jesus told his disciples to leave their things behind is that they already had what was most important. Our "money" or wealth is in the kingdom realm of God. Our "clothing" is the garment of righteousness we wear in Christ. Our "backpack" points to our past experiences, which we tend to carry as weights on our backs. We leave our past behind since it no longer exists in Christ. Our "shoes" become a picture of the good news we walk in as we experience his continual peace. Our "staff" is a symbol of authority, and we take with us no other authority but Christ's. We can leave it all behind since we take it all with us in Christ.

i 10:11 Or "worthy" or "honorable"; that is, "deserving of your confidence." The "worthy" man would be one who welcomed the disciples into his home, providing hospitality to them.

j 10:14 Implied in the historical context of shaking dust off of one's feet when leaving a city. The "uncleanness" could also refer to any bitter response to the rejection they experienced. They were to "shake it off" before they went to their next assignment.

words, on the day of judgment the wicked people who lived in the land of Sodom and Gomorrah will have a lesser degree of judgment than the city that rejects you, *for the people of Sodom and Gomorrah did not have the opportunity that was given to them!* [16] Now, remember, it is I who sends you out, even though you feel vulnerable as lambs going into a pack of wolves. So be as shrewd as snakes yet as harmless [a] as doves."

Jesus Warns His Apostles of Persecution

[17] "Be on your guard! For there will be those who will betray you before their religious councils and brutally beat you with whips in their public gatherings. [b] [18] And because you follow me, they will take you to stand trial in front of rulers and even kings as an opportunity to testify of me before them and the unbelievers. [c] [19] So when they arrest you, don't worry about how to speak or what you are to say, for the Holy Spirit will give you at that very moment the words to speak. [20] It won't be you speaking but the Spirit of your Father repeatedly speaking through you. [d]

[21] "A brother will betray his brother unto death—even a father his child! Children will rise up against their parents and have them put to death. [22] Expect to be hated by all because of my name, but be faithful to the end and you will experience life and deliverance. [c] [23] And when they persecute you in one town, flee to another. But I promise you this: you will not deliver all the cities and towns of Israel until the Son of Man will have made his appearance. [f]

[24] "A student is not superior to his teacher any more than a servant would be greater than his master. [25] The student must be satisfied to share his teacher's fate and the servant his master's. If they have called the head of the family 'lord of flies,' [g] no wonder they malign the members of his family.

[26] "Don't be afraid or intimidated by others, for God will bring everything out into the open and every secret will be told. [27] What I say to you in the dark, repeat in broad daylight, and what you hear in a whisper,

---

a 10:16 Or "innocent."

b 10:17 Although this can be translated "synagogues," it is actually a gathering of people. No one would be scourged in a synagogue building. See Luke 4:28–30. The Sinaiticus version of Matthew is "courts of justice."

c 10:18 This prophecy of Jesus was fulfilled many times over with the apostles of the Lamb.

d 10:20 See Ex. 4:12.

e 10:22 There is found here one of the agrapha, quoted from an earlier gospel manuscript that has been lost, which reads, "As often as you fall, rise up, and you will be saved." *Akolouthia of Confession* (Evans, *The Historical Jesus*; 2004, *supra*, at 213).

f 10:23 As translated from the Aramaic, which can also be translated "Those who believe [in hope] until the end will live." The Greek is somewhat ambiguous and reads, "You will not finish going through all the towns of Israel before the Son of Man comes."

g 10:25 Or *Baal-zebub*, a derisive term for Satan. There is some evidence that the Hebrew word *Baal-zebub* could also mean "lord of tricks" (or "trickster").

announce it publicly. [28] Don't be in fear of those who can kill only the body but not your soul. Fear only God, who is able to destroy both soul and body in hell. [29] You can buy two sparrows for only a copper coin, yet not even one sparrow falls from its nest without the knowledge of your Father. Aren't you worth much more to God than many sparrows? [30-31] So don't worry. For your Father cares deeply about even the smallest detail of your life. [a]

[32] "If you openly and publicly acknowledge me, I will freely and openly acknowledge you before my heavenly Father. [33] But if you publicly deny that you know me, [b] I will also deny you before my heavenly Father.

[34] "Perhaps you think I've come to spread peace and calm over the earth—but my coming will bring conflict and division, [c] not peace. [35] Because of me,

A son will turn against his father,
    a daughter her mother
    and against her mother-in-law. [d]
[36] Within your own families you will find enemies. [e]

[37] "Whoever loves father or mother or son or daughter more than me is not fit to be my disciple. [f] [38] And whoever comes to me must follow in my steps and be willing to share my cross and experience it as his own, or he cannot be considered to be my disciple. [39] All who seek to live apart from me [g] will lose it all. But those who let go of their lives for my sake and surrender it all to me will discover true life!

[40] "Whoever receives you receives me, and whoever receives me receives the One who sent me. [h] [41] Whoever receives a prophet because he is God's messenger [i] will share a prophet's reward. And whoever welcomes a good and godly man because he follows me [j] will also share in his reward. [42] And whoever gives a cup of cold water to one of my humble disciples, I promise you, he will not go unrewarded."

---

a   10:30–31 Or "even the hairs of your head are numbered."
b   10:33 The Aramaic can be translated "he who blasphemes me."
c   10:34 Or "I have not come to bring peace but a sword." The Aramaic word *harba* can mean either "sword" or "war." The Greek is "sword" (of division). Either term signifies division.
d   10:35 The Hebrew Matthew adds here, "For there will be five in a house, three against two and two against three, father against son and son against father, and they will stand alone." This is missing from the Greek manuscripts.
e   10:36 See Mic. 7:6.
f   10:37 Or "is of no use to me." The Hebrew Matthew is "I am not suitable for him."
g   10:39 Or "Anyone who clings to his own life [soul, self, being]."
h   10:40 Justin Martyr (AD 165) cited this verse but translated it, possibly from an earlier manuscript, "He who hears me hears Him who sent me" (*First Apology* LXXXII).
i   10:41 Or "in the name of a prophet." See 1 Kings 17:9–24; 2 Kings 4:9–37.
j   10:41 Or "in the name of a righteous person."

Jesus and John the Baptizer

11 After Jesus finished giving instructions to his twelve disciples, he went on to minister in different villages throughout the region.

² Now, while John the Baptizer was in prison, he heard about what Christ was doing among the people, so he sent his disciples to ask him this question: ³ "Are you really the one prophesied would come, or should we still wait for another?"

⁴ Jesus answered them, "Give John this report: ⁵ 'The blind see again, the crippled walk, lepers are cured, the deaf hear, the dead are raised back to life, and the poor and broken now hear of the hope of salvation!'ᵃ ⁶ And tell John that the blessing of heaven comes upon those who never lose their faith in meᵇ—no matter what happens!"

⁷ As they were leaving, Jesus began to speak to the crowd about John. "What kind of man did you see when you went out into the wilderness? Did you expect to see a man who would be easily intimidated?ᶜ ⁸ Who was he? Did you expect to see a man decked out in the splendid fashion of the day?ᵈ Those who wear fancy clothes live like kings in palaces. ⁹ Or did you encounter a true prophet out in the lonely wilderness? Yes, John was a prophet like those of the past, but he is even more than that! ¹⁰ He was the fulfillment of this Scripture:

> See, I am sending my prophetic messengerᵉ
>   who will go ahead of me
>   and prepare hearts to receive me.ᶠ

¹¹ "For I tell you the truth, throughout history there has never been a man who surpasses John the Baptizer. Yet the least of those who now experience heaven's kingdom realm will become even greater than he. ¹² From the moment John stepped onto the scene until now, the realm of heaven's kingdom is bursting forth, and passionate people have taken hold of its power.ᵍ ¹³ For all the prophets and the Torahʰ prophesied until John appeared. ¹⁴ If you

---

a   11:5 This fulfills many Old Testament references to the coming of the Messiah, including Isa. 29:18–19; 35:5–6; 61:1. Jesus is assuring John that the message he brings is life and salvation, not judgment and wrath.

b   11:6 Or "Blessed are those who are not offended over me."

c   11:7 Or "a reed shaken by the wind?"

d   11:8 See Matt. 3:4.

e   11:10 Or "angel."

f   11:10 This is quoted from Mal. 3:1.

g   11:12 Or "The kingdom of heaven is entered into by force, and violent ones take hold of it." This is one of the most difficult passages in Matthew to translate from the Greek. When the Greek words are translated into Hebrew it becomes a clear reference to Mic. 2:12–13 and includes the "breaking forth [Hb. *peretz*]."

h   11:13 That is, the first five books of the Bible (Genesis, Exodus, Leviticus, Numbers, and Deuteronomy).

352 of MATTHEW 11

can receive this truth, John is the Elijah who was destined to come. [15] So listen and understand what I'm telling you. [a]

[16] "Don't you understand? How could I describe the people of this generation? You're like children playing games on the playground, yelling at their playmates, [17] 'You don't like it when we want to play Wedding! And you don't like it when we want to play Funeral! You will neither dance nor mourn.' [18] Why is it that when John came to you, neither feasting nor drinking wine, you said, 'He has a demon in him!'? [19] Yet when the Son of Man came and went to feasts and drank wine, you said, 'Look at this Man! He is nothing but a glutton and a drunkard! He spends all his time with tax collectors and other affluent sinners.' [b] But God's wisdom will be visibly seen living in those who embrace it." [c]

Jesus Criticizes Unrepentant Cities

[20] Then Jesus began to openly denounce the cities where he had done most of his mighty miracles, because the people failed to turn away from sin and return to God. [21] He said, "How tragic it will be for the city of Korazin! And how horrible for the city of Bethsaida! For if the powerful miracles that I performed in Korazin and Bethsaida had been done in Tyre and Sidon, [d] they would have humbled themselves and repented, and turned from their sins. [22] Tyre and Sidon [e] will better off on judgment day than you! [23] And Capernaum—do you really think you'll be exalted because of the great miracles I have done there? No! You'll be brought down to the depths of hell [f] because of your rejection of me. For if the miracles I worked in your streets were done in Sodom, it would still be standing today! [24] But I tell you, it will be more bearable for the region of Sodom in the day of judgment than it will be for you."

Jesus Invites Everyone to Come

[25] Then Jesus exclaimed, "Father, thank you, for you are Lord, the Supreme Ruler over heaven and earth! And you have hidden the great revelation of your authority from those who are proud and wise in their own eyes. Instead, you have shared it with these who humble themselves. [26] Yes, Father, your plan delights your heart, as you've chosen this way to extend your

---

a 11:15 Or "Anyone who has ears to hear, let him hear," an idiom that means "You'd better listen!"

b 11:19 As translated from Hebrew Matthew.

c 11:19 Or more literally "Wisdom is vindicated by all her children" (Gr. *teknon*) (some manuscripts, "by her deeds"). The Aramaic word can mean either "servant" (disciple) or "works," which would explain the difference in some Greek manuscripts.

d 11:21 The Hebrew Matthew is "Sodom."

e 11:22 Tyre and Sidon were two gentile cities on the Mediterranean coast that were known for their wickedness.

f 11:23 See Isa. 14:13–15.

kingdom—*by giving it to those who have become like trusting children.* [27] You have entrusted me with all that you are and all that you have. No one fully and intimately knows the Son except the Father. And no one fully and intimately knows the Father except the Son. But the Son is able to unveil the Father to anyone he chooses.

[28] "Are you weary, carrying a heavy burden? Then come to me.[a] I will refresh your life, for I am your oasis.[b] [29] Simply join your life with mine.[c] Learn my ways and you'll discover that I'm gentle,[d] humble, easy to please. You will find refreshment and rest in me.[e] [30] For all that I require of you will be pleasant[f] and easy to bear."[g]

Jesus, Lord over the Sabbath

12 One Saturday, on the day of rest,[h] Jesus and his disciples were walking through a field of wheat. The disciples were hungry, so they plucked off some heads of grain and rubbed them in their hands[i] to eat. [2] But when some of the Pharisees saw what was happening, they said to him, "Look! Your disciples shouldn't be harvesting grain on the Sabbath!"

[3] Jesus responded, "Haven't you ever read what King David and his men did when they were hungry? [4] They entered the house of God[j] and ate the sacred bread of God's presence,[k] violating the law by eating bread that only the priests were allowed to eat.

[5] "And haven't you read in the Torah that the priests violated the rules of the Sabbath by carrying out their duties in the temple on a Saturday, and yet they are without blame? [6] But I say to you, there is one here who is even greater than the temple. [7] If only you could learn the meaning of the words

---

a 11:28 Many times Jesus said, "Come after (follow) me," but only here does he say, "Come to me." See Ex. 33:14; Matt. 23:4.

b 11:28 As translated from the Aramaic.

c 11:29 Or "Bend your neck to my yoke." The metaphor of a yoke is that it joins two animals to work as one. It is not simply work or toil that is the focus here, but union with Christ.

d 11:29 The Aramaic is "tranquil" or "peaceful."

e 11:29 As translated from the Hebrew Matthew. The Aramaic could be translated "Come to me and I will cheer [refresh] you. I am cheerful [refreshing] and humble in heart, and you will find cheer [refreshing] for your soul."

f 11:30 Or "kind" (or "delightful").

g 11:30 See Ps. 55:22.

h 12:1 The Hebrew word for Sabbath comes from *shavat*, which is the verb "to rest." What was designed to be a day of rest and intimacy with God and family was now complicated by a host of rules and traditions.

i 12:1 As found in Hebrew Matthew.

j 12:4 That is, the tabernacle. See 1 Sam. 21:1–6. Ancient Jewish tradition states that David did this on a Sabbath day. See also Lev. 24:5–9.

k 12:4 Or "loaves of presentation." See Ezek. 44:15–16.

'I want compassion more than a sacrifice,'ᵃ you wouldn't be condemning my innocent disciples. ⁸For the Son of Man exercises his lordship over the Sabbath."ᵇ

⁹Then Jesus left them and went into the synagogue where ¹⁰he encountered a man who had an atrophied, paralyzed hand.ᶜ The fault-finding Pharisees asked Jesus, "Is it permissible to perform a work of healing on the Sabbath, *when no one is supposed to work?*" They only asked him this question because they hoped to accuse him of breaking the Jewish laws.ᵈ

¹¹He answered them, "If any of you had a lamb that fell into a ditch on the Sabbath, wouldn't you reach out your hand and lift it out? ¹²Isn't a man much more valuable than a lamb? So of course, it's always proper to do miracles,ᵉ even on the Sabbath."

¹³Then he turned to the man and said, "Hold out your hand!" And as he stretched it out, it was restored, exactly like the other.

¹⁴Immediately the Pharisees went out and started to scheme about how they would do away with him. ¹⁵Jesus knew what they were thinking, so he left by another way. Massive crowds followed him from there, and he healed all who were sick. ¹⁶However, he sternly warned them not to tell others or disclose his real identity, ¹⁷in order to fulfill the prophecy of Isaiah:ᶠ

¹⁸Take a careful look at my servant,ᵍ my chosen one.
    I love him dearly
    and I find all my delight in him.ʰ
    I will breathe my Spirit upon him
    and he will decree justiceⁱ to the nations.
¹⁹He will not quarrel or be found yelling in public.
²⁰He won't brush aside the bruised and broken.
    He will be gentle with the weak and feeble,ʲ

---

a 12:7 See Hos. 6:6. Mercy is greater than ritual.

b 12:8 Jesus made three startling statements that stunned those who heard him. First he said that he was greater than the temple (v. 6), then that God didn't want sacrifices but mercy (v. 7), and finally that he, the Messiah, was the Lord of the Sabbath. Don't be surprised when Jesus shocks you with truth that is outside your understanding.

c 12:10 There is a reading given by Jerome which inserts here these words, possibly from an older manuscript of Hebrew Matthew: "I was a stonemason working with my hands. Jesus, I beg you to heal me so that I don't have to shamefully beg for food." See Jerome, *Commentary in Matthew* xii:13 (de Santos 23).

d 12:10 The Aramaic is "They were like pests who wanted to devour him."

e 12:12 As translated from the Aramaic. The Greek is "to do (morally) good."

f 12:17 See Isa. 42:1–4.

g 12:18 Or "Here is my son."

h 12:18 The Aramaic is literally "He has sun-shined my being."

i 12:18 Or "judgment."

j 12:20 Or "A bruised reed he will not break and a smoldering wick he will not extinguish."

until his victory releases justice.

[21] And the fame of his name
 will birth hope among the people. [a]

Jesus Frees a Demonized Man

[22] Then a man was brought before Jesus who had a demon spirit that made him both blind and unable to speak. Jesus healed him instantly, and he could see and talk again! [23] The crowds went wild with amazement as they witnessed this miracle. And they kept saying to one another, "Could this man be the Messiah?" [b]

[24] But when the Pharisees overheard what the people were saying about the miracle, they said, "He casts out demons by the power of Satan, [c] the prince of demons!"

[25] Now, Jesus supernaturally perceived their thoughts and motives, so he confronted them by telling them this parable: [d]

"Any kingdom that fights against itself will end up in ruins. And any family or community splintered by strife will fall apart. [26] So if Satan casts out Satan, he is making war on himself. How then could his kingdom survive? [27] So if Satan empowers me to cast out demons, who empowers your exorcists [e] to cast them out? Go ask them, for what they do proves you're wrong in your accusations. [f] [28] On the other hand, if I drive out demons by the power of the Spirit of God, then the end of Satan's kingdom has come! [g] [29] Who would dare enter the house of a mighty man and steal his property? First he must be overpowered and tied up by one who is stronger than he. Then his entire house can be plundered and every possession stolen.

[30] "So join with me, [h] for if you're not on my side you are against me. And if you refuse to help me gather the spoils, *you are making things worse.* [i] [31] This is why I warn you, for God will forgive people for every sin and blasphemy

---

The Hebrew Matthew adds a phrase here that corresponds to Isa. 42: "He will not fail or be discouraged."

a 12:21 Hebrew Matthew is "The islands will wait for his teachings."

b 12:23 Or "Could he be the Son of David," a title used for the Messiah.

c 12:24 Or "Beelzebub" (*Baal-zebub*), a title used for Satan. See footnote on Matt. 10:25.

d 12:25 As translated from the Hebrew Matthew.

e 12:27 Or "your sons," and by implication, "your followers" (who are exorcists).

f 12:27 In other words, to condemn Jesus as working by Satan's power would be to condemn their own exorcists.

g 12:28 As translated from Hebrew Matthew and implied in the Greek. The Greek text, somewhat ambiguously, reads, "then the kingdom of God has approached." The Hebrew Matthew cohesively fits Jesus' parable in making the conclusion that the end of Satan's kingdom has arrived for he has bound the mighty one (Satan) and ransacked his house (kingdom). Regardless, one indeed implies the other.

h 12:30 Jesus is saying, "This is a war with no neutrality. Join my side or you will miss the spoils of victory and be forever scattered."

i 12:30 The Hebrew Matthew is "He who does not join me denies me."

they have committed except one. There is no forgiveness for the sin of blasphemy against the Holy Spirit. [32] If anyone speaks evil of me, the Son of Man, he can be forgiven; but if anyone contemptuously speaks against the Holy Spirit, it will never be forgiven, now or ever!"

Only Good Trees Bear Good Fruit

[33] "You must determine if a tree is good or rotten. You can recognize good trees by their delicious fruit. But if you find rotten fruit, you can be certain that the tree is rotten. The fruit defines the tree. [34] But you who are known as the Pharisees are rotten to the core! You've been poisoned by the nature of a venomous snake. [a] How can your words be good and trustworthy if you are rotten within? For what has been stored up in your hearts will be heard in the overflow of your words! [b]

[35] "When virtue is stored within, the hearts of good and upright people will produce good fruit. But when evil is hidden within, those who are evil will produce evil fruit. [36] You can be sure of this: when the day of judgment comes, everyone will be held accountable for every careless word [c] he has spoken. [d] [37] Your very words will be used as evidence against you, and your words will declare you either innocent or guilty."

The Sign of Jonah

[38] Then a few Jewish scholars and Pharisees spoke up and said, "Teacher, why don't you perform a miraculous sign for us."

[39] Jesus replied, "Only evil people who are unfaithful to God would demand a sign. [e] There will be no sign given to you except the sign of the prophet Jonah. [40] For just like Jonah was in the belly of the huge sea creature for three days and three nights, so the Son of Man will be in the heart of the earth for three days and three nights. [41] The people of Nineveh will also rise up on the day of judgment to accuse and condemn this generation. [f] For they all repented when they heard the preaching of Jonah, yet you have refused to repent. And there is one greater than Jonah who is preaching to you

---

a   12:34 Or "You are the sons of snakes"; that is, their inner identity was like a striking, poisonous viper.

b   12:34 The Hebrew Matthew reads, "Truly the heart awakens and the mouth speaks."

c   12:36 Or "worthless word." The Aramaic is "every untrue word."

d   12:36 The agrapha includes a sentence here, also quoted by Justin Martyr: "In the words I find you saying, in those I will judge you." See Justin Martyr, *Dialogue* 47:5.

e   12:39 After experiencing the many miracles of Jesus' love and power, and hearing his words of grace, for them to demand a further sign is what distinguished that generation as "evil."

f   12:41 The Aramaic is "tribe." The Ninevites (modern-day Mosul, Iraq) were pagans, yet through the preaching of one prophet they converted. The people of Israel had many prophets throughout their history, and the greatest Prophet of all was now preaching to them, yet they refused to listen.

today! [42] Even the Queen of Sheba[a] will rise up on the day of judgment to accuse and condemn this generation for its unbelief! She journeyed from a far and distant land just to hear the wisdom of King Solomon. Yet now there is one greater than Solomon speaking to you, and you still refuse to listen."

Demons

[43] "When a demon is cast out of a person, it roams around a dry region, looking for a place to rest, but never finds it. [44] Then it says, 'I'll return to the house I moved out of,' and so it goes back, only to find that the house is vacant, warm, and ready for it to move back in.[b] [45] So it goes looking for seven other demons more evil than itself, and they all enter together to live there. Then the person's condition becomes much worse than it was in the beginning. This describes what will also happen to the people of this evil generation."

Jesus' True Family

[46] While Jesus was still speaking to the crowds, his mother and brothers came and stood outside, asking for him to come out and speak with them. [47] Then someone said, "Look, your mother and brothers are standing outside, wanting to have a word with you." [48] But Jesus just looked at him and said, "Let me introduce you to my true mother and brothers." [49] Then gesturing to the disciples gathered around him, he said, "Look closely, for this is my true family. [50] When you obey my heavenly Father, that makes you a part of my true family."

The Parables of Jesus

13 Later that day, Jesus left the house and sat by the lakeshore to teach the people. [2] Soon, there were so many people surrounding him that he had to teach sitting in a boat while the large crowd stood on the shore. [3] He taught them many things by using stories, parables that would illustrate spiritual truths,[c] saying:

"Consider this: There was a farmer who went out to sow seeds. [4] As he

---

a   12:42 Literally "the queen of the south." See 1 Kings 10:1–13. Sheba is modern-day Yemen.
b   12:44 As translated from the Aramaic. The Greek is "swept clean and put in order."
c   13:3 The Aramaic and Greek use a word for "parable" that means "a metaphor, allegory, simile, illustration, comparison, figure of speech, riddle, or enigmatic saying that is meant to stimulate intense thought." Throughout Hebrew history wise men, prophets, and teachers used parables and allegories as a preferred method of teaching spiritual truths. Poets would write their riddles and musicians would sing their proverbs with verbal imagery. Jesus never taught the people without using allegory and parables (Matt. 13:34). As a true prophet, one of Jesus' preferred methods of teaching was allegory. To deny the validity of allegorical teaching is to ignore the teaching methods of Jesus, the Living Word. This chapter contains seven parables of Jesus: (1) the parable of the seed, (2) the parable of the wheat and weeds, (3) the parable of the net, (4) the parable of the tiny mustard seed, (5) the parable of yeast, (6) the parable of the hidden treasure, and (7) the parable of the costly pearl.

cast his seeds, some fell along the beaten path and the birds came and ate them. ⁵ Other seeds fell onto gravel that had no topsoil. The seeds quickly shot up, ⁶ but when the days grew hot, the sprouts were scorched and withered because they had insufficient roots. ⁷ Other seeds fell among the thorns and weeds, so when the seeds sprouted, so did the weeds, crowding out the good plants. ⁸ But other seeds fell on good, rich soil that kept producing a good harvest. Some yielded thirty, some sixty, and some even one hundred times as much as he planted! ⁹ If you're able to understand this, then you need to respond." ᵃ

¹⁰ Then his disciples approached Jesus and asked, "Why do you always speak to people in these hard-to-understand parables?"

¹¹ He explained, "You've been given the intimate experience of insight into the hidden truths and mysteries ᵇ of the realm of heaven's kingdom, but they have not. ¹² For everyone who listens with an open heart will receive progressively more revelation ᶜ until he has more than enough. ᵈ But those who don't listen with an open, teachable heart, even the understanding that they think they have will be taken from them. ᵉ ¹³ That's why I teach the people using parables, because they think they're looking for truth, yet because their hearts are unteachable, they never discover it. Although they will listen to me, they never fully perceive the message I speak. ¹⁴ The prophecy of Isaiah describes them perfectly:

> Although they listen carefully to everything I speak,
>> they don't understand a thing I say.
> They look and pretend to see,
>> but the eyes of their hearts are closed.
> ¹⁵ Their minds are dull and slow to perceive, ᶠ
>> their ears are plugged and are hard of hearing,

---

a 13:9 Or "The one with ears to hear should use them." See also v. 43.

b 13:11 The Greek word *musterion* is found twenty-seven times in the New Testament and means "secrets" or "mysteries." The mysteries of heaven's kingdom realm are spiritual insights into the nature and ways of God. Jesus Christ can only be fully understood by the spirit, not merely by the intellect of man. Jesus taught his disciples using the cryptic language of parables to move them beyond intellectual abilities and engage the spirit. If the listener had a hunger to learn with an open, teachable heart, then Jesus' words brought life and understanding. We must always be those who push aside our opinions and traditions to glean the deepest meaning of all that Jesus did and taught. See also Job 15:8; Prov. 3:32; 1 Cor. 2:14; Col. 2:2; 4:3.

c 13:12 Or "To he who has, more will be given." This is an obvious ellipsis that, in the context, refers to having an open heart to receive the understanding of the mysteries of the kingdom of heaven.

d 13:12 Or "until they habitually superabound" (with understanding).

e 13:12 As translated from Hebrew Matthew.

f 13:15 The Aramaic is "waterlogged."

and they have deliberately shut their eyes to the truth.
Otherwise they would open their eyes to see,
and open their ears to hear,
and open their minds to understand.
Then they would turn to me
and let me instantly heal them. [a]

[16] "But your eyes are privileged, for they see. Delighted are your ears, for they are open to hear all these things. [b] [17] Many prophets and godly people in times past yearned to see these days of miracles that you've been favored to see. They would have given everything to hear the revelation you've been favored to hear. Yet they didn't get to see as much as a glimpse or hear even a whisper.

[18] "Now you are ready to listen to the revelation of the parable of the sower and his seeds:

[19] "The seed that fell on the beaten path represents the heart of the one who hears the message of the kingdom realm [c] but doesn't understand it. The Adversary then comes and snatches away what was sown into his heart.

[20] "The seed sown on gravel represents the person who gladly hears the kingdom message, [d] but his experience remains shallow. [e] [21] Shortly after he hears it, troubles and persecutions come because of the kingdom message he received. Then he quickly falls away, [f] for the truth didn't sink deeply into his heart.

[22] "The seed sown among weeds represents the person who receives the message, but all of life's busy distractions, his divided heart, and his ambition for wealth [g] result in suffocating the kingdom message and prevent him from bearing spiritual fruit. [h]

[23] "As for the seed that fell upon good, rich soil, it represents the hearts of people who hear and fully embrace the message of heaven's kingdom realm. Their lives bear good fruit—some yield a harvest of thirty, sixty, even one hundred times as much as was sown."

---

a 13:15 See Isa. 6:9–10.

b 13:16 As translated from the Aramaic. Or "Your eyes have a blessing resting upon them because they see, and your ears because they hear."

c 13:19 The Aramaic can be translated "He hears of the manifestation of the kingdom." It is found also in vv. 20, 21, 22, and 23.

d 13:20 Hebrew Matthew is "the word of the Mighty One."

e 13:20 Implied by the "shallow" soil, representing a shallow interest that doesn't sink spiritual roots into the truth of God.

f 13:21 Or "gets offended" or "is made to stumble."

g 13:22 Or "deceptive riches." See Prov. 23:4–5.

h 13:22 Hebrew Matthew adds a phrase here: "and the Adversary causes him to forget the word of God."

The Parable of the Weeds

²⁴ Then Jesus taught them ᵃ another parable:

"Heaven's kingdom realm can be compared to a farmer who planted good seed in his field. ²⁵ But at night, when everyone was asleep, an enemy came and planted poisonous weeds ᵇ among the wheat and ran away. ²⁶ When the wheat sprouted and bore grain, the weeds also appeared. ²⁷ So the farmer's hired hands came to him and said, 'Sir, wasn't that good seed that you sowed in the field? Where did all these weeds come from?'

²⁸ "He answered, 'This has to be the work of an enemy!'

"They replied, 'Do you want us to go and gather up all the weeds?'

²⁹ "'No,' he said. 'If you pull out the weeds you might uproot the wheat at the same time. ³⁰ You must allow them both to grow together until the time of harvest. At that time, I'll tell my harvesters to make sure they gather the weeds first and tie them all in bundles to be burned. Then they will harvest the wheat and put it into my barn.'"

The Parable of the Tiny Mustard Seed

³¹ Then Jesus taught them another parable:

"Heaven's kingdom realm can be compared to the tiny mustard seed that a man takes and plants in his field. ³² Although the smallest of all the seeds, it eventually grows into the greatest of garden plants, becoming a tree for birds to come and build their nests in its branches."

The Parable of the Yeast

³³ Then he taught them another parable:

"Heaven's kingdom realm can be compared to yeast that a woman takes and blends into three measures of flour and then waits until all the dough rises." ᶜ

Prophecy and Parables

³⁴ Whenever Jesus addressed the crowds, he always spoke in allegories. He never spoke without using parables. ³⁵ He did this in order to fulfill the prophecy:

---

a 13:24 Or "set before them." See also vv. 31 and 33.

b 13:25 Or "darnel" or "rye grass." The Greek word *zizanion* is a noxious weed (*lolium temelentum*) that appears from a distance to look like wheat, but has poisonous black seeds. See *Fauna and Flora of the Bible* (London: United Bible Societies, 1980), 194.

c 13:33 These two parables, about the tiny mustard seed and the yeast, both teach of God's kingdom having a small beginning but growing until its influence permeates and prevails into all the earth. The "three measure [Hb. *seahs*] of flour" was nearly twenty-two kilos, enough to feed three hundred people. What once looked unimpressive rises to impact and feed many. The number three always points to resurrection life.

I will speak to you in allegories.
I will reveal secrets that have been concealed
since before the foundation of the world. *ᵃ*

Jesus Explains the Parables

³⁶ Jesus left the crowds and went inside the house *where he was staying.* *ᵇ* Then his disciples approached him and asked, "Please explain the deeper meaning of the parable of the weeds growing in the field of wheat."

³⁷ He answered, "The man who sowed his field with good seed represents me, the Son of Man. ³⁸ And the field is the world. The good seeds I sow are the children of the kingdom realm. The weeds are the children of the Evil One, ³⁹ and the enemy who sows them is the devil. The harvest points to the end of this age, and the harvesters are God's messengers. *ᶜ* ⁴⁰ As the weeds are bundled up and thrown into the fire, so it will be at the close of the age. ⁴¹ The Son of Man will send his messengers, and they will uproot everything out of his kingdom. All the lawless ones and everything that causes sin will be removed. ⁴² And they will throw them into the fiery furnace, where they will experience great sorrow, pain, and anguish. *ᵈ* ⁴³ Then the godly ones will shine like the brightness of the sun *ᵉ* in their Father's kingdom realm. If you're able to understand this, then you'd better respond!"

Parables of Hidden Treasure and an Extraordinary Pearl

⁴⁴ "Heaven's kingdom realm can be illustrated like this:

"A person discovered that there was hidden treasure in a field. Upon finding it, he hid it again. Because of uncovering such treasure, he was overjoyed and sold all that he possessed to buy the entire field *just so he could have the treasure.* *ᶠ*

---

a 13:35 As translated from the Aramaic. The Hebrew Matthew is "I will speak with riddles from ancient times." See Ps. 78:2; Prov. 25:2. A parable has hidden meaning. Everything stands for something else. Jesus interprets and unlocks the meaning of the Word to us.

b 13:36 This was likely in Capernaum.

c 13:39 Or "[God's] angels." In both Greek and Hebrew the word *angels* can also refer to human messengers.

d 13:42 Or "gnashing of teeth," a metaphor for despair and torment. The Aramaic can be translated "thrown into the essence of fire." The Aramaic word *athuna* can mean either "furnace" or "essence." See also v. 50.

e 13:43 See Judg. 5:31; Song. 6:10; Isa. 60:1; Dan. 12:3.

f 13:44 See also Prov. 2:4. The most accepted interpretation of this parable is that Jesus is the treasure, but Jesus taught that the field is the world (v. 38). The allegory breaks down, for a believer doesn't sell all he has (works) and then buy the world to find Jesus (the treasure). It is more plausible to view the hidden treasure as a symbol of you and me. Jesus is the man who sold all that he owned, leaving his exalted place of glory to come and pay for the sin of the whole world with his own blood just so he could have you, his treasure. Heaven's kingdom realm is experienced when we realize what a great price Jesus places on our souls,

[45] "Heaven's kingdom realm is also like a jewel merchant in search of rare pearls. [46] When he discovered one very precious[a] and exquisite pearl, he immediately gave up all he had in exchange for it."[b]

The Parable of the Fishing Net

[47] "Again, heaven's kingdom realm is like a fisherman who casts his large net into the lake, catching an assortment of different kinds of fish. [48] When the net was filled, the fishermen hauled it up on the shore, and they all sat down to sort out their catch. They collected the good fish in baskets and threw the bad away. [49] And so it will be at the close of the age. The messengers[c] will come and separate the evil from among the godly [50] and throw them into the fiery furnace, where they will experience great sorrow, pain, and anguish. [51] Now do you understand all this?"

"Yes," they replied.

[52] He responded, "Every scholar of the Scriptures,[d] who is instructed in the ways of heaven's kingdom realm, is like a wealthy home owner with his house filled with treasures both new and old. *And he knows how and when to bring them out to show others.*"[e]

[53] Right after Jesus taught this series of parables, he left[f] from there.

Jesus Rejected in His Hometown

[54] When Jesus arrived in his hometown *of Nazareth*, he began teaching the people in the synagogue. Everyone was dazed, overwhelmed with astonishment over the depth of revelation they were hearing. They said to one another, "Where did this man get such great wisdom and miraculous powers? [55] Isn't he just the

---

for he gave his sacred blood for us. The re-hiding of the treasure is a hint of our new life, hidden in God. See Eph. 1:4; Col. 3:1–5.

a   13:46 The Aramaic is "unique." Jesus is the merchant. (See Song. 3:6.) You are the exquisite and unique pearl, as his beloved follower, that came from the wounded side of Jesus Christ. You prompted him to give up all, including his sacred blood, in exchange for having you as his very own. See also Heb. 12:2.

b   13:46 See Isa. 43:4.

c   13:49 Or "angels."

d   13:52 Or "scribe."

e   13:52 These "new treasures" speak of new insights and understandings that are revealed at the proper time. The "old treasures" speak of truths that have been established, founded upon what God has already revealed. Teachers are to bring forth the revelation of God and his word as treasures to the people. We need both new and old insights.

f   13:53 The Greek word for "left" is *metairo* and means "to depart" or "to be lifted up and taken from one place to another."

wood-worker's son?"ᵃ Isn't his mother named Mary, and his four brothers Jacob,ᵇ Joseph, Simon, and Judah? ⁵⁶ And don't his sisters all live here in Nazareth? How did he get all this revelation and power?"ᶜ ⁵⁷ And the people became offended and began to turn against him.ᵈ

Jesus said, "There's only one place a prophet isn't honored—his own hometown!" ⁵⁸ And their great unbelief kept him from doing any mighty miracles *in Nazareth.*

John the Baptizer Killed

14 At that time Herod,ᵉ the Roman ruler over Galilee, heard reports about Jesus. ² He told his officials, "This man has to be John the Baptizer who has come back from the dead. That's why he has this power to work miracles."ᶠ ³ For Herod had earlier arrested John for confronting him over taking the wife of his brother Philip. He had John thrown in prison and placed in chains ⁴ because John had repeatedly said to him, "It's not legal or proper for you to be married to Herodias, your sister-in-law!"ᵍ ⁵ So Herod wanted John dead, but he was afraid of the crowds who flocked to John because they considered him to be a prophet.

⁶ During Herod's birthday celebration, the daughter of Herodiasʰ danced before Herod and all his distinguished quests, which greatly pleased the king. ⁷ So he said to her in front of them all, "I give you my oath, ask of me anything you wish and it will be yours!"

⁸ Because she had been instructed by her mother, she said, "I want the head of John the Baptizer here on a platter!"

⁹ This grieved the king, but because of his oath in front of all of his guests,

---

ᵃ 13:55 The Hebrew Matthew is "blacksmith's son." The Greek word *tekton* can be translated "carpenter," "metal worker," "sculptor," "artisan," "stone worker," or "builder." The people of Jesus' hometown presumed that Joseph was his father, but Jesus had no earthly father, because he was "born of a woman."

ᵇ 13:55 Or "James." Translations of the Bible have substituted Jacob with James. Both Greek and Aramaic leave the Hebrew name as it is, Jacob. This translation will use Jacob throughout.

ᶜ 13:56 Implied in the context. See v. 54.

ᵈ 13:57 The Aramaic is "They were suspicious of him." The Hebrew Matthew is "They were confused about him."

ᵉ 14:1 This was Herod Antipas, the son of Herod the Great who had the infant boys killed in Bethlehem. See Matt. 2:16. Herod Antipas was the one who Jesus stood before to be judged. See Luke 23:15.

ᶠ 14:2 The Aramaic is "This is why powers are emanating from him." Herod believed that it was the spirit of John working through Jesus, not the Spirit of God.

ᵍ 14:4 Herod Antipas wanted to take his brother's wife so he divorced his wife, a Nabatean princess, and Herodias divorced Philip so they could marry each other. This was why John confronted Herod. See Lev. 18:16.

ʰ 14:6 Josephus, the Jewish historian, notes that her daughter was named Salome.

[10] he had John beheaded in prison. [11] They brought in his head and displayed it to her on a platter, and she then had it shown to her mother.

[12] John's disciples went into the prison and carried his body away and buried it. Then they left to find Jesus and tell him what had happened.

Jesus Feeds the Multitude

[13] On hearing this, Jesus slipped away privately by boat to be alone. But when the crowds discovered he had sailed away, they emerged from all the nearby towns and followed him on foot. [14] So when Jesus landed he had a huge crowd waiting for him. Seeing so many people, his heart was deeply moved with compassion toward them, so he healed all the sick who were in the crowd.[a]

[15] Later that afternoon the disciples came to Jesus and said, "It's going to be dark soon and the people are hungry, but there's nothing to eat here in this desolate place. You should send the crowds away to the nearby villages to buy themselves some food."

[16] "They don't need to leave," Jesus responded. "You can give them something to eat."

[17] They answered, "But all we have is five barley loaves and two fish."

[18] "Let me have them," Jesus replied. [19] Then he had everyone sit down on the grass as he took the five loaves and two fish. He looked up into heaven, gave thanks to God, and broke the bread into pieces. He then gave it to his disciples, who in turn gave it to the crowds. [20] And everyone ate until they were satisfied, *for the food was multiplied in front of their eyes!*[b] They picked up the leftovers and filled up twelve baskets full! [21] There were about five thousand men who were fed, in addition to many women and children!

Jesus Walks on Water

[22] As soon as the people were fed, Jesus told his disciples to get into their boat and to go to the other side of the lake while he stayed behind to dismiss the people. [23] After the crowds dispersed, Jesus went up into the hills to pray. And as night fell he was there praying alone with God.

[24] But the disciples, who were now in the middle of the lake, ran into trouble, for their boat was tossed about by the high winds and heavy seas.

[25] At about four o'clock in the morning,[c] Jesus came to them, walking on the waves! [26] When the disciples saw him walking on top of the water, they were terrified and screamed, "A ghost!"

[27] Then Jesus said, "Be brave and don't be afraid. I am here!"[d]

---

a 14:14 The Aramaic is "he nurtured them in love and cured their frailties."

b 14:20 The miracle took place as the disciples distributed what they had. Each disciple ended up with a basket full of leftovers.

c 14:25 Or "during the fourth watch of the night" (between 3:00 and 6:00 a.m.).

d 14:27 Or "I AM," which was the name of God used in Ex. 3:14.

²⁸ Peter shouted out, "Lord, if it's really you, then have me join you on the water!"

²⁹ "Come and join me," ᵃ Jesus replied.

So Peter stepped out onto the water and began to walk toward Jesus. ³⁰ But when he realized how high the waves were, he became frightened and started to sink. "Save me, Lord!" he cried out.

³¹ Jesus immediately stretched out his hand and lifted him up and said, "What little faith you have! Why would you let doubt win?"

³² And the very moment they both stepped into the boat, the raging wind ceased. ³³ Then all the disciples crouched down before him and worshiped Jesus. ᵇ They said in adoration, "You are truly the Son of God!"

³⁴ After they crossed over and landed at Gennesaret, ᶜ ³⁵ the people living there quickly recognized who he was. They were quick to spread the news throughout the surrounding region that Jesus had come to them. ³⁶ So they brought him all their sick, begging him to let them touch the fringe of his robe. And everyone who touched it was instantly healed! ᵈ

Jesus Breaks Religious Traditions

15 Then the Pharisees and religious scholars ᵉ came from Jerusalem and approached Jesus with this question: ² "Why do your disciples ignore the traditions of our elders? For example, they don't ceremonially wash their hands before they eat bread."

³ Jesus answered, "And why do you ignore the commandment of God because of your traditions? ⁴ For didn't God say, 'Honor your father and mother,' and, 'Whoever abuses or insults his father or mother must be put to death?' ᶠ

⁵ "But you teach that it's permissible to say to your parents when they are in financial need, 'Whatever gift you would have received from me I can keep for myself, since I dedicated it as an offering to God.' ⁶ This doesn't honor your father or mother. And you have elevated your tradition above the words of God. ⁷ Frauds and hypocrites! Isaiah described you perfectly when he said:

---

a 14:29 Or "Go for it!"

b 14:33 The Greek word used for "worship," *proskuneo,* includes three concepts: to bow, to kiss, and to pay homage (worship). All three are included here.

c 14:34 Gennesaret means "harp." It was known as a lovely and fertile plain south of Capernaum. Lake Galilee was also called the Lake of Gennesaret.

d 14:36 See also Matt. 9:21–22; Mark 3:10; Luke 6:19. The power of God exuding from Jesus was so incredible that merely touching his prayer shawl (or cloak) would bring instant healing. This same power is available to the church today, for Christ, the healer, lives in every believer. See also Acts 19:12.

e 15:1 Or "scribes," considered to be experts in interpreting Jewish laws.

f 15:4 See Ex. 20:12; 21:17; Lev. 20:9.

8 These people honor me only with their words,
    for their hearts are so very distant from me.
9 They pretend to worship me,
    but their worship is nothing more
    than the empty traditions of men." [a]

10 Then Jesus turned to the crowd and said, "Come, listen and open your heart to understand. 11 What truly contaminates a person is not what he puts into his mouth but what comes out of his mouth. That's what makes people defiled."

12 Then his disciples approached him and said, "Don't you know that what you just said offended the Pharisees?"

13 Jesus replied, "Every plant that my heavenly Father didn't plant is destined to be uprooted. 14 Stay away from them, [b] for they're nothing more than blind guides. Do you know what happens when a blind man pretends to guide another blind man? They both stumble into a ditch!"

15 Peter spoke up and said, "Will you explain to us what you mean by your parable?"

16 Jesus said, "Even after all that I've taught you, you still remain clueless? 17 Is it hard to understand that whatever you eat enters the stomach only to pass out into the sewer? 18 But what comes out of your mouth reveals the core of your heart. Words can pollute, not food. 19 You will find living within an impure heart evil ideas, murderous thoughts, adultery, sexual immorality, theft, lies, and slander. [c] 20 That's what pollutes a person. Eating with unwashed hands doesn't defile anyone."

A Lebanese Woman's Faith

21 Then Jesus left and went north into the non-Jewish region of Lebanon. [d] 22 He encountered there a Canaanite woman [e] who screamed out to him, "Lord, Son of David, show mercy to me! My daughter is horribly afflicted by a demon that torments her." 23 But Jesus never answered her. So his disciples said to him, "Why do you ignore this woman who is crying out to us?" [f]

---

a 15:9 See Isa. 29:13.

b 15:14 The Aramaic is "Let them remain blind! For they are nothing more than blind leaders of the blind."

c 15:19 Or "blasphemies."

d 15:21 Or "Tyre and Sidon," both cities of Lebanon.

e 15:22 The Hebrew Matthew is "a Canaanite merchant woman." Canaan included the region of modern-day Lebanon. Canaanite refers to a non-Jewish person who lived in that region. It was in this very region that an Old Testament woman named Jezebel established Baal worship. Now Jesus heals a woman and brings her into the true worship of God.

f 15:23 As translated from Hebrew Matthew. The Greek is "The disciples kept begging Jesus to send her away."

²⁴Jesus said, "I've only been sent to the lost sheep of Israel." ²⁵But she came and bowed down before him and said, "Lord, help me!"

²⁶Jesus responded, "It's not right for a man to take bread from his children and throw it out to the dogs." *ᵃ*

²⁷"You're right, Lord," she replied. "But even puppies get to eat the crumbs that fall from the prince's table."

²⁸Then Jesus answered her, "**Dear woman, your faith is strong! What you desire will be done for you.**" And at that very moment, her daughter was instantly set free from demonic torment.

Jesus Heals Many Others

²⁹After leaving Lebanon, Jesus went to Lake Galilee and climbed a hill nearby and sat down. ³⁰Then huge crowds of people streamed up the hill, bringing with them the lame, blind, deformed, mute, and many others in need of healing. They laid them at Jesus' feet and he healed them all.

³¹And the crowds marveled with rapture and amazement, astounded over the things they were witnessing with their own eyes! The lame were walking, the mute were speaking, the crippled were made well, and the blind could see. *For three days* everyone celebrated the miracles as they exalted and praised the God of Israel!

Jesus Feeds Thousands

³²Jesus called his disciples to himself and said, "**I care deeply about all these people, for they've already been with me for three days without food. I don't want to send them away fasting or else they may be overcome by weakness on their journey home.**"

³³So the disciples said to him, "Where in the world are we going to find enough food in this desolate place to feed this crowd?"

³⁴"**How many barley loaves do you have?**" Jesus asked.

"Seven," they replied, "and a few small fish."

³⁵So he gave the order, "**Have the people sit down on the grass.**" ³⁶Then he took the seven loaves and the fish and gave thanks to God. He broke the bread and gave it to his disciples, who then distributed the food to the crowds. ³⁷When everyone was full and satisfied, they gathered up the leftovers. And from what was once seven loaves and a few fish, they filled seven baskets! *ᵇ* ³⁸There were four thousand men who ate the food Jesus multiplied, and even more including the women and children!

---

a 15:26 Jesus uses a figure of speech and describes the people of Israel as "children" who view the non-Jewish people as "dogs."

b 15:37 The Greek word used here implies a very large basket, possibly the size of a person.

[39] After dismissing the crowd, Jesus got into the boat and crossed over to the region of Magdala. [a]

The Demand for a Sign from Heaven

16 One day some of the Pharisees and those of the Jewish sect known as the Sadducees [b] approached Jesus, insisting that he prove to them that he was the Messiah. "Show us a supernatural sign from heaven," they demanded.

[2] Jesus answered, "You can read the signs of the weather, for you say, 'Red sky at night, sailors delight.' [3] And, 'Red sky in the morning, sailors take warning.' You're so adept at forecasting the weather by looking at the sky, but you're absolutely clueless in reading the obvious signs of the times. [4] A wicked and wayward generation always asks for signs, but the only sign I provide for you will be the sign of Jonah the prophet." [c] Then he turned away and left them.

The Hypocrisy of the Pharisees and Sadducees

[5] Later, as Jesus and his disciples crossed over to the other side of Lake Galilee, the disciples realized they had forgotten to bring any loaves of bread. [6] Jesus spoke up and said, "Watch out for the yeast of the Pharisees and the Sadducees."

[7] Thinking Jesus was scolding them over not bringing bread, they whispered among themselves. [8] Knowing their thoughts, Jesus said to them, "You have such little faith! Why are you arguing with one another about having no bread? [9] Are you so slow to understand? Have you forgotten the miracle of feeding the five thousand families and how each of you ended up with a basket full of fragments? [10] And how seven loaves of bread fed four thousand families with baskets left over? [11] Don't you understand? I'm not talking about bread, but I'm warning you to avoid the yeast of the Pharisees and the Sadducees."

---

a 15:39 Or "Magadan." This was a place where fish were salted and preserved. Magdala means "tower." Magdala was the town that Mary Magdalene came from. Perhaps during this visit is when they first met.

b 16:1 Of the three major sects of Judaism of that day (Pharisees, Essenes, and Sadducees), the Sadducees were a small but influential group that philosophically denied the supernatural and gravitated instead toward political control of the people.

c 16:4 The "sign of Jonah" points to Jesus in many ways. Jonah being thrown into the sea points to Christ's death. Being swallowed by the fish for three days points to Christ's burial. And being expelled from the fish speaks of Christ's resurrection and triumph over death, which is the greatest "sign" God could ever give. The resurrected Jesus is the eternal sign that our sins are forgiven.

¹²Then finally they realized he wasn't talking about yeast found in bread, but the error of the teachings of the Pharisees*a* and the Sadducees.*b*

Peter's Revelation of Christ

¹³When Jesus came to Caesarea Philippi,*c* he asked his disciples this question: "What are the people saying about me, the Son of Man? Who do they believe I am?"

¹⁴They answered, "Some are convinced you are John the Baptizer, others say you are Elijah reincarnated, or Jeremiah, or one of the prophets."

¹⁵"But you—who do you say that I am?" Jesus asked.

¹⁶Simon Peter spoke up and said, "You are the Anointed One,*d* the Son of the living God!"

¹⁷Jesus replied, "You are favored and privileged Simeon, son of Jonah!*e* For you didn't discover this on your own, but my Father in heaven has supernaturally revealed it to you. ¹⁸I give you the name Peter, a stone.*f* And this

---

a 16:12 "Pharisees" means "separated ones" (separatists). It is believed that during the time of Jesus there were approximately six thousand Pharisees in Israel. They refused to have dealings with the common people, because there were separated to God. Jesus described them as religious frauds who loved money and wanted to be the final authority on all the doctrines that were taught to the people. They were not all priests, but zealous law keepers who wanted their interpretation of the Scriptures to be the standard in Israel.

b 16:12 The Sadducees (*Tzedukim*) were wealthy aristocrats with political connections to Rome. They did not believe in the afterlife or angels or demons, and they denied the miraculous. It is believed that among them were Jewish converts from the Edomites who were forced to convert to Judaism in 129 BC by John Hyrcanus, the Hasmonean leader of the second century BC. The Sadducees loved Greek (Hellenistic) culture and basically rejected the oral law of the Pharisees. The Herodians would also be considered to be of the Sadducees. You can imagine how Jesus upset both the Pharisees and the Sadducees. Jesus had no difficulty breaking the traditions, taboos, religious teachings, and political loyalties of both Pharisees and Sadducees in order to please his heavenly Father.

c 16:13 This was a beautiful area north of Lake Galilee and near Tel-Dan. Located at the foothills of Mount Hermon, it was an ancient Roman city rebuilt by Herod Philip in honor of Tiberius Caesar.

d 16:16 Or "the Christ" (Messiah).

e 16:17 Jonah means "dove." Or "Simon, son of John." Simeon means "he who hears." Peter heard the Father's whisper within that Jesus was the Christ. Simeon was his formal Hebrew name. Peter became his identity as Jesus gave him the nickname of "pebble." He is also referred to as "Simon Peter."

f 16:18 Or *Keefa*, the Aramaic word for "stone" or "pebble." See Matt. 4:18 and footnote. There is an obvious pun only found in the Hebrew Matthew. The Hebrew word for "stone" is *eben*, and the Hebrew word for "build" is *ebeneh*. The Greek text does state that Peter is the "rock" on which the church is built. However, the implication is that it is Peter's revelation from the Father and his confession of Jesus as the Son of God that becomes the "bedrock foundation" for the church. The earliest writings of the church fathers all acknowledge that the Rock is Jesus Christ, not Peter. See Deut. 32:18, 30–31; Ps. 18:46; Isa. 8:14; 17:10; 51:1–8.

truth of who I am will be the bedrock foundation on which I will build my church—my legislative assembly,[a] and the power of death[b] will not be able to overpower it![c] [19] I will give you the keys[d] of heaven's kingdom realm to forbid on earth that which is forbidden in heaven, and to release on earth that which is released in heaven."[e] [20] He then gave his disciples strict orders not to tell anyone that he was God's Anointed One.

Jesus Prophesies His Death and Resurrection

[21] From then on Jesus began to clearly reveal to his disciples that he was destined to go to Jerusalem and suffer injustice[f] from the elders, leading priests, and religious scholars. He also explained that he would be killed and three days later be raised to life again.

[22] Peter took him aside to correct him privately. He reprimanded Jesus over and over, saying to him, "God forbid, Master! Spare yourself. You must never let this happen to you!"

[23] Jesus turned to Peter[g] and said, "Get out of my way, you Satan![h] You are an offense to me,[i] because your thoughts are only filled with man's viewpoints and not with the ways of God."

[24] Then Jesus said to his disciples, "If you truly want to follow me, you should at once completely reject and disown your own life. And you must be willing to share my cross and experience it as your own,[j] as you continually

---

a 16:18 The Greek word for "church" is *ekklesia* and means "legislative assembly" or "selected ones." This is not a religious term at all, but a political and governmental term that is used many times in classical Greek for a group of people who have been summoned and gathered together to govern the affairs of a city. For Jesus to use this term means he is giving the keys of governmental authority in his kingdom to the church. See R. Scott and H. G. Liddell, *A Greek-English Lexicon*, p. 206; J. H. Thayer, *A Greek-English Lexicon of the New Testament*, p. 196; and Oskar Seyffert, *A Dictionary of Classical Antiquities*, pp. 202–203.

b 16:18 Or "the gates of hell," a metonymy for the power of death.

c 16:18 Or "all the forces of hell will never have the power to win a victory over it!" There is no power of darkness that can stop the advancing church that Jesus builds.

d 16:19 The "keys" are symbols of authority and ruling power. See Isa. 22:22.

e 16:19 Or "Whatever you bind on earth will have been bound in heaven, and whatever you loose on earth will have been loosed in heaven." Or "That which you forbid on earth must be that which is already forbidden in heaven, and that which you permit on earth must be that which is already permitted in heaven."

f 16:21 The Hebrew Matthew adds, "many scourgings and many mockings."

g 16:23 Or "He turned from Peter and said . . ."

h 16:23 Or "adversary." Jesus is equating Peter's display of character to that of Satan. Peter was not possessed by Satan, but speaking from Satan's realm and speaking demonic wisdom. See James 3:15. The Hebrew Matthew can be translated "Follow me! Don't quarrel with me, adversary!"

i 16:23 Or "You are laying a trap for me."

j 16:24 The Hebrew Matthew is "offer yourself up to death." The words Jesus spoke were shocking and must be translated as such.

surrender to my ways. ²⁵ For if you choose self-sacrifice and lose your lives for my glory, you will continually discover true life. But if you choose to keep your lives for yourselves, you will forfeit what you try to keep. ²⁶ For even if you were to gain all the wealth and power of this world with everything it could offer you—at the cost of your own life—what good would that be? And what could be more valuable to you than your own soul?ᵃ ²⁷ It has been decreed that I, the Son of Man, will one day return with my messengersᵇ and in the splendor and majesty of my Father. And then I will reward each person according to what they have done.ᶜ ²⁸ But I promise you, there are some standing here now who won't experience death until they have witnessed the coming of the Son of Man in the presence and the power of the kingdom realm of God!"ᵈ

Jesus' Glorious Transfiguration

17 Six days later Jesus took Peter and the two brothers, Jacobᵉ and John, and hiked up a high mountain to be alone. ² Then Jesus' appearance was dramatically altered. A radiant light as bright as the sun poured from his face. And his clothing became luminescent—dazzling like lightning.ᶠ He was transfiguredᵍ before their very eyes. ³ Then suddenly, Moses and Elijah appeared,ʰ and they spoke with Jesus.

⁴ Peter blurted out, "Lord, it's so wonderful that we are all here together! If you want, I'll construct three shrines,ⁱ one for you, one for Moses, and one for Elijah."ʲ

ᵃ 16:26 Or "What would a person give in exchange for his life?"

ᵇ 16:27 Or "angels."

ᶜ 16:27 See Pss. 28:4; 62:12; Prov. 24:12.

ᵈ 16:28 Or "when they see the Son of Man appearing to inaugurate his regal reign." This was a prophecy of what was about to take place with Peter, Jacob, and John on the Mountain of Transforming Glory. This promise would be fulfilled as they experienced the power of the kingdom of God and the cloud of glory. Christ's appearing is equated to the power manifested in the cloud that overshadowed Jesus on the Mount of Transfiguration.

ᵉ 17:1 Or "James." Translations of the Bible have substituted Jacob with James. Both Greek and Aramaic leave the Hebrew name as it is, Jacob. This translation will use Jacob throughout.

ᶠ 17:2 Or "white as light."

ᵍ 17:2 Moses also went up Sinai's mountain and received an impartation of glory. His face shone and had to be veiled. The transfiguration of Jesus is also part of our destiny, for the same Greek word is used twice for believers being transfigured by the renewing of our minds and by the glory of Christ within us that will complete our transformation into Christ's image. See Rom. 12:2; 2 Cor. 3:18.

ʰ 17:3 Moses represented the Law and Elijah represented the Prophets. Both Moses and Elijah were associated with Mount Sinai (Horeb), both had a ministry of performing astounding miracles, and both had unusual circumstances surrounding their passing from this life into glory.

ⁱ 17:4 Or "tabernacles," which speaks of the booths made to celebrate the Feast of Tabernacles.

ʲ 17:4 The Hebrew Matthew adds this line: "because he [Peter] did not know what he was saying."

⁵ But while Peter was still speaking, a radiant cloud composed of light spread over them, enveloping them all.ᵃ And God's voice suddenly spoke from the cloud, saying, "This is my dearly loved Son, the constant focus of my delight.ᵇ Listen to him!"ᶜ

⁶ The three disciples were dazedᵈ and terrified by this phenomenon, and they fell facedown to the ground. ⁷ But Jesus walked over and touched them, saying, "Get up and stop being afraid." ⁸ When they finally opened their eyes and looked around, they saw no one else there but Jesus.ᵉ

⁹ As they all hiked down the mountain together, Jesus ordered them, "Don't tell anyone of the divine appearanceᶠ you just witnessed. Wait until the Son of Man is raised from the dead."

¹⁰ His disciples asked him, "Why do all the religious scholars insist that Elijah must first appear before the Anointed One comes?"

¹¹ He answered them, "They're right. Elijah must come first and restore all things. ¹² But Elijah has already appeared. And yet they didn't recognize him, so they did to him whatever they pleased. And the Son of Man is destined to suffer the same abuse as what they did to him."

¹³ Then the disciples realized that Jesus was referring to John the Baptizer all along.ᵍ

Unbelief Hinders Healing

¹⁴ They came to where a large crowd had gathered *to wait for Jesus.* A man came and knelt before him ¹⁵ and said, "Lord, please show your tender mercy toward my son. *He has a demon who afflicts him.*ʰ He has epilepsy, and he suffers horribly

---

a 17:5 See Acts 5:15. The Greek word translated "overshadow" is *episkiazo,* which is used exclusively for the power of the Almighty "overshadowing," such as Mary, who conceived a child supernaturally by God. See also Mark 9:7; Luke 1:35. This was not a natural shadow created by the light of the sun, but the supernatural overshadowing of God's power. Jesus will appear again in these clouds of glory. See Matt. 16:27; 24:30; 26:64.

b 17:5 Or "He is the one on whom my favor rests."

c 17:5 Or "You must constantly listen to him." See Ps. 2:7; Isa. 42:1.

d 17:6 Implied by the Hebrew Matthew, which can be translated "They were asleep and not asleep; they were awake but not awake."

e 17:8 The Greek is quite emphatic: "They saw only him, and him alone."

f 17:9 Or "supernatural vision." The Greek word used here *(horama)* does not refer to an imaginary vision, but an actual one. It points to a theophany, an appearing of God.

g 17:13 Jesus was comparing Elijah with John the Baptist. John was not Elijah reincarnated, but the Spirit upon Elijah was the Spirit upon John. John, the forerunner, ministered in the spirit and power of Elijah. The same anointing of Elijah is present today to restore all things. (See Acts 3:21.) The Bible scholars had properly concluded that Elijah must come first, but failed to interpret it figuratively. This is often repeated today with biblical prophecies. We need the Spirit of Christ to help us understand even the basic truths of the Bible.

h 17:15 Although not in the Greek text, it is implied in the context (v. 18). The Hebrew Matthew states three times in this pericope (vv. 15, 18, 21) that the boy had a demon.

from seizures. He often falls into the cooking fire or into the river. *a* *16* I brought him to your followers, but they weren't able to heal him."

17 Jesus replied, "Where is your faith? Can't you see how wayward and wrong this generation is? *b* How much longer do I stay with you and put up with your doubts? Bring your son to me."

18 Then Jesus rebuked the demon and it came out of him and the boy was instantly healed!

19 Later the disciples came to him privately and asked, "Why couldn't we cast out the demon?"

20 He told them, "It was because of your lack of faith. I promise you, if you have faith inside of you no bigger than the size of a small mustard seed, you can say to this mountain, 'Move away from here and go over there,' and you will see it move! *c* There is nothing you couldn't do! *d* *21* But this kind of demon is cast out only through prayer and fasting." *e*

Jesus Prophesies Again of His Death and Resurrection

22 When they all gathered together *f* in Galilee, Jesus said to them, "The Son of Man is going to be betrayed and turned over to his enemies. *23* They will kill him and in three days he will be resurrected." When the disciples heard these words they were devastated.

The Miracle of a Coin in a Fish's Mouth

24 After they arrived in Capernaum, the collectors of the temple tax approached Peter and asked, "Does your teacher pay the tax for the upkeep of the temple, like the rest of us?" *g*

25 "Of course he does," Peter answered.

When Peter walked into the house, and before he had a chance to speak, Jesus spoke up and said, "Peter, I have a question for you. Who pays tolls or

---

a 17:15 The Hebrew Matthew is "He grinds his teeth and foams at the mouth."

b 17:17 The Hebrew Matthew adds a sentence here: "Woe to those who deny me!"

c 17:20 Jesus compares faith to a small seed that grows into a large shrub. Faith will grow as it feeds on spiritual truth found in the Bible. A mountain can also be a symbol of a kingdom. Mountain-moving faith brings the power of God's kingdom to the earth. See also 1 Cor. 13:2.

d 17:20 Or "Nothing will be beyond your power." The Aramaic can be translated "Nothing is higher or stronger than you."

e 17:21 As translated from the Hebrew Matthew, Aramaic, and some Greek manuscripts. Many reliable Greek manuscripts do not have this verse, and it is not included in many modern translations.

f 17:22 The Greek word is "twisted together like strands of a rope."

g 17:24 This was known as "head tax." See also Ex. 30:13–16; 38:26; Neh. 10:32–33. The word *pay* (vv. 24, 25, 27) is the same word Jesus spoke on the cross, "It is finished (*paid* in full)." Jesus paid it all so that we would be set free.

taxes to a king? Is tax collected from the king's own children, or from his subjects?"

²⁶ "From his subjects," Peter answered.

Jesus replied, "That's right. The children get off free without paying taxes. ²⁷ But so that we don't offend them, go to the lake and throw out your hook, and the first fish that rises up*ᵃ* will have a coin in its mouth. It will be the exact amount you need to pay the temple tax for both of us."*ᵇ*

Who Is the Greatest in the Kingdom Realm?

18 At that time the disciples came to ask Jesus, "Who is considered to be the greatest in heaven's kingdom realm?"*ᶜ*

²Jesus called a little one*ᵈ* to his side and said to them, ³ **"Learn this well:** Unless you dramatically change your way of thinking and become teachable, and learn about heaven's kingdom realm with the wide-eyed wonder of a child, you will never be able to enter in. ⁴Whoever continually humbles himself*ᵉ* to become like this gentle child is the greatest one in heaven's kingdom realm. ⁵And if you tenderly care for this little one*ᶠ* on my behalf, you are tenderly caring for me. ⁶But if anyone abuses*ᵍ* one of these little ones who believe in me, it would be better for him to have a heavy boulder tied around his neck and be hurled into the deepest sea *than to face the punishment he deserves!*ʰ*

⁷ "Misery will come to the one who lures people away into sin. Troubles and obstacles to your faith are inevitable, but great devastation will come to the one guilty of causing others to leave the path of righteousness! ⁸If your hand clings to sin, cut it off and throw it away. If your foot continually steps

---

a 17:27 This miracle is a picture of the death and resurrection of our Lord Jesus. The depth of the sea speaks to us of the depth of suffering Jesus passed through for us on the cross. Note that the fish rose to the surface on its own; it was not "caught." In the mouth of our Lord Jesus is the full price of our sin debt, for he has declared the work of redemption finished, and our "tax" has been paid in full. Now we have that same message in our mouths.

b 17:27 Peter made a presumptuous statement to the tax collectors that Jesus would pay the temple tax. But Peter didn't ask Jesus first; he just said to them, "Of course!" Yet Jesus still backed up Peter's word and performed a miracle to pay the tax. In this somewhat amusing account, Jesus got Peter "off the hook" by having him hook a fish with the exact amount of the tax for both Jesus and Peter. See 1 Cor. 3:16.

c 18:1 The Aramaic is "Who will reign in the kingdom realm of heaven?"

d 18:2 Or "toddler." The Greek word is *paidion,* either a boy or a girl.

e 18:4 This means "to see yourself as unimportant in your own eyes."

f 18:5 The Greek uses the word for hospitality. The "little child" becomes a representative of unimportant people in general. Treating the least with care and respect makes us truly great.

g 18:6 The Greek word is *skandalizō* and can also mean "to scandalize," "to put a stumbling block before them," "to offend," or "to cause to sin."

h 18:6 The Hebrew Matthew adds, "It would be better for him to never have been born!"

onto sin's path, cut it off and throw it away. For it is better for you to enter into heaven crippled and maimed than to have both hands and both feet and be thrown into eternal fire. [9] And if your eye is always focusing on sin, pluck it out and throw it away. For it is better for you to enter into heaven with one eye than to be thrown into hell fire with two. [a]

[10] "Be careful that you not corrupt [b] one of these little ones. For I can assure you that in heaven each of their angelic guardians [c] have instant access [d] to my heavenly Father."

A Parable of the Lost Lamb

[11] "The Son of Man has come to give life to anyone who is lost. [e] [12] Think of it this way: If a man owns a hundred sheep and one lamb wanders away and is lost, won't he leave the ninety-nine grazing on the hillside and go out and thoroughly search for the one lost lamb? [13] And if he finds his lost lamb, he rejoices over it, more than over the ninety-nine who are safe. [f] [14] Now you should understand that it is never the desire of your heavenly Father that a single one of these *humble believers* should be lost." [g]

Restoring Broken Relationships

[15] "If your fellow believer sins against you, [h] you must go to that one privately and attempt to resolve the matter. If he responds, your relationship is restored. [16] But if his heart is closed to you, then go to him again, taking one or two others with you. You'll be fulfilling what the Scripture teaches when it says, 'Every word may be verified by the testimony of two or three witnesses.' [j] [17] And if he refuses to listen, then share the issue with the entire church *in hopes of restoration*. If he still refuses to respond, disregarding the

---

a 18:9 Although the language Jesus uses is hyperbolic, the drastic measures he instructs us to take in order to stay pure remain valid. The last phrase is literally "into the Gehenna of fire."

b 18:10 As translated from the Aramaic, which uses a figure of speech ("to bring down") that is best translated "to corrupt" or "degrade." The Greek is "despise," or "look down upon."

c 18:10 As translated from the Aramaic. The Greek is simply "angels."

d 18:10 Or "who always see the face of my heavenly Father."

e 18:11 As translated from the Hebrew Matthew, the Aramaic, and a few Greek texts. Many reliable Greek manuscripts do not have this verse, and it is missing in many modern translations. See Ezek. 34:16.

f 18:13 The Aramaic is "the ninety-nine that did not go astray."

g 18:14 Implied in the context.

h 18:15 Although the words "against you," are not found in the most reliable Greek manuscripts, they are included in the Hebrew Matthew and Aramaic, along with a number of Greek texts. The Hebrew Matthew indicates that Jesus addressed these words to Peter directly: "At that time Jesus said to Simon, called Keefa . . ."

i 18:15 See Lev. 19:17.

j 18:16 See Deut. 19:16.

fellowship of his church family, you must disregard him as though he were an outsider, on the same level as an unrepentant sinner. [a]

[18] "Receive this truth: Whatever you forbid on earth will be considered to be forbidden in heaven, [b] and whatever you release on earth will be considered to be released in heaven. [19] Again, I give you an eternal truth: If two of you agree to ask God for something in a symphony of prayer, [c] my heavenly Father will do it for you. [20] For wherever two or three come together in honor of my name, [d] I am right there with them!"

Unlimited Forgiveness

[21] Later Peter approached Jesus and said, "How many times do I have to forgive my fellow believer who keeps offending me? Seven times?" [e]

[22] Jesus answered, "Not seven times, Peter, but seventy times seven times! [f]
[23] The lessons of forgiveness in heaven's kingdom realm can be illustrated like this:

"There once was a king who had servants who had borrowed money from the royal treasury. He decided to settle accounts with each of them. [24] As he began the process, it came to his attention that one of his servants [g] owed him one billion dollars. [h] So he summoned the servant before him and said to him, 'Pay me what you owe me.' [25] When his servant was unable to repay his debt, the king ordered that he be sold as a slave along with his wife and children and every possession they owned as payment toward his debt. [26] The servant threw himself facedown at his master's feet and begged for mercy. 'Please be patient with me. Just give me more time and I will repay

---

a   18:17 Or "a pagan or a tax collector." Again, this is in hope of ultimate restoration. For even pagans and tax collectors can be saved. God is able to turn the wandering one back, as Jesus taught in the parable of the lost lamb (see vv. 11–14).

b   18:18 Or "Whatever you bind [Aramaic 'harness'] on earth will have been bound in heaven." See Matt. 16:19 and footnote.

c   18:19 The Greek word used here is *sumphoneo,* from which we get our English word "symphony." The Aramaic is "if you are deserving of what you pray for." The implication is that God will not give you what you are not yet ready for, just as an earthly father would not give his eight-year-old a car to drive.

d   18:20 Or "in my name."

e   18:21 The Hebrew Matthew is "Seven times in one day?"

f   18:22 Or "seventy-seven times." This is a metaphor for an attitude of forgiveness that is limitless.

g   18:24 Although the Greek uses the word for "servant," it means someone who ruled under the king, perhaps one of his magistrates or cabinet members who had authority over finances.

h   18:24 Or "ten thousand talents," an unbelievable amount of money. A talent could be compared to the wages earned over decades. The number ten thousand is a Hebrew metaphor for "myriad." The point is, the servant owed a huge amount of money that he was simply unable to repay.

you all that I owe.' ²⁷ Upon hearing his pleas, the king had compassion on his servant, and released him, and forgave his entire debt.

²⁸ "No sooner had the servant left when he met one of his fellow servants, who owed him twenty thousand dollars ᵃ He seized him by the throat and began to choke him, saying, 'You'd better pay me right now everything you owe me!' ²⁹ His fellow servant threw himself facedown at his feet and begged, 'Please be patient with me. If you'll just give me time, I will repay you all that is owed.' ³⁰ But the one who had his debt forgiven stubbornly refused to forgive what was owed him. He had his fellow servant thrown into prison and demanded he remain there until he repaid the debt in full.

³¹ "When his associates saw what was going on, they were outraged and went to the king and told him the whole story. ³² The king said to him, 'You scoundrel!ᵇ Is this the way you respond to my mercy? Because you begged me, I forgave you the massive debt that you owed me. ³³ Why didn't you show the same mercy to your fellow servant that I showed to you?' ³⁴ In a fury of anger, the king turned him over to the prison guards to be tortured until all his debt was repaid. ³⁵ In this same way, my heavenly Father will deal with any of you if you do not release forgiveness from your heartᶜ toward your fellow believer."

Questions about Divorce

19 After Jesus finished teaching them, he left Galilee and made his way toward the district of Judea, east of the Jordan River. ² Massive crowds followed him and he healed all who were sick. ᵈ ³ The Pharisees were intent on putting Jesus to the test with difficult questions, so they approached him and asked, "Is it lawful for a man to divorceᵉ his wife for any reason?"ᶠ

⁴ "Haven't you read the Scriptures about creation?" Jesus replied. "The Creator made us male and female from the very beginning,ᵍ ⁵ and 'For this

---

a 18:28 Or "one hundred silver coins." This would be a denarii, which is about a day's wages. So the servant owed his friend about three months' wages.

b 18:32 The Hebrew Matthew is "You servant of Belial!"

c 18:35 The Hebrew Matthew is "with a perfect heart."

d 19:2 As translated from the Hebrew Matthew.

e 19:3 The Greek word used for divorce (*apolyo*) here and in this chapter can also mean "to loose," "to dismiss," "to send away."

f 19:3 This a clever test by the Pharisees. Jesus was now in Judea and under the jurisdiction of Herod Antipas, the one who had John beheaded over challenging his divorce. They were hoping Jesus would say something that could get him arrested and killed by Herod. Their question was based on Deut. 24:1. Jewish divorce law had a "for any reason" clause that made divorce legal. They were pressing Jesus for his interpretation of this "for any reason" law.

g 19:4 See Gen. 1:27; 5:2. Notice that Jesus highlights gender difference in the context of marriage.

reason a man will leave his father and mother and live with his wife.[a] And the two will become one flesh.'[b] [6] From then on, they are no longer two, but united as one. So what God unites let no one divide!"

[7] They responded, "So then why did Moses command us to give a certificate of divorce and it would be lawful?"

[8] Jesus said, "Moses permitted you to divorce because your hearts are so hard and stubborn,[c] but originally there was no such thing. [9] But I say to you, whoever leaves his wife for any reason other than immorality, then takes another wife is living in adultery. And whoever takes a divorced woman in marriage is also living in adultery."[d]

[10] His disciples spoke up and said, "If this is the standard, then it seems better to never get married."

[11] "Not everyone is meant to remain single—only those whom God gives grace to be unmarried.[e] [12] For some are born to celibacy; others have been made eunuchs by others. And there are some who have chosen to live in celibacy for the sacred purpose of heaven's kingdom realm.[f] Let those who can, accept this truth for themselves."

Jesus and Little Children

[13] Then they brought little children to Jesus so that he would lay his hands on

---

a 19:5 Or "cling to his wife."

b 19:5 See Gen. 2:24.

c 19:8 That is, in a fallen world with frail human beings, God allowed divorce to accommodate broken humanity. Jesus restates divorce as being permitted only in the case of immorality. Adultery breaks the bond of marriage and requires God's healing grace. Those testing Jesus were attempting to trap him by getting him to say something against Moses, their venerated historical leader.

d 19:9 As translated from the Hebrew Matthew, Aramaic, and some Greek manuscripts. The majority of Greek manuscripts do not include the last sentence.

e 19:11 Or "This doesn't apply to everyone, but only to those to whom it [grace for singleness] has been given."

f 19:12 Three types of "celibates" are mentioned. First, there are those who from birth have grace to remain celibate. Second, sometimes a male who has been castrated, usually before puberty, which would greatly affect the hormonal changes of a boy becoming an adult. In biblical times, these eunuchs were chosen to be male servants of a king, having been castrated in order to ensure they don't have sex with the king's harem. Third, this is a metaphorical class of people (male and female) who are like "spiritual eunuchs," having been chosen to never use the bride of Christ for their own purposes. Jesus gives us a parable of God's servants who will lead the church but never harm or use the bride of Christ for their own desires. They will always point the bride to her Bridegroom, Jesus Christ. They have made themselves "eunuchs" and are determined to extend God's kingdom, not their own. The rare Greek verb for "make themselves eunuchs" can also refer to being "always watchful, sleepless, diligent." To become a "spiritual eunuch" has nothing to do with sex, but with always watching out for the interests of our King, and not taking for ourselves what only belongs to him in order to serve our own desires.

them, bless them, and pray for them.[a] But the disciples scolded those who brought the children, saying, "Don't bother him with this now!"

[14]Jesus overheard them and said, "I want little children to come to me, so never interfere with them when they want to come, for heaven's kingdom realm is composed of beloved ones[b] like these! Listen to this truth: No one will enter the kingdom realm of heaven unless he becomes like one of these!"[c] [15]Then he laid his hands on each of them and went on his way.

A Rich Young Man Questions Jesus

[16]*Then a teenager*[d] approached Jesus and bowed before him,[e] saying, "Wonderful teacher[f]—is there a good work I have to do to obtain eternal life?"

[17]Jesus answered, "Why would you call me wonderful? God alone is wonderful.[g] And why would you ask what good work you need to do? Keep the commandments and you'll enter into the life of God."

[18]"Which ones?" he asked.

Jesus said, "Don't murder, don't commit adultery, don't steal, don't lie, [19]honor your father and mother, and love those around you as you love yourself."[h]

[20]"But I've always obeyed every one of them without fail," the young man replied. "What else do I lack?"

[21]Jesus said to him, "If you really want to be perfect,[i] go immediately and sell everything you own. Give all your money to the poor and your treasure will be transferred into heaven. Then come back and follow me for the rest of your life."

---

a 19:13 See Gen. 48:14.

b 19:14 As translated from the Aramaic, which uses the word for "beloved," found only twice in the New Testament. The Greek is "little children." God receives little children into his kingdom.

c 19:14 As translated from the Hebrew Matthew. This last sentence is missing in the Greek text.

d 19:16 This is supplied from v. 22. The Aramaic uses a word that identifies his age as a teenager.

e 19:16 As translated from the Hebrew Matthew. This is missing from the Majority Text.

f 19:16 As translated from the Aramaic, which uses the word *tawa*, meaning "wonderful, good, gifted." Some Greek manuscripts have only "teacher" (rabbi).

g 19:17 At least one of the earliest Greek manuscripts reads "There is no one good but my Father in the heavens."

h 19:19 See Ex. 20:12–17; Lev. 19:18. Notice that Jesus left out the commandment "Don't covet." He addresses this with the young man in v. 21 and exposes the need to abandon all to follow Jesus.

i 19:21 Or "fully developed morally," "mature."

²² When the young man heard these words, he walked away angry,ᵃ for he was extremely wealthy.

²³ Then Jesus turned to his disciples and said, "Listen. Do you understand how difficult it is for the rich to enter into heaven's kingdom realm? ²⁴ In fact, it's easier to stuff a heavy ropeᵇ through the eye of a needle than it is for the wealthy to enter into God's kingdom realm!"

²⁵ Stunned and bewildered, his disciples asked, "Then who in the world can possibly be saved?"

²⁶ Looking straight into their eyes, Jesus replied, "Humanly speaking, no one, *because no one can save himself.* But what seems impossible to you is never impossible to God!"

²⁷ Then Peter blurted out, "Here we are. We've given up everything to follow you. What reward will there be for us?"

²⁸ Jesus responded, "Listen to the truth: In the age of the restoration of all things,ᶜ when the Son of Man sits on his glorious throne, you who have followed me will have twelve thrones of your own, and you will governᵈ the twelve tribes of Israel. ²⁹ For anyone who has left behind their home and property,ᵉ leaving family—brothers or sisters, mothers or fathers,ᶠ or children—for my sake, they will be repaid a hundred times over and will inherit eternal life. ³⁰ But many who push themselves to be first will find themselves last. And those who are willing to be last will find themselves to be first."ᵍ

A Parable of Workers in the Vineyard

20 "This will help you understand the way heaven's kingdom operates:

"There once was a wealthy landowner who went out at daybreak to hire all the laborers he could find to work in his vineyard. ² After agreeing to pay them the standard day's wage, he put them to work. ³ Then at nine o'clock, as he was passing through the town square, he found others standing around without work. ⁴ He told them, 'Come and work for me in my vineyard

---

a 19:22 As translated from the Hebrew Matthew. The Greek reads "grieved," or "sorrowful."

b 19:24 As translated from the Aramaic. The Greek is "to stuff a camel through the eye of a needle." The Aramaic word for both "rope" and "camel" is the homonym *gamla*. This could be an instance of the Aramaic text being misread by the Greek translators as "camel" instead of "rope." Regardless, this becomes a metaphor for something impossible. It would be like saying, "It's as hard as making pigs fly!" See also Luke 18:25.

c 19:28 Or "in the second birth" (Hebrew Matthew) or "in the new realm" (Aramaic). The Greek word *palingenesia* is only used one other time in the New Testament (Titus 3:5) and refers to our rebirth. See also Acts 3:21; 2 Cor. 5:17; Rev. 3:21.

d 19:28 Or "judge."

e 19:29 Or "fields."

f 19:29 The Aramaic and a few Greek manuscripts include "or wife." The majority of reliable Greek manuscripts do not include it.

g 19:30 Or "Many of the first ones will be last and many of the last ones will be first."

and I'll pay you a fair wage.' ⁵ So off they went to join the others. He did the same thing at noon and again at three o'clock, making the same arrangement as he did with the others.

⁶ "Hoping to finish his harvest that day, he went to the town square again at five o'clock ʰ and found more who were idle. So he said to them, 'Why have you been here all day without work?'

⁷ "'Because no one hired us,' they answered.

"So he said to them, 'Then go and join my crew and work in my vineyard.'

⁸ "When evening came, the owner of the vineyard went to his foreman and said, 'Call in all the laborers, line them up, and pay them the same wages, starting with the most recent ones I hired and finishing with the ones who worked all day.'

⁹ "When those hired late in the day came to be paid, they were given a full day's wage. ¹⁰ And when those who had been hired first came to be paid, they were convinced that they would receive more. But everyone was paid the standard wage. ¹¹ When they realized what had happened, they were offended and complained to the landowner, saying, ¹² 'You're treating us unfairly! They've only worked for one hour while we've slaved and sweated all day under the scorching sun. You've made them equal to us!'

¹³ "The landowner replied, 'Friends, I'm not being unfair—I'm doing exactly what I said. Didn't you agree to work for the standard wage? ¹⁴ If I want to give those who only worked for an hour equal pay, what does that matter to you? ¹⁵ Don't I have the right to do what I want with what is mine? Why should my generosity make you jealous of them?' ⁱ

¹⁶ "*Now you can understand what I meant when I said that* the first will end up last and the last will end up being first. Everyone is invited, but few are the chosen." ʲ

Jesus Again Prophesies His Death

¹⁷ Jesus was about to go to Jerusalem, so he took his twelve disciples aside privately and said to them, ¹⁸ "Listen to me. We're on our way to Jerusalem, and I need to remind you that the Son of Man will be handed over to the religious leaders and scholars, and they will sentence him to be executed. ¹⁹ And they will hand him over to the Romans ᵏ to be mocked, tortured, and crucified. Yet three days later he will be raised to life again."

---

h 20:6 Or "in the eleventh hour" (about five o'clock).

i 20:15 Or "Is your eye evil because I am good?"

j 20:16 As translated from the Hebrew Matthew, Aramaic, and a few later Greek manuscripts. This logion is not included in the majority of the Greek manuscripts but is found in Matt. 22:14.

k 20:19 Or "gentiles." By implication, the Romans.

The Ambition of Jacob and John

[20] The wife of Zebedee approached Jesus with her sons, Jacob[a] and John. She knelt before him and asked him for a favor.

[21] He said to her, "What is it that you want?"

She answered, "Make the decree[b] that these, my sons, will rule with you in your kingdom—one sitting on your right hand, one on your left."

[22] Jesus replied, "You don't know what you are asking." Then, looking in the eyes of Jacob and John, Jesus said, "Are you prepared to drink from the cup of suffering that I am about to drink? And are you able to endure the baptism into death that I am about to endure?"[c]

They answered him, "Yes, we are able."[d]

[23] "You will indeed drink the cup of my suffering and be immersed into my death," Jesus told them. "But to be the ones who sit at the place of highest honor is not mine to decide. My Father is the one who chooses them and prepares them."[e]

[24] The other ten disciples were listening to all of this, and a jealous anger arose among them against the two brothers. [25] Jesus, knowing their thoughts, called them to his side and said, "Kings and those with great authority in this world rule oppressively over their subjects, like tyrants. [26] But this is not your calling. You will lead by a completely different model. The greatest one among you will live as the one who is called to serve others, [27] because the greatest honor and authority is reserved for the one with the heart of a servant. [28] For even the Son of Man did not come expecting to be served by everyone, but to serve everyone, and to give his life in exchange for the salvation of many."[f]

Two Blind Men Healed

[29] As Jesus approached[g] Jericho an immense crowd gathered and followed him. [30] And there were two blind men sitting on the roadside. When they heard that it was Jesus passing by, they shouted, "Son of David,[h] show us mercy, Lord!"

---

a 20:20 Or "James." Translations of the Bible have substituted Jacob with James. Both Greek and Aramaic leave the Hebrew name as it is, Jacob. This translation will use Jacob throughout.

b 20:21 Or "Give the order."

c 20:22 Or "Are you able to drink from the cup I am about to drink?"

d 20:22 The naïveté of Jacob (James) and John is glaring. Their ambition is emphasized by having their mother come to ask this favor. This event is included immediately after Jesus prophesied for the third time his coming crucifixion. Their hearts were set on their own advancement rather than intercession for their Master.

e 20:23 As translated from the Aramaic and the Hebrew Matthew.

f 20:28 As translated from the Aramaic. The Greek is "a ransom paid for many."

g 20:29 As translated from the Hebrew Matthew. The Greek is "As Jesus left Jericho." See also Luke 18:35–43, which may indicate that Luke used the Hebrew Matthew as one of his sources.

h 20:30 The term Son of David was used for the Messiah. The blind men believed Jesus was the Messiah.

³¹ Those in the crowd scolded them and told them to be quiet. But the blind men screamed out even louder, "Jesus, Son of David, show us mercy, Lord!"

³² So Jesus stopped and had them brought to him. He asked them, "What do you want me to do for you?"

³³ They said, "Lord, we want to see! Heal us!"

³⁴ Jesus was deeply moved with compassion[a] toward them. So he touched their eyes, and instantly they could see! Jesus said to them, "Your faith has healed you." And all the people praised God because of this miracle.[b] And the two men became his followers from that day onward.

Jesus' Triumphal Entry into Jerusalem

21 Now, as they were approaching Jerusalem they arrived at the place of the stables[c] near the Mount of Olives. Jesus sent two of his disciples ahead, saying, ² "As soon as you enter the village, you will find a donkey tethered along with her young colt. Untie them both and bring them to me. ³ And if anyone stops you and asks, 'What are you doing?' just tell them, 'The Lord of All needs them,' and he will let you take them."

⁴ All of this happened to fulfill the prophecy:

⁵ Tell Zion's daughter:
  "Look, your King arrives!
  He's coming to you full of gentleness,
    sitting on a donkey, riding on a donkey's colt."[d]

⁶ So the two disciples went on ahead and did as Jesus had instructed them. ⁷ They brought the donkey and her colt to him and placed their cloaks and prayer shawls on the colt, and Jesus rode on it.

⁸ Then an exceptionally large crowd gathered and carpeted the road before him with their cloaks and prayer shawls.[e] Others cut down branches from trees to spread in his path. ⁹ Jesus rode in the center of the procession—crowds going before him and crowds coming behind him, and they all shouted, "Bring the

---

a 20:34 The Aramaic is "Jesus had nurturing love toward them."
b 20:34 This and the previous sentence, "Your faith has healed you," are translated from the Hebrew Matthew. They are missing from the Greek text.
c 21:1 Or "Bethphage," which in Aramaic means "the house of stables." Transliterated into Greek it means "the house of unripe figs."
d 21:5 See Zech. 9:9. Kings rode on horses, not donkeys. He chose the young colt as a symbol of humility and gentleness.
e 21:8 See 2 Kings 9:13.

victory, Lord,[a] Son of David! He comes with the blessings of being sent from the Lord Yahweh![b] We celebrate with praises to God in the highest!"

[10] As Jesus entered Jerusalem, the people went wild with excitement—the entire city was thrown into an uproar![c] [11] Some asked, "Who is this man?" And the crowds shouted back, "This is Jesus! He's the prophet from Nazareth[d] of Galilee!"

Jesus in the Temple

[12] Upon entering Jerusalem Jesus went directly into the temple area and drove away all the merchants who were buying and selling their goods. He overturned the tables of the money changers and the stands of those selling doves.[e] [13] And he said to them, **"My dwelling place will be known as a house of prayer, but you have made it into a hangout for thieves!"**[f]

[14] Then the blind and the crippled came into the temple courts, and Jesus healed them all. And the children circled around him shouting out, "Blessings and praises to the Son of David!"

[15] But when the chief priests and religious scholars heard the children shouting and saw all the wonderful miracles of healing, they were furious.[g] [16] They said to Jesus, "Don't you hear what these children are saying? This is not right!"

Jesus answered, **"Yes, I hear them. But have you never heard the words 'You have fashioned the lips of children and little ones to compose your praises'?"**[h]

[17] Jesus then left at once for the nearby village of Bethany, where he spent the night.[i]

[18] While walking back into the city the next morning, he got hungry. [19] He noticed a lone fig tree by the side of the path and walked over to see if there

---

a 21:9 Or "Hosanna," an Aramaic word that means "O, save (bring the victory), Lord!" The crowds were recognizing Jesus as Yahweh's Messiah. By shouting out, "Son of David," they were clearly expecting Jesus to immediately overthrow the Roman oppression and set the nation free. Many want victory before the cross, but true victory comes after resurrection!
b 21:9 As translated from the Aramaic. See Ps. 118:25–26.
c 21:10 Or "The city was shaken [like with an earthquake]!"
d 21:11 The Hebrew word *Nazara* (Nazareth) can be translated "Branch" or "Victorious One." They were shouting, "This is Jesus, the Victorious One of Galilee!"
e 21:12 The revered theologian and historian Jerome was the translator of the Bible into Latin. He also wrote a commentary on Matthew, which includes a fascinating thought about Jesus overturning the tables. Jerome writes, "For a certain fiery and starry light shone from his eyes, and the majesty of God gleamed in his face."
f 21:13 See Isa. 56:5–7; Jer. 7:11.
g 21:15 The Aramaic is "it seemed evil to them."
h 21:16 See Ps. 8:2. The Greek text quoting from Ps. 8 does not agree with either the Hebrew text, the Septuagint, or the Aramaic, but seems to line up with a version found in the Dead Sea Scrolls. You might say Jesus paraphrased the Scriptures to speak to his generation.
i 21:17 The Hebrew Matthew adds, "There he was explaining the kingdom of God."

was any fruit on it, but there was none—he found only leaves. So he spoke to the fig tree and said, "You will be barren and will never bear fruit again!" Instantly the fig tree [a] shriveled up right in front of their eyes!

[20] Astonished, his disciples asked, "How did you make this fig tree instantly wither and die?"

[21] Jesus replied, "Listen to the truth. If you have no doubt of God's power and speak out of faith's fullness, you can be the ones who speak to a tree and it will wither away. Even more than that, you could say to this mountain, 'Be lifted up and be thrown into the sea' and it will be done. [b] [22] Everything you pray for with the fullness of faith you will receive!" [c]

The Authority of Jesus

[23] After this Jesus went into the temple courts and taught the people. The leading priests and Jewish elders approached him and interrupted him and asked, "By what power [d] do you do these things, and who granted you the authority to teach here?"

[24] Jesus answered them, "I too have a question to ask you. If you can answer this question, then I will tell you by what power I do these things. [25] From where did John's authority to baptize come from? From heaven or from people?"

[26] They stepped away and debated among themselves, saying, "How should we answer this? If we say from heaven, he will say to us, 'Then why didn't you respond to John and believe what he said?' But if we deny that God gave him his authority, we'll be mobbed by the people, for they're convinced that John was God's prophet."

[27] So they finally answered, "We don't know."

"Then neither will I tell you from where my power comes to do these things!" he replied.

The Parable of Two Sons

[28] Jesus said to his critics, [e] "Tell me what you think of this parable:

---

a 21:19 The fig tree is first mentioned in Gen. 3:7, with its leaves being a "covering" for fallen Adam and Eve to hide behind. It is connected to the Tree of Knowledge of Good and Evil, and became a hiding place for Zacchaeus, who climbed a sycamore-fig tree to see Jesus. Many also equate the fig tree as being a symbol of Israel.

b 21:21 The mountain and the sea are both metaphors. Mountains speak of kingdoms, and the sea represents the nations (e.g., "sea of humanity"). Faith brings the reality of the kingdom realm into the nations.

c 21:22 Jesus taught his disciples that if faith's fullness lived in them, they could speak to the physical creation around them and it would respond. Faith unlocks great authority for the believer.

d 21:23 As translated from the Hebrew Matthew. The Greek is "authority." See also vv. 24 and 27.

e 21:28 As translated from the Hebrew Matthew.

"There once was a man with two sons. The father came to the first and said, 'Son, I want you to go and work in the vineyard today.' [29] The son replied, 'I'd rather not.' But afterward, he deeply regretted what he said to his father, changed his mind, and decided to go to the vineyard. [30] The father approached the second son and said the same thing to him. The son replied, 'Father, I will go and do as you said.' But he never did—he didn't go to the vineyard. [31] Tell me now, which of these two sons did the will of his father?"

They answered him, "The first one."

Jesus said, "You're right. For many sinners, tax collectors, and prostitutes are going into God's kingdom realm ahead of you! [32] John came to show you the path of goodness and righteousness,[a] yet the despised and outcasts believed in him, but you did not. When you saw them turn, you neither repented of your ways nor believed his words."

The Parable of the Rejected Son

[33] "Pay close attention to this parable," Jesus said. "There once was an honorable man who planted a vineyard.[b] He built a fence around it,[c] dug out a pit for pressing the grapes, and erected a watchtower. Afterward he leased the land to tenant farmers and then went a distance away. [34] At harvest time he sent his servants to the tenants to collect the portion that was due him as the lord of the vineyard. [35] But the tenants seized his servants and beat one, killed another, and stoned another.[d] [36] So the landowner sent other servants, even more than at first, but they were mistreated the same way. [37] Finally, he sent his own son to them, and he said to himself, 'Perhaps with my own son standing before them they will be ashamed of what they've done.'[e] [38] But when the tenants saw the son, they said, 'This is the heir! Let's kill him and then we can have his inheritance!' [39] So they violently seized him, took him outside the vineyard, and murdered him.

[40] "You tell me, when the lord of the vineyard comes, what do you think he will do to those tenants?"

[41] They answered, "He will bring a horrible death to those who did this evil and he will completely destroy them. Then he'll lease his vineyard to different tenants who will be faithful to give him the portion he deserves."

[42] Jesus said to them, "Haven't you ever read the Scripture that says:

---

a 21:32 Or "the way of righteousness" (justice). The Aramaic is "the way of goodness." The translation includes both concepts.

b 21:33 As translated from the Hebrew Matthew. The Greek is "landowner." See Isa. 5:1–7.

c 21:33 The Aramaic can be translated "He planted a vineyard by a stream."

d 21:35 The obvious meaning of the parable is this: God is the landowner, the servants he sends are God's prophets, and the son is Jesus Christ.

e 21:37 As translated from the Aramaic. The Greek is "They will respect my son."

The very stone the builder rejected as flawed
has now become the most important
capstone of the arch. [a]
This was the Lord's plan [b]—
isn't it a miracle for our eyes to behold?

[43] "This is why I say to you that the kingdom realm of God will be taken from you and given to a people [c] who will bear its fruit. [44] The one who comes against this stone [d] will be broken, but the one on whom it falls will be pulverized!" [e]

[45] When the leading priests and the Pharisees realized that the parable was referring to them, they were [46] outraged and wanted to arrest him at once. But they were afraid of the reaction of the crowds, because the people considered him to be a prophet.

Parable of the Wedding Feast

22 As was his custom, Jesus continued to teach the people by using allegories. [2] He illustrated the reality of heaven's kingdom realm by saying, "There once was a king who arranged an extravagant wedding feast for his son. [f] [3] On the day the festivities were set to begin, he sent his servants [g] to summon all the invited guests, but they chose not to come. [4] So the king sent even more servants to inform the invited guests, saying, 'Come, for the sumptuous feast is now ready! The oxen and fattened cattle have been killed and everything is prepared, so come! Come to the wedding feast for my son and his bride!'

[5] "But the invited guests were not impressed. One was preoccupied with his business; another went off to his farming enterprise. [6] And the rest seized the king's messengers and shamefully mistreated them, and even killed

---

a 21:42 See Ps. 118:22–23. The words "capstone of the arch" could also be translated "cornerstone" or "keystone." This is an obvious metaphor of Jesus Christ. He is a Stone that many will stumble over, and a Stone that will fall upon the unbeliever.

b 21:42 The Aramaic and the Hebrew Matthew read "This came from the presence of [next to] Lord Yahweh and is a marvel in our eyes."

c 21:43 Or "nation." The Hebrew Matthew and Aramaic can be translated "gentiles." This is a prophecy of the church being given access to God's kingdom realm through faith in Jesus Christ.

d 21:44 Or "falls upon this stone." Some manuscripts do not include v. 44. The Hebrew Matthew does not have the last clause of v. 44.

e 21:44 See Isa. 8:14–15; Dan. 2:34–35.

f 22:2 See Isa. 25:6–8.

g 22:3 God is the king who prepares his kingdom feast for his Son, Jesus Christ. The messenger-servants are the prophets he sends to summon the people to enter into the love feast of Jesus. It is all about the wedding of the Lamb to the bride of Christ. What a glorious feast is prepared for us!

them. [7] This infuriated the king! So he sent his soldiers to execute those murderers and had their city burned to the ground. [a]

[8] "Then the king said to his servants, 'The wedding feast is ready, yet those who had been invited to attend didn't deserve the honor. [9] Now I want you to go into the streets and alleyways [b] and invite anyone and everyone you find to come and enjoy the wedding feast in honor of my son.'

[10] "So the servants went out into the city streets and invited everyone to come to the wedding feast, good and bad alike, until the banquet hall was crammed with people! [11] Now, when the king entered the banquet hall, he looked with glee over all his guests. But then he noticed a guest who was not wearing the wedding robe *provided for him*. [c] [12] So he said, 'My friend, how is it that you're here and you're not wearing your wedding garment?' But the man was speechless.

[13] "Then the king turned to his servants and said, 'Tie him up and throw him into the outer darkness, [d] where there will be great sorrow, with weeping and grinding of teeth.' [14] For everyone is invited [e] to enter in, but few respond in excellence." [f]

The Pharisees Try to Entrap Jesus

[15] Then the Pharisees came together to make a plan to entrap Jesus with his own words. [16] So they sent some of their disciples together with some staunch supporters of Herod. [g] They said to Jesus, "Teacher, we know that you're an honest man of integrity and you teach us the truth of God's ways. We can clearly see that you're not one who speaks only to win the people's favor, because you

---

a 22:7 This was fulfilled by the Roman prince Titus (who eventually became emperor of Rome) in the Roman war of AD 67–70.

b 22:9 The Aramaic is "go to the ends of the roads."

c 22:11 Those invited to come from the streets had no opportunity to buy wedding clothes. This wedding robe is a picture of the garment of righteousness that grace provides for us. The man without the wedding garment had one provided, but he didn't want to change into new clothes. A change is necessary, for our King provides garments of white linen for us to wear, our wedding garments. See Isa. 52:1; Rev. 19:8.

d 22:13 The Hebrew Matthew is "the lowest hell [*sheol*]."

e 22:14 Or "Many are called." This can be understood to be a Semitic figure of speech that universalizes the invitation. See also Matt. 20:28.

f 22:14 The Greek word *eklektoi* can mean "chosen," but it can also be translated "worthy," "pure," "choice," "excellent." See 2 John 1, 13.

g 22:16 The Hebrew Matthew is "They took violent men from Herod." The Aramaic is "They took men from Herod's household." By bringing with them loyalists to Rome (Herodians), the Pharisees were convinced that Jesus would offend either the Jews, who despised paying the "poll tax" required of every adult male, or those political followers of Herod who sided with the Roman occupation.

speak the truth without regard to the consequences. [a] [17] So tell us, then, what you think. Is it proper for us Jews to pay taxes to Caesar or not?"

[18] Jesus knew the malice that was hidden behind their cunning ploy and said, "Why are you testing me, you imposters who think you have all the answers? [19] Show me one of the Roman coins." So they brought him a silver coin used to pay the tax. [20] "Now, tell me, whose head is on this coin and whose inscription is stamped on it?"

[21] "Caesar's," they replied.

Jesus said, "Precisely, for the coin bears the image of the emperor Caesar. [b] Well, then, you should pay the emperor what is due to the emperor. *But because you bear the image of God,* [c] give back to God all that belongs to him."

[22] The imposters were baffled in the presence of all the people and were unable to trap Jesus with his words. So they left, stunned by Jesus' words.

Marriage and the Resurrection

[23] Some of the Sadducees, a religious group that denied there was a resurrection of the dead, [d] came to ask Jesus this question: [24] "Teacher, the law of Moses teaches that if a man dies before he has children, his brother should marry the widow and raise up children for his brother's family line. [e] [25] Now, there was a family with seven brothers. The oldest got married but soon died, leaving his widow for his brother. [26] The second brother married and also died, and the third also. This was repeated down to the seventh brother, [27] when finally the woman also died. So here's our dilemma: [28] Which of the seven brothers will be the woman's husband when she's resurrected from the dead, since they all were once married to her?"

[29] Jesus answered them, "You are deluded, because your hearts are not filled with the revelation of the Scriptures or the power of God. [30] For after the resurrection, men and women will not marry, just like the angels of heaven don't marry. [31] Haven't you read what God said: [32] 'I am the Living God, [f] the God of Abraham, the God of Isaac, and the God of Jacob'? God is not the God of the dead, but of the living." [g]

[33] When the crowds heard this they were dazed, stunned over such wisdom! [h]

---

a 22:16 Or "You don't look into the faces of men [before you speak the truth]."

b 22:21 Actual coins from that era have been found with the emperor's image and a superscription saying, "Tiberius Caesar Augustus, son of the divine Augustus."

c 22:21 The coin belongs to Caesar because it carries his image. We have an obligation to God because we carry his image.

d 22:23 The Aramaic clearly states that the Sadducees said to Jesus, "There is no life after death."

e 22:24 See Deut. 25:5–10.

f 22:32 As translated from the Aramaic and implied in the Greek.

g 22:32 The implication Jesus is making is that Abraham, Isaac, and Jacob were all alive (in glory) when God spoke to Moses in the burning bush. See Ex. 3:6.

h 22:33 As translated from the Hebrew Matthew. The Greek is "teaching."

The Greatest Commandment

³⁴ When the Pharisees heard that Jesus had silenced the Sadducees, they called a meeting to discuss how to trap Jesus. ³⁵ Then one of them, a religious scholar, posed this question to test him: ³⁶ "Teacher, which commandment in the law is the greatest?"

³⁷ Jesus answered him, "'Love[a] the Lord your God with every passion of your heart, with all the energy of your being, and with every thought that is within you.'[j] ³⁸ This is the great and supreme commandment. ³⁹ And the second is like it in importance: 'You must love your friend[k] in the same way you love yourself.'[l] ⁴⁰ Contained within these commandments to love you will find all the meaning of the Law and the Prophets."

Jesus, Son of David—Lord of David

⁴¹ While all the Pharisees were gathered together, Jesus took the opportunity to pose a question of his own: ⁴² "What do you think about the Anointed One? Whose son is he?"

"The son of David," they replied.

⁴³ Then Jesus said to them, "How is it that David, inspired by the Holy Spirit, could call his son the Lord? For didn't he say:

⁴⁴ The Lord Jehovah said to my Lord,
'Sit near me in the place of authority
until I subdue all your enemies under Your feet'?[m]

⁴⁵ "So how could David call his own son 'the Lord Jehovah'?"[n]

⁴⁶ No one could come up with an answer. And from that day on none of the Pharisees had the courage to question Jesus any longer.

Superficial Spirituality versus Genuine Humility

23 Then Jesus addressed both the crowds and his disciples and said, ² "The religious scholars and the Pharisees sit on Moses'

---

a 22:37 The Hebrew Matthew is "worship," also quoted as "worship" by Justin Martyr (ca. AD 165), *First Apology* XXI.

j 22:37 Or "with all your mind." See Deut. 6:5.

k 22:39 As translated from the Aramaic word *kareb*, which means "one who is close to you" (emotionally or by proximity). The Greek is "neighbor."

l 22:39 See Lev. 19:18.

m 22:44 See Ps. 110:1, which is the Old Testament passage of Scripture most often quoted in the New Testament.

n 22:45 As translated from the Aramaic. To those who insisted on only interpreting the Scriptures literally, Jesus was proving there was a deeper spiritual interpretation. To say the Messiah would be the Son of David means that the Anointed One would manifest the qualities and devotion that David walked in. A true "spiritual" son of David.

throne[a] as the authorized interpreters of the Law. [3] So listen and follow what they teach, but don't do what they do, for they tell you one thing and do another. [4] They tie on your backs an oppressive burden of religious obligations and insist that you carry it, but will never lift a finger to help ease your load. [5] Everything they do is done for show and to be noticed by others. *They want to be seen as holy,* so they wear oversized prayer boxes on their arms and foreheads with Scriptures inside, and wear extra-long tassels on their outer garments. [b] [6] They crave the seats of highest honor at banquets and in their meeting places. [7] And how they love to be admired by men with their titles of respect, aspiring to be recognized in public and have others call them 'Reverend.'[c]

[8] "But you are to be different from that. You are not to be called 'master,' for you have only one Master, and you are all brothers and sisters. [9] And you are not to be addressed as 'father,'[d] for you have one Father, who is in heaven. [10] Nor are you to be addressed as 'teacher,'[e] for you have one Teacher, the Anointed One.[f] [11] The greatest among you will be the one who always serves others from the heart. [12] Remember this: If you have a lofty opinion of yourself and seek to be honored, you will be humbled. But if you have a modest opinion of yourself and choose to humble yourself, you will be honored."

Jesus Pronounces Seven Woes

[13] "Great sorrow awaits[g] you religious scholars and you Pharisees—such frauds and pretenders! You do all you can to keep people from experiencing the reality of heaven's kingdom realm.[h] Not only do you refuse to enter in, you also forbid anyone else from entering in!

[14] "Great sorrow awaits you religious scholars and you Pharisees—frauds and pretenders! For you eat up the widow's household with the ladle of your prayers. Because of this, you will receive a greater judgment.[i]

[15] "Great sorrow awaits you religious scholars and you Pharisees—such

---

a 23:2 Moses' throne (Aramaic) was a special seat in the ancient synagogues where the most respected elders of the people would sit to instruct them.

b 23:5 See Num. 15:38; Deut. 22:12.

c 23:7 Or "rabbi," an Aramaic word that means "master," "chief," "great one," or "teacher."

d 23:9 As translated from the Hebrew Matthew and the Aramaic. The Greek is "Call no one father."

e 23:10 Or "leader."

f 23:10 Jesus is emphasizing the priority of God over titles of men and over all teachers, fathers, and leaders. He is not teaching us to be disrespectful to teachers, fathers, and leaders, but that God must be in first place over all others. See Deut. 17:9–10.

g 23:13 Or "woe."

h 23:13 The Hebrew Matthew is "You have hidden the keys of knowledge and shut the kingdom of heaven from the children of men."

i 23:14 As translated from the Aramaic and the Hebrew Matthew. The most reliable Greek manuscripts do not include this verse, and it is omitted by modern translations.

frauds and pretenders! For you will travel over lake and land to find one disciple, only to make him twice the child of hell[a] as yourselves.

¹⁶ "You blind guides![b] Great sorrow awaits you, for you teach that there's nothing binding when you swear by God's temple, but if you swear by the gold of the temple, you are bound by your oath. ¹⁷ You are deceived in your blindness![c] Which is greater, the gold or the temple that makes the gold sacred? ¹⁸ And you say that whoever takes an oath by swearing, 'By the altar,' it is nothing. But if you swear, 'By the gift upon the altar,' then you are obligated to keep your oath. ¹⁹ What deception! For what is greater, the gift or the altar that makes the gift sacred? ²⁰ Whoever swears by the altar swears by the altar and everything offered on it. ²¹ And whoever swears by the temple swears by it and the one who dwells in it. ²² And whoever swears by heaven swears by the throne of God and by God, who sits upon it.

²³ "Great sorrow awaits you religious scholars and Pharisees—frauds and pretenders! For you are obsessed with peripheral issues, like insisting on paying meticulous tithes on the smallest herbs that grow in your gardens.[d] These matters are fine, yet you ignore the most important duty of all: to walk in the love of God, to display mercy to others, and to live with integrity.[e] Readjust your values and place first things first. ²⁴ What blind guides! Nitpickers! You will spoon out a gnat from your drink, yet at the same time you've gulped down a camel without realizing it![f]

²⁵ "Great sorrow awaits you religious scholars and Pharisees—frauds and imposters! You are like one who will only wipe clean the outside of a cup or bowl, leaving the inside filthy. You are foolish to ignore the greed and self-indulgence that live like germs within you. ²⁶ You are blind and deaf[g] to your evil. Shouldn't the one who cleans the outside also be concerned with cleaning the inside? You need to have more than clean dishes; you need clean hearts!

²⁷ "Great sorrow awaits you religious scholars and Pharisees—frauds

---

a 23:15 Or "son of Gehenna." Gehenna is an Aramaic word for the garbage dump outside of Jerusalem, which became a metaphor for hell.
b 23:16 The Aramaic is "blind rescuers."
c 23:17 Or "you blind fools."
d 23:23 Or "You tithe on mint, dill, and cumin [caraway seed]." See Lev. 27:30; Num. 18:12; Deut. 14:22–23. The law of Moses only obligated tithing on grain, wine, and oil. The religious scholars added to the law their interpretation, which added vegetables and herbs to their list of what should be tithed.
e 23:23 Or "faithfulness." The Hebrew Matthew is "justice, loving-kindness, and truth." The Aramaic is "justice, grace, and faith." See Mic. 6:8; Zech. 7:9.
f 23:24 This is best seen as an Aramaic pun, because the Aramaic word for gnat is qamla, and the word for camel is gamla. The gnat becomes a metaphor of what is least and insignificant, for swallowing a gnat will not hurt you. But the camel becomes a picture of self-righteousness. To swallow a camel would indeed kill you.
g 23:26 As translated from the Aramaic.

and imposters! You are nothing more than tombs painted with fresh coats of white paint—tombs that look shining and beautiful on the outside, but within are found decaying corpses full of nothing but corruption. [28] Outwardly you masquerade as righteous people, but inside your hearts you are full of hypocrisy and lawlessness.

[29] "Great sorrow awaits you religious scholars and Pharisees—frauds and imposters! You build memorials for the prophets your ancestors killed and decorate the monuments of the godly people your ancestors murdered. [30] Then you boast, 'If we had lived back then, we would never have permitted[a] them to kill the prophets.' [31] But your words and deeds testify that you are just like them and prove that you are indeed the descendants of those who murdered the prophets. [32] Go ahead and finish what your ancestors started! [33] You are nothing but snakes in the grass, the offspring of poisonous vipers! How will you escape the judgment of hell if you refuse to turn in repentance?[b]

[34] "For this reason I will send you more prophets and wise men and teachers of truth. Some you will crucify, and some you will beat mercilessly with whips in your meeting houses, abusing and persecuting them from city to city. [35] As your penalty, you will be held responsible for the righteous blood spilled and the murders of every godly person throughout your history—from the blood of righteous Abel to the blood of Zechariah, son of Jehoiada,[c] whom you killed as he stood in the temple between the brazen altar and the Holy Place. [36] I tell you the truth: the judgment for all these things will fall upon this generation!"

Jesus Prophesies Judgment Coming to Jerusalem

[37] "O Jerusalem, Jerusalem—you are the city that murders your prophets! You are the city that stones the very messengers who were sent[d] to deliver you! So many times I have longed to gather a wayward people, as a hen gathers her chicks under her wings—but you were too stubborn to let me. [38] And

---

a 23:30 As translated from the Hebrew Matthew. The Greek is "we would not have joined them in killing the prophets."

b 23:33 As translated from the Hebrew Matthew.

c 23:35 As translated from the Hebrew Matthew. See 2 Chron. 24:20–21. This strengthens the argument that the original manuscript of Matthew was written in Hebrew. The Greek erroneously lists Zechariah's father as Barachiah. There was indeed a Zechariah son of Barachiah, but he didn't live until after the crucifixion of Christ and was killed in a massacre in AD 69 by zealots inside the temple. See Sabine Baring-Gould, *The Lost and Hostile Gospels* (Williams & Norgate, 1874), 138. It is also recorded by the Jewish historian Josephus that Zechariah was the son of Jehoiada. *B. J.* 4.6.4. Furthermore, Jerome, in his commentary on Matthew, says, "In the [Hebrew] Gospel [of Matthew] which the Nazarenes use, for 'son of Barachiah' we find written, 'son of Jehoiada.'" Quoted from http://www.textexcavation.com.

d 23:37 Or "apostles" (sent ones).

now it is too late, since your city will be left in ruins. [a] [39] For you will not see me again until you are able to say, 'We welcome the one who comes to us in the name of the Lord.'" [b]

Jesus Prophesies the Destruction of the Temple

24 As Jesus was leaving the temple courts, his disciples came to him and pointed out the beautiful aspects of the architecture of the temple structures. [2] And Jesus turned to them and said, "Take a good look at all these things, for I'm telling you, there will not be one stone left upon another. It will all be leveled!" [c]

[3] Later, when they arrived at the Mount of Olives, his disciples came privately to where he was sitting and said, "Tell us, when will these things happen? And what supernatural sign should we expect to signal your coming [d] and the completion of this age?" [e]

[4] Jesus answered, "At that time deception will run rampant. So beware that you are not fooled! [5] For many will appear on the scene claiming my authority or saying about themselves, 'I am God's Anointed,' and they will lead many astray.

[6] "You will hear of wars nearby and revolutions on every side, with more rumors of wars to come. Don't panic or give in to your fears, for the breaking apart of the world's systems is destined to happen. But it won't yet be the end; it will still be unfolding.

[7] "Nations [f] will go to war against each other and kingdom against kingdom. And there will be terrible earthquakes—seismic events of epic proportion, horrible epidemics [g] and famines in place after place. [8] This is how the first contractions and birth pains *of the new age will begin!*" [h]

Persecution of Believers

[9] "You can expect to be persecuted, even killed; for you will be hated by all the nations because of your love for me. [i] [10] Then many will stop following me and

---

a 23:38 See Jer. 12:7; 22:5.

b 23:39 See Ps. 118:26.

c 24:2 This prophecy of Jesus was fulfilled by the Roman prince Titus, who, in the Roman war of AD 67–70, destroyed the temple. In about AD 135 the emperor Hadrian completely destroyed the city of Jerusalem and built a new city on its foundations and named it Aelia Capitolina.

d 24:3 Or "presence" (Gr. *parousia*).

e 24:3 Although it is possible to translate this "the end of the world," the Hebraic mind-set of the end of days is a transition into a new age of the Messiah's coming when all things will be restored.

f 24:7 Or "ethnic group." See 2 Chron. 15:6; Isa. 19:2.

g 24:7 Although missing from a few Greek manuscripts, "horrible epidemics" is found in the Hebrew Matthew, the Aramaic, and the majority of Greek texts.

h 24:8 The translators are aware of distorted use of the words "new age"; however, true believers in Christ anticipate the coming of a new day (age) dawning, with Christ and his bride ruling the nations. See Joel 2; Rev. 3:21.

i 24:9 Or "because of my name."

fall away,ᵃ and they will betray one another and hate one another. ¹¹ And many lying prophets will arise, deceiving multitudes and leading them away from the path of truth. ¹² There will be such an increase of sin and lawlessness that those whose hearts once burned with passion for God and others will grow cold. ¹³ But keep your hopeᵇ to the end and you will experience life and deliverance.

¹⁴ "Yet through it all, this joyful assurance of the realm of heaven's kingdom will be proclaimed all over the world, providing every nation with a demonstration of the reality of God. And after this the end of this age will arrive."

The Detestable Idol That Brings Misery

¹⁵ "When you witness what Daniel prophesied, 'the disgusting destroyer,'ᶜ taking its standᵈ in the Holy Place [let the reader learn],ᵉ ¹⁶ then those in the land of Judah must escape to the higher ground.ᶠ ¹⁷ On that day, if you happen to be outside,ᵍ don't go back inside to gather belongings. ¹⁸ And if you're working out in the field, don't run back home to get a coat. ¹⁹ It will be especially hard for pregnant women and for those nursing their babies in those days. ²⁰ So pray that your escape will not be during the winter months or on a Sabbath. ²¹ For this will be a time of great misery beyond the magnitude of anything the world has ever seen or ever will see. Unless God limited those days, no one would escape. ²² But because of his love for those chosen to be his, he will shorten that time of trouble.

²³ "And you will hear reports from some, saying, 'Look, he has returned,' 'The Messiah is over here,' or 'The Messiah is over there!' Don't believe it. ²⁴ For there will be imposters falsely claiming to be God's 'Anointed One,' and false prophetsʰ will arise to perform miracle signs to lead astray, if possible, those God has chosen to be his. ²⁵ Remember this, for I prophesy it will happen! ²⁶ So if someone says to you, 'Look, the Anointed One has returned! He's in the desert,' don't go chasing after him. Or if they say to you, 'Look,

---

a 24:10 The Aramaic is "Many will stumble" (or take offense).
b 24:13 As translated from the Aramaic. The Greek is "endure."
c 24:15 Or "the abomination [sin] that brings desolation [desecration]." See Dan. 8:13; 9:27; 11:31; 12:11. Jesus is saying that Daniel's prophecy was not yet fulfilled in Jesus' time. Many see the fulfillment of this prophecy in AD 70, when Titus, the Roman prince, went into the temple and sacrificed animals to Jupiter.
d 24:15 The Aramaic is "the defiling sign of desolation piling up (setting up) in the Holy Place."
e 24:15 These parenthetical words were added by Matthew to encourage us to seek the Lord for the understanding of this mystery. Jesus, speaking in the role of the True Prophet, gives us truth to ponder in veiled language.
f 24:16 See Jer. 16:16; Zech. 14:5; Luke 21:20–22.
g 24:17 Or "on the roof."
h 24:24 The Aramaic is "prophets of lies."

he's here in our house,'ᵃ don't believe it. ²⁷The appearingᵇ of the Son of Man will burst forth with the brightness of a lightning strike that shines from one end of the sky to the other, illuminating the earth. ²⁸How do birds of prey know where the dead body is?ᶜ They just know instinctively, and so you will know when I appear."

The Appearing of the Son of Man

²⁹"Then immediately this is what will take place: 'The sun will be darkened and the moon give no light. The stars will fall from the sky and all the cosmic powers will be shaken.'ᵈ ³⁰Then the sign announcing the Son of Man will appear in the sky, and all the nations of the earth will mourn over him.ᵉ And they will see the Son of Man appearing in the clouds of heaven, revealed with mighty power,ᶠ great splendor, and glory. ³¹And he will send his messengers with the loud blast of the trumpet,ᵍ and with a great voiceʰ they will gather his beloved chosen ones by the four winds, from one end of heaven to the other!"

A Parable of the Fig Tree

³²"Now learn the lesson from the parable of the fig tree. When spring arrives and it sends out its tender branches and sprouts leaves, you know that ripe fruitⁱ is soon to appear. ³³So it will be with you, for when you observe all these things taking place, you will know that he is near, even at the door! ³⁴I assure you, the end of this age will not come until all I have spoken comes to pass.

---

a 24:26 Or "in the inner rooms."

b 24:27 Or "presence" (Gr. *parousia*).

c 24:28 Or "Wherever you find the corpse, there the eagles will gather." This peculiar verse is best understood as a parallel of vultures knowing where the carcass is (for example) to how instinctively believers will know when Jesus has appeared.

d 24:29 See Isa. 13:10; 34:4; Joel 2:10; Amos 8:9. This can also be viewed as a Hebraic metaphor of the lights of the natural realm being shut off and replaced with heaven's glory—lights out on the old order. Sun, moon, and stars are also representative of the governmental structures failing with great calamity. A new order, a new glory, is coming to replace the fading glories of this world.

e 24:30 See Zech. 12:10–14; Rev. 1:7.

f 24:30 The Hebrew Matthew is "mighty warriors."

g 24:31 There is always a deeper meaning to the literal understanding of the text of the Bible. This deeper meaning does not negate the literal, but gives a fuller comprehension. Clouds are metaphors of God's presence among his people. The trumpet blast is symbolic of the universal announcement that will be heard by all.

h 24:31 As translated from the Hebrew Matthew, which can also be translated "with a great shout." This is also found in the Latin Vulgate translated by Jerome, who is believed to have had access to the manuscript of the Hebrew Matthew.

i 24:32 As translated from the Hebrew Matthew. The Greek is "summer is near."

[35] The earth and sky will wear out and fade away before one word I speak loses its power or fails to accomplish its purpose."

Live Always Ready for His Appearing

[36] "Concerning that day and exact hour, no one knows when it will arrive, not even the angels of heaven[a]—only the Father knows. [37] For it will be exactly like it was in the days of Noah when the Son of Man appears.[b] [38] Before the flood, people lived their lives eating, drinking, marrying, and having children.[c] [39] They didn't realize the end was near until Noah entered the ark, and then suddenly, the flood came and took them all away in judgment. It will happen the same way when the Son of Man appears. [40] At that time, two men will be working on the farm; one will be taken away in judgment, the other left. [41] Two women will be grinding grain; one will be taken away in judgment, the other left.[d] [42] This is why you must stay alert: because no one knows the day your Lord will come.

[43] "But realize this: If a homeowner had known what time of night the burglar would come to rob his house, he would have been alert and ready, and not let his house be robbed. [44] So always be ready, alert, and prepared, because at an hour when you're not expecting him, the Son of Man will come."

The Wise and Faithful Servant

[45] "Who is the one qualified to oversee the master's house? He will be a reliable servant who is wise and faithful, one he can depend on. The master will want to give him the responsibility of overseeing others in his house, for his servant will lead them well and give them food at the right time. [46] What joy and blessing will come to that faithful servant when the master comes home to find him serving with excellence! [47] I can promise you, the master will raise him up and put him in charge of all that he owns.

[48] "But the evil servant says in his heart, 'My master delays his coming, and who knows when he will return?' *And because of the delay, the servant mistreats those in his master's household. Instead of caring for the ones he was appointed to serve,* [49] he abuses the other servants and gives himself over to eating and drinking with drunkards. [50] Let me tell you what will happen to

---

a 24:36 A few Greek manuscripts add "nor the Son." However, that phrase is missing in many Greek texts and is not found in the Hebrew Matthew, the Aramaic, or the Latin Vulgate.

b 24:37 Or "so it will be in the Lord's presence" (Gr. *parousia*).

c 24:38 As translated from the Hebrew Matthew, which is literally "being fruitful and multiplying" (having children). The Greek is "marrying and giving in marriage."

d 24:41 One of the three manuscripts of the Hebrew Matthew, known as Shem-Tob, includes additional text: "This is because the angels at the end of the age will first remove the stumbling blocks [the wicked] from the world and will separate the good from the evil." This passage is not speaking of what is known as the "rapture," for as it was in the days of Noah, the evil were "taken" and the righteous were "left."

him. His master will suddenly return at a time that surprises him, and he will remove the abusive, selfish servant from his position of trust. ⁵¹And the master will cut him in two *a* and assign him to the place of great sorrow and anguish *b* along with all the other pretenders and unbelievers."

A Parable about Ten Virgins

25 "At the time my coming draws near, heaven's kingdom realm can be compared to ten maidens who took their oil lamps and went outside to meet the bridegroom and his bride. *c* ²⁻⁴Five of them were foolish and ill-prepared, for they took no *extra* oil *d* for their lamps. Five of them were wise and sensible, for they took flasks of olive oil with their lamps. ⁵When the bridegroom didn't come when they expected, they all grew drowsy and fell asleep. ⁶Then suddenly, in the middle of the night, they were awakened by the shout 'Get up! The bridegroom is here! Come out and have an encounter with him!' *e* ⁷So all the girls got up and trimmed their lamps. ⁸But the foolish ones were running out of oil, so they said to the five wise ones, 'Share your oil with us, because our lamps are going out!'

⁹"'We can't,' they replied. 'We don't have enough for all of us. You'll have to go and buy some for yourselves!'

¹⁰"While the five girls were out buying oil, the bridegroom appeared. Those who were ready and waiting were escorted inside with him and the wedding party to enjoy the feast. And then the door was locked. ¹¹Later, the five foolish girls came running up to the door and pleaded, 'Lord, Lord, let us come in!'

¹²"But he called back, 'Go away! Do I know you? I can assure you, I don't even know you!'

¹³"That is the reason you should always stay awake and be alert, because you don't know the day or hour when the Bridegroom will appear." *f*

---

a 24:51 Most likely hyperbole. The Greek word *dichotomeō* could also mean that God "will separate him from himself" (soul and body).

b 24:51 Or "gnashing of teeth."

c 25:1 As translated from the Hebrew Matthew and a few Greek manuscripts. Most Greek manuscripts have only "bridegroom." This would mean the ten virgins were going to marry one man, a doubtful teaching from Jesus. The ten virgins were bridesmaids, ladies-in-waiting. This was not Jesus condoning polygamy. It is possible that the parable hints of Zech. 8:23.

d 25:2–4 See v. 8. Oil in the Scriptures is a metaphor of the Holy Spirit, who brings us revelation of the Word of God and power for ministry.

e 25:6 This is not simply "meet him," for it is a rare Greek noun that means to "have a meeting" or "an encounter." See also 1 Thess. 4:17.

f 25:13 As translated from the Hebrew Matthew.

A Parable about Financial Stewardship

[14] "Again, heaven's kingdom realm is like the wealthy man who went on a long journey and summoned all his trusted servants and assigned his financial management over to them. [15] Before he left on his journey, he entrusted a bag of five thousand gold coins to one of his servants, to another a bag of two thousand gold coins, and to the third a bag of one thousand gold coins, each according to his ability to manage. [a]

[16] "The one entrusted with five thousand gold coins immediately went out and traded with the money, and he doubled his investment. [17] In the same way, the one who was entrusted with two thousand gold coins traded with the sum and likewise doubled his investment. [18] But the one who had been entrusted with one thousand gold coins dug a hole in the ground and buried his master's money.

[19] "After much time had passed, the master returned to settle accounts with his servants. [20] The one who was entrusted with five thousand gold coins came and brought ten thousand, saying, 'See, I have doubled your money.'

[21] "Commending his servant, the master replied, 'You have done well, and proven yourself to be my loyal and trustworthy servant. Because you have been a faithful steward to manage a small sum, now I will put you in charge of much, much more. You will experience the delight of your master, who will say to you, "Come celebrate with me!"'

[22] "Then the one who had been entrusted with two thousand gold coins came in and said, 'See, my master, I have doubled what you have entrusted to me.'

[23] "Commending his servant, the master replied, 'You have done well, and proven yourself to be my loyal and trustworthy servant. Because you were faithful to manage a small sum, now I will put you in charge of much, much more. You will experience the delight of your master, who will say to you, "Come celebrate with me!"'

[24] "Then the one who had been entrusted with one thousand gold coins came to his master and said, 'Look, sir. I know that you are a hard man to please and you're a shrewd and ruthless businessman who grows rich on the backs of others. [b] [25] I was afraid of you, so I went and hid your money and buried it in the ground. But here it is— take it, it's yours.'

[26] "Angered by what he heard, the master said to him, 'You're an

---

a 25:15 Or "five talents . . . two talents . . . one talent." A talent, although hard to determine exactly how much it represents, is a measure of weight. King Solomon received 666 talents of gold as his yearly tribute. A talent is clearly a large sum of money. See 2 Chron. 9:13 and 1 Kings 10:14.

b 25:24 Or "that you harvest where you didn't sow and gather where you didn't plant." This is most likely a proverb, a figure of speech that reinforces the thought of the servant that his

untrustworthy[a] and lazy servant! If you knew I was a shrewd and ruthless business man who always makes a profit, why didn't you deposit my money in the bank? [27] Then I would have received it all back with interest when I returned.[b] [28] But because you were unfaithful, I will take the one thousand gold coins and give them to the one who has ten thousand. [29] For the one who has will be given more, until he overflows with abundance. And the one with hardly anything, even what little he has will be taken from him.'[c]

[30] "Then the master said to his other servants, 'Now, throw that good-for-nothing servant far away from me into the outer darkness, where there will be great misery and anguish!'"

The Judgment of the Multitudes

[31] "When the Son of Man appears in his majestic glory, with all his angels by his side, he will take his seat on his throne of splendor, [32] and all the nations will be gathered together before him.[d] And like a shepherd who separates the sheep from the goats, he will separate all the people. [33] The 'sheep' he will put on his right side and the 'goats' on his left. [34] Then the King will turn to those on his right and say, 'You have a special place in my Father's heart. Come and experience the full inheritance of the kingdom realm that has been destined for you from before the foundation[e] of the world! [35] For when you saw me hungry, you fed me. When you found me thirsty, you gave me something to drink. When I had no place to stay, you invited me in, [36] and when I was poorly clothed, you covered me. When I was sick, you tenderly cared for me, and when I was in prison you visited me.'

[37] "Then the godly will answer him, 'Lord, when did we see you hungry or thirsty and give you food and something to drink? [38] When did we see you with no place to stay and invite you in? When did we see you poorly clothed and cover you? [39] When did we see you sick and tenderly care for you, or in prison and visit you?'

[40] "And the King will answer them, 'Don't you know? When you cared

---

master was strict, harsh, and ruthless. The attitude of the servant was "You are so ruthless; you're like a man who expects a harvest from a field he didn't plant!"

a   25:26 Or "evil."

b   25:27 The Aramaic can be translated "Why didn't you throw my money into the offering? Then I would have returned to ask for what was mine together with its bounty." The implication is that money given in sacred offering to God will be returned with even more, by God's generosity. See Luke 6:38.

c   25:29 By implication the parable is stating, "The one who has [a heart of faithful stewardship] will be given more [to manage]. And the one who has very little [faithfulness, wisdom, integrity] will lose the little he has [failed to manage well]."

d   25:32 See Dan. 7:13–14.

e   25:34 Or "from before the fall" of the world.

for one of the least important of these my little ones, my true brothers and sisters, you demonstrated love for me.'

⁴¹ "Then to those on his left the King will say, 'Leave me! For you are under the curse of eternal fire that has been destined for the devil and all his demons. ⁴² For when you saw me hungry, you refused to give me food, and when you saw me thirsty, you refused to give me something to drink. ⁴³ I had no place to stay, and you refused to take me in as your guest. When you saw me poorly clothed, you closed your hearts and would not cover me. When you saw that I was sick, you didn't lift a finger to help me, and when I was imprisoned, you never came to visit me.'

⁴⁴ "And then those on his left will say, 'Lord, when did we see you hungry or thirsty and not give you food and something to drink? When did we see you homeless, or poorly clothed? When did we see you sick and not help you, or in prison and not visit you?'

⁴⁵ "Then he will answer them, 'Don't you know? When you refused to help one of the least important among these my little ones, my true brothers and sisters, you refused to help and honor me.' ⁴⁶ And they will depart from his presence and go into eternal punishment. But the godly and beloved 'sheep' will enter into eternal bliss."

Jesus Prophesies His Crucifixion

26 After Jesus had completed his teachings, he said to his disciples, ² "You know that the Feast of the Passover begins in two more days. That's when the Son of Man is to be betrayed and handed over to be crucified."

³ Meanwhile, the prominent priests and religious leaders of the nation were gathered in the palace of the high priest Caiaphas.ᵃ ⁴ That's when they made their decision to secretlyᵇ have Jesus captured and killed. ⁵ But they all agreed, "We can't do this during the Passover celebrations or we could have a riot on our hands."

A Woman Anoints Jesus

⁶⁻⁷ Then Jesus went to Bethany, to the home of Simon, a man Jesus had healed of leprosy. A woman came into the house, holding an alabaster flaskᶜ filled with fragrant and expensive oil.ᵈ *She walked right up to Jesus, and in a lavish gesture of*

---

a 26:3 Caiaphas was a Sadducee with political connections to Pilate's government. He was the son-in-law of Annas, who had been deposed from his office by the Roman procurator Valerious, but he was still viewed by the people as the high priest. In effect, Israel had two high priests at the same time, Annas and Caiaphas, thus violating Jewish law.
b 26:4 Or "deceitfully" (Aramaic "with false testimony").
c 26:6–7 Jars such as this usually had a long neck that would be broken off and the oil poured out. The woman is identified as Mary, the sister of Lazarus and Martha. See Song. 1:12; Mark 14:3; Luke 7:37; John 12:1–5.
d 26:6–7 This was spikenard (or nard), a spice taken from a plant that grows in northern

devotion, she poured out the costly oil, and it cascaded over his head as he was at the table. [8] When the disciples saw this, they were offended. "What a total waste!" they grumbled. [9] "We could have sold it for a great deal of money and given it to the poor."

[10] Jesus knew their thoughts and said to them, **"Why are you critical of this woman? She has done a beautiful act of kindness for me. [11] You will always have someone poor whom you can help, but you will not always have me. [12] When she poured the fragrant oil over me, she was preparing my body for burial.** [a] **[13] I promise you that as this wonderful gospel spreads all over the world, the story of her lavish devotion to me will also be mentioned in memory of her."** [b]

Judas Agrees to Betray Jesus

[14] One of the twelve apostles, Judas the locksmith, [c] went to the leading priests [15] and said, "How much are you willing to pay me to betray Jesus into your hands?" They agreed to pay him thirty silver coins. [d] [16] Immediately Judas began to scheme and look for an opportunity to betray him.

Jesus Celebrates Passover with His Disciples

[17] On the first day of Passover, [e] the day when any bread made with yeast was removed from every Jewish home, the disciples came to Jesus and asked, "Where should we prepare the Passover meal [f] for you?"

India near the Himalayas. This costly perfume would have been carried over land to the Middle East. Many believe this jar of spikenard would have cost the average worker a year's wages. It was a common practice among the Jews to prepare a body for burial with fragrant ointment.

a 26:12 It is entirely possible that when the Roman soldiers pierced Jesus' beautiful feet and put the crown of thorns on his lovely head, they could have smelled this fragrant oil.

b 26:13 Jesus' prophecy is that Mary would be included in the Gospel account. Her act of devotion is mentioned in three of the four Gospels. You can't read the New Testament without knowing of Mary's worship of Jesus.

c 26:14 Or "Judah Iscariot." Iscariot is not his last name or the name of a town. It means "locksmith." *Iscariot* comes from an Aramaic word for "brass lock." The one who held the key to the finances of the twelve disciples brazenly wanted to lock up Jesus.

d 26:15 See Zech. 11:12–13. Assuming the thirty pieces of silver were tetradrachms, it would represent about four months' wages of a skilled worker. If the coins were the Roman denarius, it would be about five weeks' wages. If they were Jewish shekels, it would have been a very modest sum. How could anyone put a monetary value on the life of the glorious Son of God?

e 26:17 Or "the first day of Unleavened Bread." The Aramaic reads "on the day before the Passover festival." This was the first day of an eight-day celebration to commemorate the deliverance of the Hebrew slaves out of Egypt. The Jews would eat a roasted lamb after sunset in a family group of at least ten people. The meal would include bitter herbs (in remembrance of their bitter years of slavery), unleavened bread, and four cups of wine mixed with water. See Num. 9:2–5.

f 26:17 That is, "the Passover seder."

¹⁸ He answered them, "My heart longs with great desire to eat this Passover meal with you. ª Go into Jerusalem and you will encounter a man. ᵇ Tell him that the teacher says, 'My appointed time ᶜ is near. I am coming to your home to eat the Passover meal with my disciples.'"

¹⁹ The disciples did as Jesus had instructed them, and they prepared the Passover meal. ²⁰ When evening came he took his place at the table and dined with the Twelve. ²¹ While they were eating, Jesus spoke up and said, "One of you is about to betray me."

²² Feeling deeply hurt by these words, one after another asked him, "You don't mean me, do you?"

²³ He answered, "It is one who has shared meals with me as an intimate friend. ᵈ ²⁴ All that was prophesied of me will take place, but how miserable it will be for the one who betrays the Son of Man. It would be far better for him if he had never been born!"

²⁵ Then finally, Judas the traitor spoke up and asked him, "Teacher, ᵉ perhaps it is I?"

Jesus answered, "You said it."

The Lord's Supper

²⁶ As they ate, Jesus took the bread and blessed it and broke it and gave it to his disciples. He said to them, "This is my body. Eat it." ²⁷ Then taking the cup of wine and giving praises to the Father, he entered into covenant with them, ᶠ saying, "This is my blood. Each of you must drink it in fulfillment of the covenant. ²⁸ For this is the blood that seals the new covenant. ᵍ It will be poured out for many for the complete forgiveness of sins. ²⁹ The next time we drink

---

a 26:18 As translated from the Hebrew Matthew and other external evidence. The Greek text does not include this sentence; however, it seems to be essentially the same as found in Luke 22:15, which may support the theory that part of Luke's eyewitness accounts may have included Matthew.

b 26:18 The Greek is actually "Mr. So-and-So." This was someone who would know who the teacher was and understand what it meant when Jesus said, "My time is near." The Hebrew Matthew adds this line: "He will volunteer for the task."

c 26:18 An obvious ellipsis that could mean "My time of fulfilling my destiny" is near.

d 26:23 Or "he who has dipped his hand with me in the dish." This is a figure of speech of one who was an intimate friend of Jesus. To break bread together was a sign of friendship throughout the Middle East.

e 26:25 Notice that the other eleven disciples called Jesus "Lord." Judas called him "teacher."

f 26:27 As translated from the Aramaic.

g 26:28 The Aramaic word khawdata can be translated "new," but is better rendered "renewed" covenant or "repaired" covenant. See Lev. 17:11; Jer. 31:31–37. After each disciple took the cup and drank from it, they passed it to the next one. This was a love covenant between Jesus and each of his disciples, and it sealed the affection they had for one another.

this, I will be with you and we will drink it together with a new understanding in the kingdom realm of my Father." [a]

[30] Then they sang a psalm [b] and left for the Mount of Olives.

Jesus Prophesies Peter's Denial

[31] Along the way Jesus said to them, "Before the night is over, you will all desert me. This will fulfill the prophecy of the Scripture that says:

I will strike down the shepherd
    and all the sheep will scatter far and wide! [c]

[32] "But after I am risen, I will go ahead of you to Galilee and will meet you there." [d]

[33] Then Peter spoke up and said, "Even if all the rest lose their faith and fall away, I will still be beside you, Jesus!"

[34] "Are you sure, Peter?" Jesus said. "In fact, before the rooster crows a few hours from now, you will have denied me three times."

[35] Peter replied, "I absolutely will never deny you, even if I have to die with you!" And all the others said the same thing.

Jesus Prays in Gethsemane

[36] Then Jesus led his disciples to an orchard called "The Oil Press." [e] He told them, "Sit here while I go and pray over there." [37] He took Peter, Jacob, and John with him. [f] However, an intense feeling of great sorrow plunged his soul into deep sorrow and agony. [38] And he said to them, "My heart is overwhelmed and crushed with grief. It feels as though I'm dying. Stay here and keep watch with me."

[39] Then he walked a short distance away, and overcome with grief, he threw himself facedown on the ground and prayed, "My Father, if there is any

---

a 26:29 We are now in the realm of the kingdom of God. The Holy Spirit brings us into the body of Christ and into the reality of the kingdom of God. It is growing and increasing in scope, and every time believers drink of the cup of communion, Jesus is present with us. It is the Lord's table, not ours. This was a prophecy of what would happen in just a matter of days from then, as believers would break bread together in remembrance of what Jesus did for them. See Acts 2:42. Jesus now drinks it with us in a new way, and not just once a year at Passover, but every time we worship him by taking communion.

b 26:30 Or "a hymn." The Aramaic is "They offered praise." It was the custom after celebrating the Passover seder to conclude with singing one of the Hallel psalms (Pss. 115–118).

c 26:31 See Zech. 13:7.

d 26:32 As translated from the Hebrew Matthew.

e 26:36 Or "Gethsemane," which means "oil press." This was located on the lower slope of the Mount of Olives near the brook Kidron. King David left Jerusalem weeping as he crossed the Kidron Valley and went up the Mount of Olives (2 Sam. 15:23). Now the Son of David comes into that valley with great sorrow on his way into Jerusalem to be crucified. Kidron comes from the Hebrew verb qadar, which means "to grow dark" or "to mourn."

f 26:37 Or "Peter and the two sons of Zebedee."

way you can deliver me from this suffering, *a* please take it from me. Yet what I want is not important, for I only desire to fulfill your plan for me." Then an angel from heaven appeared to strengthen him. *b*

⁴⁰ Later, he came back to his three disciples and found them all sound asleep. He awakened Peter and said to him, "Do you lack the strength to stay awake with me for even just an hour? ⁴¹ Keep alert and pray that you'll be spared from this time of testing. You should have learned by now that your spirit is eager enough, but your humanity is weak." *c*

⁴² Then he left them for a second time to pray in solitude. *He said to God,* "My Father, if there is not a way that you can deliver me from this suffering, *d* then your will must be done."

⁴³ He came back to the disciples and found them sound asleep, for they couldn't keep their eyes open. ⁴⁴ So he left them and went away to pray the same prayer for the third time.

⁴⁵ When he returned again to his disciples, he awoke them, saying, "Are you still sleeping and resting? Don't you know the hour has come for the Son of Man to be handed over to the authority of sinful men? ⁴⁶ Get up and let's go, for the betrayer has arrived."

The Betrayal and Arrest of Jesus

⁴⁷ At that moment Judas, his once-trusted disciple, appeared, along with a large crowd of men armed with swords and clubs. They had been sent to arrest Jesus by order of the ruling priests and Jewish religious leaders. ⁴⁸ Now, Judas, the traitor, had arranged to give them a signal that would identify Jesus, for he had told them, "Jesus is the one whom I will kiss. So grab him!"

---

a 26:39 Or "If possible, take away this cup of suffering." The cup becomes a metaphor of the great suffering that Jesus had to drink that night in the garden. However, Jesus was not asking the Father for a way around the cross. Rather, he was asking God to keep him alive through this night of suffering so that he could carry the cross and take away our sins. According to the prophecies of the Old Testament, Jesus was to be pierced on a cross. We learn from Heb. 5:7 that Jesus' prayer was answered that night as the cup was indeed taken from him. An angel of God came to strengthen him and deliver him from premature death. The "cup" he was asking God to let pass from him was the cup of premature death that Satan was trying to make him drink in the garden, not the death he would experience the next day on the cross. He had already sweat drops of blood, but the prophecies had to be fulfilled of being pierced on a cross for our transgressions. God answered his cry and he lived through the agony of Gethsemane so that he could be our sacrifice for sin on Calvary. Jesus did not waver in the garden. We have a brave Savior.

b 26:39 As translated from the Hebrew Matthew. See Luke 22:43, which may be evidence of Luke having access to the Hebrew Matthew account.

c 26:41 The Aramaic is "the flesh is failing."

d 26:42 See the first footnote for v. 39 and Heb. 5:7.

⁴⁹Judas quickly stepped up to Jesus and said, "Shalom, Rabbi," and he kissed him *on both cheeks.* ᵃ

⁵⁰ "My beloved friend," ᵇ Jesus said, "is this why you've come?" ᶜ

Then the armed men seized Jesus to arrest him. ⁵¹ But one of the disciples ᵈ pulled out a dagger and swung it at the servant of the high priest, slashing off his ear. ⁵² Jesus said to him, "Put your dagger away. For all those who embrace violence will die by violence. ᵉ ⁵³ Don't you realize that I could ask my heavenly Father for angels to come at any time to deliver me? And instantly he would answer me by sending twelve armies of the angelic host ᶠ to come and protect us. ⁵⁴ But that would thwart the prophetic plan of God. For it has been written that it would happen this way."

⁵⁵ Then Jesus turned to the mob and said, "Why would you arrest me with swords and clubs as though I were an outlaw? Day after day I sat in the temple courts with you, teaching the people, yet you didn't arrest me. ⁵⁶ But all of this fulfills the prophecies of the Scriptures."

At that point all of his disciples ran away and abandoned him.

Jesus Is Condemned by the Religious Leaders

⁵⁷ Those who arrested Jesus led him away to Caiaphas, the chief priest, and to a meeting where the religious scholars and the supreme Jewish council were already assembled. ᵍ ⁵⁸ Now, Peter had followed the mob from a distance all the way to the chief priest's courtyard. And after entering, he sat with the servants ʰ of the chief priest who had gathered there, waiting to see how things would unfold. ⁵⁹ The chief priests and the entire supreme Jewish council of leaders ⁱ were doing their best to find false charges that they could bring against Jesus, because they were looking for a reason to put him to death.

⁶⁰ Many false witnesses came forward, but the evidence could not be

---

a 26:49 This would have been the customary kiss among the Jews of that day.

b 26:50 As translated from the Hebrew Matthew.

c 26:50 As translated from the Aramaic. The Greek is "Do what you've come to do."

d 26:51 From John 18:10 we learn that the disciple was Peter. Matthew, although knowing it was his friend Peter, kept him from any embarrassment by not naming him in his Gospel narrative.

e 26:52 The Aramaic reads, "Those who have taken up swords against me will all die by the sword." The Aramaic is a prophecy that those armed men who came against Jesus in the garden that night would die by the sword.

f 26:53 Or "twelve legions." A legion was a detachment of six thousand Roman soldiers. Jesus could have called down seventy-two thousand angels to come to his aid. The number twelve was a reminder to the twelve disciples that God had more than enough protection for them all.

g 26:57 Or "elders." The supreme Jewish council (Sanhedrin) is made explicit in v. 59.

h 26:58 The Aramaic is "temple ushers."

i 26:59 Or "Sanhedrin" (or Great Sanhedrin), which was a council of seventy men who were appointed to serve as the leadership of the Jewish community and the affairs of the temple.

corroborated. Finally two men came forward [61] and declared, "This man said, 'I can destroy God's temple and build it again in three days!'"

[62] Then the chief priest stood up and said to Jesus, "Have you nothing to say about these allegations? Is what they're saying about you true?" [63] But Jesus remained silent before them. So the chief priest said to him, "I charge you under oath—in the name of the living God, tell us once and for all if you are the anointed Messiah, the Son of God!"

[64] Jesus answered him, "You just said it yourself. And more than that, you are about to see the Son of Man seated at the right hand of God, the Almighty.[a] And one day you will also see the Son of Man coming in the heavenly clouds!"

[65] This infuriated the chief priest, and as an act of outrage, he tore his robe and shouted, "What blasphemy! No more witnesses are needed, for you heard this grievous blasphemy." [66] Turning to the council he said, "Now, what is your verdict?"

"He's guilty and deserves the death penalty!" they answered. [67] Then they spat on his face and slapped him. Others struck him over and over with their fists. [68] Then they taunted him by saying, "Oh, Anointed One, prophesy to us! Tell us which one of us is about to hit you next?"

Peter's Denials

[69] Meanwhile, Peter was still sitting outside in the courtyard when a servant girl came up to him and said, "I recognize you. You were with Jesus the Galilean."

[70] In front of everyone Peter denied it and said, "I don't have a clue what you're talking about."

[71] Later, as he stood near the gateway of the courtyard, another servant girl noticed him and said, "I know this man is a follower of Jesus the Nazarene!"

[72] Once again, Peter denied it, and with an oath he said, "I tell you, I don't know the man!"

[73] A short time later, those standing nearby approached Peter and said, "We know you're one of his disciples—we can tell by your speech. Your Galilean accent gives you away!"[b]

[74] Peter denied it, and using profanity he said, "I don't know the man!" At that very moment the sound of a crowing rooster pierced the night. [75] Then Peter remembered the prophecy of Jesus, "Before the rooster crows you will have denied me three times." With a shattered heart, Peter went out of the courtyard, sobbing with bitter tears.

---

a 26:64 See Ps. 110:2; Dan. 7:13.
b 26:73 Peter, being from Capernaum in Galilee, spoke the northern dialect of Aramaic, while the people of Jerusalem spoke the southern dialect (Chaldean).

Jesus Condemned by the Religious Leaders

27 Before dawn that morning, all the chief priests and religious leaders resolved to take action against Jesus and decided that he should be executed. [2] So they bound him with chains and led him away to Pilate, the Roman governor.

Judas Commits Suicide

[3] Now, when Judas, the betrayer, saw that Jesus had been sentenced to death, remorse filled his heart. He returned the thirty pieces of silver to the chief priests and religious leaders, [4] saying, "I have sinned because I have betrayed an innocent[a] man."

They replied, "Why are you bothering us? That's your problem."

[5] Then Judas flung the silver coins inside the temple and went out and hanged himself.

[6] The chief priests, picking up the pieces of silver, said, "We can't keep this, for it's unlawful to put blood money into the temple treasury." [7] So after some deliberation, they decided to purchase the potter's field *of clay*,[b] to use as a cemetery for burying strangers. [8] That's why that land has been called "The Field of Blood." [9] This fulfilled the prophecy of Zechariah:[c]

They took the thirty pieces of silver,
> the price at which he was valued by the people of Israel,
> > the price of a precious man,[d]
[10] And with the silver they bought the potter's field,
> as the Lord directed.[e]

Jesus Brought before Pilate

[11] As Jesus stood in front of the Roman governor, Pilate asked him, "So, you are really the king of the Jews?"

Jesus answered, **"You have just spoken it."** [12] Then he was slandered and accused by the chief priests and religious leaders, but he remained silent.

[13] Pilate said, "Don't you hear these allegations?" [14] But Jesus offered no defense to any of the charges, much to the great astonishment of Pilate.

[15] Now, every year at Passover it was the custom of the governor to pardon

---

a 27:4 The Aramaic word for "innocent," *zakaia*, can also mean "victorious."

b 27:7 Implied in the historical context. This was the field owned by a potter, used for making clay vessels.

c 27:9 As translated from the Hebrew Matthew. See Zech. 11:12–13. The Greek manuscripts incorrectly identify the prophecy as from Jeremiah. There is no clear prophecy found in Jeremiah that is quoted here by Matthew. The Aramaic reads simply, "spoken of by the prophet." The Hebrew Matthew correctly states, "spoken through Zechariah."

d 27:9 As translated from the Aramaic.

e 27:10 Or "as the Lord directed me."

a prisoner and release him to the people—anyone they wanted. [16] And at that time, Pilate was holding in custody a notorious criminal named Jesus Barabbas. [a] [17] So as the crowds of people assembled outside of Pilate's residence, he went out and offered them a choice. He asked them, "Who would you want me to release to you today, Jesus who is called Barabbas, or Jesus who is called the Anointed One?" [18] (Now, Pilate was fully aware that the religious leaders had handed Jesus over to him because of their bitter jealousy.)

[19] Just then, as Pilate was presiding over the tribunal, [b] his wife sent him an urgent message: "Don't harm that holy man, [c] for I suffered a horrible nightmare last night about him!"

[20] Meanwhile, the chief priest and the religious leaders were inciting the crowd to ask for Barabbas to be freed and to have Jesus killed. [21] So Pilate asked them again, "Which of the two men would you like me to release for you?"

They shouted, "Barabbas."

[22] Pilate asked them, "Then what would you have me to do with Jesus who is called the Anointed One?"

They all shouted back, "Crucify him!"

[23] "Why?" Pilate asked. "What has he done wrong?"

But they kept shouting out, "Crucify him!"

Jesus Condemned to Death

[24] When Pilate realized that a riot was about to break out and that it was useless to try to reason with the crowd, he sent for a basin of water. After washing his hands [d] in front of the people, he said, "I am innocent of the blood of this righteous man. [e] The responsibility for his death is now yours!" [f]

[25] And the crowd replied, "Let his blood be on us and on our children!"

[26] So he released Barabbas to the people. He ordered that Jesus be beaten with a whip made of leather straps embedded with metal, and afterward be crucified. [27] Then the guards took him into their military compound, where a detachment of nearly six hundred soldiers surrounded him.

[28] They stripped off his clothing and placed a scarlet robe on him to make fun of him. [29] Then they braided a crown of thorns and set it on his head. After placing a reed staff in his right hand, they knelt down before him and irreverently

---

a 27:16 As translated from the Hebrew Matthew and a few Greek manuscripts. Most Greek texts have only Barabbas. The name Barabbas is Aramaic and means "son of a father" or "son who is like his father." He becomes a picture of every son of Adam, our father. Some believe this is a figure of speech, a nickname for one who was born an illegitimate son, with no known father. The true Son of the Father was crucified that day.

b 27:19 Or "sat on the judgment seat."

c 27:19 As translated from the Aramaic.

d 27:24 See Deut. 21:6–7.

e 27:24 As translated from the Hebrew Matthew and the Aramaic.

f 27:24 The Aramaic is "You do as you please!"

mocked him, saying, "Hail, king of the Jews!" [30] Then they spat in his face and took the reed staff from his hand and hit him repeatedly on his head, *driving the crown of thorns deep into his brow.* [31] When they finished ridiculing him, they took off the scarlet robe and put his own clothes back on him and led him away to be crucified. [32] And as they came out of the city, they stopped an African man named Simon, from Libya,*a* and compelled him to carry the cross for Jesus.

The Crucifixion

[33] They brought Jesus to Golgotha, which means "Skull Hill."*b* [34] And there the soldiers offered him a mild painkiller, a drink of wine mixed with gall,*c* but after tasting it, he refused to drink it.

[35] Then they crucified Jesus, nailing his hands and feet to the cross. The soldiers divided his clothing among themselves by rolling dice to see who would win them. [36] And the soldiers stood there to watch what would happen and to keep guard over him. [37] Above his head they placed a sign that read, "This is Jesus of Nazareth,*d* King of Israel."

[38] Two criminals were also crucified with Jesus, one on each side of him.*e* [39] And those who passed by shook their heads and spitefully ridiculed him, [40] saying, "We heard you boast that you could destroy the temple and rebuild it in three days! Why don't you save yourself now? If you're really God's Son, come down from the cross!"

[41] Even the ruling priests, with the Jewish scholars and religious leaders, joined in the mockery*f* [42] and kept on saying, "He saved others, but he can't even save himself! Israel's king, is he? He should pull out the nails and come

---

a 27:32 Or "from Cyrene," which is present-day Tripoli, Libya.

b 27:33 The Aramaic word *Golgotha* is, in Latin, *calvaria*, or Calvary. David brought Goliath's head (Goliath and Golgotha are taken from the same root word) and buried it outside of Jerusalem. Some believe this is where it got its name, Golgotha (the place of the skull). The cross has to pierce the place of the skull for our minds to submit to the revelation of the cross.

c 27:34 See Ps. 69:21.

d 27:37 As translated from the Hebrew Matthew. See John 19:20. The sign was written in Aramaic, Latin, and Greek. Aramaic was the language of the common people in Israel. Hebrew ceased to be their spoken language after 450 BC, when the Jews returned from Babylon. Aramaic remained the language of Israel for nearly one thousand years. Latin was the official language of the Roman Empire. The inscription was also in Greek, for the Alexandrian Jews who had come to observe the Passover in Jerusalem would be unable to read Aramaic. The words were "Jesus, the Nazarene, King of the Jews." The first letters of each of the four words written on the sign in Aramaic (Hebrew) were Y-H-W-H (*Y'shua Hanozri Wumelech a Yehudim*). To write these letters, YHWH (also known as the Tetragrammaton), was the Hebrew form of writing the sacred name "Yahweh." No wonder the chief priests were so offended by this sign and insisted that Pilate change it. This was a sign given to Israel, for over Jesus' head on the cross was written "Y-H-W-H! God, the Savior, bled to death for you."

e 27:38 See Isa. 53:12.

f 27:41 See Pss. 22:17; 109:25; Lam. 2:15.

down from the cross right now; then we'll believe in him! [43] He says he puts all his trust in God, so let's see if it's true, and see if God really wants to rescue his 'favorite son'!" [a]

[44] Even the two criminals who were crucified with Jesus began to taunt him, hurling their insults on him.

The Death of the Savior

[45] For three hours, beginning at noon, darkness came over the earth. [b] [46] And at three o'clock Jesus shouted with a mighty voice in Aramaic, "**Eli, Eli, lema sabachthani?**" [c]—that is, "**My God, My God, why have you deserted me?**" [d] [47] Some who were standing near the cross misunderstood and said, "He's calling for Elijah." [48] One bystander ran and got a sponge, soaked it with sour wine, then put it on a stick and held it up for Jesus to drink. [49] But the rest said, "Leave him alone! Let's see if Elijah comes to rescue him." [e]

[50] Jesus passionately cried out, [f] took his last breath, and gave up his spirit.

[51] At that moment the veil in the Holy of Holies was torn in two from the top to the bottom. The earth shook violently, rocks were split apart, [52] and graves were opened. Then many of the holy ones who had died were brought back to life and came out of their graves. [53] And after Jesus' resurrection, [g] they were plainly seen by many people walking in Jerusalem. [h]

[54] Now, when the Roman military officer and his soldiers witnessed what was happening and felt the powerful earthquake, they were extremely terrified. They said, "There is no doubt, this man was the Son of God!"

[55] Watching from a distance were many of the women who had followed him from Galilee and given him support. [56] Among them were Mary Magdalene; Mary, the mother of Jacob and Joseph; and the mother of Jacob and John.

---

a 27:43 As translated from the Aramaic. See also Ps. 22:8.

b 27:45 Or "the land."

c 27:46 The last words of Jesus were spoken in Aramaic. Every Greek text gives a transliteration of the Aramaic words and then translates them back into Greek.

d 27:46 See Pss. 22:1; 42:9. The Aramaic can be translated "for this purpose you have spared me."

e 27:49 A few Greek manuscripts have an additional sentence: "A soldier took a lance and pierced him in the side and blood and water poured out." It is not found in the Aramaic and many Greek texts of Matthew. If included, it would mean the soldier took Jesus' life with his lance. However, Jesus said that no man could take his life from him. The evidence is compelling that it was not part of the original text, but was taken from John 19:34 and added here.

f 27:50 See Luke 23:46 and John 19:30 to read the words he shouted out at death.

g 27:53 The Aramaic reads "after their rising."

h 27:53 Perhaps one was Joseph, for he had asked that his bones be buried in the promised land. He saw a resurrection coming and didn't want to be left out. See Heb. 11:22. Jesus' resurrection was so powerful that many were instantly raised back to life again along with him.

The Burial of Jesus

⁵⁷ At the end of the day, a wealthy man named Joseph, a follower of Jesus from the village of Ramah,ᵃ ⁵⁸ approached Pilate and asked to have custody of the body of Jesus. So Pilate consented and ordered that the body be given to him. ⁵⁹ Then Joseph wrapped the body in a shroud of fine linen and placed it in his own unused tomb, which had only recently been cut into the rock. ⁶⁰ They rolled a large stone to seal the entrance of the tomb and left.

⁶¹ Sitting across from the tomb were Mary Magdalene and the other Marys,ᵇ watching all that took place.

⁶² The next day, the day after Preparation Day for Passover, the chief priests and the Pharisees went together to Pilate. ⁶³ They said to him, "Our master, we remember that this imposter claimed that he would rise from the dead after three days. ⁶⁴ So please, order the tomb to be sealed until after the third day. Seal it so that his disciples can't come and steal the corpse and tell people he rose from the dead. Then the last deception would be worse than the first!"

⁶⁵ "I will send soldiers to guard the tomb," Pilate replied. "Go with them and make the tomb as secure as possible." ⁶⁶ So they left and sealed the stone,ᶜ and Pilate's soldiers secured the tomb.

The Resurrection of Jesus

28 After the Sabbath ended, at the first light of dawn on the first day of the week, Mary Magdalene and the other Maryᵈ went to take a look at the tomb. ²⁻⁴ Suddenly, the earth shook violently beneath their feet as the angel of the Lord Jehovahᵉ descended from heaven. Lightning flashed around him and his robe was dazzling white! The guards were stunned and terrified—lying motionless like dead men. Then the angel walked up to the tomb, rolled away the stone, and sat on top of it!

⁵ The women were breathless and terrified, until the angel said to them, "There's no reason to be afraid. I know you're here looking for Jesus, who was crucified. ⁶ He isn't here—he has risen victoriously,ᶠ just as he said! Come inside the tomb and see the place where our Lord was lying.ᵍ ⁷ Then run and tell his

---

a 27:57 As translated from the Aramaic. Ramah (formerly Ramathaim Zophim) was the village of Samuel, situated on a hill overlooking Jerusalem. The Greek is "Joseph of Arimathea." Luke tells us that he was a member of the Sanhedrin. See Luke 23:50–51. It is possible that Joseph may have lost a son the age of Jesus when Herod killed the infants.

b 27:61 As translated from the Hebrew Matthew. See v. 56 and 28:1.

c 27:66 This official seal, if broken, would bring the death penalty to the offender.

d 28:1 This was Mary, the mother of Jacob and Joseph. See Mark 16:1; Luke 24:10.

e 28:2–4 Or "the angel of YHWH," as translated from the Aramaic.

f 28:6 As translated from the Aramaic.

g 28:6 As translated from the Aramaic and some Greek texts.

disciples that he has risen from the dead! I give you his message: "I am going ahead of you in Galilee and you will see me there." [a]

[8] They rushed quickly to tell his disciples, and their hearts were deep in wonder and filled with great joy.

[9] Along the way, Jesus suddenly appeared in front of them and said, "Rejoice!" [b] They were so overwhelmed by seeing him that they bowed down and grasped his feet in adoring worship.

[10] Then Jesus said to them, "Throw off all your fears. Go and tell my brothers [c] to go to Galilee. They will find me there."

The Guards Report What They Witnessed

[11] After the women left the tomb, a few of the guards went into Jerusalem and told the chief priests everything they had seen and heard. [12] So the chief priests called a meeting with all the religious leaders and came up with a plan. They bribed the guards with a large sum of money [13] and told them, "Tell everyone, 'While we were asleep, his disciples came at night and stole his body!' [14] If Pilate finds out about this, don't worry. We'll make sure you don't get blamed." [15] So they took the money and did as they were told. (That is why the story of the guards is still circulated among the Jews to this day.)

The Great Commission

[16] Meanwhile, the eleven disciples heard the wonderful news from the women and left for Galilee, to the mountain where Jesus had arranged to meet them. [17] The moment they saw him, they worshiped him, but some still had lingering doubts.

[18] Then Jesus came close to them and said, "**All the authority of the universe has been given to me.** [d] [19] Now go *in my authority* and make disciples of all nations, baptizing them in the name of the Father, the Son, and the Holy Spirit. [20] And teach them to faithfully follow [e] all that I have commanded you. And never forget that I am with you every day, even to the completion of this age." [f]

---

a 28:7 Or "He is going ahead of you to Galilee and you will see him there. Behold, I have told you!"

b 28:9 Or "Be rejoicing!"

c 28:10 What an incredible truth! Believers are now his brothers and sisters. See Heb. 2:11.

d 28:18 There is a sentence found in the Aramaic that is missing in all but one Greek manuscript, which reads, "As my Father has sent me, so I send you."

e 28:20 The Aramaic is "keep" or "guard" (a fortress).

f 28:20 Or "I am with you all the appointed days" (Variorum Version).

MARK

Introduction

AT A GLANCE

Author: John Mark
Audience: Roman Christians
Date: AD 50–55
Type of Literature: Ancient historical biography
Major Themes: The person of Jesus, the mission of Jesus, the work of Jesus, discipleship and faith, the kingdom realm
Outline:

Prologue — 1:1–13
Jesus' Galilee Ministry: Phase 1 — 1:14–3:6
Jesus' Galilee Ministry: Phase 2 — 3:7–6:13
Jesus Leaves Galilee — 6:14–8:21
Jesus Journeys to Jerusalem — 8:22–10:52
Jesus' Jerusalem Ministry — 11:1–13:37
Jesus' Passion — 14:1–15:47
Jesus' Resurrection — 16:1–8 (9–20)

ABOUT MARK

God has given the world a treasure with the Gospel of Mark! What a beautiful description we find of Jesus, the Anointed One, within its pages. Mark unveils the Lord Jesus before our eyes as the true Servant of God, holy, harmless, and merciful! As God's Servant we find Jesus very busy in this Gospel healing, teaching, and working wonders. You will fall in love with Jesus Christ as you read this inspired account of his life.

Many believe Mark was a disciple of Peter and received much of the material given in his Gospel from Peter, for Peter describes Mark as "my son" (1 Peter 5:13). The church fathers Papias and Clement of Alexandria both state that Mark wrote a factual and inspired Gospel with the help of Peter while Peter was still living. We know for sure that Mark wrote under the inspiration of the Holy Spirit and gave us a vibrant, striking picture of the life of the Messiah, Jesus, the Servant of the Lord. It is likely that Mark wrote this Gospel about AD 50–55.

The book easily divides itself between Jesus' Galilean ministry (1:1–8:21) and his Judean ministry (8:22–16:8).

Mark omits the narrative of Jesus' birth and genealogy, for a servant needs no pedigree. But rather, he introduces Jesus as the one with a mission of love and power to change the world. Forty times Mark uses the Greek word *eutheos*, which means "immediately"! There is urgency with Jesus as he works toward completing his task of providing salvation and power to all who believe in him.

Mark records over three times as many miracles as parables. This is a Gospel of miracles! Twenty-one miracles are recorded here with two unique to Mark's Gospel. There is a freshness and vitality about this Gospel that is gripping to the reader. See if you can read the entire Gospel through in one sitting—you'll be on the edge of your seat! Although it is the briefest of the four Gospels, you'll still enjoy reading about Jesus' supreme power over both the invisible and visible worlds. He was with the wild beasts in the wilderness and subdued the even wilder nature of demon-controlled souls. He is Master over creation, man, and the devil, for he is the perfect servant who came to do the Father's will.

Mercy triumphs in every page of Mark's Gospel, for he writes as one set free from his past and as one who has discovered the divine surprise of mercy. May you also find mercy triumphant as you read the translation of this book. Today is the day for you to become a fervent follower of the Lord Jesus Christ!

PURPOSE

While John Mark likely had a variety of reasons for writing his Gospel, two broad themes stand out: (1) to confirm Jesus' messianic identity; and (2) to call believers to follow Jesus' example. The first purpose is confirmed by the dramatic moment (Mark 8:29) where Peter confesses, "You are the Messiah, the Son of the Living God!" The whole story pivots around this confirmation, though Jesus won't be confined to anyone's definition. Because while Peter and Israel expected a conquering hero Messiah, Jesus is the Suffering Servant Messiah. It is through the cross he achieves his full glory and full identity!

In his second purpose, Mark builds on his first by exhorting believers to follow Jesus' example. The disciples aren't the ones we are to model, however, for they repeatedly fail and remain relatively faithless throughout; their example is one to avoid! Instead, we are to pattern our lives after Jesus' own faithful, cross-shaped life. As Jesus said, "If you truly want to follow me, you should at once completely disown your own life. And you must be willing to share my cross and experience it as your own" (Mark 8:34).

AUTHOR AND AUDIENCE

The author of the Gospel of Mark is nearly universally recognized to be the John Mark who was related to Barnabas and lived in Jerusalem (Acts 12:12). He and Barnabas and Paul once traveled together in their missionary work (Acts 13:4) until some kind of failure took place in Mark's life and he left his team for a short period. Because of his abrupt departure, Paul refused to have Mark rejoin them from that time forward, which caused a rift between Paul and Barnabas. Even so, Barnabas the encourager still took Mark with him to advance the work of the gospel (Acts 15:36–39). It is also likely that Mark is the individual he mentions in Mark 14:51, using the common literary tool of that day when speaking of oneself by allusion.

Isn't it amazing how God does not give up on us because of our failures? It is comforting to see how God's mercy restored Mark and used him to write this inspired record, a gospel that will endure for all eternity. Later, while Paul was imprisoned, he asked Timothy to bring Mark to him, saying, "For he (Mark) is a tremendous help for me in my ministry" (2 Tim. 4:11). So we learn that none of our failures need disqualify us if we continue to love and follow Jesus Christ. When you get to heaven, ask Mark. He will tell you that mercy triumphs over judgment!

While the Gospels were written for the church at large, the writers often had specific audiences in mind and addressed needs and concerns relevant to them. Early Christian tradition closely identifies Mark's Gospel with Rome. This is supported by church fathers like Irenaeus and Clement of Alexandria. Since Mark translates Aramaic words into Greek for his readers and explains Jewish customs, a Palestinian audience seems to be ruled out. And because he uses Roman words in place of Greek ones, Christians in Rome were a likely target audience. He wrote to these Roman Christians to bring encouragement and assurance in their faith.

MAJOR THEMES

The Person of Jesus. Mark wrote his Gospel to write Jesus' story; the unfolding story itself reveals who Jesus is. He clues us into the revelation of his Person in the opening stanza: "This is the beginning of the wonderful news about Jesus the Messiah, the Son of God." These two titles, "Messiah" and "Son of God," point to what Jesus has come to do, which is key to understanding who Jesus is: He is the bearer of God's salvation, announced in words and deeds, teaching and miracles, and ultimately his sacrifice!

The Messianic Mission of Jesus. One of the most peculiar aspects of Mark's Gospel is the so-called "Messianic Secret." At various times Jesus commands his disciples not to reveal his true messianic identity. He tells others whom he's healed to keep his identity a secret too. In fact, the demons are commanded to keep the secret! Though he clearly demonstrated his identity through his miracle and teaching ministry, his full identity as Israel's awaited Messiah wouldn't be revealed until the end of Mark when he was resurrected in full glory.

The Work of Jesus. Some have said Mark is a Passion narrative with a lengthy introduction. Perhaps this is a bit of an overstatement, but Jesus' death plays a central role in this Gospel. While the work of Christ on the cross doesn't appear until the fourteenth chapter, Mark peppers references to Jesus' crucifixion throughout. He wrote to show that Jesus' death on the cross wasn't a tragedy or mistake, but God's plan from the beginning. Through suffering and death Jesus brings in the last days of God's kingdom realm. Through the crucifixion we see Jesus was both the long-awaited Messiah as well as the Son of God, which comes through the climactic confession of the Roman centurion: "There is no doubt this man was the Son of God!" (Mark 15:39).

Discipleship and Faith. At every turn in Mark's Gospel, Jesus is inviting people to follow him. This is the essence of discipleship. It's an invitation extended to everyone and anyone. Jesus taught that this kind of following involves three things: self-denial, cross bearing, and daily living. Denying oneself is about submitting to the lordship of Christ over every ounce of one's life. Taking up one's cross reminds us of Jesus' own self-denial on that cross of execution and his committal of himself fully to God's will; it is a radical and total commitment. Finally, following Jesus is a continuous, daily act that requires living out Jesus' teachings and example. This relationship is built on faith, which isn't some magical formula, but comes from a repeated hearing of Jesus' teachings and participation in his way of life.

The Kingdom Realm of God. "It is time for the realm of God's kingdom to be experienced in its fullness!" Jesus announced at the beginning of his ministry. "Turn your lives back to God and put your trust in the hope-filled gospel!" As with the other Gospels, God's kingdom realm takes center stage in Mark from the beginning where this opening stanza summarizes the good news Jesus brought. Later, in chapter four, Mark summarizes the entire ministry of Jesus and its effects with the term *kingdom*. The world is brought under "God's kingship" in and through the work of Jesus. For Mark the kingdom realm is already dynamically in the present, yet fully experienced in the future. It's surprising and small, yet powerful and great; beyond understanding for many, yet accessible to all; and calls people to a radical new way of living and challenges every human value.

MARK

Miracles and Mercy

The Wonderful News

1 This is the beginning of the wonderful news about Jesus[a] the Messiah, the Son of God. [b]

² It starts with Isaiah the prophet, who wrote:

Listen! I am sending my messenger ahead of you[c]
and he will prepare your way!
³ He is a thunderous voice of one
who shouts in the wilderness:
"Prepare your hearts
for the coming of the Lord Yahweh,[d]
and clear a straight path[e]
inside your hearts for him!"[f]

⁴ John the Baptizer[g] was the messenger who appeared in an uninhabited region, preaching a baptism of repentance[h] for the complete cancellation of sins. ⁵ A steady stream of people came to be dipped in the Jordan River as they publicly confessed their sins. They came from all over southern Israel,[i] including

---

a 1:1 The Aramaic is "the revelation of Jesus."
b 1:1 Although the words "Son of God" are missing from some Greek manuscripts, it is found in the Aramaic.
c 1:2 This line is a quotation from Ex. 23:20 and Mal. 3:1, where it is an "angel" (or "messenger") that God sends before them.
d 1:3 As translated from the Aramaic.
e 1:3 Or "Prepare the way for the Lord and make his beaten paths straight, level, and passable." This "way" is not a road, but preparing the heart, making room for the ways of the Lord.
f 1:3 See Isa. 40:3.
g 1:4 John was the son of Zechariah, a priest. As the son of a priest, John was qualified to serve in the temple but chose instead the lonely wilderness to begin his ministry of calling a nation to repentance and preparing the way for the Lord Jesus.
h 1:4 That is, "an immersion that will bring a change of heart and lead you into repentance" for the complete cancellation of sins.
i 1:5 Or "Judea."

nearly all the inhabitants of Jerusalem. [6]John wore a rough garment made from camel hair,[a] with a leather belt around his waist,[b] and he ate locusts and honey of the wilderness. [7]And this is the message he kept preaching: "There is a man coming after me who is greater and a lot more powerful than I am. I'm not even worthy to bend down and untie the strap of his sandals. [8]I've baptized you into water, but he will baptize you into the Spirit of Holiness!"

The Baptism and Testing of Jesus

[9]One day, Jesus came from the Galilean village of Nazareth[c] and had John immerse him in the Jordan River. [10]The moment Jesus rose up out of the water, John saw the heavenly realm split open, and the Holy Spirit descended like a dove and rested upon him.[d] [11]At the same time, a voice spoke from heaven, saying:

"You are my Son, my cherished one,
    and my greatest delight is in you!"[e]

[12]Immediately after this he was compelled by the Holy Spirit[f] to go into an uninhabited desert region. [13]He remained there in the wilderness for forty days,[g] enduring the ordeals of Satan's tests. He encountered wild animals, but also angels who appeared and ministered to his needs.[h]

---

a 1:6 John was not afraid to violate religious taboos. A camel was considered unclean in the Jewish tradition. He was wearing what others considered to be unclean. Those who break loose of religious tradition will often appear to be undignified, as was John. His commission was to inaugurate a new way of living according to the truths of Jesus Christ and the Holy Spirit.

b 1:6 This was considered to be the wardrobe of a prophet and was identical to what the prophet Elijah wore (2 Kings 1:8; Zech. 13:4). With a diet of locusts John points back to the four varieties of locusts mentioned in Joel 1:4. Locusts (grasshoppers) are an emblem of intimidation that will keep believers from taking their inheritance by faith. Israel thought themselves to be like grasshoppers in their own eyes because of the intimidation of the fierce inhabitants of the land. John the Baptizer arrives on the scene and makes locusts his food, eating up that symbol of intimidation (devouring the devourer). And he drank honey, which is a biblical metaphor of the revelation of God's Word that is sweeter than honey (Ps. 19:7–10). John's ministry was a prophetic statement from God that a new day had come, a day of leaving dead formalism and embracing new life in Jesus without intimidation.

c 1:9 It is possible to translate the Aramaic as "Then one day Jesus came from victorious revelation" to be baptized by John. The word Nazareth can mean "victorious one," and the word Galilee can be translated "the place of revelation."

d 1:10 The Lord Jesus was buried in baptism, symbolically into death (the Jordan) so that he might minister not in the natural way of men, but in the way of resurrection by the power of the Holy Spirit. The dove, an emblem of the Holy Spirit, pictures both meekness and purity. The implication is that the Holy Spirit came upon Jesus and never left him.

e 1:11 Although not a direct quotation, the wording is similar to Ps. 2:7.

f 1:12 Or "cast out [or "thrown," or "pushed"] into the wilderness." The Greek word ekballei is often used for driving out demons. This was a forceful compelling of the Holy Spirit.

g 1:13 The "forty days" points to Moses, Elijah, and David, who were all great champions in Israel's history. See Ex. 34:28; 1 Sam. 17:16; 1 Kings 19:8, 15.

h 1:13 Between vv. 13 and 14 there is an entire year of our Lord's life that Mark skips over.

Jesus Calls Four Fishermen to Follow Him

[14] Later on, after John the Baptizer was arrested, Jesus went back into the region of Galilee and preached the wonderful gospel of God's kingdom realm. [a] [15] His message was this: **"At last the fulfillment of the age has come! It is time for the realm of God's kingdom to be experienced in its fullness! Turn your lives back to God and put your trust in the hope-filled gospel!"** [b]

[16] As Jesus was walking along the shore of Lake Galilee, he noticed two brothers fishing: Simon and Andrew. He watched them as they were casting their nets into the sea [17] and said to them, **"Come follow me and I will transform you into men who catch people instead of fish!"** [c] [18] Immediately they dropped their nets and left everything behind to follow Jesus. [19] Walking a little farther, Jesus found two other brothers sitting in a boat, along with their father, mending their nets. Their names were Jacob [d] and John, and their father Zebedee. [e] [20] Jesus immediately walked up to them and invited the two brothers to become his followers. At once, Jacob [f] and John dropped their nets, stood up, left their father in the boat with the hired men, and followed Jesus. [g]

People Stunned by Jesus' Teachings

[21] Then Jesus and his disciples went to Capernaum, [h] and he immediately started teaching on the Sabbath day in the synagogue. [22] The people were awestruck and

---

Jesus spent most of that year in and around Jerusalem. The Gospel of John gives further details of that year in ch. 1.

a 1:14 As translated from the Aramaic and most Greek manuscripts.

b 1:15 The Greek is "believe the good news" ("the gospel"), and the Aramaic is "put your trust in the joyful message of hope." This translation merges both concepts, making it "the hope-filled gospel."

c 1:17 The metaphor of "fishers of men" simply means that they will persuade others and catch people for God.

d 1:19 Or "James." Other translations of the Bible substitute Jacob for James. Both Greek and Aramaic leave the Hebrew name as it is, Jacob. This translation will use the correct name, Jacob, throughout.

e 1:19 Zebedee means "my gift." Zebedee's gift to Jesus was his sons. A wise father will always want his children to be given to Jesus.

f 1:20 Or "James."

g 1:20 What a powerful effect Jesus had upon people! One encounter with the Son of God compelled these businessmen to leave their trade and follow Jesus. We learn from Luke 5:10 that the family of Zebedee was in business together with Simon (Peter) and Andrew. They owned the boat and had a hired crew, which makes one think they were somewhat prosperous business owners, for commercial fishermen in the time of Jesus were usually wealthy.

h 1:21 Capernaum means "the village of Nahum." Nahum means "comforted." Jesus did many miracles and made his Galilean base of ministry in "the village of the comforted."

overwhelmed *a* by his teaching, because he taught in a way that demonstrated *God's* authority, which was quite unlike the religious scholars. *b*

²³ Suddenly, during the meeting, a demon-possessed man screamed out, ²⁴ "Hey! Leave us alone! Jesus the victorious, *c* I know who you are. You're God's Holy One and you have come to destroy us!" *d*

²⁵ Jesus rebuked him, saying, "**Silence! You are bound!** *e* **Come out of him!**"

²⁶ The man's body shook violently in spasms, and the demon hurled him to the floor until it finally came out of him with a deafening shriek! ²⁷ The crowd was awestruck and unable to stop saying among themselves, "What is this new teaching that comes with such authority? With merely a word he commands demons to come out and they obey him!"

²⁸ So the reports about Jesus spread like wildfire throughout every community in the region of Galilee.

Jesus Heals Many

²⁹ Now, as soon as they left the meeting, they went straight to Simon and Andrew's house, along with Jacob *f* and John. ³⁰ Simon's mother-in-law was bedridden, sick with a high fever, so the first thing they did was to tell Jesus about her. ³¹ He walked up to her bedside, gently took her hand, and raised her up! Her fever disappeared and she began to serve them.

³² Later in the day, *just after the Sabbath ended* *g* at sunset, the people kept bringing to Jesus all who were sick and tormented by demons, ³³ until the whole village was crowded around the house. ³⁴ Jesus cured many who were sick *h* with various diseases and cast out many demons. But he

---

a 1:22 The Greek word used here, *ekplesso,* is a strong verb that means "awestruck, filled with amazement, astonished, panic stricken, something that takes your breath away (being hit with a blow), to be shocked, to expel, to drive out." Clearly, Jesus spoke with such glory and power emanating from him that his words were like thunderbolts in their hearts. May we hear his words in the same way today.

b 1:22 Or "scribes" (experts of the Law). Jesus taught from an inner knowledge of God and his Word, for his teaching emphasized obedience to God from the heart, not just outwardly keeping of laws.

c 1:24 As translated from the Aramaic. The Greek is "Jesus the Nazarene" ("Branch" or "Scion").

d 1:24 The demon knew Jesus' true identity before the people did. This is not so much a question (Have you come to destroy us?), but rather an assertive and defiant declaration. There is no question mark in the Greek text. The demonized man was apparently comfortable in the presence of the religious teachers, but when Jesus stepped into the room, he spoke out and couldn't resist the power of Jesus.

e 1:25 Or "muzzled."

f 1:29 Or "James."

g 1:32 Implied in the context.

h 1:34 The Greek word *kakos* is actually the word for "evil"; however, it is traditionally translated "sickness."

would not permit the demons to speak, because they knew who he really was. [a]

Jesus Prays, Preaches, Heals, and Casts Out Demons

[35] The next morning, Jesus got up long before daylight, left the house while it was dark, and made his way to a secluded place to give himself to prayer. [36] Later, Simon and his friends searched for him, [37] and when they finally tracked him down, they told him, "Everyone is looking for you—they want you!"

[38] Jesus replied, "We have to go on to the surrounding villages so that I can give my message to the people there, for that is my mission." [39] So he went throughout the region of Galilee, preaching in the Jewish synagogues and casting out demons.

[40] On one occasion, a leper came and threw himself down in front of Jesus, pleading for his healing, saying, "You have the power to heal me right now if only you really want to!" [41] Being deeply moved with tender compassion, [b] Jesus reached out and touched the skin of the leper and told him, "Of course I want you to be healed—so now, be cleansed!" [42] Instantly his leprous sores completely disappeared and his skin became smooth! [43] Jesus sent him away with a very stern warning, [c] [44] saying, "Don't say anything to anyone *about what just happened*, but go find a priest and show him that you've been healed. Then bring the offering that Moses commanded for your cleansing as a living testimony to everyone." [d]

[45] But no sooner did the man leave than he began to proclaim his healing publicly [e] and spread the story everywhere *of his healing*.

Jesus' growing fame prevented him from entering the villages openly, which forced him to remain in isolated places. Even so, a steady stream of people flocked to him from everywhere.

Jesus Heals a Paralyzed Man

2 Several days later, Jesus returned to Capernaum, and the news quickly spread that he was back in town. [2] Soon there were so many people crowded

---

a   1:34 Jesus wants *us* to proclaim who he is, not demons.

b   1:41 This is an intense emotion. Some Greek manuscripts have "Jesus was moved with anger" (at the leprosy, not the man). However, the Aramaic is clearly "moved with compassion." The two Aramaic words for "anger" and "compassion" are written almost identically. Perhaps both are correct. Jesus was deeply moved with compassion toward the man and angry at the disease.

c   1:43 The Greek word *embrimaomai* can mean "to sternly give a warning"; however, in John 11:33 it is translated "was deeply moved wtih tenderness and compassion." The miracle of healing this leper had a profound effect on both Jesus and the man who was healed.

d   1:44 See Lev. 14:1–32. Normally, touching a leper would make a man unclean, but in this instance, the leper was healed and Jesus was not defiled.

e   1:45 Or "preach."

inside the house to hear him that there was no more room, even outside the door.

While Jesus was preaching the word of God, [3] four men arrived, carrying a paralyzed man. [4] But when they realized that they couldn't even get near him because of the crowd, they went up on top of the house and tore away the roof above Jesus' head. And when they had broken through, they lowered the paralyzed man on a stretcher *right down in front of him!* [5] When Jesus saw the extent of their faith, he said to the paralyzed man, "**My son, your sins are now forgiven.**"

[6] This offended some of the religious scholars who were present, and they reasoned among themselves, [7] "Who does he think he is to speak this way? This is blasphemy for sure! Only God himself can forgive sins!"

[8] Jesus supernaturally perceived their thoughts and said to them, "**Why are you being so skeptical?** [9] **Which is easier, to say to this paralyzed man, 'Your sins are now forgiven,' or, 'Stand up and walk!'?**[a] [10] **But to convince you that the Son of Man has been given authority to forgive sins,** [11] **I say to this man, 'Stand up, pick up your stretcher, and walk home.'**" [12] Immediately the man sprang to his feet in front of everyone and left for home.

When the crowds witnessed this miracle, they were awestruck.[b] They shouted praises to God and said, "We've never seen anything like this before!"

Jesus Calls Levi (Matthew) to Follow Him

[13] Jesus went out to walk near Lake Galilee, and a massive crowed gathered, so he taught them. [14] As he walked along, he found Levi, the son of Alphaeus,[c] sitting at the tax booth, collecting taxes. He approached him and said, "**Come follow me.**" Immediately he got up from his booth and began to follow Jesus.

[15] Later, Jesus and his disciples went to have a meal with Levi. Among the guests in Levi's home were many tax collectors and notable sinners sharing a meal with Jesus, for there were many kinds of people who followed him. [16] But when the religious scholars and the Pharisees[d] found out that Jesus was keep-

---

a 2:9 The answer to Jesus' question is obvious. It is easy for anyone to say, "Your sins are forgiven," for that cannot be proven. But if someone were to tell a paralyzed man to stand up, and he didn't stand up, that would prove the person is a fraud. Jesus didn't do the "easy thing" without accomplishing the hard thing, the miracle of healing. Forgiveness and healing both flow from Jesus Christ.

b 2:12 The Greek word used here can also mean "shocked into wonderment" or "to be out of their minds" (with amazement). This event teaches us that salvation not only involves the forgiveness of our sins, but gives us the power to rise up and walk.

c 2:14 The name Levi means "joined," "united," and Levi is the same person as Matthew, who wrote the Gospel bearing his name. Alphaeus means "changing." It is obvious that Matthew's allegiance is changing from being a servant of Rome to being joined to Jesus as his future apostle.

d 2:16 The word *Pharisees* means "separated ones."

ing company and dining with sinners and tax collectors,[a] they were indignant. So they approached Jesus' disciples and said to them, "Why is it that someone like Jesus *defiles himself* by eating with sinners and tax collectors?"

[17] But when Jesus overheard their complaint, he said to them, "**Who goes to the doctor for a cure? Those who are well or those who are sick? I have not come to call the 'righteous,' but to call those who are sinners and bring them to repentance.**"

Jesus Questioned about Fasting

[18] One time, the disciples of John the Baptizer and the Pharisees were fasting. So they came to Jesus and asked, "Why is it that John's disciples and disciples of the Pharisees are fasting but your disciples are not?"

[19] Jesus answered, "**How can the sons of the bridal chamber fast when the bridegroom is next to them? As long as the bridegroom is with them they won't,** [20] **but the days of fasting will come when the Bridegroom is taken from them.**

[21] "**And who would mend worn-out clothing with new fabric? When the new cloth shrinks, it will rip, making the tear worse than before.** [22] **And who would pour fresh, new wine into an old wineskin? Eventually the wine will ferment and make the wineskin burst, losing everything—the wine will be spilled and the wineskin ruined. Instead, new wine is always poured into new wineskins.**"

Jesus, Lord of the Sabbath

[23] One Saturday, on the day of rest,[b] Jesus and his disciples were walking through a field of wheat. The disciples were hungry, so they plucked off some heads of grain to eat. [24] But when some of the Pharisees saw what was happening, they said to him, "Look! Your disciples shouldn't be harvesting grain on the Sabbath!"

[25] Jesus responded, "**Haven't you ever read what King David and his men did when they were hungry?** [26] **They entered the house of God**[c] **when Abiathar was high priest and ate the sacred bread of God's presence.**[d] **They violated the law by eating bread that only the priests were allowed to eat. But there is one here who is even greater than the temple.**"

[27] Then he said to them, "**The Sabbath was made for the sake of people,**

---

a 2:16 These were Jews who worked for the Roman empire to collect taxes and were empowered by Rome to profit greatly by what they collected.

b 2:23 Or "Sabbath." The Hebrew word for *Sabbath* comes from *shavat*, which is the verb "to rest." What was designed to be a day of rest and intimacy with God and family was now complicated by a host of rules and traditions.

c 2:26 That is, the tabernacle. See 1 Sam. 21:1–6. Ancient Jewish tradition states that David did this on a Sabbath day. See also Lev. 24:5–9.

d 2:26 Or "loaves of presentation." See Ezek. 44:15–16.

and not people for the Sabbath. ²⁸ For this reason the Son of Man exercises his lordship over the Sabbath."

Jesus Heals on the Sabbath

3 Then Jesus left them and went again into the synagogue, where he encountered a man who had an atrophied, paralyzed hand. ² Everyone was watching Jesus closely to see if he would heal the man on the Sabbath, giving them a reason to accuse him *of breaking Sabbath rules*.

³ Jesus said to the man with the paralyzed hand, "Stand here in the middle of the room."

⁴ Then he turned to all those gathered there and said, "Which is it? Is it against the law to do evil on the Sabbath or to do good? To destroy a life or to save one?" But no one answered him a word.

⁵ Then looking around at everyone, Jesus was moved with indignation and grieved by the hardness of their hearts and said to the man, "Now stretch out your hand!" As he stretched out his hand, it was instantly healed!ᵃ

⁶ After this happened, the Pharisees left abruptly and began to plot together with the friends and supporters of Herod Antipas on how they would kill Jesus.

Massive Crowds Follow Jesus

⁷ Once again Jesus withdrew with his disciples to the lakeside, but a massive crowd of people followed him from all around the provinces of Galilee and southern Israel. ⁸ Vast crowds came from Jerusalem, Idumea,ᵇ beyond the Jordan, and from Lebanon.ᶜ Large numbers of people swarmed in from everywhere when they heard of him and his wonderful works.

⁹ The crowd pressed so closely to Jesus that he instructed his disciples to bring him a small boat to get into and keep from being crushed by the crowd. ¹⁰ For he had healed so many that the sick kept pushing forwardᵈ just so they could touch Jesus. ¹¹ And whenever a demon saw him, it would throw the person down at Jesus' feet, screaming out, "You are the Son of God!" ¹² But Jesus would silence the demons and sternly order them not to reveal who he was.

---

a 3:5 This miracle is found in Matthew, Mark, and Luke. It contains valuable lessons for us today, for the hand symbolizes holding, giving, receiving, doing. It was his right hand (Luke 6:6), which brings the added significance of power (i.e., God's right hand, Ex. 15:6), pleasure (Ps. 16:11), approval (Heb. 1:13), and righteousness (Ps. 48:10). A crippled right hand points to the lack of all these things. Human beings are helpless before God, crippled in all our works. But the power of Jesus heals our limitations and brokenness. Religion cannot heal us, but Jesus can.
b 3:8 Or "Edom." Idumea was the region south of Beersheba, south and west of the Dead Sea, a territory of ancient Israel.
c 3:8 Or "Tyre and Sidon," which are in modern-day Lebanon.
d 3:10 Or "falling all over him." Jesus had power coming through him for healing, and everyone wanted to touch him. What a wonderful Savior who loves and heals people!

Jesus Chooses Twelve Apostles

¹³ Afterward, Jesus went up on a mountainside and called to himself the men he wanted to be his close companions, so they went up the mountainside to join him. ¹⁴ He appointed ᵃ the Twelve, whom he named apostles. ᵇ He wanted them to be continually at his side as his friends, and so that he could send them out to preach ¹⁵ and have authority to heal the sick and to cast out demons. ᶜ

¹⁶ He appointed his Twelve ᵈ and gave Simon the nickname Peter the Rock. ᵉ ¹⁷ And he gave the brothers, Jacob ᶠ and John, the sons of Zebedee, the nickname *Benay-Regah*, ᵍ which means "passionate sons." ¹⁸ The others were Andrew, Philip, Bartholomew, ʰ Matthew, Thomas, Jacob the son of Alphaeus, Thaddaeus, ᶦ ¹⁹ and Judas Iscariot, ᵏ who betrayed him.

---

a 3:14 This was not simply a passive acknowledgment, but an active setting them in place. The Greek verb *poieo* is the verb "do" or "make." Jesus "did" them; that is, he imparted his favor, blessing, and grace to set them in place as apostolic emissaries for the kingdom realm of God.

b 3:14 The Greek word *apostoles* means "sent ones."

c 3:15 As translated from the Aramaic and a few Greek manuscripts. This ordination was for a three-fold purpose: (1) that they might continually be at his side, (2) to send them out with love for others, preaching the truth of God's Word, and (3) to receive power to heal and cast out demons. This is the same for all whom Jesus calls to represent him. See Acts 4:13.

d 3:16 These twelve disciples became apostles ("sent ones"), serving God's kingdom realm. Jesus raised up twelve, and later seventy, whom he sent out to preach the message of God's kingdom. None of them were fully mature or equipped, for the Holy Spirit had not yet come to empower them. Leaders today need to raise up others and not center their ministry around themselves. The legacy of a spiritual leader is made up of those whom he or she has released and sent forth to proclaim Christ.

e 3:16 In the ancient Hebraic mind-set, to name something is to give it existence, purpose, and function. (See Gen. 32:27–28.) In the Greek mind-set, naming is simply assigning phonetic sounds to an object or a person. When Jesus gave this name to Peter, he was calling his purpose into existence. Peter would be a strong rock of faith and a leader to the other eleven apostles. Peter is always named first in all the listings of the Twelve (Matt. 10:1–4; Luke 6:13–16; Acts 1:13). The name Jesus gave him was *Keefa*, the Aramaic word for "rock." The Greek is *Petros*, which in John 1:42 is explained as the translation from Galilean Aramaic.

f 3:17 Or "James." It is unfortunate that translations of the Bible have substituted "James" for "Jacob." Both Greek and Aramaic leave the Hebrew name as it is, Jacob. This translation will use the correct name, Jacob, throughout.

g 3:17 As translated from Aramaic. The Greek transliteration is "Boanerges." *Benay-Regah* can also be translated "sons of loud shouts" (or "passionate sons") or "sons of commotion" (easily angered) or "sons of thunder." Jesus, by giving the brothers this nickname, acknowledged that they were two rowdy boys, thunderous and passionate. Jesus chose twelve men who were all different in their personality types. It was no doubt humorous to Jesus to observe how different these twelve men were and how difficult it was to form them into a band of brothers.

h 3:18 Or in Aramaic, "the son of *Tolmai*" ("discipline"). This could be another name for Nathaniel.

i 3:18 Or "Lebbaeus."

j 3:18 Or "Simon the Zealot" or "Simon the Cananaean."

k 3:19 Iscariot is taken from an Aramaic derivative for "lock" (or "locksmith").

Jesus and the Ruler of Demons

[20] Then Jesus went home,[a] but once again a large crowd gathered around him, which prevented him from even eating a meal. [21] When his own family heard that he was there, they went out to seize him, for they said, "He's insane!" [22] The religious scholars who arrived from Jerusalem were saying, "Satan[b] has possessed him! He casts out demons by the authority of the prince of demons!" [23] Jesus called them to himself and spoke to them using parables. "How can Satan cast out Satan? [24] No kingdom can endure if it is divided against itself, [25] and a splintered household will not be able to stand, for it is divided. [26] And if Satan fights against himself he will not endure, and his end has come."

[27] Jesus said to them,[c] "Listen. No one is able to break into a mighty man's house and steal his property unless he first overpowers the mighty man and ties him up.[d] Then his entire house can be plundered and his possessions taken. [28] I tell you this timeless truth: All sin will be forgiven, even all the blasphemies they speak. [29] But there can never be forgiveness for the one who blasphemes against the Holy Spirit, for he is guilty of an eternal sin!" [30] (This is because they said he was empowered by a demon spirit.)[e]

Members of Jesus' True Family

[31] Then Jesus' mother and his brothers came and stood outside and sent a message to him, asking that he come out and speak with them.[f] [32] When the crowd sitting around Jesus heard this, they spoke up, and said to him, "Jesus, your mother and brothers[g] are outside looking for you."

[33] He answered them saying, "Who is my true mother and my true brothers?" [34] Then looking in the eyes of those who were sitting in a circle around him, he said, "Here are my true family members. [35] For whoever does the will of God is my brother, my sister, and my mother!"

---

a 3:20 This was likely the house of Simon and Andrew mentioned in Mark 1:29.

b 3:22 Or "Beelzebub," another name for Satan, the ruler of demons.

c 3:27 This information is given in v. 30 and is positioned here for the sake of clarity of the English narrative.

d 3:27 Luke adds a phrase here: "The stronger one [Jesus] overpowers him." The stronger one is Jesus, who first defeated Satan in the wilderness ordeal and then destroyed him by the cross and resurrection (Heb. 2:14). Bruising his head, Jesus now has Satan under his feet and will soon consign him to the lake of fire.

e 3:30 The information found in v. 30 is included in v. 27 for the sake of the English narrative.

f 3:31 It is likely that Jesus' family did not follow him, because they feared rejection by their community. This happened in Nazareth, after Jesus publicly stated that he was the fulfillment of Isaiah's prophecy of the Messiah and the townspeople wanted to kill Jesus by throwing him off a cliff. See Luke 4:18–29.

g 3:32 Some manuscripts include the words "and sisters."

Parable of the Farmer Scattering Seed

4 Once again Jesus went to teach the people on the shore of Lake Galilee [a] and a massive crowd surrounded him. The crowd was so huge that he had to get into a boat and teach the people from there. [2] He taught them many things by using parables [b] to illustrate spiritual truths, saying:

[3] "Consider this: A farmer went out to sow seeds. [4] As he cast his seeds some of it fell along the beaten path and soon the birds came and ate it. [5] Other seeds fell onto gravel with no topsoil and the seeds quickly sprouted since the soil had no depth. [6] But when the days grew hot, the sprouts were scorched and withered because they had insufficient roots. [7] Other seeds fell among the thorns, so when the seeds sprouted so did the thorns, crowding out the young plants so that they could produce no grain. [8] But some of the seeds fell onto good, rich soil that kept producing a good harvest. Some yielded thirty, some sixty—and some even one hundred times as much as was planted! [9] If you understand this, then you need to respond." [c]

The Purpose of Parables

[10] Afterwards, Jesus, his disciples and those close to him remained behind to ask Jesus about his parables. [11] He said to them, "The privilege of intimately knowing the mystery of God's kingdom realm has been granted to you, but not to the others, [d] where everything is revealed in parables.

[12] "For even when they see what I do, they will not understand, and

---

a 4:1 Commonly known as the Sea of Galilee. It is interesting that Jesus left the house (Mark 3:20) to go to the sea. The "house" suggests the "house of Israel," and the "sea" speaks of the non-Jewish peoples (i.e., the "sea of humanity").

b 4:2 The Aramaic and Greek use a word for "parable" that means "a metaphor," "allegory," "simile," "illustration," "comparison," "figure of speech," "riddle," or "enigmatic saying that is meant to stimulate intense thought." Throughout Hebrew history, wise men, prophets, and teachers used parables and allegories as a preferred method of teaching spiritual truths. Poets would write their riddles and musicians would sing their proverbs with verbal imagery. Jesus always taught the people by using allegory and parables (Matt. 13:34; Mark 4:34). As a true prophet, one of Jesus' preferred methods of teaching was allegory. To deny the validity of allegorical teaching is to ignore the teaching methods of Jesus, the living Word.

c 4:9 Or "The one with ears to hear should use them." We usually apply portions of this parable to unbelievers, but Jesus instructs us to apply it to ourselves. The four kinds of soils speak of four kinds of hearts: hard hearts, hollow hearts, half hearts, and whole hearts. With the first soil we see the activity of Satan, the second, that of the flesh, and the third, that of the world. Bearing fruit is never a problem with the seed but with the soil it falls upon.

d 4:11 Or "to the outsiders." The Aramaic is "backward ones." Jesus spoke allegorically so that those who didn't care to understand couldn't understand. Yet he knew that the hungry ones would seek out the hidden meaning of the parables and understand the secrets of God's kingdom realm. It is still that way today. See Prov. 25:2.

when they, hear what I say, they will learn nothing, otherwise they would repent and be forgiven." [a]

[13] Then he said to them, "If you don't understand this parable, how will you understand any parable? [14] Let me explain: The farmer sows the Word as seed, [15] and what falls on the beaten path represents those who hear the Word, but immediately Satan appears and snatches it from their hearts. [16] The seed sown on gravel represents those who hear the Word and receive it joyfully, [17] but because their hearts fail to sink a deep root into the Word, they don't endure for long. For when trouble or persecution comes on account of the Word, they immediately wilt and fall away. [18] And the seed sown among thorns represents those who hear the Word, [19] but they allow the cares of this life and the seduction of wealth and the desires for other things to crowd out and choke the Word so that it produces nothing.

[20] "But the seed sown on good soil represents those who open their hearts to receive the Word and their lives bear good fruit—some yield a harvest of thirty, sixty, even one hundred times more than was sown!"

Parable of the Lamp

[21] He also gave them this parable: "No one lights a lamp [b] only to place it under a basket or under the bed. It is meant to be placed on a lampstand. [22] For there is nothing that is hidden that won't be disclosed, and there is no secret that won't be brought out into the light! [23] If you understand what I'm saying, you need to respond!" [c]

[24] Then he said to them, "Be diligent to understand the meaning behind everything you hear, for as you do, more understanding will be given to you. And according to the depth of your longing to understand, [d] much more will be added to you. [25] For those who listen with open hearts will receive more revelation. But those who don't listen with open hearts will lose what little they think they have!" [e]

---

a 4:12 See Isa. 6:9–10.

b 4:21 The Jewish people considered the Torah, God's Word, to be a lamp that gives light to see and understand. Israel was meant to be a light that gives illumination to the nations. Jesus also calls his followers those who "light up the world." See Matt. 5:14.

c 4:23 Or "The one with ears to hear should use them." The Aramaic is "If one brings a hearing ear for himself, he will hear."

d 4:24 Or "By the measure with which you measure, it will be measured to you." Some interpret this to refer to our relationships; i.e., "The way you treat others will be the way you will be treated." However the context is clearly about having an open heart to receive and live in truth, and not to hide it or have a closed heart to understand.

e 4:25 This verse contains a complicated ellipsis, which is a literary function of omitting certain information to invite discovery. The ellipsis of the text has been supplied by making explicit what is implicit in the context. The verse reads literally "More will be given to the person who has (something), but a person who doesn't have (something), even what

Parable of the Growing Seed

[26] Jesus also told them this parable: "God's kingdom realm is like someone spreading seed on the ground. [27] He goes to bed and gets up, day after day, and the seed sprouts and grows tall, though he knows not how. [28] All by itself it sprouts, and the soil produces a crop; first the green stem, then the head on the stalk, and then the fully developed grain in the head. [29] Then, when the grain is ripe, he immediately puts the sickle to the grain, because harvest time has come." [a]

Parable of the Tiny Mustard Seed

[30] And he told them this parable: "How can I describe God's kingdom realm? Let me illustrate it with this parable. [31] It is like the mustard seed, the tiniest of all the seeds, [32] yet when it springs up and grows, it becomes the largest plant in the garden. And with so many enormous spreading branches, even birds can nest in its shade." [b]

Jesus Always Taught Using Parables

[33] Jesus used many parables such as these as he taught the people, and they learned according to their ability to understand. [34] He never spoke to them without using parables, but would wait until they were alone before he explained their meanings to his disciples. [c]

Jesus Stills a Storm

[35] Later that day, after it grew dark, Jesus said to his disciples, "Let's cross over to the other side of the lake." [36] After they had sent the crowd away, they shoved off from shore with him, as he had been teaching from the boat, [d] and there were other boats that sailed with them. [37] Suddenly, as they were crossing the lake, a ferocious tempest arose, with violent winds and waves that were crashing into

---

(something) they do have will be taken from him." The translation fills the ellipsis with the theme of the context—having an open heart to receive the truth of God. The parables of the sower and of the lamp are similar in that they speak of the heart that receives truth. The Word is a "seed" that grows within us and a "lamp" that glows within us.

a 4:29 This parable is only found in Mark's Gospel. It teaches us that the reality of God's kingdom realm is like seed sown into the world that will grow through stages of maturity until the harvest.

b 4:32 Like the preceding parable, this is an allegorical way of describing the growth of God's kingdom realm. It may appear in the beginning as small and insignificant, yet it will grow until it becomes the greatest kingdom of all. Both of these parables teach us that God's kingdom is growing on the earth and not diminishing. See Ezek. 17:22–24.

c 4:34 Jesus still delights to mystify those who follow him, but he waits until we are alone with him, and then he reveals the wonders of his grace and truth to our hearts.

d 4:36 The somewhat awkward construction of the Greek sentence, "They took him along just as he was, in the boat," implies that Jesus was already in the boat where he had been sitting and teaching.

the boat until it was all but swamped.[a] [38] But Jesus was calmly sleeping in the stern, resting on a cushion. [39] So they shook him awake, saying, "Teacher, don't you even care that we are all about to die!" Fully awake, he rebuked the storm and shouted to the sea, **"Hush! Calm down!"** All at once the wind stopped howling and the water became perfectly calm.

[40] Then he turned to his disciples and said to them, **"Why are you so afraid? Haven't you learned to trust yet?"** [41] But they were overwhelmed with fear and awe and said to one another, "Who is this man who has such authority that even the wind and waves obey him?"

A Demonized Man Set Free

5 They arrived at the other side of the lake, at the region of the Gerasenes.[b] [2] As Jesus stepped ashore, a demon-possessed madman came out of the graveyard and confronted him. [3] The man had been living there among the tombs of the dead, and no one was able to restrain him, not even with chains. [4] For every time they attempted to chain his hands and feet with shackles, he would snap the chains and break the shackles in pieces. He was so strong that no one had the power to subdue him. [5] Day and night he could be found lurking in the cemetery or in the vicinity, shrieking and mangling himself with stones!

[6] When he saw Jesus from a distance, he ran to him and threw himself down before him, [7] screaming out at the top of his lungs, "Leave me alone, Jesus, Son of the Most High God! Swear in God's name that you won't torture me!" [8] (For Jesus had already said to him, **"Come out of that man, you demon spirit!"**)

[9] Jesus said to him, **"What is your name?"**

"Mob,"[c] he answered. "They call me Mob because there are thousands of us in his body!" [10] He begged Jesus repeatedly not to expel them out of the region.

[11] Nearby there was a large herd of pigs feeding on the hillside. [12] The demons begged him, "Send us into the pigs. Let us enter them!"

[13] So Jesus gave them permission, and the demon horde immediately came out of the man and went into the pigs! This caused the herd to rush madly down the steep slope and fall into the lake, drowning about two thousand pigs![d]

---

a 4:37 This gale of wind and ferocious tempest was demonic in nature, as Jesus was about to confront a powerful principality on the other side of the lake. (See Mark 5:1–20.) Jesus would not have rebuked the storm if it was from God. The devil knew that if Jesus crossed to the other side, he would cast out the demon horde that had long terrorized the entire region.

b 5:1 This was a region of non-Jewish people who were raising swine, which was considered unclean by Jewish dietary laws. Gerasenes (or Gadarenes) were people who lived in a region opposite Galilee, on the southeastern side of Lake Galilee. See Matt. 8:28–34.

c 5:9 Or "Legion" (a Roman military unit of more than six thousand men). Mark gives twelve accounts of Jesus defeating demon spirits. The demons always recognized Jesus as God's Son.

d 5:13 Depending on weight, the cost of two thousand live pigs today could be as much as $250,000. The economic cost to the community over the loss of this herd was significant.

[14] Now, the herdsmen fled to the nearby villages, telling everyone what they saw as they ran through the countryside, and everyone came out to see what had happened. [15] When they found Jesus, they saw the demonized man sitting there, properly clothed and in his right mind. Seeing what had happened to the man who had thousands of demons, the people were terrified. [16] Those who had witnessed *this miracle* reported the news to the people and included what had happened to the pigs. [17] Then they asked Jesus to leave their region. [a]

[18] And as Jesus began to get into the boat to depart, the man who had been set free from demons asked him, "Could I go with you?" [19] Jesus answered, "No," but said to him, "Go back to your home and to your family and tell them what the Lord has done for you. Tell them how he had mercy on you."

[20] So the man left and went into the region of Jordan and parts of Syria [b] to tell everyone he met about what Jesus had done for him, and all the people marveled!

Two Miracles—Healing and Resurrection

[21] After Jesus returned from across the lake, a huge crowd of people quickly gathered around him on the shoreline. [22] Just then, a man saw that it was Jesus, so he pushed through the crowd and threw himself down at his feet. His name was Jairus, [c] a Jewish official who was in charge of the synagogue. [23] He pleaded with Jesus, saying over and over, "Please come with me! My little daughter is at the point of death, *and she's only twelve years old!* [d] Come and lay your hands on her and heal her and she will live!"

[24] Jesus went with him, and the huge crowd followed, pressing in on him from all sides.

[25] Now, in the crowd that day was a woman who had suffered horribly from continual bleeding for twelve years. [e] [26] She had endured a great deal under the care of various doctors, yet in spite of spending all she had on their treatments, she

---

a 5:17 The people preferred swine to the Son of God. There is no indication that Jesus ever went back to their land.

b 5:20 Or "Decapolis," which means "Ten Cities." The region of these ten cities was Jordan and parts of Syria, including Damascus. These cities were Greek and Roman cultural centers of that day. It is a wonder of grace that Jesus used a man who once had thousands of demons to bring God's truth to thousands of people. After he was set free, he became a missionary evangelist, telling others what Jesus Christ had done for him. No wonder the people marveled when they heard his story!

c 5:22 Jairus (taken from the Hebrew name *Jair*) means "he enlightens" or "he shines the light." Some have taken it to mean "Jehovah enlightens," but God's name is not found in the name Jairus.

d 5:23 This is taken from v. 42 and is brought in at this sequence of the narrative for the sake of clarity and in contrast with the woman who suffered for twelve years (v. 25).

e 5:25 The daughter of Jairus was twelve years old; this woman had suffered for twelve years. Jesus touched the girl; the woman touched Jesus. The two intertwining miracles in this chapter speak of Jesus healing the gentiles and raising Israel back to life (Jairus' Jewish

was not getting better, but worse. [27]When she heard about Jesus' *healing power*, she pushed through the crowd and came up from behind him and touched his prayer shawl. [a] [28]For she kept saying to herself, "If only I could touch his clothes, I know I will be healed." [b] [29]As soon as her hand touched him, her bleeding immediately stopped! She knew it, for she could feel her body instantly being healed of her disease!

[30]Jesus knew at once that someone had touched him, for he felt the power that always surged around him[c] had passed through him for someone to be healed. He turned and spoke to the crowd, saying, "**Who touched my clothes?**"[d]

[31]His disciples answered, "What do you mean, who touched you? Look at this huge crowd—they're all pressing up against you." [32]But Jesus' eyes swept across the crowd, looking for the one who had touched him for healing.

[33]When the woman who experienced this miracle[e] realized what had happened to her, she came before him, trembling with fear, and threw herself down at his feet, *saying, "I was the one who touched you."* And she told him her story of what had just happened.

[34]Then Jesus said to her, "**Daughter, because you dared to believe, your faith has healed you. Go with peace in your heart, and be free from your suffering!**"

[35]And before he had finished speaking, people arrived from Jairus' house *and pushed through the crowd* to give Jairus the news: "There's no need to trouble the master any longer—your daughter has died." [36]But Jesus refused to listen

---

daughter). On his way to raise the Jewish girl, he stopped to heal the gentile woman. This is what is happening today with Jews and non-Jews.

a 5:27 Or "cloak" (or "outer garment"). As a Jewish man, Jesus would have had over his shoulders a prayer shawl ("tallit"). The blue tassel on the corner of the prayer shawl was said to symbolize all the commandments and promises of God. See Num. 15:38–40. The Hebrew word for "fringe" or "border" (of a garment) can also mean "wing." Some have interpreted Mal. 4:2 ("healing in his wings") as a reference to the tassels of the prayer shawl.

b 5:28 The Greek word is *sozo* and has many possible meanings, including "safe and sound," "healed," "delivered," "made whole," "rescued," "restored," and "saved." This is what Jesus does for us today. See Heb. 13:8.

c 5:30 This is a literal reading of a unique phrase in Greek construction. It could be translated "the power that keeps going out of him went out from him." There was a glorious power that kept going out around Jesus Christ, drawing others to him and healing those he touched, and in this case, healing a woman who touched him in faith. Jesus knew that the power of God was always emanating around him, yet it had flowed through him to someone in the crowd. This same miracle was repeated with Peter in Acts 5:15.

d 5:30 Jesus already knew the answer to his question. He wanted the woman to come forward and acknowledge her healing. There were crowds around Jesus, the living Word. Many today crowd around the written Word. But only those who "touch" the Scriptures in faith receive its promises, just like the sick woman who received her healing.

e 5:33 As translated from the Aramaic.

to what they were told[a] and said to the Jewish official, "Don't yield to fear. All you need to do is to keep on believing." [37] *So they left for his home,* but Jesus didn't allow anyone to go with them except Peter and the two brothers, Jacob and John.

[38] When they arrived at the home of the synagogue ruler, they encountered a noisy uproar among the people, for they were all weeping and wailing. [39] Upon entering the home, Jesus said to them, "Why all this grief and weeping? Don't you know the girl is not dead but merely asleep?" [40] Then everyone began to ridicule and make fun of him. But he threw[b] them all outside.

Then he took the child's father and mother and his three disciples and went into the room where the girl was lying. [41] He tenderly clasped the child's hand in his and said to her in Aramaic, "**Talitha koum**,"[c] which means, "Little girl,[d] wake up from the sleep of death." [42] Instantly the twelve-year-old girl sat up, stood to her feet, and started walking around the room! Everyone was overcome with astonishment in seeing this miracle! [43] Jesus had them bring her something to eat. And he repeatedly cautioned them that they were to tell no one about what had happened.[e]

Jesus Rejected in Nazareth

6 Afterward, Jesus left Capernaum[f] and returned with his disciples to Nazareth, his hometown. [2] On the Sabbath, he went to teach in the synagogue. Everyone who heard his teaching was overwhelmed with astonishment. They said among themselves, "What incredible wisdom has been given to him!

---

a   5:36 At times there must be a holy "deafness" to the words of others, words that would distract us from the purposes of God. See Isa. 42:19–20.

b   5:40 The Greek word *ekballo* is often used for driving out demons. It implies a forceful action of authority.

c   5:41 One of the many references in the New Testament proving that the language of Jesus was Aramaic.

d   5:41 The Aramaic word *talitha* can also mean "little lamb." The Greek word used here is *korasion,* which may be a hypocorism, similar to "sweetheart." The tenderness of this moment is obvious in the text. However, some Hebrew scholars find in the word *talitha* a Hebrew root that could point to the tallit, or prayer cloak of Jesus, which he may have placed over the girl. This would make his words to mean, "Little girl under the prayer cloak, arise." This fringed tallit had already been touched by a woman who received her healing previously in this chapter. (See Klein and Spears, *Lost in Translation Vol. 1,* p. 18, 2007.)

e   5:43 There was nothing secretive about this resurrection miracle of the twelve-year-old girl. It would be hard to keep hidden from the people. Jesus was cautioning them because of the reaction of certain religious authorities who were convinced that Jesus was working wonders by the power of Satan. Later on, the miracle of Lazarus being raised from the dead was what triggered the arrest of Jesus.

f   6:1 The healing of the woman and the resurrection of Jairus' daughter were both done in Capernaum.

Where did he receive such profound insights?[a] And what mighty miracles flow through his hands! [3] Isn't this Mary's son, the carpenter,[b] the brother of Jacob, Joseph,[c] Judah, and Simon? And don't his sisters all live here in Nazareth?" And they took offense at him.

[4] Jesus said to them, "**A prophet is treated with honor everywhere except in his own hometown, among his relatives, and in his own house.**" [5] He was unable to do any great miracle in Nazareth,[d] except to heal a few sick people by laying his hands upon them. [6] He was amazed at the depth of their unbelief![e]

Then Jesus went out into the different villages and taught the people.

Jesus Sends Out the Twelve Apostles

[7] Jesus gathered his twelve disciples and imparted to them his authority to cast out demons. Then he sent them out in pairs with these instructions: [8-9] "**Take only your staff and the sandals on your feet—no bread, no knapsack, no extra garment, and no money.**[f] [10] **And whatever house you enter, stay there until you leave the area.** [11] **Whatever community does not welcome you or receive your message, leave it behind. And as you go, shake the dust off your feet as a testimony against them.**"[g]

[12] So they went out and preached publicly that everyone should repent. [13] They cast out many demons and anointed many sick people with oil and healed them.

Death of John the Baptizer

[14] King Herod soon heard about Jesus, for the name of Jesus was on everyone's lips. Some were even saying about him, "John the Baptizer has been raised from the dead, and that's why miraculous powers flow from him!" [15] Others said, "No, he's Elijah!" While others said, "He's a prophet, like one of the prophets of old!"

[16] When Herod heard what the people were saying, he concluded, "I beheaded John, and now he's raised from the dead!" [17-18] For Herod had John

---

a 6:2 Or "Where did he get these things" (or "insights," "understanding," "ideas," "teachings")?

b 6:3 The Greek word *tekton* can be translated "carpenter," "metal worker," "sculptor," "artisan," "stone worker," or "builder."

c 6:3 Or "Joses."

d 6:5 Nazareth was the only place recorded in the Gospels that Jesus was unable (because of their unbelief) to do miracles.

e 6:6 This is one of two instances where Jesus was amazed. The other is found in Matt. 8:10. Both refer to the response of faith. Here it is the great unbelief of those who knew Jesus and lived in his hometown of Nazareth (Jews). The other is the great faith of the Roman military captain (a gentile). We have no record of Jesus ever returning to Nazareth. He made Capernaum his base of ministry while in the province of Galilee.

f 6:8–9 Or "copper coins inside your belt."

g 6:11 The Aramaic and some Greek manuscripts add a sentence: "Truly, I tell you that it will be more tolerable for Sodom and Gomorrah in the day of judgment than for that city."

arrested and thrown into prison for repeatedly rebuking him in public, saying, "You have no right to marry Herodias, the wife of your brother Philip! You are violating the law of God!"[a]

[19] This infuriated Herodias, and she held a bitter grudge against him and wanted John executed. [20] But Herod both feared and stood in awe[b] of John and kept him safely in custody, because he was convinced that he was a righteous and holy man. Every time Herod heard John speak, it disturbed his soul, but he was drawn to him and enjoyed listening to his words.

[21] But Herodias found her opportunity to have John killed—it was on the king's birthday! Herod prepared a great banquet and invited all his officials, military commanders, and the leaders of the province of Galilee to celebrate with him on his birthday. [22] On the day of the feast, his stepdaughter, the daughter of Herodias,[c] came to honor the king with a beautiful dance, and she flattered him.[d] Her dancing greatly pleased the king and his guests, so he said to the girl, "You can ask me for anything you want and I will give it to you!" [23] And he repeated it in front of everyone, with a vow to complete his promise to her: "Anything you desire and it will be yours! I'll even share my kingdom with you!"

[24] She immediately left the room and said to her mother, "What should I ask for?" Her mother answered, "The head of John the Baptizer on a platter!" [25] So she hurried back to the king and made her request: "I want you to bring me the head of John the Baptizer on a platter—and I want it right now!"

[26] Deeply grieved, the king regretted[e] his promise to her, but since he had made his vow in front of all his honored guests, he couldn't deny her request. [27] So without delay the king ordered an executioner to bring John's head, and he went and beheaded John in prison. [28] He brought his head on a platter and gave it to the girl, and the girl brought it to her mother. [29] When John's followers heard what had happened, they came and removed his body and laid it in a tomb.

Jesus Multiplies Food to Feed Five Thousand

[30] The apostles *returned from their mission*[f] and gathered around Jesus and told him everything they had done and taught.

[31] There was such a swirl of activity around Jesus, with so many people coming and going, that they were unable to even eat a meal. So Jesus said to his

---

a 6:17–18 See Lev. 18:16; 20:21.

b 6:20 The Greek text can also mean "deep respect" or that Herod "feared" John.

c 6:22 Although unnamed, church history and tradition identifies her as Salome, not to be confused with the Salome who was a witness of the crucifixion (Mark 15:40).

d 6:22 Or "she fascinated him."

e 6:26 The Aramaic is "The king was tied in a knot."

f 6:30 Jesus had sent the apostles into the Galilean villages to preach and cast out demons (6:7–13), and they are now returning to report back to him.

disciples, "Come, let's take a break and find a secluded place where you can rest a while." [32] They slipped away and left by sailboat for a deserted spot. [33] But many of the people saw them leaving and realized where they were headed, so they took off running along the shore. Then people from the surrounding towns joined them in the chase, and a large crowd got there ahead of them.

[34] By the time Jesus came ashore, a massive crowd was waiting. At the sight of them, his heart was filled with compassion,[a] because they seemed like wandering sheep who had no shepherd.[b] So he taught them many things.

[35] Late that afternoon, his disciples said, "It's getting really late and we're here in this remote place with nothing to eat. [36] You should send the crowds away so they can go into the surrounding villages and buy food for themselves."

[37] But he answered them, "You give them something to eat."

"Are you sure?" they replied. "You really want us to go buy them supper? It would cost a small fortune[c] to feed all these thousands of hungry people."

[38] "How many loaves of bread do you have?" he asked. "Go and see." After they had looked around, they came back and said, "Five—plus a couple of fish."

[39] Then he instructed them to organize the crowd and have them sit down in groups on the grass. [40] So they had them sit down in groups[d] of hundreds and fifties. [41] Then Jesus took the five loaves and two fish, gazed into heaven, and gave thanks to God. He broke the bread and the two fish and distributed them to his disciples to serve the people—*and the food was multiplied in front of their eyes!* [42] Everyone had plenty to eat and was fully satisfied. [43] Then the twelve disciples picked up what remained, and each of them ended up with a basket full of leftovers! [44] Altogether, five thousand families[e] were fed that day!

Jesus Walks on Water

[45] After everyone had their meal, Jesus instructed his disciples to get back into the boat and go on ahead of him and sail to the other side to Bethsaida.[f] [46] So

---

a 6:34 The Aramaic is "nurturing love toward them."

b 6:34 See Num. 27:17; Ezek. 34:5.

c 6:37 Or "two hundred denarii" (silver coins). A denarius was the going rate for a day's wage. This would equal nearly eight months' wages.

d 6:40 There are two Greek words used for groups in this context. In v. 39 it is the Greek word *symposion,* which is used most frequently for drinking parties (rows of guests). The word *prasai* found in v. 40 can also mean "garden plots" or "flower beds." Spread out over the hillside the people would have looked like flower beds, planted in green pastures, drinking in the miracle power of Jesus. See Ps. 23:2.

e 6:44 Or "five thousand men." There were women and children present as well, but it would have not been common for women and children to come by themselves. These five thousand men represented their households. This miracle is the only miracle recorded in all four Gospels.

f 6:45 This is *Beit-Tside,* which in Aramaic and Hebrew is "the fishing place."

he dispersed the crowd, said good-bye to his disciples, then slipped away to pray on the mountain.

[47] As night fell, the boat was in the middle of the lake and Jesus was alone on land. [48] The wind was against the disciples and he could see[a] that they were straining at the oars, trying to make headway.

When it was almost morning,[b] Jesus came to them, walking on the surface of the water, and he started to pass by them.[c] [49–50] When they all saw him walking on the waves, they thought he was a ghost and screamed out in terror. But he said to them at once, "**Don't yield to fear. Have courage. It's really me—I Am!**"[d]

[51] Then he came closer and climbed into the boat with them, and immediately the stormy wind became still. They were completely and utterly overwhelmed with astonishment [52] because they failed to learn the lesson of the *miracle*[e] of the loaves, and their hearts were unwilling to learn the lesson.[f]

Jesus the Healer

[53] They made landfall at Gennesaret and anchored there.[g] [54] The moment they got out of the boat, everyone recognized that it was Jesus, *the healer*! [55] So they ran throughout the region, telling the people, "Bring all the sick—even those too sick to walk and bring them on mats!" [56] Wherever he went, in the countryside,

---

a 6:48 Seeing them from land in the dark was an obvious miracle, for evening had come and Jesus was a great distance from them while they were in the middle of the lake. Jesus sees and knows the struggles each of us go through.

b 6:48 Or "about the fourth watch of the night."

c 6:48 To pass by them is somewhat similar to God "passing by Moses" when he was on Sinai. See Ex. 33:19, 22.

d 6:49–50 In both Greek and Aramaic, this reads, "I Am" (the living God), an obvious statement that Jesus is "the great I AM" and there is nothing to be afraid of. This is the same statement God made to Moses in front of the burning bush. See also Matt. 14:27; John 8:58.

e 6:52 Or "They didn't understand about the loaves." That is, they didn't understand the lesson that the miracle was meant to teach them—that God has the power to deliver us, no matter what the limitation. Also, the miracle was that the bread multiplied in their hands, so they likewise had the power to rebuke the stormy wind and sail through to the other side, even if Jesus were to pass them. He wanted them to see things in a new light and know the authority that they now carried. The two lessons of the multiplied loaves were the following: (1) that Jesus had all power to meet every need, and (2) that the disciples carried this power with them, for the bread multiplied in their hands. They were also a part of the miracle. See also Mark 8:14–21. The two great miracles of Israel were also duplicated here. The "crossing of the sea" and the "bread" (or "manna") that fell from heaven.

f 6:52 Or "their minds were dull" or "unwilling to learn," or "their hearts had been hardened." The implication is that they were unwilling to accept new information. Every miracle carries a message.

g 6:53 Apparently, they were blown off course, since they were headed for Bethsaida. Gennesaret is a plain not far from Capernaum on the northwest side of the lake.

villages, or towns, they placed the sick on mats in the streets or in public places[a] and begged him, saying, "Just let us touch the tassel of your prayer shawl!"[b] And all who touched him were instantly healed!

Jesus Breaks Religious Traditions

7 One day, those known as the Pharisees and certain religious scholars came from Jerusalem and gathered around Jesus. [2] They were shocked[c] to find that some of Jesus' disciples ate bread without first observing the prescribed Jewish ritual of hand washing before eating their meal. [3] (For the Pharisees, like all other Jews, will not eat without first performing a ritual of pouring water over their cupped hands[d] to keep the tradition of the elders. [4] Similarly, when returning from the marketplace, they ceremonially wash themselves before eating.[e] They also observed many other traditions, such as ceremonially washing cups, pitchers, and kettles.)[f]

[5] So the Pharisees and religious scholars asked Jesus, "Why don't your disciples live according to the age-old traditions passed down by our elders? They should first ceremonially wash their hands before eating."

[6] Jesus replied, "You are frauds and hypocrites! How accurately[g] did Isaiah prophesy about you phonies when he said:

'These people honor me with their words
    while their hearts run far away from me!
[7] Their worship is nothing more than a charade!
    For they continue to insist
    that their man-made traditions
    are equal to the instructions of God.'[h]

---

a 6:56 Or "marketplace."

b 6:56 The blue tassel on the corner of the prayer shawl was said to symbolize all the commandments and promises of God. See Num. 15:38–40. The Hebrew word for "fringe" or "border" (of a garment) can also mean "wing." Some have interpreted Mal. 4:2 ("healing in his wings") as a reference to the tassels of the prayer shawl.

c 7:2 As translated from the Aramaic.

d 7:3 Or "with a fist." Some have surmised this was a thorough washing from the hand to the elbow. But it was most likely water poured over cupped hands. This is not taught in the Torah, but was insisted on because of the tradition of the elders. A few Greek manuscripts and the Aramaic read "They do not eat unless they wash their hands carefully," with no mention of a fist.

e 7:4 The Aramaic is "If they do not bathe, they do not eat."

f 7:4 Some manuscripts add "dining couches." Some Aramaic manuscripts add "beds" (or "mats"). This ceremonial sprinkling amounted to nothing more than religious rules and customs, but none of them were commanded in the writings of Moses—they were the oral traditions of men.

g 7:6 Or "excellently."

h 7:7 See Isa. 29:13 (LXX).

[8] "You abandon God's commandments just to keep men's rituals, such as ceremonially washing utensils, cups, and other things." [a]

[9] Then he added, "How skillful you've become in rejecting God's law in order to maintain your man-made set of rules. [10] For example, Moses taught us:

'Honor your father and your mother,' [b]
    and,
'Whoever insults or mistreats his father or
    mother must be put to death.' [c]

[11] "But your made-up rules allow a person to say to his parents, 'I've decided to take the support you were counting on from me and make it my holy offering to God, and that will be your blessing instead.' [d] [12] How convenient! The rules you teach exempt him from providing for his aged parents. [13] Do you really think God will honor your traditions passed down to others, making up these rules that nullify God's Word? And you're doing many other things like that."

Jesus Explains What Truly Defiles

[14] Then Jesus called the crowd together again, saying, "Hear my words, all of you, and take them to heart. [15] What truly contaminates a person is not what he puts into his body, but what comes out. That's what makes a person defiled." [e]

[17] When Jesus went back home and away from the crowd, his disciples *acknowledged that they didn't understand the meaning of the parable and* asked him to explain it. [18] He answered them, "Are you as dull as the rest? Don't you understand that you are not defiled by what you eat? [19] For the food you swallow doesn't enter your heart, but goes into your stomach, only to pass out into the sewer." (This means all foods are clean.) [f] [20] He added, "Words and deeds pollute a person, not food. [21] Evil originates from inside a person. Coming

---

a 7:8 Some manuscripts omit the last clause. It is found in the Aramaic and the majority of Greek texts.

b 7:10 See Ex. 20:12; Deut. 5:16.

c 7:10 See Ex. 21:17; Lev. 20:9.

d 7:11 As translated from the Aramaic. The Greek is "Whatever you would have gained from me will be *corban* (an offering)." *Corban* (*qorban*) is an Aramaic word that implies that a person is pure, sincere, and pious when he makes an offering to God. In this case, people would simply speak the word *corban* over the money they were obligated to use in support of their aged parents, and that would exempt them from their duty to give it. Jesus disapproved of this practice, as it nullified God's commands. Words themselves don't count with God; he seeks justice and obedience from the heart.

e 7:15 Some Greek manuscripts and the Aramaic add v. 16, "If anyone has ears to hear, let him hear."

f 7:19 The words in parenthesis are added by the author (Mark).

out of a human heart are evil schemes,[a] sexual immorality,[b] theft, murder, [22] adultery, greed, wickedness, treachery, debauchery,[c] jealousy,[d] slander,[e] arrogance,[f] and recklessness.[g] [23] All these corrupt things emerge from within and constantly pollute a person."

Jesus and a Foreign Woman

[24] Jesus set out from there to go into the non-Jewish region of Tyre.[h] He intended to slip into a house unnoticed, but people found out that he was there. [25] But when a woman whose daughter had a demon spirit heard he was there, she came and threw herself down at his feet. [26] She was not Jewish, but a foreigner,[i] born in the part of Syria known as Phoenicia.[j] She begged him repeatedly to cast the demon out of her daughter. [27] Finally he said to her, "First let my children be fed and satisfied, for it isn't fair to take the children's bread[k] and throw it to the little dogs."[l]

[28] She answered, "How true that is, Lord. But even puppies under the family table are allowed to eat the little children's crumbs."

[29] Then Jesus said to her, "That's a good reply! Now, because you said this,

---

a 7:21 Or "depraved thoughts."

b 7:21 This is the Greek word *porneia* (the root word from which we get *pornography*). The literal meaning is "to sell off oneself" (into sexual impurity).

c 7:22 Or "indecency."

d 7:22 Or "an evil eye," which is an Aramaic idiom for stinginess.

e 7:22 The Aramaic is "blasphemy."

f 7:22 The Aramaic is "boasting."

g 7:22 Or "senselessness."

h 7:24 Or "the region of Tyre and Sidon." (Some manuscripts do not have Sidon.) These two cities are located in Lebanon on the Mediterranean coast.

i 7:26 Or "Greek." The Jews considered the word *Greek* to mean anyone who was not a Jew, not necessarily a person of Greek descent.

j 7:26 This story, in light of the culture of that time, is phenomenal. She was a foreign-born woman with a demonized daughter. Combined, these characteristics made her an unlikely candidate to seek out a Jewish healer. The racial divide of that day was quite pronounced, but love and faith overcome every barrier, including racial prejudice. In Matt. 15:22, the Hebrew Matthew text describes her as "a Canaanite merchant woman." Canaan included the region of modern-day Lebanon and parts of Syria. A "Canaanite" would refer to a non-Jewish person who lived in that region. In this region, Jezebel established Baal worship and there her body was eventually thrown to the dogs. Here Jesus heals a woman and brings her into the true worship of God.

k 7:27 "Children" is a metaphor for the Jewish people (children of Israel), and the "children's bread" becomes a metaphor for healing or casting out demons.

l 7:27 Or "little pet dogs." The term translated "dog" here is the diminutive form of the Greek *kuon*. Calling her a household pet was not meant as an ethnic slur, but was used to describe an impure (unclean) mind. See Matt. 7:6; Phil. 3:2; 2 Peter 2:22; Rev. 22:15. Using the metaphors of children, children's bread, and dogs was the way Jesus tested her faith and revealed her strong confidence in Jesus' power to heal her daughter. She saw Jesus as "Lord" and received her miracle.

you may go. The demon has permanently left your daughter." [30] And when she returned home, she found her daughter resting quietly on the couch, completely set free from the demon!

Jesus Heals a Deaf Man

[31] After this, Jesus left the coastland of Tyre and came through Sidon on his way to Lake Galilee and over into regions of Syria. [a] [32] Some people brought to him a deaf man with a severe speech impediment. They pleaded with Jesus to place his hands on him and heal him.

[33] So Jesus led him away from the crowd to a private spot. Then he stuck his fingers into the man's ears and placed some of his saliva on the man's tongue. [b] [34] Then he gazed into heaven, [c] sighed deeply, and spoke to the man's ears and tongue, "Ethpathakh," which is Aramaic [d] for "Open up, now!" [e]

[35] At once the man's ears opened and he could hear perfectly, and his tongue was untied and he began to speak normally. [36] Jesus ordered everyone to keep this miracle a secret, but the more he told them not to, the more the news spread! [37] The people were absolutely beside themselves and astonished beyond measure. [f] And they began to declare, "Everything he does is wonderful! [g] He even makes the deaf hear and the mute speak!"

Jesus Multiplies Food Again

8 During those days, another massive crowd gathered to hear Jesus, and again, there was no food and the people were hungry. So Jesus called his disciples to come near him and said to them, [2] **"My heart goes out to this crowd, for they've already been here with me for three days with nothing to**

---

a   7:31 Or "the Decapolis," which means "Ten Cities," all of which were located in Syria. (See Mark 5:20 and footnote.) Jesus headed southeast to Lake Galilee. This trek was many miles and would have taken him days to arrive.

b   7:33 The saliva of firstborn sons in the Jewish culture of Jesus' time was considered to have power to heal infirmities.

c   7:34 The Aramaic is "Then he focused on (or contemplated) heaven."

d   7:34 Aramaic was the language of Jesus and his disciples and continues to be spoken today. The spelling of *Ethpathakh* has been adjusted to fit proper Aramaic instead of the transliterated Greek text, which is unintelligible, possibly due to a scribal error.

e   7:34 The phrase "open up" is the same wording used in the Hebrew of Isa. 61:1, "Open the prison doors." It furthermore refers to the opening of the eyes of the blind and the ears of the deaf.

f   7:37 The Greek text uses an unusual construction, found nowhere else in the New Testament, to describe the utter astonishment of the people over this miracle. Jesus led the man away from the unbelief of others to work his miracle and healed him with his saliva. (Later, wicked men would spit upon him in public.) Jesus then told the man he healed not to tell others, but he did. Jesus tells us to spread the good news, and we don't.

g   7:37 Or "beautiful," "perfect," "admirable," or "marvelous." This verse can also be translated "He has made everything beautiful" or "He has made everything ideally."

eat. ³I'm concerned that if I send them home hungry, they'll be exhausted along the way, for some of them have come a long, long way just to be with me."

⁴His disciples replied, "But could anyone possibly get enough food to satisfy a crowd this size out here in this isolated place?"

⁵He asked them, "How many loaves of flatbread have you got?"

"Seven," they replied.

⁶Jesus instructed the crowd to sit down on the grass. After he took the seven loaves, he gave thanks to God, broke them, and started handing them to his disciples. They kept distributing the bread until they had served the entire crowd.

⁷They also had a few small fish, and after giving thanks for these, Jesus had his disciples serve them to the crowd. ⁸Everyone ate until they were satisfied. Then the disciples gathered up the broken pieces and filled seven large baskets *a* with the leftovers. ⁹About four thousand *b* people ate the food that had been multiplied! Then he dismissed the crowd. *c*

¹⁰Afterward, Jesus got into a boat and sailed to the vicinity of Dalmanutha. *d*

The Pharisees Demand a Sign

¹¹As soon as Jesus landed, *e* he was confronted by the Pharisees, *f* who argued with Jesus and tested him. They demanded that he give them a miraculous sign from heaven.

¹²And with a deep sigh from his spirit, he said, "**What drives this generation**

---

a 8:8 This is the same word used for Paul escaping from Damascus by being lowered down the city wall in a basket (hamper). These baskets were large enough for a man to hide in. See Acts 9:25.

b 8:9 Although four thousand people are mentioned by Mark, this does not include women and children. See Matt. 15:32–39; see also 2 Kings 4:42–44. All four Gospels record the feeding of the five thousand, but only Matthew and Mark give us the feeding of the four thousand. Many have called this the forgotten miracle. Jesus multiplied food twice with miracle power. Because of the locations of these two miracles, it is believed that the five thousand were mostly Jews and the four thousand mentioned here were mostly gentiles. First the Jew, then the gentile. First there were twelve baskets of leftovers, then seven large baskets full. Twelve is a distinctively Jewish number representing government, and seven represents fullness, indicating the fullness of blessing going out to the entire world. The Bread of Life, Jesus Christ, is now our feast.

c 8:9 The Aramaic uses an idiomatic saying that can mean "Jesus ended their fast."

d 8:10 Some scholars believe that this may have been near Magdala on the western shore of Lake Galilee. See Matt. 15:39. The Aramaic word for Dalmanutha means "the land of oppression."

e 8:11 Or "immediately."

f 8:11 Or "separated ones" who saw themselves as Jewish purists and guardians of religious orthodoxy. Although the text does not say what sign they were demanding, they were requiring proof of Jesus' divine mission and ministry. The text does imply that they were disingenuous and wanted only to discredit Jesus.

to clamor for a sign? Listen to the truth: there will absolutely be no sign given to this generation!"[a] [13] Then he turned and left them, got back into the boat, and crossed over to the opposite shore.

Jesus Warns of the Yeast of the Pharisees and of Herod

[14] Now, the disciples had forgotten to take bread with them, except for one loaf of flatbread. [15] *And as they were sailing across the lake,* Jesus repeatedly warned them, "Be on your guard against the yeast[b] inside of the Pharisees and the yeast inside of Herod!" [16] But the disciples had no clue what Jesus was talking about, so they began to discuss it among themselves, saying, "Is he saying this because we forgot to bring bread?"

[17] Knowing what they were thinking, Jesus said to them, "Why all this fussing over forgetting to bring bread? Do you still not see or understand what I say to you? Are your hearts still hard? [18] You have good eyes, yet you still don't see, and you have good ears, yet you still don't hear, neither do you remember. [19] When I multiplied the bread to feed more than five thousand people, how many baskets full of leftovers did you gather afterward?"

"Twelve," they replied.

[20] "And when I multiplied food to feed over four thousand, how many large baskets full of leftovers did you gather afterwards?"

"Seven," they replied.

[21] "Then how is it that you still don't get it?"

Jesus Heals Blind Eyes

[22] When they arrived at Bethsaida, some people brought a blind man to Jesus, begging him to touch him and heal him. [23] So Jesus led him, as his sighted guide, outside the village. He placed his saliva on the man's eyes[c] and covered them with his hands.[d] Then he asked him, "Now do you see anything?"

[24] "Yes," he said. "My sight is coming back! I'm beginning to see people, but they look like trees—walking trees."

[25] Jesus put his hands over the man's eyes a second time and made him look up. The man opened his eyes wide and he could see everything perfectly. His eyesight was completely restored! [26] Then Jesus sent him home with these instructions: "Go home, but don't tell anyone what happened, not even the people of your own village."[e]

---

a 8:12 The Greek word for "generation" can also mean "a tribe or nation."
b 8:15 The yeast Jesus is referring to here is hypocrisy. See Luke 12:1. The yeast of religious and political hypocrisy is what Jesus warned them to avoid.
c 8:23 This is not the common word for "eyes." The Greek word *omma* can refer to both physical and spiritual sight. See also Matt. 20:34.
d 8:23 The Aramaic can be translated "Jesus placed his hands over his eyes and brought light."
e 8:26 As translated from the Aramaic and some Greek manuscripts. The Greek contains many

Peter Receives Revelation from God

[27] Then Jesus and his disciples walked[a] to the villages near Caesarea Philippi.[b] On the way, he posed this question to his disciples: "Who do the people say that I am?"

[28] They replied, "Some say John the Baptizer, others say Elijah[c] the prophet, and still others say you must be one of the prophets."

[29] He asked them, "But who do you say that I am?"

Peter[d] spoke up, saying, "You are the Messiah,[e] the Son of the Living God!"[f]

[30] Then he warned them not to breathe a word of this to anyone.

Jesus Prophesies His Death and Resurrection

[31] From then on, Jesus began to tell his disciples that he, the Son of Man, was destined to go to Jerusalem and suffer great injustice[g] from the elders, leading priests, and religious scholars. He also explained that he would be killed and three days later be raised to life again. [32] Jesus opened his heart and spoke freely with his disciples, explaining all these things to them.[h]

Then Peter took him aside and rebuked him.[i] [33] But Jesus turned around,

---

variations of this statement. Other manuscripts read "Go to your house, and if you go into the village, don't tell anyone what happened." Others read "Do not even go into the village."

a 8:27 This would likely have been a two-day journey of thirty miles north from Bethsaida.

b 8:27 This was a beautiful area north of Lake Galilee near Tel-Dan. Located at the foothills of Mount Hermon, it was an ancient Roman city rebuilt by Philip the tetrarch in honor of Augustus Caesar.

c 8:28 For the Jews, the return of Elijah would signal the end of days. See Mal. 4:5.

d 8:29 The Aramaic is "Shimon" (or "Simeon"), which presents an interesting word play. *Shimon* means "he who hears." Simon Peter heard the question posed by Jesus and answered it. But he also heard the revelation from the Father that Jesus is the Messiah, God's Son. See Matt. 16:17. Simon is the first one of the disciples who truly heard the Father's revelation of the identity of Jesus Christ.

e 8:29 Or "the Christ," which means "the Anointed One" (or "Messiah").

f 8:29 As translated from the Aramaic and a small number of Greek manuscripts.

g 8:31 This great injustice refers to the beatings, mockings, rejection, and illegal trial Jesus endured. To have the Messiah suffer was contrary to every belief system among the Jews. The Messiah was to be the King of Israel, surrounded with glory, not suffering. Mark gives us three instances of Jesus prophesying his death and resurrection (8:31, 9:31, and 10:33). Each time Jesus made this prediction, the disciples were confused and unable to understand. So each time Jesus took the opportunity to explain what being his follower really entailed (8:34–38, 9:33–37, and 10:35–45).

h 8:32 Or "He spoke openly [boldly, plainly, freely, honestly] about this."

i 8:32 Although Mark does not state what Peter was saying to Jesus, he was likely rebuking him for not understanding the role of the Messiah-King, who was going to suffer and die, but who would rise to power and bring glory to Israel. Peter wanted Jesus to come up with another plan. Yet Peter was the who was mistaken, not Jesus. How many times have we assumed we had a better plan for our lives than God had? One moment Peter speaks profoundly about Jesus' identity, and the next he rebukes the Messiah for choosing the wrong path.

and glancing at all of the other disciples, ᵃ he rebuked Peter, saying, "Get out of my sight, Satan! ᵇ For your heart is not set on God's plan but man's!" ᶜ

What It Means to Be a Follower of Jesus

³⁴ Jesus summoned the crowd, along with his disciples, and had them gather around. And he said to them: "If you truly want to follow me, you should at once completely disown your own life. And you must be willing to share my cross and experience it as your own, as you continually surrender to my ways. ᵈ ³⁵ For if you let your life go for my sake and for the sake of the gospel, you will continually experience true life. ᵉ But if you choose to keep your life for yourself, you will forfeit what you try to keep. ³⁶ For what use is it to gain all the wealth and power of this world, with everything it could offer you, at the cost of your own life? ³⁷ And what could be more valuable to you than your own soul? ³⁸ So among the unfaithful and sinful people living today, if you are ashamed of me and my words, the Son of Man will also be ashamed of you when he makes his appearance with his holy messengers ᶠ in the glorious splendor of his Father!" ᵍ

The Transfiguration of Jesus

9 Jesus said to them, "I tell you the truth, there are some standing here now who won't experience death until they see God's kingdom realm manifest with power!" ʰ

² After six days, Jesus took Peter and the two brothers, Jacob and John, and hiked up a high mountain to be alone. And Jesus' appearance was dramatically altered, for he was transfigured before their very eyes! ³ His clothing sparkled and became glistening white—whiter than any bleach in the world could make

---

a 8:33 Jesus knew that Peter was merely being the spokesman for all twelve disciples, voicing their opinion to Jesus on their behalf.

b 8:33 Peter's rebuke of Jesus became, as it were, the words of Satan himself. The word used for Satan here means "adversary."

c 8:33 The Aramaic can be translated "For you never cheer God but the children of men!"

d 8:34 Or "Follow me." This powerful verse was shocking to those who heard Jesus that day. To follow Jesus is more than the dethroning of our own lives, but the enthroning of Christ.

e 8:35 Or "will save it" (his life). There is only one Greek word for both "soul" and "life." The Aramaic uses a word that can mean "breath of life," "person," "soul," or "self."

f 8:38 Or "angels."

g 8:38 See Dan. 7:13–14.

h 9:1 This manifestation of the power of God's kingdom realm could be seen in three dimensions. (1) Beginning with v. 2, the kingdom power of God was seen in Jesus' transfiguration and the appearing of Moses and Elijah on the mountain. (2) Jesus' resurrection and ascension into glory inaugurated a new era of God's kingdom power. (3) The coming of the Holy Spirit at Pentecost, which brought to birth the church of Jesus Christ, and extended God's kingdom realm to all the earth.

them. ⁴Then suddenly, right in front of them, Moses and Elijah appeared,ᵃ and they spoke with Jesus.

⁵Peter blurted out, "Beautiful Teacher,ᵇ *this is so amazing to see the three of you together!* Why don't we stay here and set up three shelters:ᶜ one for you, one for Moses, and one for Elijah?" ⁶(For all of the disciples were in total fear, and Peter didn't have a clue what to say.) ⁷Just then, a radiant cloud began to spread over them, enveloping them all. And God's voice suddenly spoke from the cloud, saying, "This is my most dearly loved Son—always listen to him!"ᵈ

⁸Suddenly, when they looked around, the disciples saw only Jesus, for Moses and Elijah had faded away.ᵉ

⁹As they all hiked down the mountain together, Jesus ordered them, **"Don't tell anyone of what you just witnessed. Wait until the Son of Man is raised from the dead."** ¹⁰So they kept it to themselves, puzzled over what Jesus meant about rising from the dead.

¹¹Then they asked him, "Why do the religious scholars insist that Elijah must come before the Messiah?"ᶠ

¹²He answered them, **"They're right. Elijah must come first to put everything in order.ᵍ And what about all that is written about the Son of Man? It is true that he must endure many sufferings and be rejected.ʰ** ¹³So Elijah has

---

a 9:4 Moses represented the Law and Elijah represented the Prophets. Both Moses and Elijah were associated with Mount Sinai (Horeb), both had a ministry of performing astounding miracles, and both had unusual circumstances surrounding their passing from this life into glory. Peter tells us clearly that what he saw that day was a preview of God's kingdom realm (2 Peter 1:16–17).

b 9:5 Or "Good Rabbi," as translated from the Aramaic. *Rabbi* is an Aramaic title that means master-teacher.

c 9:5 Or "booths," a reference to making booths for the Feast of Tabernacles. Peter wanted to celebrate that feast there on the mountaintop with Jesus, Moses, and Elijah. However, Jesus is not to be treated equally with Moses or Elijah—Jesus is the Lord of all creation, including all of humanity.

d 9:7 Or "You must constantly listen to him." See Deut. 18:15; Ps. 2:7; Isa. 42:1.

e 9:8 Or "They saw no one with them anymore except Jesus." There were two mountains in the life of Jesus that focused on his true identity and mission. On this mountain, his face shone as bright as the sun; yet on Mount Calvary, his face was beaten to a pulp. On this mountain, his clothing was glistening white; yet on Mount Calvary, his clothing was taken from him and he was bleeding crimson. On this mountain, he had at his side two of the greatest men ever to live, Moses and Elijah; yet on Mount Calvary, he had at his side two murderers. On this mountain, the glory of God overshadowed him; yet on Mt. Calvary, he was alone, forsaken, in the dark. On this mountain, we hear the Father's voice of commendation; yet on Calvary's mountain, the Father was silent. How beautiful was Jesus on both mountains!

f 9:11 Or "come first" (prior to the coming of the Messiah).

g 9:12 See Mal. 4:5–6. Jesus is obviously referring to John the Baptizer as the one who symbolized Elijah's coming. Using metaphors, symbols, and parables was Jesus' preferred way of teaching.

h 9:12 Read Ps. 22; Isa. 53.

already appeared, just as it was prophesied,[a] and they did to him whatever they pleased."

The Disciples Unable to Cast Out a Demon

[14] Now when they came down the mountain to the other nine disciples, they noticed a large crowd of people gathered around them, with the religious scholars arguing with them. [15] The crowd was astonished to see Jesus himself walking toward them, so they immediately ran to welcome him.

[16] **"What are you arguing about with the religious scholars?"** he asked them.

[17] A man spoke up out of the crowd. "Teacher," he said, "I have a son possessed by a demon that makes him mute. I brought him here to you, Jesus. [18] Whenever the demon takes control of him, it knocks him down, and he foams at the mouth and gnashes his teeth, and his body becomes stiff as a board. I brought him to your disciples, hoping they could deliver him, but they were not strong enough."[b]

[19] Jesus said to the crowd, **"Why are you such a faithless people?[c] How much longer must I remain with you and put up with your unbelief? Now, bring the boy to me."**

[20] So they brought him to Jesus. As soon as the demon saw him, it threw the boy into convulsions. He fell to the ground, rolling around and foaming at the mouth. [21] Jesus turned to the father and asked, **"How long has your son been tormented like this?"**

"Since childhood," he replied. [22] "It tries over and over to kill him by throwing him into fire or water. But please, if you're able to do something, anything—have compassion on us and help us!"

[23] Jesus said to him, **"What do you mean 'if'?[d] If you are able to believe,[e] all things are possible to the believer."**

[24] When he heard this, the boy's father cried out with tears, saying, "I do believe, Lord; help my little faith!"[f]

[25] Now when Jesus saw that the crowd was quickly growing larger, he commanded the demon, saying, **"Deaf and mute spirit, I command you to come out of him and never enter him again!"**

[26] The demon shrieked and threw the boy into terrible seizures and finally came out of him! As the boy lay there, looking like a corpse, everyone thought

---

a 9:13 Or "just as it was written about him."

b 9:18 That is, they were not able to conquer the demon.

c 9:19 Or "generation."

d 9:23 Implied by the use of the most emphatic form of "if" in the Greek text.

e 9:23 As translated from the Aramaic and the majority of Greek manuscripts. There are, however, some Greek manuscripts that leave out the words "to believe."

f 9:24 As translated from the Aramaic. The Greek is "I do believe; help my unbelief."

he was dead. [27] But Jesus stooped down, gently took his hand, and raised him up to his feet, and he stood there completely set free![a]

[28] Afterwards, when Jesus arrived at the house, his disciples asked him in private, "Why couldn't we cast out the demon?"

[29] He answered them, "This type of powerful spirit can only be cast out by fasting and prayer."[b]

Jesus Again Prophesies His Death and Resurrection

[30] They went on from there and walked through the region of Galilee. Jesus didn't want the people to know he was there, because he wanted to teach his disciples in private. [31] He said to them, "The Son of Man is destined[c] to be betrayed and turned over to those who will execute him. But after three days he will rise again." [32] But the disciples didn't have a clue what he meant and were too embarrassed to ask him to explain it.

The Disciples Argue over Who Will Be the Greatest

[33] Then they came to Capernaum. And as soon as Jesus was inside the house, he asked his disciples, "What were you arguing about on the way here?"

[34] No one said a word, because they had been arguing about which one of them was the greatest. [35] Jesus sat down, called the twelve disciples to come around him, and said to them, "If anyone wants to be first, he must be content to be last and become a servant to all." [36] Then he had a child[d] come and stand among them. He wrapped the child in his arms and said to them, [37] "Whoever welcomes a little child in my name welcomes me. And whoever welcomes me welcomes not only me, but the one who sent me."

The Name of Christ

[38] John spoke up and said, "Teacher, we noticed someone[e] was using your name to cast out demons, so we tried to stop him because he wasn't one of our group."

[39] "Don't stop him!" Jesus replied. "For the one who does miracles in the power of my name proves he is not my enemy.[f] [40] And whoever is not against us is for us. [41] Listen to the truth that I speak: Whoever gives you a cup of

---

a 9:27 Luke 9:43 adds "Everyone was awestruck. They were stunned seeing the power and majesty of God flow through Jesus."

b 9:29 As translated from the Aramaic and some Greek manuscripts. Many reliable Greek texts leave out "fasting." However, the word *fasting* was found on a fragment going back to the third century. (See also Isa. 58:6.) Our lives must be saturated with the presence of God through prayer and fasting in order to conquer the evil that is in the world and hiding in the hearts of mankind.

c 9:31 The Greek verb, a present tense with a future aspect, implies something certainly meant to be.

d 9:36 The Greek word is not gender specific.

e 9:38 Some manuscripts add here "who does not follow along with us."

f 9:39 Or "would soon speak evil of me."

water because you carry the name of Christ will never lose his reward. [42] But if anyone abuses [a] one of these little ones who believe in me, it would be better for him to have a heavy boulder [b] tied around his neck and be hurled into the deepest sea *than to face the punishment he deserves!* [c]

[43] "If your hand entices you to sin, let it go limp and useless! [d] For it is better for you to enter into life maimed than to have your entire body thrown into hell, [e] the place of unquenchable fire. [44] This is where the maggots never die and the fire never goes out. [f] [45] And if your foot leads you into sin, cut it off! For it is better to enter life crawling than to have both feet and be flung into hell. [46] This is where the maggots never die and the fire never goes out. [47] And if your eye causes you to sin, pluck it out! For it is better to enter into life with one eye than to be thrown into hell with two. [48] This is where the maggots never die and the fire never goes out! [g]

[49] "Everyone will pass through the fire and every sacrifice will be seasoned with salt. [h] [50] Salt is excellent for seasoning. But if salt becomes tasteless, [i] how can its flavor ever be restored? Your lives, like salt, are to season and preserve. [j] *So don't lose your flavor,* [k] and preserve the peace in your union with one another."

---

a 9:42 Or "entraps," "holds in bondage," "enslaves," "engages in child trafficking." The Aramaic is "confuses" or "misleads."

b 9:42 Or "the upper millstone turned by a donkey."

c 9:42 Implied in the words, "it would be better." Better than what? This is an ellipsis, which when made explicit, enhances the narrative. In the Hebrew text of Matt. 26:24 it reads, "It would be better for him not to even be born."

d 9:43 Or "cut it off." Jesus is obviously using hyperbole to help us understand how purposeful we must be to guard our lives from sin.

e 9:43 Or "the Valley of Hinnom" (or "Gehenna"), which is a metaphor for hell. Gehenna was known in the Old Testament era as the place where human sacrifice was offered to the pagan god Molech. See 2 Chron. 33:6; Jer. 7:31.

f 9:44 The oldest and most reliable manuscripts do not have vv. 44 or 46. They are included in the Aramaic. See Isa. 66:24.

g 9:48 The Aramaic can be translated "where their revenge never dies and their hatred does not subside."

h 9:49 As translated from the Aramaic and a few Greek manuscripts. The majority of reliable Greek texts have "Everyone will be salted with fire." Some manuscripts have "Every sacrifice will be salted with salt." Other manuscripts combine both statements, as does the Aramaic. The unbeliever will be thrown into the fires of Gehenna, and the believer will pass through the refining fire of God's holiness and love. The phrase "every sacrifice will be seasoned with salt" may refer to us as "living sacrifices" who are made "salty" for God. In the days of Jesus, as soon as an animal was killed, it was salted to preserve the meat. See Lev. 2:13 (LXX); Mal. 3:2–3; 4:1; 1 Cor. 3:11–15.

i 9:50 Or "loses its saltiness."

j 9:50 Or "Constantly have (hold) salt in yourselves"; that is, our lives are to become "salty" for God. Aramaic speakers refer to salt as a symbol of faithfulness in friendship. The Jews observed a "salt covenant." Jesus instructs his followers to be faithful friends to one another and to live in peace.

k 9:50 Implied by the comparison of salt losing its flavor and the disciples being like salt.

The Revolutionary Values of the Kingdom

10 Then Jesus left the region[a] and went into the district of Judea,[b] across from the Jordan River,[c] and again, massive crowds flocked to him, and Jesus, as was his custom, began to teach the people. [2] At one point, some of the Pharisees came, seeking to entrap him with a question. "Tell us," they asked, "is it lawful for a man to divorce[d] his wife?"

[3] He answered them, "What did Moses command you?"

[4] They replied, "Moses permitted us to write a certificate of separation that would be valid to complete a divorce."

[5] Jesus said, "Yes, Moses wrote this exception[e] for you because you are hardhearted. [6] But from the beginning God created male and female.[f] [7] For this reason a man will leave his parents and be wedded to his wife.[g] [8] And the husband and wife[h] will be joined as one flesh, and after that they no longer exist as two, but one flesh. [9] So there you have it. What God has joined together, no one has the right to split apart."[i]

[10] Once indoors, his disciples asked him to explain it to them again. [11] So he said to them, "Whoever divorces his wife and marries another commits adultery against her. [12] And if the wife divorces her husband and marries another, she also commits adultery."

Jesus Blesses Little Children

[13] The parents kept bringing their little children to Jesus so that he would lay his hands on them *and bless them*.[j] But the disciples kept rebuking and scolding the

---

a 10:1 Or "left that place" (Capernaum, on the shore of Lake Galilee).

b 10:1 Judea was a Roman province that included central Israel, with Jerusalem as its center. Jesus, leaving to go into Judea, began the journey he made to his destiny, to be crucified in Jerusalem.

c 10:1 The reason this is important to note is that this places Jesus in the jurisdiction of Herod Antipas, who had John the Baptizer beheaded at the request of his stepdaughter. Now the Pharisees are coming to test Jesus in hopes of setting him up for likewise being put to death by Herod. The Aramaic notes the location as "the crossing place." This could have been the place where Joshua and the Hebrews crossed the Jordan to enter into the promised land.

d 10:2 The Greek word for divorce (*apolyo*) used also in vv. 2, 4, 11, and 12 can also be translated "to dismiss," "to send away," "to loose."

e 10:5 Or "commandment."

f 10:6 See Gen. 1:27; 5:2.

g 10:7 As translated from the Aramaic and the majority of Greek manuscripts. See Gen. 2:24 (LXX).

h 10:8 Or "the two" (i.e., husband and wife).

i 10:9 See Deut. 24:1; Matt. 19:3–12. This question in v. 2 was asked in the context of an ongoing debate between two schools of rabbinical thought. The liberal view (Rabbi Hillel's) said that divorce could be made on any grounds, called "Any Matter" divorce, while the conservative viewpoint (Rabbi Shammai's) believed that divorce was only legal on the grounds of adultery. Jesus gave them God's view and used the creation of man and woman in the garden as the standard.

j 10:13 Or "touch them." The laying on of Jesus' hands was an obvious impartation of a

people for doing it. ¹⁴ When Jesus saw what was happening, he became indignant with his disciples and said to them, "Let all the little children come to me and never hinder them! Don't you know that God's kingdom realm exists for such as these? ¹⁵ Listen to the truth I speak: Whoever does not open their arms to receive God's kingdom like a teachable child will never enter it." ᵃ ¹⁶ Then he embraced each child, and laying his hands on them, he lovingly blessed each one.

A Rich Man Meets Jesus

¹⁷ As Jesus started on his way, a man came running up to him. Kneeling down in front of him, he cried out, "Good Teacher, what one thing am I required to do to gain eternal life?"

¹⁸ Jesus responded, "Why do you call me good? Only God is truly good. ¹⁹ You already know the commandments: 'Do not murder, do not commit adultery, do not steal, do not give a false testimony, do not cheat, and honor your father and mother.'" ᵇ

²⁰ The man said to Jesus, "Teacher, I have carefully obeyed these laws since my youth."

²¹ Jesus fixed his gaze upon the man, with tender love, and said to him, "Yet there is still one thing in you lacking. ᶜ Go, sell all that you have and give the money to the poor. Then all of your treasure will be in heaven. After you've done this, come back and walk with me." ᵈ

²² Completely shocked by Jesus' answer, he turned and walked away very sad, for he was extremely rich. ᵉ

²³ Jesus looked at the faces of his disciples and said, "How hard it is for the wealthy to enter into God's kingdom realm."

²⁴ The disciples were startled when they heard this. But Jesus again said to them, "Children, it is next to impossible for those who trust in their riches to find their way into God's kingdom realm. ᶠ ²⁵ It is easier to stuff a rope

---

blessing. The words "and bless them," though implied, are made explicit in v. 16. Parents should always bring their children to be blessed by Jesus. The apparent reason for Mark including this episode is to express not only Jesus' desire to bless children, but also the disciple's inability to see people the way Jesus sees them.

a 10:15 Jesus uses an emphatic negative, something similar to "never, no never enter it."

b 10:19 See Ex. 20:12–16.

c 10:21 As translated from the Aramaic. The Greek is "You lack one thing." The Greek wording used here is the same as found in Rom. 3:23, "we all have sinned and are in need of [lack] the glory of God."

d 10:21 There are a few Greek and Aramaic manuscripts that read "pick up your cross."

e 10:22 Or "he had much property." The Greek word used here implies that he was a wealthy landowner.

f 10:24 Some reliable Greek manuscripts leave out the words "who trust in their riches." However, the majority of the Greek manuscripts and the Aramaic include it. The difficulty Jesus speaks of is not because it is evil to be rich, but because the wealthy are quick to put their confidence in riches and not in God. See 1 Tim. 6:9, 17.

through the eye of a needle[a] than for a wealthy person to enter into God's kingdom realm."[b]

[26] But this left them all the more astonished, and they whispered to one another, "Then who could ever be saved?"

[27] Jesus looked at them and replied, "With people it is impossible, but not with God—God makes all things possible!"[c]

[28] Then Peter spoke up and said, "Can't you see that we've left everything we had to cling to you?"

[29] "Listen to my words," Jesus said. "Anyone who leaves his home behind and chooses me over children, parents, family, and possessions, all for the sake of the gospel, [30] it will come back to him a hundred times as much in this lifetime—homes, family, mothers, brothers, sisters, children, possessions—along with persecutions. And in the age to come, he will inherit eternal life. [31] But many who are considered to be the most important now will be the least important then. And many who are viewed as the least important now will be considered the most important then."

Jesus Again Prophesies His Death and Resurrection

[32] Jesus and his disciples were on the road that went up to Jerusalem, and Jesus was leading them forward. The disciples were filled with wonder and amazement at his bravery, but those following along with them were very afraid. As they approached the city, he took the Twelve aside privately and told them what was going to happen. [33] "I want you to know that we are going to Jerusalem, where the Son of Man will be handed over to the ruling priests and religious scholars and they will condemn him to death and hand him over to the Romans. [34] And they will mock him, spit in his face, torture him, and kill him, but three days later he will rise again."

Jacob (James) and John Ask a Favor of Jesus

[35] Jacob and John, sons of Zebedee, approached Jesus and said, "Teacher, will you do a favor for us?"[d]

---

a   10:25 As translated from the Aramaic. The Greek is "to stuff a camel through the eye of a needle." The Aramaic word for "rope" and for "camel" is the homonym *gamla*. This could be an instance of the Aramaic text being misread by the Greek translators as "camel" instead of "rope." Regardless, this becomes a metaphor for something impossible. It would be like saying, "It's as hard as making pigs fly!"

b   10:25 To enter into God's kingdom realm means more than salvation. It implies a participation in its principles and an experience of its power to change our hearts. The principles of God's kingdom are not the principles of the world. Greed is conquered by generosity. Promotion is given to the humble. The power of God's kingdom is found in the Holy Spirit. See Rom. 14:17.

c   10:27 See Gen. 18:14; Luke 1:37.

d   10:35 A better question that followers of Jesus should ask is, "What can we do to bring you glory? Anything you ask of us we will do for you if you will help us."

³⁶ "What is it you're wanting me to do?" he asked.

³⁷ "We want to sit next to you when you come into your glory," they said, "one at your right hand and the other at your left."

³⁸ Jesus said to them, "You don't have a clue what you're asking for! Are you prepared to drink from the cup of suffering*a* that I am about to drink? And are you able to endure the baptism into death*b* that I am about to experience?"

³⁹ They replied, "Yes, we are able."*c*

Jesus said to them, "You will certainly drink from the cup of my sufferings and be immersed into my death, ⁴⁰ but to have you sit in the position of highest honor is not mine to decide. It is reserved for those whom grace has prepared them to have it."*d*

⁴¹ Now the other ten disciples overheard this, and they became angry and began to criticize Jacob and John. ⁴² Jesus gathered them all together and said to them, "Those recognized as rulers of the people and those who are in top leadership positions rule oppressively over their subjects, but this is not the example you are to follow. ⁴³ You are to lead by a different model. If you want to be the greatest one, then live as one called to serve others. ⁴⁴ The path to promotion and prominence comes by having the heart of a bond-slave*e* who serves everyone. ⁴⁵ For even the Son of Man did not come expecting to be served by everyone, but to serve everyone, and to give his life as the ransom price in exchange for the salvation of many."

Jesus Heals Blind Bar-Timai

⁴⁶ When Jesus and his disciples had passed through Jericho, a large crowd joined them. Upon leaving the village, they met a blind beggar sitting on the side of

---

a 10:38 The cup is mentioned many times in the Old Testament as a metaphor of a cup of suffering. See Ps. 75:8; Isa. 51:17–22; Jer. 25:15; Ezek. 23:31–34.

b 10:38 Baptism is a metaphor for immersion into death. See Rom. 6:3–7; 1 Cor. 10:2; Col. 2:11–13.

c 10:39 How naive was this for them to say! So many times we exaggerate our spirituality and believe we are more mature than we actually are. Yet in spite of their ambition and self-confidence, Jesus affirms that they will indeed taste of the sufferings of Christ.

d 10:40 As translated from the Aramaic. Mark's Gospel records three times that Jesus prophesied of his death and resurrection. After each time he had to rebuke his disciples. The first time (Mark 8:31) he rebuked Peter for being used by Satan to try to hinder Jesus. The second time (Mark 9:31) the disciples argued over who would be the greatest. After the third time (Mark 10:33), Jesus corrected Jacob (James) and John about their ambition to be in the place of highest honor. This shows us that not only is the sacrifice of the cross difficult to understand, it also brings out the ambition that hides in our hearts. Jesus' submission to the Father to choose who sits in glory next to him becomes a rebuke to the ambition of James and John.

e 10:44 Jesus uses two Greek words for servant: *diakonos* ("minister," "servant," "deacon") in v. 43, and *doulos* ("bondslave," "bond servant") in v. 44.

the road named Timai, the son of Timai. [a] [47] When he heard that Jesus from Nazareth was passing by, he began to shout "Jesus, son of David, [b] have mercy on me now in my affliction. *Heal me!*" [c]

[48] Those in the crowd were indignant and scolded him for making so much of a disturbance, but he kept shouting with all his might, "Son of David, have mercy on me now *and heal me!*"

[49] Jesus stopped and said, "Call him to come to me." So they went to the blind man and said, "Have courage! Get up! Jesus is calling for you!" [50] So he threw off his beggars' cloak, jumped up, and made his way to Jesus.

[51] Jesus said to him, "What do you want me to do for you?"

The man replied, "My Master, [d] please, let me see again!"

[52] Jesus responded, "Your faith heals you. Go in peace, with your sight restored." [e] All at once, the man's eyes opened and he could see again, and he began at once to follow Jesus, walking down the road with him.

Jesus' Triumphal Entry into Jerusalem

11 Now, as they were approaching Jerusalem, they arrived at the place of the stables [f] near Bethany on the Mount of Olives. Jesus sent two of his disciples ahead [2] and said to them, "As soon as you enter the village ahead, you will find a donkey's colt tethered there that has never been ridden. Untie it and bring it to me. [3] And if anyone asks, 'Why are you taking it?' tell them, 'The master needs it and will send it back to you soon.'" [g]

[4] So they went and found the colt outside in the street, tied to a gate. When

---

a 10:46 The name Timai is Aramaic and means "highly prized" (or "esteemed"). Though unable to see, he was highly prized in the eyes of Jesus, who stopped to heal him. The Greek transliteration is "Bar-Timaeus, son of Timaeus," which is somewhat confusing, since the name Bar-Timaeus means "son of Timaeus." The Aramaic is to be preferred, for Timai spoke Aramaic when he cried out to Jesus (v. 51), for "Rabbi" ("master-teacher") is an Aramaic title of respect.

b 10:47 The term "son of David" was used for the Messiah. The blind man believed Jesus was the one who was fulfilling the messianic claims of restoring sight to the blind.

c 10:47 Implied in the Hebraic saying "Have mercy on me." The mark of mercy would be his healing.

d 10:51 This is the Aramaic emphatic form of Rabbi: *Rabbouni.* "My Master" is the best way to express this in English.

e 10:52 This is the Greek word *sozo* and is best defined with multiple terms: "delivered, saved, restored, healed, rescued, preserved, made whole." There is at least an implication that the man was saved, healed, and delivered, with sight restored, all at the same time.

f 11:1 Or Bethphage, which in Aramaic means "the house of stables." Transliterated into Greek it means "the house of unripe figs."

g 11:3 Only once in the Gospels do we see Jesus ever needing anything. In this case he needed a donkey. More than one commentator has seen a picture here of how the Lord "needs" every believer to be his representative in the world.

they started to untie it, [5] some people standing there said to them, "Why are untying that colt?"

[6] They answered just as Jesus had told them: *"The master needs it, and he will send it back to you soon."* So the bystanders let them go. [a]

[7] The disciples brought the colt to Jesus and piled their cloaks *and prayer shawls* [b] on the young donkey, and Jesus rode upon it. [c] [8] Many people carpeted the road in front of him with their cloaks *and prayer shawls,* [d] while others gathered palm branches and spread them before him. [9] Jesus rode *in the center* of the procession, with crowds going before him and behind him. They all shouted in celebration, "Bring the victory! [e] We welcome the one coming with the blessings of being sent from the Lord Yahweh! [f] [10] Blessings rest on this kingdom he ushers in right now—the kingdom of our father David! Bring us the victory in the highest realms *of heaven!"* [g]

[11] Jesus rode through the gates of Jerusalem and up to the temple. After looking around at everything, he left for Bethany with the Twelve to spend the night, for it was already late in the day.

Jesus and a Fruitless Fig Tree

[12] The next day, as he left Bethany, Jesus was feeling hungry. [13] He noticed a leafy fig tree in the distance, so he walked over to see if there was any fruit on it, but there was none—only leaves (for it wasn't yet the season for bearing figs). [h]

---

a   11:6 It is clear that Jesus had supernatural knowledge ahead of time about the colt, where it would be found, and what would be spoken by the bystanders. This would qualify as a "word of revelation knowledge," listed as one of the gifts of the Holy Spirit given to the church today. See 1 Cor. 12:8. As the Creator, Jesus Christ has the right to be called the "owner" of the donkey.

b   11:7 Or "garments." By cultural implication, this would include prayer shawls.

c   11:7 See Zech. 9:9. Kings rode on horses, not donkeys. Jesus chose the young colt as a symbol of humility and gentleness. It would be difficult for the people not to see the fulfillment of Zechariah's prophecy in front of their eyes.

d   11:8 The men would have been wearing their prayer shawls as they welcomed Rabbi Jesus to Jerusalem. See also 2 Kings 9:13.

e   11:9 Or *Hosanna,* an Aramaic word that means "O, save us now" (or "bring the victory")! The crowds were recognizing Jesus as Yahweh's Messiah. It is obvious that the people were expecting Jesus to immediately overthrow the Roman oppression and set the nation free. Many want victory before the cross, but true victory comes after resurrection.

f   11:9 As translated from the Aramaic. See Ps. 118:25–26.

g   11:10 Or "You who are in the highest place, save us now!"

h   11:13 The fig tree is first mentioned in Gen. 3:7, with its leaves being a "covering" for fallen Adam and Eve to hide behind. It also became a hiding place for Zacchaeus, who climbed a sycamore-fig tree to see Jesus. The tree with leaves but no fruit can also be a symbol of Israel's religious system of that day (Jer. 8:13; 24:1–10). Jesus next drives out the money changers from the temple, who were rotten fruit. The firstfruits of the harvest Jesus was looking for came on the day of Pentecost, at the end of the Feast of Firstfruits. See Acts 2.

[14] Jesus spoke[a] to the fig tree, saying, "No one will ever eat fruit from you again!" And the disciples overheard him.

Jesus Drives Merchants Out of the Temple Courts

[15] When they came into Jerusalem, Jesus went directly into the temple area and overturned all the tables and benches of the merchants who were doing business there. One by one he drove them all out of the temple courts,[b] and they scattered away, including the money changers[c] and those selling doves. [16] And he would not allow them to use the temple courts as a thoroughfare for carrying their merchandise and their furniture.

[17] Then he began to teach the people, saying, "Does not the Scripture say, 'My house will be a house of prayer for all the world to share'?[d] But you have made it a thieves' hangout!"[e]

[18] When the chief priests and religious scholars heard this, they began to hatch a plot as to how they could eliminate Jesus. But they feared him and his influence, because the entire crowd was carried away with astonishment by his teaching. [19] So he and his disciples spent the nights outside the city.

Lessons of Faith

[20] In the morning, they passed by the fig tree that Jesus spoke to and it was completely withered from the roots up. [21] Peter remembered and said to him, "Teacher, look! That's the fig tree you cursed. It's now all shriveled up and dead."

[22] Jesus replied, "Let the faith of God be in you![f] [23] Listen to the truth I speak to you: If someone says to this mountain with great faith and having no doubt,[g] 'Mountain, be lifted up and thrown into the midst of the sea,'[h]

---

a   11:14 Or "Answering (the fig tree), he spoke to it." The text does not say that Jesus cursed the tree, only that he "answered" and spoke to the tree. Peter's interpretation of this was that Jesus cursed the tree (vv. 20–21).

b   11:15 Also known as the court of the gentiles, the only place where non-Jews were allowed in the temple complex.

c   11:15 The Aramaic reads "the tables that had the firstborn ransom payments."

d   11:17 See Isa. 56:7.

e   11:17 See Jer. 7:11.

f   11:22 As translated from the Aramaic. It is possible to translate the Greek text as an adjectival phrase, "God-like faith" or "godly faith."

g   11:23 The Aramaic word for *doubt* means "to be divided (undecided) in your heart."

h   11:23 The mountain and the sea can also be metaphors. Mountains in the Bible can refer to kingdoms, and the sea represents the nations (e.g., "sea of humanity"). Faith lifts up and brings with us the "mountain" of God's kingdom realm when we go into the nations. The Greek word for mountain, *oros*, is related to a verb that means "to lift up and carry off and take with you." This truth Jesus brings us is more than hyperbole; it is the active power of faith to take and carry the power and authority of the mountain—God's kingdom realm—with us wherever we go.

and believes that what he says will happen, it will be done. [24] This is the reason I urge you to boldly believe for whatever you ask for in prayer—believe that you have received it and it will be yours. [25] And whenever you stand praying, [a] if you find that you carry something in your heart against another person, release him and forgive him [b] so that your Father in heaven will also release you and forgive you of your faults. [26] But if you will not release forgiveness, don't expect your Father in heaven to release you from your misdeeds." [c]

The Religious Leaders Question Jesus' Authority

[27] They came again into Jerusalem, and while Jesus was walking in the temple courts, the Jewish rulers—the chief priest, certain religious scholars, and the elders—approached him. They came up to him [28] and asked, "What right do you have to say and do these things? Who gave you the authority to do all this?"

[29] Jesus replied, "I too have a question to ask you. If you can answer this question, then I will tell you by what power I do all these things. [30] Where did John's authority to immerse come from? Was it from heaven or from people? Answer me now."

[31] They stepped away and debated among themselves, saying, "How should we answer this? If we say, 'from heaven,' he will say to us, 'Then why didn't you respond to John and believe what he said?' [32] But if we say, 'from the people,' we fear the crowds, for they're convinced that John was God's prophet."

[33] So they finally answered, "We don't know."

"Then neither will I tell you where my power comes from to do these things," Jesus replied. [d]

The Parable of the Tenants

12 Then Jesus began to speak to them in parables: "There once was a man who planted a vineyard [e] and put a secure fence around it. [f] He dug a pit for its winepress and erected a watch tower. Then he leased it to tenant-farmers

---

a 11:25 Most ancient Jewish prayers require that a person stand to pray.

b 11:25 The Greek word for forgiveness is *apehiemi* and means "to send away," "to take away," "to release," "to let flow" (away).

c 11:26 This verse is omitted by the Greek texts of Nestle-Aland, Wescott & Hort, and most modern translations because it is not found in some of the most reliable and earliest manuscripts. It is found in the Aramaic. Although its inclusion is dubious, this translation includes it, for it does not interfere with the understanding of this pericope and a similar saying is found in Matt. 6:15.

d 11:33 As they listened to the parable of the tenant in ch. 12, they began to understand that Jesus was the Son of God who came with heaven's authority to represent the Father.

e 12:1 The Aramaic can be translated "He planted a vineyard by a stream."

f 12:1 See Isa. 5:1–7. The vineyard is a metaphor for the promises of life and glory for Israel. The leaders of the nation were but tenants who were to tend the vineyard. The fence was God's protection and favor that surrounded them. The winepress was the Holy Spirit, who gave them the inspired revelation of Scripture. The watchtower could speak of the ministry of the prophets, who were like watchmen on the walls for God's people.

and traveled abroad. [2] When the time of harvest came, he sent one of his servants[a] to the tenants to collect the landowners' share of the harvest. [3] But the tenants seized him and beat him and sent him back empty-handed. [4] So the owner sent another servant to them. And that one they shamefully humiliated and beat over the head.[b] [5] So he sent another servant, and they brutally killed him. Many more servants were sent, and they were all severely beaten or killed. [6] The owner had only one person left to send—his only son, whom he dearly loved. So he sent him to them, saying, 'Surely they will restrain themselves[c] and respect my son.' [7] But the tenants *saw their chance* and said to one another, 'This is the heir. Come! Let's kill him, and then we'll inherit it all!' [8] So they violently seized him, killed him, and threw his body over the fence![d] [9] So what do you think the owner of the vineyard will do? He will come and put to death those tenants and give his vineyard to others.[e] [10] Haven't you read what the psalmist said?

The stone the builders examined and rejected
　　has become the cornerstone,
　　　the most important stone of all?[f]
[11] This was the Lord's plan—
　　and he[g] is wonderful for our eyes to behold!"[h]

[12] Now, the chief priests, religious scholars, and leaders realized that Jesus' parable was aimed at them. They had hoped to arrest him then and there, but they feared the reaction of the crowd, so they left him alone and went away.

Paying Taxes to Caesar

[13] Then they sent a delegation of Pharisees, together with some staunch supporters of Herod, to entrap Jesus with his own words. [14] So they approached him and said, "Teacher, we know that you're an honest man of integrity and you teach us the truth of God's ways. We can clearly see that you're not one who speaks only to win the people's favor, because you speak the truth without regard to the consequences.[i] So tell us, then, what you think. Is it proper for us to pay taxes to Caesar or not?"

---

a 12:2 These servants represent the prophets whom God commissioned to take his word to the people, but they were rejected and persecuted.

b 12:4 Some Greek manuscripts and the Aramaic read "and stoned him."

c 12:6 The Aramaic is "They'll be ashamed of what they've done."

d 12:8 Jesus was the true Heir, who was crucified outside the walls of the city. See Heb. 13:12.

e 12:9 The "others" is a hint of the gentiles who would receive the new covenant promises of God. See also John 15:1–2; Eph. 2:11–22.

f 12:10 See Ps. 118:22–23; Isa. 8:14–15; 28:16.

g 12:11 Or "it."

h 12:11 The Aramaic reads "This came from the presence of [next to] Lord Yahweh and is a marvel in our eyes."

i 12:14 Or "You don't look into the faces of men" (before you speak the truth).

[15] Jesus saw through their hypocrisy and said to them, "Why are you test-ing me? Show me one of the Roman coins." [16] They brought him a silver coin used to pay the tax.

"Now, tell me," Jesus said, "whose head is on this coin and whose in-scription is stamped on it?"

"Caesar's," they replied. [a]

[17] Jesus said, "*Precisely. The coin bears the image of the emperor Caesar,* so you should pay the emperor his portion. *But because you bear the image of God,* [b] you must give back to God all that belongs to him." And they were utterly stunned by Jesus' words.

A Question about Marriage

[18] Some of the Sadducees, a religious group that denied there was a resur-rection of the dead, came to ask Jesus this question: [19] "Teacher, the law of Moses teaches [c] that if a man dies before he has children, his brother should marry the widow and raise up children for his brother's family line. [20] Now, there was a family with seven brothers. The oldest got married but soon died, and he had no children. [21] The second brother married his oldest broth-er's widow, and he also died without any children, and the third also. [22] This repeated down to the seventh brother, none of whom had children. Finally, the woman died. [23] So here's our dilemma: Which of the seven brothers will be the woman's husband when she's resurrected from the dead, since they all were once married to her?"

[24] Jesus answered them, "You are deluded [d] because your hearts are not filled with the revelation of the Scriptures or the power of God. [25] For when they rise from the dead, men and women will not marry, just like the angels of heaven don't marry. [26] Now, concerning the resurrection, haven't you read in the Torah [e] what God said to Moses at the burning bush? 'I AM the living God, the God of Abraham, the God of Isaac, and the God of Jacob'? [f] [27] God is not the God of the dead, but of the living, and you are all badly mistaken!" [g]

The Greatest Commandment

[28] Now a certain religious scholar overheard them debating. When he saw how

---

a 12:16 Actual coins from that era have been found with the emperor's image and a super-scription saying, "Tiberius Caesar Augustus, son of the divine Augustus."

b 12:17 Implied in the text. The coin belongs to Caesar because it carries his image. We have an obligation to God because we carry his image.

c 12:19 See Deut. 25:5–10.

d 12:24 Or "You wander off the path" (of truth).

e 12:26 Or "in the book of Moses."

f 12:26 See Ex. 3:6. The implication Jesus is making is that Abraham, Isaac, and Jacob were all alive (in glory) when God spoke to Moses in the burning bush.

g 12:27 Or "you wander off the path" (of truth).

beautifully Jesus answered all their questions, he posed one of his own, and asked him, "Teacher, which commandment is the greatest of all?"

²⁹ Jesus answered him, "The most important of all the commandments is this: 'The Lord Yahweh, our God, is one!'ᵃ ³⁰ You are to love the Lord Yahweh, your God, with every passion of your heart, with all the energy of your being, with every thought that is within you, and with all your strength. This is the great and supreme commandment. ³¹ And the second is this: 'You must love your neighborᵇ in the same way you love yourself.' You will never find a greater commandment than these."

³² The religious scholar replied, "Yes, that's true, Teacher. You spoke beautifully when you said that God is one, and there is no one else besides him.ᶜ ³³ And there is something more important to God than all the sacrifices and burnt offerings: it's the commandment to constantly love God with every passion of your heart, with your every thought, and with all your strength—and to love your neighbor in the same way as you love yourself."

³⁴ When Jesus noticed how thoughtfully and sincerely the man answered, he said to him, "You're not far from the reality of God's kingdom realm."ᵈ After that, no one dared to question him again.

Jesus, Son of David—Lord of David

³⁵ While Jesus was teaching in the courts of the temple, he posed a question to those listening: "Why do the religious scholars say that the Messiah is David's son? ³⁶ Yet it was David, inspired by the Holy Spirit, who sang:

The Lord Jehovah said to my Lord,
  'Sit near me in the place of authority
    until I subdue all your enemies under Your feet.'ᵉ
³⁷ Since David calls him Lord, how can he be his son?"

The large crowd that had gathered around Jesus took delight in hearing his words.

ᵃ 12:29 As translated from the Aramaic.
ᵇ 12:31 The Aramaic is literally "your nearest," which is a figure of speech for "your friend."
ᶜ 12:32 See Deut. 4:35.
ᵈ 12:34 Jesus tells the man that God's kingdom realm is within reach. It is a present reality, not just a far-off concept. In Mark 11–12, the religious scholars (scribes) are mentioned a number of times. It was a religious scholar who questioned Jesus' authority (11:27–28), and it was a religious scholar who questioned his interpretation of Scripture (12:28). Now, in the verses that follow, Jesus shows that they had taught a theology without knowing the reality of Christ, the Messiah. Every teaching needs to be weighed by the reality of Christ, not the traditions of men.
ᵉ 12:36 See Ps. 110:1, the most quoted Old Testament verse in the New Testament. Jesus is challenging them to consider that the Christ will be both God and man (David's son and David's Lord).

462 | MARK 13

Jesus Warns Against the Religious Scholars

[38] Jesus also taught the people, "Beware of the religious scholars. [a] They love to parade around in their clergy robes and be greeted with respect on the street. [b] [39] They crave to be made the leaders of synagogue councils, [c] and they push their way to the head table at banquets. [40] For appearance's sake, they will pray long religious prayers at the homes of widows for an offering, cheating them out of their very livelihood. [d] Beware of them all, for they will one day be stripped of honor, and the judgment they receive will be severe."

The Widow's Offering

[41] Then he sat down near the offering box, watching all the people dropping in their coins. Many of the rich would put in very large sums, [42] but a destitute widow walked up and dropped in two small copper coins, worth less than a penny. [43] Jesus called his disciples to gather around and then said to them, "I tell you the truth, this poor widow has given a larger offering than any of the wealthy. [44] For the rich only gave out of their surplus, but she sacrificed out of her poverty and gave to God all that she had to live on, which was everything she had."

Jesus Prophesies the Destruction of the Temple

13 As Jesus was leaving the temple courts, one of his disciples came to him and said, "Teacher, look at these magnificent buildings! And what tremendous stones were used to build all this!" [e]

[2] Jesus turned to them and said, "Take a good look at all these enormous buildings, for I'm telling you, there will not be one stone left upon another. It will all be leveled!" [f]

---

a 12:38 The implied meaning of Jesus' teaching is that we should choose carefully those we follow. The religious scholars are not rebuked for their plans to crucify Jesus, but for their flawed character.

b 12:38 Or "marketplaces."

c 12:39 As translated from the Aramaic. The Greek is "the best seats [reserved for respected leaders] in the synagogues."

d 12:40 Translated from the Aramaic, which is literally "They eat of the household with the ladle of their tender prayers." The implication is that the religious leaders would go and pray at the homes of widows, then intimidate them by asking for offerings.

e 13:1 This is Solomon's temple, rebuilt by Herod the Great. He began the project in 19 BC, prior to the birth of Christ, using some of the greatest marble and gold ornamentation found in the Middle East. Some of the stones he used were five meters long and over one meter high.

f 13:2 This prophecy of Jesus was fulfilled by the Roman prince Titus, who, in the Roman war of AD 67–70, destroyed the temple. There is still standing in Rome today the Arch of Titus, which commemorates his conquest of Jerusalem. In about AD 135, the emperor Hadrian completely destroyed the city of Jerusalem and built a new city on its foundations.

Signs of the End of the Age

[3] Later, while Jesus was sitting on the Mount of Olives, overlooking the temple, his disciples, Peter, Jacob, John, and Andrew, came to him privately where he was sitting and said, [4] "Tell us, when will these things happen? And what supernatural sign should we expect to signal your coming and the completion of this age?" [a]

[5] Jesus answered, "At that time deception will run rampant. So beware that you're not fooled! [6] For many will appear on the scene claiming my authority [b] or saying about themselves, 'I am God's Anointed,' [c] and they will lead many astray. [7] You will hear rumors of wars nearby, with more rumors of wars to come. Make sure that you are not thrown into a panic or give in to your fears, for these things are destined to happen. Prepare for it, [d] but still the end is not yet. [8] For nations [e] will go to war against each other and kingdom against kingdom. And there will be terrible earthquakes in place after place—seismic events of epic proportion. And there will be famines and riots. [f] This is how the first contractions and birth pains of the new age will begin."

Jesus Warns of Persecution

[9] "Be on your guard! For they will repeatedly hand you over to the ruling councils, and you will be beaten in public gatherings. And you will stand trial before kings and high-ranking governmental leaders as an opportunity to testify to them on my behalf. [10] *But prior to the end of the age,* the hope of the gospel [g] must first [h] be preached to all nations.

[11] "So when they put you under arrest and hand you over for trial, don't even give one thought about what you will say. Simply speak what the Holy Spirit gives you at that very moment. And realize that it won't be you speaking but the Holy Spirit repeatedly speaking through you. [12] Brothers will betray each other unto death—even a father his child. Children will rise up to

---

a 13:4 Although it is possible to translate this "the end of the world," the Hebraic mind-set of the end of days is a transition into a new age of the Messiah's coming that would restore all things. Note also that this teaching regarding the last days was not given publicly but only to four disciples.

b 13:6 Or "making use of my name."

c 13:6 Or "I am" (the one), or "It is I."

d 13:7 As translated from the Aramaic.

e 13:8 Or "ethnic groups." Although implied in the Greek, the Aramaic text is explicit: "Peoples will rise over peoples and kingdoms over kingdoms."

f 13:8 The word *riots* (rebellious uprisings) is found only in the Aramaic manuscripts. See also 2 Chron. 15:6 and Isa. 19:2.

g 13:10 As translated from the Aramaic (lit. "hopes").

h 13:10 The chronological reference ("first") takes us back to v. 7. That is, the end will not come before the gospel is preached to all nations.

take a stand against their parents and have them put to death. [13] Expect to be hated by all because of your allegiance to the cause that bears my name. But determine to be faithful to the end and you will be saved." [a]

The Detestable Idol That Brings Misery

[14] "When you witness what Daniel prophesied, 'the disgusting destroyer,' [b] standing where it must not be [c] [Let the reader learn what it means], [d] then those in the land of Judah must escape to higher ground. [e] [15] On that day, if you happen to be outside, [f] don't go back inside to gather your belongings. [16] And if you're working out in the field, don't run back home to get a coat. [17] It will be especially hard [g] for pregnant women and for those nursing their babies when those days come. [18] So pray that your escape will not be during the winter months. [19] For this will be a time of great misery beyond the magnitude of anything the world has ever seen from the beginning of time [h] or ever will see. [20] Unless God limits those days, no one would escape. But because of his love for those chosen to be his, he will shorten that time of trouble.

[21] "And if you hear reports from people, saying, 'Look, the Messiah is over here,' or, 'The Messiah is over there!' don't believe it. [22] For there will be imposters falsely claiming to be God's 'Anointed One.' And false prophets [i] will arise to perform miracle signs, and if it were possible, they would cause God's chosen ones to wander off the right track. [23] Be alert, for I prophesy all this will happen!"

The Appearing of the Son of Man

[24] "This is what will take place after that suffering:

The sun will be darkened and the moon will reflect no light.
[25] The stars will be falling from the sky
and all the cosmic powers will be shaken. [j]

---

a 13:13 Or "you will be rescued" or "preserved" or "delivered."

b 13:14 Or "the abomination [sin] that brings desolation [desecration]." See Dan. 8:13; 9:27; 11:31; 12:11. Jesus is saying that Daniel's prophecy had not yet been fulfilled in his time. Many see the fulfillment of this prophecy in AD 70, when Titus, the Roman prince, went into the temple and sacrificed animals to Jupiter.

c 13:14 The Aramaic is "the defiling sign of desolation piling up" (setting up).

d 13:14 These parenthetical words were added by Mark to encourage us to seek the Lord for the understanding of this mystery. Jesus, speaking in the role of the true Prophet, gives us truth to ponder in veiled language.

e 13:14 See Jer. 16:16; Zech. 14:5; Luke 21:20–22.

f 13:15 Or "on the roof."

g 13:17 Or "woe." Jesus is not cursing them, but stating how dreadfully difficult it will be for them.

h 13:19 Or "such as has not been seen from the beginning of the creation that God created until now."

i 13:22 The Aramaic is "prophets of lies."

j 13:25 See Isa. 13:10; 34:4; Joel 2:10; Amos 8:9. This can also be viewed as a Hebraic metaphor

²⁶ "Then they will see the Son of Man appearing in the midst of clouds and revealed with mighty power and great glory.ᵃ ²⁷ At that time he will send his messengers,ᵇ who will gather together his beloved chosen ones from every direction—from the ends of the earth to the ends of heaven!"

The Parable of the Fig Tree

²⁸ "Now, learn the lesson from the parable of the fig tree. When spring arrives, and it sends out its tender branches and sprouts leaves, you know that summer is soon to appear. ²⁹ So also, when you observe all these things progressively taking place, you will know that heᶜ is coming near, even at the door! ³⁰ I assure you, this familyᵈ will not pass away until all I have spoken comes to pass. ³¹ The earth and sky will wear out and fade away before one word I speak loses its power or fails to accomplish its purpose."

Live Always Ready for His Appearing

³² "Concerning that day and exact hour, no one knows when it will arrive, not the angels of heaven, not even the Son—only the Father knows. ³³ This is why you must be waiting, watching and praying,ᵉ because no one knows when that season of time will come."

A Parable of a Man Who Left on a Journey

³⁴ "For those days can be compared to a man who was about to leave on a journey, but before leaving he placed his servants in charge and gave each one work to do while he was away. Then he commanded the watchmanᶠ to be on guard at all times. ³⁵ So I say to you, keep awake and alert—for you have no idea when the master of the house will return; in the evening, at midnight, at four o'clock in the morning,ᵍ or at dawn. ³⁶ Be alert, for he's coming

---

of the lights of the natural realm being shut off and replaced with heaven's glory. Lights out on the old order. Sun, moon, and stars are also representative of the governmental structures failing with great calamity. A new order, a new glory, is coming to replace the fading glories of this world.

a 13:26 See Dan. 7:13.

b 13:27 Or "angels." The Greek word for "angels" can also mean "messengers."

c 13:29 Or "it."

d 13:30 As translated from the Aramaic, which employs a homonym that can be translated either "this generation will not pass away," or "this family will not pass away." The generation in which Jesus lived on earth has indeed passed away, but the Christian "family" of believers remains and endures. Arguably one of the most difficult verses in the Gospels to interpret, "this generation" could also refer to the Jewish people (race).

e 13:33 Most Greek manuscripts do not have "and praying"; however, there are ancient authorities who make reference to its inclusion here.

f 13:34 Or "doorkeeper."

g 13:35 Or "when the rooster crows."

suddenly and may find you sleeping! [37] And what I say to the four of you, I say to everyone—be awake at all times!"

The Plot to Kill Jesus

14 Two days before the Passover and the Feast of Unleavened Bread, [a] the leading priests and religious scholars were committed to finding a way to secretly arrest Jesus and have him executed. [2] But they all agreed that their plot could not succeed if they carried it out during the days of the feast, for they said, "There could be a riot among the people."

Jesus Is Anointed for His Death and Burial

[3] Now Jesus was in Bethany, in the home of Simon, a man Jesus had healed of leprosy. [b] And as he was reclining at the table, [c] a woman came into the house, holding an alabaster flask. [d] It was filled with the highest quality of fragrant and expensive oil. [e] *She walked right up to Jesus, and with a gesture of extreme devotion, she broke the flask and poured out the precious oil over his head.* [4] But some were highly indignant when they saw this, and they complained to one another, saying, "What a total waste! [5] It could have been sold for a great sum, [f] and the money could have benefited the poor." So they scolded her harshly.

[6] Jesus said to them, "Leave her alone! Why are you so critical of this woman? She has honored me with this beautiful act of kindness. [7] For you will always have the poor, whom you can help whenever you want, but you will not always have me. [8] When she poured the fragrant oil over me, she

---

a 14:1 To commemorate the "passing over" of the death angel over the homes of the Hebrew people in Egypt, God instituted these days of celebration. It was an eight-day observance that began with the Passover and included the Feast of Unleavened Bread. See Ex. 12:15–20; 34:18. Some believe there could have been 250,000 pilgrims who flocked to Jerusalem to observe the celebrations. Jesus, our Passover Lamb, was killed on the day of Passover.

b 14:3 We are all cleansed lepers, symbolized by Simon. Christ left the religious structure of the temple and went into the house of a leper. Former "lepers" are now the true temple of God.

c 14:3 In the time of Jesus, meals were not eaten sitting at a table, but rather while reclining on one's side before a low table. There are two suppers mentioned in this chapter. At one, Jesus was a guest; at the other, he was the host.

d 14:3 An alabaster flask would itself be considered a luxury item in that day. Alabaster was a type of gypsum, very white and possibly translucent. It was found in caves and in limestone deposits.

e 14:3 This was spikenard (or nard), a spice taken from a plant that grows in northern India near the Himalayas. This costly perfume would have been carried over land to the Middle East. Many believe this jar of spikenard would have cost the average worker a year's wages. It was a common practice among the Jews to prepare a body for burial with fragrant ointment. John records that it was about twelve ounces of perfume, which would have dripped down all of Jesus' garments to his feet (John 12:3).

f 14:5 Or "three hundred denarii," which is equivalent to nearly a year's salary. Works of charity are important, but they can never replace our devotion to Christ.

was preparing my body in advance of my burial.[a] She has done all that she could to honor me. [9]I promise you that as this wonderful gospel spreads all over the world, the story of her lavish devotion to me will be mentioned in memory of her."[b]

Judas Schemes to Betray Jesus

[10]One of the twelve apostles, Judas Iscariot,[c] went to the leading priests to inform them of his willingness to betray Jesus into their hands. [11]They were delighted to hear this and agreed to pay him for it.[d] So immediately Judas began to look for an opportunity to betray him.

The Passover

[12]On the first day of Unleavened Bread, when the Passover Lamb is sacrificed, Jesus' disciples asked him, "Where would you like us to prepare the Passover meal[e] for you?"

[13]So he sent two of his disciples ahead into Jerusalem with these instructions: "Make your way into the city and watch for a man carrying an earthenware pitcher of water. Follow him, [14]and say to the owner of whatever house he enters, 'The Teacher wants to ask you: "Do you have my room ready where I can eat the Passover meal with my disciples?"' [15]And he will show you a large upstairs room ready and with a table set. Make preparations for us there."

[16]So they went into the city and found everything to be exactly like Jesus had prophesied, and they prepared for him the Passover meal.[f] [17]And when

---

a 14:8 It is possible that when the Roman soldiers pierced Jesus' feet and placed the crown of thorns on his head, they could have smelled this fragrant oil.

b 14:9 Jesus' prophecy is that her sacrifice and love would be included in the Gospel account. Her act of devotion is mentioned in three of the four Gospels. You can't read the New Testament without knowing of her passionate act of worship. The gospel will always give birth to hearts filled with passion for Jesus.

c 14:10 Or "Judas the locksmith." Judas is the name Judah. Iscariot was not his last name. There are two possibilities for the meaning of Iscariot. Some believe it is taken from a Hebrew word that means "lock." Judah the locksmith. He most likely was the one who locked the collection bag, which means he had the key and could pilfer the fund at will. It's his sad history that he wanted to lock up Jesus and control him for his own ends. Other scholars see the possibility that Iscariot actually "Ish [man] of Kerioth" (a town once situated south of Hebron). This would mean Judas was the only non-Galilean among the Twelve.

d 14:11 This was thirty pieces of silver, the going price of a slave. See Ex. 21:32 and Matt. 26:15.

e 14:12 That is, "the Passover seder."

f 14:16 This miracle account shows that Jesus had revelation knowledge and prophetic insight into the future. The disciples encountered the man, just like Jesus had said. Carrying water was a task given to women, making it easy to spot a man carrying a water jug. Also, it was somewhat of a miracle that during the feast days, with a quarter of a million pilgrims celebrating Passover in Jerusalem, there would be a large room like this unoccupied. This was the last Passover feast in God's economy, as the shadow of Passover was fulfilled at the

evening came, he entered the house and went upstairs with his twelve disciples.
¹⁸ Over dinner, while they were reclining around the table, Jesus said, "Listen to
the truth: One of you eating here with me is about to betray me."

¹⁹ Feeling deeply troubled by these words, one after another asked him,
"You don't mean me, do you?"

²⁰ He answered, "It is one of you twelve who has shared meals with me
as an intimate friend.ᵃ ²¹ All that was prophesied of me, the Son of Man,
is destined to soon take place,ᵇ but it will be disastrous for the one who
betrays the Son of Man. It would be far better for him if he had never been
born!"

Jesus Shares Communion with His Twelve

²² As they ate, Jesus took the bread and blessed it, tore it,ᶜ and gave it to his
disciples. He said to them, "Receive this; it is my body." ²³ Then taking the cup
of wine and giving praises to the Father, he declared the new covenant with
them.ᵈ And as each one drank from the cup, ²⁴ he said to them, "This is my
blood, which seals the newᵉ covenant poured out for many. ²⁵ I tell you the
truth, I will not drink again of the fruit of the vine until the day comes when
we drink it together in the kingdom realm of my Father."ᶠ ²⁶ Then they sang
a psalmᵍ and afterwards left for the Mount of Olives.

---

cross, where Jesus was crucified. Passover is now replaced for believers by the communion
we share at the Lord's Supper. See 1 Cor. 5:7–8.

a 14:20 Or "one who dips with me in the bowl." This is a figure of speech for an intimate friend.

b 14:21 Or "The Son of Man will go where it is written that he must go."

c 14:22 Although the Greek word *klao* means to "break bread," it is better understood as tearing a round loaf of flatbread in half. The symbolism of this communion meal was fulfilled
by Jesus giving us his body on the cross. Believers today now feast, not on the crucified body
of Jesus, but on the substance of the glorified body of the resurrected Christ.

d 14:23 As translated from the Aramaic.

e 14:24 A few Greek manuscripts do not have the word *new*. It is included in the Aramaic and
the majority of Greek texts. This new covenant is a better covenant because it is established
on better promises. In this new covenant, God freely gives us forgiveness, life, salvation,
and every heavenly spiritual blessing. See Eph. 1:3; Heb. 8:6–13; 9:16–17. Jesus serves his disciples the bread and the cup (the blood or wine), which means he is serving us his death and
resurrection. This is now our feast and our constant supply of life (John 6:51).

f 14:25 We are now in the realm of the kingdom of God. The Holy Spirit brings us into the
body of Christ and into the reality of God's kingdom realm. It is growing and increasing in
scope, and every time believers drink of the cup of communion, Jesus is present with us. It
is the Lord's Table, not ours. This was a prophecy of what would happen in just a matter of
days from then, as believers would break bread together in remembrance of what Jesus had
done for them. See Acts 2:42. Jesus now drinks it with us in a new way, and not just once a
year at Passover, but every time we worship him by taking communion.

g 14:26 Or "a hymn." The Aramaic is "They offered praise." It was the custom after celebrating the Passover seder to conclude with singing one of the Hallel psalms (Pss. 115–118).

Jesus Prophesies Peter's Denial

[27] Jesus said to them, "You will all fall away and desert me. [a] This will fulfill the prophecy of the Scripture that says:

I will strike down the shepherd
and all the sheep will scatter far and wide. [b]

[28] "But after I am risen, [c] I will go ahead of you to Galilee."

[29] Then Peter spoke up and said, "Even if all the rest lose their faith and fall away, I will still be beside you, Jesus!"

[30] Jesus said, "Mark my words, Peter. This very night, before the rooster crows twice a few hours from now, you will utterly deny that you know me three times."

[31] But Peter was insistent and replied emphatically, "I will absolutely not! Under no circumstances will I ever deny you—even if I have to die with you!" And all the others repeated the same thing.

Jesus Prays in Gethsemane

[32] Then Jesus led his disciples to an orchard called "The Oil Press." [d] He told them, "Sit here while I pray awhile." [33] He took Peter, Jacob, and John with him. [e] An intense feeling of great horror plunged his soul into deep sorrow and agony. [34] And he said to them, "My heart is overwhelmed with anguish and crushed with grief. [f] It feels as though I'm dying. Stay here and keep watch with me."

[35] He walked a short distance away, and being overcome with grief, he threw himself facedown on the ground. He prayed that if it were possible, he would not have to experience this hour *of suffering*. [36] He prayed, "Abba, my Father, all things are possible for you. Please—don't allow me to drink this cup of suffering! [g] Yet what I want is not important, for I only desire to fulfill your plan for me."

---

a 14:27 Or "You will all fall into a trap and be ensnared."

b 14:27 See Zech. 13:7.

c 14:28 Jesus knew he would triumph over death and be raised from the dead.

d 14:32 Or "Gethsemane," the Aramaic word for (olive) "oil press." This was located on the lower slope of the Mount of Olives near the brook Kidron. King David left Jerusalem weeping as he crossed the Kidron Valley and went up the Mount of Olives (2 Sam. 15:23). Now the Son of David comes into that valley with great sorrow on his way into Jerusalem to be crucified. Kidron comes from the Hebrew verb *qadar,* which means "to grow dark" or "to mourn."

e 14:33 Peter, Jacob (James), and John were the three disciples who were witnesses of Christ's glory when he was transfigured before their eyes. On the eve of his crucifixion, Jesus longed to have his three closest disciples nearby.

f 14:34 The Greek words used here in vv. 33–34 are unusual. The terms are extraordinarily emotional and expressive, describing the deepest feelings a person could experience.

g 14:36 The cup becomes a metaphor of the great suffering that Jesus had to endure that

[37] Then he came back to his three disciples and found them all sound asleep. He awakened Peter and said to him, "Simon, are you asleep? Do you lack the strength to stay awake with me for even just an hour? [38] Keep alert and pray that you'll be spared from this time of testing. For your spirit is eager enough, but your humanity is feeble." [a]

[39] Then he left them a second time and went to pray the same thing. [40] Afterward, he came back to the disciples and found them sound asleep, for they couldn't keep their eyes open and they didn't know what to say to him.

[41] After praying for the third time, he returned to his disciples and awoke them again, saying, "Do you plan on sleeping and resting indefinitely? That's enough sleep! The end has come and the hour has arrived [b] for the Son of Man to be handed over to the authority of sinful men. [42] Get up and let's go. Don't you see? My betrayer draws near."

Jesus' Betrayal and Arrest

[43] At that moment Judas, one of the Twelve, arrived, along with a large crowd of men armed with swords and clubs. They had been sent to arrest Jesus by order of the ruling priests, the religious scholars, and the Jewish leaders. [44] Now, Judas, the traitor, had arranged to give them a signal that would identify Jesus, for he had told them, "Jesus is the man I will kiss. So grab him and take him safely away." [45] Judas quickly stepped up to Jesus and said, "Rabbi, my Teacher!" [c] and he kissed him affectionately on both cheeks.

[46] Then the armed men seized Jesus to arrest him. [47] One of the disciples [d] pulled out a sword [e] and swung it at the servant of *Caiaphas*, the high priest, slashing off his ear.

[48] Jesus said to the mob, "Why would you arrest me with swords and

---

night in the garden. However, Jesus was not asking the Father for a way around the cross. Rather, he was asking God to keep him alive through this night of suffering so that he could carry the cross and take away our sins. According to the prophecies of the Old Testament, Jesus was to be pierced on a cross. We learn from Heb. 5:7 that Jesus' prayer was answered that night as the cup was indeed taken from him. An angel of God came to strengthen him and deliver him from premature death (Matt. 26:39). The "cup" he was asking God to let pass from him was the cup of premature death that Satan was trying to make him drink in the garden, not the death he would experience the next day on the cross. He had already sweat drops of blood (Luke 22:44), but the prophecies had to be fulfilled of being pierced on a cross for our transgressions. God answered his cry and he lived through the agony of Gethsemane so that he could be our sacrifice for sin on Calvary. Jesus did not waver in the garden. We have a brave Savior.

a 14:38 The Aramaic is "the flesh is failing."
b 14:41 Or "It is received in full; the hour has come." Although this clause is not found in the most reliable Greek texts, it is included in the Aramaic and a few Greek manuscripts (Codex D).
c 14:45 The Aramaic repeats Rabbi (my "Teacher"); the Greek has it only once.
d 14:47 Or "bystanders," which we know to have included Peter. See John 18:10.
e 14:47 This was a small sword or dagger.

MARK 14 ¢ 471

clubs as though I were an outlaw?*⁴⁹Day after day I sat with you in the temple courts, teaching the people, yet you didn't arrest me then. But all of this fulfills the prophecies of the Scriptures." ⁵⁰At that point all of his disciples ran away and abandoned him.

⁵¹There was a young man ᵇ there following Jesus, wearing only a linen sheet wrapped around him. ᶜ ⁵²They tried to arrest him also, but he slipped from their grasp and ran off naked, ᵈ leaving his linen cloth in their hands.

Jesus Condemned by the Religious Leaders

⁵³Those who arrested Jesus led him away to Caiaphas, the high priest, to a meeting where the religious scholars and Jewish leaders were assembled. ⁵⁴Now, Peter had followed him from a distance all the way to the chief priest's courtyard. He sat with the guards and was warming himself by the fire.

⁵⁵The chief priests and the entire supreme Jewish council of leaders were doing their best to find false charges that they could bring against Jesus and condemn him to death, but they could not find any. ⁵⁶Many false witnesses came forward, but the evidence could not be corroborated. ⁵⁷Some came forward and testified against him, saying, ⁵⁸"We heard him say, 'I can destroy this temple made with hands and then build another one again in three days not made with hands!'" ⁵⁹Yet even on this point the witnesses did not agree.

⁶⁰Finally, the chief priest stood up in the middle of them and said to Jesus, "Have you nothing to say about these allegations? Is what they're saying about you true?"

⁶¹But Jesus remained silent before them and did not answer. So the chief priest said to him, "Are you the anointed Messiah, the Son of the Blessed God?" ⁶²Jesus answered him, "I am. And more than that, you are about to see the Son of Man seated at the right hand of the Almighty and coming in the heavenly clouds!" ᵉ

---

a 14:48 Or "revolutionary."

b 14:51 Traditionally, this young man was thought to be Mark, the author of this Gospel. Mark may be using the common literary device of allusion when speaking of himself. The Greek text uses the word *neaniskos,* which would mean that the young man was a teenager or in his early twenties.

c 14:51 This linen sheet is from the Greek word *sindon* and occurs in the Synoptic Gospels to describe the linen sheet used for burial cloth. *Sindon* is also used for the young man (*neaniskos*) dressed in linen who announced to the women at the tomb that Jesus was alive (Mark 16:5–7). This event can be seen as a foreshadowing of the resurrection, with the symbolism of the burial cloth and the escape from their clutches (in the next verse).

d 14:52 Or "he was nearly naked," for in the Jewish culture, if you were in your undergarment, you were considered to be naked. The linen garment (tunic) would point to a family of wealth. We know the weather was somewhat cold that night, for in just a few hours Peter would be standing by a fire, warming his hands.

e 14:62 See Dan. 7:13.

[63] Then, *as an act of outrage,* the high priest[a] tore his robe and shouted, "No more witnesses are needed, [64] for you've heard this grievous blasphemy." *Turning to the council he said,* "Now, what is your verdict?"

"He's guilty and deserves the death penalty!" they all answered.

[65] Then they spat on his face[b] and blindfolded him. Others struck him over and over with their fists and taunted him by saying, "Prophesy to us! *Tell us which one of us is about to hit you next?*" And the guards took him and beat him.

Peter's Denials

[66] Meanwhile, Peter was sitting below in the courtyard when a girl, a servant of the high priest, came near the fire. [67] When she saw Peter there warming himself, she said to him, "I recognize you. You were with that Nazarene, Jesus."

[68] But Peter denied it, saying, "I don't have a clue what you're talking about." Then he went out to the gateway of the courtyard and the rooster crowed.[c]

[69] When the servant girl noticed him, she said to all the bystanders, "I know this man is one of his followers!"

[70] Once again, Peter denied it. A short time later, the bystanders said to him, "You must be one of them. You're a Galilean, like he is, for your accent proves it!"[d]

[71] Peter cursed and said, "I tell you, I don't know this man you're talking about!"

[72] At the same moment Peter spoke those words, the sound of a rooster crowing pierced the night for the second time. And Peter remembered the words Jesus had spoken to him earlier: **"Before the rooster crows twice, you will deny me three times."** *With a shattered heart,* Peter broke down and sobbed with bitter tears.

Jesus Handed Over to Pilate

15 Before dawn that morning, all the ruling priests, elders, religious scholars, and the entire Jewish council set in motion their plan against Jesus. They bound him in chains, took him away, and handed him over to Pilate.

---

a 14:63 What a dramatic scene! Two high priests are facing each other: the high priest of the Jewish system and the true High Priest. One is of the order of Aaron; the other of the order of Melchizedek (Heb. 7:11–28). One a sinful man; the other, the sinless Son of God. It is clear from Lev. 21:10 that if a high priest tears his robe he is disqualified from his office. Indeed, Caiaphas is now stepping aside and God's true High Priest is taking his place.

b 14:65 See Isa. 50:6.

c 14:68 Some manuscripts leave out the last phrase, "and the rooster crowed."

d 14:70 Or "You are also a Galilean." As a Galilean, Peter spoke a northern dialect of Aramaic that would pronounce certain words slightly differently, much like English is spoken with different accents around the world.

[2] *As Jesus stood in front of the Roman governor,*[a] Pilate asked him, "So, are you really the king of the Jews?"

Jesus answered, **"You have just spoken it."**

[3] Then the ruling priests, over and over, made bitter accusations against him, but he remained silent.[b]

[4] So Pilate questioned him again. "Have you nothing to say? Don't you hear these many allegations they're making against you?" [5] But Jesus offered no defense to any of the charges, much to the great astonishment of Pilate.

Jesus and Barabbas

[6] Every year at Passover, it was the custom of the governor to pardon a prisoner and release him to the people—anyone they wanted. [7] Now, Pilate was holding in custody a notorious criminal named Barabbas,[c] one of the assassins[d] who had committed murder in an uprising. [8] The crowds gathered in front of Pilate's judgment bench and asked him to release a prisoner to them, as was his custom.

[9] So he asked them, "Do you want me to release to you today the king of the Jews?" [10] (Pilate was fully aware that the religious leaders had handed Jesus over to him because of sheer spite and envy.)

[11] But the ruling priests stirred up the crowd to incite them to ask for Barabbas instead.

[12] So Pilate asked them, "Then what do you want me to do with this one you call the king of the Jews?"

[13] They all shouted back, "Crucify him!"

[14] "Why?" Pilate asked. "What evil thing has he done wrong?" But they kept shouting out with an deafening roar, "Crucify him at once!"

[15] Because he wanted to please the people, Pilate released Barabbas to them. After he had Jesus severely beaten with a whip made of leather straps *and embedded with metal,*[e] he sentenced him to be crucified.[f]

---

a 15:2 The Aramaic identifies him as the Roman governor; the Greek is simply Pilate.

b 15:3 See Isa. 53:7; 1 Peter 2:23.

c 15:7 The name Bar-Abbas is Aramaic and means "son of a father" or "son who is like his father." He becomes a picture of every son of Adam, our father. The true Son of the Father was crucified that day. One man wanted a political revolution, the other a revolution of love filling the hearts of all men.

d 15:7 As translated from the Aramaic. The Greek is "revolutionaries."

e 15:15 This was a tortuous beating with a leather whip that had sharp pieces of bone and metal at the end of its lashes, designed to inflict severe pain.

f 15:15 The Jewish death penalty was by stoning. It was the Roman practice to crucify only rebellious slaves and the worst of criminals. To have Jesus crucified was not only the fulfillment of Old Testament prophecies (Gal. 3:13; Isa. 53:5–8) but also the fulfillment of Jesus' own words concerning the mode of his death (John 3:14; 8:28; 12:32), which would not have been fulfilled by stoning.

The Soldiers Mock Jesus

[16] The soldiers took Jesus into the headquarters of the governor's compound[a] and summoned a military unit of nearly six hundred men.[b] [17] They placed a purple robe on him *to make fun of him.* Then they braided a victor's crown, a wreath made of thorns,[c] and set it on his head. [18] And with a mock salute they repeatedly cried out, "Hail, your majesty, king of the Jews!" [19] They kept on spitting in his face and hit him repeatedly on his head with a reed staff, driving the crown of thorns deep into his brow. They knelt down before him in mockery, pretending to pay him homage. [20] When they finished ridiculing him, they took off the purple robe, put his own clothes back on him, and led him away to be crucified.

The Crucifixion of Jesus

[21] As they came out of the city, they stopped an African man named Simon, a native of Libya.[d] He was passing by, just coming in from the countryside with his two sons,[e] Alexander and Rufus, and the soldiers forced him to carry the heavy crossbeam for Jesus. [22] They brought Jesus to the execution site called Golgotha, which means "Skull Hill."[f] [23] There they offered him a mild painkiller, a drink of wine mixed with gall,[g] but he refused to drink it.

[24] They nailed his hands and feet to the cross. The soldiers divided his clothing among themselves by rolling dice[h] to see who would win them. [25] It was nine o'clock in the morning[i] when they finally crucified him. [26] Above his head

---

a 15:16 Or "praetorium."

b 15:16 That is, a Roman cohort (battalion), which was the tenth part of a Roman legion of about six thousand men.

c 15:17 Thorns are an emblem of the curse of sin. Jesus took the curse for us. See Gen. 3:17–18; Gal. 3:13.

d 15:21 Or "from Cyrene," which is present-day Tripoli, Libya. Cyrene was a Greek colony that had a great number of Jews who had been forced to live there during the reign of Ptolemy Soter (323–285 BC). Church tradition states that Simon's two sons became powerful missionaries for Jesus Christ. Their mention here might indicate that they were notable among the early Christians. See Rom. 16:13. It is also possible that Simon himself could be linked to the "believers from Cyprus and Cyrene" who were evangelists to the Syrians, mentioned in Acts 11:20.

e 15:21 Or "the father of two sons," who, by implication, were with him at that time. Church tradition states that their names were Rufus and Alexander who became missionaries preaching the message of Christ. See Rom. 16:13.

f 15:22 The Aramaic word is "Golgotha" (Mark uses a variant dialectic form, "Gajultha"). This is *calvaria* in Latin, or "Calvary." David took Goliath's head (Goliath and Golgotha are taken from the same root word) and buried it outside of Jerusalem (1 Sam. 17:54). Some believe this is where the hill got its name, Golgotha (the place of the skull). The cross has to pierce the place of the skull for our minds to submit to the revelation of the cross.

g 15:23 See Ps. 69:21.

h 15:24 That is, they cast lots. See Ps. 22:18.

i 15:25 Or "the third hour" (of the day).

they placed a sign with the inscription of the charge against him, which read, "This is the King of the Jews." [27] Two criminals were also crucified with Jesus, one on each side of him. [28] This fulfilled the Scripture that says:

He was considered to be a criminal. [a]

[29] Those who passed by shook their heads and spitefully ridiculed him, saying, "Aha! You boasted that you could destroy the temple and rebuild it in three days. [b] [30] Why don't you save yourself now? Just come down from the cross!"

[31] Even the ruling priests and the religious scholars joined in the mockery [c] and kept laughing among themselves, [d] saying, "He saved others, but he can't even save himself! Israel's king, is he? [32] Let the 'Messiah,' the 'king of Israel,' *pull out the nails and* come down from the cross right now. We'll believe it when we see it!" Even the two criminals who were crucified with Jesus began to taunt him, hurling insults on him.

The Death of Jesus

[33] For three hours, beginning at noon, darkness came over the earth. [e] [34] About three o'clock, Jesus shouted with a mighty voice in Aramaic, [f] "Eli, Eli, lama sabachthani?"—that is, "My God, My God, why have you turned your back on me?" [g]

[35] Some who were standing near the cross *misunderstood* and said, "Listen! He's calling for Elijah." [h] [36] One bystander ran and got a sponge, soaked it with sour wine, then put it on a stick and held it up for Jesus to drink. [i] But the rest said, "Leave him alone! Let's see if Elijah comes to rescue him." [37] Just then Jesus passionately cried out with a loud voice and breathed his last. [j] [38] At that moment the veil *in the Holy of Holies* was torn in two from the top to the bottom. [k]

---

a 15:28 See Isa. 53:12. Although this verse is not found in some of the early and reliable Greek manuscripts, the majority of manuscripts do include it, and it is also found in the Aramaic.

b 15:29 Jesus never said that he would destroy the temple, but that it would be destroyed by others.

c 15:31 See Pss. 22:17; 109:25; Lam. 2:15.

d 15:31 As translated from the Aramaic.

e 15:33 See Ex. 10:22; Joel 2:30–31; Amos 8:9–10; Acts 2:16–21.

f 15:34 The last words of Jesus were spoken in Aramaic. Every Greek text gives a transliteration of the Aramaic words and then translates them back into Greek.

g 15:34 See Pss. 22:1; 42:9. The Aramaic can be translated "For this purpose you have spared me."

h 15:35 Perhaps they misunderstood because the Aramaic word *Eli* sounds similar to the name Elijah.

i 15:36 See Ps. 69:21.

j 15:37 See Luke 23:46 and John 19:30 to read the words he shouted out at death.

k 15:38 The veil torn from the top to the bottom proves that it was God who did this, for the veil was very thick, heavy, and nearly eighty feet tall. See Heb. 10:19–22.

[39] When the Roman military officer who was standing right in front of Jesus saw how he died, he said, "There is no doubt this man was the Son of God!

[40-41] Watching from a distance, *away from the crowds*, were many of the women who had followed Jesus from Galilee and had cared for him. [a] Among them were Mary Magdalene, [b] Mary the mother of Jacob the younger [c] and Joseph, [d] and Salome. Many other women who had followed him to Jerusalem were there too. [e]

Jesus' Burial

[42] Evening was fast approaching, and it was a preparation day before a Sabbath. [43] So a prominent Jewish leader named Joseph, from the village of Ramah, [f] courageously went to see Pilate and asked to have custody of the body of Jesus. Joseph was a highly regarded member of the Jewish council and a follower of Jesus [g] who had focused his hope on God's kingdom realm. [h] [44] Pilate was amazed to hear that Jesus was already dead, so he summoned the Roman officer, who confirmed it. [i] [45] After it was confirmed, Pilate consented to give the corpse to Joseph.

[46] Joseph purchased a shroud of fine linen and took the body down from the cross. Then he wrapped it in the linen shroud and placed it in a tomb quarried from out of the rock. [j] Then they rolled a large stone over the entrance to seal the tomb. [47] Mary Magdalene and Mary the mother of Joseph [k] were there and saw exactly where they laid the body of Jesus.

The Resurrection of Jesus

16 [1-2] On the first day of the week, as the Sabbath was ending, Mary Magdalene, Mary the mother of Jacob, and Salome made their way to the

---

a 15:40–41 Or "ministered to him." This most likely included financial support.

b 15:40–41 Or "Miriam of [the village of] Magdala," which was discovered beginning in 2009 on the southwestern shore of Lake Galilee. See also Luke 8:2.

c 15:40–41 Or "James, the short one."

d 15:40–41 Or "Joses," a nickname for Joseph that perhaps could best be translated "Joey."

e 15:40–41 Apparently, all the men had fled from the scene except for the apostle John. See John 19:26.

f 15:43 As translated from the Aramaic. Ramah (formerly Ramathaim Zophim) was the village of Samuel, situated on a hill overlooking Jerusalem. The Greek is "Joseph of Arimathea." Luke tells us that he was a member of the Sanhedrin. See Luke 23:50–51. It is possible that Joseph may have lost a son the age of Jesus when Herod killed the infants.

g 15:43 See Matt. 27:57.

h 15:43 The Greek text could be translated "He was habitually focusing and progressively moving toward receiving [welcoming, anticipating] God's kingdom reign." The Aramaic is "anxiously awaiting the kingdom realm of God."

i 15:44 Or "if he had died too soon."

j 15:46 This was a tomb that had been chiseled into a rock, forming a cave-like structure.

k 15:47 Or "Joses."

tomb. It was very early in the morning as the first streaks of light were beginning to be seen in the sky. They had purchased aromatic embalming spices so that they might anoint his body. ³ And they had been asking one another, "Who can roll away the heavy stone for us from the entrance of the tomb?" ⁴ But when they arrived, they discovered that the very large stone that had sealed the tomb was already rolled away! ⁵ And as they stepped into the tomb, they saw a young man sitting on the right, dressed in a long white robe. The women were startled and amazed. ⁶ But the angel ⁴ said to them, "Don't be afraid. I know that you're here looking for Jesus of Nazareth, who was crucified. He isn't here—he has risen victoriously! Look! See the place where they laid him. ⁷ Run and tell his disciples, even Peter, that he is risen. He has gone ahead of you into Galilee and you will see him there, just like he told you."

⁸ They staggered out of the tomb, awestruck, ᵇ with their minds swirling. They ran to tell the disciples, but they were so afraid and deep in wonder, they said nothing to anyone. ᶜ

Jesus Appears to Some of His Followers

⁹ Early on the first day of the week, after rising from the dead, Jesus appeared to Mary Magdalene, from whom he had cast out seven demons. ¹⁰ After she had seen Jesus, she ran to tell his disciples, who were all emotionally devastated and weeping. ¹¹ Excitedly, Mary told them, "He's alive and I've seen him!" But even after hearing this, they didn't believe her.

¹² After this, Jesus appeared to two of the disciples, who were on their way to another village, ᵈ appearing in a form they did not recognize. ¹³ They went back to Jerusalem to tell the rest of the disciples, but they didn't believe it was true.

¹⁴ Then Jesus appeared ᵉ before the eleven apostles as they were eating a meal. He corrected them for having such hard, unbelieving hearts because they did not believe those who saw him after his resurrection.

¹⁵ And he said to them, "As you go into all the world, preach openly the wonderful news of the gospel to the entire human race! ¹⁶ Whoever believes the good news and is baptized will be saved, and whoever does not believe the good news will be condemned. ¹⁷ And these miracle signs will accompany those who believe: They will drive out demons in the power of my name. They will

---

a 16:6 See Matt. 28:2.

b 16:8 Or "trembling" (with astonishment).

c 16:8 Some early manuscripts of Mark do not include vv. 9–20. They are found in the Aramaic. A shorter ending to Mark found in a few manuscripts reads, "They reported briefly to those around Peter all that they had been commanded. After these things, Jesus himself commissioned them to take the message from the east to the west—the holy and imperishable preaching of eternal salvation. Amen."

d 16:12 Or "to the country." See Luke 24:13–35.

e 16:14 Or "manifested" or "became visible" (in clear light).

speak in tongues. [18] They will be supernaturally protected from snakes and from drinking anything poisonous. [a] And they will lay hands on the sick and heal them."

[19] After saying these things, Jesus was lifted up into heaven and sat down *at the place of honor* at the right hand of God! [20] And the apostles went out announcing the good news everywhere, as the Lord himself consistently worked with them, validating the message they preached with miracle-signs that accompanied them!

---

a   16:18 Or "They will pick up snakes and be unharmed, and whatever poison they drink will not hurt them." Some scholars believe that this sentence contains two Aramaic idioms. To pick up snakes could be a picture of overcoming one's enemies ("snakes"), and drinking poison may be speaking of dealing with attacks on one's character (poisonous words). The imagery is from Ps. 91:13.

LUKE

Introduction

AT A GLANCE

Author: Luke, beloved physician, friend, and companion to Paul
Audience: Theophilus, and all "lovers of God"
Date: Late-AD 60s, though possibly 70–85
Type of Literature: Ancient historical biography
Major Themes: Jesus' person, Jesus' works, the kingdom realm, the Christian life, social dimensions, and the Holy Spirit
Outline:

Luke's Preface — 1:1–4
Jesus' Birth and Childhood — 1:5–2:52
Jesus' Ministry Preparation — 3:1–4:13
Jesus' Galilean Ministry — 4:14–9:50
Jesus Heads to Jerusalem — 9:51–19:44
Jesus Teaches in Jerusalem — 19:45–21:38
Jesus' Suffering and Death — 22:1–23:56
Jesus' Resurrection and Exaltation — 24:1–24:53

ABOUT LUKE

You are about to read the biography of the wonderful Man Jesus Christ. This glorious Gospel was penned by one of his early followers, a physician named Luke. All four Gospels in our New Testament are inspired by God, but Luke's is unique. I believe that this could be described as the loveliest book ever written.

Luke's pen was anointed by the Holy Spirit and his book is still read today by the lovers of God, because it is the mercy Gospel. It is a book for everybody, for we all need mercy. Luke writes clearly of the humanity of Jesus—as the servant of all and the sacrifice for all. Every barrier is broken down in Luke's Gospel: between Jew and gentile, men and women, rich and poor. In Luke we see Jesus as the Savior of all who come to him.

Luke, being a physician, learned the need to exhibit compassion and mercy toward others. It comes through in every chapter. Luke's Gospel is perhaps the most compassionate and love-filled account of Jesus' life ever written.

Luke shares Jesus' teachings on prayer, forgiveness, and our obligation to demonstrate mercy and grace in dealings with others. Luke provides us with rich details of Jesus' love of children and the forsaken. Luke writes more about Jesus' ministry to women than the other Gospel authors. This was somewhat controversial in the culture of his day. In fact, Luke uses an alternating narrative of one story about a man and the next story about a woman. Luke begins with the story of Zechariah, then moves to Mary. A focus on Simeon, then on Anna. The Roman centurion, then the widow of Nain. The good Samaritan, then Mary and Martha. This pattern continues throughout his Gospel.

A large amount of Luke's Gospel is not found in any other Gospel narrative. If we did not have the book of Luke, we wouldn't know about the stories of the prodigal son, the good Samaritan, the wedding banquet, and other amazing teachings. Only in the book of Luke do we find the stories of the shepherds at Bethlehem, the ten lepers who were healed, the young man from Nain who was raised from the dead, and the dying thief on the cross next to Jesus. How thankful I am for the Gospel of Luke!

My heart overflows with the joy of seeing the Word of God being translated with all its passion and fire into contemporary English. Unveiled before your eyes will be the glorious Man, Jesus Christ, and the revelation of his undying love for you.

I present to you, and to every lover of God, the Gospel of Luke.

PURPOSE

This world is a far better place because of the revelation Luke shares with us in his Gospel. He gives us a full picture of Jesus' life and ministry, applying scrupulous accuracy to all he wrote to ensure that what we read is factual. In fact, Luke uses the Greek word for "autopsy" (1:2) for investigating with firsthand knowledge those who had seen what Jesus did and heard what Jesus taught.

Dr. Luke performed an "autopsy" on the facts of Jesus' life, death, and resurrection, tracing them all back to their source to make sure what he compiled was of the highest degree of accuracy. He takes "Theophilus" through Jesus' entire ministry career to reveal how God worked to show Jesus to be true and the hope of the world. He also shows how God has been faithful to Israel and the promises he's given her, while inviting the nations to the table of Christ's love and hope.

AUTHOR AND AUDIENCE

We know little about Luke, the human author of this Gospel. He was a companion of the apostle Paul for some of his missionary journeys and was possibly one of Paul's early converts. Luke was a literary genius and writes with powerful prose. Some believe Luke was possibly the only non-Jewish writer of the New Testament. Others believe that he was a Syrian Jew who took upon himself a gentile name. It is obvious that he knew firsthand many of the early followers of Jesus, even the apostles who were chosen to preach his name throughout the nations. Near the end of the apostle Paul's life, when he was facing martyrdom, Paul wrote of his trusted friend, "only Luke [is] with me" (2 Tim. 4:11).

The opening line of the Gospel indicates Luke wrote to the "most excellent Theophilus" (see the first footnote on Luke 1:1–4). The name Theophilus means "friend of God" or "lover of God." The Greek word means "most honorable" or "mightiest." Some scholars suggest there was no individual named Theophilus mentioned in Luke's writings. Regardless, Luke's Gospel is a greeting to all the lovers of God. He especially wrote it to non-Jewish lovers of God who may have felt out of place in the originally Jewish movement.

MAJOR THEMES

The Person and Work of Jesus. As you can imagine, a historical biography of Jesus will feature him and his work, front and center! In Luke's Gospel, he is the sent one who is both Lord and Messiah. He is uniquely and intimately connected to God, transcending any portrait of him as simply a human figure and agent. He is also the one who acts, as the promised Messiah anointed by the Spirit to bring in the new era—God's heavenly kingdom realm to earth. His ultimate act was on behalf of every person on the planet, bearing the sins of the world as he hung on the Roman cross. And in the end, this Lord Messiah was vindicated by the Father through the resurrection and exalted to his right hand through the ascension.

The Promised Kingdom Realm. In Jesus Christ, all of God's promises are fulfilled. Chief among them is God's promised kingdom realm. God's kingdom realm is both present and coming. Jesus commands his disciples to proclaim that it has "come near" and is within peoples' reach in the present. The promises of the last days have started to be fulfilled, and yet those promises haven't been ultimately fulfilled. The full manifestation of the kingdom realm is still anticipated, when all the hoped-for prophecies of restoration will be realized.

Women and the Poor. Women are a crucial part of Jesus' story—now and then. In Luke's Gospel they provide examples of deep piety and devotion. They are both of humble means and wealthy. At every turn women are part of Jesus' ministry: Elizabeth, Anna, and of course Mary play important roles in his infancy; women are healed, comforted, and forgiven in Galilee; on the way to Jerusalem, we meet Mary and Martha; and during Christ's most desperate hours, women weep at his feet, stand with him faithfully; finally, they receive the first revelation of Jesus' resurrection. Then there are the poor. Throughout Luke, the poor receive special attention too, showing that God deliberately reaches out to those whom society casts away. He makes clear the good news of Jesus and his love is for people like them, which means the gospel truly is for everybody!

The Holy Spirit. The Holy Spirit plays a major role in Luke's Gospel, where he is referenced nearly twenty times. The Spirit is the driving force in the picture Luke paints of God's coming salvation. He is the architect, the maestro guiding and energizing the events that transpire throughout the life of Jesus. We find him present from the very beginning with his conception and birth on to Christ's baptism in the Spirit and through to his powerful miracle ministry. One of the most important texts in all the Gospels is Luke 3:15–16, where John says one "mightier" than he would come baptizing with "the Spirit of holiness and . . . fire." This Spirit of fire is the sign and seal of the new era of the Messiah, come to rescue and re-create the world!

LUKE

To the Lovers of God

1 [1-4] Dear friend,

I am writing for you, mighty lover of God,[a] an orderly account of what Jesus, the Anointed One, accomplished and fulfilled among us. Several eyewitness biographies have already been written,[b] using as their source material the good news preached among us by his early disciples, who became loving servants of the Living Expression.[c] But now I am passing on to you this accurate compilation of my own meticulous investigation[d] based on numerous eyewitness interviews and thorough research of the story of his life. It is appropriate for me to write this, for he also appeared to me[e] so that I would reassure you beyond any shadow of a doubt the reliability of all you have been taught of him.

Angelic Prophecy of the Prophet John's Birth

[5] During the reign of King Herod the Great over Judea, there was a Jewish priest named Zechariah[f] who served in the temple as part of the priestly order of Abijah.[g] His wife, Elizabeth, was also from a family of priests, being a direct descendant of Aaron. [6] They were both lovers of God, living virtuously and following the commandments of the Lord fully. [7] But they were childless since Elizabeth was barren, and now they both were quite old.

---

a 1:1–4 The Greek text can be translated "most excellent Theophilus." The name Theophilus means "friend of God" or "lover of God." The Greek word means "most honorable" or "mightiest." Some scholars believe there was no individual named Theophilus mentioned in Luke's writings. This becomes instead a greeting to all the lovers of God.

b 1:1–4 It is likely that Matthew and Mark are two of the Gospel accounts Luke refers to here.

c 1:1–4 Translated literally from the Aramaic text. The Greek word is *logos*. Some have translated this rich term as "Word." It could also be translated "Message" or "Blueprint." Jesus Christ is the eternal Word, the creative Word, and the Word made visible. He is the divine self-expression of all that God is, contains, and reveals in incarnated flesh. Just as we express ourselves in words, God has perfectly expressed himself in Christ.

d 1:1–4 The Greek word used here is actually "to see with the eye" or "autopsy."

e 1:1–4 Translated literally from the Aramaic text. The Greek text uses the same term for "coming from above" found in John 3:31 and 19:11. Luke is revealing that the Lord Jesus appeared to him and authorized him to compile his inspired Gospel.

f 1:5 Zechariah means "God has remembered." Elizabeth means "oath" or "covenant of God."

g 1:5 King David organized the priests into twenty-four divisions, and Abijah was the head of one of the priestly families. See Neh. 12:12, 17; 1 Chron; 24:10.

[8-9] One day, while Zechariah's priestly order was on duty and he was serving as priest, it happened by the casting of lots (according to the custom of the priesthood) that the honor fell upon Zechariah to enter into the Holy Place [a] and burn incense before the Lord. [10] A large crowd of worshipers had gathered to pray outside the temple at the hour when incense was being offered. [11] All at once an angel of the Lord appeared to him, standing just to the right of the altar of incense. [b]

[12] Zechariah was startled and overwhelmed with fear. [13] But the angel reassured him, saying, "Don't be afraid, Zechariah! *God is showing grace to you.* [c] For I have come to tell you that your prayer [d] for a child has been answered. Your wife, Elizabeth, will bear you a son and you are to name him John. [14] His birth will bring you much joy and gladness. Many will rejoice because of him. [15] He will be one of the great ones in the sight of God. He will drink no wine or strong drink, [e] but he will be filled with the Holy Spirit even while still in his mother's womb. [16] And he will persuade many in Israel to convert and turn back to the Lord their God. [17] He will go before the Lord as a forerunner, with the same power and anointing [f] as Elijah the prophet. He will be instrumental in turning the hearts of the fathers in tenderness back to their children and the hearts of the disobedient back to the wisdom of their righteous fathers. And he will prepare a *united people* [g] who are ready for the Lord's appearing."

[18] Zechariah asked the angel, "How do you expect me to believe this? I'm an old man and my wife is too old to give me a child. *What sign can you give me to prove this will happen?*"

[19] Then the angel said, "I am Gabriel. [h] I stand beside God himself. He has sent me to announce to you this good news. [20] But now, since you did not believe my words, you will be stricken silent and unable to speak [i] until the day

---

a   1:8–9 Some have said there were twenty thousand priests in Christ's time, so that no priest would ever offer incense more than once. This was a once-in-a-lifetime moment for him. The burning of incense before the Lord was done twice daily, once in the morning and once in the afternoon (Ex. 30:7–8).

b   1:11 This would be the south side of the temple, between the altar of incense and the golden lampstand.

c   1:13 Implied in the context and in the name John, which means "God is gracious" or "God shows mercy."

d   1:13 The Greek verb allows for a possible translation of "prayer you don't even pray anymore."

e   1:15 Most likely, John was to be a Nazarite from birth, one totally set apart for God and who would fulfill the Nazarite vow found in Num. 6:1–12.

f   1:17 Or "spirit."

g   1:17 The words "united people" are found in the Aramaic text.

h   1:19 The name Gabriel means "God's hero" or "God's mighty one."

i   1:20 Since Zechariah asked for a sign rather than believe the word of the Lord, he was given the sign of silence. Unbelief keeps a priest from speaking until faith arises.

my words have been fulfilled at their appointed time and a child is born to you. That will be your sign!"[a]

[21] Meanwhile, the crowds outside kept expecting him to come out. They were amazed over Zechariah's delay,[b] wondering what could have happened inside the sanctuary. [22] When he finally did come out, he tried to talk, but he couldn't speak a word, and they realized from his gestures that he had seen a vision while in the Holy Place. [23] He remained mute as he finished his days of priestly ministry in the temple and then went back to his own home. [24] Soon afterward his wife, Elizabeth, became pregnant and went into seclusion for the next five months. [25] She said with joy, "See how kind it is of God to gaze upon me[c] and take away the disgrace of my barrenness!"

Angelic Prophecy of Jesus' Birth

[26-27] During the sixth month of Elizabeth's pregnancy, the angel Gabriel was sent from God's presence to an unmarried girl[d] named Mary, living in Nazareth, a village in Galilee.[e] She was engaged[f] to a man named Joseph, a true descendant of King David. [28] Gabriel appeared to her and said, "Grace to you, young woman, for the Lord is with you[g] and so you are anointed with great favor."

[29] Mary was deeply troubled over the words of the angel and bewildered over what this may mean for her. [30] But the angel reassured her, saying, "Do not yield to your fear, Mary, for the Lord has found delight in you and has chosen to surprise you with a wonderful gift. [31] You will become pregnant with a baby boy, and you are to name him Jesus. [32] He will be supreme[h] and will be known as the Son of the Highest. And the Lord God will enthrone him as King on his ancestor David's throne. [33] He will reign as King of Israel[i] forever, and his reign will have no limit."

---

a 1:20 This is the first spoken message from heaven in more than four hundred years. The last person before Zechariah to receive a message given by angels was also named Zechariah. See Zech. 1:6.

b 1:21 They were waiting outside for the priest to come out and speak over them the customary Aaronic blessing found in Num. 6:24–26.

c 1:25 This phrase is translated from the Aramaic text.

d 1:26–27 Many translations have the word *virgin*. It is a possible translation of the Greek word *parthenos*, but its most common usage implies "a girl of marriageable age." It is made explicit in Matt. 1:25 and Luke 1:34 that Mary was indeed a virgin.

e 1:26–27 The Aramaic word translated "Galilee" here means "revealed." It is only fitting that God would first be "revealed" in a village in Galilee. Nazareth means "branch." Jesus grew up as the "Branch" of the Lord in the city of the "branch."

f 1:26–27 This betrothal period usually lasted one year, and unfaithfulness on the part of the bride during the engagement was punishable by death.

g 1:28 For Gabriel to say, "the Lord is with you," signified that Jesus, our Master, had been conceived in her womb. This was what bewildered Mary.

h 1:32 As translated from the Aramaic text.

i 1:33 Or "house of Jacob."

³⁴ Mary said, "But how could this happen? I am still a virgin!"

³⁵ Gabriel answered, "The Spirit of Holiness will fall upon you and almighty God will spread his shadow of power over you in a cloud of glory![a] This is why the child born to you will be holy,[b] and he will be called the Son of God. ³⁶ What's more, your aged aunt,[c] Elizabeth, has also become pregnant with a son. The 'barren one' is now in her sixth month. ³⁷ Not one promise from God is empty of power, for nothing is impossible with God!"[d]

³⁸ Then Mary responded, saying, "This is amazing! I will be a mother for the Lord![e] As his servant, I accept whatever he has for me. May everything you have told me come to pass." And the angel left her.

Elizabeth's Prophecy to Mary

³⁹ Afterward, Mary arose and hurried off to the hill country of Judea, to the village where Zechariah and Elizabeth lived. ⁴⁰ Arriving at their home, Mary entered the house and greeted Elizabeth. ⁴¹ At the moment she heard Mary's voice, the baby[f] within Elizabeth's womb jumped and kicked. And suddenly, Elizabeth was filled to overflowing with the Holy Spirit! ⁴² With a loud voice she *prophesied with power:*

"Mary! You are a woman given the highest favor
and privilege above all others.
For your child[g] is destined to bring God great delight.
⁴³ How did I deserve such a remarkable honor
to have the mother of my Lord[h] come and visit me?
⁴⁴ The moment you came in the door and greeted me,
my baby danced inside me with ecstatic joy!
⁴⁵ Great favor is upon you, for you have believed
every word spoken to you from the Lord."

---

a 1:35 The Greek word used as a metaphor, "spread his shadow over you," is also the word used at Jesus' transfiguration when the cloud of glory "overshadowed" Jesus on the mountain (Mark 9:7).

b 1:35 Jesus Christ is holy, born without sin in his bloodline, for his Father was God Almighty. He would become the only perfect sacrifice to take away our sin and remove its power and penalty from us.

c 1:36 The Greek word is "relative." Many scholars believe Elizabeth was Mary's maternal aunt.

d 1:37 This verse can be translated in two different ways: "There is nothing impossible with God" or "The word of God will never fail." The translator has chosen to include both for this verse.

e 1:38 As translated from the Aramaic text.

f 1:41 The Bible calls Elizabeth's yet-to-be-born son, John, a "baby."

g 1:42 Or "the fruit of your womb." This is the same word used for the "fruit" of the tree of life in Rev. 22:2. Jesus is "fruit" for us to take in as our life supply.

h 1:43 An obvious prophetic revelation was given to Elizabeth from the Holy Spirit about what had happened with Mary.

Mary's Prophetic Song

⁴⁶ And Mary sang this song:

"My soul is ecstatic, overflowing with praises to God!
⁴⁷ My spirit bursts with joy over my life-giving God! ᵃ
⁴⁸ For he set his tender gaze upon me, his lowly servant girl.ᵇ
  And from here on, everyone will know
    that I have been favored and blessed.
⁴⁹ The Mighty One has worked a mighty miracle for me;
  holy is his name!
⁵⁰ Mercy kisses all his godly lovers,
  from one generation to the next.ᶜ
⁵¹ Mighty power flows from him
  to scatter all those who walk in pride.
⁵² Powerful princes he tears from their thrones
  and he lifts up the lowly to take their place.
⁵³ Those who hunger for him will always be filled,ᵈ
  but the smug and self-satisfied he will send away empty.
⁵⁴ Because he can never forget to show mercy,
  he has helped his chosen servant, Israel,
⁵⁵ Keeping his promises to Abrahamᵉ
  and to his descendants forever."

⁵⁶ Before going home, Mary stayed with Elizabeth for about three months.ᶠ

The Birth of the Prophet John

⁵⁷ When Elizabeth's pregnancy was full term, she gave birth to a son. ⁵⁸ All her family, friends, and neighbors heard about it, and they too were overjoyed, for they realized that the Lord had showered such wonderful mercy upon her.

⁵⁹ When the baby was eight days old, according to their custom, all the family and friends came together for the circumcision ceremony.ᵍ Everyone was convinced that the parents would name the baby Zechariah, after his father. ⁶⁰ But Elizabeth spoke up and said, "No, he has to be named John!"

ᵃ 1:47 Or "Savior." The first recorded person to call Jesus Savior was his mother, Mary. She rejoices in God not simply as her Creator, but as Life Giver and Savior.

ᵇ 1:48 The Aramaic text is "He set his gaze upon the willingness of his mother."

ᶜ 1:50 Mary is quoting Pss. 103:17 and 111:9.

ᵈ 1:53 Mary is quoting Ps. 107:9.

ᵉ 1:55 Mary understood by revelation that the Christ child would fulfill the promises of mercy that God gave to Abraham. See Gen. 22:16–18.

ᶠ 1:56 The cultural practice of the Hebrews was for the mother to do nothing but rest during the first three months of pregnancy.

ᵍ 1:59 This ceremony was an important time of celebration in Jewish culture, for another child was born under the covenant of God with Israel. See Gen. 17:4–14; Lev. 12:1–3.

⁶¹ "What?" they exclaimed. "No one in your family line has that name!"

⁶² So they gestured to the baby's father to ask what to name the child. ⁶³ After motioning for a writing tablet, in amazement of all, he wrote, "His name is John." ᵃ

⁶⁴ Instantly Zechariah could speak again. And his first words were praises to the Lord.

⁶⁵ The fear of God then fell on the people of their village, and the news of this astounding event traveled throughout the hill country of Judea. Everyone was in awe over it! ⁶⁶ All who heard this news were astonished and wondered, "If a miracle brought his birth, what on earth will this child become? Clearly, God's presence is upon this child in a powerful way!"

Zechariah's Prophecy

⁶⁷ Then Zechariah was filled to overflowing with the Holy Spirit and he prophesied, saying:

⁶⁸ "Praise be to the exalted Lord God of Israel,
for he has seen us through eyes of grace,
and he comes as our Hero-God to set us free!
⁶⁹ He appears to us as a mighty Savior,
a trumpet of redemption ᵇ from the house of David, his servant,
⁷⁰ Just as he promised long ago
by the words of his holy prophets.
⁷¹ They prophesied he would come one day and save us
from every one of our enemies
and from the power of those who hate us. ᶜ
⁷² Now he has shown us the mercy promised to our ancestors,
for he has remembered his holy covenant. ᵈ
⁷³⁻⁷⁵ He has rescued us from the power of our enemies!
This fulfills the sacred oath he made with our father Abraham.
Now we can boldly worship ᵉ God with holy lives,
living in purity as priests ᶠ in his presence every day!
⁷⁶ And to you I prophesy, my little son,
you will be known as the prophet of the glorious God.

ᵃ 1:63 The name John means "God's gift" or "God is gracious."

ᵇ 1:69 Literal translation of the Aramaic. The Hebrew is "a horn of salvation," which signifies strength and fighting power.

ᶜ 1:71 Zechariah is quoting from Ps. 106:10.

ᵈ 1:72 There is amazing Hebrew poetry contained in this passage. The names of John, Zechariah, and Elizabeth are all found in this verse. "He has shown us mercy" or "God's gracious gift" is found in the name John. "He has remembered" is the name Zechariah. "His holy covenant" is the name Elizabeth.

ᵉ 1:73–75 Or "serve."

ᶠ 1:73–75 The word translated as "purity" here is a Hebraic homonym for "priesthood."

> For you will be a forerunner,
> going before the face of the Master, Yahweh, [a]
> to prepare hearts to embrace his ways. [b]
> [77] You will preach to his people the revelation of salvation life,
> the cancellation of all our sins, *to bring us back to God.*
> [78] The splendor light of heaven's glorious sunrise [c]
> is about to break upon us in holy visitation,
> all because the merciful heart of our God is so very tender.
> [79] The word from heaven will come to us [d]
> with dazzling light to shine upon those
> who live in darkness, near death's dark shadow. [e]
> And he will illuminate the path that leads to the way of peace."

[80] Afterward, their son grew up and was strengthened by the Holy Spirit [f] and he grew in his love for God. John chose to live in the lonely wilderness until the day came when he was to be displayed publicly to Israel.

The Birth of Jesus

2 [1-2] During those days, the Roman emperor, Caesar Augustus, [g] ordered that the first census be taken throughout his empire. (Quirinius was the governor of Syria at that time.) [3] Everyone had to travel to his or her hometown to complete the mandatory census. [4-5] So Joseph and his fiancé, Mary, left Nazareth, [h] a village in Galilee, and journeyed to their hometown in Judea, to the village of Bethlehem, [i] King David's ancient home. They were required to register

---

a 1:76 Literal translation of the Aramaic.

b 1:76 Zechariah quotes from Mal. 3:1.

c 1:78 Some believe this is a quote from Mal. 4:2. Jesus the Savior is the dawning light of a new day to this dark world. This "sunrise" is the appearing of Jesus, the Messiah.

d 1:79 Or "manifestation from heaven" as translated from the Aramaic.

e 1:79 Zechariah is quoting from Isa. 9:2 and 59:8.

f 1:80 Both of John's parents were full of the Holy Spirit (vv. 41, 67). John was raised in a Spirit-filled home.

g 2:1–2 It is ironic that the Roman emperors viewed themselves as "gods" while the little baby born in a feeding trough was the true God incarnate.

h 2:4–5 "Nazareth" is taken from a Hebrew word for "branch" (Isa. 11:1).

i 2:4–5 The distance from Nazareth to Bethlehem is about sixty-five miles (105 kilometers) and would have taken a number of days for them to arrive. Bethlehem, or *Byt-lehem*, means "house of bread," the prophesied birthplace of Messiah. However, the Hebrew word *lechem* is a homonym for "fighter" or "warrior." Jesus was born in "the house of fighters." This is the city of David, one of the greatest fighters in the entire Bible. Perhaps this is why the people of Jesus' day expected him to fight the Romans and free their land from foreign occupation. Jesus fulfilled both aspects of the meaning of Bethlehem in Gethsemane and on the cross, where he fought the "Goliath" of our souls and won, becoming bread for the world. God controls all events, proven by the prophecy that Jesus would be born in Bethlehem, even though his parents were living in Nazareth. See Mic. 5:2.

there, since they were both direct descendants of David. Mary was pregnant and nearly ready to give birth.

⁶⁻⁷ When they arrived in Bethlehem, Mary went into labor, and there she gave birth to her firstborn son. After wrapping the newborn baby in strips of cloth, they laid him in a feeding trough since there was no available space in any upper room in the village. ᵃ

An Angelic Encounter

⁸ That night, in a field ᵇ near Bethlehem, there were shepherds watching over their flocks. ⁹ Suddenly, an angel of the Lord appeared in radiant splendor before them, lighting up the field with the blazing glory of God, and the shepherds were terrified! ¹⁰ But the angel reassured them, saying, "Don't be afraid. For I have come to bring you good news, the most joyous news the world has ever heard! And it is for everyone everywhere! ¹¹ For today in Bethlehem ᶜ a rescuer was born for you. He is the Lord Yahweh, the Messiah. ᵈ ¹² You will recognize him by this miracle sign: You will find a baby wrapped in strips of cloth and lying in a feeding trough!" ᵉ

---

a 2:6–7 This is the Greek word *kataluma*. This is not an "inn" but simply the upstairs level of a home where guests would stay. It means there was no guest room available in Bethlehem for Mary to give birth. Since all of Joseph's and Mary's family also made the journey because of the census, every home of a relative would have been full. In that day Bethlehem was far too small of a village to have an actual inn, all the *katalumai* there were occupied. It is likely that Joseph and Mary had to sleep downstairs in the main room of a relative's house. The downstairs of a village home in that day was like an all-purpose room that served as a workshop during the day, and at night it was used to shelter frail animals, while the rest of the flock was left outdoors. The *kataluma* was not a full-fledged barn or stable, but it did contain a drinking trough or manger cut in the bedrock. This was the likely place where the baby Jesus was placed after his birth.

b 2:8 Many scholars believe that these could be the same fields where sacrificial flocks were kept for temple worship. How fitting that these shepherds would hear the announcement of the birth of the Lamb of God. Others believe these fields could have been near the field of Boaz, or the fields where David once watched over the flocks of his father, Jesse.

c 2:11 The Greek text says, "the city of David."

d 2:11 Translated literally from the Aramaic text. This is one of the most amazing statements found in the Gospels declaring the deity of Jesus Christ.

e 2:12 A baby lying in a feeding trough where animals were kept nearby, wrapped in strips of cloths, became a sign of the Man-Savior's life on earth. He entered the world as a lowly baby, and though he is the mighty God, he lived his life on earth in gentleness before all. The shepherds that night were possibly near Bethlehem at Migdal Eder, "the [watch] tower of the flock." This would fulfill both the prophecies of Mic. 5:2 and Mic. 4:8, which say, "to you it [he] will come, your dominion [kingdom] from old will arrive." It was at the lower floor of the watchtower (Migdal Eder) that the birthing of the Passover lambs would take place. Selected ewes that were about to give birth would be brought there. After the birth of the lambs, the priestly shepherds would wrap the lambs in cloth and lay them in a manger lined with soft hay to prevent them from hurting themselves, for Passover lambs must be unblemished with no bruise or broken bone. The miracle sign for these priestly shepherds would be a baby boy lying where the Passover lamb should be—in a manger, wrapped in strips of cloth. It was at the cradle of Jesus Christ that the kingdom from ancient times arrived on earth.

¹³ Then all at once, a vast number of glorious angels appeared, the very armies of heaven! And they all praised God, singing:

¹⁴ "Glory to God in the highest realms of heaven!
   For there is peace *a* and a good hope *b* given to the sons of men."

¹⁵ When the choir of angels disappeared back to heaven, the shepherds said to one another, "Let's go! Let's hurry and find this Word *c* that is born in Bethlehem and see for ourselves what the Lord has revealed to us." ¹⁶ So they ran into the village and found their way to Mary and Joseph. And there was the baby, lying in a feeding trough.

¹⁷ Upon seeing this miraculous sign, the shepherds recounted what had just happened. ¹⁸ Everyone who heard the shepherds' story was astonished by what they were told.

¹⁹ But Mary treasured all these things in her heart and often pondered what they meant.

²⁰ The shepherds returned to their flock, ecstatic over what had happened. They praised God and glorified him for all they had heard and seen for themselves, just like the angel had said.

Baby Jesus Dedicated in the Temple

²¹ On the day of the baby's circumcision ceremony, eight days after his birth, his parents gave him the name Jesus, the name prophesied by the angel before he was born. ²² After Mary's days of purification had ended, it was time for her to come to the temple with a sacrifice, according to the law of Moses after the birth of a son. *d* So Mary and Joseph took the baby Jesus to Jerusalem to be dedicated before the Lord. *e* ²³ For it is required in the law of the Lord, "Every firstborn male shall be a set-apart one for God." *f* ²⁴ And, to offer a prescribed sacrifice, "either a pair of turtledoves or two young pigeons." *g*

---

a 2:14 Luke's Gospel is the Gospel of peace. The four prominent sacrifices of the Old Testament are emphasized in the four Gospels. In Matthew we see the death of Christ in the figure of the trespass offering, in Mark the sin offering, in Luke the peace offering, and in John the burnt offering. The peace God gives us is emphasized in Luke's Gospel, which is why the angels announced peace and hope. On the day of his resurrection Jesus said, "Peace to you."

b 2:14 As translated from the Aramaic. The Greek is "good will."

c 2:15 Or "Manifestation" in the Aramaic text. The Greek is the word *rhema*.

d 2:22 This comes from Lev. 12:1–7. When a son was born, the mother went through a forty-day period of purification, and then she was to offer a sacrifice to complete the process.

e 2:22 The ark of the covenant, signifying the presence of God, had been absent from the temple since 586 BC, when the Babylonians destroyed the temple. Herod's temple had no ark of covenant until Jesus came into the temple that day. God returned to the temple when Mary carried her baby into its courts. What a dramatic moment! See Mal. 3:1–2.

f 2:23 Ex. 13:2, 12.

g 2:24 Because Joseph and Mary were rather poor, not yet having received the gifts brought by the wise men, they offered a pair of doves or pigeons instead of a lamb (Lev. 12:8). Mary

²⁵ As they came to the temple to fulfill this requirement, an *elderly* man was there waiting—a resident of Jerusalem whose name was Simeon. He was a very good man, a lover of God who kept himself pure, and the Spirit of holiness rested upon him. Simeon believed in the imminent appearing of the one called "The Refreshing of Israel." [a] ²⁶ For the Holy Spirit had revealed to him [b] that he would not see death before he saw the Messiah, the Anointed One of God. ²⁷ For this reason the Holy Spirit had moved him to be in the temple court at the very moment Jesus' parents entered to fulfill the requirement of the sacrifice.

²⁸ Simeon cradled the baby in his arms and praised God and prophesied, saying:

²⁹⁻³¹ "Lord and Master, I am your loving servant,
and now I can die content,
for your promise to me has been fulfilled.
With my own eyes I have seen your Word, [c]
the Savior you sent into the world.
³² He will be glory for your people Israel,
and the Revelation Light for all people everywhere!" [d]

³³ Mary and Joseph stood there, awestruck over what was being said about their baby.

Simeon then blessed them and prophesied over Mary, saying:

³⁴⁻³⁵ "A painful sword [e] will one day pierce your inner being,
for your child will be rejected by many in Israel.
And the destiny of your child is this:
he will be laid down [f] as a miracle sign
for the downfall [g] and resurrection of many in Israel.

---

offered a sin offering, showing her need of a Savior. Jesus would one day be offered as her true Lamb.

a   2:25 "The Refreshing of Israel" is a name for Jesus that can also be translated "The Encourager of Israel."

b   2:26 Simeon's name means "he who hears."

c   2:29–31 Or "Manifestation" in the Aramaic.

d   2:32 This is a fulfillment of many Old Testament prophecies, such as those found in Isa. 9:2; 40:5; 42:6; 49:6; 51:4; 60:1–3.

e   2:34–35 This is a unique Greek word used for "sword." Literally it means "a large broadsword."

f   2:34–35 The Greek word translated "appointed" actually means "to lie down." Jesus was laid in a tomb for us and rose again for us.

g   2:34–35 The Greek word translated "falling" can also be translated "downfall" or "destruction." Perhaps this was a prophecy of the cross of Jesus Christ, where many will rise or fall depending on what they do with Jesus' death and resurrection. We are all destined to be joined to him in his death and resurrection (Gal. 2:20). Every believer experiences both a "downfall" and a "resurrection."

Many will oppose this sign, but it will expose to all
the innermost thoughts of their hearts before God."

³⁶⁻³⁷ A prophetess named Anna was also in the temple court that day. She was from the Jewish tribe of Asher and the daughter of Phanuel.^a Anna was an aged widow who had been married only seven years before her husband passed away. After he died she chose to worship God in the temple continually. For the past eighty-four years^b she had been serving God with night-and-day prayer and fasting.

³⁸ While Simeon was prophesying over Mary and Joseph and the baby, Anna walked up to them and burst forth with a great chorus of praise to God for the child. And from that day forward she told everyone in Jerusalem who was waiting for their redemption that the anticipated Messiah had come!^c

³⁹ When Mary and Joseph had completed everything required of them by the law of Moses, they took Jesus and returned to their home^d in Nazareth in Galilee. ⁴⁰ The child grew more powerful in grace, for he was being filled with wisdom, and the favor of God was upon him.

At Age Twelve Jesus Visits the Temple

⁴¹ Every year Jesus' parents went to worship at Jerusalem during the Passover festival. ⁴² When Jesus turned twelve,^e his parents took him to Jerusalem to observe the Passover, as was their custom. ⁴³ A full day after they began their journey home, Joseph and Mary realized that Jesus was missing. ⁴⁴ They had assumed

---

a 2:36–37 The name Asher means "blessed." Phanuel means "the face of God."
b 2:36–37 Some Greek manuscripts make her age to be eighty-four. But the most reliable Greek and Aramaic texts state that she had been in the temple for eighty-four years. If so, this would make her at that time to be about one hundred six. God is faithful to those who wait in faith. Both Simeon and Anna were privileged to touch the Christ before they died in faith.
c 2:38 The Greek text literally says that Anna told everyone "who was looking for the redemption of Jerusalem." This is a figure of speech for the one who would come and set them free; i.e., the Messiah. What amazing prophetic words came through Simeon and Anna!
d 2:39 Luke omits their journey to Egypt to spare Jesus from the death decree of Herod. That information is given to us by Matthew. But none of the Gospels gives all the details of this period. Luke also has nothing about the visit of the wise men (Matt. 2:1–12), and Matthew tells nothing of the shepherds or of Simeon and Anna (Luke 2:8–28). All four Gospels supplement one another. A long period of time likely transpired between vv. 38 and 39.
e 2:42 At the age of twelve, a boy was called by the Jews a "son of the law." The number twelve is found often in the Bible and is linked to God's perfect administration and our human alignment to it. God's family of Israel was made up of twelve tribes, twelve sons of Jacob. Jesus chose twelve apostles, there are twelve months in the yearly cycle, and there are twenty-four elders around God's throne (twelve times two). Jesus coming into the house of God at age twelve points to the perfect alignment he had with his Father as the Apostle of our faith. See Heb. 3:1.

he was somewhere in their entourage, but he was nowhere to be found. After a frantic search among relatives and friends, [45] Mary and Joseph returned to Jerusalem to search for him.

[46] After being separated from him for three days, they finally found him in the temple, sitting among the Jewish teachers,[a] listening to them and asking questions. [47] All who heard Jesus speak were astounded at his intelligent understanding of all that was being discussed and at his wise answers to their questions.

[48] His parents were shocked to find him there, and Mary scolded him, saying, "Son, your father and I have searched for you everywhere! We have been worried sick over not finding you. Why would you do this to us?"

[49] Jesus said to them, "Why would you need to search for me? Didn't you know that it was necessary for me to be here in my Father's house, consumed with him?"[b]

[50] Mary and Joseph didn't fully understand what Jesus meant.

[51] Jesus went with them back home to Nazareth and was obedient to them. His mother[c] treasured Jesus' words deeply in her heart. [52] As Jesus grew, so did his wisdom and maturity. The favor of men increased upon his life, for he was loved greatly by God.[d]

John the Baptizer

3 [1-2] A powerful message from God came to John, Zechariah's son, when he was living out in the lonely wilderness.[e] This prophetic commission came to John during the fifteenth year of the reign of Emperor Tiberius, son of Caesar. Pontius Pilate was governor over Judea at that time. Antipas, son of Herod, was governor over Galilee, Herod's brother Philip was over the region of Ituraea and Trachonitis, and Lysanias was over Abilene.[f] This happened during the days of two high priests, Annas and Caiaphas.[g]

---

a 2:46 Or "rabbis."

b 2:49 The first recorded words of Jesus, when he was only twelve, are given to us here.

c 2:51 Mary was an amazing woman and should be honored as the mother of our Lord Jesus Christ. She was the only human being who was with Jesus all the way from his birth to his death. She is also mentioned in Acts 1:14.

d 2:52 We know virtually nothing about the eighteen years between ch. 2 and ch. 3, when Jesus went to the Jordan to be baptized by the prophet John. We knew he grew in favor with God and men. He served his earthly father in a carpenter's shop. It is likely that Joseph, Jesus' earthly father, died during this season of his life. This left Jesus with the responsibility as firstborn to provide for his family. Amazing mysteries surround this one who is too marvelous for words!

e 3:1-2 Some believe that John may have been a member of the Qumran community of Jewish Essenes, who lived in the wilderness because they viewed the Jewish religious system as corrupt.

f 3:1-2 A region west of Ituraea.

g 3:1-2 As the forerunner of Jesus Christ, the prophet John was a hinge of human history who forever changed the world. Luke carefully dates this event by giving us six markers. Historians have dated the reign of Tiberius Caesar as beginning in AD 14. The fifteenth year

[3]John went preaching and baptizing throughout the Jordan Valley. He persuaded people to turn away from their sins and turn to God[a] for the freedom of forgiveness.[b] [4]This was to fulfill what was written in the book of the prophet Isaiah:

"Listen! You will hear a thunderous voice in the lonely wilderness telling you to wake up and get your heart ready for the coming of the Lord Jehovah.[c] Every twisted thing in your lives must be made straight. [5-6]Every dark way must be brought to the light. Wrongs righted. Injustices removed. Every heart of pride will be humbled low before him. Every deception will be exposed and replaced by the truth so that everyone everywhere will be ready to see the Life of God!"[d, e]

[7]John kept preaching to the many crowds who came out to be baptized, "You are nothing but the offspring of poisonous snakes, full of deception! Have you been warned to repent before the coming wrath of God? [8]Then turn away from your sins, turn to God, and prove it by a changed life. Don't think for a moment that it's enough to simply be the favored descendants of Abraham. *That's not enough to save you.*[f] I'm telling you, God could make more sons of Abraham out of stones if he chose to!

[9]"Even now God's axe of judgment is poised to chop down your barren

of his reign would be AD 28–29. Regarding Annas and Caiaphas, never in Jewish history had there been two high priests. The priesthood was corrupt. Even though Caiaphas, Annas' son-in-law, was the high priest, Annas remained the real authoritative leader behind the scenes (John 18:13; Acts 4:6).

a   3:3 This is the definition of repentance, and it has two concepts. One is turning away from sin; the other is turning to God for freedom. They are linked together as one word, translated "repentance." The Aramaic word has the concept of returning to God, to unite with Unity.

b   3:3 John's message was revolutionary, for the religion of the day taught that forgiveness could only be found temporarily by offering sacrifices in the temple. John, an Essene, told the people that forgiveness of sin was a heart issue, not gained by an animal sacrifice offered in the corrupt religious system of the day. Repentance, breaking open the heart, is more important than gaining forgiveness by religious acts.

c   3:4 Translated from the Aramaic.

d   3:5–6 The Greek text, quoting from Isa. 40:3–5, is literally translated "Wake up and make lines for the Lord, make his side alleys straight. Every ravine will be filled, every mountain and hill shall be leveled, the crooked straightened, rough ways smoothed, and all flesh shall see the salvation of God." Every honest scholar recognizes this as more than a road construction project, implying a spiritual renewal in hearts.

e   3:5–6 Translated from the Aramaic. The Aramaic word translated "life" often refers to salvation.

f   3:8 God values reformation over ritual. John's ministry was to prepare people for the appearing of Jesus Christ through repentance and baptism. Repentance breaks open the heart and changes our attitudes toward God. Baptism was a burial of those who repented, preparing them for the germination of Christ coming to live within by the new birth.

tree right down to its roots! And every tree that does not produce good fruit will be leveled and thrown into the fire."

[10] The crowd kept asking him, "What then are we supposed to do?"

[11] John told them, "Give food to the hungry, clothe the poor, and bless the needy."[a]

[12] Even the despised tax collectors came to John to be baptized, and they asked him, "What are we to do to prove our hearts have changed?"

[13] "Be honest," he replied. "Don't demand more taxes than what you are required to collect."[b]

[14] "And us?" asked some soldiers.[c] "What about us?"

John answered them, "Be content with what you earn. Never extort money or terrify others by threats of violence or be guilty of accusing the innocent."

[15] During those days, everyone was gripped with messianic expectations, believing the Messiah could come at any moment, and many began to wonder if John might be the Christ.

[16] But John made it clear by telling them, "There is one coming who is mightier than I. He is supreme.[d] In fact, I'm not worthy of even being his slave.[e] I can only baptize you in this river, but he will baptize you into the Spirit of holiness and into his raging fire.[f] [17] He has in his hands a winnowing fork to clean up his threshing floor![g] He will separate the wheat from the chaff. The wheat he will gather into his barn, but he will burn the chaff in a fire that no one can ever put out!"

[18] John used many similar warnings as he preached the good news and prepared[h] the people. [19] He even publicly rebuked Antipas, son of Herod, the governor of Galilee, for the many wicked things he had done. He fearlessly reprimanded him for seducing and marrying his sister-in-law, Herodias.

[20] Adding to his many other sins, Herod had John seized and locked up in prison.

---

a 3:11 The Greek text is literally "The one with two tunics is to share with him who has none, and he who has food is to do likewise."

b 3:13 True repentance is tied to actions, a change of heart and deeds, not just words.

c 3:14 They were likely temple police.

d 3:16 The word translated "supreme" is found only in the Aramaic text. John was a true prophet who pointed others to the Supreme One. Before John came on the scene, there had not been a prophet in Israel for four hundred years.

e 3:16 Or "loose his sandal strap," which only a slave would do.

f 3:16 The Aramaic text reads "He will baptize you into the Spirit of the Holy One and in light." A baptism of light or fire would cleanse and change a life, giving new power to live for God and deal with every issue that hinders love and passion from burning in our hearts. It is the baptism of the Holy Spirit that is needed today.

g 3:17 The text is literally "a winnowing fork is in his hand." This was a small pitchfork used to separate the chaff from the grain.

h 3:18 Translated from the Aramaic text.

The Baptism of Jesus

²¹⁻²² One day Jesus came to be baptized ^a along with all the others. As he was consumed with the spirit of prayer, ^b the heavenly realm ripped open above him and the Holy Spirit descended from heaven in the visible, tangible form of a dove ^c and landed on him. Then God's audible voice was heard, saying, "My Son, you are my beloved one. ^d Through you I am fulfilled." ^e

The Ancestry of Jesus Christ

²³⁻³⁸ Jesus, assumed to be Joseph's son, was about thirty years old when he began his ministry. ^f Here are the names of Mary's ^g ancestors, from her father traced all the way back to Adam:

Eli, ^h Matthat, Levi, Melki, Jannai, Joseph, Mattathias, Amos, Nahum, Esli,

---

a 3:21–22 Jesus identified with sinners, even at his baptism. Although he had no sin, he chose to become one with sinners and was washed by John as a preview of what would happen when he became sin and was judged for our sins at the cross.

b 3:21–22 We read about Jesus praying eight times in Luke's Gospel. (1) At his baptism Jesus prayed and the heavens were opened, revealing his sonship. Jesus asked the Father to send the Holy Spirit to strengthen him for his wilderness temptations (3:21–23). (2) Jesus prayed in solitude, and miracles broke loose in his ministry (5:16–17). (3) Jesus prayed all night before he chose his twelve companions (6:12–16). (4) Jesus prayed for his apostles to receive the full revelation of who he is (9:18–22). (5) When Jesus was about to be glorified in splendor on the mountain, he prayed, and his face glowed with a flashing light (9:28–29). (6) Jesus prayed that he would be an example to every one of his disciples (11:1). (7) Jesus prayed for Peter's restoration and future ministry (22:31–32). (8) Jesus prayed in Gethsemane for strength and glory as the terrors of Calvary lay before him (22:41–46).

c 3:21–22 What a beautiful picture: a dove resting on a lamb. To have the power of the Spirit (dove), we need to have the nature of the Lamb (Jesus). Although Jesus had the Holy Spirit from his immaculate conception, at his baptism he received the abiding presence of the Holy Spirit to fulfill his ministry. God gives more and more of his Spirit to those who love him and obey him.

d 3:21–22 The heavenly voice confirms the identity of Jesus as Messiah. God quoted Ps. 2:7 and Isa. 42:1, both of which are considered as speaking of the Christ. God publicly stated that Jesus was the long-awaited and much-loved Son, the Christ. The Trinity is clearly seen in this passage: Jesus, the Holy Spirit, and the Father.

e 3:21–22 As translated from the Aramaic text. The Greek text states, "in whom I am greatly pleased." When the presence of the Holy Spirit came upon the Son of God, those around him heard the voice of the Father. We see from this a picture of the triune God, three in one.

f 3:23–38 Old Testament priests could not begin their ministry until they were thirty years old. The number thirty is the biblical number of maturity. Both Joseph and David were promoted to the place of honor when they were thirty.

g 3:23–38 Matthew gives us the genealogy of Jesus from Joseph's family, while some suggest Luke's genealogy is from Mary's side. Luke is the only Gospel writer who gives much attention to women. Neither Matthew nor Luke gives a complete genealogy.

h 3:23–38 Matthew identifies Joseph's father as Jacob (Matt. 1:16), while Luke says he was Eli's (Heli's) son (Luke 3:23). The ancient world often referred to a man's sons-in-law as his own sons. Thus it is possible that Eli was Mary's father and Joseph's father-in-law.

Naggai, Maath, Mattathias, Semein, Josech, Joda, Joanan, Rhesa, Zerubbabel, Shealtiel, Neri, Melchi, Addi, Cosam, Elmadam, Er, Joshua, Eliezer, Jorim, Matthat, Levi, Simeon, Judah, Joseph, Jonam, Eliakim, Melea, Menna, Mattatha, Nathan, David, Jesse, Obed, Boaz, Salmon, Nahshon, Amminadab, Admin, Arni, Hezron, Perez, Judah, Jacob, Isaac, Abraham, Terah, Nahor, Serug, Reu, Peleg, Eber, Shelah, Kenan, Arphaxad, Shem, Noah, Lamech, Methuselah, Enoch, Jared, Mahalaleel, Cainan, Enos, Seth, and Adam, who was created by God. *a*

Jesus Tested in the Wilderness

4 [1-2] From the moment of his baptism, Jesus was overflowing with the Holy Spirit. He was taken by the Spirit from the Jordan into the lonely wilderness of Judea *b* to experience the ordeal of testing *c* by the accuser *d* for forty days. *e* He ate no food during this time and ended his forty-day fast very hungry. [3] It was then the devil said to him, "If you are really the Son of God, command this stone to turn into a loaf of bread for you."

[4] Jesus replied, "I will not! *f* For it is written in the Scriptures, *g* 'Life does not come only from eating bread but from God. Life flows from every revelation from his mouth.'" *h*

[5] The devil lifted Jesus high into the sky *i* and in a flash showed him all the kingdoms and regions of the world. [6-7] The devil then said to Jesus, "All of this, with all its power, authority, and splendor, is mine to give to whomever I wish. Just do one thing and you will have it all. Simply bow down to worship me and it will be yours! You will possess everything!"

[8] Jesus rebuked him and said, "Satan, get behind me! *j* For it is written

---

a 3:23–38 As translated from the Aramaic. The Greek text states, "the son of God."

b 4:1–2 The Holy Spirit's leading is not always into comfort and ease. The Spirit may lead us, as he did Jesus, into places where we will be proven, tested, and strengthened for our future ministry. After Jesus' greatest affirmation from heaven came a great time of testing.

c 4:1–2 The Greek word here means "to test with a sinister motive." This test was more than proving that Jesus could overcome this ordeal. It proved that Satan was defeated by Christ's appearing.

d 4:1–2 The words *accuser* and *devil* are used interchangeably in this translation.

e 4:1–2 Jesus' baptism and the forty days of wilderness temptations that followed evoke parallels with the historical narrative of the Hebrew exodus through the Red Sea and the forty years of wilderness testing.

f 4:4 Jesus refused to turn stones to bread, yet today he transforms the stony hearts of human beings and converts us into living bread to give to the nations.

g 4:4 Jesus, the living Word, is quoting from the written Word (Deut. 8:3). If the living Word used the written Word against the enemy's temptations, how much more do we need the revelation of what has been written so we can stand against all his snares?

h 4:4 This is implied by both the Greek and Aramaic texts. Although this last clause is missing in some Greek manuscripts, it is included in the Aramaic.

i 4:5 Implied, for the Greek text simply says, "took him up," without telling us where.

j 4:8 This is found in the majority of later manuscripts. See also Matt. 4:10.

in the Scriptures, 'Only one is worthy of your adoration. You will worship before the Lord your God and love him supremely.'" [a]

[9] Next, the devil took Jesus to Jerusalem and set him on the highest point of the temple and tempted him there, saying, "If you really are the Son of God, jump down in front of all the people. [10-11] For it is written in the Scriptures, 'God has given his angels instructions to protect you from harm. For the hands of angels will hold you up and keep you from hurting even one foot on a stone.'" [b]

[12] Jesus replied, "It is also written in the Scriptures, 'How dare you provoke the Lord your God!'" [c]

[13] That finished the devil's harassment for the time being. So he stood off at a distance, retreating until the time came to return and tempt Jesus again.

[14] Then Jesus, armed with the Holy Spirit's power, returned to Galilee, and his fame spread throughout the region. [15] He taught in the synagogues [d] and they glorified him. [e]

[16-17] When he came to Nazareth, [f] where he had been raised, he went into the synagogue, as he always did on the Sabbath day. When Jesus came to the front to read the Scriptures, [g] they handed him the scroll of the prophet Isaiah. He unrolled the scroll and read where it is written, [18-19] "The Spirit of the Lord is upon me, and he has anointed me to be hope [h] for the poor, freedom for the brokenhearted, and new eyes [i] for the blind, and to preach to prisoners, [j] 'You are set free!' I have come to share the message of Jubilee, [k] for the time of God's great acceptance [l] has begun." [m]

[20] After he read this he rolled up the scroll, handed it back to the minister, and sat down. Everyone stared at Jesus, wondering what he was about to say. [21] Then he added, "These Scriptures came true today in front of you."

---

a 4:8 This is taken from Deut. 6:13; 10:20.

b 4:10–11 The devil is quoting from Ps. 91:11–12, but he misapplies it.

c 4:12 Jesus was not deceived. He quotes here from Deut. 6:16.

d 4:15 This was the meeting places for the Jewish people. Every village that had at least ten families would erect a meeting house where they would come and hear visiting teachers expound the Scriptures.

e 4:15 The Aramaic can be translated, "and he offered everyone glory!"

f 4:16–17 This is Netzaret, which is taken from the Hebrew word for "branch" or "sprout."

g 4:16–17 It was the custom of the day to read the Scriptures in Hebrew and then paraphrase it into Aramaic, the common language of that day.

h 4:18–19 Or "good news."

i 4:18–19 The Greek word is translated "looking up to heaven" in Mark 6:41.

j 4:18–19 Literally "prisoners of war."

k 4:18–19 See Lev. 25:8–17; Isa. 58:6; 61:1–2. The Isaiah passage is associated with the proclamation of the Year of Jubilee. The Greek word used here implies a cycle of time. Jesus clearly defined his mission by reading these words of the prophet Isaiah.

l 4:18–19 Or "favor." This phrase can be translated "the years when God will accept man."

m 4:18–19 This is quoted from Isa. 61:1.

²² Everyone was impressed by how well Jesus spoke, in awe of the beautiful words of grace that came from his lips. *But they were surprised at his presumption to speak as a prophet,* so they said among themselves, *"Who does he think he is?* ª This is Joseph's son, *who grew up here in Nazareth."*

²³ Jesus said to them, "I suppose you'll quote me the proverb, 'Doctor, go and heal yourself before you try to heal others.' And you'll say, 'Work the miracles here in your hometown that we heard you did in Capernaum.' ²⁴ But let me tell you, no prophet is welcomed or honored in his own hometown.

²⁵ "Isn't it true that there were many widows in the land of Israel during the days of the prophet Elijah when he locked up the heavens for three and a half years and brought a devastating famine over all the land? ²⁶ But he wasn't sent to any of the widows living in that region. Instead, he was sent to a foreign place, to a widow in Zarephath of Sidon. ᵇ ²⁷ Or have you not considered that the prophet Elisha healed only Naaman, ᶜ the Syrian, rather than one of the many Jewish lepers living in the land?"

²⁸ When everyone present heard those words, they erupted with furious rage. ᵈ ²⁹ They mobbed Jesus and threw him out of the city, dragging him to the edge of the cliff on the hill on which the city had been built, ready to hurl him off. ³⁰ But he walked right through the crowd, leaving them all stunned. ᵉ

Jesus Confronts a Demonized Man

³¹ Jesus went to Capernaum ᶠ in Galilee and taught the people on the Sabbath day. ³² His teachings stunned and dazed ᵍ them, for he spoke with penetrating words that manifested great authority.

³³ In the congregation there was a demonized man, who screamed out

---

a 4:22 This is the inferred meaning of their criticism of Jesus. His true Father was not Joseph, but Yahweh.

b 4:26 Zarephath means "the place of refining." Sidon means "fishery" and was a Phoenician seaport city.

c 4:27 Both the Aramaic and Greek texts have "Naaman the Aramean" or "descendant of Aram." The Arameans inhabited what is now Syria. Naaman means "pleasantness."

d 4:28 Jesus' listeners got the point of his sermon. His statements implied that he would take his miracle ministry to non-Jewish people. Jubilee had come, not only for them, but for those they hated. This infuriated them enough to want to kill Jesus.

e 4:30 The Greek text clearly implies it was a supernatural event. After hearing Jesus' first sermon, they wanted to throw him off a cliff!

f 4:31 Capernaum means "the village of Nahum" and Nahum means "comforted." Jesus did many miracles and made his Galilean base of ministry in "the village of the comforted."

g 4:32 The Greek word used here, *ekplesso,* is a strong verb that means "struck with amazement," "astonished," "panic stricken," "shocked" or "something that takes your breath away" (like being hit with a blow), or "to expel," "to drive out." Jesus spoke with such glory and power emanating from him that his words were like thunderbolts into their hearts. May we hear his words in the same way today.

with a loud voice, ³⁴ "Hey, you! Go away and leave us alone. I know who you are. You're Jesus of Nazareth, God's holy one. Why are you coming to meddle with us? You have come to destroy us already!" [a]

³⁵ Just then the demon hurled the man down on the floor in front of them all. But Jesus rebuked the demon, "Be quiet and come out of him!" And the demon came out of him without causing him any harm.

³⁶ Great astonishment swept over the people, and they said among themselves, "What kind of man is this who has such power and authority? With a mere word he commands demons to come out and they obey him!" ³⁷ The reports about Jesus spread like wildfire throughout every community in the surrounding region.

Jesus Heals Many

³⁸ After leaving the meeting that day, Jesus went into Simon's house, where Simon's mother-in-law was sick with a high fever. The disciples begged Jesus to help her. ³⁹ Jesus stood over her and rebuked the fever, [b] and she was healed instantly. Then she got up and began to serve them.

⁴⁰ At sunset, [c] the people brought all those who were sick to Jesus to be healed. Jesus laid his hands on them one by one, and they were all healed of different ailments and sicknesses.

⁴¹ Demons also came out of many of them. The demons knew that Jesus was the Anointed One, so they shouted while coming out, "You are the Messiah, the Son of El Shaddai!" [d] But Jesus rebuked them and commanded them to be silent.

⁴² At daybreak the next morning, the crowds came and searched everywhere for him, but Jesus had already left to go to a secluded place. When they finally found him, they held him tightly, begging him to stay with them in Capernaum. ⁴³ But Jesus said, "Don't you know there are other places I must go to and offer them the hope found in God's kingdom realm? [e] This is what I have been sent to do."

⁴⁴ Jesus continued to travel and preach in the synagogues throughout the land.

---

a 4:34 This is an assertive statement made by the demon to Jesus.

b 4:39 Five times in this chapter Jesus corrects and rebukes various things and persons. He rebuked Satan (v. 8) and the unbelieving people in his hometown (vv. 23–27). Twice he rebuked demons (vv. 35 and 41). And in this verse he rebukes fever.

c 4:40 People came before dark. The Sabbath, which was to be a day of rest for every Jew, began at sunset on Friday and ended at sunset on Saturday.

d 4:41 Or "Son of God." *El Shaddai* is used to emphasize the Hebraic word for God Almighty. See footnote on Ps. 91:1.

e 4:43 The gospel includes the hope of an eternal kingdom. Conversion is not found in believing a historical event but is found in the revelation of God's kingdom realm that changes our hearts.

The Miracle Catch of Fish

5 On one occasion, Jesus was preaching to the crowds on the shore of Lake Galilee. [a] There was a vast multitude of people pushing to get close to Jesus to hear the word of God. [2] He noticed two fishing boats at the water's edge, with the fishermen nearby, rinsing their nets. [3] Jesus climbed into the boat belonging to Simon Peter and asked him, **"Let me use your boat. Push it off a short distance away from the shore so I can speak to the crowds."**

[4] Jesus sat down and taught the people from the boat. When he had finished, he said to Peter, **"Now row out to deep water to cast your nets and you will have a great catch."**

[5] "Master," Peter replied, "we've just come back from fishing all night and didn't catch a thing. But if you insist, we'll go out again and let down our nets because of your word."

[6] When they pulled up their nets, they were shocked to see a huge catch of fish, so much that their nets were ready to burst! [7] They waved to their business partners in the other boat for help. They ended up completely filling both boats with fish until their boats began to sink! [b]

[8] When Simon Peter saw this *astonishing miracle*, he knelt at Jesus' feet and begged him, "Go away from me, Master, for I am a sinful man!"

[9-10] Simon Peter and the other fishermen—including his fishing partners, Jacob [c] and John, the sons of Zebedee—were awestruck over the miracle catch of fish.

Jesus answered, **"Do not yield to your fear, Simon Peter. From now on you will catch men for salvation!"** [d]

[11] After pulling their boats to the shore, they left everything behind and followed Jesus. [e]

Jesus, the Healer

[12] One day, while Jesus was ministering in a certain city, he came upon a man covered with leprous sores. When the man recognized Jesus, he fell on his face

---

a 5:1 Or "Gennesaret," which is known as Lake Galilee.

b 5:7 It has been estimated that this was a catch of nearly one ton of fish, what was normally caught in two weeks. The miracle is even greater when we consider that fishing was normally only done at night.

c 5:9–10 Or "James." Both Greek and Aramaic leave the Hebrew name as it is, Jacob. This translation will use Jacob throughout.

d 5:9–10 Translated literally from the Aramaic text. The Greek word *zoogreo* is a compound word of *zoos* (meaning "life") and *agreuo* (meaning "to catch"). Fishermen catch fish that die and are consumed, but Peter was to catch men and give them life and freedom.

e 5:11 When you leave everything behind to follow Jesus, you are actually in the position to have it all. Jesus will be your everything. Later, Peter will once again leave his nets behind to swim to Jesus. See John 21:4–8.

at Jesus' feet and begged to be healed, saying, "If you are only willing, you could completely heal me."

[13-14] Jesus reached out and touched him[a] and said, "Of course I am willing to heal you, and now you will be healed." Instantly the leprous sores were healed and his skin became smooth.

Jesus said, "Tell no one what has happened, but go to the priest and show him you've been healed. And to show that you are purified, make an offering for your cleansing, just as Moses commanded. You will become a living testimony to them!"

[15] After this miracle the news about Jesus spread even farther. Massive crowds continually gathered to hear him speak and to be healed from their illnesses. [16] But Jesus often slipped away from them and went into the wilderness to pray.

[17] One day many Jewish religious leaders, known as Pharisees[b] along with many religious scholars came from every village of Galilee, throughout Judea, and even from Jerusalem to hear Jesus teach. And the power of the Lord God surged through him to instantly heal.

[18] Some men came to Jesus, carrying a paraplegic man on a stretcher. They attempted to bring him in past the crowd to set him down in front of Jesus. [19] But because there were so many people crowding the door, they had no way to bring him inside. So they crawled onto the roof, dug their way through the roof tiles, and lowered the man, stretcher and all, into the middle of the crowd, right in front of Jesus.

[20] Seeing the demonstration of their faith, Jesus said to the paraplegic man, "My friend, your sins are forgiven!"

[21] The Jewish religious leaders and the religious scholars[c] whispered objections among themselves. "Who does this man think he is to speak such blasphemy? Only God can forgive sins. Does he think he is God?"

[22-23] Jesus, knowing their thoughts, said to them, "Why do you argue in your hearts over what I do and think that it is blasphemy for me to say his sins are forgiven? Let me ask you, which is easier to prove: when I say, 'Your sins are forgiven,' or when I say, 'Stand up, carry your stretcher, and walk'?"

Jesus turned to the paraplegic man and said, [24] "To prove to you all that I, the Son of Man,[d] have the lawful authority on earth to forgive sins, I say to you now, stand up! Carry your stretcher and go on home, for you are healed."

---

a 5:13–14 For the religious Jew, touching a leper was forbidden because of the contamination. Jesus was not defiled in touching the leper; rather, the leper was healed.

b 5:17 "Pharisees" means "separated ones."

c 5:21 Or "scribes." They were the experts in the law of Moses.

d 5:24 This is the title Jesus uses for himself more than any other, especially in Luke. This refers to the vision of Daniel when he saw the Ancient of Days, and walking before the Ancient of Days was one like the Son of Man who would be given the right to judge

²⁵ In an instant, the man rose right before their eyes. He stood, picked up his stretcher, and went home, giving God all the glory with every step he took.

²⁶ The people were seized with astonishment and dumbfounded over what they had just witnessed. And they all praised God, remarking over and over, "Incredible! What an unbelievable miracle ᵃ we've seen today!"

Jesus Calls Matthew to Follow Him

²⁷ Afterward, Jesus went out and looked for a man named Matthew. ᵇ He found him sitting at his tax booth, for he was a tax collector. Jesus said to him, "**Be my disciple and follow me.**" ²⁸ That very moment, Matthew got up, left everything behind, and followed him.

²⁹⁻³⁰ Matthew wanted to throw a banquet to honor Jesus. So he invited Jesus to his home for dinner, along with many tax collectors and other notable sinners. While they were all sitting together at the table, the Jewish religious leaders and experts of the law complained to Jesus' disciples, "Why would you defile yourselves by eating and drinking with tax collectors and sinners? *Doesn't Jesus know it's wrong to do that?*"

³¹ Jesus overheard their complaining and said, "**Who goes to the doctor for a cure? Those who are well or those who are sick?** ᶜ ³² **I have not come to call the 'righteous,' but to call those who fail to measure up and bring them to repentance.**"

A Question about Fasting

³³ Jesus' critics questioned him. "John the prophet is known for leading his disciples to frequently fast and pray. As the religious leaders of the land, we do the same. Why do you and your disciples spend most of your time feasting at banquets?" ᵈ

³⁴ Jesus replied, "**Should you make the sons of the bridal chamber fast while celebrating with the Bridegroom? ³⁵ But when the Bridegroom is taken away from them, then you will see them fasting.**"

³⁶ And he gave them this illustration: "**No one rips up a new garment to make patches for an old, worn-out one. If you tear up the new to make a patch for the old, it will not match the old garment. ³⁷ And who pours new wine into an old wineskin? If someone did, the old wineskin would burst and**

---

the world. Calling himself the Son of Man was Jesus' claim to heavenly authority. It was more of an exalted and heavenly concept than being a human, the "son of a man." See Dan. 7:13; Matt. 16:13–20.

a 5:26 Or "things we never expected," or "paradox."

b 5:27 The Greek text is "Levi," another name for Matthew.

c 5:31 The word used here is the Greek word for "evil." Sickness is a form of evil in God's eyes. Jesus came to heal the "evil" or sicknesses of earth.

d 5:33 It is likely that Matthew held his banquet on one of the Jewish fast days.

the new wine would be lost. [38] New wine must always be poured into new wineskins. [a] [39] Yet you say, 'The old ways are better,' and you refuse to even taste the new that I bring."

Jesus and Religious Traditions

6 One Sabbath day, Jesus and his disciples were walking through a field of ripe wheat. His disciples plucked some heads of grain and rubbed the husks off with their hands and ate it. [2] This infuriated some of the Jewish religious leaders. They said to Jesus, "Why are you allowing your disciples to harvest grain on the Sabbath day? Don't you know it's not permissible according to the law?"

[3] Jesus replied, "Haven't you read the Scriptures? Haven't you read what King David did when he was hungry? [4] He entered the sanctuary of God, took the bread of God's presence right off the sacred table, and shared it with his men. [b] It was only lawful for the priests to eat the bread of God's presence. [5] You need to know that the Son of Man is no slave to the Sabbath day, for I am master over the Sabbath."

[6-7] On another Sabbath day, Jesus was teaching in the synagogue. In the room with him was a man with a deformed right hand. Everyone watched Jesus closely, especially the Jewish religious leaders and the religious scholars, to see if Jesus would heal on a Sabbath day, for they were eager to find a reason to accuse him of breaking the Jewish laws.

[8] Jesus, knowing their every thought, said to the man with the deformed hand, "Come and stand here in the middle of the room." So he got up and came forward.

[9] Jesus said to all who were there, "Let me ask you a question. Which is better: to heal or to do harm on the Sabbath day? I have come to save a life, but you have come to find a life to destroy." [c]

[10] One by one Jesus looked into the eyes of each person in the room. Then he said to the man, "Stretch out your arm and open your hand!"

With everyone watching intently, he stretched out his arm, and his hand was completely healed!

[11] The room erupted with bitter rage because of this Sabbath-day healing. And from that moment on, the religious leaders plotted among themselves about how they might harm Jesus.

---

a 5:38 Christ is our new garment (righteousness) and our new wine that is poured into a new wineskin (our new life and divine nature). Many today are trying to patch up their old garments (self-righteousness), hoping their old lives can hold the new wine of the Spirit.

b 6:4 This incident is found in 1 Sam. 21:1–6. Jesus referred to this story to prove to the Pharisees that they were hypocrites who were willing to overlook David's "violation" of the Sabbath but not Jesus' supposed "violation."

c 6:9 Jesus knew there were some present who wanted to "destroy" his life and would soon crucify him. He came to heal; they came to kill. They were the real Sabbath breakers.

Jesus Chooses Twelve Apostles

[12] After this, Jesus went up into the high hills to spend the whole night in prayer to God. [a] [13] At daybreak he called together all of his followers and selected twelve from among them, and he appointed them to be his apostles. [b]

[14-16] Here are their names: Simon, whom he named Peter; Andrew, Peter's brother; Jacob; [c] John; Philip; Bartholomew; [d] Matthew; Thomas; Jacob the son of Alpheus; Simon, known as a fiery political zealot; Judah [e] the son of Jacob; and Judas the locksmith, [f] who later betrayed Jesus.

[17] Jesus and his apostles came down from the hillside to a level field, where a large number of his disciples waited, along with a massive crowd of people who had gathered from all over Judea, Jerusalem, and the coastal district of Tyre and Sidon. [g] [18] They had all come to listen to the Manifestation so that they could be healed of their diseases [h] and be set free from the demonic powers that tormented them. [19] The entire crowd eagerly tried to come near Jesus so they could touch him and be healed, because a tangible supernatural power emanated from him, healing all who came close to him.

Jesus Taught Them What Matters Most

[20] Looking intently at his followers, Jesus began his sermon. "How enriched [i] you become when you are poor, [j] for you will experience the reality of God's kingdom realm.

[21] "How filled you become when you are consumed with hunger and desire, for you will be completely satisfied.

---

a 6:12 This was the pattern of Jesus in the Gospel accounts. Before he made important decisions and before great events in his life, he sought the Father. Once he saw what the Father wanted, Jesus obeyed as the perfect Son. See John 5:19.

b 6:13 Apostle means "ambassador," "missionary," or "sent one." The apostles were all different in their personalities and came from different backgrounds. The people Jesus chooses today don't all look, act, or sound alike. The first ministry Jesus established was the apostolic. See 1 Cor. 12:28; Eph. 4:11.

c 6:14–16 Or "James." Both Greek and Aramaic leave the Hebrew name as it is, Jacob. This translation will use Jacob, throughout.

d 6:14–16 Many scholars believe that Bartholomew was the Nathaniel mentioned in John 1:45–46.

e 6:14–16 He is also called Thaddeus, as mentioned in Matt. 10:3 and Mark 3:18.

f 6:14–16 The name Judas is actually Judah. Iscariot is not his last name, but could be taken from the name of the town, Kerioth, twelve miles south of Hebron. More plausibly, it is from a Hebrew word meaning "lock": Judah the locksmith. Most likely he was chosen to lock the collection bag, which means he had the key and could pilfer the funds at will. Sadly, he wanted to lock up Jesus and control him for his own ends.

g 6:17 The non-Jewish people flocked to hear Jesus, and he healed them all.

h 6:18 This is the literal translation of the Aramaic text.

i 6:20 Or "blessed." The Aramaic word for "blessed" can also be translated "ripe."

j 6:20 The Aramaic word for "poor" is *miskeneh*, which means "more poverty stricken." It can also mean "meek," "humble" or "those who are poor in pride."

"How content you become when you weep *with complete brokenness,* for you will laugh with unrestrained joy.

²² "How favored you become when you are hated, excommunicated, or slandered, or when your name is spoken of as evil because of your love for me, the Son of Man.

²³ "I promise you that as you experience these things, you will celebrate and dance with overflowing joy. And the heavenly reward of your faith will be abundant, because you are being treated the same way as your forefathers the prophets.

²⁴ "But what sorrows await those of you who are rich in this life only. For you have already received all the comfort you'll ever get.

²⁵ "What sorrows await those of you who are complete and content with yourselves. For hunger and emptiness will come to you.

"What sorrows await those of you who laugh now, having received all your joy in this life only. For grief and wailing will come to you.

²⁶ "What sorrows await those of you who are always honored and lauded by others. For that's how your forefathers treated every other false prophet."

Love Your Enemies

²⁷ "But if you will listen, I say to you, love your enemies and do something wonderful ᵃ for them in return for their hatred. ²⁸ When someone curses you, bless that person in return. When you are mistreated and harassed by others, accept it as your mission to pray for them. ²⁹ To those who despise you, continue to serve them and minister to them. ᵇ If someone takes away your coat, give him as a gift your shirt as well. ³⁰ When someone comes to beg from you, give to that person what you have. When things are wrongly taken from you, do not demand they be given back. ³¹ However you wish to be treated by others is how you should treat everyone else.

³² "Are you really showing true love by only loving those who love you back? Even those who don't know God will do that. ³³ Are you really showing compassion when you do good deeds only to those who do good deeds to you? Even those who don't know God will do that.

³⁴ "If you lend money only to those you know will repay you, what credit is that to your character? Even those who don't know God do that. ³⁵ But love your enemies and continue to treat them well. When you lend money, don't despair ᶜ if you are never paid back, for it is not lost. You will receive a rich reward and you will be known as true children of the Most High God, having

---

a 6:27 As translated from the Aramaic text.

b 6:29 As literally translated from the Aramaic text. The Greek text states, "If someone strikes you on one side of your jaw, offer the other side too."

c 6:35 The Aramaic is literally "Do not cut off the hope of man."

his same nature. For your Father is famous for his kindness to heal[a] even the thankless and cruel. [36] Show mercy and compassion for others, just as your heavenly Father overflows with mercy and compassion for all."

Judging Others

[37] Jesus said, "Forsake the habit of criticizing and judging others, and then you will not be criticized and judged in return. Don't look at others and pronounce them guilty, and you will not experience guilty accusations yourself. Forgive over and over and you will be forgiven over and over. [38] Give generously and generous gifts will be given back to you, shaken down to make room for more. Abundant gifts will pour out upon you with such an overflowing measure that it will run over the top! Your measurement of generosity becomes the measurement of your return."

[39] Jesus also quoted these proverbs: "What happens when a blind man pretends to guide another blind man? They both stumble into a ditch! [40] And how could the apprentice know more than his master, for only after he is fully qualified will he be at that level. [41] Why do you focus on the flaw in someone else's life and fail to notice the glaring flaws of your own life?[b] [42] How could you say to your friend, 'Here, let me show you where you're wrong,' when you are guilty of even more than he is? You are overly critical, splitting hairs and being a hypocrite! You must acknowledge your own blind spots and deal with them before you will be able to deal with the blind spot of your friend."[c]

The Fruit of Your Life

[43] "You'll never find choice fruit hanging on a bad, unhealthy tree. And rotten fruit doesn't hang on a good, healthy tree. [44] Every tree will be revealed by the quality of fruit that it produces. Figs or grapes will never be picked off thorn trees. [45] People are known in this same way. Out of the virtue stored in their hearts, good and upright people will produce good fruit. But out of the evil hidden in their hearts, evil ones will produce what is evil. For the overflow of what has been stored in your heart will be seen by your fruit and will be heard in your words.

[46] "What good does it do for you to say I am your Lord and Master if what I teach you is not put into practice? [47] Let me describe the one who truly follows me and does what I say. [48] He is like a man who chooses the right place to build a house and then lays a deep and secure foundation. When the

---

a 6:35 Literal translation of the Aramaic text.

b 6:41 Or "Why do you see a speck in your brother's eye but fail to see the beam of wood sticking out of your own eye?"

c 6:42 Or "You hypocrite, why don't you first remove the beam sticking out of your own eye? Then you can see clearly to remove the small speck out of your brother's eye." Jesus is teaching that our blind spots prevent us from accurately evaluating the needs of others.

storms and floods rage against that house, it continues to stand strong and unshaken through the tempest, for it has been wisely built on the right foundation. [49] But the one who has heard my teaching and does not obey it is like a man who builds a house without laying any foundation whatsoever. When the storms and floods rage against that house, it will immediately collapse and become a total loss. *Which of these two builders will you be?"* [a]

Jesus Heals

7 After Jesus finished giving revelation [b] to the people on the hillside, he went on to Capernaum. [2-3] There he found a Roman military captain who had a beloved servant he valued highly, and the servant was sick to the point of death. When the captain heard that Jesus was in the city, he sent some respected Jewish elders to plead with him to come and heal his dying servant. [4] So they came to Jesus and told him, "The Roman captain is a wonderful man. If anyone deserves to have a visit from you, it is him. Won't you please come to his home and heal his servant? [5] For he loves the Jewish people, and he even built our meeting hall for us."

[6-7] Jesus started off with them, but on his way there, he was stopped by friends of the captain, who gave this message: "Master, don't bother to come to me in person, for I am not good enough for you to enter my home. I'm not worthy enough to even come out to meet one like you. But if you would just release the manifestation of healing right where you are, I know that my young servant will be healed.

[8] "Unlike you, [c] I am just an ordinary man. Yet I understand the power of authority, *and I see that authority operating through you.* I have soldiers under me who obey my every command. I also have authorities over me whom I likewise obey. So Master, just speak the word and healing will flow."

[9] Jesus marveled at this. He turned around and said to the crowd who had followed him, "**Listen, everyone! Never have I found even one among the people of God a man like this who believes so strongly in me.**" [10] Jesus then spoke the healing word from a distance. [d] When the man's friends returned to the home, they found the servant completely healed and doing fine.

Jesus Raises the Dead

[11] Shortly afterward, Jesus left on a journey for the village of Nain, [e] with a massive crowd of people following him, along with his disciples. [12] As he

---

a 6:49 This last question is an important summary implied in the context.
b 7:1 Or "teaching." The Greek word used here is *rhema.*
c 7:8 The text implies that the Roman captain acknowledged that Jesus was more than a man.
d 7:10 Implicit in the miracle was that Jesus released the word of healing for the servant.
e 7:11 *Nain* means "pleasant." The Prince of Life was about to enter the gate of the city when death came out. There at the gates where life and death meet, life wins and death is defeated. Just outside of Jerusalem one day, death and life met again, and life won forevermore.

approached the village, he met a multitude of people in a funeral procession, who were mourning as they carried the body of a young man to the cemetery. The boy was his mother's only son and she was a widow. [13] When the Lord saw the grieving mother, his heart broke for her.[a] With great tenderness he said to her, "**Please don't cry.**" [14] Then he stepped up to the coffin and touched it. When the pallbearers came to a halt, Jesus said to the corpse, "**Young man, I say to you, arise and live!**"

[15] Immediately, the young man moved, sat up, and spoke to those nearby. Jesus presented the son to his mother, alive! [16] A tremendous sense of holy mystery swept over the crowd *as they witnessed this miracle of resurrection.* They shouted praises to God, saying, "God himself has visited us to bless his people! A great prophet has appeared among us!"

[17] The news of Jesus and this miracle raced throughout Judea and the entire surrounding region.

The Prophet John's Question

[18] John's disciples reported to him *in prison* [b] about all the wonderful miracles and the works Jesus was doing. [19] So John dispatched two of his disciples to go and inquire of Jesus. [20] When they came before the Master, they asked him, "Are you the coming Messiah we've been expecting, or are we to continue to look for someone else? John the prophet has sent us to you to seek your answer."

[21] Without answering,[c] Jesus turned to the crowd and healed many of their incurable diseases. His miracle power freed many from their suffering. He restored the gift of sight to the blind, and he drove out demonic spirits from those who were tormented.

[22] Only then did Jesus answer the question posed by John's disciples. "**Now go back and tell John what you have just seen and heard here today. The blind are now seeing. The crippled are now walking. Those who were lepers are now cured. Those who were deaf are now hearing. Those who were dead are now raised back to life. The poor and broken**[d] **are given the hope of salvation.**[e] [23] **And tell John these words: 'The blessing of heaven comes upon those who never lose their faith**[f] **in me no matter what happens.'**"

---

a 7:13 The Greek word *splanchnizomai* denotes the deepest level of compassion. There is no greater word in the Greek language to describe the depth of emotion Jesus felt for this widow over the loss of her son. *Splanchnizomai* is actually the word for "intestines." Jesus' emotions fully identified with her grief and he carried her sorrow.

b 7:18 See also Matt. 11:2–19; Luke 3:20.

c 7:21 Or "at that time."

d 7:22 This fulfills many Old Testament references to the coming of the Messiah, including Isa. 29:18–19; 35:5–6; 61:1.

e 7:22 Jesus is assuring John that the message he brings is life and salvation, not judgment and wrath.

f 7:23 The Greek text is literally "Blessed are those who are not offended over me."

²⁴ After John's messengers departed, Jesus spoke about John to the audience crowded around him, saying, "What kind of man did you expect to see out in the wilderness? Did you expect to see a man who would be easily influenced and shaken by the shifting opinions of others? ²⁵ Who did you really go there to see? Did you expect to see a man decked out in the splendid fashion of the day?ᵃ They are the ones who live in the lap of luxury, embracing the values of this world. ²⁶ Or did you discover a true prophet out in the lonely wilderness? Yes, John was a legitimate prophet. Even more than that, ²⁷ he was the fulfillment of this Scripture:

'See, I am sending my prophetic messengerᵇ
    who will go ahead of me
    and prepare hearts to receive me.'ᶜ

²⁸ "Throughout history there was never found a man as great as John the Baptizer. Yet those who now walk in God's kingdom realm, though they appear to be insignificant, will become even greater than he."

²⁹ When the common and disreputable people among the audience heard Jesus say this, they acknowledged that it was the truth, for they had already experienced John's baptism. ³⁰ But the hearts of the Jewish religious leaders and experts of the law had rejected the clear purpose of God by refusing to be baptized by John.

³¹ Jesus continued, saying, "How could I describe the people of this generation? Can't you see? ³² You're like children playing games on the playground, complaining to friends, 'You don't like it when we want to play Wedding. And you don't like it when we want to play Funeral. Why will you neither dance nor mourn?'ᵈ

³³ "When the prophet John came fasting and refused to drink wine, you said, 'He's crazy! There's a demon in him.' ³⁴ Yet when the Son of Man came and went to feasts and drank wine, you said, 'Look at this man! He is nothing but a glutton and a drunkard. He spends all his time with tax collectors and other notorious sinners.'

³⁵ "Nevertheless, I say to you, the wisdom of Godᵉ will be proven true by the expressions of godliness in everyone who follows me."

---

a 7:25 See Matt. 3:4.
b 7:27 Or "angel."
c 7:27 This is quoted from Mal. 3:1.
d 7:32 Christ and John the Baptist both offered people the "wedding," yet the Pharisees didn't want to dance. They both offered a funeral to the old, dead ways of religion, yet the Pharisees refused to attend. Grace offered them salvation, but they rejected it.
e 7:35 Or "Wisdom is vindicated by all her children." The Aramaic word used here is a homonym that mean either "children" or "good works" (expressions of godliness). This may explain why there is such a variation of the Greek texts.

Extravagant Worship

[36] Afterward, a Jewish religious leader named Simon[a] asked Jesus to his home for dinner. Jesus accepted the invitation. When he went to Simon's home, he took his place at the table.

[37] In the neighborhood there was an immoral woman of the streets, known to all to be a prostitute. When she heard about Jesus being in Simon's house, she took an exquisite flask made from alabaster,[b] filled it with the most expensive perfume, went right into the home of the Jewish religious leader, and knelt at the feet of Jesus in front of all the guests. [38] Broken and weeping, she covered his feet with the tears that fell from her face. She kept crying and drying his feet with her long hair. Over and over she kissed Jesus' feet. Then she opened her flask and anointed his feet[c] with her costly perfume as an act of worship.

[39] When Simon saw what was happening, he thought, "This man can't be a true prophet. If he were really a prophet, he would know what kind of sinful woman is touching him."[d]

[40] Jesus said, "Simon, I have a word for you."

"Go ahead, Teacher. I want to hear it," he answered.

[41] "It's a story about two men who were deeply in debt. One owed the bank one hundred thousand dollars,[e] and the other only owed ten thousand dollars. [42] When it was obvious that neither of them would be able to repay their debts, the kind banker graciously wrote off the debts and forgave them all that they owed. Tell me, Simon, which of the two debtors would be the most thankful? Which one would love the banker most?"

[43] Simon answered, "I suppose it would be the one with the greatest debt forgiven."

"You're right," Jesus agreed. [44] Then he spoke to Simon about the woman still weeping at his feet.

"Don't you see this woman kneeling here? She is doing for me what you didn't bother to do. When I entered your home as your guest, you didn't think

---

a 7:36 The name Simon is supplied from v. 40.

b 7:37 This is a soft, cream-colored stone often used for jars and vases.

c 7:38 Six times in Luke we find someone at Jesus' feet (described as "beautiful" in Isa. 52:7): (1) the sinful woman mentioned in this verse who poured out her worship and tears at Jesus' feet; (2) the demonized man who worshiped at Jesus' feet (8:35); (3) Jairus, who fell at his feet pleading for a miracle for his daughter (8:41); (4) Mary, who sat at his feet and received his word (10:39); (5) the healed leper who fell at his feet in deep gratitude (17:15–16); (6) those who worshiped Jesus at his resurrection when he showed them his hands and his feet (24:39–40).

d 7:39 Simon thought Jesus should have known the sinfulness of the woman, but Simon should have known the love of the one next to him, who was ready to forgive and restore. Religion focuses on the sinfulness of a person, but faith sees the glory of the one who forgives and heals.

e 7:41 The Greek text uses the monetary term denarius. The point is that one person owed more than a year's wages, the other much less.

about offering me water to wash the dust off my feet. Yet she came into your home and washed my feet with her many tears and then dried my feet with her hair. [45] You didn't even welcome me into your home with the customary kiss of greeting, but from the moment I came in she has not stopped kissing my feet. [46] You didn't take the time to anoint my head with fragrant oil, but she anointed my head and feet with the finest perfume. [47] She has been forgiven of all her many sins. This is why she has shown me such extravagant love. But those who assume they have very little to be forgiven will love me very little."

[48] Then Jesus said to the woman at his feet, "All your sins are forgiven." [a]

[49] All the dinner guests said among themselves, "Who is the one who can even forgive sins?"

[50] Then Jesus said to the woman, "Your faith in me has given you life. Now you may leave and walk in the ways of peace."

Jesus Ministers throughout the Land

8 Soon afterward, Jesus began a ministry tour throughout the country, visiting cities and villages to announce the wonderful news of God's kingdom realm. His twelve disciples traveled with him [2] and also a number of women who had been healed of many illnesses under his ministry and set free from demonic power. Jesus had cast out seven demons from one woman. [b] Her name was Mary Magdalene, *for she was from the village of Magdala.* [c] Among the women were Susanna and [3] Joanna, the wife of Chusa, who managed King Herod's household. [4] Many other women who supported Jesus' ministry from their own personal finances also traveled with him. [e]

Mysteries of God's Kingdom Realm

[4] Massive crowds gathered from many towns to hear Jesus, and he taught them using metaphors and parables, [f] such as this:

---

a 7:48 Twice in Luke's Gospel we hear Jesus say, "All your sins are forgiven." Once he says it to a man (Luke 5:20) and here to a woman. The proof of her sins being forgiven is her love; with the healed man it was his life, for he took up his bed and walked.

b 8:2 The number seven means completeness. Mary was completely possessed by demons, but Jesus restored her true self and cast out her demons.

c 8:2 Implied by the word *Magdalene.* The ancient village of Magdala has recently been discovered near the current town of Migdol.

d 8:3 Some scholars believe that Chusa was the government official mentioned in John 4:46–53.

e 8:3 To travel with a rabbi was considered a high honor. Yet it was not permitted in the culture and time of Jesus' ministry for a woman to be mentored by a rabbi. Jesus elevated women into a place of honor and respect, in spite of the cultural limitations. It was these wealthy women who provided for Jesus' care. Luke is the one Gospel writer who brings out the many times Jesus honored women. These women would later be present at the crucifixion (Matt. 27:56; Mark 15:40–41; Luke 23:49, 55) and at the resurrection (Luke 24:1–11). Mary Magdalene was the first human being to see the risen Christ (John 20:11–18).

f 8:4 One of Jesus' preferred teaching methods was through story (Matt. 13:34). A parable

⁵"A farmer went out to sow seeds for a harvest. As he scattered his seed, some of it fell on the hard pathway and was quickly trampled down and unable to grow and became nothing but bird seed. ⁶Some fell on the gravel, and though it sprouted it couldn't take root; it withered for lack of moisture. ⁷Other seed fell where there was nothing but weeds. It too was unable to grow to full maturity, for it was choked out by the weeds. ⁸Yet some of the seed fell into good, fertile soil, and it grew and flourished until it produced more than a hundredfold harvest, a bumper crop." Then Jesus added, shouting out to all who would hear, "Listen with your heart and you will understand!"

⁹Later his disciples came to Jesus and asked him privately what deeper meaning was found in this parable. ¹⁰He said, "You have been given a teachable heart to perceive the secret, hidden mysteries of God's kingdom realm. But to those who don't have a listening heart, my words are merely stories. Even though they have eyes, they are blind to the true meaning of what I say,ᵃ and even though they listen, they won't receive full revelation.

¹¹"Here, then, is the deeper meaning to my parable: The word of Godᵇ is the seed that is sown into hearts. ¹²The hard pathway represents the hard hearts of men who hear the word of God but the slandererᶜ quickly snatches away what was sown in their hearts to keep them from believing and experiencing salvation. ¹³The seed falling on the gravel represents those who initially respond to the word with joy, but soon afterward, when a season of harassment of the enemy and difficulty come to them, they whither and fall away, for they have no root in the truth and their faith is temporary.ᵈ ¹⁴The seed that falls into the weeds represents the hearts of those who hear the word of God but their growth is quickly choked off by their own anxious cares, the riches of this world, and the fleeting pleasures of this life. This is why they never become mature and fruitful. ¹⁵The seed that fell into good, fertile soil represents those lovers of truth who hear it deep within their hearts. They respond by clinging to the word, keeping it dear as they endure all things in faith. This is the seed that will one day bear much fruit in their lives."

The Revelation Light

¹⁶"No one lights a lamp and then hides it, covering it over or putting it where

---

required the listener to be humble, teachable, and open to truth. Revelation from God can be found through the doorway of an allegory. This parable is described in the Aramaic as "the parable of the seed."
ᵃ 8:10 This is taken from Isa. 6:9–10. See also Jer. 5:21; Ezek. 12:2.
ᵇ 8:11 Or "manifestation of God."
ᶜ 8:12 Or "the devil." The Greek word *diabolos* (also translated "devil") means "the slanderer."
ᵈ 8:13 From the Aramaic text.

its light won't be seen. No, the lamp is placed on a lampstand so others are able to benefit from its brightness. [17] Because this revelation lamp now shines within you, nothing will be hidden from you—it will all be revealed. Every secret *of the kingdom* [a] will be unveiled and out in the open, made known by the revelation-light. [18] So pay careful attention to your hearts as you hear my teaching, for to those who have open hearts, even more revelation will be given to them until it overflows. And for those who do not listen with open hearts, what little light they imagine to have will be taken away." [b]

Jesus' True Family

[19] Mary, Jesus' mother, and her other sons [c] came to where Jesus was teaching, but they couldn't get through the crowd that had gathered around him. [20] So he was told, "Your mother and brothers [d] are standing outside, wanting to speak with you."

[21] Jesus told them, "These who come to listen to me are like my mothers and my brothers. They're the ones who long to hear and to put God's word into practice."

Peace in the Storm

[22-23] One day Jesus said to his disciples, "Let's get in a boat and go across to the other side of the lake." So they set sail. Soon Jesus fell asleep. The wind rose, and the fierce wind became a violent squall that threatened to swamp their boat. [24] So the disciples woke Jesus up and said, "Master, Master, we're sinking! Don't you care that we're going to drown?"

With great authority Jesus rebuked the howling wind and surging waves, and instantly they stopped and became as smooth as glass. [25] Then Jesus said to them, "Why are you fearful? Have you lost your faith *in me*?"

Shocked and shaken, they said with amazement to one another, "Who is this man [e] who has authority over winds and waves that they obey him?"

A Demonized Man Set Free

[26-29] As soon as they stepped ashore on the eastern side of the lake in the land of

---

a 8:17 Implied in the context of Jesus' teaching on the mysteries of God's kingdom realm (v. 10).

b 8:18 This verse contains a complicated ellipsis, which is a literary function of omitting certain information to invite discovery. The ellipsis of the text has been supplied by making explicit what is implicit in the context. The parables of the sower and of the lamp are similar, in that they speak of the heart that receives truth. The word of the kingdom is a "seed" that grows within us and a "lamp" that glows within us.

c 8:19 Mary had other sons and daughters. These were the half-brothers/sisters of Jesus. Jesus' father was not Joseph, but the Father of eternity. See also Mark 6:3.

d 8:20 See John 7:5

e 8:25 The answer to that question is found in Jer. 31:35, "He is the Lord of hosts!"

the Gerasenes, the disciples were confronted by a demon-possessed madman from a nearby town. Many times he had been put under guard and bound with chains, but repeatedly the many demons inside him had thrown him into convulsions, breaking his shackles and driving him out of the town into the countryside. He had been demonized for a long time and was living naked in a cemetery among the tombs. When he saw Jesus, he fell at his feet and screamed out, "What are you doing here? You are Jesus, the Son of the Most High God!"

Jesus commanded the demons to come out of him, and they shouted, "We beg you, don't torture us!"

[30] Jesus asked the man, "**What is your name?**"

"Mob," the demons answered. "We are a mob,[a] for there are many of us here in this man. [31] We beg you, don't banish us to the bottomless pit of the Abyss!"[b]

[32] On the hillside nearby, there was a large herd of pigs, and the demons pled with Jesus, "Let us enter into the pigs." [33] So Jesus ordered all the "mob" of demons to come out of the man and enter the pigs. The crazed herd of swine stampeded over the cliff into the lake and all of them drowned.

[34] When the herders tending the pigs saw what had happened, they ran off in fear and reported it to the nearby town and throughout the countryside. [35] Then the people of the region came out to see for themselves what had happened. When they came to where Jesus was, they discovered the *notorious* madman totally set free. He was clothed, speaking intelligently, and sitting at the feet of Jesus. They were shocked! [36] Then eyewitnesses to the miracle reported all that they had seen and how the demonized man was completely delivered from his torment.

After hearing about such amazing power, the townspeople became frightened. [37] Soon all the people of the region of the Gerasenes and the surrounding country begged Jesus to leave them, for they were gripped with fear. So Jesus got into the boat, intending to return to Galilee. [38] But the man who had been set free begged Jesus over and over not to leave, saying, "Let me be with you!"

Jesus sent him away with these instructions: [39] "**Return to your home and your family, and tell them all the wonderful things God has done for you.**" So the man went away and preached to everyone who would listen about the amazing miracle Jesus had worked in his life.

More Miracles of Healing

[40] When Jesus returned to Galilee, the crowds were overjoyed, for they had been waiting for him to arrive. [41-42] Just then, a man named Jairus, the leader of the

---

a 8:30 The Greek word used for "mob" is literally "legion," which was the largest unit of the Roman military and represented up to 6,800 soldiers.

b 8:31 See Rev. 9:1; 20:1–3. The Abyss is the place of imprisonment for Satan and his demons.

local Jewish congregation, fell before Jesus' feet. He desperately begged him to come and heal his twelve-year-old daughter, his only child, because she was at the point of death.

Jesus started to go with him to his home to see her, but a large crowd surrounded him. [43] In the crowd that day was a woman who had suffered greatly for twelve years [a] from slow bleeding. Even though she had spent all that she had on healers, [b] she was still suffering. [44] Pressing in through the crowd, she came up behind Jesus and touched the tassel [c] of his prayer shawl. Instantly her bleeding stopped and she was healed.

[45] Jesus suddenly stopped and said to his disciples, "**Someone touched me. Who is it?**" [d]

While they all denied it, Peter pointed out, "Master, everyone is touching you, trying to get close to you. The crowds are so thick [e] we can't walk through all these people without being jostled."

[46] Jesus replied, "**Yes, but I felt power surge through me. Someone touched me to be healed, and they received their healing.**"

[47] When the woman realized she couldn't hide any longer, she came and fell trembling at Jesus' feet. Before the entire crowd she declared, "I was desperate to touch you, Jesus, for I knew if I could just touch even the fringe of your robe [f] I would be healed."

[48] Jesus responded, "**Beloved daughter, your faith in me has released your healing. You may go with my peace.**"

[49] While Jesus was still speaking to the woman, someone came from Jairus' house and told him, "There's no need to bother the Master any further. Your daughter has passed away. She's gone."

[50] When Jesus heard this, he said, "**Jairus, don't yield to your fear. Have faith in me and she will live again.**"

[51] When they arrived at the house, Jesus allowed only Peter, John, and Jacob—along with the child's parents—to go inside. [52] Jesus told those left outside, who were sobbing and wailing with grief, "**Stop crying. She is not dead; she's just asleep and must be awakened.**"

---

a 8:43 The daughter of Jairus was twelve years old; this woman had suffered for twelve years. Jesus touched the girl; the woman touched Jesus.

b 8:43 Translated from the Aramaic text, which states literally "the house of healers." This phrase is not found in many Greek texts.

c 8:44 This was on the corner of the prayer shawl, and the tassel was meant to symbolize all of the commandments and promises of God. The woman was laying hold of a promise for healing.

d 8:45 Jesus already knew the answer to his question. He wanted the woman to come forward and acknowledge her healing.

e 8:45 There were many crowds around Jesus, the living Word. Many today crowd around the Bible, the written Word. But only those who "touch" the Scriptures in faith receive its promises, just like the sick woman received her healing.

f 8:47 She was touching the hem of the robe of our anointed High Priest, Jesus. See Ps. 133:2.

[53] They laughed at him,[a] knowing for certain that she had died.

[54] Jesus approached the body, took the girl by her hand, and called out with a loud voice, "My sleeping child, awake! Rise up!"

[55-56] Instantly her spirit returned to her body and she stood up.[b]

Jesus directed her stunned parents to give her something to eat and ordered them not to tell anyone what just happened.

Jesus Sends Out His Apostles

9 Jesus summoned together his twelve apostles[c] and imparted to them authority over every demon and the power to heal every disease. [2] Then he commissioned them to preach God's kingdom realm and to heal the sick to demonstrate that the kingdom had arrived. As he sent them out, he gave them these instructions: [3] "Take nothing extra on your journey.[d] Just go as you are. Don't carry a staff, a backpack, food, money, not even a change of clothes. [4] Whatever home welcomes you as a guest, remain there and make it your base of ministry. [5] And wherever your ministry is rejected and not welcomed, you are to leave that town and shake the dust off your shoes as a testimony before them."[e]

[6] The apostles departed and went into the villages with the wonderful news of God's kingdom realm, and they instantly healed diseases wherever they went.

Herod Perplexed

[7] Now, Herod, the governor, was confused and perplexed when he heard the reports of all the miracles of Jesus and his apostles. Many were saying, "John the Baptizer has come back to life!" [8] Others said, "This has to be Elijah who has reappeared or one of the prophets of old who has risen from the dead." These were the rumors circulating throughout the land.

---

a 8:53 They did not realize that Jesus was using "sleep" as a metaphor for death.

b 8:55–56 This chapter contains four great miracles of Jesus Christ: (1) over nature, for he stilled the wind and waves; (2) over demons, for he cast out a mob of evil spirits; (3) over disease, for he healed the hemorrhaging woman; and (4) over death, for he restored the life of this twelve-year-old girl.

c 9:1 As translated from certain Greek manuscripts and implied in the context.

d 9:3 Why did Jesus tell them to go empty-handed? To trust and walk in faith. But also because they already had the five items they were told not to bring, as their spiritual counterparts are found in him (i.e., he is our treasure, our strength, our living bread, our provider, and our righteousness).

e 9:5 Shaking the dust off their feet would be a statement against the people who had rejected the gospel, that the messengers would not be responsible for their fate. More than a metaphor, this was an actual custom of the day. However, the words "before them" can also be translated "against them." Shaking the dust off their feet did not mean they were to stomp off offended and angry, but that they would move on with no defilement or unforgiveness in their hearts toward those who rejected their message. If they did not do that, they would take the "dust" of that offense to the next place they ministered.

Herod exclaimed, [9] "Who is this Man? I keep hearing about him over and over. It can't be the prophet John; I had him beheaded!" [a] Herod was very eager to meet Jesus.

Jesus Feeds Thousands

[10] *Months later,* [b] the apostles returned from their ministry tour and told Jesus all the wonders and miracles they had witnessed. Jesus, wanting to be alone with the Twelve, quietly slipped away with them toward Bethsaida. [c] [11] But the crowds soon found out about it and took off after him. When they caught up with Jesus, he graciously welcomed them all, taught them more about God's kingdom realm, and healed all who were sick.

[12] As the day wore on, the Twelve came to Jesus and told him, "It's getting late. You should send the crowds away to the surrounding villages and farms to get something to eat and find shelter for the night. There's nothing to eat here in the middle of nowhere."

[13] Jesus responded, "**You have the food to feed them.**" [d]

They replied, "All we have are these five small loaves of bread and two dried fish. Do you really expect us to go buy food for all these people? [14] There are nearly five thousand men here, *with women and children besides!*" [e]

He told his disciples, "**Have them all sit down in groups of fifty each.**" [f]

[15-16] After everyone was seated, Jesus took the five loaves and two fish, and gazing into the heavenly realm he gave thanks for the food. Then, in the presence of his disciples, he broke off pieces of bread and fish, and kept giving more to each disciple to give to the crowd. *It was multiplying before their eyes!* [17] So everyone ate until they were filled, and afterward the disciples gathered up the leftovers—it came to exactly twelve baskets full!

Jesus Prophesies His Death and Resurrection

[18] One time, when Jesus was praying in a quiet place with his disciples nearby, he came over to them and asked, "**Who do people think I am?**"

[19] They answered, "Some are convinced you're the prophet John who has

---

a 9:9 See Mark 6:14–29.

b 9:10 Matthew infers that they had been sent north and east, possibly as far as Persia to preach to the Jewish residents there, which would take them months to return.

c 9:10 Bethsaida means "house of fishing."

d 9:13 In the Greek text, the word *you* here is emphatic. Jesus told his disciples they had food to give to others. Because Jesus lives within us, we can give others the living bread and, if need be, multiply food for others to eat. We are to focus on what we have, not on what we don't have.

e 9:14 There were likely ten thousand people whom Jesus miraculously fed that day.

f 9:14 There is an interesting correlation between seating the people in groups of fifty and the feast of Pentecost. Fifty was the number of days between Passover and Pentecost.

returned. Others say you are Elijah, or perhaps one of the Jewish prophets brought back from the dead."

²⁰ Jesus asked them, "But who do you believe that I am?"

Peter said, "You are the Anointed One, God's Messiah!"

²¹ Jesus gave them strict orders not to tell this to anyone yet, saying, ²² "The Son of Man ᵃ is destined to experience great suffering and face complete rejection by the Jewish leaders and religious hierarchy. ᵇ He will be killed and raised back to life on the third day."

What it Means to Follow Jesus

²³ Jesus said to all of his followers, "If you truly desire to be my disciple, you must disown your life completely, embrace my 'cross' ᶜ as your own, *and surrender to my ways.* ²⁴ For if you choose self-sacrifice, giving up your lives for my glory, you will embark on a discovery of more and more of true life. But if you choose to keep your lives for yourselves, you will lose what you try to keep. ²⁵ Even if you gained all the wealth and power of this world, everything it could offer you, yet lost your soul in the process, what good is that? ²⁶ So why then are you ashamed of being my disciple? Are you ashamed of the revelation-truth ᵈ I give to you?

"I, the Son of Man, will one day return in my radiant brightness, with the holy angels and in the splendor and majesty of my Father, and I will be ashamed of all who are ashamed of me. ²⁷ But I promise you this: there are some of you standing here right now who will not die until you have witnessed the presence and the power of God's kingdom realm." ᵉ

The True Glory of Jesus

²⁸ Eight days later, Jesus took Peter, Jacob, and John and climbed a high mountain to pray. ²⁹ As he prayed, his face began to glow until it was a blinding glory streaming from him. His entire body was illuminated with a radiant glory. *His brightness ᶠ* became so intense that it made his clothing blinding white, like multiple flashes of lightning.

---

a 9:22 Or "the true Man."

b 9:22 The Greek text is literally "the elders, chief priests, and scribes." These three groups were represented in the religious hierarchy of the Sanhedrin, a council of seventy-one leaders.

c 9:23 This could also mean being willing to suffer and die for Christ.

d 9:26 The Greek word is *logos.*

e 9:27 This was a prophecy of what was about to take place with Peter, Jacob (James), and John on the Mountain of Transforming Glory. This promise was fulfilled when they experienced the power of God's kingdom realm and the cloud of glory.

f 9:29 The Greek text says, "The appearance of his face was altered." The light shone through his clothing as his glorified body became brilliant with light. This is called Jesus' transfiguration.

[30-31] All at once, two men appeared in glorious splendor: Moses and Elijah. They spoke with Jesus about his soon departure[a] from this world and the things he was destined to accomplish in Jerusalem.

[32] Peter and his companions had become very drowsy, but they became fully awake when they saw the glory and splendor of Jesus standing there and the two men with him.

[33] As Moses and Elijah were about to return to heaven, Peter impetuously blurted out, "Master, this is amazing to see the three of you together! Why don't we stay here and set up three shelters: one for you, one for Moses, and one for Elijah?"

[34] While Peter was still speaking, a radiant cloud of glory formed above them and overshadowed them. As the glory cloud enveloped them, they were struck with fear. [35] Then the voice of God thundered from within the cloud, "This is my Son, my Beloved One.[b] Listen carefully to all he has to say."

[36] When the thunderous voice faded away and the cloud disappeared, Jesus was standing there alone. Peter, Jacob, and John were speechless and awestruck. But they didn't say a word to anyone about what they had seen.

The Power of Faith

[37] The next day, when they came down from the mountain, a massive crowd was waiting there to meet them. [38] And a man in the crowd shouted desperately, "Please, Teacher, I beg of you, do something about my boy. He's my only child. [39] He's possessed by an evil spirit that makes him scream out in torment and hardly ever leaves him alone. It throws him into convulsions and he foams at the mouth. And when it finally does leave him, he's left with horrible bruises. [40] I begged your disciples to drive it out of him, but they didn't have enough power to do it."

[41] Jesus responded, "You are an unbelieving people with no faith! Your lives are twisted with lies that have turned you away from doing what is right. How much longer should I remain here, offering you hope?"[c] Then he said to the man, "Bring your son to me."

[42] As the boy approached, the demon slammed him to the ground, throwing him into violent convulsions. Jesus sternly commanded the demon to come out of the boy, and immediately it left. Jesus healed the boy of his injuries and returned him to his father, *saying, "Here is your son."*

[43] Everyone was awestruck. They were stunned seeing the power and majesty of God flow through Jesus.

---

a 9:30-31 The actual word in Greek is translated "exodus."
b 9:35 Several Greek manuscripts have "my Chosen One."
c 9:41 As translated from Aramaic text. Some translate this phrase "How long must I endure you?" However, the Aramaic root word for "endure" is *sebar*, which means "hope" or "good news."

⁴⁴ While everyone marveled, trying to process what they had just witnessed, Jesus turned to his disciples and said, "This is very important, so listen carefully and remember my words. **The Son of Man is about to be betrayed and given over to the authority of men.**"

⁴⁵ But the disciples were unable to perceive what he was saying, for it was a veiled mystery to them, and they were too embarrassed to ask him to explain it.

True Greatness

⁴⁶ The disciples began to argue and became preoccupied over who would be the greatest one among them. ⁴⁷ Fully aware of their innermost thoughts, Jesus called a little child to his side and said to them, ⁴⁸ **"If you tenderly care for this little child** *ᵃ* **on my behalf, you are tenderly caring for me. And if you care for me, you are honoring my Father who sent me. For the one who is least important in your eyes is actually the most important one of all."**

⁴⁹ The disciple John said, "Master, we found someone who was casting out demons using your name and we tried to stop him, because he doesn't follow you like we do."

⁵⁰ Jesus responded, **"You shouldn't have hindered him, for anyone who is not against you is your friend."** *ᵇ*

Jesus' Journey to Jerusalem

⁵¹ Jesus passionately determined to leave for Jerusalem *and let nothing distract him from fulfilling his mission there,* for the time for him to be lifted up was drawing near. *ᶜ* ⁵² So he sent messengers *ᵈ* ahead of him as envoys to a village of the Samaritans. ⁵³ But as they approached the village, they were turned away. They would not allow Jesus to enter, for he was on his way *to worship in Jerusalem.*

⁵⁴ When the disciples Jacob and John realized what was happening, they came to Jesus and said, "Lord, if you wanted to, you could command fire to fall down from heaven just like Elijah did *ᶠ* and destroy all these wicked people."

---

a 9:48 The little child is representative of unimportant people in general. Treating the least with care and respect makes us truly great.

b 9:50 Jealousy blinds our hearts. Nine disciples combined could not cast out a demon spirit (v. 40), and they were jealous of this one who did.

c 9:51 This refers to the cross, where Jesus was lifted up on a tree to bear the sins of all humankind. His exaltation into glory was through the sacrifice of his life on Calvary's cross. Nothing would turn him aside from being our Sin-Bearer and Redeemer.

d 9:52 The most literal translation is "He sent angels before his face."

e 9:53 The Samaritans had their own place of worship on Mount Gerizim, and they were hostile toward Jews, who wanted to worship in Jerusalem. There were many cultural, religious, and ethnic hostilities between Jews and Samaritans.

f 9:54 This sentence is translated from the Aramaic. The earliest Greek manuscripts do not include "just like Elijah did." Some Greek texts state that the disciples asked, "Do you want us to call down fire and destroy them?"

[55] Jesus rebuked them sharply, saying, "Don't you realize what comes from your hearts when you say that? For the Son of Man did not come to destroy life, but to bring life to the earth."[a]

[56] So they went to another village instead.

The Cost to Follow Jesus

[57] On their way, someone came up to Jesus and said, "I want to follow you wherever you go."

[58] Jesus replied, "Yes, but remember this: even animals in the field have holes in the ground to sleep in and birds have their nests, but the Son of Man has no place here to lay down his head."

[59] Jesus then turned to another and said, "Come be my disciple."

He replied, "Someday I will, Lord, but allow me first to fulfill my duty as a good son[b] and wait until my father passes away."

[60] Jesus told him, "Don't wait for your father's burial. Let those who are already dead wait for death. But as for you, go and proclaim everywhere that God's kingdom has arrived."

[61] Still another said to him, "Lord, I want to follow you too. But first let me go home and say good-bye to my entire family."

[62] Jesus responded, "Why do you keep looking backward to your past and have second thoughts about following me? When you turn back you are useless to God's kingdom realm."

Labor Shortage

10 After this, the Lord Jesus formed thirty-five teams among the other disciples. Each team was two disciples, seventy in all,[c] and he commissioned them to go ahead of him into every town he was about to visit. [2] He released them with these instructions:

---

a 9:55 Translated from Aramaic and a few Greek manuscripts. This pericope reveals the mercy of Jesus. Although the Samaritans refused entry to Jesus and his disciples, in the next chapter Jesus uses an example of a good Samaritan who cared for a stranger. Jesus saw in the Samaritan outcasts a redemptive future (Luke 10:25–37). He knew the Father had the grace to change even the most stubborn individuals. An entire Samaritan village received Jesus through the witness of a woman (John 4:39–42), and later, as recorded in the book of Acts, the entire region of the Samaritans received the gospel (Acts 8:9–25). We can never give up on those who seem to be wayward.

b 9:59 The text is literally "Allow me first to go and bury my father." This is an idiom for waiting until his father passed away. He wanted an inheritance in this life as his security.

c 10:1 The text states they were "other" (i.e., other than the Twelve). A few Greek manuscripts have "seventy-two." The number seventy is a key numerical symbol in the Bible. Seventy nations are listed in Gen. 10, seventy of Jacob's clan went into Egypt (Ex. 1:5), seventy palm trees refreshed God's people at Elim (Ex. 15:27), seventy elders served with Moses (Ex. 24:1), seventy princes are mentioned in Judg. 9:56, seventy men sat on the council of the Sanhedrin, and Jesus sent out seventy apostles to preach the message of the kingdom.

"The harvest is huge and ripe. But there are not enough harvesters to bring it all in. As you go, plead with the Owner of the Harvest to drive out[a] into his harvest fields many more workers. ³Now, off you go! I am sending you out even though you feel as vulnerable as lambs going into a pack of wolves. ⁴You won't need to take anything[b] with you—trust in God alone. And don't get distracted from my purpose by anyone you might meet along the way.

⁵"Once you enter a house, speak to the people there and say, 'God's blessing of peace be upon this house!' ⁶If a lover of peace[c] resides there, your peace will rest upon that household.[d] But if you are rejected, your blessing of peace will come back upon you. ⁷Don't feel the need to shift from one house to another, but stay put in one home during your time in that city. Eat and drink whatever they serve you. Receive their hospitality, for you are my harvester, and you deserve to be cared for.

⁸"When you enter into a new town, and you have been welcomed by its people, follow these rules: Eat[e] what is served you. ⁹Then heal the sick, and tell them all, 'God's kingdom realm has arrived and is now within your reach!' ¹⁰But when you enter a city and they do not receive you, say to them publicly, ¹¹'We wipe from our feet the very dust of your streets as a testimony before you![f] Understand this: God's kingdom realm came within your reach and yet you have rejected God's invitation!'"

¹²Jesus continued, "Let me say it clearly: on the day of judgment the wicked people of Sodom will have a lesser degree of judgment than the city that rejects you, *for Sodom did not have the opportunity that was given to them.*"

Jesus Condemns the Unrepentant Cities

¹³"How disastrous it will be for the city of Korazin! How horrible for the city of Bethsaida! For if the powerful miracles that I performed in Korazin and Bethsaida had been done *in Tyre and Sidon*, they would have humbled themselves and repented, and turned from their sins. ¹⁴*Tyre and Sidon*[g] will

---

a 10:2 This is the term used many times in the Gospels for driving out or casting out demons. The Lord of the Harvest must cast them forth. The Holy Spirit is the Director of the Harvest.

b 10:4 The text states literally "Take no money, no knapsack, no sandals." The implication is that they were to trust in God alone for all their needs to be met.

c 10:6 Literally "son of peace," which is a way of saying, "a godly man."

d 10:6 Or as translated from the Aramaic, "Let him rest upon your peace."

e 10:8 This instruction to "eat what is served" was given twice, for the Jewish dietary laws were not meant to be a hindrance in their ministry, nor were the disciples to demand certain foods.

f 10:11 See footnote on Luke 9:5.

g 10:14 Tyre and Sidon (present-day Lebanon) were two gentile cities on the Mediterranean coast that were known for their wickedness.

face a lesser degree of judgment than you will on the day of judgment. [15] And Capernaum! Do you really think you'll be highly exalted because of the great things I have done there? No! You'll be brought down to the depths of hell[a] because of your rejection of me!"

[16] Jesus concluded his instructions to the seventy with these words: "Remember this: Whoever listens to your message is actually listening to me. And anyone who rejects you is rejecting me, and not only me but the one who sent me."

The Seventy Return

[17] When the seventy missionaries returned to Jesus, they were ecstatic with joy, telling him, "Lord, even the demons obeyed us when we commanded them in your name!"

[18] Jesus replied, "While you were ministering, I watched Satan topple until he fell suddenly from heaven like lightning to the ground. [19] Now you understand that I have imparted to you all my authority to trample over his kingdom. You will trample upon every demon before you and overcome every power[b] Satan possesses. Absolutely nothing will be able to harm you as you walk in this authority. [20] However, your real source of joy isn't merely that these spirits submit to your authority, but that your names are written in the journals of heaven and that you belong to God's kingdom. This is the true source of your authority."

[21] Then Jesus, overflowing with the Holy Spirit's anointing of joy, exclaimed, "Father, thank you, for you are Lord Supreme over heaven and earth! You have hidden the great revelation of this authority from those who are proud, those wise in their own eyes, and you have shared it with these who humbled themselves. Yes, Father. This is what pleases your heart and the very way you've chosen to extend your kingdom: to give to those who become like trusting children.

[22] "Father, you have entrusted me with all that you are and all that you have. No one fully knows the Son except the Father. And no one fully knows the Father except the Son. But the Son is able to introduce and reveal the Father to anyone he chooses."

[23] When Jesus was alone with the Twelve, he said to them, "You are very privileged to see and hear all these things. [24] Many kings and prophets of old longed to see these days of miracles that you've been favored to see. They would have given everything to hear the revelation you've been favored to hear. Yet they didn't get to see as much as a glimpse or hear even a whisper."

---

a 10:15 See Isa. 14:13–15.
b 10:19 The Greek text is literally "snakes and scorpions," which are emblems of demonic powers.

Loving God, Loving Others

[25] Just then a religious scholar stood before Jesus in order to test his doctrines. He posed this question: "Teacher, what requirement must I fulfill if I want to live forever in heaven?"

[26] Jesus replied, **"What does Moses teach us? What do you read in the Law?"**

[27] The religious scholar answered, "It states, 'You must love the Lord God with all your heart, all your passion, all your energy, and your every thought. And you must love your neighbor as well as you love yourself.'"

[28] Jesus said, **"That is correct. Now go and do exactly that and you will live."**

[29] Wanting to justify himself, he questioned Jesus further, saying, "What do you mean by 'my neighbor'?"

[30] Jesus replied, **"Listen and I will tell you. There was once a *Jewish*[a] man traveling from Jerusalem to Jericho when bandits robbed him along the way. They beat him severely, stripped him naked, and left him half dead.**

[31] **"Soon, a Jewish priest walking down the same road came upon the wounded man. Seeing him from a distance, the priest crossed to the other side of the road and walked right past him, not turning to help him one bit.**

[32] **"Later, a religious man, a Levite,[b] came walking down the same road and likewise crossed to the other side to pass by the wounded man without stopping to help him.**

[33] **"Finally, another man, a Samaritan,[c] came upon the bleeding man and was moved with tender compassion for him. [34] He stooped down and gave him first aid, pouring olive oil on his wounds, disinfecting them with wine, and bandaging them to stop the bleeding. Lifting him up, he placed him on his own donkey and brought him to an inn. Then he took him from his donkey and carried him to a room for the night. [35] The next morning he took his own money from his wallet and gave it to the innkeeper with these words: 'Take care of him until I come back from my journey. If it costs more than this, I will repay you when I return.'[d] [36] So, now, tell me, which one of the three men who saw the wounded man proved to be the true neighbor?"**

---

a 10:30 Although the text does not describe him as Jewish, it is clearly implied in the context.

b 10:32 The Levites were temple assistants, helping the priests (1 Chron. 23:28–32).

c 10:33 There was racial tension in those days between Jews and Samaritans. The Samaritans were considered to be a mixed race by the religious Jews. A Samaritan would be the most unlikely person to stop and help a Jewish man. The word *Samaritan* does not refer to people who lived in a geographical place, but is the Hebrew-Aramaic word *Samarim*, which means "keeper of the law."

d 10:35 Jesus is the Good Samaritan. He stoops down to touch us, heal us, lift us up, carry us on our journey, and pay our debts, and he promises to return and reward those who do his will.

³⁷ The religious scholar responded, "The one who demonstrated kindness and mercy."

Jesus said, "You must go and do the same as he."

Jesus Visits Martha and Mary

³⁸⁻³⁹ As Jesus and the disciples continued on their journey, they came to a village where a woman welcomed Jesus into her home. Her name was Martha and she had a sister named Mary. Mary sat down attentively before the Master, absorbing every revelation he shared. ⁴⁰ But Martha became exasperated by finishing the numerous household chores in preparation for her guests, so she interrupted Jesus and said, "Lord, don't you think it's unfair that my sister left me to do all the work by myself? You should tell her to get up and help me."

⁴¹ The Lord answered her, "Martha, my beloved Martha. Why are you upset and troubled, pulled away by all these many distractions? Are they really that important? ⁴² Mary has discovered the one thing most important by choosing to sit at my feet. She is undistracted, and I won't take this privilege from her."

Jesus Teaches about Prayer

11 One day, as Jesus was in prayer, one of his disciples came over to him as he finished and said, "Would you teach us a *model prayer* that we can pray, just like John did for his disciples?"

² So Jesus taught them this prayer: "Our heavenly Father,ᵃ may the glory of your name be the center on which our life turns.ᵇ May your Holy Spirit come upon us and cleanse us.ᶜ Manifest your kingdom on earth. ³ And give us our needed bread for the coming day.ᵈ ⁴ Forgive our sins as we ourselves release forgiveness to those who have wronged us. And rescue us every time we face tribulations."ᵉ

⁵ Then Jesus gave this illustration: "Imagine what would happen if you were to go to one of your friends in the middle of the night and pound on his door and shout, 'Please! Do you have some food you can spare? ⁶ A friend just arrived at my house unexpectedly and I have nothing to serve him.'ᶠ

---

a 11:2 Some Greek manuscripts read simply "Father." The Aramaic is *Abba*.

b 11:2 An alternate reading of the Aramaic text. The Aramaic word for "name" is *shema* (or the Hebrew word, *shem*), a word with multiple meanings. It can also be translated as "light," "sound," or "atmosphere." Placing a light in an enclosed space, like a lantern, magnifies that light. This is the meaning here of God's name being made sacred and magnified as we focus our lives on him.

c 11:2 Translated from some of the earliest Greek manuscripts.

d 11:3 This is more than asking for food, for Jesus has taught us not to worry about the needs of our body. It is the request for tomorrow's living bread to come and feed us today.

e 11:4 Or "Do not let us enter into ordeals."

f 11:6 It was the culture of the day to honor every guest and provide a meal when they arrived.

⁷But your friend says, 'Why are you bothering me? The door's locked and my family and I are all in bed. Do you expect me to get up and give you our food?' ⁸But listen—because of your shameless impudence, even though it's the middle of the night, your friend will get up out of his bed and give you all that you need. ⁹⁻¹⁰So it is with your prayers. Ask and you'll receive. Seek and you'll discover. Knock on heaven's door, and it will one day open for you. Every persistent person will get what he asks for. Every persistent seeker will discover what he needs. And everyone who knocks persistently will one day find an open door.

¹¹"Let me ask you this: Do you know of any father who would give his son a snake on a plate when he asked for a serving of fish?ᵃ Of course not! ¹²Do you know of any father who would give his daughter a spider when she had asked for an egg? Of course not! ¹³If imperfect parents know how to lovingly take care of their children and give them what they need, how much more will the perfect heavenly Father give the Holy Spirit's fullness when his children ask him."

Jesus Responds to Controversy

¹⁴One day there was a crowd gathered around Jesus, and among them was a man who was mute. Jesus drove out of the man the spirit that made him unable to speak. Once the demon left him, the mute man's tongue was loosed and he was able to speak again. The stunned crowd saw it all and marveled in amazement over this miracle!

¹⁵But there were some in the crowd who protested, saying, "He casts out demons by the power of Satan,ᵇ the demon king." ¹⁶Others were skeptical and tried to persuade Jesus to perform a spectacular display of power *to prove that he was the Messiah.*

¹⁷Jesus, well aware of their every thought, said to them, "Every kingdom that is split against itself is doomed to fail and will eventually collapse. ¹⁸If it is true that Satan casts out his own demons through me, how could his kingdom remain intact? ¹⁹If Satan gives me the power to cast out his demons, who is it that gives your exorcistsᶜ their power? Let them become your judges! Go and ask them and they will tell you. ²⁰Yet if I am casting out demons by God's mighty power,ᵈ God's kingdom realm is now released upon you—*but you still reject it!*

---

a 11:11 Some manuscripts substitute the word "fish" with "loaf" (bread) and the word "snake" with "a stone."

b 11:15 The word used here is *Beelzelbul*, which was an Aramaic word for "the prince of devils" and was worshiped by the Philistines.

c 11:19 Literally "your sons," which is a figure of speech for their followers.

d 11:20 The text literally states "in the finger of God," a Hebrew phrase denoting God's power. See Ex. 8:19; 31:18.

[21] "Satan's belongings are undisturbed as he stands guard over his fortress kingdom, strong and fully armed with an arsenal of many weapons. [22] But when one stronger than he comes to attack and overpower him, the stronger one will empty the arsenal in which he trusted. The conqueror will ransack his kingdom and distribute all the spoils of victory. [23] *This is a war,* and whoever is not on my side is against me, and whoever does not gather the spoils with me will be forever scattered.

[24] "When a demon is cast out of a person, it goes to wander in the waterless realm, searching for rest. But finding no place to rest it says, 'I will go back to the body of the one I left.' [25] When it returns, it finds the person like a house that has been swept clean and made tidy *but is empty.*[a] [26] Then it goes and enlists seven demons more evil than itself, and they all enter and possess the person, leaving that one with a much worse fate than before."[b]

[27] While he was saying all this, a woman shouted from the crowd, "God bless the one who gave you birth and nursed you as a child!"

[28] "Yes," said Jesus. "But God will bless all who listen to the word of God and carefully obey everything they hear."

The Miracle Sign of Jonah the Prophet

[29] As the crowds swelled even more, Jesus went on to say, "How evil is this generation! For when you demand a mighty display of power simply to prove who I am, *you demonstrate your unbelief.* The only sign given you will be a repeat of the miracle of Jonah. [30] For in the same way Jonah became a sign to the people of Nineveh, so the Son of Man will be a sign to this generation.[c]

[31] "The Queen of Sheba[d] will rise up on the day of judgment to accuse and condemn this generation for its unbelief. She journeyed from a far and distant land just to listen to the wisdom of King Solomon. There is one greater than Solomon speaking with you today, *but you refuse to listen.* [32] Yes, the people of Nineveh will also rise up on the day of judgment to accuse and condemn this generation.[e] For they all repented when they heard the preach-

---

a 11:25 Implied in the text is the truth that if a person is delivered from a demon but does not receive Christ and become filled with him, that individual's condition can become even worse. True conversion fills a life with Christ and his Spirit.

b 11:26 Christ's power is still available for all. Even Mary Magdalene had seven demons cast out of her. See Luke 8:2.

c 11:30 The Aramaic is "tribe." See v. 31. The Ninevites were a different Semitic tribe from the Jews.

d 11:31 Literally "the queen of the south." See 1 Kings 10:1–13. Sheba is modern-day Yemen.

e 11:32 The Aramaic is "tribe." The Ninevites were of Semitic origin, and although they were pagans, after the preaching of one prophet they converted. The people of Israel had many prophets throughout their history, and the greatest prophet of all was now preaching to them, yet they refused to listen.

ing of Jonah, but you refuse to repent. Yet there is one greater than Jonah who is preaching to you today."

Revelation Light

³³ "No one would think of lighting a lamp and then hiding it in the basement where no one would benefit. A lamp belongs on a lampstand, where all who enter may see its light. ³⁴ The eyes of your spirit allow revelation-light[a] to enter into your being. When your heart is open the light floods in.[b] When your heart is hard and closed, the light cannot penetrate and darkness takes its place. ³⁵ Open your heart and consider my words. Watch out that you do not mistake your opinions for revelation-light! ³⁶ If your spirit burns with light, fully illuminated with no trace of darkness, you will be a shining lamp, reflecting rays of truth by the way you live."

Jesus Warns Hypocrites

³⁷⁻³⁸ After Jesus finished saying this, a Jewish religious leader, one of the "separated ones," asked him to come for a meal at his home. When everyone had been seated at the table, the religious leader noticed that Jesus hadn't performed the cleansing ritual[c] before he began eating. He was shocked.

³⁹ The Lord said, "You Pharisees are religiously strict to your customs and obsessed with the peripheral issues. You are like one who will wipe clean only the outside of a cup or bowl, *leaving the inside filthy.* ⁴⁰ You are foolish to ignore the greed and wickedness within you! Shouldn't the one who cleans the outside also be concerned with cleaning the inside?[d] ⁴¹ If you free your heart of greed, showing compassion and true generosity to the poor, you have more than clean hands; you will be clean within.

⁴² "You Pharisees are hopeless frauds! For you are obsessed with peripheral issues, like paying meticulous tithes on the smallest herbs that grow in your gardens.[e] These matters you should do. Yet when you unjustly cheat others, you ignore the most important duty of all: to walk in the love of God. *Readjust* your values and place first things first.

⁴³ "You Pharisees are hopeless frauds! For you love to be honored before

---

a 11:34 The teachings of Jesus are the "revelation-light" referred to here.
b 11:34 Or "The eye is like a lamp to your body." The literal Greek text reads "Your eye is the lamp of your body. If your eye is healthy, your whole body is full of light; but if it is sick, your body is full of darkness." The eye becomes a metaphor for spiritual perception. The body is our spirit. The lamp is Jesus' teachings. The darkness is formed by the lies and opinions that blind us. These metaphors have been made explicit.
c 11:37-38 This was not required by the law of Moses, but was a rule imposed by the Pharisees.
d 11:40 Translated from the Aramaic text.
e 11:42 Literally "You pay tithes even on mint and dill and every other garden herb."

men with your titles of respect, seeking public recognition[a] as you aspire to become important among others.[b]

[44] "You Pharisees, what hopeless frauds! Your true character is hidden, like an unmarked grave that hides the corruption inside, defiling all who come in contact with you."[c]

[45] Just then a specialist in interpreting religious law blurted out, "But Teacher, don't you realize that your words insult me and those of my profession? You're being rude to us all!"

[46] Jesus responded, "Yes, and you are also hopeless frauds, you experts of the law! For you crush people beneath the burden of obeying impossible religious regulations, yet you would never even think of doing them yourselves.[d] What hypocrites! [47] What hopeless frauds! You build monuments to honor the prophets of old, yet it was your murdering ancestors who killed them. *The only prophet you'll honor is a dead one!* [48] In fact, by erecting monuments to the prophets they killed, you demonstrate your agreement with your murdering ancestors and bear witness to their deeds. You're no better than they! [49] That accounts for the wisdom of God, saying, 'I will send to them apostles and prophets though some they will murder and others they will chase away.'

[50] "This generation will be held accountable for every drop of blood shed by every murdered prophet from the beginning of time until now, [51] from the blood of Abel, who was killed by his brother, to the blood of Zechariah,[e] who was murdered in the middle of the temple court. Yes, the blood-guilt of all your ancestors will be laid before you in this generation.

[52] "You are nothing but hopeless frauds, you experts of religion! You take away from others the key that opens the door to the house of knowledge. Not only do you lock the door and refuse to enter, you do your best to keep others from the truth."

[53-54] The religious leaders and experts of the law became enraged and began to furiously oppose him. They harassed Jesus all the way out the door, spewing out their hostility, arguing over everything he said—wanting nothing more than to find a reason to entrap him with his own words.

---

a 11:43 Literally "greeted with respect in the marketplaces."

b 11:43 The Aramaic text states, "You aspire to leadership of the synagogues."

c 11:44 The strictly religious Jew could not touch a dead body or walk over a grave. It was common to whitewash the grave so no one would walk on it and be ceremonially defiled. Jesus taught that people who followed the example of the Pharisees would become morally unclean.

d 11:46 The Greek text is literally "You compel men to carry burdens that you yourselves do not touch."

e 11:51 See 2 Chron. 24:21–22. Second Chronicles is the last book in the Hebrew order of the Old Testament. So the implied time frame is from Genesis throughout the period of the Old Testament.

Jesus Warns against Hypocrisy

12 By now a crowd of many thousands had gathered around Jesus. So many people pushed to be near him, they began to trample on one another.

Jesus turned to his disciples and warned them, "Make sure you are not influenced by the hypocrisy and phoniness of the religious leaders. It permeates everything they do and teach, for they are merely serving their own interests. *a* ²Everything hidden and covered up will soon be exposed. For the facade is falling down, and nothing will be kept secret for long. ³Whatever you have spoken in private will be public knowledge, and what you have whispered secretly behind closed doors will be broadcast far and wide for all to hear.

⁴"Listen, my beloved friends, don't fear those who may want to take your life but nothing more. It's true that they may kill your body, but they have no power over your soul. ⁵The one you must fear is God, for he has both the power to take your life and the authority to cast your soul into hell. *b* Yes, the only one you need to fear is God.

⁶⁻⁷"What is the value of your soul to God? Could your worth be defined by an amount of money? God doesn't abandon or forget even the small sparrow he has made. How then could he forget or abandon you? What about the seemingly minor issues of your life? Do they matter to God? Of course they do! So you never need to worry, for you are more valuable to God than anything else in this world. *c*

⁸"I can assure you of this: If you don't hold back, but freely declare in public that I am the Son of Man, the Messiah, I will freely declare to all the angels of God that you are mine. ⁹But if you publicly pretend that you don't know me, I will deny you before the angels of God. ¹⁰If anyone speaks evil of me, the Son of Man, he can be forgiven. But if anyone scornfully speaks against the Holy Spirit, it will never be forgiven. ¹¹And remember this: When people accuse you before everyone *d* and forcefully drag you before the religious leaders and authorities, do not be troubled. Don't worry about defending yourself or be concerned about how to answer their accusations. ¹²Simply be confident and allow the Spirit of Wisdom access to your heart, and he will reveal in that very moment what you are to say to them."

---

a 12:1 "Serving their own interests" is found in the Aramaic text.

b 12:5 The Greek text is literally "the Valley of Hinnom." This was a valley along the south side of Jerusalem where excrement and rubbish were burned continually. It became a Jewish metaphor for the place of eternal punishment.

c 12:6–7 The translator has chosen to make explicit the figures of speech and metaphors of these verses. The literal Greek text reads "Do not five sparrows sell for two copper coins? Not one is overlooked before God. Indeed, the very hairs of your head are numbered. Stop fearing—you are more valuable than many sparrows."

d 12:11 The Greek text adds "in the synagogues."

Jesus Condemns Greed

[13] Just then someone spoke up from the crowd and said, "Master, you should tell my older brother that he has to divide the family inheritance and give me my fair share!"

[14] Jesus answered,[a] "My friend, you can't expect me to help you with this. It's not my business to settle arguments between you and your brother—that's yours to settle."

[15] Speaking to the people, Jesus continued, "Be alert and guard your heart from greed and always wishing for what you don't have. For your life can never be measured by the amount of things you possess."

[16] Jesus then gave them this illustration: "A wealthy land owner had a farm that produced bumper crops. In fact, it filled his barns to overflowing! [17] He thought, 'What should I do now that every barn is full and I have nowhere else to store more? [18] I know what I'll do! I'll tear down the barns and build one massive barn that will hold all my grain and goods. [19] Then I can just sit back, surrounded with comfort and ease. I'll enjoy life with no worries at all.'

[20] "God said to him, 'What a fool you are to trust in your riches and not in me. This very night the messengers of death[b] are demanding to take your life. Then who will get all the wealth you have stored up for yourself?' [21] This is what will happen to all those who fill up their lives with everything but God."

Don't Worry

[22] Jesus taught his disciples, saying, "Listen to me. Never let anxiety enter your hearts. Never worry about any of your needs, such as food or clothing. [23] For your life is infinitely more than just food or the clothing you wear. [24] Take the carefree birds as your example. Do you ever see them worry? They don't grow their own food or put it in a storehouse for later. Yet God takes care of every one of them, feeding each of them from his love and goodness. Isn't your life more precious to God than a bird? *Be carefree in the care of God!*

[25] "Does worry add anything to your life? Can it add one more year, or even one day? [26] So if worrying adds nothing, but actually subtracts from your life, why would you worry about God's care of you?

[27] "Think about the lilies. They grow and become beautiful, not because they work hard or strive to clothe themselves. Yet not even Solomon, wearing his kingly garments of splendor, could be compared to a field of lilies. [28] If God can clothe the fields and meadows with grass and flowers, can't he clothe you as well, O struggling one with so many doubts?[c] [29] I repeat

---

a 12:14 In the Jewish culture of that day, rabbis would be asked to mediate disputes such as this. However, the man did not want mediation but representation.

b 12:20 The Greek text is simply "they."

c 12:28 This Greek word means "little faiths."

it: Don't let worry enter your life. Live above the anxious cares about your personal needs. [30] People everywhere seem to worry about making a living, but your heavenly Father knows your every need and will take care of you. [31] Each and every day he will supply your needs as you seek his kingdom passionately, above all else. [32] So don't ever be afraid, dearest friends! Your loving Father joyously gives you his kingdom realm with all its promises!

[33] "So, now, go and sell what you have and give to those in need, making deposits in your account in heaven, an account that will never be taken from you. Your gifts will become a secure and unfailing treasure, deposited in heaven forever. [34] Where you deposit your treasure, that is where your thoughts will turn to—and your heart will long to be there also."

Be Ready

[35] "Be prepared for action[a] at a moment's notice. [36] Be like the servants who anticipate their master's return from a wedding celebration. They are ready to unlock and open the door for him at a moment's notice. [37] What great joy is ahead for the awakened ones who are waiting for the Master's return! He himself will become their servant and wait on them at his table as he passes by. [38] He may appear at midnight or even later, but what great joy for the awakened ones whenever he comes! [39] Of course, if they knew ahead of time the hour of the master's appearing, they would be alert, just as they would be ready if they knew ahead of time that a thief was coming to break into their house. [40] So keep being alert and ready at all times. For I can promise you that the Son of Man will surprise you and will appear[b] when you don't expect him."

The Faithful Servant

[41] "Lord," Peter asked, "does this apply only to the twelve of us, or is it for everyone else as well?"

[42] The Lord said, "A trustworthy and thoughtful manager who understands the ways of his master will be given a ministry of responsibility in his master's house, serving others exactly what they need at just the right time. [43-44] And when the master returns, he will find that his servant has served him well. I can promise you, he will be given a great reward and will be placed as an overseer of everything the master owns.

[45] "But what if that servant says in his heart, 'My master delays his coming, and who knows when he will return?' Because of the delay, the servant elevates himself and mistreats those in his master's household. Instead of caring for the ones he was appointed to serve, he abuses the other servants,

---

a 12:35 The Greek is literally "Let your loins be girded and keep your lamps burning."
b 12:40 The Greek word can also be translated "become."

both men and women. He throws drunken parties for his friends and gives himself over to every pleasure. [46]Let me tell you what will happen to him. His master will suddenly return at a time that shocks him, and he will remove the abusive, selfish servant from his position of trust. He will be severely punished and assigned a portion with the unbelievers.

[47]"Every servant who knows full well what pleases his master, yet who does not make himself ready and refuses to put his master's will to action, will be punished with many blows. [48]But the servant who does not know *his master's will* and unwittingly does what is wrong will be punished less severely. For those who have received a greater revelation from their master are required a greater obedience. And those who have been entrusted with great responsibility will be held more responsible to their master."

Jesus Brings Fire to the Earth

[49]"I have come to set the earth on fire. And how I long for every heart to be already ablaze with this fiery passion for God! [50]But first I must be immersed into the baptism *of God's judgment,*[a] and I am consumed with passion as I await its fulfillment. [51]Don't think for a moment that I came to grant peace and harmony to everyone. No, for my coming will change everything and create hostility among you. [52]From now on, even family members will be divided over me and will choose sides[b] against one another. [53]Fathers will be split off against sons and sons against fathers; mothers will be against daughters and daughters against mothers; mothers-in-law will be against brides and brides against mothers-in-law—all because of me."

Discerning the Time

[54]Jesus then said to the crowds gathered around him, "When you see a cloud forming in the west, don't you say, 'A storm is brewing'? And then it arrives. [55]And when you feel the south wind blowing, you say, 'A heat wave is on the way.' And so it happens. [56]What hypocrites![c] You are such experts at forecasting the weather, but you are totally unwilling to understand *the spiritual significance of* the time you're living in.

[57]"You can't even judge for yourselves what is good and right.

[58]"When you are wrong, it is better that you agree with your adversary

---

a 12:50 The implication of the context is that Jesus was drawing closer to his time of experiencing God's judgment for our sins on the cross. It is a "baptism" of judgment that we deserved.

b 12:52 The Greek text is literally "Among five in one house, three will be against two and two will be against three."

c 12:56 There is an amazing play on words found in the Aramaic text. The word translated "hypocrites" is literally "accepter of faces." The Aramaic states that the Pharisees looked at the "face" of the sky and the "faces" of men, living superficially, not seeing what was happening spiritually around them.

and settle your dispute before you have to go before a judge. If not, you may be dragged into court, and the judge may find you guilty and [9]throw you into prison until you have paid off your fine entirely."

The Need for True Repentance

13 Some of those present informed Jesus that Pilate had slaughtered some Galilean Jews[a] while they were offering sacrifices at the temple, mixing their blood with the sacrifices they were offering.

[2]Jesus turned and asked the crowd, "Do you believe that the slaughtered Galileans were the worst sinners of all the Galileans? [3]No, they weren't! So listen to me. Unless you all repent,[b] you will perish as they did. [4]Or what about the eighteen who perished when the tower of Siloam[c] fell upon them? Do you really think that they were more guilty than all of the others in Jerusalem? [5]No, they weren't. But unless you repent, you will all eternally perish, just as they did."

The Parable of the Barren Tree

[6]Then Jesus told them this parable: "There was a man who planted a fig tree in his orchard. But when he came to gather fruit from his tree he found none, for it was barren and had no fruit. [7]So he said to his gardener, 'For the last three years I've come to gather figs from my tree but it remains fruitless. What a waste! Go ahead and cut it down!'

[8]"But the gardener said, 'Sir, we should leave it one more year. Let me fertilize and cultivate it, then let's see if it will produce fruit. [9]If it doesn't bear fruit by next year, we'll cut it down.'"[d]

Jesus Heals on the Sabbath Day

[10]One Sabbath day, while Jesus was teaching in the synagogue, [11]he encountered a seriously handicapped woman. She was crippled and had been doubled over for eighteen years. Her condition was caused by a demonic spirit of bondage[e] that had left her unable to stand up straight.

[12-13]When Jesus saw her condition, he called her over and gently laid his

---

a 13:1 It is likely that Pilate viewed these Jews as rebellious to his rule. This was indeed an atrocious act by Pilate.

b 13:3 The Greek term for repentance means "to change your mind and amend your ways."

c 13:4 Siloam was the name of a pool or reservoir for the city of Jerusalem near the junction of the south and east walls of the city.

d 13:9 This parable was an obvious picture of the nation of Israel. The owner was the Father and the gardener was Jesus, who had come to them and for three years had longed to have true spiritual fruit from his spiritual vine (Isa. 5:1–7). The warning is that it would be cut down if it did not bear the fruits of repentance. The purpose of the parable was to warn people that they were in their last year of God's grace toward them.

e 13:11 Literally "spirit of weakness."

hands on her. Then he said, "Dear woman, you are free. I release you forever from this crippling spirit." Instantly she stood straight and tall and overflowed with glorious praise to God!

[14] The Jewish leader who was in charge of the synagogue was infuriated over Jesus healing on the Sabbath day. "Six days you are to work," he shouted angrily to the crowd. "Those are the days you should come here for healing, but not on the seventh day!"

[15] The Lord said, "You hopeless frauds! Don't you care for your animals on the Sabbath day, untying your ox or donkey from the stall and leading it away to water? [16] If you do this for your animals, what's wrong with allowing this beloved daughter of Abraham, who has been bound by Satan for eighteen long years, to be untied and set free on a Sabbath day?"

[17] When they heard this, his critics were completely humiliated. But the crowds shouted with joy over the glorious things Jesus was doing among them.

Parables of Jesus

[18] Jesus taught them this parable: "How can I describe God's kingdom realm? Let me illustrate it this way. [19] It is like the smallest of seeds that you would plant in a garden. And when it grows, it becomes a huge tree, with so many spreading branches that various birds make nests there." [a]

[20] Jesus taught them another parable: "How can I describe God's kingdom realm? Let me give you this illustration: [21] It is like something as small as yeast that a woman kneads into a large amount of dough. It works unseen until it permeates [b] the entire batch and rises high."

The Way of the Kingdom

[22] Jesus ministered in one town and village after another, [c] teaching the people as he made his way toward Jerusalem. [23] A bystander asked him, "Lord, will only a few have eternal life?"

Jesus said to the crowd, [24] "There is a great cost [d] for anyone to enter through the narrow doorway to God's kingdom realm. I tell you, there will be many who will want to enter but won't be able to. [25] For once the head of the house has shut and locked the door, it will be too late. Even if you stand outside knocking, begging to enter, and saying, 'Lord, Lord, open the door

---

a 13:19 See Ezek. 17:23. The obvious meaning of this parable is that God's kingdom realm will begin small but it will expand, grow, and mature. People from every nation will come and make a "nest" in God's kingdom realm.

b 13:21 The meaning of this parable is that something small can impact and penetrate something great. It is the pervading influence of virtue and truth that is highlighted here. A transformation takes place when the hidden yet pervasive kingdom impacts every part of culture and society around us.

c 13:22 Jesus now visits the places where his disciples had already been. See Luke 10:1–11.

d 13:24 The Greek word used here is actually "agonize."

for us,' he will say to you, 'I don't know who you are. *You are not a part of my family.'*

²⁶ "Then you will reply, 'But Lord, we dined with you and walked with you as you taught us.' ²⁷ And he will reply, 'Don't you understand? I don't know who you are, for you are not a part of my family. You cannot enter in. Now, go away from me! For you are all disloyal to me and do evil.' ᵃ

²⁸ "You will experience great weeping and great anguish when you see Abraham, Isaac, and Jacob, along with all the prophets of Israel, enjoying God's kingdom realm while you yourselves are barred from entering. ²⁹ And you will see people streaming from the four corners of the earth, accepting the invitation to feast in God's kingdom, *while you are kept outside looking in.* ³⁰ And take note of this: There are some who are despised and viewed as the least important now, but will one day be placed at the head of the line. And there are others who are viewed as 'elite' today who will become least important then."

Jesus' Sorrow for Jerusalem

³¹ Just then some Jewish religious leaders came to Jesus to inform him that Herod was out to kill him and urged him to flee from that place. ³² Jesus told them, "Go and tell that deceiver ᵇ that I will continue to cast out demons and heal the sick today and tomorrow, but on the third day I will bring my work to perfection. ³³ For everyone knows I am safe until I come to Jerusalem, for that is where all the prophets have been killed. ³⁴ O city of Jerusalem, you are the city that murders your prophets! You are the city that pelts to death with stones the very messengers ᶜ who were sent to deliver you! So many times I have longed to gather your wayward children together around me, as a hen gathers her chicks under her wings—but you were too stubborn to let me. ³⁵ And now it is too late, since your house will be left in ruins. ᵈ You will not see me again until you are able to say, 'We welcome the one who comes to us in the name of the Lord.'" ᵉ

Jesus Heals on the Sabbath

14 One day Jesus was on his way to dine with a prominent Jewish religious leader for a Sabbath meal. Everyone was watching him to see if he would heal anyone on the Sabbath. ² Just then, standing right in front of him was a man suffering with his limbs swollen with fluid.

---

a 13:27 This is quoted from Ps. 6:8. Though they were acquaintances, they had not responded to his message with repentance. The word *disloyal* is taken from the Aramaic. The question to ask is not simply, "Will the saved be few?" (v. 23) but rather, "Will it be you?"

b 13:32 Or "fox."

c 13:34 Or "apostles."

d 13:35 See Jer. 12:7.

e 13:35 See Ps. 118:26.

[3]Jesus asked the experts of the law and the Pharisees who were present, "Is it permitted within the law to heal a man on the Sabbath day? Is it right or wrong?" [4]No one dared to answer. So Jesus turned to the sick man, took hold of him, and released healing to him, then sent him on his way.

[5]Jesus said to them all, "If one of your children or one of your animals fell into a well, wouldn't you do all you could to rescue them even if it was a Sabbath day?"

[6]There was nothing they could say—all were silenced.

Humility and Hospitality

[7]When Jesus noticed how the guests for the meal were all vying for the seats of honor, he shared this story with the guests around the table:

[8]"When you are invited to an important social function, don't be quick to sit near the head of the table, choosing the seat of honor. What will happen when someone more distinguished than you arrives? [9]The host will then bring him over to where you are sitting and ask for your seat, saying in front of all the guests, 'You're in the wrong place. Please give this person your seat.' Disgraced, you will have to take whatever seat is left. [10]Instead, when you're invited to a banquet, you should choose to sit in the lowest place[a] so that when your host comes and sees you there, he may say, 'My friend, come with me and let me seat you in a better place.' Then, in front of all the other guests at the banquet, you will be honored and seated in the place of highest respect.

[11]"Remember this: everyone with a lofty opinion of who he is and who seeks to raise himself up will be humbled before all. And everyone with a modest opinion of who he is and chooses to humble himself will be raised up before all."

[12]Then Jesus turned to his host and said, "When you throw a banquet, don't just invite your friends, relatives, or rich neighbors—for it is likely they will return the favor. [13-14]It is better to invite those who never get an invitation. Invite the poor to your banquet, along with the outcast, the handicapped, and the blind—those who could never repay you the favor. Then you will experience a great blessing in this life, and at the resurrection of the godly you will receive a full reward."

[15]When they heard this, one of the dinner guests said to Jesus, "Someday God will have a kingdom feast,[b] and how happy and privileged will be the ones who get to share in that joy!"

[16]Jesus replied with this parable:

"There was a man who invited many to join him in a great feast. [17]When the day for the feast arrived, the host instructed his servant to notify all the

---

a   14:10 See Prov. 25:6–7.
b   14:15 The guest at the dinner assumed God's kingdom realm was coming one day, but Jesus' parable explained that it had already begun with the invitation to come to him, the King.

invited guests and tell them, 'Come, for everything is now ready for you!' [18] But one by one they all made excuses. One said, 'I can't come. I just bought some property and I'm obligated to go and look it over.' [19] Another said, 'Please accept my regrets, for I just purchased five teams of oxen[a] and I need to make sure they can pull the plow.' [20] Another one said, 'I can't come because I just got married.'

[21] "The servant reported back to the host and told him of all their excuses. So the master became angry and said to his servant, 'Go at once throughout the city and invite anyone you find—the poor, the blind, the disabled, the hurting, and the lonely—and invite them to my banquet.'

[22] "When the servant returned to his master, he said, 'Sir, I have done what you've asked, but there's still room for more.'

[23] "So the master told him, 'All right. Go out again, and this time bring them all back with you. Persuade the beggars on the streets, the outcasts, even the homeless. Urgently insist that they come in and enjoy the feast so that my house will be full.'

[24] "I say to you all, the one who receives an invitation to feast with me and makes excuses will never enjoy my banquet."

The Cost of Following Jesus

[25] As massive crowds followed Jesus, he turned to them and said, [26] "When you follow me as my disciple, you must put aside[b] your father, your mother, your wife, your sisters, your brothers—yes, you will even seem as though you hate your own life. This is the price you'll pay to be considered one of my followers. [27] And anyone who comes to me must be willing to share my cross and experience it as his own, or he cannot be considered to be my disciple. [28] So don't follow me without considering what it will cost you. For who would construct a house[c] before first sitting down to estimate the cost to complete it? [29] Otherwise he may lay the foundation and not be able to finish. The neighbors will ridicule him, saying, [30] 'Look at him! He started to build but couldn't complete it!'

[31] "Have you ever heard of a commander[d] who goes out to war without first sitting down with strategic planning to determine the strength of his army to win the war[e] against a stronger opponent? [32] If he knows he doesn't stand a chance of winning the war, the wise commander will send out

a 14:19 This implies he was a wealthy man who foolishly chose possessions over Christ.
b 14:26 Or "hate." This is an Aramaic and Hebraic metaphor for putting Jesus above every other relationship. The Aramaic word *sna* has several meanings and can mean "hate" or "put aside." In this case, Jesus, the King of love is not saying to hate but to put aside every other relationship into second place. The meaning becomes quite clear in the Aramaic language.
c 14:28 Or "tower."
d 14:31 Or "king."
e 14:31 The Greek text states, "With ten thousand he will be able to go up against twenty thousand."

delegates to ask for the terms of peace. ³³ Likewise, unless you surrender all to me, giving up all you possess, you cannot be one of my disciples. ³⁴ "Salt is good for seasoning. But if salt were to lose its flavor,ª how could it ever be restored? ³⁵ It will never be useful again, not even fit for the soil or the manure pile!ᵇ If you have ears opened by the Spirit, then hear the meaning of what I have said *and apply it to yourselves.*"

The Parable of the Lost Lamb

15 Many dishonest tax collectors and other notorious sinners often gathered around to listen as Jesus taught the people. ² This raised concerns with the Jewish religious leaders and experts of the law. Indignant, they grumbled and complained, saying, "Look at how this man associates with all these notorious sinners and welcomes them all to come to him!"

³ In response, Jesus gave them this illustration:

⁴⁻⁵ "There once was a shepherd with a hundred lambs, but one of his lambs wandered away and was lost. So the shepherd left the ninety-nine lambs out in the open field and searched in the wilderness for that one lost lamb. He didn't stop until he finally found it. With exuberant joy he raised it up and placed it on his shoulders,ᶜ carrying it back with cheerful delight! ⁶ Returning home, he called all his friends and neighbors together and said, 'Let's have a party! Come and celebrate with me the return of my lost lamb. It wandered away, but I found it and brought it home.'"

⁷ Jesus continued, "In the same way, there will be a glorious celebration in heaven over the rescue of one lost sinner who repents, comes back home, and returns to the fold—more so than for all the righteous people who never strayed away."

The Parable of the Lost Coin

⁸ Jesus gave them another parable:

"There once was a woman who had ten ᵈ valuable silver coins. When

---

a 14:34 Or "become foolish." Both Greek and Aramaic use a word that can mean "foolish." If salt that has lost its flavor is foolish, then the salt that keeps its flavor is equal to wisdom. Rabbinical literature equates salt with wisdom. (Eduard Schweizer," *The Good News According to Matthew*, Atlanta: John Knox Press, 1975.) After speaking of salt, Jesus, in Matthew 5:13–15, goes on to refer to lighting a lamp. It was a common practice in the time of Jesus to put salt on the wick of a lamp to increase its brightness. The "salt" of wisdom will make our light shine even brighter. (W. A. Elwell and P.W. Comfort, *Tyndale Bible Dictionary*, Tyndale reference library, Wheaton, Ill.: Tyndale House, 2001, 797–798.)

b 14:35 Followers of Jesus who are unwilling to pay the price of discipleship are like worthless salt, unable to affect anything or anyone.

c 15:4–5 What a wonderful picture this gives us of our "Good Shepherd." He doesn't beat the lost sheep for wandering away. He raises it up and carries it home!

d 15:8 The silver coin was a *zuza* (Aramaic). Although there are differing opinions as to its

she lost one of them, she swept her entire house, diligently searching every corner of her house for that one lost coin. ⁹When she finally found it, she gathered all her friends and neighbors for a celebration, telling them, 'Come and celebrate with me! I had lost my precious silver coin, but now I've found it.' ¹⁰That's the way God responds* every time one lost sinner repents and turns to him. He says to all his angels, 'Let's have a joyous celebration, for that one who was lost I have found!'"*

The Loving Father

¹¹Then Jesus said, "Once there was a father with two sons. ¹²The younger son came to his father and said, 'Father, don't you think it's time to give me the share of your estate that belongs to me?'* So the father went ahead and distributed among the two sons their inheritance.* ¹³Shortly afterward, the younger son packed up all his belongings and traveled off to see the world. He journeyed to a far-off land where he soon wasted all he was given in a binge of extravagant and reckless living.

¹⁴"With everything spent and nothing left, he grew hungry, for there was a severe famine in that land. ¹⁵So he begged a farmer in that country to hire him. The farmer hired him and sent him out to feed the pigs. ¹⁶The son was so famished, he was willing to even eat the slop given to the pigs,* because no one would feed him a thing.

¹⁷"Humiliated, the son finally realized what he was doing and he thought, 'There are many workers at my father's house who have all the food they want with plenty to spare. They lack nothing. Why am I here dying of hunger, feeding these pigs and eating their slop? ¹⁸I want to go back home to my father's house, and I'll say to him, "Father, I was wrong. I have sinned against you. ¹⁹I'll never be worthy to be called your son. Please, Father, just treat me like one of your employees."'

---

value, it could be equal in today's currency to more than twelve hundred US dollars. Notice the change of numbers in the three parables in this chapter: one out of a hundred for the sheep, one out of ten for the coins, and one out of two for the sons. This progressively shows the extraordinary value that Jesus places on every lost soul. Although the coin was lost, it never lost its value.

a 15:10 Jesus used the woman in this parable as a metaphor for God. This alone would incite anger from the Pharisees. In the next parable, God is unveiled as the extravagant Father who forgives his wayward son.

b 15:10 The silver coin had an image of Roman authority on it. We have been stamped with the image of God. Even when we are "lost," that image is still present, needing only to be "found" by grace and redeemed.

c 15:12 In the light of Middle Eastern culture, it was a great offense for a son to ask his father for his inheritance. It would be equivalent to saying, "I wish you were already dead!"

d 15:12 The Greek is literally "He gave them his life" (Greek *bios*).

e 15:16 This would be degrading to anyone, but especially to a Jew, who was forbidden to raise swine.

²⁰ "So the young son set off for home. From a long distance away, his father saw him coming, *dressed as a beggar,*ᵃ and great compassion swelled up in his heart for his son who was returning home. So the father raced out to meet him. He swept him up in his arms, hugged him dearly, and kissed him over and over with tender love.

²¹ "Then the son said, 'Father, I was wrong. I have sinned against you. I could never deserve to be called your son. Just let me be—'

"The father interrupted and said,ᵇ 'Son, you're home now!'

²² "Turning to his servants, the father said, 'Quick, bring me the best robe, my very own robe, and I will place it on his shoulders. Bring the ring, the seal of sonship,ᶜ and I will put it on his finger. And bring out the best shoesᵈ you can find for my son. ²³ Let's *prepare a great feast*ᵉ and celebrate. ²⁴ For this beloved son of mine was once dead, but now he's alive again. Once he was lost, but now he is found!' And everyone celebrated with overflowing joy.

²⁵ "Now, the older son was out working in the field when his brother returned, and as he approached the house he heard the music of celebration and dancing. ²⁶ So he called over one of the servants and asked, 'What's going on?'

²⁷ "The servant replied, 'It's your younger brother. He's returned home and your father is throwing a party to celebrate his homecoming.'

²⁸ "The older son became angry and refused to go in and celebrate. So his father came out and pleaded with him, 'Come and enjoy the feast with us!'ᶠ

²⁹ "The son said, 'Father, listen! How many years have I been working like a slave for you, performing every duty you've asked as a faithful son?ᵍ And I've never once disobeyed you. But you've never thrown a party for me because of my faithfulness. Never once have you even given me a goat that I could feast on and celebrate with my friends like he's doing now. ³⁰ But look at this son of yours! He comes back after wasting your wealth on prostitutes and reckless living, and here you are throwing a great feast to celebrate—for him!'

³¹ "The father said, 'My son, you are always with me by my side.

---

a 15:20 Implied in the context of the Greek text and stated more explicitly in the Aramaic.

b 15:21 This poetic description is made explicit from the cultural and spiritual implication of the text.

c 15:22 Culturally, this ring was an emblem of authority, giving the son authority to transact business in the father's name. This was a picture of the seal of the Holy Spirit (Eph. 1:14).

d 15:22 Or "bring sandals for his feet." Slaves were barefoot.

e 15:23 The Greek text is "kill the grain-fatted calf." This is a picture of feasting upon Christ, who was sacrificed for us.

f 15:28 In the culture of that era, hospitality was of supreme importance. To refuse to go in to the feast, when it was his responsibility culturally to cohost the event with his father, was a humiliating rejection of the father.

g 15:29 While the younger brother pursued self-discovery, the older brother believed in moral conformity, earning favor from his father. Both needed the revelation of grace.

Everything I have is yours to enjoy. [32] It's only right to celebrate like this and be overjoyed, because this brother of yours was once dead and gone, but now he is alive and back with us again. He was lost but now he is found!'" [a]

The Dishonest Manager

16 Jesus taught his disciples using this story:

"There was once a very rich man who hired a manager to run his business and oversee all his wealth. But soon a rumor spread that the manager was wasting his master's money. [2] So the master called him in and said, 'Is it true that you are mismanaging my estate? You need to provide me with a complete audit of everything you oversee for me. I've decided to dismiss you.'

[3] "The manager thought, 'Now what am I going to do? I'm finished here. I can't hide what I've done, [b] and I'm too proud to beg to get my job back. [4] I have an idea that will secure my future. It will win me favor and secure friends who can take care of me and help me when I get fired!'

[5] "So the dishonest manager hatched his scheme. He went to everyone who owed his master money, one by one, and he asked them, 'How much do you owe my master?' [6-7] One debtor owed twenty thousand dollars, so he said to him, 'Let me see your bill. Pay me now and we'll settle for twenty percent less.' The clever manager scratched out the original amount owed and reduced it by twenty percent. And to another who owed two hundred thousand dollars, he said, 'Pay me now and we'll reduce your bill by fifty percent.' And the clever manager scratched out the original amount owed and reduced it by half.

[8] "Even though his master was defrauded, when he found out about the shrewd way this manager had feathered his own nest, he congratulated the clever scoundrel for what he'd done to lay up for his future needs."

Jesus continued, "Remember this: The sons of darkness are more shrewd than the sons of light in their interactions with others. [9] It is important that you use the wealth of this world to demonstrate your friendship with God

---

a 15:32 Jesus spoke three parables unveiling and revealing how the Trinity desires to bring people back through the Son, by the Spirit, to the Father. The Son came as a shepherd, seeking and sacrificing to find the lost sinner. The Spirit seeks the lost like the woman with the light of illumination for the lost coin until she found it. And the Father welcomes the returning sinner back to his house. It is the work of the Trinity to bring us back to God. In Matt. 28:19, it is the sequence of the Father, the Spirit, and the Son. Here in Luke 15, it is the Son, the Spirit, and the Father.

b 16:3 The manager's words include an ancient Aramaic figure of speech, "I can't dig," which means it can't be buried or hidden.

by winning friends and blessing others. Then, when this world *a* fails and falls apart, your generosity will provide you with an eternal reward. *b*

¹⁰ "The one who manages the little he has been given with faithfulness and integrity will be promoted and trusted with greater responsibilities. But those who cheat with the little they have been given will not be considered trustworthy to receive more. ¹¹ If you have not handled the riches of this world with integrity, why should you be trusted with the eternal treasures of the spiritual world? ¹² And if you've not been proven faithful with what belongs to another, why should you be given wealth of your own? ¹³ It is impossible for a person to serve two masters at the same time. You will be forced to love one and reject the other. One master will be despised and the other will have your loyal devotion. It is no different with God and the wealth of this world. *c* You must enthusiastically love one and definitively reject the other."

¹⁴ Now, the Jewish religious leaders who were listening to Jesus were lovers of money. They laughed at what he said and mocked his teachings.

¹⁵ So Jesus addressed them directly. "You always want to look spiritual in the eyes of others, but you have forgotten the eyes of God, which see what is inside you. The very things that you approve of and applaud are the things God despises. ¹⁶ The law of Moses and the revelation of the prophets have prepared you for the arrival of the kingdom realm announced by John. And now, when this wonderful news of God's kingdom realm is preached, people's hearts burn with extreme passion to press in and receive it. ¹⁷ Heaven and earth will disintegrate before even the smallest detail of the word of God will fail or lose its power.

¹⁸ "It is wrong for you to divorce *d* your wife so that you can marry another—that is adultery. And when you take that one you have lusted after as your wife, and contribute to the breakup of her marriage, you are once again guilty of adultery."

The Rich Man and Lazarus

¹⁹ Jesus continued. "There once was a very rich man who had the finest things imaginable, *e* living every day enjoying his life of opulent luxury. ²⁰⁻²¹ *Outside the gate of his mansion* was a poor beggar named Lazarus. *f* He lay there every day, covered with boils, and all the neighborhood dogs would come and lick

---

a 16:9 Or "your earthly wealth."
b 16:9 Or "you will be welcomed to the tents of eternity."
c 16:13 The word used here is *Mammon*, which is money personified as a god and worshiped.
d 16:18 Or "dismiss," or "send away."
e 16:19 The Greek text is literally "He was dressed in a purple robe." This is a figure of speech that refers to the luxury that surrounded him. This was the kind of robe worn only by kings.
f 16:20–21 *Lazarus* is a form of the name Eleazar and means "God helps."

his open sores. The only food he had to eat was the garbage that the rich man threw away.

²² "One day poor Lazarus died, and the angels of God came and escorted his spirit into paradise. ͣ

²³ "The day came that the rich man also died. In hell he looked up from his torment and saw Abraham in the distance, and Lazarus the beggar was standing beside him in the glory. ²⁴ So the rich man shouted, 'Father Abraham! Father Abraham! Have mercy on me. Send Lazarus to dip his finger in water and come to cool my tongue, for I am in agony in these flames of fire!'

²⁵ "But Abraham responded, 'My friend, don't you remember? While you were alive, you had all you desired, surrounded in luxury, while Lazarus had nothing. Now Lazarus is in the comforts of paradise and you are in agony. ²⁶ Besides, between us is a huge chasm that cannot be bridged, keeping anyone from crossing from one realm to the other, even if he wanted to.'

²⁷ "So the rich man said, 'Then let me ask you, Father Abraham, to please send Lazarus to my relatives. ²⁸ Tell him to witness to my five brothers and warn them not to end up where I am in this place of torment.'

²⁹ "Abraham replied, 'They've already had enough warning. They have the teachings of Moses and the prophets, and they must obey them.'

³⁰ "'But what if they're not listening?' the rich man added. 'If someone from the dead were to go and warn them, they would surely repent.'

³¹ "Abraham said to him, 'If they won't listen to Moses and the prophets, neither would they believe even if someone ᵇ was raised from the dead!'"

Faith and Forgiveness

17 One day Jesus taught his disciples this: "Betrayals ͨ are inevitable, but great devastation will come to the one guilty of betraying others. ² It would be better for him to have a heavy boulder tied around his neck and be hurled into the deepest sea than to face the punishment of betraying one of my dear ones! So be alert to your brother's condition, ³ and if you see him going the wrong direction, cry out and correct him. If there is true repentance on his part, forgive him. ⁴ No matter how many times in one day your brother sins against you ͩ and says, 'I'm sorry; I am changing; forgive me,' you need to forgive him each and every time."

---

a 16:22 The Greek text is literally "Abraham's bosom," which is a metaphor for paradise.
b 16:31 Translated from the Aramaic. Jesus is that "someone" who rose from the grave, yet many still will not listen and believe.
c 17:1 As translated from the Aramaic. Other Greek texts use the words "temptation" or "to stumble."
d 17:4 The Greek text states explicitly "seven times." But this is used as a metaphor for unlimited forgiveness.

⁵Upon hearing this, the apostles said to Jesus, "Lord, you must increase*
our measure of faith!"

⁶Jesus responded, "If you have even the smallest measure of authentic
faith, it would be powerful enough to say to this large* tree, 'My faith will
pull you up by the roots and throw you into the sea,' *and it will respond to your
faith and obey you."* *

⁷⁻⁸Jesus continued, "After a servant has finished his work in the field or
with the livestock, he doesn't immediately sit down to relax and eat. No, a
true servant prepares the food for his master and makes sure his master is
served his meal before he sits down to eat his own. ⁹Does the true servant
expect to be thanked for doing what is required of him? ¹⁰So learn this lesson:
After doing all that is commanded of you, simply say, 'We are mere servants,
undeserving of special praise, for we are just doing what is expected of us
and fulfilling our duties.'"

Jesus Heals Ten Lepers

¹¹Jesus traveled on toward Jerusalem and passed through the border region between Samaria and Galilee. ¹²As he entered one village, ten men approached
him, but they kept their distance, for they were lepers. ¹³They shouted to him,
"Mighty Lord, our wonderful Master!* Won't you have mercy on us *and heal us?*"
¹⁴When Jesus stopped to look at them, he spoke these words: "Go to be
examined by the Jewish priests."*

They set off, and they were healed while walking along the way. ¹⁵One
of them, *a foreigner from Samaria,*/ when he discovered that he was completely
healed, turned back to find Jesus, shouting out joyous praises and glorifying
God. ¹⁶When he found Jesus, he fell down at his feet and thanked him over and
over, saying to him, "You are the Messiah."* This man was a Samaritan.

¹⁷"So where are the other nine?" Jesus asked. "Weren't there ten who
were healed? ¹⁸They all refused to return to give thanks and give glory to God
except you, a foreigner from Samaria?"

---

a 17:5 The Greek text is literally "add faith to us."

b 17:6 The Greek text is "mulberry" or "sycamore tree," which is known to grow to about
thirty-five feet high.

c 17:6 The apostles had faith; they simply needed to use it.

d 17:13 The Greek word used here for "Master" is not the usual word used for "Teacher" or
"Master." It denotes one with supernatural authority and power.

e 17:14 This was what was required. See Lev. 13:19; 14:1–11. What a step of faith for these
lepers as they stepped out on only the word Jesus spoke to them. They were to go the priest,
who would confirm their healing and declare them ceremonially clean and approved to go
into the temple to worship God.

f 17:15 For a Samaritan man to give thanks to a Jewish man was indeed peculiar. Since he
likely had no "priest," he turned to the only one he knew to be a priest for him, Jesus Christ.

g 17:16 From the Aramaic text.

[19] Then Jesus said to the healed man lying at his feet, "Arise and go. It was your faith that brought you salvation and healing."

God's Kingdom Realm within You

[20] Jesus was once asked by the Jewish religious leaders, "When will God's kingdom realm come?" [a]

Jesus responded, "God's kingdom realm does not come simply *by obeying principles* [b] or by waiting for signs. [21] The kingdom is not discovered in one place or another, for God's kingdom realm is already expanding within some of you." [c]

[22] Later, Jesus addressed this again with his apostles, saying, "The time is coming when a great passion will be awakened within you to see me again. Yes, you will long to see the beginning of the days of the Son of Man, but you won't be able to find me. [23] You will hear reports from some who will say, 'Look, he has returned,' 'He's over here,' or, 'He's over there!' Don't believe it or run after them, *for their claims will be false.* [24] The day of the Son of Man will burst forth with the brightness of a lightning strike that shines from one end of the sky to the other, illuminating the earth.

[25] "But before this takes place, the Son of Man must pass through great suffering and rejection from this generation. [26] The same things that happened in the days of Noah will take place in the days of the Son of Man. [27] They were eating, they were drinking, they were marrying, and they were given in marriage until the day Noah boarded the ark and the devastating flood came and swept them all away.

[28-30] "The days of the Son of Man can also be compared to the days of Lot. The people of that time lived their lives as normal. They got married, raised families, built homes and businesses, yet they were totally unaware of what was coming until the day Lot departed from Sodom. The sky opened up and rained fire and burning sulfur upon them, destroying everyone and everything they had built. So it will be on the day of the unveiling of the Son of Man.

[31] "In the day of my appearing, if one is outside, [d] he won't even have time to go back into the house to gather his belongings. And those toiling in their fields won't have time to run back home. [32] Don't forget the example of Lot's wife and what happened to her when she turned back. [e] [33] All who

---

a 17:20 Or "When will God's kingdom be established?"
b 17:20 Implied in the Aramaic text where it states, "observances" (of the law). The same word is found in Gal. 4:10 referring to "observances" of keeping the law.
c 17:21 Translated from the Aramaic text. The implication is that God's kingdom realm is a person, Jesus Christ. The reality of God's kingdom appears when Jesus lives within us by faith.
d 17:31 The Greek text is literally "on the roof."
e 17:32 See Gen. 19:26.

are obsessed with being secure in life will lose it all—including their lives. But those who let go of their lives and surrender them to me will discover true life. ³⁴ For in that night there will be two lying in their bed; one will be suddenly swept away while the other will be left alive. ³⁵⁻³⁶ There will be two women working together at household duties; one will be suddenly swept away while the other will be left alive." *a*

³⁷ His apostles asked, "Lord, where will this *judgment* happen?"

Jesus responded, "*It will be obvious*, for wherever there are those spiritually dead, *b* there you will find the eagles *c* circling."

Jesus Gives a Parable about Prayer

18 One day Jesus taught the apostles to keep praying and never stop or lose hope. He shared with them this illustration:

² "In a certain town there was a civil judge, a thick-skinned and godless man who had no fear of others' opinions. ³ And there was a poor widow in that town who kept pleading with the judge, 'Grant me justice and protect me against my oppressor!'

⁴⁻⁵ "He ignored her pleas for quite some time, but she kept asking. Eventually he said to himself, 'This widow keeps annoying me, demanding her rights, and I'm tired of listening to her. Even though I'm not a religious man and don't care about the opinions of others, I'll just get her off my back by answering her claims for justice and I'll rule in her favor. Then she'll leave me alone.'"

⁶ The Lord continued, "Did you hear what the ungodly judge said—that he would answer her persistent request? ⁷ Don't you know that God, the true judge, will grant justice to all of his chosen ones who cry out to him night and day? He will pour out his Spirit upon them. *d* He will not delay to answer you and give you what you ask for. ⁸ God will give swift justice to those who don't give up. So be ever praying, ever expecting, just like the widow was with the judge. Yet when the Son of Man comes back, will he find this kind of persistent faithfulness in his people?"

Humility in Prayer

⁹ Jesus taught this parable to those who were convinced they were morally

---

a 17:35–36 This Greek word can also refer to being "forgiven of sin." Some later Greek texts add, "Two men will be in the field; one will be taken and the other will be left. Those who are swept away are taken to judgment; those who are left behind remain to enter into the kingdom glory."

b 17:37 The Greek word used here is literally "corpse" and can be a metaphor for those who are spiritually dead.

c 17:37 The Greek word used here is clearly "eagles." Some translations read "vultures."

d 18:7 Translated from the Aramaic text. The Greek text has an unusual verb that means "ever tapping," signifying one who keeps knocking on the door of heaven until he receives what he came for.

upright and those who trusted in their own virtue yet looked down on others with disgust:

[10] "Once there were two men who went into the temple to pray. One was a proud religious leader, the other a despised tax collector. [11-12] The religious leader stood apart from the others and prayed, 'How I thank you, O God, that I'm not wicked like everyone else. They're cheaters, swindlers, and crooks—like that tax collector over there. God, you know that I never cheat or commit adultery; I fast from food twice a week and I give you a tenth of all I make.'

[13] "The tax collector stood off alone in the corner, *away from the Holy Place*, and covered his face in his hands, feeling that he was unworthy to even look up to God. Beating his breast,[a] he sobbed with brokenness and tears saying, 'God, please, in your mercy *and because of the blood sacrifice, forgive me*,[b] for I am nothing but the most miserable of all sinners!'

[14] "Which one of them left for home that day made right with God? It was the humble tax collector and not the religious leader! For everyone who praises himself will one day be humiliated before all, and everyone who humbles himself will one day be lifted up and honored before all."

Jesus Blesses Children

[15] The people brought their babies and small children[c] to Jesus so that he might lay his hands on them to bless them. When the disciples saw this, they scolded the parents and told them to stop troubling the Master. [16] But Jesus called for the parents, the children, and his disciples to come and listen to him. Then he told them, "Never hinder a child from coming to me. Let them all come, for God's kingdom realm belongs to them as much as it does to anyone else. *They demonstrate to you what faith is all about.* [17] Learn this well: unless you receive the revelation of the kingdom realm the same way a little child receives it, you will never be able to enter in."

Jesus Speaks with a Young, Wealthy Official

[18] One day a wealthy Jewish nobleman of high standing posed this question to Jesus: "Wonderful Teacher, what must I do to be saved and receive eternal life?"

[19] Jesus answered, "Why would you call me wonderful when there is only one who is wonderful—and that is God alone?[d] [20] You already know what is

---

a 18:13 The Greek verb *typto*, means "to strike," or "to strike dead." It is a violent term also used of the scourging of Jesus.

b 18:13 The Greek text uses a word that implies he was saying to God, "Look at me as you look at the blood-sprinkled mercy seat."

c 18:15 There is a hint in the Greek text that these children may have been sick. Jesus loves and heals children.

d 18:19 Jesus is implying that if we call him "wonderful," we are calling him "God."

right and what the commandments teach: 'Do not commit adultery, do not murder, do not steal, do not lie, and respectfully honor your father and your mother.'"

[21] The wealthy leader replied, "These are the very things I've been doing for as long as I can remember."

[22] "Ah," Jesus said. "But there's still one thing you're missing in your life."

"What is that?" asked the man.

"You must go and sell everything you own and give all the proceeds to the poor so you will have eternal treasures. Then come and follow me." [a]

[23] When the rich leader heard these words, he was devastated, for he was extremely wealthy.

[24] Jesus saw his disappointment, and looking right at him he said, "It is next to impossible for those who have everything to enter into God's kingdom realm. [25] Nothing could be harder! It could be compared to trying to stuff a rope through the eye of a needle." [b]

[26] Those who heard this said, "Then who can be saved?"

[27] Jesus responded, "What appears humanly impossible is more than possible with God. For God can do what man cannot."

[28] Peter said, "Lord, see how we've left all that we have, our houses and our careers, to follow you."

[29-30] Jesus replied, "Listen to my words: anyone who leaves his home behind and chooses God's kingdom realm over wife, children, parents, and family, it will come back to him many more times in this lifetime. [c] And in the age to come, he will inherit even more than that—he will inherit eternal life!"

Jesus Prophesies His Death and Resurrection

[31] Jesus took the Twelve aside in private and told them, "We are going to Jerusalem so that everything prophesied about the Son of Man will be fulfilled. [32] They will betray him and hand him over to the people, and they will mock him, insult him, and spit in his face. [33] And after they have abused [d] and flogged the Son of Man, they will kill him. But in three days he will rise again."

---

a 18:22 This does not teach us that salvation can be earned by giving away our possessions to the poor. Jesus was showing the young, wealthy man that he couldn't truly be a disciple until there was no competition in his heart to following Jesus.

b 18:25 As translated from the Aramaic. The Greek is "to stuff a camel through the eye of a needle." The Aramaic word for "rope" and for "camel" is the homonym *gamla*. This could be an instance of the Aramaic text being misread by the Greek translators as "camel" instead of "rope." Regardless, this becomes a metaphor for something impossible. It would be like saying, "It's as hard as making pigs fly!"

c 18:29–30 The Mark account of this passage adds, "and with persecutions." See Mark 10:30.

d 18:33 The word translated "abused" is powerful. It occurs in the Greek text in v. 32 but in the Aramaic text in v. 33.

³⁴ The disciples didn't have a clue what he was saying, for his words were a mystery that was hidden from them.

Jesus Heals a Blind Beggar

³⁵ As Jesus and his followers arrived at Jericho, there was a blind beggar sitting on the roadside. ³⁶ When he heard the crowd approaching, he asked, "What's all this commotion about?"

³⁷ "It's Jesus!" they said. "Jesus the Nazarene is passing by."

³⁸ The blind beggar shouted, "Jesus, Son of David,^a have pity and show me mercy!"

³⁹ Those who were in the front of the crowd scolded him and warned him to be quiet. But the blind beggar screamed out even louder, "Jesus, Son of David, show me mercy!"

⁴⁰ Suddenly Jesus stopped. He told those nearby, "**Bring the man over to me.**" When they brought him before Jesus, he asked the man, ⁴¹ "**What is it you want me to do for you?**"

"Lord," he said, "please, I want to see again."

⁴² Jesus said, "**Now you will see. Receive your sight this moment. For your faith in me has given you sight and new life.**"^b

⁴³ Instantly he could see again. His eyes popped opened, and he saw Jesus. He shouted loud praises to God and he followed Jesus. And when the crowd saw what happened, they too erupted with shouts of praise to God.

Jesus and Zacchaeus

19 ¹⁻³ In the city of Jericho there lived a very wealthy man named Zacchaeus,^c who was the supervisor over all the tax collectors. As Jesus made his way through the city, Zacchaeus was eager to see Jesus. He kept trying to get a look at him, but the crowd around Jesus was massive. Zacchaeus was a very short man and couldn't see over the heads of the people. ⁴ So he ran on ahead of everyone and climbed up a blossoming fig tree^d so he could get a glimpse of Jesus as he passed by.

⁵ When Jesus got to that place, he looked up into the tree and said, "Zacchaeus, hurry on down, for I am appointed to stay^e at your house today!"

⁶ So he scurried down the tree and came face-to-face with Jesus.

---

^a 18:38 The term *Son of David* was used for the Messiah. The blind man believed Jesus was the Messiah.

^b 18:42 Translated from the Aramaic. The Greek word signifies both healing and salvation.

^c 19:1–3 The name Zacchaeus means "pure."

^d 19:4 This was a sturdy sycamore-fig tree that was known to reach over forty feet high. The Aramaic text calls it a "tree in bloom."

^e 19:5 Although they had never met, Jesus knew Zacchaeus' name. This was a "word of knowledge." The Aramaic text states, "It is my duty to stay at your house." It is likely that Jesus spent the night in Zacchaeus' home.

[7] As Jesus left to go with Zacchaeus, many in the crowd complained, "Look at this! Of all the people to have dinner[a] with, he's going to eat in the house of a crook."

[8] Zacchaeus joyously welcomed Jesus[b] and was amazed over his gracious visit to his home. Zacchaeus stood in front of the Lord and said, "Half of all that I own I will give to the poor. And Lord, if I have cheated anyone, I promise to pay back four times as much as I stole."

[9-10] Jesus said to him, "This shows that today life[c] has come to you and your household, for you are a true son of Abraham. The Son of Man has come to seek out and to give life to those who are lost."[d]

The Parable of a Prince and His Servants

[11] At this time Jesus was getting close to entering Jerusalem. The crowds that followed him were convinced that God's kingdom realm would fully manifest when Jesus established it in Jerusalem. [12] So he told them this story to change their perspective:

"Once there was a wealthy prince who left his province to travel to a distant land, where he would be crowned king and then return. [13] Before he departed he summoned his ten servants together and said, 'I am entrusting each of you with fifty thousand dollars[e] to trade with while I am away. Invest it and put the money to work until I return.'

[14] "Some of his countrymen despised the prince and sent a delegation after him to declare before the royals, 'We refuse to let this man rule over us! He will not be our king!'

[15] "Nevertheless, he was crowned king and returned to his land. Then he summoned his ten servants to see how much each one had earned and what their profits came to.

[16] "The first one came forward and said, 'Master, I took what you gave me and invested it, and it multiplied ten times.'

[17] "'Splendid! You have done well, my excellent servant. Because you have shown that you can be trusted in this small matter, I now grant you authority to rule over ten fortress cities.'

[18] "The second came and said, 'Master, what you left with me has multiplied five times.'

[19] "His master said, 'I also grant you authority in my kingdom over five fortress cities.'

---

a 19:7 The Aramaic states "dinner after the fast."

b 19:8 This is supplied from v. 6, stated here for the sake of the narrative.

c 19:9–10 As translated from the Aramaic. The Greek text is "salvation." Notice that Jesus describes himself as "life" and "Son of Man." He is both divine and human.

d 19:9–10 This is a quotation taken from Ezek. 34:16.

e 19:13 Literally "ten minas."

²⁰ "Another came before the king and said, 'Master, here is the money you entrusted to me. I hid it for safekeeping. ²¹ You see, I live in fear of you, for everyone knows you are a strict master and impossible to please. You push us for a high return on all that you own, and you always want to gain from someone else's efforts.' ᵃ

²² "The king said, 'You wicked servant! I will judge you using your own words. If what you said about me is true, that I am a harsh man, pushing for a high return and wanting gain from others' efforts, ²³ why didn't you at least put my money in the bank ᵇ to earn some interest on what I entrusted to you?'

²⁴ "The king said to his other servants, 'Take the money he has and give it to the faithful servant who multiplied my money ten times over.'

²⁵ "'But master,' the other servants objected, 'why give it to him? He already has so much!'

²⁶ "'Yes,' replied the king. 'But to all who have been faithful, even more will be given them. And for the ones who have nothing, even the little they seem to have will be taken from them. ²⁷ Now, bring all those rebellious enemies of mine who rejected me as their king—bring them here before me and execute them!'"

²⁸ After saying all of this, Jesus headed straight for Jerusalem. ²⁹ When he arrived at the stables of Annia ᶜ near the Mount of Olives, ᵈ he sent two of his disciples ahead, saying, ³⁰ "When you enter the next village, ᵉ you will find tethered there a donkey's young colt that has never been ridden. Untie it and bring it to me. ³¹ And if anyone stops you and asks, 'What are you doing?' just tell them this: 'It is needed for the Lord of All.'" ᶠ

³² The two who were sent entered the village and found the colt exactly like Jesus had said. ³³ While they were untying the colt, the owners approached them and asked, "What are you doing?"

³⁴ The disciples replied, "We need this donkey for the Lord of All."

³⁵⁻³⁶ They brought the colt to Jesus. Then they placed their prayer shawls on its back, and Jesus rode it as he descended the Mount of Olives toward

---

ᵃ 19:21 The text is literally "You pick up what you didn't lay down and reap where you didn't sow." This statement is obviously not true. The opposite can be found in how the master shared his kingdom with the other more faithful servants. Today, many likewise have a misconception of the true heart of our Master. Our Master makes servants into rulers.

ᵇ 19:23 The text is literally "upon a table," a metaphor for where banking transactions took place.

ᶜ 19:29 The Greek text includes two small villages, Bethphage and Bethany. The meaning of the names combined means "the stables of Annia." This is how it is translated in the Aramaic.

ᵈ 19:29 This was a large hill less than two miles from Jerusalem and about one hundred feet higher.

ᵉ 19:30 Literally "across the valley."

ᶠ 19:31 The Lord Jesus created all things and therefore owns it all.

Jerusalem. *As he rode along, people spontaneously threw their prayer shawls on the path in front of him like a carpet. *

³⁷ As soon as he got to the bottom of the Mount of Olives, the crowds of his followers shouted with a loud outburst of ecstatic joy over all the mighty wonders of power they had witnessed. ³⁸ They shouted over and over, "Highest praises to God for the one who comes as King in the name of the Lord! Heaven's peace and glory from the highest realm *now comes to us!*" '

³⁹ Some Jewish religious leaders who stood off from the procession said to Jesus, "Teacher, you must order your followers at once to stop saying these things!"

⁴⁰ Jesus responded, "Listen to me. If my followers were silenced, the very stones would break forth with praises!"

Jesus Weeps over Jerusalem

⁴¹ When Jesus caught sight of the city, he burst into tears with uncontrollable weeping over Jerusalem, ⁴² saying, "If only you could recognize that this day peace is within your reach! But you cannot see it. ⁴³ For the day is soon coming when your enemies will surround you, pressing you in on every side, and laying siege to you. * ⁴⁴ They will crush you to pieces, and your children too! And when they leave, your city will be totally destroyed. Since you would not recognize God's day of visitation, your day of devastation is coming!"

Jesus Cleanses the Temple Courts

⁴⁵ Jesus entered the temple area and forcibly threw out all the merchants from their stalls. ⁴⁶ He rebuked them, saying, "The Scriptures declare, 'My Father's house is to be filled with prayer—a house of prayer,' not a cave of bandits!'"

⁴⁷ From then on Jesus continued teaching in the temple area, but all the while, the high priests, the experts of the law, and the prominent men of the city kept trying to find a way to accuse Jesus, for they wanted him dead. ⁴⁸ They could find no reason to accuse him, for he was a hero to the people and the crowds were awestruck by every word he spoke.

A Day of Controversy

20 One day Jesus was teaching in the temple courts and sharing with the people the wonderful news of salvation.' The high priest and the experts

---

a 19:35–36 See Zech. 9:9.
b 19:35–36 This was done to signify Jesus was King. See 2 Kings 9:13. This is an obvious reference to the coming of the promised Messiah.
c 19:38 This is a quotation of Ps. 118:26.
d 19:43 Translated from the Aramaic. The Greek text states, "They will throw up ramparts." See Isa. 29:3; Jer. 6:6; Ezek. 4:2. Jesus was the only one weeping while everyone else was rejoicing.
e 19:46 See Isa. 56:7; Jer. 7:11.
f 20:1 Translated from the Aramaic text.

of the law were there with the prominent men of the city. They confronted Jesus and asked him, [2] "We want to know right now by what authority you're doing this. Who gave you the authority to teach these things here in the temple?"

[3] Jesus responded, "First, let me ask you a question and you tell me right now. [4] Did John baptize because of a mandate from heaven or merely from men?"

[5] His interrogators pulled aside to discuss this among themselves. "What should we say? If we say that John's mandate was from heaven, he will ask us, 'Then why didn't you believe him *and get baptized*?' [6] But if we say, 'John's mandate was merely from men,' then all the people around him will stone us, for they believe John was a prophet of God." [7] So they answered Jesus, "We cannot tell where John's authority came from."

[8] Jesus said, "Then neither will I tell you where my authority comes from to do what I do."

The Story of the Vine Growers

[9] Jesus taught the people this story:

"Once there was a man who planted a vineyard, then leased it out to tenants and left to go abroad and was away for a long time. [10] When the harvest season arrived, the owner sent one of his servants to the tenants to collect the landowner's share of the harvest. But the tenants sent him away, beaten and empty-handed. [11] So the owner dispatched another one of his servants to collect his portion. But the tenants treated him the same way. They cursed him, beat him, and sent him away empty-handed. [12] Then the owner sent a third servant, but they brutalized him also with the same treatment. [13] Finally the owner of the vineyard said to his son, 'Perhaps if I send you, my own cherished son, they will be ashamed of what they've done.'[a]

[14] "But when the tenants saw the son coming, they schemed among themselves. 'This is the heir of the vineyard! If we kill him, the inheritance will be ours.' [15] So they threw the son off the property and killed him.

"I ask you, what do you think the owner of the vineyard will do to those who murdered his son? [16] He will come and destroy them and give his vineyard to another."

When the people heard this story, they all agreed, "This should never happen!"

[17] Jesus looked straight at the people and said, "What do you think this verse means: 'The worthless, rejected stone has become the cornerstone, the most important stone of all'?[b] [18] Everyone who falls *in humility* upon that stone will be broken. But if that stone falls on you, it will grind you to pieces!"

---

a 20:13 Translated from the Aramaic text.
b 20:17 This is a quotation from Ps. 118:22. See also Isa. 8:14–15; 28:16.

[19] When the high priests and experts of the law realized that this story was about them, they wanted to have Jesus arrested that very moment, but they were afraid of all the people.

Paying Taxes

[20] So they sent spies who pretended to be honest seekers, but who watched closely for an opportunity to entangle Jesus by his words. Their plan was to catch him saying something against the government, and then they could hand him over to the jurisdiction of the Roman authorities *to be killed.*

[21] At the right time they asked him this question: "Teacher, we know that all you say is straightforward and what you teach us is right, giving us the true ways of God. You're one who doesn't show favoritism to anyone's status. So we ask you—[22] is it proper or not to pay taxes *to a corrupt government?*" [a]

[23] Jesus saw right through their cunning ploy and said, "Why are you testing me? [b] [24] Show me one of the Roman coins. Whose head is on the coin? Whose title is stamped on it?"

They answered, "Why, it's Caesar's."

[25] Jesus said, "Precisely. The coin [c] bears the image of the Emperor Caesar, and you should give back to Caesar all that belongs to him. But you bear the image of God. So give back to God all that belongs to him."

[26] The imposters were left speechless and amazed in the presence of all the people, unable to trap Jesus with his words.

A Question about the Resurrection

[27] Some of the Sadducees, a religious group that denies there is a resurrection of the dead, came to ask Jesus this question: [28] "Teacher, the law of Moses [d] teaches that if a man dies before he has children, his brother should marry the widow and raise up children for his brother's family line. [29] But suppose there was a family with seven brothers, and the oldest married and died without children. [30–31] Then his brother married the widow, but he too died with no children. And so it happened, one brother after another brother, until each of the seven had married the widow and died childless. [32] Then finally, the widow died too. So here's our dilemma: [33] Whose wife will the woman be when she's resurrected from the dead? Which of the brothers will be her husband, for all seven were once married to her?"

[34] Jesus replied, "Marriage is for the sons of this world only. [35–36] But those who are worthy of the resurrection from the dead into glory become

---

a 20:22 The Greek text states, "to the emperor."
b 20:23 Although not found in most Greek manuscripts, it is included in the Aramaic text.
c 20:25 Actual coins from that era have been found with the emperor's image and a superscription saying, "Tiberius Caesar Augustus, son of the divine Augustus."
d 20:28 See Deut. 25:5–10.

immortal, like the angels, who never die nor marry. When the dead come to life again, they will be sons of God's life—the sons of the resurrection. [37] In fact, it was Moses who taught the resurrection of the dead [a] when he wrote of the Lord God who was at the burning bush and described him as 'the God of Abraham, Isaac, and Jacob.' [38] Don't you agree that God is not the God of the dead, but the God of the living? For in his eyes, Abraham, Isaac, and Jacob are alive forevermore. He must be the God who raises the dead."

[39] The experts of the law [b] chimed in, "Yes, Teacher, you speak the truth beautifully."

[40] From then on, the religious Sadducees never dared to ask Jesus a question again.

The Messiah, Both God and Man

[41] Jesus then posed this question to the people: "How can the experts of the law [c] say that Christ the Messiah is David's son? [42] Haven't you read in the Psalms where David himself wrote:

The Lord Jehovah said to my Lord, [d]
'Sit near me in the place of authority
[43] until I subdue all your enemies under Your feet!'" [e]

[44] Jesus explained, "If David calls this one 'my Lord,' how can he merely be his son?" [f]

Jesus Denounces the Experts of the Law

[45] Within earshot of all the people, Jesus warned his disciples, [46] "Don't follow the example of these pretentious experts of the law! They love to parade around in their clergy robes so that they are honored wherever they go, sitting right up front in every meeting and pushing for the head table at every banquet. [47] And for appearances' sake they will pray long religious prayers at the homes of widows for an offering, [g] cheating them out of their very

---

a 20:37 See Ex. 3:6.
b 20:39 Historically, these "experts of the law" (Pharisees) were opposed to, and argued with, the Sadducees over their disbelief of a supernatural resurrection.
c 20:41 Or "scribes," as translated from the Aramaic.
d 20:42 A Hebrew translation of this passage would read "Yahweh said to my Adonai." Paraphrased it would read "The Lord (God) said to my protecting Lord (Messiah)."
e 20:43 See Ps. 110:1. Translated from the Aramaic and one Greek manuscript. Most Greek texts have "until all your enemies become a footstool under your feet."
f 20:44 Jesus is challenging them to consider that the Christ will be both God and man (David's son and David's Lord).
g 20:47 Translated from the Aramaic. The implication is that the religious leaders would go and pray at the homes of widows, then intimidate them and ask for offerings.

livelihood. Beware of them all, for they will one day be stripped of honor, and the judgment they receive will be severe."

The Widow's Offering

21 Jesus was in the temple,ᵃ observing all the wealthy wanting to be noticed as they came with their offerings. ²He noticed a very poor widow dropping two small copper coins in the offering box. ³"Listen to me," he said. "This poor widow has given a larger offering than any of the wealthy. ⁴For the rich only gave out of their surplus, but she sacrificed out of her poverty and gave to God all that she had to live on."

The Signs of the End of the Age

⁵Some of the disciples remarked about the beauty of the temple. They pointed out all the lovely adornments and how it was built with excellence from the gifts given to God.

Jesus said, ⁶"The day will come that everything you admire here will be utterly destroyed. It will all become a heap of rubble!"

⁷"Master, tell us," they asked, "when exactly will this happen? Can you tell us what warning sign to look for when it is about to take place?"

⁸Jesus responded, "Deception will run rampant with many who will appear on the scene, saying I have sent them, or saying about themselves, 'I am the Messiah!'ᵇ And the doomsday deceivers will say, 'The end of the age is now here!' But listen to me. Don't be fooled by these imposters.

⁹"There will also be many wars and revolutions on every side, with rumors of more wars to come. Don't panic or give in to your fears, for these things are bound to happen. This is still not the end yet."

¹⁰Jesus continued, *"There will be upheavals of every kind.* Nations will go to war against each other and kingdom against kingdom— ¹¹and there will be terrible earthquakes, seismic events of epic proportion, resulting in famines in one place after another. There will be horrible plagues and epidemics, cataclysmic stormsᶜ on the earth, and astonishing signs and cosmic disturbances in the heavens. But before all of this happens, you will be hunted down and arrested, persecuted by both civil and religious authorities, and thrown into prison. ¹²⁻¹³And because you follow me, you will be on trial before kings and governmental leaders as an opportunity to testify to them in my name. ¹⁴⁻¹⁵Yet determine in your hearts not to prepare for your own defense. Simply speak with the words of wisdom that I will give you that

---

a 21:1 This would have been in the courtyard of the temple, where men and women came to deposit their contributions to the temple treasury. Historians say there were thirteen trumpet-mouthed boxes used in the courtyard for offerings.

b 21:8 Translated from the Aramaic, it literally states, "I Am! The Messiah!"

c 21:11 As translated from the Aramaic. Only one Greek manuscript adds, "great storms."

moment, and none of your persecutors will be able to withstand the grace and wisdom that comes from your mouths.

[16] "You can expect betrayal even by your parents, your brothers, your relatives and friends—and yes, some of you will die as martyrs. [17] You will be hated by all because *of my life in you.*[a] [18] But don't worry. My grace will never desert you or depart from your life.[b] [19] And by standing firm with patient endurance you will find your souls' deliverance."

The Destruction of Jerusalem

[20] "When you see Jerusalem being surrounded by armies, you will know for sure that its devastation is imminent.[c] [21] At that time all who are living in Judea must flee to the mountains. Those who live inside the city gates, go out and flee, and those who live outside the city must not enter it seeking refuge. [22] For these are the days of God's vengeance to fulfill what has been written[d] against Jerusalem. [23] It will be extremely difficult for pregnant women and for those nursing little ones in that day, for there will be great persecution and wrath against this nation. [24] Many will be cut down by the sword or scattered as prisoners in many countries. And Jerusalem shall be trampled down by nations until the days of world empires come to an end."

The Coming of the Son of Man

[25] "Expect to witness amazing and perplexing signs throughout the universe with the sun, the moon, and the stars.[e] The raging of the sea will bring desperation and turmoil to many nations. [26] Earthquakes[f] will bring panic and disaster. What men see coming to the earth will cause the fear of doom to grip their hearts, for they will even see the powers of the heavenly realm shaken!

[27-28] "And at last, when you see how the Son of Man[g] comes—surrounded with a cloud, with great power and miracles, in the radiance of his splendor,

---

a 21:17 The Greek says, "because of my name."

b 21:18 Although quite different from the Greek manuscripts, this is the literal translation of the Aramaic figure of speech, "Grace will not leave your head."

c 21:20 This was fulfilled in AD 70 when Jerusalem was left desolate by Roman armies. Some historians estimate that more than one million Jews were slaughtered at that time and up to one hundred thousand were taken captive to other nations.

d 21:22 See 1 Kings 9:6–9; Dan. 9:26; Hos. 9:7; Mic. 3:12.

e 21:25 See Isa. 13:10; Ezek. 32:7–8; Joel 2:10.

f 21:26 The word *earthquakes* is found only in Aramaic manuscripts.

g 21:27–28 The title "Son of Man" was used frequently when Jesus spoke of himself. Note that he is not the "son of a man," but the Son of God who became a man.

and with great glory and praises[a]—it will make you jump for joy! For the day of your full transformation[b] has arrived."

The Lesson of the Fig Tree

[29-30] Jesus gave his disciples this parable:

"Haven't you observed the fig tree, or any tree, that when it buds and blooms you realize that the season is changing and summer is near? [31] In the same way, when you see these prophetic signs occurring, you realize the earth is yielding to the fullness of God's kingdom realm. [32] I assure you, the end of this age will not come until all I have spoken comes to pass. [33] Earth and sky will wear out and fade away before one word I speak loses its power or fails to accomplish its purpose."

Guard Your Hearts

[34] "Be careful that you never allow your hearts to grow cold. Remain passionate[c] and free from anxiety and the worries of this life. Then you will not be caught off guard by what happens. Don't let me come and find you drunk or careless in living like everyone else. [35] For that day will come as a shocking surprise to all, like a downpour[d] that drenches everyone, catching many unaware and unprepared. [36] Keep a constant watch over your soul, and pray for the courage and grace to prevail over these things that are destined to occur and that you will stand before the presence of the Son of Man *with a clear conscience*."

[37] Each day, Jesus taught in the temple, and he spent his nights on the Mount of Olives. [38] And all the people came early to the temple courts to listen to the words[e] he taught.

Satan Entered into Judas

22 [1-2] As the celebration of the Passover Lamb[f] was approaching, the Jewish religious leaders and scholars of the law continually schemed to find a way to murder Jesus without starting a riot—for they feared the crowds.

[3] At that time Satan himself entered into Judas the locksmith,[g] who was one of the twelve apostles. [4] He secretly went to the religious hierarchy and the captains of the temple guards to discuss with them how he could betray

---

a 21:27–28 "Praises" is only found in Aramaic manuscripts.

b 21:27–28 The Greek word is "redemption" or "liberation." It speaks of the total transformation of our body, soul, and spirit when we see him as he is.

c 21:34 The Aramaic text says, "Beware that your hearts never grow cold."

d 21:35 Greek manuscripts have "like a snare." The Aramaic text states, "like a downpour."

e 21:38 The Greek text is *logos*. The Aramaic is literally "manifestation."

f 22:1–2 The Passover celebration was known as the "Feast of Bread without Yeast." The Jewish people commemorate their exodus from Egypt to this day with a weeklong Passover feast. See Ex. 12:1–20; Deut. 16:1–8.

g 22:3 See the last footnote on Luke 6:14–16.

Jesus and turn him over to their hands. [5] The religious hierarchy was elated over Judas' treachery, and they agreed to give him a sum of money in exchange for Jesus' betrayal. [6] Judas vowed that he would find them a suitable opportunity to betray Jesus when he was away from the crowds.

Jesus Prophesies the Location of the Last Supper

[7-8] On the day the sacrifice of the Passover lambs was to take place, Jesus sent for Peter and John and instructed them, "Go and prepare the Passover supper so we can eat it together."

[9] They asked him, "Where do we make the preparations to eat the meal?"

[10] Jesus gave them this sign: "When you enter the city, you will find a man[a] carrying a jug of water.[b] Follow him home [11] and say to the owner of the house, 'The Teacher told us to ask you, "Where is the room I may use to have the Passover meal with my disciples?"' [12] He will then take you to a large, fully furnished upstairs room. Make the preparations for us there."

[13] They went and found everything to be exactly like Jesus had prophesied, and they prepared the Passover meal.

Jesus and His Disciples Eat the Last Supper

[14] When Jesus arrived at the upper room, he took his place at the table along with all the apostles. [15] Then he told them, "I have longed with passion and desire to eat this Passover lamb with you before I endure my sufferings. [16] I promise you that the next time we eat this, we will be together in the banquet of God's kingdom realm."

[17] Then he raised a cup and gave thanks to God and said to them, "Take this and pass it on to one another and drink. [18] I promise you that the next time we drink this wine, we will be together in the feast of God's kingdom realm."[c]

[19] Then he lifted up a loaf, and after praying a prayer of thanksgiving to God, he gave each of his apostles a piece of bread, saying, "This loaf is my body,[d] which is now being offered to you. Always eat it to remember me."

[20] After supper was over, he lifted the cup again and said, "This cup is my

---

a 22:10 Carrying water was a task given to women; it would have been easy to spot a man carrying the water jug.

b 22:10 Jerusalem would have been filled with pilgrims coming to celebrate the feast. Every house would be filled with additional guests, so finding a room for Jesus and the Twelve would be no easy task. It is possible that this man carrying a jug of water (normally a woman's task) would be an Essene. They were the only Jewish men who culturally would carry water in this way since they were celibates. They had a community in Jerusalem that had a gate called the "Essene Gate." They also had a different calendar than the typical Jewish one, which meant they would still have guest rooms available.

c 22:18 Verses 17–18 are not found in most Aramaic texts. Most Greek texts and a fifth-century Aramaic manuscript known as "the Palestinian Syriac" include them in the narrative.

d 22:19 From here to the end of v. 20 is considered the most highly debated passage in Luke's

blood of the new covenant[a] I make with you, and it will be poured out soon for all of you. [21] But I want you to know that the hands of the one who delivers me to be the sacrifice are with mine on the table this very moment. [22] The Son of Man must now go where he will be sacrificed. But there will be great and unending doom for the man who betrays me."

[23] The apostles questioned among themselves which one of them was about to do this.

Apostles Argue over Which of Them Will Be the Greatest

[24] The disciples bickered over which one of them would be considered the greatest[b] in the kingdom. [25] Jesus interrupted their argument, saying, "The kings and men of authority in this world rule oppressively over their subjects, claiming that they do it for the good of the people. They are obsessed with how others see them.[c] [26] But this is not your calling. You will lead by a different model. The greatest one among you will live as one called to serve others without honor.[d] The greatest honor and authority is reserved for the one who has a servant heart. [27] The leaders who are served are the most important in your eyes, but in the kingdom, it is the servants who lead. Am I not here with you as one who serves you?

[28] "Because you have stood with me through all my trials and ordeals, [29] I give you your destiny: I am promising you the kingdom realm that the Father has promised me. [30] We will celebrate in this kingdom and you will feast with me at my table. And each of you will be given a throne, twelve thrones in all, and you will be made rulers on thrones to judge the tribes of Israel."

Jesus Prophesies Peter's Denial

[31] "Peter, my dear friend, listen to what I'm about to tell you. Satan has demanded to come and sift you like wheat and test your faith. [32] But I have prayed for you, Peter, that you would stay faithful to me no matter what comes. Remember this: after you have turned back to me and have been restored, make it your life mission to strengthen the faith of your brothers."

[33] "But Lord," Peter replied, "I am ready to stand with you to the very end, even if it means prison or death!"

Gospel because a few reliable Greek manuscripts do not have it. Yet there is ample internal evidence to argue for its inclusion.

a 22:20 The Aramaic word used here is literally "new testament."

b 22:24 This took place at the Lord's Passover table. Their discussion of who was the worst among them led them to argue over who was the greatest. Jesus was only hours away from the horrible death of crucifixion while his apostles argued.

c 22:25 The Aramaic is actually "They want to be called 'servants of goodness.'"

d 22:26 The Greek text uses the word here for "youngest," and the Aramaic is "small one." In Hebrew culture in the days of Jesus, the firstborn of the household had honor, while the youngest accepted the role of menial service to all the others of the house.

[34] Jesus looked at him and prophesied, "Before the rooster crows in the morning, you will deny [a] three times that you even know me."

[35] Then he said to all of them, "When I sent you out empty-handed, did you lack anything?"

"Not a thing," they answered. "God provided all we needed."

Jesus said, "But now I say to you: Take what you need. [36] If you have money, take it [b]—and a knapsack and a sword. [c] Danger is imminent. [d] [37] For the prophetic Scripture about me 'He will be accused of being a criminal' [e] will now come to pass. All that was prophesied of me will be fulfilled."

[38] The disciples told him, "Lord, we already have two swords!"

"You still don't understand," [f] Jesus responded.

The Garden of Gethsemane

[39] Jesus left the upper room with his disciples [g] and, as was his habit, went to the Mount of Olives, *his place of secret prayer*. [40] There he told the apostles, "**Keep praying for strength to be spared from the severe test of your faith that is about to come.**"

[41] Then he withdrew from them a short distance [h] to be alone. Kneeling down, he prayed, [42] "**Father, if you are willing, take this cup of agony away from me.** [i] **But no matter what, your will must be mine.**"

[43] Jesus called [j] for an angel of glory to strengthen him, and the angel appeared. [44] He prayed even more passionately, like one being sacrificed, [k] until he was in such intense agony of spirit that his sweat became drops of blood, dripping onto the ground. [l]

---

a 22:34 The Aramaic text says "blasphemed."

b 22:36 Now the disciples were to take needed items with them, including money, for they were to be a source of blessing to others with their generosity.

c 22:36 It is possible that Jesus was using symbolic speech, for we take with us the sword of the Spirit, which is the Word of God. See Eph. 6:17.

d 22:36 The text here is a Hebraic figure of speech: "If you don't have a sword, you'd better sell something and buy one," which implies that danger is imminent.

e 22:37 See Isa. 53:8–9.

f 22:38 Or "That will be enough." Jesus is saying, "Never mind. You still don't get it." He corrected their thinking about taking swords and using violent means in vv. 50–51.

g 22:39 That is, with the exception of Judas. See v. 47.

h 22:41 Literally "a stone's throw away."

i 22:42 Jesus asked the Father to be spared from death in the garden so that he could go all the way to the cross. His prayer was answered. The blood that dripped in the garden would not redeem. Jesus had to carry the cross and fulfill all that was written of him. See Heb. 5:7.

j 22:43 Translated from the Aramaic text. The Greek manuscripts state it passively: "An angel from heaven appeared."

k 22:44 The Aramaic text is literally "He prayed sacrificially."

l 22:44 Although vv. 43–44 are found in the Aramaic manuscript, many Greek texts omit them. Most of the early church fathers included them in their translations and

[45] When Jesus finished praying, he got up and went to his disciples and found them all asleep, for they were exhausted and overwhelmed with sorrow. [46] "Why are you sleeping?" he asked them. "You need to be alert and pray for the strength to endure the great temptation."

Judas Betrays Jesus

[47] No sooner had he finished speaking when suddenly a mob approached, and right in front of the mob was his disciple Judas. He walked up close to Jesus and greeted him with a kiss. For he had agreed to give the religious leaders a sign, saying, "The one I kiss is the one to seize." [a]

[48] Jesus looked at him with sorrow and said, "A kiss, Judas? Are you really going to betray the Son of Man with a kiss?"

[49] When the other disciples understood what was happening, they asked, "Lord, shall we fight them with our swords?"

[50] Just then, one of the disciples [b] swung his sword at the high priest's servant and slashed off his right ear.

[51] Jesus stopped the incident from escalating any further by shouting, "Stop! That's enough of this!" Then he touched the right side of the injured man's head and *the ear grew back* [c]—he was healed!

[52] Jesus turned to those who had come to seize him—the ruling priests, the officers of the temple police, and the religious leaders—and said, "Am I a criminal that you come to capture me with clubs and swords? Wasn't I with you day after day, teaching in the temple courts? [53] You could have seized me at any time. But in the darkness of night you have now found your time, for it belongs to you and to the prince of darkness." [d]

Peter Denies He Knew Jesus

[54] The religious leaders seized Jesus and led him away, but Peter followed from a safe distance. They brought him to the home of the high priest, where people

---

commentaries. Though very rare, the phenomenon of hematidrosis, sweating blood, is well documented. Under great emotional stress, tiny capillaries in the sweat glands can break, thus mixing blood with sweat. This process could have marked weakness and possibly shock.

a 22:47 Nearly every Greek manuscript leaves out this information. The Aramaic text includes it.

b 22:50 The unnamed disciple was Peter; the servant's name was Malchus. See John 18:10.

c 22:51 Implied in the context of this miracle. Jesus, the Creator, re-created his ear. The last thing Jesus did before they tied and bound his beautiful hands to arrest him in Gethsemane: He used his healing hands to restore the cut-off ear that Peter slashed (here and John 18:12). He was bound for hours until they loosed his hands to pierce them with nails.

d 22:53 The "prince of darkness" is Satan. This phrase is found only in the Aramaic manuscripts. The Greek text states, "the powers of darkness."

were already gathered out in the courtyard. [55] Someone had built a fire, so Peter inched closer and sat down among them to stay warm.

[56] A girl noticed Peter sitting in the firelight. Staring at him, she pointed him out and said, "This man is one of Jesus' disciples!"

[57] Peter flatly denied it, saying, "What are you talking about, girl? I don't know him!"

[58] A little while later, someone else spotted Peter and said, "I recognize you. You're one of his, I know it!"

Peter again said, "I'm not one of his disciples."

[59] About an hour later, someone else identified Peter and insisted he was a disciple of Jesus, saying, "Look at him! He's from Galilee,[a] just like Jesus. I know he's one of them."

[60] But Peter was adamant. "Listen, I don't know what you're talking about. Don't you understand? I don't even know him." While the words were still in his mouth, the rooster crowed.

[61] At that moment, the Lord, who was being led through the courtyard by his captors,[b] turned around and gazed at Peter. All at once Peter remembered the words Jesus had prophesied over him, **"Before the rooster crows in the morning, you will deny three times that you even know me."** [62] Peter burst into tears,[c] ran off from the crowd, and wept bitterly.

Jesus Is Mocked and Severely Beaten

[63] Those who were guarding Jesus mocked and beat him severely. [64] They also made fun of him, blindfolding him and slapping his face and saying, "Prove that you are a prophet and tell us which one of us hit you!" [65] They blasphemed and heaped insult after insult upon him.

Jesus before the Jewish Council

[66] At daybreak the high priests, the experts of the law, and the top religious leaders convened and had Jesus brought before their council. [67] They asked him point blank, "Tell us, are you the Christ, the Messiah, or not?"

Jesus responded, **"If I tell you the truth, you won't believe me. [68] And if I question you, you will not answer me or release me.[d] [69] But from today on, the Son of Man will be enthroned in the place of honor, power, and authority with Almighty God."**

[70] They all shouted, "Then you do claim to be the Son of God?"

He said to them, **"You are the ones who say I am."**

---

a   22:59 Peter's accent gave him away as being a Galilean. See also Mark 14:70.
b   22:61 Implied by the context, necessary for proper understanding of the narrative.
c   22:62 It is not just our sin that causes us to weep. It is seeing the Savior whom we have sinned against that brings our tears.
d   22:68 The phrase "or release me" is found only in the Aramaic text.

⁷¹ They all shouted, "We've heard it from his very lips! What further proof do we need?"

Jesus before Pilate

23 The entire council stood at once and took Jesus to Pilate, the Roman governor. ²They accused him with false testimony before the governor, saying, "This man tells us we're not to pay our taxes to Caesar. And he proclaims himself to be Christ the King and Messiah. He's a deceiver of our nation."

³Pilate asked Jesus, "Is this true? Are you their king and Messiah?"

Jesus answered, "It is true."

⁴Pilate turned to the high priests and to the gathered crowd and said, "This man has committed no crime. I find nothing wrong with him."

⁵But they yelled and demanded that Pilate do something, saying, "He has stirred up our nation, misleading people from the moment he began teaching in Galilee until he has come here to Jerusalem!"

Jesus before Herod

⁶⁻⁷When Pilate heard the word Galilee, he asked if Jesus was a Galilean, as he knew that Antipas, son of Herod, was the ruler over Galilee. When they told him yes, Pilate saw a way out of his problem. Herod happened to be in Jerusalem at that time, so Pilate sent Jesus to Antipas.

⁸When Antipas saw Jesus, he was elated, for he had heard a great deal about his ministry and wanted Jesus to perform a miracle in front of him. ⁹Antipas questioned him at length, but Jesus wouldn't even answer him.

¹⁰⁻¹¹All the while the high priests and religious leaders stood by, hatefully accusing Jesus of wrongdoing, so that Antipas and his soldiers treated him with scorn and mocking. Antipas put an elegant purple robe on Jesus and sent him back to Pilate. ¹²That day, Antipas, son of Herod, and Pilate healed the rift between themselves due to old hostilities and they became good friends.

Jesus Sentenced to Death

¹³⁻¹⁴Pilate gathered the people together with the high priests and all the religious leaders of the nation[a] and told them, "You have presented this man to me and charged him with stirring a rebellion among the people. But I say to you that I have examined him here in your presence and have put him on trial. My verdict is that none of the charges you have brought against him are true. I find no fault in him.[b] ¹⁵⁻¹⁶And I sent him to Antipas, son of Herod, who also, after questioning him, has found him not guilty. Since he has done nothing deserving

a 23:13–14 This group of religious leaders was known as the Jewish council of the Sanhedrin.
b 23:13–14 The phrase "I find no fault in him" is found in the Aramaic text.

of death, I have decided to punish him with a severe flogging and release him." [17] For it was Pilate's custom to honor the Jewish holiday by releasing a prisoner. [a]

[18] When the crowd heard this, they went wild. Erupting with anger, they cried out, "No! Take this one away and release Barabbas!" [b] [19] For Barabbas had been thrown in prison for robbery [c] and murder.

[20] Pilate, wanting to release Jesus, tried to convince them it was best to let Jesus go. [21] But they cried out over and over, "Crucify him! Crucify him!" [d]

[22] A third time, Pilate asked the crowd, "What evil crime has this man committed that I should have him crucified? I haven't found one thing that warrants a death sentence! I will have him flogged severely and then release him."

[23] But the people and the high priests, shouting like a mob, screamed out at the top of their lungs, "No! Crucify him! Crucify him!"

Finally their shouts and screams succeeded. [24] Pilate caved in to the crowd and ordered that the will of the people be done. [25] Then he released the guilty murderer Barabbas, as they had insisted, and handed Jesus over to be crucified.

The Crucifixion of Jesus

[26] As the guards led Jesus to be crucified, there was *an African man* in the crowd named Simon, from Libya. [e] He had just arrived from a rural village *to keep the Feast of the Passover*. The guards laid Jesus' cross on Simon's shoulders [f] and forced him to walk behind Jesus and carry his cross.

[27] Massive crowds gathered to follow Jesus, including a number of women, who were wailing with sorrow over him. [28] Jesus turned to them and said, "**Daughters of Jerusalem, do not weep for me. You should be weeping for yourselves and your children. [29] For the day is coming when it will not be the women with children who are blessed but the childless. Then you will say, 'The barren women are the most fortunate! Those who have never given birth and never nursed a child**—*they are more fortunate than we are, for they will never see their children put to death!*' [30] **And the people will cry out for the mountains and hills to fall on top of them to hide them from all that is to come.** [g] [31] **For if this is what they do to the living Branch,** [h] **what will they do with the dead ones?**"

---

a 23:17 Although many Greek manuscripts do not have this verse in the text, it is found in the Aramaic text.

b 23:18 There were two men, two sons. Barabbas means "son of a father." Jesus was the Son of our heavenly Father. One was a son of Adam; the other was the Son of God.

c 23:19 Most Greek manuscripts have "for insurrection." The Aramaic states "for robbery."

d 23:21 Crucifixion was the cruelest form of execution, reserved for only the worst of criminals.

e 23:26 The text is literally "from Cyrene," which is present-day Tripoli, Libya.

f 23:26 By this time Jesus had been severely beaten and flogged, had gone days without sleep, and was carrying a heavy load. Presumably this is why Simon was compelled to carry the cross for him.

g 23:30 See Hos. 10:8.

h 23:31 The Aramaic is literally "a green tree." This could be a figure of speech for "an

³² Two criminals were led away with Jesus, and all three were to be executed together. ³³ When they came to the place that is known as The Skull, the guards crucified Jesus, nailing him on the center cross between the two criminals. ³⁴ While they were nailing Jesus to the cross, he prayed over and over, **"Father, forgive them,** *a* **for they don't know what they're doing."**

The soldiers, after they crucified him, gambled over his clothing. *b*

³⁵ A great crowd gathered to watch what was happening. The religious leaders sneered at Jesus and mocked him, saying, "Look at this man! What kind of 'chosen Messiah' is this? He pretended to save others, but he can't even save himself!"

³⁶ The soldiers joined in the mockery by offering Jesus a drink of vinegar. *c*

³⁷⁻³⁸ Over Jesus' head on the cross was written an inscription in Greek, Latin, and Aramaic: *d* "This man is the king of all the Jews." And all the soldiers laughed and scoffed at him, saying, "Hey! If you're the king of Jews, why don't you save yourself?"

³⁹ One of the criminals hanging on the cross next to Jesus kept ridiculing him, saying, "What kind of Messiah are you? Save yourself and save us from this death!"

⁴⁰ The criminal hanging on the other cross rebuked the man, saying, "Don't you fear God? You're about to die! ⁴¹ We deserve to be condemned, for we're just being repaid for what we've done. But this man—he's done nothing wrong!"

⁴² Then he said, "I beg of you, my Lord Jesus, show me grace and take me with you into your *everlasting* kingdom!"

⁴³ Jesus responded, **"I promise you—this very day you will enter paradise with me."**

The Death of the Savior

⁴⁴ It was now only midday, yet the whole world became dark for three hours as the light of the sun faded away. *e* ⁴⁵ And suddenly in the temple the thick veil hanging in the Holy Place was ripped in two! ⁴⁶ Then Jesus cried out with a loud

---

innocent man." The "dead" could be a figure of speech for "an evil man."

a 23:34 The Greek text implies a repetitive action. He did not pray, "forgive me," but "forgive them." As the centurion crushed him to the ground and tied his arms to the crossbeam, Jesus prayed, "Father, forgive them." When the spikes tore through each quivering palm, he prayed again, "Father, forgive them." And when the soldiers parted his garments and gambled for the seamless robe, again Jesus prayed, "Father, forgive them." Only heaven knows how many times that prayer was spoken.

b 23:34 Many Greek manuscripts have omitted v. 34.

c 23:36 See Ps. 69:21. It was likely Jesus had had nothing to drink since the night before.

d 23:37–38 Many Greek texts omit the mention of these three languages.

e 23:44 This indicates the "day of the Lord" has now come. See Joel 2:10; Amos 8:9.

voice, "**Father, I surrender my Spirit into your hands.**" *ᵃ* And he took his last breath and died.

⁴⁷ When the Roman captain overseeing the crucifixion witnessed all that took place, he was awestruck and glorified God. Acknowledging what they had done, he said, "I have no doubt; we just killed the righteous one." *ᵇ*

⁴⁸ The crowds that had gathered to observe this spectacle went back to their homes, overcome with deep sorrow *ᶜ* and devastated by what they had witnessed. ⁴⁹ But standing off at a distance were some who truly knew Jesus, and the women who had followed him all the way from Galilee were keeping vigil.

⁵⁰⁻⁵¹ There was also a member of the Jewish council named Joseph, from the village of Ramah, *ᵈ* a good-hearted, honorable man who was eager for the appearing of God's kingdom realm. He had strongly disagreed with the decision of the council to crucify Jesus. *ᵉ* ⁵² He came before Pilate and asked permission to take the body of Jesus *and give him a proper burial, and Pilate granted his request.* ⁵³ So he took the body from the cross and wrapped it in a winding sheet of linen and placed it in a new, unused tomb chiseled out of solid rock. ⁵⁴ It was Preparation Day, and the Sabbath was fast approaching.

⁵⁵ The women who had been companions of Jesus from the beginning saw all this take place and watched as the body was laid in the tomb. ⁵⁶ Afterward they returned home and prepared fragrant spices and ointments and were planning to anoint his body after the Sabbath was completed, according to the commandments of the law.

The Resurrection of Jesus

24 Very early that Sunday morning, the women made their way to the tomb, carrying the spices they had prepared. ⁽¹⁰⁾ Among them were Mary Magdalene; Joanna; and Mary, Jesus' mother. *ᶠ* ² Arriving at the tomb they discovered that the huge stone covering the entrance had been rolled aside, ³ so they went in to look. But the tomb was empty. The body of Jesus was gone!

⁴ They stood there, stunned and perplexed. Suddenly two men in dazzling white robes shining like lightning appeared above them. *ᵍ* ⁵ Terrified, the women fell to the ground on their faces.

The men in white said to them, "Why would you look for the living One *ʰ* in

---

a 23:46 See Pss. 22:1; 31:5.

b 23:47 As translated from the Aramaic.

c 23:48 Literally "beating their breasts," which is a figure of speech for deep sorrow.

d 23:50–51 As translated from the Aramaic. Ramah (formerly Ramathaim Zophim) was the village of Samuel, only a few miles from Jerusalem. The Greek is, "Joseph of Arimathea."

e 23:50–51 One ancient Syriac manuscript adds here, "This man was one who did not take part with the mind of the devil."

f 24:1 For the sake of the English narrative, the information found in v. 10 is placed here.

g 24:4 "Above them" is found only in the Aramaic text.

h 24:5 The Aramaic text is literally "the Life."

a tomb? He is not here, for he has risen! ⁶Have you forgotten what he said to you while he was still in Galilee: ⁷'The Son of Man is destined to be handed over to sinful men to be nailed to a cross, and on the third day he will rise again'?"

⁸All at once they remembered his words. ⁹Leaving the tomb, they went to break the news to the Eleven and to all the others of what they had seen and heard. ᵃ

¹¹When the disciples heard the testimony of the women, it made no sense, and they were unable to believe what they heard. ¹²But Peter jumped up and ran the entire distance to the tomb to see for himself. Stooping down, he looked inside and discovered it was empty! There was only the linen sheet lying there. Staggered by this, he walked away, wondering what it meant.

Jesus Walks to Emmaus

¹³Later that Sunday, two of Jesus' disciples were walking from Jerusalem to Emmaus,ᵇ a journey of about seventeen miles. ¹⁴⁻¹⁵They were in the midst of a discussion about all the events of the last few days when Jesus walked up and accompanied them in their journey. ¹⁶They were unaware that it was Jesus walking alongside them, for God prevented them from recognizing him.

¹⁷⁻¹⁸Jesus said to them, "You seem to be in a deep discussion about something. What are you talking about, so sad and gloomy?"

They stopped, and the one named Cleopasᶜ answered, "Haven't you heard? Are you the only one in Jerusalem unaware of the things that have happened over the last few days?"

¹⁹Jesus asked, "What things?"

"The things about Jesus, the Man from Nazareth," they replied. "He was a mighty prophet of God who performed miracles and wonders. His words were powerful and he had great favor with God and the people. ²⁰⁻²¹But three days ago the high priest and the rulers of the people sentenced him to death and had him crucified. We all hoped that he was the one who would redeem and rescue Israel. ²²Early this morning, some of the women informed us of something amazing. ²³They said they went to the tomb and found it empty. They claimed two angels appeared and told them that Jesus is now alive. ²⁴Some of us went to see for

---

ᵃ 24:9 For the sake of the English narrative, the information of v. 10 is included in v. 1.

ᵇ 24:13 The Greek text states that the distance from Jerusalem to Emmaus was sixty stadia = seven miles in the majority of manuscripts. However some patristic writers such as Eusebius, Sozomen, and Jerome, as well as a few Greek manuscripts read one hundred sixty stadia which would be seventeen miles. There is an ancient site in modern-day Israel identified as Hamat (Emmaus) that is seventeen miles from Jerusalem and is known for its hot (burning) springs. The word *Emmaus* is taken from a Hebrew root that means "the burning place."

ᶜ 24:17–18 Cleopas means "from a renowned father." Some scholars believe this could be the Clopas mentioned in John 19:25.

ourselves and found the tomb exactly like the women said. But no one has seen him."

²⁵ Jesus said to them, "Why are you so thick-headed? Why do you find it so hard to believe every word the prophets have spoken? ²⁶ Wasn't it necessary for Christ, the Messiah, to experience all these sufferings and then afterward to enter into his glory?"

²⁷ Then he carefully unveiled to them the revelation of himself throughout the Scripture. He started from the beginning and explained the writings of Moses and all the prophets, showing how they wrote of him and revealed the truth about himself.

²⁸ As they approached the village, Jesus walked on ahead, telling them he was going on to a distant place. ²⁹ They urged him to remain there and pleaded, "Stay with us. It will be dark soon." So Jesus went with them into the village.

³⁰ Joining them at the table for supper, he took bread and blessed it and broke it, then gave it to them. ³¹ All at once their eyes were opened and they realized it was Jesus! Then suddenly, in a flash, Jesus vanished from before their eyes!

³² Stunned, they looked at each other and said, "Why didn't we recognize it was him? Didn't our hearts burn with the flames of holy passion ᵃ while we walked beside him? He unveiled for us such profound revelation from the Scriptures!"

³³ They left at once and hurried back to Jerusalem to tell the other disciples. When they found the Eleven and the other disciples all together, ³⁴ they overheard them saying, "It's really true! The Lord has risen from the dead. He even appeared to Peter!" ³⁵ Then the two disciples told the others what had happened to them on the road to Emmaus and how Jesus had unveiled himself as he broke bread with them. ᵇ

Jesus Appears to the Disciples

³⁶⁻³⁷ While they were still discussing all of this, Jesus suddenly manifested right in front of their eyes! Startled and terrified, the disciples were convinced they were seeing a ghost. Standing there among them he said, "Be at peace. I am the living God. Don't be afraid. ᶜ ³⁸ Why would you be so frightened? Don't let

---

a 24:32 As translated from the Greek text. The Aramaic manuscript reads, "Were not our hearts dull as he taught us?" This is also the translation of the Latin text. The Aramaic words for "burning" and "dull" are almost identical.

b 24:35 Luke's Gospel begins and ends with a similar story. In the beginning of Jesus' life we have the story of his parents walking off from Jerusalem and leaving him in the temple (Luke 2:41–52), unaware that they had left Jesus behind. Luke ends with the story of Jesus walking alongside two disciples and they weren't aware of who was walking next to them. Both accounts were after the Feast. In both stories they were leaving Jerusalem. And both the Jewish scholars in the temple (Luke 2) and the two Emmaus road disciples (Luke 24) were astounded at what Jesus taught them.

c 24:36–37 The words "I am the living God. Don't be afraid" are only found in the Aramaic text and the Latin Vulgate. The Greek text omits this sentence.

doubt or fear[a] enter your hearts, for I AM! [39] Come and gaze upon my pierced hands and feet. See for yourselves, it is I, standing here alive. Touch me and know that my wounds are real. See that I have a body of flesh and bone." [40] He showed them his pierced hands and feet and let them touch his wounds. [b] [41] The disciples were ecstatic yet dumbfounded, unable to fully comprehend it.

Knowing that they were still wondering if he was real, Jesus said, "Here, let me show you. Give me something to eat."

[42–43] They handed him a piece of broiled fish and some honeycomb. And they watched him eat it.

[44] Then he said to them, "Don't you remember the words that I spoke to you when I was still with you? I told you that everything written about me would be fulfilled, including all the prophecies from the law of Moses through the Psalms and the writings of the prophets—that they would all find their fulfillment."

[45] He *supernaturally unlocked their understanding* to receive the revelation of the Scriptures, [46] then said to them, "Everything that has happened fulfills what was prophesied of me. Christ, the Messiah, was destined to suffer and rise from the dead on the third day. [47] Now you must go into all the nations and preach repentance[c] and forgiveness of sins so that they will turn to me. Start right here in Jerusalem. [48] For you are my witnesses and have seen for yourselves all that has transpired. [49] And I will send the fulfillment of the Father's promise[d] to you. So stay here in the city until the mighty power of heaven falls upon you and wraps around you."

The Ascension of Jesus

[50] Jesus led his disciples out to Bethany. He lifted his hands over them and blessed them in his love. [51] While he was still speaking out words of love and blessing, *he floated off the ground into the sky*, ascending into heaven before their very eyes! [52] And all they could do was worship him.

Overwhelmed and ecstatic with joy, they made their way back to Jerusalem. [53] Every day they went to the temple, praising and worshiping God. [e]

---

a 24:38 The Aramaic reads "imaginations."

b 24:40 Verse 40 is missing in some manuscripts.

c 24:47 The Aramaic reads "grace" or "conversion."

d 24:49 The Aramaic reads "the kingdom" or "rule." The Father's promise would be the coming of the Holy Spirit to live in them and empower them. See Acts 2:1–12.

e 24:53 So ends the glorious Gospel of Luke. The one who walked with his friends on the way to Emmaus wants to walk with us. May we never walk in sadness or unbelief, for Jesus has risen from the grave and lives victorious as the living God in resurrection life! May you pause here and rejoice, believing that Jesus is the Christ, the Son of the living God and the only one who will bring us to the Father. Trust in him alone to save you, and you will spend eternity with him.

JOHN

Introduction

AT A GLANCE

Author: The apostle John
Audience: Diaspora Jews and believers.
Date: AD 80–85, though possibly 50–55.
Type of Literature: Ancient historical biography
Major Themes: The person and work of Jesus, salvation, the Holy Spirit, and the end of the age
Outline:

Prologue — 1:1–18
The Testimony of John the Baptist — 1:19–51
The New Order in Jesus — 2:1–4:42
Jesus as the Mediator of Life and Judgment — 4:43–5:47
Jesus as the Bread of Life — 6:1–71
Jesus as the Water and Light of Life — 7:1–8:59
Jesus as the Light and Shepherd to Humanity — 9:1–10:42
Jesus as the Resurrection and the Life — 11:1–54
Jesus as the Triumphant King — 11:55–12:50
Jesus' Ministry to His Disciples before Death — 13:1–17:26
Jesus' Death and Resurrection — 18:1–20:31
Epilogue — 21:1–25

ABOUT JOHN

How God longs for us to know him! We discover him as we read and study his living Word. But the "Word" is not just dead letters; it's the Living Expression of God, Jesus Christ. The Word came with skin on as the perfect Man—the One who is the divine self-expression and fullness of God's glory; he was God in the flesh!

The New Testament, at its beginning, presents four biographies to portray the four main aspects of this all-glorious Christ. The Gospel of Matthew testifies that he is the King, the Christ of God according to the prophecies of the Old Testament, the One who brings the kingdom of the heavens to earth. The Gospel of Mark presents him as the Love-Slave of God, the perfect servant who labors faithfully for God. Mark's account is the most simple, for a servant doesn't need a detailed record. The Gospel of Luke presents a full picture of Christ as the true Man and the compassionate Savior of all who come to him. And the Gospel of John unveils him as the Son of God, the very God himself, to be life to God's people.

Miracles are everywhere in the Gospel of John! Water became wine. Blind eyes were blessed with sight. Even the dead rose to walk again when Jesus lived among men. Every miracle was a sign that makes us wonder about who this man truly is. The book of John brings us a heavenly perspective filled with such wonderful revelations in every verse. Nothing in the Bible can be compared to the writings of John. He was a prophet, a seer, a lover, an evangelist, an author, an apostle, and a son of thunder.

The other three Gospels give us the history of Christ, but John writes to unveil the mystery of Christ. Jesus is seen as the Lamb of God, the Good Shepherd, the Kind Forgiver, the Tender Healer, the Compassionate Intercessor, and the great I AM. Who can resist this man when he tugs on your heart to come to him? To read John's Gospel is to encounter Jesus. Make this your goal as you read.

There are three things that are important to remember about John, the author of this Gospel: First, he was a man who was a passionate follower of Jesus Christ. He had seen the miracles of Jesus firsthand and heard the anointed words he taught. He walked with Jesus and followed him wholeheartedly, becoming one of Christ's apostolic servants.

Secondly, John describes himself as "the disciple whom Jesus loved" (John 21:7, 20). This was not a term to indicate that Jesus loved John more than the others, but rather, John saw himself as one that Jesus loved. You could also say this about yourself, "I am the disciple whom Jesus loves!" Every single believer can echo John's description of himself, as those words must become the true definition of our identity.

Love unlocks mysteries. As we love Jesus, our hearts are unlocked to see more of his beauty and glory. When we stop defining ourselves by our failures, but rather as the one whom Jesus loves, then our hearts begin to open to the breathtaking discovery of the wonder of Jesus Christ.

And thirdly, it's important to keep in mind that John did not include everything that Jesus did and taught. In fact, if you put all the data of the Gospels together and condense it, we only have information covering merely a few months of Jesus' life and ministry! We are only given snapshots, portions of what he taught, and a few of the miracles he performed. From his birth to the age of twelve, we know virtually nothing about his life; and from the age of twelve until he began his public ministry at thirty, we again have almost no information given to us about him in the Gospels. John summarizes his incomplete account in the last verse of his Gospel:

Jesus did countless things that I haven't included here. And if every one of his works were written down and described one by one, I suppose that the world itself wouldn't have enough room to contain the books that would have to be written! —John 21:25

John gives us the fourth Gospel, which corresponds to the fourth of the living creatures mentioned in the book of Revelation—the flying eagle. This brings before our hearts Christ as the One who came from heaven and reveals heaven's reality to those who love him. In Dan. 3:25, it was the fourth man walking in the fire who was in the form of the Son of God. This fourth man revealed in the fourth Gospel is the One who on the fourth day put the sun into the sky (Gen. 1:7).

According to one of the church fathers, Tertullian, John was plunged in burning oil in front of a massive crowd that had filled the Roman Coliseum in order to silence his ministry. But God was not yet finished with his aged apostle. Tertullian reports that he came out of the burning caldron alive and unharmed! This miracle resulted in the mass conversion to Christ of nearly all who witnessed it. John was later banished to the island of Patmos where he wrote the book of the Revelation of Jesus Christ.

This translation of John's good news is dedicated to every faithful evangelist and preacher of the gospel. You are a gift to the world and through your ministry millions have been brought into the kingdom of God. We are forever grateful to God for your lives and your message.

You can trust every word you read from John, for he speaks the truth. His Gospel will take you into a higher glory where Jesus now sits exalted at the right hand of God. As John's Gospel unveils Jesus before your eyes, enter into the great magnificence of his presence and sit enthroned with him. Your life will never be the same after absorbing the glory presented to you in the book of John.

PURPOSE

The Gospel of John is all about the beautiful Christ. John tells us why he wrote this amazing book:

Jesus went on to do many more miraculous signs in the presence of his disciples, which are not even included in this book. But all that is recorded here is so that you will fully believe that Jesus is the Anointed One, the Son of God, and that through your faith in him you will experience eternal life by the power of his name! —John 20:30–31

There is a twofold purpose here: he's writing to nonbelievers, mostly Jews but also gentiles, to believe that Jesus is the One through whom they will find and experience eternal life; he's also writing to believers that they would more fully believe the same, to experience the fullness of that life by Jesus' powerful name.

The word *believe* is found one hundred times in John. It is the Gospel of believing! We believe that Jesus Christ is the Living Expression of God and the Light of the World. He is the Savior, the King, the true Anointed One, the living Bread, and the loving Shepherd. This is why we continue to teach and preach from this magisterial book: that people might have faith and grow in their faith. It is the Gospel of John that reveals these truths to us.

AUTHOR AND AUDIENCE

Many believe that John penned this Gospel about AD 80–85. However, the Dead Sea Scrolls hint at an earlier date as early as AD 50–55, since some of the verses found in the Dead Sea Scrolls are nearly identical to verses found in John's Gospel. The earlier date, though contested by some, seems to be more likely. Why would John wait to write and share the good news of Jesus? It seems likely that John wrote his Gospel prior to AD 66 when the Roman war with Jews began, for he mentions the Temple as still standing and the pool, which "has" (not "had") five porticos. All of this was destroyed during the Roman war of AD 67–70.

John was called to follow Jesus while he was mending a net, which seems to point to the focus of his ministry. John's message "mends" the hearts of men and brings healing to the body of Christ through the revelation he brings us.

There is an interesting possibility that both Jacob (James) and John (sons of Zebedee) were actually cousins of Jesus. By comparing Matt. 27:56 to Mark 15:40, we learn that Zebedee's wife was Salome. And Salome was believed to be the younger sister of Mary, the mother of our Lord Jesus, which would make her sons, Jacob and John, cousins of Jesus.

MAJOR THEMES

The Person of Jesus as God. Of all the major themes in John's Gospel, the question of "Who is Jesus?" lies at its heart, especially when it comes to distinguishing it from the other three Gospels. For John, Jesus is the Son of God. He does only the things that God the Father tells and shows him to say and do. Jesus is God's unique Messenger, who claims to be God and yet submits to God. Through Jesus' obedience and dependence upon him, he becomes the center for disclosing the very words and deeds of God himself. Which means the Gospel of John is as much about God as it is about Jesus!

The Work of Jesus in Salvation. John makes it clear that God the Father is the one who alone initiates human salvation. And the one who bears the Father's salvation is the Son. Jesus is the Lamb of God, come to take away the sins of the world—which means we need to be saved from those sins. He is the Good Shepherd who lays down his life for his sheep. He is also the Bread of Life, the Light of the World, the Truth, and the Life—all names that point to the salvation found in Jesus.

It is true that faith features prominently in John's Gospel, calling people to make a decision and confirm it doing the truth. But John also teaches that such a decision merely reveals what God himself is doing in those who will eventually become his children—saving them through Jesus!

The Holy Spirit. The Spirit of God fills the pages of John in the way he fills the other Gospels: the Spirit is given to Jesus at baptism; Jesus will baptize his people in this Spirit; Jesus is uniquely endowed with the Spirit; as the only one who has and gives the Spirit, Jesus shows us the characteristics of him. Above all, in this Gospel John connects the gift of the Holy Spirit to the people of God to the death and exaltation of the Son. We have come to know the precious doctrine of the Trinity in and through much of John!

The People of God. One of the major themes of John's Gospel actually draws on the Old Testament: the formation of a people, a community that will embody and carry forth Jesus' mission. This community of God's people we call the disciples begins with a sort of commissioning, where Jesus breathes upon them, marking them as his new creation people. This act recalls the original creation of the first human when God blew his breath into Adam. And like Moses' farewell address in Deuteronomy, Jesus addresses his followers (see chs. 13–17) to fulfill his redemptive purposes.

Eternal Life Now and Later. As with the other Gospels, John's is oriented around the life, death, and resurrection of Jesus—the purpose of which is that humanity might have life—eternal life in the age to come, while experiencing a taste of it right now. Everlasting, unending life in this ultimate age is a gift given to people who believe in the redemption of Christ; the alternative is judgment. But this realty isn't merely for later, it's also for now; eternal life is both already and not yet. John emphasizes the present enjoyment of this eternal life and its blessings. But he also makes it plain Jesus will return to gather to himself his own to the dwelling he's prepared for them.

JOHN

Eternal Love

The Living Expression

1 In the very beginning[a] the Living Expression[b] was already there.
  And the Living Expression was with God, yet fully God.[c]

[2] They were together—*face-to-face*,[d] in the very beginning.[e]

[3] And through his creative inspiration
  this Living Expression made all things,[f]
  for nothing has existence apart from him!

[4] Life came into being[g] because of him,
  for his life is light for all humanity.[h]

---

a 1:1 The first eighteen verses of John are considered by most scholars to be the words of an ancient hymn or poem that was cherished by first-century believers in Christ.

b 1:1 The Greek is *logos*, which has a rich and varied background in both Greek philosophy and Judaism. The Greeks equated *logos* with the highest principle of cosmic order. God's *logos* in the Old Testament is his powerful self-expression in creation, revelation, and redemption. In the New Testament we have this new unique view of God given to us by John, which signifies the presence of God himself in the flesh. Some have translated this rich term as "Word." It could also be translated "Message" or "Blueprint." Jesus Christ is the eternal Word, the creative Word, and the Word made visible. He is the divine self-expression of all that God is, contains, and reveals in incarnated flesh. Just as we express ourselves in words, God has perfectly expressed himself in Christ.

c 1:1 The Living Expression (Christ) had full participation in every attribute of deity held by God the Father. The Living Expression existed eternally as a separate individual but essentially the same, as one with the Father.

d 1:2 The Greek word used here and the Hebraic concept conveyed is that of being before God's face. There is no Hebrew word for "presence" (i.e., the "presence" of God), only the word *face*.

e 1:2 Both Gen. 1:1 and John 1:1–2 speak of *the beginning*. In Genesis it is the beginning of time, but John speaks of eternity past, a beginning before time existed. The Living Expression is Christ who existed eternally as part of the Trinity. He had no beginning, being one with the Father.

f 1:3 Or "all things happened because of him and nothing happened apart from him." The Aramaic is, "everything was in his hand" (of power). See Ps. 33:6; Isa. 44:24.

g 1:4 The Aramaic reads "In him were lives" (plural)—not only multiple human lives, but also spiritual life, eternal life, and life in every form.

h 1:4 As translated from the Aramaic, which can also be translated "the spark of human life." Jesus Christ brings the light of eternal life and the full revelation of God. The

⁵ And this Living Expression is the Light that bursts through gloom ᵃ—
   the Light that darkness could not diminish! ᵇ

⁶ Then suddenly a man appeared who was sent from God,
   a messenger named John. ᶜ

⁷ For he came to be a witness, to point the way to the Light of Life,
   and to help everyone believe.

⁸ John was not that Light but he came to show who is.
   For he was merely a messenger to speak the truth about the Light.

⁹ For the Light of Truth ᵈ was about to come into the world
   and shine upon everyone. ᵉ

¹⁰ He entered into the very world he created,
   yet the world was unaware. ᶠ

¹¹ He came to the very people he created ᵍ—
   to those who should have recognized him,
   but they did not receive him.

¹² But those who embraced him and took hold of his name ʰ
   were given authority to become
   the children of God!

¹³ He was not born by the joining of human parents ⁱ
   or from natural means, ʲ or by a man's desire,
   but he was born of God. ᵏ

¹⁴ And so the Living Expression
   became a man ˡ and lived among us! ᵐ

Gospel of John is easily divided into three sections: life (chs. 1–7), light (chs. 8–12), and love (chs. 13–21).

a 1:5 Or "keeps on shining through."

b 1:5 The Greek has a double meaning here. Darkness could not diminish this Light, nor could it comprehend it. The darkness can also be a metaphor for the sons of darkness.

c 1:6 This is John, the Baptizer.

d 1:9 As translated from the Aramaic. The Greek is, "the True Light."

e 1:9 Or "to enlighten everyone."

f 1:10 Or "the world [of humanity] didn't perceive it."

g 1:11 Or "to his own" (things or people).

h 1:12 Or "those who are putting faith into his name." To "lay hold of his name" means to believe all that he represents and put into practice what he taught in the power of his name.

i 1:13 Or "not from streams of blood" (i.e., the blood of a father and mother).

j 1:13 Or "from the natural realm."

k 1:13 Or "born out from God." This verse could be considered John's version of the virgin birth of Christ. The Word (message) is now "humanized" (and become the messenger). However, the vast majority of translations and expositors see here not Christ's virgin birth, but the new birth of those who became "children of God" in v. 12. Both are clearly presented in the Scriptures.

l 1:14 Or "became visible."

m 1:14 This is the fulfillment of Isa. 7:14. The "God with us" is Jesus Christ our Immanuel. He is among us in that he is in human form, a man for all eternity. The Greek and Aramaic

And we gazed upon the splendor of his glory,[a]
the glory of the One and Only[b]
who came from the Father overflowing
with tender mercy[c] and truth!
[15] John taught the truth about him
when he announced to the people,
"He's the One! *Set your hearts on him!*
I told you he would come after me,
even though he ranks far above me,
for he existed before I was even born."[d]
[16] And now out of his fullness we are fulfilled![e]
And from him we receive grace heaped upon more grace![f]
[17] Moses gave us the Law, but Jesus, the Anointed One,
unveils truth wrapped in tender mercy.
[18] No one has ever gazed upon the fullness of God's splendor
except the uniquely beloved Son,
who is cherished by the Father[g]
and held close to his heart.
Now he has unfolded to us[h]
the full explanation of who God truly is!

The Ministry of John the Baptizer

[19] There were some of the Jewish leaders[i] who sent an entourage of priests and temple servants[j] from Jerusalem to interrogate John. They asked him, "Who are you?"

---

reads, "he pitched his tent among us." This takes us back into the book of Exodus where God came down and lived in the tent (tabernacle) in the wilderness. See Ex. 25:8.
a 1:14 The Aramaic is, "We gazed upon his preciousness."
b 1:14 The Aramaic is, "Unique and Beloved Son." The Greek word, *monogenes*, means "of a single [*mono*] kind [*genes*]." This word is also used for Isaac in Heb. 11:17 as Abraham's uniquely precious son, but not his only one.
c 1:14 The Aramaic word, *taybootha*, means "loving kindness or goodness." The Greek word is *charis*, which can also be translated, "grace, favor, sweetness, pleasure or delight." The translator has combined all those concepts in the words *tender mercy*. Truly, Jesus Christ is full of everything that our hearts crave.
d 1:15 This reveals the eternal nature of Jesus Christ, for John was older than Jesus. The Aramaic can be translated, "He is preferred before me, for he has priority over me."
e 1:16 As translated from the Aramaic.
f 1:16 Or "one gift after another."
g 1:18 Or "from the lap of the Father." This is an idiom for the place of closest intimacy.
h 1:18 Or "He has led the way into the knowledge of God." The Greek word, *hexegeomai*, can mean either "to lead the way" or "to explain."
i 1:19 Or simply, "Jews." This is a metonymy for "Jewish leaders." Obviously, not all Jews opposed John's ministry. Some estimate that John and his disciples baptized as many as one million people. It is possible that John was a part of the Essene community of devout Jews.
j 1:19 Or "Levites."

[20] John answered them directly,[a] saying, "I am not the Messiah!"

[21] "Then who are you?" they asked. "Are you Elijah?"

"No," John replied.

So they pressed him further, "Are you the prophet Moses said was coming, the one we're expecting?"[b] "No," he replied.

[22] "Then who are you?" they demanded. "We need an answer for those who sent us. Tell us something about yourself—anything!"

[23] So, John answered them, *"I am fulfilling Isaiah's prophecy:* 'I am an urgent, thundering voice shouting in the desert—clear the way and prepare your hearts for the coming of the Lord Yahweh!'"[c]

[24] Then some members of the religious sect known as the Pharisees[d] questioned John, [25] "Why do you baptize the people since you admit you're not the Christ, Elijah, or the Prophet?"

[26–27] John answered them, "I baptize in this river, but the One who will take my place is to be more honored than I,[e] but even when he stands among you, you will not recognize or embrace him! I am not worthy enough to stoop down in front of him and untie his sandals!" [28] This all took place at Bethany,[f] where John was baptizing at the place of the crossing of the Jordan River.[g]

The Lamb of God

[29] The very next day John saw Jesus coming to him to be baptized, and John cried out, "Look! There he is—God's Lamb![h] He will take away[i] the sins of

---

a 1:20 Or "he did not deny it."

b 1:21 See Deut. 18:15. Jesus is identified as that "Prophet" in Acts 3:22.

c 1:23 As translated from the Aramaic. See Isa. 40:3. The Aramaic is clear that the preparations are for the Lord Yahweh, signifying the deity of Jesus Christ. The Greek is, "Make straight the way for the Lord [*kurios*]."

d 1:24 Or "separated ones." They were the religious leaders of the day who considered themselves separated from sin and closer to God than other people.

e 1:26–27 As translated from the Aramaic.

f 1:28 This was a different Bethany than the one near Jerusalem, commonly referred to in the Gospels. Some Greek manuscripts have the location as "Bethabara," however, the Aramaic is clearly Bethany.

g 1:28 As translated from the Aramaic. This place of crossing is likely where the children of Israel crossed into the promised land when the Jordan River parted and they passed through on dry land. See Josh. 3. This place was a powerful reminder of crossing over into a new day, a new era for Israel. This was the place chosen by God for John to baptize.

h 1:29 As the Lamb of God, Jesus was publicly washed and proven to be without flaw or blemish, ready to become the sacrifice for all the world. Although he will become the Lion of the tribe of Judah in resurrection power, John points to him as the meek Lamb, a willing sacrifice for our sins.

i 1:29 Or "lift off" (the burden). The Greek word used here is often used for "lifting up and away" an anchor from off the ocean floor.

the world!* ³⁰ I told you that a Mighty One* would come who is far greater than I am, because he existed long before I was born! ³¹ My baptism was for the preparation of his appearing to Israel, even though I've yet to experience him."

³² Then, as John baptized Jesus he spoke these words: "I see the Spirit of God appear like a dove descending from the heavenly realm and landing upon him—and it rested upon him from that moment forward!* ³³ And even though I've yet to experience him, when I was commissioned to baptize with water God spoke these words to me, 'One day you will see the Spirit descend and remain upon a man. He will be the One I have sent to baptize with the Holy Spirit.'* ³⁴ And now I have seen with discernment. I can tell you for sure that this man is the Son of God."*

Jesus' First Followers

³⁵⁻³⁶ The very next day John was there again with two of his disciples as Jesus was walking right past them. John, gazing upon him, pointed to Jesus and said, "Look! There's God's Lamb!" ³⁷ And as soon as John's two disciples heard this, they immediately left John and began to follow a short distance behind Jesus.

³⁸ Then Jesus turned around and saw they were following him and asked, **"What do you want?"** They responded, "Rabbi (which means, Master Teacher*), where are you staying?"* ³⁹ Jesus answered, **"Come and discover for yourselves."** So they went with him and saw where he was staying, and since it was late in the afternoon, they spent the rest of the day with Jesus.

---

a 1:29 The Aramaic is "the sins of the universe." To take away our sins is a figure of speech that means "he will break sin's grip from humanity, taking away both its guilt and power from those who believe."

b 1:30 As translated from the Aramaic.

c 1:32 Jesus, the Lamb, took away our sins, and the Holy Spirit, the Dove, brings to man the life of God. Jesus didn't come to start a movement but to bring the fullness of life to us. This "Dove" points to the dove that Noah released from the ark. It found no place to rest in a fallen world. The last time Noah released the dove it flew and never returned. It flew throughout history over Abraham and the patriarchs, over the prophets and kings with no place to rest, until at last, there was a heavenly man who carried the life of heaven—upon him the dove (Holy Spirit) rested and remained. There was nothing that could offend heaven in the life of our Lord Jesus.

d 1:33 Or "the Spirit of Holiness."

e 1:34 Some Greek manuscripts have "the Chosen One of God." The Aramaic is clearly "the Son of Elohim."

f 1:38 This is the first recorded saying of Jesus in the Gospels. It is a question that should be asked to every follower of Jesus: "What do you want in following me?" Do we want something only for ourselves? A ministry? Answers to prayer? Or do we simply want to be with him? Their answer, "Where are you staying?" shows that they were seeking only him. The first question God asked to Adam and Eve was, "Where are you?" The first words of the God-man were, "What do you want?"

g 1:38 The parenthetical words are added by the author, John. *Rabbi* is an honorific term that means more than teacher. The Aramaic word is best translated "Master," or "Master Teacher."

h 1:38 Or "Where do you abide?" This is the same word used in John 15:4 where it refers to life-union, to be joined to Jesus as the living vine. Jesus wants everyone to come and discover where he "abides" in life-union with his Father.

⁴⁰⁻⁴¹ One of the two disciples who heard John's words and began to follow Jesus was a man named Andrew. ᵃ He went and found his brother, Simon,
and told him, "We have found the Anointed One!" ᵇ (Which is translated, the
Christ.) ⁴² Then Andrew brought Simon to meet him. When Jesus gazed upon
Andrew's brother, he prophesied to him, "**You are Simon and your father's
name is John.** ᶜ **But from now on you will be called Cephas**" (which means,
Peter the Rock). ᵈ

Jesus Calls Philip and Nathanael

⁴³ The next day Jesus decided to go to the region of Galilee. There he found
Philip and said to him, "**Come and follow me.**" ⁴⁴ (Now Philip, Andrew, and Peter were all from the same village of Bethsaida.) ᵉ ⁴⁵ Then Philip went to look for
his friend, Nathanael, ᶠ and told him, "We've found him! We've found the One
we've been waiting for! It's Jesus, son of Joseph from Nazareth, the Anointed
One! He's the One that Moses and the prophets prophesied would come!"

⁴⁶ Nathanael sneered, "Nazareth! What good thing could ever come from
Nazareth?" ᵍ Philip answered, "Come and let's find out!"

⁴⁷ When Jesus saw Nathanael approaching, he said, "**Now here comes a
true son of Israel—an honest man with no hidden motive!**"

⁴⁸ *Nathanael was stunned* and said, "But you've never met me—how do you
know anything about me?"

Jesus answered, "**Nathanael, right before Philip came to you I saw you
sitting under the shade of a fig tree.**" ʰ

---

a 1:40–41 *Andrew* means "brave."

b 1:40–41 Or "Messiah." The word *messiah* is taken from the Hebrew verb, "to anoint with
oil." Jesus Christ is the One anointed to deliver, to save, and to reconcile us back to God.

c 1:42 The Aramaic can also be translated "You are Simon, son of the dove." Simon means
"one who hears."

d 1:42 The Aramaic word is *keefa*, which means "rock." It is anglicized as "Peter." This parenthetical statement is not found in the Aramaic, but only in Greek manuscripts. It appears
that the Greek text is admitting it is a translation from the Aramaic.

e 1:44 Bethsaida means "place of fishing," and was a village on Lake Galilee.

f 1:45 Nathanael means "gift of God." It is commonly thought that he is the same one as the
Bartholomew mentioned as one of Christ's apostles. Almost every time Philip's name is
listed as an apostle, it is followed by Bartholomew. The word *friend* is implied.

g 1:46 Jesus and his disciples were Galileans and spoke the northern dialect of Aramaic. Galileans were considered somewhat backward. Isaiah called that region "the land of the gentile
peoples, those surrounded with great darkness." Yet this was the region where the Messiah's
light would shine forth. See Isa. 9:1–2.

h 1:48 Although we can only speculate what Nathanael was doing while sitting under the
fig tree, it had to have been something very personal to him. Perhaps he was confessing to
God his love for him and his desire to be pure and holy. Or perhaps he was meditating on
the Scriptures that speak of the coming Messiah. A fig tree is often a biblical metaphor of
God's purpose and destiny coming to fruitfulness, especially as it relates to God's kingdom
realm being established on the earth. See Mic. 4:4; Zech. 3:10. There is some speculation

⁴⁹ Nathanael blurted out, "Teacher, you are truly the Son of God and the King of Israel!"

⁵⁰ Jesus answered, "Do you believe simply because I told you I saw you sitting under a fig tree? You will experience even more impressive things than that! ⁵¹ I prophesy to you eternal truth:ᵈ From now onᵇ you will seeᶜ an open heaven and gaze upon the Son of Manᵈ like a stairway reaching into the skyᵉ with the messengers of God climbing up and down uponᶠ him!"

Jesus Comes to a Wedding

2 Now on the third dayᵍ there was a wedding feast in the Galilean village of Cana,ʰ and the mother of Jesus was there. ²⁻³ Jesus and his disciples were all invited to the banquet,ⁱ but with so many guests in attendance, they ran out of wine.ʲ And when Mary realized it, she came to him and asked, "They have no wine, *can't you do something about it?*"ᵏ

that the phrase "I saw you under the fig tree" could be an Aramaic idiom for "I knew you since you were in the cradle."

a 1:51 As translated from the Aramaic. John records Jesus using this phrase twenty-five times. The Greek is "Amen, Amen I say to you."

b 1:51 As translated from the Aramaic.

c 1:51 Or "you [plural] will spiritually see." This is a promise for every believer today.

d 1:51 This is a messianic term pointing to Christ, not as the son of *a* man, but the Son of Man (humanity). He is the true Man. He is not Joseph's son, but the Son of God.

e 1:51 This is an obvious reference to "Jacob's Ladder" as the fulfillment of his dream found in Gen. 28:10–22. Jesus Christ is that stairway that joins earth to heaven and brings heaven to earth. The word for "angels" can be translated "messengers" and could be humans given access into the heavenly realm through the blood of Jesus. Jesus, as the stairway, is both in heaven and on earth as he speaks this to Nathanael. What mysteries surround him!

f 1:51 Or "next to."

g 2:1 This was a Tuesday as counted by the Hebrew week beginning on Sunday. The "third day" was chosen as the wedding day in ancient Judaism because it is only on the third day of creation that God says "It was good" twice (see Gen. 1:10, 12). The day was considered twice blessed. Tuesdays were ideal for Jewish weddings, for that gave the guests time to get there after the Sabbath and remain for the multiple days of the wedding feast. The third day is also a picture of the day of resurrection glory, the day Jesus rose from the dead. This miracle is a revelation of going from death to resurrection life, water to wine.

h 2:1 Cana means "land of reeds," which points to the weak and fragile nature of man. See Isa. 42:3; Matt. 11:7; 12:20.

i 2:2–3 There is speculation that this wedding involved someone of Jesus' family since Mary and all his disciples were also in attendance. A Near Eastern wedding would often last between three and seven days.

j 2:2–3 Interpreting Mary's words for today we could say, "Religion has failed, it has run out of wine." The traditions of religion cannot gladden the heart, but Jesus can. Moses (the law) turned water into blood, but Jesus (grace) turned water into wine.

k 2:2–3 This is a dilemma that Mary is hoping Jesus will solve by performing a miracle. Mary has no doubt about the power and anointing of her Son. Running out of wine is a picture of how the joy of this world runs out and fades away.

[4] Jesus replied, "My dear one, don't you understand that if I do this, it won't change anything for you, but it will change everything for me! [a] My hour *of unveiling my power* has not yet come."

[5] Mary then went to the servers and told them, "Whatever Jesus tells you, make sure that you do it!"

[6] Now there were six stone water pots [b] standing nearby. They were meant to be used for the Jewish washing rituals. [c] Each one held about 20 gallons or more. [7] Jesus came to the servers and told them, **"Fill the *pots with water, right up to the very brim*."** [8] Then he said, **"Now fill your pitchers and take them to the master of ceremonies."**

[9] And when they poured out their pitcher for the master of ceremonies to sample, the water became wine! When he tasted the water that became wine, the master of ceremonies was impressed. (Although he didn't know where the wine had come from, but the servers knew.) [10] He called the bridegroom over and said to him, "Every host serves his best wine first until everyone has had a cup or two, then he serves the wine of poor quality. But you, my friend, you've reserved the most exquisite wine until now!" [d]

[11] This miracle in Cana was the first of the many extraordinary miracles Jesus performed in Galilee. This was a sign revealing his glory, and his disciples believed in him. [e]

Jesus at the Temple

[12] After this, Jesus, his mother and brothers and his disciples went to Capernaum [f] and stayed there for a few days. [13] But the time was close for the Jewish Passover to

---

a 2:4 Or literally "Woman, what is that for you and for me?" This is an Aramaic idiom meaning, "What do we have in common if I do this?" For Mary, it will change her very little, but for Jesus, this will be his first public miracle and will dramatically change his ministry from this moment on as the crowds see the power that he possesses. Jesus knows his miracle ministry will "come out of hiding" by performing a miracle. Yet with Mary's encouragement, Jesus proceeds to do just that.

b 2:6 Six is the number for man, for man was made on the sixth day. These six stone jars could represent man's method of helping others. It is nothing but water. But Jesus changes the water of the Word of God into the wine of the Spirit. True spiritual life can fill our vessel as we bring joy to the world. The fruit of the Spirit includes joy, and there is no limit to the joy available for the child of God. See Gal. 5:22–23.

c 2:6 This was an outward purification (baptism) for worshipers coming into a synagogue.

d 2:10 Jesus delights in your joy more than you know. He does not withhold joy from his people. He created between 120 and 150 gallons of the very best wine for a wedding feast! This was one of five miracles that are unique to John's Gospel. The other four are: healing the rich man's son (John 4), healing the crippled man at Bethesda (John 5), healing the blind man (John 9), and raising Lazarus from the dead (John 11).

e 2:11 Or "The disciples made known his glory and believed in him."

f 2:12 The village of Capernaum means "the village of Nahum" which means "the village of the comforted." Jesus did many miracles and made his Galilean base of ministry in "the village of the comforted."

begin, so Jesus walked to Jerusalem.ᵃ ¹⁴As he went into the temple courtyard, he noticed it was filled with merchants selling oxen, lambs, and doves *for exorbitant prices*, while others were overcharging as they exchanged currencyᵇ behind their counters. ¹⁵So Jesus found some rope and made it into a whip. Then he drove out every one of them and their animals from the courtyard of the temple, and he kicked over their tables filled with money, scattering it everywhere!ᶜ ¹⁶And he shouted at the merchants,ᵈ **"Get these things out of here! Don't you dare make my Father's house into a center for merchandise!"** ¹⁷That's when his disciples remembered the Scripture: "I am consumed with a fiery passion to keep your house pure!"ᵉ

¹⁸But the Jewish religious leaders challenged Jesus, "What authorization do you have to do this sort of thing? If God gave you this kind of authority, what *supernatural* sign will you show us to prove it?"

¹⁹Jesus answered, **"After you've destroyed this temple,ᶠ I will raise it up again in three days."**

²⁰Then the Jewish leaders sneered, "This temple took forty-six yearsᵍ to build, and you mean to tell us that you will raise it up in three days?" ²¹*But they didn't understand that* Jesus was speaking of the "temple" of his body.ʰ ²²But the disciples remembered his prophecy after Jesus rose from the dead, and believed both the Scripture and what Jesus had said.

²³While Jesus was at the Passover Feast, *the number of his followers began to grow*, and many gave their allegiance to him because of all the miraculous signs they had seen him doing! ²⁴But Jesus did not yet entrust himself to them, because he knew how fickle human hearts can be. ²⁵He didn't need anyone to tell him about human nature, *for he fully understood what man was capable of doing*.

Nicodemus

3 Now there was a prominent religious leader among the Jews named Nicodemus,ⁱ who was part of the sect called the Pharisees and a member of the Jewish ruling council. ²One night he discreetly came to Jesus and said, "Master,

---

a 2:13 This was a journey of nearly eighty miles.

b 2:14 These money changers would exchange Roman currency into Jewish currency to pay the temple tax.

c 2:15 Jesus came to end animal sacrifices and to end the financial tyranny of religion.

d 2:16 Or "the dove dealers."

e 2:17 See Ps. 69:9.

f 2:19 Or "sanctuary."

g 2:20 Our bodies (temples) have forty-six chromosomes in every cell.

h 2:21 Resurrection power would be the sign of his supreme authority. Jesus' death and resurrection effectively dismantled the need for the temple, for now his powerful gospel of the kingdom realm builds us into a holy temple not made with hands. See 1 Cor. 3:16; 6:19. This symbolic form of speaking was so different than the teachings of the Pharisees, as it is to the understanding of many Christians today. The God who was once worshiped by animal sacrifices is now to be worshiped in spirit and truth with every believer as a priest.

i 3:1 Nicodemus means "conqueror." Here we see a distinguished and moral man speaking

we know that you are a teacher from God, for no one performs the miracle signs that you do, unless God's power is with him."

[3] Jesus answered, "Nicodemus, listen to this eternal truth: Before a person can perceive God's kingdom realm, they must first experience a rebirth." [a]

[4] Nicodemus said, "Rebirth? How can a gray-headed man be reborn? It's impossible for a man to go back into the womb a second time and be reborn!"

[5] Jesus answered, "I speak an eternal truth: Unless you are born of water [b] and Spirit-wind, you will never enter God's kingdom realm. [6] For the natural realm can only give birth to things that are natural, but the spiritual realm gives birth to supernatural life!

[7] "You shouldn't be amazed by my statement, [c] 'You must be born from above!' [d] [8] For the Spirit-wind blows as it chooses. You can hear its sound, [e] but you don't know where it came from or where it's going. So it is within the hearts of those who are Spirit-born!" [f]

[9] Then Nicodemus replied, "But I don't understand, what do you mean? How does this happen?"

[10] Jesus answered, "Nicodemus, aren't you the respected teacher in Israel, and yet you don't understand this revelation? [11] I speak eternal truths about things I know, things I've seen and experienced—and still you don't accept

---

with Jesus. In the next chapter we will see an immoral woman coming to know Jesus, the woman at Jacob's well.

a 3:3 The Greek word can be translated "born from above." It is clear in the context that Nicodemus understood it as a rebirth. The Aramaic word is clearly "born from the origin." The implication is that you must be born again like Adam was born by the direct breath of God. Nicodemus came seeking knowledge; Jesus offered him life.

b 3:5 This is the water of the Word of God that cleanses and gives us life. See Eph. 5:25–26; James 1:18; 1 Peter 1:23. Some see in the water and Spirit analogy the creative beginning of Gen. 1, where God's Spirit fluttered over the chaotic waters. New creation life comes the same way. It was water and blood that came from the side of our Lord Jesus. He was the last Adam giving birth to his bride from his pierced side.

c 3:7 Or "say to you all."

d 3:7 A common poetic form of Hebraic teaching is to use a play on words, which Jesus utilizes in this poetic masterpiece with multiple words containing dual meanings. The word reborn can also be translated "born from above."

e 3:8 The word for blow can also be translated "breathe." The word sound can be translated "voice." And the same word for Spirit can also mean "wind." If our new birth is so mysterious, how much more will be the ways of living each moment by the movement of the Holy Spirit? You can then understand why Nicodemus was confused, for he took everything at face value and couldn't see a deeper meaning.

f 3:8 Or "The Spirit moves you as he chooses, and you hear his voice, but you don't know where he came from or where he goes." The Aramaic is so rich and multilayered in this passage. Perhaps it could be paraphrased as, "The wind, the breath, and the Spirit are moved by mysterious moods and in their own wonderful ways. When you feel their touch and hear their voices you know they are real, but you don't understand how they flow and move over the earth. In this same mysterious way so is the way of everyone who is born by wind, breath, and Spirit."

what I reveal. [12] If you're unable to understand and believe what I've told you about the natural realm, what will you do when I begin to unveil the heavenly realm? [13] No one has risen into the heavenly realm except the Son of Man who also exists in heaven." [a]

God's Love for Everyone

[14] "And just as Moses in the desert lifted up the brass replica of a snake on a pole *for all the people to see and be healed,* [b] so the Son of Man is ready to be lifted up, [15] so that those who truly believe in him [c] will not perish but be given eternal life. [16] For this is how much God loved the world—he gave his one and only, unique Son *as a gift.* [d] So now everyone who believes in him [e] will never perish but experience everlasting life.

[17] "God did not send his Son into the world to judge and condemn the world, but to be its Savior and rescue it! [f] [18] So now there is no longer any condemnation for those who believe in him, but the unbeliever already lives under condemnation because they do not believe in the name of God's beloved Son. [g] [19] And here is the basis for their judgment: The Light of God has now come into the world, but the hearts of people love their darkness more than the Light, because they want the darkness to conceal their evil. [20] So the wicked [h] hate the Light and try to hide from it, for their lives are fully exposed in the Light. [21] But those who love the truth [i] will come out into the Light and welcome its exposure, for the Light will reveal that their fruitful works were produced by God." [j]

---

a   3:13 Jesus shares a mystery with Nicodemus. While he was on the earth ministering, Jesus was also in heaven in the spirit realm. Being in two places at the same time is also the privilege given to every believer. We are seated with Christ in the heavenly realm and living our earthly life to please him. This is what it means to be "in Christ." See Eph. 2:6; Col. 3:1–5. In the realm of the Spirit, heaven and earth is one. Jesus is telling Nicodemus that only those who are seated in the heavenly realm will understand spiritual truths. See 1 Cor. 2:1–10. There are some Greek manuscripts that read "the Son of Man who came from heaven." But the Aramaic is clearly "who is in heaven."

b   3:14 See Num. 21:8–9. The brass snake was an emblem of sin and disease. The Hebrew uses a word, *seraph,* which means a fiery one (fiery serpent). All of humanity has been bitten by the "snake of sin," but Jesus was raised up on a cross for all people to see. We only need to look to him and believe, and we are healed and saved from sin.

c   3:15 The Aramaic participle can also be "believe on him" or "believe into him," which could explain the variations found in the Greek text.

d   3:16 Or "God proved he loved the world by giving his Son."

e   3:16 Or "believe into him." Salvation and regeneration must be by faith. True faith (Gr. *pistis*) has a number of components: acceptance, embracing something (someone) as truth, union with God and his Word, and an inner confidence that God alone is enough.

f   3:17 The Aramaic is "so that they shall live by his hand" (of power).

g   3:18 Or "one and only Son."

h   3:20 The Aramaic is "those who do hateful things."

i   3:21 Or "practice the truth."

j   3:21 Some scholars believe that vv. 16–21 are explanatory material supplied by John, the author, rather than the words of Jesus.

John, Friend of the Bridegroom

²²Then Jesus and his disciples went out for a length of time into the Judean countryside where they baptized the people. ²³At this time John was still baptizing people at Aenon,ᵃ near Salim,ᵇ where there was plenty of water. And the people kept coming for John to baptize them. ²⁴(This was before John was thrown into prison.)

²⁵An argument then developed between John's disciples and a particular Jewish man about baptism.ᶜ ²⁶So they went to John and asked him, "Teacher, are you aware that the One you told us about at the crossing place—he's now baptizing everyone with larger crowds than yours. People are flocking to him! *What do you think about that?"*

²⁷John answered them, "A person cannot receive even one thing unless God bestows it.ᵈ ²⁸You heard me tell you before that I am not the Messiah, but certainly I am the messenger sent ahead of him. ²⁹He is the Bridegroom,ᵉ and the bride belongs to him. I am the friendᶠ of the Bridegroom who stands nearby and listens with great joy to the Bridegroom's voice. And because of his words my joy is complete and overflows! ³⁰So it's necessary for him to increaseᵍ and for me to be diminished.ʰ

³¹"For the one who is from the earth belongs to the earth and speaks from the natural realm. But the One who comes from above is above everything and speaks of the highest realm of all! ³²His message is about what he has seen and experienced, even though people don't accept it. ³³Yet those who embrace his message know in their hearts that it's the truth.ⁱ

³⁴"The One whom God has sent to represent him will speak the words of God, for God has poured out upon him the fullness of the Holy Spirit without limitation.ʲ ³⁵The Father loves his Son so much that all things have been given

---

ᵃ 3:23 The Aramaic location is *Ainyon*, which in Aramaic means "the spring of doves," or "dove's eyes." The Greek manuscripts have transliterated this to *Aenon*.

ᵇ 3:23 Or in Aramaic, *Shalim*, which means "to follow." One ancient tradition refers to this location to be eight miles south of the town of Scythopolis, or *Beit She'an*.

ᶜ 3:25 Or "purification." The implication is that the Jewish man was telling John's disciples that Jesus' baptism was better than John's.

ᵈ 3:27 Or "No one of his own will can receive anything unless it comes to him from heaven."

ᵉ 3:29 See Isa. 62:5; Rev. 21:9.

ᶠ 3:29 Or "family member."

ᵍ 3:30 The increase of Christ in v. 30 is the bride of Christ in v. 29. We are the increase of Christ as his counterpart. Just as Eve was the increase of Adam, the bride is the increase of Christ on the earth.

ʰ 3:30 Or "He is destined to become greater, and I must be pruned." Some translations end John the Baptizer's words here and make vv. 31–36 the words of John the apostle.

ⁱ 3:33 The Aramaic is "Those who accept his testimony take God's true seal (upon them)."

ʲ 3:34 Or "the Spirit does not give anything in small measures." There is some textual evidence that this verse is saying, "The Son gives the Spirit [to his people] without measure."

into his hands. *[a] [36]* Those who trust in the Son possess eternal life; but those who don't obey *[b]* the Son will not see life, and God's anger will rise up against them." *[c]*

A Thirsty Savior

4 Soon the news reached the Jewish religious leaders known as the Pharisees that Jesus was drawing greater crowds of followers coming to be baptized than John. [2] (Although Jesus didn't baptize, but had his disciples baptize the people.) [3] *Jesus* *[d]* heard what was being said and abruptly left Judea and returned to the province of Galilee, [4] and he had to pass through Samaritan territory.

[5] Jesus arrived at the Samaritan village of Sychar, *[e]* near the field that Jacob had given to his son, Joseph, long ago. [6-8] Wearied by his long journey, he sat on the edge of Jacob's well. *[f]* He sent his disciples into the village to buy food, for it was already afternoon.

Soon a Samaritan woman came to draw water. Jesus said to her, **"Give me a drink of water."** *[g]*

[9] Surprised, she said, "Why would a Jewish man ask a Samaritan woman for a drink of water?"

[10] Jesus replied, **"If you only knew who I am and the gift that God wants to give you—you'd ask me for a drink, and I would give to you living water."**

[11] The woman replied, "But sir, *[h]* you don't even have a bucket and this well is very deep. So where do you find this 'living water'? [12] Do you really think that you are greater than our ancestor Jacob who dug this well and drank from it himself, along with his children and livestock?"

[13] Jesus answered, **"If you drink from Jacob's well you'll be thirsty again**

---

a 3:35 The text is simply "he has given all into his hands." The "all" can be all things, or "all authority," but can also mean "all people."

b 3:36 The Aramaic can be translated "those who do not cling to the Son."

c 3:36 As translated from the Aramaic. The Greek is "wrath rests upon them."

d 4:3 Some manuscripts have "The Lord." This is included here from v. 1 for the sake of the English narrative.

e 4:5 This is near modern-day Nablus in the northern region of the West Bank. There is a village named Askar, which was formerly known as Sychar, about one kilometer north of the well.

f 4:6-8 The well was "a spring-fed well." This becomes a picture of the "spring" of the Jacob-life inside of every one of us. Fed by Adam's fall, this spring has flowed through all of humanity. But Jesus sat as a "lid" to Jacob's well, sealing its polluted stream. In Christ, Jacob's clever striving has ended. A living well became a lid to Jacob's well as Jesus sat there ready to give his living water to all who would come and drink. A well sitting upon a well.

g 4:6-8 The "water" Jesus wanted was the refreshing, satisfying pleasure of her devotion. He says to each one of us, "Nothing satisfies me except you." The sinner drank of the Savior and the Savior drank of the sinner and both were satisfied. Neither ate or drank, but both were satisfied.

h 4:11 The woman used the Greek title *kurios* when she addressed Jesus. *Kurios* is the Greek word for "lord." However, *kurios* is not a word used for "exalted or sovereign Lord," but more like "sir."

and again, [14] but if anyone drinks the living water I give them, they will never thirst again and will be forever satisfied! For when you drink the water I give you it becomes a gushing fountain *of the Holy Spirit*, springing up and flooding you with endless life!" [a]

[15] The woman replied, "Let me drink that water so I'll never be thirsty again and won't have to come back here to draw water."

[16] Jesus said, "Go get your husband and bring him back here."

[17] "But I'm not married," the woman answered.

"That's true," Jesus said, [18] "for you've been married five times [b] and now you're living with a man who is not your husband. You have told the truth." [c]

[19] The woman said, "You must be a prophet! [20] So tell me this: Why do our fathers worship God here on this nearby mountain, [d] but your people teach that Jerusalem is the place where we must worship. Which is right?"

Jesus responded, [21] "Believe me, dear woman, the time has come when you won't worship [e] the Father on a mountain nor in Jerusalem, *but in your heart.* [22] Your people don't really know the One they worship. We Jews worship out of our experience, for it's from the Jews that salvation is made available. [f] [23-24] From here on, worshiping the Father will not be a matter of the right place but with the right heart. For God is a Spirit, [g] and he longs to have sincere worshipers who worship and adore him in the realm of the Spirit and in truth."

[25] The woman said, *"This is all so confusing,* but I do know that the Anointed One is coming—the true Messiah. And when he comes, he will tell us everything we need to know."

---

a 4:14 The Greek verb used for "springing up" is *hallomenou*, and is never used for inanimate objects (water). It is a verb used for people (living things) and means "jumping," or "leaping up." The Septuagint translates this verb elsewhere as an activity of the Holy Spirit.

b 4:18 In a sense, every one of us has been married to our five husbands: our five senses. The six men speak of our fallen humanity, for six is the number of man who was created on the sixth day. Our heart can never be satisfied with what is on this earth; we must have the living water that comes from heaven. Christ is the seventh husband, the only One who satisfies. Christ is the real husband. See 2 Cor. 11:2.

c 4:18 After offering her living water, Jesus first confronts her with her sin and steers her away from religious debates (the proper place to worship, v. 20). Then he unveils himself to her as the true Messiah. Jesus does the same thing to everyone who comes to him.

d 4:20 This is most likely Mt. Gerizim where the Samaritans had a shrine to worship God. However, Jacob's well is located at the base of Mt. Ebal, the mountain the Levites were told to curse. See Deut. 27:12–26; Josh. 8:33. Both Gerizim and Ebal are mountains in Samaria.

e 4:21 The Aramaic word for "worship," *seged*, means "to bow down" or "to surrender."

f 4:22 Or "the life-givers are from the Jews."

g 4:23–24 Or "God is breath," or "God is wind." Jesus refers to "Spirit" more than one hundred times in the four Gospels.

[26] Jesus said to her, "You don't have to wait any longer, the Anointed One is here speaking with you—I am the One you're looking for." [a]

[27] At that moment the disciples returned and were stunned to see Jesus speaking with the Samaritan woman. Yet none of them dared to ask him why or what they were discussing. [28] All at once, the woman dropped her water jar and ran off to her village and told everyone, [29] "Come and meet a man at the well who told me everything I've ever done! [b] He could be the Anointed One we've been waiting for." [30] Hearing this, the people came streaming out of the village to go see Jesus. [c]

The Harvest Is Ready

[31] Then the disciples began to insist that Jesus eat some of the food they brought back from the village, saying, "Teacher, you must eat something." [32] But Jesus told them, "Don't worry about me. I have eaten a meal [d] you don't know about."

[33] Puzzled by this, the disciples began to discuss among themselves, "Did someone already bring him food? Where did he get this meal?"

[34] Then Jesus spoke up and said, "My food is to be doing the will of him who sent me and bring it to completion."

[35] As the crowds emerged from the village, Jesus said to his disciples, "Why would you say, 'The harvest is another four months away'? Look at all the people coming—now is harvest time! For their hearts are like vast fields of ripened grain—ready for a spiritual harvest. [36] And everyone who reaps these souls for eternal life will receive a reward. And those who plant spiritual seeds and those who reap the harvest will celebrate together with great joy! [37] And this confirms the saying, 'One sows the seed and another reaps the harvest.' [e] [38] I have sent you out to harvest a field that you haven't planted, where many others have labored long and hard before you. And now you are privileged to profit from their labors and reap the harvest."

---

a 4:26 Or "I am the I AM who speaks to you."

b 4:29 No doubt, this woman was the talk of the town. Having five marriages, she was well known for what she had done. For her to say these words was an honest confession of her past. The miracle here is that the people believed her and went out to see for themselves.

c 4:30 Although unnamed in the biblical account, church tradition identifies the Samaritan woman to be Photini. An internet search of her name will yield many interesting stories about her post-conversion ministry, including her being named as an "apostle" of Jesus and her eventual martyrdom. Regardless of the validity of the extrabiblical references, she will go down in history as the first New Testament evangelist to win a city to Christ. God is faithful to use anyone to reach others when we are honest to tell others that Jesus knows everything we've ever done and still loves us.

d 4:32 There is a fascinating wordplay here in the Aramaic. The word Jesus uses isn't the common word for "food," but is actually a word that means "nutrients." It is also a homonym that is more commonly translated "kingdom." Jesus has a kingdom feast that no one else knows about. He feasts upon the devotion of his bride. See Song. 4:15; 5:1. The church is truly the "woman at the well."

e 4:37 See Job 31:8; Mic. 6:15.

[39] So there were many from the Samaritan village who became believers in Jesus because of the woman's testimony: "He told me everything I ever did!" [40] Then they begged Jesus to stay with them, so he stayed there for two days, [41] resulting in many more coming to faith in him because of his teachings.

[42] Then the Samaritans said to the woman, "We no longer believe just because of what you told us, but now we've heard him ourselves and are convinced that he really is the true Savior of the world!" [a]

Jesus Returns to Galilee

[43] On the third day Jesus left there and walked to the province of Galilee, *where he was raised.* [b] [44] Now Jesus knew that prophets are honored everywhere they go except in their own hometown. [45] Even so, as Jesus arrived in the province of Galilee, he was welcomed by the people with open arms. Many of them had been in Jerusalem during the Passover Festival and had witnessed firsthand the miracles he had performed. [c]

[46-47] Jesus entered the village of Cana of Galilee where he had transformed water into wine. And there was a governmental official in Capernaum who had a son who was very sick and dying. When he heard that Jesus had left Judea and was staying in Cana of Galilee, he decided to make the journey to Cana. [d] When he found Jesus he begged him, "You must come with me to Capernaum and heal my son!"

[48] So Jesus said to him, "You [e] never believe unless you see signs and wonders." [f]

[49] But the man continued to plead, "You have to come with me to Capernaum before my little boy dies!"

[50] Then Jesus looked him in the eyes and said, "Go back home now. I promise you, your son will live and not die."

The man believed in his heart the words of Jesus and set off for home. [51] When he was still a distance from Capernaum, his servants met him on the road and told him the good news, "Your son is healed! He's alive!"

[52] Overjoyed, the father asked his servants, "When did my son begin to recover?"

"Yesterday," they said, "at one in the afternoon. All at once his fever broke—and now he's well!"

---

a 4:42 They acknowledge Jesus not just as the Messiah, but the "Savior of the world," including the Samaritan people who were outcasts from Judaism. The word *Savior* in Aramaic is literally translated "Life-Giver."

b 4:43 See v. 44.

c 4:45 See John 2:23.

d 4:46–47 The distance from Capernaum to Cana was about twenty miles.

e 4:48 Or "You all."

f 4:48 The Samaritans believed without seeing miracles.

⁵³ Then the father realized that it was at that very same hour that Jesus spoke the words to him, **"Your son will live and not die."** So from that day forward, the man and all his family and servants believed. ⁵⁴ This was Jesus' second extraordinary miracle in Galilee after coming from Judea. ᵃ

The Healing at Bethesda

5 Then Jesus returned to Jerusalem to observe one of the Jewish holy days. ᵇ ² Inside the city near the Sheep Gate there is ᶜ a pool called in Aramaic, The House of Loving Kindness. ᵈ And this pool is surrounded by five covered porches. ᵉ ³ Hundreds of sick people were lying there on the porches—the paralyzed, the blind, and the crippled, all of them waiting for their healing. ⁴ For an angel of God would periodically descend into the pool to stir the waters, and the first one who stepped into the pool after the waters swirled would instantly be healed. ᶠ

⁵ Now there was a man who had been disabled for thirty-eight years lying among the multitude of the sick. ᵍ ⁶ When Jesus saw him lying there, he knew

---

a 4:54 There is an interesting parallel in Jesus' ministry in John with Acts 1:8. Jesus began first in Jerusalem (Nicodemus—John 3), then went to Judea (John 4:1–3), then to Samaria (the Samaritan woman—John 4:4–30), and then to the people with no Jewish heritage (the healing of the nobleman's son, a gentile—John 4:46–54).

b 5:1 Or "feast." It is difficult to determine with certainty which of the feasts it was: Passover, Tabernacles, or Purim. Most of the ancient expositors taught that it was the Feast of Pentecost. There is no mention of the other disciples being with him at this time.

c 5:2 The present tense is here in the text indicates that when John wrote his Gospel, the pool of Bethesda was still there. However, by 68–70 AD, Jerusalem had been destroyed, along with the temple, by the Roman invasion. This would indicate John's Gospel has an earlier date of origin than believed. It is likely that John wrote this prior to 67 AD.

d 5:2 Or Bethesda. In Hebrew, *Beit-Hesed*, which means "House of Loving Kindness." The name of this pool is found with many variations in different manuscripts. Some have "Bethsaida," or "Bethsatha," or "Belzetha (House of the Olive)." Archaeologists have discovered a deep double pool near St. Anne's Church in Jerusalem surrounded by five porticoes located near the Sheep Gate, confirming the validity of the biblical account. The Sheep Gate is where the sacrificial animals were brought into the temple. This points us to the Lamb of God whose cross and sacrifice brought us healing. There is a pool of mercy near the Sheep Gate.

e 5:2 Or "covered walkways," or "alcoves." The sick were under the "covering" of the Law, the five books of the Torah. But the Law cannot heal; it wounds and brings death. Christ is the healer, the living Torah.

f 5:4 The majority of manuscripts do not have v. 4, and a few Greek manuscripts do not even have v. 3. However, the absence of the data found in these verses would leave a tremendous gap in the narrative, leaving unanswered why all these sick people would have congregated at the pool of Bethesda, and making v. 7 very confusing. There remains a strong basis found in a diverse set of manuscripts, both Greek and Aramaic, to argue for the inclusion of vv. 3 and 4 here.

g 5:5 Under the shelter of religion, there are the sick and lame and blind who can't be healed unless they do the work and step into the pool. They are helpless and hopeless so near the Sheep Gate. But Jesus has none of the law's requirements to put upon us for our healing, only to believe in one who is greater than angels. The man had been sick

that the man had been crippled for a long time.ᵃ So Jesus said to him, "**Do you truly long to be healed?**"ᵇ

⁷The sick man answered him, "Sir,ᶜ there's no way I can get healed, for I have no one who will lower me into the water when the angel comes. As soon as I try to crawl to the edge of the pool, someone else jumps in ahead of me."

⁸Then Jesus said to him, "**Stand up! Pick up your sleeping mat and you will walk!**" ⁹Immediately he stood up—he was healed! So he rolled up his mat and walked again! Now this miracle took place on the Jewish Sabbath.

¹⁰When the Jewish leaders saw the man walking along carrying his sleeping mat,ᵈ they objected and said, "What are you doing carrying that? Don't you know it's the Sabbath? It's not lawful for you to carry things on the Sabbath!"

¹¹He answered them, "The man who healed me told me to pick it up and walk."

¹²"What man?" they asked him. "Who was this man who ordered you to carry something on a Sabbath?"ᵉ ¹³But the healed man couldn't give them an answer, for he didn't yet know who it was since Jesus had already slipped away into the crowd.

¹⁴A short time later, Jesus found the man at the temple and said to him, "**Look at you now! You're healed! Walk away from your sin**ᶠ **so that nothing worse will happen to you.**"

¹⁵Then the man went to the Jewish leaders to inform them, "It was Jesus who healed me!" ¹⁶So from that day forward the Jewish leaders began to persecute Jesus because of the things he did on the Sabbath.

Jesus Responds to the Jewish Leaders

¹⁷Jesus answered his critics by saying, "**Everyday my Father is at work, and I will be too!**" ¹⁸This infuriated them and made them all the more eager to devise a plan to kill him. For not only did he break their Sabbath rules,ᵍ but he called God "**my Father,**" which made him equal to God.ʰ

---

for thirty-eight years, the exact length of time Israel had wandered in the wilderness. See Deut. 2:14.

a 5:6 Jesus exercised a supernatural knowledge of this man's situation.
b 5:6 Or "Are you convinced that you are already made whole?" The Greek phrase *genesthai* is actually not a future tense ("want to be healed") but an aorist middle infinitive that indicates something already accomplished. Jesus is asking the crippled man if he is ready to abandon how he sees himself and now receive the faith for his healing.
c 5:7 The Greek word *kurios* means "lord" or "sir."
d 5:10 Or "cot" or "stretcher." The Aramaic word is "quilt" or "mat."
e 5:12 The Jewish leaders were filled with malice. They should have been filled with joy that the man was healed. They should have asked, "Who is the wonderful one who healed you?"
f 5:14 Or "Don't continue sinning any longer."
g 5:18 Jesus did not break the Sabbath, he "loosed" it (literal Aramaic). He loosed it from the bondage of tradition and man-made rules.
h 5:18 They clearly understood that Jesus was claiming God as his Father in a unique way.

[19] So Jesus said, "I speak to you timeless truth. The Son is not able to do anything from himself or through my own initiative. I only do the works that I see the Father doing, for the Son does the same works as his Father. [20] "Because the Father loves his Son so much, he always reveals to me everything that he is about to do. And you will all be amazed when he shows me even greater works than what you've seen so far! [21] For just like the Father has power to raise the dead, the Son will raise the dead and give life to whomever he wants.

[22] "The Father now judges no one, for he has given all the authority to judge to the Son, [23] so that the honor that belongs to the Father will now be shared with his Son. So if you refuse to honor the Son, you are refusing to honor the Father who sent him.

[24] "I speak to you an eternal truth: if you embrace my message and believe in the One who sent me, you will never face condemnation, for in me, you have already passed from the realm of death into the realm of eternal life!"

Two Resurrections

[25] "I speak to you eternal truth: Soon the dead will hear the voice of the Son of God, and those who listen will arise with life! [26] For the Father has given the Son the power to impart life, even as the Father imparts life. [27] The Father has transferred to the Son the authority to judge, because he is the Son of Man.

[28] "So don't be amazed when I tell you these things, for there is a day coming when all who have ever died will hear my voice *calling them back to life*, [29] and they will come out of their graves! Those who have done what is good will experience a resurrection to eternal life. And those who have practiced evil will taste the resurrection that brings them to condemnation!

[30] "Nothing I do is from my own initiative, for as I hear the judgment passed by my Father, I execute judgment. And my judgments will be perfect, because I can do nothing on my own, except to fulfill the desires of my Father who sent me. [31] For if I were to make claims about myself, you would have reasons to doubt.[a] [32] But there is another[b] who bears witness on my behalf, and I know that what he testifies of me is true."

John the Baptizer

[33] "You have sent messengers to John, and what he testified *about me* is true. [34] I have no need to be validated by men, but I'm saying these things so that you will *believe* and be rescued.

---

a 5:31 According to the Mosaic laws, a man's testimony about himself is inadmissible.

b 5:32 This is the Father (see v. 37). Some believe it to be John because of v. 33. However, Jesus states that he does not need human validation.

[35] "John was a blazing, burning torch,[a] and for a short time you basked in his light with great joy. [36] But I can provide a more substantial proof of who I am that exceeds John's testimony—my miracles! These works which the Father destined for me to complete—they prove that the Father has sent me! [37] And my Father himself, who gave me this mission, has also testified that I am his Son.[b] But you have never heard his voice nor seen his face, [38] nor does his Word truly live inside of you, for you refuse to believe in me or to embrace me as God's messenger.

[39] "You are busy analyzing the Scriptures, frantically poring over them in hopes of gaining eternal life. Everything you read points to me, [40] yet you still refuse to come to me so I can give you the life you're looking for—eternal life![c]

[41] "I do not accept the honor that comes from men, [42] for I know what kind of people you really are, and I can see that the love of God has found no home in you. [43] I have come to represent my Father, yet you refuse to embrace me in faith. But when someone comes in their own name and with their own agenda,[d] you readily accept him. [44] Of course you're unable to believe in me. For you live for the praises of others and not for the praise that comes from the only true God.

[45] "I won't be the one who accuses you before the Father. The one who will incriminate you is Moses, the very one you claim to obey, the one in whom you trust![e] [46] If you really believed what Moses has written, then you would embrace me, for Moses wrote about me! [47] But since you do not believe what he wrote, no wonder you don't believe what I say."[f]

Jesus Multiplies Food

6 After this Jesus went to the other side of the Lake of Tiberias,[g] which is also known as Lake Galilee. [2] And a massive crowd of people followed him

---

a 5:35 Or "a lantern of chasing flames."

b 5:37 Or "testified about me." This an obvious reference to the audible voice of God that spoke over Jesus at his baptism. For this reason and the reference to God's voice, the translator has chosen to make it explicit that it refers to the Father's testimony at Jesus' baptism. See Luke 3:21–22. The fourfold witness of Christ's glory is: Jesus himself, John the Baptizer, the Father who spoke over his Son, and the miracles of Jesus.

c 5:40 There were five witnesses to Christ's authority and deity in this chapter. Jesus himself (vv. 25–27), John the Baptizer (vv. 32–34), Christ's miracles (v. 36), the Father (vv. 36–38), and the Scriptures (vv. 39–40, see also Ps. 40:7).

d 5:43 Implied in the text.

e 5:45 Jesus prophesies that Moses, on the final judgment day, will be the one to accuse those who would not listen to the laws and teachings of the Torah, which point to their fulfillment in Christ.

f 5:47 Apparently this concludes Jesus' ministry in Jerusalem at this time. The text does not tell us of his return to the province of Galilee.

g 6:1 Or "which is also called the Lake of Tiberias." Tiberias was the largest Jewish city in the

everywhere. They were attracted by his miracles and the healings they watched him perform. ³Jesus went up the slope of a hill and sat down with his disciples. ⁴Now it was approaching the time of the Jewish celebration of Passover, *and there were many pilgrims on their way to Jerusalem in the crowd.*

⁵As Jesus sat down, he looked out and saw the massive crowd of people scrambling up the hill, for they wanted to be near him. So he turned to Philip and said, **"Where will we buy enough food to feed all these people?"** ⁶Now Jesus already knew what he was about to do, but he said this to stretch Philip's faith.

⁷Philip answered, "Well, I suppose if we were to give everyone only a snack, it would cost thousands of dollars[a] to buy enough food!"

⁸But just then, Andrew, Peter's brother, spoke up and said, ⁹"Look! Here's a young person[b] with five barley loaves and two small fish . . . but how far would that go with this huge crowd?"

¹⁰**"Have everyone sit down,"** Jesus said to his disciples. So on the vast grassy slope, more than five thousand hungry people sat down.[c] ¹¹Jesus then took the barley loaves[d] and the fish and gave thanks to God. He then gave it to the disciples to distribute to the people. Miraculously, the food multiplied, with everyone eating as much as they wanted![e]

¹²When everyone was satisfied, Jesus told his disciples, **"Now go back and gather up the pieces left over so that nothing will be wasted."** ¹³The disciples filled up twelve baskets of fragments, *a basket of leftovers for each disciple.*

¹⁴All the people were astounded as they saw with their own eyes the incredible miracle Jesus had performed! They began to say among themselves, "He really is the One—the true prophet[f] we've been expecting!"

Galilee province, located on the western shore of Lake Galilee. This could also be translated, "Jesus went *beyond* Tiberias to Lake Galilee."

a 6:7 Or "two hundred pieces of silver." This equates to about eight months' wages of the average person. Philip didn't answer the question and was focused on how much money it would cost, but Jesus' question was, "Where will we buy bread?" Jesus was testing Philip to see if he would look to Jesus to supply all that was needed and not consider their limited resources.

b 6:9 The Aramaic is literally translated "boy." However, the Greek uses a word, *paidarion,* which can also mean a girl or young woman.

c 6:10 The number five thousand would have likely been only the number of men in the crowd. Jesus had everyone sit down. To receive bread from Jesus, the Source, doesn't require that you stand and work hard for it, you simply sit down and rest to be fed the living bread.

d 6:11 Barley is the first crop to harvest in Israel. It is a picture of the resurrected Christ. A barley loaf becomes a picture of Christ given to us in resurrection life. He is the firstfruit of resurrection life. See Lev. 23:10; Judg. 7:13–14.

e 6:11 When tempted by the devil, Jesus refused to turn stones into bread to satisfy his own hunger. Yet here Jesus multiplies bread to satisfy the hunger of others. Philip was hoping to give each one a little to eat, but Jesus' supply is always abundant to satisfy the hunger of all.

f 6:14 See Deut. 18:15–19.

¹⁵ So Jesus, knowing that they were about to take him and make him their king by force, quickly left and went up the mountainside alone. *a*

Jesus Walks on Water

¹⁶⁻¹⁷ After waiting until evening for Jesus to return, the disciples went down to the lake. But as darkness fell, he still hadn't returned, so the disciples got into a boat and headed across the lake to Capernaum. *b* ¹⁸ By now a strong wind *c* began to blow and was stirring up the waters. ¹⁹ The disciples had rowed about halfway *d* across the lake when all of a sudden they caught sight of Jesus walking on top of the waves, coming toward them. The disciples panicked, ²⁰ but Jesus called out to them, **"Don't be afraid. You know who I am."** *e*

²¹ They were relieved to take him in, and the moment Jesus stepped into the boat, they were instantly transported to the other side!

Jesus, the Living Bread

²²⁻²³ The next morning, the crowds were still on the opposite shore of the lake, near the place where they had eaten the bread he had multiplied after he had given thanks to God. *f* Yet Jesus was nowhere to be found. They realized that only one boat had been there and that Jesus' hadn't boarded, and they concluded that his disciples had left him behind. ²⁴ So when the people saw on the shoreline a number of small boats from Tiberias and realized Jesus and the disciples weren't there, they got into the boats and went to Capernaum to search for him.

²⁵ When they finally found him, they asked him, "Teacher, how did you get here?"

²⁶ Jesus replied, **"Let me make this very clear,** *g* **you came looking for me because I fed you by a miracle, not because you believe in me.** ²⁷ **Why would you strive for food that is perishable and not be passionate to seek the food of eternal life, which never spoils?** *h* **I, the Son of Man, am ready to give you what matters most, for God the Father has destined me for this purpose."** *i*

²⁸ They replied, "So what should we do if we want to do God's work?"

---

a 6:15 Jesus knew the time of liberating Israel had not yet come. Men don't just need better government; we need new hearts.

b 6:16–17 Capernaum means "the village of Nahum." Nahum means "comfort." Or "the village of comfort."

c 6:18 Or "the Spirit stirred up on their behalf."

d 6:19 Or "three or four miles." The lake was approximately seven miles across, so they would have rowed about halfway.

e 6:20 Or "Fear not. I AM!"

f 6:22–23 This information from v. 24 is included here for the sake of the English narrative.

g 6:26 Or "Amen, amen, I say unto you," or "Timeless truth I speak unto you."

h 6:27 The Aramaic is "Why would you not seek the food that fastens you to eternal life?"

i 6:27 Or "has set his seal (of approval) upon me," or "the Father has sealed me as God with his seal of approval." The Aramaic word for "seal" can also mean "destine" or "determine."

²⁹ Jesus answered, "The work you can do for God starts with believing in the One he has sent."

³⁰⁻³¹ They replied, "Show us a miracle so we can see it, and then we'll believe in you. *Moses took care of our ancestors* who were fed by the miracle of manna ᵃ every day in the desert, just like the Scripture says, 'He fed them with bread from heaven.' ᵇ What sign will you perform for us?"

³² "The truth is," ᶜ Jesus said, "Moses didn't give you the bread of heaven. It's my Father who offers bread that comes as a dramatic sign ᵈ from heaven. ³³ The bread of God is the One who came out of heaven to give his life to feed the world."

³⁴ "Then please, sir, give us this bread every day," they replied.

³⁵ Jesus said to them, "I am the Bread of Life. ᵉ Come every day to me and you will never be hungry. Believe in me and you will never be thirsty. ³⁶ Yet I've told you that even though you've seen me, you still don't believe in me. ³⁷ But everyone my Father has given to me, they will come. And all who come to me, I will embrace and will never turn them away. ³⁸ And I have come out of heaven not for my own desires, but for the satisfaction ᶠ of my Father who sent me. ³⁹ My Father who sent me has determined that I will not lose even one of those he has given to me, and I will raise them up in the last day. ⁴⁰ For the longing of my Father is that everyone who embraces the Son ᵍ and believes in him will experience eternal life and I will raise them up in the last day!"

⁴¹ When the Jews who were hostile to Jesus heard him say, "I am the bread that came down from heaven," they immediately began to complain, ⁴² "How can he say these things about himself? We know him, and we know his parents. How dare he say, 'I have come down from heaven?'"

⁴³ Jesus responded, "Stop your grumbling! ⁴⁴ The only way people come to me is by the Father who sent me—he pulls ʰ on their hearts to embrace me. And those who are drawn to me, I will certainly raise them up in the last day."

⁴⁵ Jesus continued, "It has been written by the prophets, 'They will all be

---

a 6:30–31 *Manna* means "What is it?" This is the bread of mystery that became the wilderness food for more than thirty-eight years.

b 6:30–31 See Ex. 16:4–36; Neh. 9:15; Ps. 78:24.

c 6:32 The Aramaic is "Timeless truth I speak unto you."

d 6:32 The Aramaic can be translated "a rainbow sign." Just as Noah was given a rainbow sign of the covenant God was making with him, Jesus' earthly life was a rainbow sign from heaven of the new covenant life given to every believer today. See Gen. 9; Rev. 4:3; 10:1. The Greek is "true bread out of heaven."

e 6:35 The Aramaic can be translated "I am the living God, the Bread of Life."

f 6:38 As translated from the Aramaic.

g 6:40 Or "sees the Son."

h 6:44 The Greek word is "drag" or "pull by force." The name Moses means "pulled" (from the Nile). The Aramaic is "ransom" or "save."

taught by God himself.'ᵃ If you are really listening to the Father and learning directly from him, you will come to me. ⁴⁶For I am the only One who has come from the Father's side, and I have seen the Father!

⁴⁷"I speak to you living truth: Unite your heart to me and believe— and you will experience eternal life! ⁴⁸I am the true Bread of Life.ᵇ ⁴⁹Your ancestors ate manna in the desert and died. ⁵⁰But standing here before you is the true Bread that comes out of heaven, and when you eat this Bread you will never die. ⁵¹I alone am this living Bread that has come to you from heaven. Eat this Bread and you will live forever. The living Bread I give you is my body, which I will offer as a sacrifice so that all may live."

⁵²These words of Jesus sparked an angry outburst among the Jews. They protested, saying, "Does this man expect us to eat his body?"

⁵³Jesus replied to them, "Listen to this eternal truth: Unless you eat the body of the Son of Man and drink his blood, you will not have eternal life. ⁵⁴Eternal life comes to the one who eats my bodyᶜ and drinks my blood, and I will raise him up in the last day. ⁵⁵For my body is real food for your spirit and my blood is real drink. ⁵⁶The one who eats my body and drinks my blood lives in me and I live in him.ᵈ ⁵⁷The Father of life sent me, and he is my life. In the same way, the one who feeds upon me, I will become his life. ⁵⁸I am not like the bread your ancestors ate and later died. I am the living Bread that comes from heaven. Eat this Bread and you will live forever!"

⁵⁹Jesus preached this sermon in the synagogue in Capernaum.

Many Disciples Became Offended

⁶⁰And when many of Jesus' followers heard these things, it caused a stir. "That's disgusting!" they said. "How could anybody accept it?"ᵉ

⁶¹Without anyone telling him, Jesus knew they were outraged and told

---

a 6:45 See Isa. 54:13; Jer. 31:34.

b 6:48 Although not found in the Greek text, there are some Aramaic manuscripts that have "I am the living God, the Bread of Life."

c 6:54 To eat his flesh is to take into our life by faith all that Jesus did for us by giving his body for us. To drink his blood is to take by faith all that the blood of Jesus has purchased for us. This "eating" and "drinking" is receiving the life, power, and virtue of all that Jesus is to replace all that we were in Adam. Jesus' blood and body is the Tree of Life, which is offered to everyone who follows him.

d 6:56 The Aramaic is "He that eats my body and drinks my blood is strengthened in me and I in him."

e 6:60 Jesus knows that these words were offending the religious Jews. To eat flesh that was not kosher was a violation of the law; how much more so to eat human flesh. Drinking blood of any kind was also forbidden (Lev. 17:11–12). The imagery is similar to Ezekiel who "ate the scroll" (of the Word, Ezek. 3:1–15).

them, "Are you offended over my teaching? [62] What will you do when you see the Son of Man ascending *into the realm* from where he came? [a]

[63] "The Holy Spirit is the one who gives life, that which is of the natural realm [b] is of no help. The words I speak to you are Spirit and life. But there are still some of you who won't believe." [64] In fact, Jesus already knew from the beginning who the skeptics were and who his traitor would be.

[65] He went on to say, "This is why I told you that no one embraces me unless the Father has given you to me."

Peter's Confession of Faith

[66] And so from that time on many of the disciples turned their backs on Jesus and refused to be associated with him. [c] [67] So Jesus said to his twelve, "And you—do you also want to leave?" [68] Peter spoke up and said, "But Lord, where would we go? No one but you gives us the revelation of eternal life. [69] We're fully convinced that you are the Anointed One, the Son of the Living God, [d] and we believe in you!"

[70] Then Jesus *shocked them* with these words: "I have hand-picked you to be my twelve, knowing that one of you is the devil." [e] [71] Jesus was referring to Judas Iscariot, [f] son of Simon, for he knew that Judas, one of his chosen disciples, was getting ready to betray him.

Jesus at the Feast of Tabernacles

7 After this Jesus traveled extensively throughout the province of Galilee, but he avoided the province of Judea, for he knew the Jewish leaders in Jerusalem were plotting to have him killed. [2] Now the annual Feast of Tabernacles [g] was approaching. [3] So Jesus' brothers [h] came to advise him, saying, "Why don't

---

a 6:62 The greatest offense of all will be the cross where Jesus will soon be crucified, and they will watch him surrender his Spirit to the Father in death. See 1 Cor. 1:18–25; Gal. 5:11.

b 6:63 The Aramaic is "the body."

d 6:66 Jesus went from feeding five thousand to offending five thousand. They wanted him to feed them, but didn't want Jesus alone to be their feast.

d 6:69 As translated from the Aramaic. Although many Greek scholars believe this is borrowed from the Synoptic Gospels, and is found in variant forms in Greek texts, the Aramaic and many Greek manuscripts have, "You are the Christ, the Son of the living God."

e 6:70 The Greek word for "devil" means "slanderer" or "adversary."

f 6:71 Judas is the name Judah. *Iscariot* was not his last name. There are two possibilities for the meaning of *Iscariot*. Some believe it is taken from a Hebrew word that means "lock." Judah the "locksmith." He most likely was the one who locked the collection bag, which means he had the key and could pilfer the fund at will. It's his sad history that he wanted to lock up Jesus and control him for his own ends. Other scholars see the possibility that *Iscariot* is actually "Ish" (man) of "Kerioth" (a town once situated south of Hebron). This would mean Judas was the only non-Galilean among the Twelve.

g 7:2 Or "Tents." See Deut. 16:13.

h 7:3 These were actually Jesus' half brothers, for Joseph was his stepfather.

you leave the countryside villages and go to Judea where the crowds are, [a] so that your followers can see your miracles? [4] No one can see what you're doing here in the backwoods of Galilee. How do you expect to be successful and famous if you do all these things in secret? Now is your time—go to Jerusalem, come out of hiding, and show the world who you are!" [5] His brothers were pushing him, even though they didn't yet believe in him as the Savior. [b]

[6] Jesus responded, "My time of being unveiled hasn't yet come, but any time is a suitable opportunity for you *to gain man's approval.* [7] The world can't hate you, but it does me, for I am exposing their evil deeds. [8] You can go ahead and celebrate the feast without me—my appointed time has not yet come."

[9-10] Jesus lingered in Galilee until his brothers had left for the feast in Jerusalem. Then later, Jesus took a back road and went into Jerusalem in secret. [11] During the feast, the Jewish leaders kept looking for Jesus and asking around, "Where is he? Have you seen him?"

[12] A controversy was brewing among the people, with so many differing opinions about Jesus. Some were saying, "He's a good man!" While others weren't convinced and insisted, saying, "He's just a demagogue." [c] [13] Yet no one was bold enough to speak out publicly on Jesus' behalf for fear of the Jewish leaders.

[14] Not until the feast was half over did Jesus finally appear in the temple courts and begin to teach. [15] The Jewish leaders were astonished by what he taught and said, "How did this man acquire such knowledge? He wasn't trained in our schools—who taught him?"

[16] So Jesus responded, "I don't teach my own ideas, [d] but the truth revealed to me by the One who sent me. [17] If you want to test my teachings and discover where I received them, first be passionate to do God's will, [e] and then you will be able to discern if my teachings are from the heart of God or from my own opinions. [18] Charlatans praise themselves and seek honor from men, but my Father sent me to speak truth on his behalf. And I have no false motive, because I seek only the glory of God. [19] Moses has given you the law, but not one of you is faithful to keep it. So if you are all law-breakers, why then would you seek to kill me?"

[20] Then some in the crowd shouted out, "You must be out of your mind! [f] Who's trying to kill you?"

---

a 7:3 Or "so that your followers can see your miracles."

b 7:5 As translated from the Aramaic and implied in the Greek text. This fulfills the prophecy of Ps. 69:8–9.

c 7:12 Or "He leads the people astray."

d 7:16 Or "My doctrine is not my own."

e 7:17 The Aramaic is very poetic, "Whoever is satisfied to do God's satisfaction shall gain liberating knowledge."

f 7:20 Or "Are you demon possessed?" This is an Aramaic figure of speech for lunacy.

²¹ Jesus replied, "I only had to do one miracle,ᵃ and all of you marvel! ²² Yet isn't it true that Moses and your forefathers ᵇ ordered you to circumcise your sons even if the eighth day fell on a Sabbath?ᶜ ²³ So if you cut away part of a man on the Sabbath and that doesn't break the Jewish law,ᵈ why then would you be indignant with me for making a man completely healed on the Sabbath? ²⁴ Stop judging based on the superficial.ᵉ First you must *embrace the standards of mercy*ᶠ *and truth.*"

²⁵ Then some of the residents of Jerusalem spoke up and said, "Isn't this the one they're trying to kill? ²⁶ So why is he here speaking publicly and not one of the Jewish leaders is doing anything about it? Are they starting to think that he's the Anointed One? ²⁷ But how could he be, since we know this man is from Galilee, but no one will know where the true Messiah comes from, he'll just appear out of nowhere."ᵍ

²⁸ Knowing all of this, Jesus one day preached *boldly* in the temple courts, "So, you think you know me and where I come from? But you don't know the One who sent me—the Father who is always faithful.ʰ I have not come simply on my own initiative. ²⁹ The Father has sent me here, and I know all about him, for I have come from his presence."ⁱ

³⁰ His words caused many to want to arrest him, but no man was able to lay a hand on him, for it wasn't yet his appointed time. ³¹ And there were many people who thought he might be the Messiah. They said, "After all, when the Anointed One appears, could he possibly do more signs and wonders than this man has done?"

³² So when the Phariseesʲ heard these rumors circulating about Jesus, they went with the leading priests and the temple guards to arrest him.

³³ Then Jesus said, "My days to be with you are numbered. Then I will

---

a 7:21 Or "one deed." Although Jesus performed many miracles, it is likely he is referring to the miracle of the lame man being healed in John 5.

b 7:22 This is the patriarchs. Circumcision actually began with a sign of the covenant God instituted with Abraham. See Gen. 17.

c 7:22 A son was to be circumcised eight days after he was born. See Phil. 3:5.

d 7:23 Or "Torah." Jesus is saying, "Who are you to judge me when you don't practice what you preach?"

e 7:24 Or "Never judge as a hypocrite wearing a mask."

f 7:24 Jesus is teaching that the law of mercy (healing the lame man) overrides the laws of Moses (regulations of the Sabbath). Seeing situations and people with the lens of mercy gives us true discernment.

g 7:27 This was a Rabbinical interpretation that was common in that day. However, they knew that the Messiah would come from Bethlehem, for it was prophesied in Mic. 5:2 where the Christ would be born. So in truth, they did not know where Jesus was from.

h 7:28 Or "truthful."

i 7:29 Or "I am from next to him." The Aramaic is "from his presence I am."

j 7:32 Or "separated ones."

return to the One who sent me. [34] And you will search for me and not be able to find me. For where I am,[a] you cannot come."[b]

[35] When the Jewish leaders heard this, they discussed among themselves, "Where could he possibly go that we won't be able to find him? Is he going to minister in a different land where our people live scattered among the nations? Is he going to teach those who are not Jews?[c] [36] What did he really mean by his statement, 'You will search for me and won't be able to find me. And where I am you can't come'?"

Rivers of Living Water

[37] Then on the most important day of the feast, the last day,[d] Jesus stood and shouted out to the crowds—"All you thirsty ones, come to me! Come to me and drink! [38] Believe in me so that rivers of living water will burst out from within you, flowing[e] from your innermost being, just like the Scripture says!"[f]

[39] Jesus was prophesying about the Holy Spirit that believers were being prepared to receive.[g] But the Holy Spirit had not yet been poured out upon them, because Jesus had not yet been unveiled in his full splendor.[h]

Divided Opinions about Jesus

[40] When the crowd heard Jesus' words, some said, "This man really is a prophet!" [41] Others said, "He's the Messiah!" But others said, "How could he be the Anointed One since he's from Galilee? [42] Don't the Scriptures say that he will be one of David's descendants and be born in Bethlehem, the city of David?"[i]

---

a 7:34 In this tremendous statement, Jesus is telling them that he is about to return to the realm where I AM dwells. Of course, the Jewish leaders didn't understand the impact of what he was telling them.

b 7:34 Jesus was speaking of his approaching death on the cross, which he knew was near, and his ascension back to the Father, the realm of I AM.

c 7:35 There were many of the tribes of Israel who were scattered at that time in Assyria, Iran, Afghanistan, and other adjacent nations. These had been taken captive by the kings of Assyria in 722 BC. See 2 Kings 17–18.

d 7:37 When man's feasting is over there is still thirst. Jesus comes at the last day of the feast to satisfy the thirst of those who seek God. Only the Lord Jesus can quench the spiritual thirst of men by giving them his living water.

e 7:38 The root word used here is the same as the River Jordan, which means "flowing" (down).

f 7:38 Or "rivers of living water will flow from his throne within." See Isa. 44:3; 55:1; 58:11; Ezek. 47:1; Rev. 22:1. A drink becomes a river!

g 7:39 As translated from the Aramaic.

h 7:39 This splendor included the splendor of the cross, the splendor of his resurrection, and the glory of his ascension into heaven. Just as water poured out of the rock that was struck by Moses, so from the wounded side of Jesus living water poured out to heal, save, and bring life to everyone who believes. The Holy Spirit poured out of Christ and into the church at Pentecost.

i 7:42 They had an understanding of the Bible but still missed who Jesus was. Bible knowledge

[43] So the crowd was divided over Jesus, [44] some wanted him arrested but no one dared to lay a hand on him.

The Unbelief of Religious Leaders

[45] So when the temple guards returned to the Pharisees and the leading priests without Jesus, they were questioned, "Where is he? Why didn't you bring that man back with you?"

[46] They answered, "You don't understand—he speaks amazing things like no one else has ever spoken!"

[47] The religious leaders mocked, "Oh, so now you also have been led astray by him? [48] Do you see even one of us, your leaders, following him? [49] This ignorant rabble swarms around him because none of them know anything about the Law! They're all cursed!"

[50] Just then, Nicodemus, who had secretly spent time with Jesus, spoke up, for he was a respected voice among them. [51] He cautioned them, saying, "Does our law decide a man's guilt before we first hear him and allow him to defend himself?"

[52] They argued, "Oh, so now you're an advocate for this Galilean! Search the Scriptures, Nicodemus, and you'll see that there's no mention of a prophet coming out of Galilee!" [a] So with that their debate ended, [53] and they each went their own way.

An Adulteress Forgiven

8 Jesus walked up the Mount of Olives [b] near the city where he spent the night. [2] Then at dawn Jesus appeared in the temple courts again, and soon all the people gathered around to listen to his words, so he sat down and taught them. [3] Then in the middle of his teaching, the religious scholars [c] and the Pharisees broke through the crowd and brought a woman who had been caught in the act of committing adultery and made her stand in the middle of everyone.

[4] Then they said to Jesus, "Teacher, we caught this woman in the very act of adultery. [5] Doesn't Moses' law command us to stone to death a woman like

---

alone, without the Holy Spirit opening our hearts and bringing us to Christ, can leave us as a skeptic. They jumped to conclusions, not realizing that Jesus may have been raised in Nazareth in Galilee, but he was born in Bethlehem and was a true descendant of David. See Ps. 89:3–4; Mic. 5:2; Matt. 1:1; 2:1; Luke 2:4.

a 7:52 They apparently didn't know their own Jewish history, for the prophet Jonah, in 580 BC, came from Gathepher, a village only three miles from Nazareth. It is believed that Elijah, Nahum, and Hosea also came from Galilee. Jesus' Galilean ministry was prophesied in Isa. 9:1–2.

b 8:1 Named for the many olive trees on its slopes, the Mount of Olives was a high slope just east of Jerusalem across the Kidron Valley.

c 8:3 Or "scribes." The scribes were not merely professional copyists, they were the scholarly experts who were to be consulted over the details of the written law of Moses.

this?[a] Tell us, what do you say we should do with her?" [6] They were only testing Jesus because they hoped to trap him with his own words and accuse him of breaking the laws of Moses.

But Jesus didn't answer them. Instead he simply bent down and wrote in the dust with his finger.[b] [7] Angry, they kept insisting[c] that he answer their question, so Jesus stood up and looked at them and said, "**Let's have the man who has never had a sinful desire**[d] **throw the first stone at her.**" [8] And then he bent over again and wrote some more words in the dust.[e]

[9] Upon hearing that, her accusers slowly left the crowd one at a time, beginning with the oldest to the youngest,[f] with a convicted conscience. [10] Until finally, Jesus was left alone with the woman still standing there in front of him. So he stood back up and said to her, "**Dear woman, where are your accusers? Is there no one here to condemn you?**"

[11] Looking around, she replied, "I see no one, Lord."[g]

Jesus said, "**Then I certainly**[h] **don't condemn you either.**[i] **Go, and from now on, be free from a life of sin.**"[j]

---

a 8:5 See Lev. 20:10 and Deut. 22:22–24, where it is clear that both the man and woman were to be stoned to death.

b 8:6 This is the not the first time God wrote with his finger. See Ex. 31:18.

c 8:7 As translated from the Aramaic.

d 8:7 The Greek word *anamartetos* means more than simply sin, but is best translated "a sinful desire."

e 8:8 See Jer. 17:13. Jesus wrote in the dust to fulfill Jeremiah's prophecy that those who forsake God (spiritual adultery) will be written in the dust. All of the accusers were guilty of having forsaken God, the fountain of living water, and yet were so anxious to stone this woman to death. The same finger that wrote the Ten Commandments in stone also wrote the names of each of the accusers, or perhaps he wrote Jer. 17:13 in the dirt in front of their eyes, pointing to their hypocrisy.

f 8:9 The Aramaic can be translated "starting with the priests."

g 8:11 The Aramaic contains a powerful testimony from this woman. Apparently the woman had the revelation of who Jesus really was, for she addressed Jesus with the divine name in the Aramaic, *MarYah*, Lord Yahweh! See also 1 Cor. 12:3. The Greek texts use the word *kurios* for Lord, which can also mean "sir" or "landowner."

h 8:11 The Greek has the emphatic use of the personal pronoun.

i 8:11 The Aramaic is "Neither do I put you down" (or, "oppress you"). The Torah required two witnesses. There were none left!

j 8:11 Or "no longer be sinning." It should be noted that this entire episode (referred to commonly as the "Pericope Adulterae") is missing in the majority of the most reliable Greek manuscripts. There are some manuscripts that have this story at the end of the book of John and at least two that include it in the Gospel of Luke. Many scholars surmise that this episode in the ministry of Jesus was added after the Gospel of John had been completed. However, it is the conclusion of this translation that the above text is indeed an inspired account of the ministry of Jesus and may have been deleted by many translators and copyists who doubted that Jesus could tell an adulterer that he would not condemn her. St. Augustine, one of the early church fathers, mentioned this story and stated that many translators

Jesus, the Light of the World

[12] Then Jesus said, "I am[a] light to the world and those who embrace me will experience life-giving light, and they will never[b] walk[c] in darkness."

[13] The Pharisees were immediately offended and said, "You're just boasting about yourself! Since we only have your word on this, it makes your testimony invalid!"

[14] Jesus responded, "Just because I am the one making these claims doesn't mean they're invalid. *For I absolutely know who I am,* where I've come from, and where I'm going. But you Pharisees have no idea about what I'm saying. [15] For you've set yourselves up as judges of others based on outward appearances, but I certainly never judge others in that way. [16] For I discern the truth. And I am not alone in my judgments, for my Father and I have the same understanding in all things, and he has sent me to you.

[17] "Isn't it written in the law of Moses that the testimony of two men is trustworthy?[d] [18] Then what I say about who I am is true, for I am not alone in my testimony—my Father is the other witness, and we testify together of the truth."

[19] Then they asked, "Just who is this 'Father' of yours? Where is he?"

Jesus answered, "You wouldn't ask that question if you knew who I am, or my Father. For if you knew me, you would recognize my Father too."

[20] (Jesus taught all these things while standing *in the treasure room of the temple.*[e] And no one dared to arrest him, for it wasn't yet his time to surrender to men.)

"I Am Not from This World"

[21] One day Jesus said again, "I am about to leave you. You will want to find me, but you will still die in your sins.[f] You won't be able to come where I am going."

[22] This so confused the Jewish leaders that they began to say, "Is he planning to commit suicide? What's he talking about—'You won't be able to come where I am going'?"

[23] Jesus spoke up and said, "You are all from the earth; I am from above. I am not from this world like you are. [24] That's why I've told you that you will all die in your sins if you fail to believe that I AM who I AM."[g]

---

had removed it because they interpreted it as Jesus giving license to immorality. God's grace always seems to startle the religious (St. Augustine, *De Conjug. Adult.*, II:6.)

a 8:12 Again we see Jesus using the words "I Am," which is the name of God.

b 8:12 The Greek word is a double negative, emphatically saying, "never, no never!"

c 8:12 The Aramaic is "they will never be driven (pushed) by the darkness."

d 8:17 See Deut. 17:6.

e 8:20 Jesus unlocks that "treasure room" to us, his temple. When we receive him as our life-giving light, we see the treasures that have been given to us by grace.

f 8:21 Jesus gives a stern warning of dying before you have turned away from sin and put your faith in the Savior.

g 8:24 Believing the truth that Jesus Christ is the "I AM," God who became a man, is an essential part of our faith as followers of Christ.

²⁵ So they asked him plainly, "Who are you?"

"I am the One I've always claimed to be." Jesus replied. ²⁶ "And I still have many more things to pronounce in judgment about you. For I will testify to the world of the truths that I have heard from my Father, and the Father who sent me is trustworthy." ²⁷ (Even after all of this, they still didn't realize that he was speaking about his heavenly Father.)

²⁸ "You will know me as 'I AM' after you have lifted me up from the earth ⁿ as the Son of Man. Then you will realize that I do nothing on my own initiative, but I only speak the truth that the Father has revealed to me. ²⁹ I am his messenger and he is always with me, for I only do that which delights his heart." ᵇ ³⁰ These words caused many *respected Jews* to believe in him.

The Son Gives Freedom

³¹ Jesus said to those Jews who believed in him, "When you continue to embrace all that I teach, you prove that you are my true followers. ³² For if you embrace the truth, it will release more freedom into your lives." ᶜ

³³ Surprised by this, they said, "But we're the descendants of Abraham and we're already free. We've never been in bondage ᵈ to anyone. How could you say that we will be released into more freedom?" ᵉ

³⁴ "I speak eternal truth," Jesus said. "When you sin you are not free. You've become a slave in bondage to your sin. ³⁵ And slaves have no permanent standing in a family, like a son does, for a son is a part of the family forever. ³⁶ So if the Son sets you free from sin, then become a true son and be unquestionably free! ³⁷ Even though you are descendants of Abraham, you desire to kill me because the message I bring has not found a home in your

---

a 8:28 There is a dual meaning in these words. To honor Jesus and exalt him reveals his true identity to our hearts. The word for "lifted up" can also mean "to exalt" and therefore "to honor." However, Jesus was "lifted up" on a cross, suspended between heaven and earth, and died for the sins of all mankind. Both of these implications are found in these words of Jesus.

b 8:29 The Aramaic is "I only do what adorns [beautifies] him."

c 8:32 The truth Jesus gives us releases us from the bondage of our past, the bondage of our sins, and the bondage of religion. Jesus is speaking these words to those who were not fully free from man's traditions. Truth must be embraced and worked out through the divine process of spiritual maturity. The Greek word for "truth" is *reality*. To embrace the reality of Christ brings more freedom into your life. See the book of Galatians for a clear explanation of the freedom Jesus refers to here.

d 8:33 The Greek is translated "slavery." However, the Aramaic word used here (*abdota*) refers not to slavery but to paying off debts (indentured servants). The Jews were not forgetting their slavery in Egypt, but rather saying that they were not in bondage to serve anyone as free sons of Abraham. Jesus reminds them that ancestral lineage does not guarantee spiritual freedom.

e 8:33 The Aramaic is translated "released as children of freedom."

hearts. [38] Yet the truths I speak I've seen and received in my Father's presence. But you are doing what you've learned from your father!" [a]

[39] "What do mean?" they replied. "Abraham is our father!"

Jesus said, "If you are really Abraham's sons, then you would follow in the steps of Abraham. [40] I've only told you the truth that I've heard in my Father's presence, but now you are wanting me dead—is that how Abraham acted? [41] No, you people are doing what your father has taught you!"

Indignant, they responded, "What are you talking about? We only have one Father, God himself! We're not illegitimate!"

[42] Jesus said, "Then if God were really your father, you would love me, for I've come from his presence. I didn't come here on my own, but God sent me to you. [43] Why don't you understand what I say? [b] You don't understand because your hearts are closed to my message!

[44] "You are the offspring of your father, the devil, [c] and you serve your father very well, passionately carrying out his desires. He's been a murderer right from the start! He never stood with the One who is the true Prince, for he's full of nothing but lies—lying is his native tongue. [d] He is a master of deception and the father of lies! [45] But I am the true Prince who speaks nothing but the truth, yet you refuse to believe and you want nothing to do with me. [46] Can you name one sin that I've committed? Then if I am telling you only the truth, why don't you believe me? [47] If you really knew God, you would listen, receive, and respond with faith to his words. But since you don't listen and respond to what he says, it proves you don't belong to him and you have no room for him in your hearts."

[48] "See! We were right all along!" some of the Jewish leaders shouted. "You're nothing but a demon-possessed Samaritan!" [e]

[49] Jesus replied, "It is not a demon that would cause me to honor my Father. I live my life for his honor, even though you insult me for it. [f] [50] I never have a need to seek my own glory, for the Father will do that for me, and

---

a 8:38 Some Greek manuscripts have, "Since I'm saying what I've seen while with my Father, put my Father's words into practice."

b 8:43 The Aramaic is "Why don't you receive my manifestation?"

c 8:44 The word for "devil" in Greek means "slanderer-accuser." The Aramaic word is *akelqarsa*, or "adversary." It is taken from a root word that means "to ridicule" or "to gnaw." See v. 48 where the Jewish leaders ridiculed Jesus' words.

d 8:44 Or "when he lies he's only doing what is natural to him."

e 8:48 They are obviously scorning Jesus by calling him "a demon-possessed Samaritan." The Jews despised their northern cousins, the Samaritans, for their ancestors had come from Assyria and occupied Israel's lands. The three major groups in Israel at that time were Judeans (Jews), Galileans, and Samaritans. The Jerusalem Jews saw themselves as superior and more faithful to the God of the Hebrews than their northern neighbors. Jesus was a Galilean, having come from Nazareth. But Nazareth was part of the northern region looked down upon by the Jews. The Aramaic can be translated, "You're a crazy Samaritan."

f 8:49 The Aramaic is "you curse me."

he will judge those who do not. ⁵¹ I speak to you this eternal truth: whoever cherishes my words and keeps them will never experience death."

⁵² This prompted the Jewish leaders to say, "Now we know for sure that you're demon possessed! You just said that those who keep watch over your words will never experience death, but Abraham and all the prophets have died! ⁵³ Do you think you're greater than our father Abraham and all the prophets? You are so delusional about yourself that you make yourself greater than you are!"

⁵⁴ Jesus answered them, "If I were to tell you how great I am, it would mean nothing. But my Father is the One who will prove it and will glorify me. Isn't he the One you claim is your God? ⁵⁵ But in reality, you've never embraced him as your own. I know him, and I would be a liar, like yourselves, if I told you anything less than that. I have fully embraced him, and I treasure his every word. ⁵⁶ And not only that, Abraham, your ancestor, was overjoyed when he received the revelation of my coming to earth. Yes, he foresaw me coming and was filled with delight!" ᵃ

⁵⁷ But many of the Jewish leaders doubted him and said, "What are you talking about? You're not even fifty years old yet. You talk like you've seen Abraham!"

⁵⁸ Jesus said to them, "I give you this eternal truth: I have existed long before Abraham was born, for I AM!" ᵇ

⁵⁹ When they heard this, they picked up rocks to stone him, but Jesus concealed himself as he passed through the crowd ᶜ and went away from there.

Jesus Healed a Man Born Blind

9 Afterward, as Jesus walked down the street, he noticed a man blind from birth. ² His disciples asked him, "Teacher, whose sin caused this guy's blindness, his own, or the sin of his parents?"

³ Jesus answered, "Neither. It happened to him so that you could watch him experience God's miracle. ⁴ While I am with you, it is daytime and we

---

ᵃ 8:56 This refers to the prophetic insight God gave to Abraham about the coming Messiah. Many Hebrew scholars believe this was given to Abraham on the day of "binding." That is, the day he tied his son, Isaac, to the altar to offer him as a sacrifice. It was then that God showed him a ram that was caught in a thicket nearby to be the substitute for Isaac. See Gal. 3:16; Heb. 11:13, 17–19.

ᵇ 8:58 Proper English grammar would be, "Before Abraham was born, I Was." However, Jesus identifies himself with the "I AM that I AM" of Ex. 3:14, when Yahweh appeared to Moses in the flames of the sacred shrub.

ᶜ 8:59 Some reliable Greek texts present Jesus' exit in a less than supernatural way. But the Aramaic and many other Greek manuscripts make it clear that it was a supernatural exit from the Jewish leaders who wanted to kill him. See also Luke 4:30 for another incident of Jesus walking through a hostile crowd. Chapter 8 begins with the self-righteous wanting to stone the adulterous woman and ends with them wanting to stone the sinless Messiah.

must do the works of God who sent me while the light shines. For there is coming a dark night when no one will be able to work. [a] 5 As long as I am with you my life is the light that pierces the world's darkness."

6 Then Jesus spat on the ground and made some clay with his saliva. [b] Then he anointed the blind man's eyes with the clay. 7 And he said to the blind man, "Now go and wash the clay from your eyes in the ritual pool of Siloam." [c] So he went and washed his face and as he came back, he could see for the first time in his life! [d]

8 This caused quite a stir among the people of the neighborhood, for they noticed the blind beggar was now seeing! They began to say to one another, "Isn't this the blind man who once sat and begged?" 9 Some said, "No, it can't be him!" Others said, "But it looks just like him—it has to be him!" All the while the man kept insisting, "I'm the man who was blind!"

10 Finally, they asked him, "What has happened to you?"

11 He replied, "I met the man named Jesus! He rubbed clay on my eyes and said, 'Go to the pool named Siloam and wash.' So I went and while I was washing the clay from my eyes I began to see *for the very first time ever!*" [e]

12 So the people of the neighborhood inquired, "Where is this man?"

"I have no idea." the man replied.

13 So the people marched him over to the Pharisees to speak with them. 14 They were concerned because the miracle Jesus performed by making clay with his saliva and anointing the man's eyes happened on a Sabbath day, a day that no one was allowed to "work."

15 Then the Pharisees asked the man, "How did you have your sight restored?"

He replied, "A man anointed my eyes with clay, then I washed, and now I can see for the first time in my life!"

---

a 9:4 The Aramaic can be translated "The One who sent me is the day, and we must do his works. But the night (of mankind) will follow when no work can be accomplished."

b 9:6 John has left us a book of pictures. The picture here is the mingling of spit and clay, a picture of the Christ who is God and man. The saliva comes from the mouth, the spoken Word, God incarnate. The clay is always a picture of man, for our human vessel is a jar of clay. No doubt, the blind man had heard people spit as they walked by him, as a sign of disgust, for in that day they believed blindness was caused by a curse. But this day, as he heard Jesus spit on the ground, it was for his healing.

c 9:7 Or "the pool of apostleship." *Siloam* is a Hebrew word that means "to be sent" or "to be commissioned"—the Greek word for apostle or apostleship is the closest meaning. The apostle of our faith is the Lord Jesus Christ who was sent from the Father. To wash in the Pool of Apostleship is to recognize the healing that flows from the One who was sent from heaven.

d 9:7 In the context of Jesus' teaching on the light of the world and mankind being in the dark, this miracle of giving sight to the blind man is a powerful proof of Jesus' words. Christ, in his birth, became a man of clay. When he applies this clay over our eyes and we wash in the water of his Word, our spiritual sight is restored.

e 9:11 See also vv. 7, 16.

[16] Then an argument broke out among the Pharisees over the healing of the blind man on the Sabbath. Some said, "This man who performed this healing is clearly not from God! He doesn't even observe the Sabbath!" Others said, "If Jesus is just an ordinary sinner,ᵃ how could he perform a miracle like that?"

[17] This prompted them to turn on the man healed of blindness, putting him on the spot in front of them all, demanding an answer. They asked, "Who do you say he is—this man who opened your blind eyes?"

"He's a prophet of God!" the man replied.

[18] Still refusing to believe that the man had been healed and was truly blind from birth, the Jewish leaders called for the man's parents to be brought to them.

[19-20] So they asked his parents, "Is this your son?"

"Yes," they answered.

"Was he really born blind?"

"Yes, he was," they replied.

So they pressed his parents to answer, "Then how is it that he's now seeing?"

[21] "We have no idea," they answered. "We don't know what happened to our son. Ask him, he's a mature adult. He can speak for himself." [22] (Now the parents were obviously intimidated by the Jewish religious leaders, for they had already announced to the people that if anyone publicly confessed Jesus as the Messiah, they would be excommunicated. [23] That's why they told them, "Ask him, he's a mature adult. He can speak for himself.")

[24] So once again they summoned the man who was healed of blindness and said to him, "Swear to God to tell us the truth!ᵇ We know the man who healed you is a sinful man! Do you agree?"

[25] The healed man replied, "I have no idea what kind of man he is. All I know is that I was blind and now I can see for the first time in my life!"

[26] "But what did he do to you?" they asked. "How did he heal you?"

[27] The man responded, "I told you once and you didn't listen to me. Why do you make me repeat it? Are you wanting to be his followers too?"

[28] This angered the Jewish leaders. They heaped insults on him, "We can tell you are one of his followers—now we know it! We are true followers of Moses, [29] for we know that God spoke to Moses directly. But as for this one, we don't know where he's coming from!"

[30] "Well, what a surprise this is!" the man said. "You don't even know where he comes from, but he healed my eyes and now I can see! [31] We know that God doesn't listen to sinners, but only to godly people who do his will. [32] Yet who has

---

a 9:16 Or "a sinning man."

b 9:24 Or "Give glory to God." This has been interpreted by some as an idiomatic saying, which would put the man under oath to testify the truth.

ever heard of a man born blind that was healed and given back his eyesight? [33] I tell you, if this man isn't from God, he wouldn't be able to heal me like he has!"

[34] Some of the Jewish leaders were enraged and said, "Just who do you think you are to lecture us! You were born a blind, filthy sinner!" So they threw the man out in the street.

[35] When Jesus learned they had thrown him out, he went to find him and said to him, "Do you believe in the Son of God?" [a]

[36] The man whose blind eyes were healed answered, "Who is he, Master? Tell me so that I can place all my faith in him."

[37] Jesus replied, "You're looking right at him. He's speaking with you. It's me, the one in front of you now."

[38] Then the man threw himself at his feet and worshiped Jesus and said, "Lord, I believe in you!" [b]

[39] And Jesus said, "I have come to judge those who think they see and make them blind. And for those who are blind, I have come to make them see."

[40] Some of the Pharisees were standing nearby and overheard these words. They interrupted Jesus and said, "You mean to tell us that we are blind?"

[41] Jesus told them, "If you would acknowledge your blindness, then your sin would be removed. But now that you claim to see, your sin remains with you!" [c]

The Parable of the Kind Shepherd

10 Jesus said to the Pharisees, "Listen to this eternal truth: The person who sneaks over the wall to enter into the sheep pen, rather than coming through the gate, reveals himself as a thief coming to steal. [2] But the true Shepherd walks right up to the gate, [3] and because the gatekeeper knows who he is, he opens the gate to let him in. [d] And the sheep recognize the voice of the true Shepherd, for he calls his own by name and leads them out, for they belong to him. [4] And when he has brought out all his sheep, he walks ahead of them and they will follow him, for they are familiar with his voice. [5] But

---

a 9:35 This is a common title of the Lord Jesus in the book of John. Although there are many reliable Greek manuscripts that have "the Son of Man," the Aramaic and a few early Greek manuscripts have "the Son of Elohim [God]."

b 9:38 Although this man had never been able to read the Scriptures, he had faith in Jesus. Traditions and superficial knowledge of the Bible can actually blind our hearts if we do not believe in Jesus above all other religious dogmas. Many of those who knew the Scriptures refused to believe. The miracle of blind eyes opening is proof that God had come to us. See Isa. 35:4–5.

c 9:41 Or "your sin stands" (rises up).

d 10:3 In this parable the gatekeeper would represent John the Baptizer who recognized Jesus as the Shepherd. John opened the gate for him to be introduced to Israel at Jesus' baptism.

they will run away from strangers and never follow them because they know it's the voice of a stranger." [6] Jesus told the Pharisees this parable even though they didn't understand a word of what he meant. [a]

[7] So Jesus went over it again, "I speak to you eternal truth: I am the Gate for the flock. [b] [8] All those who broke in before me are thieves who came to steal, [c] but the sheep never listened to them. [9] I am the Gateway. [d] To enter through me is to experience life, freedom, and satisfaction. [e] [10] A thief has only one thing in mind—he wants to steal, slaughter, [f] and destroy. But I have come to *give you everything in abundance,* [g] *more than you expect* [h]—life in its fullness until you overflow! [11] I am the Good [i] Shepherd who lays down my life as a sacrifice for the sheep. [12–13] But the worker who serves only for wages is not a real shepherd. Because he has no heart for the sheep he will run away and abandon them when he sees the wolf coming. And then the wolf mauls the sheep, drags them off, and scatters them.

[14] "I alone am the Good Shepherd, and I know those whose hearts are mine, for they recognize me and know me, [15] just as my Father knows my heart and I know my Father's heart. I am ready to give my life for the sheep.

---

a 10:6 They didn't understand this allegory of the Old Testament law as the sheepfold that became the religion of Judaism, like a pen that confined the people. Christ is the gate that not only allowed everyone in, but he let them out in the New Testament to enjoy all the riches of the pasture. The Holy Spirit is the gatekeeper and the false prophets and Pharisees are the thieves and robbers. Remember that this chapter follows the healing of the blind man who was cast out of the "sheep pen" but accepted in Christ. See Gal. 3:23–26. Jesus is the shepherd, the gate, and the pasture.

b 10:7 As translated from the Aramaic. There is a word play with "I" (*ena*) and "flock" (*ana*). As the gateway, he brings us to the Father and his kingdom realm. As the shepherd, he cares for us and shows us his loving heart.

c 10:8 The Old Testament refers to the kings of Israel and Judah as "shepherds." These kings along with false prophets are shepherds who don't always have God's heart for the sheep. After the healing of the blind man, the Pharisees refused to acknowledge Jesus' rightful place as shepherd of his flock, so the *thieves coming to steal* would also refer to them.

d 10:9 A sheep pen was an enclosure with walls and no roof that would often have the sheep of an entire village kept within. After the sheep were brought in for the night, it was common for the shepherd to sleep at the entrance so he could protect his sheep. Only the shepherds of the sheep would be recognized by that gatekeeper. Jesus is the one who will remain with his flock and keep his sheep living in peace and safety. His teaching (voice) will guard us from the unreliable teachers who want to steal our hearts and bind us to themselves. They steal and rob the affection that belongs only to Jesus, our kind shepherd.

e 10:9 Or "go in and out and find pasture."

f 10:10 The Greek word *thuo* is not the usual word for "kill." It means "sacrifice," or "slaughter."

g 10:10 Implied in the Aramaic text.

h 10:10 Implied in the Greek text.

i 10:11 The word for "good" in Greek (*kalos*) can also mean "beautiful," "virtuous," "excellent," "genuine," or "better." (See *Strong's Concordance,* Gr. 2570.) Jesus is also called the "Great Shepherd" (Heb. 13:20) and the "Shepherd-King" (1 Peter 5:4).

[16] "And I have other sheep that I will gather which are not of this Jewish flock. And I, their shepherd, must lead them too, and they will follow me and listen to my voice. And I will join them all into one flock with one shepherd. [a]

[17] "The Father has an intense love for me because I freely give my own life—to raise it up again. [18] I surrender my own life, and no one has the power to take my life from me. I have the authority to lay it down and the power to take it back again. This is the destiny my Father has set before me."

[19] This teaching set off another heated controversy among the Jewish leaders. [20] Many of them said, "This man is a demon-possessed lunatic! Why would anyone listen to a word he says?" [21] But then there were others who weren't so sure: "His teaching is full of insight. These are not the ravings of a madman! How could a demonized man give sight to one born blind?"

Jesus at the Feast of Renewal

[22-23] The time came to observe the winter Feast of Renewal in Jerusalem. [b] Jesus walked into the temple area under Solomon's covered walkway [24] when the Jewish leaders encircled him and said, "How much longer will you keep us in suspense? Tell us the truth and clarify this for us once and for all. Are you really the Messiah, the Anointed One?"

[25] Jesus answered them, "I have told you the truth already and you did not believe me. The proof of who I am is revealed by all the miracles that I do in the name of my Father. [26] Yet, you stubbornly refuse to follow me, because you are not my sheep. As I've told you before: [27] My own sheep will hear my voice and I know each one, and they will follow me. [28] I give to them the gift of eternal life and they will never be lost and no one has the power to snatch them out of my hands. [29] My Father, who has given them to me as his gift, is the mightiest of all, and no one has the power to snatch them from my Father's care. [30] The Father and I are one."

[31] When they heard this, the Jewish leaders were so enraged that they picked up rocks to stone him to death. [32] But Jesus said, "My Father has empowered me to work many miracles and acts of mercy among you. So which one of them do you want to stone me for?"

[33] The Jewish leaders responded, "We're not stoning you for anything good you did—it's because of your blasphemy! You're just *a son of Adam*, but you've claimed to be God!"

[34] Jesus answered, "Isn't it written in your Scriptures that God said, 'You are

---

a 10:16 This "one flock" is the church made up of both Jews and non-Jews. See Ezek. 34:23; Eph. 2:11–14.

b 10:22–23 This is also known as the "Feast of Dedication" or "The Feast of Lights." Contemporary Judaism recognizes this as Hanukkah. The Greek is literally "The Feast of Renewing" to commemorate the miraculous renewing of oil that burned for eight days.

gods?'[a] The Scriptures cannot be denied or found to be in error. [35]So if those who have the message of the Scriptures are said to be 'gods,' then why would you accuse me of blasphemy? [36]For I have been uniquely chosen by God and he is the one who sent me to you. How then could it be blasphemy for me to say, 'I am the Son of God!' [37]If I'm not doing the beautiful works that my Father sent me to do, then don't believe me. [38]But if you see me doing the beautiful works of God upon the earth, then you should at least believe the evidence of the miracles, even if you don't believe my words! Then you would come to experience me and be convinced that I am in the Father and the Father is in me."

[39]Once again they attempted to seize him, but he escaped miraculously[b] from their clutches. [40]Then Jesus went back to the place where John had baptized him at the crossing of the Jordan. [41]Many came out to where he was and said about him, "Even though John didn't perform any miracles, everything he predicted about this man is true!" [42]And many people became followers of Jesus at the Jordan and believed in him.

Lazarus Raised from the Dead

11 [1-2]In the village of Bethany there was a man named Lazarus, and his sisters, Mary and Martha. Mary was the one who would anoint Jesus' feet with costly perfume and dry his feet with her long hair. One day Lazarus became very sick to the point of death. [3]So his sisters sent a message to Jesus, "Lord, our brother Lazarus, the one you love, is very sick. Please come!"

[4]When he heard this, he said, "This sickness will not end in death for Lazarus, but will bring glory and praise to God. This will reveal the greatness of the Son of God by what takes place."

[5-6]Now even though Jesus loved Mary, Martha, and Lazarus, he remained where he was for two more days. [7]Finally, on the third day, he said to his disciples, "Come. It's time to go to Bethany."[c]

[8]"But Teacher," they said to him, "do you really want to go back there? It was just a short time ago the people of Judea were going to stone you!"

[9-10]Jesus replied, "Are there not twelve hours of daylight in every day?[d] You can go through a day without the fear of stumbling when you walk in the One who gives light to the world. But you will stumble when the light is not in you, for you'll be walking in the dark."

---

a 10:34 See Ps. 82:6.

b 10:39 Implied in the context of being encircled by those with stones in their hands ready to kill him. It was clearly a miracle. He may have become invisible, transported himself to another location, or caused his accusers to be momentarily paralyzed or blinded as he slipped away.

c 11:7 Or "Judea."

d 11:9–10 Jesus uses a parable to respond to why he is not afraid to go where his life could be in danger. This is more than the sun, but "the One who gives light to the world."

[11] Then Jesus added, "Lazarus, our friend, has just fallen asleep.[a] It's time that I go and awaken him."

[12] When they heard this, the disciples replied, "Lord, if he has just fallen asleep, then he'll get better." [13] Jesus was speaking about Lazarus' death, but the disciples presumed he was talking about natural sleep.

[14] Then Jesus made it plain to them, "Lazarus is dead. [15] And for your sake, I'm glad I wasn't there, *because now you have another opportunity to see who I am so that you will learn to trust in me. Come, let's go and see him.*"

[16] So Thomas, nicknamed the Twin, remarked to the other disciples, "Let's go so that we can die with him."[b]

[17-18] Now when they arrived at Bethany, which was only about two miles from Jerusalem, Jesus found that Lazarus had already been in the tomb for four days. [19] Many friends[c] of Mary and Martha had come from the region to console them over the loss of their brother. [20] And when Martha heard that Jesus was approaching the village, she went out to meet him, but Mary stayed in the house.

[21] Martha said to Jesus, "My Lord, if only you had come sooner, my brother wouldn't have died. [22] But I know that if you were to ask God for anything, he would do it for you."

[23] Jesus told her, "Your brother will rise and live."

[24] She replied, "Yes, I know he will rise with everyone else on resurrection day."[d]

[25] "Martha," Jesus said, "*You don't have to wait until then. I am*[e] *the Resurrection,*[f] *and I am Life Eternal. Anyone who clings to me in faith, even though he dies, will live forever. [26] And the one who lives by believing in me will never die.*[g] *Do you believe this?*"[h]

[27] Then Martha replied, "Yes, Lord, I do! I've always believed that you

---

a 11:11 Jesus is stating an obvious euphemism. Lazarus "sleeping" means that he has died. To "awaken" him means that Jesus would raise him from the dead.

b 11:16 It is likely that Thomas was expressing pessimism about the fate of Jesus going back into the region where he was threatened with death.

c 11:19 Or "Jews."

d 11:24 Or "at the last day."

e 11:25 The words *I am* in the Aramaic are a clear statement of Christ's deity, "I am the living God, the Resurrection and the Life!"

f 11:25 The Aramaic uses a word that is related linguistically to the name Noah, who was symbolically "resurrected" from the flood as the life-giver to those who repopulated the earth. Resurrection is superior to life, for life can be defeated and ended. But resurrection overcomes. Life is the power to exist, but resurrection is the power to conquer all, even death itself. Believers must learn to live in Christ our Life, but also, Christ our Resurrection to conquer all things. See Phil. 3:10.

g 11:26 This is very emphatic in the Greek, "never die forever!"

h 11:26 John presents Jesus as the great Savior who saves us from sin (John 8), blindness (John 9–10), and death (John 11).

are the Anointed One, the Son of God who has come into the world for us!"
[28] Then she left and hurried off to her sister, Mary, and called her aside from all the mourners and whispered to her, "The Master is here and he's asking for you."[a]

[29] So when Mary heard this, she quickly went off to find him, [30] for Jesus was lingering outside the village at the same spot where Martha met him. [31] Now when Mary's friends who were comforting her[b] noticed how quickly she ran out of the house, they followed her, assuming she was going to the tomb of her brother to mourn.

[32] When Mary finally found Jesus outside the village, she fell at his feet in tears and said, "Lord, if only you had been here, my brother would not have died."

[33] When Jesus looked at Mary and saw her weeping at his feet, and all her friends who were with her grieving, he shuddered with emotion[c] and was deeply moved with tenderness and compassion. [34] He said to them, **"Where did you bury him?"**

"Lord, come with us and we'll show you," they replied.

[35] Then tears streamed down Jesus' face.

[36] Seeing Jesus weep caused many of the mourners to say, "Look how much he loved Lazarus."[d] [37] Yet others said, "Isn't this the One who opens blind eyes? Why didn't he do something to keep Lazarus from dying?"

[38] Then Jesus, with intense emotions, came to the tomb—a cave with a stone placed over its entrance. [39] Jesus told them, **"Roll away the stone."**

Then Martha said, "But Lord, it's been four days since he died—by now his body is already decomposing!"

[40] Jesus looked at her and said, **"Didn't I tell you that if you will believe in me, you will see God unveil his power?"**[e]

[41] So they rolled away the heavy stone. Jesus gazed into heaven and said, **"Father, thank you that you have heard my prayer, [42] for you listen to every word I speak. Now, so that these who stand here with me will believe that you have sent me to the earth as your messenger, *I will use the power you have given me.***" [43] Then with a loud voice Jesus shouted with authority: **"Lazarus! Come out of the tomb!"**

---

a   11:28 This is one of the most beautiful things that ever could be said to you, "The Master is here and he's asking for you." Mary's response must be ours, "she quickly went off to find him" (v. 29).

b   11:31 The Aramaic is "Mary's friends who loved her."

c   11:33 The Greek word used here (*enebrimēsato*) can also mean "indignant and stirred with anger." Was he angry at the mourners? Not at all. He was angry over the work of the devil in taking the life of his friend, Lazarus. The Aramaic, however, has no connotation of indignation, only tenderness and compassion (lit. "his heart melted with compassion").

d   11:36 The Aramaic is "how much mercy he felt for Lazarus."

e   11:40 Or "you would see the glory of God."

⁴⁴ Then in front of everyone, Lazarus, who had died four days earlier, slowly hobbled out—he still had grave clothes tightly wrapped around his hands and feet and covering his face! Jesus said to them, "Unwrap him and let him loose." *a*

⁴⁵ From that day forward many of those *b* who had come to visit Mary believed in him, for they had seen with their own eyes this amazing miracle! ⁴⁶ But a few went back to inform the Pharisees about what Jesus had done.

⁴⁷ So the Pharisees and the chief priests called a special meeting of the High Council *c* and said, "So what are we going to do about this man? Look at all the great miracles he's performing! ⁴⁸ If we allow him to continue like this, everyone will believe in him. And the Romans will take action and destroy both our country and our people!" *d*

⁴⁹ Now Caiaphas, the high priest that year, spoke up and said, "You don't understand a thing! ⁵⁰ Don't you realize we'd be much better off if this one man were to die for the people than for the whole nation to perish?"

⁵¹ (This prophecy that Jesus was destined to die *e* for the Jewish people didn't come from Caiaphas himself, *but he was moved by God* to prophesy as the chief priest. ⁵² And Jesus' death would not be for the Jewish people only, but to gather together God's children scattered around the world and unite them as one.) *f* ⁵³ So from that day on, they were committed to killing Jesus.

⁵⁴ For this reason Jesus no longer went out in public among the Jews. But he went in the wilderness to a village called Ephraim, *g* where he secluded himself with his disciples.

⁵⁵ Now the time came for the Passover preparations, and many from the countryside went to Jerusalem for their ceremonial cleansing before the feast began. ⁵⁶ And all the people kept looking out for Jesus, expecting him to come to the city. They said to themselves while they waited in the temple courts, "Do you think that he will dare come to the feast?" ⁵⁷ For the leading priests and the Pharisees had given orders that they be informed immediately if anyone saw Jesus, so they could seize and arrest him.

---

a 11:44 Burial customs in the Middle East were to wrap the corpse in white cotton cloths from the neck to the feet. The head was then covered with a large handkerchief.

b 11:45 Or "Jews."

c 11:47 Or "the Sanhedrin." This was the Great Sanhedrin, equivalent to a Jewish court, which would be comprised of seventy men who would judge Jewish religious matters.

d 11:48 As translated from the Aramaic. The Greek is translated "our place [position] and our nation." "Our place" could refer to the temple.

e 11:51 As translated from the Aramaic.

f 11:52 See Isa. 49:6.

g 11:54 The Aramaic can be translated "the fortress city of Ephraim," or "the mill called Ephraim." Ephraim means "double fruitfulness." Some believe this location is the present town of Et-Taiyibeh, which would make it about fourteen miles (twenty-two kilometers) northeast of Jerusalem.

Mary Anoints Jesus

12 Six days before the Passover began, Jesus went back to Bethany, the town where he raised Lazarus from the dead. ²They had prepared a supper for Jesus. ᵃ Martha served, and Lazarus and Mary were among those at the table. ³Mary picked up an alabaster ᵇ jar filled with nearly a liter ᶜ of extremely rare and costly perfume—the purest extract of nard, ᵈ and she anointed Jesus' feet. Then she wiped them dry with her long hair. And the fragrance of the costly oil filled the house. ᵉ ⁴But Judas the locksmith, ᶠ Simon's son, the betrayer, spoke up and said, ⁵"What a waste! We could have sold this perfume for a fortune ᵍ and given the money to the poor!"

⁶(In fact, Judas had no heart for the poor. He only said this because he was a thief and in charge of the money case. He would steal money whenever he wanted from the funds *given to support Jesus' ministry.*)

⁷Jesus said to Judas, **"Leave her alone! She has saved it for the time of my burial.** ʰ ⁸**You'll always have the poor with you;** ⁱ **but you won't always have me."**

⁹When the word got out that Jesus was not far from Jerusalem, a large crowd came out to see him, and they also wanted to see Lazarus, the man Jesus had raised from the dead. ¹⁰This prompted the chief priests to seal their plans to do away with both Jesus and Lazarus, ʲ ¹¹for his miracle testimony was incontrovertible and was persuading many of the Jews living in Jerusalem to believe in Jesus.

¹²The next day the news that Jesus was on his way to Jerusalem swept through the massive crowd gathered for the feast. ¹³So they took palm branches ᵏ and went out to meet him. Everyone was shouting, "Lord, be our Savior! ˡ Blessed is the one who comes to us sent from Jehovah-God, ᵐ the King of Israel!"

ᵃ 12:2 We see from Mark 14:3 that this took place at the house of Simon, the leper Jesus had healed.

ᵇ 12:3 As translated from the Aramaic.

ᶜ 12:3 Or "nearly a pound."

ᵈ 12:3 Nard is an extremely expensive perfume taken from the root and spike of the nard plant found in northern India. See Song. 1:12; 4:13–14.

ᵉ 12:3 This fragrance, usually associated with a king, was upon Jesus' feet as he stood before his accusers and as the soldiers pierced his feet with a nail. It is possible they would all have smelled the fragrance of this costly perfume.

ᶠ 12:4 Or "Iscariot," a word related linguistically to "a lock" or "locksmith." Judas apparently held the key to the lockbox of funds to support Jesus' ministry. See John 6:71 and footnote.

ᵍ 12:5 Or "three hundred silver coins (denarii)," which would be equal to a year's salary.

ʰ 12:7 The Aramaic could be translated, "Let her conduct my burial day ceremony." It is possible that this rare and expensive perfume could have been her family's treasure or her inheritance.

ⁱ 12:8 That is, "You will have many opportunities to help the poor, but you will not always have me." See also Deut. 15:11.

ʲ 12:10 Darkness has only one way to deal with the truth—kill it.

ᵏ 12:13 The palm tree is a symbol of triumph, victory over death. Palms grow in the desert and overcome the arid climate. Deborah sat under a palm tree as a judge in Israel and received the strategy to overcome her enemies. See Rev. 7:9.

ˡ 12:13 Or "Hosanna!"

ᵐ 12:13 See Ps. 118:25–26.

¹⁴ Then Jesus found a young donkey and rode on it to fulfill what was prophesied: ¹⁵ "People of Zion,ᵃ have no fear! Look—it's your king coming to you riding on a young donkey!"ᵇ

¹⁶ Now Jesus' disciples didn't fully understand the importance of what was taking place, but after he was raised and exalted into glory, they understood how Jesus fulfilled all the prophecies in the Scriptures that were written about him.

¹⁷ All the eyewitnesses of the miracle Jesus performed when he called Lazarus out of the tomb and raised him from the dead kept spreading the news about Jesus to everyone. ¹⁸ The news of this miracle of resurrection caused the crowds to swell as great numbers of people *welcomed him into the city with joy.*ᶜ ¹⁹ But the Pharisees were disturbed by this and said to each other, "We won't be able to stop this.ᵈ The whole world is going to run after him!"

True Seekers

²⁰ Now there were a number of foreigners from among the nations who were worshipers at the feast.ᵉ ²¹ They went to Philip (who came from the village of Bethsaida in Galilee) and they asked him, "Would you take us to see Jesus? We want to see him." ²²So Philip went to find Andrew, and then they both went to inform Jesus.ᶠ

²³ He replied to them, "Now is the time for the Son of Man to be glorified. ²⁴ Let me make this clear:ᵍ A single grain of wheat will never be more than a single grain of wheat unless it drops into the ground and dies. Because then it sprouts and producesʰ a great harvest of wheat—all because one grainⁱ died.ʲ

²⁵ "The person who loves his life and pampers himself will miss true life!

---

a 12:15 Or "Daughter of Zion."

b 12:15 See Zech. 9:9. Conquering kings would ride on a warhorse or in a golden chariot, but Jesus rode into Jerusalem on a domesticated donkey. He is the King of Peace.

c 12:18 The Greek is "the crowd went out to meet him." The Aramaic is "great crowds went in front of him."

d 12:19 The Aramaic is "See, you have lost your influence."

e 12:20 As translated from the Aramaic. The Greek text states they were "Greeks."

f 12:22 See Isa. 55:5.

g 12:24 The Aramaic is translated "Timeless truth I say to you."

h 12:24 The Aramaic has an interesting word play with "it dies" (*myta*) and "it produces" (*mytya*).

i 12:24 The "one grain" is Jesus Christ, who will within days be offered as the sacrifice for sin on Calvary's cross. He will "drop" into the ground as "a grain of wheat" and bring forth a great "harvest" of "seeds." This parable given to Philip and Andrew was meant to be Jesus' reply to the request by the non-Jewish seekers to see Jesus. Christ's answer? "They will see me through you. As you follow me, you will also experience the dying and birthing experience." The harvest among the nations will come when we follow Jesus where he goes.

j 12:24 The Aramaic is translated "if it dies, it will bring forth a great rebirth."

But the one who detaches his life from this world and abandons himself to me, will find true life and enjoy it forever! [26] If you want to be my disciple, follow me and you will go where I am going. [a] And if you truly follow me as my disciple, [b] the Father will shower his favor upon your life.

[27] "Even though I am torn within, and my soul is in turmoil, I will not ask the Father to rescue me from this hour of trial. For I have come to fulfill my purpose [c]—*to offer myself to God.* [28] So, Father, bring glory to your name!" [d] Then suddenly a booming voice was heard from the sky,

"I have glorified my name! And I will glorify it *through you* again!"

[29] The audible voice of God startled the crowd standing nearby. Some thought it was only thunder, yet others said, "An angel just spoke to him!"

[30] Then Jesus told them, "The voice you heard was not for my benefit, but for yours—*to help you believe.* [31] From this moment on, everything in this world is about to change, [e] for the ruler of this dark world [f] will be overthrown. [g] [32] *And I will do this* when I am lifted up off the ground [h] and when I draw the hearts of people [i] to gather them to me." [33] He said this to indicate that he would die by being lifted up on the cross. [j]

[34] People from the crowd spoke up and said, "Die? How could the Anointed One die? The Word of God says that the Anointed One will live with us forever, [k] but you just said that the Son of Man must be lifted up from the earth. [l] And who is this Son of Man anyway?"

[35] Jesus replied, "You will have the light shining with you for only a little

---

a 12:26 The implication in the text is that a life of full surrender to God will make us "a grain of wheat" that multiplies into a "harvest." The Greek text can be translated, "If anyone ministers to me (materially provides for me), where I am, my minister will be there too."

b 12:26 Or "materially provides for me."

c 12:27 The Aramaic is translated "to fulfill this hour I have come."

d 12:28 Some later manuscripts have "Father, bring glory to your Son." One of the oldest manuscripts reads "Father, bring glory to your name with the glory that I had with you before the world was created." The majority of reliable manuscripts have "Father, bring glory to your name."

e 12:31 Or "the time of judging the world (system) has come." The judging of the world is the overthrow of the kingdom of darkness. The preaching of the gospel of Jesus Christ is passing a sentence of judgment on this fallen world and declaring treason in the kingdom of darkness. Everything changes because of the cross—the hinge of history.

f 12:31 An obvious reference to Satan.

g 12:31 Or "driven into exile."

h 12:32 The Aramaic phrase "lifted up" is another way of saying "lifted up in crucifixion." The Greek implies being lifted up from beneath the earth (resurrection).

i 12:32 Or "I will draw all things to myself." Or "I will bundle everyone/everything next to me." Jesus also drew all our judgment to himself when he died for our sins. The Judge became the payment for the guilty.

j 12:33 Or "to clarify what kind of death he would die."

k 12:34 See Ps. 89:35–37; Isa. 9:7; Ezek. 37:25; Dan. 7:14.

l 12:34 It was obvious to the crowd that Jesus being lifted up was a reference to the cross.

while longer. While you still have me, walk in the light, so that the darkness doesn't overtake you. For when you walk in the dark you have no idea where you're going. ³⁶ So believe and cling to the light while I am with you, so that you will become children of light." After saying this, Jesus then entered into the crowd and hid himself from them.

The Unbelief of the Crowd

³⁷ Even with the overwhelming evidence of all the many signs and wonders that Jesus had performed in front of them, his critics still refused to believe. ³⁸ This fulfilled the prophecy given by Isaiah:

Lord, who has believed our message? Who has seen the unveiling of your great power? [a]

³⁹ And the people were not able to believe, for Isaiah also prophesied:

⁴⁰ God has blinded their eyes and hardened their hearts [b] to the truth. So with their eyes and hearts closed they cannot understand the truth nor turn to me so that I could instantly cleanse and heal them. [c]

⁴¹ Isaiah said these things because he had seen and experienced the splendor of Jesus [d] and prophesied about him. ⁴² Yet there were many Jewish leaders who believed in Jesus, but because they feared the Pharisees they kept it secret, so they wouldn't be ostracized by the assembly of the Jews. ⁴³ For they loved the glory that men could give them rather than the glory that came from God!

Jesus' Last Public Teaching

⁴⁴ Jesus shouted out passionately, "To believe in me is to also believe in God who sent me. ⁴⁵ For when you look at me you are seeing the One who sent me. ⁴⁶ I have come as a light to shine in this dark world so that all who trust in me will no longer wander in darkness. ⁴⁷ If you hear my words and refuse to follow them, I do not judge you. For I have not come to judge you but to save you. ⁴⁸ If you reject me and refuse to follow my words, [e] you already have a judge. The message of truth I have given you will rise up to judge you at the

---

a 12:38 Or "To whom is the arm of the Lord revealed." The arm of the Lord is a metaphor for God's great power. The word for "revealed" means "to unveil." See Isa. 53:1.

b 12:40 Or "closed their minds." The Aramaic is translated "darkened their hearts." The Aramaic indicates that they did this to themselves, rather than God doing this.

c 12:40 The Aramaic is translated "cleansed"; the Greek is translated "healed." Both are included here. See Isa. 6:10.

d 12:41 See Isa. 6:1–5. This is a profound statement that Isaiah saw Jesus Christ when he was taken into heaven and encountered the Lord Yahweh on the throne. This "Lord high and exalted" was none less than Jesus Christ before he became a man.

e 12:48 This is the plural form of the Greek word *rhema* and would refer to all that Jesus taught.

Day of Judgment. [a] [49] For I'm not speaking as someone who is self-appointed, but I speak by the authority of the Father himself who sent me, and who instructed me what to say. [50] And I know that the Father's commands result [b] in eternal life, and that's why I speak the very words I've heard him speak."

Jesus Washes Feet

13 Jesus knew that the night before Passover would be his last night on earth before leaving this world to return to the Father's side. All throughout his time with his disciples, Jesus had demonstrated a deep and tender love for them. And now he longed to show them the full measure of his love. [c] [2] Before their evening meal had begun, the accuser [d] had already planted betrayal [e] into the heart of Judas Iscariot, the son of Simon.

[3] Now Jesus was fully aware that the Father had placed all things under his control, for he had come from God and was about to go back to be with him. [4] So he got up from the meal and took off his outer robe, and took a towel and wrapped it around his waist. [5] Then he poured water into a basin and began to wash the disciples' dirty feet and dry them with his towel.

[6] But when Jesus got to Simon Peter, he objected and said, "I can't let you wash my dirty feet—you're my Lord!"

[7] Jesus replied, "**You don't understand yet the meaning of what I'm doing, but soon it will be clear to you.**" [f]

[8] Peter looked at Jesus and said, "You'll never wash my dirty feet—never!"

"**But Peter, if you don't allow me to wash your feet,**" Jesus responded, "**then you will not be able to share life with me.**"

[9] So Peter said, "Lord, in that case, don't just wash my feet, wash my hands and my head too!"

[10] Jesus said to him, "**You are already clean. You've been washed completely and you just need your feet to be cleansed—but that can't be said of all of you.**" For Jesus knew which one was about to betray him, [11] and that's why he told them that not all of them were clean.

[12] After washing their feet, he put his robe on and returned to his place at

---

a 12:48 Or "at the last day."

b 12:50 Or in the Aramaic "represent."

c 13:1 Or "he loved them to the very end."

d 13:2 Or "devil."

e 13:2 Or "that he should betray Jesus." The Aramaic is "Satan arose in the heart of Judas to betray Jesus."

f 13:7 By removing their sandals and washing their feet, Jesus was showing them that he was granting them a new inheritance—his own. The sandal is often used in covenants of inheritance in Hebrew culture. Every defilement would be removed so that they could "place the sole of their feet" upon the new covenant inheritance. See Josh. 1:3; Ruth 4:1–12. God likewise told Moses to remove his sandals (Ex. 3:5), for he was about to receive a new inheritance—the holiness of God and the authority that came with it.

the table. [a] "Do you understand what I just did?" Jesus said. [13] "You've called me your teacher and lord, and you're right, for that's who I am. [14-15] So if I'm your teacher and lord and have just washed your dirty feet, then you should follow the example that I've set for you and wash one another's dirty feet. Now do for each other what I have just done for you. [16] I speak to you timeless truth: a servant is not superior to his master, and an apostle is never greater than the one who sent him. [17] So now put into practice what I have done for you, and you will experience a life of happiness enriched with untold blessings!"

Jesus Predicts His Betrayal

[18] "I don't refer to all of you when I tell you these things, for I know the ones I've chosen—to fulfill the Scripture that says, 'The one who shared supper with me treacherously betrays me.' [b] [19] I am telling you this now, before it happens, so that when the prophecy comes to pass you will be convinced that I AM. [c] [20] "Listen to this timeless truth: whoever receives the messenger I send receives me, and the one who receives me receives the Father [d] who sent me."

[21] Then Jesus was moved deeply in his spirit. [e] Looking at his disciples, he announced, "I tell you the truth—one of you is about to betray me."

[22] Eyeing each other, his disciples puzzled over which one of them could do such a thing. [23] The disciple that Jesus dearly loved [f] was at the right of him at the table [g] and was leaning his head on Jesus. [24] Peter gestured to this disciple to ask Jesus who it was he was referring to. [25] Then the dearly loved disciple leaned into Jesus' chest and whispered, "Master, who is it?"

[26] "The one I give this piece of bread to after I've dipped it in the bowl," Jesus replied. Then he dipped the piece of bread into the bowl and handed it to Judas Iscariot, the son of Simon. [h] [27] And when Judas ate the piece of bread,

---

a 13:12 There has never been a nobleman, a teacher, or a king that loves and serves his servants like Jesus.

b 13:18 Or "has lifted up his heel against me." The Greek text preserves the idiom of Ps. 41:9, which speaks of a treacherous betrayal. In the Semitic culture it is the greatest breach of etiquette to sit and eat with a friend and then later betray them. This is why many would never eat with someone they were not on good terms with. See also footnotes on Ps. 41:9.

c 13:19 Or "I Am the One," or "I AM Who I AM." Jesus once again equates himself with Jehovah-God, the I Am.

d 13:20 Or "the One." By implication, this is the Father.

e 13:21 As translated from the Greek. The Aramaic describes Jesus' emotion as "feeling a profound tenderness," or "his spirit felt a longing." We can conclude that everything within our Lord Jesus was moved deeply by the thought of being betrayed by one of his beloved disciples.

f 13:23 The Aramaic is "the one Jesus showed mercy to." This was obviously John, the one who wrote this Gospel. Remember, you too can say, "I am the disciple who Jesus dearly loves and shows mercy to."

g 13:23 This could be a figure of speech for "the place of honor."

h 13:26 This was culturally an act of cherished friendship and intimacy, to hand over choice

Satan[a] entered him. Then Jesus looked at Judas and said, "**What you are planning to do, go do it now.**" [28]None of those around the table realized what was
happening. [29]Some thought that Judas, their trusted treasurer, was being told
to go buy what was needed for the Passover celebration, or perhaps to go give
something to the poor. [30]So Judas left quickly and went out into the dark night
to betray Jesus.

Jesus Predicts Peter's Denial

[31]After Judas left the room, Jesus said, "The time has come for the glory of
God to surround the Son of Man, and God will be greatly glorified through
what happens to me.[b] [32]And very soon God will unveil the glory of the Son
of Man.[c]

[33]"My dear friends,[d] I only have a brief time left to be with you. And
then you will search and long for me. But I tell you what I told the Jewish
leaders: you'll not be able to come where I am.[e]

[34]"So I give you now a new[f] commandment: Love each other just as
much as I have loved you. [35]For when you demonstrate the same love I have
for you by loving one another, everyone will know that you're my true
followers."

[36]Peter interjected, "But, Master, where are you going?"

Jesus replied, "**Where I am going you won't be able to follow, but one day
you will follow me there.**"

[37]Peter[g] said, "What do you mean I'm not able to follow you now? I would
sacrifice my life to die for you!"[h]

[38]Jesus answered, "**Would you really lay down your life for me, Peter?**

---

bits of food to a friend. This is the love of Christ, to give food to his enemy. It is no wonder
Satan entered his heart after Judas ate the bread handed to him by his friend. For how can
one accept the gift of true friendship and still hold on to treachery and the spirit of betrayal?

a 13:27 This is an Aramaic word that means "adversary."

b 13:31 Or "The Son of Man was glorified and the Father was glorified by him."

c 13:32 Or "Since God is glorified in him (the Son of Man) God will also glorify him in himself,
and glorify him immediately." The Greek text has the word *doxazo* ("glory" or "honor") five
times in vv. 31–32. This repetition would mean that it speaks of more than simply honor. It
is the clear statement of the exchange of glory between God and his Son, Jesus Christ.

d 13:33 Or "children."

e 13:33 See John 7:33–34.

f 13:34 Jesus sets a new standard of love before his followers. Although the Old Testament
does instruct us to love one another (Lev. 19:18, 34; Deut. 10:18), Jesus now gives the commandment to use his standard of love for us as the true measurement of love as we care for
one another.

g 13:37 The Aramaic is translated "Simon the Rock."

h 13:37 The Aramaic uses the word "consecrate," which means to offer up a sacrifice. Peter
implies that he would willingly offer himself in Jesus' place.

Here's the absolute truth: Before the rooster crows in the morning, you will say three times that you don't even know me!" [a]

Jesus Comforts His Disciples

14 "Don't worry or surrender to your fear. [b] For you've believed in God, now trust and believe in me also. [c] [2] My Father's house has many dwelling places. [d] If it were otherwise, I would tell you plainly, because I go [e] to prepare a place for you to rest. [3] And when everything is ready, I will come back and take [f] you to myself so that you will be where I am. [4] And you already know the way to the place where I'm going." [g]

[5] Thomas said to him, "Master, we don't know where you're going, so how could we know the way there?"

[6] Jesus explained, "I am the Way, I am the Truth, [h] and I am the Life. No one comes next to the Father [i] except through *union with me*. [j] To know me is to know my Father too. [7] And from now on you will realize that you have seen him and experienced him."

[8] Philip spoke up, "Lord, show us the Father, and that will be all that we need!"

[9] Jesus replied, "Philip, I've been with you all this time and you still don't know who I am? How could you ask me to show you the Father, for anyone who has looked at me has seen the Father. [10] Don't you believe that the Father

---

a 13:38 Peter, like all of us, resisted the acknowledgment of his weakness and chose to cling to the illusion of strength. Peter was given the sign of a rooster crowing, for that is what he was. He was like a crowing rooster, strutting in pride. "Rocky" got cocky and forgot where true strength is found.

b 14:1 Or "Don't let your hearts be distressed." The Aramaic is translated "Let not your heart flutter."

c 14:1 Or "Believe in God and believe in me."

d 14:2 Or "There are many resting places on the way to my Father's house." Or "There are many homes in my Father's household." The Father's house is also mentioned by Jesus in John 2:16, where it is his temple on earth, his dwelling place. This is not just heaven, but the dwelling place of God among men. There is ample room for people from every nation and ethnicity, room to spare, for the church, the body of Christ, is now the house of God. See 1 Cor. 3:16; Eph. 2:21–22; 1 Tim. 3:15; Heb. 3:6; 1 Peter 2:5. Every believer is now one of the many dwelling places that make up God's house (temple). See also v. 23.

e 14:2 Jesus' "going" was to go through death and resurrection in order to make us ready to be his dwelling place. He had to "go," not to heaven, but to the cross and pass through resurrection.

f 14:3 The Greek verb used here, *paralambano*, is the word used for a bridegroom coming to take his bride. He "takes" us as his bride through his death and resurrection. His "coming back" can also refer to his "coming" to live within believers.

g 14:4 Or "You know where I'm going and the way to get there."

h 14:6 Or "the True Reality."

i 14:6 Jesus does more than take us to heaven, he brings us next to (alongside of) the Father. The Father is the destination.

j 14:6 Or "through [faith in] me."

is living in me and that I am living in the Father? Even my words are not my own but come from my Father, for he lives in me and performs his miracles of power through me. ¹¹Believe that I live as one with my Father and that my Father lives as one with me—or at least, believe because of the mighty miracles I have done.

¹²"I tell you this timeless truth: The person who follows me in faith, believing in me, will do the same mighty miracles that I do—even greater miracles than these because I go to be with my Father! ¹³For I will do whatever you ask me to do when you ask me in my name. And that is how the Son will show what the Father is really like and bring glory to him. ¹⁴Ask me anything in my name, and I will do it for you!"

Jesus Prophesies about the Holy Spirit

¹⁵"Loving me empowers you to obey my commands.ᵃ ¹⁶⁻¹⁷And I will ask the Father and he will give you anotherᵇ Savior,ᶜ the Holy Spirit of Truth, who will be to you a friend just like me—and he will never leave you. The world won't receive him because they can't see him or know him. But you will know him intimately, because he will make his home in you and will live inside you.ᵈ

¹⁸"I promise that I will never leave you helpless or abandon you as orphans—I will come back to you!ᵉ ¹⁹Soon I will leave this world and they will see me no longer, but you will see me, because I will live again, and you will come alive too. ²⁰So when that day comes, you will know that I am living in the Father and that you are one with me, for I will be living in you. ²¹Those

---

a 14:15 Love for Christ is proven and demonstrated by our obedience to all that he says.

b 14:16–17 The Greek word *allos* means "another of the same kind." As Jesus is the Savior from the guilt of sin, the Holy Spirit is the Savior who saves us from the power of sin by living through us in fullness.

c 14:16–17 The Greek word used here is *paráklētos*, a technical word that could be translated "defense attorney." It means "one called to stand next to you as a helper." Various translations have rendered this "Counselor," "Comforter," "Advocate," "Encourager," "Intercessor," or "Helper." However none of these words alone are adequate and fall short in explaining the full meaning. The translator has chosen the word *Savior*, for it depicts the role of the Holy Spirit to protect, defend, and save us from our self and our enemies and keep us whole and healed. He is the One who guides and defends, comforts and consoles. Keep in mind that the Holy Spirit is the Spirit of Christ, our Savior. The Aramaic word is *paraqleta*, which is taken from two root words: (1) *praq*, "to end, finish, or to save," and (2) *lyta*, which means "the curse." What a beautiful word picture, the Holy Spirit comes to end the work of the curse (of sin) in our lives and to save us from its every effect! *Paraqleta* means "a redeemer who ends the curse." (See *Strong's Concordance*, Gr. 6561 and 6562; *A Compendious Syriac Dictionary*, p. 237; and *Oraham's Dictionary*, p. 250.)

d 14:16–17 Jesus is prophesying about the coming of the Holy Spirit at Pentecost, who will indwell every believer. See Acts 2.

e 14:18 There are three ways Jesus will come to them. He came after his resurrection and appeared numerous times to his disciples. He came in the person of the Holy Spirit at Pentecost to live within them (Rom. 8:9) and he will come in the *parousia*, known traditionally as the second coming.

who truly love me are those who obey my commands. Whoever passionately loves me will be passionately loved by my Father. And I will passionately love you in return and will manifest my life within you."

²² Then one of the disciples named Judas*ᵃ* (not Judas Iscariot) said, "Lord, why is it you will only reveal your identity to us and not to everyone?"

²³ Jesus replied, "Loving me empowers you to obey my word.*ᵇ* And my Father will love you so deeply that we will come to you and make you our dwelling place. ²⁴ But those who don't love me will not obey my words. The Father did not send me to speak my own revelation, but the words of my Father. ²⁵ I am telling you this while I am still with you. ²⁶ But when the Father sends the Spirit of Holiness, the One like me who sets you free,*ᶜ* he will teach you all things in my name. And he will inspire you to remember every word that I've told you.

²⁷ "I leave the gift of peace with you—my peace. Not the kind of fragile peace given by the world, but my perfect peace. Don't yield to fear or be troubled in your hearts—instead, be courageous!*ᵈ* ²⁸ "Remember what I've told you, that I must go away, but I promise to come back to you. So if you truly love me, you will be glad for me, since I'm returning to my Father, who is greater than I. ²⁹ So when all of these things happen, you will still trust and cling to me. ³⁰ I won't speak with you much longer, for the ruler of this dark world*ᵉ* is coming. But he has no power over me, *for he has nothing to use against me.* ³¹ I am doing exactly what the Father destined for me to accomplish,*ᶠ* so that the world will discover how much I love my Father. Now come with me."

Jesus the Living Vine

15 "I am a true sprouting vine, and the farmer who tends the vine is my Father. ² He cares for the branches connected to me by lifting and propping up the fruitless branches*ᵍ* and pruning*ʰ* every fruitful branch to yield a

---

a 14:22 Judas was a common name in the time of Jesus. It is actually the name Judah.

b 14:23 Love for Christ is proven and demonstrated by our obedience to all that he says.

c 14:26 The Aramaic is translated "the Redeemer from the curse." See the second footnote on John 14:16–17.

d 14:27 These are the same words Moses gave before he died and the words God spoke to Joshua as he entered into his life's plan of taking the promised land for Israel. See Deut. 31:8; Josh. 1:8–9; 10:25. God has not given us a spirit of cowardly fear. See also 2 Tim. 1:7.

e 14:30 Implied in the text and in the word *devil,* which means slanderer and accuser.

f 14:31 Or "commanded me to do."

g 15:2 The Greek phrase can also be translated "he takes up [to himself] every fruitless branch." He doesn't remove these branches, but he takes them to himself. As the wise and loving farmer, he lifts them up off the ground to enhance their growth. In the context, Christ's endless love for his disciples on the last night of his life on earth seems to emphasize God's love even for those who fail and disappoint him. Peter's denial didn't bring rejection from Jesus.

h 15:2 The Greek word for "pruning," *kathairo,* can also mean cleansing.

greater harvest. ³The words I have spoken over you have already cleansed[a] you. ⁴So you must remain in life-union with me,[b] for I remain in life-union with you. For as a branch severed from the vine will not bear fruit, so your life will be fruitless unless you live your life intimately joined to mine.

⁵"I am the sprouting vine and you're my branches.[c] As you live in union with me as your source, fruitfulness will stream from within you—but when you live separated from me you are powerless. ⁶If a person is separated from me, he is discarded; such branches are gathered up and thrown into the fire to be burned. ⁷But if you live in life-union with me and if my words[d] live powerfully[e] within you—then you can ask whatever you desire and it will be done. ⁸When your lives bear abundant fruit, you demonstrate that you are my mature disciples who glorify my Father!

⁹"I love each of you with the same love that the Father loves me. You must continually let my love nourish your hearts. ¹⁰If you keep my commands, you will live in my love, just as I have kept my Father's commands, for I continually live nourished and empowered by his love. ¹¹My purpose for telling you these things is so that the joy that I experience will fill your hearts with overflowing gladness!

¹²"So this is my command: Love each other deeply, as much as I have loved you.[f] ¹³For the greatest love of all is a love that sacrifices all. And this great love is demonstrated when a person sacrifices his life[g] for his friends.

¹⁴"You show that you are my intimate friends when you obey[h] all[i] that I command you. ¹⁵I have never called you 'servants,'[j] because a master doesn't confide in his servants, and servants don't always understand what the master is doing. But I call you my most intimate friends,[k] for I reveal to you everything that I've heard from my Father. ¹⁶You didn't choose me, but I've

---

a 15:3 Or "pruned."
b 15:4 Or "grafted into me."
c 15:5 See Isa. 4:2; 11:1–2; Rev. 1:20. The branch of the Lord is now Christ living in his people, branching out through them. The church is now his lampstand with seven branches.
d 15:7 This is the Greek word *rhema*, which refers to the spoken words, or the sayings, of God.
e 15:7 The Aramaic is translated "my words take hold (are strong) within you."
f 15:12 Because we are all branches in one vine, if we don't love one another it means that our fellowship with the vine has been cut off. To bear fruit must come from loving each other, for the same Christ-life lives within every believer. We are not branches of many trees, but of one vine.
g 15:13 Or "willingly lay down his soul for his friends." The Aramaic word for "friends" is actually "family" or "relatives."
h 15:14 The Greek verb indicates "if you keep on obeying as a habit."
i 15:14 The Aramaic is translated "all"; the Greek is translated "what I command you."
j 15:15 As translated from the Aramaic. The Greek is, "I will no longer call you servants." The Greek word for "servants" is *doulos*, which means "slaves."
k 15:15 Both the Aramaic and Greek word for "intimate friends" is actually "those cared for from the womb." You are more than a friend to him, for you were born again from his wounded side.

chosen[a] and commissioned you to go into the world[b] to bear fruit. And your fruit will last, because whatever you ask of my Father, for my sake,[c] he will give it to you! [17] So this is my parting command: Love one another deeply!"

True Disciples Can Expect Persecution

[18] "Just remember, when the unbelieving world hates you, they first hated me. [19] If you were to give your allegiance to the world, they would love and welcome you as one of their own. But because you won't align yourself with the values of this world, they will hate you. I have chosen you and taken you out of the world to be mine. [20] So remember what I taught you, that a servant isn't superior to his master.[d] And since they persecuted me, they will also persecute you. And if they obey my teachings, they will also obey yours. [21] They will treat you this way because you are mine,[e] and they don't know the One who sent me.

[22] "If I had not come and revealed myself[f] to the unbelieving world, they would not feel the guilt of their sin, but now their sin is left uncovered.[g] [23] If anyone hates me, they hate my Father also. [24] If I had not performed miracles in their presence like no one else has done, they would not feel the guilt of their sins. But now, they have seen and hated both me and my Father. [25] And all of this has happened to fulfill what is written in their Scriptures:[h] They hated me for no reason.[i]

[26] "And I will send you the Divine Encourager[j] from the very presence of my Father. He will come to you, the Spirit of Truth, emanating from the Father, and he will speak[k] to you about me. [27] And you will tell everyone the truth about me, for you have walked with me from the start."

Jesus Warns His Disciples

16 "I have told you this so that you would not surrender to confusion or doubt.[l] [2] For you will be excommunicated from the synagogues, and

---

a 15:16 The Aramaic is "I have invited you" (as dinner guests).

b 15:16 This could mean "to go on into maturity" (character), or "to go into the world" (ministry). However, the "choosing" and "commissioning" infers the latter.

c 15:16 Or "in my name."

d 15:20 Or "redeemer." See John 13:16.

e 15:21 Or "because of my name."

f 15:22 As translated from the Aramaic. The Greek is "spoken these things."

g 15:22 As translated from the Aramaic.

h 15:25 Or "written in their law."

i 15:25 See Pss. 35:19; 69:4. The Greek text can also be translated "They hated my undeserved gifts."

j 15:26 Or "Redeemer from the curse." See the second footnote on John 14:16–17.

k 15:26 Or "provide evidence."

l 16:1 Or "so that you won't have a trap laid for you." The Aramaic is translated "so that you will not be crushed."

634 ◊ JOHN 16

a time is coming when you will be put to death by misguided ones who will presume to be doing God a great service by putting you to death.[a] ³ And they will do these things because they don't know anything about the Father or me. ⁴ I'm telling you this now so that when their time comes you will remember that I foretold it. I didn't tell you this in the beginning because I was still with you. ⁵ But now that I'm about to leave you and go back to join the One who sent me, you need to be told. Yet, not one of you are asking me where I'm going. ⁶ Instead your hearts are filled with sadness because I've told you these things. ⁷ But here's the truth: It's to your advantage that I go away, for if I don't go away the Divine Encourager[b] will not be released to you. But after I depart, I will send him to you. ⁸ And when he comes, he will expose sin and prove that the world is wrong about God's righteousness and his judgments.

⁹ "'Sin,' because they refuse to believe in who I am.

¹⁰ "God's 'righteousness,' because I'm going back to join the Father and you'll see me no longer.

¹¹ "And 'judgment' because the ruler of this dark world has already received his sentence.[c]

¹² "There is so much more I would like to say to you, but it's more than you can grasp at this moment. ¹³ But when the truth-giving Spirit comes, he will unveil the reality of every truth[d] within you. He won't speak his own message, but only what he hears from the Father, and he will reveal prophetically to you what is to come. ¹⁴ He will glorify me on the earth, for he will receive from me what is mine[e] and reveal it to you. ¹⁵ Everything that belongs to the Father belongs to me—that's why I say that the Divine Encourager will receive what is mine and reveal it to you. ¹⁶ Soon you won't see me any longer, but then, after a little while, you will see me *in a new way*."[f]

¹⁷ Some of the disciples asked each other, "What does he mean, 'Soon you won't see me,' and, 'A little while after that and you will see me in a new way'? And what does he mean, 'Because I'm going to my Father'?" ¹⁸ So they kept on

---

a 16:2 The Aramaic is "those who kill you will think they are presenting a holy offering to God."

b 16:7 Or "the Redeemer of the curse." See the second footnote on John 14:16–17.

c 16:11 In essence, "sin . . . righteousness . . . and judgment are related to three persons." Sin is related to Adam, for it was through Adam that sin entered humanity (Rom. 5:12). Righteousness is related to Christ, because it comes through him, and he has become our righteousness (1 Cor. 1:30). Judgment is related to Satan, for the pure works of Christ bring judgment to the works of Satan. If we do not embrace Christ's righteousness, we will share Satan's judgment.

d 16:13 The Greek word for "truth" is "reality," not "doctrine." It is the application of truth that matters, not just a superficial knowledge.

e 16:14 As translated from the Aramaic. Or "he plants what is mine and shows it to you."

f 16:16 Jesus uses two different Greek words for "see" in this verse. The Aramaic adds "because I go to my Father."

repeating, "What's the meaning of 'a little while'? We have no clue what he's talking about!"

[19] Jesus knew what they were thinking, and it was obvious that they were anxious to ask him what he had meant,[a] so he spoke up and said, [20] "Let me make it quite clear: You will weep and be overcome with grief *over what happens to me.* The unbelieving world will be happy, while you will be filled with sorrow. But know this, your sadness will turn into joy *when you see me again!* [21] Just like a woman giving birth experiences intense labor pains in delivering her baby,[b] yet after the child is born she quickly forgets what she went through because of the overwhelming joy of knowing that a new baby has been born into the world.

[22] "So will you also pass through a time of intense sorrow *when I am taken from you,* but you will see me again! And then your hearts will burst with joy, with no one being able to take it from you![c] [23] For here is eternal truth: When that time comes you won't need to ask me for anything, but instead you will go directly to the Father and ask him for anything you desire and he will give it to you, because of your relationship with me.[d] [24] Until now you've not been bold enough to ask the Father for a single thing in my name,[e] but now you can ask, and keep on asking him! And you can be sure that you'll receive what you ask for, and your joy will have no limits!

[25] "I have spoken to you using figurative language,[f] but the time is coming when I will no longer teach you with veiled speech, but I will teach you about the Father with your eyes unveiled.[g] [26] And I will not need to ask the Father on your behalf, for you'll ask him directly because of your new relationship with me.[h] [27] For the Father tenderly loves you, because you love me and believe that I've come from God. [28] I came to you sent from the Father's presence, and I entered into the created world, and now I will leave this world and return to the Father's side."

[29] His disciples said, "At last you're speaking to us clearly and not using veiled speech and metaphors! [30] Now we understand that you know everything there is

---

a 16:19 Or "Are you asking each other what I meant when I told you, 'A little while and you will see me no more, and then after a little while you will see me'?"

b 16:21 Or "because her time [for delivery] has come." It is fascinating that Jesus speaks of the disciples in the terms of giving birth. Christ is being formed within us (Gal. 4:19). The church continues in "labor" today so that Jesus can be seen again through us. See Rev. 12:1–5.

c 16:22 Jesus is referring to the prophecy of Isa. 66:7, 14.

d 16:23 Or "he will give it to you in my name."

e 16:24 To ask in Jesus' name is to ask in the name of "I AM." We take all the fullness of Jesus (his name, his glory, his virtue) as the "I AM" of Ex. 3:14—because of our relationship with him.

f 16:25 This is the Greek word, *paroimiais,* which can mean obscure figurative speech, analogies, parables, proverbs, metaphors, or allegory. These were all utilized as Jesus' preferred teaching method while on earth. See v. 29 and Matt. 13:34.

g 16:25 As translated from the Aramaic.

h 16:26 Or "in my name."

to know, and we don't need to question you further. And everything you've taught us convinces us that you have come directly from God!"

³¹ Jesus replied, "Now you finally believe in me. ³² And the time has come when you will all be scattered, and each one of you will go your own way, leaving me alone!ᵃ Yet I am never alone, for the Father is always with me. ³³ And everything I've taught you is so that the peace which is in me will be in you and will give you great confidence as you rest in me. For in this unbelieving world you will experience trouble and sorrows, but you must be courageous,ᵇ for I have conquered the world!"ᶜ

Jesus Finished the Father's Work

17 This is what Jesus prayed as he looked up into heaven,
"Father, the time has come.
Unveil the glorious splendor of your Sonᵈ
so that I will magnify your glory!
² You have already given me authorityᵉ
over all people so that I may give
the gift of eternal life to all those that you have given to me.
³ Eternal life means to know and experience you
as the only true God,ᶠ
and to know and experience Jesus Christ,
as the Son whom you have sent.
⁴ I have glorified you on the earth
by faithfully doing everything you've told me to do.
⁵ So my Father, restore me back to the glory
that we shared together when we were face-to-face
before the universe was created."ᵍ

Jesus Prays for His Disciples

⁶ "Father, I have manifested who you really are
and I have revealed youʰ to the men and women

---

a 16:32 This will fulfill the prophecy of Zech. 13:7.
b 16:33 Or "cheer up!"
c 16:33 Jesus has taken away the power this world has to defeat us and has conquered it for us. Peace is resting in his victory.
d 17:1 Or "Glorify your Son!" The Father unveiled the glory of his Son on the cross, by the empty tomb, through his ascension into heaven, and by the mighty outpouring of the Holy Spirit upon his church.
e 17:2 The Aramaic is translated "responsibility."
f 17:3 The Aramaic is translated "the God of truth." This alludes to Deut. 6:4.
g 17:5 The Aramaic is translated "before the light of the universe."
h 17:6 Or "I have made known your name." The Greek word, phaneroo, means "to make visible," "to manifest," "to reveal," and "to be plainly recognized." (See Strong's Concordance, Gr. 5319.)

that you gave to me. [a]
They were yours, and you gave them to me,
and they have fastened your Word firmly to their hearts.
[7] And now at last they know that everything I have is a gift from you,
[8] And the very words you gave to me to speak
I have passed on to them.
They have received your words
and *carry them in their hearts*.
They are convinced that I have come from your presence,
and they have fully believed that you sent me to represent you.
[9] So with deep love, [b] I pray for my disciples.
I'm not asking on behalf of the unbelieving world, [c]
but for those who belong to you,
those you have given me.
[10] For all who belong to me now belong to you.
And all who belong to you now belong to me as well,
and my glory is revealed through *their surrendered lives*. [d]

[11] "Holy Father, I am about to leave this world [e]
to return and be with you,
but my disciples will remain here.
So I ask that by the power of your name,
protect each one that you have given me,
and watch over them so that they will be united
as one, even as we are one.
[12] While I was with these that you have given me, [f]
I have kept them safe by your name that you have given me.
Not one of them is lost,
except the one that was destined to be lost, [g]

---

a 17:6 Or "you gave to me out of the world."
b 17:9 The Aramaic can be translated "I desired (loved) them." The Greek is "I pray for them." The translator has chosen to include both concepts.
c 17:9 This is emphatic in the Greek sentence structure. How could it be that Jesus loves the world and gave himself for the sin of the world, yet emphasizes that he is praying for his disciples and not praying for the world? Jesus' coming into the world brings life to those who believe and judgment to those who do not. The implication is that the key to reaching the world is the life, maturity, unity, and love of the disciples. This does not mean that Jesus doesn't love the world, but that the world will only be reached when the disciples come into the fullness of Christ and in unity of the faith. This is what consumes the heart of Jesus as he prays for them before the cross.
d 17:10 Or "I am glorified in them."
e 17:11 Or "I am no longer in the world."
f 17:12 See footnote on v. 11.
g 17:12 Or "son of perdition," which is a Semitic idiom that means "to be destined to

so that the Scripture would be fulfilled.

[13] "But now I am returning to you so Father,
I pray[a] that they will experience
and enter into my joyous delight in you[b]
so that it is fulfilled in them and overflows.
[14] I have given them your message
and that is why the unbelieving world hates them.
For their allegiance is no longer to this world
because I am not of this world.
[15] I am not asking that you remove them from the world,
but I ask that you guard their hearts from evil,[c]
[16] For they no longer belong to this world any more than I do.

[17] "Your Word is truth! So make them holy by the truth.
[18] I have commissioned them to represent me
just as you commissioned me to represent you.
[19] And now I dedicate myself to them as a holy sacrifice
so that they will live as fully dedicated to God
and be made holy by your truth."[d]

Jesus Prays for You

[20] "And I ask not only for these disciples,
but also for all those who will one day
believe in me through their message.
[21] I pray for them all to be joined together as one[e]
even as you and I, Father, are joined together as one.
I pray for them to become one with us[f]
so that the world will recognize that you sent me.
[22] For the very glory you have given to me I have given them
so that they will be joined together as one

---

destruction." This obviously refers to Judas, the betrayer. See also Ps. 41:9; John 6:70.

a 17:13 Or "I speak these things [this prayer] in the world [before I leave]."

b 17:13 This "delight" is more than happiness. It is the complete satisfaction that comes in knowing that our lives are pleasing to the Father and that we fulfill his desires on the earth. This is the delight that Jesus shares with us and prays that we would experience.

c 17:15 Or "the Evil One" (or "Satan"). The implication is that the disciples of Jesus will influence the systems of this world but need to be preserved from evil influences.

d 17:19 The Aramaic can be translated "And in their sight I will glorify [consecrate] myself, so that they will be glorified [consecrated] by the truth."

e 17:21 Jesus prayed for the birth of the church, made up of Jewish and non-Jewish believers.

f 17:21 Or "in us."

and experience the same unity that we enjoy.[a]

23 You live fully in me and now I live fully in them
so that they will experience perfect unity,[b]
and the world will be convinced that you have sent me,
for they will see that you love each one of them
with the same passionate love that you have for me.

24 "Father, I ask that you allow everyone that you have given to me
to be with me where I am![c]
Then they will see my full glory—
the very splendor you have placed upon me
because you have loved me even before the beginning of time.

25 "You are my righteous Father,[d]
but the unbelieving world has never known you
in the perfect way that I know you!
And all those who believe in me[e]
also know that you have sent me!

26 I have revealed to them who you are[f]
and I will continue to make you even more real to them,
so that they may experience the same endless love
that you have for me,
for your love will now live in them, even as I live in them!"

Jesus in the Garden of Gethsemane

18 After Jesus finished this prayer; he left with his disciples and went across the Kidron Valley[g] to a place where there was a garden.[h] 2 Judas, the traitor, knew where this place was, for Jesus had gone there often with his disciples.

---

a 17:22 It is important to note that the key to unity among believers is experiencing the glory of God that Jesus has imparted to us. As one with God through faith in Christ, he shares his glory with us, since we are not "another," but have been made one with the triune God through the blood of Jesus. See Isa. 42:8.

b 17:23 The Aramaic is "shrink into one." When we see Jesus in one another, our vaulted opinions of ourselves will shrink.

c 17:24 This is experienced not only after we die, but also took place when the ascended Christ took us up into the heavenly realm and seated us at his side with the Father. See Eph. 2:6; Col. 3:1–4.

d 17:25 As translated from the Aramaic.

e 17:25 The Greek is simply "these" (disciples).

f 17:26 Or "I have revealed your name to them."

g 18:1 The Kidron ravine is the path David took when he was forced to flee Jerusalem because of the betrayal of his son Absalom. David went up the Mount of Olives weeping. Jesus went up also in sorrow. David went up to save himself; Jesus went up to save the people of the world.

h 18:1 This is the garden of Gethsemane, which means "olive press." Jesus not only went to

[3] The Pharisees and the leading priests had given Judas a large detachment[a] of Roman soldiers and temple police to seize Jesus. Judas guided them to the garden, all of them carrying torches and lanterns and armed *with swords and spears.*[b] [4] Jesus, knowing full well what was about to happen, went out to the garden entrance to meet them. Stepping forward, he asked, "Who are you looking for?"

[5] "Jesus of Nazareth,"[c] they replied. (Now Judas, the traitor, was among them.)

He replied, "I am he."

[6] And the moment Jesus spoke the words, "I am he," the mob fell backward to the ground![d]

[7] So once more, Jesus asked them, "Who are you looking for?"

As they stood up, they answered, "Jesus of Nazareth."

[8] Jesus replied, "I told you that I am the one you're looking for, so if you want me, let these men go home."[e]

[9] He said this to fulfill the prophecy he had spoken, "Father, not one of those you have given me has been lost."[f]

[10] Suddenly, Peter took out his sword and struck the high priest's servant, slashing off his right ear![g] The servant's name was Malchus.[h]

---

the garden to pray, but to be captured. He knew full well the Father's plan. Just as Adam fell in a garden of paradise, Jesus stood faithful in a garden of betrayal.

a   18:3 The Greek and Aramaic word used for this company of soldiers implies quite a large number, up to five to six hundred men sent to arrest Jesus. Even his enemies knew his power was great.

b   18:3 The Greek word is "foot-soldiers' weapons."

c   18:5 Or "Jesus, the Nazarene." This is the Aramaic word *nussraya,* which means "victorious one," or "heir of a powerful family." The Hebrew word for "Nazareth" comes from the root word *netzer,* which means "branch." See Isa. 4:2; 11:1.

d   18:6 This was a stunning event as the great I Am spoke his name before those who sought to seize him. It is obvious in the text that they did not trip over each other in surprise, for every one of these strong men fell backward to the ground by the power of God. Jesus was in charge that night as the captain of the host of the Lord. They could not seize him unless he permitted them to do so. What a wonderful Savior who willingly submitted to the hands of cruel men to bring us the gift of salvation.

e   18:8 "These men" were the eleven disciples who were with Jesus in the garden.

f   18:9 See John 6:39; 17:12.

g   18:10 This event is a vivid picture of what happens when we act impetuously and in anger. We hinder people's ability to hear our message (we cut off their ear) when we walk in angry offense toward others.

h   18:10 Malchus' name means "king." Perhaps at the moment of healing his ear, Jesus personally revealed himself to Malchus in a supernatural way, the King who healed a king. Jesus is the true servant to the High Priest. We can imagine Jesus reaching out his hand to help Malchus up. And in an instant, Malchus believes. Malchus' ears, both of them, are healed.

[11] Jesus ordered Peter, "Put your sword away! Do you really think I will avoid the suffering[a] which my Father has assigned to me?"

Jesus Is Taken before Annas

[12] Then the soldiers and their captain, along with the Jewish officers, seized Jesus and tied him up. [13] They took him first to Annas,[b] as he was the father-in-law of Caiaphas, the high priest that year.[c] [14] Caiaphas was the one who had persuaded the Jewish leaders that it would be better off to have one person die for the sake of the people.[d]

Peter's First Denial

[15] Peter and another disciple followed along behind them as they took Jesus into the courtyard of Annas' palace. Since the other disciple was well known to the high priest, he entered in,[e] [16] but Peter was left standing outside by the gate. Then the other disciple came back out to the servant girl who was guarding the gate and convinced her to allow Peter inside. [17] As he passed inside, the young servant girl guarding the gate took a look at Peter and said to him, "Aren't you one of his disciples?"

He denied it, saying, "No! I'm not!"

[18] Now because it was cold, the soldiers and guards made a charcoal fire and were standing around it to keep warm. So Peter huddled there with them around the fire.

Jesus Interrogated by Annas

[19] The high priest interrogated Jesus concerning his disciples[f] and his teachings.

[20] Jesus answered Annas' questions by saying, "I have said nothing in secret. At all times I have taught openly and publicly in a synagogue, in the temple courts, and wherever the people assemble. [21] Why would you ask me for evidence to condemn me? Ask those who have heard what I've taught. They can tell you."

---

a 18:11 Or "Shall I not drink the cup (of suffering) assigned me by the Father?"

b 18:13 John is the only Gospel account that inserts this pre-trial meeting with Annas. He was the retired and illegal high priest.

c 18:13 Or "close friend to the high priest." The priesthood was corrupt in the time of Jesus. It was not proper for two men to hold the office of high priest at the same time, as it apparently was done in Jesus' day. They both were called high priest in this narrative. See John 18:19, 24.

d 18:14 See John 11:49–51.

e 18:15 Although it is impossible to determine who exactly was this other disciple, some have surmised it was John himself, or Nicodemus. If it was Nicodemus, as a leader among the Pharisees, this would explain his inclusion into the proceedings taking place that night.

f 18:19 It is interesting that Annas was concerned about Jesus' disciples. The religious spirit is always concerned with impressive numbers and influence. Jesus only had twelve disciples who were always with him.

²²Just then one of the guards standing near Jesus punched him in the face with his fist *ᵃ* and said, "How dare you answer the high priest like that!"

²³Jesus replied, "If my words are evil, then prove it. But if I haven't broken any laws, then why would you hit me?"

²⁴Then Annas sent Jesus, still tied up, across the way to the high priest Caiaphas.

Peter's Second and Third Denials

²⁵Meanwhile, Peter was still standing in the courtyard by the fire. And one of the guards standing there said to him, "Aren't you one of his disciples? I know you are!" Peter swore *ᵇ* and said, "I am not his disciple!" ²⁶But one of the servants of the high priest, a relative to the man whose ear Peter had cut off, looked at him and said, "Wait! Didn't I see you out there in the garden with Jesus?" ²⁷Then Peter denied it the third time and said, "No!"—and at that very same moment, a rooster crowed nearby.

Pilate Questions Jesus' Arrest

²⁸Before dawn they took Jesus from his trial before Caiaphas to the Roman governor's palace. *ᶜ* Now the Jews refused to go into the Roman governor's residence to avoid ceremonial defilement before eating the Passover meal. ²⁹So Pilate came outside where they waited and asked them pointedly, "Tell me, what exactly is the accusation *ᵈ* that you bring against this man? What has he done?"

³⁰They answered, "We wouldn't be coming here to hand over *ᵉ* this 'criminal' to you if he wasn't guilty of some wrongdoing!"

³¹Pilate said, "Very well, then you take him yourselves and go pass judgment on him according to your Jewish laws!"

But the Jewish leaders complained and said, "We don't have legal authority to put anyone to death. *You should have him crucified!*" *ᶠ* ³²(This was to fulfill the words of Jesus when he predicted the manner of death that he would die.)

---

a 18:22 The Greek is simply "struck him." This could have been with a rod, for the verb has an etymological connection to the word for "rod." Most translators have chosen to use, "struck [or "slapped"] with his hand." Regardless, Jesus was beaten everywhere he went that night and the next morning until he was finally crucified.

b 18:25 As translated from the Aramaic. This is a very strong word that can also be translated "blasphemed." God's loving grace forgave Peter's sin—and our sin.

c 18:28 The Greek is *Praetorium*, which is the transliteration of the Latin word meaning "general's tent." It became used for the Roman governor's official residence.

d 18:29 The Aramaic word for "accusation" is similar to the word *devil* ("accuser"). Pilate is saying, "What the devil do you have against this man?"

e 18:30 The Aramaic word for "hand over" can also be translated "betray."

f 18:31 Implied in the context and made explicit to clarify the illegality of the Jews to crucify Jesus. The Jewish law permitted death by stoning, not by crucifixion. The Scriptures had prophesied that he would be pierced and crucified. This was the cruel manner of death

Pilate Interrogates Jesus

[33] Upon hearing this, Pilate went back inside his palace and summoned Jesus. Looking him over, Pilate asked him, "Are you really the king of the Jews?"

[34] Jesus replied, "Are you asking because you really want to know,[a] or are you only asking this because others have said it about me?"

[35] Pilate responded, "Only a Jew would care about this; do I look like a Jew? It's your own people and your religious leaders that have handed you over to me. So tell me, Jesus, what have you done wrong?"

[36] Jesus looked at Pilate and said, "The royal power of my kingdom realm doesn't come from this world. If it did, then my followers would be fighting to the end to defend me from the Jewish leaders. My kingdom realm authority is not[b] from this realm."

[37] Then Pilate responded, "Oh, so then you are a king?"

"You are right." Jesus said, "I was born a King, and I have come into this world to prove what truth really is. And everyone who loves the truth[d] will receive my words."

[38] Pilate looked at Jesus and said, "What is truth?"[e]

As silence filled the room, Pilate went back out to where the Jewish leaders were waiting and said to them, "He's not guilty. I couldn't even find one fault with him.[f] [39] Now, you do know that we have a custom that I release one prisoner every year at Passover—shall I release your king—the king of the Jews?"[g]

[40] They shouted out over and over, "No, not him! Give us Barabbas!"[h] (Now Barabbas was a robber and a troublemaker.)

---

used by the Romans to execute the worst of criminals. For this reason they wanted Pilate to order his crucifixion. See John 12:32–34.

a 18:34 The Aramaic is "Have you spoken this from your soul?"

b 18:36 The Aramaic is "not yet from here."

c 18:36 The Greek text is not "world," but literally "this side," or "this realm." The Aramaic word used here can be translated "not of this age."

d 18:37 Or "everyone who is not deaf to the truth." The Aramaic is "everyone who came from the truth."

e 18:38 The Aramaic could be translated "Who is truth?" or, "Who is the true prince?" This skepticism is still voiced today in postmodernism.

f 18:38 As translated from the Aramaic.

g 18:39 Pilate was not a saint. He was considered to be a corrupt and violent leader who would execute people without a trial. (Philo, De Legatione ad Caium, ed. Mangey, ii.590). He stole money from the temple treasury and brought pagan statues into Jerusalem, which caused riots and death to many. It was reported by the church father, Eusebius, (History Eccl. ii 7) that he was later banished to Vienna in Gaul, where he committed suicide.

h 18:40 Barabbas is an Aramaic name that means "son of the father." He becomes a picture of every son of Adam, our father. Some believe this is a figure of speech, a nickname for one who has no known father, an illegitimate son. Both in Greek and Aramaic the word for "thief" or "robber" can also mean one who leads an insurrection.

Jesus Is Flogged

19 Then Pilate ordered Jesus to be brutally beaten with a whip of leather straps embedded with metal.[a] ²And the soldiers also wove thorn-branches into a crown and set it on his head and placed a purple[b] robe over his shoulders. ³Then, one by one, they came in front of him to mock him by saying, "Hail, to the king of the Jews!" And one after the other, they repeatedly punched him in the face.[c]

⁴Once more Pilate went out and said to the Jewish officials, "I will bring him out once more so that you know that I've found nothing wrong with him." ⁵So when Jesus emerged, *bleeding,* wearing the purple robe and the crown of thorns on his head, Pilate said to them, "Look at him! Here is your man!"[d]

⁶No sooner did the high priests and the temple guards see Jesus that they all shouted in a frenzy, "Crucify him! Crucify him!"

Pilate replied, "You take him then and nail him to a cross yourselves! I told you—he's not guilty! I find no reason to condemn him."

⁷The Jewish leaders shouted back, "But we have the Law! And according to our Law, he must die,[e] because he claimed to be the Son of God!"

⁸Then Pilate was greatly alarmed[f] when he heard that Jesus claimed to be the Son of God! ⁹So he took Jesus back inside and said to him, "Where have you come from?" But once again, silence filled the room. ¹⁰Perplexed, Pilate said, "Are you going to play deaf? Don't you know that I have the power to grant you your freedom or nail you to a tree?"

¹¹Jesus answered, **"You would have no power over me at all, unless it was given to you from above. This is why the one who betrayed[g] me is guilty of an even greater sin."**

¹²From then on Pilate tried to find a way out of the situation and to set him free, but the Jewish authorities shouted him down: "If you let this man go,

---

a 19:1 This leather whip, embedded with sharpened pieces of bone and metal, was known as "the scorpion." Historians record that many people never survived this cruel flogging. The whips were known to break open the flesh and cut through muscle and sinew all the way to the bone. It was his love for you that enabled him to endure such treatment.

b 19:2 The color purple has long symbolized royalty. Purple's elite status stems from the rarity and cost of the dye originally used to produce it. Jesus is the true king for all eternity.

c 19:3 Or "they slapped his face" (Aramaic). He turned the other cheek and they slapped him on both sides of his face. See Isa. 53:5–7.

d 19:5 See Zech. 6:12.

e 19:7 They are most likely referring to Lev. 24:16.

f 19:8 The Aramaic is "his soul collapsed!"

g 19:11 Or "handed me over." This is the same Greek verb translated "betray" in John 6:71. It would obviously point to Judas. However, some expositors believe it was Caiaphas who handed over Jesus to Pilate, and is referred to here. But in fact, it was the evil spirits of darkness who were controlling Pilate and moving in the hearts of all involved to crucify Jesus. These dark powers would be the ones to experience the tremendous judgment unleashed on them by the power of the cross and resurrection.

you're no friend of Caesar! Anyone who declares himself a king is an enemy of the emperor!" ᵃ

¹³ So when Pilate heard this threat, he relented and had Jesus, *who was torn and bleeding,* brought outside. Then he went up the elevated stone platform and took his seat on the judgment bench—which in Aramaic is called Gabbatha, ᵇ or "The Bench." ¹⁴ And it was now almost noon. And it was the same day they were preparing to slay the Passover lambs. ᶜ

Then Pilate said to the Jewish officials, "Look! Here is your king!"

¹⁵ But they screamed out, "Take him away! Take him away and crucify him!"

Pilate replied, "Shall I nail your king to a cross?"

The high priests answered, "We have no other king but Caesar!"

¹⁶ Then Pilate handed Jesus over to them. So the soldiers seized him and took him away to be crucified.

Jesus Is Crucified

¹⁷ Jesus carried his own cross out of the city to the place called "The Skull," which in Aramaic is Golgotha. ¹⁸ And there they nailed him to the cross. He was crucified, along with two others, one on each side with Jesus in the middle. ¹⁹⁻²⁰ Pilate had them post a sign over the cross, which was written in three languages—Aramaic, Latin, and Greek. Many of the people of Jerusalem read the sign, for he was crucified near the city. The sign stated: "Jesus of Nazareth, the King of the Jews." ᵈ

---

a 19:12 In essence, these words were a form of blackmail as the Jewish authorities were reminding Pilate that it would ruin his career if he pardoned Jesus. The term "friend of Caesar" was an honorific title given only to the ruling wealthy class of Romans who would have access to the emperor's court. Many of these friends of Caesar were senators and members of the Equestrian Order, known also as the Knights. Pilate's position was a political appointment due to his being a member of this elite class of Romans who took an oath of loyalty to Caesar. They were, in effect, threatening to inform Rome that Pilate was allowing treason in Caesar's empire. As one historian remarked, "One false move and his appointment would be cancelled and his career finished" (P. Barnett, *Jesus and the Rise of Early Christianity: A History of New Testament Times,* Illinois: InterVarsity, 1999, p. 147). This overruled Pilate's desire to set Jesus free. He went on to condemn him to death. To place your career over Jesus is never wise.

b 19:13 *Gabbatha* is an Aramaic compound word meaning "on the side of the house" (*gab,* "on the side," and *batha,* "the house"). This would be a stone bench that was used by Pilate to issue sentence. See 2 Chron. 7:3; Ezek. 40:17.

c 19:14 Jesus, our Passover Lamb, would be crucified at the very moment Jewish priests were slaughtering lambs in the temple. See Ex. 12:6. Because there were so many lambs to be killed, the priesthood in that day extended the time of slaughter from noon to twilight— the very hours Jesus was on the cross.

d 19:19–20 Aramaic was the language of the common people in Israel. Hebrew ceased to be their spoken language after 450 BC, after the Jews returned from Babylon. Aramaic remained the language of Israel for nearly one thousand years. Latin was the official language of the Roman Empire. The inscription was also in Greek, for the Alexandrian Jews

²¹ But the chief priests of the Jews ᵃ said to Pilate, "You must change the sign! Don't let it say, 'King of the Jews,' but rather—'he claimed to be the King of the Jews!'" ²² Pilate responded, "What I have written will remain!"

²³ Now when the soldiers crucified Jesus, they divided up his clothes into four shares, one for each of them. But his tunic was seamless, woven from the top to the bottom ᵇ as a single garment. ²⁴ So the soldiers said to each other, "Don't tear it—let's throw dice ᶜ to see who gets it!" The soldiers did all of this not knowing they fulfilled the Scripture that says, "They divided my garments among them and gambled for my garment." ᵈ

²⁵ Mary, Jesus' mother, was standing next to his cross, along with Mary's sister, Mary the wife of Clopas, and Mary Magdalene. ᵉ ²⁶ So when Jesus looked down and saw the disciple he loved standing with her, he said, **"Mother, ᶠ look—John ᵍ will be a son to you."** ²⁷ Then he said, **"John, look—she will be a mother to you!"** From that day on, John accepted Mary into his home *as one of his own family.* ʰ

---

who had come to observe the Passover in Jerusalem would be unable to read Aramaic. The words were, "Jesus, the Nazarene, King of the Jews." The first letters of each of the four words written on the sign in Aramaic (Hebrew) were: Y-H-W-H (*Y'shua Hanozri Wumelech a Yehudim*). To write these letters, YHWH (also known as the tetragrammaton), was the Hebrew form of writing the sacred name "Yahweh." No wonder the chief priests were so offended by this sign and insisted that Pilate change it. This was a sign given to Israel, for over Jesus' head on the cross was written, Y-H-W-H! God, the Savior, bled to death for you.

a 19:21 There is obvious irony in the Greek text of these two phrases, "King of the Jews" and "the chief priests of the Jews." This is the only place John describes the priests in this way.

b 19:23 The Aramaic could be translated "his tunic was entirely woven from above." Jesus' tunic was an emblem of his perfect holiness and righteousness as one who came "from above." As believers, we are now robed in that seamless garment of righteousness in Christ.

c 19:24 Or "cast lots." See also v. 25.

d 19:24 See Ps. 22:18.

e 19:25 Many scholars believe that Mary's sister (Jesus' aunt) was Salome. This would mean she was the wife of Zebedee and the mother of Jacob (James) and John (the writer of the Gospel of John). Furthermore, that would mean that Jacob (James) and John were cousins of Jesus. See also Matt. 27:56; Mark 15:40.

f 19:26 Or "woman."

g 19:26 Although unnamed, this was most certainly John the apostle. John, the apostle of love, was the only one of the Twelve who stood near the cross and witnessed the crucifixion. Love doesn't quit, run away, or hide from pain. It endures all things, overcomes all things, and empowers us in all things. John didn't run from the suffering of the Savior. We must be those who will stand next to Jesus even if the entire world is against us.

h 19:27 Mary would be nearly fifty years old and a widow. What tenderness we see with Jesus toward his mother! Moments before his death, Jesus thought about Mary and her long journey back to Nazareth and that no one would be there to provide for her. Jesus deeply honored his mother.

Jesus' Death on the Cross

[28] Jesus knew that his mission was accomplished, and to fulfill the Scripture,[a] Jesus said: "I am thirsty."

[29] A jar of sour wine was sitting nearby, so they soaked a sponge with it and put it on the stalk of hyssop[b] and raised it to his lips. [30] When he had sipped the sour wine, he said, **"It is finished, my bride!"**[c] Then he bowed his head and surrendered his spirit to God.

[31] The Jewish leaders did not want the bodies of the victims to remain on the cross through the next day, since it was the day of preparation[d] for a very important Sabbath. So they asked Pilate's permission to have the victims' legs broken *to hasten their death*[e] and their bodies taken down before sunset. [32] So the soldiers broke the legs of the two men who were nailed there. [33] But when they came to Jesus, they realized that he had already died, so they decided not to break his legs. [34] But one of the soldiers took a spear and pierced Jesus' side, and blood and water gushed out.[f]

[35] (I, John,[g] do testify to the certainty of what took place, and I write the truth so that you might also believe.) [36] For all these things happened to fulfill the prophecies of the Scriptures:

---

a 19:28 See Pss. 22:15; 69:21. The Fountain of Living Water now thirsts for the souls of men and women to come to him. He thirsts for your friendship.

b 19:29 The hyssop branch points to the sacrificial death of Jesus. Hyssop is first mentioned in Ex. 12:22 in reference to the application of lamb's blood upon the door posts of the homes of the Hebrews the night of Passover. Hyssop was also used for the cleansing of lepers and points to the cleansing of our souls that happened when Jesus was crucified for sinners (spiritual lepers). See Ps. 51:7; Heb. 9:19.

c 19:30 This is from the Hebrew word *kalah*, a homonym that can mean "fulfilled [completed]," and "bride." Jesus finished the work of our salvation for his bride. The translation has combined both concepts. For a fascinating study of the Hebrew word used for "bride" and "finished," with its universe of meaning, see *Strong's Concordance*, Hb. 3615, 3616, 3617, 3618, and 3634. Although the completed work of salvation was finished on the cross, he continues to work through his church today to extend God's kingdom realm on the earth and glorify the Father through us. He continues to work in us to accomplish all that his cross and resurrection have purchased for us, his bride. His cross fulfilled and finished the prophecies of the Messiah's first coming to the earth. There was nothing written that was not fulfilled and now offered to his bride.

d 19:31 The Aramaic is "because it was Friday."

e 19:31 Breaking their legs would prevent the one on a cross to lift himself up and take a deep breath. The victim would die sooner by suffocation. The Roman practice was to leave the bodies of the victims on the cross for a day or more as a warning to others. See Deut. 21:22–23.

f 19:34 This becomes a picture of the cleansing by blood and the water of the Holy Spirit. However, water and blood both come forth when a baby is born. Christ gave birth on the cross to "sons." He is the everlasting Father (Isa. 9:6), and you must have children to be a Father. We are all born again by the wounded side of Jesus Christ. He not only died for his bride, but he also gave birth to her at the cross.

g 19:35 Or "the person who saw this." Although unnamed, it was John, the author of this narrative, who witnessed and testified to the truth of what happened.

"Not one of his bones will be broken," [a]
[37] and, "They will gaze on the one they have pierced!" [b]

Jesus' Burial

[38] After this, Joseph from the city of Ramah, [c] who was a secret disciple of Jesus for fear of the Jewish authorities, asked Pilate if he could remove the body of Jesus. So Pilate granted him permission to remove the body from the cross. [39] Now Nicodemus, who had once come to Jesus privately at night, accompanied Joseph, and together they carried a significant amount [d] of myrrh and aloes to the cross. [40] Then they took Jesus' body and wrapped it in strips of linen with the embalming spices [e] according to the Jewish burial customs. [41] Near the place where Jesus was crucified was a garden, and in the garden there was a new tomb where no one had yet been laid to rest. [42] And because the Sabbath was approaching, and the tomb was nearby, that's where they laid the body of Jesus. [f]

The Empty Tomb

20 Very early Sunday morning, [g] before sunrise, Mary Magdalene made her way to the tomb. And when she arrived she discovered that the stone that sealed the entrance to the tomb was moved away! [2] So she went running as fast as she could to go tell Peter and the other disciple, the one Jesus loved. [h] She told them, "They've taken the Lord's body from the tomb, and we don't know where he is!"

[3] Then Peter and the other disciple jumped up and ran to the tomb to go see for themselves. [4] They started out together, but the other disciple outran Peter and reached the tomb first. [i] [5] He didn't enter the tomb, but peeked in, and

---

a   19:36 See Ex. 12:46; Ps. 34:20.

b   19:37 See Zech. 12:10.

c   19:38 As translated from the Aramaic. Or *Arimathea* (Greek), which means "heights." This was the likely birthplace of the prophet Samuel. Keep in mind that Joseph may have lost a son the age of Jesus when Herod killed all the babies.

d   19:39 Or "approximately one hundred pounds." Some calculate this as Roman pounds weighing thirty kilograms. Others interpret the one hundred pounds to be closer to a liter, or less than one kilogram, which seems more appropriate considering the cost and weight of these valuable spices.

e   19:40 This was the myrrh and aloes, which were embalming spices.

f   19:42 See Isa. 53:9. Jesus' body was laid on a bed of spices in a garden tomb. Death came upon the first Adam in the garden of Eden, but eternal life surged through the last Adam in the garden of the cross and his tomb. Man fell in a garden, but man now finds life in that empty garden tomb.

g   20:1 Or "On the first day of the week."

h   20:2 This was obviously John the apostle, the author of this Gospel.

i   20:4 How did John outrun Peter to the tomb? Love will always "outrun" curiosity. Some are simply curious to know Jesus, but we must be those who are passionate to experience his love and power.

saw only the linen cloths lying there. ⁶Then Peter came behind him and went right into the tomb. He too noticed the linen cloths lying there, ⁷but the burial cloth that had been on Jesus' head had been rolled up and placed separate from the other cloths.

⁸Then the other disciple who had reached the tomb first went in, and after one look, he believed!ᵃ ⁹For until then they hadn't understood the Scriptures that prophesiedᵇ that he was destined to rise from the dead.ᶜ ¹⁰Puzzled, Peter and the other disciple then left and went back to their homes.

¹¹Mary arrived *back at the tomb*, broken and sobbing. She stooped to peer inside, and through her tears ¹²she saw two angels in dazzling white robes, sitting where Jesus' body had been laid—one at the head and one at the feet!ᵈ

¹³"Dear woman, why are you crying?" they asked.

Mary answered, "They have taken away my Lord, and I don't know where they've laid him."

¹⁴Then she turned around to leave, and there was Jesus standing in front of her, but she didn't realize that it was him!

¹⁵He said to her, "**Dear woman, why are you crying? Who are you looking for?**"

Mary answered, thinking he was only the gardener, "Sir, if you have taken his body somewhere else, tell me, and I will go and . . ."

¹⁶"**Mary,**" Jesus interrupted her.

Turning to face him, she said, "Rabboni!" (Aramaic for "my teacher")

¹⁷Jesus cautioned her, "**Mary, don't hold on to me now, for I haven't yet ascended to God, my Father. And he's not only my Father and God, but now he's your Father and your God! Now go to my brothersᵉ and tell them what I've told you, that I am ascending to my Father—and your Father, to my God—and your God!**"

¹⁸Then Mary Magdalene left to inform the disciples of her encounter with Jesus. "I have seen the Lord!" she told them. And she gave them his message.

---

a 20:8 It was lovers of Jesus that were the first to realize the resurrection of Christ. What did John see that caused him to believe? Perhaps it was the linen burial cloths that had not been unwrapped, but simply were empty. And the cloth that had been wrapped around his head was rolled up and placed aside. Jesus left everything pertaining to the old creation in the tomb, signified by the linen cloths and handkerchief left behind.

b 20:9 Some of these prophecies would include Pss. 2:6–8; 16:10; Isa. 53:10–12; Hos. 6:2; Jonah 1:17.

c 20:9 As translated from the Aramaic.

d 20:12 This becomes a picture of the two golden cherubim engraved on the mercy seat, peering down into the treasures of grace.

e 20:17 This is the first time in John's Gospel that Jesus calls his disciples "brothers." See Heb. 2:10–12.

Jesus Appears to His Disciples

[19] That evening,[a] the disciples gathered together. And because they were afraid of reprisals from the Jewish leaders, they had locked the doors to the place where they met. But suddenly Jesus appeared among them and said,[b] "**Peace to you!**"[c] [20] Then he showed them the wounds of his hands and his side—they were overjoyed to see the Lord with their own eyes!

[21] Jesus repeated his greeting, "**Peace to you!**" And he told them, "**Just as the Father has sent me, I'm now sending you.**" [22] Then, taking a deep breath, he blew[d] on them and said, "**Receive the Holy Spirit.**[e] [23] **I send you to preach the forgiveness**[f] **of sins—and people's sins will be forgiven. But if you don't proclaim the forgiveness of their sins, they will remain guilty.**"[g]

Jesus Appears to Thomas

[24] One of the twelve wasn't present when Jesus appeared to them—it was Thomas, whose nickname was "the Twin." [25] So the disciples informed him, "We have seen the Lord with our own eyes!"

Still unconvinced, Thomas replied, "There's no way I'm going to believe this unless I personally see the wounds of the nails[h] in his hands, touch them with my finger, and put my hand into the wound of his side where he was pierced!"

[26] Then eight days later, Thomas and all the others were in the house together. And even though all the doors were locked, Jesus suddenly stood before them! "**Peace to you,**" he said.

[27] Then, looking into Thomas' eyes, he said, "**Put your finger here in the**

---

a 20:19 Or "That Sunday evening."

b 20:19 Or "came and stood among them."

c 20:19 This is the idiomatic equivalent of saying, "Hello, everyone!"

d 20:22 The Greek word used here does not appear elsewhere in the New Testament, however, it is the same word found in the Septuagint for God "breathed" into Adam's nostrils the breath of life (Gen. 2:7). The beginning of new creation life came from the breath of Jesus. The mighty wind of Acts 2 was for power, the breath Jesus breathed into his disciples in this verse was for life.

e 20:22 Or "accept the Sacred Breath."

f 20:23 Or "removal, acquittal."

g 20:23 Or "If you forgive someone for their sins, their sins will be discharged, but if you retain their sins, their sins will be retained." Jesus was not giving absolute authority to forgive the guilt of sins, for God alone has that right (Mark 2:7), and the apostles at no time assumed that authority. What he gives them, in the context of being his sent ones, is the authority to proclaim the gospel to the nations. If they refuse to go and preach the good news, then people will have no opportunity to believe it. See Acts 10:43–44; 13:38.

h 20:25 The Aramaic is "the blossom of the nails." You can imagine a wide nail head that when struck with a heavy mallet, "blossomed" over the sacred palm of our Lord Jesus. The wound of the nail had imprinted his entire palm. His wounds are like beautiful flowers to the lovers of God.

wounds of my hands. Here—put your hand into my wounded side and see for yourself. Thomas, don't give in to your doubts any longer, just believe!"

²⁸ Then the words spilled out of his heart—"You are my Lord, and you are my God!"

²⁹ Jesus responded, "Thomas, now that you've seen me, you believe. But there are those who have never seen me with their eyes but have believed in me with their hearts, and they will be blessed even more!"

³⁰ Jesus went on to do many more miraculous signs in the presence of his disciples, which are not even included in this book. ³¹ But all that is recorded here is so that you will fully believe *a* that Jesus is the Anointed One, the Son of God, and that through your faith in him you will experience eternal life *b* by the power of his name!

Jesus Appears at Lake Galilee

21 Later, Jesus appeared once again to a group of his disciples by Lake Galilee. *c* ² It happened one day while Peter, Thomas (the Twin), Nathanael (from Cana in Galilee), Jacob, John, *d* and two other disciples were all together. ³ Peter told them, "I'm going fishing." And they all replied, "We'll go with you." *e* So they went out and fished through the night, but caught nothing.

⁴ Then at dawn, Jesus was standing there on the shore, but the disciples didn't realize that it was him! ⁵ He called out to them, saying, "Hey guys! Did you catch any fish?" *f*

"Not a thing," they replied.

⁶ Jesus shouted to them, "Throw your net over the starboard side, and you'll catch some!" And so they did as he said, and they caught so many fish they couldn't even pull in the net!

⁷ Then the disciple whom Jesus loved said to Peter, "It's the Lord!" *g* When Peter heard him say that, he quickly wrapped his outer garment around him, and because he was athletic, *h* he dove right into the lake to

---

a 20:31 Or "never stop believing."

b 20:31 As translated from the Aramaic.

c 21:1 Or "the Sea of Tiberias."

d 21:2 Or in place of Jacob (James) and John, "the sons of Zebedee."

e 21:3 According to Luke 24:49, the disciples were told to wait in Jerusalem for the day they would be clothed with power. These seven apostles were not following what they had been told, and for this reason they caught nothing until Jesus joined them. He became the eighth man.

f 21:5 Or "Have you caught anything to eat?"

g 21:7 It was John, the one whom Jesus loved, that recognized the voice of Jesus. Perhaps it was Peter's discouragement that prevented him from recognizing the voice of the Master. Peter's name was Simon (Hb. *Simeon*), which means "he who hears." Our hearing his voice is hindered when we are confused and filled with doubts.

h 21:7 As translated from the Aramaic. The Greek is literally "because he was naked." This is

go to Jesus! [8] The other disciples then brought the boat to shore, dragging their catch of fish. They weren't far from land, only about a hundred meters. [9] And when they got to shore, they noticed a charcoal fire with some roasted fish and bread. [a] [10] Then Jesus said, "**Bring some of the fish you just caught.**"

[11] So Peter waded into the water and helped pull the net to shore. It was full of many large fish, exactly one hundred and fifty-three, [b] but even with so many fish, the net was not torn.

[12] "**Come, let's have some breakfast,**" Jesus said to them.

And not one of the disciples needed to ask who it was, because every one of them knew it was the Lord. [13] Then Jesus came close to them and served them the bread and the fish. [14] This was the third time Jesus appeared to his disciples after his resurrection.

Jesus Restores Peter

[15] After they had breakfast, Jesus said to Peter, "**Simon, son of John,** [c] **do you burn with love** [d] **for me more than these?**" [e]

Peter answered, "Yes, Lord! You know that I have great affection for you!"

---

very strange and most expositors make quite a case for this not being the case, in spite of the Greek saying he was, indeed, naked. The problem is solved by the Aramaic, which says, "because Peter was athletic, he dove into the water." There is no mention of being "naked" in the Aramaic.

a 21:9 It was while standing next to a fire that Peter denied Christ; now standing next to a fire, Jesus will restore his beloved friend.

b 21:11 This speaks of the great redemption of Christ for all nations and all people. One hundred and fifty-three large fish points to a mighty harvest from among the people groups of the world. This great catch of fish begins the process of inner healing for Peter and the guilt of his denial of Christ. Peter began to follow Jesus because of a great catch of fish (Luke 5:2–10), so Jesus now repeats that miracle, inviting Peter to begin to follow him again.

c 21:15 The Aramaic is "son of the dove." See also vv. 16, 17.

d 21:15 The Aramaic word for "love" is hooba, and is taken from a root word that means "to set on fire." This was the word Jesus would have used to ask Peter, "Do you burn with love for me?" Our love for Jesus must be passionate and kindle a holy flame within our hearts. See Song. 8:6–7.

e 21:15 As often is the case, Jesus' words have more than one meaning. "These" can refer to the fish they had just caught, for Peter was a fisherman and loved to fish. He may have been counting and sorting the fish when Jesus asked him that question. But "these" most likely refers to the other disciples. It was Peter's boast that he loved Jesus more than the others, and though everyone else would leave him, Peter never would. That boast proved empty, as within hours of making the claim, Peter denied he even knew Jesus three times. So Jesus asks Peter three times if he loved him. In essence, Jesus knew how to bring healing to Peter and remove the pain of his denial. Three times Peter denied Jesus, but three times he makes his confession of his deep love for Christ. By the third time, the "crowing rooster" inside Peter had been silenced, and now he was ready to be a shepherd for Jesus' flock.

"Then take care of my lambs," ª Jesus said.

[16] Jesus repeated his question the second time, "Simon, son of John, do you burn with love for me?"

Peter answered, "Yes, my Lord! You know that I have great affection for you!"

"Then take care of my sheep," Jesus said.

[17] Then Jesus asked him again, "Peter, son of John, do you have great affection for me?"

Peter was saddened by being asked the third time ᵇ and said, "My Lord, you know everything. You know that I burn with love for you!"

Jesus replied, "Then feed my lambs! [18] Peter, listen, when you were younger you made your own choices ᶜ and you went where you pleased. But one day when you are old, ᵈ others will tie you up and escort you where you would not choose to go—and you will spread out your arms." ᵉ [19] (Jesus said this to Peter as a prophecy of what kind of death he would die, for the glory of God.) And then he said, "Peter, follow me!"

[20] Then Peter turned and saw that the disciple whom Jesus loved was following them. (This was the disciple who sat close to Jesus at the Last Supper and had asked him, "Lord, who is the one that will betray you?") [21] So when Peter saw him, he asked Jesus, "What's going to happen to him?"

[22] Jesus replied, "If I decide to let him live until I return, what concern is that of yours? You must still keep on following me!"

[23] So the rumor started to circulate among the believers that this disciple wasn't going to die. But Jesus never said that, he only said, "If I let him live until I return, what concern is that of yours?"

ª 21:15 The Aramaic is "feed my rams" (male lambs). This may refer to the other disciples. In v. 16 the Aramaic is simply "sheep." And in v. 17 in Aramaic, Jesus uses the third term, "ewes" (female lambs). Some see in these that Peter was symbolically given charge of three flocks: Jews, Samaritans, and gentiles. Regardless, men and women need to be cared for and fed by the leadership of Christ's church among the nations.

ᵇ 21:17 Three times Peter denied Christ, so Jesus gave him three opportunities to redeem himself.

ᶜ 21:18 Or "you girded yourself."

ᵈ 21:18 The Aramaic is "grayheaded."

ᵉ 21:18 Or "stretch out your hands." This was clearly a hint of the martyrdom Peter would experience in Rome one day, where historians have recorded that Peter was crucified upside down, at his request, because he said that he was unworthy to be crucified in the same way as his Lord. He once said he was willing to die for our Lord Jesus; now Christ promises that will happen.

Conclusion

²⁴ I, John,ᵃ am that disciple who has written these things to testify of the truth, and weᵇ know that what I've documented is accurate. ²⁵ Jesus did countless things that I haven't included here. And if every one of his works were written down *and described one by one,*ᶜ I suppose that the world itself wouldn't have enough room to contain the books that would have to be written!ᵈ

ᵃ 21:24 The evidence both internally and externally clearly points to John as the author of this book, thus the explicit reference here.

ᵇ 21:24 The word we implies that John had conferred with the other disciples, as he has left us an accurate account of the life of Jesus Christ.

ᶜ 21:25 Implied in the Aramaic.

ᵈ 21:25 The Aramaic is very poetic, "The world itself would be emptied out into the books that would be written." An alternate translation of the Aramaic could read "I suppose that forever is still not enough time for all the books to be written!"

ACTS

Introduction

AT A GLANCE

Author: Luke, beloved physician, friend, and companion to Paul
Audience: Theophilus, and all "lovers of God"
Date: mid- to late-AD 60s, though possibly 70–85
Type of Literature: Ancient historical biography
Major Themes: Jesus, the Holy Spirit, salvation, the church, mission, persecution, discipleship, and social dimensions
Outline:

The Church is Born — 1:1–6:7
The Church is Persecuted and Expands — 6:8–9:31
The Church and Mission to the Gentiles — 9:32–12:25
First Missionary Journey and Full Gentile Inclusion — 13:1–15:35
Second and Third Missionary Journeys — 15:36–21:16
Paul's Arrest and Journey to Rome — 21:17–28:31

ABOUT ACTS

The book of Acts provides us with the startling details of how the church of Jesus Christ began. We see the pillar of fire that led Israel through her wilderness years appearing in the upper room and splitting into 120 personal pillars of fire over the heads of the lovers of God. This inspired account of church history will awaken your soul with transforming power and give you courage to be a witness for Christ wherever he sends you!

Although many consider this book to be the "Acts of the Apostles," only two apostles are predominantly mentioned in Acts: Peter and Paul. It would be more accurate to call it the "Acts of the Holy Spirit." God indeed uses men and women to fulfill his purpose—those who are empowered, filled, anointed, and overflowing with the Holy Spirit.

Acts takes up the story where Luke left off. We begin with 120 disciples who had been in a ten-day prayer meeting. It explains the explosive beginning of the outpouring of the Holy Spirit that resulted in tongues, prophecy, miracles, salvations, and the birthing of countless churches. Acts provides us with the story of Paul's three missionary journeys, with many gentile nations hearing the gospel and believers being added to the church. Acts demonstrates the healing miracles of Peter, Paul, and the apostles. We see miracles in answer to prayers, including signs and wonders, and many deliverances. God will do what only God can do—and he is still working in power today through his yielded lovers.

We learn much about the Spirit of God in Acts. Without him there would be no church, no evangelistic impact, no miracles, and no expression of the power of God. For it is not by human means, human power, or human might, but by the limitless power of the Holy Spirit that God's kingdom realm advances on the earth. Jesus builds his church through the Holy Spirit.

PURPOSE

Like the book of Luke, Acts is a quick trip through history—this time the history of Christ's body, the church. His purpose for writing was to offer a vivid portrait of the church's birth by cataloging the historical events in the movement of those who carried the good news about Jesus far and wide throughout the Mediterranean world.

The book of Acts confirms and further defines the identity of the church as the community of people who follow Jesus. Luke paints this picture with the Holy Spirit at the foreground, not background, of the church through the impartation of gifts and the miraculous signs and wonders that are present at every turn. He wants to make crystal clear that the life and work of Jesus continues on in the life and work of the church—which means it continues on in and through you and me!

AUTHOR AND AUDIENCE

Both Luke and Acts were written by a physician named Luke. The material in Luke and Acts covers a period of about sixty years, from the birth of Christ to the birth of the church and the early years of the expansion of God's kingdom realm on the earth. You could consider Acts to be "Luke, Volume 2," since he wrote them both for the lovers of God.

Luke wrote both of his books to someone named Theophilus, which means "lover of God." You are also meant to be the recipient of Luke and Acts, for Luke wrote them to you, the lover of God. You are the most excellent and favored one. He wrote his books for you!

MAJOR THEMES

Jesus, the Exalted, Exclusive Lord of Salvation. Acts opens the way Luke closes: with the ascension and exaltation of Jesus to the right hand of the Father. In essence, the disciples pick up where Jesus left off in seeing the salvation of the world realized. Not only is he the object of the church's affection, Jesus is the content of their message! Luke makes it clear that salvation is found in no one and nothing else but Jesus and his name. Over fifty times the word *name* appears in Acts, signifying that Jesus is the exalted, exclusive Lord of salvation. Through him and him alone we are saved!

The Holy Spirit of Power. There are almost four times as many references to the Holy Spirit in Acts as there are in the book of Luke. If Jesus was front and center in Luke, the Holy Spirit takes center stage in the book of Acts! He is the promised gift dispensed to Christ's disciples and unleashed through them on the world in full power. He enables the church to carry out its mission, empowers them to bear witness to the gospel, and anoints God's people to perform mighty wonders. The Spirit isn't reserved for the select, holy few; he is the promised gift given to all whom God has called and who believe in his Son.

Salvation for the World. The book of Acts makes it clear that "everyone who calls on the name of the Lord will be saved" (2:21). One of the most moving episodes is when Simon Peter is given a vivid dream from heaven. In this dream God essentially says the non-Jewish people Peter thought were unclean are now clean and also invited to partake of the same salvation he and the Jews enjoyed. Later the full council of church leaders realized the same thing: Salvation by grace through faith in Jesus was available to the entire world!

The Church, Mission, and Persecution. In a book about the birth of the church, you'd think you'd find more references to "church" than the twenty-three times the term appears in Acts. That's because Luke has a unique word for the church, that of a community called "the Way." His point is that the church of Jesus is a distinct community who are on a love-mission by the One who loves the world with fiery passion! For Luke, the church isn't merely a "gathering" or "assembly" (the English definitions of the Greek word); she's a movement—a Spirit-fueled movement led by leaders who articulate and apply the power of the gospel. And like most movements, the church faces opposition and persecution, yet triumphs and expands through the Holy Spirit's power.

Discipleship and Ethics in the Church. Discipleship is transformed in Acts because after Pentecost believers are able to follow Jesus in ways they couldn't before they received the Spirit. Because of the Spirit, this community is an active community on an intentional mission to bear witness to the risen Christ in both word and deed. Proclamation is a central focus of this community in Acts. So too is their care for one another and the world around them in the name of Jesus. Such a commitment to the mission and message of Christ finds its expression in all their lifestyle. Through their love for neighbors and God, prayer, perseverance in suffering, watchfulness, faith, joy, and commitment to the lost, we find on-fire disciples of Jesus at every turn!

Women and the Poor. Luke continues the tone set in his Gospel here in Acts, insisting women are fully included in Jesus' work through his community of followers. They receive the Spirit of power in full measure, empowered as witnesses of who Christ is and what he did. In some contexts women teach and prophesy. Luke makes it clear that unlike many social contexts, women aren't dismissed and aren't forgotten. Neither are the poor! While the term *poor* doesn't appear in Acts, we see the church rising up to provide for and care for them. Not only do they pool their resources together to care for the poor in their city, they send food along to other cities in need. They are gospel people who give out of the abundance of grace and mercy they've received from their heavenly Father!

ACTS

To the Lovers of God

1 To Theophilus,[a] the lover of God.

I write to you again, my dear friend, *to give you further details*[b] about the life of our Lord Jesus and all the things that he did and taught.[c]

[2] Just before he ascended into heaven, he left instructions[d] for the apostles he had chosen by the Holy Spirit.[e] [3] After the sufferings of his cross, Jesus appeared alive *many times*[f] to these same apostles over a forty-day period.[g] Jesus proved to them with many convincing signs that he had been resurrected.[h] During these encounters, he taught them the truths of God's kingdom realm [4] and shared meals with them.[i]

Jesus instructed them, "Don't leave Jerusalem, but wait here until you receive the gift I told you about, the gift the Father has promised. [5] For John

---

a   1:1 Some scholars believe that Theophilus could be a symbolic name and not necessarily one individual. This is most likely not written to one individual. When the meaning of his name is translated, the sentence reads, "I wrote to you before, O lover of God." Both Luke and Acts were written to every lover of God.

b   1:1 This account was written by Luke, the human author of the Gospel of Luke. The title Lord Jesus is found only in the Aramaic. The Greek is simply "Jesus."

c   1:1 Although Jesus' work of redemption has been completed for us, there is still the unfinished work of preparing and beautifying his eternal partner, the bride of Christ. With gifts of power his church is continuing what Jesus began to do and teach through evangelism and discipleship. See Matt. 28:19–20; John 21:25; Eph. 4:11–13.

d   1:2 Or "commands."

e   1:2 As translated from the Aramaic. The Greek implies that the "instructions" (commands) he gave them were "by the Holy Spirit."

f   1:3 Jesus appeared to his followers at least eleven times and taught them the mysteries of God's kingdom realm. See also Matt. 13:11.

g   1:3 The number forty is significant, for it speaks of transformation and completeness through testing. Jesus was tempted for forty days, the deluge during Noah's day lasted forty days and nights, Moses met with God for forty days on Sinai, Israel wandered for forty years, and Elijah fasted for forty days. Jesus spent forty days appearing to his disciples to teach them that a day of completeness and transformation had arrived. It took them forty days to comprehend that Christ's kingdom was spiritual, not political.

h   1:3 The world is still waiting to see "many convincing signs" from our lives signifying that we too have been raised from the dead. Spiritual fruit and spiritual power provide these signs.

i   1:4 As translated from the Aramaic.

baptized you in water, but in a few days from now you will be baptized in the Holy Spirit!" [a]

[6] Every time they were gathered together, they asked Jesus, "Lord, is it the time now for you to free Israel and restore our kingdom?"

[7] He answered, "The Father is the one who sets the fixed dates and the times of their fulfillment. You are not permitted to know the timing of all that he has prepared by his own authority. [8] But I promise you this—the Holy Spirit will come upon you and you will be filled with power. [b] And you will be my messengers [c] to Jerusalem, throughout Judea, the distant provinces [d]—even to the remotest places on earth!" [e]

[9] Right after he spoke those words, the disciples saw Jesus lifted into the sky and disappear into a cloud! [f] [10] As they stared into the sky, watching Jesus ascend, two men in white robes suddenly appeared beside them. [11] They told the startled disciples, "Galileans, why are you staring up into the sky? Jesus has been taken from you into heaven, but he will come back the same way that you saw him ascend."

A New Apostle Is Chosen

[12] The disciples left the Mount of Olives and returned to Jerusalem, less than a mile away. [g] [13-14] Arriving there, they went into a large second-floor room to pray. [h] Those present were Peter, John, Jacob, Andrew, Philip, Thomas, Bartholomew, Matthew, Jacob (the son of Alpheus), Simon (the zealot), Judas (the son of Jacob), and a number of women, including Mary, Jesus' mother. His brothers [i]

---

a 1:5 The Aramaic implies that they would be the ones who would do the baptizing: "John baptized you in water, but you will baptize [others] in the Holy Spirit."

b 1:8 Or "You will seize power," or "You will be seized with power."

c 1:8 Or "witnesses." The Greek word can also be translated "martyrs."

d 1:8 Or "Samaria," a term used for a distant province populated by another people group.

e 1:8 See Matt. 24:14.

f 1:9 Or "A cloud came under him and took him up from their sight." The Aramaic is "A cloud accepted him and covered him from their eyes." He did not start from a cloud and ascend to outer space. He started from their visible presence, and disappeared from view in a cloud, ascending by that means into heaven. And when he returns it will be a reverse order. We will see him appearing from out of a cloud and descending back into our visible presence where we can see him and be with him.

g 1:12 The Aramaic is "seven stadia" (furlongs). A furlong is about one-eighth of a mile. The Greek uses a phrase not found in the Septuagint or elsewhere in the Greek New Testament or in any Greek literature: "of a Sabbath having away." It is rendered in most modern translations "a Sabbath's journey."

h 1:13-14 The Greek uses the definite article "the upstairs room." This was where they had met before to have the Last Supper with Jesus. In Mark's Gospel, after the disciples returned from witnessing the ascension, they preached, for Mark is the Gospel of ministry. In Luke, after Jesus' ascension, they praised, and here in Acts they prayed.

i 1:13-14 Or "siblings." Jesus' four brothers are named in Matt. 13:55 and Mark 6:3 as Jacob, Joses (or Joseph), Simon, and Judas. Even though John 7:5 records that early in Jesus'

were there as well. All of them were united in prayer, gripped with one passion,[a] interceding night and day.

[15] During this time Peter stood up among the 120 believers who were gathered and said, [16] "Fellow believers,[b] the Scripture David prophesied by the Holy Spirit concerning Judas had to be fulfilled.[c] Judas betrayed our Lord Jesus and led the mob to the garden to arrest him. [17] He was one of us, and he was chosen to be an apostle just as we were.[d] [18] He earned the wages of his sin,[e] for he fell headfirst, and his belly split open, spilling his intestines on the ground. [19] Everyone in Jerusalem knows what happened to him. That's why the field where he died is called in Aramaic[f] 'Haqel Dama,' that is, 'The Bloody Field.' [20] For it is written in the Psalms:

'Let his house be deserted and become a wasteland.
   No one will live there.'[g]

And also:

'Let another take his ministry.'[h]

[21] "So then, we must choose his replacement from among those who have been with us from the very beginning,[i] [22] from John's baptism until Jesus' ascension. And, like us, he must be a witness of his resurrection."

[23] They proposed two candidates: Joseph, who is also called Barsabbas the Just, and Matthias.[j] [24] They all prayed, "Lord Yahweh,[k] you know the heart of every man.[l] Please give us clear revelation to know which of these two men you have chosen [25] to be an apostle and take Judas' place because he renounced

---

ministry his own brothers did not believe in him, they obviously later repented and received the revelation of the resurrected Christ, their own brother, and believed in him.

a   1:13–14 The Aramaic is "They prayed with one soul."

b   1:16 Or "brothers."

c   1:16 That is, replacing Judas with another to complete the Twelve. See v. 20.

d   1:17 As translated from the Aramaic.

e   1:18 As translated from the Aramaic. The Greek is "He acquired a field with the reward of his wickedness." Judas would have had no time between his betrayal and his suicide to purchase land. This plot of land was likely purchased by the Jewish authorities. They could not use the returned blood money for temple purposes, so instead they purchased a small burial plot for Judas.

f   1:19 Or "in the language of the region." The Greek text is clear that the Jews of Jesus' day spoke Aramaic, the language that Jesus and his apostles taught in. The Greek text transliterates the name of the field into a Greek equivalent for a Greek audience.

g   1:20 See Ps. 69:25.

h   1:20 See Ps. 109:8.

i   1:21 Or "that our Lord Jesus went in and out among us."

j   1:23 Barsabbas means "son of promise." Matthias means "gift of YHWH."

k   1:24 As translated from the Aramaic. The Greek is simply "Lord."

l   1:24 The Greek is "Lord, you are the heart knower of all."

his apostleship to go where he belonged." [a] [26] They cast lots [b] and determined that Matthias was the Lord's choice, so he was added to the eleven apostles.

The Holy Spirit Comes at Pentecost

2 On the day Pentecost was being fulfilled, [c] all the disciples were gathered in one place. [2] Suddenly they heard the sound of a violent blast of wind [d] rushing into the house [e] from out of the heavenly realm. The roar of the wind was so overpowering it was all anyone could bear! [3] *Then all at once a pillar of fire appeared before their eyes.* [f] It separated into tongues of fire that engulfed [g] each one of them. [4] They were all filled and equipped [h] with the Holy Spirit and were inspired [i] to speak in tongues—empowered by the Spirit to speak in languages they had never learned!

[5] Now, at that time there were Jewish worshipers [j] who had emigrated from many different lands to live in Jerusalem. [6] When the people [k] of the city

---

a 1:25 The Aramaic is "go to his place." The Greek is "departed from this life," a euphemism for death.

b 1:26 This was similar to rolling dice. Casting lots is not mentioned again in the New Testament after the Holy Spirit was poured out. The Aramaic reads "They raised up a shaking-free and elevated Matthias," which indicates they shook free from Judas' claim to apostleship and appointed Matthias.

c 2:1 Or "came to be fulfilled." The Greek word means "to fill completely (to be fulfilled)." Pentecost was one of the main feasts of Israel. The name is derived from *pentekostos*, which means "fiftieth," since it was held on the fiftieth day after the Passover Sabbath. It was also known as the Feast of Harvest.

d 2:2 The Aramaic can also be translated "like the roar of a groaning spirit." This mighty wind is for power; the breath of Jesus breathed into his disciples in John 20:22 was for life.

e 2:2 Or "It filled the house." Although most believe this was in an upper room, it is possible to conclude from the Aramaic that it was the House of the Lord (the temple), where they all gathered to celebrate Pentecost. See also Luke 24:53.

f 2:3 This was the pillar of fire that led Israel from bondage into the promised land. The same pillar of fire manifested here to initiate a new beginning from dead religious structures into the powerful life of the Spirit. Each believer received an overpowering flame of fire, signified by the shaft of light that engulfed them. It was as though each one received his own personal pillar of fire that would empower him and lead him throughout his life. This was the promise Jesus gave to his disciples of "the one like me" (John 14:26), who would be sent by the Father and never leave them. Today every believer is indwelt by the Spirit of Christ (Rom. 8:9). This was the birthday of the church of Jesus Christ.

g 2:3 Or "rested over them."

h 2:4 There are two Greek words used here for "filled." In v. 2, it is *pleroo*, which means "filled inwardly." In v. 4 it is *pletho*, which means "filled outwardly" or "furnished and equipped." This was the anointing of the Spirit for ministry. Every believer needs the filling of the Spirit both inwardly for life and outwardly for ministry.

i 2:4 The Greek word *apotheggomai* literally means "to ring out" (like a bell). It can also mean "carried along" or "inspired."

j 2:5 Or "devout Jewish men."

k 2:6 The Greek word *andres* implies respect, such as "ladies and gentlemen."

heard the roaring sound, crowds came running to where it was coming from, stunned over what was happening, because each one could hear the disciples speaking in his or her own language. [7] Bewildered, they said to one another, "Aren't these all Galileans? [a] [8] So how is it that we hear them speaking in our own languages? [9] We are northeastern Iranians, [b] northwestern Iranians, [c] Elamites, [d] and those from Mesopotamia, [e] Judea, east central Turkey, [f] the coastal areas of the Black Sea, [g] Asia, [h] [10] north central Turkey, [i] southern Turkey, Egypt, Libyans who are neighbors of Cyrene, visitors from all over the Roman Empire, both Jews and converts to Judaism, Cretans and Arabs. [11] Yet we hear them speaking of God's mighty wonders in our own dialects!" [j] [12] They all stood there, dumbfounded and astonished, saying to one another, "What is this phenomenon?" [k]

[13] But others poked fun at them and said, "They're just drunk on new wine."

Peter's Pentecost Sermon

[14] Peter stood up with the eleven apostles [l] and shouted [m] to the crowd. "Listen carefully, my fellow Jews [n] and residents of Jerusalem. You need to clearly understand what's happening here. [15] These people are not drunk like you think they are, for it is only nine o'clock in the morning. [o] [16] This is *the fulfillment of* what was prophesied through the prophet Joel, *for God says:* [p]

---

a 2:7 It is likely they knew they were Galileans by their Aramaic dialect common in Galilee.

b 2:9 Or "Parthians."

c 2:9 Or "Medes."

d 2:9 This area is now Khuzestan and the Ilam Province, including a small part of southern Iraq.

e 2:9 The Aramaic is Beth-Nahrin, which means "land of the rivers." This would include Iraq, parts of Syria, southeastern Turkey, and southwestern Iran. The Assyrians also consider themselves to be natives of Beth-Nahrin (Mesopotamia).

f 2:9 Or "Cappadocia."

g 2:9 Or "Pontus," which is northeastern Turkey. Pontus means "sea."

h 2:9 Or "Orientals."

i 2:10 Or "Phrygia."

j 2:11 This is the universal remedy of the curse of Babel, where human beings were divided by languages (Gen. 11:9). Now, in Christ, the language of the Spirit unifies us all in him.

k 2:12 As translated from the Aramaic.

l 2:14 All of the twelve standing there would prove that they were not drunk. They stood before this massive crowd, possibly in the courts of the temple. There were three thousand converted and baptized that day, so the crowd was possibly much larger than that.

m 2:14 See footnote for v. 4. Peter was speaking under the anointing of the Holy Spirit. The tongues being spoken, along with the sound of the wind, drew the crowd. Peter would have spoken to them in the common language of Aramaic. Even with the Galilean and Judean dialects, nearly all of the Jewish people present would understand his words.

n 2:14 Or "you Jewish men." This is also used in Acts 2:22; 3:12; 5:35; 13:16; 21:28.

o 2:15 Or "the third hour," the time for Jewish morning prayer.

p 2:16 See Joel 2:28–32.

¹⁷ "This is what I will do in the last days *ᵃ*—I will pour out *ᵇ* my Spirit on everybody and cause your sons and daughters to prophesy, and your young men will see visions, *ᶜ* and your old men will experience dreams *from God*. *ᵈ* ¹⁸ The Holy Spirit will come upon all my servants, men and women alike, and they will prophesy. ¹⁹ I will reveal startling signs and wonders in the sky above and mighty miracles on the earth below. Blood and fire and pillars of clouds *ᵉ* will appear. ²⁰ For the sun will be turned dark *ᶠ* and the moon blood-red before that great and awesome appearance of the day of the Lord. ²¹ But everyone who calls on the name of the Lord *ᵍ* will be saved.'"

²² Peter continued, "People of Israel, listen to the facts. *ʰ* Jesus, the Victorious, *ⁱ* was a Man on a divine mission *ʲ* whose authority was clearly proven. For you know how God performed many powerful miracles, signs, and wonders through him. ²³ This Man's destiny was prearranged, for God knew that Jesus would be handed over to you to be crucified and that you would execute him on a cross by the hands of lawless men. Yet it was all part of his predetermined plan. ²⁴ God destroyed the cords of death *ᵏ* and raised him up, because it was impossible for death's power to hold him prisoner. ²⁵ This is the very thing David prophesied about him: *ˡ*

---

a 2:17 The New Testament term "the last days" began at Pentecost and extends until the return of Christ. We have technically been in "the last days" for over two thousand years.

b 2:17 Or "gush forth," or "run greedily." The Aramaic can be translated "I will be splashing my Spirit-Wind over all flesh" (humanity).

c 2:17 Or "divinely appointed appearances." The Greek word for "visions," *horasis*, can also mean "our eyes opened to have divine encounters and see into the spiritual realm." These are not daydreams but visions of the heavenly realm. (See *Strong's Concordance*, Gr. 3700 and 3706.)

d 2:17 This verse can be translated from the Aramaic as "Your grandparents shall see visions and your priests shall dream dreams."

e 2:19 Or "columns [plumes] of smoke." The Aramaic can be translated "the sweet smell of burning incense."

f 2:20 This could be a figure of speech similar to "Lights out on the old order." The Aramaic is "The sun will be in mourning." Perhaps this prophecy was fulfilled when Christ was crucified.

g 2:21 The Aramaic can be translated "Whoever calls on the name of Jesus as the Messiah will receive life."

h 2:22 Peter wisely begins his sermon with a recounting of Jewish history, keeping the main point of his sermon until the end. A great transformation had taken place in Peter, who had denied Christ three times only six weeks ago. Now he preaches with power and authority. This is the difference the Holy Spirit makes in the life of a believer.

i 2:22 Or "Jesus the Nazarene" (the Branch). The Aramaic word used here also implies the title of an heir of a powerful family, or one who is victorious ("Jesus, the Victorious").

j 2:22 The Aramaic is "the Man from God," which may be an idiomatic saying for "the Man born of God."

k 2:24 As translated from the Aramaic, which can also be translated "God destroyed death's destruction." The Greek is "God freed him from the travails of death." The Greek word translated "travails" is commonly used for the labor pains of childbirth.

l 2:25 See Ps. 16:8–11.

'I continually see the Lord[a] in front of me.

He's at my right hand, and I am never shaken.[b]

[26] No wonder my heart is glad and my glory celebrates![c]

My mouth is filled with his praises,

and I have hope that my body will live[d]

[27] because you will not leave my soul among the dead,[e]

nor will you allow your sacred one to experience decay.

[28] For you have revealed to me the pathways to life,

and seeing your face fills me with euphoria!'[f]

[29] "My fellow Jews, I can tell you there is no doubt that our noted patriarch has both died and been buried in his tomb, which remains to this day. *So you can see that he was not referring to himself with those words.* [30] But as a prophet, he knew God's faithful promise, made with God's unbreakable oath, that one of his descendants would take his throne.[g] [31] So when peering into the future, David prophesied[h] of the Messiah's resurrection. *And God revealed to him* that the Messiah would not be abandoned to the realm of death, nor would his body experience decay.

[32] "Can't you see it? God has resurrected Jesus, and we all have seen him![i]

[33] "Then God exalted him to his right hand upon the throne of highest honor. And the Father gave him the authority to send the promised Holy Spirit, which is being poured out[j] upon us today. This is what you're seeing and hearing!

[34] "David wasn't the one who ascended into heaven, but the one who prophesied:

'The Lord Jehovah[k] said to my Lord,

I honor you by enthroning you beside me,[l]

[35] until I make your enemies

a footstool beneath your feet.'[m]

---

a 2:25 The Hebrew-Aramaic word is *Yahweh.*

b 2:25 As translated from the Aramaic. The Greek is "so that I will not be shaken."

c 2:26 As translated from the Aramaic.

d 2:26 The Greek word for "live" (*kataskenosei*) is always used for "pitch a tent." Or "My body will pitch its tent in hope (expectation)." The Aramaic is "Even my body he will restore to hope."

e 2:27 The Aramaic is "Sheol"; the Greek is "Hades." Both refer to the realm of death.

f 2:28 This Greek word (*euphrosune*) occurs only here and in Acts 14:17. It is the spirit of joy, an ecstasy that comes from God. The Aramaic is "You will fill me, O Sweetness, with your presence."

g 2:30 See Ps. 132:11; Luke 1:32.

h 2:31 The Aramaic can be translated "David rose up after seeing a vision and he saw."

i 2:32 Or "of whom we are witnesses," which implies that they all had seen the resurrected Jesus.

j 2:33 The Aramaic is "splashed out the gift of the Holy Spirit."

k 2:34 As translated from the Aramaic.

l 2:34 Or "at my right hand."

m 2:35 See Ps. 110:1, which is the most frequently quoted Old Testament verse found in the

[36] "Now everyone in Israel[a] can know for certain[b] that Jesus, whom you crucified, is the one God has made[c] both Lord[d] and the Messiah."

The Crowd Responds to Peter's Words

[37] When they heard this they were crushed and realized what they had done to Jesus.[e] Deeply moved, they said to Peter and the other apostles, "What do we need to do, brothers?"[f]

[38] Peter replied, "Repent and return to God,[g] and each one of you must be baptized in the name of Jesus, the Anointed One,[h] to have your sins removed. Then you may take hold of the gift of the Holy Spirit. [39] For God's promise of the Holy Spirit is for you[i] and your families, for those yet to be born[j] and for everyone whom the Lord our God calls to himself."

[40] Peter preached to them and warned them with these words: "Be rescued from the wayward and perverse culture of this world!"[k]

[41] Those who believed the word that day numbered three thousand. They were all baptized and added *to the church.*[l]

The Community of Believers

[42] Every believer was faithfully devoted to following the teachings[m] of the

---

New Testament. This shows there is a continuing work of defeating Christ's enemies as his kingdom increases on earth as it is in heaven.

a 2:36 Or "all the house of Israel."

b 2:36 Or "inescapably," for no one can escape the claims of Christ.

c 2:36 The Aramaic is "Lord Yahweh made him [from birth] to be both Elohim and Messiah." The Greek verb used for "made" can also mean "brought forth." This is a clear statement of both Jesus' humanity (God brought him forth by human birth) and his deity.

d 2:36 Y'shua (Jesus) is now Lord of a new creation company, a new heaven, and a new earth— he is Lord of all. The Greek word *kurios* is not necessarily a divine title. The Aramaic text uses a clear title of Jesus' deity.

e 2:37 This Greek verb indicates the deepest sorrow and emotional agitation. It is taken from a root word that means "mortally wounded" and is found only here in all the New Testament.

f 2:37 The Aramaic contains an idiomatic figure of speech, "What do we need to do to be your brothers?"

g 2:38 The Greek word translated "repent" means both "to change the mind and direction of your life" and "to turn back to God."

h 2:38 Peter was likely saying these words from the steps of the temple. Below him were dozens of *mikveh* (immersion pools used for ceremonial cleanings of Jewish worshipers). Peter was pointing them to the cleansing that comes through the name and authority of Jesus Christ. The Aramaic is startling: "Be immersed in the name of Lord Yahweh Y'shua." Peter is clearly saying that Lord Yahweh and Jesus are one and the same.

i 2:39 The Aramaic can be translated "This outpouring is for you."

j 2:39 Or "for those who are far away (gentiles)."

k 2:40 Or "Be free from and preserved from this crooked people!"

l 2:41 Although the word *church* is not in the text, it is implied. They were converted by the message of Peter and brought into the fellowship of the believers.

m 2:42 The Greek word *didache* means "skilled instruction and training."

apostles. Their hearts were mutually linked to one another,[a] sharing communion[b] and coming together regularly for prayer.[c] [43] A deep sense of holy awe[d] swept over everyone, and the apostles performed many miraculous signs and wonders.[e] [44] All the believers were in fellowship as one body,[f] and they shared with one another whatever they had. [45] *Out of generosity* they even sold their assets to distribute the proceeds to those who were in need among them. [46] Daily they met together in the temple courts and in one another's homes to celebrate communion. They shared meals together with joyful hearts and tender humility. [47] They were continually filled with praises to God, enjoying the favor of all the people. And the Lord kept adding to their number daily those who were coming to life.[g]

Healing at the Beautiful Gate

3 One afternoon Peter and John went to the temple for the three o'clock prayer.[h] [2] As they came to the entrance called the Beautiful Gate,[i] they were captured by the sight of a man crippled from birth being carried and placed at the entrance to the temple. He was often brought there to beg for money from those going in to worship. [3] When he noticed Peter and John going into the temple, he begged them for money.

[4] Peter and John, looking straight into the eyes of the crippled man, said, "Look at us!" [5] Expecting a gift, he readily gave them his attention. [6] Then Peter said, "I don't have money, but I'll give you this—by the power of the name of Jesus Christ of Nazareth, stand up and walk!"

---

a 2:42 Or "They became partners."

b 2:42 Or "breaking of bread." This was more than sharing meals, but participating together in observing the Lord's Table. The Aramaic, which can be translated "the Eucharist" or "holy communion," makes it even more explicit.

c 2:42 Or "[all kinds of] prayers."

d 2:43 Or "Fear [of God] came upon every person."

e 2:43 The Aramaic adds, "in Jerusalem," which is missing in the Greek.

f 2:44 Or "added into one body."

g 2:47 As translated from the Aramaic. The Aramaic word for "church" is the joining of "meet" and "come." This word is an invitation to enter into fellowship with Christ and his people. The Greek word for "church" is *ekklesia*, which is "called-out ones." (See the second footnote on Matt. 16:18.)

h 3:1 Daily sacrifices were made in the temple at sunrise and about three o'clock every afternoon.

i 3:2 Or "the gate called Wonderful" in Aramaic. It is difficult to ascertain which of the many gates of the temple this might have been, and there is varying speculation with no certain conclusion. However, this Beautiful Gate points to Jesus Christ, who is the gate or entrance into the sheepfold of God. Furthermore, it hints of Ezekiel's temple (Ezek. 47), which has a river flowing out from the threshold through the gateway of the temple. This river was first measured to be ankle deep. This man, lame in his ankles, was healed by the spiritual "river" that flowed out the "Beautiful Gate" of Christ. The gateway opened up and the river poured out of Peter and John, bringing healing to the lame.

[7-8] Peter held out his right hand to the crippled man. As he pulled the man to his feet, suddenly power surged into his crippled feet and ankles. The man jumped up, stood *there for a moment stunned*, and then began to walk around! As he went into the temple courts with Peter and John, he leapt for joy and shouted praises to God.

[9] When all the people saw him jumping up and down and heard him glorifying God, [10] they realized it was the crippled beggar they had passed by in front of the Beautiful Gate. Astonishment swept over the crowd, for they were amazed over what had happened to him.

Peter Preaches to the Crowd

[11] Dumbfounded over what they were witnessing, the crowd ran over to Peter and John, who were standing under the covered walkway called Solomon's Porch. Standing there also was the healed beggar, clinging to Peter and John. [a]

[12] With the crowd surrounding him, Peter said to them all, "People of Israel, [b] listen to me! Why are you so amazed by this healing? Why do you stare at us? We didn't make this crippled man walk by our own power or authority. [c] [13] The God of our ancestors, Abraham, Isaac, and Jacob, [d] *has done this.* For he has glorified his Servant [e] Jesus, the one you denied to Pilate's face when he decided to release him—and you insisted that he be crucified. [14] You rejected [f] the one who is holy and righteous, and instead begged for a murderer to be released. [15] You killed the Prince of Life! [g] But God raised him from the dead, and we stand here as witnesses to that fact. [16] Faith in Jesus' name has healed this man standing before you. It is the faith that comes through believing in Jesus' name that has made the crippled man walk right in front of your eyes!

[17] "My fellow Jews, I realize that neither you nor your leaders realize the grave mistake you made. [18] But in spite of what you've done, God has fulfilled what he foretold through the prophets long ago about the sufferings of his Anointed One. [19] And now you must repent and turn back [h] to God so that your

---

a 3:11 What an amazing picture this makes. This scene transpired at Solomon's Porch. Lessons of wisdom, greater than the wisdom of Solomon, were uncovered by this miracle to those who had hearts of understanding.

b 3:12 The Aramaic could be translated "protectors of Israel."

c 3:12 As translated from the Aramaic. The Greek is "piety."

d 3:13 See Ex. 3:6.

e 3:13 See Isa. 52:13.

f 3:14 Or "denied." It is amazing how complete was the healing of Peter's life. Just fifty days previously, it was Peter who denied he knew Jesus three times. Now he says to his fellow Jews, "You denied the holy and righteous One!"

g 3:15 Or "Originator of Life."

h 3:19 Peter uses the Greek word *epistrepho* ("turn back to God," "be converted"). We need to not only repent but to return home to God's grace and truth. This is a Hebraic thought

sins will be removed,[a] and so that times of refreshing[b] will stream from the Lord's presence. [20] And he will send you Jesus, the Messiah, the chosen one for you.[c] [21] For he must remain in heaven until the restoration of all things[d] has taken place,[e] *fulfilling everything that God said* long ago through his holy prophets. [22] For has not Moses told us:[f]

> 'The Lord your God will raise up
>   a prophet from among you who is like me.
>   Listen to him and follow everything he tells you.
> [23] Every person who disobeys that prophet
>   will be cut off and completely destroyed.'

[24] "In fact, every prophet from the time of Samuel onward has prophesied of these very days! [25] And you are heirs of their prophecies[g] and of the covenants God made with your fathers when he promised Abraham,[h] 'Your descendant[i] will bring blessing to all the people on the earth.'

[26] "Now that God raised up his Son,[j] he has chosen to send him first to you that he might bless you by turning each one of you[k] from your wickedness."[l]

---

of returning to the Lord God (the Hebrew word *shuv*). Every Jew would know what that means: "Come back to God!" Repentance and return is more than a passive changing of one's mind.

a 3:19 The Greek word used here, *exaleipho*, means "obliterated" or "canceled."

b 3:19 Or "cooling breeze," which occurs only here in the New Testament. This hints of the time when God walked with Adam in the cooling breeze of the day. The work of the cross begins the restoration of Paradise within the hearts of Christ's followers.

c 3:20 The Aramaic can be translated "He will send you all that has been already prepared for you through Jesus, the Anointed One."

d 3:21 Or "until the time for the universal restoration."

e 3:21 Or "This one the heavens must receive until the times of universal restoration." The word *restoration* in Greek is *apokatastasis*, which infers the restoration of creation to the state of existence before the fall, but also Davidic covenant being restored. Luke's choice of the Greek word found only here in the New Testament is noteworthy. It is a medical term that means "restoration of perfect health."

f 3:22 See Lev. 23:29; Deut. 18:15, 19.

g 3:25 Or "sons of the prophets."

h 3:25 See Gen. 22:18; 26:4.

i 3:25 Or "seed" (descendants).

j 3:26 The Greek word *pais* can mean either "servant" or "son." (See *Strong's Concordance*, Gr. 3816.) The Aramaic is clearly "son." Notice how many times in the book of Acts that the followers of Christ preached the resurrection. The power and virtue of the cross can never be diminished; however, it is the resurrection of Christ that became the apostolic center of their preaching in the book of Acts.

k 3:26 The Aramaic uses the conditional clause "if you turn and repent from your evils."

l 3:26 The Greek is plural, "wickednesses" or "evil ways."

Peter and John Arrested

4 [1-2] The teaching and preaching of Peter and John angered the priests, the captain of the temple police, and representatives of the Jewish sect of the Sadducees. [a] They were furious that the people were being taught that in Jesus there is a resurrection from the dead. So while Peter and John were still speaking, the Jewish authorities came to the temple courts to oppose them. [3] They had them arrested, and since it was already evening they kept them in custody until the next day. [4] Yet there were many in the crowd who believed the message, [b] bringing the total number of men who believed [c] to nearly five thousand!

[5] The next day many Jewish leaders, religious scholars, and elders of the people convened a meeting in Jerusalem. [6] Annas the high priest was there with Caiaphas, John, Alexander, [d] and others who were members of the high priest's family. [7] They made Peter and John stand in front of the council as they questioned them, saying, "Tell us, by what power and authority have you done these things?" [e]

[8] Peter, filled with the Holy Spirit, answered, "Respected elders and leaders of the people, listen. [9] Are we being put on trial today for doing an act of kindness by healing a frail, crippled man? Well then, [10] you and everyone else in Israel should know that it is by the power of the name of Jesus that the crippled man stands here today completely healed! You crucified Jesus Christ of Nazareth, [f] but God raised him from the dead. [11] This Jesus is 'the stone that you, the builders, have rejected, and now he has become the cornerstone!' [g] [12] There is no one else [h] who has the power to save us, for there is only one name to whom God has given authority by which we must experience salvation: [i] *the name of Jesus.*"

[13] The council members were astonished as they witnessed the bold courage [j]

---

a 4:1-2 Of the three major sects of Judaism of that day (Pharisees, Essenes, and Sadducees), the Sadducees were a small but influential group that philosophically denied the supernatural and gravitated instead toward political control of the people. Their denial of the resurrection is what prompted their actions here.

b 4:4 Or "the Word" (Gr. *logos*).

c 4:4 Although the cultural way of numbering the Jewish crowd is technically "adult males," the usage of the Greek term *ton andron* is consistently found throughout Greek literature as an inclusive and formal term of respect, similar to "ladies and gentlemen." Including women and children, the early church swelled rapidly into tens of thousands.

d 4:6 There is little known about John (or Jonathan) and Alexander. It is possible that John was the son of Caiaphas, who would one day be the high priest. Or John and Alexander could have been the leaders of the Sadducees.

e 4:7 Or "In whose name did you do this?"

f 4:10 Or "the Nazarene."

g 4:11 See Ps. 118:22.

h 4:12 Peter insisted there was no man who could claim to be the Messiah other than Jesus.

i 4:12 The Aramaic is "We must experience the Life Giver" or "We must receive the covenant of life."

j 4:13 The Aramaic is "hearing the bold words of Peter and John."

of Peter and John, especially when they discovered that they were just ordinary men who had never had religious training. *a* Then they began to understand the effect Jesus had on them simply by spending time with him. [14] Standing there with them was the healed man, and there was nothing further they could say. [15] So they ordered them to leave the room while they discussed the matter. Among themselves, they said, [16] "What should we do with these men? Everyone in Jerusalem can clearly see that they've performed a notable sign and wonder—we can't deny that. [17] But to keep this propaganda from spreading any further among the people, let's threaten them severely and warn them to never speak to anyone in this name again."

[18] So they had them brought back in before the council, and they commanded them to never teach the people or speak again using the name of Jesus. [19] But Peter and John replied, "You can judge for yourselves—is it better to listen to you or to God? [20] It's impossible for us to stop speaking about all the things we've seen and heard!"

[21] Since the members of the council couldn't come up with a crime they could punish them for, they threatened them once more and let them go. All the people praised God, thrilled over the miraculous healing of the crippled man. *b* [22] And the man who received this miracle sign of healing was over forty years old. *c*

The Church Prays

[23] As soon as they were released from custody, Peter and John went to the other believers and explained all that had happened with the high priest and the elders. [24] When the believers heard their report, they raised their voices in unity and prayed, "Lord Yahweh, *d* you are the Lord of all! You created the universe—the earth, the sky, the sea, and everything that is in them. *e* [25] And you spoke by the Holy Spirit through your servant David, our forefather, saying:

'How dare the nations plan a rebellion,
    ranting and raging against the Lord Most High?
    Their foolish plots are futile!
[26] Look at how the kings of the earth take their stand,
    with the rulers scheming and conspiring together
    against God *f* and his anointed Messiah!' *g*

---

a 4:13 The Aramaic is "They did not know the scrolls." The Greek is "uneducated."

b 4:21 Made explicit from the text, "over what had happened."

c 4:22 For the significance of the number forty, see the second footnote on 1:3.

d 4:24 As translated from the Aramaic.

e 4:24 See Ex. 20:11; Ps. 146:6.

f 4:26 The Aramaic is "Lord Yahweh," and the Greek is "Lord" (*kurios*).

g 4:26 See Ps. 2:1–2.

[27] "In fact, Herod and Pontius Pilate, along with Jews and non-Jews, met together to take their stand against your holy servant, Jesus the Messiah. [28] They did to him all that your purpose and will had determined, according to the destiny you had marked out for him. [29] So now, Lord, listen to their threats to harm us. Empower us, as your servants, to speak the word of God freely and courageously. [30] Stretch out your hand of power *through us* to heal, and to move in signs and wonders by the name of your holy Son, Jesus!" [a]

[31] At that moment the earth shook beneath them, causing the building they were in to tremble. [b] Each one of them was filled with the Holy Spirit, and they proclaimed the word of God with unrestrained boldness. [c]

[32] All the believers were one in mind and heart. Selfishness was not a part of their community, for they shared everything they had with one another. [33] The apostles gave powerful testimonies about the resurrection of the Lord Jesus, and great measures of grace rested upon them all. [34-35] Some who owned houses or land sold them and brought the proceeds before the apostles to distribute to those without. Not a single person among them was needy.

[36-37] For example, there was a Levite from Cyprus named Joseph, who sold his farmland and placed the proceeds at the feet of the apostles. They nicknamed him Barnabas (or "Encourager"). [d]

The Judgment of Ananias and Sapphira

5 Now, a man named Ananias and his wife, Sapphira, [e] likewise sold their farm. [2] They conspired to secretly keep back for themselves a portion of

---

a   4:30 As translated from the Aramaic. The Greek is "your holy servant, Jesus."

b   4:31 The Aramaic is "an earthquake."

c   4:31 The Greek word is *parresia*. This involves more than confidence; it was a free-flowing, unrestrained boldness. It can also mean "freedom of speech." *Parresia* carries nuances that are not easily brought over into English. The person who speaks with *parresia* will say everything that is on his mind with no restraint, flowing out of his heart with confidence. It involves being frank and honest, hiding nothing and speaking directly to the heart. Most often it is a word used for public speaking. It refers to speech that is not tailored to make everyone happy but to speak the truth, in spite of what that may cost. It is the courage to speak truth into the ears of others. This was reserved for only the highest rank of Greek citizens, not people of other lands or slaves. The right to speak freely was an essential aspect of Athenian democracy. Although it is sometimes associated with negative speech, in this context *parresia* refers to an unrestrained boldness. There was a Greek idiom that said essentially, "If you tell me the truth no matter what that truth turns out to be, I will not punish you." This was known as the Parresiastic Contract. See M. Foucault, "Discourse and Truth: The Problematization of Parresia," six lectures given at the University of California at Berkeley, 1983, ed. by Joseph Pearson in 1985. *Parresia* is found also in Mark 8:32; John 7:4, 13, 26; 10:24; 11:14, 54; 2 Cor. 3:12; 7:4; Eph. 3:12; 6:19; Phil. 1:20; and numerous other places.

d   4:36-37 The name Barnabas means "son of encouragement," or "son of the prophet." This was the Barnabas who traveled with Paul as an apostle.

e   5:1 The Aramaic can be translated "Ananias, together with his wife, who was famous for her beauty." The Aramaic name *Shapeera* means "beauty."

the proceeds. So when Ananias brought the money to the apostles, it was only a portion of the entire sale. ³ *God revealed their secret to Peter,*ᵃ so he said to him, "Ananias, why did you let Satan fill your heart and make you think you could lie to the Holy Spirit? You only pretended to give it all, yet you hid back part of the proceeds from the sale of your property to keep for yourselves. ⁴ Before you sold it, wasn't it yours to sell or to keep? And after you sold it, wasn't the money entirely at your disposal? How could you plot such a thing in your heart? You haven't lied to people; you've lied to God!"ᵇ

⁵ The moment Ananias heard those words, he fell over dead. Everyone was terrified when they heard what had happened. ⁶ Some young men came in and removed the body and buried him.

⁷ Three hours later, his wife came into the room, with no clue what had happened to her husband.

⁸ Peter said to her, "Tell me, were the two of you paid this amount for the sale of your land?"

Sapphira said, "Yes, that's how much it was."

⁹ Peter told her, "Why have you agreed together to test the Spirit of the Lord?ᶜ I hear the footsteps of those who buried your husband at the door— they're coming here to bury you too!" ¹⁰ At that moment she dropped dead at Peter's feet.

When the young men came in, she was already dead, so they carried her out and buried her next to her husband. ¹¹ The entire church was seized with a powerful sense of the fear of God,ᵈ which came over all who heard what had happened.

The Apostles Perform Miracles, Signs, and Wonders

¹² The apostles performed many signs, wonders, and miracles among the people. ¹³ And the believers were wonderfully united as they met regularly in the temple courts in the area known as Solomon's Porch. No one dared harm them,ᵉ for everyone held them in high regard.

¹⁴ Continually more and more people believed in the Lordᶠ and were added to their number—great crowds of both men and women. ¹⁵ In fact, when people knew Peter was going to walk by, they carried the sick out to the streets and

---

ᵃ 5:3 With supernatural discernment, God revealed to Peter what had happened. The words "pretended to give it all" are not in the original text, but supplied because of the inference of the words "lie to the Holy Spirit." The true sin was more than simply telling Peter a lie, but lying to the Holy Spirit.
ᵇ 5:4 The Aramaic can be translated "You are not a phony with just men, but with God."
ᶜ 5:9 The Aramaic is "the Spirit of the Lord Yahweh."
ᵈ 5:11 Or "mega-fear fell on the church."
ᵉ 5:13 As translated from the Aramaic. The Greek is "No one else dared join them," which is somewhat confusing because of the next verse.
ᶠ 5:14 The Aramaic is "the Lord Yahweh."

laid them down on cots and mats, knowing the incredible power emanating from him would overshadow them *and heal them*.[a] [16] Great numbers of people swarmed into Jerusalem from the nearby villages. They brought with them the sick and those troubled by demons—and everyone was healed!

The Apostles Persecuted

[17] The high priest and his officials, who formed the party of the Sadducees, became extremely jealous over all that was happening, [18] so they had the apostles arrested, placed in chains,[b] and thrown into jail. [19] But during the night, the Lord[c] sent an angel *who appeared before them*. He supernaturally opened their prison doors and brought the apostles outside. [20] "Go," the angel told them. "Stand in the temple courts and preach the words that bring life!" [21] So early that morning they entered the temple courts and taught the people. The high priest and his officials, *unaware of their supernatural release from prison*, convened the members of the supreme council.[d] They sent for the apostles to be brought to them from prison. [22] But when the officers came to the prison cell, it was empty! They returned to the council and informed them, [23] "We found the jail securely locked and the guards standing by their cell, but when we opened the door, there was no one inside!"

[24] When the captain of the temple guard and the leading priests heard this report, they were perplexed and at a loss over what to make of it.

[25] Someone came and informed them, "The men you put in prison are out there standing in the temple courts, teaching the people!"

[26] So the captain of the temple guard and his officers went to arrest them once again, but without using force, for they were afraid the people would stone them.

[27] When they brought them before the council, the high priest demanded an explanation, [28] saying, "Didn't we strictly warn you that you were to never again teach in this name? But instead you have now filled all of Jerusalem with this doctrine and are committed to holding us responsible for this man's death!"[e]

[29] Peter and the apostles replied, "We must listen to and obey God more than pleasing religious leaders. [30] You had Jesus arrested and killed by crucifixion,[f] but

---

a 5:15 The Greek word translated "overshadow" is *episkiazo*, which is used exclusively for the power of the Almighty "overshadowing," such as with Mary, who conceived a child supernaturally by God. It is also used for the cloud that overshadowed Jesus on the Mount of Transfiguration. See Matt. 17:5; Mark 9:7; Luke 1:35. This was not a natural shadow created by the light of the sun, but the supernatural overshadowing of God's power coming upon the sick to bring healing.

b 5:18 As translated from the Aramaic.

c 5:19 The Aramaic is "Lord Yahweh."

d 5:21 Or "the Sanhedrin."

e 5:28 Or "bringing [the guilt of] this man's blood on us."

f 5:30 Or "by hanging him on a tree," an Aramaic idiom for crucifixion. See Deut. 21:22–23.

the God of our forefathers[a] has raised him up. [31]He's the one God has exalted and seated at his right hand as our Savior and Champion.[b] He is the provider of grace as the Redeemer of Israel.[c] [32]We are witnesses of these things,[d] and so is the Holy Spirit, whom God freely gives to all who believe in him."[e]

[33]When they heard this, they were infuriated and determined to murder them. [34]But a Pharisee named Gamaliel, a noted religious professor who was highly respected by all, stood up. He gave orders to send the apostles outside. [35]Then he said to the council, "Men of Israel, you need to be very careful about how you deal with these men. [36]Some time ago there was a man named Theudas who rose up claiming to be somebody. He had a following of about four hundred men, but when he was killed, all of his followers were scattered, and nothing came of it.

[37]"After him, in the days of the census,[f] another man rose up, Judas the Galilean, who got people to follow him in a revolt. He too perished, and all those who followed him were scattered. [38]So in this situation, you should just leave these men to themselves. For if this plan or undertaking originates with men, it will fade away and come to nothing. [39]But if this movement is of God, you won't be able to stop it. And you might discover that you were fighting God all along!"

Gamaliel's words convinced the council. [40]So they brought the apostles back in and had them severely beaten. They ordered them never again to speak in the name of Jesus and then let them go.

[41]The apostles left there rejoicing, thrilled that God had considered them worthy to suffer disgrace for the name of Jesus. [42]And nothing stopped them! They kept preaching every day in the temple courts and went from house to house, preaching the gospel of Jesus, God's Anointed One!

Servant Leaders

6 During those days the number of Jesus' followers kept multiplying greatly. But a complaint was brought against those who spoke Aramaic[g] by the Greek-speaking Jews,[h] who felt their widows were being overlooked during the daily distribution of food.

[2]The twelve apostles called a meeting of all the believers and told them, "It

---

a 5:30 See Ex. 3:15.

b 5:31 Or "Prince."

c 5:31 As translated from the Aramaic. The Greek is "He gives repentance and removal of sins to Israel."

d 5:32 Or "words." This is the Greek word *rhema*.

e 5:32 As translated from the Aramaic. The Greek is "to those who hear and obey him."

f 5:37 Or "registration for the Roman tax."

g 6:1 Or "the Hebrews" (converts from orthodox Judaism). There was one dominant language in Israel: Aramaic. However, the issue between the two groups was more than merely a language difference. Those who spoke Aramaic were natives, while the Greek-speaking minority were most likely Jews from other nations.

h 6:1 Or "Hellenists." These were Jewish converts who sought to maintain a Greek language

is not advantageous for us to be pulled away from the word of God to wait on tables. [3]We want you to carefully select[a] from among yourselves seven godly men. Make sure they are honorable, full of the Holy Spirit and wisdom, and we will give them the responsibility of this crucial ministry of serving. [4]That will enable us to give our full attention to prayer and preaching the word of God."

[5]Everyone in the church loved this idea.[b] So they chose seven men. One of them was Stephen,[c] who was known as a man full of faith and overflowing with the Holy Spirit. Along with him they chose Philip, Prochorus, Nicanor, Timon, Parmenas, and Nicholas from Antioch,[d] who had converted to Judaism. [6]All seven stood before the apostles, who laid their hands on them and prayed for them, *commissioning them to this ministry.*[e]

[7]God's word reigned supreme[f] and kept spreading. The number of Jesus' followers in Jerusalem quickly grew and increased by the day. Even a great number of Jewish priests became believers and were obedient to the faith!

[8]Stephen, who was a man full of grace and supernatural power, performed many astonishing signs and wonders and mighty miracles among the people.[g] [9]This upset some men belonging to a sect who called themselves the Men Set Free.[h] They were Libyans,[i] Egyptians,[j] and Turks.[k]

---

and culture and were predominantly Alexandrian Jews. These may have been Jews who were scattered throughout the Roman Empire, including Greece and Alexandria, Egypt.

a 6:3 The Aramaic is "select with awe," that is, in the presence of the Lord.

b 6:5 The Aramaic can be translated "This proposal appeared beautiful."

c 6:5 It is most likely that Stephen was not a gentile but a Jewish believer. His Hebrew name, *Tzephania*, is transliterated into Greek as *Astaphanos* (Stephen in English). *Tzephania* is the name of the prophet Zephaniah. Zephaniah means "Yah has treasured [him]." Stephen was not a gentile proselyte to Judaism but a Greek-speaking Hebrew. He spoke in Acts 7 and addressed his hearers as "fellow Jews and fathers." Although he was a powerful minister of the Word, Stephen was humble to accept the task of serving.

d 6:5 The Aramaic can be translated "Nicholas, the hero of Antioch."

e 6:6 The practice of laying on of hands indicates approval, impartation of authority, commissioning, and ordaining. As the Old Testament priest laid hands on a sacrifice and transferred the guilt of sins upon the animal, the New Testament apostles laid their hands on men and appointed them to ministry. See Lev. 16:21–22; Num. 27:18–20; Heb. 6:2.

f 6:7 As translated from the Aramaic.

g 6:8 Stephen was not an apostle, yet he worked miracles of power through his ministry. The miraculous is not for the few, but for the many.

h 6:9 Or "the Synagogue of the Freedmen." Although most expositors view these as former Hebrew slaves, the Aramaic is "Libertines." It is possible that these were pagan cult members who followed a Roman mythical hero named Liber. From this word we get the English word *liberty*. They emphasized drunkenness and promiscuity. They boasted in their freedom from all moral laws as the Men Set Free to do whatever they desired. They were so hedonistic that even other pagans viewed them as wicked. These Libertines were the antithesis to the true freedom that comes through Christ (John 8:36).

i 6:9 Or "Cyrene," a region of eastern Libya.

j 6:9 Or "Alexandria," a large Egyptian city on the Mediterranean.

k 6:9 Or "Cilicia" (southeastern coastal area of Turkey) and "the province of Asia" (that is,

They all confronted Stephen to argue[a] with him. [10] But the Holy Spirit gave Stephen remarkable wisdom to answer them. His words were prompted by the Holy Spirit, and they could not refute what he said. [11] So the Men Set Free conspired in secret to find those who would bring false accusations against Stephen and lie about him by saying, "We heard this man speak blasphemy against Moses and God."

[12] The Men Set Free agitated the crowd, the elders, and the religious scholars,[b] then seized Stephen and forcefully took him before the supreme council. [13] One after another, false witnesses stepped forward and accused Stephen, saying, "This man never stops denigrating our temple and our Jewish law. [14] For we have heard him teach that Jesus of Nazareth will destroy the temple and change the traditions and customs that Moses handed down to us."[c]

[15] Every member of the supreme council focused his gaze on Stephen, for right in front of their eyes, *while being falsely accused*, his face glowed as though he had the face of an angel![d]

Stephen's Sermon

7 The high priest asked, "Are these accusations true?"

[2] Stephen replied, "My fellow Jews and fathers, listen to me. The God of glory appeared[e] to our ancestor Abraham while he was living in Iraq[f] and before he moved to Haran[g] in Syria. [3] God said to him, 'Go! Leave behind your country and your relatives. Begin your journey and come to the land that I will show you.'[h]

[4] "So Abraham left southeastern Iraq[i] and began his journey. He settled in Haran in Syria and stayed there until his father passed away. Then God had him move to the land of Israel with only a promise. [5] Although God gave him no parcel of land he could call his own, not even a footprint,[j] yet he prom-

---

Asia Minor, comprised of western and southwestern Turkey). Both regions are included in the word *Turks*.

a 6:9 The Aramaic is "word wrestle."

b 6:12 Or "scribes." These were considered the experts in the law of Moses.

c 6:14 The Aramaic is "We heard him teach that Jesus the Nazarene is the one who freed our nation and changed the feasts that Moses observed."

d 6:15 As he faced persecution and martyrdom, Stephen's face lit up with heaven's light, shining as an angelic messenger. What manifests in your life when you are opposed and falsely accused?

e 7:2 The entire Hebrew family, and consequently the life of believers today, all began with a divine encounter as the God of glory appeared before Abraham. It is this same glory that calls people to faith in Christ. We, like Abraham, have been captured by the God of glory. See 2 Peter 1:3.

f 7:2 Or "Mesopotamia," or "the land between two rivers" (Euphrates and Tigris).

g 7:2 This is the city to which Abraham migrated on his way to the promised land. Haran was also the son of Caleb who claimed a mountain. Haran means "mountain climber."

h 7:3 See Gen. 12:1.

i 7:4 Or "the land of Chaldeans."

j 7:5 See Deut. 2:5.

ised Abraham that he and his descendants would one day have it all. And even though as yet Abraham had no child, [6] God spoke with him and gave him this promise:

> 'Your descendants will live in a foreign land with a people
> > who will make slaves of them
> > and oppress them for four hundred years. [a]
> [7] But I will judge the nation that enslaves them,
> > and your descendants will be set free
> > to return to this land to serve and worship me.' [b]

[8] "Then God entered into covenant with Abraham, which included the requirement of circumcision. So when he became the father of Isaac, he circumcised him eight days after his birth.

[9] "Isaac then became the father of Jacob, who was the father of our twelve patriarchs. Jacob's sons became jealous of their brother Joseph and sold him to be a slave in Egypt. But God's favor and blessing rested upon Joseph, and in time, [10] God rescued him from all his oppression and granted him extraordinary favor before Pharaoh, the king of Egypt. Pharaoh appointed him as the overseer of his nation and even of his own palace. [c]

[11] "Then a devastating famine came over all of Egypt and Canaan, bringing great misery to the people, including our ancestors, who couldn't find food. [d] [12] But when Jacob learned that there was food in Egypt, he sent his sons, our ancestors, on their first trip to purchase grain for their family. [13] On their second trip to Egypt, Joseph revealed his identity to his brothers, [e] and because of this, Pharaoh learned about Joseph's family and where he came from.

[14] "Joseph sent for his father, Jacob, and his entire family, a total of seventy-five people, to come and reside in Egypt. [15] Eventually, Jacob died there, along with all of his sons, our forefathers. [16] Their bones [f] were later carried back to the promised land and buried in Shechem, in the tomb Abraham had purchased for a sum of money from the sons of Hamor.

[17] "The time drew near for God to fulfill the prophetic promise he had made to Abraham. Our Jewish people had increased greatly in number, multiplying many times over while in Egypt.

[18] "Another [g] king, *who had forgotten how Joseph had made their nation great,*

---

a 7:6 See Gen. 15:13–14; Ex. 2:22; 12:40.

b 7:7 See Ex. 3:12.

c 7:10 See Gen. 41:37–44.

d 7:11 See Gen. 41:54; 42:5.

e 7:13 See Gen. 45:1.

f 7:16 The Aramaic is "his [Jacob's] bones," while every Greek manuscript is "their bones." Jacob was buried in Abraham's tomb according to Gen. 50:1–14. Joseph was buried in a plot purchased in Shechem for one hundred pieces of silver (Gen. 33:18–20; Josh. 24:32).

g 7:18 The Greek is "another of a different kind [or "character"]."

arose to rule over Egypt.[a] [19]He was an abusive king who exploited our people with his smooth talk. With cruelty he forced our ancestors to give up their little boys as he committed infanticide![b]

[20]"Then Moses came on the scene—a child of divine beauty.[c] His parents hid him from Pharaoh as long as they could to spare his life.[d] After three months they could conceal him no longer, [21]so they had to abandon him to his fate. But God arranged that Pharaoh's daughter would find him, take him home, and raise him as her own son. [22]So Moses was fully trained in the royal courts and educated in the highest wisdom Egypt had to offer, until he arose as a powerful prince and an eloquent orator.[e]

[23]"When Moses turned forty, his heart was stirred for his people, the Israelites. [24]One day he saw one of our people being violently mistreated, so he came to his rescue, and with his own hands Moses murdered the abusive Egyptian. [25]Moses hoped that when the people realized how he had rescued one of their own, they would recognize him as their deliverer. How wrong he was! [26]The next day he came upon two of our people engaged in a fist fight, and he tried to break it up by saying, 'Men, you are brothers! Why would you want to hurt each other?'

[27]"But the perpetrator pushed Moses aside and said, 'Who do you think you are? Who appointed you to be our ruler and judge? [28]Are you going to kill me like you did the Egyptian yesterday?'[f]

---

a   7:18 See Ex. 1:7–8.
b   7:19 The Aramaic can also be translated "forced them to abort their children."
c   7:20 Or "beautiful [well pleasing] in the eyes of God." The Aramaic is "He was loved by God." Ancient Hebrew scholars believed Moses may have had a shining of glory on his countenance when he was born, distinguishing him as a special servant of the Lord God. This shining face would later mark him as one who dwelt in the presence of the Lord (Ex. 34:29). Moses was a type or picture of the Lord Jesus Christ. No one was fairer than he; but no one was more extraordinary than our Lord. We learn from Ex. 6:20 that Moses' father was Amram and his mother was Jochebed. Amram means "family of the lofty One" and Jochebed means "Yah makes great." The sister of Moses was Miriam (the Hebrew name for Mary), which comes from the root word for "myrrh," meaning "aromatic," "fragrant," or "bitter." The name Moses means "rescued out of the water."
d   7:20 See Heb. 11:23.
e   7:22 Jewish tradition is that Pharaoh's daughter had no child of her own and she herself was an only child. Moses stood in line to receive the throne of Egypt, the great world power. God was going to prepare a servant who would do his pleasure. All the education and culture of this world dynasty with its unlimited resources was placed before Moses. See Ps. 113:7–8.
f   7:28 See Ex. 2:14. Moses missed God's timing. To know God's will doesn't mean you know God's timing. God made Moses a ruler and a judge, but it took forty years to prepare him. Moses wanted the position forty years before he was ready. No one can make himself ruler and judge—only God has authority to set leaders in place. We cannot raise ourselves up with ministry responsibilities until God releases us. See also Prov. 8:16.

[29] "Shaken by this, Moses fled Egypt[a] and lived as an exile in the land of Midian, where he became the father of two sons. [30] After forty years had passed, while he was in the desert near Mount Sinai, the Messenger of Yahweh[b] appeared to him in the midst of a flaming thorn bush.[c] [31] Moses was astonished and stunned by what he was seeing, so he drew closer to observe this marvel. Then the Lord Yahweh spoke to him out of the flames:

[32] 'I am the living God,[d] the God of your ancestors.
   I am the God of Abraham, Isaac, and Jacob.'

"Trembling in God's presence and overwhelmed with awe, Moses didn't even dare to look into the fire.

[33] "Out of the flames the Lord Yahweh said to him:

'Take the sandals off your feet,[e]
   for you are standing in the realm of holiness.[f]
[34] I have watched and seen how my people
   have been mistreated[g] in Egypt.
I have heard their painful groaning,
   and now I have come down to set them free.
So come to me, Moses,
   for I am sending you to Egypt to represent me.'[h]

[35] "So God sent back to Egypt the man our people rejected and refused to recognize by saying, 'Who appointed you to be our ruler and judge?' God sent this man back to be their ruler and deliverer, commissioned with the power of the messenger who appeared to him in the flaming thorn bush. [36] This man brought the people out from their Egyptian bondage with many astonishing wonders and miracle signs—miracles in Egypt, miracles at the Red Sea, and miracles during their forty-year journey through the wilderness. [37] This is the same Moses who said to our ancestors, 'The Lord God[i] will raise up one from among you who will be a prophet to you, like I have been. Listen to everything he will say!'[j]

---

a 7:29 See Heb. 11:24–27.

b 7:30 As translated from the Aramaic.

c 7:30 See Ex. 3:2.

d 7:32 As translated from the Aramaic.

e 7:33 Removing one's shoes indicated the highest reverence. It is symbolic of removing earthly matters from our minds and hearts in readiness to accept spiritual realities.

f 7:33 Or "you are standing on ground that is set apart" (sacred).

g 7:34 The Aramaic is "I have seen their torment."

h 7:34 See Ex. 3:6–10.

i 7:37 As translated from the Aramaic.

j 7:37 As translated from the Aramaic. See Deut. 18:15.

[38] "Moses led the congregation in the wilderness [a] and *he spoke face-to-face* with the angel who spoke with him on the top of Mount Sinai. Along with our ancestors, he received the living oracles of God that were passed down to us. [39] But our forefathers refused to obey. They pushed him away, and their hearts longed to return to Egypt.

[40] "While Moses was on the mountain, our forefathers said to Aaron, 'Make us gods to lead us, because we don't know what has become of this Moses who brought us out of Egypt.' [b]

[41] "So they made a god, an idol in the form of a bull calf. They offered sacrifices to it and celebrated with delight what their own hands had made. [c]

[42] "When God saw what they had done, he turned away from them and handed them over to the worship of the stars of heaven, [d] as recorded in the prophetic writings: [e]

'People of Israel, you failed to worship me
  when you offered animal sacrifices
  for forty years in the wilderness.
[43] Instead you worshiped the god Moloch, [f]
  and you carried his tabernacle, not mine.
  You worshiped your star-god, Rephan. [g]
  You made idols with your hands
  and worshiped them instead of me.
  So now I will cast you into exile beyond Babylon.'

[44] "God gave Moses the revelation of the pattern of the tabernacle of the testimony. By God's command, he made it exactly according to the specifications given to him for our ancestors in the wilderness. [45] The next generation received possession of it, and under Joshua's [h] leadership they took possession of the land of the nations, which God drove out in front of them. The tabernacle was carried about until [46] David found loving favor with God and prayed for a dwelling place for the God of Jacob, [47] but it was Solomon who built him a house. [i]

[48] "However, the Most High God does not live in temples made by human hands, as the prophet said: [j]

---

a 7:38 Or "Moses is the one who was in the assembly in the wilderness."
b 7:40 The Aramaic is "We don't know who this Moses is." See Ex. 32:1, 23.
c 7:41 Or "They had a party in honor of what their own hands had made."
d 7:42 This was in violation of Deut. 4:19; 17:2–5.
e 7:42 See Amos 5:25–27.
f 7:43 This was the Canaanite god of the sun and sky.
g 7:43 Or "Derphan," or "Remphan." This is the Assyrian deity also referred to as Saturn.
h 7:45 In Aramaic-Hebrew, the spelling of Joshua and Jesus is the same: *Yeshua*.
i 7:47 See 2 Chron. 5.
j 7:48 See Isa. 66:1–2.

⁴⁹ 'Heaven is my throne room and the earth
    is but a footstool for my feet.
    How could you possibly build a house
    that could contain me?' says the Lord Yahweh.
    'And where could you find a place where I could live?
⁵⁰ Don't you know that it is my hands
    that have built my house,ᵃ not yours?'

⁵¹ "Why would you be so stubborn as to close your hearts and your ears to me? You are always opposing the Holy Spirit, just like your forefathers! ⁵² Which prophet was not persecuted and murdered by your ancestors? Name just one! They killed them all—even the ones who prophesied long ago of the coming of the Righteous One! Now you follow in their steps and have become his betrayers and murderers. ⁵³ You have been given the law by the visitationᵇ of angels, but you have not obeyed it."

Stephen Is Stoned to Death

⁵⁴ When they heard these things, they were overtaken with violent rage filling their souls, and they gnashed their teeth at him. ⁵⁵ But Stephen, overtaken with great faith,ᶜ was full of the Holy Spirit. He fixed his gaze into the heavenly realm and saw the glory and splendor of God—and Jesus, who stood up at the right hand of God.

⁵⁶ "Look!" Stephen said. "I can see the heavens opening and the Son of Man standing at the right hand of God to welcome me home!"ᵈ

⁵⁷ His accusers covered their ears with their hands and screamed at the top of their lungs to drown out his voice. ⁵⁸ Then they pounced on him and threw him outside the city walls to stone him. His accusers, one by one, placed their outer garments at the feet of a young man named Saul of Tarsus.ᵉ

⁵⁹ As they hurled stone after stone at him, Stephen prayed, "Our Lord Jesus, accept my spirit into your presence." ⁶⁰ He crumpled to his knees and shouted in a loud voice, "Our Lord, don't hold this sin against them."ᶠ And then he died.

Saul Persecutes the Believers

8 Now, Saul agreed to be an accomplice to Stephen's stoning and participated in his execution. From that day on, a great persecution of the church in

---

a 7:50 Or "all these things."
b 7:53 As translated from the Aramaic. The Greek is "by angelic decrees."
c 7:55 As translated from the Aramaic.
d 7:56 Jesus sits at the right hand of God, but when he saw Stephen give his last breath for the gospel, he stood to welcome his martyr into his eternal reward.
e 7:58 That is, Saul, who would be converted and become Paul the apostle. Stephen's graduation was Paul's initiation.
f 7:60 See Luke 23:34, 46.

Jerusalem began. All the believers scattered into the countryside of Judea and among the Samaritans, except the apostles who remained behind in Jerusalem. [2] God-fearing men gave Stephen a proper burial and mourned greatly over his death. [3] Then Saul mercilessly persecuted the church of God, going from house to house into the homes of believers to arrest both men and women and drag them off to prison.

The Gospel Spreads to Samaria

[4] Although the believers were scattered by persecution, they preached the wonderful news of the word of God wherever they went. [5] Philip traveled to a Samaritan city[a] and preached to them the wonderful news of the Anointed One. [6] The crowds were eager to receive[b] Philip's message and were persuaded by the many miracles and wonders he performed. [7] Many demon-possessed people were set free and delivered as evil spirits came out of them with loud screams and shrieks, and many who were lame and paralyzed were also healed.[c] [8] This resulted in an uncontainable joy filling the city!

Simon the Sorcerer Converted

[9] Now, there was a man who lived there who was steeped in sorcery. For some time he had astounded the people of Samaria with his magic, boasting to be someone great.[d] [10] Everyone, from the least to the greatest among them, was dazzled by his sorcery,[e] saying, "This man is the greatest wizard of all! The divine power of God walks among us!" [11] For many years everyone was in awe of him because of his astonishing displays of the magic arts.

[12] But as Philip preached the wonderful news of God's kingdom realm, and the name of Jesus the Anointed One, many believed his message and were baptized, both men and women. [13] Even Simon believed and was baptized! Wherever Philip went, Simon was right by his side, astounded by all the miracles, signs, and enormous displays of power that he witnessed.

[14] When the apostles in Jerusalem heard that the Samaritans had accepted God's message of life, they sent Peter and John [15] to pray over them so that they would receive the Holy Spirit.[f] [16] For they had only been baptized in the name of the Lord Jesus and were yet to have the Holy Spirit fall upon them. [17] As soon

---

a 8:5 Or "the main city of Samaria." Many believe this was the Samaritan city of Sebaste.
b 8:6 As translated from the Aramaic, which indicates they did more than just hear the good news; they silenced those who said anything against Philip's message.
c 8:7 Healings, miracles, and deliverances were being accomplished through others, not just the apostles.
d 8:9 The Aramaic is "He boasted of himself, saying, 'I am the great god!'"
e 8:10 The Aramaic is "They were all praying to him" or "bowing down to him."
f 8:15 Or "take hold of the Holy Spirit."

as Peter and John arrived, they laid their hands on the Samaritan believers, one after another, and the Holy Spirit fell and filled each one of them![a]

[18] When Simon saw how the Holy Spirit was released through the laying on of the apostles' hands, he approached them and offered them money, [19] saying, "I want this power too. I'm willing to pay you for the anointing[b] that you have, so that I also can lay my hands on everyone to receive the Holy Spirit."

[20] Peter rebuked him and said, "Your money will go with you to destruction! How could you even think that you could purchase God's supernatural gift with money? [21] You will never have this gift or take part in this ministry,[c] for your heart is not right with God. [22] Repent this moment for allowing such wickedness to fill you. Plead with the Lord that perhaps he would forgive you the treachery of your heart. [23] For I discern that jealous envy[d] has poisoned you and binds you as a captive to sin."

[24] Simon begged, "Peter, please pray to God for me. Plead with him so that nothing you just said over me may come to pass!"

Philip and the Ethiopian

[25] After Peter and John had testified and taught the word of God in that city, they returned to Jerusalem, stopping at many Samaritan villages along the way to preach the hope of the gospel.[e]

[26] Then the Lord's angel said to Philip, "Now go south from Jerusalem on the desert road to Gaza." [27] He left immediately on his assignment.

Along the way he encountered an Ethiopian *who believed in the God of the Jews,*[f] who was the minister of finance for Candace, queen of Ethiopia. He was on his way home from worshiping God in Jerusalem. [28] As he rode along in his chariot, he was reading from the scroll of Isaiah.

[29] The Holy Spirit said to Philip, "Go and walk alongside the chariot."

[30] So Philip ran to catch up. As he drew closer he overheard the man reading from the scroll of Isaiah the prophet. Philip asked him, "Sir, do you understand what you're reading?"

[31] The man answered, "How can I possibly make sense of this without someone explaining it to me?"[g] So he invited Philip up into his chariot to sit with him.

---

a 8:17 Implied in the text. The Greek is "They took hold of the Holy Spirit." That is, the power of the Holy Spirit came upon them and filled them.

b 8:19 Or "authority."

c 8:21 Or "You have no part with us in this word" (*logos*). The Aramaic is "You have no portion in this faith."

d 8:23 Or "bitter anger."

e 8:25 As translated from the Aramaic.

f 8:27 Implied by the Aramaic word *mhymna*, a homonym that can mean "believer" or "eunuch." It is difficult to understand why a minister of finance would need to become a eunuch.

g 8:31 Or "unless someone guide me."

[32] The portion from Isaiah he was reading was this:

He was led away to the slaughter
like a lamb to be offered.
He was like a lamb that is silent
before those who sheared him—
he never even opened his mouth.
[33] In his lowliness justice was stripped away from him. [a]
And who could fully express his struggles?
For his life was taken from the earth. [b]

[34] The Ethiopian asked Philip, "Please, can you tell me who the prophet is speaking of? Is it himself or another man?"

[35] Philip started with this passage and shared with him the wonderful message of Jesus.

[36] As they were traveling down the road, the man said, "Look, here's a pool of water. Why don't I get baptized right now?"

[37] Philip replied, "If you believe with all your heart, I'll baptize you."

The man answered, "I believe that Jesus is the Anointed One, the Son of God." [c]

[38] The Ethiopian stopped his chariot, and they went down into the water [d] and Philip baptized him. [39-40] When they came up out of the water, Philip was suddenly snatched up by the Spirit of the Lord and instantly carried away to the city of Ashdod, [e] where he reappeared, preaching the gospel in that city.

The man never saw Philip again. He returned to Ethiopia full of great joy. Philip, however, traveled on to all of the towns of that region, bringing them the good news, until he arrived at Caesarea. [f]

---

a 8:33 Which means he had no one there to defend him and stand up for justice.

b 8:33 As translated from the Aramaic. Both the Greek and the Aramaic are difficult to translate. The Greek is "Who can describe his posterity?" or "Who could describe the [evil] people of his time?" The Aramaic word for "struggles" (sufferings) and "generation" is the homonym darreh. See Isa. 53:7–8.

c 8:37 Although only a few later Greek manuscripts include v. 37, it is found in one of the oldest Aramaic texts (Harklean Syriac Version, AD 616) and one Greek uncial from the eighth century. There is widespread consensus among scholars of both Greek and Aramaic texts that v. 37 was added as an ancient Christian confession of faith.

d 8:38 There was no need to go down into the water if it was a baptism of sprinkling. Philip immersed the believing Ethiopian man in baptism.

e 8:39-40 Or "Azotus." This translation of Philip was an amazing miracle, as the city of Ashdod would have been fifteen miles or more from the desert road to Gaza. This miracle of being translated also took place with Ezekiel. See Ezek. 3:12–15.

f 8:39-40 This prominent Roman city was also known as Caesarea by the Sea.

Saul Encounters Jesus

9 During those days, Saul, full of angry threats and rage,[a] wanted to murder the disciples of the Lord Jesus. So he went to ask the high priest [2] and requested a letter of authorization he could take to the Jewish leaders in Damascus,[b] requesting their cooperation in finding and arresting any who were followers of the Way.[c] Saul wanted to capture all of the believers he found, both men and women, and drag them as prisoners back to Jerusalem. [3] *So he obtained the authorization* and left for Damascus.

Just outside the city, a brilliant light flashing from heaven suddenly exploded all around him. [4] Falling to the ground, he heard a booming voice say to him, **"Saul, Saul, why are you persecuting me?"**[d]

[5-7] The men accompanying Saul were stunned and speechless, for they heard a heavenly voice but could see no one.

Saul replied, "Who are you, Lord?"

"I am Jesus, the Victorious,[e] the one you are persecuting.[f] Now, get up and go into the city, where you will be told what you are to do."

[8] Saul stood to his feet, and even though his eyes were open he could see nothing—he was blind. So the men had to take him by the hand and lead him into Damascus. [9] For three days he didn't eat or drink and couldn't see a thing.

[10] Living in Damascus was a believer named Ananias. The Lord spoke to him in a vision, calling his name. **"Ananias."**

"Yes, Lord," Ananias answered.

[11-12] The Lord said, **"Go at once to the street called Abundance[g] and look**

---

a 9:1 As translated from the Aramaic.

b 9:2 Or "synagogues of Damascus."

c 9:2 The "Way" is Jesus Christ, the way that God dispenses himself into human beings. He lives inside of those who believe in him. See John 14:6. "The Way" is also a term Luke uses throughout the book of Acts to designate believers in Jesus.

d 9:4 To persecute the church is to persecute Jesus. He is one with his beloved church. See Zech. 2:8.

e 9:5–7 As translated from the Aramaic, which uses the word *scion*. Although *scion* is often translated "branch" (Nazarene), it can also be mean "victorious" or "heir of a mighty family."

f 9:5–7 The Aramaic adds a line here that can be translated "Is it hard for you to rear up against a scorpion's stinger" (or goads)?

g 9:11–12 As translated from the Aramaic, or "Fat Street." The Greek is "Straight Street." As the straightest street in the city, this is the main east-west thoroughfare in Damascus, which is known today as Midhat Pasha Souq. Damascus, only 190 miles northeast of Jerusalem, in 2017 has a population of about two million and is considered to be the oldest continually inhabited city in the world. Many remnants of the Roman occupation, including two-thirds of the walls of the city, can still be seen today. The conversion of Saul the legalist into Paul the grace preacher has a significant lesson for us. We can be amazingly wrong while thinking we are doing right. The Holy Spirit awakens our hearts to feast on Christ, our righteousness. Religion has a deadening effect on our hearts. Like Saul, we have to fall off our "high horse" and bite the dust before our blinded eyes can see.

for a man from Tarsus^a named Saul. You will find him at Judah's house.^b While he was praying,^c he saw in a supernatural vision a man named Ananias^d coming to lay hands upon him to restore his sight."^e

¹³ "But Lord," Ananias replied, "many have told me about his terrible persecution of those in Jerusalem who are devoted to you.^f ¹⁴ In fact, the high priest has authorized him to seize and imprison all those in Damascus who call on your name."

¹⁵ The Lord Yahweh^g answered him, "Arise and go! I have chosen this man to be my special messenger.^h He will be brought before kings, before many nations, and before the Jewish people to give them the revelation of who I am. ¹⁶ And I will show him how much he is destined to sufferⁱ because of his passion for me."

¹⁷ Ananias left and found the house where Saul was staying. He went inside and laid hands on him, saying, "Saul, my brother, the Lord Jesus, who appeared to you on the road, has sent me to pray for you so that you might see again and be filled to overflowing with the Holy Spirit."

¹⁸ All at once, the crusty substance that was over Saul's eyes disappeared and he could see perfectly. Immediately, he got up and was baptized. ¹⁹ After eating a meal,^j his strength returned.^k

²⁰ Within the hour^l he was in the synagogues, preaching about Jesus and proclaiming, "Jesus is the Son of God!"^m ²¹ Those who heard him were astonished, saying among themselves, "Isn't this the Saul who furiously persecuted those in Jerusalem who called on the name of Jesus? Didn't he come here with permission from the high priest to drag them off and take them as prisoners?"

²² Saul's power increased greatly as he became more and more proficient

---

a 9:11–12 Tarsus, or Cilicia, is in southeastern Turkey. Tarsus means "a basket." See v. 25.

b 9:11–12 Or "Judas' house." (Judah's house is the house of praise).

c 9:11–12 Made explicit from the text.

d 9:11–12 Ananias means "the Lord's gracious gift." He truly was the Lord's gracious gift to Paul, who was healed by God's gracious gift. The word *grace* is found 125 times in the New Testament, and Paul uses the word 120 times.

e 9:11–12 Ananias means "Yah is merciful." This is a wonderful play on words in the Aramaic, for God is about to show mercy to Saul and is asking Ananias to live up to his name.

f 9:13 Or "your holy ones."

g 9:15 As translated from the Aramaic word for "Yahweh," *MarYah.*

h 9:15 Or "tool."

i 9:16 Or "experience."

j 9:19 Some Aramaic manuscripts add, "He accepted the message of salvation," or "He received the hope" (of the kingdom).

k 9:19 The sentence "Saul remained with the disciples for several days" has been placed in v. 22 as a concluding statement of the narrative.

l 9:20 As translated from the Aramaic.

m 9:20 Or "This Man is the Son of God."

in proving that Jesus was the anointed Messiah. Saul remained there for several days with the disciples, even though it agitated the Jews of Damascus.

Saul Escapes from Damascus

²³ As time passed, the Jews plotted together to kill Saul, ²⁴ but it was revealed to him what they were about to do. They closely guarded the gates of the city and tracked his every movement so they could kill him. ²⁵ But during the night, some of Saul's converts helped him escape by lowering him down through an opening in the wall, hiding him in a woven basket.ᵃ

Saul Returns to Jerusalem

²⁶ When Saul arrived in Jerusalem, he attempted to introduce himself to the fellowship of the believers, but everyone was afraid of him because they doubted he was a true disciple. ²⁷ Barnabasᵇ came to his defense and brought him before the apostles. Saul shared with them his supernatural experience of seeing the Lord, who spoke with him on the road to Damascus. Barnabas also told them how boldly Saul preached throughout the city in Jesus' mighty name.

²⁸ Then they accepted him as a brother and he remained with them, joining them wherever they went in Jerusalem, boldly preaching in the power and authority of Jesus.ᶜ ²⁹ He openly debated with some of the Jews who had adopted the Greek culture,ᵈ yet they were secretly plotting to murder him. ³⁰ When the believers discovered their scheme, they smuggled him out of the city and took him to Caesarea and then sent him on to Tarsus.ᵉ

³¹ After this, the church all over Judea, Galilee, and Samaria experienced a season of peace.ᶠ The congregations grew larger and larger, with the believers being empowered and encouraged by the Holy Spirit. They worshiped God in wonder and awe,ᵍ and walked in the fear of the Lord.

---

a 9:25 See 2 Cor. 11:33.

b 9:27 See Acts 4:36–37.

c 9:28 Or "in the name of Jesus."

d 9:29 Or "Hellenist Jews." These were Jews who had adopted the Greek culture and language, as opposed to the orthodox Jews, who were strictly following Hebrew culture. The respected historian Josephus writes in AD 44, in his book of Jewish wars, that Greek was not the predominant language spoken in Israel. (See *Antiquities* xx, xi, 2.) The Hellenists were Jewish immigrants who had lived in Alexandria, Greece, and in Rome. They would have learned Greek culture and language as well as Hebrew.

e 9:30 Tarsus was a city in south-central Turkey, about ten miles from the Mediterranean coast. Saul's family originated from Tarsus, but he grew up in Jerusalem as an orthodox Jew.

f 9:31 The "church" in a region is mentioned here, "Judea, Galilee, and Samaria." Even though great cultural distinctions existed between them, the Holy Spirit had made them one church.

g 9:31 Implied in the Hebraic concept of "the fear of the Lord," which means more than just dread or terror. It also includes "to worship with awe."

Peter Heals Aeneas

[32] As Peter was ministering[a] from place to place, he visited God's devoted ones in the village of Lydda.[b] [33] He met a man there named Aeneas[c] who had been paralyzed and bedridden for eight years. [34] Peter said to him, "Aeneas, Jesus the Anointed One instantly and divinely heals you. Now, get up and make your bed."

[35] All at once he stood to his feet. And when all the people of Lydda and Sharon saw him, they became believers in the Lord.[d]

Peter Raises the Dead

[36] Now, there was a follower of Jesus who lived in Joppa. Her Aramaic name, Tabitha, means "gazelle."[e] She lived her life doing kind things for others and serving the poor. [37] But then she became very ill and died. After the disciples prepared her body for burial,[f] they laid her in an upstairs room.

[38] When the believers heard that Peter was nearby in Lydda, they sent two men with an urgent message for him to come without delay. [39] So Peter went with them back to Joppa, and upon arriving they led him to the upper room.

There were many widows standing next to Peter, weeping. One after another showed him the tunics and other garments that Tabitha had made to bless others. [40] Peter made them all leave the room.[g] Then he knelt down and prayed. Turning to the dead body, he said, "Tabitha, rise up!"

At once she opened her eyes, and seeing Peter, she sat up. [41] He took her by the hand and helped her to her feet. Then he called for the believers and all the widows to come and see that she was alive!

[42] The news spread all over the city of Joppa, and many believed in the Lord. [43] Peter remained in Joppa for several more days as a guest at the house of Simon the tanner.[h]

An Angel Comes to Cornelius

10 At that time there was a Roman military officer, Cornelius, who was in charge of one hundred men stationed in Caesarea. He was the captain of the Italian regiment,[i] [2] a devout man of extraordinary character who

---

a 9:32 Or "traveling."

b 9:32 Lydda (Aramaic, *Lod*) means "strife."

c 9:33 Aeneas means "praise." "Praise" had been paralyzed for eight years. Eight is the number of a new beginning.

d 9:35 Or "they turned to the Lord."

e 9:36 Or "Dorcas," which is the Greek word for "deer." The name Dorcas is also found in v. 39 in the Greek.

f 9:37 Or "washed her body." By implication they prepared her for burial.

g 9:40 The Greek word used here is *ekballo*, a strong word that can mean "drive out" or "cast out."

h 9:43 Or "Simon Berseus."

i 10:1 Cornelius was a centurion who was in charge of a sixth of a cohort of six hundred men. It seems likely that Cornelius was a gentile who had converted to Judaism.

worshiped God and prayed regularly, together with all his family. He also had a heart for the poor and gave generously to help them.

[3] One afternoon about three o'clock, he had an open vision and saw the angel of God appear right in front of him, calling out his name, "Cornelius!"

[4] Startled, he was overcome with fear by the sight of the angel. He asked, "What do you want, Lord?"

The angel said, "All of your prayers and your generosity to the poor have ascended before God as an eternal offering.[a] [5] Now, send some men to Joppa at once. Have them find a man named Simon the Rock,[b] [6] who is staying as a guest in the home of Simon the tanner, whose house is by the sea."

[7] After the angel left, Cornelius called for two of his servants and a trusted, godly soldier who was his personal attaché. [8] He explained to them everything that had just happened and sent them off to Joppa.

Peter's Trance

[9] The next day around noon, as Cornelius' men were approaching Joppa, Peter went up to the flat roof[c] of the house to pray. [10] He was hungry and wanted to eat, but while lunch was being prepared he fell into a trance and entered into another realm.[d] [11] As the heavenly realm opened up, he saw something resembling a large linen tablecloth that descended from above, being let down to the earth by its four corners. [12] As it floated down he saw that it held many kinds of four-footed animals, reptiles, and wild birds.

[13] A voice said to him, "Peter, go and prepare them to be eaten."

[14] Peter replied, "There's no way I could do that, Lord, for I've never eaten anything forbidden or impure *according to our Jewish laws*."

[15] The voice spoke again. "Nothing is unclean if God declares it to be clean."[e]

[16] The vision was repeated three times.[f] Then suddenly the linen sheet was snatched back up into heaven.

---

a 10:4 Or "as an offering that he remembers."

b 10:5 Or "Simon, who is also called Peter" (Rock).

c 10:9 This was common when the house was filled with smoke from the cooking fires.

d 10:10 The Greek word for "trance" (*ekstasis*, from which we get the word *ecstasy*) literally means "to be taken to another place" (state or realm). (See *Strong's Concordance*, Gr. 1611.) He was actually taken into another realm as a trance came over him.

e 10:15 Or "purified." The meaning of this spiritual vision is this: God has declared every human being to be of special worth and dignity. The entire world needs the gospel. The four corners of the large tablecloth represent the four corners of the earth. The clean animals represent God's people, the Jews, and the unclean speak of the non-Jewish nations. This encounter helped Peter understand that God was about to send him off with the men who were at the door of the house, even though their religion had been labeled "unclean."

f 10:16 Peter's history contains a number of threes. Peter denied he knew Jesus three times, the Lord restored Peter by challenging his love three times, and here we have the vision repeated three times.

¹⁷ Peter was so stunned by the vision that he couldn't stop wondering about what all it meant.

Meanwhile, Cornelius' men had learned where Peter was staying and at that same moment were standing outside the gate.

¹⁸ They called out to those in the house, "Is this where Simon, the Rock,ᵃ is staying?"

¹⁹⁻²⁰ As Peter was in deep thought, trying to interpret the vision, the Spirit said to him, "Go downstairs now, for three men are looking for you. Don't hesitate to go with them,ᵇ because I have sent them."

²¹ Peter went downstairs to the men and said, "I believe I'm the one you're looking for. What brings you here?"

²² They answered, "We serve Cornelius, a Roman military captain, who sent us to find you. He is a devout man of the highest integrity who worshipsᶜ God and is respected throughout the Jewish community. He was divinely instructed through the appearance of an angel to summon you to his home and to listen to the message that you would bring him."

²³ Peter invited them to stay for the night as his guests. The next morning they departed, accompanied by some of the believers from Joppa.

²⁴ The next day they arrived in Caesarea, where Cornelius was waiting anxiously for them and had gathered together all of his relatives and close friends. ²⁵ The moment Peter walked in the door, Cornelius fell at his feet to worship him. ²⁶ But Peter pulled him to his feet and said, "Stand up, for I'm only a man and no different from you."

²⁷ They talked together and then went inside, where Peter found a large gathering *waiting to hear his words.*

²⁸ Peter said to them, "You all know that it is against the Jewish laws for me to associate with or even visit the home of one who is not a Jew. Yet God has shown me that I should never view anyone as inferiorᵈ or ritually unclean. ²⁹ So when you sent for me, I came without objection.ᵉ Now, may I ask why you sent for me?"

³⁰ Cornelius replied, "Four days ago I was fastingᶠ and praying here in my home at this very hour, three o'clock in the afternoon, when a man in glistening clothing suddenly appeared in front of my eyes. ³¹ He said, 'Cornelius, God has heard your prayers. Your generosity to the poor has been

---

a 10:18 Or "Peter."

b 10:19–20 Or "Don't let prejudice keep you from going with them." The Aramaic is literally "Don't be divided" (in your soul).

c 10:22 Or "fears God."

d 10:28 Or "forbidden."

e 10:29 The Aramaic is "I was destined to come to you."

f 10:30 As translated from the Aramaic. The Greek has no mention of Cornelius fasting.

recorded and remembered in God's presence.ᵃ ³²However, you must send for a man named Simon, the Rock, who is staying in Joppa as a guest of Simon the tanner, who lives by the sea.' ³³So I immediately sent my men to bring you here—and you were kind enough to come. And now, here we are, all of us in God's presence, anxious to hear the message that God has put into your heart to share with us."

³⁴Peter said, "Now I know for certain that God doesn't show favoritism with peopleᵇ *but treats everyone on the same basis.*ᶜ ³⁵It makes no difference what race of people one belongs to. If they show deep reverence for God, and are committed to doing what's right, they are acceptable before him. ³⁶God sent his word to the Jewish people first,ᵈ announcing the wonderful news of hope and peaceᵉ through Jesus, the Anointed One, the Lord of all.ᶠ ³⁷You are well aware of all that began in Galilee and spread throughout the land of Israel immediately after John preached his message of baptism.

³⁸"Jesus of Nazareth was anointed by God with the Holy Spirit and with great power. He did wonderful things for others and divinely healed all who were under the tyranny of the devil,ᵍ for God had anointed him. ³⁹We apostles were eyewitnesses to all the miraclesʰ that he performed throughout the land of Israel. Finally, in Jerusalem, he was crucified on a cross,ⁱ ⁴⁰but God raised him from the dead three days later, allowing him to be seen openly.ʲ ⁴¹He didn't appear to everyone, but he appeared to us, his chosen witnesses. He actually ate and drank with usᵏ after he rose from the dead!ˡ

⁴²"Jesus ordered us to preach and warn the peopleᵐ that God had appointed him to be the judge of the living and the dead. ⁴³*And not only us,* but all of the

a 10:31 The Aramaic is "Your acts of righteousness are offerings before God."
b 10:34 The Aramaic is "God is not the God of hypocrites."
c 10:34 The Greek is "God is not one who receives masks (faces)." God doesn't treat us according to externalities but according to what is in our hearts.
d 10:36 The Aramaic is "For the Living Expression was the inheritance of the Jewish people."
e 10:36 Or by inference, "peace with God through Jesus Christ." Only the Aramaic has "hope and peace."
f 10:36 The Aramaic is "who is Master Yahweh of all." That is, Jesus is Lord, not just for the Jewish people but for all people groups. The Aramaic is "who is Master Yahweh of all."
g 10:38 The Greek word for "devil" can also be translated "slanderer-liar."
h 10:39 Or "things." By inference, the miracles of healing and deliverance.
i 10:39 Or "hung him on a tree and killed him." See Deut. 21:23.
j 10:40 As translated from the Aramaic.
k 10:41 The word *sumpino* means "to drink together." It is used only here in the New Testament and refers to being refreshed by drinking the after-dinner wine together. Jesus celebrated with his disciples after his resurrection. He still longs to celebrate with us today.
l 10:41 See Luke 24:35–49.
m 10:42 Or "He commanded us to tell everyone the command."

prophets agree in their writings that everyone who believes in him receives complete forgiveness [a] of sins through the power of his name."

The Holy Spirit Falls

[44] While Peter was speaking, the Holy Spirit cascaded over all those listening to his message. [45] The Jewish brothers who had accompanied Peter were astounded that the gift of the Holy Spirit was poured out on people who weren't Jews, [46] for they heard them speaking in supernaturally given languages and passionately praising God. [b]

[47] Peter said, "How could anyone object to these people being baptized? For they have received the Holy Spirit just as we have." [48] So he instructed them to be baptized in the power of the name of Jesus, the Anointed One.

After their baptism, they asked Peter to stay with them for a few more days. [c]

Ethnic Barriers Broken

11 The news traveled fast and soon reached the apostles and the believers living in Judea that non-Jewish people were also receiving God's *message of new life.* [2] When Peter finally arrived in Jerusalem, the Jewish believers called him to task, saying, [3] "Why did you stay in the home of people who aren't Jewish? You even ate your meals with them!"

[4] Peter explained what had happened, saying, [5] "One day when I was in the city of Joppa, while I was praying I fell into an ecstatic trance and I went into another realm. [d] I saw in a vision something like a linen tablecloth descending out of heaven, being let down by its four corners, and it got close to me. [6] As I examined it I saw many four-footed animals, wild animals, reptiles, and wild birds. [7] Then I heard a voice say to me, 'Get up, Peter. Kill and eat them.'

[8] "I said, 'I can't do that, Lord! For I've never eaten anything that is forbidden or impure according to our Jewish laws.'

[9] "The voice spoke to me again, saying, 'Nothing is unclean if God declares it to be clean.'

---

a 10:43 Or "cancellation."

b 10:46 This is the gentile Pentecost as the Holy Spirit fell on gentile believers for the first time, imparting to them the gift of tongues.

c 10:48 At last the gospel broke through and penetrated into the non-Jewish cultures and people groups. The Holy Spirit was now uniting Jewish believers and non-Jewish believers into one mystical body of Christ on the earth. Because of this, there would no longer be a distinction between Jew and non-Jew, but one family of believers formed by faith in Jesus Christ. See Gal. 3:26–29. The three conversions of the Ethiopian dignitary in ch. 8, Saul of Tarsus in ch. 9, and the Roman officer Cornelius in ch. 10 prove the power of the gospel of God. One could view these three represent all of the sons of Noah: Ham (Ethiopian), Shem (Saul), and Japheth (the Roman Cornelius). A black man, a Jew, and a gentile were converted!

d 11:5 See footnote on Acts 10:10.

[10] "The vision repeated itself three times. Then suddenly the linen sheet was snatched back up into heaven. [11] At that moment three men from Caesarea, who had been sent for me, approached the house where I was staying. [12] The Spirit told me to accompany them with no questions asked. These six brothers here with me made the trip, and we entered into the home of the man who had sent for me. [13] He shared with us about the angel who appeared to him and told him to send messengers to Joppa to find Simon, the Rock. The angel had told him, [14] 'He will tell you and your family the message of how you can be saved!'

[15] "Shortly after I began to speak, the Holy Spirit was poured out upon them, just like what happened to us at the beginning. [16] And I remembered the words the Lord had told us: **'John immersed you in water, but you will be immersed in the Holy Spirit.'** [17] So I concluded that if God is pleased to give them the same gift of the Holy Spirit that he gave us after they believed in the Lord Jesus Christ, who am I to stand in the way of God?"

[18] When they heard this, their objections were put to rest and they all glorified God, saying, "Look what God has done! He's giving the gift of repentance that leads to life to people who aren't even Jews."

The Church at Antioch

[19] Because of the persecution triggered by Stephen's death in Jerusalem, many of the believers were scattered. Some reached as far as the coast of Lebanon,[a] the island of Cyprus, and Antioch of Syria, but they were still only preaching the word to Jews. [20] However, some of the believers from Cyprus and Cyrene,[b] who had come to Antioch in Syria,[c] preached to the non-Jews living there, proclaiming the message of salvation in the Lord Jesus.[d] [21] The mighty power of the Lord was with them as they ministered, and a large number of people believed and turned their hearts to the Lord.

[22] News of what was happening in Antioch reached the church of Jerusalem, so the apostles sent Barnabas to Antioch as their emissary. [23] When he got

---

a 11:19 Or "Phoenicia."

b 11:20 A city on the coast of Libya. Some have linked the man who carried the cross of Jesus, Simon of Cyrene, to this group of missionary evangelists.

c 11:20 Antioch was important from both a commercial and a military point of view. It was the seat of the Roman governor-general, with large garrisons and military supplies stored there. It was also a center of art and culture, known for its beauty and recognized as the capital of the Syrian kingdom. The church prospered greatly in Antioch, and it became a Christian hub and headquarters for the apostles. For many centuries in church history, Antioch remained a strong witness for evangelization, sending missionaries into Persia and throughout the Roman Empire.

d 11:20 In the early days of the church, every believer was a missionary. There was a great cost involved with following Christ. They laid their lives down to serve him and to make him known among the nations. Not just the apostles, but all of the believers did their part in spreading the teachings of Jesus wherever they went.

there and witnessed for himself God's marvelous grace, he was enthused and overjoyed. He encouraged[a] the believers to remain faithful and cling to the Lord with passionate hearts.[b] [24] Barnabas was a good man,[c] full of the Spirit of holiness, and he exuded a life of faith. Because of his ministry even more crowds of people were brought to the Lord!

[25] Barnabas left for Tarsus to find Saul and bring him back to Antioch. [26] Together Saul and Barnabas ministered there for a full year, equipping the growing church and teaching the vast number of new converts. It was in Antioch that the followers of Jesus were first revealed as "anointed ones."[d]

Agabus Prophesies a Coming Famine

[27] At that time there were prophets in the church of Jerusalem, and some of them came to Antioch. [28] One of them, named Agabus, stood up in one of the meetings and prophesied by the Holy Spirit that a severe famine was about to come over Israel. (This prophecy was fulfilled during the reign of Claudius Caesar.)[e] [29] So they determined that each believer, according to his or her ability, would give an offering to send as relief to the brothers living in Judea. [30] They set aside the gifts and entrusted the funds to Barnabas and Saul to take to the elders[f] of the church in Jerusalem.[g]

Peter's Miraculous Escape from Prison

12 During this period King Herod[h] incited persecution against the church, causing great harm to the believers. [2] He even had the apostle Jacob,[i] John's brother, beheaded.[j] [3-4] When Herod realized how much this pleased the Jewish leaders, he had Peter arrested and thrown into prison during the Feast of Passover.[k] Sixteen soldiers were assigned to guard him until Herod could bring

---

a 11:23 Barnabas was given the nickname "Encourager." See Acts 4:36–37.

b 11:23 The Aramaic is "He begged them to imitate the Lord with all their hearts."

c 11:24 The Aramaic is "He was a blessed man."

d 11:26 Or "Christians." The Greek word *chrematizo* means "supernaturally revealed" (imparted), more than simply "called." It was first in Antioch that the revelation came that the believers were anointed ones. See also Matt. 2:12, where the term is used as God giving revelation in a dream.

e 11:28 This would have been about AD 45–46.

f 11:30 The Aramaic is "priests."

g 11:30 Upon hearing the prophecy of a famine coming, the church of Antioch determined to receive an offering for the Judean believers, for the gospel came to them from Jerusalem. They gave back to the place where the gospel was sent to them.

h 12:1 Or "King Herod Agrippa."

i 12:2 Or "James." Both Greek and Aramaic leave the Hebrew name as it is, Jacob. According to the Gospels, Jacob (James) and John were the first two disciples of Jesus, and Jacob was the first apostle to be martyred.

j 12:2 Or "executed by the sword."

k 12:3–4 These events most likely took place in AD 42 or 43.

him to public trial, immediately after the Passover celebrations were over. [5] The church went into a season of intense intercession, [a] asking God to free him.

[6] The night before Herod planned to bring him to trial, he made sure that Peter was securely bound with two chains. Peter was sound asleep between two soldiers, with additional guards stationed outside his cell door, [7] when all at once an angel of the Lord appeared, filling his prison cell with a brilliant light. The angel struck Peter on the side [b] to awaken him and said, "Hurry up! Let's go!" Instantly the chains fell off his wrists. [8] The angel told him, "Get dressed. Put on your sandals, bring your cloak, and follow me."

[9] Peter quickly left the cell and followed the angel, even though he thought it was only a dream or a vision, for it seemed unreal—he couldn't believe it was really happening! [10] They walked unseen past the first guard post and then the second before coming to the iron gate that leads to the city—and the gate swung open all by itself right in front of them!

They went out into the city and were walking down a narrow street when all of a sudden the angel disappeared. [11] That's when Peter realized that he wasn't having a dream! He said to himself, "This is really happening! The Lord sent his angel to rescue me from the clutches of Herod and from what the Jewish leaders planned to do to me."

[12] When he realized this, he decided to go to the home of Mary [c] and her son John Mark. The house was filled with people praying. [13] When he knocked on the door to the courtyard, a young servant girl named Rose [d] got up to see who it was. [14] When she recognized Peter's voice, she was so excited that she forgot to open the door, but ran back inside the house to announce, "Peter is standing outside!"

[15] "Are you crazy?" they said to her. But when she kept insisting, they answered, "Well, it must be his angel."

[16] Meanwhile, Peter was still outside, knocking on the door. When they finally opened it, they were shocked to find Peter standing there.

[17] He signaled for them to be quiet as he shared with them the miraculous way the Lord brought him out of prison. Before he left he said, "Make sure you let Jacob [e] and all of the other believers know what has happened."

[18] At the first sign of daylight, the prison guards were in a tremendous uproar because of Peter's disappearance. [f] Herod ordered a thorough search

---

a 12:5 The Greek phrase used here for "intense intercession" means "to stretch tightly in prayer."

b 12:7 The word translated "struck" is the same Greek word used for Jesus being "struck" for our sins (Matt. 26:31). Jesus was pierced in his side to awaken hearts to God. Peter was awakened from his sleep by an angel who struck him on his side.

c 12:12 This Mary was the sister of Barnabas. See Col. 4:10.

d 12:13 Or "Rhoda."

e 12:17 This was Jacob (James), the brother of Jesus.

f 12:18 This is the last mention of Peter in the book of Acts. The remaining chapters focus on the ministry of Paul.

for him, but no one could find him. [19] After he interrogated the guards, he ordered them executed. Then Herod left the province of Judea for Caesarea and stayed there for a period of time.

[20] Now, during those days, Herod was engaged in a violent dispute with the people of Tyre and Sidon.[a] So they sent a united delegation to Caesarea to appeal to him and reconcile their differences[b] with the king, for Herod controlled their food supply. First they enlisted the support of his trusted personal assistant, Blastus, who secured them an appointment with the king.

[21] On the chosen day, Herod came before them, arrayed in his regal robes. Sitting on his elevated throne, he delivered a stirring public address to the people. [22] At its conclusion the people gave him a round of applause. The crowd shouted, "These are the words of a god, not a man!"

[23] Immediately, an angel of the Lord struck Herod with a sickness, an infestation of worms, because he accepted the people's worship and didn't give the glory to God, and he died. [24] But the hope of God's kingdom[c] kept spreading and multiplying everywhere!

[25] After Barnabas and Saul *had delivered the charitable offering for relief,* they left Jerusalem, bringing with them a disciple named Mark (who was also known as John).[d]

Saul and Barnabas Sent Out as Apostles

13 In the church at Antioch there were a number of prophets and teachers of the Word, including Barnabas, Simeon from Niger,[e] Lucius the Libyan, Manean (the childhood companion of King Herod Antipas),[f] and Saul. [2] While they were worshiping as priests[g] before the Lord in prayer and fasting, the Holy Spirit said,[h] "I have called Barnabas and Saul to do an important work

---

a 12:20 Tyre and Sidon are coastal cities in Lebanon, north of Israel.

b 12:20 The Aramaic can also be translated "They wanted cultivated land," which makes sense if their food supply was running out.

c 12:24 As translated from the Aramaic. The Greek is "the word."

d 12:25 This is the Mark who wrote the second Gospel included in our New Testament. John (or *Yochanan*) was his Jewish name; Marcus was his Roman name. Because he once abandoned Paul during a missionary journey, Paul refused to take him with him again. But later, Mark and Paul were fully restored in their ministry together. See 2 Tim. 4:11.

e 13:1 The Aramaic word *niger* means "someone who works with wood, a carpenter." The Latin word *niger* means "black."

f 13:1 Or "who was like a brother to Herod the tetrarch."

g 13:2 Or "serving the Lord." The Greek word used here is also used for priestly duties.

h 13:2 Here we see the Lord of the harvest, the Holy Spirit, sending out laborers into the harvest field. The Holy Spirit speaks in many different ways. Perhaps he spoke a prophecy through one of the prophets in the church, or a divine voice may have interrupted their worship. God's Spirit still speaks today in any way he chooses.

for me. Now, release them[a] to go and fulfill it." [3] So after they had fasted and prayed, they laid hands on them and sent them off.[b]

[4-5] So Saul and Barnabas, *and their assistant Mark (known as John),* were directed by the Holy Spirit to go to Seleucia,[c] and from there they sailed to Cyprus.[d] When they arrived at Salamis,[e] they went to the synagogues and preached the manifestation of our Lord.[f] [6] From there they crossed the island as far as Paphos,[g] where they encountered a Jewish false prophet, a sorcerer named Elymas,[h] who also went by the name of "son of Jesus."[i] [7] He had gained influence as the spiritual advisor to the regional governor, Sergius Paulus, considered by many to be a wise and intelligent leader. The governor requested a meeting with Barnabas and Saul because he wanted to hear the message of God's word.[j] [8] But Elymas, whose name means "sorcerer,"[k] stood up against them and tried to prevent the governor from believing their message.

[9] Saul, also known as Paul,[l] stared into his eyes and rebuked him. Filled with the Holy Spirit, he said, [10] "You son of the devil![m] You are full of every form of fraud and deceit and an enemy of all that is right. When will you stop perverting the truth of God into lies? [11] At this very moment the hand of God's judgment comes down upon you and you will be blind—so blind you won't even be able to see the light of the sun."[n]

---

a 13:2 Or "appoint them." The Greek word used here is found in the Septuagint of Num. 8:11 for consecrating Levites for God's service as priests.

b 13:3 Or "dispatched them" (a military term). This was the commissioning of Barnabas and Saul as apostles. The word *apostle* means "sent one." They were sent by the Holy Spirit and by the church and released as missionaries. The New Testament shows there were many other apostles besides the Twelve. See also Eph. 4:11–13.

c 13:4–5 Implied in the text. Seleucia (modern-day Samandag) was a coastal city in Syria from which Paul and Barnabas left with John Mark for their first missionary journey in AD 49. Seleucia means "white light."

d 13:4–5 Cyprus was the home of Barnabas.

e 13:4–5 Salamis is a city on the southeastern coast of Cyprus. Salamis means "in the middle of salty water."

f 13:4–5 As translated from the Aramaic. The Greek is "the word of God."

g 13:6 Paphos is a city on the southwestern coast of Cyprus. Paphos means "boiling hot."

h 13:6 Or "spiritual advisor." The Greek word *magos* is often translated "astrologer." Although the text does not give us his name, Elymas, until v. 8, it is included here for the sake of the English narrative.

i 13:6 Or "Bar-Jesus" (son of Joshua). The Aramaic is "Bar-Shuma."

j 13:7 The Aramaic can be translated "the manifestation of God."

k 13:8 The Aramaic name Elymas means "magician" or "sorcerer." This would be similar to the Arabic name Alumas, which also means "magician."

l 13:9 From here on in Acts, Saul is only referred to as Paul. Saul means "sought after," and Paul means "little." The name change is descriptive of what happened within Paul, leaving behind greatness in his own eyes and being content to be insignificant. This is the journey every believer must take.

m 13:10 Or "son of the accuser."

n 13:11 The Aramaic is "until the end of the age."

As Paul spoke these words, a shadowy mist[a] and darkness came over the sorcerer, leaving him blind and groping about, begging someone to lead him around by the hand. [12] When the governor witnessed this, he believed and was awestruck by the power of the message of the Lord.

Paul and Barnabas at Antioch in Turkey

[13] Paul and his companions sailed from the Cyprus port of Paphos to Perga in southern Turkey.[b] John left them[c] there and returned to Jerusalem [14] as they journeyed on to the city of Antioch in the region of Pisidia.[d]

On the Sabbath they went into the synagogue and took their seats. [15] After the reading from the scrolls of the books of Moses and the prophets, the leader of the meeting[e] sent Paul and Barnabas a message, saying, "Brothers, do you have a word of encouragement to share with us? If so, please feel free to give it."

[16] Paul stood and motioned that he had something to say. He said, "Listen, all of you Jews and non-Jews who worship God. [17] The God of Israel divinely chose our ancestors to be his people. While they were enslaved in Egypt, he made them great, both in numbers and in strength, until he unveiled his mighty power and led them out of bondage.[f] [18] For nearly forty years, he nourished them in the wilderness.[g] [19] He was the one who destroyed the seven nations inhabiting the land of Canaan[h] and afterward gave the land to his people as their inheritance. [20] This took about four hundred and fifty years.[i]

"Then God raised up deliverers for the people until the time of the prophet Samuel. [21] The people craved for a king, so God gave them one from the tribe of Benjamin: Saul, the son of Kish, who ruled for forty years. [22] After removing him, God raised up David to be king, for God said of him, 'I have found in David, son of Jesse, a man who always pursues my heart[j] and will accomplish all that I have destined him to do.'[k]

---

a   13:11 The Aramaic can be translated "gloom."
b   13:13 Or "Pamphylia," which may mean "a place of mingled races." It is a region in southern Turkey.
c   13:13 The sudden departure of John from the team became an issue between Paul and Barnabas. See Acts 15:36–39.
d   13:14 Antioch in the region of Pisidia is situated in the Sultandag Mountains about one hundred miles north of Perga. This would have been an arduous journey from the sea into the mountains. God was directing his missionaries where to go.
e   13:15 Or "president of the synagogue."
f   13:17 See Ex. 6:6; 12:51.
g   13:18 As translated from the Aramaic and some Greek manuscripts. See also Ex. 16:35; Num. 14:34.
h   13:19 See Deut. 7:1.
i   13:20 There is much debate over where this clause fits. It is possible that it would go with the next sentence, "For four hundred and fifty years God raised up deliverers."
j   13:22 See 1 Sam. 13:14; Ps. 89:19–29.
k   13:22 Or "he will do all my pleasure."

[23] "From David's lineage God brought Israel a Savior, just as he promised. [24] So before Jesus appeared, John preached the message of a baptism of repentance[a] to prepare all of Israel. [25] As John was about to finish his mission, he said repeatedly, 'If you think that I am the one to come, you're mistaken. He will come after me, and I don't even deserve to stoop down and untie his sandals!'

[26] "Fellow Jews, Abraham's descendants, and all those among you who worship and reverence God, this message of life[b] has been sent for us all to hear. [27] But the people of Jerusalem and their leaders didn't realize who he was, nor did they understand the prophecies written of him. Yet they fulfilled those very prophecies, which they read week after week in their meetings, by condemning him to death. [28] Even though they could come up with no legal grounds for the death sentence, they pleaded with Pilate to have him executed. [29] And they did to him all that was prophesied they would do.

"Then they took him down from the cross and laid him in a tomb. [30] But God raised him from the dead! [31] And for many days afterward he appeared on numerous occasions to his disciples who knew him well and had followed him from Galilee to Jerusalem. Those disciples are now his witnesses,[c] telling the people the truth about him.

[32] "So here we are to share with you some wonderful news! The promise God made to our forefathers [33] has now been fulfilled for us, their children. For God has raised Jesus from the dead, as it says in Psalms:

'Today I reveal you as my Son, and I as your Father.'[d]

[34] "God had promised to not let him decay in the tomb or face destruction again, so God raised him from the dead. He gave this promise in the Psalms:

'I will give to you[e] what I gave to David:
Faithful mercies[f] that you can trust.'[g]

[35] "He explains it further in another Psalm:

'You will not allow your holy one
to experience bodily decay.'[h]

[36] "This cannot be a reference to David, for after he passionately served

---

a 13:24 The Aramaic is "the baptism of grace."
b 13:26 As translated from the Aramaic. The Greek is, "the message of salvation." See Ps. 107:20.
c 13:31 The Greek word for "witnesses" can also be translated "martyrs."
d 13:33 See Ps. 2:7.
e 13:34 The Greek is plural, "you all," or "to you and yours."
f 13:34 Or "decrees." See Isa. 55:3.
g 13:34 The Aramaic is "I will give to you the grace [favor] I gave to faithful David."
h 13:35 See Ps. 16:10.

God's desires for his generation, he died. He was buried with his ancestors and his body experienced decay. [37] But the one whom God raised from the dead has never experienced corruption in any form.

[38] "So listen, friends! Through this Jesus, the forgiveness[a] of sins is offered to you. [39] Everyone who believes in him is set free from sin and guilt—something the law of Moses had no power to do. [40] So be very careful that what the prophets warned about does not happen to you:

[41] 'Be amazed and in agony, you scoffers![b]
For in your day I will do something so wonderful
  that when I perform mighty deeds among you,
  you won't even believe that it was I who did it!' "[c]

[42] As Paul and Barnabas started to leave, the people pleaded with them to share more about these things on the next Sabbath day. [43] When the meeting had finally broken up, many of those in attendance, both Jews and converts to Judaism, tagged along with Paul and Barnabas, who continued to persuade them to go deeper in their understanding of God's grace.

[44] The following week, nearly everyone in the city gathered to hear the word of God. [45] When the Jewish leaders saw the size of the crowds, vicious jealousy filled their hearts and they rose up to oppose what Paul was teaching. They insulted him[d] and argued with him over everything he said.

[46] Yet Paul and Barnabas did not back down. Filled with courage, they boldly replied, "We were compelled to bring God's message[e] first to you Jews. But seeing you've rejected this message and refuse to embrace eternal life,[f] we will focus instead on the nations and offer it to them. [47] This will fulfill what the Lord has commanded us:

'I have destined you to become
  a beacon light for the nations
    and release salvation to the ends of the earth!' "[g]

[48] When the non-Jewish people in the crowd heard these words, they were thrilled and they honored[h] the word of the Lord. All who believed that they

---

a 13:38 Or "cancellation."
b 13:41 As translated from the Aramaic. The Greek is "Be amazed and perish, you scoffers."
c 13:41 As translated from the Aramaic. The Greek text seems to quote from the Septuagint version of Hab. 1:5, "I am doing a work in your days that you won't believe even when it is announced to you."
d 13:45 Or "blasphemed."
e 13:46 Or "word."
f 13:46 Or "You view yourselves as unworthy of eternal life."
g 13:47 See Isa. 42:6; 49:6; 60:1–3.
h 13:48 Or "praised."

were destined to experience eternal life received the message. [a] [49] God's word spread like wildfire throughout the entire region.

[50] The Jewish leaders stirred up a violent mob against Paul and Barnabas, including many prominent and wealthy people of the city. They persecuted them and ran them out of town. [51] As they left, they shook the dust off their feet as a sign of protest against them, and they went on to the city of Iconium. [b] [52] They left the new converts in Antioch overflowing with the joy of the Holy Spirit.

Miracles and Revival in Iconium

14 When Paul and Barnabas arrived at Iconium, the same thing happened there. They went, as they always did, to the synagogue and preached to the people with such power that a large crowd of both Jews and non-Jews believed.

[2] Some of the Jews refused to believe, and they began to poison the minds [c] of the non-Jews to discredit the believers. [3] Yet Paul and Barnabas stayed there for a long time, preaching boldly and fearlessly about the Lord. [d] Many trusted in the Lord, for he backed up his message [e] of grace [f] with miracles, signs, and wonders performed by the apostles.

[4] The people of the city were split over the issue. Some sided with the apostles, and others with the Jews *who refused to believe*. [5] Eventually, all the opposition factions came together, with their leaders devising a plot [g] to harm Paul and Barnabas and stone them to death. [6] When the apostles learned about this, [h] they escaped to the region of Lyconia, [i] to the cities of Lystra [j] and Derbe [k] and the nearby villages. [7] And they continued to preach the hope of the gospel. [l]

---

a 13:48 As translated from the Aramaic. The Greek is "Those who were appointed to experience eternal life believed." The Greek word for "appointed" can also be translated "stationed in battle order."

b 13:51 This is present-day Konya, a large city about sixty-two miles (one hundred kilometers) from Antioch. This journey would have taken a number of days. Iconium means "small image" (idol). In Israel, Iconium is a girl's name that means "coming."

c 14:2 Or "embittered their souls."

d 14:3 The Aramaic uses the phrase "the Lord Yahweh," referring to Jesus Christ.

e 14:3 The Aramaic is "manifestation of grace."

f 14:3 The Greek word for grace, *charis*, means "that which brings delight, joy, pleasure, and sweetness." (See *Strong's Concordance*, Gr. 5485.)

g 14:5 The Aramaic is "They issued a decree" (death sentence).

h 14:6 Although not clearly stated, it is possible that it was by supernatural revelation that Paul and Barnabas learned of the plot to kill them.

i 14:6 Lyconia means "land of the wolf."

j 14:6 Lystra means "ransomed" or "set free."

k 14:6 Derbe means "tanner" or "one who covers with skins." The journey from Iconium to these cities would have been about twenty-two miles (thirty-five kilometers).

l 14:7 As translated from the Aramaic. The Greek is "the good news."

Paul and Barnabas Preach at Lystra

[8] In Lystra, Paul and Barnabas encountered a man who from birth had never walked, for he was crippled in his feet. [9] He listened carefully to Paul as he preached. All of a sudden,[a] Paul discerned that this man had faith in his heart to be healed.[b] [10] So he shouted, "You! In the name of our Lord Jesus,[c] stand up on your feet!" The man instantly jumped to his feet, stood for the first time in his life, and walked!

[11] When the crowds saw the miracle Paul had done, they shouted in their own language,[d] "The gods have come down to us as men!" [12] They addressed Barnabas as "Zeus"[e] and Paul as "Hermes,"[f] because he was the spokesman.

[13] Now, outside of the city stood the temple of Zeus. The priest of the temple, in order to honor Paul and Barnabas, brought bulls with wreaths of flowers draped on them to the gates of the courtyard where they were staying.[g] The crowds clamored to offer them as sacrifices to the apostles. He even brought flower wreaths as crowns to place on their heads.

[14] When the apostles[h] understood what was happening, they were mortified and tore their clothes as a sign of dismay. They rushed into the crowd and shouted, [15] "People, what are you doing? We're only weak human beings like everyone else. This is why we've come to tell you the good news, so that you would turn away from these worthless *myths*[i] and turn to the living God. He is the Creator of all things: the earth, the heavens, the sea, and everything they contain. [16] In previous generations he allowed the nations to pursue their own

---

a 14:9 There is an implication in the Greek that Paul was watching this man and waited until he saw faith rise in the man's heart for his healing.

b 14:9 The same phrase, "to be healed," is consistently translated elsewhere in the New Testament as "to be saved." To be saved and to be healed are synonymous.

c 14:10 As translated from the Aramaic. This clause is absent in the Greek.

d 14:11 That is, the Lyconian language.

e 14:12 The Aramaic is "the master of deities," and the Latin is "Jupiter." Also found in v. 13.

f 14:12 Hermes was considered to be the messenger god, whom the Romans called Mercury. In Ovid's famous story *Metamorphoses*, there is an account of Philemon and Baucis from Lystra, who took in two strangers (Zeus and Hermes) and welcomed them into their home. But the rest of the village rejected them, and for that the village was destroyed—only Philemon and Baucis survived. That story was no doubt in the minds of the people when they welcomed Barnabas and Paul. They did not want to make the same mistake as their ancestors. (See Ovid, *Metamorphoses* 8.611–725.) Archeologists have found a stone altar near Lystra with an inscription dedicating it to Zeus and Hermes.

g 14:13 As translated from the Aramaic. The Greek is ambiguous and could be "the gates of the temple" or "the gates of the city."

h 14:14 The book of Acts clearly states that there were more than twelve apostles who were recognized by the church. Barnabas is described multiple times as an apostle. Ephesians 4:11–13 says that apostles and prophets will minister and equip the body of Christ until we are complete and restored into Christ's fullness.

i 14:15 Implied in the text, which is simply "things."

ways, [17] yet he has never left himself without clear evidence of his goodness. For he blesses us with rain from heaven and seasons of fruitful harvests, and he nourishes us with food to meet our needs. He satisfies our lives, and euphoria[a] fills our hearts."

[18] Even after saying these things, they were barely able to restrain the people from offering sacrifices to them.

[19] Some of the Jews who had opposed Paul and Barnabas in Antioch and Iconium arrived and stirred up the crowd against them. They stoned Paul and dragged his body outside the city and left him for dead.

[20] When the believers encircled Paul's body, he miraculously stood up![b] Paul stood and immediately went back into the city. The next day he left with Barnabas for Derbe.

[21] After preaching the wonderful news of the gospel there and winning a large number of followers to Jesus, they retraced their steps and revisited Lystra, Iconium, and Antioch. [22] At each place they went, they strengthened the lives of the believers[c] and encouraged them to go deeper in their faith. And they taught them, "It is necessary for us to enter into the realm of God's kingdom, because that's the only way we will endure our many trials and persecutions."[d]

[23] Paul and Barnabas ordained leaders, known as elders, from among the congregations in every church they visited.[e] After prayer and fasting, they publicly committed them into the care and protection of the Lord of their faith.

[24] After passing through different regions of central Turkey,[f] [25] they went to the city of Perga, preaching the life-giving message of the Lord.[g] Afterward they journeyed down to the coast at Antalya,[h] [26] and from there they sailed back to Antioch.

With their mission complete, they returned to the church where they had originally been sent out as missionaries, for it was in Antioch where they had been

---

a 14:17 See footnote on Acts 2:28.

b 14:20 The Greek word used here, *anistemi*, is used twenty-seven times in the New Testament for people being raised from the dead.

c 14:22 The Aramaic is "they confirmed their spirit of discipleship."

d 14:22 That is, the only way to avoid the oppression of the age is to enter deeper into God's kingdom realm. An alternate translation would be "Through great tribulation we enter into God's kingdom realm." Neither translation of this sentence implies a future kingdom, but a kingdom realm that is presently accessible.

e 14:23 The appointment of elders among the people dates back to the days of Moses in the wilderness. See Ex. 18:21, where the word used to describe these leaders is *khayil*, or "mighty men of valor." The word *khayil* is also used for the radiant church (commonly known as the "virtuous woman" found in Prov. 31). These elders were the pastors and leaders of the churches, ordained by the apostles. See also Heb. 13:17; 1 Tim. 3; Titus 1.

f 14:24 Or "After they had passed through Pisidia, they went into Pamphylia."

g 14:25 Or "the manifestation of Lord Yahweh," as translated from the Aramaic. The Greek is "the word of the Lord."

h 14:25 Or "Attalia." Antalya is a city on the southwestern coast of Turkey.

handed over to God's powerful grace. ²⁷When they arrived in Antioch, they gathered the church together and shared with them all of the wonderful works God had done through them and how God had opened the door of faith for the non-Jews to enter in. ²⁸Afterward, Paul and Barnabas stayed there for a long time in fellowship with the believers.ᵃ

The Jerusalem Council of Apostles

15 While Paul and Barnabas were in Antioch, *some false teachers* came from Judea to trouble the believers. They taught, "Unless you are circumcised, as the law of Moses requires, you cannot be saved." ²This sparked a fierce argument between the false teachers and Paul and Barnabas. So the church appointed a delegation of believers, including Paul and Barnabas, to go to Jerusalem to meet with the apostles and elders of the church and resolve this issue. ³So the church sent them on their way.

As they passed through Lebanonᵇ and Samaria, they stopped to share with the believers how God was converting many from among the non-Jewish people.ᶜ Hearing this report brought great joy to all the churches.

⁴When they finally arrived in Jerusalem, Paul and Barnabas were welcomed by the church, the apostles, and the elders. They explained to them everything God had done among them. ⁵But some of the believers who were of the religious group called "separated ones"ᵈ were insistent, saying, "We must continue the custom of circumcision and require that the people keepᵉ the law of Moses."

⁶So the apostles and elders met privately to discuss the matter further. ⁷After a lengthy debate, Peter rose to his feet and said to them, "Brothers, you know how God has chosen meᶠ from the beginning to preach the wonderful news of the gospel to the non-Jewish nations. ⁸God, who knows the hearts of every person, confirmed this when he gave them the Holy Spirit, just like

---

a 14:28 This would have been AD 47–48, when Paul wrote his letter to the Galatians, the region they had visited during their first missionary journey. Antioch of Syria is here seen as the center of the missionary enterprise as the church hosts the anointed apostles Paul and Barnabas, who taught the church during their time there. For many centuries Antioch of Syria was considered a major Christian center. Into the fourth century, it was noted as having schools of theology and institutions of learning.

b 15:3 Or "Phoenicia."

c 15:3 The Aramaic is "the reconciliation of the gentiles."

d 15:5 Or "Pharisees." The legalism of the Pharisees continued even among some believers, who were still bound in the expressions of external religion.

e 15:5 The Aramaic is "to put a fence around the Torah"; that is, to guard the Torah and keep it as a sacred duty to man. The apostolic council of Acts 15 makes it clear that gentile believers had no obligation to keep that "fence" around the Torah (observing the Mosaic laws).

f 15:7 The wording of the Aramaic text is different, stating, "God chose the gentiles from the beginning to hear the manifestation of the gospel from my mouth and to believe."

he has given the Spirit to us. [a] [9] So now, not one thing separates us as Jews and gentiles, for when they believe he makes their hearts pure. [10] So why on earth would you now *limit God's grace* [b] by placing a yoke of religious duties on the shoulders of the believers that neither we nor our ancestors have been able to bear? [11] Don't you believe that we are introduced to eternal life through the grace of our Lord Jesus—the same grace that has brought these people new life?"

[12] Everyone became silent and listened carefully as Paul and Barnabas shared with the council at length about the signs and wonders and miracles God had worked through them while ministering to the non-Jewish people.

[13] When they had finished, Jacob took the floor and said, "Ladies and gentlemen, listen. [14] Peter has explained thoroughly that God has determined to win a people for himself from among the non-Jewish nations. [15] And the prophet's words are fulfilled:

[16] 'After these things I will return to you
    and raise up the tabernacle of David
    that has fallen into ruin.
    I will restore and rebuild what David experienced
[17] so that all of humanity will be able to encounter the Lord
    including the gentiles whom I have called
    to be my very own,' says the Lord.
[18] 'For I have made known my works from eternity!' [c]

[19] "So, in my judgment, we should not add any unnecessary burden upon the non-Jewish converts who are turning to God. [20] We will go to them as apostles [d] and teach them to be set free from offering sacrifices to idols, sexual immorality, and eating anything strangled or with any blood. [e] [21] For many generations these words of Moses have been proclaimed every Sabbath day in the synagogues."

The Apostles' Letter to the Non-Jewish People

[22] The apostles and elders and the church of Jerusalem chose delegates to go to Antioch in Syria. They chose Judas, called Barsabbas, and Silas, both leaders in the church, to accompany Paul and Barnabas. [23] They sent with them this letter:

"Greetings from the apostles and pastors, and from your fellow

---

a 15:8 This is in reference to the events of Acts 10–11.
b 15:10 The text is "testing [provoking] God"; e.g., by limiting his grace among the gentiles.
c 15:18 As translated from the Aramaic. This prophecy (vv. 16–18) is found in Amos 9:11–12 and Isa. 45:21.
d 15:20 Or "We will be apostles [sent ones] to them." As translated from the Aramaic. The Greek is "to send a message" (letter).
e 15:20 See Lev. 17:12–16.

believers—to our non-Jewish brothers and sisters living in Antioch in Syria and the nearby regions. [a]

[24] "We are aware that some have come to you from the church of Jerusalem. These men were not sent by us, but came with false teachings that have brought confusion and division, telling you to keep the law and be circumcised—things we never commanded them to teach. [b] [25-27] So after deliberation, we're sending you our beloved brothers Paul and Barnabas, who have risked their lives [c] for the glory of the name of our Lord Jesus, the Anointed One. They are accompanied by Judas and Silas, whom we have unanimously chosen to send as our representatives to you. They will validate all that we're wanting to share with you. [d]

[28] "For it pleases the Holy Spirit and us [e] that we not place any unnecessary burden on you, except for the following restrictions: [29] Stay away from anything sacrificed to a pagan idol, from eating what is strangled or with any blood, and from any form of sexual immorality. You will be beautiful believers [f] if you keep your souls from these things, and you will be true and faithful to our Lord Jesus. May God bless you!"

[30] They sent the four men off for Antioch, and after gathering the regional church together, they delivered the letter. [31] When the people heard the letter read out loud, they were overjoyed and delighted by its encouraging message. [32] Then Judas and Silas, who were both prophets, spoke to them affirming words [g] that strengthened the believers. [h]

[33] After the four men spent some time there, the church sent them off in peace to return to the apostles in Jerusalem. [i] [34-35] However, only Judas departed; [j] Paul, Barnabas, and Silas stayed in Antioch, where they and many others preached and taught the wonderful message of the word of God.

---

a 15:23 Or "Cilicia," which is the southwestern region of coastal Turkey that borders Syria.

b 15:24 As translated from the Aramaic and implied in the Greek. The Greek does not make explicit the false teaching, but says simply, "They have upset and unsettled you."

c 15:25–27 The Aramaic is "they have devoted their souls."

d 15:25–27 Significant changes in the order of the clauses in these three verses have been made for the sake of clarity of the English narrative.

e 15:28 Or "the Holy Spirit and we have determined" (decided).

f 15:29 As translated from the Aramaic.

g 15:32 The Aramaic is "an abundant word" or "a rich word."

h 15:32 The ministry of the New Testament prophet is to strengthen the church.

i 15:33 Or "sent them with peace back to those who sent them."

j 15:34–35 The most reliable Greek manuscripts do not mention Silas remaining in Antioch. However, many manuscripts include this information, such as the Aramaic, codices D and C, the Harklean Syriac Version of AD 616, the Sahidic Version of the second to third centuries, and the St. Ephraim of Syria version of the fourth century. Regardless, v. 40 indicates

Paul and Barnabas Disagree

[36] After some days, Paul said to Barnabas, "Let's travel to the regions where we've preached the word of God and see how the believers are getting along."

[37] Barnabas wished to take Mark (also known as John) along with them, [38] but Paul disagreed. He didn't think it was proper to take the one who had deserted them in south-central Turkey,[a] leaving them to do their missionary work without him. [39] It became a heated argument between them, a disagreement so sharp that they parted from each other. Barnabas took Mark and sailed to Cyprus. [40] And Paul chose Silas[b] as his partner.

After the believers prayed for them, asking for the Lord's favor on their ministry, they left [41] for Syria and southeast Turkey.[c] Every place they went, they left the church stronger and more encouraged than before.

Timothy Joins Paul and Silas

16 Paul and Silas came to the city of Derbe and then went on to Lystra,[d] the hometown of a believer named Timothy. His mother was a Jewish follower of Jesus, but his father was not a Jew.[e] [2] Timothy was well known and highly respected among all the believers of Lystra and Iconium. [3] Paul *recognized God's favor on Timothy's life* and wanted him to accompany them in ministry, but Paul had Timothy circumcised first because of the significant Jewish community living in the region, and everyone knew that Timothy's father wasn't a Jew.

[4] They went out together as missionaries, traveling to different cities where they preached and informed the churches of the decrees of the apostolic council of Jerusalem for the non-Jewish converts to observe. [5] All the churches were growing daily and were encouraged and strengthened in their faith.

Paul's Vision of the Man from Macedonia

[6] The Holy Spirit had forbidden Paul and his partners to preach the word in the southwestern provinces of Turkey,[f] so they ministered throughout the region of

---

that Silas did remain behind. An argument could be made that copyists inserted the data in v. 34 to explain the presence of Silas from v. 40.

a 15:38 Or "Pamphylia."

b 15:40 The apostle Silas was acknowledged in church history as one of the seventy apostles whom Jesus sent out. See Luke 10:1–11. After his missionary journey with Paul, he remained in Corinth and ministered there until his death.

c 15:41 Or "Cilicia."

d 16:1 Lystra is modern-day Klistra, a city in Turkey. Derbe, also in Turkey, was about sixty miles from Klistra (Lystra).

e 16:1 The Aramaic is "his father was a Syrian" (an Aramaic speaker). In the time of Paul's missionary journeys, the Aramaic language was commonly spoken in the region he traveled throughout in the Middle East. The Greek is "his father was a Greek."

f 16:6 Or "Asia." This does not refer to the continent of Asia as we know it today, but to the far western and southwestern provinces of Asia Minor (Turkey).

central and west-central Turkey.ᵃ ⁷When they got as far west as the borders of Mysia, they repeatedly attempted to go north into the province of Bithynia,ᵇ but again the Spirit of Jesus would not allow them to enter.ᶜ ⁸So instead they went right on through the province of Mysia to the seaport of Troas.

⁹While staying there Paul experienced a supernatural, ecstatic vision during the night. A man from Macedonia appeared before him, pleading with him, "You must come across the sea to Macedonia and help us!"

¹⁰After Paul had this vision, weᵈ immediately prepared to cross over to Macedonia, convinced that God himself was calling us to go and preach the wonderful news of the gospel to them.

Paul Arrives at Philippi

¹¹From Troas we sailed a straight course to the island of Samothrace, and the next day to Neapolis. ¹²Finally we reached Philippi, a major cityᵉ in the Roman colony of Macedonia, and we remained there for a number of days.ᶠ

¹³When the Sabbath day came, we went outside the gates of the city to the nearby river, for there appeared to be a house of prayer and worship there.ᵍ Sitting on the riverbank we struck up a conversation with some of the women who had gathered there. ¹⁴One of them was Lydia, a businesswoman from the city of Thyatira who was a dealer of exquisite purple clothʰ and a Jewish convert. While Paul shared the good news with her, God opened her heart to receive Paul's message.ⁱ ¹⁵She devoted herself to the Lord, and we baptized her and her entire family. Afterward she urged us to stay in her home, saying,

---

ᵃ 16:6 Or "Phrygia" and "Galatia." The modern-day capital of Turkey, Ankara, is situated in the area known as Galatia.

ᵇ 16:7 Both Mysia and Bithynia are northwestern regions of Turkey.

ᶜ 16:7 We do not know how the Holy Spirit kept them from going into Bithynia, but it could have been through a warning given by means of a dream or vision. In any case, it is obvious the Holy Spirit was guiding his missionaries. He is the Lord of the harvest who prepares, imparts gifts, anoints, and sends out his servants to gather the nations to Jesus Christ. The book of Acts is best understood as the book of Activities of the Holy Spirit. Here he is designated "the Spirit of Jesus." True and lasting fruit in ministry comes through the work and leading of the Spirit of Jesus.

ᵈ 16:10 Apparently, Luke now joins the missionary team going to Macedonia (which includes parts of modern-day Bulgaria and former Yugoslavia). This is the first instance in Acts of the gospel going to Europe. Luke likely left the group later, as he is not included in the team starting in v. 40. Portions of Acts appear to be Luke's missionary travel journal.

ᵉ 16:12 The Aramaic is "the capital city."

ᶠ 16:12 The Aramaic can be translated "In a matter of days we were well known in the city." Other versions of the Aramaic read "We were there over certain holy days."

ᵍ 16:13 Although implied in the Greek text, it is made explicit in the Aramaic, "We saw it was a house [place] of prayer."

ʰ 16:14 Or "purple dye," a rare commodity that would only be purchased by the wealthy.

ⁱ 16:14 Or "feared [worshiped] God." The implication is that Lydia was a gentile convert to Judaism.

"Since I am now a believer in the Lord, come and stay in my house." So we were persuaded to stay there.

The Python Spirit

[16] One day, as we were going to the house of prayer, we encountered a young slave girl who had an evil spirit of divination, the spirit of Python.[a] She had earned great profits for her owners by being a fortune-teller.

[17] She kept following us, shouting, "These men are servants of the Great High God, and they're telling us how to be saved!"

[18] Day after day she continued to do this, until Paul, greatly annoyed, turned and said to the spirit indwelling her, "I command you in the name of Jesus, the Anointed One, to come out of her, now!" At that very moment, the spirit came out of her!

[19] When her owners realized that their potential of making profit had vanished, they forcefully seized Paul and Silas and dragged them off to the city square to face the authorities.

[20] When they appeared before the Roman soldiers and magistrates, the slave owners leveled accusations against them, saying, "These Jews are troublemakers. They're throwing our city into confusion. [21] They're pushing their Jewish religion down our throats. It's wrong and unlawful for them to promote these Jewish ways, for we are Romans living in a Roman colony."

[22] A great crowd gathered, and all the people joined in to come against them. The Roman officials ordered that Paul and Silas be stripped of their garments and beaten with rods on their bare backs.

Miracles Can Come Out of Painful Places

[23] After they were severely beaten, they were thrown into prison and the jailer was commanded to guard them securely. [24] So the jailer placed them in the innermost cell of the prison and had their feet bound and chained.[b]

[25] Paul and Silas, undaunted, prayed in the middle of the night and sang songs of praise to God, while all the other prisoners listened to their worship.

[26] Suddenly, a great earthquake shook the foundations of the prison. All at once every prison door flung open and the chains of all the prisoners came loose.

[27] Startled, the jailer awoke and saw every cell door standing open. Assuming that all the prisoners had escaped, he drew his sword and was about to kill himself [28] when Paul shouted in the darkness, "Stop! Don't hurt yourself. We're all still here."

---

a 16:16 In the religious context of Greek mythology, she was an "oracle," a medium who had the spirit of the gods speaking through her to foretell the future. The Python spirit was the epithet of Apollo, known as the Greek god of prophecy. An individual (often a young virgin) who became the oracle of Apollo was known as the Python, or Pythia.

b 16:24 Or "placed in stocks."

²⁹ The jailer called for a light. When he saw that they were still in their cells, he rushed in and fell trembling at their feet. ³⁰ Then he led Paul and Silas outside and asked, "What must I do to be saved?"

³¹ They answered, "Believe in the Lord Jesus and you will be saved—you and all your family." ᵃ ³² Then they prophesied the word of the Lord ᵇ over him and all his family. ³³ Even though the hour was late, he washed their wounds. Then he and all his family were baptized. He took Paul and Silas into his home and set them at his table and fed them. ³⁴ The jailer and all his family were filled with joy in their newfound faith in God.

³⁵ At daybreak, the magistrates sent officers to the prison with orders to tell the jailer, "Let those two men go." ³⁶ The jailer informed Paul and Silas, "The magistrates have sent orders to release you. So you're free to go now."

³⁷ But Paul told the officers, "Look, they had us beaten in public, without a fair trial—and we are Roman citizens. ᶜ Do you think we're just going to quietly walk away after they threw us in prison and violated all of our rights? Absolutely not! You go back and tell the magistrates that they need to come down here themselves and escort us out!"

³⁸ When the officers went back and reported what Paul and Silas had told them, the magistrates were frightened, especially upon hearing that they had beaten two Roman citizens without due process. ³⁹ So they went to the prison and apologized to Paul and Silas, begging them repeatedly, saying, "Please leave our city."

⁴⁰ So Paul and Silas left the prison and went back to Lydia's house, where they met with the believers and comforted and encouraged them before departing.

A Riot Breaks Out in Thessalonica

17 After passing through the cities of Amphipolis and Apollonia, Paul and Silas arrived at Thessalonica. ᵈ ² As they customarily did, they went to the synagogue to speak to the Jews from the Torah scrolls. For three weeks ³ Paul challenged them by explaining the truth and proving to them the reality of the gospel—that the Messiah had to suffer and die, then rise again from among the dead. He made it clear to them, saying, "I come to announce to you that Jesus is the Anointed One, the Messiah!"

⁴ Some of the Jews were convinced that their message was true, so they

---

a 16:31 The implication is "you and anyone in your household who believes."

b 16:32 Or "spoke the word of the Lord." This phrase is consistently used in the Old Testament for prophetic utterance of a supernatural origin.

c 16:37 Paul didn't notify them that he and Silas were Romans prior to their beatings, when they could have escaped persecution. Instead, they endured the brutal treatment and ended up leading their jailer to Christ.

d 17:1 Known today as Salonica or Thessaloniki, it was the ancient capital of Macedonia.

joined Paul and Silas, along with quite a few prominent women and a large number of Greeks who worshiped God.[a] [5]But many of the Jews were motivated by bitter jealousy and formed a large mob out of the troublemakers, unsavory characters, and street gangs to incite a riot. They set out to attack Jason's house, for he had welcomed the apostles into his home.[b] The mob was after Paul and Silas and sought to take them by force and bring them out to the people. [6]When they couldn't find them, they took Jason instead, along with some of the brothers *in his house church,*[c] and dragged them before the city council. Along the way they screamed out, "Those troublemakers who have turned the world upside down have come here to our city. [7]And now Jason and these men have welcomed them as guests. They're traitors to Caesar, teaching that there is another king named Jesus."

[8]Their angry shouts stirred up the crowds and troubled the city and all its officials. [9]*So when Paul and Silas came before the leaders of the city,* they refused to let them go until Jason and his men posted bail.

The Gospel Received in Berea

[10]That night the believers sent Paul and Silas off to the city of Berea,[d] where they once again went into the synagogue. [11]They found that the Jews of Berea were of more noble character and much more open minded than those of Thessalonica. They were hungry to learn and eagerly received the word. Every day they opened the scrolls of Scripture to search and examine them, to verify that what Paul taught them was true. [12]*A large number of Jews became believers in Jesus,* along with quite a few influential[e] Greek women and men.

[13]When the news reached the Jews in Thessalonica that Paul was now in Berea, preaching the word of God, the troublemakers went there too and they agitated and stirred up the crowds against him. [14]The fellow believers helped Paul slip away to the coast of the Aegean Sea,[f] while Silas and Timothy remained in Berea.

[15]Those who accompanied Paul sailed with him as far as Athens. Then

---

a 17:4 It is probable that this is when Timothy arrived in Thessalonica with gifts of money and food from the church of Philippi. See Phil. 4:16; 1 Thess. 1:1; 2 Thess. 1:1.

b 17:5 This information is borrowed from v. 7 and inserted here for the sake of English narrative.

c 17:6 Although not much about Jason is given here, he is known in church history as Jason of Tarsus, who was one of the seventy apostles Jesus sent out and is named as one of Paul's ministry companions. See Luke 10:1–11; Rom. 16:21.

d 17:10 Berea (modern-day Veria) was a city in Macedonia about forty-five miles (seventy-five kilometers) from Thessalonica.

e 17:12 The Greek word *euschemon* also implies "women of high standing," "wealthy," "honorable," "elegant," and "respected." (See *Strong's Concordance,* Gr. 2158.)

f 17:14 The Greek text is simply "the sea."

Paul sent them back to Berea with instructions[a] for Silas and Timothy to hurry and join him.

The Apostle Paul in Athens

[16] While Paul was waiting for them in Athens, his spirit was deeply troubled[b] when he realized that the entire city was full of idols. [17] *He argued the claims of the gospel* with the Jews in their synagogue, and with those who were worshipers of God, and every day he preached in the public square to whomever would listen.

[18] Philosophers of the teachings of Epicurus,[c] and others called Stoics,[d] debated[e] with Paul. When they heard him speak about Jesus and his resurrection, they said, "What strange ideas is this babbler trying to present?" Others said, "He's peddling some kind of foreign religion." [19] So they brought him for a public dialogue before the leadership council of Athens,[f] known as the Areopagus. "Tell us," they said, "about this new teaching that you're bringing to our city. [20] You're presenting strange and astonishing things to our ears, and we want to know what it all means." [21] Now, it was the favorite pastime of the Athenians and visitors to Athens to discuss the newest ideas and philosophies.

Paul Speaks to the Leaders of Athens

[22] So Paul stood in the middle of the leadership council and said, "Respected leaders of Athens,[g] it is clear to me how extravagant you are in your worship of idols.[h] [23] For as I walked through your city, I was captivated by the many shrines and objects of your worship. I even found an inscription on one altar that read,

---

a 17:15 The Aramaic makes it clear that this message was written as a letter.

b 17:16 Or "deeply pained" or "irritated."

c 17:18 Epicurus was a Greek philosopher (341–270 BC) who espoused a radical materialism that claimed people should live for pleasure and materialistic gain. He denied an afterlife and asserted that the gods had little interest in or concern for humanity.

d 17:18 Stoicism, in contrast to Epicureanism, is a passive determinism of emotional indifference that elevates the virtue of self-control. By mastering human passions and emotions, one could realize peace within himself. The Greek Stoics believed that humans can only reach their full potential when they live by sheer reason and divine principle, or the spark of divinity, which they called *logos*.

e 17:18 The Aramaic is "word wrestled."

f 17:19 The Areopagus was a governing body of intellectuals who were the overseers of Athens. It was equivalent to the board of education, the city council, the ethics committee, the council of foreign relations, and leaders of the religious and philosophical community all rolled into one. The Areopagus, also known as Mars Hill (Mars, or Ares, was the Greek god of war), was not simply a location but a gathering of a council of people overseeing the spiritual atmosphere of Athens. It could best be described as the Greek temple of human thought. The Aramaic here uses the phrase "house of religion."

g 17:22 Or simply, "Athenians."

h 17:22 As translated from the Aramaic, which can also be translated "You excel in the worship of demons" (or "idols"). The Greek is "How very superstitious you are (i.e., extraordinarily religious)."

'To the Unknown God.'[a] I have come to introduce to you this God whom you worship without even knowing anything about him.

[24] "The true God is the Creator of all things. He is the owner and Lord of the heavenly realm and the earthly realm, and he doesn't live in man-made temples. [25] He supplies life and breath and all things to every living being. He doesn't lack a thing that we mortals could supply for him, for he has all things and everything he needs. [26] From one man, Adam, he made every man and woman and every race of humanity, and he spread us over all the earth. He sets the boundaries of people and nations, determining their appointed times in history.[b] [27] He has done this so that every person would long for God, feel their way to him,[c] and find him—for he is the God who is easy to discover![d] [28] It is through him that we live and function and have our identity; just as your own poets have said,[e] 'Our lineage comes from him.'[f]

[29] "Since our lineage can be traced back to God, how could we even think that the divine image could be compared to something made of gold, silver, or stone, sculpted by man's artwork and clever imagination?

[30] "In the past God tolerated[g] our ignorance of these things, but now the time of deception has passed away.[h] He commands us all to repent and turn to God.[i] [31] For the appointed day has risen, in which he is going to judge the world in righteousness by the Man he has designated. And the proof given to the world that God has chosen this Man is this: he resurrected him from among the dead!"[j]

[32] The moment they heard Paul bring up the topic of resurrection, some of them ridiculed him, *then got up and left*. But others said, "We want to hear you again later about these things." [33] So Paul left the meeting. [34] But there were some who believed the message and joined him from that day forward. Among them were Dionysius, a judge on the leadership council,[k] and a woman named Damaris.[l]

---

a 17:23 The Aramaic can be translated "To the Hidden God."

b 17:26 The Aramaic adds an interesting nuance: "He commands the separation of the seasons and sets the lifespan of every person."

c 17:27 The Aramaic is "investigating him in his creation."

d 17:27 Or "the God who is not far from each one of us."

e 17:28 Paul is quoting two classical Greek writers (ca. 270 BC): Aratus (*Phaenomena*, 5) and Cleanthes (*Hymn to Zeus*, 5).

f 17:28 Or "Our nature comes from him," as translated from the Aramaic. The Greek is "We are his offspring." The Greek word is *genos*, which means "kindred" or "family" (taken from his genes).

g 17:30 Or "deliberately paid no attention to."

h 17:30 As translated from the Aramaic.

i 17:30 That is, to turn away from idolatry and worship the true God.

j 17:31 The Aramaic is "God turns the hearts of men to faith in him [Jesus] and raises them from among the dead."

k 17:34 As translated from the Aramaic. According to the church historian Eusebius, Dionysius later became the Bishop of Athens (Eusebius, *Historia Ecclesiae* III: iv).

l 17:34 The Greek word can also mean "wife," indicating she was possibly the wife of

The Apostle Paul in Corinth

18 When Paul left Athens he traveled to Corinth,[a] [2]where he met a Jewish man named Aquila, who was originally from northeastern Turkey.[b] He and his wife, Priscilla, had recently emigrated from Italy to Corinth because Emperor Claudius had expelled all the Jews from Rome. [3]Since Paul and Aquila were both tentmakers[c] by trade, Paul moved in with them and they became business partners.

[4]Every Sabbath day Paul spoke openly in the synagogue, to both Jews and non-Jews,[d] attempting to persuade them *to believe the message of Jesus*.

[5]When Silas and Timothy finally arrived from Macedonia, Paul spent all his time preaching the word of God,[e] trying to convince the Jews that Jesus was the Messiah.

[6]When they viciously slandered him and hurled abuse on him, he symbolically shook the dust off his clothes in protest against them. He said to them, "Have it your way then! I am guiltless as to your fate, for the blood-guilt of your actions will be on your own heads, and from now on I will preach to the non-Jews."

[7]Leaving the synagogue, Paul went to the home of Titus,[f] a convert to Judaism, for he and his family attended the Jewish meetings[g] *and they had all become believers in Jesus*. [8]Crispus,[h] the leader of the synagogue, believed in the Lord, together with his entire family, and many of the Corinthians who heard what had happened believed in the Lord and were baptized.

[9]One night, the Lord spoke to Paul in a supernatural vision and said, "Don't ever be afraid. Speak *the words that I give you* and don't be intimidated, [10]because I am with you.[i] No one will be able to hurt you, for there are many in this city whom I call my own."

Dionysius. Regardless, she must have been a woman of high social standing to be included in the meeting of the leadership council.

a   18:1 Corinth is about forty-eight miles (seventy-eight kilometers) from Athens. It was a large commercial center with trade links all over the entire ancient world. It was the home of the famous Isthmian Games and the temple of Aphrodite, which held a thousand temple prostitutes. Corinth was known for its debauchery. In the midst of a depraved culture, God birthed a church to become light to the people of their city.

b   18:2 Or "Pontus," a Roman province in northeastern Asia Minor (Turkey).

c   18:3 The Aramaic can also mean "saddle makers."

d   18:4 The Aramaic is "pagans."

e   18:5 The Aramaic is "the manifestation of God."

f   18:7 The Greek text is "Titus Justus," but the Aramaic only has Titus. It is possible that he is the Titus who accompanied Paul in ministry and the one Paul addressed in the book of Titus.

g   18:7 As translated from the Aramaic. The Greek says that Titus Justus lived next door to the synagogue.

h   18:8 Crispus was one of the few people Paul baptized. See 1 Cor. 1:14. According to church tradition he became the bishop of Aegina.

i   18:10 Somewhat more explicit in the Aramaic, this is the great "I AM" who is speaking with Paul, assuring him of God's presence.

¹¹ For the next year and a half, Paul stayed in Corinth, faithfully teaching the word of God.

Paul Brought before the Roman Official Gallio

¹² Now, at that time, Gallio was the regional governor who ruled over the Roman province of Achaia, *a* and the Jews turned against Paul and came together to seize him and bring him publicly before the governor's court. *b* ¹³ They accused him before Gallio, saying, "This man is creating a disturbance by persuading people to worship God in ways that are contrary to our laws."

¹⁴ Just as Paul was about to speak in his defense, Gallio interrupted and said, "Wait! If this involved some major crime or fraud, it would be my responsibility to hear the case. ¹⁵ But this is nothing more than a disagreement among yourselves over semantics *c* and personalities *d* and traditions of your own Jewish laws. *e* Go and settle it yourselves! I refuse to be the judge of these issues." ¹⁶ So Gallio dismissed them from the court.

¹⁷ Immediately the crowd turned on Sosthenes, *f* one of the leaders *g* of the synagogue *who sided with Paul.* They seized him and beat him up right there in the courtroom! But Gallio showed no concern at all over what was happening.

Priscilla and Aquila

¹⁸ After remaining in Corinth several more days, Paul finally bid *shalom* *h* to the believers and sailed away for the coast of Syria, accompanied by Priscilla and Aquila. *i* Before they left, Paul had his head shaved at Cenchrea, *j* because he had taken a vow of dedication.

¹⁹ When they reached Ephesus, *k* Paul left Priscilla and Aquila behind, then

---

a 18:12 The province of Achaia included the three most important parts of southern Greece: Attica, Boeotia, and the Peloponnesus. Gallio was the brother of Seneca, the tutor of Nero.

b 18:12 Or "judgment seat." This was a raised platform with a marble bench where judicial and governmental decrees were issued. This bench has been discovered after excavations in the agora.

c 18:15 Or "doctrines."

d 18:15 Or "names."

e 18:15 The Aramaic is "Torah" (the first five books of Moses).

f 18:17 Sosthenes means "savior of our nation." See 1 Cor. 1:1.

g 18:17 The Aramaic word used here can mean "priest" or "elder." Crispus is mentioned as the president or leader (v. 8). Some speculate that Crispus' term of service had been completed and Sosthenes took his place.

h 18:18 *Shalom* is the Hebrew and Aramaic word for "peace and well-being." The Greek is "farewell." The Aramaic can also be translated "Paul brought peace to the brothers."

i 18:18 Priscilla means "Ancient"; Aquila means "Eagle."

j 18:18 Cenchrea was one of two major ports of Corinth, possibly where agricultural goods were exported, for Cenchrea means "millet," a grain similar to quinoa.

k 18:19 Ephesus was in the ancient world, a white marble city, one of the most beautiful in the world. It had the temple of Artemis, one of the seven great wonders of that era. It also

he went into the synagogue and spoke to the Jews. [20] They asked him to stay longer, but he refused [21] and said farewell to them, adding, "I will come back to you, if it is God's will, after I go to Jerusalem to observe the feast." [a] Then he set sail from Ephesus for Caesarea.

[22] When he arrived there he traveled on to Jerusalem to visit the church and pray for them, [b] then he left for Antioch. [23] After spending some time there, Paul continued on through the region of Galatia and Phyrgia in central Turkey. And wherever he went he encouraged and strengthened the believers. [c]

The Ministry of Apollos

[24] A Jewish man by the name of Apollos arrived in Ephesus. He was a native of Alexandria [d] and was recognized as an educated and cultured man. He was powerful in the Scriptures, [25] had accepted Jesus, and had been taught about the Lord. He was spiritually passionate [e] for Jesus and a convincing teacher, although he only knew about the baptism of John. [26] He fearlessly preached [f] in the synagogue. But when Priscilla and Aquila heard Apollos' teachings, they met with him privately [g] and revealed to him the ways of God more completely. [h]

[27] Then Apollos, with the encouragement of the believers, went to the province of Achaia. [i] He took a letter of recommendation from the brothers of Ephesus so his ministry would be welcomed in the region. He was a tremendous help to the believers and caused them to increase in grace. [j] [28] Apollos boldly and publicly confronted the Jews, vigorously debating them, proving undeniably from the Scriptures that Jesus was the Messiah.

---

had two agoras, a beautiful fountain in the city supplied by an aqueduct, the monument of Phillio, the Koressian Gates, the Bouleuterion, a large stadium, and many terraced houses. It was the capital city of the Roman province of Asia and had a population of well over one hundred thousand at the time Paul visited the city. Ephesus was known historically as the center of powerful magical practices and the casting of spells, as well as the cult center of the worship of the Ephesian goddess Artemis, known as "the supreme power." It was in this backdrop that the apostle Paul and his companions planted the renowned church of Ephesus.

a 18:21 This last clause is only found in the Aramaic.

b 18:22 Although this clause is missing in the Greek, the Aramaic can be translated "to pray for the peace of the congregation." A true spiritual father prays for believers and brings them a message of hope and peace.

c 18:23 The Aramaic can be translated "Wherever he went he made them all disciples."

d 18:24 This is, Alexandria in Egypt.

e 18:25 Or "His spirit boiled."

f 18:26 That is, boldly and powerfully. The Aramaic can be translated "with crystal clarity."

g 18:26 The Aramaic is "they took him into their home."

h 18:26 Or "more accurately." They filled in the gaps in his understanding of the Lord Jesus.

i 18:27 See the first footnote on v. 12.

j 18:27 As translated from the Aramaic. The Greek is "He helped those who believed by grace."

The Apostle Paul in Ephesus

19 While Apollos was ministering in Corinth, Paul traveled on through the regions of *Turkey* [a] until he arrived in Ephesus, where he found *a group of twelve* followers of Jesus. [b] [2] The first thing he asked them was "Did you receive the Holy Spirit when you became believers?"

"No," they replied. "We've not even heard of a holy spirit."

[3] Paul asked, "Then what was the meaning of your baptism?" [c]

They responded, "It meant that we would follow John's teaching."

[4] Paul said, "John's baptism was for those who were turning from their sins, [d] and he taught you to believe in and follow the one who was coming after him: Jesus the Anointed One." [e]

[5] When they understood this, they were baptized into the authority of Jesus, the Anointed One. [f] [6-7] And when Paul laid his hands on each of the twelve, the Holy Spirit manifested and they immediately spoke in tongues [g] and prophesied. [h]

[8] For three months Paul taught openly and fearlessly in the synagogue, arguing persuasively for them to enter into God's kingdom realm. [i] [9] But some of them hardened their hearts and stubbornly refused to believe. When they spoke evil [j] of the Way in front of the congregation, Paul withdrew from them and took the believers with him.

[10] Every day [k] for over two years, [l] he taught them in the lecture hall of

---

a 19:1 The Greek is "the upper inland country." This was a trek through certain regions of Turkey for him to arrive in Ephesus.

b 19:1 Or "some disciples." Verse 7 states there were twelve. This information is included here in v. 1 for the sake of the English narrative.

c 19:3 Or "into what [name or authority] were you baptized?"

d 19:4 The Aramaic can be translated "John's baptism was a baptism of grace to the people."

e 19:4 "The Anointed One" (or "Messiah") is found only in the Aramaic. The Greek is simply "Jesus."

f 19:5 Or "on the name of Jesus Christ," which means they were baptized into the authority of the name of Jesus, who was greater than John.

g 19:6–7 Or "supernaturally given languages."

h 19:6–7 The Aramaic is "They spoke tongue by tongue and gushed out prophecies." The impartation of the Holy Spirit and his gifts are here being transferred from Paul to these believers. See also 1 Tim. 4:14; 2 Tim. 1:6–7. Jesus taught that when the Holy Spirit comes upon us, it is to impart power for our lives and ministries. See Acts 1:8.

i 19:8 Or "about God's kingdom realm." It is a big step for both Jews and Christians to come out of their religious identity and focus on the reality of God's kingdom realm.

j 19:9 Or "cursed the Christian way of living."

k 19:10 The Greek manuscript D adds, "from the fifth hour [11:00 a.m.] to the tenth hour [4:00 p.m.]."

l 19:10 Counting the three months of focusing on ministry to the Jews, Paul's entire stay in Ephesus came to three years, which would have included a short visit to Corinth. See Acts 20:31.

Tyrannus, [a] which resulted in everyone living in the province of Asia, [b] Jews and non-Jews, hearing the prophetic word of the Lord. [c]

Extraordinary Miracles in Ephesus

[11] God kept releasing a flow of extraordinary miracles through the hands of Paul. [12] Because of this, people took Paul's handkerchiefs and articles of clothing, even pieces of cloth that had touched his skin, laying them on the bodies of the sick, and diseases and demons left them and they were healed.

[13-14] Now, there were seven itinerant Jewish exorcists, sons of Sceva the high priest, who took it upon themselves to use the name and authority of Jesus over those who were demonized. They would say, "We cast you out in the name of the Jesus that Paul preaches!"

[15] One day, when they said those words, the demon in the man replied, "I know about Jesus, and I recognize Paul, but who do you think you are?"

[16] Then the demonized man jumped on them and threw them to the ground, beating them mercilessly. [d] He overpowered the seven exorcists until they all ran out of the house naked and badly bruised.

Revival Breaks Out

[17] All of the people in Ephesus were awestruck, both Jews and non-Jews, when they heard about what had happened. Great fear fell over the entire city, and the authority of the name of Jesus was exalted. [18] Many believers publicly confessed their sins and disclosed their secrets. [19] Large numbers of those who had been practicing magic took all of their *books and scrolls of spells and incantations* and publicly burned them. When the value of all the books and scrolls was calculated, it all came to several million dollars. [e] [20] The power of God caused the word to spread, and the people were greatly impacted. [f]

---

a 19:10 This was like a college or lecture hall. Tyrannus (whose name means "sovereign") was most likely a philosopher and lecturer who had disciples whom he taught. Apparently Tyrannus welcomed Paul after he left the Jewish congregation and brought him into his school to teach the students.

b 19:10 This "school of ministry" exploded as many came to hear Paul and then went out to preach, expanding the reach of the gospel into all the "province of Asia" (Asia Minor). The province of Asia would have covered no less than one-third of Turkey. Many multitudes heard the gospel in the two-year period when Paul taught in Ephesus. The teaching of the apostles resulted in the expansion of God's kingdom realm.

c 19:10 Or simply, "the word of the Lord." However, the phrase "the word of the Lord" is a Hebrew expression consistently used for the prophetic utterances given by the prophets.

d 19:16 True authority comes from relationship with Jesus Christ, not just using formulas and techniques. Evil spirits know about the depth of our relationship with God.

e 19:19 Or "fifty thousand silver drachmas." Some historians have said that one lamb would be sold for one silver drachma. The price of a ewe lamb today is about 150 USD. A drachma was one day's wage, and fifty thousand drachmas would be one hundred years' wages. The value of the books could have been millions of dollars.

f 19:20 Chronologically, this would have been the time when Paul wrote his first letter to the Corinthians.

A Riot Breaks Out

[21] Paul had it in his heart to go to Jerusalem and, on his way there, to revisit the places in Greece where he had ministered. [a] "After that," he said, "I have to go to Rome also." [22] So he sent ahead into Macedonia two of his ministry assistants, Timothy [b] and Erastus, [c] while he remained in western Turkey. [d]

[23] At that time a major disturbance erupted in Ephesus over the people following God's way. [e] [24] It began with a wealthy man named Demetrius, who had built a large business and enriched many craftsmen by manufacturing silver shrines for the Greek goddess Artemis. [f]

[25-26] Demetrius called a meeting of his employees, along with all the various tradespeople of Ephesus, and said, "You know that our prosperous livelihood is being threatened by this Paul, who is persuading crowds of people *to turn away from our gods.* [g] We make a good living by doing what we do, but everywhere Paul goes, not only here in Ephesus but throughout western Turkey, [h] he convinces people that there's no such thing as a god made with hands. [27] Our businesses are in danger of being discredited. And not only that, but the temple of our great goddess Artemis is being dishonored and seen as worthless. [i] She is the goddess of all of western Turkey and is worshiped in all the world. But if this outrage continues, everyone everywhere will suffer the loss of her magnificent greatness."

[28] When the people heard this, they were filled with boiling rage. They shouted over and over, "Artemis, the great goddess of the Ephesians!" [29] The entire city was thrown into chaos as everyone rushed into the stadium together, [j] dragging with them Gaius [k] and Aristarchus, [l] Paul's traveling companions from Macedonia.

---

a 19:21 Or "to go through Macedonia and Achaia." The implication is that Paul wanted to revisit the area of Greece he had ministered in; therefore, that is made explicit in the translation.

b 19:22 Timothy's name means "one who honors God." He was Paul's spiritual son and later became an apostolic church planter. See 1 and 2 Timothy.

c 19:22 Erastus means "beloved." He was possibly the treasurer of the city of Corinth. See Rom. 16:23; 2 Tim. 4:20.

d 19:22 Or "the province of Asia" (Minor).

e 19:23 As translated from the Aramaic. The Greek is simply "the way."

f 19:24 Also known as Diana. She was venerated as the daughter of Zeus and the sister of Apollo.

g 19:25–26 The true worship of God threatens not only the political realm, but the spiritual and economic realm as well. Jesus compels men to adopt new values.

h 19:25–26 Or "the [Roman] province of Asia [Minor]."

i 19:27 The temple of Artemis (Diana) is one of the seven ancient wonders of the world. We must never put buildings or temples above the true worship of God. The Ephesians valued their goddess and economic standards more than truth.

j 19:29 The stadium of Ephesus has recently been discovered and is estimated to have held twenty-four thousand spectators.

k 19:29 Gaius' name is a variant form of "lord." There is speculation that he could be the man to whom the apostle John wrote his third letter (3 John).

l 19:29 Aristarchus' name means "best ruler." He was a native of Thessalonica (Acts 20:4;

[30] When Paul attempted to go in and speak to the massive crowd, the disciples wouldn't let him. [31] Some of the high-ranking governmental officials of the region, because they loved him, [a] sent Paul an urgent message, saying, "Whatever you do, don't step foot into that stadium!"

[32] The frenzied crowd shouted out one thing, and others shouted something else, until they were all in mass confusion, with many not even knowing why they were there!

[33] Some of the Jews pushed forward a Jewish man named Alexander to be their spokesman, and different factions of the crowd shouted instructions at him. He stood before the people and motioned for everyone to be quiet so he could be heard. [34] But when he began to speak, they realized that he was a Jew, so they shouted him down. For nearly two hours they shouted over and over, "Great is Artemis, the goddess of the Ephesians!" [b]

[35] Eventually the mayor of the city [c] was able to quiet them down. He said, "Fellow citizens! Who in the world doesn't know that we are devoted to the great temple [d] of Artemis and to her image that fell from Zeus out of heaven? [e] [36] Since no one can deny it, you should all just be quiet. Calm down and don't do anything hasty. [37] For you have brought these men before us who aren't guilty of any crime. They are neither temple robbers nor blasphemers of our goddess. [38] So if Demetrius and the men of his trade have a case against someone, the courts are open. They can appear before the judge and press charges. [39] But if you're looking for anything further to bring up, it must be argued before the court and settled there, not here. [40] Don't you realize we're putting our city in danger of being accused of a riot by the Roman authorities? There's no good explanation we can give them for all this commotion!"

[41] After he had said this, he dispersed the crowds and sent them away.

27:2). He traveled often with Paul and is also mentioned in Col. 4:10 and Philem. 24, called there Paul's "fellow prisoner." Church tradition states that he was martyred by Emperor Nero for loving and serving Jesus Christ.

a 19:31 As translated from the Aramaic.

b 19:34 Artemis, the great goddess of the Ephesians, has faded from history, while we fill stadiums today for conferences and revivals and say, "Great is the God Most High!"

c 19:35 The Aramaic is "the city governor." The Greek is "city clerk" or "scribe" (or "keeper of the records"). For all practical purposes he would be or represent the mayor of the city.

d 19:35 As translated from the Aramaic, the Greek is "custodians of the temple."

e 19:35 The Aramaic is "her face that fell from heaven." Much conjecture has been made over this statement. Some of the oldest translations have "fell from Zeus [Jupiter]," while most modern translations have "fell from the sky [heaven]." Some believe it was an aerolite that was fashioned into a stature of Artemis; however, Pliny the Elder, a Roman author and philosopher who died trying to save relatives from the eruption of Mount Vesuvius, says it was made from wood, possibly ebony (*Naturalis Historia* 16.79.213–14).

The Apostle Paul Goes to Macedonia and Greece

20 When the uproar finally died down, Paul gathered the believers and encouraged their hearts. He kissed them,ᵃ said good-bye, and left for Macedonia. ²At every place he passed through, he brought words of great comfort and encouragement to the believers. Then he went on to Greece ³and stayed there for three months.

Just as Paul was about to sail for Syria, he learned of a plot against him by the Jews, so he decided to return by going through Macedonia. ⁴Seven men accompanied him as far as western Turkey. They were Sopater,ᵇ son of Pyrrhusᶜ from Berea, Aristarchusᵈ and Secundusᵉ from Thessalonica, Gaiusᶠ from Derbe, and Timothy,ᵍ Tychicus,ʰ and Trophimusⁱ from western Turkey. ⁵These men went ahead and were waiting for us at Troas.ʲ

⁶As soon as all of the Passover celebrations were over,ᵏ we sailed from Philippi. After five days we joined the others in Troas, where we stayed another week.ˡ ⁷On Sunday we gathered to take communionᵐ and to hear Paul preach. Because he was planning to leave the next day, he continued speaking until past midnight. ⁸Many flickering lamps burned in the upstairs chamber where we were meeting. ⁹Sitting in an open window listening was a young man named Eutychus.ⁿ As Paul's sermon dragged on, Eutychus became drowsy and fell into a deep slumber. Sound asleep, he fell three stories to his death below.ᵒ

¹⁰Paul went downstairs, bent over the boy, and embraced him. Taking him

---

a 20:1 As translated from the Aramaic.

b 20:4 Sopater, or Sosipater, is mentioned in Rom. 16:21 as one of Paul's relatives. His name means "his father's savior."

c 20:4 Or "son of fiery red flames." This phrase is not found in the Aramaic.

d 20:4 See the third footnote on 19:29.

e 20:4 Secundus means "fortunate."

f 20:4 Many believe this is the same Gaius mentioned in 19:29. See the second footnote on 19:29.

g 20:4 The Aramaic is "Timothy of Lystra." See introductions to 1 and 2 Timothy.

h 20:4 It is likely that Tychicus was a native of Ephesus since he carried the letter Paul wrote to them as well as the letter to Colossae. See Eph. 6:21; Col. 4:7. He is also mentioned in 2 Tim. 4:12 and Titus 3:12. His name means "child of fortune."

i 20:4 Trophimus was not a Jew. He is mentioned in Acts 21:29. His name means "nutritious."

j 20:5 Notice "us," which implies Luke has now rejoined the missionary team.

k 20:6 Or "the Days of Unleavened Bread." This holiday was observed during the week immediately following Passover and was wrapped into the Passover celebration.

l 20:6 This is when the events took place mentioned by Paul in 2 Cor. 2:12–13.

m 20:7 The Aramaic is "breaking pieces of the Eucharist."

n 20:9 Or "a preteen named Eutychus," which means "fortunate" or "lucky."

o 20:9 There is no doubt that "Lucky" died because of his fall. The Greek word *nekros* can only mean that he was lifeless. This boy becomes a picture of some believers today who, because they view themselves as "well off," sit carelessly where they shouldn't, growing drowsy, falling asleep, and enduring a disastrous fall. But God has grace and power to raise even the foolish ones back to life.

in his arms, he said to all the people gathered, "Stop your worrying. He's come back to life!" [a]

[11] Paul went back upstairs, served communion, and ate a meal with them. Then he picked back up where he left off and taught until dawn. [b] [12] Filled with enormous joy, they took the boy home alive and everyone was encouraged. [c]

Paul's Voyage to Miletus

[13] Continuing our journey, we made our way to the ship and sailed for Assos. [d] Paul had previously arranged to meet us there as he traveled overland by foot. [14] So he rejoined our team there and we took him aboard and sailed for Mitylene. [e] [15] The next day we crossed over to Chios, [f] and the following day we arrived at the island of Samos. [g] We stayed at Trogyllium, [h] and on the day after that we reached Miletus. [i] [16] Paul was in a hurry to arrive in Jerusalem, hoping to make it in time for the Feast of Pentecost, so he decided to bypass Ephesus and not spend any time in that region. [j] [17] However, from Miletus Paul had sent a message to the elders of the church [k] in Ephesus and asked them to come meet with him.

[18] When they arrived, he said to them, "All of you know how I've lived and conducted myself while I was with you. From the first day I set foot in western Turkey [19] I've operated in God's miracle power [l] with great humility and served you [m] with many tears. I've endured numerous ordeals because of the plots of the Jews. [20] You know how I've taught you in public meetings and in your homes, and that I've not held anything back from you that would help you grow. [21] I urged both Jews and non-Jews to turn from sin to God and to have faith in our Lord Jesus. [22] And now I am being compelled by the Holy Spirit [n] to go to Jerusalem, without really knowing what will happen to me there. [23] Yet I

---

a 20:10 Or "His soul is in him." Paul raised him from the dead.

b 20:11 The Aramaic adds "by land" (on foot).

c 20:12 The Greek is "comforted," while the Aramaic is "overjoyed." The translation merges both concepts.

d 20:13 A coastal city in far western Turkey. Assos means "approaching."

e 20:14 A city on the Greek island of Lesbos.

f 20:15 A Greek island in the Aegean Sea off the coast of Turkey.

g 20:15 A Greek island in the Aegean Sea off the coast of Turkey.

h 20:15 As translated from the Aramaic and some Greek manuscripts. Most Greek manuscripts do not have this clause.

i 20:15 An ancient seaport of far western Turkey.

j 20:16 Or "waste any time in the province of Asia [Minor]."

k 20:17 These elders would be equivalent to pastors, leaders of the church.

l 20:19 As translated in the Aramaic, which is literally "I've performed God's miracles." The Greek is "I've served the Lord."

m 20:19 Some manuscripts add, "for more than three years." See also 1 Thess. 2:10–12.

n 20:22 Or "shackled by the Holy Spirit."

know that the Holy Spirit warns me [a] in town after town, saying, 'Chains and afflictions are prepared for you.'

[24] "But whether I live or die is not important, for I don't esteem my life as indispensable. [b] It's more important for me to fulfill my destiny and to finish the ministry my Lord Jesus has assigned to me, which is to faithfully preach the wonderful news of God's grace. [25] I've been a part of your lives and shared with you many times the message of God's kingdom realm. But now I leave you, and you will not see my face again. [26] If any of you should be lost, I will not be blamed, for my conscience is clean, [27] because I've taught you everything I could about God's eternal plan and I've held nothing back. [28] So guard your hearts. Be true shepherds [c] over all the flock and feed them well. Remember, it was the Holy Spirit who appointed you to guard and oversee [d] the churches that belong to Jesus, the Anointed One, [e] which he purchased and established by his own blood.

[29] "I know that after I leave, imposters who have no loyalty to the flock [f] will come among you like savage wolves. [30] Even some from among your very own ranks will rise up, twisting the truth [g] to seduce people into following them instead of Jesus. [31] So be alert and discerning. Remember that for three years, night and day, I've never stopped warning each of you, pouring out my heart to you with tears.

[32] "And so now, I entrust you into God's hands and the message of his grace, [h] which is all that you need to become strong. [i] All of God's blessings are imparted through the message of his grace, which he provides as the spiritual inheritance given to all of his holy ones. [j]

[33] "I haven't been after your money or any of your possessions. [k] [34] You all know that I've worked with my hands to meet my own needs and the needs of those who've served with me. [35] I've left you an example of how you should

---

a 20:23 This warning from the Holy Spirit could have come through prophecies, dreams, visions, or the voice of the Holy Spirit speaking within him.

b 20:24 Or "I do not consider my life worth a single word." That is, Paul viewed his life as not worth mentioning. We don't need to see our lives as precious in our own eyes, for they are precious in the eyes of our Lord Jesus, and that must be enough.

c 20:28 Or "pastors."

d 20:28 The Greek uses the word overseers or guardians. This is the sacred duty of his leaders in the church.

e 20:28 As translated from some Greek and Aramaic texts. Jesus is implied, for the Aramaic is simply "the Anointed One." Some Greek manuscripts and the Western Peshitta read "the church of God."

f 20:29 As translated from the Aramaic. The Greek is "they won't spare the flock."

g 20:30 Or "speaking crooked things."

h 20:32 The Aramaic is "the manifestation of grace."

i 20:32 Or "to build you up," a Greek word taken from the root word for "architect."

j 20:32 Or "sanctified"; that is, those who are devoted to holiness.

k 20:33 Or "silver, gold, or fine apparel."

serve and take care of those who are weak.[a] For we must always cherish the words of our Lord Jesus, who taught, 'Giving brings a far greater blessing than receiving.'"[b]

[36] After Paul finished speaking, he knelt down and prayed with them. [37] Then they all cried with great weeping as one after another hugged Paul and kissed him. [38] What broke their hearts the most were his words "You will not see my face again."

Then they tearfully accompanied Paul back to the ship.

Paul's Journey to Jerusalem

21 After we tore ourselves away from them, we put out to sea and sailed a direct course for the island of Kos, and on the next day to the island of Rhodes,[c] and from there to Patara.[d] [2] There we found a ship that was crossing over to Syria,[e] so we went aboard and sailed away. [3] After we sighted Cyprus and sailed south of it, we docked at Tyre[f] in Syria, where the ship unloaded its cargo.

[4] When we went ashore we found a number of believers and stayed with them for a week. *They prophesied to Paul repeatedly*, warning him by the Holy Spirit not to set foot in Jerusalem. [5] When it was time for us to leave and be on our way, everyone—men, women, and children—accompanied us out of the city down to the beach. After we all knelt *in the sand* and prayed together, [6] we kissed one another,[g] said our good-byes, and boarded the ship, while the believers went back to their homes.

[7] From Tyre we sailed[h] on to the town of Akko and greeted the believers there with peace.[i] We stayed with them for a day. [8] Then we went on to Caesarea and stayed for several days[j] in the home of Philip the evangelist, who was one of the seven deacons[k] and [9] the father of four unmarried daughters who prophesied.

---

a 20:35 Or "minister to the sick."

b 20:35 The Aramaic is an idiom that speaks of extravagant generosity. "Blessed are those who try to give more than they've been given."

c 21:1 Both Kos and Rhodes are Greek islands in the Aegean Sea.

d 21:1 A city on the Mediterranean coast of Turkey.

e 21:2 Or "Phoenicia," a Greek term for coastal Lebanon and Syria.

f 21:3 Tyre was a city in Phoenicia. They would have sailed four or five days from Patara to reach Tyre.

g 21:6 As translated from the Aramaic idiom "one to one" (kissed).

h 21:7 The text can mean either "continued our journey" or "completed our journey." If they completed their journey by boat to Akko, they would have gone by land to Caesarea. Akko, or Ptolemais, was named after the Egyptian ruler Ptolemy II Philadelphus in 261 BC (*Epistulae Aristeas* 115; 1 Macc. 5:15). See also Judg. 1:31.

i 21:7 As translated from the Aramaic.

j 21:8 This information is supplied from v. 10.

k 21:8 See Acts 6:1–7. An evangelist is simply "a preacher of the good news" or in Aramaic, "a preacher of the hope." Philip is described as both an evangelist and a deacon (servant). Every minister must become a servant.

[10] During our stay of several days, Agabus,[a] a prophet from Judea, came to visit us. [11] *As a prophetic gesture,* he took Paul's belt and tied his own hands and feet with it as he prophesied, "The Holy Spirit says, 'The one who owns this belt will be tied up in this same way by the Jews and they will hand him over to those who are not Jews.'"[b]

[12] When we heard this, both we and the believers of Caesarea begged Paul not to go on to Jerusalem. [13] But Paul replied, "Why do you cry and break my heart with your tears? Don't you know that I'm prepared not only to be imprisoned but to die in Jerusalem for the sake of the wonder of the name of our Lord Jesus?"

[14] Because we couldn't persuade him, we gave up and said nothing more except "May the will of the Lord be done."

Paul Arrives in Jerusalem

[15] Afterward we packed our bags and set off for Jerusalem, [16] with some of the believers from Caesarea accompanying us. *They brought us to a village*[c] where they introduced us to Mnason, a Cypriot, one of the original disciples,[d] and he offered us hospitality.

[17] When we finally arrived in Jerusalem, the believers welcomed us with delight. [18] The next day Paul and our team had a meeting with Jacob[e] and all the elders of the Jerusalem church. [19] After greeting everyone, Paul explained in detail what God had accomplished through his ministry among the non-Jewish people.

[20] When they heard Paul's report, they praised God. And they said to him, "You should know, brother, that there are many tens of thousands of Jews who have also embraced the faith and are passionately keeping the law of Moses. [21] But they've heard a rumor that you've been instructing the Jews everywhere to abandon Moses[f] by telling them they don't need to circumcise their children or keep our Jewish customs. [22] They will certainly hear that you've come to Jerusalem. So what is the proper way to proceed? [23] We urge you to follow our suggestion. We have four men here who have taken a vow and are ready to have their heads shaved. [24] Now go with them to the temple and sponsor them in their purification ceremony,[g] and pay all their required expenses. Then

---

a 21:10 See Acts 11:28.

b 21:11 Or "gentiles"; i.e., the Romans.

c 21:16 Implied in the text and found in a few Greek manuscripts.

d 21:16 That is, one of the first converts. He may have been one of the original converts at Pentecost or one of the first disciples converted by Paul and Barnabas. *Mnason* means "remembering."

e 21:18 That is, Jacob (James) the brother of our Lord Jesus, not the apostle Jacob who was martyred.

f 21:21 Or "apostasy from [the law of] Moses."

g 21:24 This could have been the completion of a Nazarite vow (Num. 6:1–12) or a reference

everyone will know that the rumors they've heard are false. They'll see that you are one who lives according to the law of Moses. [25] But in reference to the non-Jewish believers, we've sent them a letter with our decision, stating that they should avoid eating meat that has been offered to an idol, or eating blood or any animal that has been strangled, and to avoid sexual immorality."[a]

Paul Arrested in Jerusalem

[26] The next day, Paul took the four men to the temple and ceremonially purified himself along with them. He publicly gave notice of the date when their vows would end and when sacrifices would be offered for each of them.

[27] When the seven-day period[b] was almost over, a number of Jews from western Turkey[c] who had seen him in the temple courts stirred up the whole crowd against him. Seizing him, [28] they shouted, "Men of Israel, help us! This is the man who teaches everywhere what is contrary to our nation, our law, and this temple. And not only that, but now he brings these non-Jewish men with him into the inner courts of our temple! They have made this sacred place ritually unclean." [29] (For Trophimus, an Ephesian, had been seen previously with him, and they assumed that he entered the inner courts with Paul.)

[30] This ignited a huge riot in the city as all the people came together to seize Paul and drag him out of the temple courts, closing the gates behind him. [31] But as they were about to kill Paul, the news reached the commander of the Roman garrison[d] that the entire city was in an uproar. [32] He immediately ran out to the crowd with a large number of his officers and soldiers. When the crowd saw them coming, they stopped beating Paul. [33] The commander arrested him and ordered that he be bound with two chains. He then asked, "Who is he and what has he done wrong?"

[34] Some in the crowd shouted one thing and others something else, just adding to the confusion. Since the commander was unable to get to the truth because of the disturbance, he ordered that Paul be brought back to their headquarters. [35] When they reached the steps leading up to the fortress,[e] they had to protect Paul and carry him up because of the violent mob following them, [36] and everyone was screaming out, "Away with this man! Kill him!"

---

to the Jewish custom of when a Jew returned from a trip to a foreign (pagan) land, he would purify himself of the defilement of being with unbelievers (Mishnah *Oholoth* 2:3).
a 21:25 It seems strange that Jacob makes no mention of the offering that Paul brought for the poor saints in Jerusalem, which was the reason for leaving his missionary work to come to Jerusalem. Instead, Jacob wants to ensure the purity of Paul's message. There is at least a hint that Paul's ministry was not always well received in Judea. See Rom. 15:30–31.
b 21:27 This could also mean "the Sabbath."
c 21:27 Or "Asia (Minor)." They were possibly in Jerusalem to celebrate the Feast of Pentecost.
d 21:31 The Roman commander was in charge of about six hundred soldiers.
e 21:35 This was the Antonia Fortress (or Tower) built by Herod the Great in 19 BC.

³⁷ As Paul was being led to the entrance of the compound, he said to the commander in Greek, "May I have a word with you?"

The commander replied, "So you know Greek, do you?^{a 38} Aren't you that Egyptian fanatic who started a rebellion some time ago and led four thousand assassins^b out into the wilderness?"

³⁹ Paul answered, "I am, in fact, a Jew from Tarsus, in Cilicia, a well-known city of southern Turkey where I was born. I beg you, sir, please give me a moment to speak to these people."

⁴⁰ When the commander gave his permission, Paul stood on the steps and gestured with his hands for the people to listen. When the crowd quieted down, Paul addressed them in Aramaic^c and said:

Paul's Defense

22 "Ladies and gentlemen, fellow believers and elders^d—please listen to me as I offer my defense."^{e 2} (Now, when everyone realized he was speaking to them in their Judean Aramaic language,^f the crowd became all the more attentive.)

³ Then Paul said, "I am a Jewish man who was born in Tarsus, a city of Turkey.^g However, I grew up in this city and was properly trained in the Mosaic law and tutored by Rabbi Gamaliel according to our ancestral customs. I've been extremely passionate in my desire to please God, just as all of you are today. ⁴ I've hunted down and killed the followers of this Way. I have seized them and thrown them into prison, both men and women. ⁵ All of this can be verified by the high priest and the Supreme Council of Elders. For they even wrote letters to our fellow Jews of Damascus, authorizing me to arrest them and bring them back to Jerusalem as prisoners to be punished.

⁶ "As I was on the road approaching Damascus, about noon, a brilliant heavenly light suddenly appeared, flashing all around me. ⁷ As I fell to the ground I heard a voice say, 'Saul, Saul . . . why are you persecuting me?'

---

a 21:37 The commander was surprised that Paul could speak some Greek, for the people living in Israel at that time did not speak Greek. Paul, an educated Jew from Turkey, spoke to the commander in the common language of the Roman Empire.

b 21:38 The Greek word used here is *Sicarii*, a sect of Jewish nationalists who were violently hostile to Roman rule. They got their name from the small dagger known as a sicarii.

c 21:40 Or "Hebrew." The Hebrew language had been replaced with Aramaic during the Babylonian captivity. For more than a thousand years the Aramaic language remained the language of the Jewish people. Note that Paul did not address the Jewish people in Greek.

d 22:1 Or "fathers" (or "parents").

e 22:1 The Aramaic is literally "Listen to my soul's outburst."

f 22:2 Or "Hebrew." Throughout the Middle East, Assyria, and Babylon, Aramaic was the lingua franca, the language of the people of that day. Greek and Latin were also spoken but were not as prevalent as Aramaic.

g 22:3 Or "Cilicia," which was known as Asia Minor.

[8] "I answered, 'Who are you, my Lord?'

"He said to me, 'I am Jesus, the Victorious.[a] I am the one you are persecuting.'

[9] "Those who were with me saw the brilliant light, but they didn't hear the voice of the one who spoke to me.[b]

[10] "So I asked, 'Lord, what am I to do?'

"And the Lord said to me, 'Get up and go into Damascus, and there you will be told about all that you are destined to do.'

[11] "Because of the dazzling glory of the light, I couldn't see—I was left blind. So they had to lead me by the hand the rest of the way into Damascus.

[12] "A Jewish man living there named Ananias came to see me. He was a godly man who lived according to the law of Moses and was highly esteemed by the Jewish community. [13] He stood beside me and said, 'Saul! My brother, Saul—open your eyes and see again!' At that very instant I opened my eyes and I could see! [14] Then he said to me, 'The God of our ancestors has destined you[c] to know his plan and for you to see the Holy One[d] and to hear his voice. [15] For you will be his witness[e] to every race of people and will share with them everything that you've seen and heard. [16] So now, what are you waiting for? Get up, be baptized, and wash away your sins as you call upon his name.'

[17] "Then I returned to Jerusalem. And while I was praying in the temple, I entered another realm[f] [18] and saw him. He said to me, 'Hurry and depart from Jerusalem quickly, for the people here will not receive the truths you share about me.'

[19] "'But Lord,' I argued, 'they all know that I'm the one who went into our Jewish meetings to find those who believe in you and had them beaten[g] and imprisoned. [20] When the blood of your witness[h] Stephen was shed, I stood nearby in full approval of what was happening. I even guarded the cloaks of those who stoned him to death.'

[21] "Then he said to me, 'Go at once, for I am sending you to preach to the non-Jewish nations.'"[i]

---

a 22:8 Or "Jesus the Nazarene." The word *Nazarene* means "the branch" or "Scion." The Aramaic word implies the title of an heir of a powerful family, or one who is victorious ("Jesus, the Victorious"). Believers are now grafted-in branches of his family tree, victorious ones in Christ.

b 22:9 Some Greek manuscripts add "and they were afraid."

c 22:14 The Aramaic is "raised you up."

d 22:14 Or "the Righteous One" or "the Just One."

e 22:15 Or "martyr."

f 22:17 Or "fell into a trance." The Greek word for trance (*ekstasis*, from which we get the word *ecstasy*) literally means "to be taken to another place" (state or realm). (See *Strong's Concordance*, Gr. 1611.) He was actually taken into another realm as a trance came over him.

g 22:19 Or "beat with a whip" (flogged).

h 22:20 Or "martyr."

i 22:21 The Aramaic is "the far-away nations." See also Rom. 11:13.

[22] The crowd listened attentively to Paul up to this point. But when they heard this, all at once they erupted with loud shouts, saying, "Get rid of this man! Kill him! He doesn't deserve to live!"

The Roman Commander Interrogates Paul

[23] While the crowd was screaming and yelling, removing their outer garments, and throwing handfuls of dust in the air in protest, [24] the commander had Paul brought back into the compound. He ordered that he be whipped with a lash and interrogated to find out what he said that so infuriated the crowd.

[25] When the soldiers stretched Paul out with ropes, he said to the captain, who was standing nearby, "Is it legal for you to torture a Roman citizen like this, without a proper trial?"

[26] When the officer heard this, he immediately went to his commander and reported it, saying, "This man is a Roman citizen. What should we do now?"

[27] The commander came to Paul and asked him, "Tell me the truth, are you a Roman citizen?"

"Yes I am," he replied.

[28] The commander said, "I had to purchase my citizenship with a great sum of money."

Paul replied, "I was born as a citizen!"

[29] All of the soldiers who were about to whip Paul backed away, because they were afraid of the consequences for tying up and holding a Roman citizen against his will.

[30] The next day the commander ordered that the high priest and the supreme Jewish council[d] be convened, because he wanted to find out exactly why the Jews were accusing Paul. So he had him untied and brought out to stand before them all.

Paul before the Supreme Council

23 Paul fixed his eyes on the members of the council and said, "My brothers, up to this day I have lived my life before God with a perfectly clear conscience."[b]

[2] At that moment, Ananias[c] the high priest ordered those standing near Paul to strike him in the mouth.

[3] Paul responded, "God is going to strike you, you corrupt pretender![d] For

---

a 22:30 Or "Sanhedrin," a council of seventy of the elders of Israel.

b 23:1 The Aramaic is "I have been blessed by God in every way unto this day" or "I have been guided by God unto this day."

c 23:2 It is ironic that one Ananias was God's instrument to bring healing and sight to Paul in Damascus, but here it is a different Ananias.

d 23:3 Or "white-washed wall" (or "hypocrite"). See Ezek. 13:10–16; Matt. 23:27–28.

you sit there judging me according to the law, yet you broke the law when you ordered me to be struck."

⁴ Those standing near Paul said to him, "Do you dare insult the high priest of God?"

⁵ Paul answered, "I had no idea, brothers, that he was the high priest. ᵃ For the Scriptures say, 'Do not curse the ruler of your people.'" ᵇ

⁶ Just then Paul realized that part of the council were Sadducees, who deny the resurrection of the dead, ᶜ and others were of the separated ones. So he shouted, "My fellow Jews, I am a separated one, ᵈ and the son of a separated one. That's why I'm on trial here. It's because of the hope I have that the dead will rise to live again." ᵉ

⁷ When he said this, a heated argument started among them, dividing the council between the Sadducees and the separated ones. ⁸ *Paul knew* that the Sadducees teach there is no resurrection and do not believe in angels or spirits, but the separated ones believe in them all. ⁹ This sparked an even greater uproar among them.

Finally, some of the separated ones who were religious scholars ᶠ stood up and protested strongly, saying, "We find nothing wrong with this man. It could be that the Spirit ᵍ has spoken to him or an angel came to him."

¹⁰ When the shouting match became intense, the commander, fearing they would tear Paul to pieces, intervened and ordered his soldiers to go in to their meeting and seize him and take him back to their headquarters.

¹¹ That night our Lord appeared to Paul and stood before him and said, ʰ

---

a 23:5 It was common for priests and rabbis to wear common clothes except on holy occasions. This could be why Paul did not recognize him as the high priest. There was also uncertainty as to who the high priest was, as Paul had been away from Jerusalem for years.

b 23:5 See Ex. 22:28.

c 23:6 This clause is borrowed from v. 8 and inserted here for the sake of clarity of the English narrative. Of the three major sects of Judaism of that day (Pharisees, Essenes, and Sadducees), the Sadducees were a small but influential group that philosophically denied the supernatural (including the resurrection of the dead, angels, and spirits) and gravitated instead toward political control of the people.

d 23:6 Or "Pharisee," which means "separated one." They were strict keepers of the law and believed in angels and the resurrection.

e 23:6 Or "the hope and the resurrection from the dead." This is most likely a hendiadys. The Aramaic is "I have faith in the [miracle] of the resurrection from the dead."

f 23:9 Or "scribes" (experts in the law).

g 23:9 The Spirit referred to was obviously sent from God (the Holy Spirit).

h 23:11 The Lord Jesus works with his apostolic servants and appeared to them throughout church history to encourage and give them direction for the expansion of God's kingdom realm. See also Mark 16:15; Acts 18:9–10; 22:17–18; 27:23–24; 2 Cor. 12:1.

"Receive miracle power.[a] For just as you have spoken for me in Jerusalem, you will also speak for me in Rome."[b]

The Plot to Kill Paul

[12-13] The next day, more than forty Jews formed a conspiracy and bound themselves under an oath[c] to have no food or water until they had killed Paul. [14] They went to the high priest and the elders to divulge their plans and said to them, "We have united in a solemn oath not to eat or drink until Paul is dead. [15] So we urge you to have the commander bring him to you as though you were to determine his case with a more thorough inquiry. And we will kill him before he even gets here!"

[16] When Paul's nephew, his sister's son, overheard their plot to kill him, he came to the headquarters and informed him of their plans. [17] Paul called for one of the captains[d] and said, "Take this boy[e] to the commander, for he has something important to report to him."

[18] The captain took him to the commander and informed him, "Paul the prisoner asked me to bring this boy to you because he has something important for you to know."

[19] The commander took him by the arm and led him aside in private and asked him, "What do you have to tell me?"

[20] He replied, "The Jews have plotted to kill Paul. Tomorrow they will ask you to bring him again to the supreme council under the pretense of wanting to question him further. [21] Don't believe them, because they have forty men lying in wait to ambush Paul. These men have sworn an oath not to eat or drink until they have killed him. They're all waiting for you to agree to their request *so they can carry out their plot.*"

[22] The commander dismissed Paul's nephew after directing him, "Tell no one that you've reported these things to me." [23-24] Then he summoned two of his captains and said to them, "I want you to take Paul by horseback to Caesarea tonight at nine o'clock. Dispatch two hundred infantrymen, seventy horsemen, and another two hundred spearmen to provide security and deliver him safely to Governor Felix." [25] He sent with them a letter that read:

[26] From Claudias Lysias, to His Excellency, Governor Felix:[f]

---

a 23:11 As translated from the Aramaic. The Greek is "Have courage."

b 23:11 The Aramaic is "You are destined to speak for me in Rome also."

c 23:12–13 Or "with a curse." That is, they pronounced a curse upon themselves, calling down heaven's punishment if they did not murder Paul. One wonders what happened to them when their plot failed.

d 23:17 Or "centurions." See also v. 18.

e 23:17 The Aramaic is "preteen boy." The Greek is "young man."

f 23:26 This was Antonius Felix, the governor of Caesarea who had jurisdiction over Israel and parts of Syria. He was known as a corrupt and cruel tyrant. However, he was married to a

Dear Governor,

[27] I rescued this man, who was seized by the Jews as they were about to put him to death. I intervened with my troops because I understand that he is a Roman citizen. [28] I was determined to learn exactly what charge they were accusing him of, so I brought him to stand before the Jewish supreme council. [29] I discovered that he was being accused with reference to violating controversial issues about their law, but I found no charge against him that deserved death or imprisonment. [30] When I was informed of an imminent plot to kill him, I sent him to you at once, and I have ordered his accusers to also come before you and state their charges against him.

Sincerely,

Claudius Lysias

[31] The soldiers carried out their orders and escorted Paul during the night until they reached the city of Antipatris.[a] [32] The next day the horsemen continued on with Paul and the rest of the soldiers were dismissed to return to their headquarters.

[33] Upon their arrival in Caesarea, they presented the letter to the governor and brought Paul before him. [34] After reading the letter, he asked Paul what province he was from.

Paul answered, "Southeast Turkey."[b]

[35] The governor said, "I will give you a full hearing when your accusers arrive here also." Then he ordered that Paul be kept under guard in Herod's palace.

Paul's Trial before Felix

24 Five days later, Ananias the high priest arrived in Caesarea, accompanied by some Jewish elders and Tertullus, their prosecuting attorney.[c] They were brought before the governor to present formal charges against Paul. [2] After Paul was summoned, Tertullus accused him, saying, [3] "Your Excellency Felix, under the shadow of your wise leadership[d] we Jews have experienced a long period of peace. Because of your wise foresight, many reforms are coming to pass in our nation because of you, Most Honorable Felix. We deeply appreciate this and thank you very much.

Jewish woman and was well acquainted with Jewish laws and traditions. It was important that Paul, a Roman citizen, be tried by Roman authorities.
a 23:31 This was over halfway from Jerusalem to Caesarea.
b 23:34 Or "Cilicia."
c 24:1 Or "an orator" or "a public speaker." He was a professional advocate representing the high priest and Jewish elders. Tertullus means "triple-hardened."
d 24:3 As translated from the Aramaic, "under your shade" (or "shadow") or "tent."

⁴ "So that I won't weary you with a lengthy presentation, I beg you to hear our brief summary, with your customary graciousness. ⁵For we have found this man to be a contagious plague,ᵃ a seditious man who continually stirs up riots among the Jews all over the world. He has become a ringleader of the sect known as the Nazarenes.ᵇ ⁶He has even attempted to desecrate our temple, which is why we had him arrested. We sought to judge him according to our law, ⁷but Commander Lysias came with great force, snatched him away from our hands, and sent him here to you. ⁸He has ordered his accusers to come to you so that you could interrogate him and ascertain for yourself that all these charges we are bringing against him are true."ᶜ

⁹ All the Jews present joined in the verbal attack, saying, "Yes, it's true!"

Paul's Defense before Felix

¹⁰ The governor motioned that it was Paul's turn to speak, so he began to answer the accusations.

"Because I know that you have been a judge over this nation for many years, I gladly respond in my defense. ¹¹You can easily verify that about twelve days ago, I went to Jerusalem to worship. ¹²No one found me arguing with anyone or causing trouble among the people in the synagogues or in the temple or anywhere in the city. ¹³They are completely unable to prove these accusations they make against me.

¹⁴ "But I do confess this to you: I worship the God of our Jewish ancestors as a follower of the Way, which they call a sect. For I believe everything that is written in the Law and the Prophets. ¹⁵And my hope is in God, the same hope that even my accusers have embraced, the hope of a resurrection from the dead of both the righteous and the unrighteous. ¹⁶That's why I seek with all my heart to have a clean conscience toward God and toward others.

¹⁷ "After being away from Jerusalem for several years, I returned to bring to my people gifts for the poor.ᵈ ¹⁸I was in the temple, ritually purified and presenting my offering to God, when they seized me. I had no noisy crowd around me, and I wasn't causing trouble or making any kind of disturbance whatsoever. ¹⁹It was a group of Jews from western Turkeyᵉ who were being unruly; they are the ones who should be here now to bring their charges if

---

ᵃ 24:5 As translated literally from the Greek. The Aramaic is "He is an assassin."

ᵇ 24:5 The word *Nazarene* means "the branch" or "Scion." The Aramaic word implies the title of an heir of a powerful family, or one who is victorious ("Jesus, the Victorious"). Believers are now grafted-in branches of his family tree, victorious ones in Christ (Nazarenes). Many modern-day Arabic speakers still use the term *Nazarenes* when speaking of believers in Jesus.

ᶜ 24:8 Verse 7 and parts of vv. 6 and 8 are missing in most reliable Greek manuscripts. They are a part of the Aramaic text and included here.

ᵈ 24:17 The Aramaic is "For many years I brought to my people gifts for the poor."

ᵉ 24:19 Or "Asia" (Minor).

they have anything against me. [20] Or at least these men standing before you should clearly state what crime they found me guilty of when I stood before the Jewish supreme council, [21] unless it's the one thing I passionately spoke out when I stood among them. I am on trial today only because of my belief in the resurrection of the dead."

[22] Felix, who was well acquainted with the facts about the Way, concluded the hearing with these words: "I will decide your case after Commander Lysias arrives." [23] He then ordered the captain to keep Paul in protective custody, but to give him a measure of freedom, he allowed any of his friends to visit him and help take care of his needs.

Paul Speaks to Felix and Drusilla

[24] Several days later, Felix came back with his wife, Drusilla,[a] who was Jewish. They sent for Paul and listened as he shared with them about faith in Jesus, the Anointed One. [25] As Paul spoke about true righteousness, self-control, and the coming judgment, Felix became terrified and said, "Leave me for now. I'll send for you later when it's more convenient."[b]

[26] He expected to receive a bribe from Paul for his release, so for that reason he would send for Paul from time to time to converse with him.

[27] Two years later, Felix was succeeded by Porcius Festus. Before he left office he decided to leave Paul in prison as a political favor to the Jews.

Paul Appeals to Caesar

25 Three days after Festus assumed his duties in Caesarea, he made the journey to Jerusalem.[c] [2] Religious authorities and prominent leaders among the Jews brought formal charges against Paul before Festus. [3] They came asking him for a favor—that he would transfer Paul from Caesarea to Jerusalem—all the while plotting to ambush and kill Paul along the way.

[4] Festus responded to their request by informing them that he planned to return to Caesarea shortly. [5] He told them, "Your leaders can come with me to Caesarea. If this man has broken any laws, you can bring charges against him there."

[6] After Festus had stayed in Jerusalem no more than eight to ten days, he left for Caesarea. The day after he arrived, he convened the court and took his seat on the bench as judge over the proceedings. After he ordered Paul brought into the courtroom, [7] the Jewish leaders who came from Jerusalem encircled him and leveled against him many serious charges, which they were unable to substantiate.

---

a 24:24 Drusilla was the youngest daughter of Herod Agrippa I and sister of Agrippa II. As a Jewess, she was likely the source of Felix's understanding of the Way.

b 24:25 The Aramaic can be translated "When my conscience is clear I will call for you."

c 25:1 This was a journey of about sixty-five miles (over one hundred kilometers).

⁸ In his defense, Paul said by the Holy Spirit, ᵃ "I have done nothing wrong. ᵇ I've committed no offense against Jewish law, or against the temple, or against Caesar."

⁹ Festus, because he wanted to curry favor with the Jews, asked Paul, "Are you willing to go with me to Jerusalem and be tried for these charges?"

¹⁰ Paul replied, "I am standing here before Caesar's tribunal. This is where I should be tried. As you well know, I have done no harm to the Jews. ¹¹ If I have committed a crime worthy of death, I won't seek to escape the death penalty. But if none of their charges are true, no one has the right to hand me over to them. I appeal to Caesar!"

¹² After conferring with the members of his council, Festus replied, "Since you have appealed to Caesar, to Caesar you will go!"

Festus and King Agrippa

¹³ Several days later, King Agrippa and Bernice ᶜ arrived at Caesarea for a visit with Festus. ¹⁴ During their stay of many days, Festus explained Paul's situation to the king to get his opinion on the matter, saying, "There is a man here whom Felix left as a prisoner. ¹⁵ When I was in Jerusalem, the leading priests and Jewish elders pressed charges against him and demanded that I issue a guilty verdict against him. ¹⁶ I explained to them that it is not our Roman custom to condemn any man before he has an opportunity to face his accusers and present his defense. ¹⁷ So they returned here with me. I didn't postpone the trial, but convened the court the very next day and ordered the man to be brought before me. ¹⁸ I listened to their accusations against him, but they were not what I expected to hear, for he had committed no crime. ¹⁹ Rather, their issues centered around disagreements with him over their religion, and about a dead man named Jesus, who Paul claimed was alive. ²⁰ Because I was perplexed about how to proceed, I asked him if he would be willing to go to Jerusalem to stand trial on these charges. ²¹ When Paul appealed his case to the emperor for a decision, I ordered him to be held in custody until I could send him to Caesar."

²² King Agrippa said to Festus, "I would like to listen to this man myself."

"Tomorrow," he replied, "you will have that opportunity."

Paul before King Agrippa

²³ The next day King Agrippa and Bernice entered the audience hall with much pomp and pageantry. Accompanying them were the senior military officers and prominent citizens. Festus ordered that Paul be brought before them all.

²⁴ Then Festus said, "King Agrippa, and esteemed guests, here is the man

---

a 25:8 As translated from the Aramaic.

b 25:8 Or "I have not sinned in anything."

c 25:13 Bernice, a Jewess, was the sister of King Agrippa and the older sister of Drusilla, wife of Felix (Acts 24:24).

whom the entire Jewish community, both here and in Jerusalem, has asked me to condemn to death. They have screamed and shouted at me, demanding that I end his life. ²⁵ Yet upon investigation I couldn't find one thing that he has done to deserve the death penalty. When he appealed to His Majesty the emperor, I determined to send him. ²⁶ But I have nothing concrete to write to His Majesty, so I have now brought him before you all, and especially before you, King Agrippa. After this preliminary hearing I should have something to write, ²⁷ for it seems absurd to me to send a prisoner without specifying the charges against him."

Paul's Defense before King Agrippa

26 King Agrippa said to Paul, "You may now state your case." Paul motioned with his hand for silence, then began his defense. ᵃ

² "King Agrippa, I consider myself highly favored to stand before you today and answer the charges made against me by the Jews. ³ Because you, more than anyone else, are very familiar with the customs and controversies among the Jewish people, I now ask for your patience as I state my case. ᵇ

⁴ "All the Jews know how I have been raised as a young man, living among my own people from the beginning and in Jerusalem. ⁵ If my accusers are willing to testify, they must admit that they've known me all along as a Pharisee, a member of the most strict and orthodox sect within Judaism. ᶜ ⁶ And now, here I am on trial because I believe in the hope ᵈ of God's promises made to our ancestors. ⁷ This is the promise the twelve tribes of our people hope to see fulfilled as they sincerely strive to serve God with prayers night and day. ᵉ

"So, Your Highness, it is because of this hope that the Jews are accusing me. ⁸ And how should you judge this matter? ᶠ Why is it that any of you think it unbelievable that God raises the dead? ⁹ I used to think that I should do all that was in my power to oppose the name of Jesus of Nazareth. ¹⁰ And that's exactly what I did in Jerusalem, for I not only imprisoned many of the holy believers by the authority of the chief priests, I also cast my vote against them, sentencing them to death. ¹¹ I punished them often in every Jewish meeting hall and attempted to force them to blaspheme. I boiled with rage against them, hunting them down in distant foreign cities to persecute them.

¹² "For that purpose I went to Damascus, with the authority granted to me by the chief priests. ¹³ While traveling on the road at noon, Your Highness, I

---

a 26:1 An alternate reading of the Aramaic is "The [Holy] Spirit issued from his mouth."

b 26:3 An alternate reading of the Aramaic is "I beg you to allow the Spirit to flow so that you can hear me."

c 26:5 The Aramaic is "I have lived by the elite knowledge of the Pharisees."

d 26:6 The Aramaic can also be translated "good news."

e 26:7 As translated from the Aramaic.

f 26:8 As translated from the Aramaic.

saw a light brighter than the sun flashing from heaven all around me and those who were with me. [14] We all fell to the ground, and I heard a voice speaking to me in Aramaic, saying, 'Saul, Saul, why are you persecuting me? You are only hurting yourself when you resist your calling.'[a]

[15] "I asked, 'Who are you, Lord?'

"And the Lord replied, 'I am Jesus,[b] the one you are persecuting. [16] Get up and stand to your feet, for I have appeared to you *to reveal your destiny and to commission you* as my assistant.[c] You will be a witness to what you have seen and to the things I will reveal whenever I appear to you.[d] [17] I will rescue you from the persecution of your own people and from the hostility of the other nations that I will send you to. [18] And you will open their eyes to their true condition, so that they may turn from darkness to the Light[e] and from the power[f] of Satan to the power of God. By placing their faith in me they will receive the total forgiveness[g] of sins and be made holy, *taking hold of the inheritance that I give to my children!*'

[19] "So you see, King Agrippa, I have not been disobedient to what was revealed to me from heaven. [20] For it was in Damascus that I first declared the truth. And then I went to Jerusalem and throughout our nation,[h] and even to other nations, telling people everywhere that they must repent and turn to God and demonstrate it with a changed life.[i] [21] That's why the Jews seized me when I was in the temple and tried to murder me.

[22] "But in spite of all this, I have experienced the supernatural help of God up to this very moment. So I'm standing here saying the same thing that I've shared with everyone, from the least to the greatest. For I teach nothing but what [23] Moses and the prophets have said was destined to happen: that our Messiah had to suffer and die and be the first to rise from the dead,[j] to release the bright light of truth both to our people and to the non-Jewish nations."[k]

---

a 26:14 Or "Why are you hurting yourself by kicking against the ox-goads?"

b 26:15 The Aramaic is "Jesus, the Victorious." See Acts 22:8 and footnote.

c 26:16 The Greek word *hypēretēs* is also used for John Mark as the "assistant" to Barnabas in Acts 13:5.

d 26:16 As translated from the Aramaic, which is literally "a witness that you have seen me and are going to see me again." The Greek is "to what shall yet appear before your eyes" or "to the things in which I will appear to you." Both Greek and Aramaic are somewhat combined in the translation of this verse. Jesus promised future appearances to Paul.

e 26:18 See Isa. 35:5; 42:6–7, 16.

f 26:18 Or "authority" or "dominion."

g 26:18 Or "cancellation of sins."

h 26:20 Or "Judea."

i 26:20 Or "with fruits in keeping with repentance."

j 26:23 The Aramaic is "to inaugurate [or "be the origin of"] the resurrection from the dead."

k 26:23 See Luke 2:32.

²⁴Festus interrupted Paul's defense,ᵃ blurting out, "You're out of your mind! All this great learning of yours is driving you crazy."ᵇ

²⁵Paul replied, "No, Your Excellency Festus, I am not crazy. I speak the words of truth and reason.ᶜ ²⁶King Agrippa, I know I can speak frankly and freely with you, for you understand these matters well, and none of these things have escaped your notice. After all, it's not like it was a secret! ²⁷Don't you believe the prophets, King Agrippa? I know that you do."

²⁸Agrippa responded, "In such a short time you are nearly persuading me to become a Christian."

²⁹Paul replied, "I pray to God that both you and those here listening to me would one day become the same as I am, except, of course, without these chains."

³⁰The king, the governor, Bernice, and all the others got up. ³¹As they were leaving the chamber, they commented to one another, "This man has done nothing that deserves death or even imprisonment."

³²King Agrippa said to Festus, "If he hadn't appealed to Caesar, he could have been released."

Paul Sails to Italy

27 When it was decided that weᵈ were to sail for Italy, Festus handed over Paul and a number of other prisoners to the custody of a Roman officer named Julius, a member of the imperial guard. ²We went on board a ship from the port of Adramyttiumᵉ that was planning to stop at various ports along the coast of southwestern Turkey.ᶠ We put out to sea and were accompanied by Aristarchusᵍ from Thessalonica in Macedonia.

³The next day we docked at Sidon,ʰ and Julius, being considerate of Paul, allowed him to disembark and be refreshed by his friends living there. ⁴From there we put out to sea, but because the windsⁱ were against us, we sailed under the lee of Cyprus.ʲ ⁵After sailing across the open sea off Cilicia and Pamphylia, we docked at the port of Myra in Lycia. ⁶While we were there, the

---

a 26:24 The Aramaic can be translated "As the Holy Spirit spoke through Paul, Festus interrupted."
b 26:24 Or "So much Scripture has made you senseless!"
c 26:25 Or "words of sober truth."
d 27:1 It is likely that Luke rejoined Paul here and sailed with him to Rome.
e 27:2 Adramyttium (modern-day Edrimit, Turkey) was a seaport in the Roman colony of Mysia. Adramyttium means "I will abide in death."
f 27:2 Or "the coast of the province of Asia" (Minor).
g 27:2 Aristarchus means "the best leader."
h 27:3 A Phoenician city now in modern-day Lebanon.
i 27:4 The Aramaic can be translated "the spirits were against us."
j 27:4 That is, east and north of the island.

commanding officer found an Egyptian ship from Alexandria that was bound for Italy, and he put us on board.

[7] We made little headway for several days, and with difficulty we made it to Knidus. [a] The strong winds kept us from holding our course, so from there we sailed along the lee of Crete, [b] opposite Cape Salome. [8] Hugging the coast, we struggled on to a place called Fair Havens, near the town of Lasea. [9] We remained there a long time, until we passed the day of the Jewish fast. [c]

Paul advised the frightened sailors that they should not put out to sea in such dangerous weather, [d] saying, [10] "Men, I can see that our voyage would be disastrous for us and bring great loss, not only to our ship and cargo but also to our own lives. *We should remain here.*" [e]

[11] But the officer in charge was persuaded more by the ship's helmsman and captain [f] than he was by Paul. [12] So the majority decided to put out to sea, since Fair Haven was an exposed harbor and not suitable to winter in. They had hoped to somehow reach the Cretan port of Phineka, [g] which was a more suitable port because it was facing south. [h]

[13] When a gentle south breeze began to blow, they assumed they could make it, so they pulled up anchor and sailed close to Crete. [14] But it wasn't long before the weather abruptly worsened and a storm of hurricane force called the Nor'easter [i] tore across the island and blew us out to sea. [15] The sailors weren't able to turn the ship into the wind, so they gave up and let it be driven by the gale winds. [j]

[16] As we passed to the lee of a small island called Cauda, [k] we were barely able to get the ship's lifeboat under control, [17] so the crew hoisted the dinghy aboard. The sailors used ropes and cables to undergird the ship, [l] fearing they would run aground on the shoals of Syrtis. [m] They lowered the drag anchor to slow its speed and let the ship be driven along.

---

a 27:7 Or "Cnidus," an ancient port city on the Gulf of Gökova on the coast of Turkey.

b 27:7 The Aramaic is "we circled Crete."

c 27:9 This was possibly the Day of Atonement, when every Jew fasts.

d 27:9 As translated from the Aramaic. This was the season the Romans called *mare clausum*, the closed sea, when the Mediterranean was not navigable.

e 27:10 This was clearly prophetic revelation given to the apostle Paul.

f 27:11 Or "ship's owner."

g 27:12 Or "Phoenix."

h 27:12 As translated from the Aramaic. The Greek is "looking toward Lips and Choros." *Lips* was the Greek term for the "winds from the southwest," and *Choros* the word for "winds from the northwest."

i 27:14 The Aramaic is "Euroclydon's typhoon."

j 27:15 The Aramaic is "we surrendered to its power."

k 27:16 Or "Gaudos."

l 27:17 The Aramaic is "They tied down the lifeboat on the ship, lest it fall into the sea."

m 27:17 This was a shallow region full of reefs and sandbars off the coast of Libya between Benghazi and Tripoli.

[18] The next day, because of being battered severely by the storm, the sailors jettisoned the cargo, [19] and by the third day they even threw the ship's tackle and rigging overboard. [20] After many days of seeing neither the sun nor the stars, and with the violent storm continuing to rage against us, all hope of ever getting through it alive was abandoned.

[21] After being without food for a long time, Paul stepped before them all and said, "Men, you should have obeyed[a] me and avoided all of this pain and suffering by not leaving Crete. [22] Now listen to me. Don't be depressed, for no one will perish—only the ship will be lost. [23] For God's angel visited me last night, the angel of my God, the God I passionately serve. He came and stood in front of me [24] and said, 'Don't be afraid, Paul. You are destined to stand trial before Caesar. And because of God's favor on you, he has given you the lives of everyone who is sailing with you.' [25] So men, keep up your courage! I know that God will protect you, just as he told me he would. [26] But we must run aground on some island to be saved."

[27] On the fourteenth night of being tossed about the Adriatic Sea, about midnight, the sailors sensed we were approaching land. [28] So they took soundings and discovered that the water was about 120 feet deep.[b] After sailing a short distance, they again took soundings and found it was only ninety feet deep.[c] [29] Fearing we would be dashed against a rocky coast, they dropped four anchors from the stern and waited for morning to come.

[30] Some sailors pretended to go down to drop anchors from the bow when in fact they wanted to lower the lifeboat into the sea and escape, abandoning ship. [31] Paul said to the Roman officer and his soldiers, "Unless you all stay together onboard the ship, you have no chance of surviving." [32] At the moment they heard this, the soldiers cut the ropes of the dinghy and let it fall away.

[33] Just before daybreak, Paul urged everyone to eat. He said, "Today makes two full weeks that you've been in fearful peril and hunger, unable to eat a thing. [34] Now eat and be nourished. For you'll all come through this ordeal without a scratch."[d]

[35] Then Paul took bread and gave thanks to God[e] in front of them, broke it and began to eat. [36-37] There were 276 people who ate until they were filled, and were strengthened and encouraged.[f] [38] After they were satisfied, they threw the grain into the sea to lighten the ship.

a 27:21 The Greek word *peitharkheo* means "to obey one who is in authority." Paul was the true captain of the ship and carried the weight of authority.
b 27:28 Or "twenty fathoms."
c 27:28 Or "fifteen fathoms."
d 27:34 Or "Not one hair of your heads will perish."
e 27:35 The Aramaic is "glorified God."
f 27:36–37 Paul served communion on board the ship and fed every passenger and crew member. (Did God multiply the bread?) The language used is vividly eucharistic. There is a variation among many Greek manuscripts as to the total of those who were fed. Some have as few as sixty-nine or seventy. The majority of reliable manuscripts in Greek and Aramaic have 276.

Paul Is Shipwrecked

[39] When daylight came, the sailors didn't recognize the land, but they noticed a cove with a sandy beach, so they decided to run the ship ashore. [40] They cut away the anchors, leaving them in the sea, untied the ropes holding the rudders, and hoisted the foresail to the breeze to head for the beach. [41] But they drifted into the rocky shoals between two depths of the sea, causing the ship to flounder still a distance from shore. The bow was stuck fast, jammed on the rocks, while the stern was being smashed by the pounding of the surf.

[42] The soldiers wanted to kill all the prisoners to prevent them from escaping. [43] But the Roman officer was determined to bring Paul safely through, so he foiled their attempts. He commanded the prisoners and crew who could swim to jump overboard and swim ashore. [a] [44] The rest all managed to survive by clinging to planks and broken pieces of the ship, so that everyone scrambled to the shore uninjured.

Paul on the Island of Malta

28 After we had safely reached land, we discovered that the island we were on was Malta. [2] The people who lived there showed us extraordinary kindness, for they welcomed us around the fire they had built because it was cold and rainy.

[3] When Paul had gathered an armful of brushwood and was setting it on the fire, a venomous snake was driven out by the heat and latched onto Paul's hand with its fangs. [4] When the islanders saw the snake dangling from Paul's hand, they said to one another, "No doubt about it, this guy is a murderer. Even though he escaped death at sea, Justice [b] has now caught up with him!"

[5] But Paul shook the snake off, flung it into the fire, and suffered no harm at all. [6] Everyone watched him, expecting him to swell up or suddenly drop dead. After observing him for a long time and seeing that nothing unusual happened, they changed their minds and said, "He must be a god!"

[7] The Roman governor of the island, named Publius, had his estate nearby. He graciously welcomed us as his houseguests and showed us hospitality for the three days that we stayed with him. [8] His father lay sick in bed, suffering from fits of high fever and dysentery. So Paul went into his room, and after praying, placed his hands on him. He was instantly healed. [9] When the people of the island heard about this miracle, they brought all the sick to Paul, and they were

---

a 27:43 As translated from the Aramaic.

b 28:4 The implication in the Greek text is that they were referring to a "goddess of justice," perhaps a local deity.

also healed. *a* [10] The islanders honored us greatly, *b* and when we were preparing to set sail again, they gave us all the supplies we needed for our journey.

Paul Reaches Rome

[11] After three months we put out to sea on an Egyptian ship from Alexandria that had wintered at the island. The ship had carved on its prow as its emblem the "Heavenly Twins." *c*

[12] When we landed at Syracuse, *d* we stayed there for three days. [13] From there we set sail for the Italian city of Rhegium. The day after we landed, a south wind sprang up that enabled us to reach Puteoli *e* in two days. [14] There we found some believers, who begged us to stay with them for a week. Afterward, we made our way to Rome.

[15] When the believers were alerted we were coming, they came out to meet us at the Forum of Appius *while we were still a great distance from Rome.* *f* *Another group met us* at the Three Taverns. *g* When Paul saw the believers, his heart was greatly encouraged and he thanked God.

[16] When we finally entered Rome, Paul was turned over to the authorities and was allowed to live where he pleased, with one soldier assigned to guard him.

Paul Speaks to Prominent Jews of Rome

[17] After three days Paul called together all the prominent members of the Jewish community of Rome. *h* When they had all assembled, Paul said to them, "My fellow Jews, while I was in Jerusalem, I was handed over as a prisoner of the Romans for prosecution, even though I had done nothing against any of our people or our Jewish customs. [18] After hearing my case, the Roman authorities wanted to release me since they found nothing that deserved a death sentence. [19] When the Jews objected to this, I felt it necessary, with no malice against them, *i* to appeal to Caesar. [20] This, then, is the reason I've asked to speak with

---

a 28:9 Although Paul was technically a prisoner, he was the one setting everyone free. No doubt he preached the gospel with signs and wonders, leaving the island healed in more ways than one.

b 28:10 Or "They honored us with many honors."

c 28:11 These were the twin sons of Zeus, Castor and Pollux. The Aramaic is "flying the flag of Gemini." This was a widespread cult in Egypt in that era.

d 28:12 This was the city on the eastern coast of Sicily.

e 28:13 This was on the western coast of Italy, with a road leading to Rome, about 145 miles to the north.

f 28:15 The Forum of Appius was about forty-three miles away from Rome.

g 28:15 Three Taverns was about thirty-three miles from Rome.

h 28:17 Some believe there could have been as many as fifty thousand Jews living in Rome at the time of Paul's visit.

i 28:19 Or "not that I had any feud against my own nation."

you, so that I could explain these things. It is only because I believe in the Hope of Israel that I am in chains before you."

[21] They replied, "We haven't received any letters from the Jews of Judea, nor has anyone come to us with a bad report about you. [22] But we are anxious to hear you present your views regarding this Christian sect we've been hearing about, for people everywhere are speaking against it."

[23] So they set a time to meet with Paul. On that day an even greater crowd gathered where he was staying. From morning until evening Paul taught them, opening up the truths of God's kingdom realm. With convincing arguments from both the Law and the Prophets, he tried to persuade them about Jesus.[a] [24] Some were converted, but others refused to believe. They argued back and forth, [25] still unable to agree among themselves. They were about to leave when Paul made one last statement to them: "The Holy Spirit stated it well when he spoke to your ancestors through the prophet Isaiah:[b][c]

[26] 'I send you to this people to say to them, "You will keep learning,[d] but not understanding. You will keep staring at truth but not perceiving it. [27] For your hearts are hard and insensitive to me—you must be hard of hearing! For you've closed your eyes so that you won't be troubled by the truth, and you've covered your ears so that you won't have to listen and be pierced by what I say. For then you would have to respond and repent, so that I could heal your hearts."'

[28] "So listen well. This wonderful salvation given by God is now being presented to the non-Jewish nations, and they will believe and receive it!"[e]

[30] Paul lived two more years in Rome, in his own rented quarters, welcoming all who came to visit. [31] He continued to proclaim to all the truths of God's kingdom realm, teaching them about the Lord Jesus, the Anointed One, speaking triumphantly and without any restriction.[f]

---

a 28:23 That is, about the purpose of Jesus' coming, which would include his life, ministry, death for our sins, and glorious resurrection.

b 28:25 The Aramaic can be translated "The Holy Spirit spoke beautifully through the mouth of Isaiah the prophet."

c 28:25 See Isa. 6:9–10.

d 28:26 Or "listening."

e 28:28 Verse 29 is not included in the oldest and most reliable Greek manuscript, and it is omitted from almost every modern translation, including the Aramaic. Verse 29, if included, would read "After hearing this, the Jews left with a heated argument among themselves."

f 28:31 Tradition says that Paul was eventually released from house arrest and traveled to Spain. But the inspired account ends here, with Paul ministering to all who came to him. This completes the Acts of the Holy Spirit as recorded by Luke. Although the book of Acts is finished, the acts of God continue to be accomplished through his apostolic company of surrendered lovers. Every believer has the same Holy Spirit and can do the works of Jesus on the earth today.

ROMANS

Introduction

AT A GLANCE

Author: The apostle Paul

Audience: The church of Rome

Date: AD 55–57

Type of Literature: Ancient historical letter and theological essay

Major Themes: The gospel, salvation, the love of God, justification, God's righteousness, the law, life in the flesh versus the Spirit, the destiny of Israel

Outline:

ABOUT ROMANS

What you are about to read is a two thousand-year-old letter, penned by the apostle Paul and inspired by the Holy Spirit. You will be stirred, challenged, perhaps even corrected, as you read this enlightening letter. Paul's gospel was the gospel of grace and glory. When you receive the grace of God by faith, righteousness is birthed within your life.

The love of God is so rich; it leaves our hearts full of heaven. When we believe in Jesus Christ he pours his Holy Spirit into our hearts until every sense of abandonment leaves us. We become children of God, sons and daughters of glory, who follow the Lamb.

Do you want to be enriched and discover the heavenly treasures of faith, grace, true righteousness, and power? Plug into the book of Romans and you'll never feel the same again. Truth always sets the heart free, and nothing can free you more than the truth found in Romans. Grace and glory are waiting for you to unwrap and make your own. Live in the truths of Romans and watch how God's love sets you free!

The Protestant Reformation and the Wesleyan Revival both were born out of the revelation of righteousness found in Romans. Catch the fire of truth and grace as you read through Paul's masterpiece. While preaching in Corinth, Paul dictated the letter to Tertius (16:22) and entrusted it to Phoebe (16:1) to deliver it to the Roman believers. Phoebe was one of the outstanding women in the church of Cenchrea, a port city very near Corinth. We can date this letter to about AD 56. You can imagine the joy that came over the church at Rome when they read Paul's letter!

I encourage you to read Romans a portion at a time, first overlooking the footnotes. Then go back and make a personal study with the hundreds of study notes we have included. You will be blessed as you read the anointed words found herein. The romance of Romans will fill you with freedom. Freedom from sin! Freedom from self! Freedom from dead works! A new freedom is coming into your spirit as you embrace the truth of Romans!

> And you did not receive the "spirit of religious duty," leading you back into the fear of never being good enough. But you have received the "Spirit of full acceptance," enfolding you into the family of God. And you will never feel orphaned, for as he rises up within us, our spirits join him in saying the words of tender affection, "Beloved Father [Abba]!" For the Holy Spirit makes God's fatherhood real to us as he whispers into our innermost being, "You are God's beloved child!"—Romans 8:15–16

PURPOSE

Paul wrote Romans to communicate the grand themes of God's grace and glory encapsulated in the gospel! No one comes into glory except by the grace of God that fills believers with his righteousness. Our clumsy attempts to please God and our works of religion are totally unable to make us holy. But God is so kind, compassionate, and gracious that he shares his righteousness with all who receive his Son, Jesus Christ. He causes his faith-filled ones to be made holy by his grace and glory! Paul wrote his letter to clearly articulate this message, to explain why he preached it, and to show how it should impact Christians in their daily life and community.

AUTHOR AND AUDIENCE

Rome was the power center of the known world when Paul penned this letter. It was the most influential city on earth at that time. Although Paul had not yet been to Rome, he would one day be martyred there. So Paul wrote to these Roman Christians an important epistle filled with rich doctrines of our faith that reveal God's heart for his people, and what must be our proper response to such sacrificial love. Paul's theology flows from the romance of God toward us. Intimacy longs for understanding and oneness. And to be intimate with the God of glory requires that we understand his heart and join him in every way.

MAJOR THEMES

The Gospel. Arguably the central focus of Paul's teaching ministry is what Christians call "the gospel." It's also the major focus of his letter to the church of Rome. In the opening sentence Paul explains that God had set him apart with the mission to unveil "God's wonderful gospel" (1:1). This is one way of explaining the gospel. Here are some others: the revelation of God's Son; the wonderful message of Jesus; the joyful message of God's liberating power unleashed within us through Christ; the message of Christ's goodness, good news, and joyful news.

The Greek word for gospel is *euangelion,* which simply means "good news." Paul uses this word as shorthand for the amazing, joyful message of God's saving work in Jesus Christ. The entire Christian message is wrapped up in this one word. The gospel is the message about how God has acted in the world to rescue humanity from sin and death through the life, death, and resurrection of Jesus. So when Paul says gospel, he means all that!

Salvation. God's wonderful salvation is presented to us in this letter—a salvation not of works or religious efforts, but the joyous salvation that comes to everyone who believes the good news of Jesus Christ. He has come to save us and set us free. This salvation is seen in Romans as comprehensive and complete, restoring our souls to wholeness and glory, through God's endless grace.

The Love of God. Paul sings of God's love throughout the book of Romans! He writes that right now we "experience the endless love of God cascading into our hearts through the Holy Spirit who lives in us!" (5:5). And this love is all because of Jesus: "Christ proved God's passionate love for us by dying in our place while we were still lost and ungodly!" (5:8). If you ever doubt God's love for you, plug into Romans to be overpowered by it, realizing we will never be deprived of this gift we have in Christ Jesus!

Justification. One of the most powerful words Paul uses to describe our new reality in Christ is the word *justified.* This is a legal term that basically means "to acquit." This is God's grace at its sweetest and most potent power! While we were all at some point under God's wrath because of our sin, because Jesus paid the price of our sin in our place, we have been acquitted of all the charges against us and declared "not guilty" in heaven's courtroom!

The Righteousness of God. One of the most important themes of Paul in his letter to Roman Christians is righteousness, as it relates to both God and believers. He uses the word *righteousness* numerous times to refer to what we receive from God. Not only are we declared to be in the right, we are actually made right by God when we believe in Jesus. In fact, his righteousness is transferred to us through faith so that when we stand before God, that is who we really are: righteous!

The Law. Many have noted that Paul's relationship with the law is complicated (the Jewish law given by God to Moses for his people). In Romans, Paul says the law is "holy and its commandments are correct and for our good" (7:12). It was given to us for our benefit and intended to bring life, but instead it brought death (7:10). Paul concluded, "God achieved what the law was unable to accomplish, because the law was limited by the weakness of human nature" (8:3). Through Christ, God achieved what we could not: Christ perfectly fulfilled every requirement of the law so that now "we are free to live, not according to our flesh, but by the dynamic power of the Holy Spirit!" (8:4).

The Flesh versus the Spirit. One of the most interesting comparisons Paul makes is between our old life in "the flesh" versus our new life in the "life-giving Spirit." He offers this comparison as an exhortation to live the kind of life God desires from his children—not in the morally fallen way we once lived, but in the new way as true children of God "who are moved by the impulses of the Holy Spirit" (8:14).

The Destiny of Israel. From the very beginning Paul makes it clear that his joyful message of what Christ has done is for every single person on the planet: "the Jew first, and then people everywhere!" (1:16). Jews and non-Jews alike are under the same curse because of sin. Paul says the same solution to that problem is available for everyone by the same faith. While the Jewish people were given this promise first, people from every nation were later "grafted in" to share in their wonderful riches. And though Jews have fallen into unbelief, Paul makes it clear God will bring all of Israel to salvation once the full number of non-Jews have come into God's family!

PAUL'S LETTERS

Romans is the first of Paul's letters written to churches to encourage, inspire, and instruct. No one demonstrated more care for the churches than Paul. Many of them existed because of Paul's ministry.

Each of the Pauline letters focuses on two major themes: the importance of right doctrine and the importance of right living. For example, Rom. 1–11 contain many instructions and teaching on having a proper belief system regarding sin, salvation, the work of the cross in our lives, God's endless love for us, and the place of Israel in the plan of God. It is only after Paul instructs the church that he encourages them to live holy lives. In other words, right understanding of truth is paramount in having a right understanding of how we are to live our lives for the glory of God.

Below is a list of the thirteen letters of Paul and the book of Hebrews (the author is anonymous, but traditionally the book is attributed to Paul). These letters, viewed as Scripture from the time they were written, account for over half the New Testament that we have today.

- Romans
- 1 Corinthians
- 2 Corinthians
- Galatians
- Ephesians
- Philippians
- Colossians
- 1 Thessalonians
- 2 Thessalonians
- 1 Timothy
- 2 Timothy
- Titus
- Philemon
- Hebrews

Although each letter was written to a specific church or person or group, they were meant to be circular letters read by all the churches. Scholars believe they were all written within a span of less than fourteen years and are meant to bring all believers into the beautiful discovery of God's plan for their lives. They empower us today to live our lives with deep conviction of truth, faith, and love—overcoming every enemy and being victorious in Christ in all things. Amen!

ROMANS

Grace and Glory

1 Paul, a loving and loyal servant*a* of the Anointed One, Jesus. He called me to be his apostle*b* and set me apart*c* with a mission to reveal God's wonderful gospel. *(7)* I write this letter to all his beloved chosen ones in Rome, for you have been divinely summoned to be holy in his eyes. *d* May his joyous grace and total well-being, flowing from our Father and the Lord Jesus Christ, rest upon you.

2 My commission is to preach the good news. Yet it is not entirely new, but the fulfillment of the hope promised to us through the many prophecies found in the sacred Scriptures.*e* *3* For the gospel is all about God's Son. As a man he descended from David's royal lineage,*f* *4* but as the mighty Son of God he was raised from the dead and miraculously set apart*g* with a display of triumphant power supplied by the Spirit of Holiness.*h* And now Jesus is our Lord and our Messiah. *5* Through him a joy-producing grace cascaded into us, empowering us with the gift of apostleship,*i* so that we can win people from every nation

---

a 1:1 The Greek word *doulos* signifies more than a servant; it is one who has chosen to serve a master out of love, bound with cords so strong that it could only be severed by death.

b 1:1 Or "his called apostle." Paul was a servant before he was an apostle.

c 1:1 Or "permanently separated." There is an interesting wordplay here. The Aramaic word for "separated" is the root word for "Pharisee," a separated one. Paul is saying that God is the one who separated him as uniquely God's, as opposed to a self-righteous superiority. See also Gal. 1:15.

d 1:1 This sentence, although found in v. 7, has been placed here in Paul's introduction for purposes of clarity.

e 1:2 This would include the types, shadows, and prophecies of the entire Old Testament. Paul quotes from the Hebrew Scriptures (the Tanakh) more than eighty times in Romans.

f 1:3 Or "the seed of David." Jesus was the "seed of the woman" in Gen. 3:15, the "seed of Abraham" in Gal. 3:16, and here in Rom. 1, the "seed of David." See also Acts 13:16–41.

g 1:4 Or "marked [appointed] as God's Son immersed in power." The Greek word for "set apart" comes from *horizo*, meaning "the horizon." It means "to mark out the boundaries," "to decree," or "to define." The horizon we move toward is Jesus!

h 1:4 Or "the Holy Spirit."

i 1:5 Note that grace comes before service or ministry. This is likely a hendiadys: "We received the grace-gift of apostleship." See also 1 Cor. 15:9–10; Eph. 4:7–13.

into a faithful commitment to Jesus,[a] to bring honor to his name.[b] And you are among the chosen ones who received the call to belong to Jesus, the Anointed One.[b]

Paul's Desire to Visit Rome

[8] I give thanks to God for all of you,[c] because it's through your conversion to Jesus Christ, that the testimony of your strong, persistent faith is spreading throughout the world. [9] And God knows that I pray for you continually and at all times. For I passionately serve and worship him with my spirit in the gospel of his Son.

[10] My desire and constant prayer is that I would be able to come and visit you,[d] according to the plan and timing of God.[e] [11] I yearn to come and be face-to-face with you and get to know you. For I long to impart to you[f] the gift of the Spirit[g] that will empower you to stand strong in your faith. [12] Now, this means that when we come together and are side by side, something wonderful will be released. We can expect to be co-encouraged and co-comforted by each other's faith!

[13] So, my dear brothers and sisters, please don't interpret my failure to visit you as indifference, because many times I've intended to come but have not been released[h] to do so up to now. For I long to enjoy a harvest of spiritual fruit[i] among you, like I have experienced among the nations. [14] Love obligates me to preach to everyone, to those who are among the elite and those who are among the outcasts,[j] to those who are wise and educated as well as to those who are foolish and unlearned. [15] This is why I am so excited[k] about coming to preach the wonderful message of Jesus[l] to you in Rome!

---

a 1:5 Or "the obedience of faith." The Greek text is ambiguous and can mean "the obedience to the faith" or "the obedience that springs from faith" or "the obedience that faith produces." To obey the gospel is simply to believe it!

b 1:6 Verse 7 has been merged into the text of verse 1 to enhance clarity.

c 1:8 It was Paul's constant habit to thank God for any grace he found within any believer.

d 1:10 As translated from the Aramaic. The Greek is "that I may have a smooth and prosperous journey to you." But in fact, Paul had a very difficult journey to Rome, first traveling by ship, enduring a shipwreck, and being bitten by a snake. See Acts 27–28. One can only imagine what would have happened if Paul had not prayed for a smooth and prosperous journey!

e 1:10 Or "as God prospers me along the path of his will."

f 1:11 Or "share with you."

g 1:11 As translated from the Aramaic. The Greek is "a spiritual gift." See also Rom. 15:29.

h 1:13 Or "have been hindered" (due to missionary work). There is no implication that the devil hindered Paul from coming, but rather, the missionary work of ministering in Turkey (Asia Minor) hindered him.

i 1:13 This "fruit" would imply both converts and bringing the believers into maturity.

j 1:14 Or "to the Greek speakers and to the barbarians." By implication, Paul is obligated by love to preach to the cultured Greek speakers and to those who are uncultured foreigners.

k 1:15 Or "To my very uttermost I am eager."

l 1:15 Or "good news" (or "gospel") or "message of goodness" (well-being).

The Gospel of Power

[16] I refuse to be ashamed of sharing the wonderful message of God's liberating power unleashed in us through Christ! For I am thrilled to preach that everyone who believes is saved—the Jew first, [a] and then people everywhere! [17] This gospel unveils a continual revelation of God's righteousness—a perfect righteousness given to us when we believe. [b] And it moves us from *receiving life through faith,* to *the power of living by* faith. [c] This is what the Scripture means when it says:

"We are right with God through life-giving faith!" [d]

God Reveals His Wrath

[18] For God in heaven unveils his holy anger [e] breaking forth against every form of sin, both toward ungodliness that lives in hearts and evil actions. For the wickedness of humanity deliberately smothers the truth and keeps people from acknowledging the truth about God. [19] In reality, the truth of God is known instinctively, [f] for God has embedded this knowledge inside every human heart. [20] *Opposition to truth cannot be excused on the basis of ignorance,* [g] because from the creation of the world, the invisible qualities [h] of God's nature have made visible, such as his eternal power and transcendence. He has

---

a 1:16 Salvation comes to us through the Jewish people in our Lord Jesus Christ. The promised salvation message came historically to the Jew first, but by priority and privilege our obligation of love continues to bring the sweet message of Yeshua's grace to our Jewish friends.

b 1:17 Although the full meaning of the Greek words *dikaiosynē theou* is greatly debated, this refers to the power of the gospel that imparts to believers God's righteousness. This is the justifying power that comes through faith. The word *of* (righteousness of God) is a genitive of source or cause. It is the righteousness *from* God coming into us who believe. See 2 Cor. 5:21, where *dikaiosynē theou* is also found. However, to insist that the gospel be preached in this day first to the Jew is to deny the truth that there is no distinction between Jew and gentile. See Gal. 4:12; Rom. 3:22.

c 1:17 Ancient expositors taught that we move from what we once believed in to believing in God alone for righteousness. For the Jew it means moving from faith in Torah and doing well to a faith in the works of Yeshua, the Living Torah, who alone brings us into salvation's power. For those in any religion, it means moving from an impotent faith into the explosive faith of the gospel of Christ.

d 1:17 Or "It is through faith that the righteous enter into life" (salvation). See Hab. 2:4.

e 1:18 Or "wrath." God's wrath is his action in punishing evil, a holy disapproval of all that is seen as wicked in the eyes of his holiness. In this first chapter, both righteousness and wrath are revealed. Righteousness is revealed in the gospel, and wrath is revealed as an activity God takes to uphold his glory.

f 1:19 Or "The knowability of God is manifest in them."

g 1:20 Implied by the immediate context and by the use of the conjunction *because.* This form of ellipsis needs to be supplied for the sake of clarity.

h 1:20 The Aramaic can be translated "his holy attributes."

made his wonderful attributes easily perceived,[a] for seeing the visible makes us understand the invisible.[b] So then, this leaves everyone without excuse.

[21] *Throughout human history*[c] the fingerprints of God were upon them,[d] yet they refused to honor him as God or even be thankful for his kindness. Instead, they entertained corrupt and foolish thoughts about what God was like.[e] This left them with nothing but misguided hearts, steeped in moral darkness. [22] Although claiming to be super-intelligent,[f] they were in fact shallow fools.[g] [23] For only a fool would trade the unfading splendor of the immortal God to worship the fading image of other humans, idols made to look like people, animals, birds, and even creeping reptiles!

[24] This is why God lifted off his restraining hand and let them have full expression of their sinful and shameful desires. They were given over to moral depravity, dishonoring their bodies *by sexual perversion* among themselves—[25] all because they traded the truth of God for a lie.[h] They worshiped and served the things God made rather than the God who made all things—glory and praises to him for eternity of eternities![i] Amen!

[26-27] For this reason God gave them over to their own disgraceful and vile passions.[j] Enflamed with lust for one another, men and women ignored the natural order and exchanged normal sexual relations for homosexuality. Women engaged in lesbian conduct, and men committed shameful acts with men,[k] receiving in themselves the due penalty for their deviation.[l]

[28] And because they thought it was worthless to embrace the true knowledge of God, God gave them over[m] to a worthless mind-set, to break all rules of proper conduct. [29] Their sinful lives became full of every kind of evil,[n] wicked

---

a 1:20 Or "lies plainly before their eyes." The literal Greek is "being intellectually apprehended by reflection."

b 1:20 That is, what the eye sees becomes revelation to the conscience. See Ps. 19:1–4.

c 1:21 This phrase is implied by the use of the Greek aorist verb tense and is important for clarity as Paul continues to describe the brokenness of fallen humanity.

d 1:21 Or "They instinctively knew (there was a) God."

e 1:21 Or "they became futile in their reasoning."

f 1:22 Or "wise."

g 1:22 The Aramaic can be translated "they became insane."

h 1:25 An obvious metonymy, equating an idol with "a lie." See 2 Thess. 2:11.

i 1:25 As translated from the Aramaic.

j 1:26–27 The Aramaic can be translated "disgraceful diseases."

k 1:26–27 See Lev. 18:22.

l 1:26–27 Some see an inference here to sexually transmitted diseases.

m 1:28 This is the third time that it states, "God gave them over." See vv. 24, 26–27, and here in v. 28.

n 1:29 There are twenty-two Greek nouns and adjectives used for evil listed in vv. 29–32. Injustice (selfishness), destructiveness, covetousness, malice, envy, murder, strife, guile, hostility, slander (the hissing sound of a snake charmer), gossip, hateful to God, insolent, arrogant, disobedient to parents, without moral understanding, without faith, without natural affections, hostilities, without mercy.

schemes,[a] greed,[b] and cruelty. Their hearts overflowed with jealous cravings, and with conflict and strife, which drove them into hateful arguments and murder. They are deceitful liars full of hostility. They are gossips [30] who love to spread malicious slander. With inflated egos they hurl hateful insults at God, yet they are nothing more than arrogant boasters. They are rebels against their parents and totally immoral. [31] They are senseless, faithless,[c] ruthless, heartless, and completely merciless. [d] [32] Although they are fully aware of God's laws and proper order, and knowing that those who do all of these things deserve to die, yet they still go headlong into darkness, encouraging others to do the same and applauding them when they do!

God Judges Sin

2 No matter who you are, before you judge the wickedness of others, you had better remember this: you are also without excuse, for you too are guilty of the same kind of things! When you judge others, and then do the same things they do, you condemn yourself.[e] [2] We know that God's judgment falls upon those who practice these things. God is always right, because he has all the facts.[f] [3] And no matter who you think you are, when you judge others who do these things and then do the same things yourself, what makes you think that you will escape God's judgment?

[4] Do the riches of his extraordinary kindness make you take him for granted and despise him? Haven't you experienced how kind and understanding he has been to you? Don't mistake his tolerance for acceptance. Do you realize that all the wealth of his extravagant kindness[g] is meant to melt your heart and lead you into repentance?[h] [5] But because of your calloused heart and refusal to change direction, you are piling up wrath for yourself in the day of wrath, when God's righteous judgment is revealed.

[6] For:

He will give to each one in return for what he has done.[i]

---

a 1:29 The Aramaic and some Greek manuscripts have "immorality."

b 1:29 Or "unrestrained selfishness."

c 1:31 Or "covenant-breakers."

d 1:31 The Aramaic can be translated "They have no stability in themselves, neither love, nor peace, nor compassion."

e 2:1 The Aramaic can be translated "Because of this, O human, the Spirit is not speaking through you as you judge another, for against what you judge, you will also revert."

f 2:2 Or "It [judgment] is based on truth."

g 2:4 The Aramaic word for kindness can be translated "sweetness."

h 2:4 The Aramaic can be translated "Do you now know that it is the fulfillment of God to bring you blessings?"

i 2:6 See Ps. 62:12; Prov. 24:12; Matt. 16:27.

[7] For those living in constant goodness and doing what pleases him, [a] seeking an unfading glory and honor and imperishable virtue, will experience eternal life. [8] But those governed by selfishness and self-promotion, whose hearts are unresponsive to God's truth and would rather embrace unrighteousness, will experience the fullness of wrath. [b]

[9] Anyone who does evil can expect tribulation and distress—to the Jew first and also to the non-Jew. [10] But when we do what pleases God, we can expect unfading glory, true honor, and a continual peace—to the Jew first and also to the non-Jew, [11] for God sees us all without partiality.

[12] When people who have never been exposed to the laws of Moses commit sin, they will still perish for what they do. And those who are under the law of Moses and fail to obey it are condemned by the law. [13] For it's not merely knowing the law [c] that makes you right with God, but doing all that the law says that will cause God to pronounce you innocent. [d]

God's Judgment

[14] For example, whenever people who don't possess the law [e] as their birthright commit sin, it still confirms that a "law" is present in their conscience. For when they instinctively do what the law requires, that becomes a "law" to govern them, even though they don't have Mosaic law. [15] It demonstrates that the requirements of the law are woven into their hearts. They know what is right and wrong, for their conscience validates this "law" in their heart. Their thoughts correct [f] them in one instance and commend them in another. [16] So this judgment will be revealed on the day when God, through Jesus the Messiah, judges the hidden secrets of people's hearts. And their response to the gospel I preach will be the standard of judgment used in that day.

The Jewish Religion Will Not Save You

[17] Now, you claim to be a Jew because you lean upon your trust in the law [g] and boast in your relationship with God. [18] And you claim to know the will of God, and to have the moral high ground because you've been taught the law of Moses. [19] You are also confident that you are a qualified guide to those who are

---

a 2:7 Doing what pleases God comes from faith. We must first believe in Jesus, the Anointed One. Then our life and works will bring honor to him. See also v. 10; John 6:28–29; Heb. 11:6

b 2:8 God's wrath is mentioned twelve times in Romans (1:18; 2:5, 8; 3:5; 4:15; 5:9; 9:22; 12:19; 13:4, 5).

c 2:13 Every Sabbath day the Mosaic law, the Torah, was read in the Jewish meeting house.

d 2:13 Or "righteous." See Deut. 18:5. No one keeps the law in every part; this is why Yeshua (Jesus) came to redeem and save us. See also Rom. 3:20.

e 2:14 Or "Torah" (the first five books of Moses).

f 2:15 Or "accuse."

g 2:17 The Aramaic can be translated "you take comfort from the law."

"blind," a shining light to those who live in darkness. [20] You are confident that you are a true teacher of the foolish and immature,[a] all because you have the treasury of truth and knowledge in the law of Moses. [21] So let me ask you this: Why don't you practice what you preach? You preach, "Don't steal!" but are you a thief? [22] You are swift to tell others, "Don't commit adultery!" but are you guilty of adultery? You say, "I hate idolatry and false gods!" but do you withhold from the true God what is due him?[b] [23] Even though you boast in the law, you dishonor God, the Lawgiver, when you break it! [24] For your actions seem to fulfill what is written:

"God's precious name is cursed among the nations because of you."[c]

[25] You trust in the covenant sign of circumcision,[d] yet circumcision only has value if you faithfully keep the teachings of the law. But if you violate the law, you have invalidated your circumcision.[e] [26] And if the uncircumcised one faithfully keeps the law, won't his obedience make him more "Jewish" than the actual rite of circumcision? [27] And won't the one who has never had the knife cut his foreskin be your judge when you break the law? [28] You are not a Jew if it's only superficial—for it's more than the surgical cut of a knife that makes you Jewish. [29] But you are Jewish because of the inward act of spiritual circumcision—a radical change that lays bare your heart. It's not by the principle of law,[f] but by power of the Holy Spirit. For then your praise will not come from people, but from God himself!

God's Righteousness

3 So then what is the importance of circumcision, and what advantage is there of being a Jew? [2] Actually, there are numerous advantages.[g] Most important, God distinguished the Jews from all other people by entrusting them with the revelation of his prophetic promises.[h] [3] But what if some were unfaithful to their divine calling? Does their unbelief weaken God's faithfulness? [4] Absolutely not! God will always be proven faithful and true to his word, while people are proven to be liars. This will fulfill what was written in the Scriptures:

---

a 2:20 Or "little children," a metaphor for the untutored or the immature.
b 2:22 Or "do you rob temples?" The Aramaic can be translated "you plunder the Holy Place."
c 2:24 See Isa. 52:5 (LXX); Ezek. 36:20.
d 2:25 Implied by the immediate context and by the use of the conjunction yet. This form of ellipsis needs to be supplied for the sake of clarity.
e 2:25 Or "your circumcision has become uncircumcision."
f 2:29 Or "by the letter."
g 3:2 The Aramaic can be translated "They have increased [prospered] in every way."
h 3:2 These prophetic promises ("messages," "oracles," or "sayings") include the entire scope of revelation given to the Jews through the teachings of the Torah and the many prophecies of the coming Messiah, all finding their fulfillment in Jesus, the Anointed One.

Your words will always be vindicated
   and you will rise victorious
   when you are being tried by your critics![a]

[5] But what if our wrong shows how right God is? Doesn't our bad serve the purpose of making God look good? (Of course, I'm only speaking from a human viewpoint.) Would that infer that God is unfair when he displays his anger against wrongdoing? [6] Absolutely not! For if that were the case, how could God be the righteous judge of all the earth?

[7] So, if my lie brings into sharp contrast the brightness of God's truth, and if my lie accentuates his glory, then why should I be condemned as a sinner? [8] Is it proper for us to sin, just so we can be forgiven?[b] May it never be! Yet there are some who slander us and claim that is what we teach. They deserve to be condemned for even saying it!

Universal Sinfulness

[9] So, are we to conclude then that we Jews are superior to all others? Certainly not! For we have already proven[c] that both Jews and gentiles are all under the bondage of sin. [10] And the Scriptures agree, for it is written:

There is no one who always does what is right,
   no, not even one!
[11] There is no one with true spiritual insight,
   and there is no one who seeks after God alone.
[12] All have deliberately wandered from God's ways.
   All have become depraved and unfit.
   Kindness has disappeared from them all,
   not even one is good.[d]
[13] Their words release a stench,[e]
   like the smell of death—foul and filthy![f]
   Deceitful lies roll off their tongues.
   The venom of a viper drips from their lips.[g]
[14] Bitter profanity flows from their mouths,
   only meant to cut and harm.[h]

---

a 3:4 Or "You will prevail when judged." See Ps. 51:4.

b 3:8 As translated from the Aramaic and implied in the Greek, which reads "to do evil so that good may come."

c 3:9 Or "accused" or "drawn up an indictment."

d 3:12 This is quoted from the Greek Septuagint of Pss. 14:1–3 and 53:3.

e 3:13 Or "Their throats are open graves," a metonymy for their speech.

f 3:13 See Ps. 5:9.

g 3:13 See Ps. 140:3.

h 3:14 See Ps. 10:7.

¹⁵ They are infatuated with violence and murder. ^a
¹⁶ They release ruin and misery wherever they go.
¹⁷ They never experience the path of peace. ^b
¹⁸ They shut their eyes to the awe-inspiring God! ^c

¹⁹ Now, we realize that everything the law says is addressed to those who are under its authority. This is for two reasons: So that every excuse will be silenced, *with no boasting of innocence.* ^d And so that the entire world will be held accountable to God's standards. ^e ²⁰ For by the merit of observing the law no one earns the status of being declared righteous before God, for it is the law that fully exposes and unmasks the reality of sin.

The Gospel Reveals God's Righteousness

^{21–22} But now, independently of the law, the righteousness of God is tangible and brought to light through Jesus, the Anointed One. This is the righteousness that the Scriptures prophesied would come. ^f It is God's righteousness made visible through the faithfulness of Jesus Christ. ^g And now all who believe in him receive that gift. For there is really no difference between us, ²³ for we all have sinned and are in need of the glory of God. ²⁴ Yet through his powerful declaration of acquittal, God freely gives away his righteousness. His gift ^h of love and favor now cascades over us, all because Jesus, the Anointed One, has liberated us from *the guilt, punishment, and power of* sin!

²⁵ Jesus' God-given destiny ⁱ was to be the sacrifice to take away sins, and now he is our mercy seat ^j because of his death on the cross. We come to him for mercy, for God has made a provision for us to be forgiven by faith in

---

a 3:15 Or "Their feet are swift to shed blood."

b 3:17 Verses 15–17 are quoted from Isa. 59:7–8.

c 3:18 See Ps. 36:1. Paul lists a total of fourteen truths that describe all of humanity from the Old Testament.

d 3:19 "every excuse will be silenced" means that there will be no one boasting that they are innocent before God.

e 3:19 Or "may be liable to judgment by God."

f 3:21–22 Or "attested to by the Law and the Prophets."

g 3:21–22 Or "through faith in Jesus Christ."

h 3:24 The Greek word is *dorean,* which means "present," "gift," "legacy," "privilege."

i 3:25 The Aramaic can be translated "God ordained in advance an atonement by faith in his [Jesus'] blood."

j 3:25 Or "propitiation." The *mercy seat* becomes a metonymy for the sacrificial, redemptive work of Christ. The mercy seat was the lid to the ark of the covenant, which was carried throughout the wilderness for years and finally found a home in the temple in Jerusalem. "Blood of mercy" was sprinkled on the mercy seat (or "place of satisfaction") yearly on the Day of Atonement, which covered the sins of the people until Jesus sprinkled his blood on the mercy seat in the heavens. The mercy seat was not seen by the people; only the high priest went into the holy of holies to sprinkle blood upon the mercy seat. Yet Jesus was publicly offered as the satisfaction for sin's consequences.

the sacred blood of Jesus. This is the perfect demonstration of God's justice, because until now, he had been so patient—holding back his justice out of his tolerance for us. So he covered over[a] the sins of those who lived prior to Jesus' sacrifice. [26] And when the season of tolerance came to an end, there was only one possible way for God to give away his righteousness and still be true to both his justice and his mercy—to offer up his own Son. So now, because we stand on the faithfulness of Jesus,[b] God declares us righteous in his eyes!

[27] Where, then, is there room for boasting? Do our works bring God's acceptance? Not at all! It was not our works of keeping the law but our faith[c] in his finished work *that makes us right with God.* [28] So our conclusion is this: God's wonderful declaration that we are righteous[d] in his eyes can only come when we put our faith in Christ, and not in keeping the law.

The God of All the People

[29] After all, is God the God of the Jews only, or is he equally the God for all of humanity? Of course, he's the God of all people! [30] Since there is only one God, he will treat us all the same—he eliminates our guilt and makes us right with him by faith no matter who we are.[e] [31] Does emphasizing our faith invalidate the law? Absolutely not. Instead, our faith establishes the role the law should rightfully have.[f]

Abraham's Faith

4 Let me use Abraham as an example. It is clear that humanly speaking, he was the founder of Judaism. What was his experience of being made right with God? [2] Was it by his good works of keeping the law? No. For if it was by the things he did, he would have something to boast about, but no one boasts before God. [3] Listen to what the Scriptures say:

> Because Abraham believed God's words, his faith
> transferred God's righteousness into his account.[g]

[4] When people work, they earn wages. It can't be considered a free gift, because they earned it. [5] But no one earns God's righteousness. It can only be transferred when we no longer rely on our own works, but believe in the one

---

a 3:25 Or "passed over," "released" (let it be). This is the only place the Greek word *paresis* is found in the New Testament.

b 3:26 Or "faith in Jesus."

c 3:27 The Aramaic can be translated "It was not our works of keeping Torah, but the Torah of faith." The Greek is "the law [principle] of faith."

d 3:28 Or "continually made righteous."

e 3:30 Or "whether they are circumcised or uncircumcised."

f 3:31 Or "upholds the law." The rightful role of the law is to bring conviction of sin (vv. 19–20) and to present God's standard of holiness, now fulfilled in Christ (8:4).

g 4:3 See Gen. 15:6.

who powerfully declares the ungodly to be righteous [a] in his eyes. It is faith that transfers God's righteousness into your account!

David's Faith

[6] Even King David himself speaks to us regarding the complete wholeness that comes inside a person when God's powerful declaration of righteousness is heard over our life. Apart from our works, God's work is enough. [7] Here's what David says:

> What happy fulfillment is ahead for those [b]
> > whose rebellion has been forgiven
> > and whose sins are covered by blood. [c]
> [8] What happy progress comes to them
> > when they hear the Lord speak over them,
> > "I will never hold your sins against you!" [d]

[9] Now, think about it. Does this happiness come only to the Jews, or is it available to all who believe? [e] Our answer is this: faith was credited to Abraham as God's righteousness! [f]

[10] How did he receive this gift of righteousness? Was he circumcised at the time God accepted him, or was he still uncircumcised? Clearly, he was an uncircumcised gentile when God said this of him! [11] It was later that he received the external sign of circumcision as a seal to confirm that God had already transferred his righteousness to him by faith, while he was still uncircumcised. So now this qualifies him to become the father of all who believe among the non-Jewish people. And like their "father of faith," Abraham, God also transfers his righteousness to them by faith. [12] Yes, Abraham is obviously the true father of faith for the Jewish people who are not only circumcised but who walk in the way of faith that our father Abraham displayed before his circumcision.

---

a 4:5 Or "calculated [reckoned] to be righteous." The Greek word logizomai is used eleven times in this chapter. This teaches us that our faith is considered or calculated as righteousness before God.

b 4:7 See Ps. 32:1. The Hebrew word for "blessed" or "happy" is asher, which carries the meaning of "a happy progress." See also v. 8.

c 4:7 When David wrote this Psalm, it was during the days of covering sin by the blood of sacrifice. Today our sins are no longer simply covered, but removed forever.

d 4:8 The Greek uses the word logizomai, which means to take an inventory and settle accounts. God has taken inventory of the virtue of Christ, and through our faith in him, his perfect righteousness is now deposited in our account. It is settled; we are declared righteous by faith.

e 4:9 Or "Is this happiness then for those who are the circumcision or also for the uncircumcision?"

f 4:9 See Gen. 15:6.

The Promise of Faith versus Keeping the Law

[13] God promised Abraham and his descendants that they would have an heir who would reign over the world. [a] This royal promise was not fulfilled because Abraham kept all the law, but through the righteousness that was transferred by faith. [14] For if keeping the law earns the inheritance, then faith is robbed of its power and the promise becomes useless. [15] For the law provokes punishment, and where no law exists there cannot be a violation of the law.

[16] The promise depends on faith so that it can be experienced as a grace-gift, and now it extends to all the descendants of Abraham. This promise is not only meant for those who obey the law, but also to those who enter into the faith of Abraham, the father of us all. [17] That's what the Scripture means when it says:

> "I have made you the father of many nations." [b]

He is our example and father, for in God's presence he believed that God can raise the dead and call into being things that don't even exist yet. [c] [18] Against all odds, when it looked hopeless, Abraham believed the promise and expected God to fulfill it. [d] He took God at his word, and as a result he became the father of many nations. God's declaration over him came to pass:

> "Your descendants will be so many
> that they will be impossible to count!" [e]

[19] In spite of being nearly one hundred years old when the promise of having a son was made, his faith was so strong that it could not be undermined by the fact that he and Sarah [f] were incapable of conceiving a child. [20-21] He never stopped believing God's promise, for he was made strong in his faith [g] *to father a child*. And because he was mighty in faith and convinced that God had all the power needed to fulfill his promises, Abraham glorified God!

---

a 4:13 As translated from the Aramaic. The Greek is "for the promise made to Abraham or to his descendants that he would inherit the world," and is somewhat confusing since there is no promise in Scripture that Abraham would inherit "the whole world." This is an obvious statement about Abraham's heir Jesus Christ, who is given the dominion over the whole world.

b 4:17 See Gen. 17:5.

c 4:17 This is perfectly illustrated with God speaking to Abraham about nations coming from him and his wife even though they had no children and were beyond the age of childbearing. The God who creates out of nothing could give children, and eventually nations, to Abraham and Sarah.

d 4:18 Or "who beyond hope in hope believed."

e 4:18 Although only a portion of Gen. 15:5 is quoted here, the entire text is supplied to bring clarity to the English narrative.

f 4:19 Or "and the deadness of Sarah's womb."

g 4:20–21 Or "he was empowered in faith."

²²So now you can see why Abraham's faith was credited to his account as righteousness before God. [a] ²³And this declaration was not just spoken over Abraham, ²⁴but also over us. For when we believe and embrace the one who brought our Lord Jesus back to life, perfect righteousness will be credited to our account as well. ²⁵Jesus was handed over to be crucified for the forgiveness of our sins and was raised back to life to prove that he had made us right with God! [b]

Our New Life

5 Our faith in Jesus transfers God's righteousness to us and he now declares us flawless in his eyes. [c] This means we can now enjoy true and lasting peace [d] with God, all because of what our Lord Jesus, the Anointed One, has done for us. ²Our faith guarantees us permanent access into this marvelous kindness [e] that has given us a perfect relationship with God. What incredible joy bursts forth within us as we keep on celebrating our hope of experiencing God's glory!

³But that's not all! Even in times of trouble we have a joyful confidence, knowing that our pressures will develop in us patient endurance. ⁴And patient endurance will refine our character, and proven character leads us back to hope. ⁵And this hope is not a disappointing fantasy, [f] because we can now experience the endless love of God cascading into our hearts through the Holy Spirit who lives in us! [g]

⁶For when the time was right, the Anointed One came and died *to demonstrate his love* for sinners who were entirely helpless, weak, and powerless to save themselves.

⁷Now, who of us would dare to die for the sake of a wicked person? [h] We can all understand if someone was willing to die for a truly noble person. ⁸But Christ proved God's passionate love for us by dying in our place while we were still lost and ungodly!

⁹And there is still much more to say of his unfailing love for us! For

---

a 4:22 See Gen. 15:6.

b 4:25 In this poetic verse we discover that the blood of the cross is the means of our justification and the resurrection is the proof that God now sees believers as righteous in his eyes.

c 5:1 Or "having already been declared righteous." What bliss! We are declared righteous in the eyes of the Holy God. This is the wonder of grace!

d 5:1 Or "Let us enjoy peace with God." The Greek word for peace is *eirene* and can also mean "to join" (as in a dove-tail joint). We have entered into the union of our lives with God's peace and enjoy lasting friendship with God. The Hebrew word is *shalom*, which means abundant peace and well-being.

e 5:2 Or "grace."

f 5:5 Or "This hope does not put one to shame."

g 5:5 Or "was given to us."

h 5:7 As translated from the Aramaic. The Greek reads, "Rarely would anyone die for a righteous person."

through the blood of Jesus we have heard the powerful declaration, "You are now righteous in my sight." And because of the sacrifice of Jesus, you will never experience the wrath of God. [10] So if while we were still enemies, God fully reconciled[a] us to himself through the death of his Son, then something greater than friendship is ours. Now that we are at peace with God, and because we share in his *resurrection* life, how much more we will be rescued from sin's dominion![b]

[11] And even more than that, we overflow with triumphant joy[c] in our new relationship of living in harmony[d] with God—all because of Jesus Christ!

The Gift of Grace Greater Than Sin

[12] When Adam sinned, the entire world was affected. Sin entered human experience, and death was the result. And so death followed this sin,[e] casting its shadow over all humanity, because all have sinned. [13] Sin was in the world before Moses gave the written law, but it was not charged against them where no law existed.[f] [14] Yet death reigned[g] as king from Adam to Moses even though they hadn't broken a command *the way Adam had*. The first man, Adam, was a picture[h] of the Messiah, who was to come.[i]

[15] Now, there is no comparison between Adam's transgression and the gracious gift that we experience. *For the magnitude of the gift far outweighs the crime.*[j] It's true that many died because of one man's transgression, but how much greater will God's grace and his gracious gift of acceptance overflow[k] to many because of what one Man, Jesus, the Messiah, did for us!

[16] And this free-flowing gift imparts to us much more than what was given to us through the one who sinned. For because of one transgression, we are all facing a death sentence with a verdict of "Guilty!" But this gracious gift leaves

---

a 5:10 The Greek verb for reconciled is actually "exchanged." That is, he exchanged our sins for his righteousness and thus reconciled us to God. The reign of death is caused by the guilt of sin.

b 5:10 See also John 14:19; Heb. 7:25.

c 5:11 Or "boasting" (in God).

d 5:11 As translated from the Aramaic, which can also be translated "By him [Jesus] we now accept his door-opening." The Greek is "reconciled."

e 5:12 "This sin" is translated from the Aramaic.

f 5:13 That is, there was no ability to be charged and found guilty of breaking the law.

g 5:14 Death is a temporary monarch that exercises dominion over humanity, but one day it will be completely deposed and defeated through Jesus Christ.

h 5:14 Or "imprint."

i 5:14 The actions of both Adam and Christ affect the entire world. Death passes to all who are in Adam; life passes to all who are in Christ. Each is a corporate head of a race of people. God sees every person as in Adam or in Christ.

j 5:15 Although clearly implied in the text, this summary of explanation is necessary as it makes explicit Paul's contrast between Adam's transgression and Christ's redemption.

k 5:15 Or "multiply" or "superabound."

us free from our many failures[a] and brings us into the perfect righteousness of God—acquitted with the words "Not guilty!"

[17] Death once held us in its grip, and by the blunder of one man, death reigned as king over humanity. But now, how much more[b] are we held in the grip of grace and continue reigning as kings in life, enjoying our regal freedom through the gift of perfect righteousness[c] in the one and only Jesus, the Messiah!

[18] In other words, just as condemnation came upon all people through one transgression, so through one righteous act *of Jesus' sacrifice*, the perfect righteousness that makes us right with God and leads us to a victorious life[d] is now available to all. [19] One man's disobedience opened the door for all humanity to become sinners. So also one man's obedience opened the door for many to be made perfectly right with God and acceptable to him. [20] So then, the law was introduced into God's plan to bring the reality of human sinfulness out of hiding. And yet, wherever sin increased, there was more than enough of God's grace to triumph all the more![e] [21] And just as sin reigned through death, so also this sin-conquering grace will reign as king through righteousness, imparting eternal life through Jesus, our Lord and Messiah!

The Triumph of Grace over Sin

6 So what do we do, then? Do we persist in sin so that God's kindness and grace will increase? [2] What a terrible thought! We have died to sin once and for all, as a dead man passes away from this life. So how could we live under sin's rule a moment longer? [3] Or have you forgotten that all of us who were immersed into union with Jesus, the Anointed One, were immersed into union with his death?

[4] Sharing in his death by our baptism means that we were co-buried and entombed with him, so that when the Father's glory raised Christ from the dead, we were also raised with him. We have been co-resurrected with him so that we could be empowered to walk in the freshness of new life. [5] For since we are permanently grafted into him[f] to experience a death like his, then we are

---

a 5:16 Or "falls," or "trespasses."

b 5:17 There are four "much mores" in this chapter. Two point to our future deliverance (vv. 9, 10), and two point to the abundance of grace which we now experience (vv. 15, 17).

c 5:17 Or "the gift of covenant membership."

d 5:18 As translated from the Aramaic. The Greek is "which brings righteousness of life."

e 5:20 Paul speaks of God's grace in v. 17 as superabundant, but then adds the prefix, *huper* ("hyper"), making grace *huperperisseuō*, which could be translated super-hyperabundant grace! There is an endless fountain of grace that has been opened for us in Christ!

f 6:5 Or "if we have become grown together as one with him."

permanently grafted into him to experience a resurrection like his and the new life that it imparts.

[6] Could it be any clearer[a] that our former identity[b] is now and forever deprived of its power? For we were co-crucified with him to dismantle the stronghold of sin within us,[c] so that we would not continue to live one moment longer submitted to sin's power.[d]

[7] Obviously, a dead person is incapable of sinning. [8] And if we were co-crucified with the Anointed One, we know that we will also share in the fullness of his life. [9] And we know that since the Anointed One has been raised from the dead to die no more, his resurrection life has vanquished death and its power over him is finished. [10] For by his sacrifice he died to sin's power once and for all,[e] but he now lives continuously for the Father's pleasure. [11] So let it be the same way with you! Since you are now joined with him, you must continually view yourselves as dead and unresponsive to sin's appeal while living daily for God's pleasure in union with Jesus, the Anointed One.

Sin's Reign Is Over

[12] Sin is a dethroned monarch; so you must no longer give it an opportunity to rule over your life, controlling how you live and compelling you to obey its desires and cravings. [13] So then, refuse to answer its call to surrender your body as a tool for wickedness. Instead, passionately answer God's call to keep yielding your body to him as one who has now experienced resurrection life! You live now for his pleasure, ready to be used for his noble purpose.[f] [14] Remember this: sin will not conquer you, for God already has! You are not governed by law but governed by the reign of the grace of God.

Grace Frees Us to Serve God

[15] What are we to do, then? Should we sin to our hearts' content since there's no law to condemn us anymore? What a terrible thought! [16] Don't you realize that grace frees you to choose your own master? But choose carefully, for you surrender yourself to become a servant—bound to the one you choose to obey. If you choose to love sin, it will become your master, and it will own you and

---

a 6:6 Or "Coming to know this," or "Coming to the realization."

b 6:6 The Aramaic can be translated "our old son of Adam."

c 6:6 Or "body of sin would no longer have dominion over us."

d 6:6 Or "that the body of sin might be annulled" (put out of business). To beg God for victory over sin is a refusal to understand that we have already died to sin. Our joyful task is to believe the good news, rather than to seek to "crucify ourselves." Sin is not suppressed by the cross; it is eliminated. Upon this "water" God commands us to step out and walk upon it, for we are now in him.

e 6:10 See also Heb. 9:26–28.

f 6:13 Or "For the members of your body will be used as weapons for the righteousness of God."

reward you with death. But if you choose to love and obey God, he will lead you into perfect righteousness.

[17] And God is pleased with you,[a] for in the past you were servants of sin, but now your obedience is heart deep, and your life is being molded by truth through the teaching you are devoted to.[b] [18] And now you celebrate your freedom from your former master—sin. You've left its bondage, and now God's perfect righteousness holds power over you as his loving servants.

[19] I've used the familiar terms of a "servant" and a "master" to compensate for your weakness to understand. For just as you surrendered your bodies and souls to impurity and lawlessness, which only brought more lawlessness into your lives, so now surrender yourselves as servants of righteousness, which brings you deeper into true holiness. [20] For when you were bound as servants to sin, you lived your lives free from any obligation to righteousness.

[21] So tell me, what benefit ensued from doing those things that you're now ashamed of? It left you with nothing but a legacy of shame and death. [22] But now, as God's loving servants, you live in joyous freedom from the power of sin. So consider the benefits you now enjoy—you are brought deeper into the experience of true holiness that ends with eternal life! [23] For sin's meager wages is death,[c] but God's lavish gift is life eternal, found in your union with our Lord Jesus, the Anointed One.

Joined to God's Anointed One

7 I write to you, dear brothers and sisters, who are familiar with the law. Don't you know that when a person dies, it ends his obligation to the law? [2] For example, a married couple is bound by the law to remain together until separated by death. But when one spouse dies, the other is released from the law of the marriage. [3] So then if a wife is joined to another man while still married, she commits adultery. But if her husband dies, she is obviously free from the marriage contract and may marry another man without being charged with adultery.[d]

[4] So, my dear brothers and sisters, the same principle applies to your relationship with God. For you died to *your first husband*, the law, by being co-crucified with the body of the Messiah. So you are now free to "marry" another—the one who was raised from the dead so that you may now bear spiritual fruit[e] for God.

---

a 6:17 As translated from the Aramaic. The Greek is "Thanks be to God."
b 6:17 As translated from the Aramaic. The Greek is "the type of teaching into which you were handed over."
c 6:23 The Greek word translated "meager wages" actually means "the wages of a foot soldier." This Greek word, *opsonion*, is taken from the word used for a piece of dried fish: *opsarion*. The Aramaic can be translated "The business of sin is death."
d 7:3 Or "if joined to another man, she is not an adulteress."
e 7:4 Or "offspring."

⁵When we were merely living natural lives,ᵃ the law, *through defining sin*, actually awakened sinful desires within us, which resulted in bearing the fruit of death. ⁶But now that we have been fully released from the power of the law, we are dead to what once controlled us. And our lives are no longer motivated by the obsolete way of following the written code,ᵇ so that now we may serve God by living in the freshness of a new life in the power of the Holy Spirit.ᶜ

The Purpose of the Law

⁷So, what shall we say about all this? Am I suggesting that the law is sinful? Of course not! In fact, it was the law that gave us the clear definition of sin. For example, when the law said, "Do not covet,"ᵈ it became the catalyst to see how wrong it was for me to crave what belongs to someone else. ⁸It was through God's commandment that sin was awakened in me and built its base of operationᵉ within me to stir up every kind of wrong desire. For in the absence of the law, sin hides dormant.ᶠ

⁹⁻¹⁰I once lived without a clear understanding of the law, but when I heard God's commandments, sin sprang to life and brought with it a death sentence. The commandment that was intended to bring life brought me death instead. ¹¹Sin, by means of the commandment, built a base of operation within me, to overpower meᵍ and put me to death. ¹²So then, we have to conclude that the problem is not with the law itself, for the law is holy and its commandments are correct and for our good.

Life under the Law

¹³So, did something meant to be good become death to me? Certainly not! It was not the law but sin unmasked that produced my spiritual death. The sacred commandment merely uncovered the evil of sin so it could be seen for what it is. ¹⁴For we know that the law is divinely inspired and comes from the spiritual realm,ʰ but I am a human being made of flesh and trafficked as a slave under sin's authority.ⁱ

¹⁵I'm a mystery to myself,ʲ for I want to do what is right, but end up doing

---

a 7:5 That is, before we came to know Jesus Christ.
b 7:6 Or "the oldness of the letter."
c 7:6 Or "by a new, Holy Spirit-empowered life."
d 7:7 See Ex. 20:17; Deut. 5:21.
e 7:8 Or "a starting point."
f 7:8 Or "is lifeless."
g 7:11 Or "deceive me" or "lead me astray."
h 7:14 Or "is spiritual."
i 7:14 Or "sold and ruined under sin." The Greek word *piprasko* refers to a slave who is "sold for exportation, betrayed and ruined."
j 7:15 Paul's use of "I" is most likely his identification with the people of Israel under the law prior to receiving Christ. It is not merely an autobiographical statement that Paul

what my moral instincts condemn. [16] And if my behavior is not in line with my desire, my conscience still confirms the excellence of the law. [17] And now I realize that it is no longer my true self doing it, but the unwelcome intruder of sin in my humanity. [18] For I know that nothing good lives within the flesh of my fallen humanity. The longings to do what is right are within me, but will-power is not enough to accomplish it. [a] [19] My lofty desires to do what is good are dashed when I do the things I want to avoid. [20] So if my behavior contradicts my desires to do good, I must conclude that it's not my true identity doing it, but the unwelcome intruder of sin *hindering me from being who I really am.*

[21] Through my experience of this principle, I discover that even when I want to do good, evil is ready to sabotage me. [22] Truly, deep within my true identity, I love to do what pleases God. [23] But I discern another power operating in my humanity, waging a war against the moral principles of my conscience [b] and bringing me into captivity as a prisoner to the "law" of sin—this unwelcome intruder in my humanity. [24] What an agonizing situation I am in! So who has the power to rescue this miserable man from the unwelcome intruder of sin and death? [c] [25] I give all my thanks to God, for his mighty power has finally provided a way out through our Lord Jesus, the Anointed One! So if left to myself, the flesh is aligned with the law of sin, but now my renewed mind is fixed on and submitted to God's righteous principles. [d]

Living by the Power of the Holy Spirit

8 *So now the case is closed.* There remains no accusing voice of condemnation against those who are joined in life-union with Jesus, the Anointed One. [e] [2] For the "law" of the Spirit of life flowing through the anointing of Jesus has liberated us [f] from the "law" of sin and death. [3] For God achieved what the law was unable to accomplish, because the law was limited by the weakness of human nature. [g]

Yet God sent us his Son in human form to identify with human weakness. Clothed with humanity, God's Son gave his body to be the sin-offering so that

---

experienced all of these things, but a rhetorical device of solidarity with the experience of those who live under the law. Romans ch. 7 is not the present experience of any one person, but the testimony of a delivered person describing the condition of an undelivered one.

a   7:18 Some Greek manuscripts have "but I don't know how to do it."
b   7:23 As translated from the Aramaic. The Greek is "warring against the law of my mind."
c   7:24 Or "Who will free me from this body of death?"
d   7:25 Or "God's law."
e   8:1 Or "Those who are in Christ Jesus cannot be condemned." Although there are some manuscripts that add to this verse, "for those who do not walk according to the flesh but according to the Spirit," the addition is not supported by the oldest and most reliable Greek manuscripts.
f   8:2 Some Greek manuscripts have "sets me free" or "sets you [singular] free."
g   8:3 Or "weakness of the flesh."

God could once and for all condemn the guilt and power of sin. [4] So now every righteous requirement of the law can be fulfilled through the Anointed One living his life in us. And we are free to live, not according to our flesh, but by the dynamic power of the Holy Spirit![a]

[5] Those who are motivated by the flesh only pursue what benefits themselves. But those who live by the impulses of the Holy Spirit are motivated to pursue spiritual realities.[b] [6] For the mind-set of the flesh is death, but the mind-set controlled by the Spirit finds life and peace.

[7] In fact, the mind-set focused on the flesh fights God's plan and refuses to submit to his direction,[c] because it cannot! [8] For no matter how hard they try, God finds no pleasure with those who are controlled by the flesh. [9] But when the Spirit of Christ empowers your life,[d] you are not dominated by the flesh but by the Spirit. And if you are not joined to the Spirit of the Anointed One, you are not of him.[e]

[10] Now Christ lives his life in you! And even though your body may be dead because of the effects of sin, his life-giving Spirit imparts life to you because you are fully accepted by God.[f] [11] Yes, God raised Jesus to life! And since God's Spirit of Resurrection lives in you, he will also raise your dying body to life by the same Spirit that breathes life into you!

[12] So then, beloved ones, the flesh has no claims on us at all, and we have no further obligation to live in obedience to it. [13] For when you live controlled by the flesh, you are about to die. But if the life of the Spirit puts to death the corrupt ways of the flesh, we then taste his abundant life.

Sons and Daughters Destined for Glory

[14] The mature children of God are those[g] who are moved by the impulses of the Holy Spirit. [15] And you did not receive the "spirit of religious duty,"[h] leading you back into the fear *of never being good enough.*[i] But you have received the

---

a 8:4 What joyous truths are found in Rom. 8! All that God requires of us has been satisfied by the sacrifice of Jesus Christ. The life of Jesus in us is enough to satisfy God. The power of our new life is not the works of our weak humanity, but the dynamic power of the Holy Spirit released in us.

b 8:5 Or "the things of the [Holy] Spirit"; that is, doing what pleases God. The Aramaic can be translated "Those who are in the flesh see him only in the flesh, but those who are in the Spirit see him in the Spirit."

c 8:7 Or "refuses to submit to his law."

d 8:9 Or "makes his home in you."

e 8:9 This is an unusual Greek clause that can be translated "If anyone is not joined to the Spirit of Christ, he cannot be himself." A similar construction is used in Luke 15:17: "The prodigal son came to himself."

f 8:10 The Aramaic can be translated "for the cause of righteousness."

g 8:14 The Greek is quite emphatic: "those and only those."

h 8:15 Or "spirit of slavery.""

i 8:15 Implied in both the text and the greater context of finding our true life in the "Spirit

"Spirit of full acceptance," [a] enfolding you into the family of God. And you will never feel orphaned, for as he rises up within us, our spirits join him in saying the words of tender affection, "Beloved Father!" [b] 16 For the Holy Spirit makes God's fatherhood real to us as he whispers into our innermost being, "You are God's beloved child!"

17 And since we are his true children, we qualify to share all his treasures, for indeed, we are heirs of God himself. And since we are joined to Christ, we also inherit all that he is and all that he has. [c] We will experience being co-glorified with him provided that we accept his sufferings [d] as our own. [e]

A Glorious Destiny

18 I am convinced that any suffering we endure is less than nothing compared to the magnitude of glory [f] that is about to be unveiled within us. [g] 19 The entire universe is standing on tiptoe, [h] yearning to see the unveiling of God's glorious [i] sons and daughters! 20 For against its will the universe itself has had to endure the empty futility [j] resulting from the consequences of human sin. But now, with eager expectation, 21 all creation longs for freedom from its slavery to decay

---

of full acceptance." It can also refer to the fear of judgment that has been removed from us through Christ.

a 8:15 Or "spirit of adult [complete] sonship." The Aramaic can be translated "the spirit of consecrated children."

b 8:15 Abba is not a Greek word, but an Aramaic word transliterated into Greek letters. Abba is the Aramaic word for "father." It is also found in Mark 14:36 and Gal. 4:6. Abba is also a word used for devotion, a term of endearment. This is why some have concluded that Abba could be translated as "Daddy" or "Papa." It is hard to imagine a closer relationship to have with God than to call him "Abba, our Beloved Father."

c 8:17 Or "we are joint-heirs with Christ." Nothing in the Bible could be more amazing than this. Grace has made former rebels into princes and princesses, royal ones that share in the inheritance of Christ.

d 8:17 Or "accept his feelings" (of pain), or "things" (he experiences). By implication, "sufferings."

e 8:17 Or "if we suffer jointly we will enjoy glory jointly."

f 8:18 The Greek word doxa can also be translated "radiant beauty," "splendor," "perfection."

g 8:18 The Aramaic can be translated "with the glory which is to be perfected in us." The Greek participle eis can be translated "into us," "upon us," or "to us."

h 8:19 The Greek word used here means "intense anticipation," or "anxiously anticipating what is about to happen" (with an outstretched neck).

i 8:19 Or "the manifestation of the sons of God." Interestingly, the Greek word used for "unveiling" (apokalypsis) is the same word for the full title of the last book of the Bible, "The Revelation [Unveiling] of Jesus Christ." The created universe is but the backdrop for the dramatic appearing of God's sons and daughters unveiled with the glory of Jesus Christ upon them. The verb tense in the Greek text is clear that this "unveiling" is imminent, soon to happen, and destined to take place. Christ's glory will come to us, enter us, fill us, envelop us, and then be revealed through us as partakers of the glory. Although God will not share his glory with any other, we are no longer "another," for we are one with the Father, Son, and Holy Spirit through faith in Christ. See John 17:21–23.

j 8:20 Or "the purposelessness" or "the frustration" (or "chaos").

and to experience with us the wonderful freedom coming to God's children. [22] To this day we are aware of the universal agony and groaning of creation, as if it were in the contractions of labor for childbirth. [23] And it's not just creation. We who have already experienced the firstfruits of the Spirit[a] also inwardly groan as we passionately long to experience our full status as God's sons and daughters—including our physical bodies being transformed. [24] For this is the hope of our salvation.

But hope means that we must trust and wait for what is still unseen. For why would we need to hope for something we already have? [25] So because our hope is set on what is yet to be seen, we patiently keep on waiting for its fulfillment.

[26] And in a similar way, the Holy Spirit takes hold of us in our human frailty to empower us in our weakness. For example, at times we don't even know how to pray, or know the best things to ask for. But the Holy Spirit rises up within us to super-intercede[b] on our behalf, pleading to God with emotional sighs[c] too deep for words.

[27] God, the searcher of the heart, knows fully our longings,[d] yet he also understands the desires of the Spirit, because the Holy Spirit passionately pleads before God for us, his holy ones, in perfect harmony with God's plan and our destiny.

[28] So we are convinced that every detail of our lives is continually woven together to fit into God's perfect plan of bringing good into our lives, for we are his lovers who have been called to fulfill his designed purpose. [29] For he knew all about us before we were born and he destined us[e] from the beginning to share the likeness of his Son. This means the Son is the oldest among a vast family of brothers and sisters who will become just like him.

[30] Having determined our destiny ahead of time, he called us to himself and transferred his perfect righteousness to everyone he called. And those who possess his perfect righteousness he co-glorified with his Son!

---

a 8:23 The "firstfruits of the Spirit" would include his indwelling presence, his gifts, his wisdom, and his transforming power. Imagine what the full harvest of the Spirit will bring to us! The Aramaic can be translated "the awakening of the Spirit."

b 8:26 The Greek word *hupererentugkhano* is best translated "super [or hyper]-intercede for us." We can only imagine how many blessings have poured into our lives because of the hyper-intercession of the Holy Spirit for us!

c 8:26 Or "groanings." We find three groanings in this chapter. Creation groans for the glorious freedom of God's children (v. 22), we groan to experience the fullness of our status as God's children (v. 23), and the Holy Spirit groans for our complete destiny to be fulfilled (here).

d 8:27 Or "God, the heart-searcher." God searches our hearts not just to uncover what is wrong, but to fulfill the true desire of our hearts to be fully his. Grace triumphs over judgment.

e 8:29 The Aramaic can be translated "sealed us" (with God's mark upon us). See also Col. 3:4; Heb. 2:11.

The Triumph of God's Love

[31] So, what does all this mean? If God has determined to stand with us, tell me, who then could ever stand against us? [32] For God has proved his love by giving us his greatest treasure, the gift of his Son. And since God freely offered him up as the sacrifice for us all,[a] he certainly won't withhold from us anything else he has to give.

[33] Who then would dare to accuse those whom God has chosen in love to be his? God himself is the judge who has issued his final verdict over them—"Not guilty!"[b]

[34] Who then is left to condemn us? Certainly not Jesus, the Anointed One! For he gave his life for us, and even more than that, he has conquered death and is now risen, exalted, and enthroned by God at his right hand. So how could he possibly condemn us since he is continually praying *for our triumph*?[c]

[35] Who could ever separate us from the endless love of God's Anointed One? *Absolutely no one!* For nothing in the universe has the power to diminish his love toward us. Troubles, pressures, and problems are unable to come between us and heaven's love. What about persecutions, deprivations,[d] dangers, and death threats? No, for they are all impotent to hinder omnipotent love, [36] even though it is written:

All day long we face death threats for your sake, God.
We are considered to be nothing more
than sheep to be slaughtered![e]

[37] Yet even in the midst of all these things, we triumph over them all, for God has made us to be more than conquerors,[f] and his demonstrated love is our glorious victory over everything![g]

---

a   8:32 This is an intentional echo of Gen. 22:16. Although God spared Abraham's son, Isaac, he would not spare his own Son, Jesus Christ.

b   8:33 See Isa. 50:8.

c   8:34 Not only does the Holy Spirit pray for us, so does Jesus Christ. Two divine intercessors are praying for you each day. Two-thirds of the Trinity are actively engaged in intercession for us. This is typified by the incident of Moses interceding on the mountain for Israel's victory with one hand held high by Aaron (the high priest, a type of Jesus, our High Priest) and Hur (or "light," a metaphor for the Holy Spirit, who prays with divine illumination for our good). See Ex. 17:9–13; Heb. 7:25; 9:24.

d   8:35 Or "hunger and nakedness."

e   8:36 See Ps. 44:22.

f   8:37 Love has made us more than conquerors in four ways: (1) No situation in life can defeat us or dilute God's love. (2) We know that divine love and power work for us to triumph over all things. (3) We share in the victory spoils of every enemy we face (Isa. 53:12). (4) We have conquered the Conqueror with merely a glance of our worshiping eyes. We have won his heart (Song. 4:9; 6:5).

g   8:37 Clearly implied in the text with the Greek word *hupernikao*. The love of God gives us "a glorious hyper-victory," more than can be described or contained in one word. God's love

[38] So now I live with the confidence that there is nothing in the universe with the power to separate us from God's love. I'm convinced that his love will triumph over death, life's troubles,[a] fallen angels, or dark rulers in the heavens. There is nothing in our present or future circumstances that can weaken his love. [39] There is no power above us or beneath us—no power that could ever be found in the universe that can distance us from God's passionate love, which is lavished upon us through our Lord Jesus, the Anointed One!

Paul's Love for the Jewish People

9 [1-2] O Israel, my Jewish family,[b] I feel such great sorrow and heartache for you that never leaves me! God knows these deep feelings within me as I long for you to come to faith in the Anointed One. My conscience will not let me speak anything but the truth. [3-4] For my grief is so intense that I wish that I would be accursed, cut off from the Messiah, if it would mean that you, my people, would come to faith in him!

You are Israelites, my fellow citizens, and God's chosen people.[c] To you belong God's glorious presence, the covenants, the Torah, the temple with its required sacrifices, and the promises of God. [5] We trace our beginnings back to the patriarchs, and through their bloodline is the genealogy of the Messiah, who is God over everything. May he be praised through endless ages! Amen!

[6] Clearly, God has not failed to fulfill his promises to Israel, for that will never happen! But not everyone who has descended from Israel belongs to Israel. [7] Physical descent from Abraham doesn't guarantee the inheritance, because God has said:

"Through Isaac your descendants will be counted *as part of your lineage*."[d]

[8] This confirms that it is not merely the natural offspring of Abraham who are considered the children of God; rather, the children born because of God's promise[e] are counted as descendants. [9] For God promised Abraham:

"In nine months from now your wife, Sarah, will have a son!"[f]

---

and grace has made us hyper-conquerors, empowered to be unrivaled, more than a match for any foe!

a 8:38 Or "life"; by implication, the troubles and pressures life may bring.

b 9:1–2 Although implied here, Paul indeed calls them "my people" in v. 3.

c 9:3–4 Or "to you belong the adoption as sons."

d 9:7 See Gen. 21:12.

e 9:8 The Aramaic can be translated "the children of the kingdom." By implication, it is those who can be traced back to a supernatural birth who are regarded as the children of God.

f 9:9 See Gen. 18:10, 14.

God's Freedom of Choice

[10] Now, this son was our ancestor, Isaac, who, with his wife, Rebekah, conceived twins. [11-12] And before her twin sons were born, God spoke to Rebekah and said:

"The oldest will serve the younger." [a]

God spoke these words before the sons had done anything good or bad, which proves that God calls people not on the basis of their good or bad works, but according to his divine purpose. [13] For in the words of Scripture:

"Jacob I have chosen, but Esau I have rejected." [b]

[14] So, what does all this mean? Are we saying that God is unfair? Of course not! [15] He had every right to say to Moses:

"I will be merciful to whomever I choose and I will show compassion to whomever I wish." [c]

[16] Again, this proves that God's choice doesn't depend on how badly someone wants it or tries to earn it, [d] but it depends on God's kindness and mercy. [17] For just as God said to Pharaoh:

"I raised you up [e] as ruler of Egypt for this reason, that I might make you an example of how I demonstrate my miracle power. For by the example of how I deal with you, my powerful name will be a message proclaimed throughout the earth!" [f]

[18] So again we see that it is entirely up to God to show mercy or to harden [g] the hearts of whomever he chooses.

[19] Well then, one might ask, "If God is in complete control, how could he blame us? For who can resist whatever he wants done?"

[20] But who do you think you are to second-guess God? How could a human being molded out of clay say to the one who molded him, "Why in the world

---

a 9:11–12 See Gen. 25:23.

b 9:13 Or "Jacob I loved, Esau I hated." The love/hate contrast is not merely a matter of God's emotions, but God's actions of choosing Jacob and excluding Esau. This Semitic idiom is also found in Jesus' words of "hating our father, mother . . . even our own life." It is a "hatred" compared to the love we demonstrate by choosing to follow Jesus. See Mal. 1:2–3; Luke 14:26.

c 9:15 See Ex. 33:19.

d 9:16 Or "not of the one willing nor of the one running."

e 9:17 The Aramaic can be translated "For this reason I ruined you."

f 9:17 See Ex. 9:16.

g 9:18 Although the Greek implies God hardens hearts, the Aramaic is more of a Hebrew idiom, "God gives permission for them to be hardened." This implies the hardening the heart is from within the individual.

did you make me this way?"[a] [21] Or are you denying the right of the potter to make out of clay whatever he wants? Doesn't the potter have the right to make from the same lump of clay an elegant vase or an ordinary pot?

[22] And in the same way, although God has every right to unleash his anger and demonstrate his power, yet he is extremely patient with those who deserve wrath—vessels prepared for destruction. [23] And doesn't he also have the right[b] to release the revelation of the wealth of his glory to his vessels of mercy, whom God prepared beforehand to receive his glory? [24] Even for us, whether we are Jews or non-Jews, we are those he has called to experience his glory. [25] Remember the prophecy God gave in Hosea:

"To those who were rejected and not my people,
    I will say to them: 'You are mine.'
And to those who were unloved I will say:
    'You are my darling.'"[c]

[26] And:

"In the place where they were told, 'You are nobody,'
    this will be the very place where they will be renamed
    'Children of the living God.'"[d]

[27] And the prophet Isaiah cries out to Israel:

Though the children of Israel
    are as many as the sands of the seashore,
    only a remnant will be saved.
[28] For the Lord Yahweh[e] will act
    and carry out his word on the earth,
    and waste no time to accomplish it![f]

[29] Just as Isaiah saw it coming and prophesied:

---

a 9:20 By implication Paul is speaking of people who have been made from clay in the hands of the divine Potter. See Isa. 29:16; 45:9.

b 9:23 Or "This he did to make known." Although this sentence presents an anacoluthon and is missing the conditional clause, it is more likely that Paul is contrasting "the vessels prepared for destruction" with "the vessels of mercy." Thus, "And doesn't he also have the right?"

c 9:25 See Hos. 2:23.

d 9:26 See Hos. 1:10.

e 9:28 As translated from the Aramaic, "Lord YHWH."

f 9:28 Or "cutting it short," a Greek word found only here in the New Testament. See Isa. 10:23.

> If the Lord God of angel armies[a]
>   had not left us a remnant,[b]
> we would have been destroyed like Sodom
>   and left desolate like Gomorrah!

Israel's Unbelief

[30] So then, what does all this mean? *Here's the irony*: The non-Jewish people, who weren't even pursuing righteousness, were the ones who seized it—a perfect righteousness that is transferred by faith. [31] Yet Israel, even though pursuing a legal righteousness,[c] did not attain to it. [32] And why was that? Because they did not pursue the path of faith but insisted on pursuing righteousness by works,[d] as if it could be seized another way. *They were offended by the means of obtaining it* and stumbled over the stumbling stone,[33] just as it is written:

> "Be careful! I am setting in Zion a stone
>   that will cause people to stumble,
> a rock[e] of offense that will make them fall,
>   but believers in him will not experience shame."[f]

Faith-Righteousness

10 My beloved brothers and sisters, the passionate desire of my heart and constant prayer to God is for my fellow Israelites to experience salvation. [2] For I know that although they are deeply devoted to God, they are unenlightened. [3] And since they've ignored the righteousness God gives, wanting instead to be acceptable to God because of their own works, they've refused to submit to God's faith-righteousness. [4] For the Christ is the end of the law.[g] And because of him, God has transferred his perfect righteousness to all who believe.

---

a 9:29 As translated from the Aramaic, "Lord YHWH of hosts" (of angel armies).

b 9:29 Or "descendants." See Isa. 1:9.

c 9:31 Or "a righteousness based on the law."

d 9:32 Or "works of the law."

e 9:33 There is a play on words here that is lost in translation. The Aramaic word for "rock" (*keefa*) is also the word for "teaching" or "faith." Aramaic speakers today still say that to stand in faith means to stand on a rock. To speak of the message of faith for salvation (versus works) is hidden in the word *rock*.

f 9:33 See Isa. 8:14; 28:16. The Hebrew of Isa. 28:16 is "Let the one who believes not expect it soon." That is, even if a promise delays, we will not be disheartened but will remain steadfast in faith.

g 10:4 Or "Christ is the goal of the law."

[5] Moses wrote long ago about the need to obey every part of the law in order to be declared right with God:

"The one who obeys these things must always live by them." [a]

[6] But we receive the faith-righteousness that speaks an entirely different message:

"Don't for a moment think you need to climb into the heavens to find the Messiah and bring him down, [7] or to descend into the underworld to bring him up from the dead." [b]

[8] But the faith-righteousness we receive speaks to us in these words of Moses:

"God's living message is very close to you, as close as your own heart beating in your chest and as near as the tongue in your mouth." [c]

[9] And what is God's "living message"? It is the revelation of faith for salvation, [d] which is the message that we preach. For if you publicly declare with your mouth that Jesus is Lord and believe in your heart that God raised him from the dead, you will experience salvation. [10] The heart that believes in him receives the gift of the righteousness of God—and then the mouth gives thanks [e] to salvation. [11] For the Scriptures encourage us with these words:

"Everyone who believes in him will never be disappointed." [f]

Good News for All People

[12] So then faith eliminates the distinction between Jew and non-Jew, for he is the same Lord Jehovah [g] for all people. And he has enough treasures to lavish generously upon all who call on him. [13] And it's true:

"Everyone who calls on the name of the Lord Yahweh
    will be rescued and experience new life." [h]

[14] But how can people call on him for help if they've not yet believed? And how can they believe in one they've not yet heard of? And how can they hear the message of life if there is no one there to proclaim it? [15] And how can the message be proclaimed if messengers have yet to be sent? That's why the Scriptures say:

---

a 10:5 Or "Whoever obeys these things will find life." See Lev. 18:5.
b 10:7 See Deut. 30:12–13.
c 10:8 See Deut. 30:14.
d 10:9 Or "word of faith."
e 10:10 As translated from the Aramaic. The Greek is "the mouth confesses to salvation."
f 10:11 See Isa. 28:16.
g 10:12 As translated from the Aramaic.
h 10:13 As translated from the Aramaic. See Joel 2:32.

How welcome is the arrival[a]
> of those proclaiming the joyful news of peace
> and of good things to come!

[16] But not everyone welcomes[b] the good news, as Isaiah said:

Lord, is there anyone who hears
> and believes our message?[c]

[17] Faith, then, is birthed in a heart that responds to God's anointed utterance of the Anointed One.

[18] Can it be that Israel hasn't heard the message? No, they have heard it, for:

The voice has been heard throughout the world,
> and its message has gone to the ends of the earth![d]

[19] So again I ask, didn't Israel already understand that God's message was for others as well as for themselves?[e] *Yes, they certainly did understand*, for Moses was the first[f] to state it:

"I will make you jealous of a people who are 'nobodies.'
> And I will use people with no understanding
> to provoke you to anger."[g]

[20] And Isaiah the fearless prophet dared to declare:

"Those who found me weren't even seeking me.
> I manifested[h] myself before those
> who weren't even asking to know me!"[i]

[21] Yet regarding Israel Isaiah says:

---

a 10:15 Or "how beautiful the feet." The Greek word implies their arrival comes at just the right time. See Isa. 52:7; Nah. 1:15.

b 10:16 Or "obeys."

c 10:16 See Isa. 53:1.

d 10:18 See Ps. 19:4.

e 10:19 Paul is confirming that God's plan from the beginning was to give the message of salvation to all the nations.

f 10:19 Or "First Moses . . . then Isaiah (v. 20) confirms it."

g 10:19 See Deut. 32:21. Those who are "nobodies" and the "people with no understanding" both refer to the gentile believers among the nations that have by faith entered into new life in Jesus.

h 10:20 The compound Greek word *emphanes* means "to make manifest," "to appear in shining light," "to be bright," "to shine light upon," "to come into view."

i 10:20 See Isa. 65:1.

"With love I have held out my hands day after day,
offering myself to this unbelieving
and stubborn people!" [a]

God Will Not Forget His Promises to Israel

11 So then I ask you this question: did God really push aside and reject his people?[b] Absolutely not! For I myself am a Jew, a descendant of Abraham, from the tribe of Benjamin.[c] [2] God has not rejected his chosen, destined people![d] Haven't you heard Elijah's testimony in the Scriptures, and how he prays to God, agonizing over Israel?

[3] "Lord, they've murdered your prophets; they've demolished your altars. Now I'm the only one left and they want to kill me!"[e]

[4] But what was the revelation[f] God spoke to him in response?

"You are not alone. For I have preserved a remnant for myself—seven thousand others who are faithful and have refused to worship Baal."[g]

[5] And that is but one example of what God is doing in this age of fulfillment, for God's grace empowers his chosen remnant. [6] And since it is by God's grace, it can't be a matter of their good works; otherwise, it wouldn't be a gift of grace, but earned by human effort.

[7] So then, Israel failed to achieve what it had strived for, but the divinely chosen remnant receives it by grace, while the rest were hardened *and unable to receive the truth.* [8] Just as it is written:

God granted them a spirit of deep slumber.[h]
He closed their eyes to the truth

---

a 10:21 See Isa. 65:2.

b 11:1 See 1 Sam. 12:22; Ps. 94:14.

c 11:1 Benjamin was the only son of Jacob born in the promised land, and his was the first tribe to give Israel a king in Saul. And his was the only tribe to remain with Judah in the restored nation after the exile. Paul is saying that he is about as Jewish as anyone could ever be. See Phil. 3:5.

d 11:2 Or "his people whom he foreknew."

e 11:3 See 1 Kings 19:10–14.

f 11:4 Or "divine utterance." This is the only place in the New Testament this Greek word appears. It could imply the audible voice of God that spoke to Elijah.

g 11:4 See 1 Kings 19:18.

h 11:8 The Aramaic can be translated "a spirit of frustration."

and prevented their ears from hearing[a]
up to this very day.

[9] And King David also prophesied this:

May their table[b] prove to be a snare
and a trap to cause their ruin.
Bring them the retribution they deserve.
[10] Blindfold their eyes and don't let them see.
Let them be stooped over continually.[c]

The Restoration of Israel

[11] So, am I saying that Israel stumbled so badly that they will never get back up? Certainly not! Rather, it was because of their stumble that salvation now extends to all the non-Jewish people, in order to make Israel jealous and desire the very things that God has freely given them. [12] So if all the world is being greatly enriched through their failure, and through their fall great spiritual wealth is given to the non-Jewish people, imagine how much more will Israel's awakening[d] bring to us all!

[13] Now, I speak to you who are not Jewish, since I am an apostle to reach the non-Jewish people. And I draw attention to this ministry as much as I can when I am among the Jews, [14] hoping to make them jealous of what God has given to those who are not Jews, winning some of my people to salvation.

[15] For if their *temporary* rejection released the reconciling power of grace into the world, what will happen when Israel is reinstated and reconciled to God? It will unleash resurrection power throughout the whole earth!

A Warning to Non-Jewish Believers

[16] Since Abraham and the patriarchs are consecrated and set apart for God, so also will their descendants be set apart.[e] If the roots of a tree are holy and set apart for God, so too will be the branches.

---

a 11:8 Or "He gave them eyes that could not see and ears that could not hear." See Deut. 29:4; Isa. 6:10; 29:10–13.

b 11:9 This could also be a metaphor for their false security, being in a place of well-being and favor. King David's son Absalom held a banquet as a pretense to murder his brother Amnon. See 2 Sam. 13:23–31.

c 11:10 This could also be a metaphor of asking God to punish them. See Ps. 69:22–23 (LXX).

d 11:12 Or "fullness" (of restoration), or "full inclusion," or "full number." An ellipsis in the Greek text allows for different translations of this verse.

e 11:16 Paul uses a metaphor that is better understood when made explicit. The Greek is literally "If the first portion of the dough [Abraham and the patriarchs] is consecrated, so too is the entire batch of dough [those descended from Abraham and the patriarchs]." The principle is that if the first portion is dedicated to God, the rest belongs to him too and is

¹⁷ However, some of the branches have been pruned away. And you,ᵃ who were once nothing more than a wild olive branch in the desert,ᵇ God has grafted in—inserting you among the remaining branches as a joint partner to share in the wonderful richness of the cultivated olive stem. ¹⁸ So don't be so arrogant as to believe that you are superior to the natural branches. There's no reason to boast, for the new branches don't support the root, but you owe your life to the root that supports you!

¹⁹ You might begin to think that some branches were pruned or broken off just to make room for you. ²⁰ Yes, that's true.ᶜ They were removed because of their unbelief. But remember this: you are only attached by your faith. So don't be presumptuous, but stand in awe and reverence. ²¹ Since God didn't spare the natural branches that fell into unbelief, perhaps he won't spare you either!

²² So fix your gaze on the simultaneous kindnessᵈ and strict justiceᵉ of God. How severely he treated those who fell into unbelief! Yet how tender and kind is his relationship with you. So keep on trusting in his kindness; otherwise, you also will be cut off.

²³ God is more than ready to graft back in the natural branches when they turn from clinging to their unbelief to embracing faith. ²⁴ For if God grafted you in, even though you were taken from what is by nature a wild olive tree, how much more can he reconnect the natural branches by inserting them back into their own cultivated olive tree!

The Mystery of Israel's Restoration

²⁵ My beloved brothers and sisters, I want to share with youᶠ a mysteryᵍ concerning

---

also considered consecrated for God's use. The Aramaic can be translated "If the crust is holy, so also is the dough."

ᵃ 11:17 Every time "you" is used in vv. 17–24 it is singular. God has lovingly and personally grafted you in as a branch in his tree of life. See John 15:1–17.

ᵇ 11:17 As translated from the Aramaic.

ᶜ 11:20 The Aramaic can be translated "Yes, it's beautiful!" Non-Jewish believers are to be grateful for the Jewish roots of our faith. Our Messiah is Jewish and the Scriptures we read were given to the beloved Jewish people. We feast on the new-covenant riches that have been handed down to us through the "olive tree" of Judaism.

ᵈ 11:22 The Aramaic word for "kindness" can also be translated "sweetness."

ᵉ 11:22 The Greek word *apotomia* is used only here in the New Testament. It is a play on words, for *apotomia* is a homonym that can mean "strict justice" or "cut off."

ᶠ 11:25 The Greek text contains a litotes, a double negative: "I don't want you to not know."

ᵍ 11:25 The Greek word for mystery, *mystērion*, is found twenty-eight times in the New Testament. It means a sacred secret, something that God has hidden from ancient times and that can only be revealed by God. Jesus teaches us that these mysteries are meant for us to perceive as part of our kingdom birthright. See Matt. 13:11. The mystery Paul unfolds for us here is the partial insensitivity of Israel, as well as her future salvation as part of God's eternal plan for the nations.

Israel's future. For understanding this mystery will keep you from thinking you already know everything.

A partial and temporary hardening[a] to the gospel has come over Israel, which will last until the full number of non-Jews has come into God's family. [26] And then God will bring all of Israel to salvation! The prophecy will be fulfilled that says:

"Coming from Zion will be the Savior,
and he will turn Jacob away from evil.[b]
[27] For this is my covenant promise with them
when I forgive their sins."[c]

[28] Now, many of the Jews are opposed to the gospel, but their opposition has opened the door of the gospel to you who are not Jewish. Yet they are still greatly loved by God because their ancestors were divinely chosen to be his. [29] And when God chooses someone and graciously imparts gifts to him, they are never rescinded.[d]

[30] You who are not Jews were once rebels against God, but now, because of their disobedience, you have experienced God's tender mercies. [31] And now they are the rebels, and because of God's tender mercies to you, you can open the door to them to share in and enjoy what God has given to us!

[32] Actually, God considers all of humanity to be prisoners of their unbelief, so that he can unlock our hearts and show his tender mercies to all who come to him.

[33] Who could ever wrap their minds around the riches of God, the depth of his wisdom, and the marvel of his perfect knowledge? Who could ever explain the wonder of his decisions[e] or search out the mysterious way he carries out his plans?

[34] For who has discovered how the Lord thinks
or is wise enough to be the one
to advise him in his plans?[f]

---

a 11:25 The Greek word for hardening, *porosis,* can also mean stubbornness, an unwillingness to learn something new.
b 11:26 The Aramaic can also mean "the evil one." See Isa. 59:20–21.
c 11:27 See Isa. 27:9.
d 11:29 Or "the grace-gifts and calling of God are void of regret and without change in purpose." See Isa. 27:9; Jer. 31:33–34.
e 11:33 Or "judgments," which does not necessarily imply something negative.
f 11:34 See Isa. 40:13.

[35] Or:

"Who has ever first given something to God
that obligates God to owe him something in return?" [a]

[36] And because God is the source and sustainer of everything, everything finds fulfillment in him. May all praise and honor be given to him forever! Amen!

The Transforming Power of the Gospel

12 Beloved friends, what should be our proper response to God's marvelous mercies? I encourage you to surrender yourselves to God to be his sacred, living sacrifices. And live in holiness, experiencing all that delights his heart. For this becomes your genuine expression of worship.

[2] Stop imitating the ideals and opinions of the culture around you, [b] but be inwardly transformed by the Holy Spirit through a total reformation of how you think. This will empower you to discern God's will as you live a beautiful life, satisfying and perfect in his eyes.

Your Proper Role in the Body of Christ

[3] God has given me grace to speak a warning about pride. I would ask each of you to be emptied of self-promotion and not create a false image of your importance. Instead, honestly assess your worth by using your God-given faith as the standard of measurement, and then you will see your true value with an appropriate self-esteem.

[4] In the human body there are many parts and organs, each with a unique function. [5] And so it is in the body of Christ. For though we are many, we've all been mingled into one body in Christ. This means that we are all vitally joined to one another, with each contributing to the others.

[6] God's marvelous grace imparts to each one of us varying gifts and ministries that are uniquely ours. So if God has given you the grace-gift of prophecy, you must activate your gift by using the proportion of faith you have to prophesy. [7] If your grace-gift is serving, then thrive in serving others well. If you have the grace-gift of teaching, then be actively teaching and training others. [8] If you have the grace-gift of encouragement, [c] then use it often to encourage others. If you have the grace-gift of giving to meet the needs of others, then may you prosper in your generosity without any fanfare. If you have the gift of leadership, be passionate about your leadership. And if

---

a   11:35 See Job 41:11.
b   12:2 Or "Don't be squeezed into the mold of this present age."
c   12:8 Or "exhortation." This is the Greek word *parakaleo*, which means "to be alongside of someone to comfort, encourage, console, strengthen, exhort, and stir up faith."

you have the gift of showing compassion,[a] then flourish in your cheerful[b] display of compassion.

Transformed Relationships

[9] Let the inner movement of your heart always be to love one another, and never play the role of an actor wearing a mask. Despise evil and embrace everything that is good and virtuous.

[10] Be devoted to tenderly loving your fellow believers *as members of one family*. Try to outdo yourselves in respect and honor of one another.

[11] Be enthusiastic to serve the Lord, keeping your passion toward him boiling hot! Radiate with the glow of the Holy Spirit and let him fill you with excitement as you serve him.

[12] Let this hope burst forth within you, releasing a continual joy. Don't give up in a time of trouble,[c] but commune with God at all times.

[13] Take a constant interest in the needs of God's beloved people and respond by helping them. And eagerly welcome people as guests into your home.

[14] Speak blessing, not cursing, over those who reject and persecute you.

[15] Celebrate with those who celebrate, and weep with those who grieve. [16] Live happily together in a spirit of harmony, and be as mindful of another's worth as you are your own. Don't live with a lofty mind-set, thinking you are too important to serve others, but be willing to do menial tasks and identify with those who are humble minded.[d] Don't be smug or even think for a moment that you know it all.

[17] Never hold a grudge or try to get even, but plan your life around the noblest way to benefit others. [18] Do your best to live as everybody's friend.[e]

[19] Beloved, don't be obsessed with taking revenge, but leave that to God's righteous justice.[f] For the Scriptures say:

"If you don't take justice in your own hands,
    I will release justice for you," says the Lord.[g]

---

a 12:8 Or "if you are a caregiver."

b 12:8 The Greek word *hilarotes* is used only here in the New Testament and can be translated "cheerful" or "hilarious."

c 12:12 The Aramaic can be translated "Bear your afflictions bravely."

d 12:16 Since the Greek text is ambiguous and can mean either "be willing to do menial tasks" or "associate with the lowly," the translation incorporates both. The Berkeley Translation renders this "adjust yourselves to humble situations."

e 12:18 Or "to live at peace with all people."

f 12:19 Or "wrath."

g 12:19 As translated from the Aramaic. See Deut. 32:35.

[20] And:

If your enemy is hungry, buy him lunch!
    Win him over with kindness. [a]
For your surprising generosity will awaken his conscience,
    and God will reward you with favor. [b]

[21] Never let evil defeat you, but defeat evil with good. [c]

Our Relationship to Civil Authorities

13 Every person must submit to and support the authorities over him. For there can be no authority in the universe except by God's appointment, which means that every authority that exists has been instituted by God. [2] So to resist authority is to resist the divine order of God, which results in severe consequences. [3] For civil authorities don't intimidate those who are doing good, but those who are doing evil. So do what is right and you'll never need to fear those in authority. They will commend you for your good citizenship.

[4] Those in authority are God's servants for the good of society. But if you break the law, you have reason to be alarmed, for they are God's agents of punishment to bring criminals to justice. Why do you think they carry weapons? [5] You are compelled to obey them, not just to avoid punishment, but because you want to live with a clean conscience.

[6] This is also the reason you pay your taxes, for governmental authorities are God's officials who oversee these things. [7] So it is your duty to pay all the taxes and fees that they require and to respect those who are worthy of respect, honoring them accordingly. [d]

[8] Don't owe anything to anyone, except your outstanding debt to continually love one another, [e] for the one who learns to love has fulfilled every requirement of the law. [9] For the commandments, "Do not commit adultery, do not murder, do not steal, do not covet," [f] and every other commandment can be summed up in these words:

"Love and value others the same way you love and value yourself." [g]

---

a 12:20 Or "If he thirsts, give him a drink."

b 12:20 Or "You will heap coals of fire on his head," an obvious figure of speech. It means that by demonstrating kindness to him, his heart will be moved and his shame exposed. See Prov. 25:21–22.

c 12:21 Or "Don't be conquered by the evil one, but conquer evil through union with the good One."

d 13:7 Jesus was often maligned for being "the friend of tax-collectors" (publicans).

e 13:8 There is a pronounced play on words in the Aramaic. The Aramaic word for "owe" is *khob*, and the word for "love" is *khab*.

f 13:9 See Ex. 20:13–17.

g 13:9 See Lev. 19:18; 1 Cor. 13:4–6; Gal. 5:6.

[10] Love makes it impossible to harm another, so love fulfills all that the law requires.

Living in the Light

[11] To live like this is all the more urgent, for time is running out and you know it is a strategic hour in human history. It is time for us to wake up! For our full salvation[a] is nearer now than when we first believed.

[12] Night's darkness is dissolving away as a new day of destiny dawns.[b] So we must once and for all strip away what is done in the shadows of darkness, *removing it like filthy clothes*.[c] And once and for all we clothe ourselves with the radiance of light as our weapon. [13] We must live honorably,[d] surrounded by the light of this new day, not in the darkness of drunkenness[e] and debauchery,[f] not in promiscuity and sensuality,[g] not being argumentative or jealous of others.

[14] Instead fully immerse yourselves into[h] the Lord Jesus, the Anointed One, and don't waste even a moment's thought on your former identity to awaken its selfish desires.

Unity in the Midst of Diversity

14 Offer an open hand of fellowship to welcome every true believer, even though their faith may be weak and immature. And refuse to engage in debates with them concerning nothing more than opinions.

[2] For example, one believer has no problem with eating all kinds of food, but another with weaker faith will eat only vegetables.[i] [3] The one who eats freely shouldn't judge and look down on the one who eats only vegetables. And the vegetarian must not judge and look down on the one who eats everything. Remember, God has welcomed him and taken him as his partner.

[4] Who do you think you are to sit in judgment of someone else's household servant?[j] His own master is the one to evaluate whether he succeeds or

---

a 13:11 Or "perfect wholeness." There is a full salvation ready to be unveiled and unfolded in the last days. See 1 Peter 1:5.

b 13:12 See 1 John 2:8.

c 13:12 Implied in the text and supplied to show the contrast of "clothe ourselves" in the next sentence.

d 13:13 The Aramaic can be translated "We walk with the Designer."

e 13:13 This word includes intoxication by any substance.

f 13:13 Or "festive processions" (often to celebrate false deities), "orgies," "revelries," "carousings."

g 13:13 Or "outrageous behavior," "loose conduct," "indecencies."

h 13:14 Or "fully clothed with."

i 14:2 It is possible that the one with "weaker faith" refused to eat meat because it was offered to idols or was considered unclean.

j 14:4 We are all "household servants" in the body of Christ, for we each belong to him. When believers begin to judge other believers over our opinions or preferences, we are taking the role that belongs only to Jesus.

fails. And God's servants will succeed, for God's power[a] supports them and enables them to stand.

[5] In the same way, one person regards a certain day as more sacred than another, and another person regards them all alike. There is nothing wrong with having different personal convictions about such matters.[b] [6] For the person who observes one day as especially sacred does it to honor the Lord. And the same is true regarding what a person eats. The one who eats everything eats to honor the Lord, because he gives thanks to God, and the one who has a special diet does it to honor the Lord, and he also gives thanks to God.

[7] No one lives to himself and no one dies to himself. [8] While we live, we live for our Master, and in death we must bring honor to him. So dead or alive we belong to our Master.[c] [9] For this very reason the Anointed One died and was brought back to life again, so that he would become the Lord God[d] over both the dead and the living.[e]

[10] Why would you judge your brothers or sisters because of their diet, despising them for what they eat or don't eat? For we each will have our turn to stand before God's judgment seat.[f] [11] Just as it is written:

"As surely as I am the Living God, I tell you:
    'Every knee will bow before me
    and every tongue will confess the truth[g]
    and glorify me!'"[h]

[12] Therefore, each one must answer for himself and give a personal account of his own life before God.

Walking in Love

[13] So stop being critical and condemning of other believers, but instead determine to never deliberately cause a brother or sister to stumble[i] and fall because of your actions.

[14] I know and am convinced by personal revelation from the Lord Jesus that there is nothing wrong with eating any food. But to the one who considers it

---

a 14:4 Some Greek manuscripts have "the Lord."

b 14:5 Or "Each one must be fully convinced in his own mind." The Aramaic can be translated "Every human being justifies himself through his own perspective."

c 14:8 The Aramaic twice uses "our Master" (Lord), while the Greek is "the Lord."

d 14:9 Or "Lord Jehovah" (Aramaic). The Greek is *kurios* ("Lord").

e 14:9 That is, he exercises lordship over all believers: those living in faith and those who die in faith.

f 14:10 The Aramaic can be translated "We are all destined to stand before the podium of the Messiah."

g 14:11 Or "will fully agree" (or "speak from the same source").

h 14:11 See Isa. 45:23; 49:18; Phil. 2:10–12.

i 14:13 Or "set before them an obstacle or trap to make them stumble."

to be unclean, it is unacceptable. [15] If your brother or sister is offended because you insist on eating what you want, it is no longer love that rules your conduct. Why would you wound someone for whom the Messiah gave his life, just so you can eat what you want? [16] So don't give people the opportunity to slander what you know to be good. [a] [17] For the kingdom of God is not a matter of rules about food and drink, but is in the realm of the Holy Spirit, [b] filled with righteousness, [c] peace, and joy. [18] Serving the Anointed One by walking in these kingdom realities pleases God [d] and earns the respect of others.

[19] So then, make it your top priority to live a life of peace with harmony in your relationships, [e] eagerly seeking to strengthen and encourage one another. [20] Stop ruining the work of God by insisting on your own opinions about food. You can eat anything you want, [f] but it is wrong to deliberately cause someone to be offended over what you eat. [21] *Consider it an act of love* [g] to refrain from eating meat or drinking wine or doing anything else that would cause a fellow believer to be offended or tempted to be weakened in his faith. [h] [22] Keep the convictions you have about these matters between yourself and God, *and don't impose them upon others.* You'll be happy when you don't judge yourself in doing what your conscience approves. [23] But the one who has misgivings feels miserable if he eats meat, because he doubts and doesn't eat in faith. For anything we do that doesn't spring from faith is, by definition, sinful.

---

a 14:16 Even today in many cultures of the world, there are two things that cause division and spark debates among religious people. The observance of "special days" (fasts, feasts, Sabbaths, days of prayer, etc.) and dietary restrictions (kosher versus non-kosher). Paul addresses both of these cultural issues as examples of things that can divide us. In every culture there are religious traditions that are observed in varying degrees. As believers, our one tradition must be to love and not offend by deliberate actions that demonstrate insensitivity to others. The overarching message Paul brings in Rom. 14 is that we are obligated to walk in love and not put our preferences above love's calling to honor others. These principles are to be applied in every cultural distinction in the body of Christ.

b 14:17 The kingdom of God is entered into by the Holy Spirit, and not by observing feasts and ritual meals. We must be born of the Spirit in order to enter into God's kingdom realm. To have the Holy Spirit is to have the realities of God's kingdom.

c 14:17 *Righteousness* means, both in the context and in the Hebraic mind-set, kindness in our relationships. Paul is speaking of putting others first and expressing goodness in having right relationships with others as well as right living.

d 14:18 The Aramaic can be translated "beautiful to God."

e 14:19 See Ps. 34:15; Heb. 12:14.

f 14:20 Or "All [food] is [ceremonially] clean [acceptable to eat]."

g 14:21 Implied in the context of Rom. 14–15, and is meant to clarify the motivation to limit our liberties among believers.

h 14:21 A few manuscripts do not have the last phrase, or "to be weakened in his faith."

Love Is the Key to Unity

15 Now, those who are mature[a] in their faith can easily be recognized, for they don't live to please themselves but have learned to patiently embrace others in their immaturity.[b] [2] Our goal must be to empower others to do what is right and good for them, and to bring them into spiritual maturity. [3] For not even *the most powerful one of all*, the Anointed One, lived to please himself. His life fulfilled the Scripture that says:

All the insults of those who insulted you fall upon me.[c]

[4] Whatever was written beforehand is meant to instruct us in how to live. The Scriptures impart to us encouragement and inspiration so that we can live in hope and endure all things.

[5] Now may God, the source of great endurance and comfort, grace you with unity among yourselves, which flows from your relationship with Jesus, the Anointed One.[d] [6] Then, with a unanimous rush of passion, you will with one voice glorify God, the Father of our Lord Jesus Christ. [7] You will bring God glory when you accept and welcome one another as partners, just as the Anointed One has fully accepted you and received you as his partner.

The God of Hope for Jews and Non-Jews

[8] I am convinced that Jesus, the Messiah, was sent as a servant to the Jewish people[e] to fulfill the promises God made to our ancestors and to prove God's faithfulness. [9] And now, because of Jesus, the non-Jewish people of the world can glorify God for his kindness to them, fulfilling the prophecy of Scripture:

Because of this I will proclaim you among the nations
　　and they will hear me sing praises to your name.[f]

[10] And in another place it says:

"You who are not Jewish,
　　celebrate life right alongside his Jewish people."[g]

[11] And again:

---

a 15:1 The Aramaic can be translated "powerful."
b 15:1 Or "not just please themselves."
c 15:3 See Ps. 69:9.
d 15:5 The Aramaic can be translated "that you may value one another equally in Jesus, the Messiah."
e 15:8 Or "a servant of the circumcision," which is a figure of speech for the Jewish people.
f 15:9 See Ps. 18:49.
g 15:10 See Deut. 32:43.

Praise the Lord Yahweh,[a] all you who are not Jews,
and let all the people of the earth
raise their voices in praises to him.[b]

[12] And Isaiah prophesied:

"An heir to David's throne[c] will emerge,
and he will rise up as ruler
over all the non-Jewish nations,
for all their hopes will be met in him."[d]

[13] Now may God, the inspiration and fountain of hope, fill you to overflowing with uncontainable joy and perfect peace as you trust in him. And may the power of the Holy Spirit continually surround your life with his super-abundance until you radiate with hope!

Paul's Ministry and His Plans

[14] My dear brothers and sisters, I am fully convinced of your genuine spirituality. I know that each of you is stuffed full of God's goodness, that you are richly supplied with all kinds of revelation-knowledge, and that you are empowered to effectively instruct[e] one another. [15] And because of the outpouring of God's grace on my life to be his minister and to preach Jesus, the Anointed One, to the non-Jewish people, I have written rather boldly to you on some themes, reminding you of their importance. [16] For this grace has made me a servant of the gospel of God, constantly doing the work of a priest, for I endeavor to present an acceptable offering to God; so that the non-Jewish people of the earth may be set apart and made holy by the Spirit of holiness.

[17] Now then, it is through my union with Jesus Christ, that I enjoy an enthusiasm and confidence in my ministry for God. [18-19] And I will not be presumptuous to speak of anything except what Christ has accomplished through me. For many non-Jewish people are coming into faith's obedience by the power of the Spirit of God, which is displayed through mighty signs and amazing wonders, both in word and deed. Starting from Jerusalem I went from place to place as far as the distant Roman province of Illyricum,[f] fully preaching the wonderful

---

a 15:11 As translated from the Aramaic.
b 15:11 See Ps. 117:1.
c 15:12 Or "[a sprout from] the root of Jesse," which is a Hebrew idiom for King David, the son of Jesse, who was promised to have an heir to his throne who would rule over not only Israel but all the nations.
d 15:12 Or "their hopes will be placed on him." See Isa. 11:10.
e 15:14 Or "warn."
f 15:18–19 Illyricum (modern-day Croatia) was the Roman province that comprises parts of the western Balkan Peninsula.

message of Christ. *ᵃ,²⁰* It is my honor and constant passion to be a pioneer who preaches where no one has ever even heard of the Anointed One, instead of building upon someone else's foundation. ²¹ As the Scriptures say:

> Those who know nothing about him will clearly see him,
>> and those who have not heard will respond. *ᵇ*

Paul's Intention to Visit Rome

²² My pursuit of this mission has prevented me many times from visiting you, ²³ but there is now nothing left to keep me in these regions. So many years I have longed to come and be with you! ²⁴ So on my way to Spain I hope to visit you as I pass through Rome. And after I have enjoyed fellowship with you for a while, I hope that you would help me financially on my journey. ²⁵ But now I'm on my way to Jerusalem to encourage God's people and minister to them.

²⁶ I am pleased to inform you that the believers of Macedonia and Greece *ᶜ* have made a generous contribution for the poor among the holy believers in Jerusalem. ²⁷ They were thrilled to have an opportunity to give back to the believers in Jerusalem. For indeed, they are deeply grateful for them and feel indebted because they brought them the gospel. Since the ethnic multitudes have shared in the spiritual wealth of the Jewish people, it is only right that the non-Jewish people share their material wealth with them.

²⁸ So, when I have completed this act of worship and safely delivered the offering *ᵈ* to them in Jerusalem, I will set out for Spain and visit you on my way there. ²⁹ I am convinced that when I come to you, I will come packed full and loaded *ᵉ* with the blessings of the Anointed One!

³⁰ That's why I plead with you, because of our union with our Lord Jesus Christ, to be partners with me in your prayers to God. My dear brothers and sisters in the faith, with the love we share in the Holy Spirit, fight alongside me in prayer. *ᶠ* ³¹ Ask the Father to deliver me from the danger I face from the unbelievers in Judea. For I want to make sure that the contribution I carry for Jerusalem will be favorably received by God's holy ones. ³² Then he will send

---

a 15:18–19 The apostle Paul thoroughly preached the good news with much evidence that God was working through him. This resulted in many non-Jewish people coming to faith in Jesus Christ. The signs and wonders were a part of the message, validating Paul's apostolic mandate to evangelize and plant churches.

b 15:21 As translated from the Aramaic. The Greek is "understand." See Isa. 52:15.

c 15:26 Or "Achaia," a region in western Greece.

d 15:28 The Greek word is actually "fruit." Paul was delivering to them a "spiritual fruit basket." It is an act of worship every time we consider the poor and serve others.

e 15:29 The Greek word *pleroma* is also used for a cargo ship packed full of people and goods.

f 15:30 Although Paul was an esteemed and powerful apostle of Jesus, he was not too proud to ask other believers to pray for him.

me to you with great joy in the pleasure of God's will, and I will be spiritually refreshed by your fellowship.

[33] And now may the God who gives us his peace and wholeness[a] be with you all. Yes, Lord, so let it be!

Paul Sends His Loving Greetings

16 Now, let me introduce to you our dear and beloved sister in the faith, Phoebe, a shining minister[b] of the church in Cenchrea.[c] [2] I am sending her with this letter and ask that you shower her with your hospitality when she arrives. Embrace her with honor, as is fitting for one who belongs to the Lord and is set apart for him. I am entrusting her to you,[d] so provide her whatever she may need, for she's been a great leader and champion[e] for many—I know, for she's been that for even me!

[3] Give my love[f] to Prisca and Aquila,[g] my partners in ministry serving the Anointed One, Jesus, [4] for they've risked their own lives to save mine. I'm so thankful for them, and not just I, but all the congregations among the non-Jewish people respect them for their ministry. [5] Also give my loving greetings to all the believers in their house church.

---

a 15:33 Or "May the God who is peace be with you all."

b 16:1 Or "deaconess" or "servant," which would imply she may have held an office in the church. The name Phoebe means "shining," "radiant," "bright," "prophetic." It is likely that the church in Cenchrea was a house church.

c 16:1 Or modern-day Kenchreai, which in the days of Paul was a large port city about four miles (seven kilometers) southeast of Corinth in Greece. See also Acts 18:18.

d 16:2 As translated from the Aramaic and implied in the Greek.

e 16:2 The Greek word *prostatis* means "the one who goes first," "a leading officer presiding over many," "a protecting patroness who oversees the affairs of others," "a champion defender." It is clear that Phoebe was considered a leader, a champion, a heroic woman who was most likely quite wealthy and brought blessings to others. The term *prostatis* implies a great status (as used in classical Greek) and denotes a high position in the church. Paul honors a total of thirty-seven people in this last chapter of Romans. Their names have gone down in church history as wonderful servants of Jesus. Their names are recorded for eternity here in God's eternal Word. Church tradition states that most of those named here were martyred for their faith. Imagine dear sister Phoebe carrying with her a letter to Rome that contained the greatest wealth of Christian theology. A copy of that letter she carried is the letter you are now reading!

f 16:3 The Aramaic word used throughout this chapter for "greetings" or "love" is "send peace."

g 16:3 *Prisca* was a diminutive form of Priscilla ("long life"). She and her husband, Aquila ("eagle"), were tentmakers like Paul. They were not only business partners, but partners with him in ministry. See Acts 18:2, 18, 26; 1 Cor. 16:19; 2 Tim. 4:19.

And greet Epenetus,[a] who was the first convert to Christ in the Roman province of Asia,[b] for I love him dearly.

[6] And give my greetings to Miriam,[c] who has toiled and labored extremely hard to beautify you.[d]

[7] Make sure that my relatives Andronicus and Junia[e] are honored, for they're my fellow captives[f] who bear the distinctive mark of being outstanding and well-known apostles,[g] and who were joined into the Anointed One before me.

[8] Give my regards to Ampliatus,[h] whom I love, for he is joined into the Lord.

[9] And give my loving greetings to Urbanus,[i] our partner in ministry serving the Anointed One, and also to Stachus,[j] whom I love.

[10] Don't forget to greet Apelles[k] for me, for he's been tested and found to be approved by the Anointed One.[l]

And extend warm greetings to all those of Aristobolos's house church.[m]

---

a 16:5 Or "Epaenetus," which means "praiseworthy."

b 16:5 Or "the firstfruit [convert] of Asia" (Minor). The Roman province of Asia is modern-day Turkey. The Aramaic has Epenetus as the first convert from Achaia, a region of Greece.

c 16:6 Or "Mary." The Hebrew name Miriam is taken from the Hebrew root and Ugaritic noun *mrym*, which means "height," "summit," "exalted" (excellent).

d 16:6 As translated from the Aramaic. The Greek is "to benefit you."

e 16:7 Throughout the first twelve hundred years of church history, Andronicus ("victorious one") and Junia ("youthful") were considered to be husband and wife. A small number of manuscripts have "Julia." Paul calls them his relatives, or "[Jewish] kinsmen." The Aramaic meaning of Junia is "little dove."

f 16:7 Or "prisoners." It is possible that Paul is using this term as a metaphor; that is, they were prisoners of the love of Christ. See Song. 8:6, which uses the Hebrew word for "prison cell" or "seal."

g 16:7 It is clear in the text that Junia, along with her husband, Andronicus, was a well-known apostle. (The Greek word *episemos* means "famous, prominent, outstanding.") Jesus chose twelve men and called them apostles, but the Twelve were not the only ones identified in the New Testament as apostles ("sent ones"). There are others, including Matthias, Paul, Barnabas, Andronicus, and Junia. See Acts 14:13; Eph. 4:11–13.

h 16:8 Ampliatus was a common name given to slaves, and it means "large one." The Eastern Orthodox Church recognizes him as one of the seventy disciples whom Jesus sent out. He is believed to have become the bishop of Bulgaria.

i 16:9 Urbanus was also a common name given to slaves. It means "polite one."

j 16:9 Or Stachys ("head of grain"). He is said to have been one of the seventy disciples Jesus sent out. He eventually became the bishop of Byzantium.

k 16:10 *Apelles* means "called one."

l 16:10 Or "the Lord knows, not we, the tests he endured."

m 16:10 Or "those of Aristobolos"; by implication, those connected to Aristobolos, or, his "house church." The word *household* is not found in the Greek text. *Aristobolos* means "best counselor." Traditionally he is known as one of the seventy disciples Jesus sent out, and he brought the gospel to Britain.

¹¹ Give my love to my relative Herodion,ª and also to all those of the house church of Narcissus,ᵇ for they too are joined into the Lord.

¹² Please greet Tryphenaᶜ and Tryphosa,ᵈ for they are women who have diligently served the Lord.

To Persis,ᵉ who is much loved and faithful in her ministry for the Lord, I send my greetings.

¹³ And Rufus,ᶠ for he is especially chosen by the Lord. And I greet his mother, who was like a mother to me.

¹⁴ I cannot forget to mention my esteemed friends Asyncritus,ᵍ Phlegon,ʰ Hermes,ⁱ Patrobas,ʲ Hermas,ᵏ and all the brothers and sisters who meet with them.

ª 16:11 Herodion's name means "heroic." He was traditionally considered as one of Jesus' seventy disciples. He later became the bishop of Neoparthia (Iraq), where he was beaten to death by the Jews but was resurrected and continued to preach the gospel. It is believed that he was eventually beheaded in Rome on the same day Peter was martyred.

ᵇ 16:11 Or "those of Narcissus." Although nearly every translation adds the word *household*, it is not found in the text. By implication, this would be those meeting as a church in his house. Narcissus' name means "astonished" (or "stupefied"). Some have identified him as a close friend of Emperor Claudius.

ᶜ 16:12 *Tryphena* means "living luxuriously." Some have identified her as Antonia Tryphaena (10 BC—AD 55), the princess of the Bosporan kingdom of eastern Crimea, and connected to the queen of Thrace. This would mean that she was royal and wealthy.

ᵈ 16:12 *Tryphosa* can also mean "living luxuriously" or "triple [three-fold] shining." Some scholars believe that Tryphena and Tryphosa were twin sisters born into royalty.

ᵉ 16:12 *Persis* means "to take by storm." She was a woman from Persia (Iranian background) who was a godly servant and passionate follower of Jesus.

ᶠ 16:13 *Rufus* means "red." It is believed that he was the son of Simon of Cyrene (Libya) who helped Jesus carry his cross to Calvary. See Mark 15:21.

ᵍ 16:14 *Asyncritus* means "incomparable." The Orthodox Church recognizes him as an apostle. He became the bishop of the church of Hyracania (Turkey). In this verse Paul joins five men together. They could have represented the five-fold ministry of Eph. 4:11, or they may have been leaders of house churches, for there were others who were "with" them and connected to them.

ʰ 16:14 *Phlegon* means "burning one." He was considered to be one of the seventy disciples Jesus sent out. The Orthodox Church recognizes him as an apostle who became the bishop of Marathon in Thrace.

ⁱ 16:14 *Hermes* means "preacher of the deity." He was considered to be one of the seventy sent out by Jesus and later became the bishop of Dalmatia.

ʲ 16:14 *Patrobas* means "fatherly" (paternal). He likewise was one of the seventy sent by Jesus and later became the bishop of Neapolis (Naples).

ᵏ 16:14 Hermas was one of the seventy and later became the bishop of Philipopoulis (Bulgaria). There are interesting traditions surrounding Hermas. It is said that he was a very wealthy man but fell into poverty because of his sins. He was visited by an "angel of repentance," who accompanied him for the rest of his life until he was martyred. There are writings known as "The Shepherd of Hermas" that some scholars attribute to him.

¹⁵ Give my regards to Philologus, Julia, Nereus and his sister, and also Olympas ᵃ and all the holy believers who meet with them.

¹⁶ Greet each other with a holy kiss *of God's love.* ᵇ All the believers in all the congregations of the Messiah send their greetings to all of you.

Paul's Final Instructions

¹⁷ And now, dear brothers and sisters, I'd like to give one final word of caution: Watch out for those who cause divisions and offenses among you. When they antagonize you by speaking of things that are contrary to the teachings that you've received, don't be caught in their snare! ¹⁸ For people like this are not truly serving the Lord, our Messiah, but are being driven by their own desires for a following. ᶜ Utilizing their smooth words and well-rehearsed blessings, they seek to deceive the hearts of innocent ones.

¹⁹ I'm so happy when I think of you, because everyone knows the testimony of your deep commitment of faith. So I want you to become scholars of all that is good and beautiful, and stay pure and innocent ᵈ when it comes to evil. ²⁰ And the God of peace will swiftly pound Satan to a pulp ᵉ under your feet! And the wonderful favor of our Lord Jesus will surround you.

²¹ My ministry partner, Timothy, ᶠ sends his loving greetings, along with Luke, ᵍ Jason, ʰ and Sosipater, ⁱ my Jewish kinsmen. ʲ

²² (I, Tertius, ᵏ am the one transcribing this letter for Paul, and I too send my greetings to all of you, as a follower of the Lord.)

---

a 16:15 *Philologus* means "talkative." He was recognized by the Orthodox Church as an apostle of Christ. It is likely that Julia was his wife and Nereus and his sister were their children. Olympas means "heavenly." The Orthodox Church recognizes Olympas as an apostle who was mentored by Peter and was beheaded the same day Peter was martyred in Rome. Philologus and Olympas apparently had a measure of influence over a number of "holy believers" in the faith. The majority of the people named in this chapter were not Jewish, and many of their names indicate that they were former slaves. God can bless and anoint anyone who turns to him in faith.

b 16:16 What makes a kiss holy is that it comes from the love of God. See Song. 1:2.

c 16:18 Or "they are slaves of their bellies." The metaphor used here is that they are driven by their desires to pull others into their group and thus divide the church.

d 16:19 Or "unmixed."

e 16:20 The Greek word *suntribo* means "to beat up someone to a jelly" (or pulp). See also Ps. 60:12.

f 16:21 Timothy was a spiritual son and ministry partner to the apostle Paul. See Acts 16:1–3.

g 16:21 Or "Lucius." This seems to be the Luke who wrote Luke and Acts, but there remains considerable debate surrounding who that "Luke" may be.

h 16:21 Jason also appears in Acts 17, where he opened his home to Paul, Silas, and Timothy while they were in Thessalonica. Tradition states that Jason was one of the seventy disciples sent out by Jesus and was appointed the bishop of Tarsus by Paul.

i 16:21 According to church tradition, he was recognized as one of the seventy disciples and became the bishop of Iconium.

j 16:21 See Acts 20:4.

k 16:22 Tertius, the copyist for Paul, was recognized in church history as one of the seventy

²³ My kind host here in Corinth, Gaius, ᵃ likewise greets you, along with the entire congregation of his house church. Also, the city administrator Erastus ᵇ and our brother Quartus ᶜ send their warm greetings.

²⁴ May the grace and favor of our Lord Jesus, the Anointed One, continually rest upon you all. ᵈ

Paul Praises God

²⁵ I give all my praises and glory ᵉ to the one who has more than enough power to make you strong and keep you steadfast through the promises found in the wonderful news that I preach; that is, the proclamation of Jesus, the Anointed One. This wonderful news includes the unveiling of the mystery kept secret ᶠ from the dawn of creation until now. ²⁶ This mystery is understood through the prophecies of the Scripture and by the decree of the eternal God. And it is now heard openly by all the nations, igniting within them a deep commitment of faith.

²⁷ Now to God, the only source of wisdom, be glorious praises for endless ages through Jesus, the Anointed One! Amen!

(Paul's letter was transcribed by Tertius in Corinth and sent from Corinth and carried to Rome by Phoebe.) ᵍ

---

disciples of Jesus. He became the bishop of Iconium after Sosipater and was eventually martyred.

a 16:23 This is most likely the Gaius whom Paul baptized (1 Cor. 1:14) and who became a ministry partner with Paul (Acts 19:29). Gaius means "happy," "jolly."

b 16:23 Erastus was a political appointee who was undoubtedly of a high social status in the city of Corinth. His duties would have included being the treasurer of the city. Church tradition holds that he was one of the seventy disciples of Jesus and that he served as a minister (deacon) of the church in Jerusalem and later in Paneas. An excavation in Corinth uncovered a street with an ancient inscription dated to the first century AD. It read "Erastus . . . laid the pavement at his own expense." His name means "loveable."

c 16:23 Quartus is recognized in church history as one of the seventy disciples sent by Jesus. He became the bishop of Beirut. Nikolai Velimirovic wrote that Quartus suffered greatly for his faith and won many converts to Christ through his ministry (*Prologue from Ohrid*).

d 16:24 The vast majority of Greek manuscripts have v. 24; however, some manuscripts, including the Aramaic, place this verse after v. 27. There is some external evidence that this verse was copied from v. 20 and placed here. Many scholars are divided over where or if this verse is to be placed in the text.

e 16:25 Implied in the text and supplied from v. 27 for the sake of English sentence length. This doxology of Paul (vv. 25–27) is found in three separate locations in different Greek manuscripts with a total of five variations. Most reliable manuscripts place it here. Some have it after 14:23, and a few place it after 15:33. Some include it twice in different placements.

f 16:25 Or "kept in [God's] silence."

g 16:27 As translated from the Aramaic.

1 CORINTHIANS

Introduction

AT A GLANCE

Author: The apostle Paul
Audience: The church of Corinth
Date: AD 53–55
Type of Literature: A letter
Major Themes: The gospel, the church, spiritual gifts, holiness, love, and the resurrection
Outline:

Letter Opening — 1:1–9
Causes and Cures of Division — 1:10–4:21
Moral Issues and Marriage — 5:1–7:40
Condemnation of Idolatry — 8:1–11:1
Affirmation of Worship and Gifts — 11:2–14:40
The Resurrection of the Dead — 15:1–58
Letter Closing — 16:1–24

ABOUT 1 CORINTHIANS

The once influential seaport city of Corinth was strategically located at the crossroads of the world. Prosperous, powerful, and decadent, it was a city that God wanted to reach with the power of the gospel. God sent the apostle Paul to Corinth on his third missionary journey to establish a church in a city that desperately needed love and truth. Paul spent a year and a half in Corinth and saw the church grow, with more believers being added to their number daily. But they needed wisdom from their spiritual father, Paul. So he wrote this letter to encourage them to carry on in their faith and to remain steadfast to the truths of the gospel.

Written while Paul was in Ephesus, this letter had a powerful effect on the Corinthian believers. In his second letter to them, he was able to take them even further into the truths of our new covenant reality and the power of the gospel to overcome sufferings. While Paul was ministering in Corinth, he met two people who would become his coworkers: Aquila and Priscilla, a husband-and-wife team.

Perhaps this book is best remembered for the so-called love chapter. In 1 Corinthians 13 we have the clearest and most poetic masterpiece of love in the New Testament. God's unending love always sustains us and gives us hope. Think how many of the problems in your life could be solved by embracing the revelation of love found in this anointed letter of Paul! May the love of God win every battle in your heart, bringing a full restoration of your soul into the image of God, for God is love.

We are so enriched by having this inspired letter, written to Paul's spiritual sons and daughters. How grateful we are that God has given us the treasures found in 1 Corinthians!

PURPOSE

Many see 1 Corinthians as a letter of correction. Indeed, many errors had crept into the belief system of the church of Corinth and the spiritual walk of its members. Some of the issues Paul needed to address include: living godly in a corrupt culture, being unified as one body without competition, maintaining the priority of sexual and moral purity within the church, understanding more completely the role of spiritual gifts in the context of the church, embracing love as the greatest virtue that must live within our hearts, maintaining orderly worship with proper respect toward one another, and keeping the hope of the resurrection burning brightly in our hearts.

But 1 Corinthians is not all correction. Paul gave many wonderful teachings to the young church that will impact your life as well. Like the Corinthian believers, you possess every spiritual gift, you are fully equipped to minister to others, you are capable of demonstrating love to all, and the hope of a future resurrection brings meaning to your life today.

AUTHOR AND AUDIENCE

The apostle Paul wrote to the church of Corinth not as an outsider but as one who was intimately involved in their affairs as a founding father (see Acts 18). He composed this letter about AD 53–55, while living in Ephesus. He was responding to certain issues and problems in the Corinthian church. Apparently, a delegation had arrived from Corinth and notified Paul of what was taking place and asked for his advice. First Corinthians was his response.

While this letter was directed to a specific congregation in a specific Roman city, we are as much of the audience today, given how we mirror many of the characteristics that defined Corinth. It was considered a modern, cosmopolitan city; its people were staunch individualists; their behaviors reflected this individualism; their spirituality was polytheistic; and believers accommodated the gospel in ways that made it palatable to the surrounding culture. These characteristics could also be said of us.

Corinth was the New York, London, and Sydney of the ancient world. We need the voice of Paul and the Spirit of God to speak into our lives today. May we hear them clearly.

MAJOR THEMES

The Nature of the Gospel. This letter is gospel drenched! Not only in what it reveals about our story in Christ, but in what it reveals about his story too. In 8:6 we find revelation-truth about Christ that hadn't been understood before: "For us there is only one God—the Father. He is the source of all things, and our lives are lived for him. And there is one Lord, Jesus, the Anointed One, through whom we and all things exist." Here Paul equates the one true God of Israel, Yahweh, with Jesus. Jesus is Yahweh, the only true God.

Paul also revealed the nature of our story, the story each of us has committed to by believing the gospel. Paul shared the core message that had been part of the church from the beginning: "The Messiah died for our sins, ... He was buried in a tomb and was raised from the dead after three days, as foretold in the Scriptures. Then he appeared to Peter the Rock and to the twelve apostles" (15:3–5). This is the essence of the gospel, the good news about our forgiveness from sins, freedom from shame and guilt, and new life in Christ. Like Paul, God's amazing grace has made us who we are.

The Church of Christ. One of the central issues Paul addressed was what we call ecclesiology, the nature of the church. What does it mean to be the people of God? What does it mean to gather as God's holy people—in Corinth, throughout America, or in Australia? One commentator declares these teachings on the church to be this letter's greatest theological contribution. As a church planter this makes sense. Paul was deeply concerned for his spiritual children and how they publicly professed and lived out the gospel in a gathered community.

In this anointed letter, Paul confronted the nature of church leadership and pastoral ministry. He addressed lawsuits that were tearing believers apart. He confronted head-on the toleration of sexual immorality within the community. And he addressed the nature of worship, particularly the expression of God's supernatural gifts that God has imparted to every believer. No stone is left unturned as Paul shapes our understanding of what it means to be "God's inner sanctuary" (3:16), literally "the body of Christ" (10:16) living and breathing in the world!

Holy and Ethical Living. In two of his other letters, Romans and Galatians, Paul made it clear that we are saved by grace through faith. In this letter, he makes it equally clear that we are "God's expensive purchase, paid for with tears of blood," and in response are called to "use your body to bring glory to God" (6:20). We do this by "following God's commandments" (7:19) and obeying "the law of Christ" (9:21).

No aspect of our new Christian ethics and holy living is left unaddressed.

"People who continue to engage in sexual immorality, idolatry, adultery, sexual perversion, homosexuality, fraud, greed, drunkenness, verbal abuse, or extortion—these will not inherit God's kingdom realm" (6:9–10). We may be saved by grace, but Paul makes it clear that as Christians we are to live our lives in a way that glorifies and honors God (10:31).

Love, the Motivation of Our Lives. Each of Paul's letters seems to have an ethical high note. In his second letter to the Corinthians, it is generosity. In Ephesians, one could say it's humility. And Galatians emphasizes the fruit produced by the Spirit life. In this letter Paul uncovers the beautiful ethical prize after which we are to run: love. The so-called love chapter expounds upon the virtues of loving both God and neighbor, as Christ commanded. According to Paul, love is more worthy than speaking eloquently "in the heavenly tongues of angels" (13:1), better than having "unending supernatural knowledge" (13:2), and far more important than giving away everything to the poor (13:3). As Paul says, "Love never stops loving"; it never fails (13:8).

Issues of "the End." By "the end" we mean both our personal end at death and also our world's end when Christ returns. While we often think our end hope is in heaven, it isn't. Our ultimate Christian hope is in the resurrection. Paul spent fifty-eight verses and an entire chapter making this clear. In fact, this was his main message. Jesus' resurrection from the dead paved the way for our own resurrection. He is "the firstfruit of a great resurrection harvest of those who have died" (15:20). Because Jesus is alive, we have a bright hope for tomorrow. For this reason we can confidently declare, along with Paul, "Death is swallowed up by a triumphant victory! So death, tell me, where is your victory? Tell me death, where is your sting?" (15:54–55).

1 CORINTHIANS

Love and Truth

Paul's Greeting

1 From Paul, divinely appointed according to the plan of God, to be an apostle of the Anointed One, Jesus. Our fellow believer Sosthenes[a] joins me [2]in writing you this letter addressed to the community of God[b] throughout the city of Corinth. For you have been made pure, set apart in the Anointed One, Jesus. And God has invited you to be his devoted and holy people, and not only you, but everyone everywhere who calls on the name of our Lord Jesus Christ as their Lord, and ours also.

[3]May joyous grace[c] and endless peace be yours continually from our Father God and from our Lord Jesus, the Anointed One!

Made Wonderfully Rich

[4]I am always thanking my God for you because he has given you such free and open access to his grace through your union with Jesus, the Messiah. [5]In him you have been made extravagantly rich in every way. You have been endowed with a wealth of inspired utterance[d] and the riches that come from your intimate knowledge of him. [6]For the reality of the truth of Christ is seen among you and strengthened[e] through your experience of him. [7]So now you aren't

---

a 1:1 *Sosthenes* means "savior of his nation." He was the Jewish synagogue ruler in Corinth who had converted to Christ and had been beaten for his faith (Acts 18:12–17).

b 1:2 Or "church." This is the Greek word *ekklēsia*, which means "a summoned people, called to assemble, a legislative body." It is also a word used in Greek culture to "assemble an army."

c 1:3 The Greek word *charis*, in its original sense, is descriptive of that which brings pleasure and joy to the human heart, implying a strong emotional element. God's grace includes favor and supernatural potency, and it is meant to leave us both charming and beautiful. In classical Greek it was meant to convey the attitude of favor shown by royalty. See Torrance, *The Doctrine of Grace in the Apostolic Fathers*, pp. 1–5.

d 1:5 Or "in every kind of speaking." By implication, Paul is commending them for their speaking gifts (prophecy, tongues and interpretation of tongues, preaching, and teaching the word of God). This will be developed further in chs. 12–14.

e 1:6 Or "validated" or "confirmed." The word used here is found in classical Greek in the context of establishing (building) communities.

lacking any spiritual gift[a] as you eagerly await the unveiling[b] of the Lord Jesus, the Anointed One. [8] He will keep you steady and strong to the very end, making your character mature so that you will be found innocent on the day of our Lord Jesus Christ. [9] God is forever faithful and can be trusted to do this in you, for he has invited you to co-share the life of his Son,[c] Jesus, the Anointed One, our King![d]

Paul Addresses Divisions in the Church

[10] I urge you, my brothers and sisters, for the sake of the name of our Lord Jesus Christ, to agree to live in unity with one another[e] and put to rest any division that attempts to tear you apart.[f] Be restored[g] as one united body living in perfect harmony. Form a consistent choreography among yourselves, having a common perspective with shared values.

[11] My dear brothers and sisters, *I have a serious concern I need to bring up with you,*[h] for I have been informed by those of Chloe's *house church*[i] that you have been destructively arguing among yourselves. [12] And I need to bring this up because each of you is claiming loyalty to different preachers. Some are saying,

---

a 1:7 Or "You don't fail to receive any gift of the Holy Spirit." God wants his church to receive every gift the Holy Spirit has to give us. This may be a figure of speech called a litotes, which means it could also be translated, "You have every spiritual gift."

b 1:7 Or "eagerly accept" or "eagerly await." The Greek word *ekdechomai* is a compound word, *ek* (out of, from) and *dechomai* (to accept or receive or take hold of).

c 1:9 Or "a life of communion with his Son." That is, a co-participation (communion, fellowship) of the Son. The Aramaic can be translated "You have been called to the (wedding) feast of his Son." We see a clear picture here that believers are called to share in the sonship of Jesus. By God's grace, we will share in the Son's standing and position before the Father. We are not only blameless but made holy by the co-sharing of the life of God's Son.

d 1:9 Or "Lord."

e 1:10 Or "that you all speak the same thing"; that is, to have a united testimony. The Aramaic can be translated "that you may all be of one word."

f 1:10 The congregation of believers in Corinth was sorely divided. They had divided over which leader or apostle they followed (chs. 1–3), over the limits of their freedom (chs. 6–8), over their socio-economic status (ch. 11), and over spiritual gifts (chs. 12–14). Division among believers grossly hinders our message and ministry to the world of unbelievers. Paul is pleading with them to unite around the love of God for one another (ch. 13).

g 1:10 Or "fully equipped."

h 1:11 Before Paul brought correction to the Corinthians, he first affirmed the work of God in their midst. See vv. 4–9. Perhaps we should look at confused and messed-up Christians differently and speak to how God sees imperfect believers.

i 1:11 Or "Chloe's people." The word *household* or *family* is not in the Greek text. By implication, it refers to those who are meeting with Chloe, as the one they are connected to (Chloe's people; i.e., house church, or Chloe's congregation). She was obviously a trusted leader in Paul's estimation and had influence in the church of Corinth. Her name means "green [tender] sprout." Those who informed Paul of the problems in Corinth may have been Stephanas, Fortunatus, and Achaicus, mentioned in 1 Cor. 16:17.

"I am a disciple of Paul," or, "I follow Apollos," or, "I am a disciple of Peter the Rock,"[a] and some, "I belong *only* to Christ." [13] But *let me ask you*, is Christ divided up into groups? Did I die on the cross for you? At your baptism did you pledge yourselves to follow Paul?[b]

[14] Thank God I only baptized two from Corinth—Crispus and Gaius![c] [15] So now no one can say that in my name I baptized others.[d] [16] (Yes, I also baptized Stephanus and his family. Other than that, I don't remember baptizing anyone else.) [17] For the Anointed One has sent me on a mission, not to see how many I could baptize,[e] but to proclaim the good news. And I declare this message stripped of all philosophical arguments that empty the cross of its true power. For I trust in the all-sufficient cross of Christ alone.

The True Power of the Cross

[18] To preach the message[f] of the cross seems like sheer nonsense to those who are on their way to destruction, but to us who are on our way to salvation, it is the mighty power of God released within us.[g] [19] For it is written:

I will dismantle the wisdom of the wise
    and I will invalidate the intelligence of the scholars.[h]

[20] So where is the wise philosopher *who understands*? Where is the expert scholar *who comprehends*? And where is the skilled debater of our time *who could win a debate with God*? Hasn't God demonstrated that the wisdom of this world system is utter foolishness?

[21] For in his wisdom, *God designed that all* the world's wisdom would

---

a 1:12 Or "Cephas," the Aramaic word for rock (*keefa*) transliterated into Greek. Paul is comfortable in calling Peter by his Aramaic nickname, Keefa.

b 1:13 Or "Were you baptized in the name of Paul?"

c 1:14 Before converting to faith in Christ, Crispus was likely the ruler of the synagogue in Corinth mentioned in Acts 18:18. Gaius was most likely the one who hosted Paul when he came to Rome (Rom. 16:23). Since they had become believers before Paul's assistants, Timothy and Silas, arrived from Macedonia, Paul went ahead and baptized them.

d 1:15 As translated from the Aramaic. The Greek is "so that no one can say that they were baptized in my name."

e 1:17 In the broader context of Paul's teaching, both baptism and the Lord's Table proclaim the Lord Jesus (Rom. 6:3–11; 1 Cor. 11:24–27). Therefore, viewing Paul's statement as somewhat hyperbolic, it is taken to mean that he was not sent just to baptize but also to preach the gospel.

f 1:18 Or "expression [Gr. *logos*]" or "the act of proclaiming."

g 1:18 The "message of the cross" becomes the ignition point where God's power becomes operative and actualized with the ability to convert, transform, and save. The Aramaic can be translated "For he [rather than the message] is the power of God."

h 1:19 See Isa. 29:14 (LXX). Paul uses the prophecy of Isaiah as a warning against leaning upon human wisdom to understand spiritual matters. True wisdom comes from above and is given by divine revelation to those who are teachable and humble before God.

be insufficient to lead people to the discovery of himself. He took great delight in baffling the wisdom of the world by using the simplicity of preaching the story of the cross [a] in order to save those who believe it. [22] For the Jews constantly demand to see miraculous signs, while those who are not Jews [b] constantly cling to the world's wisdom, [c] [23] but we preach the crucified Messiah. The Jews stumble over him and the rest of the world sees him as foolishness. [24] But for those who have been chosen to follow him, both Jews and Greeks, he is God's mighty power, God's true wisdom, and our Messiah. [d] [25] For the "foolish" things of God have proven to be wiser than human wisdom. And the "feeble" things of God have proven to be far more powerful than any human ability. [e]

God's Calling

[26] Brothers and sisters, consider who you were when God called you *to salvation*. Not many of you were wise scholars by human standards, nor were many of you in positions of power. Not many of you were considered the elite *when you answered God's call*. [27] But God chose those whom the world considers foolish to shame those who think they are wise, and God chose the puny and powerless to shame [f] the high and mighty. [28] He chose the lowly, the laughable [g] in the world's eyes—nobodies—so that he would shame the somebodies. For he chose what is regarded as insignificant in order to supersede what is regarded as prominent, [29] so that there would be no place for prideful boasting in God's presence. [30] *For it is not from man that we draw our life* but from God as we are being joined to Jesus, the Anointed One. And now he is our God-given wisdom, our virtue, our holiness, and our redemption. [31] And this fulfills what is written:

---

a 1:21 Or simply "the foolishness of preaching." However, it is not the act of preaching but the content of what is preached that brings salvation to those who believe.

b 1:22 The Aramaic uses the term Arameans for gentiles. It means "Aramaic-speaking people."

c 1:22 To paraphrase, the gentiles seek for success in the world's eyes, or a wisdom that leads them to succeed. Christ crucified is both a miracle sign and the wisdom that will lead one to reign in life.

d 1:24 Christ is the supreme manifestation of God's power to save us from sin, to work miracles, and to defeat evil. Christ is the supreme manifestation of wisdom, for he carries out the eternal plan of God and brings it to completion.

e 1:25 Although the cross seemed to be the foolishness of God, it reveals his transcendent wisdom. And though God the Son was crucified in weakness, he has risen through the divine power that transforms lives today. God has no weakness or foolishness whatsoever. Yet what looks like weakness is actually his strength, and what looks like foolishness is actually his wisdom.

f 1:27 The Greek word *kataischynō* can also be translated "embarrass," "confuse," "baffle," or "frustrate."

g 1:28 Or "despised," "disgusting," "outcasts," "perceived with contempt."

If anyone boasts, let him only boast
in all that the Lord has done![a]

Paul's Reliance on Spiritual Power

2 My brothers and sisters,[b] when I first came to proclaim to you the secrets[c] of God, I refused to come *as an expert*, trying to impress you with my eloquent speech and lofty wisdom. [2] For while I was with you I was determined to be consumed with one topic—Jesus, the crucified Messiah.[d] [3] I stood before you feeling inadequate, filled with reverence for God,[e] and trembling *under the sense of the importance of my words*.[f] [4] The message I preached and how I preached it was not an attempt to sway you with persuasive arguments but to prove to you the almighty power of God's Holy Spirit. [5] For God intended that your faith not be established on man's wisdom but by trusting in his almighty power.

Wisdom from God

[6] However, there is a wisdom that we continually speak of when we are among the spiritually mature.[g] It's wisdom that didn't originate in this present age, nor did it come from the rulers of this age who are in the process of being dethroned.[h] [7] Instead, we[i] continually speak of this wonderful wisdom that comes

---

a 1:31 Or "He who triumphs, let him triumph in the Lord God!" See Jer. 9:24.

b 2:1 Or "brothers."

c 2:1 As translated from the Aramaic. Some Greek manuscripts have "testimony." Paul, as a steward of the mysteries of God (1 Cor. 4:1), comes to them bringing a clear revelation of God's mysteries. The Greek word *mustērion* (secret, or mystery) is found twenty-eight times in the New Testament.

d 2:2 Paul could have easily impressed the Corinthians with his vast knowledge of the Torah and the Jewish laws. But he was resolved to forget every other topic and stay focused on Christ and his cross. He wanted the power of the Spirit to work through his singular message.

e 2:3 As translated from the Aramaic. The Greek is "I was with you in fear and trembling."

f 2:3 Paul was not simply filled with dread or fear, but filled with how important it was to present the gospel clearly to the Corinthians. See also 2 Cor. 10:10; 11:6.

g 2:6 Or "those who have reached perfection." The Greek term for "spiritually mature" in this verse is found in classical Greek, describing those who have been initiated into mysteries. It most likely refers in this context to those who believed Paul's message containing the mysteries of God (2:1). Paul uses the word *wisdom* sixteen times in the first three chapters of 1 Corinthians.

h 2:6 Or "rulers who are doomed to come to nothing" or "the nullified overlords of this present age." This does not refer merely to human governments, but to the dethroned rulers of darkness that know nothing of God's secret wisdom.

i 2:7 Many times in 1 and 2 Corinthians when Paul uses the pronoun *we*, he is referring to the apostles of the church, gifts of Christ who are sent to teach the mysteries of God. See 1 Cor. 4:1; Eph. 4:11–13.

from God, hidden before now in a mystery.[a] It is his secret plan, destined[b] before the ages, *to bring* us into glory.[c] [8] None of the rulers of this present world order understood it,[d] for if they had, they never would have crucified the Lord of shining glory.[e] [9] This is why the Scriptures say:

Things never discovered or heard of before,
  things beyond our ability to imagine[f]—
these are the many things God has in store
  for all his lovers.[g]

[10] But God now unveils these profound realities to us by the Spirit.[h] Yes, he has revealed to us his inmost heart and deepest mysteries through the Holy Spirit, who constantly explores all things. [11] After all, who can really see into a person's heart and know his hidden impulses except for that person's spirit? So it is with God. His thoughts and secrets are only fully understood by his Spirit, the Spirit of God.

[12] For we did not receive the spirit of this world system but the Spirit of God, so that we might come to understand and experience all that grace has lavished upon us. [13] And we[i] articulate these realities with the words imparted to us by the Spirit and not with the words taught by human wisdom. We join together Spirit-revealed truths with Spirit-revealed words.[j] [14] Someone living

---

a 2:7 That is, something so profound it is beyond the scope of human ingenuity and unattainable by human reasoning. Wisdom comes from above and is given to those who love God and live in awe of him.

b 2:7 Or "decreed." The Greek word *proorizo* means "to mark out the boundaries." It is a form of the word *horizon*. God has marked out ahead of time the horizon of the ages and will finish his predetermined plan perfectly.

c 2:7 The Aramaic can be translated "for our glorification" or "so that glory may be ours."

d 2:8 Although it is possible that this refers to human rulers, it is hard to imagine how Herod, Pilate, and the Jewish authorities could be equated to the words "rulers of [over] this present world order (*aeon*)." It seems clear that Paul is speaking of the principalities and powers of darkness, who were clueless about the efficacy of Christ's crucifixion to realign the universe and initiate a new kingdom under our Lord Jesus Christ.

e 2:8 Or a genitive of quality, "the Lord, to whom glory belongs." This is the only place in the New Testament with the term "Lord of shining glory." The church father Augustine translated this "the Lord who dispenses glory" (an objective genitive: Augustine, *On the Trinity*, 1:12:24).

f 2:9 Or "entered the heart."

g 2:9 See Isa. 64:4.

h 2:10 Or "God has provided us with a revelation through the Spirit." This difficult-to-translate Greek sentence may contain an ellipsis, which would render it "Yet *we speak* [or *we know*] what God has revealed to us by the Spirit."

i 2:13 It is possible that Paul uses "we" in reference to apostles.

j 2:13 Or "We explain spiritual realities to spiritual people" or "We interpret spiritual truths by spiritual faculties."

on an entirely human level[a] rejects[b] the revelations of God's Spirit, for they make no sense to him. He can't understand the revelations of the Spirit because they are only discovered by the illumination of the Spirit. [15]Those who live in the Spirit are able to carefully evaluate all things, and they are subject to the scrutiny of no one *but God*. [16]For

Who has ever intimately known the mind of the Lord Yahweh[c] well
enough to become his counselor?[d]

Christ has, and we possess Christ's perceptions.[e]

A Call to Spiritual Maturity

3 Brothers and sisters, when I was with you I found it impossible to speak to you as those who are spiritually mature people, for you are still dominated by the mind-set of the flesh. And because you are immature infants in Christ, [2]I had to nurse you and feed you with "milk,"[f] not with the solid food *of more advanced teachings*, because you weren't ready for it. In fact, you are still not ready to be fed solid food, [3]for you are living your lives dominated by the mind-set of the flesh. Ask yourselves: Is there jealousy among you? Do you compare yourselves with others? Do you quarrel *like children* and end up taking sides? If so, this proves that you are living your lives centered on yourselves, dominated by the mind-set of the flesh, and behaving like unbelievers. [4]For when you divide yourselves up in groups—a "Paul group" and an "Apollos group"[g]—you're acting like people without the Spirit's influence.[h]

[5]Who is Apollos, really? Or who is Paul? Aren't we both just servants through whom you believed our message? Aren't each of us doing the ministry the Lord has assigned to us? [6]I was the one who planted the church and Apollos

---

a 2:14 Or "the natural man" or "the one without the Spirit." The Aramaic can be translated "A man in his natural self cannot receive spiritual concepts."

b 2:14 Or "does not have access to."

c 2:16 As translated from the Aramaic.

d 2:16 See Isa. 40:13.

e 2:16 That is, we believers possess the Holy Spirit, who reveals the thoughts and purposes of Christ. The revelation of the kingdom of God that Jesus preached was not understood by the intellect of men but by those who welcomed his truth. Humanly speaking, no one can understand the mysteries of God without the Holy Spirit. Those who have the Holy Spirit now possess the perceptions of Christ's mind and can implement his purposes on the earth.

f 3:2 This "milk" would include the basic teachings of our faith. Even so, every newborn needs milk to survive and be sustained. See 1 Peter 2:2. The more advanced teachings Paul describes are spiritual "solid food"—something we can "sink our teeth into" and look for deeper meaning in.

g 3:4 Apollos was a brilliant, educated Alexandrian Jew and a follower of John the Baptizer. While in Ephesus, Apollos met Priscilla and Aquila, who directed him into deeper teachings of Christ (Acts 18:24–26). Apparently the church of Corinth was deeply divided and in need of wisdom and unity.

h 3:4 Or "Are you [merely] men?"

came and cared for it, but it was God who caused it to grow. ⁷This means the one who plants is not anybody special, nor the one who waters, for God is the one who brings the supernatural growth.

⁸Now, the one who plants and the one who waters are *equally important* and on the same team, but each will be rewarded for his own work. ⁹We are coworkers with God*ᵃ* and you are God's cultivated garden, the house he is building. ¹⁰God has given me unique gifts*ᵇ* as a skilled master builder*ᶜ* who lays a good foundation. Afterward another craftsman comes and builds on it. So builders beware! Let every builder do his work carefully, according to God's standards. ¹¹For no one is empowered to lay an alternative foundation other than the good foundation that exists, which is Jesus Christ!

¹²⁻¹³The quality of materials used by anyone building on this foundation will soon be made apparent, whether it has been built with gold, silver, and costly stones,*ᵈ* or wood, hay, and straw. Their work will soon become evident, for the Day*ᵉ* will make it clear, because it will be revealed by blazing fire! And the fire will test and prove the workmanship of each builder. ¹⁴If his work stands the test of fire, he will be rewarded. ¹⁵If his work is consumed by the fire, he will suffer great loss. Yet he himself will barely escape destruction, like one being rescued out of a burning house.

The Church, God's Inner Sanctuary

¹⁶Don't you realize that together you have become God's inner sanctuary*ᶠ* and that the Spirit of God makes his permanent home in you?*ᵍ* ¹⁷Now, if someone

---

a 3:9 Workers have different gifts and abilities, but true growth of God's kingdom is through divine power. No one is a superstar; we are all members on God's team.

b 3:10 Or "grace" (for the task).

c 3:10 Or "wise, first-class architect." We would say in today's English, "a top-notch general contractor."

d 3:12–13 Paul's language seems to be anticipating his next subject: the church as God's true temple. There is here an allusion to the temple of Solomon, which was built using gold, silver, and costly stones. Wisdom will build her house with divine substance (gold), redemption's fruit (silver), and transformed lives (costly stones). See 1 Chron. 22:14–16; 29:2. Wood, hay, and straw are emblems of the works of the flesh, the building materials of men, not of God. They grow up from the ground, which God cursed (Gen. 3:17). It is both quality and durability that God commends. Fire will cause the better material to glow brighter, but the inferior material will be consumed. How we build and what we build matters to God. Note that it is possible to build on the true foundation of Christ but with wrong materials. We need God's work done in God's way.

e 3:12–13 See Rom. 2:16; 1 Cor. 1:8; 4:5; 5:5; 2 Cor. 5:9–10; 2 Thess. 1:10.

f 3:16 Or "temple." The plural *you* (you all) shows that Paul is referring to the church, the body of believers, the holy dwelling place of God on earth. Later, in 1 Cor. 6:19, he refers to individual believers (our human bodies) as the dwelling place of God. Ten times in 1 Corinthians Paul uses the phrase "Don't you know" (or realize)?

g 3:16 God revealed his presence in the Old Testament temple by filling it with a cloud of

desecrates[a] God's inner sanctuary, God will desecrate him, for God's inner sanctuary is holy, and that is exactly who you are.

True Wisdom

[18] So why fool yourself and live under an illusion?[b] Make no mistake about it, if anyone thinks he is wise by the world's standards, he will be made wiser by being a fool for God![c] [19] For what the world says is wisdom is actually foolishness in God's eyes. As it is written:

> The cleverness of the know-it-alls
> > becomes the trap[d] that ensnares them.

[20] And again:

> The Lord sees right through
> > the clever reasonings of the wise
> > and knows that it's all a sham.[e]

[21] So don't be proud of your allegiance to any human leader. For actually, you already have everything! It has all been given for your benefit, [22] whether it is Paul or Apollos or Peter the Rock,[f] or whether it's the world[g] or life or death,[h] or whether it's the present or the future—everything belongs to you! [23] And now you are joined to the Messiah, who is joined to God.

---

glory. The New Testament inner sanctuary is now the church, where God dwells among us by his Spirit.

a 3:17 Or "If someone destroys God's temple, God will destroy him." The Aramaic uses the word deface or shatter.

b 3:18 For every verse that warns us of being deceived by others, there is verse to warn us about being self-deceived. Having a teachable heart and learning wisdom from above is the best way to guard from self-deception.

c 3:18 As translated from the Aramaic. The Greek is "If anyone thinks he is wise by the world's standards, he must first become ignorant [or silly] and then he can become truly wise."

d 3:19 The Greek word drassomai means "to close the fist on" or, by implication, "to trap" or "to firmly grasp" (a slippery object). See Job 5:13.

e 3:20 See Ps. 94:11.

f 3:22 Or "Cephas," which is the Latin spelling of keefa, the Aramaic word for "rock." God places all of his servants at the disposal of the church. Leaders come and go, but God's work continues. Every gift and every leader is meant to serve the body of Christ and bring her into the fullness of Christ.

g 3:22 The Aramaic can be translated "the universe." That is, the church is not of this world; it is to bring heaven's kingdom into the forefront of all the world. The wisdom of the world is subdued by God's wisdom given to the church.

h 3:22 That is, the pressures of life and death are beneath the rule of Christ in our hearts. See Rom. 14:9. The days of our present life, as well as the future glory, belong to us already. We are not victims in life, for as believers we share in the lordship of Christ today and forever.

Apostolic Ministry

4 So then you must perceive us—*not as leaders of factions*, but as servants[a] of the Anointed One, those who have been entrusted[b] with God's mysteries. [2] The most important quality of one entrusted with such secrets is that they are faithful and trustworthy. [3] But personally, I'm not the least bit concerned if I'm judged by you or any verdict I receive from any human court. In fact, I don't even assume to be my own judge, [4] even though my conscience is clear. But that doesn't mean I stand acquitted before the Lord,[c] for the only judge I care about is him!

[5] So resist the temptation to pronounce premature judgment on anything before the appointed time *when all will be fully revealed*. Instead, wait until the Lord makes his appearance, for he will bring all that is hidden in darkness to light[d] and unveil every secret motive of everyone's heart. Then, *when the whole truth is known*, each will receive praise from God.[e]

The Ministry of True Apostles

[6] Dear brothers and sisters, I've been referring allusively to myself and Apollos in order to illustrate what I've been saying. It is futile to move beyond what is written in the Scriptures and be inflated with self-importance by following and promoting one leader in competition with another. [7] For what makes a distinction between you and someone else?[f] And what do you have that grace has not given you?[g] And if you received it *as a gift*, why do you boast as though there is something special about you?[h]

---

a 4:1 Paul uses an unusual Greek word, *huperetes*, which means "subordinate" or "personal assistant." The compound word *huperetes* literally means "under-rowers," and it is used in classical Greek to describe those who sit on benches in the lower parts of the ship rowing. Apostolic ministry does not mean that an apostle is seen as important and in first place, but as one who will often be in a hidden role of moving a church and region forward as a subordinate of our captain, Jesus Christ.

b 4:1 Or "stewards" ("estate managers," "trustees"). Paul is here referring to the apostles who helped establish and set in order the church at Corinth.

c 4:4 Both here and in v. 5, the Aramaic can be translated "Lord Yahweh."

d 4:5 The Aramaic can be translated "He will pour light upon the hidden things of darkness."

e 4:5 The clear inference is that God will bring to light the secret motives of love, faithfulness, righteousness, kindness, etc.—not only evil motives, but the pure motives of believers. When the Lord judges his godly lovers, their secret devotion and sacrifices will all be brought into the light and God will praise them for their faithful love. The reward of eternity will be that God affirms them. The word for "praise" can actually be translated, "thanks from God." Can you imagine the day coming when God praises his faithful servants? See also 1 John 4:17–19.

f 4:7 Or "Who sees anything different in you?" The answer to this rhetorical question is "God."

g 4:7 Or "What do you have that you have not received?" The answer to this rhetorical question is "Nothing."

h 4:7 Or "Why do you boast as though you did not receive it because of grace?" The church at

⁸Oh, I know, you already have all you need!ᵃ Since when did you become so content and rich without us? You've already crowned yourselves as royalty, reigning on your thrones, leaving us *lowly apostles* far behind!ᵇ How I wish indeed that you really were reigning as kings already, for that would mean we would be reigning as kings alongside of you.ᶜ

Apostolic Model of Ministry

⁹It seems to me that God has appointed us apostles to be at the end of the line. We are like those on display at the end of the procession, as doomed gladiators soon to be killed. We have become a theatrical spectacle to all creation, both to people and to angels. ¹⁰We are fools for Christ, but you are wise in Christ! We are the frail; you are the powerful. You are celebrated;ᵈ we are humiliated. ¹¹If you could see us now, you'd find that we are hungry and thirsty, poorly clothed,ᵉ brutally treated,ᶠ and with no roof over our heads.ᵍ ¹²We work hard, toiling with our own hands. When people abuse and insult us, we respond with a blessing, and when severely persecuted, we endure it with patience. ¹³When we are slandered incessantly, we always answer gently,ʰ ready to reconcile. Even now, in the world's opinion, we are nothing but filthⁱ and the lowest scum.

A Father's Warning

¹⁴I'm not writing this to embarrass you or to shame you, but to correct you

---

Corinth was split into different factions, each following a different leader. Apparently, each clique thought they had the truth because they had a more anointed leader. But Paul exhorts them not to put their confidence in their hero-leader, because each leader is nothing more than a servant who receives God's grace to minister according to his or her gift. No leader has a greater status than another.

ᵃ 4:8 The Greek text uses a metaphor of overfed farmyard animals. They were stuffed with self-importance.

ᵇ 4:8 See Rev. 3:17. A smug, religious self-satisfaction is to have no place in our hearts. We must continually thirst for more of God. We have all things in Christ, but not all that he has given us has filled our hearts. Though we have every blessing, we must walk it out in our daily lives. With biting irony Paul uncovers their pride in thinking they have left the poor apostles behind and have become independent—greater and with more kingdom wealth than they. The deprivations and struggles of the apostles were looked down upon by the Corinthians. See also 2 Cor. 11:12–12:1. Although v. 8 is in the form of posing rhetorical questions (irony), it is possible to translate it this way: "You have already become full [like at a feast] and fully satisfied. You are already suddenly rich. You suddenly reign as kings apart from us."

ᶜ 4:8 The Aramaic continues the irony. "Come, share your royal reign with us so we too can rule with you!"

ᵈ 4:10 Or "famous."

ᵉ 4:11 Or "wearing rags" (tattered and threadbare).

ᶠ 4:11 Or "brutally beaten" (hit with fists). See Matt. 26:67; 2 Cor. 11:26.

ᵍ 4:11 Or "homeless."

ʰ 4:13 Or "We appeal to them" (directly).

ⁱ 4:13 Or "scapegoats."

as the children I love. ¹⁵ For although you could have countless babysitters*a* in Christ *telling you what you're doing wrong*, you don't have many fathers *who correct you in love*. But I'm a true father to you, for I became your father when I gave you the gospel and brought you into union with Jesus, the Anointed One. ¹⁶ So I encourage you, my children, to follow the example that I live before you.*b*

¹⁷ That's why I've sent my dear son Timothy, whom I love. He is faithful to the Lord Yahweh*c* and will remind you of how I conduct myself as one who lives in union with Jesus, the Anointed One, and of the teachings that I bring to every church everywhere.

¹⁸ There are some among you who have exalted themselves as if I were not coming back to you. ¹⁹ But I will come soon, if it pleases the Lord, and I will find out not only what these arrogant ones are saying, but also if they have power to back up their words! ²⁰ For the kingdom realm of God comes with power, not simply impressive words. ²¹ So which would you prefer? Shall I come carrying the rod of authority to discipline or with an embrace in love with a gentle spirit?

Immorality in the Church

5 ¹⁻² It's been widely reported that there is gross sexual immorality among you—the kind of immorality that's so revolting it's not even tolerated by the social norms of unbelievers.*d* Are you proud of the fact that one of your men is having sex with his stepmother?*e* Shouldn't this heartbreaking scandal bring you to your knees in tears? You must remove the offender from among you!

³ Even though I am physically far away from you, my spirit is present with you. And as one who is present with you, I have already evaluated and judged the perpetrator. ⁴ So *call a meeting*, and when you gather together in the name of our Lord Jesus, and you know my spirit is present with you in the infinite power of our Lord Jesus,*f* ⁵ release this man over to Satan*g* for the destruction

---

a 4:15 Or "guardians" (or "tutors").

b 4:16 Or "imitate me." The Aramaic can be translated "I want you to resemble me." Paul is saying, "Prove your parentage by your conduct; follow me like a father."

c 4:17 As translated from the Aramaic. The Greek is "He is faithful [dependable] in the Lord."

d 5:1–2 Or "pagans" (gentiles).

e 5:1–2 Or "his father's wife." This incestuous relationship was forbidden by the law. See Lev. 18:8. The sin is more than the illicit acts of this unnamed man, but the tolerance of a church that refused to correct and deal with the sin in their midst. Indeed, this chapter implies that the church was somewhat smug and arrogant ("puffed up") over conduct that violated sensibility.

f 5:4 God had given Paul exceptional ability to have his spirit present, along with the power of God, in their meetings together.

g 5:5 Satan means "accusing adversary." When one is put out of the fellowship of the church family, the accuser has access to harass and oppress. There is a blessed protection in the fellowship of God's people, for the Lord is present with us when we gather in his name.

of his *rebellious* flesh, in hope that his spirit may be rescued and restored in the day of the Lord. *a*

⁶Boasting *over your tolerance of sin* is inappropriate. Don't you understand that even a small compromise with sin permeates the entire fellowship, just as a little leaven permeates a batch of dough? ⁷So remove every trace of your "leaven" of compromise with sin so that you might become new and pure again. For indeed, you are clean *b* because Christ, our Passover Lamb, has been sacrificed for us. *c* ⁸So now we can celebrate our continual feast, not with the old "leaven," the yeast of wickedness or bitterness, but we will feast on the freshly baked bread of innocence and holiness. *d*

Correcting a Misunderstanding

⁹I wrote you *in my previous letter* *e* asking you not to associate with those who practice sexual immorality. *f* ¹⁰Yet in no way was I referring to avoiding contact with unbelievers who are immoral, or greedy, or swindlers, or those who worship other gods—for that would mean you'd have to isolate yourself from the world entirely! *g* ¹¹But now I'm writing to you so that you would exclude from your fellowship anyone who calls himself a fellow believer and practices sexual immorality, or is consumed with greed, or is an idolater, or is verbally abusive or a drunkard or a

---

a 5:5 Or "Turn this man over to Satan for the destruction of your fleshly works so that your spirit may be saved in the day of the Lord." Verses 3–5 comprise one long, complicated Greek sentence. Many see this difficult passage as a prescription for ex-communication from the church. Aramaic speakers see in this passage the words "Turn him over to the accuser," as a figure of speech meaning "Let him suffer the consequences of his actions." We have similar sayings in English. "Let him stew in his own juices." Or "Give him enough rope to hang himself." Or "Let him learn his lesson the hard way." Regardless, it is not a light thing to be handed over to Satan. Apparently this man learned his lesson and repented, for Paul instructs the Corinthians in his second letter to forgive and comfort him. See 2 Cor. 2:6–11.

b 5:7 Or "unleavened." Paul uses encouragement here to stir them to embrace a lifestyle that is already theirs. We are all made "clean" by the blood of the Lamb.

c 5:7 Verses 6 and 7 contain the interesting metaphor of yeast and its effect on a batch of dough. It is literally "Don't you know that a little yeast affects the whole batch of dough? You must clean out the old yeast so that you can become a new batch of dough. For you are without yeast, because Christ, our Passover Lamb, has been sacrificed." Leaven is most often used as a metaphor for corrupting influence, especially false teaching.

d 5:8 As translated from the Aramaic. The Greek is "the unleavened bread of sincerity and unhidden reality."

e 5:9 Paul is referring to a previous letter to the Corinthians, known as the lost letter, because a manuscript has never been found.

f 5:9 In the Greek culture of that day, the word *pornos* referred to male prostitution or paramour, although in this context it is not limited to one form of sexual immorality but includes all sexual acts forbidden by Scripture.

g 5:10 Or "leave the world." Our Lord Jesus has commanded his disciples to go into all the world and preach the gospel. We do not isolate ourselves from unbelievers but seek opportunities to share the gospel with them.

swindler. Don't mingle with them or even have a meal with someone like that. [12-13] What right do I have to pronounce judgment on unbelievers? That's God's responsibility. But those who are inside the church family are our responsibility to discern and judge. So it's your duty to remove that wicked one from among you. [a]

Lawsuits between Believers

6 Furthermore, how dare you take a fellow believer to court! It is wrong to drag him before the unrighteous to settle a legal dispute. Isn't it better to take him before God's holy believers to settle the matter? [2] Don't you realize that we, the holy ones, will judge the universe? [b] If the unbelieving world is under your jurisdiction, you should be fully competent to settle these trivial lawsuits among yourselves. [3] For surely you know that we will one day judge [c] angels, let alone these everyday matters. [4] Don't you realize that you are bringing your issues before civil judges appointed by people who have no standing within the church? [d] [5] What a shame that there is not one within the church [e] who has *the spirit of* wisdom who could arbitrate these disputes and reconcile the offended parties! [6] *It's not right for* a believer to sue a fellow believer—and especially to bring it before the unbelievers.

[7] Don't you realize that when you drag another believer into court you're providing the evidence that you are already defeated? Wouldn't it be better to accept the fact that someone is trying to cheat and take advantage of you, and simply *choose the high road*? *At times it is better to* just accept injustice and even to let someone take advantage of you, *rather than to expose our conflicts publicly before unbelievers.* [f] [8] But instead you keep cheating and doing wrong to your brothers and sisters, *and then request that unbelievers render their judgment!*

---

a 5:12–13 The Aramaic can be translated "Remove wickedness from among you." See Deut. 17:7. The local church has the authority to discipline erring believers who persist in sin. Under the old covenant, that discipline was physical (execution by stoning), but under the new covenant, church discipline is spiritual. See Matt. 18:15–17.

b 6:2 As translated from the Aramaic.

c 6:3 The meaning of this is that believers will one day govern over and judge the angelic realm. Our position in Christ is higher than the angels. They are servants; we are sons. Sons rule over servants.

d 6:4 The Greek verb *kathizete* can be interpreted as an ironic imperative instead of a question. This would change the verse to read "Appoint as judges those who have no standing in the church to arbitrate ordinary lawsuits." However, it is more likely a question since *kathizete* is found at the end of the sentence.

e 6:5 This chapter is loaded with irony. Paul here argues that the church must have someone who could discern, sift, weigh, and judge these everyday matters within the body. The irony is that the word for church is *ekklēsia*, which means "governing body," similar to a senate. It was a Greek term used for the gathering of a governing body to promote the welfare of a city. To be a part of an *ekklēsia* (church) implies that there is wisdom and leadership among the group to govern and bring blessing to a city.

f 6:7 Paul does not mean that we should passively acquiesce to abuse from others. Rather,

Christian Morality and the Kingdom Realm of God

[9] Surely you must know that people who practice evil cannot possess God's kingdom realm. Stop being deceived![a] People who continue to engage in sexual immorality, idolatry, adultery, sexual perversion,[b] homosexuality, [10] fraud, greed, drunkenness, verbal abuse,[c] or extortion—these will not inherit God's kingdom realm. [11] It's true that some of you once lived in those lifestyles, but now you have been purified from sin,[d] made holy, and given a perfect standing before God—all because of the power of the name of the Lord Jesus, the Messiah, and through our union with the Spirit of our God.

[12] It's true that our freedom allows us to do anything, but that doesn't mean that everything we do is good for us. I'm free to do as I choose, but I choose to never be enslaved to anything. [13] Some have said, "I eat to live and I live to eat!" But God will do away with it all. The body was not created for illicit sex, but to serve and worship our Lord Jesus, who can fill the body with himself.

[14] Now the God who raised up our Lord from the grave will awaken and raise us up through his mighty power!

The Body of Christ

[15] Don't you know that your bodies belong to Christ as his body parts? Should one presume to take the members of Christ's body and make them into members of a harlot? Absolutely not! [16] Aren't you aware of the fact that when anyone sleeps with a prostitute he becomes a part of her, and she becomes a part of him? For it has been declared:

> The two become a single body.[e]

[17] But the one who joins[f] himself to the Lord is mingled into one spirit with him. [18] *This is why* you must keep running away from sexual immorality. For every other sin a person commits is external to the body, but immorality involves sinning against your own body.

---

he brings before us a higher principle: It is better to suffer personal injustice than to bring disgrace to Christ by bringing our conflicts before unbelievers. The Spirit of wisdom (Eph. 1:17) is one of the graces that God pours out upon his people. This anointing of wisdom will empower the body of Christ to bring justice and righteousness into our churches. Most scholars conclude that these disputes were not criminal but issues related to business, personal property, inheritances, default in loan payments to other believers, and the like. See also Matt. 5:25–26; 18:15–17.

a 6:9 Or "Make no mistake!"
b 6:9 Or "catamites" or "pederasts" or "child molesters."
c 6:10 Or "slanderers."
d 6:11 Or "washed clean."
e 6:16 See Gen. 2:24. Paul is teaching that sexual intercourse causes an interpersonal union that goes beyond a physical relationship.
f 6:17 The Greek verb *kallaō* means "to unite," "to knit or weld together," "to mingle," or "to join together," and "to make two into one."

[19] Have you forgotten that your body is now the sacred temple of the Spirit of Holiness, who lives in you? You don't belong to yourself any longer, for the gift of God, the Holy Spirit, lives inside your sanctuary.[a] [20] You were God's expensive purchase, paid for with tears of blood,[b] so by all means, then, use your body[c] to bring glory to God!

Sex and Marriage

7 Now for my response concerning the issues you've asked me to address. *You wrote saying,* "It is proper for a man to live in celibacy."[d] [2] Perhaps. But because of the danger of immorality,[e] each husband should have sexual intimacy with his wife and each wife should have sexual intimacy with her husband. [3] A husband has the responsibility of meeting the sexual needs of his wife, and likewise a wife to her husband.[f] [4] Neither the husband nor the wife have exclusive rights to their own bodies, but those rights are to be surrendered to the other. [5] So don't continue to refuse your spouse those rights, except perhaps by mutual agreement for a specified time so that you can both be devoted to prayer.[g] And then you should resume your physical pleasure so that the Adversary cannot take advantage of you because of the desires of your body.[h] [6] I'm not giving you a divine command, but my godly advice.[i] [7] I would wish that all of you could live *unmarried*, just as I do.[j] Yet I understand that we are all decidedly different, with each having a special grace for one thing or another.[k]

[8] So let me say to the unmarried and those who have lost their spouses, it is fine for you to remain single as I am. [9] But if you have no power over your

---

a 6:19 Or "the in-you Holy Spirit." The Greek word Paul uses for "temple" is actually *naos*, "sanctuary." See Eph. 2:19–22; 1 Peter 2:4–5.
b 6:20 As translated from the Aramaic.
c 6:20 The Aramaic and the Textus Receptus adds "and in your spirit."
d 7:1 Or "not to marry." The Aramaic can be translated "It is proper for a husband not to have intimacy with his wife at times." Paul now responds to a series of questions posed by the church of Corinth.
e 7:2 Or "because of immoralities" or "because of prostitutions."
f 7:3 The Aramaic (and a few of the oldest Greek manuscripts) can be translated "The husband should pay back the love he owes to his wife and the wife to her husband."
g 7:5 Some later manuscripts add "and fasting."
h 7:5 Or "[lack of] self-control."
i 7:6 Or "concession." There are at least two ways this could be interpreted: (1) Paul is saying that to be married is advisable but not commanded. This seems the most likely because of v. 7. (2) Paul is referring to the preceding paragraph, especially regarding the advice of abstinence during seasons of prayer.
j 7:7 The Aramaic can be translated "I wish that all humanity lived in purity as I do." It is possible that Paul was once married and became a widower. Some suggest he had to have been married at the time he persecuted the early church, since only married men could be part of the Sanhedrin and cast a vote. However, there is evidence that some Jewish leaders during his time were committed to celibacy. See Acts 26:10.
k 7:7 Both being single and being married require a special grace from God.

passions, then you should go ahead and marry, for marriage is far better than a continual battle with lust. [a]

Divorce

[10] And to those who are married, I give this charge—which is not mine, but the Lord's [b]—that the wife should not depart from her husband. [11] But if she does, then she should either remain unmarried or reconcile with her husband. And a husband must not divorce his wife. [12] To the rest I say, which is not a saying of the Lord, if a brother has an unbelieving wife and she is content to live with him, he should not divorce her. [13] And if a woman has a husband who is not a believer and he is content to live with her, she should not divorce him. [14] For the unbelieving husband has been made holy by his believing wife. And the unbelieving wife has been made holy by her believing husband *by virtue of his or her sacred union to a believer.* [c] Otherwise, the children from this union would be unclean, but in fact, they are holy. [d] [15] But if the unbelieving spouse wants a divorce, then let it be so. In this situation the believing spouse is not bound [e] *to the marriage*, for God has called us to live in peace.

[16] And wives, for all you know you could one day lead your husband to salvation. Or husbands, how do you know for sure that you could not one day lead your wife to salvation? [f]

Living the Life God Has Assigned

[17] May all believers continue to live the wonderful lives God has called them to live, according to what he assigns for each person, for this is what I teach

---

a 7:9 Or "better than to have a fire ever smoldering within them."

b 7:10 Paul is not stating that there is an opposition between what he says, in his teaching as an apostle, and what the Lord says. He is taking our Lord's own teaching from Mark 10:5–12 and bringing it to the people.

c 7:14 Or "The unbelieving husband is made holy because of the wife, and the unbelieving wife because of her husband." By implication, Paul is making the point that in marriages where one is a believer and one an unbeliever, the spouses should remain together, for the righteous faith of a believer makes the marriage holy. Apparently, because of their desire to serve Christ, some of the Corinthians who had pagan spouses thought it would be best to divorce their spouses and find believing ones. Paul corrects that error and affirms the marriage covenant.

d 7:14 In the concepts of the Old Testament, the entire family is in covenant with God. Therefore, the children of even one believing parent are set apart for God.

e 7:15 Or "enslaved."

f 7:16 Translators are almost equally divided over making this an optimistic possibility versus a pessimistic one. If the pessimistic choice of grammar is chosen, the verse could be translated "Wife, how do you know that you will save your husband? And husband, how do you know that you will save your wife?" Which would infer "It's no use hanging on to a marriage with no hope of converting the unbelieving spouse, for how do you know it would ever happen?" Though both are possible, the translator has chosen the optimistic possibility.

to believers[a] everywhere. [18] If when you were called *to follow Jesus* you were circumcised, it would be futile to try to undo the circumcision. And if you were called while yet uncircumcised, there is no need to be circumcised. [19] Your identity *before God* has nothing to do with circumcision or uncircumcision.[b] What really matters is following God's commandments. [20] So everyone should continue to live *faithful* in the situation of life in which they were called *to follow Jesus*.[c] [21] Were you a slave when you heard the call *to follow Jesus*? Don't let that concern you. Even if you can gain your freedom, make the most of the opportunity. [22] For truly, if you are called to a life-union with the Lord, you are already a free man! And those who were called to follow Jesus when they were free are now the Messiah's slaves. [23] Since a great price was paid for your redemption, stop having the mind-set of a slave. [24] Brothers and sisters, we must remain in close communion with God, no matter what our situation was when we were first called to follow Jesus.

Instructions to the Single and Widowed

[25] Now let me address the issue of singleness.[d] I must confess, I have no command to give you that comes directly from the Lord. But let me share my thoughts on the matter, as coming from one who has experienced the mercy[e] of the Lord to keep me faithful to him. [26] Because of the severe pressure we are in,[f] I recommend you remain as you are. [27] If you are married, stay in the marriage. If you are single,[g] don't rush into marriage. [28] But if you do get married, you haven't sinned.[h] It's just that I would want to spare you the problems you'll face with the extra challenges of being married.

[29] My friends, what I mean is this. The urgency of our times mean that from now on, those who have wives should live as though without them. [30] And those who weep should forget their tears. And those who rejoice will have no

---

a 7:17 Or "in all the churches."

b 7:19 Or "Circumcision is nothing and uncircumcision is nothing." No doubt this statement was a tremendous shock to the Corinthians. To the Jews it would be earthshaking, for circumcision was the outward sign of God's covenant with Abraham and his descendants. Paul, as elsewhere, places the emphasis not on outer things but on an inward transformation that longs to please God.

c 7:20 Paul is teaching that no matter what a person's situation is in life, the real change needed is not just in circumstances, but in a heart that is willing to be faithful to God in all things. We often wish we could be in different circumstances instead of looking for opportunities to serve God where we are.

d 7:25 Or "virgins."

e 7:25 Or "one who has been mercied."

f 7:26 Or "impending crisis." Some scholars believe this severe pressure could refer to the great famine of AD 51, while others view it as imminent persecution.

g 7:27 The Aramaic can be translated "If you are divorced, don't seek marriage."

h 7:28 Or "If you [men] do get married it is not sin, and if a [female] virgin marries, she hasn't sinned." The translation combines both statements with brothers and sisters.

time to celebrate. And those who purchase items will have no time to enjoy them. [31] We are to live as those who live in the world system but are not absorbed by it, for the world as we know it is quickly passing away. [32] Because of this, we need to live as free from anxiety as possible.

For a single man is focused on the things of the Lord and how he may please him. [33] But a married man is pulled in two directions, for he is concerned about both the things of God and the things of the world in order to please [a] his wife. [34] And the single woman is focused on the things of the Lord so she can be holy both in body and spirit. But a married woman is concerned about the things of the world and how she may please her husband. [35] I am trying to help you and make things easier for you and not make things difficult, but so that you would have undistracted devotion, serving the Lord constantly with an undivided heart.

[36] However, if a man has decided to serve God as a single person, yet changes his mind and finds himself in love with a woman, although he never intended to marry, let him go ahead and marry her; it is not a sin to do so. [b] [37] On the other hand, if a man stands firm in his heart to remain single, and is under no compulsion to get married but has control over his passions and is determined to remain celibate, he has chosen well. [38] So then, the one who marries his fiancée does well and the one who chooses not to marry her does better.

Remarriage

[39] A wife is bound *by the marriage covenant* as long as her husband is living. But if the husband dies, she is free to marry again as she desires—but, of course, he should be a believer in the Lord. [40] However, in my opinion (and I think that I too have the Spirit of God), she would be happier if she remained single.

Love Is Greater Than Knowledge

8 Now let me address the issue of food offered in sacrifice to idols. It seems that everyone believes his own opinion is right on this matter. [c] How easily we get puffed up over our opinions! But love builds up the structure *of our new life.* [d] [2] If anyone thinks of himself as a know-it-all, he still has a lot to

---

a 7:33 The Aramaic can be translated "to beautify."

b 7:36 This is arguably one of the most difficult verses to translate in all the New Testament. You will find many possible translations and interpretations of this passage, which is loaded with cultural implications for the first-century church. Consulting a variety of translations is recommended.

c 8:1 Or "we all have knowledge."

d 8:1 That is, knowledge may make a person look important, but it is only through love that we reach our full maturity. It is simply "Love builds up." It builds up our lives, our churches, our families, and others. Love is the most powerful substance for building what will last forever.

learn. ³But if a person passionately loves God, he will possess the knowledge of God. *ª*

⁴Concerning food sacrificed as offerings to idols, we all know that an idol is nothing, for there is no God but one. *ᵇ* ⁵Although there may be many so-called gods in this world, and in heaven there may be many "gods," "lords," and "masters," ⁶yet for us there is only one God—the Father. He is the source of all things, and our lives are lived for him. And there is one Lord, Jesus, the Anointed One, through whom we and all things exist.

⁷But not everyone has this revelation. For some were formerly idolaters, who consider idols as real and living. That's why they consider the food offered to that "god" as defiled. And their weak consciences become defiled if they eat it. ⁸Yes, we know that what you eat will not bring you closer to God. You are no better if you don't eat certain foods and no better if you do. ⁹But you must be careful that the liberty you exercise in eating food offered to idols doesn't offend the weak believers. ¹⁰For if a believer with a weak conscience sees you, who have a greater understanding, dining in an idol's temple, won't this be a temptation to him to violate his own conscience *ᶜ* and eat food offered to idols? ¹¹So, in effect, by exercising your understanding of freedom, you have ruined this weak believer, *ᵈ* a brother for whom Christ has died! ¹²And when you offend weaker believers by wounding their consciences in this way, you also offend *ᵉ* the Anointed One!

¹³So I conclude that if my eating certain food deeply offends *ᶠ* my brother and hinders his advance in Christ, I will never eat it again. I don't want to be guilty of causing my brother or sister to be wounded and defeated.

Paul's Apostolic Freedom

9 Am I not completely free and unrestrained? *Absolutely!* Am I not an apostle? *Of course!* Haven't I had a personal encounter with our Jesus face-to-face—

---

a 8:3 Explicit in the Aramaic and implied in the Greek, which can also be translated, "is known [acknowledged] by God."

b 8:4 See Deut. 6:4.

c 8:10 Or "have his conscience built up." Ironically, this is the same Greek word Paul used in v. 1 for love "builds up." The implication is that the weak believer will be emboldened to violate his conscience by watching a more mature believer freely eating food offered to idols.

d 8:11 This is because the "freedom" of the mature could lead the immature believer back into what he feels is idol worship.

e 8:12 That is, "They bring an offense against the teachings of Christ," as translated from the Aramaic. The Greek is "When you sin against a weaker believer . . . you also sin against Christ."

f 8:13 The Greek word *skandalizō* (from which we get our English word *scandal*) means "to throw a snare in front of someone purposely to trip them up."

and continue to see him? *ᵃ Emphatically yes!* Aren't you all the proof of my ministry in the Lord?*ᵇ Certainly!* ²If others do not recognize me as their apostle, at least you are bound to do so, for now your lives are joined to the Lord. You are the *living proof,* the certificate of my apostleship.

³So to those who want to continually criticize my apostolic ministry, here's my statement of defense.*ᶜ* ⁴Don't we apostles have the right to be supported financially?*ᵈ* ⁵Don't we have the right to travel accompanied by our believing wives *and be supported as a couple,* as do the other apostles, such as Peter the Rock and the Lord's brothers?*ᵉ* ⁶*Of course we do!ᶠ* Or is it only Barnabas and I who have no right to stop working for a living?*ᵍ*

Responsibility to Financially Support God's Servants

⁷Who serves in the military at his own expense? Who plants a vineyard and does not enjoy the grapes for himself? Who would nurture and shepherd a flock and never get to drink its fresh milk? ⁸Am I merely giving you my own opinions, or does the Torah teach the same things? ⁹For it is written in the law of Moses:

> You should never put a muzzle over the mouth of an ox
> while he is treading out the grain. *ʰ*

Tell me, is God only talking about oxen here? ¹⁰Doesn't he also give us this principle so that we won't withhold support from his workers?*ⁱ* It was written

---

a 9:1 As implied by the perfect active indicative. Paul has seen the Lord, but the effects of that "seeing" continue on in full force (i.e., "I continue to have him in my sight").

b 9:1 These four forceful rhetorical questions are emphatic in the Greek construction, which means they each demand an answer in the affirmative. Although some commentators view these four questions as qualifications of an apostle, there is no indication that this is indeed the purpose of his questions. Paul is defending his apostleship, not listing qualifications of apostles. The seven arguments he makes in defense of his apostleship are the following: (1) He enjoys freedom from all bondage, both from the world and religion (v. 1). (2) He had face-to-face encounters with Jesus (v. 1; 15:8). (3) The formation of the church of Corinth validates his apostleship (vv. 1–2; Acts 18). (4) His unselfish lifestyle resulted in not demanding to be paid for his ministry (vv. 3–15). (5) He was given a divine stewardship (vv. 16–18). (6) He was determined to win everyone through the gospel of Christ (vv. 19–23). (7) He lived a disciplined life in order to succeed in the obstacle course of ministry for Christ (vv. 24–27).

c 9:3 The Aramaic is quite blunt: "Those who judge me I rebuke in [the] spirit."

d 9:4 Or "to eat and drink," a euphemism to describe financial support.

e 9:5 See Mark 6:3; John 2:12.

f 9:6 Made explicit from the Greek disjunctive particle.

g 9:6 Apostles were usually cared for and financially supported by the church so they didn't have to engage in secular work for their wages, although Paul and Barnabas, on different occasions, supported themselves without being a burden to the congregations (see vv. 12–15).

h 9:9 See Deut. 25:4; 1 Tim. 5:18.

i 9:10 Or "Doesn't he say this for our sake [as apostles]?"

so that we would understand that the one *spiritually* "plowing" and *spiritually* "treading out the grain" also labors with the expectation of enjoying the harvest. [11] So, if we've sowed many spiritual gifts[a] among you, is it too much to expect to reap material gifts from you? [12] And if you have supported others, don't we rightfully deserve this privilege even more?

But as you know, we haven't used that right. Instead, we have continued to support ourselves[b] so that we would never be a hindrance to the spread of the gospel of Christ. [13] Don't you know that the priests[c] employed in sacred duty in the temple[d] are provided for by temple resources? And the priests who serve at the altar receive a portion of the offerings?[e] [14] In the same way, the Lord has directed those who proclaim the gospel to receive their living by the gospel. As for me, I've preferred to never use any of these rights for myself. [15] And keep in mind that I'm not writing all this because I'm hinting that you should support me.

Paul Renounces His Rights for the Sake of the Gospel

Actually, I'd rather die than to have anyone rob me of this joyous reason for boasting![f] [16] For you see, even though I proclaim the good news, I can't take the credit for my labors, for I am compelled to fulfill my duty by completing this work. It would be agony to me if I did not constantly preach the gospel! [17] If it were my own idea to preach as a way to make a living, I would expect to be paid. Since it's not my idea but God's, who commissioned me, I am entrusted with the stewardship of the gospel *whether or not I'm paid.* [18] So then, where is my reward? It is found in continually depositing the good news *into people's hearts,* without obligation, free of charge, and not insisting on my rights to be financially supported.

Paul, a Servant to All

[19] Now, even though I am free from obligations to others,[g] I *joyfully* make myself a servant to all in order to win as many converts as possible. [20] I became Jewish to the Jewish people in order to win them *to the Messiah.* I became like one under

---

a 9:11 The Greek word *pneumatikos* is often used for spiritual gifts, not just spiritual blessings. See 1 Cor. 12:1; 14:1. The Aramaic is explicit: "Since we have planted the Spirit in you, we should harvest financially from you."

b 9:12 Or "We have endured all things."

c 9:13 Or "those who work with sacred things."

d 9:13 The Aramaic word for *temple* is "house of blessing."

e 9:13 Or "what is offered on the altar." See Lev. 6:9–11, 19.

f 9:15 Paul uses the rhetorical device of abruptly breaking off his statement ("I would rather die than—"). This is known as an aposiopesis, meant to intensify the importance of having the joy of boasting in the fact that Paul provided for his own needs in ministry.

g 9:19 That is, Paul lived free from the obligation of pleasing those who paid him a salary. He lived by faith, yet he still became the servant of all.

the law to gain the people who were stuck under the law, even though I myself am not under the law. [21] And to those who are without the Jewish laws, I became like them, as one without the Jewish laws, in order to win them, although I'm not outside the law of God but under the law of Christ. [22] I became "weak" to the weak to win the weak. I have adapted to the culture of every place I've gone [a] so that I could more easily win people to Christ. [23] I've done all this so that I would become God's partner for the sake of the gospel. [b]

Paul's Disciplined Lifestyle

[24] Isn't it obvious that all runners on the racetrack [c] keep on running to win, but only one receives the victor's prize? Yet each one of you must run the race to be victorious. [25] A true athlete will be disciplined in every respect, practicing constant self-control in order to win a laurel wreath that quickly withers. But we run our race to win a victor's crown that will last forever. [26] For that reason, I don't run just for exercise [d] or box like one throwing aimless punches, [27] but I train like a champion athlete. I subdue my body [e] and get it under my control, so that after preaching the good news to others I myself won't be disqualified.

Learning from Israel's Failures

10 My dear fellow believers, you need to understand that all of our Jewish ancestors *who walked through a wilderness long ago* were under the glory cloud [f] and passed through the waters of the sea on both sides. [2] They were all baptized [g] into the cloud of glory, into the fellowship of Moses, and into the sea. [3] They all ate the same heavenly manna [h] [4] and drank water from the same

---

a 9:22 Or "I have become all things to all different kinds of people"; that is, he adapted culturally wherever he ministered.

b 9:23 Paul is declaring the five motivating principles for his ministry: (1) Always start by finding common ground with those you want to reach. (2) Avoid projecting to others that you are a know-it-all. (3) Accept everyone regardless of his or her issues. (4) Be sensitive to the culture of others. (5) Use every opportunity to share the good news of Jesus Christ with people.

c 9:24 Or "the runners in a stadium." This refers to the Pan-Hellenic stadium near Corinth where the Isthmian games were held.

d 9:26 Or "I don't run aimlessly." That is, Paul ran with his eyes on the goal of ending well.

e 9:27 Or "I beat my body black and blue." This is an obvious metaphor of placing the desires of one's body as second place to the desires of the Holy Spirit. See Rom. 8:13.

f 10:1 The cloud of glory is a picture of the Holy Spirit.

g 10:2 Or "baptized themselves." There are at least eight distinct baptisms mentioned in the New Testament: (1) the baptism of John (John 1:31–33), (2) Christ's baptism (John 3:22), (3) a baptism of suffering (Luke 12:50), (4) a baptism into the cloud of glory (1 Cor. 10:2), (5) a baptism into the sea (a picture of redemption—1 Cor. 10:2), (6) believer's baptism in water (Matt. 28:19; Acts 2:38–41), (7) baptism into Christ and into his body (1 Cor. 12:13; Gal. 3:27), and (8) baptism in the Holy Spirit (Matt. 3:11–14; Acts 1:5; 11:16; 19:2–3). See also Heb. 6:2.

h 10:3 Or "spiritual food." See Ex. 16; Ps. 78:24–25; John 6:31–48.

spiritual rock[a] that traveled with them—and that Rock[b] was Christ himself. [5] Yet God was not pleased with most of them, and their dead bodies were scattered around the wilderness.[c]

[6] Now, all these things serve as types and pictures for us—lessons that teach us not to fail in the same way by callously craving worthless things [7] and practicing idolatry, as some of them did. For it is written:

The people settled in to their unrestrained revelry, with feasting and drinking, then they rose up and became wildly out of control![d]

[8] Neither should we commit sexual immorality, as some of them did, which caused the death of twenty-three thousand[e] on a single day. [9] Nor should we ever provoke the Lord,[f] as some of them did by putting him to outrageous tests that resulted in their death from snakebites day after day.[g] [10] And we must not embrace their ways by complaining—grumbling with discontent, as many of them did,[h] and were killed by the destroyer![i]

[11] All the tests they endured on their way through the wilderness are a symbolic picture, an example that provides us with a warning so that we can learn through what they experienced. For we live in a time when the purpose of all the ages past is now completing its goal within us.[j] [12] So beware if you think it could never happen to you, lest your pride becomes your downfall.

The Way of Escape

[13] We all experience[k] times of testing,[l] which is normal for every human being.

---

a 10:4 See Ex. 17:6; Num. 20:7–21; Ps. 78:15.
b 10:4 Christ is the anointed Rock of truth and the Rock of shelter. The people drank of his living water. The miracle of the Rock of Christ provided them with water wherever they journeyed. He is a fountain that never runs dry, for he will never leave us alone in a wilderness.
c 10:5 The Aramaic can be translated "They failed [the test] in the wilderness."
d 10:7 Although most translations have "They rose up to play," this is misleading. To translate the Greek word *paizō* in this context is extremely difficult. However, because of the next verse, it appears Paul is saying that they rose up after feasting and drinking to fall into immorality. Although *paizō* could be translated "They rose up to sport" or "They rose up to hilarity," it seems that sexual immorality is the more likely inference here. The Aramaic word can be translated "carouse."
e 10:8 Some manuscripts have "twenty-four thousand." See Num. 25:9.
f 10:9 Some manuscripts have "Christ."
g 10:9 See Num. 21:5–9.
h 10:10 In the Pentateuch there are at least sixteen occasions of the people of Israel murmuring. Believers today have even more spiritual blessings than Israel experienced in the wilderness, which would make our complaining even more odious.
i 10:10 Or "the destroying angel."
j 10:11 As translated from the Aramaic. The Greek is "The end of the ages has arrived upon us."
k 10:13 Or "which has fastened onto you."
l 10:13 Or "temptation."

But God will be faithful to you. He will screen and filter the severity, nature, and timing of every test or trial you face [a] so that you can bear it. And each test is an opportunity to trust him more, for along with every trial God has provided for you a way of escape [b] that will bring you out of it victoriously. [c]

Communion

[14] My cherished friends, keep on running far away from idolatry. [15] I know I am writing to thoughtful people, so carefully consider what I say. [16] For when we pray for the blessing of the communion cup, isn't this our co-participation with the blood of Jesus? [d] And the bread that we distribute, isn't this the bread of our co-participation with the body of Christ? [e] [17] For although we're many, we become one loaf of bread and one body as we feast together [f] on one loaf.

[18] Consider the people of Israel *when they fell into idolatry*. When they ate the sacrifices offered to the gods, weren't they becoming communal participants in what was sacrificed? [19] Now, am I saying that idols and the sacrifices offered to them have any value? [20] Absolutely not! However, I am implying that when an unbeliever offers a sacrifice to an idol, it is not offered to the true God but to a demon. I don't want you to be participants with demons! [21] You can't drink from the cup of the Lord and the cup of demons. You can't feast at the table of the Lord and feast [g] at the table of demons. [22] Who would ever want to arouse the Lord's jealousy? Is that something you think you're strong enough to endure? [h]

Living for God's Glory

[23] *You say*, "*Under grace* there are no rules and we're free to do anything we please." Not exactly. Because not everything promotes growth in others. Your slogan, "We're allowed to do anything we choose," may be true—but not everything causes the spiritual advancement of others. [24] So don't always seek what is best for you at the expense of another. [25] Yes, you are free to eat anything

---

a 10:13 That is, God's faithfulness and grace will limit the severity of every test and prevent you from being tested beyond your ability to cope. Unlimited grace is available for every believer who faces hardship, temptations, and seasons of difficulty.

b 10:13 Or "an exodus." Trust in God's faithfulness is the way of escape that empowers us to overcome every difficulty we may experience. We are not told that every difficulty will be removed from our lives, but that God's grace provides an exit path.

c 10:13 Or "God bears up under you to take you out of danger" (Gr. *hupophero*) or "God provides a way of escape so that you may be empowered to endure it." God's faithfulness gives us both a way of escape and the power to endure.

d 10:16 The Aramaic can be translated "the presence of the blood of Jesus."

e 10:16 The Aramaic can be translated "the presence of the body of the Messiah."

f 10:17 The Aramaic can be translated "We are nourished by that one loaf of bread."

g 10:21 Or "participate," which is the Greek word *metaecho*, or "echo with."

h 10:22 Or "Are we really stronger than he is?"

without worrying about your conscience, [26] for the earth and all its abundance belongs to the Lord. [a]

[27] So if an unbeliever invites you to dinner, go ahead and eat whatever is served, without asking questions concerning where it came from. [b] [28] But if he goes out of his way to inform you that the meat was actually an offering sacrificed to idols, then you should pass, not only for his sake but because of his conscience. [29] I'm talking about someone else's conscience, not yours. What good is there in doing what you please if it's condemned by someone else?

[30] So if I voluntarily participate, why should I be judged for celebrating my freedom? [c] [31] Whether you eat or drink, live your life in a way that glorifies and honors God. [32] And make sure you're not offending Jews or Greeks or any part of God's assembly *over your personal preferences*. [33] *Follow my example*, for I try to please everyone in all things, rather than putting my liberty first. I sincerely attempt to do anything I can so that others may be saved.

Head Coverings

11 I want you to pattern your lives after me, just as I pattern mine after Christ. [2] And I give you full credit for always keeping me in mind as you follow carefully the substance of my instructions [d] that I've taught you. [3] But I want you to understand that Christ is the source [e] of every human alive, and Adam was the source of Eve, [f] and God is the source of the Messiah.

[4] Any man *who leads public worship*, [g] and prays or prophesies with a shawl hanging down over his head, shows disrespect to his head, *which is Christ*.

---

a 10:26 See Pss. 24:1; 50:12; 89:11.

b 10:27 Or "questions of conscience."

c 10:30 Or "eating food that I gave thanks for."

d 11:2 Or "traditions" or "guidelines." It is likely that the instructions Paul refers to here are regarding their public worship. This would include cultural customs about church order and not necessarily doctrinal matters.

e 11:3 Or "head." Although the Greek word *kephale*, found three times in this verse, can be "head," it is used figuratively. It is not used in Greek literature or Scripture as "head over," "chief," or "ruler." To say that Christ is the head of every man means that he is the source of our life and faith as the head of the body of Christ. Christ is the "head" as in the head of a river. See also vv. 8–9, which support this. The source of the woman is man, for Eve was taken from Adam. The source of the Messiah is God, for he provided a virgin birth for Christ and formed his body and fulfilled the prophecies God spoke about him. Another possible translation of v. 3 is "Christ has responsibility over all men, as the husband has responsibility for his wife, and God the Father has responsibility over Christ."

f 11:3 As translated from the Aramaic.

g 11:4 Implied in both the Aramaic and the Greek, as also in v. 5. This section (vv. 3–16) is not focused on marriage or the role of women in the church, but on proper attitudes of reverence and conduct in public worship. Paul's discussion here would have made obvious sense within the cultural standards of the Corinthians. It is a continuation of Paul's teaching that if our conduct offends and divides the church, we are to change our ways in order to promote unity among the believers. See 1 Cor. 10:27–33.

⁵ And if any woman *in a place of leadership* within the church prays or prophesies *in public* with her long hair disheveled, *ᵃ* she shows disrespect to her head, *which is her husband*, for this would be the same as having her head shaved. ⁶ If a woman who wants to be in leadership will not conform to the customs of what is proper for women, *ᵇ* she might as well cut off her hair. But if it's disgraceful for her to have her hair cut off *ᶜ* or her head shaved, let her cover her head.

⁷ A man *in leadership* is under no obligation to have his head covered *in the public gatherings*, because he is the portrait of God and reflects his glory. The woman, on the other hand, reflects the glory of her husband, ⁸ for man was not created from woman but woman from man. *ᵈ* ⁹ By the same token, the man was not created because the woman needed him; the woman was created because the man needed her. *ᵉ* ¹⁰ For this reason she should have authority over the head because of the angels. *ᶠ*

¹¹ So then, I have to insist that in the Lord, neither is woman inferior to man nor is man inferior to woman. *ᵍ* ¹² For just as woman was taken from the

---

a 11:5 Or "unbound," as translated from the Aramaic. The Greek is "with her head uncovered." The Greek word *akatakalyptos* is commonly translated as "unveiled" or "uncovered." However, the Greek Septuagint of Lev. 13:45 uses the word *akatakalyptos* in saying that a person who has "leprosy" signals to the world his disease by staying dirty and keeping his hair "disheveled." Notice also that Paul affirms the right of women to pray and prophesy in public worship services.

b 11:6 Or "So, if a women will not wear a head covering, . . ."

c 11:6 That is, "having her hair cut off [like a prostitute]," which was the common practice in Corinth. For the public worship of that era, a woman would have her long hair braided and covered up so she would not be mistaken as a cult priestess of Isis or Dionysus.

d 11:8 See Gen. 2:21–23; 1 Tim. 2:13.

e 11:9 See Gen. 2:18. In Christ, there is no fundamental difference between man and woman, as both were created by God with different roles and personalities. Although the first woman, Eve, came from Adam, every other man came from a woman (mother). To use Gen. 2:18 to say that women are inferior to men is equal to saying that all men are inferior to their mothers.

f 11:10 This literal translation is one of the most difficult verses in all the New Testament to translate and to interpret properly. Scholars and translators are divided in how to express this verse with proper meaning. First, Paul uses the Greek word *exousia* (authority), which is used for the authority of God, kings, and rulers, and can be translated "might" or "right." It never occurs as a metaphor speaking of a piece of apparel. This is not a symbol of authority, but true authority on "the" (not her) head under which she ministers. Before Pentecost, the woman was not seen as anyone with authority, but at Pentecost the Holy Spirit fell upon men and women, giving each person the authority to take the gospel with power to the ends of the earth and prophesy under the direction of the Holy Spirit. The Gospels both begin and end with a visitation of angels to women. The angel Gabriel came to Mary and the angels of God greeted the women at the empty tomb. However, the Aramaic word used here is a homonym that can mean both "power" and "covering/veil." This may explain the variation of the Greek texts.

g 11:11 As translated from the Aramaic and implied in the Greek.

side of man, in the same way man is taken from the *womb of* woman. God, as the source of all things, *designed it this way.*

[13] So then you can decide for yourselves—is it proper for a woman to pray to God with her hair unbound?[a] [14] Doesn't our long-established cultural tradition teach us that if a man has long hair that is *ornamentally arranged* it invites disgrace, but if a woman has long hair that is *ornamentally arranged* it is her glory? [15] This is because long hair is the endowment that God has given her as a head covering.[b]

[16] If someone wants to quarrel about this, I want you to know that we have no intention[c] to start an argument, neither I nor the congregations of God.

The Lord's Table

[17] Now, on this next matter, I wish I could commend you, but I cannot, because when you meet together as a church family it is doing more harm than good! [18] I've been told many times that when you meet as a congregation, divisions and cliques emerge—and to some extent, this doesn't surprise me. [19] Differences of opinion are unavoidable, yet they will reveal which ones among you truly have God's approval.[d]

[20] When all of *your house churches*[e] gather as one church family, you are not really properly celebrating the Lord's Supper.[f] [21] For when it comes time to eat, some gobble down their food before anything is given to others—one is left hungry while others become drunk![g] [22] Don't you all have homes where you can eat and drink? Don't you realize that you're showing a superior attitude by humiliating those who have nothing? Are you trying to show contempt for God's beloved church? How should I address this appropriately? If you're looking for my approval, you won't find it!

[23] I have handed down to you what came to me by direct revelation from the Lord himself. The same night in which he was handed over,[h] he took bread

---

a 11:13 As translated from the Aramaic. The Greek is "with her head uncovered."

b 11:15 Or "prayer shawl." The Greek word *peribolaion* is translated in the Deut. 22:12 (LXX) as "prayer shawl."

c 11:16 Or "custom."

d 11:19 Differences of opinion between believers expose our hearts. Mature ones will overlook offenses and faults in order to maintain the precious unity of the body of Christ. Immature ones will cause splits, divisions, and cliques around their respective opinions. The ones whom God approves are those whose hearts remain pure in spite of petty differences.

e 11:20 Implied both in the text and by the cultural context of the day.

f 11:20 Paul is implying that it is the Lord's Supper, not merely a meal for favored ones. Jesus is hosting the meal for the benefit of all every time we gather for communion.

g 11:21 Apparently, the church of Corinth was divided between the "haves" and the "have nots." Those who were wealthy would feast and become drunk, while those who had very little went hungry. The precious unity of the church was spoiled by this behavior. These shared meals were called "love feasts" (Jude 12).

h 11:23 Or "betrayed." Paul is using a play on words in the Greek text. He "handed down" to us the instructions for the Lord's Table, but the Lord was "handed over" to his accusers.

[24] and gave thanks. Then he distributed it to the disciples and said, "Take it and eat your fill. [a] It is my body, which is given for you. Do this to remember me." [25] He did the same with the cup *of wine* after supper and said, "This cup seals the new covenant with my blood. Drink it—and whenever you drink this, do it to remember me."

[26] Whenever you eat this bread and drink this cup, you are retelling the story, proclaiming our Lord's death until he comes. [27] For this reason, whoever eats the bread or drinks the cup of the Lord in the wrong spirit will be guilty of dishonoring the body and blood of the Lord. [28] So let each individual first evaluate his own attitude and only then eat the bread and drink the cup. [29] For continually eating and drinking with a wrong spirit [b] will bring judgment upon yourself by not recognizing the body. [c] [30] This insensitivity is why many of you are weak, chronically ill, and some even dying. [d] [31] If you do not sit in judgment of others, you will avoid judgment yourself. [e] [32] But when we are judged, it is the Lord's training so that we will not be condemned along with the world.

[33] So then, my fellow believers, when you assemble as one to share a meal, show respect for one another and wait for all to be served. [f] [34] If you are that hungry, eat at home first, so that when you gather together you will not bring judgment upon yourself.

When I come to you, I will answer the other questions you asked me *in your letter.*

Spiritual Gifts

12 My fellow believers, I don't want you to be confused about spiritual realities. [g] [2] For you know full well that when you were unbelievers you were often led astray [h] in one way or another by your worship of idols, which are incapable of talking with you. [3] Therefore, I want to impart to you an understanding of the following:

---

a 11:24 As translated from the Aramaic, which means "Eat and be satisfied."

b 11:29 Or "unworthily" or "irreverently."

c 11:29 Some manuscripts have "the Lord's body." This can be understood in at least two ways. It may refer to not recognizing the bread as Christ's body given in sacrifice, or not recognizing Christ's body on earth, the church. To properly discern the Lord's body, which was beaten and bruised for our healing, would mean we would not be weak or sick or die prematurely.

d 11:30 Or "asleep," a metaphor for death.

e 11:31 As translated from the Aramaic. The Greek is "If we have examined ourselves, we should not be judged."

f 11:33 The Aramaic can be translated "strengthen [encourage] one another."

g 12:1 The Greek word *pneumatikos* is "spiritual" (things), with the implication of spiritual realities or spiritual gifts. Some scholars believe that "spiritual" may refer to spiritual persons.

h 12:2 Or "carried [or snatched] away."

No one speaking by the Spirit of God[a] would ever say, "Jesus is the accursed one."

No one can say, "Jesus is the Lord Yahweh,"[b] unless the Holy Spirit is speaking through him.[c]

[4] It is the same Holy Spirit who continues to distribute many different varieties of gifts.[d]

[5] The Lord Yahweh is one,[e] and he is the one who apportions to believers different varieties of ministries.[f]

[6] The same God distributes different kinds of miracles[g] that accomplish different results through each believer's gift and ministry as he energizes and activates them.

[7] Each believer is given continuous revelation[h] by the Holy Spirit to benefit not just himself but all.[i]

Varieties of Spiritual Gifts

[8] For example:

The Spirit gives to one the gift of the word of wisdom.[j]

---

a 12:3 Some scholars believe this "speaking by the Spirit of God" refers to speaking in tongues.

b 12:3 As translated from the Aramaic. The Greek language has no equivalent for "Lord Yahweh" and uses the word kurios, which means "sir, master, wealthy landowner, boss" and is sometimes used for demons. The Aramaic is preferred. It is by divine revelation that one begins to see that the Lord Yahweh is none other than our Lord Jesus Christ.

c 12:3 Or "except by union with the Holy Spirit."

d 12:4 The nine gifts distributed by the Holy Spirit listed here include: the word of wisdom, the word of knowledge, the gift of faith, gifts of healing, miraculous powers, prophecy, discerning of spirits, speaking in different kinds of tongues, and interpretation of tongues. See vv. 7–11.

e 12:5 As translated from the Aramaic. See also Deut. 6:4.

f 12:5 See Eph. 4:7–16. The ministries Jesus apportions by grace are apostles, prophets, evangelists, pastors, and teachers.

g 12:6 As translated from the Aramaic, which can also be translated "powers."

h 12:7 As translated from the Aramaic and implied in the Greek word phanerosis ("the clear display in light," or "public manifestations").

i 12:7 To summarize, God the Father, the Son, and the Spirit delights to give spiritual gifts to his people, the bride of Christ. These gifts are imparted by God to every believer upon conversion as the Holy Spirit chooses (v. 11). They will confirm the Word of God and expand the kingdom of God. Spiritual gifts can be neglected and misused, but they remain the divine power source for Christ's body on the earth. Through teaching, evangelizing, prophesying, and demonstrating the miraculous, God uses his people to expand his kingdom and to establish righteousness on the earth through the proper use of the gifts he has given. There is no place in Scripture or church history where these gifts were taken away or removed from the body of Christ. The church moves forward through these divine gifts. Spiritual gifts do not replace the Word of God, but the Word of God will spread and flourish as the fully equipped body of Christ operates in the wise use of God's enabling power.

j 12:8 Or "the message [Gr. logos] of wisdom." This is a revelation gift of the Holy Spirit to impart an understanding of strategy and insight that only God can give. This is more than

To another, the same Spirit gives the gift of the word of revelation knowledge.[a]

[9] And to another, the same Spirit gives the gift of faith.[b]

And to another, the same Spirit gives gifts of healing.[c]

[10] And to another the power to work miracles.[d]

And to another the gift of prophecy.[e]

And to another the gift to discern what the Spirit is speaking.[f]

And to another the gift of speaking different kinds of tongues.

And to another the gift of interpretation of tongues.

[11] Remember, it is the same Holy Spirit who distributes, activates, and operates these different gifts as he chooses for each believer.[g]

One Body with Many Parts

[12] Just as the human body is one, though it has many parts that together form one body, so too is Christ.[h] [13] For by one Spirit we all were immersed and

---

simply wisdom, but the clearly crafted "word of wisdom" to unlock the hearts of people and free the corporate body to move forward under God's direction. This gift will express the wisdom of the Holy Spirit, not of man. The best examples of this gift were (1) when Jesus saw Nathanael under the fig tree and knew his true character as a man without guile and (2) when Jesus spoke to the woman at the well and unlocked her heart with the words "Go get your husband." See John 1:4.

a 12:8 The gift of the message (Gr. *logos*) of revelation knowledge has been defined by some as the Holy Spirit's impartation through an impression, a vision, or his voice that gives understanding of a person or situation that cannot be known through the natural mind of man. It may be exercised in the prayer for healing. This revelation knowledge is seen in Saul's healing of blindness in Acts 9 and in Acts 10–11 with Peter's revelation knowledge of Cornelius' servants outside his door and the subsequent salvation of Cornelius and his household. The word of revelation knowledge could also include knowing facts that are unknown to the speaker, such as names, dates, or events to come.

b 12:9 This is the supernatural power of faith released in a believer to do the miracle works of God on the earth.

c 12:9 This is the supernatural power of God released through a believer to heal the sick.

d 12:10 This includes the divine ability to still a storm, feed a multitude, walk on water, cast out demons, turn water into wine, and raise the dead. This gift was one of the distinctive marks of an apostle. See 2 Cor. 12:12.

e 12:10 This gift is a supernatural ability, given by the Holy Spirit, to speak the word of God in proclamation and at times in predicting the future. This is one gift that every believer should desire and never despise. See 1 Cor. 14:1; 1 Thess. 5:19–20; 1 Tim. 1:18; 4:14.

f 12:10 This gift imparts divine discernment to know if a prophetic message is from the Holy Spirit or from a human or demonic source. See Acts 5:3. Discernment is greatly needed in the church today to hear the voice of the Lord clearly and to know when defilement is attempting to enter the assembly.

g 12:11 Spiritual gifts are given by the Holy Spirit at any time to anyone he chooses.

h 12:12 Christ is now a body with many parts. The human body of Jesus is glorified and enthroned in heaven. So also is the body of Christ. We are co-enthroned with him (Rom. 8:29–30; Eph. 2:6; Col. 3:1–4), but we continue to exist on earth to represent him to the world.

mingled into one single body. ⁿ And no matter our status—whether we are Jews or non-Jews, oppressed or free—we are all privileged to drink deeply of the same Holy Spirit. ᵇ

¹⁴ In fact, the human body is not one single part but rather many parts *mingled into one.* ¹⁵ So if the foot were to say, "Since I'm not a hand, I'm not a part of the body," it's forgetting that it is still a vital part of the body. ¹⁶ And if the ear were to say, "Since I'm not an eye, I'm not really a part of the body," it's forgetting that it is still an important part of the body.

¹⁷ *Think of it this way.* If the whole body were just an eyeball, how could it hear sounds? And if the whole body were just an ear, how could it smell different fragrances? ¹⁸ But God has carefully designed each member and placed it in the body to function as he desires. ᶜ ¹⁹ *A diversity is required,* for if the body consisted of one single part, there wouldn't be a body at all! ²⁰ So now we see that there are many differing parts and functions, but one body.

No Competition for Importance within the Body

²¹ It would be wrong for the eye to say to the hand, "I don't need you," and equally wrong if the head said to the foot, "I don't need you." ²² In fact, the weaker our parts, the more vital and essential they are. ᵈ ²³ The body parts we think are less honorable we treat with greater respect. And the body parts that need to be covered in public we treat with propriety and clothe them. ²⁴ But some of our body parts don't require as much attention. Instead, God has mingled the body parts together, giving greater honor to the "lesser" members who lacked it. ²⁵ *He has done this intentionally* so that every member would look after the others with mutual concern, and so that there will be no division in the body. ²⁶ In that way, whatever happens to one member happens to all. If one suffers, everyone suffers. If one is honored, everyone rejoices.

One Body with Different Gifts

²⁷ You are the body of the Anointed One, and each of you is a unique and vital part of it. ²⁸ God has placed in the church the following:

---

a 12:13 This is not a baptism into the Spirit (Matt. 3:6) but a baptism into the body of Christ. Upon conversion, the Holy Spirit does four things for every believer: (1) He gives us new birth (regeneration—see John 3:5; Titus 3:5). (2) He comes to live inside us (indwelling—see Rom. 8:9). (3) He places us into the body as a member of Christ's body on the earth (spiritual baptism—see 1 Cor. 12:13). (4) He seals us as the possession of Christ until the redemption of our human body (see Eph. 1:13–14; 4:30).

b 12:13 To "drink deeply" of the Spirit is the same as receiving his power and gifts until rivers of living water flow from the inside of us. See John 3:34; 7:37.

c 12:18 Every believer should be content with the place within the body God has placed him. And God is pleased when we serve him with joy in every activity or ministry that we engage in for the sake of the body.

d 12:22 Paul is, no doubt, speaking of our internal organs: liver, heart, lungs, etc.

First apostles,
second prophets,
third teachers,
then those with gifts of miracles, gifts of divine healing,
gifts of revelation knowledge, [a] gifts of leadership, [b]
and gifts of different kinds of tongues.

[29] Not everyone is an apostle or a prophet or a teacher. Not everyone performs miracles [30] or has gifts of healing or speaks in tongues or interprets tongues. [31] But you should all constantly boil over with passion in seeking the higher gifts.

And now I will show you a superior way to live that is beyond comparison! [c]

Love, the Motivation of Our Lives

13 If I were to speak with eloquence in earth's many languages, and in the heavenly tongues of angels, [d] yet I didn't express myself with love, [e] my words would be reduced to the hollow sound of nothing more than a clanging cymbal.

[2] And if I were to have *the gift of* prophecy [f] with a profound understanding of God's hidden secrets, and if I possessed unending supernatural knowledge, and if I had the greatest gift of faith that could move mountains, [g] but have never learned to love, then I am nothing.

[3] And if I were to be so generous as to give away everything I owned to feed the poor, and to offer my body to be burned *as a martyr*, [h] without the pure motive of love, I would gain nothing of value.

---

a 12:28 Most translations render the Greek word *antilēmpsis* (a hapax legomenon) as "helps." However, it is literally "laying hold of" (revelation) or "apprehending" (perception).

b 12:28 This is a hapax legomenon that can be translated "guidance" or "one who steers the ship."

c 12:31 Or "a path corresponding to transcendence."

d 13:1 The implication is that the angels speak a distinct language among themselves that is not known on earth.

e 13:1 The Aramaic word for love is *hooba*, and it is a homonym that also means "to set on fire." It is difficult to fully express the meaning of this word and translate it into English. You could say the Aramaic concept is "burning love" or "fiery love," coming from the inner depths of the heart as an eternal energy, an active power of bonding hearts and lives in secure relationships. The Greek word is *agapē*, which describes the highest form of love. It is the love God has for his people. It is an intense affection that must be demonstrated. It is a loyal, endless, and unconditional commitment of love. Feelings are attached to this love. It is not abstract, but devoted to demonstrating the inward feelings of love toward another with acts of kindness and benevolence.

f 13:2 Or "prophetic powers."

g 13:2 The Greek present infinitive indicates a continuous aspect, which means a faith to keep on removing mountains or to remove one mountain after another.

h 13:3 The Aramaic word used here is a homonym that can mean either "to burn" or "to boast." Because of this, some Greek manuscripts have "I offer my body in order to boast [glory]."

[4]Love is *large and* incredibly patient.[a] Love is gentle and consistently kind to all. It refuses to be jealous[b] *when blessing comes to someone else.* Love does not brag about one's achievements nor inflate its own importance. [5]Love does not traffic in shame and disrespect, nor selfishly seek its own honor. Love is not easily irritated[c] or quick to take offense.[d] [6]Love joyfully celebrates honesty[e] and finds no delight in what is wrong.[f] [7]Love is a safe place of shelter,[g] for it never stops believing the best for others.[h] Love never takes failure as defeat, for it never gives up.

Perfect Love

[8]Love never stops loving.[i] It extends beyond the gift of prophecy, which eventually fades away.[j] It is more enduring than tongues, which will one day fall silent. Love remains long after *words of* knowledge are forgotten.[k] [9]Our present knowledge and our prophecies are but partial,[l] [10]but when love's perfection arrives, the partial will fade away.[m] [11]When I was a child, I spoke about childish matters, for I saw things like a child and reasoned like a child. But the day came when I matured, and I set aside my childish ways.

[12]For now we see but a faint reflection of riddles and mysteries[n] as though

---

a 13:4 Or "Love patiently endures mistreatment" could mean that love is incredibly patient *even in difficult relationships.* The Aramaic can be translated "Love transforms the spirit."

b 13:4 Or "boil with jealousy."

c 13:5 Or "overly sensitive" (having sharp edges).

d 13:5 Or "resentful" or "does not keep score." The Aramaic can be translated "Love does not stare at evil." Love will overlook offenses and remain focused on what is good, refusing to hold resentment in our hearts.

e 13:6 Or "reality" (or "truth").

f 13:6 Or "injustice" or "unrighteousness."

g 13:7 Or "Love bears all things." Although commonly understood to mean that love can bear hardships of any kind, the nominalized form of the verb (*stego*) is actually the word for "roof" found in Mark 2:4. Paul is saying that love covers all things, like a roof covers the house. See 1 Peter 4:8. Love does not focus on what is wrong but will bear with the shortcomings of others. And like a roof protects and shields, you could say that love springs no leak. It is a safe place that offers shelter, not exposure.

h 13:7 Or "it never loses faith."

i 13:8 Or "Love never, not even once, fails [lapses]" or "Love never falls down" (it keeps going higher).

j 13:8 The Aramaic can be translated "prophecy comes to pass."

k 13:8 That is, the gift of the word of knowledge (1 Cor. 12:8). Knowledge itself will not pass away or be set aside, for we will learn of God's mercies throughout eternity. This is the gifts of knowledge Paul refers to.

l 13:9 Or "in fragments."

m 13:10 Perfect love diminishes the importance of prophecy and tongues. Paul could be saying that they will cease being important when compared with perfect love. That which is perfect is love and is greater than the gifts. Perfect love puts everything else in second place, for God is love. See 1 John 4:8, 18. Paul is contrasting spiritual gifts with love, saying, "Gifts will fail, but love will never fail." Like leaves falling to the ground, something greater will one day take their place: the love of God.

n 13:12 The Greek word *ainigma* used here is equal to our English word *enigma.*

reflected in a mirror, but one day we will see face-to-face.[a] My understanding is incomplete now, but one day I will understand everything, just as everything about me has been fully understood. [13]Until then, there are three things that remain: faith, hope, and love—yet love surpasses them all.[b] So above all else, let love be the beautiful prize for which you run.[c]

Proper Use of Spiritual Gifts

14 It is good that you are enthusiastic and passionate about spiritual gifts, especially prophecy.[d] [2]When someone speaks in tongues, no one understands a word he says, because he's not speaking to people, but to God—he is speaking intimate mysteries in the Spirit.[e] [3]But when someone prophesies, he speaks to encourage people, to build them up, and to bring them comfort.[f] [4]The one who speaks in tongues advances his own spiritual progress,[g] while the one who prophesies builds up the church. [5]I would be delighted if you all spoke in tongues, but I desire even more that you impart prophetic revelation to others. Greater gain comes through the one who prophesies than the one who speaks in tongues, unless there is interpretation so that it builds up the entire church.

[6]My dear friends, what good is it if I come to you always speaking in tongues? But if I come with a clear revelation from God, or with insight,[h] or with a prophecy, or with a clear teaching, *I can enrich you.*[i] [7]Similarly, if musical instruments, such as flutes or stringed instruments, are out of tune and don't play the arrangement clearly, how will anyone recognize the melody? [8]If the bugle

---

a 13:12 Paul is referring to God speaking to Moses "face-to-face" (Hebrew "mouth-to-mouth"), and not using dreams and figures of speech (Num. 12:8). Transforming love will bring us all face-to-face, mouth-to-mouth with God.

b 13:13 Faith and hope both spring from love, which makes love the greatest virtue of all. Faith and hope are temporary, but love is eternal. Paul gives us ten characteristics of divine love in this chapter. Love (1) is patient under stress, (2) is kind at all times, (3) is generous, not envious, (4) is humble, not self-promoting, (5) is never rude, (6) does not manipulate by using shame, (7) is not irritable or easily offended, (8) celebrates honesty, (9) does not focus on what is flawed, and (10) is loyal to the end.

c 13:13 Unfortunately, there is a chapter break before this line. Chapter headings are not part of the inspired text. The translator has chosen to insert the partial text of 14:1 here in conclusion to Paul's masterful treatise on love.

d 14:1 Or "that you crave spiritual things" or "that you crave spiritual realities."

e 14:2 This verse makes it clear that the tongues Paul refers to are not known languages but Spirit-inspired utterances.

f 14:3 The Greek word *paramythia* (a hapax legomenon) could also be translated "soothing, calming speech" or "affirmation." Paul does not describe prophecy here as predictive, but as influential to advance the spiritual welfare of the body.

g 14:4 See Rom. 8:26.

h 14:6 Or "intimate knowledge through experience."

i 14:6 Paul uses these four ministries as examples of what builds up the church. Every congregation needs to focus on all four (revelation from God, insights of truth, prophecy, and teaching), as they are all necessary today.

makes a garbled sound, who will recognize the signal to show up for the battle? [9] So it is with you. Unless you speak in a language that's easily understood, how will anyone know what you're talking about? You might as well save your breath!

[10] I suppose that the world has all sorts of languages, and each conveys meaning to the ones who speak it. [11] But I am like a foreigner if I don't understand the language, and the speaker will be like a foreigner to me. [12] And that's what's happening among you. You are so passionate[a] about embracing the manifestations of the Holy Spirit! Now become even more passionate about the things that strengthen the entire church.

[13] So then, if you speak in a tongue, pray for the interpretation to be able to unfold the meaning of what you are saying. [14] For if I am praying in a tongue, my spirit is engaged in prayer but I have no clear understanding of what is being said.

[15] So here's what I've concluded. I will pray in the Spirit, but I will also pray with my mind engaged. I will sing rapturous praises in the Spirit, but I will also sing with my mind engaged. [16] Otherwise, if you are praising God in your spirit, how could someone without the gift participate by adding his "amen" to your giving of thanks, since he doesn't have a clue of what you're saying? [17] Your praise to God is admirable, but it does nothing to strengthen and build up others.

[18] I give thanks to God that I speak in tongues more than all of you, [19] but in the church setting I would rather speak five words that can be understood than ten thousand exotic words in a tongue. That way I could have a role in teaching others.

The Function of the Gifts

[20] Beloved ones,[b] don't remain as immature children in your reasoning. As it relates to evil, be like newborns, but in your thinking be mature adults.

[21] For it stands written in the law:

I will bring my message to this people with strange tongues and foreign lips, yet even then they still will not listen to me, says the Lord.[c]

[22] So then, tongues are not a sign for believers, but a miracle for unbelievers. Prophecy, on the other hand, is not for unbelievers, but a miracle sign for believers.

[23] If the entire church comes together and everyone is speaking in tongues, won't the visitors say that you have lost your minds? [24] But if everyone is prophesying, and an unbeliever or one without the gift enters your meeting, he will be convicted by all that he hears and will be called to account, [25] for the intimate secrets of his heart will be brought to light. He will be mystified and fall facedown in worship and say, "God is truly among you!"[d]

---

a 14:12 The Greek word implies a boiling over with affection and emotion.
b 14:20 Or "brothers and sisters."
c 14:21 See Deut. 28:49; Isa. 28:11–12.
d 14:25 Or "Truly God is in you."

Guidelines for Use of the Gifts

[26] Beloved friends,[a] what does all this imply? When you conduct your meetings, you should always let everything be done to build up the church family. Whether you share a song of praise,[b] a teaching, a divine revelation, or a tongue and interpretation, let each one contribute what strengthens others.

[27] If someone speaks in a tongue, it should be two or three,[c] one after another, with someone interpreting. [28] If there's no one with the interpretation, then he should remain silent in the meeting, content to speak to himself and to God.

[29] *And the same with prophecy.* Let two or three prophets prophesy and let the other prophets carefully evaluate and discern what is being said. [30] But if someone receives a revelation while someone else is still speaking, the one speaking should conclude *and allow the one with fresh revelation the opportunity to share it.*[d] [31] For you can all prophesy in turn and in an environment where all present can be instructed, encouraged, and strengthened. [32] Keep in mind that the anointing to prophesy doesn't mean that the speaker is out of control[e]—he can wait his turn.[f] [33] For God is the God of harmony, not confusion,[g] as is the pattern in all the churches of God's holy believers.

[34] The women[h] should be respectfully silent *during the evaluation of prophecy in the meetings.*[i] They are not allowed to interrupt,[j] but are to be in a support role, as in fact the law teaches.[k] [35] If they want to inquire about something,

---

a 14:26 Or "brothers and sisters."

b 14:26 Or "a psalm."

c 14:27 This could be a Greek idiom (lit. by twos and threes) meaning "just a few."

d 14:30 God wants a fresh word spoken to his people. The churches must allow God's "now" voice to be heard and evaluated by the written Word.

e 14:32 Or "The spirits of the prophets are subject to the prophets." The Aramaic allows for this translation: "The prophecies (spiritual words) of the prophets are subject to the prophets," which could imply that the prophet is to be accountable with his/her prophecies.

f 14:32 From the context it appears that the Corinthians were speaking in tongues and prophesying without regarding others in the body who also had prophetic words to share or a tongue and interpretation. This caused disorder and confusion in the church meetings, with people speaking up and giving their opinions about what was spoken.

g 14:33 Or "instability."

h 14:34 Or "wives."

i 14:34 Implied in the greater context. The theme Paul is addressing is unity and mutual edification, not simply the role of women. Women are permitted to speak in church, to prophesy, and to minister the gospel. See 1 Cor. 11:2–16; 14:31. Paul is apparently prohibiting interrupting the leaders as they evaluate prophetic utterances. It is likely that Paul was addressing a specific issue taking place in the church fellowship of Corinth with women interrupting the meetings with their opinions and questions about the prophetic words just spoken, possibly even words spoken by their husbands.

j 14:34 Or "speak." Interrupting the meeting is implied when compared with 1 Cor. 11:2–16; 14:31; Acts 2:16–21; 21:9.

k 14:34 See Gen. 2:18–24; 3:16.

let them ask their husbands when they get home, for a woman embarrasses herself when she constantly interrupts the church meeting. [a]

[36] Do you actually think that you were the starting point for the Word of God going forth? Were you the only ones it was sent to? *I don't think so!* [b] [37] If anyone considers himself to be a prophet or a spiritual person, [c] let him discern that what I'm writing to you carries the Lord's authority. [38] And if anyone continues not to recognize this, he should not be recognized!

[39] So, beloved friends, [d] with all this in mind, be passionate [e] to prophesy and don't forbid anyone from speaking in tongues, [40] doing all things in a beautiful [f] and orderly way. [g]

The Resurrection of Christ

15 Dear friends, [h] let me give you clearly the heart of the gospel that I've preached to you—the good news that you have heartily received and on which you stand. [2] For it is through the revelation of the gospel that you are being saved, if you fasten your life firmly to the message I've taught you, unless you have believed in vain. [3] For I have shared with you what I have received and what is of utmost importance:

The Messiah died for our sins,
    fulfilling the prophecies of the Scriptures.

---

a 14:35 One interpretation of this passage is that Paul is quoting from a letter written by the Corinthians to him. They were the ones saying a woman should remain silent and Paul is responding to their questions. In other words, they were imposing a rule in the church that Paul refutes in v. 36. Some manuscripts move vv. 34–35 to after v. 40, which causes a few scholars to consider this as evidence of an early introduction into the text by Jewish scribes. The only two places in the New Testament where Paul writes about women being quiet or not teaching in the church are in his letters to the church of Ephesus (1 Timothy) and Corinth. Both cities were centers of worship to the goddess Artemis (Diana), where women had the leading roles of teaching and temple prostitution was commonplace. To the Galatians Paul writes that there is no distinction between believing men and women (Gal. 3:28).

b 14:36 Inferred by the rhetorical question and the disjunctive particle.

c 14:37 Or "a spiritually gifted person."

d 14:39 Or "brothers and sisters."

e 14:39 The Greek word *zēloō* means "a boiling fervor."

f 14:40 Or "respectably." The Aramaic can be translated "with the right design."

g 14:40 This is the Greek word *taxis*, which can also mean "in battle array." Here are some summary observations concerning believers' gatherings: (1) When the believers gathered, they ate together and frequently observed the Lord's Table. See 1 Cor. 11:7–33. (2) Men and women participated together and used their spiritual gifts. See 1 Cor. 11:2–16; 12. (3) The main purpose of gathering together was the mutual building up and encouragement of one another. See 1 Cor. 14:1–26. (4) Several people would speak in the meetings, and the leaders would discern and direct. See 1 Cor. 14:26–40. (5) Expressing love was more important than gifts, teachings, or prophecies. See 1 Cor. 13. (6) Everything was to be done in a beautiful way and in order. See 1 Cor. 14:40.

h 15:1 Or "brothers."

⁴He was buried in a tomb
    and was raised from the dead after three days,
       as foretold in the Scriptures. *ᵃ*
  ⁵Then he appeared to Peter the Rock *ᵇ*
    and to the twelve apostles. *ᶜ*

⁶He also appeared to more than five hundred of his followers at the same time, most of whom are still alive as I write this, though a few have passed away. *ᵈ* ⁷Then he appeared to Jacob *ᵉ* and to all the apostles. ⁸Last of all he appeared in front of me, like one born prematurely, ripped from the womb. *ᶠ* ⁹Yes, I am the most insignificant of all the apostles, unworthy even to be called an apostle, because I hunted down believers and persecuted God's church. ¹⁰But God's amazing grace has made me who I am! *ᵍ* And his grace to me was not fruitless. In fact, I worked harder than all the rest, *ʰ* yet not in my own strength but God's, for his empowering grace is poured out upon me. ¹¹So this is what we all have taught you, and whether it was through me or someone else, you have now believed the gospel.

The Importance of the Resurrection

¹²The message we preach is Christ, who has been raised from the dead. So how could any of you possibly say there is no resurrection of the dead? ¹³For if there is no such thing as a resurrection from the dead, then not even Christ has been raised. *ⁱ* ¹⁴And if Christ has not been raised, all of our preaching has been for

---

a   15:4 See Ps. 16:9–10; Luke 24:25–27, 44–46.

b   15:5 Or "Cephas." Paul includes the bodily appearance of Jesus to his followers as part of the gospel to be believed. What Paul states as the heart of the gospel is (1) Christ's death, (2) the fulfillment of prophecies, (3) Christ's burial, (4) Christ's resurrection, and (5) Christ supernaturally appeared (manifested) to his followers. More than 515 followers of Jesus saw him after his resurrection, including those mentioned by Paul and Miriam (Mary) at the garden tomb.

c   15:5 Most scholars conclude that vv. 3–5 represent an early creed of the apostles on which our Christian faith is based.

d   15:6 Or "Some have fallen asleep," a Hebrew euphemism for death when referring to believers.

e   15:7 See also Gal. 1:19. Jacob was the half brother of our Lord Jesus. It is unfortunate that other translations of the Bible have substituted James for Jacob. Both Greek and Aramaic leave the Hebrew name as it is, Jacob. At first Jacob did not believe that his brother was the Messiah (John 7:5). Yet after he believed, he wrote what many have come to know as the book of James (or Jacob) and he became the leading elder of the church of Jerusalem (Acts 15:13).

f   15:8 Or "as one born at the wrong time." The Greek word *ektroma* is used to describe a premature birth or miscarriage or abortion. This means Paul's call to be an apostle was not normal; it was sudden and unexpected. Paul never claimed to be part of the Twelve, but an apostle chosen by the resurrected Lord Jesus. See also Eph. 4:11.

g   15:10 Or "By the grace of God, I am what I am."

h   15:10 See 2 Cor. 11:16–28.

i   15:13 Paul is showing us that the resurrection of Jesus cannot be separated from the coming

nothing and your faith is useless. [15]Moreover, if the dead are not raised, that would mean that we are false witnesses who are misrepresenting God. And that would mean that we have preached a lie, stating that God raised him from the dead, if in reality he didn't.

[16]If the dead aren't raised up,[a] that would mean that Christ has not been raised up either. [17]And if Christ is not alive, you are still lost in your sins and your faith is a fantasy. [18]It would also mean that those believers in Christ who have passed away[b] have simply perished. [19]If the only benefit of our hope in Christ is limited to this life on earth, we deserve to be pitied more than all others![c]

[20]But the truth is, Christ is risen from the dead, as the firstfruit[d] of a great resurrection harvest of those who have died. [21]For since death came through a man, Adam,[e] it is fitting that the resurrection of the dead has also come through a man, Christ. [22]Even as all who are in Adam die, so also all who are in Christ will be made alive. [23]But each one in his proper order: Christ, the firstfruits, then those who belong to Christ in his presence.[f]

[24]Then the final stage of completion comes, when he will bring to an end every other rulership, authority, and power, and he will hand over his kingdom to Father God. [25]Until then he is destined to reign[g] as King until all hostility has been subdued and placed under his feet.[h] [26]And the last enemy to be subdued and eliminated is death itself.[i]

[27]The Father has placed all things in subjection under the feet of Christ.[j] Yet when it says, "all things," it is understood that the Father does not include himself, for he is the one who placed all things in subjection to Christ. [28]However, when everything is subdued and in submission to him, then the Son

---

resurrection of believers. To remove the truth of Christ's resurrection is to destroy the message of the gospel of hope.

a 15:16 The Aramaic can be translated "if there is no life after death."

b 15:18 Or "those who have fallen asleep in Christ." In the Hebraic mind-set, this is a euphemism for believers who have died.

c 15:19 Why would we be the most pitiable people of all? Because we live a life that contains a measure of hardship and suffering and, at times, possible martyrdom, with no hope of an afterlife. The Aramaic places the emphasis on the apostles who preached the gospel: "If through these [false pretenses] we have preached life eternal through the Messiah, then we [apostles] are the most miserable of all humanity."

d 15:20 The first part of the harvest is called the firstfruits. Jesus' resurrection is the firstfruit of those who will be raised in resurrection power, never to die again.

e 15:21 See Rom. 5:12–21.

f 15:23 Or "appearance" (Gr. parousia).

g 15:25 As translated from the Aramaic.

h 15:25 See Ps. 110:1.

i 15:26 See Rev. 20:14.

j 15:27 Or "under his [the Messiah's] feet." See Ps. 8:6.

himself will be subject to the Father, who put all things under his feet.[a] This is so that Father God will be everything in everyone!

Implications of the Resurrection

[29] If there is no resurrection, what do these people think they're doing when they are baptized for the dead? If the dead aren't raised, why be baptized for them?[b] [30] And why would we be risking our lives every day?

[31] My brothers and sisters, I continually face death.[c] This is as sure as my boasting of you[d] and our co-union together in the life of our Lord Jesus Christ, who gives me confidence to share my experiences with you. [32] Tell me, why did I fight "wild beasts"[e] in Ephesus if my hope is in this life only? What was the point of that? If the dead do not rise, then

Let's party all night, for tomorrow we die![f]

[33] So stop fooling yourselves! Evil companions will corrupt good morals and character.[g] [34] Come back to your right senses and awaken to what is right.

a 15:28 Christ and the Father are equally one. The work of the Son and the work of the Father may differ, but both will result in all evil being overcome on the earth and the kingdom being given to God.

b 15:29 This is one of the most puzzling verses in all the New Testament. Bible scholars are divided over its meaning, with nearly two hundred interpretations offered. Paul is not condemning nor commending this practice, but merely using it as evidence that the hope of resurrection life after death for the believer is widely believed. Apparently, some believers were baptized in hopes of benefitting those who died before receiving baptism. This practice is not mentioned anywhere else in the Bible nor in other writings of the earliest church fathers.

c 15:31 Some translations render this "I die daily," implying a dying to sin. Yet this is not in the context at all. Paul faces death day by day because of the danger of preaching the gospel in a hostile culture. He is not referring to dying to sin daily, for our death to sin took place on the cross. We died once and for all to sin. See Rom. 6:6–11; Gal. 2:20.

d 15:31 Or "I affirm [swear] by the act of boasting in you." Paul uses a Greek particle that is reserved for taking an oath or swearing to the truth of a statement. This statement by Paul may contain an ellipsis that could be supplied by saying, "I swear by the confidence I have of your salvation *that I am confident also of a coming resurrection.*"

e 15:32 It does not appear that these wild beasts were animals. Rather, Paul is referring figuratively to beastly men and their savage opposition that Paul had to endure in Ephesus (Acts 19:28–31). Elsewhere in the Bible wicked men are called beasts (Titus 1:12; 2 Peter 2:12; Jude 10). The author of Ps. 73 described himself as a "brute beast" when he wandered away from God (Ps. 73:22). When naming all of the hardships that he endured, Paul did not mention fighting wild beasts (2 Cor. 11:23–28).

f 15:32 See Isa. 22:13; Luke 12:19.

g 15:33 This is likely a quotation from the Athenian poet Menander (*Thras.* 218). Paul is using this quote to encourage the believers to stay away from those who deny the resurrection.

Repent from your sinful ways. [a] For some have no knowledge of God's wonderful love. [b] You should be ashamed that you make me write this way to you! [c]

Our Resurrection Body

[35] I can almost hear someone saying, "How can the dead come back to life? And what kind of body will they have when they are resurrected?" [36] Foolish man! Don't you know that what you sow in the ground doesn't germinate unless it dies? [37] And what you sow is not the body that will come into being, but the bare seed. And it's hard to tell whether it's wheat or some other seed. [38] But when it dies, God gives it a new form, a body to fulfill his purpose, and he sees to it that each seed gets a new body of its own *and becomes the plant he designed it to be.* [d]

[39] All flesh is not identical. Animals have one flesh and human beings another. Birds have their distinct flesh and fish another. [40] In the same way there are earthly bodies and heavenly bodies. There is a splendor of the celestial body and a different one for the earthly. [41] There is the radiance of the sun and differing radiance for the moon and for the stars. Even the stars differ in their shining. [42] And that's how it will be with the resurrection of the dead.

[43] The body is "sown" in decay, but will be raised in immortality. It is "sown" in humiliation, but will be raised in glorification. [e] [44] It is "sown" in weakness but will be raised in power. If there is a physical body, there is also a spiritual body. [45] For it is written:

The first man, Adam, became a living soul. [f]

The last Adam [g] became the life-giving Spirit. [46] However, the spiritual didn't come first. The natural precedes the spiritual. [47] The first man was from the dust of the earth; the second Man is the Lord Jehovah, [h] from the realm of heaven. [i] [48] The first one, made from dust, has a race of people just like him, who are also made from dust. The One sent from heaven has a race of heavenly

---

a 15:34 Or "Stop sinning."

b 15:34 As translated from the Aramaic. The Greek is "Some have not the knowledge of God."

c 15:34 The motivation of Paul giving them the exhortation in this verse is the resurrection from the dead. We have a glorious hope of resurrection awaiting us, and for that reason, we live our lives with eternity in view.

d 15:38 Paul is teaching us of the resurrected body every believer will one day possess. Our bodies will then be perfect, renewed, transformed, indestructible, and not limited to the laws of nature. We will never get sick and never experience death again. We will still have our personalities as individuals but without any hint of sin. See Phil. 3:21.

e 15:43 The Aramaic can be translated "They are buried in agony, but raised in glory."

f 15:45 See Gen. 2:7.

g 15:45 The last Adam is Jesus Christ. As the last Adam, he ended Adam's race and began a new species of humans who are indwelt by the Holy Spirit and carry the life of Christ within them.

h 15:47 As translated from the Aramaic.

i 15:47 In God's eyes there are only two men, Adam and Christ. Every human being is a copy

people who are just like him. [49] Once we carried the likeness of the man of dust, but now let us[a] carry the likeness of the Man of heaven.[b]

Transformation

[50] Now, I tell you this, my brothers and sisters, flesh and blood are not able to inherit God's kingdom realm, and neither will that which is decaying be able to inherit what is incorruptible.

[51] Listen, and I will tell you a divine mystery: not all of us will die, but we will all be transformed. [52] It will happen in an instant[c]—in the twinkling of his eye. For when the last trumpet is sounded, the dead will come back to life. We will be indestructible and we will be transformed. [53] For we will discard our mortal "clothes" and slip into a body that is imperishable. What is mortal now will be exchanged for immortality. [54] And when that which is mortal puts on immortality, and what now decays is exchanged for what will never decay, then the Scripture will be fulfilled that says:

> Death is swallowed up by a triumphant victory![d]
> [55] So death, tell me, where is your victory?
> Tell me death, where is your sting?[e]

[56] It is sin that gives death its sting and the law that gives sin its power.[f] [57] But we thank God[g] for giving us the victory as conquerors through our Lord Jesus, the Anointed One.[h] [58] So now, beloved ones,[i] stand firm and secure. Live your lives with an unshakable confidence. We know that we prosper and excel in every season by serving the Lord,[j] because we are assured

---

of one or the other. To be in Adam is to be lost and merely human, but to be in Christ is to be wrapped into the Anointed One as one who carries the life of Christ within.

a 15:49 The Aramaic word can be translated either "let us" or "we shall." This may explain the variation among Greek manuscripts.

b 15:49 That is, just as Jesus now has an earthly body transformed into a spiritual body, so we will have our bodies transformed into heavenly bodies.

c 15:52 Or "in an atom of time [Gr. en atomo]."

d 15:54 See Isa. 25:8.

e 15:55 The Aramaic can be translated "your scorpion sting." See Hos. 13:14.

f 15:56 In reading vv. 55 and 56 together, we can see that the victory of v. 55 is the total victory over sin at the cross where we were co-crucified with Jesus Christ. The sting of v. 55 that is removed is the empowering of sin by the law.

g 15:57 The Aramaic can be translated "Accept God's grace."

h 15:57 What an amazing summary of what Jesus Christ has accomplished for us! Although Satan seemed to be victorious, the cross of Christ defeated him, defeated death, and defeated sin, making us into victorious conquerors who have hope beyond the grave.

i 15:58 Or "dear brothers and sisters."

j 15:58 As translated from the Aramaic. The Greek can be translated "Always have the Lord's possessions in abundance."

that our union with the Lord makes our labor productive with fruit that endures. [a]

An Offering for Believers in Jerusalem

16 Now, concerning the collection I want you to take for God's holy believers *in Jerusalem who are in need,* [b] I want you to follow the same instructions I gave the churches of Galatia. [c] [2] Every Sunday, each of you make a generous offering by taking a portion of whatever God has blessed you with and place it in safekeeping. Then I won't have to make a special appeal when I come. [3] When I arrive, I will send your gift to the poor in Jerusalem along with a letter of explanation, carried by those whom you approve. [4] If it seems advisable for me to accompany them, I'll be glad to have them travel with me.

Paul's Plans to Visit Corinth

[5] I plan to be traveling through Macedonia, and afterward I will visit you [6] and perhaps stay there for a while, or even spend the winter with you. Afterward you can send me on my journey, wherever I go next, with your financial support. [7] For it's not my desire to just see you in passing, but I would like to spend some time with you if the Lord permits. [8] Regardless, I will remain in Ephesus until *the feast of* Pentecost. [9] There's an amazing door of opportunity standing wide open for me to minister here, even though there are many who oppose and stand against me. [d]

[10] When Timothy arrives, make sure that he feels at home while he's with you, for he's advancing the Lord's work just as I am. [11] Don't let anyone disparage or look down on him, but kindly help him on his way with financial support so that he may come back to me, for I am waiting for him and the brothers to return.

[12] Now, about our brother Apollos. I've tried hard to convince him to come visit you with the other brothers, [e] but it's simply not the right time for him now. But *don't worry,* he'll come when he has the opportunity.

Paul's Final Instructions and Greetings

[13] Remember to stay alert and hold firmly to all that you believe. Be mighty

---

a 15:58 Or "Your labor in the Lord is not without effect." This final clause is litotes, a double negative, which is best conveyed in a positive form.

b 16:1 Although it is implied here, it is made explicit in v. 3 that the offering was for those in Jerusalem.

c 16:1 Galatia is a region of the Anatolia province of central Turkey.

d 16:9 See Acts 19.

e 16:12 The other brothers may have been those who carried the letter from the Corinthians to Paul, Stephanas, Fortunatus, and Achaicus (1 Cor. 16:17).

and full of courage. [14] Let love and kindness be the motivation behind all that you do. [15] Dear brothers and sisters, I have a request to make of you. Give special recognition to Stephanas and his family, for they were the first converts in Achaia,[a] and they have fully devoted themselves to serve God's holy people.[b] [16] I urge you to honor and support them, and all those like them who work so diligently for the Lord.

[17] I was delighted when Stephanas,[c] Fortunatus,[d] and Achaicus[e] arrived, for they've made up for your absence. [18] They have refreshed my spirit in the same way they've refreshed yours. Be sure to honor people like this.

[19] All the churches of western Turkey[f] send their loving greetings to you. Aquila and Prisca[g] greet you warmly in the Lord with those of their house church. [20] All of your fellow believers *here in Ephesus* send their greetings. Greet one another with a sacred kiss.[h]

[21] In my own handwriting, I, Paul, add my loving greeting.

[22] If anyone doesn't sincerely love the Lord, he deserves to be doomed as an outcast.[i] Our Lord has come![j] [23] May the grace and favor of our Lord Jesus be with you. [24] I send my love to all who are joined in the life of Jesus, the Anointed One.

---

a 16:15 At the time Paul wrote to the Corinthians, Achaia was a Roman province in southern Greece.

b 16:15 Whenever we minister to God's people, we are ministering to the Lord. See Matt. 25:34–46.

c 16:17 *Stephanas* means "crowned." Some believe that he was the Philippian jailor who, along with his household, became the first believers in Philippi.

d 16:17 *Fortunatus* means "blessed." He is recognized in the Orthodox Church as one of the seventy disciples sent out by Jesus as an apostle.

e 16:17 *Achaicus* means "a native of Achaia." He is recognized in church history as one of the seventy disciples sent out by Jesus as an apostle.

f 16:19 Or "[the Roman province] of Asia."

g 16:19 *Prisca* was a diminutive form of Priscilla ("long life"). She and her husband, Aquila ("eagle"), were tentmakers like Paul. They were not only business partners but partners with him in ministry. See Acts 18:2, 18, 26; 2 Tim. 4:19.

h 16:20 What makes a kiss holy is that it comes from the love of God. See Song. 1:2.

i 16:22 Or "accursed."

j 16:22 Or "Maranatha!" This is an Aramaic word that can be translated in two ways, "Come, our Lord" or "Our Lord has come."

2 CORINTHIANS

Introduction

AT A GLANCE

Author: The apostle Paul
Audience: The church of Corinth
Date: AD 56–57
Type of Literature: A letter
Major Themes: The person and work of Jesus, the gospel, the new covenant, Paul's apostolic ministry, Christian living, and generosity
Outline:

Letter Opening — 1:1–11
Paul's Rift with the Corinthians — 1:12–2:13
Paul's Apostolic Ministry — 2:14–7:16
Paul's Collection Effort — 8:1–9:15
Paul's Ministry Defense — 10:1–18
Paul Speaks as a Fool — 11:1–12:10
Paul's Final Warning — 12:11–13:14

ABOUT 2 CORINTHIANS

You are about to read a book written by a man who suffered for the cause of Christ, a man who knew trouble and how to overcome in victory. In 2 Corinthians you'll find a letter written by an apostle to a church that he planted—a church that was in need of a father's advice. In many ways, this letter serves as an apostolic manual for the body of Christ, replete with supernatural encounters, glory, love, and truth. This book is full of spiritual encouragement and revelation!

The church of Corinth had already received at least two prior letters from Paul. What we have in our New Testament as 1 Corinthians was Paul's second letter, making 2 Corinthians his third. The church had received Paul's rebuke in his prior letters, and now they were tender, open, and ready to receive all that their spiritual father had to impart. Although influenced by those who had claimed to be "super-apostles," their hearts were bound in love to Paul and the grace of God that was upon him.

How the church today needs the truth and love from this anointed apostle!

As you read, picture yourself in the congregation in Corinth, hearing the letter read publicly. Let its truth penetrate your heart and stir you, as a new creation, to a greater passion to follow Jesus. Here you will find the wonderful secrets Paul learned about how to turn troubles into triumph. May you find more than you expected as you read through 2 Corinthians. Enjoy!

PURPOSE

Paul's letter to the church of Corinth is one of his most personal letters. In it, he wrote to defend his apostleship in the face of rival "super-apostles," as he called them, who were threatening the spiritual ground Paul had so carefully, paternally tilled. In defending his ministry Paul wrote to address a deeper issue with the Corinthian believers. He clarified how the gospel should impact every ounce of their lives, encouraging them to stay faithful to the truth and love that had been deposited in their hearts.

One truth the Corinthians had not yet grasped, which informed the purpose behind this letter, was their inability to fully embrace the scandal of the cross. The glory of the cross is the glory of the one who was crucified upon it. They had neglected to appreciate the self-suffering nature of the cross-centered life. So Paul passionately pointed to the glory that lies ahead, especially in the midst of weakness and suffering, stirring them to keep their eyes on the prize. What wonderful insights fill the pages of this letter, magnifying the majesty of Christ, which shatters the darkness, reconciles the lost, and recreates us anew!

AUTHOR AND AUDIENCE

Paul wrote this letter to a needy congregation in the Roman city of Corinth to bring them comfort, wisdom, and insight. Many believe that this letter is actually a compilation of two: a so-called "tearful" letter that makes up the ending (chs. 10–13), which was possibly sent before the main "reconciliation" letter (chs. 1–9). Apparently, a number of people had infiltrated the church of Corinth and challenged Paul's apostolic credentials and the gospel he preached, which had bearing on what they believed.

In this letter, we get a glimpse into Paul's own trials and the path of continual triumph that he discovered. He opens his heart to us in this book, sharing his deep emotions, perhaps more here than in any of his other writings. We learn of the magnitude of his sufferings as he informs us of the trials he experienced, which informed his understanding of the gospel. As a minister of reconciliation, Paul brings tremendous energy to the church through his letters. He is a true hero of the faith!

MAJOR THEMES

The Incarnation and Crucifixion of Christ. One of the major themes of this letter is the incarnate presence of Christ on earth. As Paul wrote, "Although he was infinitely rich, he impoverished himself for our sake" (8:9). Christ's coming and condescension to our lives reveals his "gentleness and self-forgetfulness" (10:1), but Christ is also clearly God (1:2). Christ's incarnation wasn't meaningless; there was a purpose to his impoverishment.

The Son of God came to earth "so that by his poverty, we could become rich beyond measure" (8:9). Jesus, who knew no sin, became sin for us, "so that we *who did not know righteousness* might become the righteousness of God through our union with him" (5:21). He was "crucified as a 'weakling,'" (13:4) yet he "now lives again" (5:15). Because he was, and because he does, "All that is related to the old order has vanished. Behold, everything is fresh and new" (5:17).

The Call of the Gospel. One of the clearest descriptions of the gospel's call on our lives is found in 5:18, "God has made all things new, and reconciled us to himself." Paul opens up the mystery of our being made right with God through the finished work of Christ on the cross. This call has gone out from God into the hearts of all his lovers: "Turn back to God and be reconciled to him." (5:20).

This gospel call is also heard in and through the ministry that God has entrusted to us, "the ministry of opening the door of reconciliation to God" (5:19). Amazingly, we are all "ambassadors of the Anointed One who carry the message of Christ to the world" (5:20). Through our words and deeds, it's "as though God were tenderly pleading with them directly through our lips" (5:20). Our motivation is to honor God and love Christ, while petitioning people on Christ's behalf to turn back to God and be made new.

Christian Ministry. This letter is one of Paul's most personal, because in it he exhibits the characteristics of a spiritual father who has been entrusted by God as a caretaker of his children. From the beginning he roots the compassion and comfort he passes along to others in God himself (1:3). His generosity as a laborer on behalf of the Corinthians flows from God's own generous hand (chs. 8–9). Paul is paternally devoted to his children, so much so that he feels their weaknesses and burns with zeal for their restoration (11:29). Like all parents, Paul's affection was clear: he was willing to "gladly spend all that I have and all that I am for you" (12:15). In many ways Paul outlines a theology of pastoral service that should be modeled and adopted by all ministers of the gospel.

The Christian Life. At the center of Paul's letter is a strong call to live a life of holiness; the Christian life is a holy life. He tells us not to "team up with unbelievers in mismatched alliances" (6:14). Which doesn't mean that we are to avoid befriending the world, but to avoid living like the world. We are to "come out from among them and be separate" (6:17). Holy living is deliberate living, for as Christians, we are called to "remove everything from our lives that contaminates body and spirit" and develop holiness within us (7:1).

Another aspect of the Christian life Paul addresses is the paradox of our Christian existence. We are comforted, yet afflicted; we are secure, yet we suffer; we are both strong and weak; we experience joy and sorrow; we die yet live. God "comes alongside us to comfort us in every suffering" (1:4). When we are at our weakest, we "sense more deeply the mighty power of Christ living in me" (12:9). And though "we continually share in the death of Jesus," his "resurrection life . . . will be revealed through our humanity" (4:10).

Christian Generosity. One aspect of Christian living that Paul highlighted is that of generosity. During his apostolic ministry, Paul spent a good amount of energy over the course of five years collecting resources for "the poor among the holy believers in Jerusalem" (Rom. 15:26). In this letter Paul made one more appeal to the church of Corinth. He attempted to stir them to greater love by issuing a challenge of generous giving. He compared Christian generosity to the "extravagant grace of our Lord Jesus Christ" (8:9). It is an "act of worship" (8:11) and maintains "a fair balance" (8:14) between believers. Christian generosity should "flow from your heart, not from a sense of religious duty" (9:7) and should be marked by enthusiasm and "joy," because "God loves hilarious generosity" (9:7).

2 CORINTHIANS

Our New Life

Paul's Greeting

From Paul to God's called ones, his church in Corinth.

I have been chosen by Jesus Christ to be his apostle according to God's perfect plan. Our brother Timothy joins me in writing to you and all the holy believers throughout the Roman province of Achaia. *a* 2 May undeserved favor and endless peace be yours continually from our Father God and from our Lord Jesus, the Anointed One!

3 All praises belong to the God and Father of our Lord Jesus Christ. For he is the Father of tender mercy and the God of endless comfort. *b* 4 He always comes alongside us to comfort us in every suffering so that we can come alongside those who are in any painful trial. We can bring them this same comfort that God has poured out upon us. 5 And just as we experience the abundance of Christ's own sufferings, *c* even more of God's comfort will cascade upon us through our union with Christ.

6 If troubles weigh us down, that just means that we will receive even more comfort to pass on to you for your deliverance! For the comfort pouring into us empowers us to bring comfort to you. And with this comfort upholding you, you can endure *victoriously* the same suffering that we experience. 7 Now our hope for you is unshakable, *d* because we know that just as you share in our sufferings you will also share in God's comforting strength.

8 Brothers and sisters, you need to know about the severe trials we experienced while we were in western Turkey. *e* All of the hardships we passed

---

a 1:1 Although this letter was addressed primarily to the Corinthians, it was intended to be read by the churches in southern Greece (Achaia).

b 1:3 Unlike Paul's other letters, he skips over making his customary pleasant greeting to the Corinthians and begins this letter bursting with exuberant praise to God, who had delivered him from all of his painful ordeals. Tender mercy and compassion originate with God. As a kind father has compassion on his children, so God tenderly cares for each one of us. When suffering greets us, the God of mercy sustains us. His comfort is permanent and endless. See Mic. 7:18–19.

c 1:5 That is, "the sufferings we endure because of faithfully following Christ."

d 1:7 Or "firmly guaranteed."

e 1:8 Or "Asia." This was not the continent of Asia known today, but the Roman province of Asia comprised of western Turkey.

through crushed us beyond our ability to endure, and we were so completely overwhelmed that we were about to give up entirely.[a] [9] It felt like we[b] had a death sentence written upon our hearts, *and we still feel it to this day*. It has taught us to lose all faith in ourselves and to place all of our trust in the God who raises the dead. [10] He has rescued us from terrifying encounters with death. And now we fasten our hopes on him to continue to deliver us from death yet again, [11] as you labor together with us through prayer.[c] *Because there are so many interceding for us*, our deliverance will cause even more people to give thanks to God. What a gracious gift of mercy surrounds us because of your prayers!

Apostolic Integrity

[12] We rejoice in saying with complete honesty and a clear conscience[d] that God has empowered us to conduct ourselves[e] in a holy manner and with no hidden agenda.[f] God's marvelous grace enables us to minister to everyone with pure motives, not in the clever wisdom of the world. This is especially true in all of our dealings with you. [13] We write to you with words that are clearly understood, and there is no need for you to try to read between the lines of what we write in hopes that you can completely and accurately understand *our hearts*. [14] We know you have already understood us in a measure and that you will eventually come to understand us fully.[g] Then you'll be able to boast of us even as we will boast of you in the day of our Lord Jesus.

Paul Explains His Changed Plans

[15-16] With this confidence, I'm wanting to visit you before and after my trip *to Macedonia*[h] so that you enjoy a second experience of grace.[i] Afterward, I'm hoping you

---

a 1:8 We are not told exactly what overwhelming suffering Paul endured that caused him to write these words with such honest emotion. Some believe he had escaped an assassination attempt or perhaps a mob who had gathered to kill him. Regardless, the sufferings Paul endured were many. See 2 Cor. 11:23–33.

b 1:9 The Greek text is extremely emphatic: "It felt like we ourselves, within our very beings, had received the verdict of death!"

c 1:11 Or "as you lift up your faces to God in prayer." Paul knew that intercessory prayer has the power to change the future.

d 1:12 Or "indeed, our boasting and the testimony of our conscience."

e 1:12 Paul regularly uses "we" and "our" in 2 Corinthians to refer to apostles and apostolic ministry.

f 1:12 Or "We have behaved in the world with holiness and godly sincerity" (Aramaic, "purity"). Our boast and joy in ministry is not what we have done or how many followers we have, but that our conscience is clean and our motives unmixed. Paul is not taking credit for himself but stating clearly that God's grace was his source of strength and purity.

g 1:14 Or "to the end."

h 1:15–16 Implied and made explicit from v. 15.

i 1:15–16 Or "a second pleasure." It is possible Paul is using a figure of speech for his second trip to visit them.

will be able to aid me on my journey to Israel.[a] [17] When I revised my itinerary, was I vacillating? Or do I make my plans with unprincipled motives,[b] ready to flip-flop with a "yes" and a "no" in the same breath? *Of course not!*[c] [18] For as God is true to his word, my promise[d] to you was not a *fickle* "yes" when I meant "no."

[19] Jesus Christ is the Son of God, and he is the one whom Timothy, Silas, and I have preached to you—and he has never been both a "yes" and a "no." He has always been and always will be for us a resounding "YES!" [20] For all of God's promises find their "yes" of fulfillment in him.[e] And as his "yes" and our "amen"[f] ascend to God, we bring him glory![g]

[21] Now, it is God himself who has anointed us. And he is constantly strengthening both you and us in union with Christ. [22] *He knows we are his* since he has also stamped his seal of love[h] over our hearts and has given us the Holy Spirit like an engagement ring is given to a bride—a down payment of the blessings to come!

A Change in Paul's Travel Plans

[23] Now, I call upon this faithful God as a witness against me *if I'm not telling*

---

a 1:15–16 Or "Judea."

b 1:17 Or "according to the [ways of the] flesh."

c 1:17 The change of Paul's plans was used by his detractors as a sign of him being untrustworthy. But Paul explains that his itinerary change was not an indication of a lack of concern for them, but because he didn't want to come and have to rebuke them. He wanted to give the Holy Spirit time in their lives to help work out their issues. His longing was to come with joy and to impart his joy to them, rather than causing more pain. This is why he wrote an emotional letter to them pleading with them to change their ways.

d 1:18 Or "my message."

e 1:20 The Aramaic can be translated "All of the kingdoms of God are in him."

f 1:20 The Hebrew word for "amen" means "That's right!"

g 1:20 This elliptical sentence could imply the following: (1) It is through Christ that we hear and believe God's promises and say the declaration of our faith, "Amen," or (2) it is Christ who speaks through us the "Amen" (of faith).

h 1:22 The Greek word for seal is *sphragizō*. God has sealed believers with a seven-fold seal: (1) a seal of security, sealed tightly and kept secure in God's love (Deut. 32:34; Job 14:17; Matt. 27:66), (2) a seal of authentication that marks us as God's very own (1 Kings 21:8; Est. 8:10; John 6:27), (3) a seal to certify genuineness (Est. 8:8, 10; John 3:33), (4) a seal of ownership (Neh. 10:1; Jer. 32:44; 2 Cor. 1:22), (5) a seal of approval (Eph. 1:13–14), (6) a seal of righteousness (Rom. 4:11), and (7) a seal denoting a promise to be fulfilled (2 Cor. 5:5; Eph. 1:13–14; 4:30). The mark given by the beast is upon the forehead and hand, but the "seal" of Christ is over our hearts. Jesus, our Bridegroom, invites us to place him over our hearts like a fiery seal of love, the jealous flame of God that burns continually in our hearts (Song. 8:6). We are born of the Spirit, sealed with the Spirit, indwelt by the Spirit, baptized in the Spirit, filled with the Spirit, made one (unity) in the Spirit, given gifts of the Spirit, and given ministries by the Spirit. He is a promise, a seal, and a guarantee of receiving our full inheritance. The Greek word for "down payment" is *arrabōn* and is used in Greek culture for "engagement ring." Notice in vv. 21–22 that the Trinity (Father, Son, and Holy Spirit) is involved in bringing all this to pass.

you the absolute truth. It was because I hold you in my heart that I decided not to return to Corinth, in order to spare you *the humiliation of my rebuke.* [24] But I don't want to imply that *as leaders* we coerce you or somehow want to rule over your faith. [a] Instead, we are your partners who are called to increase your joy. [b] And we know that you already stand firm because of your *strong faith.* [c]

Paul's Previous Letter

2 So *until these issues were settled,* [d] I decided against paying you another painful visit. [e] [2] For if I brought you pain, you would be unable to bring me joy. [3] And this was the very point I made in my letter, for I didn't want to come and find sadness filling the very ones who should give me cheer. But I'm confident *that you will do what's right* so that my joyous delight will be yours.

[4] I wrote you previously sobbing and with a broken heart. [f] I was filled with anguish and deep distress. I had no intention of causing you pain but to convey the overwhelming measure of my love for you. [5] For the one who has caused me grief has not only grieved me but, to some extent, has caused you all grief as well. [6] I believe that your united rebuke [g] has been punishment enough for him. [7] Instead of more punishment, what he needs most is your encouragement through your gracious display of forgiveness. [8] I beg you to reaffirm your deep love for him.

[9] You see, I wrote previously in order to see if your hearts would pass the test and if you were willing to follow my counsel in everything. [10] If you freely forgive anyone for anything, then I also forgive him. And if I have forgiven anything, I did so for you before the face of Christ, [11] so that we would not be exploited [h] by the adversary, Satan, for we know his clever schemes.

[12] When I arrived at Troas, bringing the wonderful news of Christ, the Lord opened a great door of opportunity to minister there. [13] Still, I had no peace of mind, because I couldn't find my dear brother Titus [i] anywhere. So after saying goodbye to the believers, I set out for Macedonia to look for him.

---

a 1:24 Or "dictate what you must believe."

b 1:24 The Aramaic can be translated "We are helpers of your joy." True ministry in God's kingdom is to be coworkers with those we serve, laboring to see them overflow with joy. There is no control that leaders are to have over the people they serve; rather, they are to inspire lives to be filled with the joy of knowing Jesus.

c 1:24 The Aramaic can be translated "For it is through faith that you stand."

d 2:1 See 2 Cor. 2:4–11.

e 2:1 Paul implies that he had already paid them one painful visit (1:15–17).

f 2:4 Paul is referring here (and in v. 3) not to 1 Corinthians but to a letter he had written them after they received 1 Corinthians and failed to properly respond to what he wrote. This painful letter (see also 7:8) was a reprimand that powerfully impacted them. God has sovereignly chosen that we would not have this painful letter included in the New Testament, but its impact on the Corinthians is noteworthy. See also Prov. 27:6.

g 2:6 The Aramaic can be translated "Your triple rebuke is enough punishment."

h 2:11 The Aramaic can be translated "so that Satan will not overtake us."

i 2:13 Titus was a spiritual son to Paul whom he greatly loved. This is the Titus Paul wrote

Apostolic Ministry

[14] God always makes his grace visible[a] in Christ, who includes us as partners of his endless triumph.[b] Through our yielded lives he spreads[c] the fragrance of the knowledge of God everywhere we go. [15] We[d] have become the unmistakable aroma *of the victory* of the Anointed One to God[e]—a perfume of life to those being saved and the odor of death[f] to those who are perishing. [16] The unbelievers smell a deadly stench that leads to death, but believers smell the life-giving aroma that leads to abundant life. And who of us can rise to this challenge?[g] [17] For unlike so many, we are not peddlers[h] of God's Word who water down the message. We are those sent from God with pure motives, who speak in the sight of God[i] from our union with Christ.

Servants of the New Covenant

3 Are we beginning to sound like those who speak highly of themselves? Do you really need letters of recommendation *to validate our ministry*, like others do?[j] Do we really need your letter of endorsement? *Of course not!* [2] For your very lives are our "letters of recommendation," permanently engraved on our hearts, recognized and read by everybody. [3] As a result of our ministry, you are living letters written by Christ, not with ink but by the Spirit of the living God—not carved onto stone tablets[k] but on the tablets of tender hearts. [4] We carry this confidence in our hearts because of our union with Christ before God. [5] Yet we

---

his letter to (book of Titus). He was responsible to collect and distribute an offering for the church in Jerusalem (2 Cor. 8:6). It is possible that Titus was the one who carried the painful letter to Corinth. After finding Titus in Macedonia, Paul sent him back to Corinth to deliver this letter.

a 2:14 As translated from the Aramaic. The Greek is "Thanks be to God."

b 2:14 Or "who always leads us as captives in his triumphant procession." This difficult-to-translate passage may be an allusion to the Roman victory procession in celebration of their military triumphs. See also Col. 2:15.

c 2:14 Or "manifests."

d 2:15 Although this is true of every believer, Paul, throughout this section, uses "we" in reference to apostles.

e 2:15 Or "We are Christ's sweet fragrance [of sacrifice] that ascends to God."

f 2:15 That is, a sacrifice ready to be offered.

g 2:16 As challenging as our ministry may be, God empowers us to overcome by his Holy Spirit. He empowers everyone he calls.

h 2:17 The Greek word *kapēleuō* (a hapax legomenon) means "retailer," but in classical Greek it comes with a negative connotation ("one who sells at an illegitimate profit"). The adverbial form of the noun is "cheating" or "deceitful."

i 2:17 Paul states that his ministry of teaching and preaching happened while he was in the presence of God. His eyes were set on God, not on the people's response.

j 3:1 Apparently, there were some insecure and phony ministers who would carry forged letters of recommendation in an attempt to validate their ministry. Paul's supernatural ministry needed no such letter of recommendation.

k 3:3 See Ex. 24:12; 31:18; 34:1; Deut. 9:10–11; Jer. 38:33 (LXX).

don't see ourselves as capable enough to do anything in our own strength, for our true competence flows from God's *empowering presence.* [6] He alone makes us adequate ministers who are focused on an entirely new covenant. Our ministry is not based on the letter of the law but through the *power of the* Spirit. The letter of the law kills, but the Spirit pours out life. [a]

The Glorious Ministry of the Spirit

[7] Even the ministry that was characterized by chiseled letters on stone tablets came with a dazzling measure of glory, though it produced death. The Israelites couldn't bear to gaze on the glowing face of Moses [b] because of the radiant splendor shining from his countenance—a glory destined to fade away.

[8] Yet how much more radiant is this new and glorious ministry of the Spirit *that shines from us!* [9] For if the former ministry of condemnation was ushered in with a measure of glory, how much more does the ministry that imparts righteousness far excel in glory. [c] [10] What once was glorious no longer holds any glory because of the increasingly [d] greater glory that has replaced it. [11] The fading ministry came with a portion of glory, but now we embrace the unfading ministry of a permanent impartation of glory. [12] So then, with this amazing hope living in us, we step out in freedom and boldness to speak the truth.

[13] We are not like Moses, who used a veil to hide the glory to keep the Israelites from staring at him as it faded away. [e] [14] Their minds were closed and hardened, for even to this day that same veil comes over their minds when they hear the words of the former covenant. The veil has not yet been lifted from them, for it is only eliminated when one is joined to the Messiah. [15] So until now, whenever the Old Testament [f] is being read, the same blinding comes over their hearts. [16] But the moment one turns to the Lord [g] with an open heart, the veil is lifted *and they see.* [h] [17] Now, the "Lord" *I'm referring to* is the Holy Spirit, [i] and wherever he is Lord, there is freedom.

[18] We can all draw close to him with the veil removed from our faces. And

---

a 3:6 To illustrate this, on the day when the law was given by Moses, three thousand people were killed, but on the day the Spirit was poured out at Pentecost, three thousand people received new life. See Ex. 32:28; Acts 2:41.

b 3:7 See Ex. 34:29.

c 3:9 The contrast here is between a ministry that brings awareness of sin and leads to condemnation and a new ministry that confirms to us that we are made righteous and innocent by the work of the cross and the grace of the Spirit.

d 3:10 As translated from the Aramaic and implied contextually in the Greek.

e 3:13 Or "the end of what was fading."

f 3:15 Or "Moses," an obvious metonymy.

g 3:16 The Aramaic can be translated "Lord Yahweh."

h 3:16 See Ex. 34:34.

i 3:17 Paul is teaching us that not every time the word *Lord* appears does it mean Jesus Christ. Here we see that "the Lord" refers to the Holy Spirit. When the Holy Spirit is ruling, speaking, convincing us of truth, there is freedom. Jesus calls the Holy Spirit the Lord of

with no veil we all become like mirrors who brightly reflect the glory of the Lord *Jesus.* [a] We are being transfigured [b] into his very image as we move from one brighter level of glory to another. [c] And this glorious transfiguration comes from the Lord, who is the Spirit. [d]

New Covenant Ministry

4 Now, it's because of God's mercy [e] that we have been entrusted with the privilege of this *new covenant* ministry. And we will not quit or faint with weariness. [2] We reject every shameful cover-up and refuse to resort to cunning trickery or distorting the Word of God. [f] Instead, we open up our souls to you [g] by presenting the truth to everyone's conscience in the sight and presence of God. [3] Even if our gospel message is veiled, it is only veiled to those who are perishing, [4] for their minds have been blinded by the god of this age, [h] leaving them in unbelief. Their blindness keeps them from seeing the dayspring light [i] of the wonderful news of the glory of Jesus Christ, who is the *divine* image of God.

[5] We don't preach ourselves, but rather the lordship of Jesus Christ, for we are your servants for Jesus' sake. [6] For God, who said,

> "Let brilliant light shine out of darkness," [j]

---

the harvest who prepares the workers and the harvest fields, sending them out into specific places for the reaping of souls. See Matt. 9:38.

a 3:18 Or "We all, with unveiled faces, behold the glory of the Lord as in a mirror."

b 3:18 The Greek verb *metamorphoō* is the same word used for Jesus' being transfigured on the mountain (Matt. 17:2; Mark 9:2) and for our transfiguration through the renewing of the thoughts of our minds (Rom. 12:2).

c 3:18 The source of our transformation comes from Christ's glory, and the destination we are brought to is more glory. The transforming glory is the result of gazing upon the beauty and splendor of Jesus Christ.

d 3:18 Notice the ten aspects of New Testament ministry given by Paul: (1) It is based on the triumph of Christ over every power of darkness (2:14). (2) It diffuses the fragrant aroma of Christ everywhere (2:15–16). (3) It refuses to water down the Word of God (2:17). (4) It produces living letters of Christ (3:3). (5) It is not based on the clever abilities of men but God's empowering presence (3:6). (6) It imparts life (3:6). (7) It flows from the Holy Spirit (3:8, 17–18). (8) It imparts righteousness (3:9). (9) It contains a greater glory than the law (3:10–11). (10) It brings the transfiguration of believers into greater levels of glory (3:18).

e 4:1 Or "God has mercied us." The Aramaic can be translated "God's mercy rests on us."

f 4:2 Or "handle the word of God dishonestly."

g 4:2 As translated from the Aramaic. The Greek is "we commend ourselves."

h 4:4 Satan is called the god of this age. He uses trickery, deceit, accusation, and slander to blind people's hearts. See John 8:44; 12:31; 14:30; Eph. 2:2.

i 4:4 The Aramaic can be translated "the flame of the good news."

j 4:6 Paul helps us to understand that "light" is both literal and a metaphor for spiritual revelation, and shows that the creation narrative provides us with an allegory pointing to the experience of new birth in Christ. See Gen. 1:3; Isa. 9:2.

is the one who has cascaded his light into us—the brilliant dawning light of the glorious knowledge of God as we gaze into the face of Jesus Christ. [a]

Treasure in Clay Jars

[7] We are like common clay jars that carry this glorious treasure within, so that the extraordinary overflow of power will be seen as God's, not ours. [b] [8] Though we experience every kind of pressure, we're not crushed. At times we don't know what to do, but quitting is not an option. [c] [9] We are persecuted by others, but God has not forsaken us. We may be knocked down, but not out. [10] We continually share in the death of Jesus in our own bodies [d] so that the resurrection life of Jesus will be revealed through our humanity. [11] We consider living to mean that we are constantly being handed over to death for Jesus' sake so that the life of Jesus will be revealed through our humanity. [12] So, then, death is at work in us but it releases life in you.

[13] We have the same Spirit of faith that is described in the Scriptures when it says,

"First I believed, then I spoke in faith." [e]

So we also first believe then speak in faith. [14] We do this because we are convinced that he who raised Jesus will raise us up with him, and together we will all be brought into his presence. [15] Yes, all things work for your enrichment [f] so that more of God's marvelous grace will spread to more and more people, resulting in an even greater increase of praise [g] to God, bringing him even more glory!

[16] So no wonder we don't give up. For even though our outer person gradually wears out, our inner being is renewed every single day. [17] We view our slight, short-lived troubles in the light of eternity. We see our difficulties as the substance that produces for us an eternal, weighty glory far beyond all comparison, [18] because we don't focus our attention on what is seen but on what is unseen. For what is seen is temporary, but the unseen realm is eternal.

---

a 4:6 Or "in the face-to-face presence of Christ."

b 4:7 This verse begins a long and complicated Greek sentence that ends with v. 10. Paul uses figurative language to say that we are common clay jars (created from dust/clay) yet we possess the brilliant light of God's glory, Jesus Christ, and carry him as treasure in our being. The outward vessel is not as important as the glorious treasure within. The metaphors here may allude to Gideon's clay pots that had burning torches inside (Judg. 7:16).

c 4:8 Or "perplexed but not thoroughly perplexed." The Aramaic can be translated "We are corrected but not condemned."

d 4:10 Or "carry about in the body the death of Jesus."

e 4:13 See Ps. 116:10.

f 4:15 See Rom. 8:28.

g 4:15 Or "to cause thanksgiving to superabound."

Living by Faith

5 We are convinced that even if these bodies we live in are folded up at death like tents, we will still have a God-built home that no human hands have built, which will last forever in the heavenly realm. [2] We inwardly sigh[a] *as we live in these physical "tents,"* longing to put on a new body for our life in heaven, [3] in the belief that once we put on our new "clothing" we won't find ourselves "naked." [4] So, while living in this "tent," we groan under its burden, not because we want to die but because we want these new bodies. We crave for all that is mortal to be swallowed up by *eternal* life. [5] *And this is no empty hope,* for God himself is the one who has prepared us for this wonderful destiny. And to confirm this promise, he has given us the Holy Spirit, like an engagement ring, as a guarantee.[b]

[6] That's why we're always full of courage. Even while we're at home in the body, we're homesick to be with the Master—[7] for we live by faith, not by what we see with our eyes. [8] We live with a joyful confidence, yet at the same time we take delight in the thought of leaving our bodies behind to be at home with the Lord. [9] So whether we live or die[c] we make it our life's passion[d] to live our lives pleasing to him.[e] [10] For one day we will all be openly revealed before Christ on his throne[f] so that each of us will be duly recompensed for our actions done in life,[g] whether good or worthless.

The Message of Reconciliation

[11] Since we are those who stand in holy awe of the Lord,[h] we make it our passion to persuade others *to turn to him.* We know that our lives are transparent before the God who knows us fully, and I hope that we are also well known to your consciences. [12] Again, we are not taking an opportunity to brag, *but giving you information* that will enable you to be proud of us, and to answer those who esteem outward appearances while overlooking what is in the heart.

---

a 5:2 The Aramaic uses the phrase "to sigh and yearn."

b 5:5 By giving us the Holy Spirit, God is making us a promise, a guarantee of receiving our full inheritance. The Greek word for "down payment" (or "pledge") is *arrabōn* and is used in Greek culture for "engagement ring."

c 5:9 Or "at home or away from home."

d 5:9 Or "our driving ambition."

e 5:9 Or "in full agreement with him."

f 5:10 Or "judgment seat."

g 5:10 Or "done in the body" or "time spent in the body." The judgment for our sins fell upon Christ on the cross, and the believer will never be judged for his sins. This judgment (scrutinizing) is for rewards. There will be different levels of reward given to believers after death. For some, there will be no reward, yet they will still be saved. See Rom. 14:10–12; 1 Cor. 3:10–15.

h 5:11 Although the Greek word *phobos* is usually associated with fear or dread, the classic use of the word is "deepest awe/respect." See 1 John 4:18.

¹³ If we are out of our minds in a blissful, divine ecstasy,^a it is for God, but if we are in our right minds, it is for your benefit. ¹⁴ For it is Christ's love that fuels our passion and motivates us,^b because we are absolutely convinced that he has given his life for all of us. This means all died with him, ¹⁵ so that those who live^c should no longer live self-absorbed lives but lives that are poured out for him—the one who died for us and now lives again. ¹⁶ So then, from now on, we have a new perspective that refuses to evaluate people merely by their outward appearances. For that's how we once viewed the Anointed One, but no longer do we see him with limited human insight.^d

¹⁷ Now, if anyone is enfolded into Christ, he has become an entirely new creation. All that is related to the old order has vanished.^e Behold, everything is fresh and new.^{f 18} And God has made all things new,^g and reconciled^h us to himself, and given us the ministry of reconciling others to God. ¹⁹ In other words, it was through the Anointed One that God was shepherding the world,ⁱ not even keeping records of their transgressions, and he has entrusted to us the ministry of opening the door of reconciliation to God.^{j 20} We are ambassadors^k of the

---

a 5:13 The Greek word *existēmi* means to be outside of one's self in a state of blissful ecstasy and filled with pleasure. It is to come into another state of consciousness of being lost in wonder and amazement.

b 5:14 Paul uses the Greek word *synechō* (*syn* = "together with"; *echō* is where we get our English word *echo*), which is translated as "seize," "compel," "urge," "control," "lay hold of," "overwhelm," "completely dominate." Paul is stating that the motivating passion of his life is Christ's love filling his heart, leaving him no choice but to surrender everything to God. Paul gives us seven empowering motivations by which we are to live our lives: (1) the Holy Spirit—v. 5, (2) faith—v. 7, (3) a joyful confidence that we have new bodies waiting for us in heaven—v. 8, (4) our life's passion to live for Christ—v. 9, (5) the knowledge of our appointment to stand before Christ—v. 10, (6) our holy awe of God—v. 11, (7) Christ's endless love for us—v. 14.

c 5:15 Or "and he died for all so that those who live." The repetitive phrase from v. 14 has been enfolded into the verse for the sake of English clarity.

d 5:16 From man's point of view, Christ was a blasphemer and false teacher. Yet when we see him from the eyes of faith, we view him as the pure and holy one, God's Son.

e 5:17 This would include our old identity, our life of sin, the power of Satan, the religious works of trying to please God, our old relationship with the world, and our old mind-sets. We are not reformed or simply refurbished, we are made completely new by our union with Christ and the indwelling of the Holy Spirit.

f 5:17 Or "Behold, a new order has come!"

g 5:18 As translated from the Aramaic and implied in the Greek.

h 5:18 Or "who has restored us to friendship with God."

i 5:19 As translated from the Aramaic. The Greek is "God was reconciling the world to himself, not counting their trespasses against them."

j 5:19 As translated from the Aramaic.

k 5:20 To be ambassadors for Christ means that we are his diplomatic agents of the highest rank sent to represent King Jesus and authorized to speak on his behalf. We are the voice of heaven to the earth, invested with royal power through the name of Jesus and authority of his blood.

Anointed One who carry the message of Christ to the world, as though God were tenderly pleading[a] with them directly through our lips. So we tenderly plead with you on Christ's behalf, "Turn back to God and be reconciled to him." [21] For God made[b] the only one who did not know sin to become sin for us,[c] so that we *who did not know righteousness* might become the righteousness of God through our union with him.[d]

Paul's Ministry

6 Now, since we are God's coworkers, we beg you not to take God's marvelous grace for granted, *allowing it to have no effect on your lives.*[e] [2] For he says,

I listened to you at the time of my favor.
And the day when you needed salvation,
I came to your aid.[f]

So can't you see? Now is the time to respond to his favor! Now is the day of salvation! [3] We will not place obstacles[g] in anyone's way that hinder them *from coming to salvation* so that our ministry will not be discredited. [4] Yet, as God's servants, we prove ourselves authentic[h] in every way. *For example:*

We have great endurance[i] in hardships
    and in persecutions.
We don't lose courage in a time of stress and calamity.
[5] We've been beaten many times,
    imprisoned,
    and *found ourselves* in the midst of riots.
We've endured many troubles,[j]

---

a 5:20 Or "begging."

b 5:21 The Greek word Paul uses is *poieō*, a verb that, when nominalized, is *poiema* (poem, or poetry). Christ is God's poetic masterpiece who became the glorious sacrifice for sin. Though disturbing to the eyes of man, God saw the work of redemption culminated in the masterful poetry of his Son suspended on a cross to give us heaven's righteousness. Read Isa. 52:10–53:12.

c 5:21 Or "the sin offering." See Ex. 29:14; Lev. 4:3; Num. 8:8; Eph. 5:2.

d 5:21 This one verse is perhaps the greatest verse in the New Testament to describe our salvation through the sinless Savior and his substitutionary death on the cross. A wonderful divine exchange took place at the cross. All of our sins were left there, our guilt was removed and forever gone, and we walked away with all of God's righteousness. What bliss is ours! Every believer today possesses the perfect and complete righteousness of Christ. We are seen by the Father as righteous as his Son.

e 6:1 Or "not to receive God's grace in vain."

f 6:2 See Isa. 49:8.

g 6:3 Or "scandals that cause people to stumble."

h 6:4 The Aramaic can be translated "reveals our inner souls."

i 6:4 The Aramaic can be translated "profound hope."

j 6:5 Or "labors." The Aramaic can be translated "tortures."

had sleepless nights,
and gone hungry. [a]

[6] *We have proved ourselves* by our lifestyles of purity,
by our spiritual insights,
by our patience,
and by showing kindness,
by the Spirit of holiness
and by our uncritical love for you. [b]

[7] *We commend ourselves to you* by our truthful teachings, [c]
by the power of God *working through us*,
and with the mighty weapons [d] of righteousness—
a sword in one hand and *a shield* in the other. [e]

[8] Amid honor or dishonor, [f]
slander or praise—
even when we are treated as deceivers and imposters—
we remain steadfast and true.

[9] We are unknown nobodies whom everyone knows.
We are frequently at death's door,
yet here we are, still alive!
We have been severely punished
yet not executed.

[10] We may suffer,
yet in every season [g] we are always found rejoicing.
We may be poor,
yet we bestow great riches on many.
We seem to have nothing,
yet in reality we possess all things. [h]

[11] My friends at Corinth, our hearts are wide open to you and we speak freely, holding nothing back from you. [12] If there is a block in our relationship, it is not with us, for we carry you in our hearts with great love, yet you still

---

a 6:5 Or "fastings."

b 6:6 The Aramaic can be translated "love without scheming."

c 6:7 Or "the word of truth [Gr. *logos*]."

d 6:7 Or "armor."

e 6:7 Or "weapons of righteousness for the right hand and for the left." By implication, this would mean a shield and a sword—every warrior's weapons.

f 6:8 The Aramaic can be translated "cursed" (by others).

g 6:10 As translated by the Aramaic.

h 6:10 What an amazing list of characteristics of true apostolic ministry. These are the virtues that endeared Paul and his ministry companions to the churches and validated his authority as an example to them of God's true servant.

withhold your affections[a] from us. [13] So I speak to you as our children. Make room in your hearts for us as we have done for you.

The Temple of the Living God

[14] Don't continue to team up with unbelievers in mismatched alliances,[b] for what partnership is there between righteousness and rebellion? Who could mingle light with darkness? [15] What harmony can there be between Christ and Satan?[c] Or what does a believer have in common with an unbeliever? [16] What friendship does God's temple[d] have with demons?[e] For indeed, we are the temple of the living God, just as God has said:

> I will make my home in them and walk among them.
> I will be their God, and they will be my people.[f]

[17] For this reason,

> "Come out from among them and be separate," says the Lord.
> "Touch nothing that is unclean, and I will embrace you.[g]
> [18] I will be a true Father to you,[h]
>   and you will be my beloved sons and daughters,"
>   says the Lord Yahweh Almighty.[i]

Living Holy Lives

7 Beloved ones, with promises like these, and because of our deepest respect and worship of God, we must remove everything from our lives[j] that contaminates body and spirit, and continue to complete the development of holiness within us.

---

a 6:12 Or "tender mercies." Second Corinthians is Paul's most intimate and descriptive letter. He writes of his inner feelings here more than in any other letter.

b 6:14 Paul's teaching here includes marital, business, and personal relationships. We never abandon our responsibility to reach the world (1 Cor. 5:9–10), but we must steer clear of relationships that will divide our loyalty to Christ.

c 6:15 Or "Belial" (the worthless one), a term for Satan.

d 6:16 The temple in Jerusalem was still standing when Paul wrote this.

e 6:16 As translated from the Aramaic. The Greek is "idols."

f 6:16 See Lev. 26:12; Jer. 32:38; Ezek. 37:27.

g 6:17 Or "I will welcome you" (within). See Isa. 52:11; Ezek. 20:41.

h 6:18 God himself will assume the role of caring for us and meeting our needs, giving himself eternally to us. See Ps. 103:18; Mal. 1:6.

i 6:18 As translated from the Aramaic. See 2 Sam. 7:14; Isa. 43:6. Paul is paraphrasing Old Testament texts, changing phrases and combining them to make his point. Jesus likewise often paraphrased Old Testament verses as he taught the people.

j 7:1 Or "purify ourselves." Believers today must take an active and disciplined approach to spiritual maturity and living holy lives. Grace never removes our responsibility to be faithful to God. Grace empowers us to do what pleases God (Phil. 2:13).

[2]Again, I urge you, make room for us in your hearts, for we have wronged[a] no one, corrupted[b] no one, and taken advantage[c] of no one. [3]I'm not saying this to condemn you, for I already told you that we carry you permanently in our hearts—and you'll stay there throughout our lives, for we will live together and die together. [4]With an open heart let me freely say how very proud I am of you and how often I boast about you. In fact, *when I think of you* my heart is greatly encouraged and overwhelmed with joy, despite our many troubles.

Paul in Macedonia

[5]Even after we came into the province of Macedonia,[d] we found no relief. We were restless and exhausted; troubles met us at every turn. Outwardly I faced conflicts and inwardly emotional turmoil.[e] [6]But God, who always knows how to encourage the depressed, encouraged us greatly by the arrival of Titus. [7]We were relieved not only to see him but because of the report he brought us of how you refreshed his heart. He told us of your affection toward me, your deep remorse, and how concerned you were for me. This truly made my heart leap for joy!

Godly Remorse over Sin

[8]Even if my letter made you sorrowful, I don't regret sending it (even though I felt awful for a moment when I heard how it grieved you). [9]Now I'm overjoyed—not because I made you sad, but because your grief led you to a deep repentance. You experienced godly sorrow, and as God intended, it brought about gain for you, not loss, so that no harm has been done by us. [10]God designed us to feel remorse over sin in order to produce repentance that leads to victory.[f] This leaves us with no regrets. But the sorrow of the world works death.

---

a   7:2 The Aramaic can be translated "We have hated no one."
b   7:2 That is, they had not led people astray from right doctrine. They corrupted no one's faith.
c   7:2 Or "We have cheated no one" (for financial gain). These are the three goals every minister should set for his or her calling: (1) to do no wrong to another nor to "hate" anyone, (2) to not corrupt or lead anyone astray, and (3) to never use his or her authority to take advantage of anyone by cheating for personal gain. Paul had a blameless history in ministry.
d   7:5 This was after Paul left Troas and where he wrote his severe letter to the Corinthians (2 Cor. 2:12–13).
e   7:5 Or "fears." The Aramaic can be translated "on the outside battles and on the inside surrendering." With great honesty, Paul discloses his feelings while in Macedonia. He was beset with adversaries who opposed him, problems and arguments within the church, and persecution at every turn. Paul was emotionally torn by all the conflicts among the believers and feared for Titus' safety. He was worried about how the Corinthians would receive his severe letter, plus there is a hint in his words that his concern was wearing him down both physically and emotionally. Being honest about our emotions is the first step in finding comfort and peace. Paul's example of a leader opening his heart to his people should not be missed by this generation.
f   7:10 Or "deliverance (salvation)."

¹¹ Can't you see the good fruit that has come, as God intended, because of your remorse over sin?[a] Now you are eager to do what is right! Look at the indignation you experienced over what happened and how alarmed you became. What holy longing it awakened, what passion *for God*, and how ready you were to bring justice to the offender. Your response has proved that you are free of blame in this matter.

¹² So I wrote you not simply to correct the one who did the wrong or on the behalf of the one who was wronged, but to help you realize in God's sight how loyal you are to us. ¹³ Your response leaves us so encouraged! You've made us even more joyful upon hearing of how you refreshed Titus, for his mind was set at ease by all of you. ¹⁴ I have not been embarrassed by you, for the things I bragged about you to Titus were not proven false. Just as everything we said to you was true, so our boasting to Titus about you has proven to be true as well. ¹⁵ His affection toward you has grown as he remembers your obedience and how warmly you welcomed him with fear and trembling. ¹⁶ I'm beside myself with joy! I am so confident in you!

Generosity of the Churches

8 Beloved ones, we must tell you about the grace God poured out upon the churches of Macedonia. ² For even during a season of severe difficulty and tremendous suffering, they became even more filled with joy. From the depths of their extreme poverty, super-abundant joy overflowed into an act of extravagant generosity. ³ For I can verify that they spontaneously gave, not only according to their means but far beyond what they could afford. ⁴ They actually begged us for the privilege of sharing in this ministry of giving to God's holy people *who are living in poverty.* ⁵ They exceeded our expectations by first dedicating themselves fully to the Lord and then to us, according to God's pleasure.[b] ⁶ That is why we appealed to Titus, since he was the one who got you started and encouraged you to give, so he could help you complete this generous undertaking

---

a 7:11 Both the Hebraic and Greek concepts of repentance are literally "to turn from sin and come back to God"; that is, "to have a change of mind/direction." This involves the "sorrow" or "remorse" of our hearts before God. Repentance is not a sterile, feeling-less act of changing direction. Paul makes it clear that godly remorse is a "God-intended" feeling that moves the heart back to God. Our repentance is not a work of the flesh but the result of God's Spirit stirring our conscience. Peter's godly remorse over his denial of Christ eventually led him to experience a complete inner healing, while Judas' remorse led him to suicide.

b 8:5 Under persecution and desperately poor, the churches of Macedonia (Philippi, Thessalonica, and Berea) gave more than just an extravagant offering. They fully surrendered themselves to the Lord and gave out of a longing to fulfill God's pleasure. This is the key to generous giving. First we dedicate our hearts to God, which includes our finances, then we give to God's work as he directs us. Throughout 2 Corinthians, giving is described as a "grace" that God places on our lives, which empowers our generosity.

on your behalf. ⁷You do well and excel in every respect—in unstoppable faith, in powerful preaching, in revelation knowledge, in your passionate devotion, and in sharing the love we have shown to you. So make sure that you also excel in grace-filled generosity.ᵃ

⁸I'm not saying this as though I were issuing an order but to stir you to greater love by mentioning the enthusiasm *of the Macedonians* as a challenge to you.ᵇ ⁹For you have experienced the extravagant grace of our Lord Jesus Christ, that although he was infinitely rich, he impoverished himself for our sake, so that by his poverty, we could become rich beyond measure.

¹⁰So here are my thoughts concerning this matter, and it's in your best interests. Since you made such a good start last year, both in the grace of giving and in your longing to give, ¹¹you should finish what you started.ᶜ You were so eager in your intentions to give, so go do it. Finish this act of worship according to your ability to give. ¹²For if the intention and desire are there, *the size of the gift doesn't matter*. Your gift is fully acceptable to God according to what you have, not what you don't have. ¹³I'm not saying this in order to ease someone else's load by overloading you, but as a matter of fair balance. ¹⁴Your surplus could meet their need, and their abundance may one day meet your need. This equal sharing of abundance will mean a fair balance.ᵈ ¹⁵As it is written:

> The one who gathered much didn't have too much,
>> and the one who gathered little didn't have too little.ᵉ

Titus Sent to Corinth

¹⁶We give thanks to God for putting the same devotion I have for you into the heart of Titus. ¹⁷Of course, he enthusiastically accepted our request to go to Corinth, but because he carries you in his heart, he'd already planned on coming. ¹⁸So we're sending with him the brotherᶠ who is greatly honored and

---

a 8:7 Notice the features of godliness in this verse that should be seen in our lives and ministries: (1) We excel in everything. (2) We have unstoppable faith. (3) We have an anointing of grace to speak the Word. (4) We have revelation knowledge. (5) We have passionate devotion. (6) We show love. (7) We are generous.

b 8:8 Or "to test your love by the eagerness of others."

c 8:11 Or "Get on with it and finish the job!"

d 8:14 Apparently, the Corinthian church was not poor. They had intended, a year prior to receiving this letter, to make a generous offering to the believers in Jerusalem living in poverty. Paul encourages them to now follow through with their pledge. Note the principles of giving Paul teaches them in vv. 10–15: (1) A willing, cheerful offering is more important than the amount. (2) Financial commitments of giving are to be taken seriously. (3) We are to share our substance with those in need, because the time may come when we may need their gifts. (4) Our giving reflects our devotion to Christ. (5) We are to give what we are able and not stress about what we cannot give. We are to give in proportion to our income.

e 8:15 See Ex. 16:18.

f 8:18 This brother and the one mentioned in v. 22 were identified as apostles. Many have tried

respected in all the churches for his work of evangelism. [19] Not only that, he has been appointed by the churches to be our traveling companion as we carry and dispense this generous gift that glorifies the Lord and shows how eager we are to help. [20] *We are sending a team* in order to avoid any criticism over how we handle this wonderfully generous gift, [21] for we intend to do what is right and we are totally open both to the Lord's inspection and to man's. [22] So we're sending with them another brother who is faithful and proven to be a man of integrity. He is passionate to help you now more than ever, for he believes in you.

[23] Concerning the credentials of Titus, he's my partner and coworker in ministry for you. As for the brothers coming with him, they are apostles of the churches, which are the glory of the Anointed One. [a] [24] So demonstrate to them how much you love, and prove that our boasting of you is justified.

The Offering for Needy Believers

9 Actually, there's no need to write you about this contribution for the holy believers *in Jerusalem,* [2] for I already know that you are on board and eager to help. [b] I keep boasting to the churches of Macedonia about your passion to give, telling them that the believers of Corinth [c] have been preparing to give for a year. Your enthusiasm is contagious—it has stirred many of them to do likewise. [3] Still, I thought it would be best to send these brothers to receive the offering that you've prepared, so that our boasting about how you were ready to give would not be found hollow. [4] For if, after boasting of our confidence in you, some of the Macedonians were to come with me and find that you were not prepared, we would be embarrassed—to say nothing of you. [5] That's why I've requested that the brothers come before I do and make arrangements in advance for the substantial offering you pledged. Then it will be seen as a matter of generosity and not under pressure, as something you felt forced to do.

Hilarious Generosity

[6] Here's my point. A stingy sower [d] will reap a meager harvest, but the one who sows from a generous spirit will reap an abundant harvest. [7] Let giving flow from

---

unsuccessfully to identify whom they might have been. Some of the names considered include Timothy, Luke, Barnabas, Apollos, Mark, Erastus, Silas, Sopater, Aristarchus, Secundus, Gaius, Tychicus, and Trophimus. Regardless of these apostles' identities, we know that Titus was the leader of this delegation and that all three were apostles of the church. See Eph. 4:11.

a 8:23 Although ambiguous in the Greek text, the clause "which are the glory of the Anointed One" most likely refers to the churches. God's church is his glorious bride on the earth, which brings him glory through all the ages. If referring to Titus and his delegation, this verse would mean that the apostles are the glory of the Anointed One.

b 9:2 The Aramaic can be translated "I know the goodness of your impulses" (or "intentions"). Paul was not hesitant to point out the obvious qualities and virtues of others.

c 9:2 Or "Achaia," the Roman province where Corinth was situated.

d 9:6 The Aramaic can be translated "the one who sows with a storehouse of seed"

your heart, not from a sense of religious duty. Let it spring up freely from the joy of giving—all because God loves hilarious generosity![a] [8] Yes, God is more than ready to overwhelm you with every form of grace, so that you will have more than enough of everything[b]—every moment and in every way. He will make you overflow with abundance in every good thing you do. [9] Just as the Scriptures say *about the one who trusts in him*:

Because he has sown extravagantly and given to the poor,
    his kindness and generous deeds will never be forgotten.[c]

[10] This generous God who supplies abundant seed[d] for the farmer, *which becomes* bread for our meals,[e] is even more extravagant toward you. First he supplies[f] every need, plus more. Then he multiplies the seed *as you sow it*, so that the harvest of your generosity[g] will grow. [11] You will be abundantly enriched in every way as you give generously on every occasion,[h] for when we take your gifts to those in need,[i] it causes many to give thanks to God.

[12] The priestly ministry[j] you are providing through your offering not only supplies what is lacking for God's people, it inspires an outpouring[k] of praises and thanksgiving to God himself. [13] For as your extremely generous offering meets the approval[l] *of those in Jerusalem*, it will cause them to give glory to God—all because of your loyal support and allegiance to the gospel of Christ, as well as your generous-hearted partnership with them toward those in need. [14] Because of this extraordinary grace, which God has lavished on you, they will

---

(remaining). This describes a farmer who is stingy with his sowing. Since he has a storehouse of seed, he can afford to sow liberally.

a 9:7 See Prov. 22:8 (LXX). There are seven things in the Bible that God loves: (1) the resident foreigner or immigrant (Deut. 10:19), (2) righteousness in our affairs with others (Ps. 11:7), (3) justice (Ps. 37:28), (4) the gates of Zion (Ps. 87:2), (5) his righteous people (Ps. 146:8), (6) a hilarious or cheerful giver (2 Cor. 9:7), and (7) those he disciplines (Heb. 12:6).

b 9:8 The Greek word Paul uses is *autarkeia*, and it is found in classical Greek as meaning "independently wealthy, needing nothing." See Aristotle, *Pol.* 1. 8, 14.

c 9:9 See Ps. 112:9.

d 9:10 The Greek word *epichorēgeo* is used in Greek literature for someone who pays all expenses for the drama / choir (production), plus more, providing income for those who take part. God is seen as the leader of the divine choir, orchestrating everything and providing all that is needed to bring forth the sounds of his glory on the earth.

e 9:10 See Isa. 55:10.

f 9:10 The Greek word is *chorēgeo* (see the first footnote on this verse).

g 9:10 Or "righteousness," used in this context as "generosity" (or "righteous works" of benevolence).

h 9:11 Or "You will always be rich enough to be generous at all times."

i 9:11 Or "through us."

j 9:12 The Greek word *leitourgia* (similar to "liturgy") is used in Luke 1:23 for the priestly ministry of Zechariah in the temple.

k 9:12 Or "a superabounding."

l 9:13 Or "passes the test."

affectionately remember you in their prayers. [15] Praise God for his astonishing gift, which is far too great for words![a]

Paul's Defense of His Ministry

10 Now, please listen, for I need to address an issue. I'm making this personal appeal to you by the gentleness[b] and self-forgetfulness of Christ. I am the one who is "humble and timid" when face-to-face with you but "bold and outspoken" when a safe distance away.[c] [2] Now I plead with you that when I come, don't force me to take a hard line with you (which I'm willing to do) by daring to confront[d] those who mistakenly believe that we are living by the standards of the world, *not by the Spirit's wisdom and power*. [3-4] For although we live in the natural realm, we don't wage a military campaign employing human weapons, *using manipulation to achieve our aims*. Instead, our *spiritual* weapons are energized with divine power to effectively dismantle the defenses *behind which people hide*.[e] [5] We can demolish every deceptive fantasy[f] that opposes God and break through every arrogant attitude that is raised up in defiance of the true knowledge of God. We capture, like prisoners of war, every thought[g] and insist that it bow in obedience to the Anointed One. [6] *Since we are armed with such dynamic weaponry*, we stand ready to punish[h] any trace of rebellion, as soon as you choose complete obedience.[i]

---

a 9:15 The Greek and Aramaic texts have a clean break at this point. This has caused some scholars to conclude that chs. 10–13 may have originally been separated from the earlier chapters, which could imply that the following four chapters make up the missing letter of Paul to the Corinthians. If this is so, when reading 2 Corinthians, one could begin with chs. 10–13 (Paul's missing letter), then read from chs. 1–9. The term for this is "appending"; that is, taking an earlier document and adding a later manuscript to it. Yet in this case, the earlier document is appended.

b 10:1 The Aramaic can be translated "peace" or, literally "by the oasis rest."

c 10:1 Paul is apparently quoting their own words that they used to describe him.

d 10:2 Literally "Don't force me to be severe with the confidence with which I reckon to dare." Paul pleads with them not to mistake his humility as weakness or an unwillingness to act with authority.

e 10:3–4 Or "strongholds." The Aramaic word for strongholds can also be translated "rebellious castles." Paul seems to be referring to demonic strongholds or centers of opposition to the light of the gospel.

f 10:5 Or "citadels of argumentations," which include fantasies.

g 10:5 Or "every scheme." Paul is using the concept of taking prisoners of war, but in this case the prisoners held captive are faulty patterns of thought that defy God's authority.

h 10:6 Or "court martial."

i 10:6 This completes one long, complicated Greek sentence that began in v. 3. In this passage Paul describes four arenas of our warfare: (1) We are empowered by grace and with the gospel to dismantle strongholds. (2) We demolish arguments, opinions, theories, and philosophies. (3) We take captive every thought to insist that it become obedient to the mind of Christ. (4) We stand ready and willing to wage war and defeat the enemy (Eph. 6:10–18).

Paul Responds to Criticism

[7] You seem to always be looking at people by their outward appearances.[a] If someone is confident that he belongs to Christ, he should remind himself of this: we belong to Christ no less than he does. [8] I am not ashamed, even if I've come across as one who has overstated the authority given to us by the Lord. For it is the authority to help build you up, not tear you down. [9] I don't want to seem as though I'm trying to bully you with my letters. [10] For I can imagine some of you saying, "His letters are authoritative and stern, but when he's with us he's not that impressive[b][c] and he's a poor speaker." [11] Such a person should realize that when we arrive, there will be no difference in the actions we take and the words we write.

Paul's Apostolic Mandate

[12] Of course, we wouldn't dare to put ourselves in the same class or compare ourselves with those who rate themselves so highly. They compare themselves to one another[d] and make up their own standards to measure themselves by, and then they judge themselves by their own standards. What self-delusion! [13] But we are those who choose to limit our boasting to only the measure of the work[e] to which God has appointed us—a measure that, by the way, has reached as far as you. [14] And since you are within our assigned limits, we didn't overstep our boundaries of authority by being the first to announce to you the wonderful news of the Anointed One. [15] We're not trying to take credit for the ministry done by others, going beyond the limits God set for us. Instead, our hope soars as your faith continues to grow, causing a great expansion of our ministry among you. [16] Then we can go and preach the good news in the regions beyond you without trespassing on the ministry sphere of other laborers and what they have already done. [17] For:

> The one who boasts must boast in the Lord.[f]

---

a 10:7 The Aramaic can be translated "You focus on people's faces."

b 10:10 Or "he's weak."

c 10:10 Greece was known as a land of eloquent speakers. Orators were professionally trained to address crowds. It seems some people were judging Paul by comparing his speaking gift to the eloquent speeches of others. Yet Paul was a brilliant teacher, not a trained orator. True leadership is much more than our speaking ability. Our influence is not limited to a rousing sermon, but we will affect the lives of many if we walk in purity, led by the Holy Spirit. Both Moses and Jeremiah saw themselves as poor speakers. See Ex. 4:10–12; Jer. 1:6.

d 10:12 The Aramaic can be translated "copying one another." God has made each of us unique and given us spiritual gifts that are unique. It is never wise to copy or compare yourself to another believer. Pride will result if we see ourselves as better than someone else, or discouragement if we see ourselves as less valuable than someone else. We don't live by comparison to others but by Christ's life in us.

e 10:13 Or "the sphere of the allocation" (given to us). Paul uses the Greek word *metron*, which was the length of a race course (Gr. *dromos*). It was the word used to define the boundaries of a Greek stadium. One could say that Paul stayed within his lane and knew the limits of his measure (*metron*) of spiritual authority.

f 10:17 See Jer. 9:24.

[18] *So let's be clear.* To have the Lord's approval and commendation is of greater value than bragging about oneself.

The Virgin Bride of Christ

11 Now, please bear with some of my "craziness" for a moment. Yes, please be patient with me.

[2] *You need to know that* God's passion[a] is burning inside me for you, because, like a loving father, I have pledged your hand in marriage to Christ, your true bridegroom. I've also promised that I would present his fiancée to him as a pure virgin bride.[b] [3] But now I'm afraid that just as Eve was deceived by the serpent's clever lies, your thoughts may be corrupted and you may lose your single-hearted devotion and pure love for Christ. [4] For you seem to gladly tolerate anyone[c] who comes to you preaching a pseudo-Jesus, not the Jesus we have preached. You have accepted a spirit and gospel that is false, rather than the Spirit and gospel you once embraced. How tolerant you have become of these imposters!

Super-Apostles?

[5] Now, I believe that I am not inferior in any way to these special "super-apostles"[d] you are attracted to. [6] For although I may not be a polished or eloquent speaker, I'm certainly not an amateur in revelation knowledge. Indeed, we have demonstrated this to you time and again.

[7] Have I committed a sin by degrading myself to dignify you? Was I wrong to preach the gospel of God to you free of charge?[e] [8] I received ample financial support from other churches just so that I could *freely* serve you. [9] Remember, when I was with you I didn't bother anyone when I needed money, for my needs were always supplied by my Macedonian friends.[f] So I was careful, and will continue to be careful, that I never become a burden to you in any way.

[10] As the reality of Christ lives within me, my glad boast *of offering the gospel free of charge* will not be silenced throughout the region of Achaia.[g] [11] Why? Is it because I have no love for you? God knows how much I love you! [12] But in order

---

a 11:2 Or "godly jealousy."

b 11:2 Paul uses the imagery of a bride and bridegroom to describe our relationship to Christ. See Hos. 2:19–20; John 3:29–30; Eph. 5:25–27; Rev. 19:6–8; 21.

c 11:4 Or possibly a reference to "the serpent."

d 11:5 Or "hyper-apostles."

e 11:7 Paul received financial support for preaching the gospel and could have asked the Corinthians to support him (Matt. 10:10). But while among them, he refused to receive their gifts and relied on other churches to support him. He did this to set himself apart from the "super-apostles" in Corinth and to demonstrate that his ministry would not be bought.

f 11:9 Or "the brothers." This was most likely from the church of Philippi. See Phil. 4:15–16.

g 11:10 That is, the region where Corinth was located.

to eliminate the opportunity for those "super-apostles" to boast that their ministry is on the same level as ours I will continue this practice. [13] For they are not true apostles but deceitful[a] ministers who masquerade as "special apostles"[b] of the Anointed One. [14] That doesn't surprise us, for even Satan transforms himself to appear as an angel of light![c] [15] So it's no wonder his servants also go about pretending to be ministers of righteousness. But in the end they will be exposed and get exactly what they deserve.

Paul Speaks as a "Fool"

[16] So I repeat. Let no one think that I'm a fool. But if you do, at least show me the patience you would show a fool, so that I too may boast a little. [17] Of course, what I'm about to tell you is not with the Lord's authority, but as a "fool." [18] For since many love to boast about their worldly achievements,[d] allow me the opportunity to join them. [19] And since you are so smart and so wise to gladly put up with the foolishness of others, *now put up with mine*. [20] You actually allow these imposters to put you into bondage, take complete advantage of you, and rob you blind! How easily you endure those who, in their arrogance, destroy your dignity or even slap you in the face. [21] I must admit, to our shame that we were too "weak" to relate to you the way they do. But now let me dare to boast like a "fool."

Paul Boasts in His Sufferings for Christ

[22] Are these "super-apostles" of yours Hebrews? I am too. Are they Israelites? So am I. Are they descendants of Abraham? Me too! [23] Are they servants of the Anointed One? I'm beside myself when I speak this way, but I am much more of a servant than they. I have worked much harder for God, taken more beatings, and been dragged to more prisons than they. I've been flogged excessively, multiple times, even to the point of death.[e]

[24] Five times I've received thirty-nine lashes from the Jewish leaders.[f] [25] Three times I experienced being beaten with rods.[g] Once they stoned me.[h] Three times I've been shipwrecked;[i] for an entire night and a day I was

---

a 11:13 Or "dishonest."

b 11:13 Or "who change their form into super-apostles."

c 11:14 In the Jewish pseudepigraphical book, *Apocalypse of Moses*, the temptation of Eve is given, and it includes Satan masquerading himself as an angel of light. In the same way, these false apostles were claiming to be sent from Christ but were peddling another gospel.

d 11:18 Or "after the flesh" (according to earthly distinctions).

e 11:23 See 1 Cor. 15:31; 2 Cor. 4:11.

f 11:24 Or "forty lashes minus one." Paul received a total of 195 lashings in his lifetime. It was the custom that if anyone was sentenced to lashings, the punishers must ensure that they did not exceed forty, so they only struck the victim thirty-nine times. See Deut. 25:3.

g 11:25 See Acts 16:22–23.

h 11:25 See Acts 14:19.

i 11:25 Since the shipwreck mentioned in Acts 27:39–44 happened after Paul wrote to the

adrift in the open sea. ²⁶ In my difficult travels I've faced many dangerous situations: perilous rivers, robbers, foreigners, and even my own people. I've survived deadly peril in the city, in the wilderness, with storms at sea, and with spies posing as believers. ²⁷ I've toiled to the point of exhaustion and gone through many sleepless nights. I've frequently been deprived of food and water, left hungry and shivering out in the cold, lacking proper clothing. *

²⁸ And besides these painful circumstances, I have the daily pressure of my responsibility for all the churches, with a deep concern weighing heavily on my heart for their welfare. ²⁹ I am not aloof, for who is *desperate and* weak and I do not feel their weakness? Who is led astray into sin and I do not burn with zeal *to restore him?* ᵇ

³⁰ If boasting is necessary, I will boast about examples of my weakness. ³¹ The God and Father of the Lord Jesus, who is eternally praised, knows that I am speaking the truth. ³² Once, when I was in Damascus, the governor ᶜ under King Aretas ᵈ had his troops searching for me to have me arrested, ³³ but I was stuffed in a basket ᵉ and lowered down through a window and managed to escape.

Paul's Visions and Revelations

12 Although it may not accomplish a thing, I need to move on and boast about supernatural visions and revelations of the Lord. ᶠ ² Someone I'm acquainted with, who is in union with Christ, was swept away fourteen years ago in an ecstatic experience. He was taken into the third heaven, ᵍ but I'm not sure if he was in his body or out of his body—only God knows. ³ And I know that this man ʰ (again, I'm not sure if he was still in his body or taken out of his

---

Corinthians, his total shipwrecks were four. Apparently the three he mentions here took place during his earlier missionary journeys. Some have calculated that Paul had made eight or nine voyages at the time of this writing.

a 11:27 In vv. 23–27 Paul uses his experiences of enduring suffering and hardships as the validation of his apostolic ministry. He would one day sacrifice his life for the gospel while in Rome. In ch. 12 Paul will use visions and spiritual encounters from God to further validate his role as an apostle of Christ.

b 11:29 Or "ablaze with anger."

c 11:32 Or "ethnarch," a politically appointed leader over a specific ethnic group, who represents the king.

d 11:32 He was the father-in-law of Herod Antipas.

e 11:33 This was a large, braided wicker basket. Humiliated by this ordeal, one could say that Paul was a "basket case."

f 12:1 Or "from the Lord."

g 12:2 Although there are Jewish traditions that present a cosmology of seven levels of heaven, most scholars conclude that the third heaven is the highest realm of the immediate presence of God.

h 12:3 There are a number of compelling reasons to conclude that the "man" Paul refers to in vv. 2–4 is himself: (1) He knew the exact time this ecstatic experience took place. (2) He knew

body—God knows) [4] was caught up in an ecstatic experience and brought into paradise,[a] where he overheard many wondrous and inexpressible secrets[b] *that were so sacred* that no mortal is permitted to repeat them.[c] [5] I'm ready to boast of such an experience, but for my own good I refuse to boast unless it concerns my weaknesses.[d] [6] However, if I were to boast, it wouldn't be ridiculous at all, for I would be speaking the truth. Yet I will refrain, lest others think higher of me than what I demonstrate with my life and teaching.

Paul's "Thorn"

[7] The extraordinary level of the revelations I've received is no reason for anyone to exalt me.[e] For this is why a thorn in my flesh was given to me, the Adversary's messenger sent to harass me,[f] keeping me from becoming arrogant. [8] Three times I pleaded with the Lord to relieve me of this. [9] But he answered me, **"My grace is always more than enough for you,[g] and my power finds its full**

---

that what was overheard in the third heaven was "inexpressible" and not to be repeated. (3) He was not certain about what state he was in (embodied/disembodied). (4) In v. 7 he uses the first-person pronoun *me* ("a thorn in the flesh was given to me") as a counterbalance to the high level of revelation that Paul had received. It was a common literary device, a rhetorical ploy, to avoid speaking of oneself directly in this fashion and by using the phrase "Someone I'm acquainted with" (v. 2) when he, in fact, was referring to himself. It is a sign of Paul's humility and integrity that he did not "boast" of this event that took place fourteen years earlier. Many today who have experiences with God are quick to tell what happened. Paul veiled his heavenly encounters with God and waited to share them only when it was appropriate and faith-building for others. Not every experience we have is meant to be shared immediately. This is what got Joseph the dreamer thrown into a pit by his jealous brothers.

a 12:4 What Paul described as the third heaven in v. 3 is now called paradise. It is possible that Paul is recounting two different experiences, or possibly one experience in which he ascended into two levels or two realms of encounter (third heaven and then paradise/seventh heaven). The third possibility is that it was one and the same place, described with different terms. For more on the term *paradise* (Hb. *pardes*, Aramaic *pardesa*, Gr. *paradeisos*), see Gen. 2:9; Luke 23:43; Rev. 2:7.

b 12:4 Or "words" or "matters" or "things." Paul was privileged to see and hear of mysteries that are beyond the reach of human language and unable to be spoken by human lips.

c 12:4 See also Rev. 10:4.

d 12:5 The Aramaic can be translated "afflictions."

e 12:7 The true character of spiritual revelations is that they exalt Christ, not people. It is a paradox that the greater our understanding of God, the less we truly know and the more humble we become. Paul refused to be exalted in the eyes of others. This is the nature of true apostolic ministry.

f 12:7 Or "to slap my face" or "to box my ears." Paul did not have a demon, though it was possible that a demon followed him to harass and hinder. This is more likely a metaphor of the harassment he endured, the constant misunderstanding and persecution that came to him because of his faith in Jesus. There is no indication that this "thorn" was a sickness. In Paul's list of hardships (2 Cor. 11:23–27) he does not mention a sickness or disease.

g 12:9 Or "My grace is continuously sufficient in you" (to ward it off).

expression through your weakness." So I will celebrate my weaknesses, for when I'm weak I sense more deeply the mighty power of Christ living in me.[a] [10] So I'm *not defeated* by my weakness, but delighted! For when I feel my weakness and endure mistreatment—when I'm surrounded with troubles on every side and face persecution *because of my love* for Christ—I am made yet stronger. For my weakness becomes a portal to God's power.

The Signs of an Apostle

[11] I have become foolish *to boast like this*, but you have forced me to do it, when you should have boasted in me instead. For there is nothing I lack compared to these "super-apostles" of yours, even though I am nothing. [12] The things that distinguish a true apostle were performed among you with great perseverance—supernatural signs, startling wonders, and awesome miracles.

[13] Furthermore, how were you treated worse than the other churches, except that I didn't burden you financially—forgive me for depriving you![b] [14] And now here I am, ready to come to you for the third time,[c] and I still refuse to be a burden to you. For what I really want is your hearts, not your money. After all, children should not have to accumulate resources for their parents, but parents do this for their children. [15] *And as a spiritual father to you*, I will gladly spend all that I have and all that I am for you![d] If I love you more, will you respond by loving me less?[e]

[16] Be that as it may, I haven't been a burden to you at all, yet you say of me, "He's a scoundrel and a trickster!" [17] *But let me ask you this.* Did I somehow cheat or trick you through any of the men I sent your way? [18] I was the one who insisted that Titus and our brother come *and help you.* Did Titus take advantage of you? Didn't we all come to you in the same spirit, *following in the ways of integrity*?

[19] I hope that you don't assume that all this time we have simply been justifying ourselves in your eyes? Beloved ones, we have been speaking to you in the sight of God as those joined to Christ, and everything we do is meant to build

---

a 12:9 Or "The power of Christ rests upon me like a tent or tabernacle" (providing me shelter).

b 12:13 Paul appears to be addressing a complaint that he had treated the Corinthians differently than the other churches when, in fact, he had refused their financial support and was helped instead by the Philippians, who aided him financially while in Corinth, and for this he should have been commended by them. The five marks of Paul being a true apostle are (1) supernatural signs attesting to God's presence and authority, (2) wonderful deeds that could be explained only by a supernatural God, (3) powerful miracles that point to Christ, (4) treating the churches with respect and not wanting to burden them if at all possible, and (5) becoming a true spiritual father to the churches (see v. 15).

c 12:14 It was during Paul's third visit to Corinth that he wrote the letter to the Romans.

d 12:15 Or "for your souls."

e 12:15 Some manuscripts indicate that this is not a rhetorical clause but make it into a concessive clause subordinate to the first half of the verse, effectively changing the meaning to "I will gladly spend all that I am for you, even though you love me less for doing so." Sacrificial love is always the key to opening the hearts of people we minister to and serve.

you up and make you stronger in your faith. [20] Now I'm afraid that when I come to you I may find you different than I desire you to be, and you may find me different than you would like me to be. I don't want to find you in disunity, with jealousy and angry outbursts, with selfish ambition, slander, gossip, arrogance, and turmoil. [21] I'm actually afraid that on my next visit my God will humble me in front of you as I shed tears over those who keep sinning without repenting of their impurity, sexual immorality, and perversion.

Weakness and God's Power

13 This will be my third trip to you. And I will make sure that by the testimony of two or three witnesses every matter will be confirmed. [a] [2-3] Since you are demanding proof that the Anointed One is speaking through me, *I will give you proof by exercising discipline among you.* For just as I told you the last time I was there—and now, though absent, I say it again—that when I come I will not go easy on those whom I've already warned and those who continue to persist in their sin. Christ is not weak or feeble in his dealings with you but mighty and powerful within you. [4] For although he was crucified as a "weakling," now he lives *robed* with God's power. And we also are "weak ones" *in our co-crucifixion* with him, but now we live in God's triumphant power together with him, which is demonstrated on your behalf.

[5] Now your souls will be strengthened and healed if you hold steadfast to your faith. [b] Haven't you already experienced Jesus Christ himself living in you? If not, you are deficient. [c] [6] I hope you understand that we cannot be devalued. [d] [7] But we pray to God that you will be flawless, [e] not to validate our ministry among you but so that you may continue on the path of righteousness even if we are denigrated. [f] [8] For in reality, the power we have is used in support of the truth, not against it. [9] And we claim before God [g] that you will be fully equipped and mature, for it brings us great joy when you are strong, even if we seem weak and denigrated.

Paul's Farewell

[10] I'm writing my honest feelings to you from afar so that when I arrive I won't have to correct you by using the authority the Lord has given me, for I want to build you up and not tear you down.

---

a 13:1 See Deut. 19:15; Matt. 18:16; 1 Tim. 5:19.

b 13:5 As translated from the Aramaic. The Greek is "Examine yourselves to see if you are indeed in the faith."

c 13:5 As translated from the Aramaic. The Greek is "unless you are disqualified."

d 13:6 As translated from the Aramaic. The Greek is "You know that we are not disqualified."

e 13:7 See Song. 4:7.

f 13:7 As translated from the Aramaic. The Greek is "even if we appear as disapproved."

g 13:9 The Greek word *eukhomai* (accusative and infinitive construction) means more than prayer; it is to make a claim before God in prayer. The verb is *eukhe*, which means a votive obligation and is translated "make a vow" in Acts 18:18.

¹¹ Finally, beloved friends,ᵃ be cheerful! Repair whatever is broken among you, as your hearts are being knit together in perfect unity. Live continually in peace, and God, the source of love and peace, will mingle with you. ¹²Greet and embrace one another with the sacred kiss.ᵇ ¹³ All of God's holy people send their greetings.

¹⁴Now, may the grace and joyous favor of the Lord Jesus Christ, the unambiguous love of God, and the precious communion that we share in the Holy Spirit be yours continually. Amen!ᶜ

a 13:11 Or "brothers (and sisters)."
b 13:12 What makes a kiss holy or sacred is that it comes from the love of God. See Song. 1:2; Rom. 16:16.
c 13:14 The Aramaic ends with this concluding statement: "The end of the second letter to the Corinthians that was written from Philippi of Macedonia and sent by the hand of Titus."

GALATIANS

Introduction

AT A GLANCE

Author: The apostle Paul
Audience: The church of Galatia
Date: AD 47–48, or early 50s
Type of Literature: A letter
Major Themes: Grace gospel, justification, the law, legalism, freedom and behavior, and Jesus Christ
Outline:

Letter Opening — 1:1–10
Paul Defends His Ministry and Message — 1:11–2:21
Paul Defends His Theology and Gospel — 3:1–4:31
Paul Applies His Message Practically — 5:1–6:10
Letter Closing — 6:11–18

ABOUT GALATIANS

Heaven's freedom! This "grace gospel" brings heaven's freedom into our lives—freedom to live for God and serve one another, as well as freedom from religious bondage. We can thank God today that Paul's gospel is still being preached and heaven's freedom is available to every believer. We are free to soar even higher than keeping religious laws; we have a grace-righteousness that places us at the right hand of the throne of God, not as servants, but as sons and daughters of the Most High!

When Paul wrote his letter, the grace gospel was under attack. So too was his apostolic ministry—it was also debunked by those who wanted to mix grace with the keeping of Jewish law. Paul begins his letter to the Galatians by making it clear that it was not a group of men who commissioned him; instead, he was a "sent one" by the direct commissioning of our Lord Jesus Christ. And the message of grace that he preached was not a secondhand truth that he got from someone else, for he received it through a direct encounter with Jesus. Paul's ministry can be trusted and his gospel can be believed.

Who was this man, Paul? He was born with the name Saul in the city of Tarsus, the once prosperous capital of Cilicia in southern Turkey. Apparently there was a large Jewish colony in that region. Yet Saul was raised in Jerusalem and tutored by the venerated Jewish rabbi Gamaliel.

Before Saul was converted through a divine encounter, he was considered one of the most brilliant Jewish Pharisees of his day. After his conversion to Christ, however, his name became Paul and his ministry began. Reaching the non-Jewish nations with the glorious gospel of Christ was Paul's passion and pursuit. We can thank God that this brilliant man has left us his inspired letters to the churches.

PURPOSE

What a wonderful purpose is found in this letter from heaven! Shortly after the Holy Spirit was poured out upon Jewish believers in Yeshua (Jesus), the gospel spread to other ethnicities as well. By the apostolic mandate given to Jesus' disciples, they were sent into every nation. The first converts among the non-Jewish people needed clarity as to the "Jewishness" of the gospel. Was the gospel revelation to be based upon grace or upon keeping the law of Moses? Galatians was written by the apostle Paul to put those questions to rest.

AUTHOR AND AUDIENCE

The chronological order of the books of the New Testament is somewhat certain. However, the first book Paul wrote is often debated; some say it was 1 Thessalonians and others claim it was Galatians. It is my conclusion that Galatians was the first book he penned, possibly around AD 47–48, in order to passionately defend the gospel of grace from those who would confuse and twist the truth. The apostolic burden is always for purity, both in doctrine and in practice, which is why he confronted those who were distorting the gospel of Christ and reminded the Galatian church of the true message of grace.

MAJOR THEMES

Grace Gospel. When Paul wrote his letter proclaiming heaven's freedom, there were people perverting his original message of rescue from sin and death by grace through faith in Christ alone. These Judaizers, as they were called, added religious works to Paul's gospel, which placed non-Jewish believers under the thumb of religious bondage to Jewish laws. Thanks to Paul, we are reminded that a Christ-plus-something-gospel is no gospel at all; it is Christ-plus-nothing all the way!

Justification. One of the central issues for Paul in Galatians—and throughout his "Letters from Heaven"—is the issue of how people become right with God and find a "not guilty" verdict for their rebellion against him. The Reformation leader Martin Luther said that justification by grace through faith was the belief by which the church stands or falls. He's right! And Paul explains how it's possible a person can stand before a holy God without being condemned.

The Law and Legalism. The message of Galatians is clear: Christ's redemptive work on the cross prevents Jews and non-Jews alike from trying to become right with God through religious works; rescue and re-creation come on the basis of faith in Jesus alone. Through his grace, we are freed from the religious bondage that comes from laws and rituals.

Freedom and Behavior. The grace gospel brings heaven's freedom from religious bondage. Yet while Christians are free from the law, we are not free to live as we please. Instead, we are called to use that freedom to produce fruit, the "fruit of the Spirit," as Paul says. And it is through the Spirit of God that we not only find freedom but are also empowered to please God with our behavior.

Jesus Christ. As you might expect in a letter about salvation, Jesus Christ stands at the center of this letter. We see that Jesus is fully divine and should alone be worshiped. His cross also plays a pivotal role in Paul's grace-letter, for it is through his sacrifice alone that believers are made right with God.

GALATIANS

Heaven's Freedom

Introduction

1 *Dear friends,*

    My name is Paul[a] and I have been commissioned as an apostle[b] of the Lord Jesus, the Messiah. My apostleship was not granted to me by any council of men, for I was appointed by Jesus, the Anointed One, and God the Father, who raised him from the dead. [2] I am joined by all the brothers and sisters[c] who are here with me as I write you this letter, which is to be distributed to the churches throughout the region of central Turkey.[d]

    [3–4] *I pray over you a release of* the blessings of God's undeserved kindness and total well-being[e] that flows from our Father-God and from the Lord Jesus.[f] He's the Anointed Messiah who offered himself as the sacrifice for our sins! He

---

a 1:1 The name Paul means "little." His name before his conversion was Saul, which means "significant one" or "sought after." What great transformation takes place when we experience a profound change like Saul did! God transforms us from being "important" to being "small" in our own eyes. This is what qualifies God's apostolic servants.

b 1:1 The word *apostle* means "one who is sent on a mission" or "an ambassador." By implication, an apostle carries the delegated authority of the one who sends him. Paul was chosen by Jesus Christ as an apostle to plant churches and impart the revelation of Christ and his true gospel. There are more references in the New Testament about the gift of apostle than all the other gifts (prophet, evangelist, pastor, and teacher) combined. See Eph. 4:11.

c 1:2 The Greek word *adelphos* is used throughout the New Testament for brothers (and sisters). It is used in classical Greek by physicians to describe "those who came from the same womb." We are all truly born from the same "womb" of the Father's heart and the wounded side of Jesus Christ. In the time of Alexander the Great, the word *adelphos* was used not only for brothers (and sisters), but for "faithful soldiers." How wonderful it is in our journey to know that we have those fighting for the faith alongside of us who are born from the same womb and faithful partners in our battles.

d 1:2 Or "Galatia." This was the region in Asia Minor (modern-day Turkey) that Paul visited during his first and second missionary journeys. See Acts 16:1–5.

e 1:3–4 This is the word *peace*, which in the Hebraic mindset means "health, prosperity, peace, and total well-being."

f 1:3–4 Grace was not just a "message" that Paul taught; it was the way he dealt with deceived people. Even over the confused churches that were mixing works and grace, Paul spoke words of blessing and peace. When we learn to bless and release "undeserved kindness" and "well-being" over those who oppose us, perhaps then they will listen to us.

has taken us out of this evil world system [a] and set us free through our salvation, just as God desired. [5] All the glory will go to God alone, throughout time and eternity. Amen!

One Gospel

[6] I am shocked over how quickly you have strayed away from the Anointed One who called you to himself by his loving mercy. I'm frankly astounded that you now embrace a distorted gospel! [7] That is a fake "gospel" that is simply not true. There is only one gospel—the gospel of the Messiah! Yet you have allowed those who mingle law with grace to confuse you with lies.

[8] Anyone who comes to you with a different message than the grace gospel that you have received will have the curse of God come upon them! For even if we or an angel appeared before you, to give you a different gospel than what we have already proclaimed, God's curse will be upon them.

[9] I will make it clear: Anyone, no matter who they are, that brings you a different gospel than the grace gospel that you have received, let them be condemned and cursed!

[10] I'm obviously not trying to flatter you or water down my message to be popular with men, but my supreme passion is to please God. For if all I attempt to do is please people, I would not be the true servant of the Messiah.

How Paul Became an Apostle

[11] Beloved ones, let me say emphatically that the gospel entrusted to me was not given to me by any man. [12] No one taught me this revelation, for it was given to me directly by the unveiling of Jesus the Anointed One.

[13] By now you have heard stories of how severely [b] I harassed and persecuted Christians and did my best to systematically destroy God's church, all because of my radical devotion to the Jewish religion. [14] My zeal and passion for the doctrines of Judaism distinguished me among my people, for I was far more advanced in my religious instruction than others my age.

[15] But then God called me by his grace; and in love, he chose me from my birth to be his. [16] God's grace unveiled his Son in me so that I would proclaim him to the non-Jewish people of the world. After I had this encounter I kept it a secret for some time, sharing it with no one. [17] And I chose not to run to Jerusalem to try to impress those who had become apostles before me. Instead, I went away into the Arabian Desert for a season until I returned to Damascus, *where I had first encountered Jesus.* [18] I remained there for three years until I eventually went up to Jerusalem and met the apostle Peter [c] and stayed with him for

---

a 1:3–4 This "evil world system" would include the religious system that is based on duty and performance instead of love and grace.

b 1:13 The Aramaic can be translated "beyond measure."

c 1:18 The Aramaic name of Peter is *kefa*, which means "rock."

a couple of weeks so I could get to know him better. [19] The only other apostle I met during that time was James,[a] the Lord's brother.

[20] Everything I'm describing to you I confess before God is the absolute truth. [21] After my stay in Jerusalem, I went to Syria and southeast Turkey,[b] [22] but remained unknown to the Jewish believers in Judea. [23] The only thing they heard about me was this: "Our former enemy, who once brutally persecuted us, is now preaching the good news of the faith that he was once obsessed with destroying!" [24] *Because of the transformation that took place in my life, they praised God even more!*[c]

Church Leaders Accept Paul as an Apostle

2 Fourteen years later I returned to Jerusalem, this time with Barnabas[d] and Titus,[e] *my coworkers.* [2] God had given me a clear revelation[f] to go and confer with the other apostles concerning the message of grace I was preaching to the non-Jewish people. I spoke privately with those who were viewed as senior leaders of the church. I wanted to make certain that my labor and ministry for the Messiah had not been based on a false understanding of the gospel.[g]

[3] They even accepted Titus[h] without demanding that he follow strict Jewish customs[i] before they would receive him as a brother[j] since he was a Syrian[k] and not a Jew.

[4] I met with them privately and confidentially because false "brothers" had been secretly smuggled into the church meetings. They were sent to spy on the wonderful liberty and freedom that we have in Jesus the Anointed One. Their agenda was to bring us back into the legalistic bondage of religion. [5] But you must know that we did not submit to their religious shackles[l] not even for a moment, so that we might keep the gospel of grace unadulterated for you.

[6] Even the most honored and esteemed among the brothers were not able to

---

a 1:19 Or "Jacob."

b 1:21 Or "Cilicia," which was the southeastern province of Asia Minor, directly adjoining Syria.

c 1:24 The Aramaic text states "they glorified God for having me."

d 2:1 Barnabas is an Aramaic name that means "son of encouragement."

e 2:1 Titus was a Gentile convert to Christ and was a frequent companion of Paul's. Later Paul wrote a beautiful letter to Titus. Titus' name means "nurse."

f 2:2 Although we don't know exactly what the "clear revelation" might have been, it is possible it came in the form of a dream, a vision, a prophecy, or an angel that appeared to Paul.

g 2:2 The Greek text states "running the race for nothing."

h 2:3 Titus was converted through Paul's ministry and was later sent out by Paul as an apostolic church planter. The book of Titus was written by Paul to his spiritual son to give him encouragement and revelation for his ministry.

i 2:3 Or "be circumcised."

j 2:3 "Receive him as a brother," although not in the text, is implicit within the context.

k 2:3 Or "Aramean," which is an Aramaic-speaking gentile. Syrians are Arameans, but Greeks are not. Most Greek manuscripts identify Titus as a Greek when, in fact, he was Syrian. It is believed that the Greek copies of the manuscript changed Titus' ethnicity to Greek, but the Aramaic text correctly identifies him as a Syrian.

l 2:5 Or in Aramaic "their efforts to enslave us" or "their oppression."

add anything to my message. Who they are before men makes no difference to me, for God is not impressed by the reputations[a] of men. [7] So they concluded that I was entrusted with taking the gospel to the non-Jewish people just as Peter was entrusted with taking it to the Jews. [8] For the same God who anointed Peter to be an apostle to the Jews also anointed me as an apostle to those who are not Jewish.

[9] When they all recognized this grace operating in my ministry, James, Peter, and John, the esteemed followers[b] of Jesus, extended to me the warmth of Christian fellowship and honored[c] my calling to minister to the non-Jewish people. [10] They simply requested one thing of me: that I would remember the poor and needy, which was the burden I was already carrying in my heart.

Paul Confronts Peter

[11] But when Peter visited Antioch,[d] he began to mislead the believers *and caused them to stumble over his behavior*, so I had to confront him to his face over what he was doing. [12] He enjoyed being with the non-Jewish believers who didn't keep the Jewish customs, eating his meals with them—up until the time the Jewish friends of James arrived from Jerusalem. When he saw them, he withdrew from his non-Jewish friends and separated himself from them, acting like an orthodox Jew—fearing how it would look to them if he ate with the non-Jewish believers.[e]

[13] And so because of Peter's hypocrisy,[f] many other Jewish believers followed suit, refusing to eat with non-Jewish believers. Even Barnabas was led astray by their poor example and condoned this legalistic, hypocritical behavior!

[14] So when I realized they were acting inconsistently with the revelation of grace, I confronted Peter in front of everyone:

"You were born a Jew and yet you've chosen to disregard Jewish regulations and live like a gentile.[g] Why then do you force those who are not Jews to conform to the regulations of Judaism?

Jews and Non-Jews Are Saved by Faith

[15] "Although we're Jews by birth and not non-Jewish 'sinners,' [16] we know full well that we don't receive God's perfect righteousness as a reward for keeping

---

a 2:6 Or "masks."

b 2:9 Or "pillars."

c 2:9 The Aramaic can be translated "they gave me the right to proceed."

d 2:11 Antioch was a large city in Syria with a significant Jewish population. It was in Antioch that believers were first called Christians and it was the first church to send out missionaries to the nations. See Acts 11:25; 13:1–3.

e 2:12 Or "those who were not of the circumcision."

f 2:13 The incident of Acts 10–11 happened before this account in Gal. 2. Peter was shown by a heavenly vision that God views the non-Jewish believers as "clean." This amplifies Peter's hypocrisy. Even Jesus' apostles had conflicts that needed to be worked out and healed.

g 2:14 Some Aramaic translators translate this word "Syrian" or "Aramean."

the law, but by the faith of Jesus, the Messiah![a] His faithfulness, not ours, has saved us, and we have received God's perfect righteousness. Now we know that God accepts no one by the keeping of religious laws!

[17] "If we are those who desire to be saved from our sins through our union with the Anointed One, does that mean our Messiah promotes our sins if we still acknowledge that we are sinners? How absurd! [18] For if I start over and reconstruct the old religious system that I have torn down with the message of grace, I will appear to be one who turns his back on the truth.

[19] "But because the Messiah lives in me, I've now died to the law's dominion over me so that I can live for God.

[20] "My old identity has been co-crucified with Messiah and no longer lives; *for the nails of his cross crucified me with him.* And now the essence of this new life is no longer mine, for the Anointed One lives his life through me—*we live in union as one*! My new life is empowered by the faith of the Son of God who loves me so much that he gave himself for me, and dispenses his life into mine![b]

[21] "So that is why I don't view God's grace as something minor or peripheral. For if keeping the law could release God's righteousness to us, the Anointed One would have died for nothing."

Faith Brings Freedom

3 What has happened to you Galatians to be acting so foolishly? You must have been under some evil spell![c] Didn't God open your eyes to see the meaning of Jesus' crucifixion? Wasn't he revealed to you as the crucified one?[d]

[2] So answer me this: Did the Holy Spirit come to you as a reward for keeping all the Jewish laws? No, you received him as a gift because you believed in the Messiah. [3] Your new life in the Anointed One began with the Holy Spirit giving you a new birth. Why then would you so foolishly turn from living in the Spirit by trying to finish by your own works?[e]

[4] Have you endured all these trials and persecutions for nothing?

[5] Let me ask you again: What does the lavish supply of the Holy Spirit in your life, and the miracles of God's tremendous power,[f] have to do with you keeping religious laws? The Holy Spirit is poured out upon us through the revelation and power of faith, not by keeping the law!

---

a 2:16 The Aramaic and Greek is clearly "the faith of Jesus, the Messiah." It is not simply our faith, but his—the faithfulness of Jesus to fulfill the Father's pleasure in his life and the sacrifice for our sins in his death. Salvation is found in the "faith of Jesus."
b 2:20 The last sentence of this verse in Aramaic is plural, "us."
c 3:1 The Greek word used here means "to cast a spell using the evil eye." Paul uses a pun here in the Greek text. He goes on to say, "Didn't God *open* your *eyes*?"
d 3:1 The great revelation of the cross had been supernaturally given to them; but they were diluting the glorious work of the cross by adding to it the works of religion.
e 3:3 As translated from the Aramaic.
f 3:5 As translated from the Greek. The Aramaic text states "God's covenant of power."

[6] Abraham, our father of faith, led the way as our pioneering example. He believed God and the substance of his faith released God's righteousness to him. [a] [7] So those who are the true children of Abraham will have the same faith as their father! [8] God's plan all along was to bring this message of salvation to the nations through the revelation of faith. Long ago God prophesied over Abraham, as the Holy Scriptures say:

"Through your example of faith all the nations will be blessed!" [b]

[9] And so the blessing of Abraham's faith is now our blessing too! [10] But if you choose to live in bondage under the legalistic rule of religion, you live under the law's curse. For it is clearly written:

"Utterly cursed is everyone who fails to practice every detail and requirement that is written in this law!" [c]

[11] *For the Scriptures reveal,* and it is obvious, that no one achieves the righteousness of God by attempting to keep the law, for it is written:

"Those who have been made holy will live by faith!" [d]

[12] But keeping the law does not require faith, *but self-effort.* For the law teaches,

"If you practice the principles of law, you must follow all of them." [e]

[13] Yet, Christ paid the full price to set us free from the curse of the law. He absorbed it completely as he became a curse in our place. For it is written:

"Everyone who is hung upon a tree is doubly cursed." [f]

[14] Jesus, our Messiah, was cursed in our place and in so doing, dissolved the curse from our lives, so that all the blessings of Abraham can be poured out upon even non-Jewish believers. And now God gives us the promise of the wonderful Holy Spirit who lives within us when we believe in him.

The Law versus God's Promises

[15] Beloved friends, let me use an illustration that we can all understand. Technically, when a contract is signed, it can't be changed after it has been put into effect; it's too late to alter the agreement. [g]

---

a 3:6 See Gen. 15:6.
b 3:8 See Gen. 12:3; 18:18; 22:18.
c 3:10 See Deut. 27:26.
d 3:11 See Hab. 2:4.
e 3:12 See Lev. 18:5.
f 3:13 See Deut. 21:23.
g 3:15 The most ancient Aramaic manuscript has a different meaning for this verse. It could

[16] Remember the royal proclamation[a] God spoke over Abraham and to Abraham's child? God said that his promises were made to pass on to Abraham's "Child,"[b] not children. And who is this "Child?" It's the Son of promise, Jesus, the anointed Messiah!

[17-18] This means that the covenant between God and Abraham was fulfilled in Messiah and cannot be altered. Yet the written law was not even given to Moses until 430 years later, after God had "signed" his contract with Abraham! The law, then, doesn't supersede the promise[c] since the royal proclamation was given before the law.[d]

If that were the case, it would have nullified what God said to Abraham. We receive all the promises because of the Promised One—not because we keep the law!

[19] Why then was the law given? It was meant to be an intermediary agreement added after God gave the promise of the coming One! It was given to show men how guilty they are, and it remained in force until the Seed was born to fulfill the promises given to Abraham. When God gave the law, he didn't give it to them directly, for he gave it first to the angels; they gave it to *Moses*, his mediator,[e] who then gave it to the people. [20] Now, a mediator does not represent just one party alone, but God fulfilled it all by himself![f]

[21] Since that's true, should we consider the written law to be contrary to the promise of new life? How absurd![g] Truly, if there was a law that we could keep which would give us new life, then our salvation would have come by law-keeping. [22] But the Scriptures make it clear that since we were all under the power of sin, we needed Jesus! And he is the Savior who brings the promise to those who believe.

God's Sons Inherit the Promises

[23] So until the revelation of faith for salvation was released, the law was a jailer, holding us as prisoners under lock and key until the "faith," which was destined to be revealed, *would set us free*. [24] The law becomes a gateway to lead us to the

---

also be translated, "The covenant of the Son of Man that I reference should never be denigrated or changed in any way by men."

a 3:16 As translated literally from the Greek. It can also mean "covenant."

b 3:16 Or "seed."

c 3:17–18 The concept of the "promise" is that all we need is faith to believe it. This is the revelation of grace that saves us, for the "promise" is enough.

d 3:17–18 This last sentence is the implied conclusion of Paul's logic.

e 3:19 This would be Moses. However, the Aramaic can be translated "the one who was able."

f 3:20 Or "but God is one."

g 3:21 The law and the promise (grace) each have a distinct function. The law brings conviction of sin, which unveils grace as the way to salvation. The law moves us, even compels us, to reach for grace. And grace will cause one to soar even higher than the demands of the law.

Messiah so that we would be saved by faith. [25] But when faith comes the law is no longer in force, since we have already entered into life.

[26] You have all become true children of God by the faith of Jesus the Anointed One! [a] [27] It was faith that immersed you into Jesus, the Anointed One, and now you are covered and clothed with his anointing. [28] And we no longer see each other in our former state—Jew or non-Jew, rich or poor, [b] male or female—because we're all one through our union with Jesus Christ *with no distinction between us.*

[29] And since you've been united to Jesus the Messiah, you are now Abraham's "child" and inherit all the promises of the kingdom realm!

From Slavery to Sonship

4 In a similar way, God has promised our ancestors something better, but as long as an heir is a minor, he's not really much different than a servant, although he's the master over all of them. [2] For until the time appointed by the father when he comes of age, the child is under the domestic supervision of the guardians of the estate.

[3] So it is with us. When we were juveniles we were enslaved under the hostile spirits of the world. [4] But when that era came to an end and the time of fulfillment had come, God sent his Son, born of a woman, [c] born under the written law. [d] [5] Yet all of this was so that he would redeem and set free all those held hostage to the written law so that we would receive our freedom and a full legal adoption as his children.

[6] And so that we would know for sure that we are his true children, God released the Spirit of Sonship into our hearts—moving us to cry out intimately, "My Father! [e] You're our true Father!"

[7] Now we're no longer living like slaves *under the law*, but we enjoy being God's very own sons and daughters! And because we're his, we can access everything our Father has—for we are heirs of God through Jesus, the Messiah!

[8] Before we knew God as our Father and we became his children, we were unwitting servants to the powers that be, which are nothing compared to God. [9] But now that we truly know him and understand how deeply we're loved by him, why would we, even for a moment, consider turning back to those weak and feeble principles of religion, *as though we were still subject to them?*

---

a 3:26 It is the "faith of Jesus," or what he believes about you, that makes you his very own.

b 3:28 Or "enslaved or free."

c 4:4 Every child has a mother; but for Jesus to be "born of a woman" meant there was no human father, no male counterpart. Jesus' true Father is the Father of Eternity. No other child has had a virgin birth, "born of a woman," except him. All the rest of us are born from a father and a mother.

d 4:4 Or "under the law."

e 4:6 This is the Aramaic word *Abba* which means "my father." *Abba* was borrowed by the Greeks and is found in the Greek manuscripts as well.

¹⁰ Why *would we want to go backwards into the bondage of religion*—scrupulously observing rituals like special days,ᵃ celebrations of the new moon, annual festivals, and sacred years?ᵇ ¹¹ I'm so alarmed about you that I'm beginning to wonder if my labor in ministry among you was a waste of time!

Paul's Personal Appeal

¹² Beloved ones, I plead with you, follow my example and *become free from the bondage of religion.* I once became as one of you,ᶜ *a gentile, when I lived among you*—now become free like me. When I first came to minister to you, you did me no wrong. *I can't believe you would do wrong to me now!*

¹³ You are well aware that the reason I stayed among you to preach the good news was because of the poor state of my health.ᵈ ¹⁴ And yet you were so kind to me and did not despise me in my weakness,ᵉ even though my physical condition put you through an ordeal while I was with you.

Actually, you received me and cared for me as though I were an angel from God, as you would have cared for Jesus, the Messiah himself! ¹⁵ Some of you were even willing, if it were possible, to pluck out your own eyes to replace mine! Where is that kindhearted and free spirit now? ¹⁶ Have I really become your enemy because I tell you the truth?

¹⁷ Can't you see what these false teachersᶠ are doing? They want to win you over so you will side with them. They want you divided from me so you will follow only them. Would you call that integrity? ¹⁸ Isn't it better to seek excellence and integrity always, and not just only when I'm with you?

¹⁹ You are my dear children, but I agonize in spiritual "labor pains" once again, until the Anointed One will be fully formed in your hearts! ²⁰ How I wish I could be there in person and change my toneᵍ toward you, for I am truly dumbfounded over what you are doing!

ᵃ 4:10 Or "Sabbaths." There is no requirement for gentiles to become like Jews and observe Jewish ordinances in order to draw closer to God. Our approach to God is always on the basis of grace and faith in the blood of Jesus Christ, the Lord of the Sabbath.

ᵇ 4:10 These terms could also apply to following astrological signs.

ᶜ 4:12 Or "imitated you." Paul is using sarcasm and saying, "I imitated you; now you should imitate me!"

ᵈ 4:13 Paul's ministry in Antioch began when he became sick and had to delay his missionary journey to other regions. He may have been afflicted with an illness that normally aroused disgust by reason of its repulsive nature. Many surmise that Paul contracted an ophthalmic disorder (an eye disease), which was prevalent in the region. The illness can cause one to have a repugnant appearance. Other scholars think he was simply very ill as a result of his treatment by his enemies on his first missionary journey. Still the Galatians did not reject him; instead they welcomed him with open arms, and his gospel message with open hearts.

ᵉ 4:14 The Aramaic word can also mean "sickness."

ᶠ 4:17 Or "whispering enemies."

ᵍ 4:20 The Aramaic word can be translated "echo."

An Old Testament Allegory

[21-22] Tell me, do you want to go back to living strictly by the law? Haven't you ever listened to what the law really says? Have you forgotten that Abraham had two sons; one by the slave girl, and the other by the freewoman?[a]

[23] *Ishmael*, the son of the slave girl, was a child of the natural realm. But *Isaac*, the son of the freewoman, was born supernaturally by the Spirit—a child of the promise of God! [24] These two women and their sons express an allegory and become symbols of two covenants. The first covenant was born on Mt. Sinai, birthing children into slavery—children born to Hagar. [25] For "Hagar" represents the law given at Mt. Sinai in Arabia. *The "Hagar" metaphor* corresponds to the earthly Jerusalem of today who are currently in bondage.

[26] In contrast, there is a heavenly Jerusalem above us, which is our true "mother." She is the freewoman, birthing children into freedom![b] [27] For it is written:

"Burst forth with gladness,
O barren woman with no children!
Break through with the shouts of joy and jubilee,
for you are about to give birth!
The one who was once considered desolate and barren
now has more children than the one who has a husband!"[c]

[28] Dear friends, just like Isaac, we're now the true children who inherit the kingdom promises.[d] [29] And just as the son of the natural world at that time harassed the son born of the power of the Holy Spirit, so it is today. [30] And what does the Scripture tell us to do?

"Expel the slave mother with her son![e]
The son of the slave woman will not be a true heir—
for the true heir of the promises is the son of the freewoman."[f]

[31] It's now so obvious! We're not the children of the slave woman; we're the supernatural sons of the freewoman—sons of grace!

---

a 4:21–22 See Gen. 16:15; 21:2.

b 4:26 Paul is showing that the law is a system of works that brings bondage and that the promise is a system of grace that brings true freedom.

c 4:27 See Isa. 54:1.

d 4:28 Or "royal proclamation."

e 4:30 See Gen. 21:10. This is showing that the two "sons" are not meant to live together. You cannot mingle law and grace, for only grace is based upon the promise of new life.

f 4:30 See Gen. 21:10–12; John 8:35.

A Life of Freedom

5 Let me be clear, the Anointed One has set us free—not partially, but completely and wonderfully free! We must always cherish this truth and stubbornly refuse to go back into the bondage of our past.

[2] I, Paul, tell you: If you think there is benefit in circumcision and Jewish regulations, then you're acting as though Jesus the Anointed One is not enough. [3] I say it again emphatically: If you let yourselves be circumcised you are obliged to fulfill every single one of the commandments and regulations of the law!

[4] If you want to be made holy by fulfilling the obligations of the law, you have cut off more than your flesh—you have cut yourselves off from the Anointed One and have fallen away from the revelation of grace!

[5] But the Holy Spirit convinces us that we have received by faith the glorious righteousness of the Anointed One. [6] When you're placed into the Anointed One and joined to him, circumcision and religious obligations can benefit you nothing. All that matters now is living in the faith that is activated and brought to perfection by love.

[7] Before you were led astray, you were so faithful to Messiah. Why have you now turned away from what is right and true? Who has deceived you?

[8] The One who enfolded you into his grace is not behind this false teaching that you've embraced. Not at all! [9] Don't you know that when you allow even a little lie into your heart, it can permeate your entire belief system?[a]

[10] Deep in my heart I have faith that the Lord Jesus the Anointed One, who lives in you, will bring you back around to the truth. And I'm convinced that those who agitate you, whoever they think they are, will be brought under God's judgment!

[11] Dear friends, why do you think the religious system persecutes me? Is it because I preach the message of being circumcised and keeping all the laws of Judaism? Not at all! Is there no longer any offense over the cross? [12] To tell you the truth, I am so disgusted with all your agitators—I wish they would go even further and cut off their legalistic influence from your lives![b]

[13] Beloved ones, God has called us to live a life of freedom in the Holy Spirit. But don't view this wonderful freedom as an opportunity to set up a base of operations in the natural realm. Freedom means that we become so completely free of self-indulgence that we become servants of one another, expressing love in all we do.

[14] For love completes the laws of God. All of the law can be summarized in one grand statement:

---

a 5:9 Literally "A little yeast goes through the whole lump of dough." The text uses a metaphor of "yeast" that has effects that cannot be hidden when it is folded into dough. The yeast is the lie of legalism.

b 5:12 Or "castrate themselves."

"Demonstrate love to your neighbor, even as you care for and love yourself." *a*

[15] But if you continue to criticize and come against each other over minor issues, you're acting like wild beasts trying to destroy one another! *b*

The Holy Spirit, Our Victory

[16] As you yield freely and fully to the dynamic life and power of the Holy Spirit, you will abandon the cravings of your self-life. *c* [17] For your self-life craves the things that offend the Holy Spirit *and hinder him from living free within you!* And the Holy Spirit's intense cravings hinder your old self-life from dominating you! So then, the two incompatible and conflicting forces within you are your self-life of the flesh and the new creation life of the Spirit. *d*

[18] But when you are brought into the full freedom of the Spirit *e* of grace, you will no longer be living under the domination of the law, *but soaring above it!*

[19] The cravings of the self-life are obvious: Sexual immorality, lustful thoughts, pornography, [20] chasing after things instead of God, *f* manipulating others, *g* hatred of those who get in your way, senseless arguments, resentment when others are favored, temper tantrums, angry quarrels, only thinking of yourself, being in love with your own opinions, [21] being envious of the blessings of others, murder, uncontrolled addictions, *h* wild parties, and all other similar behavior.

Haven't I already warned you that those who use their "freedom" for these things *i* will not inherit the kingdom realm of God!

[22-23] But the fruit *j* produced by the Holy Spirit within you is divine love in all its varied expressions: *k*

joy *that overflows*, *l*

peace *that subdues*,

---

a 5:14 See Lev. 19:18.

b 5:15 Both Aramaic and Greek manuscripts read "biting and devouring," which is a metaphor for critical attitudes that will destroy the fellowship. These terms were often found in classical Greek literature to describe wild animals fighting each other in deadly conflict.

c 5:16 Or "the natural realm."

d 5:17 The concept of the "new creation life of the Spirit" is implied in the greater context of Galatians, and referred to explicitly in 6:15–16.

e 5:18 The word for Spirit is actually "Spirit-Wind."

f 5:20 Literally "idolatry."

g 5:20 Literally "witchcraft." The Greek word for "witchcraft" can imply drug usage.

h 5:21 Literally "drunken binges."

i 5:21 The Aramaic can be translated "those who devote themselves to these things."

j 5:22–23 The Greek word here can be translated "harvest."

k 5:22–23 There is clear textual inference that the "fruit" (singular) of the Holy Spirit is love, with the other virtues displaying aspects of the greatest quality of Spirit-life, *agape* love.

l 5:22–23 The translator has chosen to supply action to these virtues, for they are not meant to be abstract virtues, but made visible with actions.

patience *that endures,*
kindness *in action,*
a life full of virtue, *
faith *that prevails,*
gentleness *of heart,* and
strength *of spirit.* *

Never set the law above these qualities, for they are meant to be limitless. *

²⁴ Keep in mind that we who belong to Jesus, the Anointed One, have already experienced crucifixion. For everything connected with our self-life was put to death on the cross and crucified with Messiah. ²⁵ We must live in the Holy Spirit and follow after him. ²⁶ So may we never be arrogant, or look down on another, *for each of us is an original.* We must forsake all jealousy that diminishes the value of others. *

Carry Each Other's Burdens

6 My beloved friends, if you see a believer who is overtaken with a fault, * may the one who overflows with the Spirit * seek to restore him. Win him over with gentle words, *which will open his heart to you* and will keep you from exalting yourself over him. * ² *Love empowers us to* fulfill the law of the Anointed One as we carry each other's troubles. ³ If you think you are too important to stoop down to help another, you are living in deception.

⁴ Let everyone be devoted to fulfill the work God has given them to do with excellence, and their joy will be in doing what's right and being themselves, and not in being affirmed by others. ⁵ Every believer is ultimately responsible for his or her own conscience. *

We Harvest What We Plant

⁶ And those who are taught the Word must share all good things with their teacher; a sharing of wealth takes place between them.

⁷ Make no mistake about it, God will never be mocked! For what you

---

a 5:22–23 The Greek word for patience is taken from a verb that means "ever tapping" or "never quitting."
b 5:22–23 The Aramaic word can be translated "sweetness."
c 5:22–23 Or "goodness."
d 5:22–23 Although the word *self* is not found in this verse, most translations render this as "self-control." The word is actually "lordship," or by implication "spirit-strength."
e 5:22–23 Literally "there is no law set against these things" or "there is no conflict with Jewish laws."
f 5:26 As translated from the Aramaic.
g 6:1 Or "mistake."
h 6:1 Literally "those who are in the Spirit."
i 6:1 Or "keep you from being harassed by the enemy."
j 6:5 As translated from the Aramaic.

plant will always be the very thing you harvest. [8] The harvest you reap reveals the seed that was planted. If you plant the corrupt seeds of self-life into this natural realm, you can expect to experience a harvest of corruption. If you plant the good seeds[a] of Spirit-life you will reap the beautiful fruits that grow from the everlasting life of the Spirit.

[9] And don't allow yourselves to be weary or disheartened in planting good seeds, for the season of reaping the wonderful harvest you've planted is coming! [10] Take advantage of every opportunity to be a blessing to others,[b] especially to our brothers and sisters in the family of faith!

Summary and Conclusion

[11] I've written this letter to you with my own handwriting—see how large I have to make the letters?[c] [12] All those who insist that you be circumcised are recruiting you so they can boast in their own works. They are attempting to avoid the persecution that comes with preaching the liberating message of the cross of Messiah! [13] Not even those who are circumcised keep every detail of the written law. Yet they push you to be circumcised so that they can boast that you have become like them.[d]

[14] My only boast is in the crucifixion of the Lord Jesus, our Messiah. In him I have been crucified to this natural realm; and the natural realm is dead to me and no longer dominates my life.

[15] Circumcision doesn't mean a thing to me. The only thing that really matters is living by the transforming power of this wonderful new creation life. [16] And all those who live in agreement with this standard will have true peace and God's delight, for they are the Israel of God.

[17] From now on, let no one bring me trouble or criticism, for I am carrying the very scars[e] of our Lord Jesus in my body. [18] Finally my beloved ones—may the wonderful grace of our Lord Jesus, the Anointed One, be flowing in your spirit.[f] So shall it be!

In Messiah's love,
Paul

---

a 6:8 These "good seeds" would include prayer, Bible study, speaking wise words, giving, loving, and dropping "seeds" every day from a life lived in our new creation life.

b 6:10 The Greek text implies giving finances.

c 6:11 Some Greek texts imply that only beginning with v. 11 does Paul write in his own handwriting. The Aramaic indicates the entire letter was written in his handwriting.

d 6:13 Or "so that they can boast about your flesh."

e 6:17 The Aramaic word for "scars" can also mean "death marks" or "stigmata."

f 6:18 Or "with your spirits."

EPHESIANS

Introduction

AT A GLANCE

Author: The apostle Paul

Audience: The church of Ephesus, and surrounding area churches

Date: AD 60–62

Type of Literature: A letter

Major Themes: Salvation and grace, God's power, church unity, and Christian conduct and identity

Outline:

Letter Opening — 1:1–2

The Church's Heavenly Calling — 1:3–3:21

The Church's Earthly Conduct — 4:1–6:20

Letter Closing — 6:21–24

ABOUT EPHESIANS

What you are about to read is meant to be taught to every church. It is the constitution of our faith, the great summary description of all that is precious and esteemed in Christian doctrine and Christian living. Paul firmly plants the cornerstone of our faith in this powerful letter, cementing, in its few pages, the position and authority of the church over every other force. In it, Paul brings before every believer the mystery of the glory of Christ.

The theme of Ephesians is that God will one day submit everything under the leadership of Jesus Christ. He is the Head of the church and the fullness of God in human flesh. He gives his church extraordinary power to walk filled with the Holy Spirit, revealing the nature of God in all things. Jesus loves the church and cherishes everything about her. He is the one who brings Jews and non-Jews into one body. The church is God's new humanity—one new man. It is the new temple where God's glory dwells. And the church is the bride of Christ, the beloved partner who is destined to rule with him.

How wonderfully he blesses his bride with gifts from above. He gives us, both men and women, the grace to be apostles, prophets, evangelists, pastors, and teachers who will feed and encourage the church to rise higher. The greatness of God streams from Jesus Christ into the hearts of every believer. These are the grand themes of Ephesians.

I have always loved the apostolic prayers of Paul, especially those found in Ephesians. I have prayed nearly every day for forty years that God would impart to me the spirit of revelation and the spirit of wisdom to guide my life, my family, and my ministry. God is good to give the Holy Spirit's fullness to those who ask with sincere hunger for more.

PURPOSE

What an exciting letter Paul has written to us! Ephesians is full of life and its words reach higher in Christian thought than any letter in our New Testament. Full of living revelation, it simply drips with the anointing of the Holy Spirit. Where most of Paul's letters are addressed to churches facing specific issues dealing with belief and practice, this isn't the case with Ephesians. There is a more general, theologically reflective tone to this letter that is meant to ground, shape, and challenge believers (mainly gentile) in their faith.

AUTHOR AND AUDIENCE

Paul wrote this letter about AD 60, while in a prison cell in Rome, and sent it with Tychicus as a circular letter that was to be read to all the churches.

Originally, there were no titles on Paul's letters. They were gathered and the titles were assigned according to where they were sent; then they were published for the churches as a group. In none of the earliest Greek manuscripts did the words *Ephesus* or *Ephesians* occur. It was simply added in the margin next to the main text in the first copies made. The conclusion by some scholars is that this letter to the Ephesians may possibly be the lost letter of the Laodiceans mentioned in Col. 4:16: "Once you've read this letter publicly to the church, please send it on to the church of the Laodiceans, and make sure you read the letter that I wrote to them." Others believe it was intended for Ephesus as it stands today.

Scholars are not sure on this point; it is the only letter Paul wrote that did not contain any personal greetings to specific people. Since these greetings easily identified the other letters, many now believe this letter was written not only for the Ephesians but for Christians in the surrounding area too.

MAJOR THEMES

Salvation by Grace through Faith. Paul paints a very bleak picture of who we were before God stepped in to rescue us: "you were once like corpses, dead in your sins and offenses" (2:1). Yet he goes on: "Even when we were dead and doomed in our many sins, he united us into the very life of Christ and saved us by his wonderful grace!" (2:5). Paul makes it clear we don't earn or work for this rescue; rather, it's God's undeserved favor from beginning to end!

Power of God over All Others. One of the leading themes in this letter from heaven is the theme that God's power trumps that of all other principalities, powers, and authorities in this world. For Paul, any threat of the spiritual powers of this world should be seen in light of the superior power of God and the power we have as his children.

Christian Unity. Another leading theme in Paul's letter is the unity that Jews and non-Jews share in Christ. Paul's strong encouragement for unity and love within the body work together to encourage believers to overcome any and all cultural pressures of animosity on the basis of Jesus' work uniting all believers into one community of people.

Christian Conduct. Most of chs. 3–6 focus on how Christians should live, especially new believers, which is summed up with Paul's appeal in 4:17 to "not live like the unbelievers around you who walk in their empty delusions." Paul urges new believers—and really all believers—to cultivate a lifestyle consistent with their new life in Christ—a life free from drunkenness, sexual immorality, lying, stealing, bitterness, and other ungodly behaviors.

Christian Identity. One of the major themes of Paul's teachings is the fact that believers are now "in Christ," an idea that impacts every aspect of believers' identity. We exist in a personal, energizing relationship of unity with the risen Christ! This identity is crucial in our ongoing struggle with spiritual darkness and powers, maintaining Christian unity, overcoming our former lifestyle, and living as God has called us to live.

EPHESIANS

Heaven's Riches

Paul's Introduction

1 *Dear friends,*

My name is Paul, and I was chosen by God to be an apostle of Jesus, the Messiah. [2] I'm writing this letter to all the devoted believers*a* who have been made holy*b* by being one with Jesus, the Anointed One.

May God himself, the heavenly Father of our Lord Jesus Christ, release grace over you and impart total well-being*c* into your lives.

Our Sonship and the Father's Plan

[3] Every spiritual blessing in the heavenly realm has already been lavished upon us as a love gift from our wonderful heavenly Father, the Father of our Lord Jesus—all because he sees us wrapped into Christ. This is why we celebrate him*d* with all our hearts!

[4] And he chose us to be his very own, joining us to himself even before he laid the foundation of the universe!*e* Because of his great love, he ordained*f* us, so that we would be seen as holy in his eyes with an unstained innocence.

---

a 1:2 Recent manuscripts add the words "those who are in Ephesus." The oldest manuscripts have "to the Ephesians" written in the margin. This would reinforce the theory that it is meant to be read and distributed to all the churches. Although the book bears the name "Ephesians," some scholars believe that this letter could be the missing letter to the Laodiceans mentioned in Col. 4:16. Regardless, Ephesians contains crucial truths for believers worldwide.

b 1:2 Or "to the saints [holy ones] and the faithful in Christ Jesus." Notice that God is the one who makes us holy, but our response is to be "faithful" (or "devoted").

c 1:2 Or "peace." The Hebrew concept of peace means much more than tranquility.

d 1:3 Or "bless" (or "blessed be God").

e 1:4 As translated from the Aramaic. There is an alternate Greek translation of the unique wording of this verse that could be translated "He chose us to be a 'word' before the fall of the world." The Greek word for "chose" is *eklegomai*, which is a form of *lego* (speak). The word for "fall" (Adam's fall) is *kataboles*, which can mean "falling down," but is usually translated as "foundation" (of the world).

f 1:4 As translated from the Aramaic. One Eastern Aramaic text can be translated "He marked us with his love." The Greek text states "predestined us" or "set us apart."

[5-6] For it was always in his perfect plan[a] to adopt[b] us as his delightful children, through our union with Jesus, the Anointed One, so that his tremendous love that cascades over us would glorify his grace[c]—for the same love he has for his Beloved One, Jesus, he has for us. And this unfolding plan brings him great pleasure!

[7] Since we are now joined to Christ, we have been given the treasures of redemption by his blood—the total cancellation[d] of our sins—all because of the cascading riches[e] of his grace. [8] This superabundant grace is already powerfully working in us,[f] releasing within us all forms of wisdom and practical understanding. [9] And through the revelation of the Anointed One, he unveiled his secret desires to us—the hidden mystery of his long-range plan, which he was delighted to implement from the very beginning of time. [10] And because of God's unfailing purpose, this detailed plan will reign supreme through every period of time until the fulfillment of all the ages finally reaches its climax—when God makes all things new[g] in all of heaven and earth through Jesus Christ.

[11] Through our union with Christ we too have been claimed by God as his own inheritance.[h] Before we were even born, he gave us our destiny;[i] that we would fulfill the plan of God who always accomplishes every purpose and plan in his heart. [12] God's purpose was that we Jews, who were the first to long for the messianic hope, would be the first to believe in the Anointed One and bring great praise and glory to God!

[13] And because of him, when you who are not Jews heard the revelation[j] of truth, you believed in the wonderful news of salvation. Now we have been stamped with the seal of the promised Holy Spirit.[k]

[14] He is given to us like an engagement ring[l] is given to a bride, as the first

a 1:5–6 Or "He marked out our horizon [destiny] beforehand."
b 1:5–6 The Aramaic reads "to establish us."
c 1:5–6 Or "to the praise of the glory of his grace."
d 1:7 Or "forgiveness." The Greek word aphesis, means "to send away" or "to set free" (from bondage).
e 1:7 The Greek word for riches (ploutos) is also used to describe God's wisdom and knowledge in Rom. 11:33. Just as God is all-knowing and has all-wisdom, so he has untold riches of grace available for his children.
f 1:8 Or "lavished on us."
g 1:10 As translated from the Aramaic. The Greek text states "God will gather together all things in fulfillment in Christ." That is, God will unite all things under the headship of Christ.
h 1:11 The Greek construction of this phrase can mean either that God appointed us (Gr. klēroō, chosen by casting lots) to be his inheritance, or that we have been appointed an inheritance.
i 1:11 Or "estate."
j 1:13 The Greek text is logos or "word of God."
k 1:13 Some Aramaic manuscripts add here "who was announced by the angels."
l 1:14 The Greek word used here can be translated "pledge," "down payment" or "engagement ring."

installment of what's coming! He is our hope-promise of a future inheritance[a] which seals us until we have all of redemption's promises and experience complete freedom—all for the supreme glory and honor of God!

Paul Prays for the Spirit of Wisdom and Revelation

[15] Because of this, since I first heard about your strong faith in the Lord Jesus Christ and your tender love toward all his devoted ones, [16] my heart is always full and overflowing with thanks to God for you as I constantly remember you in my prayers.[b] [17] I pray that the Father of glory, the God of our Lord Jesus Christ, would impart to you the riches of the Spirit of wisdom and the Spirit of revelation[c] to know him through your deepening intimacy with him.

[18] I pray that the light of God will illuminate the eyes of your imagination,[d] flooding you with light, until you experience the full revelation of the hope of his calling[e]—that is, the wealth of God's glorious inheritances that he finds in us, his holy ones!

[19] I pray that you will continually experience the immeasurable greatness of God's power made available to you through faith. Then your lives will be an advertisement of this immense power as it works through you! This is the mighty power [20] that was released when God raised Christ from the dead and exalted him[f] to the place of highest honor and supreme authority[g] in the heavenly realm! [21] And now he is exalted as first above every ruler, authority, government, and realm of power in existence! He is gloriously enthroned over every name that is ever praised,[h] not only in this age,[i] but in the age that is coming![j]

[22] And he alone is the leader and source of everything needed in the church. God has put everything beneath the authority of Jesus Christ[k] *and has given him the highest rank above all others.* [23] And now we, his church, are his body on the earth and that which fills him who is being filled by it![l]

---

a 1:14 The Aramaic word used for "inheritance" can also be translated "dividend."

b 1:16 The literal Aramaic text can be translated "I began confessing on your behalf and praying."

c 1:17 Or "discovery."

d 1:18 Or "innermost" (heart).

e 1:18 Or "to which he is calling you."

f 1:20 Or "he seated him" (enthroned).

g 1:20 Or "at his right hand," a metaphor for the place of honor and authority.

h 1:21 As translated from the Aramaic.

i 1:21 The Aramaic word can be translated "universe."

j 1:21 As translated from the Aramaic.

k 1:22 Both Greek and Aramaic texts use the figure of speech "under his feet," which means he has conquered, subdued, and now rules over them.

l 1:23 That is, as we are those who are filled (completed) by Christ, we also complete (fill) him. What a wonderful and humbling mystery is revealed by this verse.

God's Power Raised Us from the Dead

2 *And his fullness fills you,* even though you were once like corpses,[a] dead in your sins and offenses. [2] It wasn't that long ago that you lived in the religion, customs, and values[b] of this world,[c] obeying the dark ruler of the earthly realm who fills the atmosphere with his authority, and works diligently in the hearts of those who are disobedient to the truth of God. [3] The corruption that was in us from birth was expressed through the deeds and desires of our self-life. We lived by whatever natural cravings and thoughts our minds dictated, living as rebellious children subject to God's wrath like everyone else.

[4] But God still loved us with such great love. He is so rich in compassion and mercy. [5] Even when we were dead and doomed in our many sins, he united us into the very life of Christ and saved us by his wonderful grace! [6] He raised us up with Christ the exalted One, *and we ascended with him into the glorious perfection and authority* of the heavenly realm, for we are now co-seated[d] as one with Christ!

[7] Throughout the coming ages[e] we will be the visible display of the infinite, limitless riches of his grace and kindness, which was showered upon us in Jesus Christ. [8] For it was only through this wonderful grace that we believed in him. Nothing we did could ever earn this salvation, for it was the gracious gift from God that brought us to Christ! [9] So no one will ever be able to boast, for salvation is never a reward for good works or human striving.

[10] We have become his poetry,[f] a re-created people that will fulfill the destiny he has given each of us, for we are joined to Jesus, the Anointed One. Even before we were born, God planned in advance *our destiny* and the good works[g] we would do *to fulfill it!*

A New Humanity

[11-12] So don't forget that you were not born as Jews and were uncircumcised (circumcision itself is just a work of man's hands); you had none of the Jewish covenants and laws; you were foreigners to Israel's incredible heritage;[h] you were without the covenants and prophetic promises of the Messiah, the promised hope, and without God.

---

a 2:1 As translated literally from the Greek.

b 2:2 The Aramaic can be translated "the worldliness of this world."

c 2:2 The Aramaic phrase can also refer to the authority of secular governments.

d 2:6 To be "placed" or "seated" in heaven means we have been given the perfection and authority to be there.

e 2:7 The Aramaic can be translated "universes."

f 2:10 The beautiful Greek word used here is translated "poem" or "poetry." Our lives are the beautiful poetry written by God that will speak forth all that he desires in life.

g 2:10 Although implied, these good works make up our destiny. As we yield to God, our prearranged destiny comes to pass and we are rewarded for simply doing what he wanted us to accomplish.

h 2:11–12 Or "freedom," or "commonwealth."

[13] *Yet look at you now! Everything is new!* Although you were once distant and far away from God, now you have been brought delightfully close to him through the sacred blood of Jesus—you have actually been united to Christ!

[14] Our reconciling "Peace" is Jesus! He has made Jew and non-Jew one *in Christ. By dying as our sacrifice,* he has broken down every wall of prejudice that separated us *and has now made us equal through our union with Christ.* [15] Ethnic hatred has been dissolved by the crucifixion of his precious body on the cross. The legal code that stood condemning every one of us has now been repealed *by his command.* His triune essence has made peace between us by starting over—forming[a] one new race of humanity,[b] Jews and non-Jews fused together!

[16] Two have now become one, and we live restored to God and reconciled in the body of Christ. Through his crucifixion, hatred died. [17] For the Messiah has come to preach this sweet message of peace to you,[c] the ones who were distant, and to those who are near. [18] And now, because we are united to Christ, we both have equal and direct access in the realm of the Holy Spirit to come before the Father!

[19] So, you are not foreigners or guests, but rather you are the children of the city of the holy ones,[d] with all the rights as family members of the household of God. [20] *You are rising like the perfectly fitted stones of the temple;*[e] and your lives are being built up together upon the ideal foundation laid by the apostles and prophets, and best of all, you are connected to the Head Cornerstone of the building, the Anointed One, Jesus Christ himself!

[21] This entire building is under construction and is continually growing under his supervision until it rises up completed as the holy temple of the Lord himself. [22] This means that God is transforming each one of you into *the Holy of Holies,* his dwelling place, through the power of the Holy Spirit living in you!

The Divine Mystery

3 Beloved friends, *because of my love for Jesus Christ,* I am now his prisoner for the sake of all of you who are not Jews, [2] so that you will hear the gospel that God has entrusted to me to share with you. [3] For this wonderful mystery, which I briefly described, was given to me by divine revelation, [4] so that whenever you read it you will be able to understand my revelation and insight into the secret mystery of the Messiah.

[5] There has never been a generation that has been given the detailed understanding of this glorious and divine mystery until now. He kept it a secret until

---

a 2:15 As translated from the Aramaic. The Greek is "to create in himself one new man."

b 2:15 Or "one new man."

c 2:17 This is Paul's paraphrase of Isa. 57:19.

d 2:19 As translated from the Aramaic.

e 2:20 The "temple" is not found in the text here, but is explicitly mentioned in v. 21.

this generation. God is revealing it only now to his sacred apostles and prophets by the Holy Spirit. [6] Here's the secret: The gospel of grace has made you, non-Jewish believers, into coheirs of his promise through your union with him. And you have now become members of his body—one with the Anointed One!

[7-8] I have been made a messenger of this wonderful news by the gift of grace that works through me. Even though I am the least significant of all his holy believers, this grace-gift was imparted when the manifestation of his power came upon me. Grace alone empowers me so that I can boldly preach this wonderful message to non-Jewish people, sharing with them the unfading,[a] inexhaustible riches of Christ, which are beyond comprehension.

[9] My passion is to enlighten every person to this divine mystery. It was hidden for ages past until now, and kept a secret in the heart of God, the Creator of all. [10] The purpose of this was to unveil before every throne and rank of angelic orders in the heavenly realm God's full and diverse wisdom revealed through the church.[b] [11] This perfectly wise plan was destined from eternal ages and fulfilled completely in our Lord Jesus Christ, so that now [12] we have boldness through him,[c] and free access as kings[d] before the Father because of our complete confidence in Christ's faithfulness.

[13] My dear friends, I pray that you will remain strong and not be discouraged or ashamed by all that I suffer on your behalf, for it is for your glory.

Paul Prays for Love to Overflow

[14] So I kneel humbly in awe before the Father of our Lord Jesus, the Messiah, [15] the perfect Father of every father and child[e] in heaven and on the earth. [16] And I pray that he would unveil within you the unlimited riches of his glory and favor until supernatural strength floods your innermost being with his divine might and explosive power.

[17] Then, by constantly using your faith, the life of Christ will be released deep inside you, and the resting place of his love will become the very source and root of your life.

[18-19] Then you will be empowered to discover what every holy one

---

a 3:7–8 The word *unfading* comes from an Aramaic word which can also be translated "unquestionable" or "without fault." The Greek uses the word *unsearchable*.

b 3:10 The church is the "university of the angels" and every believer is a "professor" teaching the heavenly realm the mysteries and wonders of the grace of God. The angels investigate through our lives the treasures of grace, like the cherubim who gaze upon the mercy seat. See 1 Peter 1:12.

c 3:12 The Greek words used here can be translated, "freedom of speech to say whatever you want with boldness."

d 3:12 The Aramaic text can be translated "we have kingship."

e 3:15 Translated from the Aramaic. It could also be translated "the perfect Father of every people group." The Greek word for "father" and the word for "family" are quite similar, which indicates that every family finds its source in the Father.

experiences—the great magnitude[a] of the astonishing love of Christ in all its dimensions. How deeply intimate and far-reaching is his love! How enduring and inclusive it is! Endless love beyond measurement that transcends our understanding—this extravagant love pours into you until you are filled to overflowing with the fullness of God!

²⁰ *Never doubt* God's mighty power to work in you and accomplish all this. He will achieve infinitely more than your greatest request, your most unbelievable dream, and exceed your wildest imagination! He will outdo them all, for his miraculous power constantly energizes you.

²¹ Now we offer up to God all the glorious praise that rises from every church in every generation through Jesus Christ—and all that will yet be manifest through time and eternity. Amen!

Our Divine Calling

4 As a prisoner of the Lord,[b] I plead with you to walk holy, in a way that is suitable to your high rank, given to you in your divine calling. ² With tender humility and quiet patience, always demonstrate gentleness and generous[c] love toward one another, especially toward those who may try your patience. ³ Be faithful to guard the sweet harmony of the Holy Spirit among you in the bonds of peace, ⁴ being one body and one spirit, as you were all called into the same glorious hope *of divine destiny.*

⁵ For the Lord God is one, *and so are we,* for we share in one faith, one baptism, and one Father. ⁶ And He is the perfect Father who leads us all, works through us all, and lives in us all!

The Grace-Gifts of Christ

⁷ And he has generously given each one of us supernatural grace, according to the size of the gift of Christ. ⁸ This is why he says:

"He ascends into the heavenly heights
    taking his many captured ones with him,[d]
    and gifts were given to men."[e]

⁹ He "ascended" means that he returned to heaven, after he had first descended from the heights of heaven, even descending as far as the lowest parts of the earth. ¹⁰ The same one who descended is also the one who ascended above the heights of heaven, in order to begin the restoration and fulfillment[f] of all things.

---

a 3:18–19 Or "excellence."
b 4:1 Paul wrote this letter while a prisoner in Rome because of his faith in Christ. See Song. 8:6 TPT.
c 4:2 The Aramaic word literally means "stretching."
d 4:8 Or "he captured captivity."
e 4:8 Or "men were given as gifts." See Ps. 68:18.
f 4:10 As translated from the Aramaic. The Greek text says "that he might fill all things."

[11] And he has appointed some *with grace* to be apostles, and some *with grace* to be prophets, and some *with grace* to be evangelists,[a] and some *with grace* to be pastors,[b] and some *with grace* to be teachers.[c] [12] And their calling is to nurture and prepare all the holy believers to do their own works of ministry, and as they do this they will enlarge and build up the body of Christ. [13] *These grace ministries will function* until we all attain oneness in the faith, until we all experience the fullness of what it means to know the Son of God,[d] and finally we become one perfect man[e] with the full dimensions of spiritual maturity and fully developed in the abundance of Christ.

[14] And then our immaturity will end! And we will not be easily shaken by trouble, nor led astray by novel teachings or by the false doctrines of deceivers[f] who teach clever lies. [15] But instead we will remain strong and always sincere in our love as we express the truth. *All our direction and ministries will flow* from Christ and lead us deeper into him, the anointed Head of his body, the church.

[16] For his "body" *has been formed in his image* and is closely joined together and constantly connected as one. And every member *has been given divine gifts* to contribute to the growth of all; and as *these gifts* operate effectively throughout the whole body, we are built up and made perfect in love.

Our New Life in Christ

[17] So with the wisdom given to me from the Lord I say: You should not live like the unbelievers around you who walk in their empty delusions.[g] [18] Their corrupted logic has been clouded because their hearts are so far from God—their blinded understanding and deep-seated moral darkness keeps them from the true knowledge of God. [19] Because of spiritual apathy, they surrender their lives to lewdness, impurity, and sexual obsession.

[20] But this is not the way of life that Christ has unfolded within you. [21] If you have really experienced the Anointed One, and heard his truth, *it will be seen in your life*; for we know that the ultimate reality[h] is embodied in Jesus!

[22] And he has taught you to let go of the lifestyle of the ancient man,[i] the old self-life, which was corrupted by sinful and deceitful desires that spring from delusions. [23] Now it's time to be made new by every revelation that's been given to

---

a 4:11 The Aramaic can be translated "preachers."
b 4:11 Or "shepherds."
c 4:11 The Aramaic can be translated "wise orators."
d 4:13 The Greek literally means "until we have the full knowledge of the Son of God."
e 4:13 The Hebrew and Aramaic word for perfect is *gamar,* and the word implies that perfection cannot come to the body of Christ without the example and teaching of these five ministries—apostles, prophets, evangelists, pastors, and teachers.
f 4:14 The Greek literally means "dice-playing gamblers."
g 4:17 Or "opinions."
h 4:21 Or "ultimate learning."
i 4:22 As translated from the Aramaic.

you.[a] 24 And to be transformed as you embrace the glorious Christ-within as your new life and live in union with him! For God has re-created you all over again in his perfect righteousness, and you now belong to him in the realm of true holiness. 25 So discard every form of dishonesty and lying *so that you will be known as one* who always speaks the truth, for we all belong to one another.

26 But don't let the passion of your emotions[b] lead you to sin! Don't let anger control you *or be fuel for revenge*, not for even a day. 27 Don't give the slanderous accuser, the Devil, an opportunity to manipulate you! 28 If any one of you has stolen from someone else, never do it again. Instead, be industrious, earning an honest living, and then you'll have enough to bless those in need.

29 And never let ugly or hateful words come from your mouth, but instead let your words become beautiful gifts[c] that encourage others; do this by speaking words of grace to help them.

30 The Holy Spirit of God has sealed you in Jesus Christ until you experience your full salvation. So never grieve the Spirit of God or take for granted his holy influence in your life.[d] 31 Lay aside bitter words, temper tantrums, revenge, profanity, and insults. 32 But instead be kind[e] and affectionate toward one another. Has God graciously forgiven you? Then graciously forgive one another in the depths of Christ's love.

Living in God's Love

5 Be imitators of God in everything you do,[f] for then you will represent your Father as his beloved sons and daughters. 2 And continue to walk surrendered to the extravagant love of Christ, for he surrendered his life as a sacrifice for us. His great love for us was pleasing to God, like an aroma of adoration—a sweet healing fragrance.[g]

3 And have nothing to do with sexual immorality, lust, or greed—for you are his holy ones *and let no one be able to accuse you of them in any form.* 4 Guard your speech. Forsake obscenities and worthless insults; these are nonsensical words that bring disgrace and are unnecessary. Instead, let worship fill your heart and spill out in your words.

5 For it has been made clear to you already that the kingdom of God cannot be accessed by anyone who is guilty of sexual sin, or who is impure or

---

a 4:23 Or "in the spirit of your revelation."

b 4:26 The Aramaic word *ragza* means "to shake" or "to tremble." It is a word used for any strong emotion, but usually refers to anger.

c 4:29 Or "constructive."

d 4:30 The Greek manuscripts have "do not grieve," while the Aramaic text reads "do not limit his scope." This translation includes both concepts.

e 4:32 The Aramaic word for "kind" can also be translated "sweet."

f 5:1 The Greek word *mimetes* frequently depicts an actor playing a role. God wants us to mimic him and be filled with his thoughts, his love, his deeds, and his character.

g 5:2 The Aramaic word "fragrance" can also be translated "healing balm."

greedy—for greed is the essence of idolatry. How could they expect to have an inheritance in Christ's kingdom *while doing those things?*

Living in God's Light

⁶Don't be fooled by those who speak their empty words and deceptive teachings telling you otherwise. This is what brings God's anger upon the rebellious! ⁷Don't listen to them or live like them at all. ⁸Once your life was full of sin's darkness, but now you have the very light of our Lord shining through you because of your union with him. Your mission is to live as children flooded with his revelation-light! ⁹And the supernatural fruits of his light*ᵃ* will be seen in you—goodness, righteousness, and truth. ¹⁰Then you will learn to choose what is beautiful to our Lord.

¹¹And don't even associate with the servants of darkness because they have no fruit in them; instead, reveal truth to them. ¹²The very things they do in secret are too vile and filthy to even mention. ¹³Whatever the revelation-light exposes, it will also correct, and everything that reveals truth is light to the soul.*ᵇ* ¹⁴This is why the Scripture says,

> "Arise, you sleeper! Rise up from the dead and the Anointed One will shine his light into you!"*ᶜ*

Living in God's Wisdom

¹⁵⁻¹⁶So be very careful how you live, not being like those with no understanding, but live honorably with true wisdom, for we are living in evil times. Take full advantage of every day as you spend your life for his purposes. ¹⁷And don't live foolishly for then you will have discernment to fully understand God's will. ¹⁸And don't get drunk with wine, which is rebellion;*ᵈ* instead be filled with the fullness of the Holy Spirit.*ᵉ* ¹⁹*And your hearts will overflow with* a joyful song to the Lord Jehovah. Keep speaking to each other with words of Scripture, singing the Psalms with praises and spontaneous songs given by the Spirit!*ᶠ* ²⁰Always give thanks to Father God for every person*ᵍ* *he brings into your life* in the name of our Lord Jesus Christ. ²¹And out of your reverence for Christ be supportive of each other in love.

---

a 5:9 Some Greek manuscripts have "Spirit."

b 5:13 Or "everything revealed becomes light."

c 5:14 See Isa. 26:19; 51:17; 52:1; 60:1.

d 5:18 The Aramaic can be translated "the wine of the prodigal." The Greek is "reckless living," or "debauchery."

e 5:18 Or "be inebriated in the Spirit's fullness."

f 5:19 Or "spiritual songs." There is no other song more spiritual than the Song of Songs. Perhaps Paul was encouraging the church to sing and rejoice in the greatest of all songs.

g 5:20 The Greek text is ambiguous; it can mean "give thanks for all things" or "for all people." The Aramaic is quite specific—"for all people."

Loving Relationships

[22] For wives, this means being supportive[a] to your husbands like you are tenderly devoted to our Lord, [23] for the husband provides leadership for the wife, just as Christ provides leadership for his church, as the Savior and Reviver[b] of the body. [24] In the same way the church is devoted to Christ, let the wives be devoted to their husbands in everything.

[25] And to the husbands, you are to demonstrate love for your wives with the same tender devotion that Christ demonstrated to us, his bride.[c] For he died for us, sacrificing himself [26] to make us holy and pure, cleansing us through the showering of the pure water of the Word of God. [27] *All that he does in us is designed* to make us a mature church for his pleasure, until we become a source of praise to him—glorious and radiant,[d] beautiful and holy, without fault or flaw.[e]

[28] Husbands have the obligation of loving and caring for their wives the same way they love and care for their own bodies, for to love your wife is to love your own self. [29] No one abuses his own body, but pampers it—serving and satisfying its needs. That's exactly what Christ does for his church! [30] *He serves and satisfies us*[f] as members of his body.

[31] For this reason a man is to leave his father and his mother and lovingly hold to his wife, since the two have become joined as one flesh.[g] [32] Marriage is the beautiful design of the Almighty,[h] a great and sacred mystery—*meant to be a vivid example* of Christ and his church. [33] So every married man should be gracious to his wife just as he is gracious to himself. And every wife should be tenderly devoted to her husband.

Love in Our Families and Workplaces

6 Children, *if you want to be wise*, listen to your parents and do what they tell you, and the Lord[i] will help you.

[2] For the commandment, "Honor your father and your mother," was the

---

a 5:22 The Greek word for "submit," or "supportive," is not found in v. 22. It is literally "Wives, with your husbands."

b 5:23 The Aramaic word used here can be translated "Savior" or "Reviver." This translation includes both concepts.

c 5:25 Or "church."

d 5:27 The Greek word for radiance (*endoxos*) can also mean "gorgeous," "honorable," "esteemed," "splendid," "infused with glory." This is what Christ's love will do to you. (See *Strong's Concordance*, Gr. 1741.)

e 5:27 The Greek text has "without any wrinkle." The Aramaic can be translated "without chips or knots."

f 5:30 Inferred from v. 29 and made explicit here.

g 5:31 See Gen. 2:24.

h 5:32 As translated from the Aramaic

i 6:1 Or "through our Lord."

first of the *Ten Commandments* with a promise attached: [3] "You will prosper[a] and live a long, full life *if you honor your parents.*"

[4] Fathers, don't exasperate your children,[b] but raise them up with loving discipline and counsel that brings the revelation of our Lord.

[5] Those who are employed should listen to their employers[c] and obey their instructions with great respect and honor.[d] Serve them with humility in your hearts as though you were working for the Master.[e]

[6] Always do what is right and not only when others are watching, so that you may please Christ as his servants by doing his will. [7] Serve[f] your employers wholeheartedly and with love, as though you were serving Christ and not men. [8] Be assured that anything you do that is beautiful and excellent will be repaid by our Lord, whether you are an employee or an employer.

[9] And to the caretakers of the flock[g] I say, do what is right with your people by forgiving them when they offend you, for you know there is a Master in heaven that shows no favoritism.

Spiritual Warfare

[10] Now my beloved ones, I have saved these most important truths for last: Be supernaturally infused with strength through your life-union with the Lord Jesus. Stand victorious with the force[h] of his explosive power flowing in and through you.

[11] Put on God's complete set of armor[i] provided for us, so that you will be protected as you fight against the evil strategies of the accuser![j] [12] Your hand-to-hand combat is not with human beings, but with the highest principalities and authorities operating in rebellion under the heavenly realms.[k] For they are a powerful class of demon-gods[l] and evil spirits that hold[m] this dark world in

---

a 6:3 Or "it will go beautifully for you."

b 6:4 In other words, fathers should show consideration for the different levels of understanding and experience that children possess, dealing with them at their level, or risk causing them loads of heartache.

c 6:5 Literally "servants should obey their caretakers."

d 6:5 Or "with trembling."

e 6:5 Or "the Messiah."

f 6:7 Or "minister to them."

g 6:9 As translated literally from the Aramaic. The "caretakers of the flock" can refer to both leadership in the church and in the workplace. The Greek text states "masters, do the same things to them, and give up threatening."

h 6:10 Or "weapons."

i 6:11 See Isa. 59:17.

j 6:11 Or "the devil."

k 6:12 Or literally "under heaven."

l 6:12 The classical Greek word used here is often used to refer to conjuring up pagan deities—supreme powers of darkness mentioned in occult rituals.

m 6:12 Or "possessors of this dark world."

bondage. [13] Because of this, you must wear all the armor that God provides so you're protected as you confront the slanderer,[a] for you are destined for all things[b] and will rise victorious.

[14] Put on truth as a belt to strengthen you to stand in triumph. Put on holiness as the protective armor that covers your heart. [15] Stand on your feet alert, then you'll always be ready to share the blessings of peace.

[16] In every battle, take faith as your wrap-around shield, for it is able to extinguish the blazing arrows coming at you from the Evil One! [17-18] Embrace the power of salvation's full deliverance, like a helmet *to protect your thoughts from lies*. And take the mighty razor-sharp Spirit-sword[d] of the spoken Word of God.

Pray passionately[e] in the Spirit, as you constantly intercede with every form of prayer at all times. Pray the blessings of God upon all his believers.[19] And pray also that God's revelation would be released through me every time I preach the wonderful mystery of the hope-filled gospel. [20] Yes, pray that I may preach the wonderful news of God's kingdom with bold freedom at every opportunity. Even though I am chained as a prisoner, I am his ambassador.

The Messenger, Tychicus

[21-22] I am sending you a dear friend, Tychicus.[f] He is a beloved brother and trustworthy minister in our Lord Jesus. He will share with you all the concerns that I have for your welfare and will inform you of how I am getting along. And he will also prophesy over you[g] to encourage your hearts. [23] So may God shower his peace upon you, my beloved friends. And may the blessings of faith and love fill your hearts from God the Father and from our Lord Jesus, the Messiah. [24] Abundant grace will be with you all as each of you love our Lord Jesus Christ without corruption. Amen!

Love in Christ,
Paul

---

a 6:13 Or "devil."

b 6:13 As translated from the Aramaic. The Greek text can be translated "after you have conquered, you can stand in victory."

c 6:16 The poetic language Paul uses here is likely a reference to Ps. 91:4–5.

d 6:17–18 This is the Greek word, *machaira*, which was a razor sharp Roman sword used in close combat.

e 6:17–18 Or "all desires."

f 6:21–22 Tychicus, whose name means "child of fortune," is believed to be an Ephesian who took this letter, as Paul's representative, to the churches throughout Turkey. He is mentioned four other times in the New Testament. See Acts 20:4; Col. 4:7; 2 Tim. 4:12; and Titus 3:12.

g 6:21–22 Translated from the Aramaic. Prophecy in the local church will always encourage, edify, and enlighten. See 1 Cor. 14:3.

PHILIPPIANS

Introduction

AT A GLANCE

Author: The apostle Paul

Audience: The church of Philippi

Date: AD 60–62

Type of Literature: A letter

Major Themes: The gospel, Christ's lordship, Christian conduct, and Christ's community and identity

Outline:

ABOUT PHILIPPIANS

What joy and glory came out of Paul's prison cell! Most of us would be thinking of ourselves and how we could get out; but Paul wanted to send to the Philippian church the revelation of joy!

The church of Philippi began because of a supernatural vision experienced by Paul while he was ministering at Troas (Acts 16:8–10). He had a vision in the night of a man from Macedonia who stood at his bedside pleading with him to come and give them the gospel.

It was in Philippi that Paul was arrested for preaching the gospel. Thrown in a prison cell and beaten, he and his coworker Silas began to sing songs of joy and praise to the Most High God! This caused a tremendous miracle as the prison doors were flung open and they escaped—but not before leading their jailor to Christ! Perhaps the jailor was the very man Paul had seen in his vision.

Philippi is where Paul met Lydia, a businesswoman who apparently led an import/export business from that city. The miracles of God birthed a church among the Philippians, and Paul longs to encourage them to never give up and to keep rejoicing in all things.

Paul's words point us to heaven. He teaches us that our true life is not only in this world, but it is in the heavenly calling, the heavenly realm, and in our heavenly life that was given to us through Christ, the heavenly Man. He left heaven to redeem us and reveal the heart of God, the heart of a servant. He gave us new birth that we would be heavenly lights in this dark world as witnesses of Christ's power to change our lives.

There is a good and glorious work that Christ has begun in our hearts and promises to complete once he is fully unveiled. Philippians teaches us how important it is to be joyful throughout our journey of becoming like Christ. The words *joy* and *rejoicing* occur eighteen times in this book. So read this heavenly letter of joy and be encouraged.

PURPOSE

This could be considered a letter written to friends. Throughout his Philippian letter, Paul speaks of unity and teaches how the church should live as one in the fellowship of Jesus Christ. We also discover in this, the warmest of Paul's letters, many truths about Jesus Christ, his humiliation and exaltation on high. Paul tells us that God seated us in the heavenly realm in his place of authority and power. No wonder we should have joy in our hearts!

AUTHOR AND AUDIENCE

Paul wrote this letter of heavenly joy about AD 60, while Timothy was visiting him in prison. Carried by one of the Philippian church leaders, Epaphroditus, it was delivered to the believers to be read publicly to all. He also wrote it to friends, to partners in the gospel, in the city of Philippi. Paul was motivated to write to these friends because of concerns he had over their disunity, suffering, and opponents. There were also two aspects of his imprisonment that cause him to write the letter: the gospel's advance while he was kept in chains, as well as the gift from the Philippian church. He wrote this letter to express his joyful faith in Christ Jesus while in prison and to communicate his appreciation and love for his generous friends in Philippi.

MAJOR THEMES

The Gospel of Christ. Paul's main theme in this letter is the gospel, a word that appears more often in this letter than any of his other letters. He is specifically concerned with believers' ongoing relationship with Christ on the other side of their acceptance of the gospel. He is also concerned with the advancement of the gospel, that Jesus' story of rescue and forgiveness goes out into all the world.

The Lordship of Christ. At the heart of this letter is the famed *Christ Hymn* (2:6–11)—a soaring melody of worship, adoration, and revelation of the majesty and superiority of Christ as Lord over all. This hymn expresses in lofty, lyrical language the story of Jesus from his preexistent glory to the universal praise of him as Lord paved by his obedience to death on the cross.

The Conduct of Christ. Those who have received and believed the gospel are called to live according to the gospel, to conduct their lives in such a way that they live for Christ. For Paul, such a life is a process of seizing the surpassing worth of Christ and being seized by him. It is also a progressive pursuit of Christ in which we daily die with him in order to experience the fullness of his new life.

The Community of Christ. The community of Christ is the new people of God. Paul contrasts this new people with those in the old community who tried to bring non-Jewish Christians into the circle of Judaism. He also contrasts this community with the world, reminding believers that we are citizens of heaven who submit to the lordship of Christ. Finally, he reminds believers of their unity as brothers and sisters within God's household.

PHILIPPIANS

Heaven's Joy

Introduction

1 *Dear friends* in Philippi,

¹⁻² *My name is* Paul and I'm joined by Timothy,ᵃ both of us servants of Jesus, the Anointed One. We write this letter to all his devoted followers in your city, including your pastors,ᵇ and to all the servant-leadersᶜ of the church.

May the blessings of divine grace and supernatural peace that flow from God our wonderful Father, and our Messiah, the Lord Jesus, be upon your lives.

Paul Prays for the Philippians

³⁻⁴ My prayers for you are full of praise to God as I give him thanks for you with great joy! *I'm so grateful for our union* ⁵ and our enduring partnership that began the first time I presented to you the gospel. ⁶ *I pray with great faith for you*, because I'm fully convinced that the One who began this glorious workᵈ in you will faithfully continue the process of maturing youᵉ and will put his finishing touches to it until the unveilingᶠ of our Lord Jesus Christ!

⁷ It's no wonder I pray with such confidence, since you have a permanent place in my heart!ᵍ You have remained partners with me in the wonderful grace *of God* even though I'm here in chains for standing up for the truth of the gospel.ʰ

ᵃ 1:1–2 Timothy was Paul's convert, coworker, and spiritual son. See 1 Tim. 1:2.

ᵇ 1:1–2 Or "guardians," as translated from the Greek. The Aramaic text uses the word *priests*, and could refer to Jewish priests who had received Jesus as the Messiah.

ᶜ 1:1–2 As translated from the Aramaic. The Greek text is "deacons." The word for deacon is actually taken from a Greek compound of the words *dia* and *kovis* that means "to kick up the dust," referring to a servant who is so swift to accomplish his service that he stirs up the dust of the street running to fulfill his duty.

ᵈ 1:6 Or "good [worthwhile] work." Paul uses language here that sounds similar to Gen. 1:2. When God created the heavens and the earth, he declared it to be "good." And now with the new creation life within us, God again sees our growth in grace as something good.

ᵉ 1:6 Or "he will see to it that you remain faithful."

ᶠ 1:6 Literally "day of Christ." This is the day of his unveiling, his appearing.

ᵍ 1:7 Or "since you have given me a permanent place in your hearts."

ʰ 1:7 The Aramaic can be translated "the truth of God's revelation." The Greek can also be translated "for the defense and proof (a possible hendiadys) of the gospel."

[8] Only God knows how much I dearly love you with the tender affection[a] of Jesus, the Anointed One.

[9] I continue to pray for your love to grow and increase beyond measure, bringing you into the rich revelation of spiritual insight[b] in all things.

[10] This will enable you to choose[c] the most excellent way of all[d]—becoming pure and without offense until the unveiling of Christ.[e] [11] And you will be filled completely with the fruits of righteousness[f] that are found in Jesus, the Anointed One—bringing great praise and glory to God!

Paul's Imprisonment

[12] I want you to know, dear ones,[g] what has happened to me has not hindered, but helped my ministry of preaching the gospel, causing it to expand and spread to many people. [13] For now the elite Roman guards and government officials[h] overseeing my imprisonment have plainly recognized that I am here because of my love for the Anointed One. [14] And what I'm going through has actually caused many believers[i] to become even more courageous in the Lord and to be bold and passionate to preach the Word of God, all because of my chains.

[15] It's true that there are some who preach Christ out of competition and controversy, for they are jealous *over the way God has used me.* Many others *have purer motives*—they preach with grace and love filling their hearts,[j] [16] because they know I've been destined for the purpose of defending the revelation of God.[k]

[17] Those who preach Christ with ambition and competition are insincere—they just want to add to the hardships of my imprisonment. [18] Yet in spite of

---

a 1:8 Or "mercies."

b 1:9 The Greek word for "insight" (*aisthēsis*) is a hapax legomenon in the New Testament and used numerous times in the Septuagint referring to practical understanding linked to life. It is a word that implies walking out the truth that insight reveals. It could also be translated "experience." Many translations render it "discernment," yet it is more than discerning something—it means to experience the reality of something and apply it to life.

c 1:10 The Greek word for "choose" (*dokimazō*) means "to examine, to discern, or approve after testing." It comes from a root word that means "accepted" or "pleasing." So discernment becomes the path to finding what God approves, not simply what God forbids. When love, revelation, and insight overflow into our discernment, we will always be looking for what is excellent and pleasing in God's eyes. We choose what is best, not by law or rules, but by loving discernment.

d 1:10 As translated from the Greek. The Aramaic can be translated "choose those things that bring contentment."

e 1:10 Or "in preparation for the day of Christ." This is the day of his unveiling at his appearing.

f 1:11 Or "the fruit that is righteousness."

g 1:12 Or "my brothers."

h 1:13 Or "Caesar's court."

i 1:14 Or "brothers."

j 1:15 Or "with goodwill." The translation has borrowed the term "love" from v. 16 and made it explicit here as the purest motive for preaching the gospel.

k 1:16 As translated from the Aramaic. The Greek is "the gospel." The implication from the Aramaic is that some of these preachers (v. 15) had been ordained by Paul.

all of this I am overjoyed! For what does it matter as long as Christ is being preached? If they preach him with mixed motives or with genuine love, the message of Christ is still being preached. *And I will continue to rejoice* [19] because I know that the lavish supply [a] of the Spirit of Jesus, the Anointed One, and your intercession for me will bring about my deliverance. [b] [20] No matter what, I will continue to hope and passionately cling [c] to Christ, so that he will be openly revealed through me before everyone's eyes. [d] So I will not be ashamed! [e] In my life or in my death, Christ will be magnified in me. [21] My true life is the Anointed One, and dying means gaining more of him.

[22-24] *So here's my dilemma*: Each day I live means bearing more fruit in my ministry; yet I fervently long to be liberated from this body [f] and joined fully to Christ. That would suit me fine, but the greatest advantage to you would be that I remain alive. So you can see why I'm torn between the two—I don't know which I prefer.

[25] Yet deep in my heart I'm confident that I will be spared so I can add to your joy and further strengthen and mature your faith. [g] [26] When I am freed to come to you, my deliverance will give you a reason to boast even more in Jesus Christ.

[27] Whatever happens, keep living your lives based on the reality of the gospel of Christ, *which reveals him to others*. Then when I come to see you, or hear good reports of you, I'll know that you stand united in one Spirit and one passion—celebrating together as conquerors [h] in the faith of the gospel. [i] [28] And then you will never be shaken or intimidated by the opposition that rises up against us, for your courage will only prove as a sure sign from God of their coming destruction *and that you have found a new life*. [29] For God has graciously given you the privilege not only to believe in Christ, but also to suffer for him. [30] For you have been called by him to endure the conflict in the same way I have endured it—for you know I'm not giving up.

---

a 1:19 The Greek word for "supply" can also be translated "festive chorus."

b 1:19 A quotation from Job 13:16 (LXX).

c 1:20 The Greek word is *apokaradokia* and can be translated "with the deepest and intense yearnings," or "the concentrated desire that abandons all other interests with outstretched hands in expectation." It is possible that Paul uses the words "passionately cling," and "hope" as a hendiadys (i.e., "my hope-filled intense expectation"). Romans 8:19 is the only other place in the New Testament where *apokaradokia* is found.

d 1:20 Literally "with uncovered faces." Some interpret it to mean without shame.

e 1:20 See also Rom. 1:16; 2 Cor. 10:8; 1 Peter 4:16; 1 John 2:28.

f 1:22–24 The Greek uses the word *analyō*, which means "to fold up a tent and depart." Sailors used this word to say, "loose the ship and set sail." And farmers used *analyō* to mean "to unyoke an oxen" (set it free).

g 1:25 Or "that I could help with your pioneer advance and joy in faith." Paul was excited to help them make new pioneer advances in their faith and joy.

h 1:27 As translated literally from the Aramaic. The Greek states "striving side by side with one mind."

i 1:27 Or "his revelation."

Joined Together in Perfect Unity

2 Look at how much encouragement[a] you've found in your relationship with the Anointed One! You are filled to overflowing with his comforting love. You have experienced a deepening friendship with the Holy Spirit and have felt his tender affection and mercy.[b]

² So I'm asking you, my friends, that you be joined together in perfect unity—with one heart, one passion, and united in one love. Walk together[c] with one harmonious purpose and you will fill my heart with unbounded joy.

³ Be free from pride-filled opinions, *for they will only harm your cherished unity.* Don't allow self-promotion to hide in your hearts, but in authentic humility put others first and view others as more important than yourselves. ⁴ Abandon every display of selfishness. Possess a greater concern for what matters to others instead of your own interests. ⁵ And consider the example that Jesus, the Anointed One, has set before us. Let his mindset become your motivation.

The Example of Jesus Christ

⁶ He existed in the form of God, yet he gave no thought to seizing equality with God as his supreme prize.[d] ⁷ Instead he emptied himself of his outward glory by reducing himself to the form of a lowly servant. He became human! ⁸ He humbled himself and became vulnerable, choosing to be revealed as a man and was obedient.[e] *He was a perfect example,* even in his death—a criminal's death by crucifixion![f]

⁹ Because of that obedience, God exalted him and multiplied his greatness! He has now been given the greatest of all names!

¹⁰ The authority of the name of Jesus causes every knee to bow in reverence! Everything and everyone will one day submit to this name—in the heavenly realm, in the earthly realm, and in the demonic realm.[g] ¹¹ And every tongue will proclaim in every language: "Jesus Christ is Lord Yahweh,"[h] bringing glory and honor to God, his Father![i]

---

a 2:1 The Greek word *paraklesis* can also mean "exhortation" or "comfort."

b 2:1 Or "sympathies." The Aramaic can be translated "your heart flutters with his compassion."

c 2:2 Or "Be like-minded."

d 2:6 Or "as something to be exploited."

e 2:8 See also John 5:19.

f 2:8 Notice the seven steps Christ took from the throne to the cross in vv. 7–8: (1) He emptied himself. (2) He became a servant. (3) He became human. (4) He humbled himself. (5) He became vulnerable and revealed as a Man. (6) He was obedient until his death. (7) He died a criminal's death on the cross.

g 2:10 Or "heaven, earth, and under the earth."

h 2:11 As translated from the Aramaic. The Greek text uses the word *kurios,* which is not the highest name for God. *Yahweh* (Hebrew) or *Jehovah* (Latin) is the highest name. *Kurios* is a title also used for false gods, land owners, merchants, and nobles. The Greek language has no equal to the sacred name (the tetragrammaton—*YHWH*), Yahweh. Only Hebrew and Aramaic have that equivalent. This verse makes it clear that the name given to Jesus at his exaltation was "Lord Jehovah" or "Lord Yahweh." The Hebrew name for Jesus is *Yeshua* (lit. "God is a Saving-Cry"), which bears and reveals the name Yahweh. Jesus carries the name and reputation of his Father, Yahweh, within him. See John 17:11.

i 2:11 Note the seven steps of exaltation that God gave Jesus after the cross: (1) God exalted

Believers Shine Like Lights in the World

¹² My beloved ones, just like you've always listened to everything I've taught you in the past, I'm asking you now to keep following my instructions as though I were right there with you. Now you must continue to make this new life fully manifested as you live *a* in the holy awe of God—which brings you trembling into his presence. ¹³ God will continually revitalize you, implanting within you the passion to do what pleases him. *b*

¹⁴ Live a cheerful life, without complaining or division among yourselves. ¹⁵ For then you will be seen as innocent, *c* faultless, and pure children of God, even though you live in the midst of a brutal and perverse culture. *d* For you will appear among them as shining lights *e* in the universe, ¹⁶ offering them the words of eternal life. *f*

I haven't labored among you for nothing, for *your lives are the fruit of my ministry* and will be my glorious boast at the unveiling *g* of Christ!

¹⁷ But I will rejoice even if my life is poured out like a liquid offering to God over your sacrificial and surrendered lives of faith. *h* ¹⁸ And so no matter what happens to me, you should rejoice in ecstatic celebration with me!

The Example of Timothy

¹⁹ Yet I'm trusting in our Lord Jesus that I may send Timothy to you soon, so I can be refreshed when I find out how you're doing. ²⁰ Timothy is like no other. He carries the same passion for your welfare that I carry in my heart. ²¹ For it seems as though everyone else is busy seeking what is best for themselves instead of the things that are most important to our Lord Jesus Christ. ²² You already know about his excellent reputation, since he has served alongside me as a loyal son in the work of ministry. ²³ After I see what transpires with me he's the one I will send to you to bless you. ²⁴ And I'm trusting in my Lord to return to you in due time.

---

him and multiplied his greatness. (2) He possess the greatest name of all. (3) His sovereign authority will cause every knee to bow. (4) God decreed that everyone in heaven will bow in worship of the God-Man. (5) God decreed that every demonic being will bow to the God-Man. (6) God decreed that every tongue will proclaim that Jesus Christ is Lord Yahweh! (7) God received the glory and honor of sharing his throne with the God-Man.

a 2:12 The Aramaic can be translated "push through the service of your life" or "work the work of your life."

b 2:13 The Aramaic can be translated "to accomplish the good things you desire to do."

c 2:15 Or "mature."

d 2:15 See Deut. 32:5–6.

e 2:15 The Aramaic can be translated "the enlightened ones."

f 2:16 The Aramaic can be translated "you stand in the place of life to them." The Greek text means "holding out to them the word of life."

g 2:16 Or "day."

h 2:17 The interpretation of this verse is difficult; it is speaking about Paul's willingness to be a love offering for the Philippians if that's what God desired. There is a powerful figure of speech contained in the Aramaic, literally translated as "though I imbibe the wine poured over the offering." This is a metaphor of Paul shedding his blood one day because of his love for the Philippians. Indeed, Paul was later martyred for his faith.

²⁵ But for now, I feel a stirring in my heart to send Epaphroditus[a] back to you immediately. He's a friend to me and a wonderful brother and fellow soldier who has worked with me *as we serve as ministers of the gospel*. And you sent him as your apostle to minister to me in my need. ²⁶ But now he is grieved to know that you found out he had been sick, so he longs to return and comfort you in this.

²⁷ It's true he almost died, but God showed him mercy and healed him. And I'm so thankful to God for his healing, as I was spared from having the sorrow of losing him on top of all my other troubles! ²⁸ So you can see why I'm delighted to send him to you now. I know that you're anxious to see him and rejoice in his healing, and it encourages me to know how happy you'll be to have him back.

²⁹ So warmly welcome him home in the Lord,[b] with joyous love, and esteem him highly, for people like him deserve it. ³⁰ Because of me, he put his life on the line, despising the danger, so that he could provide for me with what you couldn't, since you were so far away. And he did it all because of his ministry for Christ.

A Call to Rejoice and a Warning

3 My beloved ones, don't ever limit your joy or fail to rejoice in the wonderful experience of knowing our Lord Jesus!

I don't mind repeating what I've already written you because it protects you— ² beware of those religious hypocrites[c] who teach that you should be circumcised to please God. ³ For we have already experienced "heart-circumcision," and we worship God in the power and freedom of the Holy Spirit, *not in laws and religious duties*. We are those who boast in what Jesus Christ has done, and not in what we can accomplish in our own strength.

⁴ It's true that *I once relied on all that I had become*. I had a reason to boast and impress people with my accomplishments—more than others—for my pedigree was impeccable.

The Example of Paul

⁵ I was born a true Hebrew of the heritage of Israel[d] as the son of a Jewish man from the tribe of Benjamin.[e] I was circumcised eight days after my birth

---

a 2:25 His name means "charming."

b 2:29 Or "Lord Yahweh."

c 3:2 Literally "dogs," which is a figure of speech for religious hypocrites

d 3:5 This meant that he could trace his family line all the way back to Abraham. There is also an inference that Paul spoke Hebrew-Aramaic as his native tongue and did not adopt Greek customs.

e 3:5 The tribe of Benjamin was honored as the tribe most loyal to the house of David. *Benjamin* means "son of my right hand."

and *was raised in the strict tradition of Orthodox Judaism*, living a separated[a] and devout life as a Pharisee. [6]And concerning the righteousness of the Torah,[b] no one surpassed me; I was without a peer. Furthermore, as a fiery defender of the truth, I persecuted the messianic believers with religious zeal.

[7]Yet all of the accomplishments that I once took credit for, I've now forsaken them and I regard it all as nothing compared to the delight of experiencing Jesus Christ as my Lord! [8]To truly know him meant letting go of everything from my past and throwing all my boasting on the garbage heap. It's all like a pile of manure to me now, so that I may be enriched in the reality of knowing Jesus Christ and embrace him as Lord in all of his greatness.

[9]My passion is to be consumed with him and not clinging to my own "righteousness" based in keeping the written Law. My "righteousness" will be his, based on the faithfulness of Jesus Christ—the very righteousness that comes from God. [10]And I continually long to know the wonders of Jesus more fully and to experience the overflowing power of his resurrection working in me. I will be one with him in his sufferings and I will be one with him in his death. [11]Only then will I be able to experience complete oneness with him in his resurrection from the realm of death.

[12]I admit that I haven't yet acquired the absolute fullness that I'm pursuing, but I run with passion *into his abundance* so that I may reach the purpose that Jesus Christ has called me to fulfill and wants me to discover. [13]I don't depend on my own strength to accomplish this;[c] however I do have one compelling focus: I forget all of the past as I fasten my heart to the future instead. [14]I run straight for the divine invitation of reaching the heavenly goal and gaining the victory-prize through the anointing of Jesus. [15]So let all who are fully mature have this same passion, and if anyone is not yet gripped by these desires,[d] God will reveal it to them. [16]And let us all advance together to reach this victory-prize, following one path with one passion.

[17]My beloved friends, imitate my walk with God and follow all those who walk according to the way of life we modeled before you. [18]For there are many who live by different standards. As I've warned you many times (I weep as I write these words), they are enemies of the cross of the Anointed One and [19]doom awaits them. Their god has possessed them and made them mute.[e] Their boast is in their shameful lifestyles and their minds are in the dirt.[f]

---

a 3:5 A Pharisee was known as a "separated one," who religiously followed all the laws of Judaism.

b 3:6 Or "the written law."

c 3:13 This phrase is translated from the Aramaic. The Greek text states "I, myself, have not taken possession of it."

d 3:15 The Aramaic can be translated "those who don't run this way, God will reveal it to them."

e 3:19 Translated from the Aramaic. The Greek states "their god is their belly," which is meaningless to the average English speaker.

f 3:19 Translated from the Aramaic. It literally means "their conscience is in the ground."

[20] But we are a colony[a] of heaven on earth as we cling tightly to our life-giver, the Lord Jesus Christ, [21] who will transform our humble bodies[b] and transfigure us into the identical likeness of his glorified body. And using his matchless power, he continually subdues everything to himself.[c]

Living in Harmony with One Another

4 My dear and precious friends, whom I deeply love, you have truly become my glorious joy and crown of reward. Now arise[d] in the fullness of your union with our Lord.

[2] And I plead with Euodia and Syntyche to settle their disagreement and be restored with one mind in our Lord.[e] [3] I would like my dear friend and burden-bearer[f] to help resolve this issue, for both women have diligently labored with me for the prize and helped in spreading the revelation of the gospel,[g] along with Clement[h] and the rest of my coworkers. All of their names are written in the Book of Life.

[4] Be cheerful with joyous celebration in every season of life. Let joy overflow, *for you are united with the Anointed One!* [5] Let gentleness[i] be seen in every relationship, for our Lord is ever near.[j]

[6] Don't be pulled in different directions or worried about a thing. Be saturated in prayer throughout each day, offering your faith-filled requests before God with overflowing gratitude. Tell him every detail of your life, [7] then God's wonderful peace that transcends human understanding, *will make the answers known to you* through Jesus Christ.[k] [8] So keep your thoughts continually fixed on all that is authentic and real, honorable and admirable, beautiful and respectful, pure and holy, merciful and kind. And fasten your thoughts on every glorious

---

a 3:20 Or "citizenship," or "commonwealth."

b 3:21 Or "the body of our humility."

c 3:21 The Aramaic can be translated "everyone is in submission to him."

d 4:1 The Aramaic word *arise* implies "resurrection." The Greek is "stand fast."

e 4:2 In every church there is often found conflict in relationships. Paul seeks to encourage these two dear women to resolve all their disagreements. Their names give us a clue. Euodia comes from a word that means "a fair journey." Syntyche comes from a word that can mean "an accident." Along our fair journey we may collide with another, but God always has grace for restoration.

f 4:3 Or "Syzygos," possibly a name, however there is no record of anyone in classical or biblical Greek with this name. Some believe that Syzygos was one of the pastors of the church at Philippi.

g 4:3 The Aramaic can also be translated "God's kingdom realm."

h 4:3 Clement was one of the men who led the church in Philippi. His name means "mild" or "merciful."

i 4:5 The Greek word means "fairness;" the Aramaic "humility."

j 4:5 Or "approaching."

k 4:7 As translated from the Aramaic. The Greek is "guard your heart and your mind in Christ Jesus."

work of God, *a* praising him always. *9 Follow the example* of all that we have imparted to you and the God of peace will be with you in all things.

Paul Thanks the Philippians for Their Support

10 My heart overflows with joy when I think of how you showed your love to me *by your financial support of my ministry*. For even though you have so little, you still continue to help me at every opportunity. 11 I'm not telling you this because I'm in need, for I have learned to be satisfied in any circumstance. *b* 12–13 I know what it means to lack, *c* and I know what it means to experience overwhelming abundance. For I'm trained in the secret of overcoming all things, whether in fullness or in hunger. And I find that the strength of Christ's explosive power infuses me to conquer every difficulty. *d*

14 You've so graciously provided for my essential needs during this season of difficulty. 15 For I want you to know that the Philippian church was the only church that supported me in the beginning as I went out to preach the gospel. You were the only church that sowed into me financially, *e* 16 and when I was in Thessalonica, you supported me for well over a year. *f*

17 I mention this not because I'm requesting a gift, but so that the fruit of your generosity may bring you an abundant reward. 18 I now have all I need—more than enough—I'm abundantly satisfied! For I've received the gift you sent by Epaphroditus and viewed it as a sweet sacrifice, perfumed with the fragrance *of your faithfulness*, which is so pleasing to God!

19 I am convinced that my God will fully satisfy every need you have, *for I have seen* the abundant riches of glory *revealed to me* through the Anointed One, Jesus Christ! 20 And God our Father will receive all the glory and the honor throughout the eternity of eternities! Amen!

21 Give my warm greetings to all the believers in the Anointed One, Jesus. 22 All the brothers and sisters in Christ that are here with me send their loving greetings, especially the converts from Caesar's household.

23 May every one of you overflow with the grace and favor of our Lord Jesus Christ! *g*

Love in Christ,
Paul

---

a 4:8 The Aramaic can be translated "acts of glorification."
b 4:11 Or "to give up everything I have."
c 4:12–13 Or "be humbled."
d 4:12–13 Or "to master all things."
e 4:15 The Aramaic can be translated "accounts of planting and giving."
f 4:16 As translated from the Aramaic. The Greek means "twice you sent gifts."
g 4:23 As translated from the Aramaic. The Greek states "with your spirit."

COLOSSIANS

Introduction

AT A GLANCE

Author: The apostle Paul
Audience: The church of Colossae
Date: AD 60–61
Type of Literature: A letter
Major Themes: Christ, the church, the gospel, and the Christian life
Outline:

Letter Opening — 1:1–2:5
Letter Theme: Christ-Centered Living — 2:6–7
Threats to Christ-Centered Living — 2:8–23
Living a Christ-Centered Life — 3:1–4:6
Letter Closing — 4:7–18

ABOUT COLOSSIANS

What a glorious hope lives within us! This is the theme of Paul's masterpiece written to the church of Colossae—our hope of glory!

The beauty and revelation that comes into us when we receive the truth of this letter is astounding. The Holy Spirit hands to us many wonderful nuggets of gold here. The heavenly hope of glory, the mystery hidden and reserved for this generation, is Jesus our anointed Messiah.

Paul penned this letter while in a prison cell. When hope was absent in his environment, Paul rediscovered it in his enjoyment of Christ within himself. No matter where you live or what surrounds you in this moment, there is a burning hope inside your soul that does more than just carry you through—it releases the heavenly Christ within. Great comfort and encouragement can be found by reading the letter to the Colossians.

Written about AD 60, Paul seeks to focus on the wonderful hope of the gospel and reminds the believers to not turn aside or fall victim to those who would minimize Christ and lead the church into empty philosophies and humanism. Already, there were many false teachers and cults that were forming and deceiving new believers and drawing them away from the supremacy of

Christ. Many have noted that of all Paul's letters, Colossians speaks more of the importance of Christ than any other.

Nearly everyone who has studied Colossians would agree that the summary of this letter can be found in 1:18–19: "He is the Head of his body, which is the church. And since he is the beginning and the firstborn heir in resurrection, he is the most exalted One, holding first place in everything. For God is satisfied to have all his fullness dwelling in Christ."

We can never be moved away from our glorious Head, Jesus Christ! To see him is to see the fullness of the Father and the fullness of the Holy Spirit. How we love this firstborn heir of all things!

PURPOSE

The major reason why Paul wrote this letter was to equip the Colossian church to fend off false teaching and help them resist false teachers within the community. It seems as though certain Christians in the city had believed and were promoting a version of Christianity that threatened orthodox beliefs and practices that stood in contrast to what the Colossian church had received from Epaphras. Paul judged this version to not only be deficient but dangerous. He penned this letter to remind believers of the wonderful hope of the gospel and not to turn aside or fall victim to those who would minimize Christ and lead the church into empty philosophies and humanism.

AUTHOR AND AUDIENCE

Although the apostle Paul wrote this letter to the church of Colossae, we do not believe he was the one who started this church, nor had he ever been to the city. It was most likely the result of Paul's three-year ministry in Ephesus, which was less than a hundred miles away. So effective was Paul's preaching and teaching that his converts spread the message out of Ephesus throughout the region known as Asia Minor. Most likely it was Epaphras who was the church planter in the Lycus Valley, which included the cities of Laodicea, Hieropolis, and Colossae.

Although Paul had never visited their city, he had heard of the believers of Colossae and began to pray for them that they would advance and become the fullness of Christ on the earth. Perhaps the new converts had met first in the home of Philemon until they outgrew the "house church." How tenderly Paul speaks to them, as a father in the faith, to motivate them to keep their hearts and beliefs free from error. The church today needs to hear these truths.

MAJOR THEMES

The Supremacy and Centrality of Christ. The key theme to Paul's letter to the church at Colossae is the supremacy and centrality of Christ. One of the clearest pictures we have of this theme is the famed "Christ Hymn" of 1:15–20.

Colossians makes it clear that in reigning supreme Jesus is himself God. As God he reigns over all creation. Paul also makes it clear that Jesus is all sufficient for our spiritual life, and should reign supreme at its center.

The Body of Christ. One of the most unique aspects of this letter is Paul's description of the church as Christ's "body." He presents Christ as the church's ruler, who has authority over her and who also sustains her. And as Christ's body, we are the continuing presence of Christ on the earth; through the church the mission of Christ is revealed and advanced.

The True Gospel. The major purpose for Paul's letter was to confront false teachers and their false gospel. Apparently, they were adding to the gospel Epaphras taught—mixing Jewish legalism, human tradition, and angel worship. Paul urges the Colossians to reject this religious enslavement and remember the true message of Christ and his lasting hope: "Never be shaken from the hope of the gospel you have believed in" (Col. 1:23).

The Christian Life. Using the metaphor of a body, Paul teaches that our life as Christians must be rooted in Christ—he is the Head, after all. He is the one who empowers us and renews us; we have our entire existence in him! Since it is through Christ we live as Christians, a "rules-oriented" lifestyle dictated by humans will not lead to spiritual growth.

COLOSSIANS

Heaven's Hope

Introduction

1 Dear friends in Colossae,
¹⁻² My name is Paul and I have been chosen by Jesus Christ to be his apostle, by the calling and destined purpose of God. My colleague, Timothy, and I send this letter to all the holy believers who have been united to Jesus as beloved followers of the Messiah. May God, our true Father, release upon your lives the riches of his kind favor and heavenly peace through the Lord Jesus, the Anointed One.

Paul Prays for the Colossians

³ Every time we pray for you our hearts overflow with thanksgiving to Father God, the Father of our Lord Jesus Christ. ⁴ For we have heard of your devoted lives of faith in Christ Jesus and your tender love toward all his holy believers. ⁵ Your faith and love rise within you as you access all the treasures of your inheritance *ᵃ* stored up in the heavenly realm. For the revelation of the true gospel is as real today as the day you first heard of our glorious hope, now that you have believed in the truth of the gospel.

⁶ *This is the wonderful message that* is being spread everywhere, powerfully changing hearts throughout the earth, just like it has changed you! Every believer of this good news bears the fruit of eternal life as they experience the reality of God's grace.

⁷ Our beloved coworker, Epaphras, *ᵇ* was there from the beginning to thoroughly teach you the astonishing revelation of the gospel, and he serves you faithfully as Christ's representative. ⁸ He's informed us of the many wonderful ways love is being demonstrated through your lives by the empowerment of the Holy Spirit.

⁹ Since we first heard about you, we've kept you always in our prayers that you would receive the perfect knowledge of God's pleasure *ᶜ* over your lives, making you reservoirs of every kind of wisdom and spiritual understanding.

---

a 1:5 Or "hope."

b 1:7 The church of Colossae was not planted by Paul but by Epaphras. His name means "lovely." He imparted to the church faith and love, praying always for them. See Col. 4:12.

c 1:9 Or "experience God's will for your lives." The Greek word *thelema*, can also mean "desire" or "pleasure."

[10] We pray that you would walk in the ways of true righteousness, pleasing God in every good thing you do. Then you'll become fruit-bearing branches, yielding to his life, and maturing in the rich experience of knowing God in his fullness! [11] And we pray that you would be energized with all his explosive power from the realm of his magnificent glory, filling you with great hope. [a]

[12] *Your hearts can soar with* joyful gratitude when you think of how God made you worthy to receive the glorious inheritance freely given to us by living in the light. [b] [13] He has rescued us completely from the tyrannical rule [c] of darkness and has translated us into the kingdom realm of his beloved Son. [14] For in the Son all our sins are canceled and we have the release of redemption *through his very blood.*

The Supremacy of Christ

[15] He is the divine portrait, the true likeness of the invisible God, and the first-born heir of all creation. [16] For through the Son everything was created, both in the heavenly realm and on the earth, all that is seen and all that is unseen. Every seat of power, realm of government, principality, and authority— it was all created through him and for his purpose! [17] He existed before anything was made, and now everything finds completion in him.

[18] He is the Head of his body, which is the church. And since he is the beginning and the firstborn heir in resurrection, [d] he is the most exalted One, holding first place [e] in everything. [19] For God is satisfied to have all his fullness [f] dwelling in Christ. [20] And by the blood of his cross, everything in heaven and earth is brought back to himself—*back to its original intent, restored to innocence again!* [g]

Made Holy through Christ

[21–22] Even though you were once distant from him, living in the shadows of your evil thoughts and actions, he reconnected you back to himself. *He released his supernatural peace to you* through the sacrifice of his own body as the sin-payment on your behalf so that you would dwell in his presence. And now there is nothing between you and Father God, for he sees you as holy, flawless, and restored, [h] [23] if indeed you continue to advance in faith, assured of a firm foundation to grow upon. Never be shaken from the hope of the gospel you have believed in. And this is the glorious news I preach all over the world.

---

a 1:11 As translated from the Aramaic. The Greek text means "patient endurance."
b 1:12 Or "by enlightening us."
c 1:13 Or "authority."
d 1:18 Literally "from the dead."
e 1:18 In the Greek text this is a title, "the Holder of First Place" or "the Superior One."
f 1:19 This includes all the fullness of God, the fullness of his plan for our lives, and the full image of God being restored into our hearts.
g 1:20 It literally means "back to himself." Some scholars believe that Col. 1:15–20 is actually lyrics of an ancient hymn sung in the churches.
h 1:21–22 Or "without an indictment."

The Divine Mystery

[24] I can even celebrate the sorrows I have experienced on your behalf; for as I join with you in your difficulties, it helps you to discover what lacks *in your understanding*[a] of the sufferings Jesus Christ experienced for his body, the church. [25] This is the very reason I've been made a minister by the authority of God and a servant to his body, so that in his detailed plan I would fully equip you with the Word of God.

[26] There is a divine mystery—a secret surprise that has been concealed from the world for generations, but now it's being revealed, unfolded and manifested for every holy believer to experience. [27] Living within you is the Christ who floods you with the expectation of glory! This mystery of Christ, embedded within us, becomes a heavenly treasure chest of hope filled with the riches of glory for his people, and God wants everyone to know it!

[28-29] Christ is our message! We preach to awaken hearts and bring every person into the full understanding of truth. It has become my inspiration and passion in ministry to labor with a tireless intensity, with his power flowing through me, to present to every believer the revelation of being his perfect one in Jesus Christ.

Paul's Love for the Colossians

2 I wish you could know how much I have struggled[b] for you and for the church in Laodicea, and for the many other friends I've yet to meet. [2] I am contending for you that your hearts will be wrapped in the comfort of heaven and woven together into love's fabric. This will give you access[c] to all the riches of God as you experience the revelation of God's great mystery—Christ.

[3] For our spiritual wealth is in him, like hidden treasure waiting to be discovered—heaven's wisdom and endless riches of revelation knowledge.

[4] I want you to know this so that no one will come and lead you into error[d] through their persuasive arguments and clever words. [5] Even though I'm separated from you geographically, my spirit is present there with you. And I'm overjoyed to see how disciplined[e] and deeply committed you are because you have such a solid faith in Christ, the Anointed One.

---

a 1:24 The text contains an ellipsis that is completed by the translation. The sufferings of Christ were complete, sufficient to transfer righteousness and forgiveness to every believer. Paul's sufferings were meant to be an example of Christ and a testimony to his converts that his ministry was sincere.

b 2:1 The Greek word *agon* (from which we get "agony") means an intense conflict and struggle. This could imply Paul's apostolic intercession for them.

c 2:2 Or in the Aramaic "approach."

d 2:4 By implication, this "error" would be the teaching that Jesus is not enough, adding something to the all-sufficient Christ.

e 2:5 The Greek text literally means "unbroken battle formation." The Aramaic can be translated "organized" or "principled."

New Life in Christ

⁶ In the same way you received Jesus our Lord and Messiah by faith, continue your journey of faith, progressing further into your union with him! ⁷ Your spiritual roots go deeply into his life as you are continually infused with strength, encouraged in every way. For you are established in the faith you have absorbed and enriched by your devotion to him!ᵃ

⁸ Beware that no one distracts you or intimidates youᵇ *in their attempt to lead you away from Christ's fullness* by pretending to be full of wisdom when they're filled with endless arguments of human logic. For they operate with humanistic and clouded judgments based on the mindset of this world system, and not the anointed truths of the Anointed One.

⁹ For he is the complete fullness of deity living in human form. ¹⁰ And our own completeness is now found in him. We are completely filled *with God* as Christ's fullness overflows within us. He is the Headᶜ of every kingdom and authority in the universe!

¹¹ Through our union with him we have experienced circumcision of heart. All of the guilt and power of sinᵈ has been cut away and is now extinct because of what Christ, the Anointed One, has accomplished for us.

¹² For we've been buried with him into his death. Our "baptism into death" also means we were raised with him when we believed in God's resurrection power, the power that raised him from death's realm. ¹³ This "realm of death" describes our former state, for we were held in sin's grasp.ᵉ But now, we've been resurrected out of that "realm of death" never to return, for we are forever alive and forgiven of all our sins!

¹⁴ He canceled out every legal violation we had on our record and the old arrest warrant that stood to indict us. He erased it all—our sins, our stainedᶠ soul—he deleted it all *and they cannot be retrieved*! Everything we once were in Adamᵍ has been placed onto his cross and nailed permanently there as a public display of cancellation.

¹⁵ Then Jesus made a public spectacle of all the powers and principalities of darkness, stripping away from them every weapon and all their spiritual authority

---

a 2:7 As translated from the Aramaic. The Greek states "overflowing with gratitude."

b 2:8 The Aramaic can be translated "strips you naked." The Greek states "takes you captive."

c 2:10 Or "Source."

d 2:11 The Aramaic can be translated "flesh of sin." The Greek means "body of the natural realm."

e 2:13 Literally "the uncircumcision of your flesh."

f 2:14 This "stained soul" has been erased of its filth. The word "erased" explicitly holds the concept of removal of stains. This would mean the nature of Adam has been erased and the nature of Christ has been embedded into us. We are totally set free from every trace of sin by the power of the blood of Jesus Christ.

g 2:14 The Aramaic can be translated "from our midst." This would refer to all that was within us—the core of our past life and its memories of failure and disobedience. A new DNA has been embedded now within us through the cross and resurrection life of Christ.

and power[a] to accuse us. And by the power of the cross, Jesus led them around as prisoners in a procession of triumph. *He was not their prisoner; they were his![b]*

Liberty in Christ

[16] So why would you allow anyone[c] to judge you because of what you eat or drink, or insist that you keep the feasts, observe new moon celebrations, or the Sabbath? [17] All of these were but a prophetic shadow and the evidence of what would be fulfilled,[d] for the body[e] is now Christ!

[18] Don't let anyone disqualify you from your prize! Don't let their pretended sincerity fool you as they deliberately lead you into their initiation of angel worship.[f] For they take pleasure in pretending to be experts of something they know nothing about. Their reasoning is meaningless and comes only from their own opinions. [19] They refuse to take hold of the true source.

But we receive directly from him, and his life supplies[g] vitality into every part of his body through the joining ligaments connecting us all as one. *He is the divine Head who guides his body* and causes it to grow by the supernatural power of God.[h]

---

a 2:15 Literally "governments and authorities."

b 2:15 Implied by the obvious irony in the Greek. The Aramaic text has a phrase that is not found in Greek manuscripts. The Aramaic can be translated "having *put off his body*, he stripped principalities and powers and shamed them openly." This implies that between the day of crucifixion and the day of resurrection while in the spirit-realm, Jesus destroyed death, the powers of darkness, and every work of the enemy through the blood of his cross. All the enemy's weapons have been stripped away from him and now the church has authority in Christ to enforce this triumph upon the dethroned rulers of this world. However, an alternate translation of the Aramaic could be "after *sending out his body* [apostles, prophets, evangelists, pastors, teachers, believers], they enforced his triumph to all the thrones and authorities, putting them all to public shame by the manifestation of himself [in them]."

c 2:16 The Aramaic text implies "any unbeliever."

d 2:17 The revelation of the Old Testament is so rich when we understand that its shadow is displaced by the body of Christ, the full revelation of who he is. The shadow only reflects the substance of what has now been fulfilled.

e 2:17 Or "substance."

f 2:18 In the first century AD, there was a mystical Jewish religion called Merkabah Mysticism, or Chariot Mysticism, in which the initiate would seek to go into the palace of God through meditation and enter into his chariot-throne. His was the innermost palace of seven concentric heavenly palaces surrounding his chariot-throne. At each "palace" or level there would be a fierce protecting angel, acting as a mediator who had to be placated by angel worship, which would enable the worshiper to enter the next level. There were also ancient polytheistic folk religions that worshiped and invoked angels. These were entirely forbidden paths for believers in Jesus, and Paul warned them of that in this letter.

g 2:19 The Greek word used here is *epichoregeo*, which interestingly can be translated as "to lead the chorus," or "choir director." It was used to denote a person who paid for the expenses of a Greek drama, and who supplied all their needs throughout its production. Similarly, Jesus tunes us up to heaven's notes, and draws out of us the melody of his divine symphony. He supplies the music to us, and imparts the wisdom for us to play it under his direction. This is the artful picture of how Jesus orchestrates his body with its many members.

h 2:19 Or "makes it grow with the discipline from God."

[20] For you were included in the death of Christ and have died with him to the religious system and powers of this world. Don't retreat back to being bullied by the standards and opinions of religion— [21] *for example, their strict requirements,* "You can't associate with that person!" or, "Don't eat that!" or, "You can't touch that!" [22] These are the doctrines of men and corrupt customs that are worthless to help you spiritually. [23] For though they may appear to possess the promise of wisdom in their submission to God through the deprivation of their physical bodies, it is actually nothing more than empty rules rooted in religious rituals!

One with Christ in Glory

3 Christ's resurrection is your resurrection too. This is why we are to yearn for all that is above, for that's where Christ sits enthroned at the place of all power, honor, and authority![a] [2] Yes, *feast on all the treasures of the heavenly realm* and fill your thoughts with heavenly realities, and not with the distractions of the natural realm.

[3] Your crucifixion[b] with Christ has severed the tie to this life, and now your true life is hidden away in God in Christ. [4] And as Christ himself is seen for who he really is, who you really are will also be revealed, for you are now one with him in his glory!

New Creation Life

[5] Live as one who has died to every form of sexual sin and impurity. Live as one who died to diseases,[c] and desires for forbidden things,[d] including the desire for wealth, which is the essence of idol worship. [6] When you live in these vices you ignite the anger of God against these acts of disobedience.[e]

[7-8] That's how you once behaved, characterized by your evil deeds. But now it's time to eliminate them from your lives once and for all—anger, fits of rage, all forms of hatred,[f] cursing,[g] filthy speech, [9] and lying.[h] Lay aside[i] your old Adam-self with its masquerade and disguise.

[10] For you have acquired new creation life which is continually being

---

a 3:1 The "right hand of God," is an obvious metaphor for the place of power, authority, honor, and glory.

b 3:3 The Aramaic could be translated "Your death and your life are both hidden with the Messiah in God."

c 3:5 This is only found in the Aramaic manuscripts. It is omitted in the Greek.

d 3:5 The Aramaic word implies "magic."

e 3:6 As translated from the Aramaic. The Greek states "the sons of disobedience," but it is actually the "deeds" which are punished as seen in verses 7–9. The Aramaic word used here is a homonym that can mean either "sons" or "deeds," which may explain the variation within Greek manuscripts.

f 3:7–8 Including self-hatred.

g 3:7–8 As translated from the Aramaic. The Greek means "slander."

h 3:9 Or "living a lie."

i 3:9 As translated from the Greek. The Aramaic has a command, "take off the old life."

renewed into the likeness of the One who created you; giving you the full revelation of God. [11] In this new creation life, your nationality makes no difference, or your ethnicity, education, or economic status—*they matter nothing.* For it is Christ that means everything as he lives in every one of us![a]

Love One Another

[12] You are always and dearly loved by God! So robe yourself *with virtues of God,* since you have been divinely chosen to be holy. Be merciful as you endeavor to understand others, and be compassionate, showing kindness toward all. Be gentle and humble, unoffendable in your patience with others. [13] Tolerate the weaknesses of those in the family of faith, forgiving one another in the same way you have been graciously forgiven by Jesus Christ. If you find fault with someone, release this same gift of forgiveness to them. [14] For love is supreme and must flow through each of these virtues. Love becomes the mark[b] of true maturity.[c]

[15] Let your heart be always guided[d] by the peace of the Anointed One, who called you to peace as part of his one body. And always be thankful.

[16] Let the word of Christ live[e] in you richly, flooding you with all wisdom. *Apply the Scriptures* as you teach and instruct one another with the Psalms, and with festive praises,[f] and with prophetic songs given to you spontaneously by the Spirit, so sing to God with all your hearts!

[17] Let every activity[g] of your lives and every word[h] that comes from your lips be drenched with the beauty of our Lord Jesus, the Anointed One. And bring your constant praise to God the Father *because of what Christ has done for you!*

Loving Relationships

[18] Let every wife be supportive and tenderly devoted[i] to her husband, *for this is a beautiful illustration* of our devotion to Christ. [19] Let every husband be filled with cherishing love for his wife and never be insensitive[j] toward her.

[20] Let the children respect and pay attention to their parents in everything for this pleases our Lord Jesus. [21] And fathers, don't have unrealistic expectations[k] for your children or else they may become discouraged.

---

a 3:11 Or "there is neither Jew or Scythians, circumcision or uncircumcision, neither Greek nor barbarian, neither slave nor free, but the Messiah is all and in all."

b 3:14 The Aramaic can be translated "the girdle of maturity."

c 3:14 Or "perfection."

d 3:15 The Greek literally means "let peace be the umpire of your minds."

e 3:16 Or "grow."

f 3:16 Or "hymns."

g 3:17 The Aramaic can be translated "commitment."

h 3:17 The Aramaic can be translated "oath."

i 3:18 The Greek word, *hupotasso,* can be translated "submitted," "attached," or "supportive."

j 3:19 Or "bitter."

k 3:21 Or "exasperate your children."

[22] Let every employee listen well and follow the instructions of their employer, not just when their employers are watching, and not in pretense, but faithful in all things. For we are to live our lives with pure hearts in the constant awe and wonder of our Lord God.

[23] Put your heart and soul into every activity you do, as though you are doing it for the Lord himself and not merely for others.

[24] For we know that we will receive a reward, an inheritance from the Lord, as we serve the Lord Yahweh,[a] the Anointed One! [25] A disciple will be repaid for what he has learned and followed,[b] for God pays no attention to the titles or prestige of men.

4 Employers, treat your workers with equality and justice as you know that you also have a Lord and Master in heaven *who is watching you*.

A Life of Prayer

[2] Be faithful to pray as intercessors who are fully alert and giving thanks *to God*. [3] And please pray for me, that God will open a door of opportunity for us to preach the revelation of the mystery of Christ, for whose sake I am imprisoned. [4] Pray that I would unfold and reveal fully this mystery, for that is my delightful assignment.[c]

[5] Walk in the wisdom of God as you live before the unbelievers,[d] and make it your duty[e] to make him known. [6] Let every word you speak be drenched with grace[f] and tempered with truth and clarity.[g] For then you will be prepared to give a respectful answer to anyone who asks about your faith.

Paul's Coworkers

[7-8] Tychicus will tell you about what is happening with me. I have sent him to you so that he could find out how you are doing in your journey of faith,[h] and bring comfort and encouragement to your hearts. For he is a beloved brother in Christ, a faithful servant of the gospel and my ministry partner in our Master Yahweh's[i] work.

---

a 3:24 Although absent in the Greek manuscripts, the Aramaic text makes it abundantly clear that it is Jesus Christ who is the Lord God (Yahweh). See also Luke 2:11 TPT.

b 3:25 This clause is translated from the Aramaic. The Greek text reads "He who does wrong will receive the consequences for what he has done."

c 4:4 Or "as I should."

d 4:5 The Aramaic could be translated "as you live in the wilderness."

e 4:5 The Aramaic can be translated "sell your last crust of bread," which is a metaphor for making a full commitment (i.e., giving all you've got).

f 4:6 The Aramaic word could also be translated "compassion."

g 4:6 Literally "seasoned with salt." This is an idiom that means "friendly, clear, and making people thirsty for truth."

h 4:7–8 Or "that I may know your affairs."

i 4:7–8 Again, the Aramaic title for Jesus is Lord (Master) Yahweh; this is the clearest title that could be stated to prove the deity of Jesus Christ.

⁹ I have also sent Onesimus,ᵃ who is from your city,ᵇ and is also a beloved and faithful brother who will inform you of all that we're enduring.

¹⁰⁻¹¹ Aristarchus, a fellow prisoner here with me, sends you his love. And Joshua (who is also called Justus) along with Mark, the cousin of Barnabas, also send you their loving greetings. You have already been informed that if Mark comes to you, receive him warmly. These three men are the only ones of the circumcision who have aided me here in the work of the kingdom of God, and they have been a great blessing to me.

¹²⁻¹³ Epaphras, who is also from Colossae, sends his loving greetings. I can tell you that he is a true servant of Christ, who always labors and intercedes for you. His prayers are filled with requests to God that you would grow and mature, standing complete and perfect in the beauty of God's plan for your lives. Epaphras has such great zeal and passion for you and for those who are from Laodicea and from Hierapolis.

¹⁴ And Luke, the beloved physician, sends his warm greetings to you, and Demas also. ¹⁵ Give my greetings to all the believers in Laodicea. And pray for dear Nymphas and the church that gathers in herᶜ home.

¹⁶ Once you've read this letter publicly to the church, please send it on to the church of the Laodiceans,ᵈ and make sure you read the letter that I wrote to them. ¹⁷ Be sure you give Archippus this message: "Be faithful to complete the ministry you received from our Lord Jesus!"ᵉ

¹⁸ Now finally, I, Paul, write this with my own handwriting, and I send my loving greetings to you! Remember me in my imprisonment. May the blessings of God's grace overwhelm you!

Love in Christ,
Paul

ᵃ 4:9 This was the slave who ran away from his master, Philemon, who was a friend to the apostle Paul. See Philem. 10–12

ᵇ 4:9 Or "he is one of you."

ᶜ 4:15 There is some debate about the gender of Nymphas. It may be that many of those who translated this in the early church had difficulty with a church being led by a woman. There are some manuscripts in Greek that have "the church that meets in *her* house."

ᵈ 4:16 As stated in the introduction to Ephesians, it is most likely that this missing letter to the Laodiceans is, in fact, the letter to the Ephesian church. However, the tradition of the Eastern Church is that the letter to the Laodiceans was actually 1 and 2 Thessalonians.

ᵉ 4:17 It is believed that Archippus was a spiritual leader in the region of Colossae, perhaps the bishop of Laodicea; he is also mentioned in Philem. 2. We can only speculate why Paul wanted this exhortation to be made to him. Some believe he was a minister of Christ who was discouraged and needed to be exhorted to not abandon his calling.

1 THESSALONIANS

Introduction

AT A GLANCE

Author: The apostle Paul
Audience: The church of Thessalonica
Date: AD 50–51
Type of Literature: A letter
Major Themes: The gospel and faith, pleasing God, and the future
Outline:

Letter Opening — 1:1
Thanksgiving for Faith — 1:2–10
Ministry Explained, Thanksgiving Renewed — 2:1–3:13
Exhortation to Christian Living — 4:1–5:11
Letter Closing — 5:12–28

ABOUT 1 THESSALONIANS

What a fascinating letter! Full of encouragement and exhortation, 1 Thessalonians will leave you richer in your spiritual life. The apostle Paul brought the gospel to the important city of Thessalonica, with an estimated population of 100,000. Originally named Thermai ("hot springs"), the city was renamed Thessalonica, after Alexander the Great's half sister. The city was home to a Jewish community as well as many cults and false religions.

After leaving Philippi, during his second apostolic journey, Paul and his team arrived at the wealthy city of Thessalonica, the capital of Macedonia. As he preached and taught in the synagogue, many Jews and a large number of God-fearing non-Jews became believers and formed a congregation of Christ-followers. (See Acts 17:4.) But Paul and his companions had to cut short their stay, for their lives were in danger.

Shortly after leaving the city, Paul sent Timothy back to make sure the believers were doing well and living faithfully by the truths of the gospel. When Timothy returned, he informed Paul of the great faith, hope, and love that still burned in their hearts. So he wrote them this letter, about two years after the church had been established, in order to comfort and strengthen their hearts. The Thessalonians had let Paul know that they had questions about the appearing of Christ, so Paul addressed that subject in his letter. This was a young church that needed to hear from Paul.

Many scholars have concluded that 1 Thessalonians is one of the earliest known writings of the apostle Paul (along with the books of Galatians and 2 Thessalonians), which makes it perhaps the oldest Christian writing we have. It is dated back to AD 50–51, only twenty years or so after Jesus was crucified and raised from the dead.

In this deeply personal letter, Paul gives us wise and practical advice on how to live our lives with gratitude, grace, and glory. He speaks to the recipients as their "father" (2:11) and their "mother" (2:7). Eight times he addresses the Thessalonian believers as his beloved "brothers and sisters." He even describes them as his "exhilarating joy" (2:19).

Such a treasure is found in the few pages of this letter!

PURPOSE

Writing as a concerned "father" and longing "mother," Paul coauthored this letter with his fellow missionaries Silas and Timothy, to remind these dear believers in Thessalonica of what they had previously taught them and to reinforce what they already knew. After hastily departing them and finding no way to return, Paul dictated this letter to encourage them to maintain their hope in God by persevering, remaining pure, pursuing God's pleasure, and living in a way that prepared them for Christ's return. This concern is captured at the center of this letter:

Then your hearts will be strengthened in holiness so that you may be flawless and pure before the face of our God and Father at the appearing of our Lord Jesus with all his holy ones. (3:13)

Although Paul was encouraged by the Thessalonians' faith, hope, and love, he was still mindful of their vulnerability. So along with his trusted companions Silas and Timothy, Paul sent them this letter to build their spiritual muscles, help them live faithfully, and encourage them as they waited for Christ's return.

AUTHOR AND AUDIENCE

There is little doubt that Paul the apostle dictated the contents of the letter that was later sent to the Christian community at Thessalonica. In fact, many New Testament scholars consider it to be not only one of Paul's earliest letters but one of the earliest New Testament books. And yet Paul isn't the only author, for the letter opens with this: "From Paul, Silas, and Timothy. We send our greetings to you, the congregation of believers in Thessalonica." Paul and his coworkers jointly spoke into the situation faced by their audience, even though the letter was dictated by Paul.

Paul and Silas had a particularly special bond with the Thessalonians, for they had traveled to this Roman city from Philippi during their second missionary journey, after Paul received a vision of a man pleading with them to come. (See Acts 16:9–10.) During this evangelistic mission, a large number of God-fearing non-Jews, as well as many pagan idol-worshipers, turned to faith in Jesus Christ. Paul wrote these baby Christians and this infant church to encourage them to persevere, remain pure, and prepare for the coming of the Lord.

MAJOR THEMES

Faith and the Gospel, Explained and Personalized. While 1 Thessalonians isn't an apologia for the gospel, like Romans or Galatians, we still discover much about its essence. Paul speaks of it as a power (1:4) and as the Lord's message—a message not derived from the words of men but the very word of God (2:13), which was entrusted to the apostles (2:4). The gospel results in our being chosen and called by God (1:4; 4:7). The key verses of 1 Thessalonians are 1:9–10: "You turned to God from idols to serve the true and living God. And now you eagerly expect his Son from heaven—Jesus, the deliverer, whom he raised from the dead and who rescues us from the coming wrath."

Turning from idolatry and sin, toward God in faith and service, was their response to the gospel message that Paul, Silas, and Timothy preached—the good news that Jesus, our deliverer, rose from the dead, rescues us from God's wrath, and will one day return from heaven. This is reaffirmed near the end of the letter: "For God has not destined us to experience wrath but to possess salvation through our Lord Jesus, the Anointed One. He gave his life for us so that we may share in resurrection life in union with him" (5:9–10). There you have it: God's good news explained!

One of the more striking aspects of this letter is Paul's commendation of the believers' faith and the outworking of it in love and hope (1:3). He goes so far as to say that because of their faith, they had "become an example for all the believers to follow" (1:7). They had received the gospel "wholeheartedly," not as a "fabrication of men but as the word of God" (2:13), resulting in their lives being impacted by the gospel's power. Because of this faith, the Thessalonian believers were persecuted yet remained steadfast (3:7). You get the sense that Paul is inviting us to follow in their steps.

Living to Please God. The theme of living in a way that is worthy of the name "Christian" and in a way that pleases God runs strong through Paul's letters. First Thessalonians is no different. From the start, Paul commends these dear believers for putting their faith into practice (1:3). Yet he goes further, reminding them that as God's holy, set-apart people, they are called to live in a particular way.

First he challenges them "to adopt a lifestyle worthy of God" (2:12). When Paul first evangelized this community, this was part of what he taught them.

So he reminds them of these teachings here and makes an appeal: "Keep faithfully growing through our teachings even more and more" (4:1). Why? Because "God's will is for you to be set apart for him in holiness" (4:3).

Finally, he reminds them that they are to live differently because they are different: "For you are all children of the light and children of the day. We don't belong to the night nor to darkness" (5:5). While living to please God can be difficult, especially in a culture that lives the exact opposite, it's something we're called to, something God desires from us.

Hopeful Preparation for the Day of the Lord. Paul wants us to be prepared in hope for the day when Christ returns in full glory. The main portion of Paul's letter is framed by this sense of waiting for, expecting, and being prepared for Christ's return. Paul praised the Thessalonians for eagerly expecting God's Son from heaven to rescue them (1:10). He exhorted them to be prepared for the day when he does return, keeping themselves completely flawless until his appearing.

In between waiting and keeping, Paul encourages the believers that those who have already passed away have not died in vain but died in hope—for God will bring with Christ those who have died in a declaration of victory!

He also wants them, and us, to "stay alert and clearheaded" (5:8) as we wait, for we don't know when it will happen. The Lord's return will come unexpectedly and as a complete surprise (5:2). Yet, though we may have questions about the end, we can be encouraged and encourage one another in the hope that we will "share in resurrection life in union with him" (5:10).

1 THESSALONIANS

Faithfulness to Christ

Paul Gives Thanks for the Thessalonians

1 From Paul, Silas,[a] and Timothy.[b] We send our greetings to you, the congregation[c] of believers in Thessalonica,[d] which is in God the Father and the Lord Jesus Christ.[e] May God's delightful grace[f] and peace rest upon you.[g]

[2] We are grateful to God for your lives[h] and we always pray for you. [3] For we remember before our God and Father how you put your faith into practice, how your love motivates you to serve others, and how unrelenting is your hope-filled patience in our Lord Jesus Christ.[i]

---

a 1:1 Or "Silvanus," whom most scholars believe is the Silas mentioned as a prophet in the Jerusalem church and Paul's coworker in Macedonia (Acts 15:22–40; 16:19–40; 17:1–16). The name Silas is the Aramaic form of the Hebrew name Saul. Both Silas and Timothy had been with Paul when he first visited Thessalonica (Acts 17:4, 14). There are only four of Paul's letters in the New Testament in which he does not call himself an apostle (1 and 2 Thessalonians, Philippians, and Philemon), most likely because of the deep relationship he already had with them.

b 1:1 Ministry requires teamwork. Paul saw himself as part of a church-planting team made up of three men with wonderful giftings: Paul, Silas, and Timothy.

c 1:1 The Greek word *ekklēsia* is best translated in this context as "congregation." It means "called-out ones." In Greek culture the *ekklēsia* were members of society who were given the duties of legislating on behalf of a city, similar to a city council. They were both "called out" and "called together" to function as those who have the responsibilities of shaping societal norms and the morality of culture.

d 1:1 Thessalonica was the largest city in Macedonia and may have had a population of 200,000 when Paul wrote this letter.

e 1:1 The church is both "in" God the Father and "in" Jesus Christ. The Trinity is making room for the bride.

f 1:1 The usage of *charis* (grace) in ancient classical Greek carries the connotation of something that awakens joy and pleasure. The Greek concept of grace imparts delight, often attached to a strong emotional element. Paul uses the term *grace* as a joyous delight that rests upon the people of God (Thomas F. Torrance, *The Doctrine of Grace in the Apostolic Fathers*, 1–2).

g 1:1 Some manuscripts add "from God our Father and the Lord Jesus Christ."

h 1:2 Starting with v. 2 Paul begins one long and complicated Greek sentence that ends with v. 10.

i 1:3 Paul mentions the three invaluable qualities of a believer's life: faith, love, and

⁴Dear brothers and sisters, ᵃ you are dearly loved by God and we know that he has chosen you to be his very own. ᵇ ⁵For our gospel came to you not merely in the form of words but in mighty power infused with the Holy Spirit and deep conviction. ᶜ Surely you remember how we lived our lives transparently before you to encourage you. ᵈ

⁶And you became followers ᵉ of my example and the Lord's when you received the word with the joy of the Holy Spirit, even though it resulted in tremendous trials and persecution. ᶠ ⁷Now you have become an example for all the believers to follow throughout the provinces of Greece. ᵍ

⁸The message of the Lord has sounded out from you not only in Greece, but its echo has been heard in every place where people are hearing about your strong faith. We don't need to brag on you, ⁹for everyone tells the story of the kind of welcome you showed us when we first came to you. And everyone knows how wonderfully you turned to God from idols to serve the true and living God. ¹⁰And now you eagerly expect his Son from heaven—Jesus, the deliverer, whom he raised from the dead and who rescues us from the coming wrath. ʰ

---

hope. The Thessalonians put their faith into practice by turning away from all that was false (v. 9). They demonstrated their motive of love by serving God and others (v. 9). And they lived with undying hope that was centered upon the future appearing of Christ (v. 10).

a 1:4 Although the Greek uses the term *brothers* (*adelphoi*), it is intended to express the group identity of those who follow Christ and not meant to be gender exclusive. Paul uses the term eighteen times in five chapters. First Thessalonians could be called Paul's friendliest letter. He describes himself as a "father" and "mother" to them (2:7, 11) and calls them his "joy" and "trophy" (2:19).

b 1:4 The perfect tense of the verb implies that God loved them in the past and continues to love them in the same way.

c 1:5 True gospel ministry will be expressed by the word of God and characterized by mighty power, releasing the unmistakable presence of the Holy Spirit, and through sincere conviction of truth will be found in those who present it.

d 1:5 Or "for your sakes" (benefit).

e 1:6 Or "imitators."

f 1:6 True conversion delivers us from many things, but is not an assurance that we will never face painful trials or persecution for our faith.

g 1:7 Or "Macedonia and Achaia." Greece was divided into two provinces: the northern region known as Macedonia and the southern one, Achaia. Thessalonica was located in Macedonia, and Corinth, where Paul wrote this letter, was the leading city of Achaia. Although the believers of Thessalonica were novices, their testimony had spread throughout the region.

h 1:10 The gospel of power will change lives. The Thessalonians had renounced the worship of false gods and turned wholeheartedly to the true God and become faithful servants. Every time true conversion (repentance) takes place, a life is changed. The Thessalonians were famous for these four things: (1) They turned wholeheartedly to God. (2) They abandoned worshiping false gods (idols). (3) They became passionate servants of Christ. (4) They were eagerly anticipating the heavenly Son, Jesus.

Godly Character of Jesus' Servants

2 My dear brothers and sisters, it's obvious that our ministry among you has proven to be fruitful. [a] [2] And though we had already suffered greatly in Philippi, where we were shamefully mistreated, [b] we were emboldened *by faith* in our God to fearlessly preach his wonderful gospel to you in spite of incredible opposition.

[3] Our coming alongside you to encourage you was not out of some delusion, or impure motive, or an intention to mislead you, [4] but we have been approved by God to be those who preach the gospel. So our motivation to preach is not pleasing people but pleasing God, who thoroughly examines our hearts. [5] God is our witness that when we came to encourage you, we never once used cunning compliments as a pretext for greed, [6] nor did we crave the praises of men, whether you or others. [c] [7] Even though we could have imposed upon you our demands as apostles of Christ, [d] instead we showed you kindness and were gentle among you. [e] We cared for you in the same way a nursing mother cares for her own children. [8] With a mother's love and affectionate attachment to you, we were very happy to share with you not only the gospel of God but also our lives—because you had become so dear to us. [f]

[9] Beloved brothers and sisters, surely you remember how hard we labored among you. We worked night and day so that we would not become a burden to you while we preached the wonderful gospel of God. [10] With God as our witness you saw how we lived among you—in holiness, in godly relationships, [g] and without fault. [11] And you know how affectionately we treated each one of you, like a loving father cares for his own children. [12] We comforted and encouraged you and challenged you to adopt a lifestyle worthy of God, who invites you into his kingdom and glory. [h]

---

a 2:1 Or "Our coming to you has not been in vain" (empty). See Acts 17:1–9.

b 2:2 Paul and Silas had been beaten and imprisoned in Philippi. See Acts 16:11–17:1.

c 2:6 Paul never watered down his message in preaching the gospel. His fearless courage serves as an example to us today to keep our message uncompromised.

d 2:7 The Aramaic can be translated "Although we could have been honored as apostles of the Messiah." See also 1 Cor. 9:1–18; Philem. 8.

e 2:7 Some reliable manuscripts have "We became like little children (infants) among you."

f 2:8 Or "You had become our beloved." Just a few months before, the Thessalonians were complete strangers to Paul. Now he states how dear they had become to his heart. True ministry is caring for others with a father's love and a mother's love—not exerting control or abusive authority over those whom we serve.

g 2:10 Or "righteousness." The Hebraic concept of righteousness extends toward our relationships and how we treat others. Paul stated that he lived in holiness toward God and purity in his relationships with others, so that no one could blame him for wrongdoing.

h 2:12 Our calling is a summons from God to enter into his glory. A possible hendiadys, "his own glorious kingdom."

The Faithfulness of the Thessalonians

[13] This is why we continually thank God *for your lives*, because you received our message *wholeheartedly*. You embraced it not as the fabrication of men but as the word of God. And the word continues to be an energizing force in you who believe.

[14] *My dear* brothers and sisters, the same thing happened to you as happened to God's churches in Christ Jesus that are in Judea. For you received the same kind of mistreatment from your fellow countrymen as they did from theirs, the Jews [15] who killed both the Lord Jesus and the prophets and ran us out of town. They are offending God and hostile to everyone else [16] by hindering us from speaking to the unbelievers[a] so that they might be saved. By so doing they are constantly filling up to the brim the measure of their guilt,[b] and punishment[c] has come upon them at last![d]

Paul's Concern for the Thessalonians

[17] Beloved friends, we may have been torn away[e] from you physically for a season, but never in our hearts. For we have had intense longings and have endeavored to come and see in your faces the reflection of this great love.[f] [18] We *miss you badly*, and I personally wanted to come to you, trying again and again, but our adversary,[g] Satan, blocked our way. [19] For what will be our *confident* hope, our *exhilarating* joy, or our *wonderful* trophy[h] that we will boast in before our Lord Jesus at his appearing?[i] It is you! [20] Yes, you are our glorious *pride and* joy![j]

---

a 2:16 Or "the gentiles."

b 2:16 That is, they are filling up to the limit of their sins before God.

c 2:16 Or "wrath," a metonymy for the punishment resulting from their sins.

d 2:16 Or "completely" (to a full extent). This could be a prophetic word from Paul regarding the soon destruction of Jerusalem in the Roman war of AD 67–70. Paul is not referring to all Jews, for many had become converts and made up the early church. God rejected the empty rituals of Judaism but not the Jewish people. See Rom. 9–11.

e 2:17 Or "We have been [like] orphans."

f 2:17 As translated from the Aramaic. How poetic are the Semitic languages!

g 2:18 The Greek word *satanas* means "adversary," "accuser," "opposer," and it is the title for Satan. In some way Satan worked to hinder Paul from returning to Thessalonica, possibly through the Jews who opposed him.

h 2:19 Or "crown of boasting."

i 2:19 This is the Greek word *parousia*, which can be translated "coming" or "appearing." Paul uses it six times in his letters to the Thessalonians (3:13; 4:15; 5:23; 2 Thess. 2:1, 8).

j 2:20 The true reward of ministry is not money or fame but the souls of men and women we can influence for the glory of God.

Timothy's Mission

3 When we could bear it no longer, we decided that we would remain in Athens [2] and send Timothy *in our place*.[a] He is our beloved brother and coworker with God[b] in preaching the gospel. *We knew* he would strengthen your faith and encourage your hearts [3] so that no one would be shaken by these persecutions, for you know that we are destined for this.[c] [4] In fact, when we were with you we forewarned you: "Suffering and persecution is coming." And so it has happened, as you well know. [5] For this reason, when I could endure it no longer, I sent *our brother* to find out if your faith was still strong, for I was concerned that the tempter[d] had somehow enticed you and our labor would have been in vain.

[6] But now, Timothy has just returned to us and brought us the terrific news of your faith and love. He informed us that you still hold us dear in your hearts and that you long to see us as much as we long to see you. [7] So, our dear brothers and sisters, in the midst of all our distress and difficulties, your steadfastness of faith has greatly encouraged our hearts. [8] We feel alive again as long as we know that you are standing firm in the Lord.

[9] How could we ever thank God enough for all the wonderful joy that we feel before our God because of you? [10] Every night and day we sincerely and fervently pray that we may see you face-to-face and furnish you with whatever may be lacking in your faith.

[11] Now may our Father God and our precious Lord Jesus[e] guide our steps on a path straight back to you. [12] And may the Lord increase your love until it overflows[f] toward one another and for all people, just as our love overflows toward you. [13] Then your hearts will be strengthened[g] in holiness so that you may be flawless and pure before *the face of* our God and Father at the appearing of our Lord Jesus with all his holy ones.[h] Amen!

Holiness and Love

4 And now, *beloved* brothers and sisters, since you have been mentored by us with respect to living for God and pleasing him, I appeal to you in the name of the Lord Jesus with this request: keep faithfully growing through our

---

a 3:2 This may have been when Paul sent the letter of 2 Thessalonians with Timothy, which would make it earlier than 1 Thessalonians.
b 3:2 Some manuscripts have "servant of God."
c 3:3 That is, the sufferings of persecution are included in God's destined purpose for those who love God and faithfully follow Christ. See Acts 14:22.
d 3:5 Or "harasser," an obvious title for Satan, our adversary.
e 3:11 Some manuscripts add "the Anointed One."
f 3:12 Or "May the Lord make you increase and your love superabound."
g 3:13 The Aramaic can be translated "He will lift up your hearts without contention."
h 3:13 Or "at the coming of the Lord of us, Jesus Christ, with all of the holy myriads of himself."

teachings even more and more. [2] For you already know the instructions we've shared with you through the Lord Jesus.

[3] God's will is for you to be set apart for him in holiness and that you keep yourselves *unpolluted* from sexual defilement. [4] Yes, each of you must guard your sexual purity[a] with holiness and dignity, [5] not yielding to lustful passions like those who don't know God. [6] Never take selfish advantage[b] of a brother or sister in this matter, for we've already told you and solemnly warned you that the Lord is the avenger in all these things. [7] For God's call on our lives is not to a life of *compromise and* perversion but to a life surrounded in holiness. [8] Therefore, whoever rejects this instruction isn't rejecting human authority but God himself, who gives[c] us his precious gift—his Spirit of holiness.

Loving Others

[9] There's no need for anyone to say much to you about loving your fellow believers, for God is continually teaching you to unselfishly love one another.[d] [10] Indeed, your love is what you're known for throughout Macedonia. We urge you, beloved ones, to let this unselfish love increase *and flow through you* more and more. [11] Aspire[e] to lead a calm and peaceful life as you mind your own business[f] and earn your living, just as we've taught you. [12] By doing this you will live an honorable life, influencing others and commanding respect of even the unbelievers. Then you'll be in need of nothing and not dependent upon others.[g]

The Appearing of the Lord

[13] Beloved brothers and sisters, we want you to be quite certain about the truth concerning those who have passed away,[h] so that you won't be overwhelmed with grief like many others who have no hope. [14] For if we believe that Jesus died and rose again, we also believe that God will bring with Jesus those who died while believing in him.[i] [15] This is the word of the Lord:[j] we who are alive

---

a 4:4 Or "Each of you must possess your vessel equipment." Some see the "equipment" as a wife, but in the context it is sexual purity, not marriage, that is in view. The "vessel" is our body, including sexual urges that must be kept pure and holy with self-respect.

b 4:6 Although technically Paul uses a term for a business transaction, it is more likely, due to the context, a warning about cheating others by enticing them to sexual immorality.

c 4:8 This is in the present tense.

d 4:9 This "God-teaching" (Gr. *theodidaktos*) of divine love came to us through Christ. God taught us to love by his example of giving us his Son.

e 4:11 Or "Make it your driving ambition."

f 4:11 The Aramaic can be translated "Keep your covenants" (promises).

g 4:12 That is, self-supporting (financially).

h 4:13 Or "about those who have fallen asleep." Paul uses sleep as a euphemism for death.

i 4:14 Or "Through Jesus God will bring with him those who have fallen asleep [died] in Jesus."

j 4:15 This phrase ("the word of the Lord") is used in both the Old and New Testament for inspired prophetic speech. See Gen. 15:1; Isa. 1:10; Jonah 1:1; Luke 22:61; Acts 11:16; 16:32;

in *him* and remain *on earth* when the Lord appears will by no means have an advantage over those who have already died, [a] *for both will rise together.*

[16] For the Lord himself will appear with the declaration of victory, the shout of an archangel, and the trumpet blast of God. He will descend from the heavenly realm [b] and *command* those who are dead in Christ to rise first. [17] Then we who are alive will join them, transported together in clouds [c] to have an encounter [d] with the Lord in the air, and we will be forever joined with the Lord. [18] So encourage one another with these truths.

God's Times and Seasons

5 Now, beloved brothers and sisters, concerning the question of *God's* precise times and specific seasons, [e] you don't need me to write anything to you. [2] For you already know quite well that the day of the Lord [f] will come unexpectedly and as a complete surprise. [g] [3] For while some are saying, "Finally we have peace and security," sudden destruction will arrive at their doorstep, like labor pains seizing a pregnant woman—and with no chance of escape!

[4] But you, beloved brothers and sisters, are not living in the dark, allowing that day to creep up on you like a thief *coming to steal.* [5] For you are all children of the light and children of the day. We don't belong to the night nor to darkness. [6] This is why we must not fall asleep, as the rest do, but keep wide awake and clearheaded. [7] For those who are asleep sleep the night away, and drunkards get drunk at night. [h] [8] But since we belong to the day, we must stay alert and clearheaded by placing the breastplate of faith and love *over our hearts,*

19:20. It is possible that this was spoken to Paul in his heavenly encounter, for he had never met the Lord Jesus, and what Paul reveals here is not found in any of the Gospels.

a 4:15 Or "those who have fallen asleep," a euphemism for death.

b 4:16 Or "The Lord himself will continue habitually descending from heaven within the midst of a declaration of victory, the chief angel's shout, and God's trumpet blast, and the dead in union with Christ will continue raising themselves up first [or one after another]."

c 4:17 There is no definite article before clouds. It is literally "in clouds." Where the identifying article is missing, it often speaks of quality, or it is used as a descriptive term. The Greek word for "cloud" is often used in the Greek classics of a large body of individuals, and it is so used in this symbolic way in Heb. 12:1–2, speaking of the "great witnesses who encircle us like clouds."

d 4:17 The Greek word *apantēsis* is not a verb (go to meet) but a feminine noun (to meet or have an encounter), and in this context it is the bride of Christ rising to be with Jesus to have an encounter or "[bridal] meeting." This rarely used Greek word is also used in the parable of the ten virgins, referring to the virgins rising up to meet (have a meeting) with the bridegroom. See Matt. 25:1, 6.

e 5:1 That is "the specific intervals of time and the epoch [hinge] periods of time."

f 5:2 See Jer. 30:7; Joel 1:15; 2:1–2; Amos 5:18; Zech. 1:4–18.

g 5:2 Or "like a thief comes in the night" (as unexpected as a home invasion). See Matt. 24:3–25:46; Mark 13:3–37; Luke 21:5–36; 2 Peter 3:10; Rev. 3:3; 16:15.

h 5:7 See John 3:9–20.

and a helmet of the hope of salvation *over our thoughts.*[a] [9]For God has not destined us to experience wrath but to possess salvation through our Lord Jesus, the Anointed One. [10]He gave his life for us so that we may share in resurrection life[b] in union with him—whether we're awake or asleep. [11]Because of this, encourage the hearts of your fellow believers and support one another, just as you have already been doing.

[12]Dear brothers and sisters, make sure that you show your deep appreciation for those who cherish you and diligently work as ministers among you. For they are your leaders who care for you, teach you, and stand before the Lord on your behalf. [13]They value you with great love. Because of their service to you, let peace reign among yourselves.[c]

[14]We appeal to you, dear brothers and sisters, to instruct those who are not in their place of battle.[d] *Be skilled at* gently encouraging those who feel themselves inadequate.[e] *Be faithful* to stand your ground. Help the weak to stand again. Be *quick to* demonstrate patience with everyone. [15]Resist revenge, and make sure that no one pays back evil in place of evil but always pursue doing what is beautiful to one another and to all *the unbelievers.*

[16]Let joy be your continual feast.[f] [17]Make your life a prayer. [18]And in the midst of everything be always giving thanks, for this is God's perfect plan for you in Christ Jesus.[g]

[19]Never *restrain or* put out the fire of the Holy Spirit. [20]And don't be one who scorns prophecies,[h] [21]but be faithful to examine them by putting them

---

a 5:8 The Aramaic can be translated "be clearheaded in our vision as we are deployed on the battlefield for faithfulness and love, and set apart with the shield of the hope of everlasting life." See Isa. 59:17; Eph. 6:10–17.

b 5:10 As translated from the Aramaic and implied in the Greek.

c 5:13 Verses 12–13 are translated from the Aramaic. The Greek is "Brothers and sisters, we appeal to you to respect [recognize] those who labor among you and have oversight of your lives in the Lord and admonish you. Show them as much respect as possible with great love because of all they do for you. Be at peace among yourselves." Church leaders deserve our financial support and love because of the work they do for our benefit.

d 5:14 Or "those who are disorderly," or "those who are idle." The Greek word *ataktos* is often used for troops that are not in battle formation (unarranged).

e 5:14 Or "those who are losing heart [fainthearted]."

f 5:16 The Aramaic can be translated "Be joyous in every season."

g 5:18 Verses 16–18 identify three areas our lives we must focus on: (1) unbounded joy, (2) praying continually, and (3) giving thanks to God no matter happens in our lives. These three virtues combine to form the wonderful expression of Christ's life within us.

h 5:20 There is an implication in the context of vv. 19–20 that we put out the Spirit's fire when we scorn prophecy. Prophecy is a valid gift of the Holy Spirit needed by the church today. There is no place in Scripture or in church history that indicates the gift of prophecy has ceased or disappeared. It is an active function of the Holy Spirit in the church around the world. We must not ignore, despise, or scorn any true gift of the Holy Spirit. Putting out the fire of the Holy Spirit (v. 19) is connected to scorning the prophetic ministry. We need

to the test, and afterward hold tightly to what has proven to be right. [a] [22] Avoid every appearance of evil.

[23] Now, may the God of peace and harmony set you apart, making you completely holy. And may your entire being—spirit, soul, and body—be kept completely flawless in the appearing of our Lord Jesus, the Anointed One. [24] The one who calls you by name is trustworthy and will thoroughly complete his work in you.

[25] Now, beloved ones, pray for us.

[26] Greet every brother and sister with a sacred kiss.

[27] I solemnly [b] plead with you before the Lord to make sure that every holy believer among you has the opportunity to hear this letter read to them.

[28] Grace from our Lord Jesus Christ be with you. Amen!

---

prophets and prophecy to keep the fire (inspiration) of the Holy Spirit burning in our hearts. See 1 Cor. 12–14.

a 5:21 The Aramaic can be translated "Regard everything seriously and choose what is best."

b 5:27 Or "I put you under oath" (a serious obligation).

2 THESSALONIANS

Introduction

AT A GLANCE

Author: The apostle Paul
Audience: The church of Thessalonica
Date: AD 51
Type of Literature: A letter
Major Themes: Faith, perseverance, justice, Christ's return, laziness, and disunity
Outline:

    Letter Opening — 1:1–2
    Thanksgiving and Prayer — 1:3–12
    The Day of the Lord — 2:1–17
    Idle and Disruptive Believers — 3:1–15
    Letter Closing — 3:16–18

ABOUT 2 THESSALONIANS

What will it be like to live in the last days before Jesus appears? What words of encouragement and warning would God want to give us? Paul's second letter to the Thessalonians gives us some answers. With only forty-seven verses, this book is packed with prophetic insight that will strengthen and prepare us for the coming days. Not only does 2 Thessalonians give us information about what is ahead, it is also a map to guide us through anything that might assail us as we approach the grand finale of all time—the appearing of our Lord Jesus Christ with his glorious messengers of fire!

Although we spend our lives watching and waiting for his appearing, we must live every day for his glory. We are to be alert, awake, and filled with his holiness as we draw closer to the fulfillment of the ages.

In this letter we find encouragement for us to stand our ground, be faithful to the end, and always make the message of Christ beautiful by our lives. We must do more than combat evil; we must live for Christ and expect his coming to find us as passionate lovers of God, abandoned to him with all our hearts.

Paul wrote this letter from Corinth around AD 51 (less than a year after writing 1 Thessalonians) to his beloved friends in the city of Thessalonica. They were followers of Jesus who looked to Paul as their apostolic father and were asking him to clarify the events surrounding "the day of the Lord." A faulty understanding of eschatology (the study of the last days) will lead to faulty conduct and even a detachment from our duties in this world. So Paul writes to inspire those who are idle to engage themselves with making a living and presenting the gospel of Christ through the holy example of their changed lives.

We all need the truth of 2 Thessalonians today to keep our lives focused on what is truth as we look to Christ alone to be our strength, no matter how difficult the future may appear. One day we will each be able to personally thank the apostle Paul for writing this inspired letter! May you be blessed as you read 2 Thessalonians.

PURPOSE

Building off of his first letter to the Thessalonian church, which he sent just a year or so prior, Paul gets down to business. It seems the situation had deteriorated in the short time between planting this Christian community along with his coworkers in the gospel and his first letter. So he wrote to encourage them in three main areas: to hold fast to their faith, despite opposition, knowing that God will act on their behalf with promised justice; to live faithfully as they awaited the coming of Jesus in glory; and to confront a group of "busybodies" (3:11) who were burdening and disrupting the life of the community.

Reading this letter, written to this threatened community, will remind us of the gospel's ultimate outcome—the glorious return of Jesus Christ—while helping us remain worthy of our calling by living our faith with conviction every day.

AUTHOR AND AUDIENCE

Although some have suggested 2 Thessalonians was written pseudonymously (written by someone other than Paul, who used Paul's name as his own), there are striking similarities between Paul's first letter and this one. Both contain an extended thanksgiving and a wish prayer, and both close with a prayer of peace. Although this letter lacks the warmth of 1 Thessalonians, it's clear the author already had a personal relationship with his readers. That makes sense if Paul was writing this as a follow-up letter to members of a community he founded, after a short period of time. Given how urgent the situation had become, Paul would have launched straight into his vital words of encouragement and exhortation.

This infant congregation of former pagans in the heart of the eastern region of the Roman Empire was struggling to understand their identity in Christ as well as how to live as God's people in a hostile culture. Knowing they faced a dire situation and confusion about vital issues related to the gospel and

Christian discipleship, Paul addressed these dear believers with the care of a spiritual father.

MAJOR THEMES

Perseverance of Faith through Persecution. In his first letter to the Thessalonians, Paul acknowledged the suffering they were experiencing at the hand of a persecuting culture. He didn't want them to be unsettled by their trials, and he worried that might disrupt the gospel work he began among them and destroy their faith. Now he returns to this theme, praising them for their "unwavering faith" and boasting in their "unflinching endurance" (1:4) through all of the persecutions and painful trials they had experienced.

We aren't given specifics, but it seems persecution against these believers had ratcheted up significantly, so Paul wanted to encourage them that it wouldn't be in vain. Their perseverance of faith through persecution stands as a model for all the church, one we are urged to follow in endurance, to be counted "worthy of inheriting the kingdom of God" (1:5).

The Promise of God's Justice. In light of their persecution and trials, Paul wrote to encourage them that God hadn't forgotten about them. He would act on their behalf by judging their persecutors in the person of Jesus Christ (1:5–2:12).

Consider all that God has promised to do on our behalf to put things right: he will trouble our troublers, giving rest to those who are troubled. "He will bring perfect and full justice to those who don't know God and on those who refuse to embrace the gospel of our Lord Jesus" (1:8). The ungodly will suffer eternal destruction as a just penalty for their wicked ways, being banished from the Lord's presence. All believers will be adorned with glory. With this in mind, "live worthy of all that he has invited you to experience" (1:11).

Confusion about Christ's Coming Clarified. One reason Paul had written the believers in his first letter was to bring clarity as to what happens to believers at death and what will happen when Christ returns. Apparently, that letter didn't lessen their confusion! "Don't you remember that when I was with you I went over all these things?" Paul sarcastically writes. Apparently not! Therefore, Paul unveils further revelation-truth about what we should watch for and expect in these last days as we await the coming of our Lord in full glory.

As we wait, we're exhorted to "stand firm with a masterful grip of the teachings" we've been given, an "eternal comfort and a beautiful hope that cannot fail" (2:15–16).

The Lazy, Unruly, and Undisciplined. One might not expect believers who are lazy and disruptive, undisciplined and unruly, to be called out by Paul in such a short letter, yet they are. There's a reason: they "stray from all that we have taught you" (3:6), becoming a burden to the church. Such people refuse to work—"These people are not busy but busybodies" (3:11). The example of diligent, earnest work that Paul and his companions had set, and the teachings he laid out, were lifted up as a model for these believers. Since they themselves didn't sponge off the church, neither should anyone else. Since they worked hard to provide food and lodging for themselves, so should every believer. Paul's rule still stands: "Anyone who does not want to work for a living should go hungry" (3:10).

2 THESSALONIANS

Living in the Last Days

God's Times and Seasons

1 From Paul, Silas,[a] and Timothy.[b] *We send our greetings to you,* the Thessalonian congregation[c] of believers, which is in God our Father and the Lord Jesus Christ.[d] 2 May God's delightful grace[e] and peace rest upon you.[f]

3 We feel a personal responsibility to continually be thanking God for you, our spiritual family,[g] every time we pray. And we have every reason to do so because your faith is growing marvelously beyond measure. The unselfish love each of you share for one another is increasing and overflowing! 4 *We point to you as an example of* unwavering faith[h] for all the churches of God. We boast about how you continue to demonstrate unflinching endurance[i] through all the persecutions and painful trials you are experiencing.[j] 5 All of this proves that God's judgment is always perfect and is intended to make you worthy of *inheriting* the kingdom of God, which is why you are going through these troubles.

Encouragement of Christ's Appearing

6 It is right and just for God to trouble your troublers 7 and give rest to the

---

a 1:1 See the first footnote on 1 Thess. 1:1.

b 1:1 See the second footnote on 1 Thess. 1:1.

c 1:1 See the third footnote on 1 Thess. 1:1.

d 1:1 The church is both "in" God the Father and "in" Jesus Christ. The Trinity is making room for the bride.

e 1:2 The usage of *charis* (grace) in ancient classical Greek carries the connotation of something that awakens joy and pleasure. The Greek concept of grace imparts delight, often attached to a strong emotional element. Paul uses the term *grace* as a joyous delight that rests upon the people of God. See Thomas F. Torrance, *The Doctrine of Grace in the Apostolic Fathers*, 1–2.

f 1:2 Some manuscripts add "from God our Father and the Lord Jesus Christ."

g 1:3 Or "brothers and sisters."

h 1:4 Or "perseverance and faith," a likely hendiadys.

i 1:4 The Aramaic can be translated "your hope," making it their faith, their love, and their hope that Paul lauds them for.

j 1:4 No matter what difficulty we may pass through, a growing faith in Christ, an increasing love for others, and unwavering hope will be the keys to coming through it victoriously.

troubled, both to you and to us, at the unveiling *a* of the Lord Jesus from heaven with his messengers of power *8* within a flame of fire. He will bring perfect and full justice to those who don't know God *b* and on those who refuse to embrace the gospel of our Lord Jesus. *9* They will suffer the penalty of eternal destruction, banished from the Lord's presence *c* and from the manifestation of his glorious power. *d* *10* *This will happen* on that day when he outwardly adorns his holy ones with glory, *e* and they will be marveled at among all believers—including you, since in fact, you believed our message. *f*

11 With this in mind, we constantly pray that our God will empower you to live worthy of all that he has invited you to experience. *g* And we pray that by his power all the pleasures of goodness and all works inspired by faith would fill you completely. *h* *12* By doing this the name of our Lord Jesus will be glorified in you, and you will be glorified in him, by the *marvelous* grace of our God and the Lord Jesus Christ. *i*

The Coming of the Lord

2 Now, regarding the coming *j* of our Lord Jesus Christ and our gathering together to him, *k* we plead with you, beloved friends, *2* not to be easily confused or disturbed in your minds by any kind of spirit, rumor, or letter allegedly from us, claiming that the day of the Lord *l* has already come. *3* Don't let anyone deceive you in any way. Before that day comes the rebellion *m* must occur and the "outlaw" *n*—the destructive son—will be revealed *in his true light*. *4* He is the opposing counterpart who exalts himself over everything that is

---

a 1:7 Or "uncovering" or "revelation."
b 1:8 Or "inflicting vengeance upon those who do not know God." See Ps. 79:6; Isa. 66:15; Jer. 10:25.
c 1:9 Or "face."
d 1:9 See Isa. 2:10, 19, 21.
e 1:10 Or "is glorified in his holy ones."
f 1:10 Or "testimony."
g 1:11 Or "that our God would make you worthy [or considered worthy] of your calling."
h 1:11 This sentence is translated from the Aramaic. The Greek is "By his power he will fulfill your every resolve for goodness and works of faith."
i 1:12 Or "our God and Lord, Jesus Christ."
j 2:1 Or "presence."
k 2:1 The noun form of the Greek word for "gathering together" (*episunagoge*) is found twice in the New Testament, here and in Heb. 10:25. It is used as a verb (*episunago*) in Matt. 23:37; 24:31.
l 2:2 This is a common term that describes the day of the Lord's judgment. (See Jer. 30:7; Joel 1:15; 2:1–2; Amos 5:18; Zech. 1:14–18.)
m 2:3 Or "apostasy" or "abandonment" (falling away).
n 2:3 A few manuscripts have "the man who missed the mark" (i.e., Adam), while others have "the person owned by [associated with] lawlessness."

called "God" or is worshiped[a] and who sits enthroned in God's temple[b] and makes himself out to be a god.[c] Don't you remember that when I was with you I went over all these things?

[6] Now you are aware of the ruling power[d] so that he may be fully revealed when his time comes. [7] For the mystery of lawlessness[e] is already active, but the one who prevails[f] will do so until he is separated from out of the midst.[g] [8] Then the "outlaw" will be openly revealed, and the Lord will overthrow him by the breath of his mouth[h] and bring him to an end[i] by the dazzling manifestation of his presence.[j]

[9] The presence[k] of the "outlaw" is apparent by the activity of Satan, who uses all kinds of *counterfeit* miracles, signs, spurious wonders, [10] and every form of evil deception in order to deceive those who are perishing because they rejected the love of the truth[l] that would lead them to being saved. [11] Because of this, God sends them a powerful delusion[m] that leads them to believe what is false. [12] So then all who found their pleasure in unrighteousness and did not believe the truth will be judged.

Chosen for Wholeness

[13] We always have to thank God for you, brothers and sisters, for you are *dearly* loved by the Lord. He proved it by choosing you from the beginning for salvation[n] through the Spirit, who set you apart for holiness, and through your belief

---

a 2:4 See Dan. 11:36.
b 2:4 Some see this prophecy fulfilled in AD 70 during the Roman war, when foreigners came into the temple and desecrated it and declared themselves the true rulers of the Jewish people. Roman emperors were considered to be gods. But the one who sits in God's temple, which was not made with hands, is the sin of man, a sinful nature that is traced back to Adam.
c 2:4 See also Ezek. 28:2.
d 2:6 An intransitive verb meaning "to rule" or "to hold sway" or "to possess." The Aramaic likewise is "Now you know that which controls." The neuter form of the Greek participle suggests a principle, not a person, which could be referring to the mystery of lawlessness in human hearts (v. 7). However, some see "it" as the god of this world (Satan) or the Roman Empire, which ruled the world in the days of Paul's writings.
e 2:7 Or "the secret power of lawlessness/wickedness."
f 2:7 Or "restrains."
g 2:7 Or "until he is removed."
h 2:8 Figuratively, this is the word spoken from his mouth, the Word of God. See also Rev. 19:15, 21.
i 2:8 Or "deactivate."
j 2:8 Or "coming."
k 2:9 Or "coming."
l 2:10 Or "did not welcome the love for the truth."
m 2:11 Or "a [power] working of error." The Aramaic can be translated "God will dispatch to them servants of deception."
n 2:13 Or "He has chosen you as firstfruits [in the harvest] for salvation."

in the truth.[a] [14] To this end he handpicked you for salvation through the gospel so that you would have[b] the glory of our Lord Jesus Christ.[c]

[15] So then, dear family, stand firm with a masterful grip of the teachings[d] we gave you, either by word of mouth or by our letter.[e]

[16] Now may the Lord Jesus Christ and our Father God, who loved us and in his wonderful grace gave us eternal comfort and a beautiful hope that cannot fail, [17] encourage your hearts and inspire you with strength to always do and speak what is good and beautiful *in his eyes*.[f]

Paul Requests Their Prayers

3 Finally, dear brothers and sisters, pray for us that the Lord's message will continue to spread rapidly and its glory be recognized everywhere, just as it was with you. [2] And pray that God will rescue us from wicked[g] and evil people, for not everyone believes *the message*. [3] But the Lord Yahweh[h] is always faithful[i] to place you on a firm foundation and guard you from the Evil One.[j] [4] We have complete confidence in the Lord concerning you[k] and we are sure that you are doing and will continue to do what we have told you.

[5] Now may the Lord move your hearts into *a greater understanding of* God's pure love for you and into Christ's steadfast endurance.[l]

---

a 2:13 Or "by sanctifying your spirits and convincing you of his truth."

b 2:14 Or "share in" or "possess." This is the Greek word *peripoiēsis*, which means "an encompassing," "a surrounding" or "encircling." Believers are brought within the perimeter of the glory of God through Jesus Christ. There is nothing in the context to imply it is a future event, but rather a present enjoyment and participation in the glory of the Lord Jesus Christ (John 17:10, 22).

c 2:14 These two verses (13–14) contain some of the most wonderful truths of the New Testament. Read them over again slowly and think about all that God the Father, God the Son, and God the Spirit have done for us (e.g., his eternal love, the drawing work of the Holy Spirit, sanctification or being set apart for holiness, faith in Jesus, and much more). Paul states in v. 14 that the purpose of our salvation is more than being set free from guilt; it is so that we would share in and possess the glory of Christ (John 17:10, 22).

d 2:15 Or "traditions."

e 2:15 The "letter" Paul refers to is likely 1 Thessalonians.

f 2:17 The Aramaic can be translated "He will comfort your hearts and will stand by all [your] words and by all (your) beautiful deeds." Another possible Aramaic translation of this verse is "He will make your hearts a well of prophecy and he will stand you in every word and in every beautiful deed."

g 3:2 The Greek word *atopos* can also be translated "weird," "irrational," "absurd," "disgusting."

h 3:3 As translated from the Aramaic.

i 3:3 Twelve times in the Bible the Lord is described as faithful. (See Deut. 7:9; Isa. 49:7; 1 Cor. 1:9; 10:13; 2 Thess. 3:3; Heb. 10:23; 11:11; 1 Peter 4:19; 1 John 1:9; Rev. 1:5; 3:14; 19:11.)

j 3:3 Or "guard you from evil" (the unproductive and sinful ways of the past).

k 3:4 Or "The Lord gives us confidence in you."

l 3:5 Or "the faithful endurance of [all things] for Christ." Either translation is grammatically possible as a subjective genitive or an objective genitive. The Aramaic can be translated "the hope of the Messiah."

A Warning about Laziness and Disunity

[6] Beloved brothers and sisters, we instruct you, in the name of our Lord Jesus Christ, to stay away from believers who are unruly [a] and who stray from all that we have taught you. [b] [7] For you know very well that you should order your lives after our example, because we were not undisciplined when we were with you. [8] We didn't sponge off of you, but we worked hard night and day to provide our own food and lodging and not be a burden to any of you. [9] It wasn't because we don't have the right to be supported, [c] but we wanted to provide you an example to follow. [10] For when we were with you we instructed you with these words: "Anyone who does not want to work for a living should go hungry."

[11] Now, we hear rumors that some of you are being lazy [d] and neglecting to work—that these people are not busy but busybodies! [12] So with the authority of the Lord Jesus Christ, we order them to go back to work in an orderly fashion and exhort them to earn their own living. [e] [13] Brothers and sisters, don't ever grow weary in doing what is right. [f]

[14] Take special note of anyone who won't obey what we have written and stay away from them, so that they would be ashamed and get turned around. [g] [15] Yet don't regard them as enemies, but caution them as fellow believers.

Conclusion

[16] Now, may the Lord himself, the Lord of peace, pour into you his peace in every circumstance and in every possible way. The Lord's *tangible* presence be with you all. [h]

---

a 3:6 Or "undisciplined" or "lazy" or "not in battle order" or "not in your duty station." There is an implication that there were believers who refused to work for a living. Paul is implying that the church should not financially support those who refuse to work. Personal responsibility is a common theme in Paul's teachings.

b 3:6 Or "don't live according to the traditions they received from us."

c 3:9 Those who preach the gospel have the right to be supported financially and deserve their wages (1 Cor. 9:6–18). However, it seems that Paul's custom was to earn his own way when he went into a city for the first time to show the truth of the gospel without mixed motives. His ministry in Thessalonica was somewhat of an anomaly. Because there were believers who were lazy and not working for a living, Paul gave up his right to have financial support from them and chose to work "night and day" (v. 8) to be an example to them.

d 3:11 Or "not showing up for the war" (battle).

e 3:12 Or "eat their own bread."

f 3:13 Doing right in this context is not growing tired of honest work. The Hebrew word for "work" (*avodah*) is the same Hebrew word (a homonym) for worship. Our work can be a form of worship. Our lives are to be a seamless expression of offering to God all of our activities as things we do with all our might for the glory of God.

g 3:14 The passive Greek verb *entropē* means "to be turned" (around); that is, to be changed. This was not punishment but an attempt to draw wayward individuals into repentance and bring them back into restored fellowship with the church.

h 3:16 Paul is longing for the guidance, influence, and power that comes from God's presence to be real to them.

¹⁷⁻¹⁸ So now, in my own handwriting, I add these words:

Loving greetings to each of you. And may the grace of our Lord Jesus Christ be with you all.

Paul

The above is my signature and the token of authenticity in every letter I write. *a*

---

a 3:17–18 See 1 Cor. 16:21; Gal. 6:11; Col. 4:18; Philem. 19. The Aramaic ends with "The end of Paul's second letter to the Thessalonians, written from Laodicea [Pisidian]."

1 TIMOTHY

Introduction

AT A GLANCE

Author: The apostle Paul

Audience: Timothy, Paul's spiritual son in the faith

Date: AD 62–63

Type of Literature: A letter

Major Themes: False teachers, false doctrine, church leadership, and God's household

Outline:

Letter Opening — 1:1–2

Ordering and Organizing the Church, Part 1 — 1:3–3:16

Ordering and Organizing the Church, Part 2 — 4:1–6:19

Letter Closing — 6:20–21

ABOUT 1 TIMOTHY

First and 2 Timothy have been recognized as "Pastoral Epistles"—letters written by Paul for pastors and leaders to help them bring order and ordain elders (pastors) for the churches he planted. In fact, Timothy was an apostolic apprentice to Paul, mentored by a spiritual father who poured into his life, even after being sent out to establish churches and bring them to maturity. Timothy was the extension of Paul's apostolic ministry. Perhaps we should view these two letters more as "Apostolic Epistles" instead of Pastoral Epistles.

One reason we know that Timothy's ministry was unlike the pastoral ministry of today is that Timothy was an itinerant apostle who planted and brought healing and truth to the churches in which he ministered. Some of the locations he ministered in would include Thessalonica (1 Thess. 3:2–6), Corinth (1 Cor. 4:17; 16:10; 2 Cor. 1:19), Philippi (Phil. 2:19–23), Berea (Acts 17:14), and Ephesus (1 Tim. 1:2). His ministry eventually brought him imprisonment, much like his apostolic mentor, Paul (Heb. 13:23).

Timothy's name means "honored by God." He was from the city of Lystra, the place where Paul was stoned to death and then raised from the dead (see Acts 14:19–20). It may have been that Timothy witnessed what happened to Paul and was converted through what he saw. Paul recruited young Timothy and raised him up to take the message of the gospel to the nations. He soon began to travel with Paul in his missionary journeys and was eventually trusted with great responsibilities to teach and instruct the church.

Timothy was the son of a mixed marriage with a Greek father and a Jewish mother, whose name was Eunice ("joyous victory"). His mother was a convert to Christ and was distinguished by her faith. Timothy was likely in his thirties when Paul wrote him this challenging letter.

Timothy's ministry was in more than one location, for he was told to do the "work of an evangelist" in planting churches and winning souls to Christ. He was Paul's faithful representative to the churches of Thessalonica (1 Thess. 3:2), Corinth (1 Cor. 4:17), Philippi (Phil. 2:19), and Ephesus (1 Tim. 1:3)—yet it was in Ephesus where Paul left him to keep watering the seeds that had been planted to help the church there mature.

Paul instructs Timothy about the administration of the church and encourages him to hold up a high standard for those who lead. The qualifications for church leadership are spelled out in 1 Timothy (and Titus). And we are given clear instructions about caring for widows and for supporting the leaders of the church financially. Generally speaking, 1 Timothy could be seen as a manual for church planting. The key verse is found in 3:15: "But if I'm delayed in coming, you'll already have these instructions on how to conduct the affairs of the church of the living God, his very household, the supporting pillar and firm foundation of the truth."

What heavenly principles are revealed in this letter!

PURPOSE

The clear purpose of 1 Timothy is to reveal and emphasize the glorious truths of God. False teachers had begun to infiltrate the church of Ephesus, and Timothy was given the mission of preserving the truth and cleansing the church of error. Good relationships and spiritual growth can only come when the church grows in maturity and knows the difference between truth and error. There are wonderful revelations waiting for us in 1 Timothy that will focus our hearts on Christ, his glory, and his resurrection.

AUTHOR AND AUDIENCE

What beautiful words Paul shares with his spiritual son, Timothy! We are about to overhear the intimate words of encouragement and inspiration that a first-century apostle shared with his protégé. If we have any example at all of mentoring in the Bible, it is seen here in the relationship Paul had with Timothy. Written about AD 62–63, Paul imparts to Timothy the wisdom and revelation that is required to plant churches and lead an entire region into spiritual breakthrough.

MAJOR THEMES

False Teachers and Doctrine. Every generation has seen its fair share of false teaching; ours is no different, and neither was Timothy's. Paul commands him to confront false teachers and oppose unorthodox doctrines that "emphasize nothing more than the empty words of men" (1:6). He exhorts him to maintain his personal faith and warns against falling away, like others.

Qualifications for Church Leaders. In this letter to his ministry coworker, Paul has provided the church throughout the ages a helpful list of qualifications for two offices: overseers/elders and deacons. Both church officers are called to a similar standard of high moral and personal conduct, which includes integrity, peace, temperateness, generosity, and a well-managed household.

The Household of God. Throughout this letter from heaven, Paul explains what it means to live in the household of God. He outlines the proper treatment for widows, and he lays out the expectations for slaves, which can apply to workers too. He even says how the church should disciple its own. Paul gives Timothy the task of teaching Christ's vision for how his household should exist in the world.

1 TIMOTHY

Heaven's Truth

Introduction

1 From Paul, an apostle in Christ Jesus, for it was Jesus himself, our living hope, who sent me as his servant by the command of God, our life-giver. [a]
[2] Timothy, you are my true spiritual son in the faith. May abundant grace, mercy, and total well-being[b] from God the Father and the Anointed One, our Lord Jesus, be yours!

Timothy's Ministry in Ephesus

[3] As I urged you when I left for Macedonia,[c] I'm asking that you remain in Ephesus to instruct them not to teach or follow the error of deceptive doctrines, [4] nor pay any attention to cultural myths, traditions, or the endless study of genealogies.[d] Those digressions only breed controversies and debates. They are devoid of power that builds up and strengthens the church in the faith of God.

[5] For we reach the goal of fulfilling all the commandments when we love others deeply with a pure heart, a clean conscience, and sincere faith. [6] Some believers have been led astray by teachings and speculations that emphasize nothing more than the empty words of men. [7] They presume to be expert teachers of the law,[e] but they don't have the slightest idea of what they're talking about and they simply love to argue!

Paul's Use of the Law

[8] We know that the moral code of the law is beautiful when applied as God intended, [9] but actually, the law was not established for righteous people, but to bring conviction of sin to the unrighteous. The law was established to bring the revelation of sin to the evildoers and rebellious, the sinners without

---

a 1:1 Or "Savior."
b 1:2 The Hebrew concept of peace includes health, prosperity, and peace of mind.
c 1:3 As translated from the Aramaic.
d 1:4 The Jewish people have always been diligent to carefully record their genealogies; yet, the reference to genealogies here may also include the apocryphal writings of Jewish mysticism, detailing the origins of angelic beings involved in creation.
e 1:7 Or "Torah."

God, those who are vicious and perverse, and to those who strike their father or their mother, *a* sinners, murderers, [10] rapists, those who are sexually impure, homosexuals, *b* kidnappers, liars, those who break their oaths, and all those who oppose the teaching of godliness and purity in the church! *They are the ones the law is for.*

[11] I have been commissioned to preach the wonderful news of the glory of the exalted God. [12] My heart spills over with thanks to God for the way he continually empowers me, and to our Lord Jesus, the Anointed One, who found me trustworthy and who authorized me to be his partner in this ministry.

Empowering Mercy

[13] Mercy kissed me, even though I used to be a blasphemer, a persecutor of believers, and a scorner of what turned out to be true. I was ignorant and didn't know what I was doing. [14] I was flooded with such incredible grace, *like a river overflowing its banks,* *c* until I was full of faith and love for Jesus, the Anointed One!

[15] I can testify that the Word is true and deserves to be received by all, for Jesus Christ came into the world to bring sinners back to life—even me, the worst sinner of all! [16] Yet I was captured by grace, so that Jesus Christ could display through me the outpouring of his Spirit *d* as a pattern to be seen for all those who would believe *e* in him for eternal life.

[17] Because of this my praises rise to the King of all the universe *f* who is indestructible, *g* invisible, and full of glory, the only God *h* who is worthy of the highest honors throughout all of time and throughout the eternity of eternities! Amen!

Paul Encourages Timothy to Remain Faithful

[18-19] So Timothy, my son, I am entrusting you with this responsibility, in keeping with the very first prophecies that were spoken over your life, and are now in the process of fulfillment in this great work of ministry, in keeping with the prophecies spoken over you. With this encouragement *use your prophecies* as weapons as you wage spiritual warfare by faith and with a clean conscience. For there are

---

a 1:9 As translated from the Aramaic. The Greek reads "those who murder their father or murder their mother."

b 1:10 The Aramaic can be translated "molesters of male children."

c 1:14 Paul uses the Greek word *pleonazō,* which means "superabounding grace."

d 1:16 As translated from the Aramaic. The Greek text reads "that Jesus would demonstrate his perfect patience."

e 1:16 Or "destined to believe."

f 1:17 Or "King of the ages."

g 1:17 The Aramaic word used here is a direct reference to the physical body of Christ that did not decompose in the tomb, but was raised in resurrection.

h 1:17 As translated from the Aramaic. Some Greek texts have "the only wise God."

many who reject these virtues and are now destitute of the true faith, [20] such as Hymenaeus[a] and Alexander[b] who have fallen away. I have delivered them both over to Satan to be rid of them and to teach them to no longer blaspheme!

Instruction on Prayer

2 Most of all, I'm writing to encourage you to pray with gratitude to God. Pray for all men with all forms of prayers and requests as you intercede with intense passion. [2] And pray for every political leader[c] and representative,[d] so that we would be able to live tranquil, undisturbed lives, as we worship the awe-inspiring God with pure hearts. [3] It is pleasing to our Savior-God *to pray for them.* [4] He longs for everyone to embrace his life and return to the full knowledge of the truth.

[5] For God is one, and there is one Mediator between God and the sons of men—the true man, Jesus, the Anointed One. [6] He gave himself as ransom-payment for everyone. Now is the proper time for God to give the world this witness. [7] I have been divinely called as an apostle to preach this revelation, which is the truth. God has called me to be a trustworthy teacher to the nations.

[8] Therefore, I encourage the men to pray on every occasion[e] with hands lifted to God in worship with clean hearts, free from frustration or strife.[f]

Conduct of Women

[9] And that the women *would also pray*[g] with clean hearts, dressed appropriately and adorned modestly and sensibly, not flaunting their wealth.[h] [10] But *they should be recognized* instead by their beautiful deeds of kindness, suitable as one who worships God.

[11] Let the women *who are new converts*[i] be willing to learn with all submission to their leaders and not speak out of turn.[j] [12] I don't advocate that the *newly*

---

a 1:20 The name Hymenaeus is also the name of the pagan god of the bridal song sung by the attendants of the bride during the ceremony. He was invoked by the bride's friends in hope that he would come and manifest himself. Perhaps Hymenaeus was attempting to mix the worship of false gods into the church. See also 2 Tim. 2:17.

b 1:20 Alexander's name means "protector of men," or "man pleaser." When the church attempts to please men, we can quickly fail to please God.

c 2:2 Or "kings."

d 2:2 Or "magistrates."

e 2:8 Or "wherever you pray."

f 2:8 Or "anger or scheming."

g 2:9 Prayer is implied, but made explicit from the context of v. 8.

h 2:9 Literally "not with braids of gold, or with pearls, or gorgeous robes."

i 2:11 Implied and understood by the cultural context of that day.

j 2:11 Literally "quietly." In the context of that day, it referred to women arguing with their male congregational leaders. In the temple worship of Diana, the goddess of the Ephesian people, it was most common to have female leadership. For the women who converted to

converted [a] women be the teachers in the church, assuming authority over the men, but to live in peace. [13] For God formed Adam first, [b] then Eve. [14] Adam did not mislead Eve, but Eve misled him and violated the command of God. [c] [15] Yet a woman shall live in restored dignity by means of her children, receiving the blessing that comes from raising them as consecrated children nurtured in faith and love, walking in wisdom. [d]

Leaders in the Church

3 If any of you [e] aspires to be an overseer [f] in the church, you have set your heart toward a noble ambition, for the word is true! [2] Yet an elder needs to be one who is without blame before others.

He should be one whose heart is for his wife alone *and not another woman.* [g] He should be recognized as one who is sensible, and well-behaved, and living a disciplined life. He should be a "spiritual shepherd" who has the gift of teaching, [h] and is known for his hospitality.

[3] He cannot be a drunkard, or someone who lashes out at others, [i] or

---

Christ, their only cultural context of worship was that the women were the leaders. In the church, however, it was the men who more commonly made up the leadership of the congregations. Paul telling the women to "be willing to learn" means he was instructing them to take a respectful posture of a disciple in this new way of worshiping the true God. When Paul instructs them not to be teachers, he was apparently referring to their old religious system where it was the women who were the temple leaders and teachers of their goddess religion in Ephesus. This entire passage from 1 Tim. 2:9–15 is arguably one of the more difficult texts to translate in Paul's writings, and has a number of plausible translations and interpretations. However, the translator has chosen to make clear what was implicitly understood by the early Christians in Ephesus, making it explicit for those of us from another culture and another era.

a 2:12 Implied and understood by the cultural context of that day.

b 2:13 One of the prevailing Gnostic heresies of that era was that Eve was formed first, then Adam. Paul puts that debate to rest with this verse.

c 2:14 As translated from the Aramaic. The Greek says "Adam was not deceived but the woman was beguiled and has come into transgression."

d 2:15 As translated from the Aramaic. The Greek is "she shall be saved by childbearing," which could be misleading. The Aramaic makes it clear that the woman is honored and restored to dignity by her children (and spiritual children) who have faith in Christ, serving God. Some have interpreted the Greek text to imply that it was Mary who gave birth to Jesus and that he is the Child that saves us all and redeems womanhood.

e 3:1 Some translations have "men," however, the Greek word is not gender specific.

f 3:1 There are a number of terms that are synonymous for elder, such as: pastor, shepherd, presbyter, bishop, overseer, or guardian. These all describe the one office of pastor mentioned in Eph. 4:11.

g 3:2 This literally means "a one woman kind of man" or "faithful to your woman [wife]," which implies much more than simply not being a polygamist. It was culturally common for men to have more than one wife or concubines in that era.

h 3:2 Or "able to teach."

i 3:3 The Aramaic can be translated "not swift to strike."

argumentative, or someone who simply craves more money,[a] but instead, recognized by his gentleness.

[4] His heart should be set on guiding his household with wisdom and dignity;[b] bringing up his children to worship with devotion and purity. [5] For if he's unable to properly lead his own household well, how could he properly lead God's household?

[6] He should not be a new disciple[c] who would be vulnerable to living in the clouds of conceit and fall into pride, making him easy prey for Satan.[d] [7] He should be respected by those who are unbelievers, having a beautiful testimony among them[e] so that he will not fall into the traps of Satan and be disgraced.

[8] And in the same way the deacons[f] must be those who are pure and true to their word, not addicted to wine, or with greedy eyes on the contributions.[g] [9] Instead, they must faithfully embrace the mysteries of faith while keeping a clean conscience. [10] And each of them must be found trustworthy according to these standards before they are given the responsibility to minister as servant-leaders without blame.

[11] And the women[h] also who serve the church should be dignified,[i] faithful in all things,[j] having their thoughts set on truth, and not known as those who gossip.

[12] A deacon's heart must be toward his wife alone, leading his children and household with excellence. [13] For those who serve in this way will obtain an honorable reputation[k] for themselves and a greater right to speak boldly in the faith that comes from the anointing of Jesus!

[14] I'm writing all this with the expectation of seeing you soon. [15] But if I'm delayed in coming, you'll already have these instructions on how to conduct the affairs of the church of the living God, his very household and the supporting pillar and firm foundation of the truth.

---

a 3:3 The Aramaic can be translated "merciful to money." Some see in this the concept of not showing favoritism because of someone's economic status.

b 3:4 Literally "beautifully."

c 3:6 The Aramaic can be translated "a new plant," which implies shallow roots.

d 3:6 The Greek literally means "fall into Satan's court of law."

e 3:7 As translated from the Greek. The Aramaic uses a metaphor, "a beautiful testimony from the wilderness." This means he has passed through his wilderness journey and is now seen as tested and proven.

f 3:8 The Aramaic can be translated "ministers."

g 3:8 Or "corrupt profits."

h 3:11 The word used here can mean "women" or "wives." This may refer to women deacons. Phoebe is called a deacon in Rom. 16:1.

i 3:11 As translated from the Greek, the Aramaic can be translated "modest."

j 3:11 Or "temperate."

k 3:13 Or "a good rank."

The Mystery of Righteousness

[16] For the mystery of righteousness is truly amazing!
He was revealed as a human being,
  and as our great High Priest in the Spirit![a]
Angels gazed upon him *as a man*
  and the glorious message of his kingly rulership
  is being preached to the nations!
Many have believed in him
  and he has been taken back to heaven,
  and has ascended into the place of exalted glory
  in the heavenly realm.
Yes, great is this mystery of righteousness!

Warning against False Teachers

4 The Holy Spirit has explicitly revealed:[b] At the end of this age, many will depart from the true faith one after another, devoting themselves to spirits[c] of deception and following demon-inspired revelations and theories. [2] Hypocritical liars[d] will deceive many, and their consciences won't bother them at all! [3] They will require celibacy and dietary restrictions that God doesn't expect, for he created all foods to be received with the celebration of faith by those who fully know the truth. [4] We know that all creation is beautiful to God and there is nothing to be refused if it is received with gratitude. [5] All that we eat is made sacred by the Word of God and prayer.

[6] If you will teach the believers these things, you will be known as a faithful

---

a 3:16 As translated by the implication of the Aramaic. The Greek says "justified in the Spirit." Although some interpret it to mean his resurrection, that seems indefinite and with little meaning to today's reader. There is deep and beautiful poetic artistry here in this passage. The word order of the Aramaic lines is convincing that glorious and hidden truths are tucked into these verses; they are full of Jewish word plays and symbolism, and read like a poem. Many have concluded that this passage was an ancient hymn sung by the early church. Two different Aramaic words for "righteousness" are used in v. 16. The first word is *kanota* which is clearly connected to the word for "priest" or *kahna*. An Aramaic or Hebrew reader would clearly connect this "righteousness" to the priestly ministry. In poetic and perhaps subtle linguistic form, this points us to the High Priest of our faith. The second word used that is most often translated "righteousness" is *atzaddaq*; the word in the line before used for messenger (angels) is *malaka*, which is a form of the word for king (*malak*). To summarize, you have the words "great [high] priest," "king," and "righteousness," which is the name for Melchizedek, (King of Righteousness). Truly, this mystery of righteousness is great!

b 4:1 The Greek text could be translated "the Spirit says publicly." This is most likely through prophetic utterance in the church. God's Spirit still speaks to his people today through gifts of prophecy, tongues and interpretation of tongues, and in many other forms. Paul is likely quoting a prophecy.

c 4:1 Aramaic and Hebrew speakers would view this as an idiom for "deceiving prophecies."

d 4:2 The Aramaic can be translated "they will seduce with false appearances."

and good minister of Jesus, the Anointed One. Nurture others in the living words of faith and in the knowledge of grace which you were taught.

[7] Be quick to abstain from senseless traditions[a] and legends,[b] but instead be engaged in the training of truth that brings righteousness.

Conduct of God's Servants

[8] For athletic training only benefits you for a short season, but righteousness brings lasting benefit in everything; for righteousness contains the promise of life, for time and eternity. [9] Faithful is the Word, and everyone should accept him![c]

[10] For the sake of this ministry, we toil tirelessly and are criticized continually,[d] simply because our hope is in the living God. He is the wonderful life-giver[e] of all the children of men, and even more so to those who believe.

[11] Instruct and teach the people all that I've taught you. [12] And don't be intimidated by those who are older than you; simply be the example they need to see by being faithful and true in all that you do. Speak the truth[f] and live a life of purity and authentic love as you remain strong in your faith.

[13] So until I come, be diligent in devouring the Word of God, be faithful in prayer, and in teaching the believers.

[14] Don't minimize the powerful gift that operates in your life, for it was imparted to you by the laying on of hands of the elders and was activated through the prophecy they spoke over you. [15] Make all of this your constant meditation and make it real with your life so everyone can see that you are moving forward. [16] Give careful attention to your spiritual life and every cherished truth you teach, for living what you preach will then release even more abundant life inside you and to all those who listen to you.

Conduct toward Others

5 Don't be harsh or verbally abusive to an older man;[g] it is better to appeal to him as a father. And as you minister to the younger men it is best to encourage them as your dear brothers. [2] Honor the older women[h] as mothers, and the younger women, treat as your dear sisters with utmost purity.[i]

---

a 4:7 Or "fables."
b 4:7 Or "the fiction of old wives' tales."
c 4:9 As translated from the Aramaic. The Greek text reads "this is a faithful saying and is worthy to be fully accepted."
d 4:10 As translated from the Aramaic. In place of "criticized continually" the Greek text has "contend for the [athletic] prize."
e 4:10 As translated from the Aramaic. The Greek word is "Savior."
f 4:12 As translated from the Greek.
g 5:1 Or "elder" (one who is given responsibility within the church).
h 5:2 Or "woman elders."
i 5:2 Or "holiness."

³ The church needs to honor and support the widows, especially those who are in dire need. ⁴ But if they have children or grandchildren at home, then it is only proper to let them provide for the ones who raised them when they were children, for kindness begins at home and it pleases God.

⁵ For the true widow^a is all alone and has placed her complete hope in God. She is Messiah's missionary^b *and will need the support of the church* as one who remains in prayer day and night. ⁶ But the widow who serves only herself lives a life of self-indulgence and is wasting her life away.

⁷ Be sure to give clear instruction concerning these matters so that none of them will live with shame. ⁸ For if a believer fails to provide for their own relatives when they are in need, they have compromised^c their convictions of faith *and need to be corrected*, for they are living worse than the unbelievers.

⁹ The widows who are worthy to be supported by the church should be at least sixty years old and not remarried. ¹⁰ They should have a beautiful testimony of raising their families, practicing hospitality, encouraging other believers, comforting troubled ones,^d and have a reputation for doing good works.

¹¹ But you need not concern yourself with the younger widows, for some will depart from the Messiah because of their desire to remarry.^e ¹² For they will face their own punishment^f of living with a disturbed conscience for invalidating their former faith. ¹³ Those widows who go around from house to house as busybodies^g are only learning to be lazy, making their situation even worse by talking too much, gossiping, and speaking things they shouldn't. They become far too obsessed with empty things that will not bear good fruit.

¹⁴ For this reason, teach the younger women to remarry and bear children and care for their household. This will keep them from giving our adversary a reason to gloat. ¹⁵ For there are already those who have begun to turn aside from their faith and are influenced by Satan.

¹⁶ So if any believer has a widow in their family, instruct them to support her financially so that the church will not be burdened with her care. This will leave finances available for those widows who are truly in need.

---

a 5:5 There is an implication in the Aramaic that the "true widow" is one whose husband was killed due to persecution of believers.

b 5:5 As translated from the Aramaic.

c 5:8 Or "denied."

d 5:10 Or "paying the expenses of those who are persecuted."

e 5:11 There is a sexual connotation implied in the text.

f 5:12 Or "judgment."

g 5:13 The Greek word used for "busybodies" can also imply "gaining illegal knowledge of the supernatural." See Acts 19:19 where the same Greek word is used for black magic.

Respect toward Church Leaders

[17] The pastors[a] who lead the church well should be paid well. They should receive double honor for faithfully preaching and teaching the revelation of the Word of God. [18] For the Scriptures have taught us: "Do not muzzle an ox or forbid it to eat while it grinds the grain."[b] And also, "The one who labors deserves his wages."[c]

[19] Refuse to listen to suspicious accusations against the pastors who lead the flock unless you have two or three witnesses *to confirm the accusations.* [20] But if indeed you find that they have sinned, bring correction to them before the congregation so that the rest of the people will respect you.[d]

[21] Timothy, in the presence of God and our Lord Jesus Christ, and before the chosen messengers,[e] I solemnly charge you to put into practice all these matters without bias, prejudice, or favoritism.

[22] Don't be hasty to ordain them with the laying on of hands, or you may end up sharing in their guilt should they fall. Keep yourself pure and holy with your standards high. [23] (If drinking the water causes you to have stomach ailments,[f] drink some wine instead.)

[24] The sins of some people stand out and are well known. Yet there are others whose sins are not as obvious, but the truth of who they really are will eventually be seen and will bring them judgment.[g] [25] It is the same way with good works, even if they are not known at first, they will eventually be recognized and acknowledged.

6 Instruct every employee[h] to respect and honor their employers,[i] for this attitude presents to them a clear testimony of God's truth and renown. Tell them to never provide them with a reason to discredit God's name because of their actions. [2] Especially honor and respect employers who are believers and don't despise them, but serve them all the more, for

---

a 5:17 Or "elders," also v. 19.

b 5:18 See Deut. 25:4.

c 5:18 See Lev. 19:13; Deut. 24:15.

d 5:20 Or "fear." That is, the congregation will see proper correction and fear falling into sin.

e 5:21 This word can refer to angels or men.

f 5:23 The Greek text literally means "bladder frequency." The translator has chosen to bracket this parenthetical verse to show it is inserted in the middle of Paul's words regarding the topic of ordination (laying on of hands). Paul does not encourage the drinking of wine, nor does he condemn its moderate use.

g 5:24 An alternate Aramaic translation is "there are some who confess their sins and bring them [their sins] to judgment, and there are those whose sins follow them."

h 6:1 Or "those under the yoke of performance" (servitude or slavery). The Greek text clearly refers to slaves and masters, but the Aramaic is somewhat ambiguous and could still be referring to the topic of ch. 5. "Those" would refer to the leadership of the church instead—pastors, deacons, and deaconesses.

i 6:1 Or "masters," also in v. 2.

they are fellow believers. They should be at peace with them as beloved members of God's family. Be faithful to teach them these things as their sacred obligation.

False Teachers and True Riches

³ But if anyone spreads false teaching that does not agree with the healthy instruction of our Lord Jesus, teaching others that holy awe of God[a] is not important, then they prove they know nothing at all! It's obvious they don't value or hold dear the healing words of our Lord Jesus Christ. ⁴ They are covered with the clouds of conceit. They are loaded[b] with controversy, and they love to argue their opinions and split hairs. The fruit of their ministry is contention, competition, and evil suspicions.

⁵ They add misery to many lives by corrupting their minds and cheating them of the truth. They equate the worship of God with making great sums of money.[c]

⁶ We have a "profit" that is greater than theirs—our holy awe of God! To have merely our necessities is to have enough.

⁷ Isn't it true that our hands were empty when we came into the world, and when we leave this world our hands will be empty again?

⁸ Because of this, food and clothing is enough to make us content.

⁹ But those who crave the wealth of this world slip into spiritual snares. They become trapped by the troubles that come through their foolish and harmful desires, driven by greed and drowning in their own sinful pleasures. And they take others down with them into their corruption and eventual destruction.

¹⁰ Loving money[d] is the first step toward all kinds of trouble. Some people run after it so much that they have given up their faith. Craving more money pushes them away from the faith into error, compounding misery[e] in their lives!

Paul's Final Exhortation to Timothy

¹¹ Timothy, you are God's man, so run from all these errors. Instead, chase after true holiness, justice, faithfulness, love, hope,[f] and tender humility. ¹² So fight

---

a 6:3 The Aramaic here and in v. 6 literally means "the doctrine of the fear of God." The fear of God is one of the seven spirits of God, the spirit of the fear of God (Isa. 11:2–3). To teach there is no fear of God would be leading people away from the Holy Spirit. The fear of God is more than simply loving and respecting God. There are over one hundred references in both the Old and New Testaments that speak of "the fear of God."

b 6:4 The Aramaic can be translated "sick with controversy."

c 6:5 Or "to be godly is the way to get rich."

d 6:10 Or "insatiable greed for money."

e 6:10 As translated from the Aramaic. The word *misery* can also mean "demon."

f 6:11 Or "patience."

with faith for the winner's prize! Lay your hands upon eternal life, for this is your calling—celebrating in faith before the multitude of witnesses![a]

[13] So now, I instruct you before the God of resurrection life[b] and before Jesus, the Anointed One, who demonstrated a beautiful testimony even before Pontius Pilate, [14] that you follow this commission faithfully with a clear conscience[c] and without blemish until the appearing of our Lord Jesus, the Messiah.

[15] Yes, God will make his appearing in his own divine timing,[d] for he is the exalted God, the only powerful One, the King over every king, and the Lord of power! [16] He alone is the immortal God,[e] living in the unapproachable light of divine glory! No one has ever seen his fullness, nor can they, for all the glory and endless authority of the universe belongs to him, forever and ever. Amen!

[17] To all the rich of this world, I command you not to be wrapped in thoughts of pride over your prosperity, or rely on your wealth, for your riches are unreliable and nothing compared to the living God. Trust instead in the one who has lavished upon us all good things, fulfilling our every need.[f]

[18] Remind the wealthy to be rich in good works of extravagant generosity, willing to share with others. [19] This will provide a beautiful foundation for their lives and secure for them a great future, as they lay their hands upon the meaning of true life.

[20] So, my son Timothy,[g] don't forget all that has been deposited within you. Escape from the empty echoes of men[h] and the perversion of twisted reasoning.[i] [21] For those who claim to possess this so-called knowledge have already wandered from the true faith.

May God's grace empower you always!

Love in Christ,
Paul

---

a 6:12 As translated from the Aramaic.
b 6:13 Or "the God who resurrects all."
c 6:14 Or "without defilement."
d 6:15 By implication, the second coming of Jesus.
e 6:16 Or "incorruptible God."
f 6:17 Or "pleasure."
g 6:20 Paul uses an endearing variation of Timothy's name; it could almost be read "Oh Timmy." The translation includes the words, *my son*, to make this explicit.
h 6:20 This is an Aramaic figure of speech that means literally "daughters of the voice [echoes] of vanity." The Greek text reads "profane and vain babblings."
i 6:20 As translated from the Aramaic, which also means, "false doctrines." The Greek is "false [so-called] science."

2 TIMOTHY

Introduction

AT A GLANCE

Author: The apostle Paul

Audience: Timothy, Paul's spiritual son in the faith

Date: AD 65–67

Type of Literature: A letter

Major Themes: False teachers, false doctrine, suffering, perseverance, and faithfulness

Outline:

Letter Opening — 1:1–2

Thanksgiving for Timothy's Faith — 1:3–5

Encouragement to Timothy — 1:6–2:13

Instructions for Timothy — 2:14–4:8

Letter Closing — 4:9–22

ABOUT 2 TIMOTHY

This could be called the last will and testament of Paul the apostle. Filled with warnings of the troubles that were ahead, this letter speaks to our generation with an unusual urgency. The outward display of religion must not entice the passionate and hungry, turning them away from the truth of the gospel. Paul's heart burns as he looks to the end of his journey and knows that death is near. He stirs our conscience with his emotional letter.

The urgency of this letter is Paul's revelation of the last days. Mentioned here in 2 Timothy more than any other letter, Paul warns, instructs, and challenges all of us to live a life of purity as the days grow evil. He gives us six analogies of the last days' servant of the Lord. The believer is compared to a soldier (2:3), an athlete (2:5), a farmer (2:6), a minister (2:15), a container (2:21), and a servant (2:24).

I believe there are many verses that could be considered the most important themes of the book, but perhaps 4:7–8 would contain the summary theme of the letter:

I have fought an excellent fight. I have finished my full course and I've kept my heart full of faith. There's a crown of righteousness waiting in heaven for me, and I know that my Lord will reward me on his day of righteous judgment. And this crown is not only waiting for me, but for all who love and long for his unveiling.

As you read 2 Timothy, try to picture Paul sitting in a prison cell. He misses his wonderful disciple Timothy. Picture Timothy reading this letter with a longing deep within to hear these final words from his spiritual dad. Their love is deep, their commitment to the gospel is powerful, and their desire to see the world reached with the love of Christ is real.

PURPOSE

Writing from prison and awaiting execution, Paul seeks to impart his final words of wisdom to his spiritual son Timothy. He carries some of the concerns over from his first letter, such as dealing with false teachers. In this letter, however, Paul weaves together the themes of suffering, perseverance, and vindication in relation to his own experience and Christ's. Paul gives Timothy this example to encourage him in his own ministry, and also his Christian life.

AUTHOR AND AUDIENCE

Written in AD 65 shortly before his martyrdom at the order of the Roman Emperor Nero, Paul wants to make sure Timothy is instructed about serving the church as God's man. There is a spiritual inheritance found in 2 Timothy for every true minister of the gospel and for every lover of God.

Many have recognized this letter as the most personal and heartfelt of all of Paul's writings. He names twenty-three individuals—both friends and foes. He opens his heart and gives intimate details of his life, and he shares his desire to see Timothy advance in his calling.

Apparently, Timothy is still in Ephesus fulfilling the mandate Paul gave him in his first letter. Paul writes to his spiritual son knowing that death is near. He longed to see Timothy again and desired to make sure he was encouraged to finish his race to the end.

MAJOR THEMES

False Teachers and Doctrine. Apparently the same situation of unorthodox teaching Paul addressed in his first letter was still a problem. This time Paul calls these false teachers out by name: Hymenaeus and Philetus "are like gangrene," he says, who "have already spread their poison to many" (2:17). He urges Timothy to unapologetically preach the Word of Truth and stay away from their foolish arguments.

Suffering and Perseverance. From a Roman prison, waiting to be executed, Paul urges his gospel coworker to suffer as he has for the gospel. Paul calls Timothy into such living not only because of his own willingness to suffer but also because of Christ's own experience of death. He drives home this calling for courage by offering shameful examples of believers who've betrayed such a calling. Instead, Timothy—and we—are called to persevere through suffering like Paul, and like Christ, in order to receive their reward.

Faithfulness in Life and Ministry. As you might expect from a last will and testament, Paul instructs Timothy to pick up where he left off by carrying out his ministry with dedication and faithfully preaching the apostolic message. Paul offers his own life as an example of the kind of faithfulness to ministry and godliness he is urging Timothy to follow.

2 TIMOTHY

Heaven's Urgency

Introduction

1 From Paul, an apostle of Jesus the Messiah, appointed by God's pleasure to announce the wonderful promise of life found in Jesus, the anointed Messiah.

2 My beloved son, I pray for a greater release of God's grace, love, and total well-being to flow into your life from God our Father and from our Lord Jesus Christ!

3 You know that I've been called to serve the God of my fathers with a clean conscience. Night and day I pray for you, thanking God for your life! 4 I know that you have wept for me, your spiritual father, and your tears are dear to me. I can't wait to see you again! I'm filled with joy 5 as I think of your strong faith *that was passed down through your family line*. It began with your grandmother Lois, who passed it on to your dear mother, Eunice. And it's clear that you too are following in the footsteps of their godly example.

Timothy and the Holy Spirit

6 I'm writing to encourage you to fan into a flame and rekindle*a* the fire of the spiritual gift God imparted to you when I laid my hands *upon you*. 7 For God will never give you the spirit of fear,*b* but the Holy Spirit who gives you mighty power, love, and self-control.*c* 8 So never be ashamed of the testimony of our Lord, nor be embarrassed over my imprisonment, but overcome every evil by the revelation of the power of God!*d* 9 He gave us resurrection life*e* and drew us to himself by his holy calling on our lives. And it wasn't because of any good we have done, but by his divine pleasure and marvelous grace that confirmed our union with the anointed Jesus, even before time began!*f* 10 This truth is now being unveiled by the revelation of the anointed Jesus, our life-giver, who has

---

a 1:6 Literally "excite the gift" or "awake the gift."
b 1:7 That is, fearing men. The fear of God prevents us from fearing others.
c 1:7 The Aramaic can also be translated "revelation-light," or "instruction."
d 1:8 Or "with the gospel and the power of God."
e 1:9 Or "He is our life-giver."
f 1:9 Literally "before the time of the ages."

dismantled death, *obliterating all its effects on our lives*, and has manifested his
immortal life in us by the gospel.

Paul and His Gospel Ministry

[11] And he has anointed[a] me as his preacher, his apostle, and his teacher of truth
to the nations. [12] The confidence of my calling enables me to overcome every
difficulty without shame, for I have an intimate revelation of this God. And my
faith in him convinces me that he is more than able to keep all that I've placed
in his hands safe and secure until the fullness of his appearing.

[13] Allow the healing words you've heard from me to live in you and make
them a model for life as your faith and love for the Anointed One *grows even
more.* [14] Guard well this incomparable treasure by the Spirit of Holiness living
within you.

[15] Perhaps you've heard that Phygelus,[b] and Hermogenes[c] and all the believers of Asia have deserted me because of my imprisonment. [16] Nevertheless,
so many times Onesiphorus[d] was like a breath of fresh air to me and never
seemed to be ashamed of my chains. May our Lord Jesus bestow compassion
and mercy upon him and his household. [17] For when he arrived in Rome, he
searched and searched for me until he found out *where I was being held, so that
he could minister to me,* [18] just like he did so wonderfully as I rested in his house[e]
while in Ephesus, as you well know.

May Jesus, our Master, give him abundant mercy in the day he stands before him.

Grace to Overcome

2 Timothy, my dear son,[f] live your life empowered by God's free-flowing
grace, which is your true strength, found in the anointing of Jesus *and your
union with him!* [2] And all that you've learned from me, confirmed by the integrity
of my life,[g] pass on to faithful leaders who are competent to teach the congregations the same revelation.

---

a 1:11 Or "consecrated."
b 1:15 His name means "fugitive."
c 1:15 His name means "born of Hermes," a pagan god.
d 1:16 His name means "one who brings profit" or "profitable" or "help-bringer." The Orthodox tradition recognizes Onesiphorus as one of the seventy disciples chosen and sent by
   Jesus to preach. He became a bishop at Colophon (Asia Minor) and later at Corinth. Both
   the Orthodox and Roman Catholic churches hold that he died a martyr outside of Ephesus
   in the city of Parium.
e 1:18 This is an alternate translation of the Aramaic words found in v. 16. The translator has
   placed them here for the sake of the English narrative.
f 2:1 The Greek text literally means "my little child," and is used as a term of endearment.
g 2:2 Or "by way of many witnesses." These "witnesses" could be those people who also

³Overcome every form of evil^a as a victorious soldier of Jesus the Anointed One. ⁴For every soldier called to active duty must divorce himself from the distractions of this world so that he may fully satisfy the one who chose him.

⁵An athlete who doesn't play by the rules will never receive the trophy, *so remain faithful to God!*^b

⁶The farmer who labors to produce a crop should be the first one to be fed from its harvest.

⁷Carefully consider all that I've taught you, and may our Lord inspire you with wisdom and revelation *in everything you say and do.* ⁸But make Jesus, the Anointed One, your focus in life and ministry. For he came to earth as the descendant of David and rose from the dead, according to the revelation of the gospel that God has given me. ⁹This is the reason I am persecuted and imprisoned *by evildoers,*^c enduring the suffering of these chains—but the Word of God can never be chained! ¹⁰I endure all these hardships for the benefit of the chosen ones^d in Christ so that they may also discover the overcoming life that is in Jesus Christ, and experience a glory that lasts forever!

¹¹You can trust these words:

If we were joined with him in his death, then we are joined with him in his life! ¹²If we are joined with him in his sufferings,^e then we will reign together with him in his triumph. But if we disregard him, then he will also disregard us. ¹³But even if we are faithless, he will still be full of faith, for he never wavers in his faithfulness to us!^f

¹⁴Be committed to teach the believers all these things *when you are with them in the presence of the Lord.* Instruct them to never be drawn into meaningless arguments, or tear each other down with useless words that only harm others.

¹⁵Always be eager^g to present yourself before God as a perfect and mature minister, without shame, as one who correctly explains the Word of Truth.

---

heard Paul's teaching, or it may refer to the prophetic confirmations of the truth he taught to Timothy.
a 2:3 As translated from the Aramaic. The Greek says "suffer hardships."
b 2:5 Supplied by the context to complete the ellipsis.
c 2:9 The Greek text means "imprisoned as a criminal." However, the Aramaic word used here for "persecuted" can also be translated "crucified." Perhaps Paul is giving a prophecy of what would come. Later, Paul was indeed martyred either by crucifixion or beheading for his faith in Christ.
d 2:10 The Greek word here for "chosen" has embedded within it the word *logos*. God's chosen ones have been chosen by the word of God to become a living word sent from his mouth to reveal the message of their destiny.
e 2:12 An alternate Aramaic translation could read "If we preach the kingdom, we shall rule with him."
f 2:13 Or "he will not be unfaithful to himself."
g 2:15 An alternate Aramaic translation is "Don't become frustrated." The Greek word is *spoudazo*, an aorist imperative verb that could be translated, "Hurry and keep on hurrying,"

Avoid False Teachings

[16] And avoid empty chatter and worthless words,[a] for they simply add to the irreverence of those who converse in that manner. [17] For the words of Hymenaeus[b] and Philetus are like gangrene, *they have already spread their poison to many.* [18] They are lost to the truth *and teach gross error when* they teach that the resurrection of the dead has already passed.[c] They are guilty of subverting[d] the faith of some believers.

[19] But the firm[e] foundation of God has written upon it these two inscriptions: "The Lord God recognizes those who are truly his!"[f] and, "Everyone who worships the name of the Lord Jesus[g] must forsake wickedness!"[h]

Be a Pure Container of Christ

[20] In a palace you find many kinds of containers and tableware for many different uses. Some are beautifully inlaid with gold or silver, but some are made of wood or earthenware; some of them are used for banquets and special occasions, and some for everyday use. [21] But you, Timothy, must not see your life and ministry this way. *Your life and ministry must not be disgraced,* for you are to be a pure container of Christ and dedicated to the honorable purposes of your Master, prepared[i] for every good work that he gives you to do.

[22] Run as fast as you can from all the ambitions and lusts[j] of youth; and chase after all that is pure. Whatever builds up your faith and deepens your love must become your holy pursuit. And live in peace with all those who worship our Lord Jesus with pure hearts.

[23] Stay away from all the foolish arguments of the immature, for these disputes will only generate more conflict. [24] For a true servant of our Lord Jesus will not be argumentative[k] but gentle toward all and skilled in helping others see the truth, having great patience toward the immature. [25] Then with meekness you'll be able to carefully enlighten those who argue with you so they can

---

or "Consider it a serious matter and keep on considering it something serious to present yourself before God."

a 2:16 The Greek text could be translated "avoid corrupt and useless speakers," referring not to the words themselves, but to those who teach the flock. See v. 18.

b 2:17 See the first footnote for 1 Tim. 1:20.

c 2:18 The Aramaic can be translated "never going to happen."

d 2:18 The Greek literally means "turning upside down the faith of some."

e 2:19 Or "true." An alternate Aramaic translation of this verse could read "that resurrection is the firm foundation," referring to v. 18.

f 2:19 See Num. 16:5.

g 2:19 Or "Lord." By implication it is the Lord Jesus.

h 2:19 An alternate Aramaic translation could read "He will save from wickedness."

i 2:21 The Aramaic can be translated "appreciated."

j 2:22 The Greek text literally means "revolutionary desires."

k 2:24 An alternate Aramaic translation could read "You should not be argumentative with a true servant of the Lord."

see God's gracious gift of repentance and be brought to the truth. [26] This will cause them to rediscover themselves[a] and escape from the snare of Satan who caught them in his trap so that they would carry out his purposes.

Characteristics of the Last Days

3 But you need to be aware that in the final days the culture of society *will become extremely fierce and difficult for the people of God.* [2] People will be self-centered lovers of themselves[b] and obsessed with money. They will boast of great things as they strut around in their arrogant pride and mock all that is right. They will ignore their own families.[c] They will be ungrateful[d] and ungodly.

[3] They will become addicted to hateful and malicious slander.[e] Slaves to their desires, they will be ferocious, belligerent haters of what is good and right. [4] With brutal treachery, they will act without restraint, bigoted and wrapped in clouds of their conceit. They will find their delight in the pleasures of this world more than the pleasures of the loving God.

[5] They may pretend to have a respect for God, but in reality they want nothing to do with God's power. Stay away from people like these! [6] For they are the ones who worm their way into the hearts of vulnerable women,[f] spending the night with those who are captured by their lusts and steeped in sin. [7] They are always learning but never discover the revelation-knowledge of truth.

[8] *History has given us an example of this with the Egyptian sorcerers* Jannes and Jambres,[g] *who stood against Moses in their arrogance.* So it will be in the last days with those who reject the faith with their corrupt minds and arrogant hearts, standing against the truth of God.

[9] But they will not advance, for everyone will see their madness, just as they did with *Jannes and Jambres!*[h]

---

a 2:26 Or "come to their senses."

b 3:2 The Aramaic can be translated "men will look out only for themselves."

c 3:2 Or "disloyal to their people." The Greek is "disobedient to parents."

d 3:2 The Aramaic can be translated "rejecters of grace."

e 3:3 Because this phrase is also the description of the devil (the accuser or slanderer), it could be translated "they will be devils."

f 3:6 An alternate Greek translation could read "they intrude into households and by their heresies, take prisoners of those who are led astray by desires and sins." The Aramaic, however, is clearly speaking of the gross immorality of the last days.

g 3:8 This is a fascinating verse, for Jannes and Jambres are never mentioned by name in Exodus. It simply mentions the sorcerers who wanted to compete with Moses and his authority. These two names are, however, mentioned by Origen, one of the church fathers, who makes reference to the Book of Jannes and Jambres, but no complete copies of these books have ever been found.

h 3:9 Implied in the conclusion of Paul's argument.

Timothy's Loyalty

[10] But you, Timothy, have closely followed my example and the truth that I've imparted to you. You have modeled your life after the love and endurance *I've demonstrated in my ministry by not giving up*. The faith I have, *you now have*. What I have hungered for in life has now become *your longing as well*. The patience I have with others, *you now demonstrate*. [11] And the same persecutions and difficulties I have endured, *you have also endured*. Yes, you know all about what I had to suffer while in Antioch, Iconium, and Lystra. You're aware of all the persecution I endured there; yet the Lord delivered me from every single one of them! [12] For all who choose to live passionately and faithfully as worshipers of Jesus, the Anointed One, will also experience persecution.

[13] But the evil men and sorcerers[a] will progress from bad to worse, deceived and deceiving, as they lead people further from the truth. [14] Yet you must continue to advance in strength with the truth wrapped around your heart, being assured by God that he's the One[b] who has truly taught you all these things.

[15] Remember what you were taught from your childhood from the Holy Scrolls[c] which can impart to you wisdom to experience everlasting life through the faith of Jesus, the Anointed One! [16] Every Scripture[d] has been written by the Holy Spirit, the breath of God. It will empower you by its instruction and correction, giving you the strength to take the right direction and lead you deeper into the path of godliness. [17] Then you will be God's servant, fully mature and perfectly prepared to fulfill any assignment God gives you.

Paul's Farewell Message

4 Timothy, in the presence[e] of our great God and our Lord Jesus Christ, the One who is destined to judge both the living and the dead by the revelation of his kingdom—I solemnly instruct you to [2] proclaim the Word of God *and stand upon it no matter what!* Rise to the occasion and preach when it is convenient and when it is not. Preach in the full expression of the Holy Spirit[f]—with wisdom and patience as you instruct and teach the people.

[3] For the time is coming when they will no longer listen and respond to the healing words of truth *because they will become selfish and proud*. They will seek out teachers with soothing words that line up with their desires, saying just what they want to hear. [4] They will close their ears to the truth and believe

---

a 3:13 Or "deceivers." The Greek word is "sorcerers."
b 3:14 By implication "God." However, some interpret this as his teachers.
c 3:15 Or "sacred Scriptures."
d 3:16 Keep in mind that when Paul wrote this he was referring to the Torah and all the Old Testament writings. Today, "every Scripture" would include the New Testament as well.
e 4:1 Or "before the eyes of God." The Greek word is *enopion*, which could be translated "within eyesight of." Imagine looking into heaven and seeing the eyes of God gazing at you. This is the strength of Paul's charge to Timothy.
f 4:2 As translated from the Aramaic.

nothing but fables and myths. [a] [5] So be alert to all these things and overcome every form of evil. Carry in your heart the passion of your calling as *a church planter*[b] and evangelist, and fulfill your ministry calling.[c]

[6] And now the time is fast approaching for my release from this life and I am ready to be offered as a sacrifice.[d] [7] I have fought an excellent fight. I have finished my full course and I've kept my heart full of faith. [8] There's a crown of righteousness waiting in heaven for me, and I know that my Lord will reward me on his day of righteous judgment. And this crown is not only waiting for me, but for all who love and long for his unveiling.[e]

[9] Please come as soon as you can [10] since Demas deserted me and has left to go to Thessalonica, for he loves his own life.[f] Crescens has gone to Galatia, and Titus has gone to Dalmatia. [11] That leaves only Luke with me, so find Mark and bring him with you, for he is a tremendous help for me in my ministry.

[12] I have also dispatched Tychicus to Ephesus to minister there. [13] When you come, please bring the leather book bag[g] along with the books I left in Troas with Carpus—especially the parchment scrolls.

[14] You need to know that Alexander,[h] the jeweler,[i] has done me great harm. May our Lord give him what he deserves for all he has done. [15] Be careful of him, for he arrogantly opposes our ministry.

[16] At first there was no one I could count on to faithfully stand with me— they all ran off and abandoned me—but don't hold this against them. [17] *For in spite of this,* my Lord himself stood with me, empowering me to complete my ministry of preaching to all the non-Jewish nations so they all could hear the message and be delivered from the mouth of the lion![j] [18] And my Lord will continue to deliver me from every form of evil and give me life in his heavenly kingdom. May all the glory go to him alone for all the ages of eternity!

---

a 4:4 The Aramaic can be translated "ritualistic ceremonies."

b 4:5 Implied in the concept of being a New Testament evangelist. Apostolic missionaries sent out to evangelize were to plant churches wherever they ministered. Our contemporary concept of an evangelist is quite different than in Paul's day.

c 4:5 Or "being confident in your ministry."

d 4:6 Or "poured out as a drink offering."

e 4:8 Or "sudden appearance."

f 4:10 Or "he loves the world."

g 4:13 The Aramaic can be translated "carrying case." This would have been a bag made of leather or woolen cloth. The Greek text reads "bring the cloak." The Aramaic words for "book" and "cloak" are nearly identical, which would explain the Greek mistranslation using "cloak." It is fascinating that the aged Paul, nearing death, found his heart attached to the manuscripts and books that undoubtedly expounded on the Old Testament writings. He knew Jesus intimately, yet longed for more revelation of the written Word until his death.

h 4:14 *Alexander* means "protector of men" or "man-pleaser."

i 4:14 The word used here can also be "silversmith," "blacksmith" or "coppersmith."

j 4:17 Or "that they will hear that I have been delivered from the mouth of the lion." By implication, the lion is a metaphor for the devil.

[19] Please give my warm regards[a] to Prisca and to Aquila[b] and to Onesiphorus and his family.

[20] Erastus has remained in Corinth, but Trophimus I had to leave in Miletus due to his illness.[c]

[21] Do your best to come before winter.

Eubulus sends his greetings, along with Pudens, Linus,[d] and Claudia, and all those in prison with me.

[22] May the anointing of our Lord Jesus be with your spirit and his grace overflow to you!

Love in Christ,
Paul

---

a 4:19 The Aramaic can be translated "give peace."

b 4:19 *Prisca* is a diminutive form of Priscilla ("long life"). She and her husband, Aquila ("eagle"), were tentmakers like Paul. They were not only business partners with Paul, but also partners with him in ministry. See Acts 18:2, 18, 26; Rom. 16:3; 1 Cor. 16:19.

c 4:20 The Greek word used here can refer to physical or spiritual ailments.

d 4:21 In church history it was widely accepted and stated by Irenaeus that Linus was a disciple of Peter and became the bishop of Rome.

TITUS

Introduction

AT A GLANCE

Author: The apostle Paul
Audience: Titus, Paul's "true son"
Date: AD 57, possibly 62–63
Type of Literature: A letter
Major Themes: Salvation, church leadership, and right living
Outline:

    Letter Opening — 1:1–4
    Instructions to Titus — 1:5–16
    Instructions for Godly Living — 2:1–3:11
    Letter Closing — 3:12–15

ABOUT TITUS

Who was this friend of Paul named Titus? He was a Greek convert from Antioch and an apostolic church planter, much like Timothy, his peer. Paul describes him as a "true son" (1:4). He was likely a convert of Paul's ministry during his visit to Cyprus. Legend has it that Titus was a poet and a student of Greek philosophy when he had a prophetic dream that led him to study the Word of God and to become a Christ-follower. As God's faithful servant he traveled with Paul on his third missionary journey (2 Cor. 2:12–13; 7:5–15; 8:6–24). Paul commends him for his love, for his steadfast faith, and for bringing comfort to God's people.

After leaving Timothy in Ephesus, Paul accompanied Titus to Crete and left him there to establish the young church and set things in order. Believers who had been in the upper room had returned to Crete (Acts 2:11) and were in need of guidance and leadership from Titus.

Some say Paul wrote his letter to Titus as early as AD 57 from Nicopolis, prior to writing 2 Timothy. Others posit that he wrote this letter around the same time as he wrote his first letter to another young pastor, Timothy, around 62–63.

Titus is one of three letters commonly known as the Pastoral Epistles, which also include 1 and 2 Timothy. Paul wrote them as an older pastor to his younger colleagues, Timothy and Titus, to encourage their ministries among God's people and to give further instructions to the churches he had planted.

The theme of Titus is that right living will always accompany right doctrine. Good words will flow from a solid understanding of God's Word. In today's culture, it is easy to say that we follow Christ, but our faith in him will be demonstrated by godly living. An understanding of truth will bring a demonstration of purity through our lives. God's saving grace is the same grace that empowers us to live for him.

The book of Titus reminds us that right beliefs should impact every area of our lives: family, relationships, work, and community.

PURPOSE

Like his letters to Timothy, Paul wrote this letter to Titus in order to give him instructions for building churches and raising up leaders. It was to be considered as a church-planting manual, helping this young apostle to encourage godly living and to establish godly churches.

It appears that Paul's first letter to Timothy and this one to Titus were both written around the same time, given the close parallels in the themes addressed. From church administration to confronting false teaching to maintaining the purity of personal conduct, Paul offered sage advice and pastoral wisdom to these young ministers. In the case of Titus, Paul wrote to address basic catechesis relevant to new believers, as well as the kinds of problems expected of a young church in a pagan culture. He also wrote his former companion to ask him to remain in Crete and care for the young church in Paul's absence, as well as to encourage the two companions accompanying the letter.

AUTHOR AND AUDIENCE

As with the two letters to Timothy, Paul's letter to Titus is a deeply personal one, for it was written from mentor to mentee—from an older, wiser, seasoned pastor to a younger, inexperienced minister. It's a letter between former colleagues on the frontline of missions, as Paul sought to give roots to the work they had started together by nurturing the community of believers through Titus's leadership.

Like Timothy, Paul had left Titus among his own ethnic people to continue the work they had started as a team; in this case, on the Greek island of Crete. As a convert of Paul, his "true son in the faith" (1:4), Titus became a trusted colleague in his gospel work. In fact, many believe the two made a missionary journey to Crete to evangelize the Greek island, occurring after the events of Acts 28 and before writing 2 Timothy, when Paul was imprisoned. As a young pastor stewarding a young church plant, Titus must have viewed Paul's letter as a welcomed breeze inflating the sails of his ministry!

MAJOR THEMES

Faith and Salvation in Jesus Christ. You would expect a letter from one ministry colleague to another to center on the good news of salvation in Christ. And Titus is indeed infused with it! After laboring alongside each other to proclaim the gospel, Paul recognized that their work was unfinished. He wanted Titus "to further the faith of God's chosen ones and lead them to the full knowledge of the truth that leads to godliness" (1:1) by discipling the young church in their shared salvation.

Part of how Paul emphasized this faith and salvation was by calling on Titus to appoint godly leaders to serve as examples to teach the faith, lead people to salvation, refute false teachings that destroy faith and distract from this salvation, and imitate the practical results of this faith: godly living resulting from salvation.

He also offered a basic catechism, or summary of primary Christian beliefs. He reminded them of the grace manifested in Jesus and the salvation he brought for all. He also reminded them of their previous fallen nature, how they "were easily led astray as slaves to worldly passions and pleasures" and "wasted [their] lives in doing evil" (3:3). And he shared with them a royal "hymn of salvation by grace," which declared the wonders of God's compassion, his overflowing love, and our new birth through our salvation by faith.

Appointing Church Leadership. The work of salvation among God's people and sharing the gospel within culture requires leaders who are of sound character and judgment. As he did with Timothy, Paul instructed Titus to appoint church leaders (elders or overseers) who were blameless, faithful in marriage and had well-behaved children, gentle and patient, and never drunk, violent, or greedy. They were to set an example for the rest of the community of believers in how they should live the truth of the gospel through godly living. They were also to firmly grasp the gospel message taught to them, in order to teach other believers the essential truths of the faith and how to respond to false teaching. This rubric for spirit-anointed leaders still serves as a trusted guide for church leadership.

Right Living for the Sake of the Gospel. Right living (orthopraxy) and right believing (orthodoxy) go hand in hand in Paul's letter to Titus. For when we believe in the gospel, and experience the joys of salvation, how else could we live other than in light of this mercy?

One thing Paul emphasizes, however, is that the gospel's grace actually trains us to live rightly. "This same grace," says Paul, "teaches us how to live each day as we turn our backs on ungodliness and indulgent lifestyles, and it equips us to live self-controlled, upright, godly lives in this present age" (2:12). Paul also emphasizes the need for godly men and women within the church to come alongside others to teach them to live rightly. May our right believing never excuse wrong living. And may our right living be evidence of our right believing.

TITUS

A Godly Life

Introduction

From Paul, God's willing slave[a] and an apostle of Jesus, the Anointed One, *to Titus.*[b] I'm writing you to further the faith[c] of God's chosen ones and lead them to the full knowledge of the truth that leads to godliness, [2] which rests on the hope of eternal life. God, who never lies, has promised us this before time began. [3] In his own time he unveiled his word through the preaching *of the gospel*, which was entrusted to me by the command of God our Life Giver.[d]

[4] Titus, you are my true son in the faith we share. May grace and peace descend to you from God the Father and our Savior, the Anointed One, Jesus!

Qualities of Church Leaders

[5] The reason I stationed you in Crete[e] was so that you could set things in order and complete what was left unfinished,[f] and *to raise up and* appoint *church* elders[g] in every city, just as I had instructed you. [6] Each of them must be above reproach, devoted solely to his wife,[h] whose children are believers and not rebellious or out of control. [7] The overseer, since he serves God's household,[i] must be someone of blameless character and not be opinionated or short-tempered. He must

---

a 1:1 Or "bondservant."

b 1:1 Although the name Titus is not found until v. 4, it is included here to enhance the understanding of Paul's introduction.

c 1:1 Or "according to the faith of God's elect."

d 1:3 As translated from the Aramaic. The Greek is "Savior."

e 1:5 A Greek island in the Aegean Sea. Paul's ship had stopped on the way to Rome at Fair Havens, a small harbor on the southern coast of Crete (Acts 27:7–12).

f 1:5 The unfinished work would be bringing believers into maturity in Christ and raising up godly, qualified leaders who could teach the church and lead it forward.

g 1:5 Or "ordain elders." This is the Greek word *presbyteros,* which means "senior leaders." These are church elders who would function as overseers, teachers, and shepherds of God's flock. The same Greek word is used for women in 1 Tim. 5:2. Although generally assumed to be male in the cultural context of that day, there is nothing to indicate that *presbyteros* is gender exclusive. The church elder is called an "overseer" (or "bishop") in v. 7, which indicates that both terms speak of the same office and are synonymous.

h 1:6 Or "the husband of one wife" or "married only once."

i 1:7 Or "God's steward."

not be a drunkard or violent or greedy. [8] Instead he should be one who is known for his hospitality and a lover of goodness. [a] He should be recognized as one who is fair-minded, pure-hearted, and self-controlled. [9] He must have a firm grasp of the trustworthy message that he has been taught. This will enable him to both encourage others with healthy teachings and provide convincing answers to those who oppose his message.

False Teachers

[10] There are many wayward people, smooth talkers, and deceivers—especially the converts from Judaism. [b] [11] They must be silenced [c] because they are disrupting entire families with their corrupt teachings, all for their dishonest greed. [12] A certain one of them, one of their own prophets, [d] said, "Those Cretans are nothing but liars, worthless beasts, and lazy gluttons." [e] [13] He certainly knew what he was talking about! For this reason, correct them thoroughly so that their lives will line up with the truths of our faith. [14] Instruct them not to pay any attention to Jewish myths or follow the teachings of those who reject the truth.

[15] *It's true that* all is pure to those who have pure hearts, but to the corrupt unbelievers nothing is pure. Their minds and consciences are defiled. [16] They claim to know God, but by their actions they deny him. They are disgusting, disobedient, and disqualified from doing anything good.

Character Consistent with Godliness

2 Your duty is to teach them to embrace a lifestyle that is consistent with sound doctrine. [2] Lead the male elders [f] into disciplined lives full of dignity and self-control. Urge them to have a solid faith, generous love, and patient endurance.

[3] Likewise with the female elders, [g] lead them into lives free from gossip and drunkenness and to be teachers of beautiful things. [h] [4] This will enable them to teach the younger women [i] to love their husbands, to love their children, [5] and

---

a 1:8 The Aramaic can be translated "one who nurtures goodness" (in others). We would say, "one who brings out the best in others."

b 1:10 Or "those of the circumcision" (group), i.e., Jewish converts. Paul is pointing to three types of people who will refute and argue with church leaders: rebels, empty talkers, and deceivers. The leaders (elders) must be faithful to the Scriptures in order to correct them and set them in order.

c 1:11 Or "reined in." The Greek word *epistomizo* is used for the reins of a horse.

d 1:12 Although the Greek uses the word *prophet*, it is not used here in the biblical sense of a "prophet" of God, for the author of this proverb was a pagan.

e 1:12 A quote from the Oracles of Epimenides, a six-century BC poet. The first line is quoted from The *Hymn to Zeus* by Callimachus.

f 2:2 Or "old men."

g 2:3 Or "old women."

h 2:3 As translated from the Aramaic. The Greek is "good things."

i 2:4 Paul is contrasting the "elders" with the "younger" (Gr. *neos*) and could possibly be referring to those who are newly converted.

to be self-controlled and pure, taking care of their household and being devoted to[a] their husbands. By doing these things the word of God will not be discredited. [6]Likewise, guide the younger men into living disciplined lives *for Christ*.

Be an Example

[7]Above all, set yourself apart as a model of a life nobly lived. With dignity, demonstrate integrity in all that you teach.[b] [8]Bring a clear, wholesome message[c] that cannot be condemned, and then your critics will be embarrassed, with nothing bad to say about us.[d]

[9]Servants[e] are to be supportive of[f] their masters and do what is pleasing in every way. They are not to be argumentative [10]nor steal[g] but prove themselves to be completely loyal and trustworthy. By doing this they will advertise[h] through all that they do the beautiful teachings of God our Savior.

God's Grace, Our Motivation

[11]God's marvelous grace[i] has manifested *in person*, bringing salvation for everyone.[j] [12]This same grace teaches us how to live each day as we turn our backs on ungodliness and indulgent lifestyles,[k] and it equips us to live self-controlled, upright, godly lives in this present age.[l] [13]For we continue to look forward to the joyful fulfillment of our hope in the dawning splendor[m] of the glory of our great

---

a 2:5 Or "supportive of."

b 2:7 "Integrity in all that you teach" would imply serious study of God's Word and its personal application in our lives, and not teaching impulsively from one's opinion, which only leads to arguments and divisions. This kind of integrity gives someone the right to be heard.

c 2:8 Or "with sound speech."

d 2:8 Paul and Timothy were a team. If one were to err, it would affect the other.

e 2:9 Or "bondservants."

f 2:9 Or "submitted to."

g 2:10 Businesses today lose millions of dollars to employee theft. Believers are to be meticulously honest in the workplace.

h 2:10 Or "adorn [beautify] the doctrine of God."

i 2:11 Grace extends God's kindness and love to us every moment and makes us "worthy" of his acceptance. Grace is unconditional, unmerited, indescribable favor from God.

j 2:11 That is, grace has revealed a salvation available for everyone. Or "God's marvelous grace has appeared to all, bringing salvation."

k 2:12 The Greek word for "ungodliness" is singular, while the word for "indulgent lifestyles" is plural. This has led some scholars to believe that we are to turn our backs on both the root principle of ungodliness and the specific acts that result from ungodliness.

l 2:12 These three adjectives—"self-controlled," "upright," and "godly"—refer to our behavior, our behavior toward others and toward God.

m 2:13 The Greek word is *epiphaneia* (epiphany) and is a nominalized verb that means "a brightness shining all around." It was through *epiphaneia*, the beautiful appearing of Christ as a baby, that a wonderful hope was brought to all the world.

God and Savior, Jesus, the Anointed One. [a] [14] He sacrificed himself for us that he might purchase our freedom from every lawless deed and to purify for himself a people who are his very own, [b] passionate to do what is beautiful in his eyes.

[15] So preach these truths and exhort others to follow them. Be willing to expose sin in order to bring correction with full authority, [c] without being intimidated [d] by anyone.

Believers' Conduct in Society

3 Remind people to respect [e] their governmental leaders on every level as law-abiding citizens and to be ready to fulfill their civic duty. [2] *And remind them* to never tear down anyone with their words or quarrel, [f] but instead be considerate, humble, and courteous to everyone. [3] For it wasn't that long ago that we behaved foolishly in our stubborn disobedience. We were easily led astray as slaves to worldly passions and pleasures. We wasted our lives in doing evil, and with hateful jealousy we hated others.

The Hymn of Salvation by Grace

[4] When the extraordinary compassion of God our Savior [g]
and his overpowering love suddenly appeared *in person,*
as the brightness of a dawning day, [h]
[5] he came to save us.
Not because of any virtuous deed that we have done
but only because of his extravagant mercy.
[6] He saved us,

---

a 2:13 Or "our great God and our Savior, Jesus Christ." Note the four great truths of grace in vv. 11–13: (1) Grace is a person—"our great God and Savior, Jesus, the Anointed One." (2) Grace brings salvation for all. (3) Grace educates us on how to live pure lives. (4) Grace brings a hope of the manifestation (appearing) of Christ. This is a hope worth waiting for.
b 2:14 We are a people encircled by God himself. The compound Greek word *periousios* is translated from "around," as a circle, and the verb "to be." It can mean something surrounded by something. It can be charted by a dot within a circle. As the circle surrounds the dot, so God is around each one of his saints. The circle has the dot all to itself. So God has his very own all to himself. We are unique in that we belong only to him. Uniquely his, we are monopolized by God, taken into himself by grace through faith and surrounded by his love.
c 2:15 Or "Speak these things; exhort or rebuke [speak in order to expose sin and bring correction] with all authority."
d 2:15 Or "disregarded."
e 3:1 Or "be subject to."
f 3:2 Or "strive with others." The implication is that we accept the differences of others and allow people to be who they are and not try to make them over into our image of who we think they should be.
g 3:4 Many scholars believe that vv. 4–7 are ancient Christian poetry or perhaps the words to a hymn.
h 3:4 Implied in the Greek word *epiphainō* (epiphany), which means "to shine forth [brightly] in an appearing."

resurrecting us[a] through the washing of rebirth.
We are made completely new by the Holy Spirit,[b]
whom he splashed over us richly
by Jesus, the Messiah, our Life Giver.
[7] So as a gift of his love,
and since we are faultless—
innocent before his face—
we can now become heirs *of all things*,
all because of an overflowing hope of eternal life.

[8] How true and faithful is this message!

Faith Produces Good Works

I want you to especially emphasize[c] these truths, so that those who believe in God will be careful to devote themselves to doing good works. It is *always* beautiful and profitable *for believers* to do good works.

[9] But avoid useless controversies,[d] genealogies,[e] pointless quarrels, and arguments over the law, which will get you nowhere.[f] [10] After a first and second warning, have nothing more to do with a divisive person *who refuses to be corrected*. [11] For you know that such a one is entwined with his sin and stands self-condemned.

Paul's Coworkers

[12] When I send Artemas[g] or Tychicus[h] to you, be sure to meet me at the City of Victory,[i] for I've decided to spend the winter there.

[13] Give a generous send-off to Zenas the scribe[j] and Apollos,[k] and send them on their journey with what they need.

---

a 3:6 As translated from the Aramaic.

b 3:6 All three members of the Trinity are mentioned in vv. 4–6 and are seen as active participants in our salvation.

c 3:8 Or "affirm strongly," a hapax legomenon.

d 3:9 The Aramaic can be translated "offensive debates."

e 3:9 The Aramaic can be translated "tribal traditions."

f 3:9 See also Heb. 13:9.

g 3:12 Artemas, or "Artemas of Lystra," was considered to be one of the seventy disciples whom Jesus sent out.

h 3:12 Tychichus, an Ephesian, was a beloved coworker of Paul and is mentioned five times in the New Testament (here; Acts 20:4; Eph. 6:21; Col. 4:7; 2 Tim. 4:12). He was listed among the seventy disciples whom Jesus sent out according to Hippolytus of Rome. See Francis Mershman, "St. Tychicus" (1913) *Catholic Encyclopedia*, Charles Herbermann, editor.

i 3:12 Or "Nicopolis," a Greek city on the western shore. Nicopolis means "the City of Victory."

j 3:13 Or "lawyer." The word translated "lawyer" can be used for either Greek or Roman law. Zenas is considered to be one of the seventy whom Jesus sent out.

k 3:13 Apollos was a powerful preacher and coworker of Paul, who was very influential in the church of Corinth. He is listed ten times in the New Testament (Acts 18:24; 19:1; 1 Cor. 1:12; 3:4–6, 22; 4:6; 16:12). Jerome states that Apollos, after Paul's letters brought healing

Conclusion

[14] Encourage the believers to be passionately devoted to beautiful works of righteousness by meeting the urgent needs of others and not be unfruitful.

[15] Everyone here with me sends their loving greetings to you. Greet the believers who love us in the faith. May God's wonderful grace be with you all!

Love in Christ,
Paul [a]

---

to the divisions of the church in Corinth, returned and became an elder (overseer) in the church. See Jerome, *Commentary on the Epistle of Titus.*

a 3:15 The Aramaic adds, "The end of the letter written by Paul to Titus from Nicopolis, sent by the hand of Zenas and Apollos."

PHILEMON

Introduction

AT A GLANCE

Author: The apostle Paul

Audience: Philemon, a slave owner

Date: AD 60–61

Type of Literature: A letter

Major Themes: Christian love, Christian belonging, fellowship, and slavery

Outline:

    Letter Opening — 1–3

    Paul's Appreciation for Philemon — 4–7

    Paul's Appeal on Behalf of Onesimus — 8–21

    Letter Closing — 22–25

ABOUT PHILEMON

Paul's letter to Philemon is perhaps one of the most fascinating portions of our New Testament. It is a letter written with one purpose—to bring reconciliation between two brothers in Christ. It is a letter that promotes forgiveness as the key to unity and reconciliation. Everyone has experienced being offended, and everyone has offended another person. Yet in Christ, there is enough love to cover all sin and enough forgiveness to reconcile with those who have hurt or wounded us.

Here's the backstory of this intriguing letter: Philemon had been one of Paul's numerous coworkers in ministry. There was much history between Paul and Philemon, a person Paul considered a dear and trusted friend. It is believed that Philemon was wealthy and, along with his wife, led a dynamic house church in the city of Colossae, a city in Asia Minor (modern-day Turkey). Although Paul had never visited Colossae, there remained a strong bond of friendship between Philemon and Paul.

Apparently, Philemon owned a slave who stole from him and ran away. His name was Onesimus. (Onesimus means "useful" or "valuable." See Col. 4:9. This reference of Onesimus in Colossians suggests that Colossians was written shortly after Philemon.) By events that only God could orchestrate, the fugitive Onesimus found himself imprisoned next to Paul. Through the ministry of the Holy Spirit, Paul led his fellow prisoner to the Lord.

Paul sent the runaway slave back to Philemon carrying this letter in his hand asking his former master to fully receive Onesimus and be restored to him as a fellow believer. A slave who ran away could be punished by death according to the Roman laws of this era, yet Paul not only said Philemon should forgive him, but also love him as a brother returning home. This made-for-a-movie plot is contained in this very short letter you are about to read.

Orthodox Church tradition tells us that Onesimus served Christ faithfully throughout his life and became the bishop of the church of Ephesus after Timothy's death. The slave-turned-bishop was later taken once again as a prisoner to Rome where he testified before his judge Tertylus. He was condemned to death by stoning, and afterwards his corpse was beheaded in AD 109.

We should be grateful to God for gifting us this letter, because the dignity of every human being is brought forth powerfully in the story of Philemon and Onesimus—a story of forgiving love!

PURPOSE

The apostle Paul wrote his friend Philemon, a slave owner, mainly to encourage him to forgive and restore his slave Onesimus—and to do so no longer as a slave but as a brother in Christ. The theme of the book of Philemon is forgiving love. Love forgives, restores, covers sin, and heals broken relationships. The sweetness of reconciliation is an incomparable joy. Only the love of Christ has the power to perform such a glorious restoration of relationships. We can thank God that he has given us this amazing letter to bring hope that forgiveness is waiting—waiting for all of us to experience for ourselves.

AUTHOR AND AUDIENCE

While a prisoner for the sake of the gospel, the apostle Paul wrote to a slave owner named Philemon. Although four names are listed in the letter's opening, it was customary in ancient letters to list the primary addressee first. It is clear throughout the main body of the letter that Paul singled out a single individual in his appeal: Philemon. This letter was a precious piece of correspondence between brothers bound by Christian love.

And yet it wasn't entirely private, for two other names and "the church" were also included, revealing the important bond between brothers and sisters in their activities through their common faith in Christ. This letter becomes a window into the heart of God for Christ's community, urging generous forgiving love.

MAJOR THEMES

Christian Belonging in a Common Faith. Mentioning Apphia and Archippus, as well as Philemon's house church, turned what might have been a private conversation into a public appeal. Though Paul may have been seeking to exert some sort of social pressure on Philemon, one of the enduring, relevant teachings of this letter is that our private business is a matter for the believing community since we belong to one another in a common faith.

Paul's use of *koinōnia* (Gr. for "fellowship") in v. 6 captures this reality. When people commit themselves to Christ, they are also committing themselves to a community. They bind themselves and become identified with one another so that they receive both the benefits and responsibilities of that "belonging." Paul invited Philemon and Onesimus, in addition to the house church, to think through the radical implications of their belonging to one another as slave and master, as well as a believing community.

The Love of Christ Performed. It is clear from Paul's entire work, as well as the general tone of this letter, that his appeal was rooted in the love of Christ. Paul wanted Philemon to respond to Onesimus in forgiveness and restoration in the same way Christ has responded to us. The manner in which Paul wrote his appeal and advocated for Onesimus—his tone and tenor, his words and arguments—also reflected the tender love of Christ.

We perform the same love that Christ himself performed. Paul performed Christ's love when he advocated for Onesimus, and in the way he appealed to Philemon. And he wanted Philemon to follow his performance with his slave-turned-brother.

Slavery and Brotherhood. There's an obvious facet to the relationship between Philemon and Onesimus: slavery. To our modern ears we think of the antebellum South and the injustices of the eighteenth and nineteenth centuries. Yet slavery looked quite different in the first century, so Paul wouldn't have necessarily viewed it as sinister, and he didn't seem to offer a treatise on abolitionism in his letter.

Still Paul is clearly interested that "we no longer see each other in our former state—Jew or non-Jew, [enslaved or free] . . . because we're all one through our union with Jesus Christ with no distinction between us" (Gal. 3:28). He wanted Philemon to reflect this common union in how he treated Onesimus: "welcome him no longer as a slave, but more than that, as a dearly loved brother" (v. 16). Onesimus had gone from being a valuable slave to a valuable brother in Christ (vv. 10–11).

This letter, then, seems to be less about slavery and more about the relationship between a slave and his master, now brothers in the Lord, both of whom Paul wants to experience forgiving love.

PHILEMON

Forgiving Love

¹⁻² From Paul, a prisoner[a] of the Anointed One, Jesus, and Timothy our brother, to Philemon,[b] our precious friend and companion in this work, and to the church that meets in his house, along with our dear sister Apphia and our fellow soldier Archippus.[c]

³ May God our Father and the Lord Jesus Christ pour out his grace and peace upon you.

Philemon's Faith and Love

⁴ I am always thankful to my God as I remember you in my prayers ⁵ because I'm hearing reports about your faith in the Lord Jesus and how much love you have for all his holy followers. ⁶ I pray for you that the faith we share[d] may effectively deepen your understanding of every good thing that belongs to you in Christ. ⁷ Your love *has impacted me* and brings me great joy and encouragement, for the hearts of the believers have been greatly refreshed through you, dear brother.

Paul's Request on Behalf of Onesimus

⁸ Even though I have enough boldness in Christ that I could command you to do what is proper, ⁹⁻¹⁰ I'd much rather make an appeal because of our friendship. So here I am, an old man,[e] a prisoner for Christ, making my loving appeal to

---

a 1–2 In other letters from Paul, he describes himself as an apostle, but here, writing to his dear friend, there is no need to remind Philemon of his apostleship.

b 1–2 *Philemon* means "affectionate" and is derived from the Greek word *philema*, which means "kiss."

c 1–2 *Apphia* means "fruitful one" and is believed to be the name of Philemon's wife. Archippus means "master of the horse" and was possibly their son's name. See also Col. 4:17.

d 6 This is somewhat ambiguous, for the Greek is literally "for the sharing of the faith of you." It can mean a number of things, including the common faith that Paul and Philemon shared, or it could mean the faith that Philemon shared with others through evangelism. The Aramaic can be translated "May your association [fellowship] of believers [Philemon's house church] be fruitful in works and in the knowledge of all that you possess in Jesus, the Messiah."

e 9–10 Some manuscripts have "an ambassador" in place of "an old man."

you. It is on behalf of my child, whose spiritual father I became[a] while here in prison; that is, Onesimus.[b] [11] Formerly he was not useful or valuable to you, but now he is valuable to both of us. [12] He is my very heart,[c] and I've sent him back to you *with this letter*.

[13] I would have preferred to keep him at my side so that he could take your place as my helper during my imprisonment for the sake of the gospel.[d] [14] However, I did not want to make this decision without your consent, so that your act of kindness[e] would not be a matter of obligation but out of willingness.

[15] Perhaps *you could think of it this way*: he was separated from you for a short time so that you could have him back forever. [16] So welcome him no longer as a slave, but more than that, as a dearly loved brother. He is that to me especially, and how much more so to you, both humanly speaking and in the Lord.

[17] So if you consider me your friend and partner, accept him the same way you would accept me. [18] And if he has stolen anything[f] from you or owes you anything, just place it on my account.

[19] I, Paul, have written these words in my own handwriting. I promise to pay you back everything, to say nothing of the fact that you owe me your very self.[g]

[20] Yes, my brother, enrich my soul[h] in the Lord—refresh my heart in Christ! [21] I'm writing to you with confidence that you will comply with my request and do even more than what I'm asking.

[22] And would you do one more thing for me? Since I'm hoping through your prayers to be restored to you soon, please prepare a guest room for me.

[23] Epaphras, my fellow prisoner in the Anointed One, Jesus, sends his

---

a   9–10 The Aramaic can be translated "whom I birthed with my chains (while in prison)."

b   9–10 Paul employs a masterful play on words, for the name Onesimus means "useful" or "valuable." The book of Philemon is a masterpiece of grace, tact, and love.

c   12 The Aramaic can be translated "for he is my son." It would be hard to imagine a more powerful way to describe the affection between Paul and his spiritual son, Onesimus. The one who gave us the love chapter (1 Cor. 13) demonstrated that love in his relationships, even with those who were much younger than he.

d   13 Or "in the chains of the gospel." The Aramaic changes the object of the phrase to Onesimus: "I took him to serve me, chained to God's message, on your behalf."

e   14 By implication, this act of kindness refers to Philemon receiving the fugitive slave back with love and forgiveness.

f   18 Although the Greek verb *adikeō* means "to do wrong" or "to defraud," the clear implication is that Onesimus had stolen from his master.

g   19 By implication, it was Paul who had brought the message of life to Philemon and became his "spiritual father" as well.

h   20 Or "benefited" or "profited." This is a play on words that would not be lost on the educated Philemon, for it is taken from the root word for "Onesimus" ("profitable").

greetings of peace[a] to you, [24] and so does Mark,[b] Aristarchus,[c] Demas,[d] and Luke, my companions in this ministry.

[25] May the unconditional love[e] of the Lord Jesus, the Anointed One, be with your spirit![f]

---

[a] 23 The cultural greeting of that day would be peace or "shalom."

[b] 24 That is, "John Mark." See Acts 15:36–40. This shows that John Mark was fully restored in his relationship and partnership with the apostle Paul. Since Mark's death was in Alexandria in AD 62, the book of Philemon was obviously written before then. This is the only place in the New Testament that records Mark and Luke being in the same place. Paul had two Gospel writers who traveled with him.

[c] 24 *Aristarchus* means "best prince" ("ruler"). He was also known as Aristarchus of Thessalonica and is identified in church history as one of the seventy whom Jesus sent out. He was both a ministry companion of Paul and Paul's "fellow prisoner" (Col. 4:10).

[d] 24 *Demas* means "governor of the people." Demas would later desert Paul and turn back to the world. See 2 Tim. 4:10.

[e] 25 Or "grace."

[f] 25 The Aramaic adds a postscript: "End of the letter of Philemon, which was written from Rome and sent by the hands of Onesimus."

HEBREWS

Introduction

AT A GLANCE

Author: Unknown, but possibly Paul, Barnabas, Apollos, or Priscilla
Audience: Christians converted from Judaism
Date: AD 50–64
Type of Literature: A sermon in the form of a letter
Major Themes: Jesus, the Old Testament, faith, perseverance, and heaven
Outline:

Prologue — 1:1–3
Jesus' Superiority over Angels and Moses — 1:4–4:13
Jesus' Superior Priesthood — 4:14–7:28
Jesus' Superior Sacrifice and Covenant — 8:1–10:18
A Call to Persevere — 10:19–12:29
Final Instructions and Greetings — 13:1–25

ABOUT HEBREWS

The book of Hebrews presents the magnificent Jesus on every page!

The light of the Messiah brings truth out from the shadows and it shines brightly for all to see. Hebrews is written for every believer today, for we have crossed over from darkness to light and from doubt to faith. The name Hebrews means, "those who crossed over." We have passed from shadows to substance and from doubt to the reality of faith. What once was a symbol has now become substance, for all the pictures of the Old Testament have found their fulfillment in Jesus.

Hebrews takes us into the holy of holies as we come to him as priests, lovers, and worshipers. You will never be the same again when you absorb the light of God that shines from every chapter.

Jesus is the theme of Hebrews. You must learn from him and draw closer to him in order to understand the depth of this book, for Jesus is the language of God! When God now speaks to us, he speaks in the vocabulary of Jesus Christ. All of the Bible points to him. Can we truly understand the Bible if we don't come to him?

Hebrews is a divinely inspired composition given to show us the magnificence of Jesus as our glorious High Priest. He is greater than the law, the angels, the system of temple worship, and greater than any high priest or religious structure. Because our royal Priest gave his sacred blood for us, we now have unrestricted access to the holiest place of all. With no veil and nothing hindering our intimacy with God, we can come with an unbelievable boldness to his mercy-throne where we encounter enough grace to empower us through every difficulty. We find our true life in his presence.

Heaven's words are now before you, so read them with spiritual hunger and a passion to embrace truth, and live them out by the grace of Jesus, our Messiah.

God will help you!

PURPOSE

The purpose of the pastor's sermon is evident the further you read his letter: he is trying to prevent those he's addressing from abandoning their Christian faith and returning to Judaism. Along the way, the author teaches them—and us—about the superiority of Christ above the religious institutions of Moses and the Old Testament. The sermon-letter is filled with references to the old sacrificial system and priesthood of ancient Israel and explains how Jesus' death has replaced this old religious system—making it the perfect book to understand how Jesus' story fulfills Israel's story!

AUTHOR AND AUDIENCE

The book of Hebrews was most likely written sometime around AD 50–64. It had to have been written prior to Clement of Rome citing it as inspired (AD 95) and before the Roman war that destroyed the temple in AD 67–70. Though Hebrew's true authorship is unknown, the earliest church fathers taught that Hebrews was written in Hebrew by Paul for the Jewish people. Eusebius (AD 260–339) refers to an even earlier apostolic father, Clement of Alexandria (AD 150–211), who confirms without question that Paul wrote Hebrews in the Hebrew language for the Hebrew people. (See Eusebius, *History*, Book VI: XIV.) More recent scholarship, however, has begun to question this and speculate that it was written by Barnabas, Apollos, Priscilla, or another one of Paul's close associates.

Regardless of who wrote it, we are more certain about who read it—or rather, who first heard it read out loud, because Hebrews seems to be more of a sermon contained in a letter. The inscription placed on the original document is "To the Hebrews," and the major themes point to a group of Jewish Christians who may have been getting cold feet, wondering if they should return to Judaism. This sermon-letter is so steeped in ancient Jewish practices that it seems very likely the author is addressing Christians converted from Judaism. And yet, the letter still speaks to us today as those who enter into a better covenant by faith in Jesus Christ.

MAJOR THEMES

Christology: Christology is the study of the Christ, the Messiah, and this letter is a full-on course about our heavenly Savior! The revelation of Jesus fills the pages of Hebrews and it will set you free! He is our magnificent High Priest who is greater than Moses, greater than any sacrifice ever offered, greater than any prophet of old. He perfects our faith until we rise with him into the heavenly realm of priestly ministry. He warns us of turning back into ritual and religion, forgetting all the treasures of our faith. He stirs us to enter into the full rest by seeing Jesus alone as our perfection before the Father.

The Old Covenant Fulfilled: One of the central themes of Hebrews is the relationship of the new covenant established by the blood of Jesus, the Messiah to the old or "first covenant." Look at all the Old Testament imagery the pastor uses: Moses, the high priest, Melchizedek, the priestly order of Aaron, offerings and sacrifices, the ark of the covenant, and the Most Holy Place. Even though we are far removed from the original religious system of rules and rituals found in the Old Testament, we cannot afford to ignore the pastor's message: The high priesthood of Jesus is inherent to his identity as our all-sufficient Rescuer and Revealer!

The Reality of Heaven: The Hebrews sermon often speaks about heaven's reality. The pastor reveals it's the place where God keeps his throne; to be in heaven means to be in God's very presence; in it are the names of everyone whom God calls his own; and it is the place where our ultimate redemption and atonement took place. This last revelation of heaven is especially important, because Hebrews explains the old religious order of rules and rituals is no longer necessary because of the final sacrifice made for all people. All God commanded under the first covenant on earth became obsolete and disappeared thanks to what Jesus accomplished in heaven! The heavenly temple is where our ultimate salvation was accomplished, of which the earthly one could not.

Definition and Practice of Faith: Nowhere is there a better definition and explanation of faith in the New Testament than in the sermon-letter of Hebrews: "Now faith brings our hopes into reality and becomes the foundation needed to acquire the things we long for. It is all the evidence required to prove what is still unseen" (11:1). This is a far cry from the traditional understanding that faith is merely belief. Biblical faith claims a confidence beyond our own because it rests in the character of God, the foundation of our faith. Part of practicing faith is persevering in it. Despite the fact we live in a world that refuses to acknowledge God and opposes the church, we are called to persevere in our faith in him, just like the "great witnesses who encircle us like clouds" (12:1)! Hebrews warns against turning away in rebellion and unbelief, telling us the very divine message that saved us is the same one that will condemn us if we turn away.

HEBREWS

Living Faith

Jesus, the Language of God

1 Throughout our history God has spoken to our ancestors by his prophets in many different ways. The revelation he gave them was only a fragment at a time, *building one truth upon another.* [a] [2] But to us living in these last days, [b] God now speaks to us openly in the language of a Son, [c] the appointed Heir of everything, for through him God created the panorama of all things and all time. [d]

[3] The Son is the dazzling radiance of God's splendor, [e] the exact expression of God's true nature—his mirror image! [f] He holds the universe [g] together and expands it [h] by the mighty power of his spoken word. [i] He accomplished for us the complete cleansing of sins, [j] and then took his seat on the highest throne at the right hand [k] of the majestic One. [l]

---

a   1:1 The Greek is "God spoke in different times in different parts." That is, he reveals one piece and then another, like pieces of a puzzle, with one piece complementing the other. The Aramaic can be translated "God spoke to our ancestors by all methods and at any price" or "in every way, shape, and form." That is, by sample and by example God reveals his ways progressively, building on previous understandings, leading us into Christ's fullness.

b   1:2 This phrase, often used by the prophets of the Old Testament, speaks of our current time in human history between Acts 2 (Pentecost) and the coming again of Christ.

c   1:2 Or "he has spoken through a Son." We speak in English; God speaks in "Son," for Jesus is the language of God. The Sonship of Jesus is the language he now uses to speak to us.

d   1:2 Or "the complete period of all existence." The Aramaic can be translated "universes." Both the concept of "all things," and "all time" (the ages), are implied in the text.

e   1:3 Or "the out-shining [effulgence] of God's glory." The Aramaic can be translated "He is the Sprout of God, the image of his glory."

f   1:3 Or "the Son is God's mirror image and exact expression" (the reflection of God).

g   1:3 The Aramaic can be translated "He is almighty."

h   1:3 The Greek word *phero*, has as its primary meaning "to carry along" or "to move [something] forward." Forward motion is implied. (See *Strong's Concordance*, Gr. 5342.)

i   1:3 This is the Greek word *rhema*, which is the sayings of the Son, or "his spoken word."

j   1:3 Or "Because he had accomplished our purification from sins" (atonement).

k   1:3 That is, the place of highest honor and authority. See Ps. 110:1. Some have proposed that v. 3 is an ancient Christian hymn that summarizes our faith.

l   1:3 Or "the Majesty," a periphrasis for God.

Jesus, Greater than Angels

[4] He is infinitely greater than angels, for he inherited a rank and a Name[a] far greater than theirs. [5] For God has never said to any angel what he said to Jesus:

"You are my favored Son, today I have fathered you."[b]

And this:

"I will be the Father to him, and he will be the Son to me."[c]

[6] And again, when he brought his firstborn Son into the world:

"Let all my angels bow down before him
and kiss him in worship."[d]

[7] And about his angels he says,

"I make my angels swift winds,
and my ministers[e] fiery flames."[f]

[8] But about his Son, he called him "God,"[g] saying,

"Your throne, O God, endures forever and ever
and you will rule your kingdom
with justice and righteousness,[h]
[9] For you have cherished righteousness
and detested lawlessness.
For this reason, God, your God, has anointed you[i]
and poured out the oil of bliss on you[j]
more than on any of your friends."

---

a 1:4 This is *Ha-Shem*, in the Aramaic, the common title for God. This elevates the meaning of the passage much clearer than Greek, for Jesus is now given the "Name," that is, he has the title of God (*Ha-Shem*, the Name).

b 1:5 The Aramaic can be translated "Every day I beget you." See Ps. 2:7, 12.

c 1:5 See 2 Sam. 7:14; 1 Chron. 17:13.

d 1:6 See Ps. 97:7. The Greek word used for worship, *proskuneo*, includes three concepts: "to bow," "to kiss," and "to pay homage (worship)." All three are included here. This seems to be referring to Christ's birth, however, some interpret this to be when Jesus was exalted and ascended into heaven.

e 1:7 The Greek word *leitourgos* means "those who read the liturgy" or "priests."

f 1:7 See Ps. 104:4.

g 1:8 Clearly implied in the text and made explicit.

h 1:8 The Greek used here can mean either justice or righteousness; this translation includes both. The text is literally "the righteous scepter is the scepter of your kingdom."

i 1:9 The word *Messiah* means "Anointed One." There is a clear and unmistakable poetic play on words by reading the Aramaic (*Mashkhakh Alaha Alahakh Meshka*, almost a complete reversing of the sounds of the first into the second), that is lost in the Greek.

j 1:9 Or "the oil of rejoicing." See Ps. 45:6–7.

[10] And he called him Lord, [a] saying,

"Lord, you formed the earth in the beginning [b]
    and with your own hands you crafted the cosmos. [c]
[11] They will both one day disappear,
    but you will remain forever!
    They will all fade like a worn-out garment,
[12] And they will be changed like clothes,
    and you will fold them up and put them away.
    But you are 'I AM.' [d]
    You never change, years without end!" [e]

[13] And God has never said this to any of his angels:

"Take your seat next to me at my right hand
    until I force your whispering enemies [f]
    to be a rug under your feet." [g]

[14] What role then, do the angels have? The angels are spirit-messengers sent by God to serve those who are going to be saved. [h]

A Warning Not to Drift from Truth

2 This is why it is so crucial that we be all the more engaged and attentive to the truths [i] that we have heard so that we do not drift off course. [2] For if the message of the law spoken and confirmed by angels [j] brought a just penalty to every disobedient violation; [3] then how would we expect to escape *punishment* if we despise the very truths that give us life? [k] The Lord himself was the first

---

a 1:10 Clearly implied in the text and made explicit.

b 1:10 See Ps. 102:25–27.

c 1:10 See Ps. 8:1–3.

d 1:12 As translated from the Aramaic, which is literally "you are as you are." This is a variation of the name of God revealed to Moses in Ex. 3:14, "I AM who I AM." There is an obvious connection here to that incident and endorses the truth that the preincarnate Christ was the One who appeared in the burning bush.

e 1:12 The Aramaic can be translated "the years will not age you."

f 1:13 As translated from the Aramaic.

g 1:13 Or "a footstool for your feet." See Ps. 110:1. Placing the feet on a defeated enemy was a gesture of triumph. See Josh. 10:24; 1 Kings 5:3.

h 1:14 The Aramaic can be translated "The angels are spirit-winds-of-ministry sent to minister to those destined to receive salvation." The angels are glad to minister to us, for they see us "in Christ."

i 2:1 Or "things," by implication "truths."

j 2:2 See Deut. 33:2; Ps. 68:17; Acts 7:38, 53. Angels participated in the giving of the Torah.

k 2:3 As translated from the Aramaic. This appears to be a quote from Deut. 32:47. The Greek is "how will we escape if we neglect such a great salvation." There are six significant warnings in Hebrews: (1) Here in 2:1–4 we are warned not to drift away from the power of

to announce these things, and those who heard him firsthand confirmed their accuracy. [4] Then God added his witness to theirs. He validated their ministry with signs, astonishing wonders, all kinds of powerful miracles, [a] and by *the gifts of* the Holy Spirit, [b] which he distributed as he desired.

Jesus, and the Destiny of Believers

[5] For God will not place the coming world, of which we speak, under the government of angels. [6] But the Scriptures affirm:

> What is man that you would even think about him,
>> or care about Adam's race.
> [7] You made him lower than the angels for a little while. [c]
>> You placed your glory and honor
>> upon his head as a crown.
>> And you have given him dominion
>> over the works of your hands, [d]
> [8] For you have placed everything under his authority. [e]

This means that God has left nothing outside the control of his Son, even if presently we have yet to see this accomplished. [9] But we see Jesus,

---

our great salvation. (2) In 3:7–4:13 we are warned about failing to enter into the faith-rest life with the failure of the Israelites in the wilderness as an example. (3) In 5:11–6:12 we are warned to be devoted to the full assurance of our hope until life's end. (4) In 10:23–39 we are warned of not sinning willfully after we have received the truth. (5) In 12:1–17 we are given the warning of God's correction as our faithful Father. (6) In 12:25–29 we are warned not to close our hearts to the voice of the One who speaks from heaven.

a 2:4 Signs, wonders, and miracles, were all components of the ministries of the New Testament believer. There is no place in Scripture to indicate that any of the works of Jesus or his apostles should not be seen today. See John 14:12; Acts 2:22, 43; 5:12; 6:8; 8:13; Rom. 15:19; 2 Cor. 12:12; Gal. 3:5.

b 2:4 Or "by distributions of the Holy Spirit." The Greek word for "distribution" is often used for dividing an inheritance. The word *gifts* is implied in the text and made explicit.

c 2:7 See Ps. 8:4–6. The Aramaic can be translated "Who is man that you would give a thought toward him, for whom the Son of Man should be pledged [to be offered for them]." The phrase "son of man" is used in the New Testament consistently for Jesus Christ, the "Son of Man." The Hebrew text of Ps. 8 refers to man being made a little lower than *Elohim* (God), which can also mean "mighty angels." This seemed to be a problem to the translators of the Septuagint, so they rendered it "lower than angels." Hebrews seems to closely follow the Septuagint; however, the Greek text of Hebrews changes the quotation to read "a little while lower."

d 2:7 This last sentence is missing in some Greek manuscripts; however early and important ones include it, as well as the Aramaic.

e 2:8 Or "you subjected all things under his feet." The command given to both Adam and Eve to "take dominion" (Gen. 1:28) has never been rescinded. The planet will one day be under the rulership of men and women who are under the rulership of Christ.

who as a man, lived for a short time lower than the angels and has now been crowned with glorious honor because of what he suffered in his death. For it was by God's grace [a] that he experienced death's bitterness on behalf of everyone! [b]

Jesus Brings Many Sons to Glory

[10] For now he towers above all creation, for all things exist through him and for him. [c] And that God made him, pioneer [d] of our salvation, perfect through his sufferings, for this is how he brings many sons and daughters to share in his glory. [e] [11] Jesus, the Holy One, makes us holy. And as sons and daughters, we now belong to his same Father, [f] so he is not ashamed or embarrassed to introduce us as his brothers and sisters! [g] [12] For he has said,

> "I will reveal who you really are [h] to my brothers and sisters,
>   and I will glorify you with praises
>   in the midst of the congregation."

[13] And,

> "My confidence rests in God!" [i]

And again he says,

> "Here I am, *one with* [j] the children Yahweh has given me." [k]

[14] Since all his "children" have flesh and blood, so Jesus became human to fully identify with us. He did this, so that he could experience death and annihilate the effects of the intimidating accuser who holds against us the power [l]

---

a 2:9 A few manuscripts and some external evidence has instead "he, apart from God [separated from God], tasted death." This could be taken to mean that he experienced death only in his humanity and not in his divinity. The Aramaic can be translated "God himself, by his grace, experienced death in the place of every person."

b 2:9 Or "everything," that is, he redeems humanity and restores creation to his original plan.

c 2:10 The Greek word *prepo* means "to stand out and tower above."

d 2:10 Or "trailblazer" or "forerunner." His perfection through sufferings implies that all his sons will come to glorious perfection through hardships. The Aramaic can be translated "the Prince of Life."

e 2:10 Or "bring many children into his glorious state." Grace gives us the glory that Jesus has. Although it is true that God will not share his glory with another (Isa. 42:8), but in Christ, we are not "another," we are one with him. See also John 17:22; Rom. 8:29–30.

f 2:11 Or "we are all from [out of] one." That is, we are all out of one Source, God the Father.

g 2:11 See Song. 4:9–10; 5:1–2.

h 2:12 Or "I will announce your name." This quote is taken from Ps. 22:22.

i 2:13 See Ps. 31:14; Isa. 8:17.

j 2:13 Jesus is one with us, his children.

k 2:13 By implication "Here I am, in the midst of the sons and daughters you have given me."

l 2:14 Or "dominion."

of death. [15] By embracing death Jesus sets free those who live their entire lives in bondage[a] to the tormenting dread of death. [16] For it is clear that he didn't do this for the angels, but for all the sons and daughters of Abraham. [b] [17] This is why he had to be a Man and take hold of our humanity in every way. He made us his brothers and sisters and became our merciful and faithful King-Priest[c] before God; as the One who removed our sins to make us one with him. [18] He suffered and endured every test and temptation, so that he can help us every time we pass through the ordeals of life. [d]

Jesus, Greater than Moses

3 And so, dear brothers and sisters, you are now made holy, and each of you is invited to the feast[e] of your heavenly calling.[f] So fasten your thoughts fully onto Jesus,[g] whom we embrace[h] as our Apostle and King-Priest. [i] [2] For he was faithful to the Father who appointed him, in the same way that Moses was a model of faithfulness in what was entrusted to him.[j] [3] But Jesus is worthy to receive a much greater glory than Moses, for the one who builds a house deserves to be honored more than the house he builds. [4] Every house is built by someone, but God is the Designer and Builder of all things.

[5] Indeed, Moses served God faithfully in all he gave him to do. [k] His work

---

a 2:15 Or "slavery."

b 2:16 See Isa. 41:8.

c 2:17 The Aramaic can be translated "so that he would be the nurturing Lord of the king-priests."

d 2:18 This chapter gives us the 8 victories Christ won for us at Calvary: (1) He is crowned with glory and honor. (2) He brings many sons into his glory. (3) He is made perfect through his sufferings. (4) We are made holy. (5) By his death he destroyed the devil, who held the power of death over us. (6) He delivers us completely from the fear of death. (7) He is now our faithful High Priest. (8) He helps us in every temptation.

e 3:1 Or "sharers of the feast."

f 3:1 Or "you participate as partners in the heavenly calling." The Greek phrase, "heavenly calling" implies an invitation to a celestial feast. It could also be translated "you are called to share the life of heaven." This calling originates in heaven and draws us into heaven. However, in the Aramaic this phrase can be translated "called with a calling [from heaven]," which is the Aramaic title of the third book of the Torah, Leviticus, and refers to the calling of the Levites as priests.

g 3:1 Or "you have discovered this Jesus." The Aramaic can be translated "Jesus, the Messiah."

h 3:1 Or "with whom is our legally binding agreement."

i 3:1 God joins the apostolic and priestly ministries together in Christ. An apostle will always release God's people into their priestly calling of entering into the holy of holies without going through a system, a church or a person. The word "King-Priest" is from the Aramaic, which uses a word for a priest not of the Levitical order. Jesus could not be a "High Priest" for he was not born in the tribe of Levi, or a descendant of Aaron, but was of the tribe of Judah. So the word here for priest is not, *cohen*, but the Aramaic word, *kumrea*, the word used for Jethro and Melchizedek. See Gen. 14:18; Ex. 2:16; 3:1; 18:1.

j 3:2 Or "who was faithful in all his house." See Num. 12:7.

k 3:5 Or "in all God's house."

prophetically illustrates[a] things that would later be spoken and fulfilled.[b] 6 But Christ is more than a Servant, he was faithful as the Son in charge of God's house. And now we are part of his house if we continue courageously to hold firmly to our bold confidence and our victorious hope.[c]

Secrets from Psalm 95

7 This is why the Holy Spirit says,[d]

"If only you would listen to his voice this day![e]
8 Don't make him[f] angry by hardening your hearts,
    like your ancestors did during the days of their rebellion,[g]
    when they were tested in the wilderness.
9 There your fathers tested me and tried my patience[h]
    even though they saw my miracles[i] for forty years
    they still doubted me![j]
10 This ignited my anger with that generation
    and I said about them, 'They wander in their hearts
    just like they do with their feet,
    and they refuse to learn my ways.'
11 My heart grieved[k] over them so I decreed:
    'They will never enter into the calming rest of my Spirit!'"

12 So search your hearts every day,[l] my brothers and sisters, and make sure that none of you has evil or unbelief hiding within you. For it will lead you

---

a 3:5 Or "to testify." The Aramaic can be translated "he believed all the evidence in the house" (or "tabernacle"). That is, Moses saw and believed that the tabernacle and all its furnishings were an illustration of something greater that God would unveil later on.

b 3:5 Or "to give testimony to things that would be spoken."

c 3:6 As translated from the Aramaic. The Greek is "the pride [rejoicing] of our hope."

d 3:7 See Ps. 95:7–11. Notice the truth that the Bible is the Holy Spirit of God speaking to us.

e 3:7 The Aramaic can be translated "the echo of his voice." See also v. 15.

f 3:8 As translated from the Aramaic.

g 3:8 The Aramaic could be translated "just like the bitterness at Marah."

h 3:9 This refers to incidents that took place at Massah [testing] and Meribah [strife]. See Ex. 17:7; Num. 20:13. The Septuagint, instead of transliterating those names, translates their meanings and includes them here in the text. A Hebrew reader would have no difficulty in understanding the obvious inference of the rebellion that took place in the desert.

i 3:9 Or "works," however, these works are miracles, when considering the plagues of Egypt, the Passover miracle, the parting of the Red Sea, the manna falling from the sky, water from the rock, etc.

j 3:9 The Greek is taken from the Septuagint and is literally "There they tested me by trial." That is, they continually doubted God's faithfulness to them. We must never doubt God, even in a season of difficulty.

k 3:11 The Greek word orge is used for any emotion of extreme passion, usually anger.

l 3:12 As translated from the Aramaic. The Greek is "Take care."

astray,[a] and make you unresponsive to the living God. [13] This is the time to encourage[b] each other to never be stubborn or hardened by sin's deceitfulness.[c] [14] For we are mingled with the Messiah,[d] if we will continue unshaken in this confident assurance[e] from the beginning until the end.

[15] For again, the Scriptures say,[f]

If only today you would listen to his voice.
Don't make him angry[g] by hardening your hearts,
as you did in the wilderness rebellion.

[16] The same people who were delivered from bondage and brought out of Egypt by Moses, were the ones who heard and still rebelled. [17] They grieved God for forty years[h] by sinning in their unbelief, until they dropped dead in the desert. [18] So God swore an oath that they would never enter into his calming place of rest all because they disobeyed him. [19] It is clear that they could not enter *into their inheritance* because they wrapped their hearts in unbelief.

The Faith-Rest Life

4 Now God has offered to us the same promise of entering into his realm of resting in confident faith. So we must be extremely careful to ensure that we all embrace the fullness of that promise and not fail to experience it. [2] For we have heard the good news of deliverance just as they did, yet they didn't join their faith with the Word.[i] Instead, what they heard didn't affect them deeply, for they doubted. [3] For those of us who believe, faith activates the promise and we experience the realm of confident rest! For he has said,[j]

"I was grieved[k] with them and made a solemn oath,
'They will never enter into the calming rest of my Spirit.'"

---

a 3:12 Or "rebel against."

b 3:13 Or "warn."

c 3:13 The Aramaic can be translated "the sin of the deceiver." The deceiver could be referring to the devil, or to our own ability to be self-deceived.

d 3:14 Or "We are all business partners of Christ." The Aramaic can be translated "We are all sewn [together] with Christ."

e 3:14 The Aramaic can be translated "we are joined [leavened] in the resurrection through him."

f 3:15 See Ps. 95:7–8.

g 3:15 As translated from the Aramaic.

h 3:17 See Num. 14:33–34.

i 4:2 Or "because they did not join in with those who heard the message with faith" (Joshua and Caleb).

j 4:3 See Ps. 95:11; Heb. 3:11.

k 4:3 The Greek word *orge* is used for any emotion of extreme passion, usually anger.

God's works have all been completed from the foundation of the world,[a] [4] for it says in the Scriptures,[b]

And on the seventh day God rested from all his works.

[5] And again, as stated before,

They will never enter into my calming place of rest.

[6] Those who first heard the good news of deliverance failed to enter into that realm of faith's-rest because of their unbelieving hearts. Yet the fact remains that we still have the opportunity to enter into the faith-rest life and experience the fulfillment of the promise! [7] For God still has ordained a day for us to enter into called "Today." For it was long afterwards that God repeated it in David's words,

"If only today you would listen to his voice
    and do not harden your hearts!"

[8] Now if this promise of "rest" was fulfilled when Joshua brought the people into the land,[c] God wouldn't have spoken later of another "rest" yet to come. [9] So we conclude that there is still a full and complete "rest"[d] waiting for believers[e] to experience. [10] As we enter into God's faith-rest life we cease from our own works, just as God *celebrates his finished works and* rests in them.[f] [11] So then we must give our all and be eager to experience this faith-rest life, so that no one falls short by following the same pattern of doubt and unbelief.

[12] For we have the living Word of God, which is full of energy,[g] and it pierces more sharply than a two-edged sword.[h] It will even penetrate to the

---

a   4:3 Or "God's works have been completed, even though the world has fallen." The Greek word *katabole* means "to fall down," "to throw down." It is most often used for "laying down a foundation," but it can imply the fall of humanity through sin. Even though the world has fallen, God's works have already been accomplished, unhindered by the sin of man. God's finished works supersede the brokenness of our planet.

b   4:4 See Gen. 2:2.

c   4:8 See Josh. 21:44; 22:4.

d   4:9 Or "Sabbath." The Aramaic can be translated "He arose to be the Sabbath for the people of God."

e   4:9 Or "the people of God."

f   4:10 The word used for "Sabbath" in v. 9 is not the usual word, it is the celebratory aspects of the Sabbath that are emphasized in the Greek word *sabbatismos*.

g   4:12 The Aramaic can be translated "all effective." There is a hint here of the spinning sword of fire, held by the angel guarding the way to the Tree of Life. To come eat its fruit, you must pass through the mighty sword of fire. The context implies we pass through this "fire-sword" on our way into the holy of holies. When the veil was split in two, the cherubim embroidered on the veil parted, as it were, to allow every worshiper to enter into the unveiled presence of God. See Gen. 3:24; Matt. 27:51.

h   4:12 Or "than a two-mouthed sword." God speaks his word, then we, in agreement, also speak his word and it becomes a two-mouthed sword.

very core of our being where soul and spirit, bone [a] and marrow meet! [b] It interprets and reveals the true thoughts and secret motives of our hearts. [13] There is not one person who can hide their thoughts from God, for nothing that we do remains a secret, and nothing created is concealed, but everything is exposed and defenseless before his eyes, to whom we must render an account. [c]

Jesus, Our Compassionate King-Priest

[14] So then, we must cling in faith to all we know to be true. For we have a magnificent King-Priest, [d] Jesus Christ, the Son of God, who rose into the heavenly realm for us, and now sympathizes with us in our frailty. [e] [15] He understands humanity, for as a Man, our magnificent King-Priest was tempted in every way just as we are, and conquered sin. [f] [16] So now we come freely and boldly to where love is enthroned, [g] to receive mercy's kiss and discover the grace we urgently need to strengthen [h] us in our time of weakness. [i]

A King-Priest like Melchizedek

5 For every High Priest was chosen from among the people and appointed to represent them before God by presenting their gifts to God and offering sacrifices on their behalf. [2] Since the High Priest is also one who is clothed in weakness, he humbles himself [j] by showing compassion to those who are ignorant of God's ways and stray from them. [3] And for this reason, he has to not only present the sin offerings of others, but also to bring a sin offering for himself. [4] And no one takes this honor upon himself by being self-appointed, but God is the one who calls each one, just as Aaron was called.

[5] So also, Christ was not self-appointed and did not glorify himself by

---

a 4:12 As translated from the Aramaic, the Greek is "joint."

b 4:12 Soul and spirit are the immaterial parts of every person that make us who we are, joint and bone marrow are the physical aspects of our existence. All of this combined forms our humanity. God's Word has the ability to uncover our hidden aspects and make them known.

c 4:13 The word used here is *logos*. The Greek could also be translated "in his view the Word is our responsibility."

d 4:14 As translated from the Aramaic, which uses a word for a priest not of the Levitical order. The Aramaic word here for priest is not *cohen* but *kumrea*.

e 4:14 The Aramaic can be translated "who has sorrow with us in our affliction."

f 4:15 As translated from the Aramaic. The Greek is "He was without sin" (sinless).

g 4:16 Or "the throne of grace."

h 4:16 The Greek word *boetheia* means "urgent help," and is often used as "reinforcing" (a ship in a storm). See Acts 27:17.

i 4:16 The Aramaic can be translated "tribulation."

j 5:2 As translated from the Aramaic. There is an alternate translation of the Aramaic which reads "He [Christ] humbled himself and took the sorrows of those who knew nothing and were lost, for he was also clothed in frailty [humanity]."

becoming a high priest, but God called and glorified him![a] For the Father said to him,

> "You are my favored Son. Today I have fathered you."[b]

[6] And in another Scripture he says about this new priestly order,

> "You are a Priest like Melchizedek,[c] a King-Priest forever!"

[7] During Christ's days on earth[d] he pleaded with God, praying with passion and with tearful agony that God would spare him from death.[e] And because of his perfect devotion his prayer was answered and he was delivered. [8] But even though he was a wonderful Son,[f] he learned to listen[g] and obey through all his sufferings. [9] And after being proven perfect in this way he has now become the source of eternal salvation to all those who listen to him and obey. [10] For God has designated him as the King-Priest who is over the priestly order of Melchizedek.[h]

Moving On into Full Maturity

[11] We have much to say about this topic although it is difficult to explain,[i] because you have become too dull and sluggish to understand. [12] For you should already be professors instructing others by now; but instead, you need to be

---

a 5:5 Apparently, many Jewish believers were having difficulty with Jesus being our High Priest, since he was not of Aaron's lineage from the tribe of Levi. The Holy Spirit is showing us that his priesthood is not on the basis of lineage, but the supernatural calling of God, much like Melchizedek. The meaning of the name Melchizedek is "king of righteousness."

b 5:5 The Aramaic can be translated "Every day I beget you." See Ps. 2:7, 12; Heb. 1:5.

c 5:6 Or "in the succession of Melchizedek." See Ps. 110:4.

d 5:7 Or "During the days when Christ wore flesh."

e 5:7 That is, from a premature death in Gethsemane. The text clearly states that Jesus was spared from death. What death? He gave his life on the cross for us. This seems to reveal that Jesus prayed in the garden to be spared from death that night and live long enough to die on the cross, and not prematurely die in the garden. Most expositors believe this was the "cup" of God's wrath that was the sin payment. Yet it is possible that the "cup" he was asking God to let pass from him was the cup of premature death in the garden, not the death he would experience the next day on the cross. He had already sweat drops of blood, but the prophecies had to be fulfilled of being pierced on a cross for our transgressions. God answered his cry and he lived through the agony of Gethsemane so that he could be our sacrifice for sin on Calvary. Jesus did not waver in the garden. We have a brave Savior! See John 18:11.

f 5:8 As translated from the Aramaic.

g 5:8 The Greek word for obedience, *hupakoe*, means "to hearken" or "to listen for the knock on the door" or "to pay attention." Also in v. 9. (See *Strong's Concordance*, Gr. 5218 and 5219.) Jesus' sufferings were seen as lessons of listening to and obeying God.

h 5:10 As translated from the Aramaic. Jesus, our magnificent King-Priest, has made us kings and priests that serve him and extend his kingdom on the earth. See 1 Peter 2:9–10; Rev. 5:8–10.

i 5:11 The Aramaic can be translated "We have so much more to say about Melchizedek, but his manifestation overwhelms us and makes it difficult to explain."

taught from the beginning the basics of God's prophetic oracles![a] You're like children[b] still needing milk and not yet ready to digest solid food. [13] For every spiritual infant who lives on milk is not yet pierced[c] by the revelation of righteousness.[d] [14] But solid food is for the mature, whose spiritual senses perceive *heavenly matters*. And they have been adequately trained by what they've experienced to emerge[e] with understanding of the difference between what is truly excellent and what is evil and harmful.

Moving On to Deeper Truth

6 Now is the time for us to progress beyond the basic message of Christ[f] and advance into perfection. The foundation has already been laid for us to build upon: turning away from our dead works[g] to embrace faith in God, [2] teaching about different baptisms,[h] impartation by the laying on of hands,[i] resurrection of the dead, and eternal judgment. [3] So with God's enablement[j] we will move on to deeper truths.

A Warning to Never Turn Away

[4] It is impossible to restore an apostate.[k] For once a person has come into God's light, and tasted the gifts of the heavenly realm, and has received the Holy

---

a 5:12 Or "the elements of the beginnings of the oracles of God." That is, how Jesus is the substance and fulfillment of the oracles (message) of God.

b 5:12 The Greek word *nepios* means "still unfit to bear arms," that is, unprepared for battle.

c 5:13 Or "inexperienced." The Greek word *apeiros* means "unpierced." (See *Strong's Concordance*, Gr. 552, 586, 3984, and 4008.)

d 5:13 The Aramaic can be translated "they are not unversed in the language [manifestation] of righteousness."

e 5:14 As translated from the Aramaic.

f 6:1 Or "the Word [*Logos*] of the beginning of Christ."

g 6:1 Or "useless deeds." "Dead works" are the attempts of people to please God through religion, keeping religious laws and traditions, and serving others to gain influence with God. There was one "work" that brings life to all, that was the work of Christ on the cross.

h 6:2 The New Testament speaks of seven baptisms, including the baptism of fire, the baptism of the Holy Spirit, the baptism of suffering (Jesus' cross), the baptism into the cloud, the baptism into Moses, the baptism of repentance, and water baptism.

i 6:2 This was done in the Old and New Testaments to heal, to bless others, to impart the Holy Spirit and his gifts, to identify with a person (or sacrifice), and to release others to their calling and ministry.

j 6:3 Or "If God entrusts it to us." The Aramaic uses here the title for God "the Lord YHWH."

k 6:4 That is, one who has abandoned their faith. Because of the extraordinary length of the Greek sentence, this summary statement implied in the text is given here at the beginning of the paragraph for the sake of English narrative. To say it is impossible does not mean that God cannot bring them to repentance, but that he chooses to leave them in their hardened state, much like Pharaoh who hardened his heart to God. The Aramaic is very clear, "they cannot be renewed to conversion."

Spirit,[a] [5] and feasted on the good Word of God, and has entered into the power of the age that is breaking in,[b] [6] if he abandons his faith, there is no use even trying to lead him to repentance. By their sin of apostasy[c] they re-crucify the Son of God,[d] and have publicly repudiated him.[e]

[7] *For men's hearts* are just like the soil that drinks up the showers which often fall upon it. Some soil will yield crops as God's blessing upon the field. [8] But if the field continues to produce only thorns and thistles[f] a curse hangs over it and it will be burned.

[9] Having said that, beloved, we are fully convinced that there are more beautiful and excellent things, which flow from your salvation.[g]

[10] For God, the Faithful One, is not unfair.[h] How can he forget[i] the work you have done for him? He remembers the love you demonstrate as you continually serve[j] his beloved ones[k] for the glory of his name. [11] But we long to see you passionately advance until the end and you find your hope fulfilled. [12] So don't allow your hearts to grow dull[l] or lose your enthusiasm, but follow the example of those who fully received what God has promised[m] because of their strong faith and patient endurance.[n]

God's Faithful Promise

[13] Now when God made a promise to Abraham, since there was no one greater than himself, he swore an oath on his own integrity[o] to keep the promise as sure as God exists! [14] So he said,

> "Have no doubt, I promise to bless you over and over,
>   *and give you a son* and multiply you without measure!"

[15] So Abraham waited patiently in faith and succeeded in seeing the promise

---

a 6:4 Or "has been in [business] partnership with the Holy Spirit."

b 6:5 Or "the age that is about to come."

c 6:6 As translated from the Aramaic and implied in the Greek.

d 6:6 Or "it is impossible to crucify the Son of God again for them to change their own minds!"

e 6:6 Or "have made a public spectacle of him." The Aramaic can be translated "insulted the Son of God."

f 6:8 These are the consequences of sin from the time of Adam. See Gen. 3:18.

g 6:9 Or "things which cling to salvation."

h 6:10 The Aramaic can be translated "God is not evil."

i 6:10 He won't remember our sins, but will remember our works of loving service to others.

j 6:10 The Greek text implies financially providing for others.

k 6:10 Or "saints" (or "holy ones").

l 6:12 The Greek word for "dull of heart" is *nothros*, which is taken from a root word meaning "illegitimate child." The implication is that we don't see ourselves as a child of illegitimacy, but as a child of intimacy, and that keeps our relationship fervent and passionate.

m 6:12 The Aramaic can be translated "to those who were heirs of the royal proclamation."

n 6:12 The Aramaic can be translated "because of their faith and the outpouring of the Spirit."

o 6:13 See Gen. 22:16–17.

fulfilled. [a] [16] It is very common for people to swear an oath by something greater than themselves, for the oath will confirm their statements and end all dispute. [17] So in the same way, God wanted to end all doubt and confirm it even more forcefully to those who would inherit his promises. His purpose was unchangeable, so God added his vow to the promise. [18] So it is impossible for God to lie for we know that his promise and his vow will never change!

And now we have run into his heart to hide ourselves in his faithfulness. This is where we find his strength and comfort, for he empowers us to seize what has already been established ahead of time—an unshakeable hope! [19] We have this certain hope like a strong, unbreakable anchor holding our souls to God himself. Our anchor of hope is fastened *to the mercy seat* [b] which sits in the heavenly realm beyond the sacred threshold, [c] [20] and where Jesus, our forerunner, [d] has gone in before us. He is now and forever our royal Priest like Melchizedek. [e]

The Melchizedek Priesthood

7 [1-2] Melchizedek's name means "king of righteousness." He was the King of Peace, because the name of the city he ruled as king was Salem, which means "peace." And he was also a priest of the Most High God. Now when Abraham was returning from defeating many kings in battle, Melchizedek went out to meet him and blessed him. Then Abraham took a tenth of everything he had won in battle and gave it to Melchizedek. [f] [3] This Melchizedek has no father or mother, and no record of any of his ancestors. He was never born and he never died, but his life is like a picture [g] of the Son of God, a King-Priest forever! [4] Now let me show you proof of how great this Melchizedek is:

— Even though Abraham was the most honored and favored patriarch of all God's chosen ones, [h] he gave a tithe of the spoils of battle

---

a 6:15 That is, through the birth of Isaac. The Aramaic is fascinating, for the name of Abraham is not in the Greek text in this verse: "And he [God] bestowed his Spirit and he [Abraham] received the kingdom."

b 6:19 Implied in the text and made explicit as that which is found inside the innermost chamber.

c 6:19 As translated from the Aramaic, which is literally "beyond the faces of the door."

d 6:20 Or "trailblazer." Jesus has blazed a trail for us to enter into the sacred chamber and seize the hope that has been fulfilled in his eyes already, to have a company of king-priests who will dwell with him in the holiest of holies and minister from there out to the nations of the earth. The clear implication of vv. 19–20 is that he takes us in to share his throne and his ministry as the royal Priest.

e 6:20 Or "in the order [likeness] of Melchizedek."

f 7:1–2 See Gen. 14:17–20.

g 7:3 Or "made to resemble."

h 7:4 Implied in the text with the comparison made explicit.

to Melchizedek. [5] It would be understandable if Melchizedek had been a Jewish priest, for later on God's people were required by law to support their priests financially, because the priests were their relatives and Abraham's descendants. [6] But Melchizedek was not Abraham's Jewish relative, [a] and yet Abraham still paid him a tithe.

- Melchizedek imparted a blessing on mighty Abraham, who had received the promises of God. [7] And no one could deny the fact that the one who has the power to impart a blessing is superior to the one who receives it.

- [8] Although the Jewish priests received tithes, they all died—they were mortal. But Melchizedek lives on!

- [9] It could even be said that Levi, the ancestor of every Jewish priest who received tithes, actually paid tithes to Melchizedek through Abraham. [10] For although Levi was yet unborn, the seed from which Levi came was present in Abraham [b] when he paid his tithe to Melchizedek.

- [11] If any of the Levitical priests who served under the law had the power to bring us into perfection, then why did God send Christ as Priest after the likeness of Melchizedek? He should have said, "After the likeness of Aaron."

- [12] And furthermore, for God to send a new and different rank of priest, meant a new law would have had to be instituted even to allow it!

Jesus and the Priesthood of Melchizedek

[13] Yet the One these things all point to, was from a different tribe and no one from that tribe ever officiated at God's altar, [14] for we all know that our Lord didn't descend from the tribe of Levi, but shined from the tribe of Judah. [c] And Moses himself never said anything of a priest in connection with Judah's tribe.

[15] And all this is made even clearer if there was another King-Priest raised up with the rank of Melchizedek. [16] This King-Priest did not arise because of a genealogical right under the law to be a priest, but by the power of an indestructible, *resurrection* life! [d]

[17] For it says in the Psalms,

---

a 7:6 Or "does not share their ancestry."

b 7:10 Or "Levi was in the loins of his father Abraham." In effect, Abraham submitted all his sons to the priesthood of Melchizedek.

c 7:14 As translated from the Aramaic.

d 7:16 The word *indestructible* comes from a word that means, "tied together in unity," that is, "a united life" (or "union with God"). Resurrection life is implied, for the priestly ministry of Jesus began after he was raised from the dead. The Aramaic can be translated "He has life-giving power that has no beginning." Jesus' ministry of Prophet, Priest, and King flows from his unlimited life of resurrection power!

You are like Melchizedek, a King-Priest forever!

[18] The old *order of priesthood* has been set aside as weak and powerless. [a] [19] For the law [b] has never made anyone perfect, but in its place is a far better hope which gives us confidence to experience intimacy with God! [20] And he confirmed it to us with his solemn vow. [c] For the former priests took their office without an oath, [21] but with Jesus, God affirmed his royal-priesthood with his promise, saying,

The Lord has made a solemn oath
and will never change his mind,
"You are a King-Priest forever!" [d]

[22] So all of this magnifies the truth that we have a superior covenant with God than what they experienced, for Jesus himself is its guarantor! [e] [23] As additional proof, we know there were many priests under the old system, for they eventually died and their office had to be filled by another. [24] But Jesus permanently holds his priestly office, since he lives forever and will never have a successor! [f]

[25] So he is able to save fully from now throughout eternity, [g] everyone who comes to God through him, because he lives to pray continually for them. [26] He is the High Priest who perfectly fits our need—holy, without a trace of evil, without the ability to deceive, incapable of sin, [h] and exalted beyond the heavens!

[27] Unlike the former high priests, he is not compelled to offer daily sacrifices. They had to bring a sacrifice first for their own sins, [i] then for the sins of the people, but he finished the sacrificial system, once and for all, when he offered himself. [28] The law appointed flawed men as high priests, but God's promise, sealed with his oath, which succeeded the law, appoints a perfect Son who is complete forever!

---

a 7:18 Or "useless."

b 7:19 Or in Aramaic "Torah."

c 7:20 As translated from the Aramaic. The Greek is "Since this was not done with a solemn oath, for the others became priests without a sworn oath."

d 7:21 See Ps. 110:4; Heb. 5:6; 6:20; 7:17.

e 7:22 The Aramaic can be translated "through which we gained Jesus."

f 7:24 As translated from the Aramaic and implied in the Greek.

g 7:25 The Greek text is somewhat ambiguous, an alternative translation could be "He is able to save for all time" or "He is able, now and always, to completely [fully] save," or "He is able to save into the always."

h 7:26 As translated from the Aramaic. The Greek is "separate from sinners."

i 7:27 See Lev. 16:6–16.

Our Better Covenant

8 Now this is the crowning point of what we are saying: We have a magnificent King-Priest who ministers for us at the right hand of God. He is enthroned with honor next to the throne of the Majesty on high. ²He serves in the holy sanctuary in the true heavenly tabernacle[a] set up by God, and not by men. ³Since every high priest is appointed to offer both gifts and sacrifices, so the Messiah also had to bring some sacrifice. ⁴But since he didn't qualify to be an earthly priest, and there are already priests who offer sacrifices[b] prescribed by the law, *he offered in heaven a perfect sacrifice.*

⁵The priests on earth serve in a temple that is but a copy modeled after the heavenly sanctuary; a shadow of the reality. For when Moses began to construct the tabernacle God warned him and said,

"You must precisely follow the pattern I revealed to you on
Mt. Sinai."[c]

⁶But now Jesus the Messiah[d] has accepted a priestly ministry which far surpasses theirs, since he is the catalyst[e] of a better covenant which contains far more wonderful promises! ⁷For if that first covenant had been faultless no one would have needed a second one to replace it. ⁸But God revealed the defect and limitation of the first when he said to his people,[f]

"Look! The day will come, declares the Lord,
    when I will satisfy the people of Israel and Judah
    by giving them a new covenant.[g]
⁹It will be an entirely different covenant
    than the one I made with their fathers
    when I led them by my hand out of Egypt.
    For they did not remain faithful to my covenant,
    so I rejected them, says the Lord God.
¹⁰For here is the covenant I will one day establish with the people
    of Israel:
    I will embed my laws within their thoughts

---

a 8:2 Or "tent."
b 8:4 Or "gifts." The present tense of the verb used here shows that there was still a temple with sacrifices being offered at the time of the writing of Hebrews. This sets the date as before 70 AD when the temple was destroyed by the Roman war.
c 8:5 See Ex. 25:40.
d 8:6 As translated from the Aramaic. The Greek is simply "he."
e 8:6 As translated from the Aramaic. The Greek is "the covenant that he mediates (as intermediary and guarantor)."
f 8:8 Some Greek manuscripts have "because he found fault with them" (Israelites).
g 8:8 As translated from the Aramaic. The Greek is "I will complete a new covenant with the house of Israel and the house of Judah."

and fasten them onto their hearts.
I will be their loyal God and they will be my loyal people.

[11] And the result of this will be
that everyone will know me as Lord!
There will be no need at all to teach their fellow-citizens
or brothers by saying,
'You should know the Lord Jehovah,'
since everyone will know me *inwardly*,
from the most unlikely to the most distinguished. [a]

[12] For I will demonstrate my mercy to them
and will forgive [b] their evil deeds,
and never remember again their sins."

[13] This proves that by establishing this new covenant the first is now obsolete, ready to expire, and about to disappear. [c]

The Old Pattern of Worship

9 Now in the first covenant there were specific rules for worship including a sanctuary on earth to worship in. [2] When you entered the tabernacle you would first come into the holy chamber where you would find the lampstand [d] and the bread of his presence on the fellowship table. [e] [3] Then as you pass through the next curtain [f] you would enter the innermost chamber called, the holiest sanctuary of all. [g] [4] It contained the golden altar of incense and the ark of covenant mercy, which was a wooden box covered entirely with gold. And placed inside the ark of covenant mercy was the golden jar with mystery-manna inside, [h] Aaron's resurrection rod, which had sprouted, and the stone tablets engraved with the covenant laws. [5] On top of the lid of the ark were two cherubim, angels of splendor, with outstretched wings overshadowing the throne of mercy. [i] But now is not the time to discuss further the significant details of these things.

[6] So with this prescribed pattern of worship the priests would routinely go in and out of the first chamber to perform their religious duties. [7] And the high priest was permitted to enter into the Holiest Sanctuary of All only once

---

a 8:11 The Aramaic can be translated "from the youngest to the oldest."

b 8:12 The Aramaic can be translated "I will make atonement for their evil."

c 8:13 Or "is near obliteration." The old which is "about to disappear," can also refer to our old life and its old ways of pleasing flesh, the sinful disposition of our hearts. The Aramaic verb for "disappear" can also mean "to give birth."

d 9:2 See Ex. 25:31–40; Lev. 24:1–4.

e 9:2 See Ex. 25:23–30; 39:36. This fellowship table had twelve loaves of sacred bread. See also Lev. 24:5–9.

f 9:3 See Ex. 26:31–35.

g 9:3 Or "holy of holies," that is, the holiest place of all.

h 9:4 The Hebrew word for "manna," the wilderness bread, means "mystery" or "What is it?"

i 9:5 Or "the place of atonement." See Ex. 25:18–22.

a year and he could never enter without first offering sacrificial blood for both his own sins and for the sins of the people.

[8] Now the Holy Spirit uses the symbols of this pattern of worship to reveal that the perfect way of holiness[a] had not yet been unveiled. For as long as the tabernacle stood [9] it was an illustration[b] *that pointed to our present time of fulfillment*, demonstrating that offerings and animal sacrifices had failed to perfectly cleanse the conscience of the worshiper. [10] For this old pattern of worship was a matter of external rules and rituals concerning food and drink and ceremonial washings which was imposed upon us until the appointed time of heart-restoration had arrived.[c]

The Heavenly Pattern of Worship

[11] But now the Anointed One has become the King-Priest of every wonderful thing that has come.[d] For he serves in a greater, more perfect heavenly tabernacle[e] not made by men. [12] And he has entered once and forever into the Holiest Sanctuary of All, not with the blood of animal sacrifices, but the sacred blood of his own sacrifice. And he alone has made our salvation[f] secure forever!

[13] Under the old covenant the blood of bulls, goats, and the ashes of a heifer were sprinkled on those who were defiled and effectively cleansed them outwardly from their ceremonial impurities. [14] Yet how much more will the sacred blood of the Messiah thoroughly cleanse our consciences! For by the power of the eternal Spirit he has offered himself to God as the perfect[g] Sacrifice that now frees[h] us from our dead works[i] to worship and serve the living God.

[15] So Jesus is the One who has enacted a new covenant with a new relationship with God so that those who accept the invitation[j] will receive the eternal inheritance he has promised to his heirs. For he died to release us from the guilt of the violations committed under the first covenant.

[16-17] Now a person's last will and testament can only take effect after one has been proven to have died; otherwise the will cannot be in force while the person who made it is still alive. [18] So this is why not even the first covenant was

---

a 9:8 As translated from the Aramaic. The Greek is "the way into the Holy Place."

b 9:9 The Aramaic can be translated "mystery."

c 9:10 The Greek word *diothosis* is used only here in the New Testament. It means "to set things right," or "to snap a broken bone back into place," by implication *restoration*.

d 9:11 The Aramaic can be translated "the good things that he did." Some Greek manuscripts have "good things that are coming."

e 9:11 Or "not of this creation" (world).

f 9:12 Or "He has paid the ransom [redemption] forever."

g 9:14 Or "unblemished."

h 9:14 Or "purifies."

i 9:14 Or "what we did when we were corpses."

j 9:15 Or "those who are called."

inaugurated without the blood of animals. [19] For Moses ratified the covenant after he gave the people all the commandments of the law. He took the blood of calves and goats, with water, scarlet wool, and a hyssop branch, and sprinkled both the people and the book of the covenant,[a] [20] saying,

"This is the blood of the covenant that God commands you to keep."[b]

[21] And later Moses also sprinkled the tabernacle with blood and every utensil and item used in their service of worship. [22] Actually, nearly everything under the law was purified with blood, since forgiveness only comes through an outpouring of blood.

[23] And so it was necessary for all the earthly symbols[c] of the heavenly realities to be purified with these animal sacrifices, but the heavenly things themselves required a superior sacrifice than these. [24] For the Messiah did not enter into the earthly tabernacle made by men, which was but an echo of the true sanctuary, but he entered into heaven itself to appear before the face[d] of God in our place. [25] Under the old system year after year the high priest entered the most holy sanctuary with blood that was not his own. But the Messiah did not need to repeatedly offer himself year after year, [26] for that would mean he must suffer repeatedly ever since the fall of the world.[e] But now he has appeared at the fulfillment of the ages to abolish[f] sin once and for all by the sacrifice of himself!

[27] Every human being is appointed to die once, and then to face God's judgment.[g] [28] *But when we die we will be face-to-face with Christ*, the One who experienced death once for all to bear the sins of many![h] And now to those who eagerly await him, he will appear a second time; not to deal with sin, but to bring us the fullness of salvation.[i]

---

a 9:19 See Ex. 24:3, 7.
b 9:20 See Ex. 24:8. The blood of Jesus gave birth to the new covenant for the forgiveness of sins. See Matt. 26:28.
c 9:23 Or "outlines" or "sketches."
d 9:24 As translated from the Aramaic (Hebrew), which has no word equivalent for "presence," only "face." To come into God's presence meant that you come before his *face*.
e 9:26 Or "from the foundation of the world." The Greek word *katabole* can also mean "laying down" or "falling down" (of the world through sin), which by implication means Adam's sin.
f 9:26 The Aramaic can be translated "annihilate sin."
g 9:27 The Greek is literally "a court trial."
h 9:28 The Aramaic can be translated "to burn away [obliterate] the sins of many." See Isa. 53:12.
i 9:28 There is a salvation that is yet to be unveiled. See 1 Peter 1:5.

Christ's Eternal Sacrifice

10 The old system of living under the law presented us with only a faint shadow, a crude outline of the reality of the wonderful blessings to come. Even with its steady stream of sacrifices offered year after year, there still was nothing that could make our hearts perfect before God. ²⁻³ For if animal sacrifices could once and for all eliminate sin, they would have ceased to be offered and the worshipers would have clean consciences. Instead, once was not enough so by the repetitive sacrifices year after year, the worshipers were continually reminded of their sins, with their hearts still impure. ⁴ For what power does the blood of bulls and goats*ᵃ* have to remove sin's guilt?

⁵ So when Jesus the Messiah came into the world he said,

"Since your ultimate desire was not another animal sacrifice,
  you have clothed me with a body *ᵇ*
  that I might offer myself instead!
⁶ Multiple burnt offerings and sin-offerings
  cannot satisfy your justice.
⁷ So I said to you, 'God—
  I will be the One to go and do your will,
  to fulfill all that is written of me in your Word!'"*ᶜ*

⁸ First he said, "Multiple burnt-offerings and sin-offerings cannot satisfy your justice" (even though the law required them to be offered). ⁹ And then he said, "God, I will be the One to go and do your will." *So by being the sacrifice that removes sin,* he abolishes animal sacrifices*ᵈ* and replaces that entire system with the new covenant.*ᵉ* ¹⁰ By God's will we have been purified and made holy once and for all*ᶠ* through the sacrifice of the body of Jesus, the Messiah!

¹¹ Yet every day priests still serve, ritually offering the same sacrifices again and again— sacrifices that can never take away sin's guilt. ¹² But when this Priest had offered the one supreme sacrifice for sin for all time he sat down on a throne at the right hand of God, ¹³ waiting until all his whispering enemies are subdued and turn into his footstool. ¹⁴ And by his one perfect sacrifice he made us perfectly holy*ᵍ* and complete for all time!

¹⁵ The Holy Spirit confirms this to us by this Scripture, for the Lord says,

---

a 10:4 The Aramaic can be translated "bulls and birds."
b 10:5 As translated from the Aramaic. See also Ps. 40:6–8. The Hebrew of Ps. 40:6 has, "My ears you have pierced." The Clementine Septuagint has "My ears you have prepared."
c 10:7 Or "in the scroll of the Book." The Aramaic can be translated "from the beginning of your writings [the Torah] it is spoken of me."
d 10:9 Or "he abolishes the first."
e 10:9 Or "the second" (covenant).
f 10:10 Or "made holy through the offering up of the body of Jesus Christ once and for all."
g 10:14 Or "we are being made holy."

[16] "Afterwards, I will give them this covenant: I will embed my laws into their hearts and fasten my Word to their thoughts."

[17] And then he says,

"I will not ever again remember their sins and lawless deeds!" [a]

[18] So if our sins have been forgiven and forgotten, why would we ever need to offer another sacrifice for sin?

Our Confidence before God

[19] And now we are brothers and sisters in God's family because of the blood of Jesus, and he welcomes us to come right into the most holy sanctuary in the heavenly realm—boldly and with no hesitation. [20] For he has dedicated a new, [b] life-giving way for us to approach God. For just as the veil was torn in two, Jesus' body was torn open to give us free and fresh access to him!

[21] And since we now have a magnificent King-Priest to welcome us into God's house, [22] we come closer to God and approach him [c] with an open heart, fully convinced by faith that nothing will keep us at a distance from him. For our hearts have been sprinkled with blood to remove impurity and we have been freed from an accusing conscience and now we are clean, unstained, and presentable to God inside and out! [d]

[23] So now we must cling tightly to the hope that lives within us, knowing that God always keeps his promises! [e] [24] Discover creative ways to encourage others [f] and to motivate them toward acts of compassion, doing beautiful works as expressions of love. [25] This is not the time to pull away and neglect [g] meeting together, as some have formed the habit of doing, because we need each other! In fact, we should come together even more frequently, eager to encourage and urge each other onward as we anticipate that day dawning.

Another Warning

[26] For if we continue to persist in deliberate sin after we have known and received the truth, there is not another sacrifice for sin to be made for us. [27] But this would qualify one for the certain, terrifying expectation of judgment and the raging

---

a 10:17 See Jer. 31:33–34.

b 10:20 Or "newly slain."

c 10:22 Or "draw near to God," or "offer a true sacrifice. The Hebrew verbs "to draw near" (*lehitkarev*) and "to offer a sacrifice" (*lehakriv*) are nearly identical and both are taken from the same root word.

d 10:22 Or "our bodies washed with pure water."

e 10:23 The Aramaic can be translated "Faithful is the One who sent us this message of hope."

f 10:24 The Aramaic can be translated "Let us look on one another with the excitement of love."

g 10:25 Or "abandon." The Greek implies a person who is extremely discouraged.

fire ready to burn up his enemies![a] [28] Anyone who disobeyed Moses' law died without mercy on the simple evidence of two or three witnesses. [29] How much more severely do you suppose a person deserves to be judged who has contempt for God's Son, [b] and who scorns the blood of the new covenant that made him holy, and who mocks the Spirit who gives him grace?

[30] For we know him who said,

"I have the right to take revenge
and pay them back for their evil!"

And also,

"The Lord God will judge his own people!" [c]

[31] It is the most terrifying thing of all to come under the judgment[d] of the Living God!

[32] Don't you remember those days right after the Light shined in your hearts?[e] You endured a great marathon season of suffering hardships, yet you stood your ground. [33] And at times you were publicly and shamefully mistreated, being persecuted for your faith;[f] then at others times you stood side by side with those who preach the message of hope.[g]

[34] You sympathized with those in prison[h] and when all your belongings were confiscated you accepted that violation with joy; convinced that you possess a treasure growing in heaven[i] that could never be taken from you. [35] So don't lose your bold, courageous faith, for you are destined for a great reward![j]

[36] You need the strength of endurance to reveal the poetry[k] of God's will and then you receive the promise in full. [37] For soon and very soon,

"The One who is appearing will come without delay!" [l]

[38] And he also says, [m]

---

a 10:27 See Isa. 26:11.
b 10:29 Or "who tramples the Son of God under his feet."
c 10:30 See Deut. 32:35–36.
d 10:31 Or "to fall into the hands."
e 10:32 The Aramaic can be translated "after you were baptized."
f 10:33 The Aramaic can be translated "so that you would become seers" or "develop vision."
g 10:33 As translated from the Aramaic. The Greek is "partners with those who were similarly abused."
h 10:34 Or "my [Paul's] imprisonment."
i 10:34 As translated from the Aramaic. The Greek is "you possess greater heavenly things."
j 10:35 As translated from the Aramaic. The Greek is "your faith yields a great reward."
k 10:36 Or "to do God's will." The Greek word for "do" is taken from the Greek word *poeima* (poem or poetry).
l 10:37 That is, time is not relevant in the realm of the Spirit. See Isa. 26:20; Hab. 2:3–4.
m 10:38 Supplied for clarity of the English narrative.

"My righteous ones will live from my faith. *a*
        But if fear holds them back,*b*
        my soul is not content with them!"

[39] But we are certainly not those who are held back by fear and perish; we are among those who have faith and experience true life!*c*

The Power of Bold Faith

11 Now faith brings our hopes into reality and becomes the foundation needed to acquire the things we long for. It is all the evidence required to prove what is still unseen. [2] This testimony of faith is what previous generations*d* were commended for. [3] Faith empowers us to see that the universe was created and beautifully coordinated*e* by the power of God's words! He spoke and the invisible realm gave birth to all that is seen.

[4] Faith moved Abel*f* to choose a more acceptable sacrifice to offer God than his brother Cain, and God declared him righteous because of his offering of faith. By his faith, Abel still speaks instruction to us today, even though he is long dead.

[5] Faith lifted Enoch from this life and he was taken up into heaven! He never had to experience death; he just disappeared from this world because God promoted him. For before he was translated to the heavenly realm his life had become a pleasure to God. *g*

[6] And without faith living within us it would be impossible to please God. *h* For we come to God in faith*i* knowing that he is real and that he rewards the faith of those who give all their passion and strength into seeking him.

[7] Faith opened Noah's heart to receive revelation and warnings from God about what was coming, even things that had never been seen. But he stepped out in reverent obedience to God and built an ark that would save him and his family. By his faith the world was condemned, but Noah received God's gift of righteousness that comes by believing.

---

a 10:38 As translated from the Aramaic, and the Septuagint of Hab. 2:4.

b 10:38 The Greek word *hupostello* (aroist subjunctive middle, used absolutely), does not mean "to draw back" but "to cower in fear."

c 10:39 Or "faith to the preservation of the soul." The Aramaic can be translated "faith that fulfills our soul."

d 11:2 Or "elders."

e 11:3 Or "the ages were completely equipped."

f 11:4 Although Abel is the subject of the Greek sentence, faith is the emphasis and focus of this chapter. Nothing would have been accomplished by the figures mentioned in vv. 4–29 without faith. It is assumed that it is the faith of the person mentioned, not merely an abstraction of faith.

g 11:5 Or "he had the reputation of pleasing God." See Gen. 5:24.

h 11:6 Or "we are powerless to please God." The Greek word *adynatos* means impotent or powerless.

i 11:6 Or "Anyone who approaches God must believe."

Faith of the Patriarchs

[8] Faith motivated Abraham to obey God's call and leave the familiar to discover the territory he was destined to inherit from God. So he left with only a promise and without even knowing ahead of time where he was going, Abraham stepped out in faith. [9] He lived by faith as an immigrant in his promised land as though it belonged to someone else. [a] He journeyed through the land living in tents with Isaac and Jacob who were persuaded that they were also co-heirs of the same promise.

[10] His eyes of faith were set on the city[b] with unshakable foundations, whose architect and builder is God himself. [11] Sarah's faith embraced the miracle power to conceive even though she was barren and was past the age of childbearing, for the authority of her faith[c] rested in the One who made the promise, and she tapped into his faithfulness.

[12] In fact, so many children were subsequently fathered by this aged man of faith—one who was as good as dead, that he now has offspring as innumerable as the sand on the seashore and as the stars in the sky!

[13] These heroes all died still clinging to their faith, not even receiving all that had been promised them. But they saw beyond the horizon the fulfillment of their promises and gladly embraced it from afar. They all lived their lives on earth as those who belonged to another realm.[d]

[14] For clearly, those who live this way[e] are longing for the appearing of a heavenly city.[f] [15] And if their hearts were still remembering what they left behind, they would have found an opportunity to go back. [16] But they couldn't turn back for their hearts were fixed on what was far greater, that is, the heavenly realm![g]

So because of this God is not ashamed in any way to be called their God, for he has prepared a heavenly city for them.

Abraham, Isaac, and Jacob

[17] Faith operated powerfully in Abraham for when he was put to the test he offered up Isaac. Even though he received God's promises[h] of descendants, he was willing[i] to offer up his only son! [18] For God had promised,

---

a 11:9 Or "a foreign country."
b 11:10 Or "He was continually receiving the city."
c 11:11 As translated from the Aramaic and some Greek manuscripts. Arguably, a difficult passage to translate from the Greek; variations of the text are focused on Abraham's faith, not Sarah's. Other manuscripts seem to have the focus on "their faith" (both Sarah's and Abraham's).
d 11:13 Or "as strangers and nomads on earth."
e 11:14 Or "speak this way."
f 11:14 As translated from the Aramaic. The Greek is "homeland" (country).
g 11:16 It should be noted that there is no mention of "land" or "country" in the Greek text of vv. 15–16.
h 11:17 The Aramaic can be translated "he received the royal-proclamation," the Aramaic word for "promise."
i 11:17 Or "he attempted to offer up."

"Through your son Isaac your lineage will carry on your name." [a]

[19] Abraham's faith made it logical to him that God could raise Isaac from the dead, and symbolically, [b] that's exactly what happened.

[20] The power of faith prompted Isaac to impart a blessing to his sons, Jacob and Esau, concerning their prophetic destinies.

[21] Jacob worshiped in faith's reality at the end of his life, and leaning upon his staff he imparted a prophetic blessing upon each of Joseph's sons. [c]

[22] Faith inspired Joseph and opened his eyes to see into the future, for as he was dying he prophesied about the exodus [d] of Israel out of Egypt, [e] and gave instructions that his bones were to be taken from Egypt with them. [f]

Moses

[23] Faith prompted the parents of Moses at his birth to hide him for three months, [g] because they realized their child was exceptional [h] and *they* refused to be afraid of the king's edict.

[24] Faith enabled Moses to choose God's will, for although he was raised as the son of Pharaoh's daughter, he refused to make that his identity, [25] choosing instead to suffer mistreatment with the people of God. Moses preferred faith's certainty above the momentary enjoyment of sin's pleasures. [26] He found his true wealth in suffering abuse for being anointed, [i] more than in anything the world could offer him, [j] for his eyes looked with wonder not on the immediate, but on the ultimate—faith's great reward! [k] [27] Holding faith's promise Moses abandoned Egypt and had no fear of Pharaoh's rage because he persisted in faith as if he had seen God who is unseen. [l]

---

a 11:18 Or "in Isaac seed will be named for you." See Gen. 21:12.

b 11:19 Or "Isaac was given to him as a parable."

c 11:21 See Gen. 49.

d 11:22 Or "remembering the exodus." This is amazing, since the exodus had not yet happened, so how could Joseph "remember" it? This is the eye of faith that imparts prophetic vision of the future.

e 11:22 See Gen. 50:24–25.

f 11:22 See Gen. 47:29–30.

g 11:23 See Ex. 2:2.

h 11:23 Or "elegant." This can mean pleasing in appearance and / or good character.

i 11:26 Or "the reproach of Christ." The Greek text can be translated with either Moses as the one anointed, or Christ, the Anointed One. Moses saw the messianic hope and esteemed it greater than momentary affliction. He believed in the coming Anointed One and held the promise dear.

j 11:26 Or "the storehouses of Egypt."

k 11:26 The Aramaic can be translated "he was paid back in the reward of a Messiah!"

l 11:27 As translated from the Aramaic. The Greek does not have "God" but can be translated "Moses was patient for the invisible as though he were able to see it come to be."

²⁸ Faith stirred Moses to perform ᵃ the rite of Passover and sprinkle lamb's blood, ᵇ to prevent the destroyer from harming their firstborn. ᶜ

²⁹ Faith opened the way for the Hebrews to cross the Red Sea as if on dry land, but when the Egyptians tried to cross they were swallowed up and drowned!

Jericho and Rahab

³⁰ Faith pulled down Jericho's walls after the people marched around them for seven days!

³¹ Faith provided a way of escape for Rahab the prostitute, avoiding the destruction of the unbelievers, because she received the Hebrew spies in peace.

More Faith Champions

³² And what more could I say to convince you? For there is not enough time to tell you of the faith of Gideon, Barak, Samson, Jephthah, David, Samuel, and the prophets. ³³ Through faith's power they conquered kingdoms and established true justice. Their faith fastened onto their promises and pulled them into reality! It was faith that shut the mouth of lions, ³⁴ put out the power of raging fire, and caused many to escape certain death by the sword. In their weakness their faith imparted power to make them strong! ᵈ Faith sparked courage within them and they became mighty warriors in battle, pulling armies from another realm into battle array. ᵉ ³⁵ Faith-filled women saw their dead children raised in resurrection power.

Yet it was faith that enabled others to endure great atrocities. They were stretched out on the wheel and tortured, ᶠ and didn't deny their faith in order to be freed, because they longed for a more honorable and glorious resurrection!

³⁶ Others were mocked and experienced the most severe beating with whips; they were in chains and imprisoned. ³⁷ Some of these faith champions were brutally killed by stoning, being sawn in two or slaughtered by the sword. These lived in faith as they went about wearing goatskins and sheepskins for clothing. They lost everything they possessed, they endured great afflictions, and they were cruelly mistreated. ³⁸ They wandered the earth living in the desert wilderness, in caves, on barren mountains and in holes in the earth. Truly, the world was not even worthy of them, not realizing who they were.

³⁹ These were the true heroes, commended for their faith, yet they lived in

---

a 11:28 This is the perfect tense of the Greek, implying that the Passover is still observed.
b 11:28 Or "pouring out of [lamb's] blood."
c 11:28 That is, "firstborn people and animals."
d 11:34 The Aramaic can be translated "They were restored (healed) from sickness."
e 11:34 See Judg. 7; 16:19–30. Although most translate this "causing enemy armies to flee" the Greek is literally "wheeling ranks drawn up in battle order, ranks which belonged to another." The implication is that through their faith, angelic warriors *wheeled* into battle formation ready to fight with them in battle.
f 11:35 Or "tortured with clubs" (beaten to death).

hope without receiving the fullness of what was promised them. [40] But now God has invited us to live in something better than what they had—faith's fullness! This is so that they could be brought to finished perfection alongside of us.

The Great Cloud of Witnesses

12 As for us, we have all of these great witnesses[a] who encircle us like clouds. So we must let go of every wound that has pierced us[b] and the sin we so easily fall into.[c] Then we will be able to run life's marathon race[d] with passion and determination, for the path has been already marked out before us.[e]

[2] We look away from the natural realm and we fasten our gaze onto Jesus who birthed faith within us and who leads us forward into faith's perfection.[f] His example is this: Because his heart was focused on the joy of knowing that you would be his,[g] he endured the agony of the cross and conquered its humiliation,[h] and now sits exalted at the right hand of the throne of God!

[3] So consider carefully how Jesus faced such intense opposition from sinners who opposed their own souls,[i] so that you won't become worn down and cave in under life's pressures. [4] After all, you have not yet reached the point of sweating blood[j] in your opposition to sin. [5] And have you forgotten his encouraging words spoken to you as his children? He said,

> "My child, don't underestimate the value
>   of the discipline and training of the Lord God,
>   or get depressed when he has to correct you.[k]
> [6] For the Lord's training of your life
>   is the evidence of his faithful love.[l]

---

a 12:1 Or "martyrs."

b 12:1 Or "get rid of every arrow tip in us." The implication is carrying an arrow tip inside, a wound that weighs us down and keeps us from running our race with freedom.

c 12:1 Or "the sin that so cleverly entangles us." The Aramaic can be translated "the sin that is ready [and waiting] for us." If this is speaking of one sin, the context would point to the sin of unbelief and doubting God's promises.

d 12:1 Or "obstacle course." The Greek word *agona* means agony or conflict. The assumption is this race will not be easy, but the proper path to run has been set before us.

e 12:1 The Aramaic can be translated "the race [personally] appointed to us." God has a destiny for each of us that we are to give ourselves fully to reach.

f 12:2 Or "He is the pioneer and perfecter of faith."

g 12:2 This was the joy of our salvation. He placed before his eyes the bliss we would forever share together with him, which empowered him to go through his agony.

h 12:2 As translated from the Aramaic. The Greek is "thinking nothing of its shame."

i 12:3 Or "those who were their own stumbling block." As translated from the Aramaic.

j 12:4 Or "resisting until blood."

k 12:5 Or "when he puts you under scrutiny." The Aramaic can be translated "Don't let your soul tremble [with dread] when your loyalty strays from him."

l 12:6 The Aramaic word used here means nurturing love, a mother's love. This passage shows both the strength of a father's love in how God disciplines us and the nurturing care of

> And when he draws you to himself,
> it proves you are his delightful child." [a]

[7] Fully embrace God's correction as part of your training, [b] for he is doing what any loving father does for his children. For who has ever heard of a child who never had to be corrected? [c] [8] We all should welcome God's discipline as the validation of authentic sonship. For if we have never once endured his correction it only proves we are strangers [d] and not sons.

[9] And isn't it true that we respect our earthly fathers even though they corrected and disciplined us? Then we should demonstrate an even greater respect for God, our spiritual Father, as we submit to his life-giving discipline. [e] [10] Our parents corrected us for the short time of our childhood as it seemed good to them. But God corrects us throughout our lives for our own good, giving us an invitation to share his holiness. [11] Now all discipline [f] seems to be more pain than pleasure at the time, yet later it will produce a transformation of character, bringing a harvest of righteousness and peace [g] to those who yield to it. [h]

[12] So be made strong even in your weakness by lifting up your tired hands *in prayer and worship*. And strengthen your weak knees, [i] [13] for as you keep walking forward on God's paths [j] all your stumbling ways will be divinely healed!

[14] In every relationship be swift to choose peace over competition, [k] and run swiftly toward holiness, for those who are not holy will not see the Lord. [l] [15] Watch over each other to make sure that no one misses the revelation of God's grace. And make sure no one lives with a root of bitterness [m]

---

a mother's love. The Aramaic could be translated, "The Lord shows his nurturing love [mercy] to those he is sanctifying."

a 12:6 The Aramaic word for "draws you to himself" is *nagad,* which can mean "scourge" (severely punish) or "to attract," "to draw," or "tug the heart." The Greek is "The Lord scourges [chastises] every son he receives." See also Prov. 3:11–12.

b 12:7 Or "What you endure is meant to educate you."

c 12:7 The Aramaic can be translated "Who has ever heard of a child not approved by a father?"

d 12:8 As translated from the Aramaic. The Greek is "illegitimate."

e 12:9 See Prov. 6:23.

f 12:11 Throughout this passage the word *discipline* can also be translated "correction," "instruction," and "training."

g 12:11 See James 3:18.

h 12:11 Or "those who have endured its [gymnastic] training."

i 12:12 The Greek word used here can also mean "paralyzed knees."

j 12:13 See Isa. 35:3; Prov. 4:26.

k 12:14 See Ps. 34:14.

l 12:14 The Aramaic can be translated "no man will see into the Lord."

m 12:15 Or "resentment."

sprouting within them which will only cause trouble and poison the hearts of many.

¹⁶ Be careful that no one among you lives in immorality, becoming careless about God's blessings, like Esau who traded away his rights as the firstborn for a simple meal. ¹⁷ And we know that later on when he wanted to inherit his father's blessing, he was turned away, even though he begged for it with bitter tears, for it was too late then to repent. *ᵃ*

Entering into God's Presence

¹⁸ For we are not coming, *as Moses did*, to a physical mountain with its burning fire, thick clouds of darkness and gloom, and with a raging whirlwind. *ᵇ* ¹⁹ We are not those who are being warned by the jarring blast of a trumpet and the thundering voice;*ᶜ* the fearful voice that they begged to be silenced. ²⁰ They couldn't handle God's command that said,

> "If so much as an animal approaches the mountain it is to be stoned to death!"

²¹ The astounding phenomena Moses witnessed caused him to shudder with fear and he could only say, "I am trembling in terror!" *ᵈ*

²² By contrast, we have already come*ᵉ* near to God in a totally different realm, the Zion-realm,*ᶠ* for we have entered the city of the Living God, which

---

a 12:17 The Aramaic can be translated "he found no place of restoration."

b 12:18 See Ex. 19; Deut. 4:11 (LXX); Amos 5:20.

c 12:19 Or "the sound of words."

d 12:21 See Deut. 9:19.

e 12:22 The Greek verb is in the perfect tense indicating that the fullness of our salvation and our entrance into God's heavenly realm has already taken place. See also Rom. 8:29; Eph. 2:6; Col. 3:1–4.

f 12:22 Or "Mount Zion," which is not a literal mountain but an obvious metaphor for the realm of God's manifest presence. Mount Zion was once a Jebusite stronghold conquered by David (2 Sam. 5:6–9) who made it the capital for his kingdom. This is inside the walls of present-day Jerusalem. Zion is used in both the Old and New Testaments as more than a location. Zion is referred to as the place of God's dwelling (Pss. 9:11; 48:1–2; 74:2; Isa. 8:18). God's people are called "Zion maidens" (Song. 3:11; Zech. 9:9) or "people of Zion" (John 12:15). Zion is the heavenly realm where God is manifest (Pss. 84:7; 102:16; 110:1–2; Rev. 14:1).

is the New Jerusalem in heaven![a] We have joined the festal gathering of myriads of angels[b] in their joyous celebration![c]

[23] And as members of the church[d] of the Firstborn[e] all our names have been legally registered[f] as citizens of heaven! And we have come before God who judges all, and who lives among the spirits of the righteous who have been made perfect in his eyes![g]

[24] And we have come to Jesus who established a new covenant with his blood sprinkled upon the mercy seat; blood that continues to speak from heaven, "forgiveness," a better message than Abel's blood that cries from the earth, "justice."[h]

[25] Make very sure that you never refuse to listen to God when he speaks![i] For the God who spoke on earth from Sinai is the same God who now speaks from heaven. Those who heard him[j] speak his living Word on earth found nowhere to hide, so what chance is there for us to escape if we turn our backs on God and refuse to hear his warnings as he speaks from heaven?

[26] The earth was rocked at the sound of his voice from the mountain, but now he has promised,

---

a 12:22 This is the fulfillment of Abraham's vision (Heb. 11:10) and what Israel's ancestors had seen from afar (Heb. 11:13). The New Jerusalem is not only a place, but a people who dwell with God in their midst. It is a city that is a bride or a bridal-city coming out of heaven to the earth (Rev. 21:9–14). We are not going to the New Jerusalem; we are going to be the New Jerusalem! The breastplate worn by the high priest over his heart with its precious stones was a miniature scale model of the New Jerusalem. The New Jerusalem is the amplification of that breastplate, a metaphor of transformed sons with their names engraved upon the precious stones. See Rev. 21:2–4. The Aramaic can be translated "You have already received communion on Mount Zion."

b 12:22 See Deut. 33:2; Dan. 7:10; Jude 14; Rev. 5:11.

c 12:22 This is much more than an assembly of angels. The Greek word panēgyris was used in classic Greek literature for civic festivals and celebrations which drew people from all parts of the empire and included all the various social classes. These were times of great joy and festivities with people wearing white robes and with garlands on their heads. (See Philo, Gaius 12; Isocrates, Panegyricus 43, 46.) This verse teaches that we have already entered into the festival of angelic bliss through Jesus Christ.

d 12:23 This is the Greek word ekklēsia, which is commonly used for church. However, ekklēsia means more than a church meeting, for it signified in Greek culture the governing assembly which had the authority to make decisions for the entire city. See Matt. 16:18.

e 12:23 This is Jesus who is God's uniquely Firstborn (Heb. 1:6). In Christ we are all the firstborn and have all the rights and blessings that Jesus has.

f 12:23 Or "whose names are written in heaven." There are many books in heaven. See Ex. 32:32; Pss. 69:28; 87:6; Dan. 12:1; Luke 10:20; Phil. 4:3; Rev. 3:5; 13:8; 17:8; 20:12,15; 21:27.

g 12:23 The Aramaic can be translated "and to the Spirit who has perfected the righteous ones."

h 12:24 See Gen. 4:10.

i 12:25 Or "don't turn your back on the speaker."

j 12:25 The Greek is somewhat ambiguous with the possibility that it is Moses or even Christ who is speaking. The context seems to imply however that it is God himself who speaks both from Sinai and from heaven.

"Once and for all I will not only shake the systems of the world,ᵃ
but also the unseen powers in the heavenly realm!"ᵇ

²⁷ Now this phrase "once and for all" clearly indicates the final removal of things that are shaking, that is, the old order,ᶜ so only what is unshakeable will remain. ²⁸ Since we are receiving our rightsᵈ to an unshakeable kingdomᵉ we should be extremely thankful and offer God the purest worship that delights his heartᶠ as we lay down our lives in absolute surrender, filled with awe.ᵍ ²⁹ For our God is a holy, devouring fire!ʰ

Live Pleasing to God

13 No matter what, make room in your heart to love every believer. ² And show hospitality to strangers, for they may be angels from God showing up as your guests.ⁱ ³ Identify with those who are in prison as though you were there suffering with them, and those who are mistreated as if you could feel their pain.ʲ

⁴ Honor the sanctity of marriage and keep your vows of purity to one another, for God will judge sexual immorality in any form, whether single or married.

⁵ Don't be obsessed with money but live content with what you have, for you always have God's presence. For hasn't he promised you,

"I will never leave you alone, never! And I will not loosen my gripᵏ on your life!"

---

a 12:26 Or "earth." Although earthquakes are prophesied to come (Matt. 24:7; Mark 13:8; Luke 21:11; Rev. 8:5; 11:13, 19; 16:18) the prophet is most likely using a metaphoric term for the world's systems (finance, military, governments, religious, etc.). The message of the gospel has shaken the world's foundations as it includes an unshakeable kingdom rising on the earth. Kings of the earth have placed their crowns down before the cross of a Man who was crucified as a common criminal. The power of the gospel is still shaking the world.

b 12:26 It is not God's power or throne being shaken, but invisible forces of darkness in the heavenly realm. See Hag. 2:6; Eph. 6:12.

c 12:27 Or "things that have been made."

d 12:28 The Greek word *paralambano* is often used in classical Greek literature for heirs who have the "rights of succession" (to a throne). (See Aristotle, *Pol.* 3.14.12; Herodotus, 2.120.)

e 12:28 See Dan. 7:18.

f 12:28 Or "offer pleasing service to God."

g 12:28 The Aramaic can be translated "We have received grace to serve and we please God in awe and tender devotion" (submission).

h 12:29 The Aramaic can be translated "consuming light." See also Deut. 4:24; 9:3.

i 13:2 The Aramaic can be translated "for this is how you are worthy to receive angels while awake." See also Matt. 25:35.

j 13:3 The Aramaic can be translated "as if you were people who wear their bodies" (vulnerable to their pain).

k 13:5 Or "hand" as translated from the Aramaic. See also Deut. 31:6, 8.

⁶ So we can say with great confidence:

> "I know the Lord is for me
> and I will never be afraid of what people may do to me!" ª

⁷ Don't forget the example of your spiritual leaders who have spoken God's messages to you, take a close look at how their lives ended, ᵇ and then follow their walk of faith.

⁸ Jesus, the Anointed One, is always the same—yesterday, today, and forever. ᶜ ⁹ So don't let anyone lead you astray with all sorts of novel and exotic teachings. It is more beautiful to feast on grace and be inwardly strengthened than to be obsessed with dietary rules ᵈ which in themselves have no lasting benefit.

¹⁰ We feast on a sacrifice at our spiritual altar, but those who serve as priests in the old system of worship have no right to eat of it. ¹¹ For the high priest carries the blood of animals into the holiest chamber as a sacrifice for sin, and then burns the bodies of the animals outside the city. ᵉ ¹² And Jesus, our sin-sacrifice, also suffered death outside the city walls to make us holy by his own blood.

¹³ So we must arise and join him outside the religious "walls" and bear his disgrace. ᶠ ¹⁴ For we have no city here on earth to be our permanent home, but we seek the city that is destined to come. ᵍ ¹⁵ So we no longer offer up a steady stream of blood sacrifices, but through Jesus, we will offer up to God a steady stream of praise sacrifices—these are "the lambs" ʰ we offer from our lips that celebrate his name! ⁱ

¹⁶ We will show mercy to the poor ʲ and not miss an opportunity to do acts of kindness for others, for these are the true sacrifices that delight God's heart.

¹⁷ Obey your spiritual leaders and recognize their authority, for they keep watch over your soul without resting ᵏ since they will have to give an account to God for their work. So it will benefit you when you make their work a pleasure and not a heavy burden.

¹⁸ And keep praying for us that we continue to live with a clear conscience,

---

a 13:6 See Ps. 118:6–7.

b 13:7 Or "consider the outcome [spiritual fruit] of the way they lived."

c 13:8 The Aramaic can be translated "Jesus the Messiah is the fulfillment of yesterday, today, and forever."

d 13:9 Or "ceremonial foods."

e 13:11 See Lev. 16:14, 27.

f 13:13 Or "carry his insults" or "endure the abuse he suffered."

g 13:14 Or "the city that is intended." The Aramaic can be translated "the city which is anxiously awaited."

h 13:15 As translated from the Aramaic. The Greek is "the fruit of" our lips.

i 13:15 See Ps. 50:14, 23.

j 13:16 As translated from the Aramaic.

k 13:17 The Greek word *agrypnein* is often used for staying awake through the night.

for we desire to live honorably in all that we do. [19] And I especially ask you to pray that God would send me back to you very soon.

Apostolic Blessing and Conclusion

[20] Now may the God who brought us peace by raising from the dead our Lord Jesus Christ so that he would be the Great Shepherd of his flock; and by the power of the blood of the eternal covenant [21] may he work perfection into every part of you giving you all that you need to fulfill your destiny. And may he express through you all that is excellent and pleasing[a] to him through your life-union with Jesus the Anointed One who is to receive all glory forever! Amen!

[22] My dear brothers and sisters, I urge you to let your spirits flow through this message of love[b] that I've written to you in these few words. [23] I want you to know that our brother Timothy is free again and as soon as he arrives here we'll come together to see you. We extend our greetings to all your leaders and all the holy believers. [24] The Italian believers also send their greetings.[c] [25] Now may God's wonderful grace be poured out upon you all! Amen!

---

a   13:21 The Aramaic can be translated "beautiful."
b   13:22 As translated from the Aramaic.
c   13:24 The Aramaic has this sentence at the end, "The end of the letter to the Hebrews written from Italy."

JAMES (JACOB)

Introduction

AT A GLANCE

Author: James, brother of Jesus
Audience: Jewish Christians
Date: AD 45–47
Type of Literature: A wisdom letter
Major Themes: Wisdom, trials, the law, faith and works, poverty and wealth
Outline:
    Greeting — 1:1
    Introducing the Three Themes: Wealth, Wisdom, Trials — 1:2–27
    Theme 1: Riches and Poverty — 2:1–26
    Theme 2: Wisdom and Speech — 3:1–4:12
    Theme 3: Trials and Temptation — 4:13–5:18
    Closing — 5:19–20

ABOUT JAMES (JACOB)

The Holy Spirit speaks through the Bible, God's Holy Word. His life-giving expression comes through each verse, and we are changed by receiving the Word of God. The book of James (Jacob) is rich with life-changing revelation, a feast to strengthen you and keep you on course. We thank God that this book is included in our Bibles for it gives us the understanding of the power of faith to produce good works. Faith works!

Actually, this letter is titled "Jacob." By calling this book James instead of Jacob the church loses a vital component of our Jewish beginnings. There is no "James" in Greek; it is Jacob. We would never say that God is the God of Abraham, Isaac, and James. Neither should we call this letter James, when it is in fact, the letter of Jacob!

Most scholars don't believe that he was a believer until after Jesus died and rose again (see John 7:5). Can you imagine growing up with the Son of God and not knowing it? Yet today many are able to see the works of Jesus all around them and still remain unconvinced. However, Jacob (James) did become a powerful voice in the early church as the presiding apostle of the church of Jerusalem. And like his older brother, Jesus, he also was killed for his faith, in AD 62 according to the Jewish historian Josephus.

The book of Jacob (James) and the book of Galatians are considered to be the first letters penned by the apostles most likely sometime between AD 45–47. So when we read this letter we are reading the earliest insights of the first generation of followers of Jesus who were mostly Jews.

Jacob (James) gives us practical truths about what it means to be declared righteous by God. He gives us many clear insights on faith and walking in the truth. You might want to view this book as the New Testament version of Proverbs, for much of his writings speak of God's heavenly wisdom that can transform us.

I have fallen in love with Jesus! And I love his brother Jacob (James). I think you will too.

PURPOSE

Although the book of Jacob (James) is a letter, it reads more like a wisdom sermon addressing a number of crucial topics relevant to Jewish Christians using familiar language from the Old Testament. His letter was similar to so-called "diaspora letters" from ancient times written to the scattered Jewish people. Like those, it offers comfort and hope during persecution and trials, encourages faithful obedience to God, and provides spiritual instruction and encouragement on important matters relating to the unity and life of the church.

AUTHOR AND AUDIENCE

Although debated by some, it is believed that the Jacob (James) who wrote this book (also known as James the Just) was the half brother of our Lord Jesus referred to in Galatians 1:19 and in Mark 6:3. This is amazing to think that the actual half brother of our Lord and Savior gives us truth to live by. We should listen to what Jacob (James) has to say and take it to heart!

Given the dominant Jewish flavor of the letter, it appears he originally targeted Jewish Christians. Jacob (James) said, "I'm writing to all the twelve tribes of Israel who have been sown as seeds among the nations." His thoughts were meant to reach out to all the Christians who converted from Judaism who were scattered throughout the Roman Empire, calling their attention to the fulfillment of the promises for a Messiah in Jesus.

MAJOR THEMES

Wisdom from Above: The Greek word for wisdom, *sophia*, occurs four times in Jacob's (James') letter. His letter could be considered a wisdom sermon, for the style of the letter is similar to the Proverbs. Throughout his letter Jacob taps into the long tradition of Jewish wisdom and applies it to various practical topics for wise Christian living. He recognizes wisdom is necessary for trying circumstances; it involves insight into God's purposes and leads to spiritual maturity; and God is the source of all true wisdom.

Testing and Trials: In many ways, the wisdom letter of Jacob (James) is written to help guide those whose faith in God is being threatened by daily struggles and hardship. The kinds of testing and trials Jacob speaks of can range from religious persecution to financial difficulties, from health problems to even spiritual oppression. Jacob is clear such experiences are never a waste, there's a goal: Spiritual maturity born through perseverance.

The Law of Moses: While Jacob (James) doesn't directly refer to the law of the Old Testament, he does refer to "the royal law of love as given to us in this Scripture: 'You must love and value your neighbor'" (2:8). Of course Jesus Christ himself gave us this royal law, which he said summed up all the Law and Prophets. And for Jacob, anything that violates this law is as serious as violating any of the Ten Commandments. The law is relevant to Christian living not as legalistic rules and rituals, but as love of neighbor and God.

Faith and Good Deeds: One of the ongoing debates with Jacob's (James') letter is whether it contradicts the teachings of Paul and his theology of salvation by faith alone. While some of what Jacob says may seem like a contradiction, it isn't. Instead of undermining and opposing Paul's teaching that works cannot save, Jacob explains the kind of faith that does. "Faith that doesn't involve action is phony," Jacob argues. Faith that saves is a faith that works!

Poverty and Wealth: One of the major concerns of Jacob (James) seemed to be the huge gap between the rich and poor, even within the church. He encourages poor believers that they have been blessed with every privilege from God, though society may dismiss them. And to the rich he reminds them no amount of wealth from below could buy what they've been given from above. Jacob also writes against favoritism in the church of any kind, especially based on the size of one's pocketbook or the brand of their clothes.

JAMES (JACOB)

A Life of Good Works

Faith and Wisdom

1 Greetings! My name is Jacob,[a] and I'm a love-slave of God and of the Lord Jesus Christ. I'm writing to all the twelve tribes of Israel who have been sown as seeds[b] among the nations.

[2] My fellow believers, when it seems as though you are facing nothing but difficulties see it as an invaluable opportunity to experience the greatest joy that you can! [3] For you know that when your faith is tested[c] it stirs up power within you to endure all things. [4] And then as your endurance grows even stronger it will release perfection into every part of your being until there is nothing missing and nothing lacking.

[5] And if anyone longs to be wise, ask God for wisdom and he will give it! He won't see your lack of wisdom as an opportunity to scold you over your failures but he will overwhelm your failures with his generous grace.[d] [6] Just make sure you ask empowered by confident faith without doubting that you will receive. For the ambivalent person believes one minute and doubts the next. Being undecided makes you become like the rough seas driven and tossed by the wind. You're up one minute and tossed down the next. [7-8] When you are half-hearted and wavering it leaves you unstable.[e] Can you really expect to receive anything from the Lord when you're in that condition?

[9] The believer who is poor still has reasons to boast, for he has been placed on high. [10] But those who are rich should boast in how God has brought them low and humbled them, for all their earthly glory will one day fade away like a wildflower in the meadow. [11] For as the scorching heat of the sun causes the

---

a 1:1 James is actually the Hebrew name Jacob, the name of the man who had twelve sons that formed the twelve tribes of Israel.

b 1:1 As translated from the Aramaic, which was the language spoken by Jesus and his disciples.

c 1:3 Or "when faith passes the test."

d 1:5 Or "with an open hand."

e 1:7–8 Or "restless" or "disengaged."

petals of the wildflower to fall off and lose its appearance of beauty,ᵃ so the rich in the midst of their pursuit of wealth will wither away.

¹²If your faith remains strong, even while surrounded by life's difficulties, you will continue to experience the untold blessings of God! True happiness comes as you pass the test with faith, and receive the victorious crown of life promised to every lover of God!

¹³When you are tempted don't ever say, "God is tempting me," for God is incapable of being tempted by evil and he is never the source of temptation. ¹⁴Instead it is each person's own desires and thoughts that drag them into evil and lure ᵇ them away into darkness. ¹⁵Evil desires give birth to evil actions. And when sin is fully mature it can murder you! ¹⁶So my friends, don't be fooled by your own desires!

¹⁷Every gift ᶜ God freely gives us is good and perfect,ᵈ streaming down from the Father of lights,ᵉ who shines from the heavens with no hidden shadow or darknessᶠ and is never subject to change. ¹⁸God was delightedᵍ to give us birth by the truth of his infallible Wordʰ so that we would fulfill his chosen destiny for us and become the favorite ones out of all his creation!ⁱ

¹⁹My dearest brothers and sisters, take this to heart: Be quick to listen,ʲ but slow to speak. And be slow to become angry, ²⁰for human anger is never a legitimate tool to promote God's righteous purpose.ᵏ ²¹So this is why we abandon

---

a 1:11 In the land of the Bible there were many deserts with arid land. The rainy season is quite short and the burning heat of the sun scorched the earth until the next season of rain arrived. We live in a constantly changing world with riches and beauty quickly fading. Our hope is set on things above.

b 1:14 Or "hooked by the bait of evil from their own desires."

c 1:17 Or "legacy."

d 1:17 The Aramaic word used here, *mshamlaita,* means "complete, wholesome, abundant, sufficient, enough, and perfect."

e 1:17 Jesus calls us the light of the world (Matt. 5:14–16) and Paul describes believers as "shining lights" (Phil. 2:15) in this world. God is our Father, he created angels but he brought us into new birth. The Greek word *anōthen* ("from above") is used by Jesus in describing to Nicodemus that we are born from above. We are lights born from above. See also John 3:7.

f 1:17 Or "shadow of turning." The implication is there is nothing that you will find wrong with God, nothing in him that could even remotely appear to be evil hiding. The more you get to know him the more you realize how beautiful and holy he is.

g 1:18 Or "God having decided gave us birth." The comparison in this passage is striking. Sin gives birth to death, God from his pure desires gives us birth to bring him glory.

h 1:18 The Aramaic can be translated "the word of the rainbow-sign." That is, the unbreakable new covenant promises we have as new creatures in Christ.

i 1:18 Or "a kind of firstfruits of his creations" or "the pledge [down-payment] of a still further creation [a more complete harvest]."

j 1:19 Although the Greek does not supply an object we are to listen to, it is obvious in the context that we should listen to one another, to God's voice, and to his Word. May God give us listening hearts.

k 1:20 Or "God's righteousness will never attach itself to human anger."

everything morally impure[a] and all forms of wicked conduct.[b] Instead, with a sensitive spirit[c] we absorb God's Word, which has been implanted within our nature, for the Word of Life has power to continually deliver us.[d]

[22] Don't just listen to the Word of Truth and not respond to it, for that is the essence of self-deception. So always let his Word become like poetry written and fulfilled by your life![e]

[23] If you listen to the Word and don't live out the message you hear, you become like the person who looks in the mirror of the Word to discover the reflection of his face in the beginning.[f] [24] *You perceive how God sees you in the mirror of the Word,*[g] but then you go out and forget[h] your divine origin. [25] But those who set their gaze deeply into the perfecting law of liberty[i] are fascinated by and respond to the truth they hear and are strengthened by it—they experience God's blessing in all that they do![j]

[26] If someone believes they have a relationship with God but fails to guard his words then his heart is drifting away and his religion is shallow and empty.[k]

[27] True spirituality[l] that is pure in the eyes of our Father God is to make a difference in the lives of the orphans,[m] and widows in their troubles, and to refuse to be corrupted by the world's values.

The Royal Law of Love Excludes Prejudice

2 My dear brothers and sisters, fellow believers in our glorious Lord Jesus Christ—how could we say that we have faith in him and yet we favor one group of people above another?[n] [2] Suppose an influential man comes into your worship meeting wearing gold rings and expensive clothing, and also a homeless

---

a 1:21 The Aramaic word used here can mean "demonic activities."

b 1:21 Or "excesses of evil."

c 1:21 Due to the Greek sentence construction, this clause may refer to what preceded it, "abandon . . . all forms of wicked conduct with a gentle [meek] heart."

d 1:21 Or "save our souls." The Greek uses the effective aorist active infinitive σωσαι (sōsai) from σωζω (sōzō) and could refer to the ultimate salvation of our souls (personality, emotions, thoughts) and/or our eternal salvation.

e 1:22 Or "be a poet [doer] of the Word."

f 1:23 Or "realizing his beginning [genesis] face" or "studying the face he was born with."

g 1:24 For the believer, seeing the man "in the mirror" is seeing how God sees us from the beginning, even before the fall of Adam which resulted in sin's devastation to human hearts. The man in the mirror is the new creation man.

h 1:24 The Aramaic can be translated "drift away from."

i 1:25 This is referred to as the "royal law of love" in 2:8 and the "law of liberty" in 2:12.

j 1:25 See Luke 11:28.

k 1:26 As translated from the Aramaic. The Greek is "If one presumes to be religious but doesn't guard his tongue, he deceives himself and his religion is useless."

l 1:27 The Aramaic can be translated "True ministry."

m 1:27 The Greek word orphanos means "the fatherless" or "the comfortless."

n 2:1 The Aramaic can be translated "Don't be taken in by the face mask of people, but hold to the faith in the glory of our Lord Jesus the Messiah."

man in shabby clothes comes in. [3] If you show special attention to the rich man in expensive clothes and say, "Here's a seat of honor for you right up front!" but you turn and say to the poor beggar dressed in rags, "You can stand over here," or "Sit over there on the floor in the back," [a] [4] then you've demonstrated gross prejudice among yourselves and used evil standards of judgment!

[5] So listen carefully, my dear brothers and sisters, hasn't God chosen [b] the poor in the world's eyes to be those who are rich in faith? And won't they be the heirs of the kingdom-realm he promised to those who love him? [6] But yet you insult and shun the poor *in your efforts to impress the rich!* [d] Isn't it the wealthy who exploit you and drag you into court? [7] Aren't they the very ones who blaspheme the beautiful name of the One you now belong to? [e]

[8] Your calling is to fulfill the royal law of love [f] as given to us in this Scripture: "You must love and value your neighbor as you love and value yourself!" [g]

For keeping this law is the noble way to live. [9] But when you show prejudice you commit sin and you violate this royal law of love!

[10] For the one who attempts to keep all of the law of Moses but fails in just one point has become guilty of breaking the law in every respect! [11] For the same One who tells us, "Do not commit adultery," also said, "Do not murder." [h] Now if you don't commit adultery but do commit murder, you are still guilty as a law-breaker. [12] So we must both speak and act in every respect like those who are destined to be tried by the perfect law of liberty, [13] and remember that judgment is merciless for the one who judges others without mercy. So by showing mercy you take dominion over judgment! [i]

Faith Works

[14] My dear brothers and sisters, what good is it if someone claims to have faith but demonstrates no good works to prove it? How could this kind of faith save anyone? [15] For example, if a brother or sister in the faith is poorly clothed and hungry [16] and you leave them saying, "Good-bye. I hope you stay warm and have plenty to eat," but you don't provide them with a coat or even a cup of soup, what good is your faith? [17] So then faith that doesn't involve action is phony. [j]

---

a 2:3 The Aramaic can be translated "Sit on the floor before our footstool."
b 2:5 The Greek word for "chosen" is *eklegomai*, which is a form of *lego* (speak).
c 2:5 See 1 Cor. 1:27–28.
d 2:6 See also 1 Cor. 11:22.
e 2:7 Or "the worthy name which was invoked over you (at your baptism)."
f 2:8 It is a royal law because it is given by our King, but since he has made us kings and priests, it becomes the royal law of love given to his royal sons and daughters who are heirs with him.
g 2:8 See Lev. 19:18; Matt. 19:19; 22:39; Mark 12:31; Luke 10:27; Rom. 13:9; Gal. 5:14.
h 2:11 See Ex. 20:13–14.
i 2:13 As translated from the Aramaic. The Greek is "Mercy triumphs over judgment."
j 2:17 Or "dead (fruitless)." See also v. 20.

¹⁸ But someone might object and say, "One person has faith and another person has works." ᵃ Go ahead then and prove to me that you have faith without works and I will show you faith by my works as proof that I believe. ¹⁹ You can believe all you want that there is one true God, ᵇ that's wonderful! But even the demons know this and tremble with fear before him, ᶜ yet they're unchanged—*they remain demons.*

²⁰ O feeble sons of Adam, ᵈ do you need further evidence that faith divorced from good works is phony? ²¹ Wasn't our ancestor Abraham found righteous before God because of his works when he offered his son Isaac on the altar? ²² Can't you see how his action cooperated with his faith and by his action faith found its full expression? ²³ So in this way the Scripture was fulfilled:

> Because Abraham believed God, his faith was exchanged for God's righteousness. ᵉ

So he became known as the lover of God! ᶠ ²⁴ So now it's clear that a person is seen as righteous in God's eyes not merely by faith alone, but by his works.

²⁵ And the same is true of the prostitute named Rahab who was found righteous in God's eyes by her works, for she received the spies into her home and helped them escape from the city by another route. ᵍ ²⁶ For just as a human body without the spirit is a dead corpse, so faith without the expression of good works is dead!

The Power of Your Words

3 My dear brothers and sisters, don't be so eager to become a teacher in the church since you know that we who teach are held to a higher standard of judgment. ² We all fail in many areas, but especially with our words. Yet if we're able to bridle the words we say we are powerful enough to control ourselves in every way, and that means our character is mature and fully developed. ³ Horses have bits and bridles in their mouths so that we can control and guide their large body. ⁴ And the same with mighty ships, though they are massive and driven by fierce winds, yet they are steered by a tiny rudder at the direction of the person at the helm.

⁵ And so the tongue is a small part of the body yet it carries great power! ʰ

---

a 2:18 Many scholars conclude that the ambiguity of the Greek text makes this the most difficult verse in all of James and perhaps in all of the New Testament to translate.

b 2:19 Or "that God is one," which is the Jewish *Shema* (see Deut. 6:4).

c 2:19 The Aramaic can be translated "they writhe on their bellies in the dirt!"

d 2:20 As translated from the Aramaic. The Greek is "O empty man."

e 2:23 Or "Abraham's faith was credited to his account for righteousness." See Gen. 15:6.

f 2:23 As translated from the Aramaic. Although the Greek text is most often translated "friend of God," the Greek word *philos* can also be used as the love that bonds friends together. See also 2 Chron. 20:7; Isa. 41:18; Dan. 3:35 (LXX).

g 2:25 See Josh. 2.

h 3:5 Or "boasts of great things." The Aramaic can be translated "the tongue has dominion."

Just think of how a small flame can set a huge forest ablaze. ⁶And the tongue is a fire! It can be compared to the sum total of wickedness ᵃ and is the most dangerous part of our human body. It corrupts the entire body ᵇ and is a hellish flame! ᶜ It releases a fire that can burn throughout the course of human existence. ᵈ

⁷For every wild animal on earth including birds, creeping reptiles, and creatures of the sea and land ᵉ have all been overpowered and tamed by humans, ⁸but the tongue is not able to be tamed. It's a fickle, unrestrained evil that spews out words full of toxic poison! ⁹We use our tongue to praise God our Father ᶠ and then turn around and curse a person who was made in his very image! ᵍ ¹⁰Out of the same mouth we pour out words of praise one minute and curses the next. My brothers and sister, this should never be!

¹¹⁻¹²Would you look for olives hanging on a fig tree or go to pick figs from a grapevine? Is it possible that fresh and bitter water can flow out of the same spring? So neither can a bitter spring produce fresh water. ʰ

Wisdom from Above

¹³If you consider yourself to be wise and one who understands the ways of God, advertise it with a beautiful, fruitful ⁱ life guided by wisdom's gentleness. Never brag or boast about what you've done and you'll prove that you're truly wise. ¹⁴But if there is bitter jealousy or competition hiding in your heart, then don't deny it and try to compensate for it by boasting and being phony. ¹⁵For that has nothing to do with God's heavenly wisdom but can best be described as the wisdom of this world, both selfish ʲ and devilish. ᵏ ¹⁶So wherever jealousy ˡ

---

a 3:6 As translated from the Latin Vulgate. The Greek is "a world of wrongdoing."

b 3:6 It is possible that the body James refers to here is the body of believers (a local church).

c 3:6 Or "is set ablaze by gehenna [hell]." The Aramaic does not mention *gehenna* but is simply "burns with fire." Gehenna is taken from the concept of "The Valley of Hinnom" where rubbish was burned outside the city of Jerusalem, becoming a Hebrew metaphor for the fires of hell.

d 3:6 The Aramaic can be translated "a fire that passes through successive generations, rolling on like wheels."

e 3:7 Implied in the Greek and made explicit in the Aramaic.

f 3:9 Some Greek manuscripts have "Lord and Father." The Aramaic can be translated "Lord God (*MarYah*, the Aramaic equivalent to Yahweh).

g 3:9 The Aramaic can be translated "we curse a person and pretend to be God!"

h 3:11–12 As translated from the Aramaic.

i 3:13 As translated from the Aramaic.

j 3:15 Or "unspiritual."

k 3:15 Or "behaves like a demon."

l 3:16 The Greek word for jealousy implies an obsession to promote one's self at the expense of others.

and selfishness are uncovered, you will also find many troubles[a] and every kind of meanness.

[17] But the wisdom from above is always pure,[b] filled with peace, considerate and teachable.[c] It is filled with love[d] and never displays prejudice or hypocrisy[e] in any form [18] and it always bears the beautiful harvest of righteousness! Good seeds of wisdom's fruit will be planted with peaceful acts by those who cherish making peace.

Living Close to God

4 What is the cause of your conflicts and quarrels with each other? Doesn't the battle begin inside of you as you fight to have your own way and fulfill your own desires? [2] You jealously want what others have so you begin to see yourself as better than others. You scheme with envy and harm[f] others to selfishly obtain what you crave—that's why you quarrel and fight. And all the time you don't obtain what you want because you won't ask God for it! [3] And if you ask, you won't receive it for you're asking with corrupt motives,[g] seeking only to fulfill your own selfish desires. [4] You have become spiritual adulterers who are having an affair, an unholy relationship with the world. Don't you know that flirting with the world's values places you at odds with God? Whoever chooses to be the world's friend makes himself God's enemy!

[5] Does the Scripture mean nothing to you that says, "The Spirit that God breathed into our hearts is a jealous Lover who intensely desires to have more and more of us"?[h]

[6] But he continues to pour out more and more grace[i] upon us. For it says,

God resists you when you are proud
but continually pours out grace when you are humble."[j]

[7] So then, surrender to God. Stand up to the devil and resist him and he

---

a 3:16 The Aramaic can be translated "chaos." The Greek can be translated "instability" or "disorder."

b 3:17 Or "holy."

c 3:17 A beautiful concept that means "easy to correct" or "ready to be convinced" or "willing to yield to others." Is this true of your life?

d 3:17 As translated from the Aramaic. The Greek is "mercy."

e 3:17 Or "never wears a mask."

f 4:2 Or "kill," however, the Greek words for "kill" and "envy" are almost the same.

g 4:3 The Greek word for corrupt motives is kakos and can be translated "sick," or "sickly." James is exhorting us not to pray "sickly prayers."

h 4:5 Although it is difficult to find a verse from the Old Testament that reads exactly how James quotes it, the possibility remains that it becomes a general statement of what the Bible teaches, or even a quotation from an older translation not available today. We must always realize that the Holy Spirit pursues us relentlessly and takes it very personally when we turn from him to pursue friendship with the world.

i 4:6 Or "he gives us a greater gift" or "the grace [favor] he gives us is stronger."

j 4:6 See Prov. 3:34.

will turn and run away from you. ⁸ Move your heart closer and closer to God, and he will come even closer to you. *ᵃ* But make sure you cleanse your life, you sinners, and keep your heart pure and stop doubting. *ᵇ* ⁹ Feel the pain of your sin, be sorrowful and weep! Let your joking around *ᶜ* be turned into mourning and your joy into deep humiliation. ¹⁰ Be willing to be made low before the Lord and he will exalt you!

¹¹ Dear friends, as part of God's family, never speak against another family member, for when you slander a brother or sister you violate *ᵈ* God's law *of love*. And your duty is not to make yourself a judge of the law *of love ᵉ* by saying that it doesn't apply to you, *ᶠ but your duty is to obey it! ᵍ* ¹² There is only one true Lawgiver and Judge, the One who has the power to save and destroy—so who do you think you are to judge your neighbor?

¹³ Listen, those of you who are boasting, "Today or tomorrow we'll go to another city and spend some time and go into business and make heaps of profit!" ¹⁴ But you don't have a clue what tomorrow may bring. For your fleeting life is but a warm breath of air that is visible in the cold only for a moment and then vanishes! ¹⁵ Instead you should say, "Our tomorrows are in the Lord's hands and if he is willing we will live life to its fullest and do this or that." ¹⁶ But here you are, boasting in your ignorance, for to be presumptuous about what you'll do tomorrow is evil!

¹⁷ So if you know of an opportunity to do the right thing today, yet you refrain from doing it, you're guilty of sin.

Warning to the Rich

5 Listen all you who are rich, for it's time to weep and howl over the misery *ʰ* that will overtake you! ² Your riches lie rotting, your fine clothing eaten by moths, ³ and your gold and silver are corroded as a witness against you. You have hoarded up treasure for the last days but it will become a fire to burn your flesh. ⁴ Listen! Can't you hear the cries of the laborers *ⁱ* over the wages you fraudulently held back from those who worked for you? *ʲ* The cries for justice of those you've cheated have reached the ears of the Lord of armies! *ᵏ*

⁵ You have indulged yourselves with every luxury and pleasure this world

---

a 4:8 The Aramaic can be translated "and he will be touching you."
b 4:8 Or "you double-minded."
c 4:9 As translated from the Aramaic.
d 4:11 Or "speak against."
e 4:11 See also Lev. 19:18; James 4:8.
f 4:11 Or "to be a judge of the law."
g 4:11 Implied in the argument James makes to refrain from being a judge of the law.
h 5:1 The Aramaic word can refer to demonic torment.
i 5:4 Or "the reapers" (of your fields).
j 5:4 Or "those who worked in your fields."
k 5:4 Or "Lord Sabaoth."

offers, but you're only stuffing your heart full for a day of slaughter. [6] You have condemned and murdered good and innocent people[a] who had no power to defend themselves.[b]

[7] Meanwhile, brothers and sisters, we must be patient and filled with expectation as we wait for the appearing[c] of the Lord. Think about the farmer who has to patiently wait for the earth's harvest as it ripens because of the early and latter rains. [8] So you also keep your hopes high and be patient, for the presence of the Lord is drawing closer.[d] [9] Since each of you are part of God's family never complain or grumble about each other[e] so that judgment will not come on you, for the true Judge is near and very ready to appear![f]

[10] My brothers and sisters, take[g] the prophets as your mentors. They have prophesied in the name of the Lord[h] and *it brought them great sufferings*, yet they patiently endured. [11] We honor them as our heroes[i] because they remained faithful even while enduring great sufferings. And you have heard of all that Job went through and we can now see that the Lord ultimately treated him with wonderful kindness, revealing how tenderhearted he really is![j]

[12] Above all we must be those who never need to verify our speech as truthful by swearing by the heavens or the earth or any other oath.[k] But instead we must be so full of integrity that our "Yes" or "No" is convincing enough and we do not stumble into hypocrisy.[l]

Prayer for the Sick

[13] Are there any believers in your fellowship suffering great hardship and distress? Encourage them to pray![m] Are there happy, cheerful ones among you?

---

a 5:6 Or "the righteous one," a possible reference to the death of Jesus.

b 5:6 Or "will not (God) resist you?"

c 5:7 This is the abstract Greek word *parousia* which can mean "arrival, presence, becoming manifest, appearing." *Parousia* is taken from the present participle *pareina* a compound word of *para* (beside) and *einai* (to be seen, made visible). It has little to do with distance or space, but with becoming visible, such as an uncovering or revealing what is nearby. It is commonly used for the return of our Lord Jesus Christ.

d 5:8 Or "near at hand." The Greek word *engizo* is taken from the word *eggus*, which means to take by the hand, to throttle, or to hold the reins. (See *Strong's Concordance*, Gr. 1448 and 1451.)

e 5:9 Or "don't blame others" (for your troubles).

f 5:9 Or "at the gate."

g 5:10 Or "receive."

h 5:10 That is, by the Lord's authority. See also v. 14.

i 5:11 Or "we regard them as blessed."

j 5:11 See Ex. 34:6; Ps. 86:15.

k 5:12 See Matt. 5:34.

l 5:12 Some Greek manuscripts read "stumble into hypocrisy," while others have, "stumble into judgment."

m 5:13 See Luke 18:1; 1 Cor. 14:14–15.

Encourage them to sing out their praises![a] [14] Are there any sick among you? Then ask the elders of the church to come and pray over the sick and anoint them with oil in the name of our Lord. [15] And the prayer of faith[b] will heal the sick[c] and the Lord will raise them up,[d] and if they have committed sins[e] they will be forgiven.[f]

[16] Confess and acknowledge how you have offended one another[g] and then pray for one another to be instantly healed,[h] for tremendous power is released through the passionate, heartfelt prayer[i] of a godly believer!

[17] Elijah was a man with human frailties, just like all of us, but he prayed and received supernatural answers.[j] He actually shut the heavens over the land so there would be no rain for three and a half years! [18] Then he prayed again and the skies opened up over the land so that the rain came again and produced the harvest.

[19] Finally, as members of God's beloved family, we must go after the one who wanders from the truth and bring him back. [20] For the one who restores the sinning believer back to God from the error of his way, gives back to his soul[k] life from the dead, and covers over countless sins[l] *by their demonstration of love!*

---

a 5:13 Or "pluck the strings of a harp" or "sing a psalm."

b 5:15 Or "the claim of faith."

c 5:15 This is not the Greek usually used for sickness or disease. The word *kamno* can also mean "those who are weary and worn down," and in the context could possibly refer to believers who have been arguing with each other, leaving them spiritually weak.

d 5:15 That is, restore them to health. This could be a subtle hint of a resurrection.

e 5:15 Or "doer of sin." There is a clear implication in this passage that the sickness (weakness) referred to is the result of sin. See also 1 Cor. 11:18–32.

f 5:15 This may be speaking of the church elders who are forgiving the arguing believers and restoring them back into fellowship.

g 5:16 As translated from the Aramaic, which uses a word that can be translated "faults" or "folly" or "offenses." The Critical Greek text is "confess your sins."

h 5:16 Or "restored."

i 5:16 Or "energized prayer," a prayer within a prayer.

j 5:17 Or "he prayed with prayer" (intensity).

k 5:20 As translated from the Aramaic. The Greek is similar, meaning "save his soul from death."

l 5:20 That is, bring about forgiveness of many sins through restoring the person back to God. To cover sins is a Hebrew concept of atonement.

1 PETER

Introduction

AT A GLANCE

Author: The apostle Peter
Audience: Churches in northwestern Asia Minor, modern-day Turkey
Date: AD 62–65
Type of Literature: A letter
Major Themes: God's nature, salvation, the church, the Christian life, and suffering
Outline:

Letter Opening — 1:1–2
Identity as God's Chosen People and Foreigners — 1:3–2:10
Living Honorably as Foreigners — 2:11–3:12
Responding to Hostility as Foreigners — 3:13–4:6
Living in Christian Solidarity as Foreigners — 4:7–19
Suffering Together as Foreigners — 5:1–11
Letter Closing — 5:12–14

ABOUT 1 PETER

Everyone needs grace to overcome life's hurdles. For some, they need to overcome a difficult marriage, or the frustration of children who have wandered away. For others it may be their limitations and hardships. First Peter is the book of strengthening grace and triumphant hope. There is an abundance of hopeful grace found within the verses of this book to set you free. You are a victorious overcomer, and God's grace is our fuel to empower our hearts to soar!

Peter was the first preacher to bring the gospel of Christ to the Jews in Jerusalem. At Pentecost he stood fearlessly and told the thousands gathered around him that they had denied the Holy One of God and crucified their Messiah. Yet just fifty days earlier, the apostle Peter, while Jesus was being tried by Pilate, denied that he even knew Jesus. Three times he succumbed to the weakness of his flesh. But Jesus had prophesied all this beforehand and gave him both a promise and a commission:

"I have prayed for you, Peter, that you would stay faithful to me no matter what comes. Remember this: after you have turned back to me and have been restored, make it your life mission to strengthen the faith of your brothers." (Luke 22:32)

Jesus told Peter that his life mission after his resurrection would be to strengthen the faith of believers worldwide. So you will discover that there is an unusual grace upon Peter's letters (known as part of the General Epistles) to strengthen you in your faith. Don't be surprised if after reading these letters you become emboldened to persevere, empowered to overcome, and encouraged to remain faithful to Christ. For the grace that restored Peter after his fall is also on Peter's letters to restore every believer and impart to them overcoming grace.

The Roman historian Eusebius informs us that Peter was crucified in Rome by Nero. The church tradition records that when Peter was being crucified, he pleaded with them to turn the cross upside down, stating that he was not worthy to be crucified in the same way as Jesus. Because of their respect for the godly Peter, the soldiers complied with his request. Peter turned the world upside down with the gospel power he carried, then he died on an upside-down cross. Peter experienced the triumph of grace. Our prayer for you is that the truth you read in the following pages will release within you this same amazing grace and triumphant hope!

PURPOSE

There is rich teaching found in 1 Peter, showing us that the community of Christ is a holy nation made up of kings and priests and lovers of God. And Peter teaches us the ways of purity and righteousness, and how to remain faithful to God all the days of our lives as members of a kingdom that chafes against the values of the world. He wrote this letter to Christians undergoing persecution for living in a way that was different from their unbelieving neighbors. His letter was meant to encourage them in their suffering and give it purpose as a vital aspect of Christian living.

This is a letter about God and living for him—no matter what the costs. Some of the themes of 1 Peter include holiness and being faithful in the midst of persecution. When others turn away from us, the presence of Christ grows stronger in our lives. It pushes our souls deeper into God's overcoming grace. No matter what you face and no matter what you may be passing through in your life today, there is a power from on high to make you into an overcomer. Let Peter's letter show you the way!

AUTHOR AND AUDIENCE

Written about AD 62 from "Babylon" (a cryptic term for Rome), Peter longed to encourage and strengthen the faith of those who were being persecuted for following Christ. Although Aramaic was his first language, the fisherman Peter's refined use of Greek has caused some scholars to even doubt that he wrote this first epistle. We do know however that every good writer has a brilliant editor. Peter's editor for this letter was Silvanus (5:12), who no doubt helped Peter with the more elegant Greek words (much like the vocabulary of Paul), which are found in these five chapters.

Peter was the first missionary to go to the gentiles. After a divine trance he experienced on the rooftop in Joppa, Peter took the keys of the kingdom and opened the door of faith for the gentiles. He broke the religious limitation that the gospel was only meant for the Jews. Peter found his way to the house of Cornelius, a Roman gentile, and he and all his family became followers of Jesus. He continued this mission by writing to Christians living in the Roman regions of northeastern Asia Minor (modern-day Turkey), to encourage them in their suffering, provoke holy living and growth in God, and explain their new birth through Christ's blood. We all have a debt of love to the apostle Peter. Enjoy his letter as you read it with an open and thankful heart.

MAJOR THEMES

God the Father, God the Son, God the Holy Spirit. Who God is and what God is like is front and center in Peter's letter, because all of the teachings relate to him in some way. He's referred to as "Father God" or "God the Father," which should tell us something about how we encounter him: as a Father! He's also described as the mighty and powerful Creator and Judge, but also as our merciful and gracious Redeemer.

Of course as Redeemer, the Son of God is also featured prominently in this letter. One of the most important names Peter uses for Jesus is "Anointed One." This is a deeply Hebrew idea for the Messiah, the One whom God the Father destined "before the foundation of the earth was laid" (1:20) to be sacrificed for us "like a spotless, unblemished lamb" (1:19). It is this suffering that forms the basis for his saving work; our salvation was achieved through his crucifixion! While Jesus was fully revealed while he was on earth, he will be ultimately revealed on the last day, bringing with him the full revelation of our salvation and God's grace.

Then there is the Holy Spirit, who is vital for our ongoing Christian life, for a number of reasons: he's the One who has set us apart to be God's holy ones in the first place; he is the source of the gospel revelation, which goes out from us and draws people into God's family; and he lives in us to help us obey God as his chosen ones. Peter unveils before us the revelation-truth that he is our power as we live in this world as resident aliens and foreigners, awaiting Christ's return when he comes to make all things new.

The Nature of Our Salvation. Peter uses a number of images and words to convey to his readers the breadth and depth of their salvation in Jesus Christ. Followers of Christ have been "gloriously sprinkled with his blood" (1:2), have been redeemed once and for all through the precious blood of Christ (1:18–19), have been purified through obedience (1:22), have tasted "of the goodness of the Lord Jehovah and have experienced his kindness" (2:3), have been brought near to God (3:18).

This language reflects two ways in which believers have been changed: through Christ's sacrifice, and being born again. First, Peter uses sacrificial metaphors to explain what's happened to us. These are drawn from the ancient temple cultic practices of blood-shedding and purification. Second, Peter explains that our salvation is to be reborn into a new family, and we've inherited all of the benefits of that royal birth. So when we say we've been "born again," we are reflecting the language that Peter himself used to talk about what's happened to us!

Life in God's Family as a Spiritual "Nation." The inevitable outgrowth of our salvation and new birth in Christ is a new way of living and in concert with our new family and a spiritual "nation." We are to practice hope and holiness, fear of God, and growth in the knowledge of God. The reason why we devote ourselves to these pursuits is because we've been bought by the blood of Jesus. Without this new birth, there is no reason to obey; without the hope of salvation the Christian life is pointless.

What's interesting about Peter's letter is that he doesn't envision this kind of life as a solitary endeavor. Life in God's family is just that—a family affair! First, those in God's family are described as being "chosen" and "elect" (see the first footnote at 1:1), which recalls the story of ancient Israel. This is intentional, as the church is the continuation and culmination of Israel as the new, true people of God. This idea of family frames the whole letter, appearing in the first verse and the last. They are the ones who've received God's grace and favor. It also frames how we are to live: we are to live as "obedient children" (1:14); we are to be holy as the Father is holy; we are to live within a new familial structure, accepting the authority of elders; and we are to love one another as siblings, wrapping ourselves with "the apron of a humble servant" (5:5).

Suffering and Persecution. Inevitably, when we live as obedient children of God, and the believing community takes seriously its role as "priests who are kings, a spiritual 'nation' set apart as God's devoted ones" (2:9), there's going to be conflict with the surrounding world. But Peter wants believers, who are "resident aliens and foreigners in this world" (2:11), to take heart: "the grief of many trials . . . reveal the sterling core of your faith" (1:6–7). Persecution is a refiner's fire that unfolds the brilliance of authentic faith. And when we do suffer for Christ, Jesus is praised, glorified, and honored. Ultimately, persecution is a privilege, for we "carry the Anointed One's name!" (4:16). God will never fail those who suffer for him!

1 PETER

Triumphant Hope

Our Living Hope

From Peter, an apostle of Jesus the Anointed One, to the chosen ones[a] who have been scattered abroad like "seed" into the nations living as refugees,[b] to those living in Pontus,[c] Galatia, Cappadocia,[d] and throughout *the Roman provinces of* Asia and Bithynia.[e] [2] *You are not forgotten*, for you have been chosen and destined by Father God. The Holy Spirit has set you apart to be God's holy ones, obedient followers of Jesus Christ who have been *gloriously* sprinkled with his blood. May God's delightful grace and peace cascade over you many times over![f]

[3] Celebrate with praises the God and Father of our Lord Jesus Christ, who has shown us his extravagant mercy. For his *fountain of* mercy has given us a new life— we are reborn[g] to experience a living, energetic hope[h] through the resurrection of Jesus Christ from the dead.[i] [4] We are reborn into a perfect inheritance[j] that can

---

a 1:1 Or "elect" (believers). As God's chosen people, this would also refer to the faithful within unfaithful Israel.

b 1:1 First Peter, Hebrews, and James were all written to believers who had been scattered like "seed" among the nations due to persecution. Exile is the way the original audience would have described the situation in their day. "Refugees" is a modern equivalent in ours.

c 1:1 Pontus is the region of the Turkish coast of the Black Sea.

d 1:1 Galatia and Cappadocia are regions of central Turkey.

e 1:1 The provinces of Asia (Minor) and Bithynia are modern-day western Turkey.

f 1:2 Or "be multiplied to you." Notice all three members of the Trinity are mentioned in this verse: Father God, the Holy Spirit, and Jesus Christ. We are chosen by the Father, set apart (or sanctified) by the Holy Spirit, and submitted to Christ.

g 1:3 This is the only place in the New Testament where the Greek verb *anagennaō* is found (a hapax legomenon). This shows that God himself is the one who gives us new birth as newborn believers filled with the life of Christ. God is truly our Father, who gives us new life through his living mercy.

h 1:3 Some Greek manuscripts and the Aramaic read "the hope of life."

i 1:3 Peter states that the first result of our new birth is that we are brought into a living hope in the power of God, based on the resurrection of Christ. The God of resurrection gives us a powerful hope to excel in life.

j 1:4 The second result that comes from our new birth is an eternal inheritance, which is available now by faith, and will also be reserved in heaven for us when we pass from death

never perish, never be defiled, and never diminish. It is promised and preserved forever in the heavenly realm for you![a]

[5] Through our faith, the mighty power of God constantly guards[b] us until our *full* salvation[c] is ready to be revealed[d] in the last time. [6] May the thought of this cause you to jump for joy,[e] even though lately you've had to put up with the grief of many trials.[f] [7] But these only reveal the sterling core[g] of your faith, which is far more valuable than gold that perishes, for even gold is refined by fire. *Your authentic faith* will result in even more praise, glory, and honor when Jesus the Anointed One is revealed.[h]

[8] You love him passionately although you did not see him, but through believing in him you are saturated with an ecstatic joy, indescribably sublime and immersed in glory.[i] [9] For you are reaping the harvest of your faith—the full salvation promised you—your souls' victory![j]

Overcoming Grace

[10] This salvation was the focus of the prophets who prophesied of this *outpouring of* grace that was destined for you. They made a careful search and investigation of the meaning *of their God-given prophecies* [11] as they probed into *the mysteries* of who would fulfill them and the time period when it would all take place. The Spirit of the Anointed One was in them[k] and was pointing prophetically to the sufferings that Christ was destined to suffer and the glories that

---

to life. Paul describes it as "every spiritual blessing" that has already been given to us by God (Eph. 1:3).

a   1:4 This would no doubt encourage those believers who had scattered from their homelands and been deprived of what they once possessed. Their blessings (and ours) are not only material, but spiritual, from a transcendent reality.

b   1:5 The Greek word for "guards us" is *phrouroumenous*, which comes from a military term (*phrouria*) meaning "a fort" or "an army garrison stationed to defend a city." You are continually being watched over and protected by God's mighty power.

c   1:5 The third result of our new birth that Peter mentions is our full salvation (or deliverance) that will come when Christ is unveiled. It is ready to be revealed and waits for our discovery.

d   1:5 The Greek verb *apokalyptō* means "to unveil and disclose." Peter is saying that there is a more complete salvation awaiting us when Christ is unveiled in the last days. The nominalized form of *apokalyptō* is the title of the last book of the Bible, Revelation: The Unveiling of Jesus Christ. In just a few verses Peter will tell us that a "grace" will also be revealed to us in the last days (1:13).

e   1:6 Or "exult in joy." The Aramaic can be translated "rejoice for eternity."

f   1:6 Peter speaks of believers suffering difficulties and persecutions four times in his first letter (1:6–7; 3:13–17; 4:12–19; 5:9).

g   1:7 Or "proven character."

h   1:7 Or "comes out of his concealment."

i   1:8 The Aramaic can be translated "a glorification that cannot be described."

j   1:9 Or "the salvation of your souls."

k   1:11 The Spirit of Christ was in the prophets of the Old Testament. This means that Enoch, Abraham, Jacob, Moses, Elijah, Elisha, Isaiah, Jeremiah, and all the prophets who prophesied would be released afterward. [12] God revealed to the prophets that their ministry was not for their own benefit [a] but for yours. And now, you have heard these things from the evangelists [b] who preached the gospel to you through *the power of* the Holy Spirit sent from heaven—the gospel *containing wonderful mysteries* that even the angels long to get a glimpse of. [c]

A Call to Holiness

[13] So then, prepare your *hearts and* minds for action! [d] Stay alert and fix your hope firmly on the marvelous grace that is coming to you. For when Jesus Christ is unveiled, [e] *a greater measure of* grace will be released to you. [14] As God's obedient children, never again shape your lives by the desires that you followed when you didn't know better. [15] Instead, shape your lives to become like the Holy One who called you. [16] For Scripture says:

> "You are to be holy, because I am holy." [f]

[17] Since you call on him as your heavenly Father, the impartial Judge who judges according to each one's works, [g] live each day with holy awe and

---

did so by the Holy Spirit living in them. Today every believer has the Holy Spirit within him or her and everyone may prophesy. See Rom. 8:9; 1 Cor. 12; 14.

a 1:12 That is, the prophets understood that their prophecies were not only for their generation but for generations to come.

b 1:12 The Aramaic can be translated "extenders of hope."

c 1:12 Heavenly angels are fascinated with God's mercy shown toward us. His wise plan of making former rebels into lovers has mystified the angelic realm. The church is the University of Angels and every believer a professor. Angels long to peer into the mysteries of God's grace, which have been lavished upon us. How much more should we be fascinated explorers of the mercy of God, for we have received it and are now redeemed. See also Eph. 3:10.

d 1:13 We would say today, "Roll up your sleeves," or, "Fasten your seat belt!"

e 1:13 Or "to come out of concealment, appear, be made manifest, revealed." Peter uses the Greek word *apokálypsis,* which is the title of the last book in the Bible, Revelation: The Unveiling of Jesus Christ. The Aramaic can be translated "Stay alert and share the news about the joy that came to you with the revelation of Jesus the Messiah."

f 1:16 See Lev. 11:44; 19:2. Everything about God is holy. True holiness includes justice, mercy, truth, and righteousness. To be holy is to be absolutely devoted to God in all that we do, demonstrating who he is to the world. Holiness surrounds God's throne and we are seated with him in heavenly places (Eph. 2:6). The Hebraic concept of holiness is "set apart"; that is, we are a people set apart for God, even as God is "set apart" from all gods. Grace has imbedded holiness into our lives, yet we are to make right choices and to yield to Christ and God's Word as the Holy Spirit lives in us. Holiness is not merely actions we perform, but what we absorb and manifest as we live our lives in God's presence. Christ is our holiness (1 Cor. 1:30).

g 1:17 The Aramaic can be translated "no one will put on a face mask before him." Believers in Jesus will not be judged for their sins, since that happened once and for all when Jesus was crucified to redeem us. We will be judged, however, for our works in order to determine

reverence throughout your time on earth.[a] [18] For you know that your lives were ransomed once and for all from the empty and futile way of life handed down from generation to generation. It was not a ransom payment of silver and gold, which eventually perishes, [19] but the precious blood of Christ—who like a spotless, unblemished lamb was *sacrificed for us*.[b]

[20] *This was part of God's plan*, for he was chosen and destined for this before the foundation of the earth was laid,[c] but he has been made manifest in these last days for you. [21] It is through him that you now believe in God,[d] who raised him from the dead and glorified him,[e] so that you would fasten your faith and hope in God *alone*.

Love and Purity

[22] Now, because of your obedience to the truth,[f] you have purified your very souls, and this empowers you to be full of love for your fellow believers. So express this sincere love toward one another passionately and with a pure heart.[g] [23] For through the eternal and living Word of God[h] you have been born again. And this "seed" that he planted within you can never be destroyed but will live *and grow* inside of you forever. For:

> [24] Human beings[i] are *frail and temporary*, like grass,
>   and the glory of man *fleeting*
>   like blossoms of the field.[j]
>   The grass dries and withers and the flowers fall off,
> [25] but the Word of the Lord endures forever![k]
>
> And this is the Word[l] that was announced to you!

---

the reward (or lack of reward) that God gives to those who believe in Christ. See Isa. 53:4–5; Rom. 14:10–12; 1 Cor. 3:12–15; 1 Peter 2:24.

a 1:17 Or "throughout the time of your exile."
b 1:19 See Ex. 12; Lev. 22:20–25; Isa. 53:7; John 1:29; Heb. 4:15; 7:26–27.
c 1:20 Or "before the fall of the world." The Greek word *kataboles* can possibly mean "lay a foundation," or "a fall," or "casting down." See also Eph. 1:4.
d 1:21 Or "You believe in him."
e 1:21 As translated from the Aramaic. The Greek is "and gave him glory."
f 1:22 Most later manuscripts have "through the Spirit." It is generally recognized by scholars today that this was likely an addition to the text.
g 1:22 This verse is packed with the virtues that should be seen in the lives of believers: obedience, truth, purification of our souls, authentic (sincere) love, fervent (passionate) expressions of love, and heart purity.
h 1:23 Or "the Word of the living and enduring God."
i 1:24 Or "All flesh."
j 1:24 As translated from the Aramaic.
k 1:25 See Isa. 40:6–8.
l 1:25 As translated from the Aramaic. This reveals that Jesus is the Word proclaimed to the world. See John 1:1. The Greek is "This is the good news announced to you."

Growing in Holiness

2 So abandon*a* every form of evil, deceit, hypocrisy,*b* feelings of jealousy and slander. ²In the same way that nursing infants cry for milk, you must intensely crave the pure*c* spiritual milk *of God's Word.*ᵈ For this "milk" will cause you to grow into maturity, fully nourished and strong for life*e*—³especially now that you have had a taste of the goodness of the Lord Jehovah and have experienced his kindness.*f*

⁴So keep coming to him who is the Living Stone*g*—though he was rejected and discarded by men but chosen by God and is priceless in God's sight. ⁵Come and be his "living stones"*h* who are continually being assembled into a sanctuary for God. For now you *serve as* holy priests,*i* offering up spiritual sacrifices that he readily accepts through Jesus Christ. ⁶For it says in Scripture:

> Look! I lay a cornerstone in Zion,*j*
> a chosen and priceless stone!
> And whoever believes in him
> will certainly not be disappointed.*k*

---

a 2:1 Or "rid yourselves." The Aramaic uses an interesting word that could be translated "oasis rest." The thought is that we must be completely free from evil and be at rest within. Purity is an oasis rest for the people of God.

b 2:1 The Greek word *hupokrisis* (the behavior of a hypocrite) can also be translated "a hypercritical attitude of pulling things apart for judgmental analysis." The Aramaic can be translated "wearing a face mask."

c 2:2 Or "unadulterated, guileless milk." The nourishment contained in the milk of the Word is like an antibiotic for guile. This milk contains an element that can eliminate our guile. Therefore, the Word is guileless, unadulterated milk.

d 2:2 Implied by the Greek word for "spiritual" (*logikos*), which seems to be a play on words with what Peter says in 1:23–25 concerning the living Word (*logos*) of God. The "pure spiritual milk" is the sustaining power of God's Word coming from his very breast, as it were, to nourish and strengthen our inner being. From v. 3 we can see that this "milk" is the Lord himself dispensed to us in the Word of God. Our craving for this "milk" is not only because of necessity but of delight. He is the Seed, the Word, the Milk, the Lord, and the Living Stone.

e 2:2 As translated from the Aramaic. The Greek is "grow into salvation."

f 2:3 See Ps. 34:8; Luke 1:53.

g 2:4 The church is built on Christ, "the Living Stone." See Ps. 118:22; Isa. 28:16.

h 2:5 To be identified as Christ's living stones means that we are in union with him and share his nature, for he is the Living Stone.

i 2:5 Or "priesthood" (or "community of priests"). See Rev. 1:6; 5:10; 20:4–6.

j 2:6 Mount Zion was once a Jebusite stronghold conquered by David (2 Sam. 5:6–9), who made it the capital for his kingdom. This is inside the walls of present-day Jerusalem. Zion is used in both the Old and New Testaments as more than a location. Zion is referred to as the place of God's dwelling (Pss. 9:11; 48:1–2; 74:2; Isa. 8:18). God's people are called "Zion maidens" (Song. 3:11; Zech. 9:9) or "people of Zion" (John 12:15). Zion is the heavenly realm where God is manifest (Pss. 84:7; 102:16; 110:1–2; Heb. 12:22; Rev. 14:1).

k 2:6 Or "put to shame." See Isa. 28:16.

[7] As believers you know his great worth—indeed, his preciousness is *imparted* to you.[a] But for those who do not believe:

The stone that the builders rejected and discarded
    has now become the cornerstone[b]

[8] And

A stone that makes them stumble
    and a rock to trip over.[c]

They keep stumbling over the message because they refuse to believe it. And this they were destined to do. [9] But you are God's chosen treasure[d]—priests who are kings,[e] a spiritual "nation" set apart as God's devoted ones. He called you out of darkness to experience his marvelous light, and now he claims you as his very own. He did this so that you would broadcast his glorious wonders *throughout the world.*[f] [10] For at one time you were not God's people, but now you are. At one time you knew nothing of God's mercy, because you hadn't received it yet, but now you are drenched with it![g]

Living Godly Lives

[11] My divinely loved friends, since you are resident aliens and foreigners in this world, I appeal to you to divorce yourselves from the evil desires that wage war within you.[h] [12] Live honorable lives as you mix with unbelievers, even though they accuse you of being evildoers. For they will see your beautiful works and have a reason to glorify God in the day he visits us.[i]

[13] In order to honor the Lord, you must respect and defer to the authority

---

a 2:7 Or "Unto you who believe is the preciousness." That is, all that Jesus is before the Father has now been transferred into our account. We stand before the Father in the "preciousness" of the Son. You are as precious to God as Jesus Christ is.

b 2:7 Or "capstone." See Ps. 118:22; Matt. 21:42; Mark 12:10; Luke 20:17; Acts 4:11.

c 2:8 Or "a rock of scandal." The Greek word *skandalon* means "a trap stick." See Isa. 8:14.

d 2:9 This is taken from Ex. 19:5–6 and Mal. 3:17. The Hebrew word is *sègulla*, which means "a special treasure" (possession). It is used to describe "guarded wealth," indicating the placement of the king's jewels, treasures, etc., in a safe, protected place because of their extraordinary value. God says that each believer is a priest and king, his unique and special treasure of great importance—a treasure above all other treasures. See also Titus 2:14.

e 2:9 The nouns are in apposition ("a group of kings, a priesthood" or "a king's household, a priesthood"). There are other possible ways to translate this, such as "a priesthood of kings" or "a kingdom of priests."

f 2:9 See Isa. 42:12 (LXX) and 43:20–21 (LXX), where it is translated as "praises" or "worship." The Greek can also be translated "God's excellences" (virtues) or "wonders."

g 2:10 Or in Aramaic, "mercies cascade over you." See Hos. 1:6, 9; 2:23. Both Israel and the church have been divinely chosen and showered with mercy.

h 2:11 Or "that wage war against your soul."

i 2:12 See Matt. 5:16; 18:20.

of every human institution,[a] whether it be the highest ruler[b] [14] or the governors he puts in place to punish lawbreakers and to praise those who do what's right. [15] For it is God's will for you to silence the ignorance of foolish people[c] by doing what is right.

[16] As God's *loving* servants, you should live in complete freedom, but never use your freedom as a cover-up for evil. [17] Recognize the value of every person and continually show love to every believer. Live your lives with great reverence and in holy awe of God. Honor your rulers.

The Example of Christ's Sufferings

[18] Those who are servants,[d] submit to[e] the authority of those who are your masters—not only to those who are kind and gentle but even to those who are hard and difficult. [19] You find God's favor by deciding to please God even when you endure hardships because of unjust suffering. [20] For what merit is it to endure mistreatment for wrongdoing? Yet if you are mistreated when you do what is right, and you faithfully endure it, this is commendable before God. [21] In fact, you were called to live this way, because Christ also suffered in your place, leaving you his example for you to follow.

> [22] He never sinned
> and he never spoke deceitfully.[f]

[23] When he was verbally abused, he did not return with an insult; when he suffered, he would not threaten retaliation.[g] Jesus faithfully entrusted himself into the hands of God, who judges righteously. [24] He himself carried our sins[h] in his body on the cross[i] so that we would be dead to sin[j] and live for righteousness. Our instant healing flowed from his wounding.[k] [25] You were like sheep

---

a 2:13 Or "every authority instituted by men."

b 2:13 Or "emperor." At the time Peter wrote this letter, the Roman emperor was the infamous Nero, known for his tyranny and corruption.

c 2:15 That is, the unbelievers. The Aramaic makes it even more explicit: "the foolish who do not know God."

d 2:18 Or "slaves."

e 2:18 The Greek word *hupotasso* means "to support, uphold, be under (authority)."

f 2:22 See Isa. 53:9.

g 2:23 See Isa. 53:7.

h 2:24 See Isa. 53:4, 12.

i 2:24 Or "the tree."

j 2:24 The Greek word *apoginomai*, a hapax legomenon, means "to die" or "die to something." Although not the usual word for "to die," Peter is using this metaphorically for "dying to sin."

k 2:24 This healing includes the body, soul, and emotions. It was fulfilled in two ways: first, by the healing ministry of Jesus, and second, by the blood of Christ's wounds. See Matt. 8:16–17; Isa. 53:5.

that continually wandered away,[a] but now you have returned to the *true* Shepherd of your lives—the *kind* Guardian who *lovingly* watches over your souls.

The Marriage Relationship

3 And now let me speak to the wives. Be devoted to your own husbands,[b] so that even if some of them do not obey the Word of God, your kind conduct may win them over without you saying a thing. [2] For when they observe your pure, godly life before God, *it will impact them deeply.* [3-4] Let your true beauty come from your inner personality, not a focus on the external. For lasting beauty comes from a gentle and peaceful spirit, which is precious in God's sight *and is much more important* than the outward adornment of elaborate hair, jewelry,[c] and fine clothes.

[5] Holy women of long ago who had set their hopes in God beautified themselves with lives lived in deference to their own husbands' authority. [6] For example, our *"mother,"* Sarah, devoted herself[d] to her husband, Abraham, and even called him "master." And you have become her daughters when you do what is right without fear and intimidation.[e]

[7] Husbands, you in turn must treat your wives with tenderness,[f] viewing them[g] as feminine[h] partners who deserve to be honored, for they are co-heirs with you of the *"divine* grace of life,"[i] so that nothing will hinder your prayers.

Love One Another

[8] Now, this is the goal: to live in harmony with one another and demonstrate affectionate love,[j] sympathy,[k] and kindness toward other believers. Let humility

---

a 2:25 See Isa. 53:6.
b 3:1 As translated from the Aramaic. The Greek is "defer to the authority of your husbands" (patiently accept, submit).
c 3:3–4 Or "braiding of hair or gold ornaments."
d 3:6 As translated from the Aramaic. The Greek is "obeyed."
e 3:6 That is, the wife is not inferior and should never be intimidated by her husband. The Aramaic can be translated "without being terrified by any fear."
f 3:7 Or "with intimate insight" ("realistically," "with considerateness"). That is, with consideration of what they desire and delight in, not ignorant of their preferences.
g 3:7 Or "make a home as equals."
h 3:7 Or "weaker vessel," which is a possible idiom for "weaker livelihood." Widows and female orphans were horribly disadvantaged in the time this was written. Without an advocate, women were often oppressed by corrupt political officials. Peter instructs married men to treat their wives with respect, as those who are often disadvantaged. It is also possible to interpret this as weaker physically.
i 3:7 This unique New Testament phrase describes the joyous grace that husband and wife share as a married couple, as coheirs of eternal life. But there is more than a hint of the life they give birth to—that is, the wonderful grace of giving life to a child, "the divine grace of life."
j 3:8 Or "brotherly love."
k 3:8 The Aramaic can be translated "suffer with those who are suffering."

describe who you are as you dearly love one another. [9] Never retaliate when someone treats you wrongly, nor insult those who insult you, but instead, respond by speaking a blessing over them—because a blessing is what God promised to give you. [a] [10] For the Scriptures tell us:

Whoever wants to embrace true life
    and find beauty in each day
[11] must stop speaking evil, hurtful words
    and never deceive in what they say.
Always turn from what is wrong
    and cultivate what is good;
eagerly pursue peace in every relationship,
    making it your prize.
[12] For the eyes of the Lord Yahweh [b] rest upon the godly,
    and his heart responds to their prayers.
But he turns his back on those who practice evil. [c]

Persecuted for Doing Good

[13] Why would anyone harm [d] you if you're passionate and devoted [e] to pleasing God? [14] But even if you happen to suffer for doing what is right, you will have the *joyful* experience of the blessing of God. [f] And

Don't be intimidated or terrified
    by those who would terrify you. [g]

[15] But give reverent honor in your hearts to the Anointed One and treat him as the holy Master [h] *of your lives.* And if anyone asks [i] about the hope living

---

a 3:9 Every believer is blessed by God. There are eight virtues found in vv. 8–9 that should characterize our fellowship as believers who follow Christ: (1) a sublime harmony, (2) demonstration of affectionate (brotherly) love, (3) sympathy, (4) kindness, (5) humility, (6) fervent love, (7) never retaliating evil for evil or insult for insult, and (8) speaking blessings over those who mistreat us.

b 3:12 As translated from the Aramaic. The Greek is *kurios* (lord).

c 3:12 Or "He sets his face against evildoers." See Ps. 34:12–16.

d 3:13 The Aramaic can be translated "do evil to you."

e 3:13 Or "eager to do good." The Aramaic word used for "passionate and devoted" is a homonym that can also mean "imitators." For this reason some Greek manuscripts have "followers / imitators of what is good."

f 3:14 There are three things to remember when you suffer mistreatment or persecution for the cause of Christ: (1) The eyes of God rest upon you, v. 12; (2) God's heart responds to your prayers, v. 12; (3) You will experience the blessing of God in spite of your enemies, with nothing to fear, v. 14.

g 3:14 As translated from the Aramaic. See Isa. 8:12–13.

h 3:15 The Aramaic can be translated "Lord Yahweh." This is a clear statement that Christ is the Lord Yahweh.

i 3:15 Or "repeatedly asks."

within you, always be ready to explain your faith [16] with gentleness and respect. Maintain a clean conscience, so that those who slander you for living a pure life in Christ will have to lie about you and will be ashamed because of their slander. [a] [17] For it is better to suffer for doing good, if it is in God's plan, than for doing evil.

Christ's Victory

[18] Christ suffered and died [b] for sins once and for all—the innocent for the guilty [c]—to bring you near to God by his body [d] being put to death and by being raised to life by the Spirit. [19] He went in the spiritual realm [e] and made a proclamation to the spirits in prison [f] [20] because of their disobedience of long ago. [g] For during the time of Noah God patiently waited while the ark was being prepared, but only a few were brought safely through the floodwaters: a total of eight souls. [21] This was a prophetic picture [h] of the immersion that now saves you—not a bathing of the physical body but rather the response of a good conscience before God [i] through the resurrection of Jesus Christ, [22] who is now in heaven at the place of supreme authority next to God. [j] The very powers of heaven, including every angel and authority, now yield in submission to him.

---

a 3:16 Or "be ashamed when they accuse you." We cannot prevent people from slandering us, but when they do, they should be forced to lie.

b 3:18 There is great variation among reliable texts of this phrase. Some have "Christ suffered," and others read "Christ died." The translation has included both concepts.

c 3:18 Or "the just for the unjust." See Isa. 53:11–12.

d 3:18 Or "by being put to death in/by the flesh." The passive verb ("having been put to death") implies that this was something done to him "by flesh" (or "humanity"). The contrast is this: humanity put him on the cross, but the Spirit raised him up to life.

e 3:19 Or "through the [Holy] Spirit."

f 3:19 The Aramaic can be translated Sheol ("Hades").

g 3:20 The early church fathers cited this passage, along with others, in the belief that Jesus "descended into hell" (e.g., the Apostles' Creed, although the earliest versions of it do not include the words "descended into hell"). In this context, between his death and resurrection, Jesus is said to have gone into the underworld and preached (the victory of the cross) to the spirits (fallen angels) who are bound. See also Gen. 6:1–4; 2 Peter 2:4. However, Augustine, Aquinas, and others argue that the proclamation Jesus made was through Noah by the Holy Spirit to the people of Noah's day who were disobedient. Nearly every scholar concludes that this passage in 1 Peter is one of the most difficult in the New Testament to interpret.

h 3:21 The Greek word antitypos means "a picture," "a type," "a symbol," "a pattern," or "a counterpart."

i 3:21 Or "by the response of a good conscience." The word often translated "conscience" (syneidēsis) actually means "a joint knowing," "a virtuous co-knowledge," or "co-perception."

j 3:22 Or "at the right hand of God."

Living in the Grace of God

4 Since Christ, *though innocent,* suffered in his flesh for you,[a] now you also must be a prepared soldier,[b] having the same mind-set,[c] for whoever has died in his body is done with sin.[d] ² So live the rest of your earthly life no longer concerned with human desires but *consumed* with what brings pleasure to God. ³ For you have already spent enough time doing what unbelievers[e] love to do— living in debauchery, sensuality, partying, drunkenness, wild drinking parties,[f] and the worship of demons.[g] ⁴ They marvel that you no longer rush to join them in the excesses of their corrupt lifestyles, and so they vilify you. ⁵ But one day they will have to give an account to the one who is destined to judge the living and the dead. ⁶ This is the reason the gospel was preached to the *martyrs before they gave their lives.*[h] Even though they were judged by human standards, now they live in spirit by God's standards.

Prayer, Love, and Gifts of Grace

⁷ Since we are approaching the end of all things, be intentional, purposeful,[i] and self-controlled so that you can be given to prayer.

⁸ Above all, constantly echo[j] God's intense love for one another, for love will be a canopy over a multitude of sins.[k]

⁹ Be compassionate to foreigners[l] without complaining.

---

a 4:1 As translated from the Aramaic and most Greek manuscripts. A few Greek manuscripts have "for us," while some reliable Greek texts read simply "Christ suffered in his flesh." Variants of both the Greek and Aramaic text read "Christ died for us."

b 4:1 The Greek word *hoplisasthe,* a hapax legomenon, means "to arm yourself" (like a foot soldier). It is used metaphorically to describe the battle we experience for moral purity in a decadent world. See also 1 Peter 2:11.

c 4:1 Or "attitude." That is, learn to think like him. The Aramaic can be translated "you also are nourished by him as you mediate on these things."

d 4:1 As translated from the Aramaic. The Greek is "for the one who suffers in the flesh is done with sin." See Rom. 6:7.

e 4:3 Or "gentiles."

f 4:3 Or "orgies."

g 4:3 As translated from the Aramaic. The Greek is "idolatries."

h 4:6 Or "to those who are dead." Most scholars believe that this refers to those who heard the gospel and eventually suffered and died for Christ. However, some believe it is preaching to the dead (the entire human family), giving them the opportunity to believe.

i 4:7 Though the Greek uses only one word (*sōphroneō*), it is best defined by the two English words *intentional* and *purposeful.*

j 4:8 The Greek verb *echō* can also mean "to maintain," "to possess," "to keep," or "to be so closely joined to something that you become its echo." In this case, we join ourselves so closely to God's love that we "echo" his forgiving, fervent love toward one another.

k 4:8 As translated from the Aramaic. See Prov. 10:12; 1 Cor. 13:4–7.

l 4:9 As translated from the Aramaic and implied in the Greek, which can also be translated "Show hospitality to the stranger."

¹⁰ Every believer has received grace gifts, so use them to serve one another as faithful stewards of the many-colored tapestry of God's grace.

¹¹ *For example*, if you have a speaking *gift*, speak as though God were speaking his words through you. *ᵃ* If you have *the gift of* serving, do it *passionately* with the strength God gives you, *ᵇ* so that in everything God *alone* will be glorified through Jesus Christ. For to him belong the power and the glory forever throughout all ages! Amen. *ᶜ*

Suffering and Glory

¹² Beloved friends, if life gets extremely difficult, with many tests, *ᵈ* don't be bewildered as though something strange were overwhelming you. *ᵉ* ¹³ Instead, continue to rejoice, for you, in a measure, have shared in the sufferings of the Anointed One so that *you can share in* the revelation of his glory and celebrate with *even greater* gladness! *ᶠ* ¹⁴ If you are insulted because of the name of Christ, you are greatly blessed, *ᵍ* because the Spirit of glory and power, *ʰ* who is the Spirit of God, rests upon you. *ⁱ*

¹⁵ Let none of you merit suffering as a murderer, or thief, or criminal, or as one who meddles in the affairs of others. ¹⁶ If you suffer for being a Christian, don't consider it a disgrace but *a privilege*. Glorify God because you carry the Anointed One's name. *ʲ* ¹⁷ For the time is ripe for judgment to begin in God's own household. And if it starts with us, what will be the fate of those who refuse to obey the gospel of God?

---

a 4:11 The Greek text is simply "If anyone speaks—as God's words." This would include preaching, teaching, and prophesying.

b 4:11 The Greek can also be translated "The one who provides finances should do it with the strength of God, who supplies all things."

c 4:11 Peter exhorts us in vv. 7–11 to do five things as we see the end drawing closer: (1) be given to prayer, (2) be devoted to loving our fellow believers, (3) be compassionate to the stranger and foreigner, (4) use spiritual gifts to serve one another, and (5) give God glory in all things.

d 4:12 Or "when the burning of a fiery trial is occurring among you."

e 4:12 The Aramaic adds a clause here, "because these things are your communion in the inheritance."

f 4:13 The Greek verb tenses can imply either present or future. There is a glory unveiled in us as we focus on Christ in our difficulties. This brings immediate joy and rejoicing when we pass through suffering. Yet the greatest joy will be as we are free from mortal pain and see the revelation of his glory throughout eternity.

g 4:14 See Matt. 5:11.

h 4:14 Some Greek manuscripts have "and of power." The Aramaic can be translated "the [Shekinah] glory of the Spirit."

i 4:14 See Isa. 11:2. A few manuscripts, deemed unreliable, add "On their part he is evil spoken of, but on your part he is glorified."

j 4:16 Or "that you bear this name." The word *Christian* means "anointed one." Christ is the Anointed One, and as his followers who are joined in life union to him, we too are "anointed ones."

[18] And:

> If the righteous are barely saved, [a]
>> what will become of the wicked and godless? [b]

[19] So then, those who suffer for following God's will should enfold their lives into the Creator, who will never fail them, and continue to always do what is right. [c]

Elders and the Victor's Crown of Glory

5 Now, I encourage you as an elder, [d] an eyewitness of the sufferings of Christ, and one who shares in the glory that is about to be unveiled. I urge my fellow elders among you [2] to be *compassionate* shepherds who *tenderly* care for God's flock and who feed them well, for you have the responsibility to guide, protect, and oversee. Consider it a joyous pleasure [e] and not merely a religious duty. Lead from the heart under God's leadership—not as a way to gain finances dishonestly but as a way *to* eagerly and cheerfully *serve*. [3] Don't be controlling tyrants [f] but lead others by your beautiful examples to the flock. [g] [4] And when the Shepherd-King [h] appears, you will win the victor's crown of glory that never fades away. [i]

[5] In the same way, the younger ones should willingly support [j] the leadership of the elders. In every relationship, each of you must wrap around yourself the apron of a humble servant. Because:

> God resists you when you are proud
>> but multiplies grace and favor when you are humble. [k]

---

a 4:18 The Aramaic can be translated "if the righteous are harvested to salvation."

b 4:18 See Prov. 11:31 (LXX).

c 4:19 It is interesting that Peter points us to the Creator when we suffer. The faithful Creator, who keeps all things in order and feeds his creation, will never fail to be with us and supply grace and glory in all that we face.

d 5:1 Peter had already identified himself as an apostle (1:1), but now he takes a humble position equal to that of local church elder. Peter's identification with the church elders becomes a powerful example of true spiritual leadership.

e 5:2 As translated from the Aramaic.

f 5:3 Or "masters of the flock" (elevated above all others).

g 5:3 As translated from the Aramaic.

h 5:4 Or "Chief Shepherd." The Aramaic can be translated "Lord of the shepherds."

i 5:4 In these few verses Peter gives us the seven qualities of true shepherds who serve as elders for the flock: (1) They understand that they serve God's flock, not their own. (2) They lovingly guide and care for God's people. (3) They take the responsibilities of oversight willingly. (4) They are eager to serve, not eager for financial gain. (5) They feed and nurture God's people. (6) They reject a domineering leadership model. (7) They lead by examples of godliness and humility.

j 5:5 Although the Greek word *hupotasso* can be translated "submit," it is more often used for "support." See also Eph. 5:21.

k 5:5 See Prov. 3:34; James 4:6.

Humility and Faith

[6] If you bow low in God's awesome presence, [a] he will eventually exalt you as you leave the timing in his hands.

[7] Pour out all your worries and stress upon him *and leave them there*, for he always tenderly cares for you. [b]

[8] Be well balanced and always alert, because your enemy, [c] the devil, roams around incessantly, like a roaring lion looking for its prey to devour. [d] [9] Take a decisive stand against him and resist his every attack with strong, vigorous faith. For you know that your believing brothers and sisters around the world are experiencing the same kinds of troubles you endure. [e] [10] And then, after your brief suffering, [f] the God of all loving grace, who has called you to share in his eternal glory in Christ, [g] will personally and powerfully restore you and make you stronger than ever. Yes, he will set you firmly in place and build you up. [h] [11] And he has all the power needed to do this [i]—forever! [j] Amen.

Concluding Remarks

[12] I, Peter, with the help of Silas, [k] whom I consider a trustworthy, faith-filled

---

a 5:6 Or "under his mighty hands."

b 5:7 Or "Load upon him your every anxiety, for he is always watching over you with tender care." See also Ps. 55:22.

c 5:8 The Greek word *antidikos* is a legal term for one who presses a lawsuit that must be defended.

d 5:8 The implication in the context is that if you do not bring your worries and cares to God, the devil will use depression and discouragement to devour you. Just as lions go after the feeble, the young, and the stragglers, so the enemy of our souls will always seek out those who are isolated, alone, or depressed to devour them.

e 5:9 Suffering, in part, comes from the activity of the devil. There are sufferings that must be resisted in faith, as part of an attack from our adversary.

f 5:10 The Aramaic can be translated "slight suffering." When we are in the midst of suffering, we are convinced it will never end. Peter reminds us that all of our trials are slight, brief, and temporary, but the glory we experience is eternal.

g 5:10 Some manuscripts have "Christ Jesus." The calling of every believer is to share in the glory of God unveiled in Christ. See John 17:22–24; Rom. 8:18–21, 28–30; 2 Cor. 4:17; 2 Tim. 2:10.

h 5:10 Peter knows what he is talking about. After his ordeal of denying three times that he even knew Jesus, God restored him and made him strong. Jesus prophesied to Peter that he would "strengthen the faith of [his] brothers." See Luke 22:31–32. Both of Peter's letters are anointed by the Holy Spirit to give you strong faith that will not give up.

i 5:11 Or "To him belongs all the power" (to do this).

j 5:11 Or "May power be to him forever!" That is, all the power needed to strengthen and build up God's people belongs to him.

k 5:12 Or "through Silvanus." This could mean that Silas (Silvanus) assisted Peter in writing this letter and/or that he was the courier who brought it to the churches. In the book of Acts, Silas was a ministry partner of Paul who accompanied him on his first and second missionary journeys (Acts 15:22) and was imprisoned with Paul in Philippi (Acts 16). However, in the epistles, Silas is named Silvanus (the Latin form of Silas). It is believed that Silas was

brother, have written you this short letter so that I might encourage you and personally testify that this is the true, dependable grace of God. [a] Stand fast in this grace.

[13] She who is in Babylon, [b] who is co-elect with you, sends her greetings, along with Mark, my son. [c]

[14] Greet one another with a kiss of peace. [d]

Peace to all who are in life union with Christ. Amen.

---

one of the seventy disciples Jesus sent out and that he became the bishop of Thessalonica and was eventually martyred for his faith. The name Silas is the Greek form of the Aramaic name Saili (Saul).

a   5:12 The Aramaic adds a clause, "by which you have been resurrected."

b   5:13 Or "Your true sister in Babylon." This is a literal reference to the church of Babylon, according to the Aramaic. Since the Greek feminine pronoun is used here, many scholars have concluded that this is an allusion to the church, although some believe it could have been a reference to Peter's wife. Furthermore, Babylon may be a metaphor for the Roman Empire or even the city of Rome.

c   5:13 A possible reference to one of Peter's spiritual disciples, his spiritual "son" is most likely John Mark, a relative of Barnabas (Col. 4:10), who was the author of the Gospel that bears his name. Many believe that Peter was the literary source for much of Mark's Gospel. See also Acts 12:25–14:25; 15:36; 18:22; 2 Tim. 4:11; Philem. 24.

d   5:14 See also Rom. 16:16; 1 Thess. 5:26.

2 PETER

Introduction

AT A GLANCE

Author: The apostle Peter
Audience: Churches in northwestern Asia Minor, modern-day Turkey
Date: AD 64–66
Type of Literature: A letter
Major Themes: God, humanity, salvation, ethics, eschatology, the church, and
doctrine
Outline:
Letter Opening — 1:1–11
Peter's Reason for Writing — 1:12–15
Issue 1: The Power and Appearing of Our Lord — 1:16–18
Issue 2: The Reliable and Valid Prophetic Message — 1:19–21
Issue 3: False Teachers and Their Sure Destruction — 2:1–22
Issue 4: The Delay and Destruction of the Lord's Day — 3:1–13
Letter Closing — 3:14–18

ABOUT 2 PETER

God has given us a treasure through the writings of the fisherman turned apostle, Simon Peter. With descriptive terms, this tremendous man writes a letter
that will guard our souls through the revelation of God's triumphant grace.
Not long before Peter was martyred he took up the quill to write to those who
shared with him the glorious hope of eternal life. Read these three chapters to
learn, to grow, and to be warned. We can accept all that he tells us, for it is the
Word of God.

Peter, the one who was asked three times, "Do you burn with love for
me," has filled his letter with multiple references to love. It is the perfect expression of the life of Christ within every believer. Love triumphs over troubles
and pain. It perseveres in the truth when false teaching surrounds us. A fiery,
endless love for Christ is the antidote to stagnancy in our spiritual lives. Peter
will not let you forget the importance of this love, especially when it comes to
your growth in Christ.

Spiritual growth is a process of learning to love, so Peter speaks about growing in God's triumphant grace and becoming fully mature as those who share the divine nature with Christ (1:4). It begins with faith and virtue but it ends with love. Our diligence to hold to our faith will be rewarded in time with a greater love for God and for his people.

And finally, Peter brings the return of Christ to prominence. He speaks of the end of time and what will happen. He points us to the sure word of prophecy, rising like a daystar in our hearts, affirming within us that Christ is coming back. Be prepared to find ample reasons in 2 Peter for your faith to grow, even if it means enduring hardships. We thank God for the words Peter has left us— words that will never fade away.

PURPOSE

Peter writes as one who is facing imminent death. He describes being an eyewitness to the transfiguration of Christ. The two major themes of 2 Peter that outline his purpose for writing could be described as *truth triumphant* and *love unending*. It is necessary to address false teaching wherever it may be found. But have no fear, truth will triumph every time—especially when we speak the truth in love.

The burden that motivated Peter to write this letter seems to be the multiple false teachings that were beginning to threaten the health of the churches. Apparently, the false teachers taught the people that our freedom in Christ meant that sexual immorality was not an issue that should trouble us (2:14). They even made a mockery of the second coming of Christ (3:3–4). How we need Peter's wise exhortation today to stay pure until the coming of the Lord! As such, one could view 2 Peter as his farewell letter to the churches he loved, urging them to stay the course until Christ's coming.

AUTHOR AND AUDIENCE

Although the authorship of 2 Peter is the most contested of all the New Testament books in our Bible, there should be no doubt that the beloved Peter the "rock" is the human author of this inspired letter. In the third century Origen was the first of the church fathers to state that Peter was indeed the author, yet he did acknowledge that it was disputed by others. The stylistic differences are quite different between his first and second letter, but some scholars attribute this to a different amanuenses (secretary). Depending on the exact year Peter was martyred, we can approximate the date of writing this letter to AD 64–66.

It is believed that Peter was writing to churches within northwest Asia Minor, which is modern-day Turkey. These communities included the Roman regions of Pontus, Galatia, Cappadocia, Asia, and Bithynia. Based on the content of the letter and purpose that drove Peter to write it, a number of false teachers had begun influencing them in a moral direction that ran contrary to their calling as God's children in Christ. Peter was concerned they were vulnerable to these teachers. So he wrote to them as a pastor, to stimulate them to whole-some, Christ-centered thinking, believing, and living.

MAJOR THEMES

God the Father, God the Son, God the Holy Spirit. Unlike 1 Peter, God the Father is only mentioned a handful of times. Peter reveals he has created the cosmos and inspired the prophets; he is the ruler of angelic beings and human beings; the final judgment is described as "the coming of the day of God" (3:12), yet he is also patient and merciful. However, where God the Father was prominent in letter one, in letter two he is more in the background.

Not true of God the Son! Jesus is clearly in the foreground in Peter's second letter, yet in a way that's unique: Jesus is most often mentioned with a corresponding descriptive expression. He is "our God and Savior" (1:1); he is "our Lord" (1:2); he is "our Lord and Savior," as well as "the Messiah" (1:11); and he is described as "the Master," our sovereign Lord (2:1). He is the God-Savior, anointed by the Father, who reigns as supreme Lord.

Peter mentions the Holy Spirit only explicitly in 1:21, but he is also implied in 1:20. Though he occupies a small role in the letter, it isn't a minor one. For Peter's aim is to counter the false prophets affecting what these communities believed and how they lived. He wrote to remind the believers of their need to live a godly life and to confirm their calling. How are we to do that? We have "been given the prophetic word . . . reliable and fully validated" (1:19). And we can trust that message to guide our believing and behaving because those prophets were "inspired by the moving of the Holy Spirit" (1:21).

Entrapped Humanity and Divine Deliverance. Peter reveals something im-portant about our human condition: humanity is entrapped by corrupt desires, and God's goodness has opened a way to escape that corruption through deliv-erance. First, Peter makes known in his letter the reality that the world is filled with "corrupt desires" (1:4). In fact, these desires are so powerful that they become entangled and defeated by them once again, to the point of losing the deliverance they'd gained and turning their backs against "the sacred obligation that was given to them" in Christ (2:21).

And yet, Peter also makes known the revelation-truth that everything you need to "keep you from being inactive or fruitless in your pursuit of knowing Jesus Christ more intimately" and fully experiencing his deliverance has "already [been] planted deep within" (1:8). That's because through his divine initiative and by his divine power, God has called each of us by name and invited us to the rich experience of knowing Christ personally! For Peter, the idea of "knowing" is a crucial aspect of salvation. The Greek work *epi-gnosis* carries with it the idea of acknowledging and recognizing Jesus as Lord and Savior, which leads to grace and peace, and the blossoming of Christian virtue.

Living in Light of the End. In 2 Peter, ethics (how we live) and eschatology (the end of the world) are intimately connected. In his final chapter, Peter draws our attention to the judgment that God will unfold on this reality, in preparation for a whole new one. But we aren't just waiting for the end; we're called to live in these "last days" in light of the end, the coming "day of God." Why? Because, as Peter reveals, in the end "every activity of man will be laid bare" (3:10). In light of this coming revelation and destruction he asks rhetorically, "don't you see how vital it is to live a holy life?" Which is why "We must be consumed with godliness" (3:11), and why he urges his readers to "be eager to be found living pure lives when you come into his presence, without blemish and filled with peace" (3:14).

False Teachers and False Teaching. One of the main reasons Peter wrote his letter was to urge the believing communities to guard against false teachers who would slip into their churches, secretly infiltrating them in order to divide and confuse them with destructive false teaching. Such people deny the sovereign Lord, live and teach immoral lifestyles, exploit true believers for their greedy gain, and pervert all kinds of Christian teachings and practices. While Peter does promise that "in their destruction they will be destroyed" (2:12), he also forewarns us not to be led astray by their lawlessness. Because for Peter, there is a very real threat of believers returning back to the very corrupt world system they escaped from in Christ! Peter believes right teachings are vital to the ongoing purity of the church and our individual godly lives.

2 PETER

Triumphant Grace

Introduction and Greeting

1 *This letter is from* Simeon[a] Peter, a *loving* servant[b] and an apostle of Jesus Christ. I am writing to those who have been given a faith[c] as equally precious as ours through the righteousness of our God and Savior, Jesus Christ.[d] 2 May grace and perfect peace cascade over you[e] as you *live* in the rich knowledge of God and of Jesus our Lord.

God's Generous Grace

3 Everything we could ever need for life and complete devotion[f] to God has already been deposited in us by his divine power. *For all this was lavished upon us* through the rich experience of knowing him who has called us by name and invited us to come to him through a glorious manifestation of his goodness.[g] 4 As a result of this, he has given you[h] magnificent promises[i] that are beyond

---

a 1:1 Or "Simon," the Greek form of the Hebrew-Aramaic name Simeon. Simeon means "he who hears." Peter (the Rock) was the nickname given to him by Jesus; Simeon was his real name.

b 1:1 Or "bond-servant." From a Hebraic mind-set, this would imply a choice of remaining a servant even when freedom was offered. Thus, "a *loving* servant."

c 1:1 Even our faith has been given to us from a loving Father. Because our faith is equally precious as that of the apostles, we share an equal standing in the privileges and blessings of the kingdom realm of God.

d 1:1 In his opening verse, Peter points us to the deity of Jesus Christ—"God and Savior, Jesus Christ"—referring to one person. Some have described Peter's words to be the most clear and direct testimony to the truth of Christ's equality with God.

e 1:2 Or "May grace and peace be multiplied to you."

f 1:3 It is possible that this is a hendiadys, which would then mean "a life of godliness" (complete devotion). Everything we need to reflect God's true nature has already been given to us. See Eph. 1:3.

g 1:3 Or "called us by his glory and goodness."

h 1:4 As translated from the Aramaic. The Greek is plural, "us."

i 1:4 The Greek sentence that extends from vv. 3–5 is somewhat ambiguous. It could also be read as "Through a glorious manifestation of his goodness he has imparted to us his magnificent promises."

all price, so that through *the power of* these tremendous promises[a] you can experience partnership[b] with the divine nature, by which you have escaped[c] the corrupt desires that are of the world.

Faith's Ladder of Virtue

[5] So devote yourselves[d] to lavishly supplementing[e] your faith with goodness,[f]
  and to goodness add understanding,
    [6] and to understanding add the strength of self-control,
    and to self-control add patient endurance,
    and to patient endurance add godliness,[g]
      [7] and to godliness add mercy toward your brothers and sisters,[h]
      and to mercy toward others add unending love.[i]

[8] Since these virtues are already *planted* deep within,[j] and you possess them in abundant supply,[k] they will keep you from being inactive or fruitless in your pursuit of knowing Jesus Christ more intimately. [9] But if anyone lacks these

---

a   1:4 That is, by claiming these tremendous promises as our very own. Faith always releases the power of the Word of God.

b   1:4 The Greek word *koinonos* means "to participate as a partner, to partake of, to be a companion with, to have fellowship with" the divine nature. This is one of the great mysteries of our faith, that God shares his nature with us. We are given birth by the Holy Spirit to be God's true sons and daughters, and every father imparts his DNA and his "nature" to his children. The Greek word *physis* (nature) is taken from the word *phyō*, which means "to give birth, produce, bring forth, or to grow up." Christ lives in us and transforms us into his very own likeness. In Christ we share with him the divine nature. We will all bear the image of the Man from heaven, Jesus Christ. See Rom. 8:9–25; 1 Cor. 15:12–57.

c   1:4 The Greek word *apopheugō* also carries the connotation of being "acquitted."

d   1:5 Or "by having added your intense effort." The Aramaic can be translated "by being under the weight of all these gifts."

e   1:5 The Greek word *epichorēgeo* means "to fully support the chorus" or "to completely choreograph."

f   1:5 Or "integrity, virtues of courage, nobleness, and moral valor."

g   1:6 Or "reverence."

h   1:7 As translated from the Aramaic and implied in the Greek. This mercy would include forgiveness and forbearance to those who fail.

i   1:7 It is possible to view this passage like an unfolding of faith. "Out of your faith will emerge goodness, and out of goodness will emerge understanding (of God), and out of understanding (of God) will emerge inner strength (self-control), and out of inner strength will emerge patient endurance, and out of patient endurance will emerge godliness, and out of godliness will emerge mercy toward your brothers and sisters, and out of mercy will emerge love." It is also possible to view this passage as a mathematical equation. Faith + goodness = understanding. Goodness + understanding = inner strength. Understanding + inner strength = patience. Inner strength + patience = godliness. Patience + godliness = mercy. And godliness + mercy = love.

j   1:8 The Greek word *hyparchō* means to "begin below" (or "within," like a plant growing beneath the ground).

k   1:8 Or "abounding" (repeatedly being more than enough).

things, he is blind, constantly closing his eyes to the mysteries of our faith,[a] and forgetting *his innocence*—for his past sins have been washed away.[b]

[10] For this reason, beloved ones,[c] be eager to confirm and validate[d] that God has invited you *to salvation*[e] and claimed you[f] as his own. If you do these things, you will never stumble. [11] As a result, the kingdom's gates will open wide to you as God choreographs[g] your triumphant entrance into the eternal kingdom of our Lord and Savior, Jesus the Messiah.

Divine Revelation

[12] I won't hesitate to continually remind you of these truths, even though you are aware of them and are well established in the present measure of truth you have already embraced.[h] [13] And as long as I live[i] I will continue to awaken you with this reminder, [14] since our Lord Jesus, the Anointed One, has clearly revealed that my departure is near.[j] [15] Indeed, I'm passionate[k] to share these things with you so that you will always remember them after my exodus from this life.

Jesus' Transfiguration

[16] We were not retelling some masterfully crafted legend when we informed you

---

a 1:9 Although the Greek word *myōpazō* can mean "nearsighted," it is a compound word taken from the base word *mystērion* (mystery), and *optonomai* (to look upon, to behold). The implication is that when the virtues of the divine nature are not flourishing in believers, it is because they are "closing [their] eyes" to the mysteries of our faith, i.e., Christ in us, the hope of glory. See Col. 1:27.

b 1:9 The Aramaic can be translated "he is still searching for the purification of his original sins."

c 1:10 Or "brothers [and sisters]."

d 1:10 The Aramaic adds the phrase "by your good deeds." The implication is that by developing the virtues Peter has spoken of in vv. 3–7, we validate God's calling and choice of us.

e 1:10 We have a confident assurance that we have been chosen and called to salvation by God himself. This is a firm foundation on which to build our lives. We can grow in that confidence as we see the work of the Spirit bearing spiritual fruit through our lives. See Gal. 5:22–23; 2 Tim. 2:19; 1 John 3:10, 14. The Greek for "invited you" is *klēsis*, which means "to invite [summon] to a feast."

f 1:10 The Greek word for "claimed as his own" is *eklogē* (from his *logos* word). God spoke and you were his. You are meant to be a "chosen word" from his mouth, and you will not return to him void, but you will accomplish what he has destined for you to do.

g 1:11 This is the Greek word *epichorēgeo*, which can mean "richly provide" (for the choir) or "choreograph." The Lord of the dance will richly welcome you into his eternal kingdom. See Zech. 3:17.

h 1:12 Or "in the measure of truth that has reached you." The implication is that there is yet more truth for every follower of Jesus to learn and embrace.

i 1:13 Or "as long as I am in this tent."

j 1:14 Or "that the removal of my tent is soon," a euphemism for Peter's death. See John 21:18–19. The apostle Peter knew that death was coming soon for him. Indeed, in AD 68 he was crucified upside down in Rome, at his own request, so as not to die in the same manner as Jesus.

k 1:15 Or "make every effort."

of the power and appearing of our Lord Jesus Christ, *a* for we saw his magnificence and splendor *unveiled* before our very eyes. *b* 17 Yes, Father God lavished upon him radiant glory and honor when his distinct voice spoke out of the realm of majestic glory, *c* endorsing him with these words: This is my cherished Son, marked by my love. All my delight is found in him! *d* 18 And we ourselves heard that voice resound from the heavens while we were with him on the holy mountain.

Prophecy

19 And so we have been given the prophetic word—the *written* *e* message of the prophets, made more reliable and fully validated *by the confirming voice of God on the Mount of Transfiguration.* *f* And you will continue to do well if you stay

---

a 1:16 A possible hendiadys, "the powerful coming of our Lord Jesus Christ in power" or "the appearing of our powerful Lord Jesus Christ." The Aramaic can be translated "the power and comingness of our Master, Jesus Christ."

b 1:16 See Matt. 17:1–8; Mark 9:1–7; Luke 9:27–36.

c 1:17 A possible periphrastic reference to God, "the transcendent glory."

d 1:17 Or "On him my favor rests." The Aramaic can be translated "in whom I am fulfilled."

e 1:19 The phrase *prophetic word,* or "word of prophecy," when found in Christian writing through the second century is used only for Old Testament Scriptures. See Peter Davids, *The Letters of 2 Peter and Jude* (Grand Rapids, MI: Eerdmans, 2006), 207; Gene Green, *Jude and 2 Peter* (Grand Rapids, MI: Baker Academic, 2008), 227; David Walls and Max Anders, *The Holman New Testament Commentary: 1 and 2 Peter; 1, 2 and 3 John and Jude* (Nashville, TN: B&H Publishing, 1999), 113. See also Isa. 8:20; Luke 24:25; John 6:45.

f 1:19 The comparative adjective *bebaioteron* (more reliable) serves as a predicate adjective. "And we have the prophetic word as more certain," meaning that the transfiguration confirmed (made more certain) the witness of the Old Testament Scriptures to Jesus as Messiah, the Son of God, who brought his eternal kingdom on earth (2 Peter 1:11). The witness of God's Spirit through the transfiguration complements the witness of the Old Testament Scriptures in 2 Peter 1:19—both confirm that Jesus is the Messiah, God's Son, who will return to rule on earth. See Peter Davids, *The Letters of 2 Peter and Jude* (Grand Rapids, MI: Eerdmans, 2006), 207. What is said to be made more certain or reliable is "the written message of the prophets." This has bothered some commentators in that it places experience ahead of the prophetic word, so they argue that the prophetic word makes the transfiguration more certain, citing later Jewish opinion that even a voice (*bat qol*) from heaven could not overrule a Scripture. That, however, is not what the grammar of the text indicates. Instead, we see that "the written message of the prophets" is what is made more certain/reliable. See also M. Zerwick and M. Grosvenor, *A Grammatical Analysis of the Greek New Testament,* 3rd rev. edition (Rome: Editrice Pontificio Istituto Biblico, 1988), 719; Lewis R. Donelson, *1 and 2 Peter and Jude* (Louisville, KY: Westminster John Knox, 2010), 234: "This means that the account of the transfiguration makes OT prophecy more reliable. . . . The giving of honor and glory to Jesus at the transfiguration reinforces the credibility of OT prophecies about the messiah"; D. P. Senior and D. J. Harrington, *1 Peter, Jude and 2 Peter* (Collegeville, MN: Liturgical Press, 2008), 257: "The idea seems to be that the transfiguration and all that pertains to Jesus fulfills and thus confirms what the prophets said and so makes them even 'all the more reliable'"; the same view was also held by the well-known Greek scholar of the early twentieth century; A. T. Robertson, *Word Pictures of the New Testament,* vol. 6 (Nashville, TN: Broadman Press, 1931), p. 157.

focused on it. *For this prophetic message* is like a piercing light[a] shining in a gloomy place[b] until the dawning of a new day,[c] when the Morning Star[d] rises in your hearts.[e]

[20] You must understand this at the outset: Interpretation of scriptural prophecy *requires the Holy Spirit*, for it does not originate from someone's own imagination.[f] [21] No true prophecy comes from human initiative but is inspired by the moving of the Holy Spirit upon those[g] who spoke the message that came from God.[h]

Warning about False Teachers

2 In the past there arose false prophets[i] among *God's* people, just as there will continue to be false teachers who will secretly infiltrate in your midst *to divide you*, bringing with them their destructive heresies.[j] They will even deny the Master, who paid the price for them, bringing swift destruction on themselves. [2] Many will follow immoral lifestyles.[k] Because of these *corrupt false teachers*, the way of truth[l] will be slandered. [3] They are only out for themselves,[m] ready to exploit you for their own gain through their cunning arguments. Their condemnation has been a long time coming. But their destruction does not slumber[n] or sit idly by, *for it is sure to come*.

---

a 1:19 Or "lamp." See Ps. 119:105.

b 1:19 This dismal or dark/murky place can be both the world in which we live and the human heart bathed in the light of truth, displacing gloom and darkness. See Isa. 9:1.

c 1:19 See Luke 1:78.

d 1:19 Or "Light Bearer." The Aramaic can be translated "until the sun rises in your hearts." See Rev. 22:16.

e 1:19 This is not simply a far-off future event of Christ's coming but the internal promise of his light and power subduing our hearts, as Christ rises within us like the dawning of the new day and like the morning star. The dawn conquers the night, and the morning star promises the new day appearing.

f 1:20 The Greek text is somewhat ambiguous and can be translated in three ways: (1) No prophecy can be interpreted by the prophet's own imagination; that is, they didn't make things up. (2) No prophecy can be interpreted by itself, for other Scriptures are needed to understand and interpret biblical prophecy. (3) No prophecy can be interpreted by one's own imagination, for the help of the Holy Spirit, who inspired it, is needed to interpret it. The Aramaic can be translated "No prophecy is ever fulfilled as soon as it is written."

g 1:21 Some Greek manuscripts have "holy men" (and women).

h 1:21 This is a clear reference to the doctrine of the inspiration of the Scriptures. It is God's words spoken (prophecy) and written, as given by the Holy Spirit. God speaks through people his inspired and trustworthy words. See also 2 Tim. 3:16–17.

i 2:1 Or "Pretend prophets birthed themselves."

j 2:1 Or "destructive ways of thinking" (viewpoints).

k 2:2 Or "sensualities" (outrageous behaviors).

l 2:2 Or "the true Way." Some manuscripts have "the glory of the truth."

m 2:3 Or "with greed."

n 2:3 The Aramaic can be translated "Abaddon never slumbers." *Abaddon* is a Hebrew term for the realm of the dead and symbolizes the bottomless pit.

[4] Now, *don't forget,* God had no pity for the angels when they sinned[a] but threw them into the lowest, darkest dungeon of gloom[b] and locked them in chains, where they are firmly held until the judgment of torment.[c]

[5] And he did not spare the former world[d] *in the days of Noah* when he sent a flood to destroy a depraved world[e] (although he protected Noah, the preacher of righteousness, along with seven members of his family).[f]

[6] And *don't forget that* he reduced to ashes the cities of Sodom and Gomorrah, condemning them to ruin and destruction.[g] God appointed them to be examples as to what is coming to the ungodly.[h] [7] Yet he rescued a righteous man, Lot, suffering the indignity of the unbridled lusts of the lawless.[i] [8] For righteous Lot lived among them day after day, distressed in his righteous soul by the rebellious deeds he saw and heard.

[9] If the Lord Yahweh *rescued Lot,* he knows how to continually rescue the godly from their trials and to reserve the ungodly for punishment on the day of judgment.[j] [10] And this especially applies to those who live their lives despising authorities[k] and who abandon themselves to chasing the depraved lusts of their flesh.

The Arrogance of False Teachers

They are willfully arrogant and insolent, unafraid to insult the glorious ones.[l] [11] Yet even angels, who are greater than they in power and strength, do not dare slander

---

a 2:4 Because of the context of Noah's flood, these were possibly the "Watchers," angels who sinned and rebelled against God's laws by having sexual relations with women, thus producing offspring (Gen. 6:1–4). They are mentioned in Dan. 4:13, 17, 23; Jude 6–7; the *Book of 1 Enoch* 6–10; the *Book of Jubilees* 5; and the Dead Sea Scrolls (The Book of Giants). God put them in chains (ropes) and bound them in Tartarus (the deepest pit of gloom) until their final judgment.

b 2:4 The Greek uses the term *Tartarus,* a Hellenistic mythical term for the subterranean underworld, the lowest pit (of hell).

c 2:4 As translated from the Aramaic and two older Greek uncials.

d 2:5 Or "original world."

e 2:5 Or "a world devoid of awe."

f 2:5 See Gen. 6–8; 1 Peter 3:20.

g 2:6 See Gen. 19.

h 2:6 Or "as an example to the ungodly of coming generations." After seeing these three examples (fallen angels, people who lived at the time of the flood, Sodom and Gomorrah), it is difficult to believe that everyone will ultimately be saved. There is a doom that awaits the ungodly (those who do not believe in Jesus Christ, the Savior).

i 2:7 As translated from the Aramaic.

j 2:9 Or "to keep the unrighteous under punishment until the day of judgment," which implies that the wicked are living under God's punishment even before they are ultimately judged.

k 2:10 Or "despising realms of power" (authority). The Aramaic can be translated "They do not tremble with awe while they blaspheme."

l 2:10 Or "slandering reputations" or "blaspheming glories" (dignitaries). Because of the

them before the Lord.[a] [12] These individuals are nothing but brute beasts—irrational creatures, born in the wild to be caught and destroyed—and they will perish like beasts. They are professional insulters, who slander whatever they don't understand, and in their destruction they will be destroyed. [13] For all the evil they have done will come crashing down on them. They consider it their great pleasure to carouse in broad daylight. When they come to your love feasts[b] they are but stains and blemishes, reveling in their deceptions as they feast with you. [14] They are addicted to adultery, with eyes that are insatiable,[c] with sins that never end. They seduce the vulnerable and are experts in their greed—they are but children of a curse!

The Example of Balaam

[15] They have wandered off the main road and have gone astray, because they are prophets who love profit—the wages they earn by wrongdoing. They are following the example of Balaam, son of Beor,[d] [16] who was rebuked for evil by a donkey incapable of speech yet that spoke with a human voice and restrained the prophet's madness.[e]

[17] These people are dried-up riverbeds, waterless clouds pushed along by stormy winds—the deepest darkness of gloom has been prepared for them. [18] They spout off with their grandiose, impressive nonsense. Consumed with the lusts of the flesh, they lure *back into sin* those who recently escaped from their error. [19] They promise others freedom, yet they themselves are slaves to corruption, for people are slaves to whatever overcomes them.

[20] Those who escape the corrupting forces of this world system through the experience of knowing about our Lord and Savior, Jesus the Messiah, then go back into entanglement with them and are defeated by them, becoming worse off than they were to start with. [21] It would have been much better for them never to have experienced the way of righteousness than to know it and then turn away from the sacred obligation[f] that was given to them. [22] They become illustrations of the true proverb:

A dog will return to his own vomit[g]
and a washed pig to its rolling in the mud.

---

context, most believe this is speaking of "glorious" celestial beings in heaven (e.g., archangels). See Jude 8–10.
a   2:11 Some manuscripts do not have "before the Lord."
b   2:13 Peter equates the gatherings of believers as "love feasts." Our true purpose in coming together is to magnify and feast on the love of Christ, sharing his love with all.
c   2:14 Or "Their eyes are full of an adulteress."
d   2:15 Or "Bosor."
e   2:16 See Num. 22–24.
f   2:21 Or "holy command."
g   2:22 See Prov. 26:11. The rest of the proverb is believed to be a quote from Heraclitus of Ephesus, known as the "weeping philosopher" (535–475 BC).

The Coming of the Lord

3 Beloved friends, this is now the second letter I have written to you [a] in which I've attempted to stir you up and awaken you to a proper mind-set. [b] ² So never forget both the prophecies spoken by the holy prophets of old and the teaching [c] of our Lord and Savior spoken by your apostles. [d]

³ Above all, you must understand that in the last days mockers [e] will multiply, chasing after their evil desires. ⁴ They will say, "So what about this promise of his coming? [f] Our ancestors are dead and buried, yet everything is still the same as it was since from the beginning of time until now."

⁵ But they conveniently overlook that from the beginning, the heavens and earth were created by God's word. *He spoke* and the dry ground separated from the waters. ⁶ Then long afterward he destroyed the world with a tremendous flood by those very waters. [g] ⁷ And now, by the same *powerful* word, the heavens and the earth are reserved for fire, [h] being kept for judgment day, when all the ungodly will perish.

⁸ So, dear friends, don't let this one thing escape your notice: a single day counts like a thousand years to the Lord Yahweh, [i] and a thousand years counts as one day. [j] ⁹ This means that, *contrary to man's perspective*, the Lord is not late with his promise *to return*, as some measure lateness. But rather, his "delay" simply reveals his loving patience toward you, because he does not want any to perish but all to come to repentance. [k]

¹⁰ The day of the Lord will come and take everyone by surprise—as unexpected as a home invasion. The atmosphere will be set on fire and vanish

---

a 3:1 This would indicate that Peter is writing to the same people as his first letter (Galatia, Cappadocia, and the Roman province of Asia).

b 3:1 Or "a pure mind" or "sincere intention." The Aramaic can be translated "awaken your beautiful memories."

c 3:2 Or "commandment."

d 3:2 Peter places "your apostles" on the same level as the Old Testament prophets as to their trustworthiness and in setting the standard for living a life of purity for God.

e 3:3 Or "deceivers."

f 3:4 This is the Greek word *parousia*, which can also mean "presence" or "arrival" or "visitation." The Aramaic can be translated "Where is the kingdom that he brought?"

g 3:6 Verses 5–6 are translated from the Aramaic. The Greek could be translated "The word of the Lord formed the heavens and the earth out of water and by means of water. And it was destroyed by the submerging of the world of that day—destroyed by water."

h 3:7 The Aramaic can be translated "the earth is being kept as a hayloft (or pile of hay) for the fire."

i 3:8 As translated from the Aramaic.

j 3:8 Peter gives us an incredible interpretive key to understand time from the Lord's perspective. A day and a thousand years can both be symbolic. See also Ps. 90:4.

k 3:9 The Aramaic is quite different and can be translated "The Lord does not treat his kingdom like a dutiful chore, as some people consider it, like the treatment of a temporary laborer. But he pours out his Spirit on your behalf, since he does not wish that anyone should perish but that everyone should come into grace."

with a horrific roar, and the heavenly bodies [a] will melt away as in a tremendous blaze. The earth and every activity of man will be laid bare. [b] [11] Since all these things are on the verge of being dismantled, don't you see how vital it is to live a holy life? We must be consumed with godliness [12] while we anticipate and help to speed up the coming of the day of God, [c] when the atmosphere will be set on fire and the heavenly bodies consumed in a blaze. [13] But as we wait, we trust in God's royal proclamation to be fulfilled. There are coming [d] heavens new in quality, and an earth new in quality, where righteousness will be fully at home. [e]

Preparation for the Coming of the Lord

[14] So, my beloved friends, with all that you have to look forward to, may you be eager to be found living pure lives *when you come into his presence*, [f] without blemish and filled with peace. [15] And keep in mind that our Lord's extraordinary patience simply means *more opportunity for* salvation, [g] just as our dear brother Paul wrote to you with the wisdom that God gave him. [16] He consistently speaks of these things in all of his letters, even though he writes some concepts that are overwhelming to our understanding, which the unlearned and unstable love to twist to their *spiritual* ruin, as they do to other Scriptures. [h]

---

a 3:10 Or "elements."

b 3:10 The Aramaic can be translated "The earth and its works will be refined."

c 3:12 Peter is teaching us that the church has the ability to speed up (and, by implication, slow down) the coming of the day of God. The closer we get to Christ, the closer will be his coming. "The day of God" is an equivalent phrase to the "day of the Lord."

d 3:13 As translated from the Aramaic. The Aramaic word for promise is best translated "royal proclamation."

e 3:13 See Isa. 65:17; 66:22. There is coming a day when all will live according to God's perfect will for their lives and righteousness will be at home on earth and in every heart. This will be the day when justice reigns on earth. The Aramaic can be translated "We expect from his promise a new sky and a new earth in which the virtuous people will dwell."

f 3:14 Although this is clearly implied, it is based on the dative pronoun *autō*, which does not indicate agency (by him), but in his presence (before him).

g 3:15 See 2 Peter 3:9. The Aramaic can be translated "Consider the Lord's outpouring of [his] Spirit as salvation."

h 3:16 This is not meant to imply that we cannot understand the Bible, but that there are certain concepts that are difficult to understand. The Bible is the only book whose Author is present every time it is read. The Holy One is the Divine Author of Scripture (2 Tim. 3:16) and is the one who can open our hearts to understand truth. It is when we twist the Scriptures to fit our understanding that we are distorting its truth. Note also that Peter places Paul's letters in the same category as the "other [inspired] Scriptures."

Grow in God's Grace

[17] As for you, divinely loved ones, since you are forewarned of these things, be careful that you are not led astray by the error of the lawless and lose your firm grip *on the truth*. [18] But continue to grow and increase in God's grace and intimacy with our Lord and Savior, Jesus Christ. [a] May he receive all the glory both now and until the day eternity begins. Amen!

---

a 3:18 The Aramaic does not use the imperative but makes it more of a decree: "You continue to be nourished in grace and in the intimate knowledge of our Lord and Savior, Jesus the Messiah, and of God the Father." Spiritual growth is yielding to the grace of God and having passion to know Jesus Christ intimately. In time, we grow into his beautiful image.

1 JOHN

Introduction

AT A GLANCE

Author: The apostle John

Audience: Communities in Asia Minor experiencing schisms

Date: AD 85

Type of Literature: A letter

Major Themes: Preserving truth, false teaching, God's character, Christ's centrality, and Christian discipleship

Outline:

Letter Opening —1:1–4

Walk in God's Light, Keep God's Commands —1:5–2:11

New Status, New Love —2:12–17

Believing and Living as God's Children — 2:18–3:24

Test the Spirits — 4:1–6

Love for Another, Love for God — 4:7–5:12

Letter Closing — 5:13–21

ABOUT 1 JOHN

God is love! Let these words live within you! The glorious God of love is revealed in John's three letters. Written by the same John who penned his Gospel, the reader is taken into the Light of God. These beautiful words should be read over and over by every person on earth. God is love, and you can come to him by faith!

Everyone needs assurance from God that they are loved and cherished. The apostle John wrote this letter to assure us of the truths of God's love and mercy toward us. And when we receive his love, we are free to share it with others. As we love one another, we have the assurance that we are God's true spiritual children and that God's love is perfected in us. What joy John's words bring to our hearts!

Although the author is not named, it was clearly John the beloved who wrote this letter. (Only the New Testament books of Hebrews and 1 John do not directly name their authors.) He once walked on the shore of Lake Galilee—a fisherman, who left all to follow Jesus. And he taught all about life—eternal life, glorious life, abundant life! In Christ we find life, so John will always point us to Christ and our fellowship with him. In fact, John tells us four reasons why he wrote his letters: (1) to bring us into life-union (fellowship) with God (1 John 1:3); (2) that we might experience the fullness of joy (1 John 1:4); (3) that we might not sin (1 John 2:1); (4) that we might have the full assurance of our salvation (1 John 5:13).

The beloved apostle of Jesus reveals to us the revelation knowledge of who Jesus is and who we have become in him. John is the apostle of love. This letter is saturated with the love of God, which has been lavished upon us in Christ. And this love must be seen, made visible as we express his love toward one another. John reinforces this truth: we are to be ministers of love in how we walk in this life, demonstrating truth and kindness to all.

John's letter will bring a fresh understanding of God to your heart. Let him speak to you through his faithful servant John. Enjoy!

PURPOSE

John the beloved wrote his magisterial letter to bring the churches back into unity and clarity of faith, and beckon them to hold fast to the tradition and values they had already committed themselves to in Christ. There were false teachers who had come in and divided the flock with doctrines that diminished the glory of Christ. John's teachings always take us deeper into the truth and ways of God, and deeper into love for Jesus Christ. Anything that moves the heart away from loving Christ and loving others is to be viewed as suspect and diversionary. We can thank God for John's three letters to consistently point us back to the Light!

AUTHOR AND AUDIENCE

Although some contest it, there should be little doubt that the apostle John was responsible for writing this letter of passion, probably while he was in Ephesus around AD 85. The opening of the letter itself bears striking similarity to the Gospel that bears his name, extolling the Living Expression of God in almost poetic language. There are at least twelve other passages that have direct connection in both language, style, and scope with the fourth Gospel—showing that the beloved disciple of Jesus was the author of this beloved letter.

Unlike his other two letters, 1 John is not addressed to certain ones but to everyone. No particular audience is addressed in this letter, although there was a community over which John was an overseer in spiritual authority and fatherhood. Many believe John wrote this letter to clarify what he wrote earlier about the truth of Christ and to correct misinterpretations and misapplication of his testimony, especially by false teachers who had infiltrated this community. It was meant to encourage the believers who had been scattered by the Roman War of AD 67–70, and serve to encourage them in their understanding of their faith.

MAJOR THEMES

Preserving and Discerning Truth. In John's Gospel, he wrote his account of Jesus' life "so that you will fully believe that Jesus is the Anointed One, the Son of God" (20:31). He testified to the same truth in this letter so that those who believed wouldn't be led astray and would be "assured and know without a doubt that you have eternal life" (5:13). Such assurance and knowledge comes through the truth about Jesus, the Anointed One and Son of God, that John sought to preserve and help believers discern.

John was writing to a community troubled by false teachers who had distorted the truth of the gospel. For John, *truth* and *gospel* are equated, for the good news is about the one who was the Truth. So he defined a number of truths that one must believe in order to know eternal life, and encouraged ongoing discernment of the truth. Discernment is a major theme in this letter, and it is the task of the church to test the spirits, to "carefully examine what they say to determine if they are of God" (4:1).

Warning against Antichrists. John warns us that we must set our hearts firmly on the truths of Jesus Christ and his Word as protection from those whom John called *antichrists*. These people opposed the teachings of Christ, led people astray, and separated from the true community of Christ followers. John refuted antichrists in his day in a number of ways: he appealed to the teachings that had been with the church from the beginning, referenced early confessed creeds, pointed to the teachings and example of Jesus, appealed to the guidance of the Holy Spirit for all truth, and referenced our personal experience with God's heart through salvation. We guard against false teachers in these last days when we heed John's warnings and follow his guidance.

The Character of God. One of the more profound unveilings in 1 John is the character of God. Take a look at all we learn about him in John's Spirit-anointed letter: God is pure light, without a trace of darkness or impurity; faithfully forgives us of our sins, cleansing us from all unrighteousness; the essence of love, for he continually exists being love; the reality of all that is true; and the Father God who saves, having sent his Son into the world as its Savior. Ultimately, everything that is true about God is ours, because we have been born of God and enjoy unbroken fellowship with him.

The Centrality of Christ. It's only when we properly understand who Jesus Christ is that we can experience the heart of God. A distorted picture of Christ distorts how we live, which is why Christ takes center stage in John's letter. Every chapter is fixed on him: he is unveiled as the Living Expression of God; he is our atoning sacrifice, the one who shed his blood for our sins; he is our paraclete who advocates before the Father's throne on our behalf; he is our standard for living, the one in whom we are to actively remain; he will transform us into himself when he appears; he has come in real life flesh, not merely as a spirit-presence; and our new birth depends on believing in him, for he is the center of our believing as much as our faith.

Walking as Disciples of Christ. John's letter is largely concerned with preserving and discerning the truth about Jesus. Yet truth isn't only something to know in the head; it's something that we do with our whole self. John uses the metaphor of "walking" for the kind of life we're called to live—an image from the Hebrew Scriptures suggesting a manner and style of living that one is fully committed to. We are to walk in the pure light, not the realm of darkness; we are to walk in self-sacrificing love, not hate. Disciples of Christ walk the truth, which manifests itself as love. Of course, we know what love is because of Jesus: "This is how we have discovered love's reality: Jesus sacrificed his life for us" (3:16). John says the essence of our Christian life is emulating this love, which results in fellowship with God.

1 JOHN

God Is Love

The Living Expression

1 We saw him with our very own eyes. [a]
    We gazed upon him [b] and heard him speak. [c]
    Our hands actually touched him, [d]
    the one who was from the beginning,
    the Living Expression of God. [e]
[2] This Life-Giver was made visible
    and we have seen him.
    We testify to this truth:
    the eternal Life-Giver
    lived face-to-face with the Father
    and has now dawned upon us.
[3] So we proclaim to you
    what we have seen and heard
    about this Life-Giver
    so that we may share and enjoy
    this life together.

---

a   1:1 Or "We perceived [experienced] him with our eyes."

b   1:1 The apostles gazed upon Jesus both during Christ's earthly life and in resurrection glory.

c   1:1 The Aramaic text yields an interesting thought. By using the words *one* and *heard* in the same context, we're taken back to the ancient prayer of the Hebrews known as the Shema: "Hear, O Israel, the Lord our God is one." John is stating that he has heard the One that Israel was commanded to listen to, and that One is Jesus Christ. See Deut. 6:4.

d   1:1 The word for touch is poetic. It comes from a sensory verb meaning "to pluck the strings of an instrument." It can also be translated "to feel" (see Acts 17:27). It is as though John is saying, "We have plucked the chords of his being and felt what motivated him, his melody within."

e   1:1 Or "Word [*Logos*] of life." See the second footnote on John 1:1. This verse in both Greek and Aramaic breaks many rules of grammar and is used as a poetic tool to pack deep revelation in as few words as possible.

> For truly our fellowship [a] is with the Father
> and with his Son, Jesus, the Anointed One. [b]

[4] We are writing these things to you because we want to release to you our fullness of joy. [c]

God Is Light

[5] This is the life-giving message [d] we heard him share *and it's still ringing in our ears*. We now repeat his words to you: God is pure light. You will never find even a trace of darkness in him. [e]

[6] If we claim that we share life with him, [f] but keep walking in the realm of darkness, we're fooling ourselves and not living the truth. [7] But if we keep living in the pure light that surrounds him, [g] we share *unbroken* fellowship with one another, [h] and the blood of Jesus, his Son, continually cleanses us from all sin.

Purified from Sin

[8] If we boast that we have no sin, we're only fooling ourselves and are

---

a 1:3 The Greek word *koinōnia* means "to share in partnership; a reality shared in common." Through Christ, our shared reality is now with the Father. See also 2 Peter 1:4.

b 1:3 It is believed that these first three verses comprised an early hymn sung by the church.

c 1:4 Or "that our joy may be fulfilled." The first four verses form one Greek sentence, somewhat awkward in its construction, with three parenthetical interruptions in the sequence of the Greek sentence, which would be confusing if left in a literal form. This translation attempts to make one long, complicated Greek sentence into a meaningful translation of what John wrote.

d 1:5 The Greek word for "life-giving message" (promise) is *angelia* and is found only twice in the New Testament. It is related semantically to *euangelion,* which means "to evangelize or preach the [life-giving] gospel." The Aramaic can be translated "This is the hope that we heard from him and gives you hope because God is light and there is absolutely no darkness in him."

e 1:5 Or "no darkness at all can find any place in him." Although we do not have these exact words in any of the four Gospels, it is clear that John and the apostles attributed these words to Jesus Christ. Not everything Jesus said or did is recorded in the Gospels. If all of the events given in Matthew, Mark, Luke, and John were condensed, we would only have details recorded of but a few months of Jesus' entire life of over thirty-three years. See John 21:25.

f 1:6 Or "We share in fellowship with him" (Gr. *koinōnia*, "having things in common," "sharing in what he has and who he is"). This is the first of six conditional "if" clauses that extend through 2:1.

g 1:7 Or "as he [Christ] is in the light."

h 1:7 That is, God and the believer enjoy fellowship on the basis of walking in the light of God. Fellowship is maintained with God as we continue walking in the light he reveals to us. To walk in the light also involves being open, transparent, and honest, acknowledging any darkness the Lord might reveal in us. The blood of Jesus will cleanse us from all known sin, and if we continue to be open to God's pure light his blood will cleanse us from all unknown sin as well, enabling imperfect believers to walk in fellowship with a holy God. Freedom from sin (which is mentioned seventeen times in 1 John) is equated to walking in the pure light of God—not simply a fleshly struggle but a desire to walk in fellowship with God in his light.

strangers to the truth. [9] But if we freely admit our sins *when his light uncovers them,*[a] he will be faithful to forgive us every time. God is just to forgive us our sins *because of Christ,* and he will continue to cleanse us from all unrighteousness.[b]

[10] If we claim that we're not guilty of sin *when God uncovers it with his light,*[c] we make him a liar and his word is not in us.

Christ, Our Answer for Sin

2 You are my dear children, and I write these things to you so that you won't sin. But if anyone does sin, we continually have a forgiving Redeemer[d] who is face-to-face with the Father:[e] Jesus Christ, the Righteous One. [2] He is the atoning sacrifice[f] for our sins, and not only for ours but also for the sins of the whole world.[g]

The New Commandment

[3] Here's how we can be sure that we've truly come to know God: if we keep his commands.[h] [4] If someone claims, "I have come to know God *by experience,*" yet

---

a 1:9 Confession of sin is the way to find restoration and unbroken fellowship with God. It cleanses the conscience and removes every obstacle from communion with Christ. Confession does not gain God's acceptance, for that was won for us forever by the sacrifice of Christ. It is on the basis of being his dearly loved children that we restore intimacy with God through our tenderhearted confession before him. God will always be faithful to restore our first-love passion for him. There is no need to confess the same sins over and over, for that is ignoring the blood of Jesus that cleanses us. All of our sins were paid for on the cross and we can do nothing to remove them, but confession acknowledges God's faithfulness to restore our intimacy with him. Our Father and our forgiving Redeemer fill the heavens with grace toward every believer, even when we sin.

b 1:9 "Unrighteousness," in this context, means the sins we're not aware of. Confession cleanses known sin and restores fellowship with God, but God's faithfulness, in seeing Christ as our Sin-Bearer, cleanses us from all unknown sin as well. If we do but one thing (confess our sin), God will do four things: (1) demonstrate his faithful love, (2) demonstrate justice by counting our sins paid for by Christ, (3) forgive us every sin, and (4) continue a deeper work of cleansing from all aspects of sin's defilement.

c 1:10 We can only confess what God has revealed to us in his light. But when he shows that a thought or life pattern is sinful, we must agree with him in order to be restored. We cannot hide or conceal our sin, but confess our failure to him and move forward in faith. This is like a "rebound" for a missed shot.

d 2:1 Or "Advocate." The Aramaic can be translated "the Redeemer who ends the curse." See John 14:16 and the second footnote.

e 2:1 He is still our Father even when we sin.

f 2:2 Or "satisfaction for our sins."

g 2:2 In these two verses we find three things that Christ is to us: (1) our forgiving Redeemer/Intercessor, (2) the Righteous One who suffered in our place, and (3) the atoning sacrifice for our sins, which cleanses and shelters us.

h 2:3 Keeping God's commands is the proof and evidence of coming to know God, not the means of knowing God.

doesn't keep God's commands, he is a phony and the truth finds no place in him. ⁵ But the love of God will be perfected within the one who obeys God's Word. We can be sure that we've truly come to live in *intimacy with* God, ⁶ not just by saying, "I am intimate with God," but by walking in the footsteps of Jesus.

⁷ Beloved, I'm not writing a new commandment to you, but an old one that you had from the beginning, and you've already heard it. *ᵃ* ⁸ Yet, in a sense, it is a new commandment, *ᵇ* as its truth is made manifest both in Christ and in you, because the darkness is disappearing and the true light is already blazing. *ᶜ*

⁹ Anyone who says, "I am in the light," while holding hatred in his heart toward a fellow believer is still in the darkness. ¹⁰ But the one who truly loves a fellow believer lives in the light, and there is nothing in him that will cause someone else to stumble. *ᵈ* ¹¹ But whoever hates a fellow believer lives in the darkness—stumbling around in the dark with no clue where he is going, for he is blinded by the darkness. *ᵉ*

Three Stages of Spiritual Maturity

¹² I remind you, dear children: *ᶠ* your sins have been permanently removed because of the power of his name. *ᵍ*

¹³ I remind you, fathers *and mothers:* *ʰ* you have a relationship with the One who has existed from the beginning. *ⁱ*

And I remind you, young people: you have defeated the Evil One. *ʲ*

¹⁴ I write these things to you, dear children, because you truly have a relationship with the Father. I write these things, fathers *and mothers,* because you have had a true relationship with him who is from the beginning. And I write

---

a 2:7 See John 13:34–35.

b 2:8 This commandment to love one another is both old and new. It is found in the Old Testament (Lev. 19:18), but it is made radically new and fresh by the teaching of Christ and its application through our lives.

c 2:8 See John 1:5, 9; 8:12. The true light is the revelation of God that shines through Christ. The Aramaic can be translated "The new commandment I write to you became realized in him [Christ] and is in you, destroying the darkness and revealing the light of truth anew."

d 2:10 Or "no fear of stumbling haunts him" or "there is no trap laid for him."

e 2:11 John is equating darkness with the absence of love. To love is to walk in God's light. To hate is to walk in darkness.

f 2:12 The Greek word for "child," *teknion,* is a child still in training (under instruction), with an implication of servanthood.

g 2:12 That is, through faith in who Christ is and what he has done to redeem us through the blood of his sacrifice.

h 2:13 Fathers and mothers (parents) are not necessarily "old men" and "old women," but those who reproduce and raise children.

i 2:13 That is, Christ. See John 1:1; 1 John 1:1–3. Nothing more is said about fathers and mothers other than knowing Christ, for what could be more important than that?

j 2:13 Our enemy, Satan, is defeated through our union with Christ as we share in the triumphs of his cross and resurrection, the word of our testimony, the blood of the Lamb, and by not loving our own lives. See Rev. 12:10.

these things, young people, because you are strong, the Word of God is treasured in your hearts, and you have defeated the Evil One. [a]

A Warning Not to Love the World

[15] Don't set the affections of your heart on this world [b] or in loving the things of the world. The love of the Father and the love of the world are incompatible. [c] [16] For all that the world can offer us—the gratification of our flesh, the allurement of the things of the world, and the obsession with status and importance [d]—none of these things come from the Father but from the world. [17] This world [e] and its desires are in the process of passing away, but those who love to [f] do the will of God live forever. [g]

Believing in Jesus

[18] Dear children, the end of this age is near! You have heard that Antichrist is arising, [h] and in fact, many enemies of Christ have already appeared, and this is how we know that we are living in the closing hour of this age. [i] [19] For even

---

a 2:14 John gives young people (in Hebrew culture this would be anyone under forty) the three main components of spiritual growth: (1) courageous faith, (2) loving the Word of God, and (3) defeating the Evil One through our union with Christ.

b 2:15 Or "Stop loving the world system" (the ways of the world).

c 2:15 Or "If anyone persists in loving the world, there is no love for the Father in him."

d 2:16 These are the three areas of temptation that the serpent used with Adam and Eve in the garden to pull them away from the Father and what the devil used to tempt Jesus in the wilderness. He is an expert at using these cravings to dilute our love for the Father and cause us to turn our affections to the things of this life. See Gen. 3:6; Matt. 4:1–11. But the values of the kingdom of God are setting our affections on things above, living in the fruit of the Spirit (self-control), and humility, which always waits for God's timing for promotion.

e 2:17 That is, the world system and the desire to be in a world system that leaves God out of the picture are disappearing. Planet earth is not fading away here, but the systems, structure, and world order are.

f 2:17 Implied in the Greek present-tense verb, which means "to continually [habitually] do the will of God."

g 2:17 There is an interesting word play in the Aramaic in this verse. The Aramaic word for "world" is alma, and the word for "forever" is alam.

h 2:18 The Greek verb erchomai can be translated "to come," "to become known," "to be established," "to appear," "to show oneself," "to arise."

i 2:18 The final hour is John's description of what Paul describes as the "last days." The final hour or last days began at Pentecost (Acts 2:16–17; Heb. 1:2). We have been living in the last days for more than two thousand years. In these last days many antichrists will come. They oppose the teachings of Christ, lead people astray, and separate from the true community of Christ followers. There is no one individual named "the antichrist" (or enemy of Christ) in the Bible. (The definite article the is never used in connection to antichrist [or "anti-anointing"].) John tells us that the "spirit of antichrist" has already been in the world (1 John 4:3) and that many antichrists (false teachers who oppose the truth of Christ and have a following) have already come. John's warning is that we must set our hearts firmly on the truths of Jesus Christ and his Word as protection from the multiple lies that will

though they were once a part of us, they withdrew from us because they were never really of our number. For if they had truly belonged to us they would have continued with us. [a] By leaving our community of believers they made it obvious that they never really belonged to us. [b]

[20] But the Holy One has anointed you and you all know *the truth.* [c] [21] So I'm writing you not because you don't know the truth, but because you do know it, and no lie belongs to the truth. [d]

The Power of the Truth

[22] Who is the real liar but the one who denies that Jesus is the Christ. He is the real antichrist, the one who denies the Father and the Son. [e] [23] Whoever rejects the Son rejects the Father. Whoever embraces [f] the Son embraces the Father also. [24] So you must be sure to keep the message burning [g] in your hearts; that is, the message *of life* you heard from the beginning. If you do, you will always be living in close fellowship with the Son and with the Father. [25] And he himself has promised us the never-ending life of the ages to come!

[26] I've written these things about those who are attempting to lead you astray. [27] But the wonderful anointing you have received from God [h] *is so much greater than their deception and* now lives in you. There's no need for anyone to keep teaching you. [i] His anointing teaches you all that you need to know, for it will lead you into truth, not a counterfeit. So just as the anointing has taught you, remain in him. [j]

---

increasingly try to deceive believers. The words *antichrist* and *antichrists* are not found in the book of Revelation but only in 1 and 2 John.

a   2:19 The Aramaic can be translated "they would have clung to us" or "remained tied to us."

b   2:19 Or "all of them do not belong to us." Apparently they were not thrown out of the church or excommunicated but left of their own accord. See also 1 John 4:5.

c   2:20 Or "you [have the capacity to] know all things."

d   2:21 Jesus is the new reality and the truth. See John 14:6.

e   2:22 We have here the definition of "antichrist." It is anyone who denies the Son (or denies that Jesus is the anointed Messiah). To deny Christ is to reject the Father, who gave him to us to reveal who the Father truly is. The Father and the Son are one; you cannot receive one and reject the other.

f   2:23 Or "confesses."

g   2:24 Or "residing in you."

h   2:27 Although absent in the Greek, the words "from God" are found in the Aramaic manuscripts. It is clear from the context that the "anointing" is the Holy Spirit poured into us, bringing life, illumination, wisdom, fruit, and power from the indwelling life of Christ.

i   2:27 Or "There is no need for anyone to keep teaching you his opinions [deceptions]." John is not telling them not to continue to be taught the Word of God, for God has placed teachers in the church to instruct us and equip us and bring us into the fullness of Christ (1 Cor. 12:28; Eph. 4:11; Heb. 13:7, 17). John's warning concerns those who lead us astray by the false doctrines of men. The bride of Christ will always need Holy Spirit-filled teachers who illuminate us in the ways of Christ.

j   2:27 The Greek can be translated "remain in it" (the anointing).

[28] And now, dear children, remain in him, so that when he is revealed we may have joyful confidence and not be ashamed when we stand before him at his appearing. [a]

[29] If you know that he is righteous, you may be sure that everyone who lives in righteousness has been divinely fathered by him. [b]

Divine Sonship

3 Look with wonder at the depth of the Father's marvelous love that he has lavished on us! He has called us and made us his very own *beloved* children. [c] The reason the world doesn't recognize who we are is that they didn't recognize him. [d] [2] Beloved, we are God's children right now; however, it is not yet apparent what we will become. But we do know that when it [e] is finally made visible, [f] we will be just like him, for we will see him as he truly is. [3] And all who focus their hope on him will always be purifying [g] themselves, [h] just as Jesus is pure. [i]

The Character of God's Children

[4] Anyone who indulges in sin [j] lives in moral anarchy, for *the definition of* sin is breaking God's law. [k] [5] And you know without a doubt that Jesus was revealed to eradicate sins, and there is no sin in him. Anyone who continues to live in union with him will not sin. [6] But the one who continues sinning [l] hasn't seen him *with discernment* or known him *by intimate experience.*

[7] Delightfully loved children, don't let anyone divert you from this truth.

---

a 2:28 See also Luke 16:3; 2 Cor. 10:8; Phil. 1:20; 1 Peter 4:16.

b 2:29 Or "born of him." Living in righteousness, or doing what is right before God, is the proof that we have been fathered by God himself.

c 3:1 As translated from the Aramaic. The Greek reads "that we should be called God's children, and indeed we are." See Rom. 8:14–17; Gal. 3:26–27; 4:6–7.

d 3:1 That is, Jesus, God incarnated in human form.

e 3:2 The Aramaic can be translated "It has not been revealed until now what we are destined to be." Many translations view the subject of the Greek verb *phanerōthē* to be Christ ("when *he* is revealed"), but in the immediate context, "what we will become" is the subject and makes better grammatical sense.

f 3:2 The Greek word *phaneroō* means "to make clear, to be made visible," and it comes from the verb *phainō*, which means "to shine." John is saying we are not yet shining as we will one day. We are both children of God and reflections of God. See Dan. 12:3.

g 3:3 The Greek word *hagnizo* is found only twice in the New Testament. John uses the term in John 11:55 to refer to ritually cleansing ourselves in order to be morally undefiled as we come into God's presence.

h 3:3 There is a purifying hope that transforms us. This is more than the second coming. This is the hope of glory, that we will be revealed as fully like Christ. See Col. 1:25–27.

i 3:3 Or "as that one [Jesus] is pure." The beautiful purity of Jesus' life is the model for our lives.

j 3:4 Or "who habitually sins."

k 3:4 The Aramaic can be translated "Whoever commits sin commits evil, for sin is absolutely evil."

l 3:6 The present tense of the Greek verb throughout this section indicates a behavior that

The person who keeps doing what is right *proves that he* is righteous before God, even as the Messiah[a] is righteous. [8] But the one who indulges in a sinful life is of the devil,[b] because the devil has been sinning from the beginning. The reason the Son of God was revealed was to undo and destroy the works of the devil.

[9] Everyone who is truly God's child will refuse to keep sinning[c] because God's seed[d] remains within him, and he is unable to continue sinning because he has been fathered by God himself.[e] [10] Here is how God's children can be clearly distinguished from the children of the Evil One.[f] Anyone who does not demonstrate righteousness[g] and show love to fellow believers is not living with God as his source.[h]

Love One Another

[11] The beautiful message you've heard right from the start is that we should walk in self-sacrificing love toward one another. [12] We should not be like Cain, who yielded to the Evil One and brutally murdered his own brother, *Abel*.[i] And why did he murder him? Because his own actions were evil and his brother's righteous.

[13] So don't be shocked, beloved brothers and sisters, if you experience the world's hatred. [14] Yet we can be assured that we have been translated from *spiritual* death into *spiritual* life because we love the family of believers. A loveless life remains spiritually dead. [15] Everyone who keeps hating a fellow believer is a murderer,[j] and you know that no murderer has eternal life residing in him.

[16] This is how we have discovered love's reality: Jesus sacrificed his life for us.[k] Because of this great love, we should be willing to lay down our lives for one another. [17] If anyone sees a fellow believer in need and has the means

---

is persistent and habitual. John is not speaking of those who are yet to walk in complete victory, but those who continue sinning and find ways to excuse and justify it.

a   3:7 As translated from the Aramaic.

b   3:8 Or "is operating under the influence of the devil." That is, belonging to the devil, not to Christ.

c   3:9 The Aramaic can be translated "never serves sin."

d   3:9 This is the Greek word *sperma*, "male seed." See 2 Peter 1:4.

e   3:9 Or "born of God." We have been fathered by God himself and we carry his DNA, his genes.

f   3:10 Or "children of the devil" (or "the Adversary"). This is the only place in the New Testament that refers to those who have never experienced salvation as the devil's children. See also John 8:44.

g   3:10 Or "justice."

h   3:10 Or "is not of God."

i   3:12 See Gen. 4:8–10.

j   3:15 See Matt. 5:21–22.

k   3:16 Or "that he [Jesus] placed his soul over us and we are constantly indebted to place our souls over our brothers and sisters."

to help him, yet shows no pity and closes his heart against him, how is it even possible that God's love lives in him?[a]

[18] Beloved children, our love can't be an abstract theory we only talk about, but a way of life demonstrated through our loving deeds. [19] We know that the truth lives within us[b] because we demonstrate love in action, which will reassure[c] our hearts in his presence.[d]

[20] Whenever our hearts make us feel guilty *and remind us of our failures*, we know that God is much greater *and more merciful* than our conscience, and he knows everything there is to know *about us.*[e] [21] My delightfully loved friends, when our hearts don't condemn us, we have a bold freedom to speak face-to-face with God. [22] And whatever we ask of him we receive,[f] because we keep his commands. And by our beautiful intentions[g] we continue to do what brings pleasure to him.

[23] So these are his commands: that we continually place our trust in the name of his Son, Jesus Christ, and that we keep loving one another, just as he has commanded us. [24] For all who obey his commands find their lives joined in union with him, and he lives and flourishes in them. We know and have proof that he constantly lives and flourishes in us, by the Spirit that he has given us.

A Warning against False Teaching

4 Delightfully loved friends, don't trust every spirit, but carefully examine what they say[h] to determine if they are of God, because many false prophets have mingled into the world. [2] Here's the test for those with the genuine Spirit of God: they will confess Jesus as the Christ who has come in the flesh.[i] [3] Everyone who does not acknowledge that Jesus is from God has the spirit of antichrist, which you heard was coming and is already active in the world.

[4] Little children, you can be certain that you belong to God and have conquered them,[j] for the One who is living in you is far greater than the one who

---

a 3:17 Real love is an action. Think of God's love, which rescues, saves, and empowers. Love is more like a verb than a noun. Love is seen by actions, not just words.

b 3:19 Or "that we are of [belong to] the truth."

c 3:19 Or "tranquilize our hearts."

d 3:19 The Aramaic can be translated "By this we recognize that we are of the truth and make our hearts confident [or "deliver our hearts"] before he comes."

e 3:20 There is a higher courtroom for the human heart: it is where grace is enthroned. The very worst that is in us is known by God and he still showers mercy, love, and acceptance upon us. This is the greatness of God's grace. He sees beyond the sin of a moment and sees the holy affections of love in those who refuse to turn away from him. See John 21:17.

f 3:22 See Matt. 7:7; 21:22; John 9:31; 14:13–14; 15:7.

g 3:22 As translated from the Aramaic.

h 4:1 Although "what they say" is implied, it is clear that John is speaking of those who prophesy, and it is made explicit by the mention of "false prophets."

i 4:2 Or "confesses that Jesus Christ has come in the flesh."

j 4:4 That is, the antichrists who deny that Jesus is the Christ.

is in the world. [a] [5] They belong to this world and they articulate the spirit of this world, and the world listens to them. [6] But we belong to God, and whoever truly knows God listens to us. Those who refuse to listen to us do not belong to God. That is how we can know the difference between the spirit of truth and the spirit of deceit. [b]

God Is Love

[7] Those who are loved by God, let his love continually pour from you to one another, because God is love. Everyone who loves is fathered by God and experiences an intimate knowledge of him. [8] The one who doesn't love has yet to know God, for God is love. [c] [9] The light of God's love shined within us [d] when he sent his matchless [e] Son into the world so that we might live through him. [f] [10] This is love: [g] He loved us *long before we loved him*. It was his love, not ours. He proved it by sending his Son to be the pleasing sacrificial offering to take away our sins. [h]

---

a 4:4 That is, the devil. We have the Word of God, the Holy Spirit, the favor of God, and Jesus Christ. Within us is more than enough power to overcome the evil in this world. John uses the word *world* (Gr. *kosmos*) more than any other New Testament writer (104 times) to convey the concept of this world system or world order. One could describe it as "the culture of the world."

b 4:6 The New Testament gives us a number of ways we can discern true prophets from false ones. John gives us eight here: (1) They must confess that Jesus the Messiah has come in bodily form (vv. 2–3). (2) They must not come in the spirit of this world (v. 5). (3) They must listen to the truth (v. 6). (4) They must demonstrate love (vv. 7–21). (5) The Spirit of Truth must be in them (vv. 4–6). (6) They must remain true to the written Word of God (v. 6; 5:10; 2 Tim. 3:16). (7) They must be overcomers who have the greater One living in them (v. 4). (8) They must have a commitment to the body of Christ (2:19).

c 4:8 Or "God continually exists, being love."

d 4:9 Or "God's love was revealed among us." The base word for "revealed" is *phainō*, "to shine light."

e 4:9 Or "only begotten." That is, Jesus had no beginning and was the eternal Son of God as part of the triune essence or Godhead.

f 4:9 The Aramaic can be translated "that we might live in his hand," considered to be an idiom for living by his grace.

g 4:10 The Aramaic can be translated "This is how love was born."

h 4:10 The Greek term *hilasmos* can be described as "a cleansing, satisfying sacrifice that provides a covering shelter." A form of the word is used for "mercy seat" in Heb. 9:5. God's love provides the answers for life's greatest questions: (1) Why was I created? To receive and experience God's love. (2) Does God care about me? God's love is indiscriminate; he loves everyone and cares about every detail of our lives. (3) Am I really free to choose or reject God's love? Yes—love must be a choice, freely and without compulsion. (4) What is the way of salvation? Love became a man, Jesus Christ, who died as our sacrificial offering and by believing in him we receive the gift of salvation. (5) How can I really know that I am saved? When we respond with faith to God's loving invitation and then demonstrate it by loving others, we have the assurance of our salvation. (6) How can I know that God loves me? His love prompted him to send his unique and beautiful Son to the earth to be our Savior and

[11] Delightfully loved ones, if he loved us with such tremendous love, then "loving one another" should be our way of life! [12] No one has ever gazed[a] upon the fullness of God's splendor.[b] But if we love one another, God makes his permanent home in us, and we make our permanent home in him, and his love is brought to its full expression in us. [13] And he has given us his Spirit within us so that we can have the assurance that he lives in us and that we live in him.

[14] Moreover, we have seen with our own eyes and can testify to the truth that Father God has sent his Son to be the Savior of the world. [15] Those who give thanks[c] that Jesus is the Son of God live in God, and God lives in them. [16] We have come into an intimate experience with God's love, and we trust in the love he has for us.[d]

God is love![e] Those who are living in love are living in God, and God lives through them. [17] By *living in God*,[f] love has been brought to its full expression in us[g] so that we may fearlessly face the day of judgment,[h] because all that Jesus now is,[i] so are we in this world. [18] Love never brings fear, for fear is always related to punishment. But love's perfection drives the fear *of punishment far* from our hearts. Whoever walks constantly afraid of *punishment*[j] has not reached love's perfection. [19] Our love for others is *our grateful response* to the love God first demonstrated to us.[k]

[20] Anyone can say, "I love God," yet have hatred toward another believer. This makes him a phony, because if you don't love a brother or sister, whom you can see, how can you truly love God, whom you can't see? [21] For he has

---

Redeemer. He offers to everyone the invitation to experience even deeper measures of his love. And he gives us his Holy Spirit as confirmation that he loves and cherishes us and gives us the power to love others. See Eph. 3:14–21.

a 4:12 Or "watched." The Greek verb *theaomai* is used in classical Greek for "watching a play or spectator sport."

b 4:12 See John 1:18; 5:37; 6:46.

c 4:15 As translated from the Aramaic.

d 4:16 Or "in us."

e 4:16 Or "God continually exists, being love."

f 4:17 Or "By this" (relationship with God).

g 4:17 Or "love has reached its goal / destiny within us."

h 4:17 The Aramaic can be translated "we will have open faces on the day of judgment." For the true believer filled with God's love, the day of judgment is not to be feared but looked forward to, for perfect love will have made us completely like Christ. Love provides us with no reason to fear the future or to fear punishment from God. See 1 Cor. 4:5.

i 4:17 Or "because we are what he is in this world." The verb tense is important. We are not like Jesus *was*, but because of grace, we are like he is *now*: pure and holy, seated in heaven, and glorified. See Rom. 8:30; Eph. 2:6; Col. 3:1–4. Faith has transferred his righteousness to us.

j 4:18 The immediate context shows that it is the fear of correction, "punishment," or rejection. The Aramaic can be translated "Fear is suspicious."

k 4:19 Or "We [continue to] love because God first loved us." Some manuscripts read "We love God because he first loved us."

given us this command: whoever loves God must also demonstrate love to others. [a]

The Proof of Love and the Victory of Faith

5 Everyone who believes that Jesus is the Messiah is God's spiritual child and has been fathered by God himself. And everyone who loves Father God loves his children as well. [2] This is how we can be sure that we love the children of God: by having a passionate love for God and by obedience to his commands. [3] True love for God means obeying his commands, and his commands don't weigh us down as heavy burdens. [b] [4] *You see*, every child of God overcomes [c] the world, for our faith is the victorious power that triumphs over the world. [5] So who are the world conquerors, *defeating its power?* Those who believe that Jesus is the Son of God.

The Spirit, the Water, and the Blood

[6] Jesus Christ is the One who was revealed *as God's Son* by his water *baptism* and by the blood *of his cross*—not by water only, but by water and blood. [d] And the Spirit, who is truth, confirms this with his testimony. [7] So we have these three constant witnesses giving their evidence: [e] [8] the Spirit, the water, and the blood. And these three are in agreement. [9] If we accept the testimony of men, *how much more should we accept* the more authoritative testimony of God that he has testified concerning his Son?

[10] Those who believe in the Son of God have the *living* testimony in their hearts. Those who don't believe have made God out to be a liar by not believing the testimony God has confirmed about his Son. [11] This is the true testimony:

---

a 4:21 The real proof of our love for God must always be in how we express love and treat others with dignity and respect, esteeming them in love.

b 5:3 God's grace empowers us to love, which makes his commands a delight instead of a duty. The spontaneity of love is never crushed by the commands of a loving God.

c 5:4 The Greek verb tense indicates continuous action, "continually conquers the world" (system).

d 5:6 At Jesus' baptism the voice of the Father acknowledged him as his beloved Son. At the cross his blood was shed to bring the reality of Christ to those who believe in him. The majority view of current scholarship is this passage refers to Jesus' baptism and the cross. It is possible, however, that John is referring to the blood and water that spilled from the side of Jesus after his death.

e 5:7 There is considerable historical and theological debate surrounding vv. 7–8. Some later, less reliable manuscripts have for vv. 7–8: "There are three that testify in heaven: the Father, the Word, and the Holy Spirit. And these three are one." This is known as the *Comma Johanneum*. But there has been a nearly complete agreement of scholars that this reading was added by copyists, with many theories of who it was. Although there is nothing heretical about this addition, it seems to have been inserted to reinforce the doctrine of the Trinity. It is not included in modern versions nor in the Aramaic.

that God has given us eternal life, and this life has its source in his Son. [a] [12] Whoever has the Son has *eternal* life; whoever does not have the Son does not possess *eternal* life.

Assurance of Eternal Life

[13] I've written this letter to you who believe in the name of the Son of God so that you will *be assured and* know without a doubt that you have eternal life.

[14] Since we have this confidence, we can also have great boldness before him, for if we present any request agreeable to his will, he will hear us. [15] And if we know that he hears us in whatever we ask, we also know that we have obtained the requests we ask of him.

[16] If anyone observes a fellow believer habitually sinning in a way that doesn't lead to death, [b] you should keep interceding in prayer that God will give that person life. Now, there is a sin that leads to death, and I'm not encouraging you to pray for those who commit it. [17] All unrighteousness is sin, but there is sin that does not result in death.

[18] We are convinced that everyone fathered by God does not make sinning a way of life, because the Son of God protects the child of God, and the Evil One cannot touch him. [19] We know that we are God's children and that the whole world lies under the misery and influence of the Evil One. [20] And we know that the Son of God has made our understanding come alive so that we can know by experience the One who is true. And we are in him who is true, God's Son, Jesus Christ—the true God and eternal life!

[21] So, little children, guard yourselves from worshiping anything but him. [c]

---

a 5:11 Or "this life is in [as connected to him as source] his Son." It can also mean that God has placed us in life union with his Son to manifest eternal life in us.

b 5:16 That is, if the sinning is persisted in, it may lead to death. Some believe this may refer to the unforgivable sin of blasphemy of the Holy Spirit (Matt. 12:31–32; Mark 3:28–30; Luke 12:8–10), or possibly the sin that brings death in taking communion "unworthily" (1 Cor. 11:27–30), or lying to the Holy Spirit (Acts 5:1–11). However, John speaks in this letter about the gross apostasy of those who turn away from the truth and depart from the fellowship of believers and follow the teaching of antichrists.

c 5:21 Or "keep yourselves from idols." The Aramaic can be translated "Keep your souls from fear of idols."

2 JOHN

Introduction

AT A GLANCE

Author: The apostle John
Audience: Communities in Asia Minor experiencing schisms
Date: AD 85–90
Type of Literature: A letter
Major Themes: Truth, brotherly love, and false teachers
Outline:

Letter Opening — 1–3
An Exhortation to Walk in Truth and Love — 4–6
A Warning against False Teachers — 7–11
Letter Closing — 12–13

ABOUT 2 JOHN

The book of 2 John points us to the truth and encourages us to hold it fast and never let it go. The theme of John's second letter could be described as "loving truth." Truth generates love, and love will always be faithful to the truth. To love God is to love his truth and cherish it in our hearts.

Some scholars believe that John penned what we've called his second letter actually first, before 1 John. Given that it addresses the same heartbreaking situation of schisms over false teaching that were wrecking the fragile churches under John's care in Asia Minor, some see this as a quick, almost hurriedly written note from the heart of a spiritual father to his children in trouble. Then he followed up his initial warnings with a second letter (which we know as 1 John) to make a greater appeal and guard their ongoing spiritual lives. Others see in this letter a follow-up to the first one, possibly written to a more distant audience, or even as a cover letter to 1 John given its personal greetings.

Regardless, what's evident is that John was deeply burdened about the chaos being caused in his network of churches. This beloved disciple of Jesus wanted his disciples to experience the pure love and truth that had already been birthed in their hearts. He also wanted them to walk in love, for to walk in love is to walk in the truth of God.

John's letter will bring a fresh understanding of God to your heart. Let him speak to you through his faithful servant John. Enjoy!

PURPOSE

As with his first letter, John wrote to the communities to which he was an overseer ("the elder" is a title suggesting spiritual authority) with one singular purpose: to guard and protect them from the false teachers who had gone among them and were deceiving them. These were itinerant teachers who were bearing a "truth" contrary to the received Spirit-anointed truth of the gospel. He writes as a spiritual father who was concerned about schisms wreaking havoc among his beloved children.

AUTHOR AND AUDIENCE

While the letter only identifies the author as "the elder," it's clear he was in a position of spiritual authority over his community and wrote in a similar manner and tone as both 1 John and the Gospel of John. Given this, it's no surprise that the tradition from the earliest days of the church assumed the apostle John authored the letter. Though the text doesn't bear his name, early leaders like Polycarp and Papias both ascribed it to him.

Possibly written earlier than his first letter, John addressed this one to the "chosen woman and her children." Most commentators see this as a metaphor for the church with its spiritual believers (children), believing that John the Elder wrote the letter to a church or network of churches. Some have viewed it more literally as written to an unnamed woman or a woman named Elekta or Kyria (feminine of *kurios*, "lord"). Regardless of who the letter was written to, it is inspired of God to bring truth to our hearts and keep us from evil.

MAJOR THEMES

Walking and Staying in the Truth. As with his first letter, John is concerned with the truth of the gospel—not only that believers guard it, but also walk in it and stay in it. The living truth of Christ has a permanent home in our lives, and will stay with us for all eternity. But we're also commanded to actively walk in the truth and stay in the truth—because as John says, "Anyone who wanders away and does not remain faithful to the teaching of Christ has no relationship with God" (9). For it's only when we continue in the truth that we have intimate connection with both the Father and the Son.

Loving One Another. Not only are we to love truth, we're to love each other. After all, this isn't a new command but one we've had from the beginning of time—and one our Lord and Savior Jesus Christ himself gave us. Loving one another means following the commands of Christ, which are always directed both upward (to God) and outward (to others). When we love our neighbor as ourselves, we are also loving the God who made them and saved them!

Warning about False Teachers. Finally, John warned against "deceivers" who might come into our midst and go beyond the teachings of Christ—trying to drag us with them. Early on, some believers thought this letter had either been a cover letter to 1 John, or an appendix added to its end. This makes sense given its close connection with John's first letter warning against false teachers. John reiterates our need to watch out for such antichrists—going so far as to instruct us not even to show hospitality to them, for anyone who welcomes them shares in their wicked work.

2 JOHN

Loving Truth

Loving Truth

From the elder[a] to God's chosen woman[b] and her children:

I love you all *as those who are* in the truth.[c] And I'm not the only one, for all who come to know the truth[d] share my love for you [2]because of the *living* truth that has a permanent home in us and will be with us forever.[e]

[3]God our Father and Jesus Christ, his Son, will release to us *overflowing* grace, mercy, and peace, filled with true love.[f]

[4]I was delighted and filled with joy when I learned that your children are

---

a   1 Or "presbyter." This was obviously a self-designated term for the apostle John. He was an elder because of being the only living apostle who was chosen by Jesus.

b   1 The letter is addressed to the *eklekte kuria* ("elect/chosen/excellent lady"). Most commentators see this as a metaphor for the church and her spiritual children, believing that John wrote this letter to a sister congregation or network of congregations. This has been the majority view since it was first noted by Jerome (Jerome, *Ep. Xi. ad Ageruchiam*). Still, others see it as a letter to a specific woman, with the conjecture that her name was either Elekta or Kyria. This is a possibility, since one way to read the letter is that John knew this woman and was acquainted with her sister and her children (v. 13). If this was indeed written to Kyria (feminine of "lord," meaning a woman in authority), there is a possibility that she was the pastor or overseer of a specific church. But who was the most especially "chosen woman" in the entire Bible? It was Mary, the mother of our Lord Jesus. John was given the commission by Jesus himself in his last moments on earth to care for Mary as his mother, and we know that Mary had a sister (John 19:25–27, cf. v. 13). What other woman is chosen and loved, not only by John but all the church? Every believer in Jesus rightly honors and reveres his mother, Mary. Throughout church history there have been a few scholars who believe that Mary was the recipient of this letter. (See Knauer, *Stud. U. Krit.*, 1833, Part 2, p.452ff.; q.v. J. E. Huther, *Critical and Exegetical Handbook to the General Epistles of James, Peter, John, and Jude*, translated from the German, 11 vols., Funk and Wagnalls, 1884.)

c   1 Or "whom I love in truth." John uses the word *love* sixty-two times in the New Testament, while all the other New Testament writers combined use it a total of 116 times.

d   1 It is possible that John is using the word *truth* as he uses *word* (Gr. *logos*), as a title for Jesus Christ ("all who know the Truth").

e   2 Or "into the age." The Aramaic can be translated "because the truth sustains us to the end of the eternity."

f   3 Or "in truth and love."

consistently living in the truth, just as we have received the command from the Father.

⁵ Dearest woman, I have a request to make of you. It is not a new commandment but a repetition of the one we have had from the beginning: that we constantly love one another. ⁶ This love means living in obedience to whatever God commands us. For to walk in love toward one another is the unifying commandment we've heard from the beginning.

Warning about False Teachers

⁷ Numerous deceivers have surfaced *from among us* and gone out into the world, *a* people who will not acknowledge Jesus Christ coming as a man. These deceivers are antichrists! ⁸ Be on your guard so that you do not lose all that we *b* have *diligently* worked for but receive a full reward.

⁹ Anyone who wanders away *c* and does not remain faithful to the teaching of Christ has no relationship with God. But those who remain in the teaching of Christ have a *wonderful* relationship with both the Father and the Son. ¹⁰ So if anyone comes *into your fellowship claiming to be a true believer* yet doesn't bring this teaching, you are not to consider him as a fellow believer, *d* nor should you welcome him into your homes. *e* ¹¹ For if you welcome him as a believer, *f* you will be partnering with him in his evil agenda.

¹² Although I have many more subjects I'd like to discuss with you, I'd rather not include them in this letter. *g* But I look forward to coming to visit and speaking with you face-to-face *h*—for being together will complete our joy!

¹³ The children of your sister, whom God has chosen, send you their loving greetings. Amen. *i*

---

a 7 In the context of love, John now mentions false teachers. This shows us that love is the safeguard against error. The more that love flows through us as we honor God's commands, the more we are kept from deception. Our unity, produced by love, enables us to recognize and resist false teachers.

b 8 Some manuscripts have "you."

c 9 Or "goes beyond" (the teaching of Christ). The Aramaic implies a visiting minister or itinerant speaker, "whoever passes through."

d 10 Or "don't give him any greeting" (as a believer). Hospitality was such a cultural virtue in the time of John that he actually had to warn them not to show hospitality to false teachers.

e 10 Or possibly "house [church]."

f 11 Or "If you give him a [public] greeting [as a believer]."

g 12 Or "I'd rather not write with ink [pen] and paper."

h 12 The Aramaic can be translated "mouth to mouth."

i 13 Most manuscripts do not include "Amen."

❦

3 JOHN

Introduction

AT A GLANCE

Author: The apostle John
Audience: Gaius, a friend of John
Date: AD 85–90
Type of Literature: A letter
Major Themes: Truth, hospitality, divisiveness, and doing good
Outline:

Letter Opening — 1–4
An Exhortation to Show Hospitality — 5–8
An Example of Inhospitality — 9–11
Letter Closing — 12–15

ABOUT 3 JOHN

Though it is almost the smallest of the New Testament letters, this piece of ancient correspondence offers us a glimpse into a problem every modern church should consider: hospitality, especially for those called and anointed by Christ as ministers of his gospel.

There's a good chance that one of the characters in the letter, Demetrius, was himself a missionary who was associated with the apostle John and actually carried it as a sort of letter of introduction to the letter's recipient, Gaius. This dear man was known to John as a faithful host for missionaries who were spreading the gospel in the region. One can imagine Gaius rolling out the red carpet, breaking out the fine china, and making up an extra bed for Christ's emissaries who were tirelessly working on behalf of the Lord. Oh to be known for being a welcoming spirit, and for pouring out love and support for the sake of others! And woe to the one who denies hospitality and stirs up trouble within the body, which is exactly what one of the other characters had done.

John's motivation for penning and sending his letter to the small community in modern-day Turkey (Asia Minor) was to commend hospitality as a way of expressing Christian love. John was thrilled at how Gaius had welcomed traveling evangelists throughout the region, and he wanted him to continue this show of support. John's letter will bring a fresh understanding of God to your heart. Let him speak to you through his faithful servant John. Enjoy!

PURPOSE

John's third letter, similar in structure and vocabulary as his second letter, was more of a general letter sent to the churches scattered throughout Turkey (Asia Minor), even as it was addressed to one leader of one local community. John wrote to them to encourage them to welcome itinerant minsters who would travel and teach the different congregations—commending a particularly hospitable church leader, Gaius. He also warned against allowing pride and self-centeredness to get in the way of showing such love and support. It is a letter of hospitality and carries John's trademark truths of showing love and grace to all.

AUTHOR AND AUDIENCE

This intimate letter between Christian brothers addressing a situation in a local church involved four people: the elder, who sent the note; Gaius, who received the letter; and Diotrephes and Demetrius, church leaders in the region mentioned in the letter. Though various suggestions have been offered as to the identity of this elder, as with 2 John early Christians identified him as the apostle John, beloved disciple of Jesus. Although he wrote to one church leader in Asia Minor, the letter may have been intended for a wider audience to encourage them to continue to support missionaries bearing the gospel of Christ with open-armed hospitality.

MAJOR THEMES

Walking in the Truth. This is a common theme in John's letters, walking in the truth of Christ. Such walking is not only a joyful experience for those who are spiritually responsible for others (like parents when they see their children walking with Christ); it's also a joyful experience for believers, whose souls get along well in spiritual health as they maintain their commitment to Jesus in words and deeds.

Showing Christian Hospitality. True hospitality is a lost art in some churches today and must be valued. Gaius stands as an example to all of how it looks to faithfully demonstrate loving hospitality to our fellow brothers and sisters in Christ—especially when it comes to ministers of the gospel, who deserve our full, generous support. True Christian commitment to truth means a commitment to love through support.

Divisiveness within the Body. One of the greatest toxins to the body of Christ is divisiveness—whether that's a division in truth that false teachers bring, or a division in love that some believers create. Such an attitude manifests itself in pride, inhospitality, gossip, slander, malice, and obstruction. Not only did John warn against such people, he warned against imitating them within the body. We should name them and call such people out—just as John did with Diotrephes.

Doing and Imitating Good. "Don't imitate what is evil," John wrote, "but imitate that which is good" (11). John reveals something important about what we are to imitate: the *good* here is not just any good, but godly good. It's goodness reflecting God's good character and good acts, built on his inspiring love. Such people prove they are of God, and those who don't imitate good prove they've never been in relationship with him in the first place.

3 JOHN

Love in Action

Love in Action

From the elder[a] to my dearly loved brother Gaius,[b] whom I truly love:[c] [2] Beloved friend, I pray that you are prospering in every way[d] and that you continually enjoy good health, just as your soul is prospering.[e] [3] I was filled with joy and delight when the brothers arrived and informed me of your *faithfulness to the* truth. They told me how you live continually in the truth *of Christ.*[f] [4] It is the greatest joy of my life to hear that my children are consistently living their lives in the ways of truth!

Financially Supporting Missionaries

[5] My beloved friend, *I commend you for your demonstration* of faithful love by all that you have done for the brothers *on their journey*, even though they were

---

a 1 Or "presbyter." This was obviously a self-designated term for the apostle John. He was an elder because of being the only living apostle who was chosen by Jesus.

b 1 Gaius was a convert of John's and a close friend who likely had a leadership position in the church (location not given). Church tradition states that he was one of the seventy whom Jesus sent out and was later ordained by John as the bishop of Pergamum. See *Apostolic Constitutions* (7.46.9; Funk 1, 454). However, there was also a Gaius who became the bishop of Ephesus. There are four mentions of Gaius in the New Testament, although it is unlikely that they were the same person (Acts 19:29; Rom. 16:23; 1 Cor. 1:14). The name Gaius means "joyful or happy." The Latin form of *Gaius* can be translated "lord."

c 1 Or "continually love in truth" (reality).

d 2 The Greek word *eudoomai* means "to be brought along to a smooth and prosperous journey" or "to be continually prospered [unto success] in every way." The Aramaic can be translated "as much as succeeds you." See Josh. 1:8.

e 2 John is praying that Gaius' physical health would match his spiritual health. God is concerned for both our physical health (he gave our bodies an immune system) and our souls (emotional and spiritual well-being). If physical health and soul "prosperity" were not the will of God, why would John pray that for Gaius?

f 3 Although the words *Jesus*, or *Christ*, do not appear anywhere in the text of 3 John, they are clearly implied.

strangers at the time. *[a]* [6] They have shared publicly with the congregation *[b]* about the beautiful acts of love you have shown them. *[c]* Now, if you would be so kind, send them on their way *with a generous gift*, in a manner that would honor God. *[d]* [7] You see, it was their passion for *the glory of* the name *of Christ* that launched them out, and they've not accepted financial support from unbelievers. *[e]* [8] They are deserving of all the support we can give them, *because through our giving* we can partner with them for the truth. *[f]*

Domineering Diotrephes

[9] I have already written you once about this, *[g]* but Diotrephes, *[h]* who loves to be in charge and recognized as first among you, does not acknowledge our authority. [10] So if I come, I will address what he's doing—spreading his malicious slander against us. *[i]* And not content with that, he refuses to welcome our brothers, *[j]* and he stands in the way of those who want to receive them and show them hospitality by throwing them out of the church!

[11] Delightfully loved ones, don't imitate what is evil, but imitate that which is good. *[k]* Whoever does good is of God; whoever does evil has not seen God. *[l]*

---

a 5 These are traveling missionaries and itinerant speakers who were shown hospitality by Gaius. True hospitality is a lost art in some churches today and needs to be valued anew.

b 6 This would likely have been the church where John was ministering (Ephesus, Pergamum, or another unnamed location).

c 6 As translated from the Aramaic.

d 6 Or "equal to God's value of them." Apparently, these missionaries had reported to John, returned to the area where Gaius was living, and then continued on with their missionary journey. The Aramaic is quite different: "You outfitted them like a plank billboard for God"; that is, "The gifts you gave them made them an advertisement for God."

e 7 Or "from the gentiles."

f 8 By giving to those who preach the gospel and nurture the people of God, we are partnering with them in their ministry.

g 9 This refers to a lost letter, possibly destroyed by Diotrephes. So the letter we now have is actually 4 John.

h 9 Diotrephes was most likely an elder in the congregation who saw himself as the most important one, pushing himself forward with a controlling leadership style. He refused the apostolic authority of John and would not accept guest speakers who may have been sent by John. His name means "nourished by Jupiter." Leaders must view other leaders not as threats but as coworkers. Love is not controlling or tyrannical. It is clear in the New Testament that the local church must have God-appointed ministry in the congregation from pastors, prophets, teachers, evangelists, and apostles (Eph. 4:11). Additionally, there were itinerant ministers that—if proven authentic—were to be received by the local church authorities and given both opportunities to minister and generous gifts to send them on their way.

i 10 Or "with evil words talking nonsense about us."

j 10 These would be the itinerant ministers, missionaries who visited their assembly to minister in the region.

k 11 The Aramaic gives an entirely different slant to this verse. It can be translated "Beloved, don't treat him with malice but with blessing" (good deeds).

l 11 This last clause is asyndetic in order to add emphasis.

Devoted Demetrius

¹² As for Demetrius, everyone speaks very highly of him, *ᵃ* and even the truth itself stands by his side. We too wholeheartedly endorse him, and you know that our recommendation is reliable.

¹³ Although I have many more subjects I'd like to discuss with you, I'd rather not include them in this letter. *ᵇ* ¹⁴ Instead, I hope to visit you and speak with you face-to-face. *ᶜ*

¹⁵ Peace to you, *my friend*. Your friends here send their loving greetings to you. Please greet each one of our friends there by name.

---

a 12 It is possible that Demetrius was one of the "brothers" (v. 3) who was now coming to visit the church and that he was the one who carried this letter to Gaius. This letter served the purpose of being a "letter of recommendation" of Demetrius and his ministry.

b 13 Or "I'd rather not write with ink [pen] and paper."

c 14 The Aramaic can be translated "mouth to mouth."

JUDE (JUDAH)

Introduction

AT A GLANCE

Author: The apostle Judah, also known as Jude
Audience: Eastern Mediterranean Christians, all God's lovers
Date: AD 58–60
Type of Literature: A letter
Major Themes: Christian faith, Christian life, God's character, salvation, and judgment
Outline:

    Letter Opening — 1–2
    Jude's Reason for Writing — 3
    Jude's Arguments against the False Teachers — 4–16
    Jude's Call to Persevere — 17–23
    Letter Closing — 24–25

ABOUT JUDE (JUDAH)

The name of this book from the Greek text is *Judas*, which is taken from the Hebrew/Aramaic name Judah. The actual name of this book is Judah! One of the most neglected letters in the New Testament, Judah carries a message for every believer today: there is a truth worth fighting for. It is not only written to you, as one who loves the truth; it is also entrusted to you—to preserve, defend, contend, and struggle for.

Though Judah wrote to a specific community who had been influenced by false teachers and foreign ideas to the gospel, his warning to persevere in both believing in our faith and living out our faith is timeless—for the church has always had to contend with false teachers who have tried to pervert the message of God's grace and distort the nature of our salvation.

The one striking fact you'll discover in reading Judah's letter is that he likely refers to two extrabiblical books, *The Assumption of Moses* (v. 9), and the *Book of 1 Enoch* (vv. 14–15). (Or "The Testament of Moses." Some scholars believe *The Assumption of Moses* and *The Testament of Moses* are one in the same. Others see them as different pseudephraphical books.) This has led some to reject Judah entirely, but there is no law against quoting from non-inspired books or borrowing thoughts and including them in an inspired text. They teach us some important revelation-truths about corruption and ungodliness.

By the last half of the first century there were already many false teachers who had infiltrated the ranks of the believers. Judah writes to warn and identify them as those who cause divisions and distort the truths of our faith. Yet you'll find some of the most beautiful treasures in his book, such as praying in the spirit, and the duty of keeping our hearts burning with passion for Jesus. Today, almost two thousand years after Judah wrote his short letter, we still need to guard our hearts and our churches from being led astray from the simplicity of the gospel. After all, these are truths worth fighting for!

PURPOSE

Judah's reason for writing his letter is clear: he needed to urge believers "to vigorously defend and contend for the beliefs that we cherish" (v. 3). Intruders had sown the seeds of false teaching among the believers, creating chaos and confusion. So Judah urged them to preserve, contend for, struggle for, and defend the body of truth we've received from the inspired Word of God, through the teaching ministry of the apostles.

Perhaps to combat and prevent the dangers of the sown heresy from fully blooming, Judah ended his letter by giving seven commands: (1) Keep building up your inner life on the foundation of faith. (2) Pray in the Holy Spirit. (3) Fasten your life to the love of God. (4) Receive more mercy from our Lord Jesus Christ. (5) Have compassion on the wavering. (6) Save the lost. (7) Hate any compromise that will stain our lives. It's when we live the truth of the gospel that we are sure to defend and contend for it most effectively.

AUTHOR AND AUDIENCE

Judah (Jude) is one of the two New Testament books written by half brothers of Jesus—James and Jude. Judah was possibly the youngest of the four brothers of Jesus (Matt. 13:55). Many scholars believe that Judah may have written his letter only twenty to twenty-five years after the life and resurrection of Jesus (AD 58–60). Although the exact audience is unclear, he most likely was addressing believers who lived in a Greek-speaking area not far from Palestine in the eastern Mediterranean region, including Syria and Egypt. All we know is they had received the gospel from the apostles, and were being disrupted by outsiders who brought ideas foreign to that received teaching.

MAJOR THEMES

Defend and Contend for the Faith. Judah's message reminds us to defend and contend for the faith entrusted to us. It is clear that he is not speaking of faith as simply believing in God, but *the (Christian) faith.* This encompasses the body of truth we receive from the inspired Word of God, delivered by the apostles—the gospel. Judah used an athletic metaphor to drive home the point that we need to struggle as in a great contest, exerting great effort to promote the noble cause of the gospel's advance—while defending these core beliefs (transmitted through generations of Christians) from the threat of false teachers.

Live the Faith. Not only is Judah concerned about the content of the believer's faith, he's also concerned about its expression—for right beliefs and right living go hand-in-hand. The false teachers who had sneaked into the churches were teaching a faith that had "perverted the message of God's grace into a license to commit immorality" (v. 4). Judah feared this perverted message would destroy their beliefs, which would in turn cause them to live ungodly lives. After warning of such examples, he urged believers to live their faith through discipleship, prayer, remaining in God's love, accepting Christ's mercy, being compassionate, evangelistic, and with discernment. Living our faith by showing it is the surest way to preserve and contend for it!

The Character of God. Judah offers us a rich understanding of the character and person of God—beginning with the words "chosen," "wrapped in the love," and "kept and guarded." This is what God has done for us who have believed! He is also the God who reveals, for he has entrusted to us revelation-truths through his apostles, leading to our salvation. Then there are shades of the Trinity: he urges believers to pray in the Holy Spirit, remain in God's (the Father's) love, and receive the mercy of Jesus Christ (vv. 20–21). Finally, we find one of the most vibrant, almost hymnic descriptions of God at the end in vv. 24–25: God keeps us from sin, revealing us as faultless; is heralded as Savior; and possesses endless glory and majesty, power and authority.

Coming Salvation and Judgment. Judah had wanted to write to the believers "about our amazing salvation we all participate in" (v. 3) for that is what we possess right now! Yet we are also waiting for our final salvation when Christ comes bearing eternal life. This is why Judah's theme of defending and contending for the faith is so important, for we are to preserve and persevere in our salvation until the end. There's another reason: judgment. For along with his salvation, the Lord will bear judgment for all the ungodly. Judah reveals that God destroys those who are guilty of unbelief and who give themselves to immorality, slander heavenly beings, and corrupt his church. Judgment makes the issue of false teaching that much more important, for such people sow seeds of division and doubt. This is why we're called to come alongside those who doubt their salvation and offer Christ's saving work in order to snatch people from the fires of judgment.

JUDE (JUDAH)

Truth Worth Fighting For

Truth Worth Fighting For

From Judah,[a] a loving servant[b] of Jesus, the Anointed One, and brother of James.[c] *I'm writing* to the chosen ones who are wrapped in the love of Father God—kept and guarded for[d] Jesus, the Messiah. [2] May God's mercy, peace, and love[e] cascade over you![f]

[3] Dearly loved friend, I was fully intending to write to you about our *amazing* salvation we all participate in, but felt the need instead to challenge you to vigorously defend and contend for[g] the beliefs that we cherish.[h] For God, *through the apostles*, has once for all entrusted these truths to his holy believers.

Warning against False Teachers

[4] There have been some who have sneaked in among you unnoticed.[i] They are depraved people whose judgment was prophesied in Scripture[j] a long time

---

a 1 Or Jude. The Greek is *Judas*. This was a common Hebrew / Aramaic name during the time of Jesus, and there were two of the Twelve who had this name.
b 1 The Greek word *doulos* implies a close and lasting relationship to a master; love is implied.
c 1 This James was the brother of our Lord Jesus. Jude is not asserting his family ties to Jesus but to James, as a sign of his humility. Instead of introducing himself as the half-brother of Jesus, he chose to describe himself simply as a "loving servant of Jesus . . . and brother of James." Jude is not boasting of a physical commonality with Jesus but a spiritual relationship he has with the risen Christ. See Matt. 13:55, where he is named as a (half) brother of Jesus.
d 1 Or "by."
e 2 Jude adds the word *love* to the typical greeting of mercy and peace.
f 2 Or "be multiplied in you."
g 3 Or "keep adding to the contest" or "repeatedly participate fully in the race course."
h 3 Although the Greek here is "the faith" or "on behalf of the faith," it is clear that Jude is not speaking of faith as simply believing in God. The Christian faith encompasses the body of truth we receive from the inspired Word of God. It is possible that Jude wrote his letter after the death of Peter and was referring to 1 and 2 Peter, a few of Paul's early letters, or even Mark's Gospel.
i 4 See Acts 20:29–30; 2 Peter 2:1.
j 4 Or "written." It is possible that Jude is referring not only to Old Testament prophecies but also to the New Testament book of 2 Peter.

ago. They have perverted *the message of* God's grace into a license to commit immorality[a] and turn against[b] our only absolute Master,[c] our Lord Jesus Christ.

[5] I need to remind you, even though you are familiar with it all, that *the Lord* Jesus[d] saved his people out of Egypt but subsequently destroyed those who were guilty of unbelief.

[6] In the same way, there were heavenly messengers *in rebellion* who went outside their rightful domain of authority[e] and abandoned their appointed realms.[f] God bound them in everlasting chains and is keeping them in the dark abyss of the *netherworld* until the judgment of the great day.

[7] In a similar way, the cities of Sodom and Gomorrah and nearby towns[g] gave themselves to sexual immorality and the unnatural desire of different flesh.[h] Now they all serve as examples of those who experience the punishment of eternal fire.[i]

---

a 4 Or "debauchery." See Rom. 6:1; Titus 2:11–14. The gospel of grace is beautiful to our ears. God's grace empowers and equips us to live an ascended life so that we are not distracted or detoured by our former life of sin.

b 4 Or "deny."

c 4 Or "Sovereign" (God). They deny the authority, glory, and sovereignty of our Master (God) and our Lord Jesus Christ.

d 5 Some reliable manuscripts have "the Lord," while other very reliable early manuscripts have "Jesus." This translation, for the sake of clarity, includes both Lord and Jesus. This is an incredible reference of the preincarnate Jesus, who powerfully delivered the Hebrew people before he was even born.

e 6 Or "their own principality" or "their native state."

f 6 See Gen. 6:1–4; 2 Peter 2:4–8. This episode is referring to angels who abandoned the heavenly realm to come to earth to have intercourse with women in order to corrupt the godly lineage of Seth. Cain had already gone into the darkness of sin, but the godly line of Seth would one day bring forth Noah, and from his seed (Shem) Jesus would eventually be born. The rebellious rank of angels mentioned here had sex with women who then gave birth to the Nephilim (mighty giants). Ancient references to this can be found in the writings of early Jewish writers, including Josephus and Philo of Alexandria, as well as early church fathers, such as Justin Martyr, Irenaeus, Clement of Alexandria, Ambrose of Milan, Athenagoras, Tertullian, Eusebius, Lactantius, Jerome, Augustine of Hippo, and Sulpicius Severus. All of them, along with the Septuagint, identified these sons of God as the offspring of angels. See also 1 *Enoch* 10. This sin was one of the significant causes for the flood.

g 7 This would include Admah and Zeboyim (Deut. 29:23).

h 7 Or "strange flesh." This is homosexuality, but it includes any sexual deviation or immorality. In the pseudepigraphal book The Testament of Naphtali, 3.3.4–5 refers to sexual relations between the women of Sodom and these fallen angels, called "Watchers." The *Book of Jubilees* makes mention of holy angels sent by God to punish the "Watchers." *Second Enoch* describes the people of Sodom as committing abominations such as pedophilia, sorcery, magic enchantments, and the worship of many gods. *First Enoch* 6–10 indicates there were two hundred of these "Watchers" who came to earth, lusting after the women of Sodom who had offspring (Nephilim) from their sexual relations with them. Both humanity and angels violated the boundaries God had set in place.

i 7 Jude gives us three examples from ancient history in vv. 5–7, pointing to those who experienced wonderful privileges from God but terribly abused God's grace and so were

The Fate of Apostates

[8] In the same way, these sensual "dreamers" corrupt and pollute the natural realm, while on the other hand they reject the *spiritual* realms of governmental power and repeatedly scoff at heavenly glories. [a] [9] Even the archangel Michael, [b] when he was disputing with the devil over the body of Moses, [c] dared not insult or slander him, but simply said, "The Lord Yahweh [d] rebuke you!" [e]

[10] These people insult anything they don't understand. They behave like irrational beasts by doing whatever they feel like doing. [f] Because they live by their animal instincts, they corrupt themselves and bring about their own destruction. [11] How terrible it is for them! [g] For they have followed in the steps of Cain. [h] They have abandoned [i] themselves to Balaam's error because of their greedy pursuit of financial gain. [j] *And since they have rebelled like Korah rebelled,* they will experience the same fate of Korah and likewise perish. [k]

[12] These false teachers are like dangerous hidden reefs at your love feasts, [l]

---

punished. Sodom and Gomorrah was described as fertile, fruitful, "like the garden of the Lord" (Gen. 13:10). Each example cited (Israel's exodus, angels that sinned, and the cities of sexual perversion) serves as an example and a warning that God judges sin. There is an eternal punishment of fire awaiting all who refuse to hide themselves in the love and grace of God, which is expressed through Christ toward us.

a   8 Or "blaspheming reputations"; that is, angelic beings.

b   9 See Dan. 10:13, 21; 12:1; Rev. 12:7. Michael is one of the highest angelic messengers, who is seen as leading the angelic host in war against the devil and his angels.

c   9 Moses' death is mentioned in Deut. 34:5–6.

d   9 As translated from the Aramaic.

e   9 See 2 Peter 2:10–12. It is obvious here that Michael the archangel had a measure of respect for spiritual powers, even toward the devil. A possible translation of the Greek word *epitimao* is "to hold in high regard" or "to respect." Most scholars believe that Jude is quoting from the book of *The Assumption of Moses,* as cited also by some church fathers (Clement of Alexandria and Origen).

f   10 There is an implication that they are like animals in heat, following their natural instincts.

g   11 Or "A curse is on them."

h   11 See Gen. 4:3–8. The way of Cain was to reject the blood sacrifice that God desired and instead offer the fruit of his own labors (works). False teachers will insist on adding something to the gospel, polluting it with human works.

i   11 Or "poured out" (themselves).

j   11 Balaam's error was an abuse of the prophetic gift for financial gain. See Num. 22–24; 31:16.

k   11 See Num. 16. Korah led 250 men in rebellions against the leadership of Moses. The earth opened up and swallowed Korah alive. In a similar way, the "things of this earth" enticed these false teachers and they would be "swallowed up" by their greed for what this world can offer. Jude gives us three illustrations of wicked men who did as they pleased and suffered greatly: Cain, Balaam, and Korah.

l   12 "Love feasts"! What a beautiful description of what our church gatherings are meant to be. We celebrate the love of Christ through our communion, worship, teaching, prophesying, and fellowship together in our love for one another.

lying in wait to shipwreck the immature. They feast among you without reverence,[a] having no shepherd but themselves.[b] They are clouds with no rain,[c] swept along by the winds.[d] Like fruitless late-autumn trees[e]—twice dead,[f] barren, and plucked up by the roots! [13] They are wild waves of the sea, flinging out the foam of their shame and disgrace.[g] They are *misleading* like wandering stars,[h] for whom the complete darkness of eternal gloom has been reserved.[i]

Enoch's Prophecy

[14] Enoch, the seventh direct descendant from Adam,[j] prophesied of their doom[k] when he said, "Look! Here comes the Lord Yahweh[l] with his countless myriads of holy ones. [15] *He comes* to execute judgment against them all and to convict each one of them for their ungodly deeds and for all the terrible words that ungodly sinners have spoken against him."[m]

[16] These people are always complaining and never satisfied—finding fault with everyone. They follow their own evil desires and their mouths speak scandalous things. They *enjoy* using seductive flattery to manipulate others.[n]

A Call to Remain Faithful

[17] But you, *my* delightfully loved friends, remember the prophecies of the apostles of our Lord Jesus, the Anointed One. [18] They taught you, "In the last days[o]

---

a 12 See 1 Cor. 11:17–22.
b 12 Or "shepherds who care for only themselves." The Aramaic can be translated "they submit their souls to no one."
c 12 Rain in the Bible is often a symbol of revelatory teaching (Deut. 32:2).
d 12 Both in Hebrew and in Aramaic, the word Jude uses for "winds" is *spirits*—"swept along by the spirits."
e 12 Autumn trees are often quite stunning in beauty, but these false teachers are bearing no fruit. They have the appearance of being true, but there is no fruit connected to their lives and ministries.
f 12 They are dead in appearance and dead in reality—dead through and through.
g 13 The Aramaic can be translated "They manifest their confusion."
h 13 Stars were seen as navigational tools for seamen. But these false teachers could not be depended on and would give disastrous guidance. The word *misleading* is found in the Aramaic.
i 13 This is an Hebraic expression that is meant to convey the place of future eternal punishment, the farthest away from God that anyone could ever be.
j 14 That would be Adam, Seth, Enosh, Kenan, Mahalalel, Jared, and Enoch.
k 14 Or "prophesied against them."
l 14 As translated from the Aramaic. The Greek can also be translated "The Lord has come" (proleptic [or futuristic] aorist).
m 15 See 1 Enoch 1:9.
n 16 Or "admiring faces [of the rich] for their own [financial] gain."
o 18 The last days began at Pentecost and have continued for more than two thousand years. We have been living in the last days since the Holy Spirit was poured out. See Acts 2:17; Heb. 1:2.

there will always be mockers, motivated by their own ungodly desires." [a] [19] These people cause divisions and are followers of their own natural instincts, devoid of *the life of* the Spirit.

[20] But you, *my* delightfully loved friends, constantly and progressively build yourselves up on the foundation of your most holy faith [b] by praying every moment in the Spirit. [c] [21] Fasten your hearts to the love of God and receive the mercy of our Lord Jesus Christ, who gives us eternal life. [d]

[22] Keep being compassionate to those who still have doubts, [e] [23] and snatch others out of the fire to save them. Be merciful over and over to them, but always couple your mercy with the fear of God. Be extremely careful to keep yourselves free from the pollutions of the flesh. [f]

[24] Now, to the one with enough power to prevent you from stumbling *into sin* [g] and bring you faultless before his glorious presence to stand before him with ecstatic delight, [25] to the only God our Savior, through our Lord Jesus Christ, be *endless* glory and majesty, great power and authority—from before he created time, now, and throughout all the ages of eternity. Amen! [h]

---

a 18 See Acts 20:29; 1 Tim. 4:1; 2 Tim. 3:1–5; 2 Peter 3:2–3; 2 John 7.

b 20 Or "faithfulness."

c 20 Paul uses this phrase "praying . . . in the Spirit" to refer to praying in tongues. See Rom. 8:26; 1 Cor. 14:15; Eph. 6:18. It can also mean "pray as led by the Spirit," "pray in the Spirit's realm," or "pray by means of/power of the Spirit."

d 21 Or "By constantly and progressively building each other up on the foundation of your most holy faith, and by praying every moment in the Spirit's power, you will keep yourselves in the love of God, awaiting the mercy of our Lord Jesus, who gives eternal life."

e 22 Or "Show mercy to those who are still undecided."

f 23 Or "hating even the garment ['snake skin' or 'coating'] of the pollution of the flesh [the natural realm]." In other words, we do all we can to bring others to Christ, but not at the expense of becoming like them in ignoring sin. Jude, in closing, gives us seven commands: (1) Keep building up your inner life on the foundation of faith. (2) Pray in the Holy Spirit. (3) Fasten your life to the love of God. (4) Receive more mercy from our Lord Jesus Christ. (5) Have compassion on the wavering. (6) Share the gospel with those who are lost. (7) Hate any compromise that will stain our lives.

g 24 The Greek word *aptaistos*, a hapax legomenon, is translated in classical Greek as "to keep from harm."

h 25 The Aramaic adds "The end of the letter of the apostle Judah, the brother of Jacob and Joseph."

REVELATION

Introduction

AT A GLANCE

Author: The apostle John
Audience: Every church and believer in every age
Date: AD 64–68 or 92–95
Type of Literature: Prophetic apocalyptic literature
Major Themes: spiritual symbols, Jesus Christ, the church, perseverance, judgment and destruction, rescue and re-creation
Outline:

ABOUT REVELATION

Do you long for the fullness of Christ and desire to know him intimately as a friend? Do you want more than anything else to be consumed with the glory of Jesus Christ? All this and more is waiting for you to discover in the pages of the book of Revelation!

The most deeply spiritual book of the New Testament is before you now. Revelation is a book written to satisfy your craving to be one with Jesus Christ. It is something that must be "eaten" (Rev. 10:9) if it is to be understood. It has the power to profoundly change a generation who gives heed to what has been written.

Of all the sixty-six books that comprise our Bible, the last book is meant to thrill and exhilarate the believer. A beautiful Christ is unveiled, and an overcoming company of saints is seen rising into his fullness. The book of Revelation is exciting, powerful, dynamic, and more than meets the eye. It can be more to us than merely an unveiling of events to come; it can be an experience of encountering Christ. Revelation is a glory book and requires a glory heart to receive it.

God is ready to unveil this book to those who are ready to embrace it, eat it, and live fully in the splendor of Christ. This is more than a vision given to John; it is meant to be an inward discovery, a delightful unveiling within us. This is not a drama of Satan's worst, but a supernatural drama of God's best, pouring through his beautiful Son, Jesus Christ.

Revelation is the unique deposit of the fullness of every truth in the Scriptures wrapped up in the person and glory of Jesus Christ. Genesis is the book of beginnings. Revelation is the book of consummation. All things are made new as we are given a new name (nature), a new song (message), a New Jerusalem (a realm of union with God), a new heaven (government), and a new earth (order, expression). The Bible ends with the passing away of all that is old and the establishment of all that is new. These symbols of deeper realities require ears to hear and hearts to discern, as with the "unveilings" Christ himself taught.

When Jesus unveiled the deep spiritual truths of the heart of God, he spoke in parables (Matt. 13:34), using symbols to teach us. In fact, when Jesus spoke clearly, his disciples were amazed (John 16:29). Today, he continues to teach us through the language of the heart—through pictures, parables, and allegories.

We must allow the Lord to transform our natural ears into spiritual ones if the truths of this book are to be heard and received in our spirits. Without a deep and abiding desire to see Christ, and not just have a preview of what's coming, we are all in the dark. The key that unlocks the book of Revelation is a passion to know Jesus Christ. To those who have this passion to know him, more will be given. Jesus is the only one worthy to open the seals of the book. And his Spirit is present today to break open those seals and bring deep understanding to our hearts.

God's glory is found when truth touches the heart and strikes us with light. Understanding comes when humility and revelation meet. As our hearts are touched by truth, our minds are filled with light. This revelation enabled Daniel to interpret dreams, Paul to teach heavenly truths, and John to write the Revelation. With unveiled faces we come to the well of the Word and drink deeply, not merely to seek answers, but to discover him.

May the Lord himself, who inspired John to write the Revelation, inspire your heart as you read it to love Jesus more. And may this book be more than a manual of coming events, but also an unveiling of the coming King!

PURPOSE

Why was the book of Revelation written? This is an important question given there have been multiple views on the book's purpose over the ages. Some view it as a fascinating piece of first-century writing with little or no relevance for us today. Others see Revelation as a code book describing a specific outline of history written in advance. Many have tried to decode the book from a historical perspective to find the major world events of the past two thousand years, or to prove that most of the book has already been fulfilled. Others interpret it as a handbook that predicts the cataclysmic events that will bring the nations to Armageddon and the end of the world.

But perhaps there is yet another viewpoint to guide us through this incredible book of mysteries. We must stop and allow the Holy Spirit to unveil its treasures to us. Only the Holy Spirit can unveil Christ to the unbeliever, and only the Holy Spirit can unveil the glory of Christ to those who know him. The purpose of the Revelation is to unveil Christ to our hearts like no other book in the Bible.

This is the book of Revelation, not the book of revelations (plural). It emphasizes one revelation alone: Christ unveiled to his people. To read this book with any other focus is to miss the center of its meaning. There are other truths waiting for us to discover, but only after centering our gaze on this one—our Magnificent Obsession.

AUTHOR AND AUDIENCE

It was to the "beloved" disciple, John, that this revelation was first imparted. John was the apostle of love. In his later years he taught us the importance of love, "for God is love" (1 John 4:8). John wrote for us an incredible book full of symbols and intriguing insights into the heart of God. It takes us behind the veil into the holy of holies. It spills forth with puzzling information about the mark of the beast, Armageddon, the four horsemen, Babylon the great, and a woman clothed with the sun. Through the ages the images found in this book—images of terror and catastrophe—have significantly influenced the thinking of millions of Christians. Yet despite nearly two thousand years of fascination with this book, the meaning of John's masterpiece continues to be debated.

It is generally believed that this book was written during two possible periods: between AD 64–68 under the reign of Emperor Nero, and during his persecution and terror; or between AD 92–95 under the reign of Emperor Domitian, who similarly launched a campaign of persecution to destroy the church. Regardless of when it was written, what's more important is to whom this letter was written: Revelation was written for every church, every lover of God in every generation. It is for *today*! It is for *you* to understand and embrace as much as it was for the early churches who received John's letter of Christ's unveiling.

INTERPRETING THE BOOK OF REVELATION

There are levels to understanding God's Word. When the transcendent, glorious God gives us an inspired book, it compels us to dig deeper and look beyond the cursory meaning of words. Yes, there is a plain and literal surface meaning to all that God has given us, but we know there is yet more to discover. The Bible is full of symbols, poetry, metaphors, and figurative language that engages our spirits, not merely our minds.

The prophetic writings of the Bible, including the book of Revelation, require that we look at them like gazing upon the finest piece of art. They beg us to ponder, to inquire, to study further until they yield their beauty and meaning. With eyes opened by the Holy Spirit we find a spiritual application to all that is written, for that is where we touch the reality of God through his Word.

As we grow up into more of Christ in all things, the Word of God will become richer and more delightful to our hearts. It will speak to us out of our relationship with Christ, for intimacy is always where revelation begins to come into our spirit.

Every commentator on the book of Revelation agrees that it is rooted in the symbolism of the Old Testament, as it is full of allusions to the prophetic writings of Scripture. Without understanding the other sixty-five books of the Bible, the last book becomes too mysterious and unknowable to the heart of man. Indeed, the mind of man is incapable of receiving the mysteries and ways of God. Revelation must come to our spirits before we can crack open the Revelation (unveiling) of Jesus Christ. The same Spirit who inspired the book will unveil the meaning of the book to those who trust him.

Several views have dominated how Christians have interpreted and understood the symbols of this divine unveiling over the generations, known in these ways: preterist, futurist, historicist, and idealist.

Preterist Re-viewing of History. This view insists that we look at most of the book (chs. 1–18) as having been already fulfilled early in the church's history. This means many of the symbols of this unveiling relate to the events of the first century instead of a future one. Those who hold this view believe Revelation addresses faithfulness to God in the face of pagan persecution, and offers hope for God's ultimate, eventual victory.

Futurist Pre-viewing of History. This view goes in the other direction: it interprets the events as largely happening in the future. The symbols are prophetic pointers to the end of the world, previewing what will take place leading up to the return of Christ. Rather than having relevance strictly to first-century believers, it offers believers in every age assurance of evil's destruction and ultimate rescue.

Historicist Identifying of History. This approach sees John's Revelation as identifying the major movements of church history, and then reading them back into the symbols and prophecies of the book. Some also consider how current events fulfill New Testament apocalyptic symbolism. A prime example is identifying the Beast with various dictators through history, like Napoleon or Hitler or Saddam Hussein. The seals, trumpets, bowls, and plagues are identified as being a series of successive events, with the hope of Christ's return being very near.

Idealist Symbolizing of History. This model of interpretation finds significance in the symbols of deeper meaning embedded throughout Revelation for the church between Christ's first and second comings. These symbols offer every church and believer in every age timeless spiritual truths unrelated to specific historical events. It is concerned with the battle between good and evil, and between the church and the world at all periods in Christian history, depicting the continuous victory of believers and Christ.

This translation of Revelation agrees with many interpreters that all of these models have validity; measures of truth get unlocked by each one. Yet as you read through the Bible, you will find time after time that symbols, parables, and pictures are the true language of God, imparting revelation-truth regardless of historical periods of circumstances. The same is true for Revelation. In it we must look for the prophetic images and ask for an understanding of the spiritual viewpoints that help believers be overcomers today.

We can read the book of Revelation as a preterist re-viewing of human history, as a futurist pre-viewing of what is to come, and also as a dynamic super-viewing of the unveiling of Christ in his people. The Revelation of Jesus Christ is something that is unveiled *in* us, not just to us. Christ in us is our hope of glory. We must see the indwelling Christ within us as the hope that moves us into fullness and expectancy. Christ is the hope of God expressing himself through us to all his creation, which is groaning and waiting for the "unveiling" of the sons of God. (The same Greek word used in Rom. 8:19–20 is also found in the title of the last book of Scripture, the "Unveiling of Jesus Christ.")

MAJOR TOPICS

The Spiritual Language of Symbols. To discover all of God within his written Word is to learn the language of symbols. How much we miss when we ignore the poetic symbolism of the Bible! The Scriptures are full of symbols, such as wheat, tares, pearls, doors, veils, along with numbers, dimensions, and colors. God's language includes pictures and symbols, which point us to a greater reality. God will hide levels of truth from superficial seekers until we become those who hunger and thirst for true treasure—the revelation of God.

Revelation is not something that can be described; it must be *discovered*. God delights when he sees us seeking with all our hearts. We become like kings in his eyes, for "God conceals the revelation of his Word in the hiding place of his glory. But the honor of kings is revealed by how they thoroughly search out the deeper meaning of all that God says" (Prov. 25:2). God's glory is found in how he hides the treasure of his Word. Our glory is seen in how we seek it out.

Those who did not love our Lord Jesus when he walked the earth were blinded to who he was and to what he taught. They consistently misinterpreted his words. When he said, "After you've destroyed this temple, I will raise it up again in three days" (John 2:19), he caused a major controversy, all because they thought he was speaking literally. Yet we know he was speaking of the temple of his physical body. This controversy remained with him throughout the rest of his life and ministry. In fact, one of the issues that led to his crucifixion was his spiritualizing the meaning of the temple (see Mark 14:58). This misunderstanding was hurled at Jesus by the jeering crowd who watched his torturous death on the cross (see Matt. 27:39–40). It would be a mistake to miss truth because of a refusal to interpret some Scripture symbolically.

Another instance of this would be when Jesus spoke of eating his flesh and drinking his blood (see John 6:53). No one today would consider these words to be literal. We know the spiritual meaning of the text is to feast upon the sacrifice of Christ and commune with him through his Word, his blood, and his Spirit. Indeed, if we view the Bible as a spiritual book, yet refuse to look for the deep spiritual meaning in the text, we are closing our eyes to reality. The Word of God is a spiritual book that will feed our spirits, for the words he speaks into our hearts are truly *spirit* and *life* (see John 6:63)!

Jesus Christ Unveiled. We have in the Gospels the glorious story of our Lord Jesus as he walked this earth. We see his marvelous ministry of teaching, healing, delivering, and loving all. He was veiled in weak flesh, humiliated by others, and rejected. The last view we have of him in the Gospels is the resurrected Jesus ascending to heaven surrounded with clouds. But what happened after that? What is he like now? We need our eyes unveiled to see him as he now is. What you read in this book will present him in his present glory.

Some have described the book of Revelation as "the sixth gospel." We have the four Gospels in the beginning of our New Testament, and with the book of Acts we find the "fifth gospel," which demonstrates the power of the resurrected Jesus working through those who follow him. And in the last book of the Bible we discover the "sixth gospel," with yet another view of Jesus as the ascended, glorified God-Man who is unveiled before our eyes as Prophet, Priest, and King of kings.

As the Prophet, Jesus is the Faithful Witness who only speaks the Father's words. As the High Priest, Jesus is the Firstborn from the dead, who intercedes for us and releases mighty power to us. And as the King, Jesus is the Ruler of the kings of the earth. Each of these clues into his identity show forth his authority. Through the victory of Christ's death and resurrection he now holds the keys of death and the unseen world. There is nothing to fear, for he holds all authority (the keys). He rides forth to conquer everything within us that hinders the life of Christ emerging in our transformation. All the universe will one day be conquered by the One riding this white horse!

Jesus' Church Unveiled. The unveiling of Jesus Christ will also be our "unveiling" as those who believe in him, for we are his body on the earth. To receive a revelation of Christ, the head of the body, is to receive the revelation of the members of his body, the radiant ones who follow him. Christ is unveiled in heaven, and he is unveiled in his body. When he is unveiled, we are unveiled, for we are one with him in his glory (see Eph. 1:23; Col. 3:4).

Christ's letter to the churches imparts especially important revelation-truths to every believer, for he calls us to burn with light as his lampstands—a powerful metaphor for bringing illumination to the world as witnesses for God. This revelation also shows forth the church as God's temple, his dwelling place. And as Jesus' lovely bride, our co-reign with him has already begun where we are commissioned to do greater works of Jesus and spread the brilliance of his glory throughout the earth. Though the powers of the Abyss may come against us, we can be sure Jesus cares for both his church and its leaders, who are intimately bound to him.

The Judgment and Destruction of Old Order. From the opening of the first of the seven seals, many have understood the revelation-truth unveiled in this book as showing forth the earth's destruction. And yet, while traditionally this destruction has been taken literally, we understand it must also be taken symbolically. The old order of the natural realm is passing away and a new order is being established. Progressively, the superior light of the kingdom of God will make dim the light of the old.

The judgment of John's Revelation, another major theme alongside destruction, is also often misunderstood. For the anger and wrath of the Lamb is corrective and redemptive—not beastly rage, but fiery passion to judge whatever gets in the way between the Lamb and his bride. Further, we find the winds of judgment are being held back until the sons of God have the thoughts and mind of Christ. We are "sealed," which means we are protected from judgment. In Revelation, an angel carries the seal of the living God, speaking powerfully of God's grace and mercy, which will always triumph over judgment.

And yet, in the end, the world will experience a final judgment—where everything and everyone destructive to God's wonderful world will be cast into the lake of fire. Until then, we now enforce the judgment that took place on Calvary, where Satan was bound through Christ's death and resurrection. During the "thousand years" in which we live (since the death and resurrection of Jesus; see Rev. 20:2 and footnote) we are given the authority to bind the strongman (Satan) and plunder his goods until evil is eventually and decisively destroyed.

The Rescue and Renewal of the Lamb. The end of the world as we know it isn't ultimately about judgment and destruction. It's about rescue and renewal, for the Lamb of God has won, and so have we! Though we have to pass through tribulation to enter the kingdom of God, we do so through the blood of Christ, knowing that our victory is sure. This unveiling shows the ultimate vindication of the people of God: we experience salvation from sin and death; we inherit the Holy City and its fount of living water.

One of the primary characteristics of prophetic apocalyptic writing is the exhortation to persevere. Endurance and faithfulness, conquering and obedience are all hallmarks of John's Revelation. It is the one who is victorious over the "beast" of the self-life who finds ultimate rescue and renewal. This isn't salvation by works. Rather, as we overcome by the power of the cross and take on the life of Christ for ourselves, we qualify as overcomers who sing the sacred song of Moses (15:3–4), sung as our final victory song.

Ultimately, as the Lord of Glory, Jesus is the bright Morning Star who signals the end of night and the beginning of God's perfect day, the end of the old order dominated by our self-life and the beginning of God's brand new order of righteousness, peace, and pure love. And he is coming quickly to finally make everything new and fresh!

REVELATION

The Unveiling of Jesus Christ

John's Introduction

1 This is the unveiling of Jesus Christ, *a* which God gave him to share with his loving servants *b* what must occur swiftly. *c* He clearly made it known *d* by sending his angel *e* to his loving servant John. *f* ² I, John, bore witness to the word of God and the testimony of Jesus Christ. ³ A joyous blessing *g* rests upon the one who reads *this message* and upon those who hear and embrace the words of this prophecy, for the appointed time is in your hands. *h*

---

a 1:1 The Greek noun *apokalypsis* is a compound word found eighteen times in the New Testament. It combines *apo* (to lift) with *lypsis* (veil, covering), and so could be translated "the lifting of the veil" or "the unveiling." The implication could be stated as simply, "Here he is!" It is not primarily lifting the veil off coming events, but the unveiling of Jesus.

b 1:1 This is the Greek word *doulos*, which means "bond servant," a slave who willingly remains with his master even after being given his freedom.

c 1:1 This does not necessarily mean "soon" from the writer's perspective, but that once the time comes it will quickly happen. The Greek phrase *en tachos* (similar to "tachometer") means that once something starts, it will take place swiftly.

d 1:1 The Greek is "signified" or "miracle-sign." The word for miracle-sign is the Greek verb *sēmainō*, which means "to give a sign." The noun form is *sēmeion* and is the word used most often (seventy-seven times) in the New Testament for "miracle." In the Septuagint of Dan. 2:45 the word *sēmainō* is used, which indicates the meaning of "to symbolize." The Aramaic likewise can be translated "symbolized." The book of Revelation is a book full of symbols.

e 1:1 Angels were instrumental in imparting divine revelation to Abraham, Moses, Joshua, the judges, the prophets, the kings, and the apostles of Jesus. This angel sent from Jesus was on a mission to give John insights into the meaning of the visions within the book of Revelation (22:6, 8, 16).

f 1:1 Notice the chain of communication: (1) God gave the revelation directly to Jesus. (2) Jesus gave it to an angel. (3) The angel explained it to John. (4) John gives it to us (v. 2), God's servants. Many don't realize that the book of Revelation came from a direct encounter with an angel sent by Jesus to give the contents to John.

g 1:3 Or "happiness to one who reads." The book of Revelation is the only book in the Bible that promises a rich blessing to those who read and obey what it states. The word *blessing* can mean "happiness." There are six other "blessings" found in Revelation (14:13; 16:15; 19:9; 20:5; 22:7, 14).

h 1:3 Or "at hand." The Greek adverb *eggus* is taken from a primary verb *agcho,* which means "to squeeze" (in your hands) or "to hold the reins" (or "throttle" in your hands). There is a sense in which the full understanding of the book of Revelation is ready to be unveiled

⁴From John to the seven churches ᵃ in western Turkey: ᵇ May *the kindness of God's* grace and peace *overflow to you* from him who is, and who was, and who is to come, ᶜ and from the seven spirits ᵈ who are in front of his throne, ⁵and from Jesus Christ the Faithful Witness, ᵉ the Firstborn from among the dead ᶠ and the ruling King, who rules over the kings of the earth! ᵍ

Now to the one who *constantly* loves us and has loosed us from our sins ʰ by his own blood, ᶦ ⁶*and to the one who* has made us to rule as a kingly priesthood ʲ to serve his God and Father—to him be glory and dominion throughout the eternity of eternities! Amen!

⁷Behold! He appears ᵏ within the clouds, ˡ and every eye will see him, even those who pierced him. ᵐ And all the people groups of the earth will weep with sorrow because of him. And so it is to be! Amen.

⁸"I am the Aleph and the Tav," ⁿ says the Lord God, "who is, who was, and who is to come, the Almighty."

---

when the reader is ready to receive it. The time for this revelation is now, not the past nor the distant future. See also 1 Peter 1:5.

a 1:4 The seven churches become a representation of all the churches, for the number seven denotes completeness, fullness, wholeness, and perfection.

b 1:4 Or "Asia" (Minor), which is modern-day western Turkey.

c 1:4 The God who dwells in these three realms (present, past, and future) is described by John as "who is, who was, and who is to come."

d 1:4 Or "the seven-fold Spirit"; that is, the Holy Spirit. If God is three in one, the Holy Spirit can be seven in one. See Isa. 11:2–3; Zech. 4:1–10; Rev. 3:1; 4:5; 5:6.

e 1:5 Jesus was a Faithful Witness to the truth while on earth (John 18:37) and is now a Faithful Witness to all that he revealed to John in this book.

f 1:5 Or "the First Begotten from the dead." He is the Firstborn who conquers death.

g 1:5 As the *Prophet*, Jesus is the Faithful Witness who only speaks the Father's words. As the *High Priest*, Jesus is the Firstborn from the dead, and as the *King*, Jesus is the Ruler of the kings of the earth.

h 1:5 Or "washed us from our sins."

i 1:5 Or "in his own blood."

j 1:6 Or "a kingdom of priests" or "kings and priests." We have the nature of both a king and a priest embedded within us in Christ. Christ is the one who "made us" into this holy order and union. It is already done. See also Rev. 5:10.

k 1:7 Or "comes." The Greek verb tense of *erchomai* ("appears" or "comes") is in the third-person singular, present indicative, which is a present-tense reality, not a distant one. It can be translated "He is now coming" or "He is in the act of coming and continues to come."

l 1:7 Or "He will appear [be surrounded] with [Gr. *meta*] clouds," or "He appears by means of clouds" or "with clouds" or "between clouds." See also Isa. 60:8; Dan. 7:13–14; Heb. 12:1. The cloud of glory is now plural—clouds, a company of clouds (Dan. 7:13–14; Matt. 26:64; 1 Thess. 4:17).

m 1:7 Every one of us has "pierced" his side with the spear of our unbelief and sin.

n 1:8 As translated from the Hebrew and Aramaic. The Greek is "the Alpha and Omega," Alpha being the first letter of the Greek alphabet and Omega the last letter. Jesus affirms that he has all knowledge and is the sum of all truth.

⁹I, John, am your brother and companion in tribulation,ᵃ the kingdom,ᵇ and the patience that are *found* in Jesus.ᶜ I was *exiled* on the island of Patmosᵈ because of *the ministry of* the word of God and the testimony of Jesus. ¹⁰I was in the spirit realmᵉ on the Lord's day,ᶠ and I heard behindᵍ me a loud voice sounding like a trumpet,ʰ ¹¹saying to me:

> Write in a book what you see and send it to the seven churches:ⁱ to Ephesus, to Smyrna, to Pergamum, to Thyatira, to Sardis, to Philadelphia, and to Laodicea.

¹²When I turnedʲ to see the voice that was speaking to me, I saw seven golden lampstands.ᵏ ¹³And walking among the lampstands, I saw someone like a son of man,ˡ wearing a full-length robeᵐ with a golden sash over his chest.ⁿ

---

a 1:9 Or "persecution." The Greek word for tribulation is *thlipsis* and means "great pressure." It refers to the pressure (tribulation) that all believers experience.

b 1:9 As a fellow companion in the kingdom, John verifies that the kingdom of God formally began after Christ was raised from the dead and continues to expand until now (Isa. 9:7). John was *on* Patmos but *in* the kingdom. See Acts 14:22.

c 1:9 Or "the one who co-shares [joint partner] with you in Jesus."

d 1:9 Patmos was a small, rocky island in the Aegean Sea roughly ten miles long and five miles wide, believed to be a Roman penal colony. This vision came to John while he was an exile on Patmos, which means "my crushing" or "my killing." But we must remember, our "killing" took place on the cross (Gal. 2:20).

e 1:10 Or "I came to be in [with] spirit" or "I became in union with the Spirit." This was John's "rapture," most likely a trance. The realm of the Spirit was John's vantage point. The same Spirit that inspired this book must interpret it, for it is what the Spirit is saying to the churches. See Job 32:8.

f 1:10 This was not Sunday, nor a twenty-four-hour day, but "the Lord's day." Nowhere in Scripture is Sunday called "the Lord's day." The Aramaic can be translated "on the lordly [majestic] day."

g 1:10 A voice "behind" us can be that which speaks about our past—about all that God has already done for us.

h 1:10 Or "shofar." The trumpet sound always carries a message (1 Cor. 14:8). The voice sounding like a trumpet blast would point us to a fresh proclamation heralding a new message to us today.

i 1:11 The number seven is the number of God and his perfection. The seven churches make up one perfect and complete church in his eyes. These seven churches speak of completeness or fullness; just like the seven Spirits are full and complete so the church is full and complete in Christ. We are the "seven in one" bride, just as the Holy Spirit is "seven in one."

j 1:12 John was in the spirit. This was more than a physical turning, but an inward turning to withdraw from the natural and see into the spiritual. The same Greek word is used for "converted" in Acts 3:19.

k 1:12 These seven golden lampstands represent seven churches (Rev. 1:20). The "lampstand" (or menorah) becomes a symbol of the burning presence of Christ. They are golden, for Christ has purified and made holy his church.

l 1:13 See Dan. 7:13. This is the ascended Christ appearing as King and High Priest. Part of the priestly duties involved tending the lampstands, filling them with fresh oil.

m 1:13 The Aramaic can be translated "the robe of the ephod" (priest's robe).

n 1:13 The Greek word used here is *mastos* and is used exclusively for a woman's breasts. Over

¹⁴His head and his hair were white like wool—white as glistening snow.ᵃ And his eyes were like flames of fire!ᵇ ¹⁵His feet were gleaming like bright metal,ᶜ as though they were glowing in a fire,ᵈ and his voice was like the roar of many rushing waters.ᵉ ¹⁶In his right hand he held seven stars, and out of his mouth was a sharp, double-edged sword.ᶠ And his face was shining like the brightness of the blinding sun!ᵍ ¹⁷When I saw him, I fell down at his feet as good as dead,ʰ but he laid his right hand on meⁱ and *I heard his reassuring voice* saying:

Don't yield to fear. I am the Beginning and I am the End, ¹⁸the Living One! I was dead, but now look—I am alive forever and ever. And I hold the keysʲ that unlock death and the unseen world.ᵏ ¹⁹Now I want you to write what you have seen, what is, and what will be after the things *that I reveal to you.* ²⁰The mystery of the lampstandsˡ and the seven stars is this: the seven lampstands are the seven churches,

---

the heart of the glorified Jesus is a golden sash of compassionate love for his bride. The Aramaic can be translated "between his breasts a golden harness." It was made of pure gold, for the divine nature holds everything together in divine order.

a 1:14 The head (or headship) speaks of Christ's authority. White speaks of the righteousness of God and an emblem of his wisdom, omniscience, justice, and leadership. This is similar to Dan. 7:9, which would equate Jesus with the Ancient of Days.

b 1:14 See Dan. 10:6.

c 1:15 Or "burnished [fine] brass." However, the Greek is somewhat confusing with a feminine noun and genitive case. The Aramaic can be translated "the brass of Lebanon." Lebanon was known for the quality of its fine brass. Brass is a biblical symbol of passing through judgment. Jesus went through judgment for our sins, and with feet on fire he is now kindling fires wherever he walks.

d 1:15 See Ezek. 1:27; Dan. 3:25.

e 1:15 See Ps. 29:3; Ezek. 1:24; 43:2. Waters are emblematic of "multitudes of people" (Rev. 17:15). It is not simply a voice of "waters," but the voices of many sons coming into his likeness (Rev. 14:1–3).

f 1:16 The sword from his mouth is a metaphor for the Word of God (Eph. 6:17; Heb. 4:12). The message of Revelation comes as a sword from the mouth of Jesus. The Aramaic can be translated "a fervent spirit came from his mouth."

g 1:16 See Ps. 84:11; Matt. 17:1–2; John 8:12.

h 1:17 John had walked with Jesus for nearly three years and even leaned upon his chest. Now he sees Jesus not as he was, but as he is, and seeing him in his glory John fell at his feet "as good as dead."

i 1:17 In v. 16 Jesus holds the seven stars in his right hand, and now he lays his right hand upon John. The right hand speaks of power, authority, and blessing (Pss. 16:11; 118:15–16; Isa. 41:10; Col. 3:1).

j 1:18 Through the victory of Christ's death and resurrection he now holds the keys of death and the unseen world. There is nothing to fear, for he holds all authority (keys).

k 1:18 Or "Hades." Originally used in Greek as the god of the underworld, Hades became identified simply with "the unseen world" (Aramaic for Hades) or "the place of the dead." See *A Greek-English Lexicon of the New Testament and Other Early Christian Literature.* 3rd ed.

l 1:20 The lampstand becomes a powerful metaphor of the churches of Jesus. They burn, bringing light and illumination to the city as a witness of God's glory (Matt. 5:14–16). It

and the seven stars in my right hand are the seven messengers[a] of the seven churches.[b]

Christ's Letter to Ephesus

2 Write the following to the messenger of the congregation in Ephesus.[c] For these are the words of the one who holds the seven stars firmly in his right hand,[d] who walks among the seven golden lampstands:

[2] I know all that you've done for me—you have worked hard and persevered. I know that you don't tolerate evil. You have tested those who claimed to be apostles and *proved* they are not, *for they were imposters.* [3] I also know how you have bravely endured *trials and persecutions* because of my name, yet you have not become discouraged.[e] [4] But I have this against you: you have abandoned the passionate love you had for me at the beginning.[f] [5] Think about how far you have fallen! Repent[g]

---

stood in the Holy Place, giving light for the priests to minister. Even with their problems these seven churches were "golden" (v. 12) in God's eyes.

a 1:20 It is likely that these "messengers" represent the human leadership of the churches, who would be accountable to God to ensure that this message was presented to the churches. Heavenly angels would have no need for letters as a form of communication, nor would the reprimands in these letters apply to angels. See Beasley-Murray, *Revelation,* 69; Robert L. Thomas, *Revelation 1–7 Exegetical Commentary* and *Revelation 8–22 Exegetical Commentary* (Chicago: Moody Press, 1992), 1995; R. C. H. Lenski, *The Interpretation of St. John's Revelation,* 1963.

b 1:20 The messages to the seven churches from Jesus Christ found in chs. 2–3 have at least four applications: (1) a local application to the specific cities and believers in the church; (2) to all the churches of all generations; (3) a prophetic application unveiling seven distinct phases of church history from the days of the apostle John until today; (4) a personal application to individual believers who have ears to hear what the Spirit is saying.

c 2:1 The meaning of *Ephesus* is "desirable" or "darling." Every church and every believer is desirable to Jesus Christ, for we are his bride. This is the word a Greek bridegroom would use for the girl he desired to marry. See Song of Songs.

d 2:1 It is good to remember that church leaders are "stars" who are firmly held in the right hand (authority and power) of Jesus Christ. He cares for both his churches and his leaders.

e 2:3 The Aramaic can be translated "You endured suffering without complaining." Every church should be known for these five qualities: (1) working for the kingdom, (2) persevering, (3) not being tolerant of sin, (4) examining the claims of ministries, and (5) enduring trials bravely. Yet doing all this without a passionate love for Jesus Christ weakens our power and witness in the world.

f 2:4 Or "you have abandoned your first love." The Greek word for "first" (*protos*) means "foremost," "best," "paramount," "supreme," "crowning," "number one." Jesus is referring to exclusive love that has first place in our hearts above all else.

g 2:5 The Greek word for "repent" is *metanoia* and means more than simply changing one's mind. It means "to take another mind." Every believer needs to turn from his or her error and take "another mind," the mind of Christ.

and do the works *of love* you did at first.[a] I will come to you and re-move your lampstand from its place *of influence* if you do not repent. [6] Although, to your credit, you despise the practices of the Nicolai-tans, which I also despise.[b] [7] The one whose heart is open let him listen carefully to what the Spirit is saying now to all the churches.[c] To the one who overcomes[d] I will give access to feast on the fruit of the Tree of Life that is found in the paradise of God.[e]

Christ's Letter to Smyrna

[8] Write the following to the messenger of the congregation in Smyrna.[f] For these are the words of the one who is the Beginning and the End, the one who became a corpse, but came back to life:[g]

[9] I am aware of all the painful difficulties you have passed through and your financial hardships, even though, in fact, you possess rich treasure.[h] And I am fully aware of the slander[i] that has come against you from those who claim to be Jews but are really not, for they are a satanic congregation.[j] [10] Do not yield to fear in the face of the suffering to come, but be aware of this: the devil[k] is about to have some of you thrown into prison[l] to test your faith.

---

a 2:5 That is, "Return to your passion for me that motivated you at the first."

b 2:6 The Greek meaning of "Nicolaitans" is "to rule [conquer] over people." Many see in this term the beginning of the movement of every believer from being a priest to being part of a special class of clergy who ruled over the church. There is also a case to be made that the Aramaic word *niaqleidto* can be translated "the performing of rituals," which would make the verse read "You despise the performing of rituals, which I also despise."

c 2:7 This shows that the message to these seven churches is for everyone today, not just a specific church or for a specific period of church history.

d 2:7 Or "subdues," "vanquishes," "prevails," "experiences victory."

e 2:7 The paradise of God is now found within the hearts of Jesus' loving followers. See Song. 4:11–15. The Tree of Life is Christ within us, the hope of glory. The fruit of that tree is reserved for those who overcome.

f 2:8 *Smyrna* (present-day Izmir, Turkey) means "sweet smelling" and comes from the word for "myrrh," an embalming spice. It is seen throughout Scripture as an emblem for suffering. Like myrrh, the Smyrna church, known as the suffering church, was crushed by Roman persecution but gave off the most fragrant perfume.

g 2:8 Jesus writes to the church of Smyrna as the Overcomer who overcame death for us (Heb. 2:14).

h 2:9 See 2 Cor. 8:9.

i 2:9 Or "blasphemy."

j 2:9 That is, they were serving Satan's purposes. Satan means "adversary." These people, known as Judaizers, attempted to impose Jewish rules upon new converts. See Acts 15; Rom. 2:28–29; Phil. 3:2–3.

k 2:10 *Devil* means "slanderer-accuser."

l 2:10 The Aramaic can be translated "torture house."

For ten days[a] you will have distress, but remain faithful to the day you die and I will give you the victor's crown of life.[b] [11]The one whose heart is open let him listen carefully to what the Spirit is presently saying to all the churches. The one who conquers will not be harmed by the second death.[c]

Christ's Letter to Pergamum

[12]Write the following to the messenger of the congregation in Pergamum.[d] For these are the words of the one whose words pierce the hearts of men:[e]

[13]I know where you live—where Satan sits enthroned, yet you still cling faithfully to the power of my name. You did not deny your faith in me even in the days of my faithful martyr Antipas,[f] who was executed in your city, where Satan lives. [14]Nevertheless, I have a few things against you. There are some among you who hold to the teachings of Balaam, who taught Balak to entice the Israelites to eat things that

---

a 2:10 It is recorded that a tremendous persecution took place in Smyrna that eventually resulted in the death of Polycarp, one of the leading church fathers, whom Tertullian described as a disciple of John. Some view the ten days as ten time periods representing ten waves of identifiable persecutions under ten Roman emperors. See John F. Walvoord, *The Revelation of Jesus Christ*, 1966.

b 2:10 Or "the victor's crown, which is life." This is a symbol of ruling and reigning in the power and nature of divine life. See James 1:12.

c 2:11 See Rev. 21:8.

d 2:12 The word *Pergamum* means "married" or "elevation." Pergamum was the center of Roman emperor worship, which demanded absolute allegiance to the god-like emperor. Additionally, it had, on a cliff overlooking the city, a throne-like altar to the Greek god Zeus. For these reasons it was described as the place of Satan's throne. See Robert L. Thomas, *Revelation 1–7 Exegetical Commentary* (Chicago: Moody Press, 1992); Robert H. Mounce, *The Book of Revelation*, revised ed.; *The New International Commentary on the New Testament*, edited by F. F. Bruce and Gordon D. Fee (Grand Rapids: Eerdmans, 1977); F. F. Bruce, *The Revelation to John: A New Testament Commentary*, edited by G. C. D. Howley (Grand Rapids: Zondervan, 1969).

e 2:12 Or "the one who has the sharp, double-edged sword," which is an emblem of the Word of God. This sword is not meant to destroy his beloved church, it is meant to pierce and circumcise our hearts. It has two edges, for it both blesses and corrects us.

f 2:13 Ancient church tradition states that Antipas was a disciple of John who was ordained by John to be the bishop of Pergamum during the reign of the emperor Domitian. He was believed to have been martyred in AD 92 after refusing to deny his faith and make a sacrifice to the gods. He was dragged to the temple of Diana and placed inside a bronze, bull-like altar and roasted alive. Eastern tradition states that Antipas was one of the seventy disciples whom Jesus sent out.

were sacrificed to idols[a] and to commit sexual immorality.[b] [15] Furthermore, you have some who hold to the doctrines of the Nicolaitans.[c] [16] So repent, then, or I will come quickly to war against them with the sword of my mouth. [17] But the one whose heart is open let him listen carefully to what the Spirit is presently saying to all the churches. To everyone who is victorious I will let him feast on the hidden manna[d] and give him a shining white stone.[e] And written upon the white stone is inscribed his new name, known only to the one who receives it.[f]

Christ's Letter to Thyatira

[18] Write the following to the messenger of the congregation in Thyatira.[g] For these are the words of the Son of God, whose eyes are blazing fire and whose feet are like burnished brass:[h]

[19] I know all that you've done for me—your love and faith, your ministry and steadfast perseverance. In fact, you now excel in these virtues even more than at the first. [20] But I have this against you:

---

a 2:14 Balaam was a prophet who was hired by Balak the king to curse the Israelites. Later, Balaam taught the people to turn to idol worship and commit immorality. See Num. 22–24; Acts 15:20; 2 Peter 2:15; Jude 11.

b 2:14 See 1 Cor. 6:13.

c 2:15 See footnote on v. 6.

d 2:17 This refers to the glorious relationship we have with the mystery of Christ within, the hope of glory (Col. 1:26–27), which is in contrast to eating meat that was sacrificed to idols. There was manna hidden within the ark of the covenant, and there is now hidden manna within the heart of the overcomer. See also Ex. 16:4, 15, 31–34.

e 2:17 The Greek word *leukos* can be translated either "shining" or "bright [white]." It is possible that this stone shines brightly from within (i.e., a glowing stone). See G. H. R. Horsley and S. R. Llewelyn, *New Documents Illustrating Early Christianity* I–VI (North Ryde: Ancient History Documentary Research Centre, 1981–92). This would remind us of the stones on the ephod-breastplate of the high priest (Ex. 28:9–12) or the Urim and Thummim that glowed as God responded to the questions of his people. Jewish tradition has held that precious stones also fell from heaven with the manna (cf. Midrash Ps. 78:4). Some scholars see this white shining stone as a reference to a vote of acquittal in a court case (Acts 26:10). Others as the burning white coal from off the altar that purged Isaiah's lips (Isa. 6:1–7). Whatever this "shining white stone" is, it is to be prized as the victor's reward. Every believer is a "living stone" (1 Peter 2:5).

f 2:17 We see that there are personal mysteries imparted to God's people; that is, secrets that are between the believer and Jesus. Only someone devoted to God is to know the meaning of the shining white stone and the name written upon it.

g 2:18 *Thyatira* comes from two Greek words: "sacrifice" and "that which goes on continually." Perhaps "a continual sacrifice" would be a good definition of Thyatira. Sadly, some Christians observe a continual sacrifice of Christ through communion rather that celebrating a "once for all" sacrifice that is sufficient to bring us to God. Other scholars have studied the etymology of the word *thyatira* and believe it means "the odor of affliction."

h 2:18 Or "polished brass." Brass, forged in flames, is an emblem of judgment.

you tolerate that woman Jezebel,[a] who calls herself a prophetess and is seducing my loving servants. She is teaching that it is permissible to indulge in sexual immorality and to eat food sacrificed to idols.[b] [21] I have waited for her to repent from her vile immorality, but she refuses to do so. [22] Now I will lay her low[c] with terrible distress along with all her adulterous partners if they do not repent.[d] [23] And I will strike down her followers with a deadly plague.[e] Then all the congregations will realize that I am the one who thoroughly searches the most secret thought[f] and the innermost being.[g] I will give to each one what their works deserve. [24] But to the rest of you in Thyatira who don't adhere to the teachings of Jezebel and have not been initiated into deep satanic secrets,[h] I say to you (without laying upon you any other burden): [25] Cling tightly[i] to all that you have until I appear. [26] To everyone who is victorious and continues to do my works to the very end I will give you authority over the nations [27] to shepherd them with a royal scepter.[j] And the rebellious will be shattered as clay pots—[k] [28] even

---

a 2:20 Jezebel, King Ahab's wicked queen, was immoral and practiced idolatry. She released into Israel a spirit of darkness that hindered God's faithful ones by attempting to mix the worship of Baal with the worship of the true God. She becomes a symbol of a spirit of tolerance and compromise, which teaches that God's loving servants can sin and not experience any consequence. See 1 Kings 16:29–31; 18:4.

b 2:20 See Acts 15:29.

c 2:22 This may be an idiom for a severe illness. The Aramaic can be translated "I will throw her down into a coffin."

d 2:22 Thyatira was known as the center of many guilds or trade societies that required their members to participate in idolatry (often involving sexual immorality). This would make it very difficult for the believers to remain morally pure in an immoral and idolatrous culture.

e 2:23 Or "I will strike dead her children." Her "children" would be a metaphor for her followers. Although the Greek word thanatos means death, in some contexts it refers to deadly disease and is often translated "pestilence" in the Septuagint. See A Greek-English Lexicon of the New Testament and Other Early Christian Literature, 3rd ed., 443.

f 2:23 Or "every emotion" (or "affection").

g 2:23 The Aramaic can be translated "I am the guardian of hearts and souls."

h 2:24 Or "have not known the deep things of Satan."

i 2:25 Or "Take into your power what you have."

j 2:27 Or "to govern them with a staff made of iron" or "a shepherd's club" (capped with iron). See Robert H. Mounce, The Book of Revelation, revised ed.; The New International Commentary on the New Testament, edited by F. F. Bruce and Gordon D. Fee (Grand Rapids: Eerdmans, 1977); Henry Barclay Swete, Commentary on Revelation (Grand Rapids: Kregel Publications, 1977); Leon Morris, The Book of Revelation, An Introduction and Commentary, Tyndale New Testament Commentaries, revised Edition (Grand Rapids: Eerdmans, 1987); Robert L. Thomas, Revelation 1–7 Exegetical Commentary, vol. 1 (Chicago: Moody Press, 1992).

k 2:27 See Ps. 2:9.

as I also received authority from the presence of my Father.[a] I will give the morning star[b] to the one who experiences victory. [29] So the one whose heart is open let him listen carefully to what the Spirit is presently saying to all the churches.

Christ's Letter to Sardis

3 Write the following to the messenger of the congregation in Sardis,[c] for these are the words of the one who holds the seven Spirits of God[d] and the seven stars:

I know all that you do and I know that you have a reputation for being really "alive," but you're actually dead! [2] Wake up and strengthen all that remains before it dies, for I haven't found your works to be perfect in the sight of my God. [3] So remember all the things you've received and heard, then turn back to God and obey them. For if you continue to slumber, I will come to you like a thief, and you'll have no idea at what hour I will come. [4] Yet there are still a few in Sardis who have remained pure,[e] and they will walk in fellowship with me in brilliant light,[f] for they are worthy. [5] And the one who experiences victory will be dressed in white robes and I will never, no never erase your name from the Book of Life. I will acknowledge your name before my Father and his angels. [6] So the one whose heart is open let him listen carefully to what the Spirit is now saying to all the churches.

Christ's Letter to Philadelphia

[7] Write the following to the messenger of the congregation in Philadelphia,[g]

---

a 2:28 Christ shares with every conqueror his own rank before the Father, and we will participate in his eternal reign.

b 2:28 Or "the star of the dawn." See Dan. 12:3; 2 Peter 1:19; Rev. 22:16.

c 3:1 Sardis can mean "those who have escaped" or "red ones" (jewels). How we need to escape every form of religious bondage on our journey into Christlikeness. By the blood of Christ, we are redeemed and set free to be his fiery (red) ones, like jewels before God. Twice in the history of Sardis it had fallen to its enemies because it was not alert and watching. It was conquered once in 549 BC by King Cyrus of Persia, and again in 214 BC by Antiochus the Great. For this reason, the people of Sardis were asleep and needed an awakening.

d 3:1 Or "the seven-fold Spirit of God." See 1:16.

e 3:4 Or "You have a few names in Sardis who have not soiled their garments" (with sin).

f 3:4 Or "in white."

g 3:7 Philadelphia means "brotherly love." A powerful earthquake nearly leveled the city in AD 17, so hearing these words of encouragement from Christ would have greatly helped them. To be made into "pillar[s]" of the temple (v. 12) would give them security in the world shaking around them.

for these are the solemn words of the Holy One, the true one, who has David's key,[a] who opens doors that none can shut and who closes doors that none can open:

> [8] I know all that you've done. Now I have set before you a wide-open door[b] that none can shut.[c] For I know that you possess only a little power, yet you've kept my word and haven't denied my name.[d] [9] Watch how I deal with those of the synagogue of Satan who say that they are Jews but are not, for they're lying. I will make them come and bow down[e] at your feet and acknowledge how much I've loved you. [10] Because you've passionately kept my message of perseverance, I will also keep you from the hour of proving that is coming to test every person on earth. [11] But I come swiftly, so cling tightly to what you have, so that no one may seize your crown of victory. [12] For the one who is victorious, I will make you to be a pillar in the sanctuary of my God,[f] permanently secure.[g] I will write on you the name of my God and the name of the city of my God—the New Jerusalem, descending from my God out of heaven.[h] And I'll write my own name on you. [13] So the one whose heart is open let him listen carefully to what the Spirit is now saying to all the churches.

Christ's Letter to Laodicea
[14] Write the following to the messenger of the congregation in Laodicea,[i] for

---

a 3:7 The key of David unlocks intimacy and prayer. David was a man who lived in grace centuries before the gospel of God's grace was unveiled. In that sense, the key of David allowed him to view the future and live in the grace it would reveal.

b 3:8 Or "a door having been opened in your sight." This open door is likely an invitation to come into the fullness of God's kingdom of joy and power in the Holy Spirit (Rom. 14:17; Rev. 4:1). Or it may refer to an open door of opportunity to give witness to others of God's power and grace (1 Cor. 16:9; Col. 4:3).

c 3:8 See Isa. 22:22.

d 3:8 Note that it takes "little power" to keep (obey) God's word and not deny his name. Imagine what having great power would look like!

e 3:9 Or "worship [God] at your feet."

f 3:12 Since the image of a secure pillar is figurative, the sanctuary (temple) is also figurative, for there is no temple in the New Jerusalem reality (21:22). The word for "pillar" is also used for a pillar of fire. The emblem of a pillar points to a sure and fixed position upholding and supporting the kingdom purposes of God.

g 3:12 Or "never again will he leave it."

h 3:12 We are not going up to the New Jerusalem; this heavenly "city" is coming down to us on earth. It's new in quality, not simply new in time.

i 3:14 *Laodicea* means "human rights" or "self-righteousness."

these are the words of the Amen,ᵃ the faithful and true witness, the rulerᵇ
of God's creation:

¹⁵ I know all that you do, and I know that you are neither frozen in
apathy nor fervent with passion.ᶜ How I wish you were either one
or the other! ¹⁶ But because you are neither cold nor hot, but luke-
warm, I am about to spit you from my mouth.ᵈ ¹⁷ For you claim, "I'm
rich and getting richer—I don't need a thing."ᵉ Yet you are clueless
that you're miserable, poor, blind, barren, and naked! ¹⁸ So I counsel
you to purchase goldᶠ perfected by fire, so that you can be truly
rich. Purchase a white garment to cover and clothe your shameful
Adam-nakedness.ᵍ Purchase eye salve to be placed over your eyes so
that you can truly see. ¹⁹ All those I dearly love I unmask and train.ʰ
So repent and be eager *to pursue what is right.* ²⁰ Behold, I'm standing
at the door, knocking.ⁱ If your heart is open to hear my voice and
you open the door *within,* I will come in to you and feast with you,
and you will feast with me.ʲ ²¹ And to the one who conquersᵏ I will

---

a 3:14 There is only one other place in the Bible that "the Amen" or "the God of Amen" is
   found. See Isa. 65:16.
b 3:14 Or "the beginning [originator, source] of God's creation." The Greek Septuagint uses
   this word (*archē*) for ruler/authority in Gen. 40:13, 21; 41:13. See also *A Greek-English Lexicon
   of the New Testament and Other Early Christian Literature,* 3rd ed.
c 3:15 Or "you are neither cold nor hot."
d 3:16 This is not a complete rejection, for Jesus gives them a call to repent and return to a
   place of being passionate and zealous for God. The Aramaic uses an idiom that can mean
   "I am about to reprimand you (lit. "give you of my mouth")."
e 3:17 Although Laodicea was known as a very prosperous city, a financial center of the
   region, Christ's estimation of them was that they were spiritually poor. Only in Christ are
   we made rich (2 Cor. 8:9).
f 3:18 That is, Christ will be our gold. The wealth of Christ is not purchased with money but
   by faith. See Job 22:25; Prov. 23:23; Isa. 55:1–3.
g 3:18 Or "so that the shame of the nakedness of you will not be exposed." Christ will be our
   white garment and our eye salve that helps us to see things as they truly are.
h 3:19 Or "rebuke and discipline."
i 3:20 The Aramaic can be translated "I have been standing at the door, knocking." Jesus knocking on the door points us to the process of an ancient Jewish wedding invitation. In the days
   of Jesus, a bridegroom and his father would come to the door of the bride-to-be carrying the
   betrothal cup of wine and the bride-price. Standing outside, they would knock. If she fully
   opened the door, she was saying, "Yes, I will be your bride." Jesus and his Father, in the same
   way, are knocking on the doors of our hearts, inviting us to be the bride of Christ.
j 3:20 This is likely taken from Song. 5:1–2, where the king knocks on the door of the heart
   of the Shulamite, longing to come in and feast with her.
k 3:21 Each of the seven churches is given a wonderful promise to the one who "conquers" (or
   "overcomes," or "is victorious"). The Greek verb tense in each of the seven instances is "one
   who continually, repeatedly, and habitually conquers." The seven churches at seven locations
   indicates that believers are at that stage in their growth as overcomers. *Ephesus* means "desirable" (deeply loved by the Lord). *Smyrna* means "myrrh" (the trials and troubles we all go

give the privilege of sitting with me on my throne, just as I conquered and sat down with my Father on his throne. ²² The one whose
heart is open let him listen carefully to what the Spirit is saying now
to the churches.

John's Vision of the Throne Room

4 Then suddenly, after I wrote down these messages, I saw a heavenly portal
open before me, ᵃ and the same trumpet-voice I heard speaking with me
at the beginning ᵇ *broke the silence* and said, "Ascend into this realm! ᶜ I want to
reveal to you what must happen ᵈ after this."

² Instantly I was taken into the spirit realm, ᵉ and behold—I saw a heavenly
throne ᶠ set in place and someone seated upon it. ³ His appearance was *sparkling
like crystal* ᵍ and *glowing* like a carnelian gemstone. ʰ Surrounding the throne

---

through). *Pergamum* means "elevated place" (seasons of praises and favor). *Thyatira* means
"the incense [odor] of affliction" (learning to praise and overcome hardships). *Sardis* means
"those who escape" (breaking free of our past). *Philadelphia* means "brotherly love" (learning
lessons of loving others). *Laodicea* means "people's rights" (surrendering our rights to him).

a 4:1 Or "Behold! I saw a door in the heavenly realm that had been opened."

b 4:1 See Rev. 1:10.

c 4:1 John did not simply watch these things happen through an open door, he was taken
through the open door into the heavenly realm. In 3:20 Jesus stood knocking on a closed
door; now John passes through an open door.

d 4:1 Or "come to be" as in "give birth." The Greek word for "happen" is *ginomai* (similar to
our English word *genome*) and is translated three times in Rom. 7:3–4 as "married."

e 4:2 Or "I came to be [Gr. *ginomai*] within Spirit." Four times John uses this phrase (1:10; 4:2;
17:3; 21:10). Although some commentators believe John was in his human spirit, John went
into an ecstatic state or prophetic trance and was shown these things in the spirit realm.
The implication is that he was taken into the heavenly realm as these pictures were unveiled
before him. After seeing the first vision of Jesus walking among the lampstands and the
messages to the seven churches, John was taken into heaven for more revelation. See R. H.
Mounce, *Revelation, New International Commentary on the New Testament*, 75; G. B. Caird, *A
Commentary on the Revelation of St. John the Divine*, Black's New Testament Commentaries,
edited by Henry Chadwick (London: Adam & Charles Black, 1966); George Eldon Ladd, *A
Commentary of the Revelation of John* (Grand Rapids: William B. Eerdmans, 1972); David E.
Aune, *Revelation*, Word Biblical Commentary, vols. 52a and 52b, edited by Ralph P. Martin
(Nashville: Thomas Nelson, 1997 and 1998).

f 4:2 John uses the word *throne* forty times in the book of Revelation. God's throne is the
governmental center of the universe.

g 4:3 Or "jasper," an aggregate of microgranular quartz. It is likely that the word used here is
not identical to our modern jasper, but instead refers to a clear stone like crystal (cryptocrys-
talline jasper). Revelation 21:11 describes it as being clear like crystal. The most common
Hebrew word for jasper is *yashĕpheh*, as found in Ex. 28:20 and 39:13, which describes the last
or twelfth jewel on the breastplate of Aaron, the high priest. The word *yashĕpheh* literally
means "polished." Jasper is recognized as a symbol of the glory of God in all his splendor,
brightness, and beauty.

h 4:3 "Carnelian" (also known as "sard") is a mineral red in color and commonly described as

was a *circle of green light,* ᵃ like an emerald rainbow.ᵇ ⁴Encircling the great throne were twenty-four thrones with eldersᶜ in *glistening* white garments seated upon them, each wearing a golden crown of victory. ⁵And *pulsing* from the throne were *blinding* flashes of lightning,ᵈ crashes of thunder, and voices.ᵉ And burning before the throne are seven blazing torches, which represent the seven Spirits of God.ᶠ ⁶And in front of the throne there was *pavement*ᵍ like a crystal sea of glass. ʰ

Worship around the Throne

Around the throne and on each sideⁱ stood four living creatures, full of eyes

---

a glassy, translucent, semiprecious gemstone. The etymological origin of *carnelian* comes from the Latin word *cornum*, used for the cornel cherry. Assuming it to be cherry-red (blood red) in color, translucent light was glowing from the one seated on the throne. The sardius (carnelian) stone was placed first in order upon the high priest's breastplate.

a 4:3 Or possibly "halo."

b 4:3 See Ezek. 1:28. This was not a typical rainbow, for a rainbow has seven colors. This was more like a halo of light, shining all around the throne. It was a full circle, not a half-circle. It could have been horizontally or vertically around the throne. The Greek also allows for the translation "a rainbow made of emerald." The emerald rainbow points to God's mercy and covenant love, for he gave the sign of a rainbow to Noah, signifying that he would never again destroy the world through a flood. The rainbow around the throne would be a clear symbol that everything God does (coming from his throne of majesty) is surrounded with grace and mercy. The Hebrew word for "emerald" is *bareqeth,* which can also be translated "flashing of light" (Ex. 28:17). God's glory is represented by these three stones: jasper, carnelian, and emerald.

c 4:4 Scholars are divided over who these twenty-four elders are, either (1) the union of Jew (twelve tribes of Israel) and the church (twelve apostles of Jesus), (2) a rank of heavenly beings serving as God's cabinet officers, (3) a symbol of the twenty-four prophetic books of the Old Testament, or (4) an actual council of elders (believers) who are subordinate to God but ruling with authority and wisdom. They are enthroned and have crowns, which would speak of regal authority. Made up from the overcomers from among the community of the redeemed, the twenty-four elders are robed in Christ's righteousness (white garments), enthroned with him (Eph. 2:6; Rev. 3:21), and crowned with glory.

d 4:5 Lightning is often an emblem of the revelation-word of God breaking forth on the earth (Ps. 97:4), which dismantles the works of Satan (Luke 10:18). As God's Word goes forth, there will always be voices to carry the fresh revelation of heaven.

e 4:5 Or "sounds." See also Ex. 19:16; Ps. 77:18.

f 4:5 Or "the seven-fold Spirit of God."

g 4:6 See Ex. 24:10; Ezek. 1:22, 26.

h 4:6 The blazing torches reflected off the glassy crystal sea would appear to be heaven's analogue to the Red Sea. See also 15:2–4. One of the miracles of the Red Sea crossing was that the waters congealed and became like glass (Ex. 15:8). John is seeing a hint of the chaotic "sea of humanity" (Dan. 7:2; Ezek. 32:2) being calmed before God's sovereign throne.

i 4:6 A possible inference in the Greek is that the four living creatures are supporting the throne; that is, the throne (chariot of God) rested upon them. See Ezek. 1:15–26. The number four points to the four winds and the four seasons (the whole created order).

in front and behind. [a] [7] The first living creature resembled a lion, the second an ox, the third had a human face, and the fourth was like an eagle in flight. [8] Each of the four living creatures had six wings, full of eyes all around and under their wings. They worshiped without ceasing, day and night, singing,

"Holy, holy, holy is the Lord God, the Almighty! [b]
The Was, [c] the Is, [d] and the Coming!" [e]

[9] And whenever the living creatures gave glory, honor, and thanks to the One who is enthroned and who lives forever and ever, [10] the twenty-four elders fell facedown before the one seated on the throne and they worshiped the one who lives forever and ever. And they surrendered their crowns before the throne, singing:

[11] "You are worthy, our Lord and God,
to receive glory, honor, and power, [f]
for you created all things,
and by your plan they were created and exist." [g]

The Unopened Scroll

5 And I saw that the one seated on the throne was holding in his right hand an unopened scroll with writing on the inside and on the outside, [h] and it was sealed with seven seals. [2] Then I saw an incredibly powerful angel [i] proclaiming with a great, loud voice, "Who is worthy to open the scroll and break [j] its *seven* seals?" [3] But no person could be found, living or dead, in all of creation [k]—no one was worthy to open the scroll and read its contents. [4] So I broke down weeping with intense sorrow, because there was found no one worthy to break open the scroll and read its contents. [l]

[5] Then one of the elders said to me, "Stop weeping. Look! The mighty

---

a 4:6 They had eyes to see into different realms and into times past and future (in front and behind).

b 4:8 See Isa. 6:1–3.

c 4:8 See John 1:1; 2 Cor. 5:19; 1 Tim. 3:16.

d 4:8 He who was (Christ in his early life) is now the one who *is* within us. See 1 Cor. 14:25.

e 4:8 Or "the coming one." He is coming to be all that he is within us. See 2 Thess. 1:10.

f 4:11 Or "praise."

g 4:11 Or "they existed and were created," an obvious figure of speech called *hysteron proteron*.

h 5:1 See Isa. 29:11; Ezek. 2:9–10; Dan. 12:4. The revelation God gave to Daniel was to be sealed, but what John saw was a book that is to be broken open.

i 5:2 There are twenty-six unidentified angels mentioned in the book of Revelation. Additionally, there are possibly fifteen angels identified as men.

j 5:2 Or "release" or "untie."

k 5:3 Or "on heaven or on earth or under the earth."

l 5:4 Or "look into it." Some see this scroll as the title deed of the universe that contains the right of ownership and the timing and plans of fulfilling the eternal destiny of all creation.

Lion of Judah's tribe,[a] the root of David—he has conquered! He is the worthy one who can open the scroll and its seven seals."

[6] Then I saw a young Lamb[b] standing in the middle of the throne, encircled by the four living creatures and the twenty-four elders. He appeared to have been slaughtered *but was now alive!*[c] He had seven horns[d] and seven eyes, which are the seven Spirits of God sent out to the ends of the earth.

[7] I saw the young Lamb approach the throne and receive the scroll from the right hand of the one who sat there. [8] And when the twenty-four elders and the four living creatures saw the Lamb had taken the scroll, they fell facedown at the feet of the Lamb and worshiped him. Each of them had a harp and golden bowls brimming full of sweet fragrant incense—which are the prayers of God's holy lovers. [9] And they were all singing this new song *of praise to the Lamb*:

> "Because you were slaughtered for us,
>> you are worthy to take the scroll and open its seals.
>> Your blood was the price paid to redeem us.
>> You purchased us to bring us to God
>> out of every tribe, language, people group, and nation.
> [10] You have chosen us to serve our God
>> and formed us into a kingdom of priests
>> who reign[e] on the earth."

Angelic Worship of the Lamb

[11] Then I looked, and I heard the voices of myriads of angels in circles around the throne, as well as the voices of the living creatures and the elders—myriads and myriads![f] [12] And as I watched, all of them were singing with thunderous voices:

> "Worthy is Christ the Lamb who was slaughtered to receive great
>> power and might, wealth and wisdom, and honor, glory, and praise!"

[13] Then every living being joined the angelic choir. Every creature in heaven

---

a 5:5 See Gen. 49:10.

b 5:6 Jesus is both a fierce Lion and a gentle Lamb. The Lamb holds the scroll.

c 5:6 This is our Lord Jesus Christ with the marks of sacrifice still upon him.

d 5:6 Horns are a picture of power and authority (Ps. 89:17; Dan. 7:8), while seven is the number of perfection. Perfect authority now belongs to the Lamb who was slain.

e 5:10 The present tense of the Greek verb indicates that the reign of believers on earth has already begun. See Henry Alford, *Alford's Greek Testament: An Exegetical and Critical Commentary*, vol. 4, 1875 (Grand Rapids: Baker, 1980); Henry Barclay Swete, *Commentary on Revelation* (Grand Rapids: Kregel Publications, 1977); G. K. Beale, *The Book of Revelation, A Commentary on the Greek Text*, The New International Greek Testament Commentary (Grand Rapids: Eerdmans, 1999).

f 5:11 Or "ten thousands of ten thousands, and thousands of thousands." If taken literally, this would exceed 110 million angels.

and on earth, under the earth, in the sea, and everything in them, were *worshiping* with one voice, saying:

> "Praise, honor, glory, and dominion
>> be to God-Enthroned
>> and to Christ the Lamb
>> forever and ever!"

[14] Then the four living creatures responded:

> "Amen!"

And the twenty-four elders threw themselves facedown to the ground and worshiped. [a]

Breaking Open the Sealed Scroll

6 Then I watched as the Lamb broke open the first of the seven seals. [b] Immediately I heard one of the four living creatures call out with a powerful voice of revelation sounding like thunder, saying, "Come forth!" [c] [2] So I looked, and behold, there was a bright white horse. [d] Its rider had a bow [e] and was given a crown of victory. He rode out as a conqueror ready to conquer. [f]

[3] When he broke open the second seal, I heard the second living creature call out: "Come forth!" [g] [4] And there appeared another horse, red *like fiery flames,* [h]

---

a 5:14 This powerful scene of heavenly worship begins near the throne and then races outwardly to every being in heaven until it extends even further, cascading upon the earth like a waterfall.

b 6:1 The breaking open of the seal would allow a portion of the scroll to be read.

c 6:1 Or "Go forth!"

d 6:2 The horse is an emblem of overcoming, invincible power in battle. The color white is found throughout Revelation, always associated with Christ or spiritual victory.

e 6:2 A bow without arrows shows that he is coming to conquer, not militarily but spiritually. He holds a bow to shoot the arrows of truth into our hearts.

f 6:2 Or "He went out continually conquering so that he might conquer." This is Christ coming forth as King in authority and power, riding out to conquer everything within us that hinders the life of Christ emerging in our transformation (Ps. 45:3–4). The words "Come forth" reflect the groaning of creation to see the unveiling of the sons of God. See Henry Alford, *Alford's Greek Testament: An Exegetical and Critical Commentary,* vol. 4, 1875 (Grand Rapids: Baker, 1980); Henry Barclay Swete, *Commentary on Revelation* (Grand Rapids: Kregel Publications, 1977). This is the calling forth of Christ by the power of his Spirit to conquer us fully. All the universe will one day be conquered by the one riding this white horse. Here he rides alone, but in Rev. 19:11 he does not come alone but with those whom he has conquered. John uses this word *conquer* more than any other New Testament writer. See Rev. 2–3.

g 6:3 Or "Go forth!"

h 6:4 See Mal. 3:1–3. The Greek word for "fiery" or "flames" comes from the word for "pure," or "to purify." Christ rides this fiery red horse as one robed in the flames of God to bring purity to his priestly people. See also Ps. 12:6.

and its rider was given a great sword and the power to take peace from earth,[a] causing one to put to death another.[b]

[5] Then he broke open the third seal, and I heard the third living creature call out, "Come forth!"[c] And behold, I saw a black horse right in front of me, and its rider was holding measuring scales. [6] And I heard what seemed to be a voice from among the living creatures[d] saying, "A small measure[e] of wheat for a day's pay, and three measures of barley for a day's pay,[f] but don't harm[g] the olive trees producing oil and the vines producing wine."

[7] When he broke open the fourth seal, I heard the fourth living creature call out, "Come forth!"[h] [8] And behold, I saw a green[i] horse, and its rider's name was Death, and Death's Domain[j] followed him. They were given authority over a fourth of the earth, to kill with sword,[k] famine,[l] death,[m] and by the wild beasts.

[9] When the Lamb broke open the fifth seal, I saw gathered under the altar

---

a 6:4 See Matt. 10:34; Heb. 4:12; Eph. 6:17.

b 6:4 See Col. 3:5.

c 6:5 Or "Go forth!"

d 6:6 This is likely the voice of the Lord, who dwells in the midst of the living creatures. See Rev. 4:6 and 5:6. These commands are for the four horses to come from the throne room. The Lamb who was slain is giving these decrees. He who gave his life now speaks of four commodities that bring life to us: wheat, barley, oil, and wine (Deut. 8:8). These four commodities point us to the promised land of God's blessings. The wheat and barley point to the Passover Feast. The second day of the feast was the Feast of Unleavened Bread (wheat). The third day of the feast, a sheaf of barley representing the first grain harvested in the land was waved before the Lord (Lev. 23:9–11). Jesus was crucified on Passover, and on the third day, Jesus, God's firstfruit (three measures of barley), was raised up from the dead and waved before the Father (1 Cor. 15:20, 23). To truly feed upon him will cost us all we have each day (a day's pay). See also Prov. 23:23; Rev. 3:18.

e 6:6 Or "a choenix," a dry measure slightly less than a quart. It would be equal to the food supply of one man for one day. See Herodotus, Histories 7.187.

f 6:6 Or "a denarius," equal to a day's wage for a laborer.

g 6:6 Or "damage" or "do wrong to." The oil and wine will not be limited. We are in the day of the oil and wine being given in fullness to the sons and daughters of God.

h 6:7 Or "Go forth!"

i 6:8 The Greek word kloros always means "green," not "pale green." It is used four times in the New Testament and always refers to grass (green grass) or green living things. The color of the horse speaks of life, but the rider's name is Death. Death rides on life (life comes through death—Gal. 2:10). The death is his death.

j 6:8 Or "Hades."

k 6:8 This is the sword from his mouth, the word of God that kills and makes alive.

l 6:8 To kill with hunger is the Lord's method of starving to death our old ways, desires, and lusts. His resurrection life emerging in us overcomes (starves to death) what we cannot overcome. To hunger and thirst for righteousness is the key to being filled (Matt. 5:6; Col. 3:1–10).

m 6:8 This is not pestilence, but death. To kill with death is not trying to die to flesh, for that is a form of suicide, but to see that the death of Christ is our death too (Gal. 2:20). We cannot kill ourselves or by self-effort bring our flesh to death; it must be wholly the work of Christ.

the souls of those who had been slain because of the Word of God and because they had the testimony of the Lamb.[a] [10] They cried out with a loud voice, saying, "Sovereign Lord, holy and dependable, how long before you judge those who live on the earth and vindicate[b] our blood on them?"[c]

[11] Each one was given a glistening white robe.[d] And they were told to rest a little longer, until the full number was fulfilled of both their fellow servants and brothers and sisters who were going to be killed just as they had been.

[12] And behold! I saw the Lamb break open the sixth seal, which released a powerful earthquake. I saw the sun become pitch black[e] and the full moon become bloodred. [13] The stars fell from heaven to the earth, as a fig tree shaken by a stormy wind sheds its unripe figs. [14] The sky receded with a snap—as a scroll rolls itself up.[f] And every mountain and island was moved from its place.[g] [15] Then the kings of the earth and its great princes[h] and generals, the rich and powerful, and everyone, whether they were slave or free, ran for cover and

---

To kill by death is a death by death. Jesus rides into our lives on the green horse to put to death all of Adam through the life poured out by his (Jesus') death.

a 6:9 As translated from the Aramaic. The Greek is "because of their testimony." These souls gathered under the altar (an emblem of sacrifice unto death), died to every soulish way, and were offered as love sacrifices to God.

b 6:10 Although the Greek word *ekdikeo* can mean "avenge" or "render a fair verdict," its primary meaning is to "validate" or "vindicate."

c 6:10 This was a vision and is full of symbolism. We are like the souls "under the altar," for we are under the shelter of the altar where Christ has been sacrificed on our behalf. We are those who cry out for a powerful move of God that will deal with the nature of man and bring the glory of God. This is not simply a cry for revenge but a cry for revival among the nations to break loose.

d 6:11 These symbolize the robes of the priesthood, the clothing of Christ upon our souls.

e 6:12 Or "black as sackcloth made of [goat] hair." This may represent our outward reasoning. What once gave us light is now turned into blackness.

f 6:14 Scrolls were equal to today's books. They were unrolled and read, then rolled back up. To have the sky rolled up like a scroll is equal to saying, "The book is closed!" The old heavens must be removed to make room for a new heaven. When Jesus was baptized, the new heavens were opened up to him like a scroll, inaugurating this era of an open heaven through Christ.

g 6:14 Upon opening the sixth seal, the scene changes to earth. The power of God is released, which shakes every continent and every island. Yet is this destruction meant to be taken literally? Great earthquakes throughout the Bible were a regular feature of divine visitation. Methods, movements, governments, and structures (mountains and islands) will all be shaken by God in this wonderful visitation. Stars do not literally fall to the earth. Some of them are so huge they are larger than our solar system. If they were to fall, it would destroy all that we know. Yet, as we read further into the book of Revelation, we find that the earth continues to exist. So this scene must be taken symbolically. The old order of the natural realm is passing away and a new order is being established. There are many prophecies of the Old Testament referring to the lights going out on the old order as something new is set in place (Isa. 24:23; 34:4; Jer. 15:9; Joel 2:30–31; Mic. 3:6). A superior light of the kingdom of God will make dim the light of the old covenant.

h 6:15 Or "high-ranking officers" or "heads of thousands." The heart of each person is being

hid in the caves and among the mountain boulders. [16] They called out to the mountains and the boulders, saying, "Fall on us at once![a] Hide us quickly from the glorious face of the one seated on the throne and from the wrath of the Lamb,[b] [17] for the great day of their wrath has come, and who is able to stand?"

John's Vision of 144,000 Servants of God

7 After this[c] I saw four angels standing at the four corners of the earth, and they were restraining the four winds so that no wind would blow on the land, on the sea, or on any tree.[d] [2] Then I saw another angel ascending from the east,[e] who had the seal of the living God.[f] He shouted out with a loud voice to the four angels who had been given power to damage earth and sea, [3] saying, "Do not damage the earth, the sea, or the trees until we[g] have marked the loving servants of our God with a seal on their foreheads."[h]

---

laid bare by the light and glory of Christ rising upon his people. It was Adam who first wanted to hide from the face of God, but for the believer we hide only in the Father's love.

a 6:16 See Hos. 10:8.

b 6:16 Few phrases in the Bible could seem more contradictory than "the wrath [anger] of the Lamb" (not the anger of the Lion). This is corrective and redemptive—not beastly rage but fiery passion to judge whatever gets in the way between the Lamb and his bride. The Greek word *orge* means "to reach out with passionate desire and take hold of." The simplest definition of the Greek word *orge* could be "fiery passion."

c 7:1 That is, after the sixth seal was broken open. Judgment is temporarily held back by these four angels of mercy.

d 7:1 The number four represents universality (the four corners of the earth), and winds speak of divine agents that bring either blessing or judgment. The trees may point to what is deeply rooted within our souls.

e 7:2 Or "from the sun rising." The east is often associated with blessings and the place from which God appears (Gen. 2:8; Ezek. 43:1–4; Matt. 2:1). The messenger was not descending from the east, but ascending. The star of Jesus was rising in the east. This sealing messenger represents the living God and points to Christ, who is rising in his people, bringing the light of a new day. It is a company of messengers arising out of the light of the sunrise to bring the seal of God upon his people.

f 7:2 This seal is the mind of Christ, for it goes on the forehead (thoughts). Until we have the mind of Christ, we are incapable of discerning properly. Partaking of Christ's mind empowers us to be righteous judges, righteous kings, and righteous priests. This seal is more than a seal of protection from the coming judgments, but a seal that qualifies them to bring the righteous judgments of God to the earth. This is the nature of God being written upon the foreheads and minds of his holy ones.

g 7:3 This is not one messenger; "he" has become "we."

h 7:3 This mighty angel has more authority than the four (the number for worldwide or universality) who would damage the earth, sea, and trees. It is the angel carrying the seal of God that speaks of God's grace and mercy, which will always triumph over judgment (James 2:13). The seal on their foreheads is the mind of Christ, the mark of the Christ. The winds of judgment are being held back until the sons of God have the thoughts and mind of Christ. To be "sealed" means to be protected from judgment (Ezek. 9:4–6). The seal of lamb's blood on the doors of the Israelites protected them from the death angel. The new covenant seal is the Holy Spirit (the mind of Christ) that opens our hearts to the restoration

⁴And I discovered the number of those who were sealed. It was one hundred and forty-four thousand, ᵃ sealed out of every tribe of Israel's people. ᵇ

⁵Twelve thousand were sealed from the tribe of Judah.ᶜ

Twelve thousand were sealed from the tribe of Reuben. ᵈ

Twelve thousand were sealed from the tribe of Gad.ᵉ

⁶Twelve thousand were sealed from the tribe of Asher.ᶠ

Twelve thousand were sealed from the tribe of Naphtali.ᵍ

Twelve thousand were sealed from the tribe of Manasseh.ʰ

⁷Twelve thousand were sealed from the tribe of Simeon.ⁱ

---

of heaven. We are the seven-sealed scroll that is broken open so that the all-conquering life of Christ will subdue all things (Phil. 3:21). We are living letters, written not with ink but by the Spirit of God writing truth upon our hearts. In the volume of the book (scroll) it is written about Christ (Ps. 40:7).

a 7:4 One hundred and forty-four thousand is 12 x 12 x 1,000. This speaks of completeness and represents God raising up sons and daughters who carry fully his image and likeness. It is not meant to be "a literal head count," but showing us who they are. It is the number of Christ multiplied in his sons and daughters coming into the likeness of the Son.

b 7:4 "Israel's people" are those who have wrestled with their nature and have been given a new name, a new nature, and have become princes with God. See Gen. 28:24–28; Gal. 3:29. The names of the twelve tribes of princes with God speak of the virtues of their names. Just as the twelve tribes were not birthed at the same time, so they become a picture of our progression in spiritual life from one "tribe" to another, from glory to glory.

c 7:5 *Judah* means "praise." In every list of the twelve tribes, Reuben, the firstborn, is always listed first—but not here. Judah is listed first, not because he was the firstborn but because he was the tribal head of King David and King Jesus, the Lion of the tribe of Judah. Israel begins with the spiritual, not the natural. Judah is the spiritual head of Israel (Gen. 49:2) and points to Christ, the true firstborn of creation and the firstborn of many brothers (the church). As we are sealed into the tribe of Judah, we are given the revelation of our sonship in him.

d 7:5 *Reuben* means "Behold, a son!" Once we have seen Judah's Lion as heaven's firstborn Son, we move to beholding that Son living in us and fully being formed in us.

e 7:5 *Gad* means "a troop." Jacob gave his son Gad this prophecy: "A troop will troop upon him, but he will troop on their heels and overcome the troop at last" (literal Hebrew of Gen. 49:19). Gad symbolizes the beginning of the victorious life of an overcomer breaking forth. Throughout Israel's history, the Gadites were tremendous warriors (1 Chron. 5:18–20; 12:8).

f 7:6 *Asher* means "happy." The kingdom of God is full of righteousness, peace, and joy in the Holy Spirit. Our journey into becoming overcomers takes us on a path of endless bliss. A joy unspeakable and full of glory becomes our strength and our song. See John 15:11.

g 7:6 *Naphtali* means "wrestling." This points to the struggle of warfare between flesh and spirit, between living in the natural realm and in the sonship realm of the Spirit.

h 7:6 *Manasseh* means "causing me to forget." There is a realm of grace, where we forget the pain of our struggles and betrayals and enter into the vibrant, victorious life of Christ. We then can say like Manasseh's father Joseph, "Others meant to harm me, but God meant to bless me and bring good out of all I've gone through."

i 7:7 *Simeon* means "a hearing ear" or "one who hears." Our ears are to be pierced open to continually hear the voice of our Shepherd, Jesus Christ. See Isa. 50:4–5.

Twelve thousand were sealed from the tribe of Levi. *a*

Twelve thousand were sealed from the tribe of Issachar. *b*

⁸Twelve thousand were sealed from the tribe of Zebulun. *c*

Twelve thousand were sealed from the tribe of Joseph. *d*

Twelve thousand were sealed from the tribe of Benjamin. *e*

A Vast Multitude from Every Nation

⁹After this I looked, and behold, right in front of me I saw a vast multitude of people—an enormous multitude so huge that no one could count—made up of *victorious* ones from every nation, tribe, people group, and language. They were all in *glistening* white robes, standing before the throne and before the Lamb with palm branches *f* in their hands. ¹⁰And they shouted out with a passionate voice:

---

a 7:7 *Levi* means "joined" (to the Lord) or "union." Because of Levi's zeal for the Lord when he refused to worship the golden calf after Israel's deliverance from Exodus, God rewarded the tribe of Levi by calling them to be his priests so that they would be "joined" to God and find God alone as their inheritance. Today there are those who realize they are the bride of Christ and are determined to live in union with him, joined to his heart (Rom. 7:4; 1 Cor. 6:17; 2 Cor. 11:2).

b 7:7 *Issachar* means "reward" or "compensation." Every obedient son and daughter of God will be rewarded with an indescribable inheritance full of blessings (Eph. 1:3; 2 Peter 1:3–4).

c 7:8 *Zebulun* means "dwelling" or "habitation." As we pass through these twelve stages of our sonship, we will become a Zebulun people, his habitation. We don't just receive things from God; we become his dwelling place, his holy of holies on the earth.

d 7:8 *Joseph* means "May he add" (another). As Rachel gave birth to Joseph, ending her season of barrenness, she exclaimed, "May he [God] add another son" (Gen. 30:22–24). Although she rejoiced in having a son, she longed for another one. In the same way, God has chosen through Christ to bring many sons to glory, for Jesus is the Firstborn among many (Rom. 8:29).

e 7:8 *Benjamin* means "son of my right hand." The cry of Rachel for another son was answered with the birth of Benjamin. As she died in childbirth, her last act was to name her son Benomi, "son of my sorrow." But Jacob renamed the boy Benjamin, "son of my right hand." Through the travail of our difficulties, a true son of God's right hand will come forth. We are now a "right hand" people, given the privilege of sitting enthroned with Christ at the right hand of God (Eph. 2:6; Rev. 3:21). In Benjamin we find the completion of our journey into the fullness of our inheritance (sonship) in Christ. At God's right hand are a Benjamin company, mature in the fullness of Christ. The above list of the twelve tribes is unlike other lists, showing it to be a symbolic list of God's people who are brought into the fullness of Christ. The tribe of Ephraim is often listed among the tribes of Israel but is missing in this list because of his (their) rebellion. The tribe of Dan is not listed due to its rebellion and idolatry. Dan means "judge." Judgment is missing from the list, for Dan is not found among them. Although Dan was removed, Levi was added. The tribe of Levi, although not given an allotment with the other tribes because of their priestly calling, is listed here because of his (their) faithfulness to serve God.

f 7:9 The palm tree is a biblical symbol of victory.

"Salvation belongs to our God
    seated on the throne
    and to the Lamb!"

[11] All the angels were standing in a circle around the throne with the elders
and the four living creatures, and they all fell on their faces before the throne
and worshiped God, [12] singing:

"Amen! Praise and glory,
    wisdom and thanksgiving,
    honor, power, and might
belong to our God forever and ever! Amen!"

[13] Then one of the elders asked me, "Who are these in glistening white
robes, and where have they come from?"

[14] I answered, "My lord—you must know."

Then he said to me, "They are ones who have washed their robes[a] and
made them white in the blood of the Lamb and have emerged from the midst
of great pressure and ordeal.[b] [15] For this reason they are before the throne of
God, ministering to him as priests[c] day and night, within his cloud-filled sanctuary. And the enthroned One spreads over them his tabernacle-shelter.[d] [16] Their
souls will be completely satisfied.[e] And neither the sun nor any scorching heat
will affect them.[f] [17] For the Lamb at the center of the throne continuously shepherds them unto life[g]—guiding them to the everlasting fountains of the water
of life.[h] And God will wipe from their eyes every last tear!"[i]

---

a 7:14 The implication is that their robes were defiled and needed to be washed. The world
    and the religious system must be removed from our "robes."

b 7:14 Or "the great [or "major"] oppression [persecution, tribulation]." Each of the white-
    robed saints had to pass through tribulation. This phrase "great tribulation" occurs twice
    in the book of Revelation and refers only to believers, never to the world. It is the true fol-
    lowers of the Lamb who pass through this "tribulation." This comes from the Latin word
    tribulum, a hollowed-out rock that was used to separate wheat (or other grains) from the
    chaff. We must pass through *tribulum* (tribulation) to enter into the kingdom of God. See
    Acts 14:22.

c 7:15 The word used for "ministering" as priests is *latreuo* and can mean both "worship" and
    "serve" (as priests).

d 7:15 A vivid figure of speech for God dwelling with them, making his very residence with
    them. The Aramaic can be translated "The enthroned One leans over them."

e 7:16 Or "They will never again experience hunger or thirst," a figure of speech for being
    completely satisfied.

f 7:16 See Isa. 49:10. This scorching heat is most likely a figure of speech representing that
    demonic power will never afflict them.

g 7:17 As translated from the Aramaic. The sacrificial heart of Christ as the Lamb will guide
    them and be their path of life.

h 7:17 Some manuscripts have "to living springs of water."

i 7:17 The Greek word for "anoint" is "to wipe" or "smear." It is possible to translate this "He

The Lamb Breaks Open the Seventh Seal

8 When the Lamb broke open the seventh seal, heaven fell silent for about half an hour. [a] [2] And then I saw the seven angels who stand before God, and each was given a trumpet. [b]

[3] Then the eighth angel with a golden incense burner came and took his place at the incense altar. [c] He was given a great quantity of incense to offer up, consisting of the prayers of God's holy people, [d] upon the golden altar that is before the throne. [4] And the smoke of the incense with the prayers of the holy ones billowed up before God from the hand of the angel. [e] [5] Then the angel filled the golden incense burner with *coals of* fire from the altar and hurled it onto the earth, releasing great peals of thunder, voices, [f] lightning flashes, and an earthquake. [g]

The Trumpets

[6] Then the seven angels prepared to sound their trumpets. [7] When the first angel sounded his trumpet, there came forth hail and fire mixed with blood, [h] and it

---

will anoint every tear shed from their eyes." See Isa. 25:8.

a 8:1 When the first seal was broken open, it released thunder, but when the seventh seal was opened, it released the silence of the awe of God. The period of silence is because of the enormity and revelation that will be released through the last seal, bringing fullness to God's work. *Silence* also points to perfect peace. The opening of the seventh seal will bring heaven's peace into the created realm, for there is no time (half an hour, a compound Greek word taken from *half* and *kairos*, or a fixed, appointed time) in the eternal realm.

b 8:2 These may be a special class of angelic beings (archangels) named in Jewish tradition and given in 1 *Enoch* as Raphael, Uriel, Michael, Raguel, Sariel, Gabriel, and Remiel. A trumpet represents sounding out a specific and clear word from the Lord, bringing revelation to the hearts of his people.

c 8:3 This eighth (or "another") messenger taking his place at the golden altar is Christ, our Great High Priest, and the great quantity of incense is his intercession, which he mingles with ours. See Ps. 141:2; Heb. 3:1; 7:25; 8:1–2; 9:11. No angel is ever seen doing the work of the high priest as in this chapter.

d 8:3 Or "to offer up incense, which is the prayers of God's holy ones."

e 8:4 There are six specific items found in vv. 3–4, and they are all related to a heavenly, priestly ministry: an angel (messenger), an altar, a golden incense burner, incense, prayers, and smoke. See Lev. 16:11–14.

f 8:5 Or "sounds."

g 8:5 As our prayers, mixed with the intercession of our High Priest, Jesus, ascend in the Spirit, the very coals of fire from the altar are cast into the earth, which releases mighty power. The voices carry the word of the Lord. The thunder manifests God's power (Job 26:14; Ps. 29:3–4). The lightning strikes illuminate divine truth (Ps. 97:4) as a great earthquake shakes the kingdoms of men to their foundations. These are not just acts of judgment, but purification (Isa. 6:6–7; Luke 12:49).

h 8:7 The Aramaic can be translated "mixed with water."

was hurled to the earth. *a* A third of the earth was burned up, destroying a third of the trees *b* and all green grass. *c*

⁸ When the second angel sounded his trumpet, something like a huge mountain burning with *flames of* fire was thrown into the sea, *d* destroying a third of the ships. *e* ⁹ A third of the sea turned into blood, destroying a third of all sea creatures.

¹⁰ The third angel sounded his trumpet, and a megastar, *f* blazing like a torch, *g* descended from heaven upon a third of the rivers and fountains. *h* ¹¹ The name of the star is Bitterness. *i* A third of the waters became so bitter that many people died.

¹² The fourth *j* angel sounded his trumpet and a third of the sun was struck, and a third of the moon, and a third of the stars, so that a third of their light was darkened, and there was no light for a third of the day and likewise the night. *k* ¹³ Then I saw and heard an eagle flying overhead, crying out with a loud voice, "Woe, woe, woe, to the people of the earth, because of the next three trumpets about to be sounded by the other three angels!"

The Fifth Trumpet

9 Then the fifth angel sounded his trumpet, and I saw a star that fell from heaven to earth, and he was handed the key to the shaft leading down to

---

a 8:7 This corresponds to the plague sent upon Egypt (a type of the world system; see Ex. 9:23–25). Hail may be a picture of the word of God that destroys the hiding place of lies and false doctrines (Isa. 28:17).

b 8:7 Trees may speak of what is deeply rooted in human nature that will be destroyed by "blood mixed with fire." Christ's blood and Spirit-fire will purify our lives.

c 8:7 Grass is consistently used in Scripture as a picture of our flesh (nature). Grass is a surface covering and can be a mask that hides what is beneath.

d 8:8 See Matt. 17:20. The kingdom of God is like a mountain (Isa. 2:1–3). The sea is a frequent metaphor for humanity (the sea of humanity). This is the mountain kingdom of God and his Spirit-fire cast into the sea of our lives. The sea creatures being destroyed (v. 9) can refer to the ungodly desires and activities of the flesh that live in the depths of our hearts. What once was life to us becomes undrinkable. See also Ex. 15:22–26; Jer. 23:13–15.

e 8:8 See Rev. 18:9–10, 17–19. The ships are all part of the activities of the system of Babylon.

f 8:10 The great or megastar is identified in Rev. 22:16 as Jesus. See also Num. 24:17–19.

g 8:10 Or "lamp." See Ps. 119:105. The burning torch is the burning Word of God.

h 8:10 Rivers and fountains are also within the believer (Ps. 36:7–9; John 4:14; 7:37–38.)

i 8:11 Or "wormwood" or "poisonwood," a bitter herb (absinthe) known for its medicinal value in killing intestinal worms.

j 8:12 It was on the fourth day of creation that the moon, sun, and stars were set in place. They were meant to "rule," so they speak of governmental authority. It was to the fourth church that Jesus promised the overcomers that they will be given the Morning Star. See Dan. 12:3; Mal. 4:2.

k 8:12 The old order is dimming and passing away as all things become new and a new "exodus" is upon us. See Ex. 10:21–23.

the pit of the deep. *ᵃ* ² He opened the shaft of the bottomless pit and a *blanket of smoke* began to rise out of it, like the smoke of a giant furnace. The sun and the atmosphere were darkened with the smoke rising from the shaft.

³ And out of smoke appeared locusts *ᵇ swarming* onto the earth, and they were given authority like that of scorpions *to inflict pain.* ⁴ They were told not to harm the grass, or any green growth or any tree, but only to afflict those who did not have the seal of God on their foreheads. *ᶜ* ⁵ The locusts were given authority to torment them for five months, but not to kill them. Their painful torment *ᵈ* is like the scorpion's sting, ⁶ and during that time people will seek death but will not find it; they will long to die but death will elude them. *ᵉ*

⁷ The locusts had the appearance of horses equipped for battle. On their heads were what seemed like golden crowns. And their faces were like human faces. *ᶠ* ⁸ Their hair *was long,* like women's hair, and their teeth like lion's teeth. ⁹ They wore breastplates that seemed like iron, and their wings made a sound

---

a 9:1 Or "the well of the abyss." This is the same Greek word found throughout the Septuagint for "the deep." (See Gen. 1:2; 8:2; Deut. 8:7; 33:13; Pss. 104:2–6; 107:23–26.) Jesus is the one who holds the keys of death and Hades (Rev. 1:18), for he unlocked both and walked out triumphantly in resurrection power. Many things are opened in Revelation (heaven, doors, books) with the purpose of releasing a new understanding or revelation. There is a deep place in the human heart, like a pit, that Jesus opens so that we can see what has been there inside us.

b 9:3 Locusts emerged from the smoke. The smoke of the abyss is a picture of deception. The lies of the enemy are a "smoke screen." The locusts are a picture of the words, actions, and lies of the religious system that dominates and intimidates others (Nah. 3:17). It causes others to feel inferior, like "grasshoppers" (or "locusts"). See Num. 13:33; Joel 2:1–10; Matt. 3:4.

c 9:4 The forehead is a metaphor for our thoughts, our minds. We must have the seal of sonship on our thoughts, the seal of God as our Father, or we will be tormented in our minds over our true identity in Christ.

d 9:5 The Greek word used for "torment" (*basanizo*) is derived from the word *touchstone,* or "to examine and test" (the purity of gold and silver). Our thoughts must be examined and made pure in the truth of our sonship and identity before God, which gives us power over the "locusts" that sting like scorpions (demonic power).

e 9:6 As believers, we don't seek to die, for we have already been crucified with Christ (Gal. 2:20). This is difficult to interpret literally. How strange it would be if those with mangled bodies still lived after trying to kill themselves. This is a picture of believers who try to put themselves to death, not recognizing that God has done so already through our co-crucifixion with Christ. Many today still suffer the sting of a scorpion (erroneous concepts of God and tormenting thoughts of self-hatred) until they see the glory of Christ's empty tomb and the resurrection life that is available to us.

f 9:7 These are not literal horses wearing literal crowns. The words *like, as,* and *appearing as* are found nine times in the Greek text in vv. 7–8. They come appearing as battle horses to intimidate with counterfeit crowns, looking like they are on a mission from God, but they are not genuine. They have what appears to be human faces, pointing to the fact that they are false teachers and false apostles with their fake crowns of gold. With hair like that of women and teeth like those of a lion, they will seduce and tear apart those who come into their religious bondage.

like the noise of horses and chariots rushing into battle. [10] They had tails[a] and stingers like scorpions, with power to injure people for five months. [b] [11] The angel of the bottomless pit was king over them, and his name in Hebrew is Destruction[c] and in Greek Destroyer. [d] [12] This is but the first woe; there are still two more to come.

The Sixth Trumpet

[13] Then the sixth angel sounded his trumpet, and I heard a voice from the four horns of the golden altar before God, [14] responding to the sixth angel, who blew his trumpet, "Set free the four angels who are confined at the great river Euphrates."[e]

[15] So the four angels were released, who had been prepared for the right hour, day, month, and year, to kill a third of humanity. [16] I heard the number of soldiers on horseback—it was twice ten thousand times ten thousand.[f] [17] And in my vision I saw the horses with riders wearing breastplates of fire and of sapphire[g] and of sulfur. [h] The horses had lions' heads breathing out fire and smoke and sulfur. [18] They killed a third of humanity by these three plagues—the fire, the smoke, and the sulfur that came from their mouths.[i] [19] For the lethal power of the horses was in their mouths and their tails, and their tails had snakes' heads that inflict injuries.

---

a 9:10 See Isa. 9:14–15. The tail is a symbol of false teaching, the lies of the enemy.
b 9:10 The life span of a locust in the region of Israel is about five months. And there are five months from the last day of Passover to the first day of the Feast of Tabernacles. Noah's ark floated upon the floodwaters for five months.
c 9:11 Or "Abaddon," which means "destruction."
d 9:11 Or "Apollyon," which means "destroyer." The Aramaic has "in Hebrew, 'Servant,' and in Aramaic, 'Prince.'" The devil holds no keys, for Christ has destroyed the works of the devil and holds the keys of every realm, including death and hell. Christ is the "angel" referred to in this passage. Notice the work of Christ to "destroy" in the following Scriptures: 1 Cor. 1:18–19; 15:25–26; 2 Thess. 2:3–8; Heb. 2:14; 1 John 3:8; Rev. 11:18; 20:1–3.
e 9:14 "The great river Euphrates" is referred to over and over in Scripture as the boundary of Israel's inheritance (Gen. 15:18; Josh. 1:4; 1 Kings 4:21). It becomes a symbol for us of the boundary of our spiritual inheritance, that which separates our "promised land" and religious "Babylon." Many believers are "bound" at the boundary and living in less than what they are called to, but they will be loosed in the last days to enter their full inheritance (Eph. 1:10–11).
f 9:16 Or "two myriads of myriads," a symbolic number, an incalculable number of enormous proportions. The Aramaic and some Greek manuscripts have "twice ten thousand" or "twenty thousand." It is clear by reading vv. 14–16 that the four messengers become the myriad of horsemen. They are the overcoming ones who are ready to wage war for the Lamb. The locust army and the army of horsemen are two armies facing each other and both are prepared for battle. See Joel 1:4; 2:1–3, 11.
g 9:17 Or "hyacinth."
h 9:17 The Greek word for "sulfur," theiōdēs, comes from the word theios, which means "divine in character" or "godlike." The verb form of this word is theioo and means "to hallow," "to make divine," or "to dedicate to a god."
i 9:18 That is, their burning words carried great power and authority.

[20] Those not killed by these plagues did not repent of their deeds so that they would stop worshiping demons and idols of gold, silver, bronze, stone, and wood—blind and mute idols that have to be carried around.[a] [21] And they did not repent of their murders or their sorceries[b] or their thefts or their immorality.

The Rainbow Angel

10 Then I saw another extremely powerful angel coming out of heaven, robed in a cloud. There was *a halo* over his head like a rainbow;[c] his face *shined bright* like the sun, and his legs like pillars of fire.[d] [2] He held a little opened scroll in his hand. He set his right foot on the sea and his left foot on the land [3] and gave a tremendous shout, like a lion's roar. When he shouted, the seven thunders responded, rumbling out *their messages*.[e] [4] I was about to write the messages of the seven thunders, but I heard a heavenly voice[f] say to me:

> Don't write a word, but place a seal on what the seven thunders have spoken.

[5] Then the mighty angel whom I saw astride the sea and the land raised his right hand to heaven [6] and swore an oath by him who lives for an eternity of eternities, the Creator of heaven and earth and sea and all that is in them:

> No more delay![g] [7] For in the day when the seventh angel is to sound his trumpet, the mystery of God will be fulfilled,[h] just as he announced to his servants the prophets.

John Eats the Scroll

[8] Then the heavenly voice spoke to me again:

> Go, take the open scroll from the hand of the angel who is standing on the sea and on the land.

[9] I went up to the angel who stood on the sea and the land and told him to

---

a 9:20 Or "cannot walk about."

b 9:21 The Greek word *pharmakeia* implies drug usage.

c 10:1 The Aramaic can be translated "a rainbow of heaven was over his head."

d 10:1 This extremely powerful messenger is Christ (Dan. 10:5–6; Rev. 1:12–16). He holds the scroll (Rev. 5–8) and now gives it to John. He is like the roaring Lion of Judah (Isa. 31:4–5; Jer. 25:29–36; Hos. 11:10–11; Joel 3:16; Amos 3:8) and will give the two witnesses their power (Rev. 11:3).

e 10:3 Or "with their own voices." See Ps. 29. The seven thunders are the complete message of God sent out by the seven Spirits of God.

f 10:4 The Aramaic can be translated "I heard a voice from the seventh heaven."

g 10:6 Or "You will not have to wait any longer" or "Time's up!"

h 10:7 Or "accomplished." The mystery of God is a description of the whole content of the book of Revelation.

give me the little scroll. Then he said to me, "Take it, and eat it. It will be sour in your stomach[a] but sweet as honey in your mouth."

[10] I took the little scroll from the hand of the mighty angel and ate it. Indeed, it was sweet as honey to taste,[b] but after I had eaten it, my stomach turned bitter.

[11] Then they[c] said to me, "You must *go back and* prophesy again to many peoples, and nations, and languages, and kings!"[d]

Measuring the Temple

11 Then a measuring rod, like a staff, was given to me and I was told:

Rise and measure God's temple[e] and the altar and count those who worship in it. [2] But exclude the courtyard outside the temple, for it has been given over to the nations, and for forty-two months[f] they will trample on the holy city. [3] And I will authorize my two witnesses to prophesy, wearing sackcloth for one thousand two hundred and sixty days.[g]

The Two Witnesses

[4] These *two witnesses*[h] are the two olive trees and the two lampstands that stand before the Lord God of the whole earth. [5] If anyone attempts to harm them, fire will flow out of their mouths and consume their foes. All who seek to harm them will die in this way. [6] They have authority to shut the heavens so that no rain will fall during the days of their prophesying. They have authority over the waters to turn them into blood and to strike the earth with every plague imaginable, as often as they desire.

[7] When their testimony is completed, the beast that comes up from the sea[i] will wage war against them and conquer them and kill them. [8] Their dead

---

a 10:9 Or "innermost being" or "womb." The message of the unrolled scroll would be bittersweet.

b 10:10 Honey is a picture of revelation-knowledge (Ps. 19:7–13). See also Ezek. 2:8–9; 3:1–3.

c 10:11 Some Greek manuscripts read "he."

d 10:11 See Jer. 1:10. This was an encouragement to John that he would be freed from his exile on Patmos to yet prophesy to us today through his writings.

e 11:1 The church is God's temple, his dwelling place. Presumably, when John wrote this there was no longer a temple standing in Jerusalem. But if John wrote this book earlier, during the time of Nero, it would point to the events of AD 67–70 during the Roman war, which lasted three and a half years.

f 11:2 This was the length of Jesus' earthly ministry.

g 11:3 That is, three and a half years, or forty-two months.

h 11:4 See Zech. 4. The two witnesses are interpreted by some scholars to be symbols of the Word and the Spirit. Some see the two olive trees as the Law and the Prophets or Moses and Elijah; others view them as believing Jews and gentiles.

i 11:7 As translated from the Aramaic. The Greek is "the beast that ascends from the abyss."

bodies will lie on the street[a] of the great city that is symbolically[b] called Sodom and Egypt,[c] where their Lord was also crucified. [9] For three and a half days people from every ethnicity, tribe, nation, and language will see their corpses, because no one is permitted to bury them. [10] The entire world will gloat over them and celebrate and exchange gifts, because these two prophets had condemned[d] those who dwell on the earth.

[11] After three and a half days God's breath of life[e] entered them and they stood to their feet, terrifying all who saw them.[f] [12] Then they heard a loud shout from heaven saying to them:

Come up here!

The two prophets climbed up into heaven in a cloud while their enemies watched. [13] At that very moment there was a powerful earthquake and a tenth of the city collapsed, killing seven thousand people. The rest were terrified and gave glory to the God of heaven.

[14] Now the second woe has passed and the third is coming swiftly.

The Seventh Trumpet

[15] Then the seventh angel sounded his trumpet, and a loud voice broke forth in heaven, saying:

"The kingdom of the world[g]
    has become the kingdom of our God[h]
    and of his Anointed One![i]
He will reign supreme for an eternity of eternities!"

[16] Then the twenty-four elders who sit on their thrones before God fell facedown before him and worshiped him, [17] saying:

"We give thanks to you, Lord God Almighty,
    who is, and who was,
    because you have established[j]
    your great *and limitless* power and begun to reign!

---

a 11:8 Or "plaza."
b 11:8 Or "spiritually."
c 11:8 This is viewed as the great city of Jerusalem, where our Lord was crucified, symbolically called Sodom (Isa. 1:9–26) and Egypt. It can also represent the corrupt religious systems of the world.
d 11:10 Or "tormented."
e 11:11 Or "spirit of lives."
f 11:11 The Aramaic can be translated "total paralysis fell on those who saw them."
g 11:15 That is, the kingdom of finance, culture, and government, both religious and secular.
h 11:15 As translated from the Aramaic. The Greek is "the kingdom of our Lord."
i 11:15 Or "Christ" (or "Messiah").
j 11:17 As translated from the Aramaic. The Greek is "you have taken your great power."

[18] The nations were furious, and you became furious, [a]
and the time for judging the dead has come.
The time has come to reward your servants, the prophets
and the holy ones and all who reverence your name,
both small and great. [b]
And the time has come to destroy those
who corrupt [c] the earth!"

[19] Then God's temple was opened in heaven and the ark of his covenant was *clearly* visible inside his temple. And there were blinding flashes of lightning, voices roaring, startling thunderclaps, a massive earthquake, and a great hailstorm! [d]

The Woman Clothed with the Sun

12 Then an astonishing miracle-sign appeared in heaven. *I saw* a woman [e] clothed with *the brilliance of* the sun, and the moon was under her feet. She was wearing on her head a victor's crown of twelve stars. [2] She was pregnant and was crying out in labor pains, in the agony of giving birth.

[3] *Consider this*: another astonishing miracle-sign appeared in heaven! I saw a huge, fiery-red dragon with ten horns and seven heads, [f] each wearing a royal crown. He was wearing seven royal crowns. [4] The dragon's *massive* tail [g] swept across the sky and dragged away a third of the stars of heaven and cast them to the earth. And the dragon crouched before the woman who was about to give birth—poised to devour the baby the moment it was born.

[5] She gave birth to a man-child who is about to rule and shepherd every nation with an iron scepter, [h] and her son was caught up to God and to his throne. [6] The woman fled into the wilderness, where God had already prepared a *safe* place for her, and there they nourished her for one thousand two hundred and sixty days.

---

a 11:18 Or "and your wrath has come."
b 11:18 The Aramaic can be translated "lords of plenty."
c 11:18 Or "deprave" or "destroy."
d 11:19 Or "heavy hailstones."
e 12:1 The church is figuratively spoken of as a woman. The description of her "clothed with . . . the sun, and the moon [powers of darkness] . . . under her feet" points to the victorious church about to give birth to a company of believers who will do the great works of Jesus and spread the brilliance of his glory throughout the earth. The overcoming bride of Christ is also seen as a woman "clothed with the sun." See Gen. 37:9–10; Song. 6:10.
f 12:3 See Dan. 7:7. A reference symbolizing the ferocious, cruel, and wicked power of the devil.
g 12:4 See Isa. 9:15.
h 12:5 See Pss. 2:8–9; 110:1–2.

The Dragon Defeated

[7] Then a terrible war broke out in heaven. Michael[a] and his angels fought against the great dragon. The dragon and his angels fought back. [8] But the dragon did not have the power to win and they could not regain their place in heaven. [9] So the great dragon was thrown down once and for all. He was the serpent, the ancient snake called the devil,[b] and Satan,[c] who deceives the whole earth. He was cast down into the earth and his angels along with him.

[10] Then I heard a triumphant voice in heaven proclaiming:

"Now salvation and power are set in place,
  and the kingdom reign of our God
  and the ruling authority of his Anointed One
  are established.
For the accuser of our brothers and sisters,
  who *relentlessly* accused them
  day and night before our God,
  has now been *defeated*—cast out once and for all!
[11] They conquered him completely
  through the blood of the Lamb
  and the powerful word of his testimony.[d]
They triumphed because they did not love and cling
  to their own lives, even when faced with death.
[12] So rejoice, you heavens,
  and every heavenly being!
But woe to the earth and the sea,
  for the devil has come down to you
  with great fury, because he knows
  his time is short."

The Dragon Fights the Woman

[13] Now, when the dragon realized that he had been cast down to the earth, he set off in pursuit of the woman who had given birth to the man-child.[e] [14] But the two wings of the great eagle were given to the woman so that she could fly and escape into the wilderness to her own special place, where she was nourished for a time, and times, and half a time, away from the face of the dragon.

  [15] Then the dragon spewed from his mouth a *raging* river of water to sweep

---

a 12:7 The name Michael means "one who is like God."
b 12:9 Or "lying slanderer."
c 12:9 Or "Adversary."
d 12:11 As translated from the Aramaic. The Greek is "the word of their testimony." It is the faithful testimony of Jesus that has the power to destroy the works of the devil.
e 12:13 The man-child is a company of believers who have overcome the dragon. They are the symbolic 144,000 victorious ones. See Rom. 8:17; 1 Cor. 4:8; 6:2; 2 Tim. 2:12.

her away with the flood. ¹⁶But the earth came to the rescue of the woman and at once opened its mouth and swallowed the river that the dragon had poured from his mouth.

¹⁷Then the dragon became enraged at the woman and went off to make war[a] against the remnant of her offspring who follow the commands of God and have the testimony of Jesus.[b] ¹⁸And the dragon stood[c] on the sand of the seashore.

The Beast Out of the Sea

13 Then I saw a wild beast[d] rising from the sea with ten horns and seven heads. On its horns were ten royal crowns, and on its heads were blasphemous names. ²It was like a leopard with feet like a bear's,[e] and its mouth like the mouth of a lion. The dragon shared his power, throne, and great authority with the wild beast.

³One of the heads of the wild beast seemed to have received a deathly wound, but the wound had been healed. After this, the whole world was filled with fascination and followed the wild beast. ⁴They worshiped the dragon because he had given the beast its ruling authority. They also worshiped the wild beast, saying, "Who is like the wild beast? And who is able to make war against him?"

⁵The wild beast was given a mouth to speak boastful and blasphemous words, and he was permitted to exercise authority for forty-two months. ⁶So the wild beast began to blaspheme against God, blaspheming his *holy* name and his dwelling place;[f] that is, those who dwell in heaven.[g] ⁷The beast was given the authority to wage war against the holy believers.[h] And he was given authority over every tribe, people, language, and nation. ⁸Everyone on earth will worship the wild beast—those who names have not been written from the foundation[i] of the world in the Book of Life of the Lamb who was slain.[j]

---

a 12:17 See Eph. 6:10–12.

b 12:17 That is, they have the character and nature of Jesus. It is the power of the faithful testimony of Jesus (not ours) that has power to overcome the devil.

c 12:18 Or "And I stood."

d 13:1 The word beast (*therion*) is also used in the Bible for an evil person or in describing the sinful nature of man. See Eccl. 3:18; Pss. 22:12–13; 73:22; 1 Cor. 15:22. *Therion* is found extensively in classical Greek describing wicked or pathetic people. Plato (*Phaedrus*, 204b) applies it to people: "A flatterer is a horrid creature [*therion*] who does great harm." See also Aristophanes, *Clouds*, 184.

e 13:2 The Aramaic can be translated either a "wolf" or a "bear."

f 13:6 Or "tabernacle."

g 13:6 Or "those who continually tabernacle in heaven."

h 13:7 Some manuscripts add "and conquered them."

i 13:8 The Greek word for "foundation," *katabole*, can also mean "overthrow" or "cast down," which would be a reference to the "fall" of man.

j 13:8 Or "those whose names were not written in the Lamb's Book of Life, who was slain from the foundation of the world."

⁹ If anyone has been given ears to hear, he'd better listen! ¹⁰ For the one who leads *others* into captivity, into captivity he goes. The one who kills *others* by the sword, by the sword he will be put to death. *ᵃ* This is a call for the endurance and faithfulness of the holy believers.

The Beast from the Earth

¹¹ Then I saw another wild beast coming up from the ground. It had two horns like a ram, *ᵇ* but it spoke like the dragon. ¹² It operated in all the authority of the first beast on its behalf, causing the earth and its inhabitants to worship the first beast, whose mortal wound had been healed. ¹³ It performed great miracle-signs, even publicly causing fire to fall out of heaven to the earth. ¹⁴ And through these startling miracles that he performed on behalf of the first beast, he deceived the world, telling the people to erect a statue in the image of the beast that had been wounded by the sword and yet lived. ¹⁵ The beast from the earth was empowered to breathe life *ᶜ* into the image of the first beast so that it could speak and kill those who refused to worship its image. ¹⁶ It also caused everyone, small and great, rich and poor, free and bound, to be marked *ᵈ* on the right hand or on the forehead. ¹⁷ This meant no one could buy or sell unless they had the mark; that is, the name of the beast or its number.

¹⁸ This will require wisdom to understand: Let the one with insight interpret the number of the wild beast, for it is humanity's number *ᵉ*—666.

The Lamb and His 144,000

14 Then I looked, and behold—there was the Lamb *ᶠ* standing on Mount Zion. *ᵍ* Gathered with him were 144,000 who had his name and his

---

a 13:10 This is one of the more difficult verses in Revelation to translate and interpret, with many variations found in differing manuscripts. It could also be translated "If anyone is destined for captivity, into captivity he goes. If anyone is destined to be killed by the sword, by the sword he will be killed." See also Jer. 15:2.

b 13:11 Or "lamb."

c 13:15 Or "spirit."

d 13:16 The Greek word used here for "marked" (or "engraved") is same root word from which we get the word *character*. The character of the beast is now upon the people.

e 13:18 Or "man's number." The Aramaic can be translated "the son of Adam's number." There is no reference to the Antichrist in the book of Revelation. The beast is equated to the nature of humanity. The number 666 is the number of man; not an incarnation of the devil, but human nature. The number six is always equated with man, for man was created on the sixth day. The wild beast rising out of the ground (which man was made from) is the sin of man that wars against our souls and prevents the image of Christ from emerging in fullness within believers. The number 666 cannot be literal, for a literal number would need no wisdom to interpret. Both the mark of the beast and the mark on the foreheads of God's faithful followers is a metaphor of the character of the beast revealed by thoughts (foreheads) and by actions (the hands).

f 14:1 Nothing but the Lamb must draw our attention when we gaze into the heavenly realm.

g 14:1 Mount Zion is not merely a place, but a realm where God's people are clothed with

Father's name written on their foreheads. ²And I heard a tremendous sound coming out of heaven, like the roar of a waterfall and like the earsplitting sound of a thunderclap. The sound *of music* that I heard was like the sound of many harpists playing their harps. ³And they were singing a *wonderful* new song before the throne, in front of the four living creatures, and in front of the *twenty-four* elders.

⁴No one could learn that song except the 144,000 who had been redeemed free from the earth. These are the ones who have not defiled themselves with women, ͣ for they are virgins, ͨ and they join themselves to the Lamb wherever he goes. They have been *redeemed,* purchased from humanity and brought forth as the firstfruits ͨ for God and the Lamb. ⁵Their words are always true; ͩ they are without flaw. ͤ

The Message of the Three Angels

⁶Then I witnessed another angel flying in the sky, carrying a message of eternal good news ͤ to announce to the earth—to every tribe, language, people, and nation. ⁷With a loud voice he shouted, "You must reverence God and glorify him, for the time has come for him to judge. ⁸ Worship at the feet of the Creator of heaven, earth, sea, and springs of water."

⁸Then a second angel followed, declaring, "She fell! She fell! Babylon the great is fallen! She once seduced the nations and made them all drink the wine of the passion of her harlotry!" ͪ

⁹Then a third angel followed them, shouting with a mighty voice, "Whoever worships the wild beast and its image, and receives a mark on his forehead or on his hand, ¹⁰will also drink the wine of God's wrath. This wine has been poured out ͥ and mixed in the cup of his indignation. They will be tormented ͪ

---

glory and beauty. See Pss. 2:6; 50:2; 87:5; 110:2; Heb. 12:22.

a 14:4 These women become a metaphor for the daughters of the harlot of Babylon, with its false religious system (Rev. 17:5).

b 14:4 See 2 Cor. 11:2. Like Mary the virgin, these are pure, obedient, and willing to do the will of God and will bring forth an expression of Christ to the earth.

c 14:4 That is, they are the first parts of the harvest of Christ's life within the believer. Set apart for God and the Lamb, they become examples for all others to follow.

d 14:5 Or "Falsehood was not found in their mouths."

e 14:5 See Song. 4:7.

f 14:6 Or "having a message of goodness for eternal ages." The Aramaic can be translated "carrying a message with blood, for he had the everlasting good news to proclaim."

g 14:7 Or "the time of his deciding came."

h 14:8 As translated from the Aramaic. The Greek is "immorality," which becomes a metaphor for idolatry. See also Isa. 21:9, where the reference is to Babylon's idolatry.

i 14:10 Or "undiluted."

j 14:10 Although the Greek word *basanizō* can be translated "tormented" (tortured), its primary meaning is "to test," "to scrutinize with the touchstone," "to examine or test its mettle" and is used for testing the purity of gold or silver.

with sulfur[a] and fire in the presence of holy angels and of the Lamb. [11]And the smoke of their severe suffering ascends into ages upon ages. Those who worship the wild beast and its image and receive the mark of its name will have no rest day or night." [12]This is a call for the endurance and faithfulness of the holy believers—those who follow God's commands and cling to the faith of Jesus.

[13]Then I heard a voice from the heavenly realm, saying, "Write this: Blessed are the dead—the ones dying in the Lord[b] from now on."

"Yes," says the Holy Spirit,[c] "they will rest from their trouble,[d] for their deeds will live on!"[e]

The Harvest of the Earth

[14]I looked and behold—I saw a white cloud, and sitting upon it was one like the Son of Man, wearing a golden crown and holding a sharp sickle. [15]Another angel came out of the temple, shouting out to the one sitting upon the cloud, "Take your sickle and reap, for the time of reaping the harvest has come and the harvest of the earth is ripe!" [16]So the one sitting upon the white cloud gave his sickle a mighty swing over the earth and reaped its harvest.

[17]Then another angel came out of the heavenly temple, and he too had a sharp sickle. [18]And another angel came out from the altar *of incense*—the angel with authority over fire. He shouted out with a loud voice to the one who had the sharp sickle, saying, "Take now your sharp sickle and harvest the clusters of the vine of the earth, for its grapes are ripe."

[19]So the angel gave his sickle a mighty swing over the earth and gathered the grapes from the vine of the earth and threw them into the great winepress of the wrath[f] of God. [20]And the winepress was trodden outside the city[g] until blood poured out of the winepress as high as the horse's bridle[h] for a distance of one thousand six hundred stadia.[i]

---

a   14:10 The Greek word for sulfur, *theion*, comes from the word *theios*, which means "divine in character" or "godlike," and is believed to originate from a word meaning "flashing" (like the flashing of burning incense). An alternate translation of this could be "in union with divine qualities and with fire."

b   14:13 The Aramaic can be translated "Master Yahweh."

c   14:13 The Holy Spirit speaks twelve times in Revelation (1:10; 2:7, 11, 17, 29; 3:6, 13, 22; 4:2; 14:13; 17:3; 21:10; 22:17).

d   14:13 Or "hard work."

e   14:13 Or "Their good deeds will follow [accompany] them."

f   14:19 Or "strong passion."

g   14:20 That is, the New Jerusalem.

h   14:20 This would be about five feet high.

i   14:20 There is variation over the exact measurement of a "stade." Some calculate it to be about 600 feet, which would make it over 180 miles. But in the Aramaic, a stadia (race track) is measured at about 1/8 of a mile, which would make nearly 140 miles. It is impossible to view this as literal, for that much blood of human beings would be over ten thousand times the population of earth. The number forty is the number of testing/trial and 1,600 is forty

The Song of Moses and of the Lamb

15 Then I witnessed another great and astonishing sign in heaven: seven angels bringing the last seven plagues, for with them the wrath[a] of God is finished.

[2] Then I saw what looked like a vast sea of glass blended with fiery flames. Standing beside the sea were those who continually conquer the wild beast, his image and the number of his name.[b] [3] They each held the harps of God and they were singing the song of Moses, God's servant, and the song of the Lamb:[c]

"Mighty and marvelous are your miracles,
　　Lord Yahweh, God Almighty![d]
Righteous and true are your ways,
　　O Sovereign King of the ages![e]
[4] Who will not reverence you with awe, O Lord,
　　and bring glory to your name?
For you alone are holy,
　　and all nations will come
　　and bow in worship before you,
　　as your blessings have revealed."[f]

Seven Angels

[5] After these things I looked, and behold, the inner sanctuary of the heavenly "tabernacle of testimony"[g] was opened before my eyes. [6] The seven angels with

---

squared. It becomes a picture of severe testing, even to the point of blood, for the people of God.

a 15:1 Or "strong passion." See also Mic. 7:18.

b 15:2 All those who are one day victorious over the "beast" will learn to sing this eternal song of thanksgiving and praise. The "beast" is our self-life (Ps. 73:22). We are called to overcome this beast through the life of Jesus within us. As we overcome by the power of the cross and borrow the life of Christ for ourselves, we qualify as overcomers who sing the sacred song of Moses. All that is of the beast must be laid aside as we take up the Christ nature and live in his strength. He can change each of us from a beast to a lamb (Isa. 11:6–10; Phil. 3:21; Rev. 12:11).

c 15:3 The song of Moses was sung in a victory celebration of Israel's deliverance from Egypt (Ex. 15); the song of the Lamb is sung in a victory celebration of believers who conquered the beast (the nature of man).

d 15:3 As translated from the Aramaic.

e 15:3 Some manuscripts have "King of the nations." The Aramaic can be translated "King of the universe."

f 15:4 As translated from the Aramaic. The Greek is "for your righteous works [judgments] are revealed."

g 15:5 Or "tent of witness." This phrase is found 130 times from Exodus through Deuteronomy and refers to the innermost place of the tabernacle (holy of holies) where God's testimony (the Ten Commandments) was kept inside the ark of glory.

the seven last plagues came out of the sanctuary in glistening robes of bright linen and golden sashes around their chests.[a]

[7] Then one of the four living creatures gave each of the seven angels a golden bowl full of the wrath[b] of God, who lives forever and ever. [8] The sanctuary was filled with the thick cloud of smoke[c] billowing out from the glory and power of God—and no one could even enter the sanctuary[d] until the seven plagues of the seven angels were completed.

Seven Bowls Are Poured Out

16 Then I heard a loud voice from within the sanctuary telling the seven angels, "Go and pour out on the earth the seven bowls of the wrath[e] of God."

[2] So the first angel poured his bowl upon the earth, causing ugly and painful sores to break out on the people who had the mark of the wild beast and worshiped his image.

[3] Then the second angel poured his bowl into the sea, and it became like the blood of the dead—every living thing in the sea died.

[4] The third angel poured his bowl into the rivers and springs of water, and they became blood. And I heard the angel of the waters say:

[5] "O holy One, who are and were, you are righteous,
　　for you have judged these things,[f]
[6] because they shed the blood of your saints and prophets.
　　They got what they deserved,
　　for you gave them blood to drink!"
[7] Then I heard *a voice from before* the altar reply:
　　"Yes, O Lord God, the Almighty!
　　Every judicial verdict you make is just and right."

[8] Then the fourth angel poured out his bowl on the sun, and it began to burn the people with a scorching heat. [9] Though they endured the fierce heat, yet the people continued to blaspheme God. They cursed the name of God, who had authority over these plagues, and refused to repent and give him glory.

[10] The fifth angel poured his bowl on the throne of the wild beast, and its kingdom was plunged into darkness. People were in agony and gnawed their

---

a 15:6 Or "across their chests." Just as we will be clothed in the garments of our High Priest, these seven messengers are robed in pure garments and free from corruption.
b 15:7 Both the Greek and the Aramaic can be translated "the strong passion of God."
c 15:8 The Aramaic can be translated "incense."
d 15:8 See Ex. 40:34–35; 1 Kings 8:10–11. The Aramaic can be translated "no one was able to depart the sanctuary."
e 16:1 The Aramaic word can be translated "passion."
f 16:5 Or "because you have passed these judgments."

tongues [11] and cursed the God of heaven because of their painful sores,[a] refusing to repent of their deeds.

[12] The sixth angel poured his bowl on "the good and abounding river,"[b] and it completely dried up in order to prepare the way for the kings of the east.[c] [13] Then I saw three unclean spirits like frogs belched from the mouths of the dragon, the wild beast, and the false prophet. [14] They were demonic spirits[d] performing signs, and they entered into the kings of the world to draw them into battle on the great day of God, the Almighty.

[15] "Behold, I come[e] like a thief! God's blessing is with the one who remains awake and fully clothed *in me* and will not walk about naked, exposed to disgrace."

[16] The demonic spirits assembled the kings together at the place called in Hebrew the "Mount of the Governor."[f]

[17] The seventh angel poured out his bowl into the air, and a loud voice came out from the temple and from the throne, saying:

"Here it comes!"[g]

[18] Then there were flashes of lightning, voices, crashes of thunder, and a massive earthquake—the most severe to shake the earth since the creation of man, so tremendous was that earthquake! [19] It split the great city *Babylon* into three parts, and other cities of the nations collapsed. For God remembered great Babylon and her winecup filled with his fiery wrath. [20] Every island fled away and the mountains were no more. [21] Enormous hailstones, each weighing nearly one hundred pounds,[h] fell from the sky and struck the people, yet they continued to curse God because of the horrendous plague of hail.

The Judgment of the Harlot, Babylon

17 Then one of the seven angels with the seven bowls approached me and said, "Come, and I will show you the judgment of the great prostitute who sits *enthroned* on many waters. [2] The kings of the earth have fornicated with her, and the people of earth are drunk on the wine of her prostitution."[i]

---

a 16:11 Or "because of their pains and sores."

b 16:12 Or "Euphrates," which means "the good and abounding river."

c 16:12 Or "for the kings from the rising of the sun."

d 16:14 Or "demon-gods."

e 16:15 Or "continually [repeatedly] come."

f 16:16 Or "Armageddon." The Greek word for "Armageddon" comes from the word *meged*, which can be translated "precious fruit," "excellent," "choice things," "pleasant things." Armegeddon can also be viewed as a realm where both good and evil is gathered together. The battle on God's great day includes the war within the hearts of mankind.

g 16:17 Or "It has come to be" as in "to give birth." The Greek word is *ginomai* (similar to our English word *genome*) and is translated three times in Rom. 7:3-4 as "married."

h 16:21 Or "weighing about a talent." A talent was a monetary measure of gold, silver, or brass, believed to weigh about ninety-five pounds.

i 17:2 A metaphor for idolatry. See Isa. 1:21.

³ Then the angel carried me away in the Spirit into a wilderness, and I saw a woman sitting on a wild, bloodred beast with seven heads and ten horns, and it was covered with blasphemous names. ⁴ The woman was robed in purple and scarlet and was glittering with gold, precious stones, and pearls. She was holding in her hand a golden chalice brimming full with defiling obscenities and the filth of her lewdness. ᵈ ⁵ On her forehead was written these mysterious titles: "The great Babylon, mother of prostitutes and of the abominations of the earth."

⁶ I saw the woman was drunk with the blood of God's holy believers— drunk on the blood of the loyal martyrs of Jesus. And when I saw her, I was utterly astonished!

The Interpretation of John's Vision

⁷ But the angel said to me, "Why are you so astonished? I will reveal to you the mystery of the woman, and of the wild beast with seven heads and ten horns that carries her. ⁸ The wild beast you saw once was, now is not, and is destined to ascend out of the deep and go to destruction. All those whose names have not been written in the Book of Life from the foundation of the world will be utterly astonished when they see the wild beast because he once was, now is not, and is about to rise.

⁹ "This requires a mind that has wisdom to interpret: The seven heads of the beast are seven mountains the woman sits upon; they are also seven kings. ¹⁰ Five kings have fallen, one is, ᵇ and the other has not yet come—and when he comes he must remain only a little while. ᶜ ¹¹ The wild beast ᵈ that was but now is not represents an eighth king who is from one of the seven, and he is going to destruction.

¹² "The ten horns that you saw represent ten kings who have not yet received a kingdom, ᵉ but they and the wild beast are destined to receive authority as kings for a short reign of one hour. ¹³ They are united in yielding their power and authority to the wild beast. ¹⁴ They will wage war against the Lamb, but the Lamb will conquer them, for he is Lord of lords and King of kings! Those who are with him will also conquer them, and they are called 'chosen ones' and 'faithful ones.'"

¹⁵ And he said to me, "The waters that you saw, upon which the great prostitute is seated, represent peoples, multitudes, nations, and languages. ¹⁶ The ten horns and the wild beast will hate the great prostitute and will make her a ruin. They will reduce her to nakedness, and they will devour her flesh and

---

a 17:4 See Jer. 51:7.
b 17:10 Scholars who believe in an earlier date of Revelation see these as the emperors of Rome, for Nero (the one who now "is") was Rome's sixth Caesar of Rome (AD 54–68).
c 17:10 The Aramaic can be translated "he will have little desire to rule."
d 17:11 The Aramaic can be translated "the dragon and the wild beast it brought."
e 17:12 Or "royal power."

burn her up with fire. ¹⁷For God has put it in their hearts to carry out his purpose for her by agreeing to give their kingdom*ᵃ* to the wild beast until the words of God are fulfilled. ¹⁸As for the woman you saw, she is the great city *Babylon*, which rules*ᵇ* over the kings of the earth."

The Destruction of Babylon

18 After these things, I saw another angel coming from the heavenly realm with great authority, and the earth was flooded with the brilliance of his splendor. ²He shouted out with a thunderous voice:

> "Fallen, fallen is Babylon the great!
> She has become a demonic dwelling place,
> a prison for every unclean spirit, unclean bird,
> and every unclean, detestable beast.*ᶜ*
> ³All the nations have drunk*ᵈ*
> of the wine of her immoral passion,
> and the kings of the earth
> have committed fornication*ᵉ* with her,
> and merchants of the earth have grown wealthy
> because of her power and luxury."

⁴Then I heard another voice from heaven saying:

> "My people, come out from her
> so that you don't participate in her sins
> and have no share with her in her plagues,
> ⁵because her sins are heaped as high as heaven*ᶠ*
> and God has remembered her vileness.*ᵍ*
> ⁶So repay to her double the same treatment
> that she has treated others with—
> pay her back double for all her deeds
> and make her drink twice the brew she gave to others!*ʰ*
> ⁷With the same measure she exalted herself
> and lived luxuriously,
> give her that measure of torment and grief,
> because she said in her heart,

---

a 17:17 Or "their royal power."
b 17:18 Or "has royal dominion [sovereignty] over."
c 18:2 See Isa. 13:21; 34:11.
d 18:3 Or "have fallen because of the wine of her wrath."
e 18:3 A metaphor for idolatry.
f 18:5 Or "her sins have touched the heaven."
g 18:5 Or "iniquities."
h 18:6 Or "Mix a double amount for her in the cup she mixed."

'I am no widow; I rule as a queen!
I will never experience grief.'
[8] Therefore, her plagues will fall on her in one day—
disease, famine and mourning.
She will be burned with fire.
For mighty is the Lord God who judges her!"

[9] The kings of the earth who fornicated with her and lived in luxury with her will weep and wail over her when they see the smoke of the fire that burns her up. [10] And they will stand far off, in fear of her torment, saying:

"Oh no! *You who were once*
the great and powerful city Babylon,
now in one hour your complete devastation has come!"

[11] The earth's merchants weep and mourn for her because no one buys their merchandise[a] anymore: [12] their gold, silver, jewels, and pearls, their fine linen, purple cloth, silk, and scarlet cloth, all kinds of things made from expensive wood,[b] ivory, bronze, iron, and marble, [13] quantities of the finest cinnamon, spice, incense, frankincense, and myrrh, wine, olive oil, wheat, and the finest flour, sheep, cattle, horses, and their four-wheeled carriages, and the trafficking of the bodies and souls of people. [14] And they will say:

The splendid delicacies[c] for which your soul craved have departed from you. All your elegance and splendor have disappeared, never to be seen again.

[15] Those who sold these things and grew wealthy through their business with her will stand far off, terrified over her torment. They will weep and mourn, saying:

[16] "How horrible!
The great city that once clothed herself
with fine linen and purple and scarlet cloth
glittering with gold, with jewels and with pearls—
[17] in one brief moment such vast wealth is now laid waste!"

Every ship's captain and his crew, every seafarer and mariner, watched from far away [18] and cried out as they saw her go up in flames:

"What city was ever like the great city *Babylon*?"

---

a 18:11 Or "ship's cargo."
b 18:12 Or "citron wood."
c 18:14 Or "ripe fruit," a metaphor for life's delicacies.

¹⁹ *As a sign of their dismay,* they threw dust on their heads
and shouted with sobs and grief:
"How horrible, so horrible, O great city Babylon!
For in one moment you suffered such destruction—
you who once made the merchants on the sea
so very wealthy.
²⁰ Rejoice over her, O heaven
You apostles and prophets and holy believers, rejoice!
For on your behalf
God pronounced the judgment against her
that she wanted to bring upon you!

²¹ Then a mighty angel took up a stone, like a huge millstone, and threw it
into the sea, saying:

"With this kind of sudden violence, the great city Babylon
will be thrown down and exist no more.
²² The music of harps, minstrels, flutes, and trumpets *ᵃ*
will never grace your city again.
No artisan of any trade will ever be found in you again,
and the noise of factories *ᵇ* falls silent.
²³ The light of a lamp will never shine in you again,
Nor will the joyous laughter of a wedding *ᶜ* be heard in you.
Your merchants were once the tycoons of the world,
But you deceived all the nations by your sorcery. *ᵈ*
²⁴ For the bloodstains of the holy believers and the prophets
and all who were slaughtered were all over you!" *ᵉ*

Heaven Rejoices

19 After this I heard what seemed to be the roar of a great multitude of voices, saying:

"Hallelujah!
Salvation and glory and power to our God!
² All his judgments are right and true,
For he has judged the great prostitute

---

a 18:22 Or "the sound of harpists, minstrels, flutists, and trumpeters."
b 18:22 Or "the noise of a mill."
c 18:23 Or "the voice of bridegroom and bride."
d 18:23 Or "magic" (spells), which often involved drug usage.
e 18:24 Or "her."

who corrupted the earth with her sexual immorality.
He has avenged on her the blood of his *loving* servants."

³ And again they shouted:

"Hallelujah!
    The smoke from her *destruction* goes up
    forever and ever!"

⁴ The twenty-four elders and the four living creatures fell facedown and worshiped God, who sits on the throne, saying in *agreement*:

"Amen! Hallelujah!"

⁵ Then a voice came from the throne, saying:

"Praise our God, all you his *loving* servants
    and all who reverence and honor him—
    those who are lowly and those who are great!"

⁶ Then I heard what seemed to be the thunderous voice of a great multitude, like the sound of a massive waterfall and mighty peals of thunder, crying out:

"Hallelujah!
    For the Lord our God, the Almighty, reigns!ᵃ
⁷ Let us rejoice and exalt him and give him glory,
    because the wedding celebration of the Lamb has come.ᵇ
    And his bride has made herself ready.ᶜ
⁸ Fine linen, shining bright and clear,
    has been given to her to wear,
    and the fine linen represents
    the righteous deeds of his holy believers."ᵈ

⁹ Then the angel said to me, "Write these words: Wonderfully blessed are those who are invited to feast at the wedding celebration of the Lamb!" And then he said to me, "These are the true words of God."

¹⁰ At this I fell facedown at the angel's feet to worship him, but he stopped me and said, "Don't do this! For I am only a fellow servant with you and one of

---

a 19:6 The Aramaic adds a clause that is missing in the Greek: "the One and Only for all."
b 19:7 The imagery of the wedding celebration of the Lamb reinforces and expresses the beautiful intimacy that Jesus shares with his beloved bride. See Hos. 2:19; Eph. 5:26–27.
c 19:7 The Aramaic can be translated "And his bride loves him!"
d 19:8 The Aramaic can be translated "and the fine linens are the blessings of the holy ones."

your brothers and sisters who cling to what Jesus testifies. Worship God. The testimony of Jesus is the spirit of prophecy." [a]

The Bridegroom-King on the White Horse

[11] Then I saw heaven opened, and suddenly a white horse appeared. The name of the one riding it was Faithful and True, [b] and with pure righteousness he judges and rides to battle. [12] He wore many regal crowns, [c] and his eyes were flashing like flames of fire. He had a *secret* name inscribed on him that's known only to himself. [d] [13] He wore a robe dipped in blood, and his title is called the Word of God. [14] Following him on white horses were the armies of heaven, wearing white fine linen, pure and bright. [15] A sharp sword came from his mouth with which to conquer [e] the nations, and he will shepherd them with an iron scepter. [f] He will trample out the wine in the winepress of the wrath [g] of God. [16] On his robe and on his thigh he had inscribed a name: King of kings and Lord of lords.

The Wild Beast Defeated

[17] Then I saw an angel standing in the sun, shouting to all the flying birds of the sky, "Come and gather for God's great supper! [18] Come and devour the flesh of the kings, generals, and soldiers, the flesh of horses and their riders, the flesh of all people, slave or free, lowly or famous."

[19] Then I saw the wild beast and the kings of the earth with their armies gathered to wage war against the rider on the *white* horse and against his armies. [20] The wild beast was captured, as was the false prophet who had performed miracle-signs in his presence. (It was by these miracle-signs that he had deceived those with the mark of the wild beast and those who worshiped its image.) The wild beast and the false prophet were both thrown alive into the lake of fire burning with sulfur, [21] and their armies were killed by the sharp sword that came from the mouth of the rider on the *white* horse. And all the birds gorged themselves with their flesh.

Binding Satan

20 Then I saw a *mighty* angel descending from the heavenly realm, holding a heavy chain and a key—the key of the deep. [h] [2] He seized the dragon, that ancient serpent known as the devil and Satan, and bound him for a thousand

---

a 19:10 That is, the essence of prophecy.
b 19:11 See Rev. 1:5; 3:14.
c 19:12 Jesus has absolute sovereignty over every nation and every heart.
d 19:12 See Rev. 3:12.
e 19:15 Or "to strike down."
f 19:15 See Ps. 2:9; Rev. 2:27 and the first footnote; 12:5.
g 19:15 Or "strong passion."
h 20:1 Or "abyss."

years. [a] ³ The mighty angel threw him into the pit, locked it, and sealed it so that he could no longer deceive the nations until the thousand years were over. (After that he must be loosed for a brief time.)

⁴ Then I saw thrones, and those who sat on them were given the authority to judge. I also saw the souls of those who had been beheaded because of the testimony of Jesus and for the Word of God. They had refused to worship the wild beast or its image and did not have their foreheads or hands marked by the wild beast. They lived and reigned with the Christ for one thousand years. ⁵ This is the first resurrection. [b] (The rest of the dead did not come to life until the thousand years were ended.) ⁶ Wonderfully blessed and holy are those who share in the first resurrection! The second death holds no power over them, but they will be priests of God and of the Christ. And they will reign as kings with him [c] a thousand years!

The Final Destruction of Satan

⁷ After the thousand years are over, Satan will be let loose from his prison ⁸ and will go out and deceive the nations of the four corners of the earth, Gog and Magog. [d] He will bring them together for battle, and they will be as numerous as grains of sand on the seashore.

⁹ They spread out over the earth and surrounded the camp of God's holy believers and the beloved city. But fire came down from heaven and completely destroyed them. ¹⁰ Then the devil who had deceived them was thrown into the same place with the wild beast and the false prophet—the lake of fire and sulfur—where they will be tormented day and night forever and ever.

Judgment Day

¹¹ Then I saw a great, dazzling-white throne and the One who sits on it. Heaven and earth fled from his presence and they were no more. [e] ¹² I saw the dead, the lowly and the famous alike, standing before the throne. Books were opened, and then another book was opened: the Book of Life. The dead were judged by what they had done as recorded in the books. ¹³ And the sea gave up the dead *souls* that were in it. Then death and the underworld gave up their dead, and all were judged according to what they had done. ¹⁴ Then death and the realm of

---

a 20:2 Satan has been bound since the death and resurrection of Jesus. We now enforce the judgment that took place on Calvary. The thousand years is an obvious metaphor of the time in which we live (2 Peter 3:8). We are given the authority to "overpower the mighty man and tie him up" and plunder his goods (Mark 3:27). See also Matt. 12:29; John 12:31; Col. 2:15.

b 20:5 The first resurrection took place when every believer was raised together with Christ. See Eph. 1:19; 2:6.

c 20:6 The first resurrection took place when Christ was raised from the dead, for he raised with him every believer and seated us in him in the heavenly realm. See Eph. 1:3–23.

d 20:8 See Ezek. 38–39.

e 20:11 Or "no place was found for them."

the dead were cast into the lake of fire, for the lake of fire is the second death. [15] And anyone whose name was not recorded in the Book of Life was cast into the lake of fire.

A New Heaven, a New Earth, the New Jerusalem

21 Then *in a vision* I saw a new heaven and a new earth. The first heaven and earth had passed away, and the sea no longer existed. [2] I saw the Holy City, the New Jerusalem, descending out of the heavenly realm from the presence of God, like a pleasing[a] bride that had been prepared for her husband, *adorned for her wedding.* [3] And I heard a thunderous voice from the throne, saying:

> "Look! God's tabernacle is with human beings.
> And from now on he will tabernacle with them as their God.
> Now God himself will have his home with them—
> 'God-with-them' will be their God![b]
> [4] He will wipe away[c] every tear from their eyes
> and eliminate death entirely.
> No one will mourn or weep any longer.
> The pain of wounds will no longer exist,
> for the old order[d] has ceased."

[5] And God-Enthroned spoke to me and said, "Consider this! I am making everything to be new and fresh. Write down at once all that I have told you, because each word is trustworthy and dependable."

[6] Then he said to me, "It has been accomplished! For I am the Aleph and the Tav,[e] the beginning and the end. I will give water to all who are thirsty. As my gracious gift, they will continuously drink from the fountain of living water. [7] The conquering ones will inherit these gifts from me. I will continue to be their God and they will continue being children for me.[f] [8] But as for the cowardly,[g] the faithless, the despicable, the murderers, the perverts,[h] the sorcerers, the idolaters, and all deceivers,[i] they will find their place in the lake of fire and sulfur, which is the second death."

---

a 21:2 As translated from the Aramaic.

b 21:3 See Lev. 26:11–12; Isa. 7:14; 8:8–10; Jer. 31:33; Ezek. 37:27.

c 21:4 Or "anoint."

d 21:4 Or "the first things."

e 21:6 See footnote for Rev. 1:8.

f 21:7 Or "in me."

g 21:8 The Aramaic can be translated "fearmongers."

h 21:8 Or "fornicators" or "male prostitutes."

i 21:8 Or "pretenders."

The New Jerusalem

⁹Then one of the seven angels who had the seven bowls full of the last seven plagues came to me and said, "Come. I will show you the beautiful bride, the wife of the Lamb." ¹⁰He carried me away in *the realm of* the Spirit to the top of a great, high mountain. There he showed me the holy city, Jerusalem, descending out of heaven from God. ¹¹It was infused with the glory of God, and its radiance was like that of a very rare jewel, like a jasper,ᵃ clear as crystal. ¹²It had a massive, high wall with twelve gates, and each gate had an angel. Each gate had written upon it a name of one of the twelve tribes of Israel— ¹³three gates on the east, three gates on the north, three gates on the south, and three gates on the west. ¹⁴The city wall had twelve foundations, and on them were the names of the twelve apostles of the Lamb.

¹⁵The angel who spoke with me had a gold measuring rod to measure the city, its gates and walls. ¹⁶The city was laid out in a perfect square;ᵇ its length, width, *and height* were equal. So he measured the city with his rod, and it was 12,000ᶜ stadia,ᵈ with equal dimensions for its width, length, and height. ¹⁷He also measured the wall at 144 cubits, according to the measure of a man, which is angelic.

¹⁸The city was pure gold, clear as crystal,ᵉ and its wall was made of jasper.ᶠ ¹⁹The twelve foundations of the wallᵍ were adorned with every kind of precious stone—the first was jasper,ʰ the second sapphire,ⁱ the third agate,ʲ the fourth emerald, ²⁰the fifth onyx,ᵏ the sixth carnelian,ˡ the seventh chrysolite,ᵐ the eighth beryl,ⁿ the ninth topaz,ᵒ the tenth chrysoprase,ᵖ the eleventh

---

a 21:11 See the first footnote for Rev. 4:3.
b 21:16 Proportionately, the New Jerusalem is the same shape as the holy of holies.
c 21:16 The number 12,000 (12 x 1,000) is found twenty-five times in the Bible. In Revelation, every measurement of the New Jerusalem is a multiple of twelve. We find twelve gates with twelve messengers, twelve tribes, twelve jewels, twelve foundations, and measuring 12,000 stadia. The walls of the "city" were 144 cubits (12 x 12).
d 21:16 Or "race courses."
e 21:18 Or "as pure glass."
f 21:18 See the first footnote for Rev. 4:3.
g 21:19 That is, there were twelve layers of the foundation going all around the wall, or perhaps twelve sections of the wall were made of a corresponding precious stone.
h 21:19 See the first footnote for Rev. 4:3.
i 21:19 Or "lapis lazuli."
j 21:19 Or "chalcedony."
k 21:20 Or "sardonyx."
l 21:20 A bloodred gemstone.
m 21:20 Or "a yellow quartz."
n 21:20 A semiprecious gemstone usually aqua (blue-green) in color.
o 21:20 A transparent stone that is colored by its impurities, with many different possibilities in coloring.
p 21:20 A greenish quartz.

turquoise,^a and the twelfth amethyst.^{b 21} The twelve gates are twelve pearls—each gate made of one pearl. And the street of the city was pure gold, clear as crystal.^c

²² I saw no temple in the city, for its temple is the Lord God, the Almighty, and the Lamb.

²³ The city has no need for the sun or moon to shine, for the glory of God is its light, and its lamp is the Lamb.^d

²⁴ The people^e will walk by its light and the kings of the earth will bring their wealth^f into it.

²⁵ Its gates will never be shut by day—standing always open—because there is no night there.

²⁶ People will bring the glory and wealth of the nations into it.

²⁷ Evil^g will not enter, nor anyone who does what is abhorrent or deceitful, but only those whose names are written in the Book of Life of the Lamb.

Eden Restored

22 Then the angel showed me the river of the water of life,^h flowing with water clear as crystal, continuously pouring out from the throne of God and of the Lamb. ² The river was flowing in the middle of the street of the city, and on either side of the river was the Tree of Life,ⁱ with its twelve kinds of *ripe* fruit according to each month *of the year*. The leaves of the Tree of Life are for the healing^j of the nations.

³ And every curse will *be broken and* no longer exist, for the throne of God and of the Lamb will be there *in the city*.

His loving servants will serve^k him; ⁴ they will see constantly his face, and his name will be on their foreheads.

⁵ Night will be no more. They will never need the light of the sun or a lamp, because the Lord God will shine on them.

And they will reign as kings forever and ever!^l

---

a 21:20 Or "jacinth."

b 21:20 A purple quartz. The Greek word literally means "not intoxicated." This list of jewels matches the twelve stones on the breastplate of the high priest. What once was only on the breastplate is now a part of the new creation life (New Jerusalem) of the believer.

c 21:21 Or "pure as glass." Note that the city only has one street and it is pure gold, an obvious metaphor for the "highway of holiness" (pure gold). See Isa. 35:8.

d 21:23 See Isa. 60:19–20.

e 21:24 Or "nations."

f 21:24 Or "glory."

g 21:27 Or "any unclean [defiling] thing."

h 22:1 See Gen. 2:10–14; Ps. 46:4; Ezek. 47:1–12; Joel 3:18; John 4:10–14.

i 22:2 See Gen. 2:9.

j 22:2 Or "are given for service" (nurture and care) of the nations.

k 22:3 Or "worship."

l 22:5 Verses 1–5 show us that the garden of Eden will be fully restored, and it is described as the heavenly Jerusalem.

The Testimony of the Angel

[6] Then the angel said to me, "These words are entirely trustworthy and true, for the Lord, the God of the spirits of the prophets, has sent his angel to show his loving servants what must occur swiftly."[a]

The Testimony of Jesus

[7] "Behold, I come quickly![b]
Wonderfully blessed is the one
who carefully guards the words
of the prophecy of this book!"

The Testimony of John

[8] I, John, am the one who heard and saw these things, and when I heard and saw it all, I fell facedown to worship the messenger who showed me these things. [9] But he said to me, "Don't do it! I am but a fellow servant with you and your brothers, the prophets, and with those who cling to the words of this book. Worship God!"

[10] And he said to me, "Don't keep secret the prophetic words of this book, for the time is near. [11] Let the evildoers be at their worst and the morally filthy continue in their depravity—yet the righteous will still do what is right, and the holy will still be holy."[c]

Jesus' Final Words and John's Final Testimony

[12] "Behold, I am coming quickly![d]
I bring my reward with me
to repay everyone according to their works.
[13] I am the Aleph and the Tav,[e]
the First and the Last,
the Beginning and the Completion."

[14] Wonderfully blessed are those who wash their robes white so they can access the Tree of Life and enter the city of bliss by its open gates. [15] Those not

---

a 22:6 Or "what must soon be." This does not necessarily mean soon from the writer's perspective, but that once the time comes it will happen quickly. The Greek phrase *en tachos* (similar to "tachometer") means that once something starts it will take place swiftly. See also Rev. 1:1.

b 22:7 Or "I am continuously coming swiftly."

c 22:11 Or "let the righteous still do what is right, and let the holy ones still be holy."

d 22:12 See footnote for v. 6.

e 22:13 See footnote for Rev. 1:8.

permitted to enter are outside: the malicious hypocrites,[a] the sexually immoral, sorcerers,[b] murderers, idolaters, and every lover of lies.

[16] "I, Jesus, sent my angel to you to give you this testimony[c] to share with the congregations. I am the bright Morning Star, both David's *spiritual* root[d] and his descendant."[e]

[17] "Come,"[f] says the Holy Spirit and the Bride *in divine duet*. Let everyone who hears *this duet* join them in saying, "Come." Let everyone gripped with *spiritual* thirst say, "Come." And let everyone who craves the gift of living water[g] come and drink it freely. *"It is my gift to you!* Come."

[18] I testify to everyone who hears the prophetic words of this book: If anyone adds to them, God will add to him the plagues described in this book. [19] And if anyone subtracts from the prophetic words of this book, God will remove his portion from the Tree of Life and in the holy city, which are described in this book.

[20] The one who testifies to these things says, **"Yes, I am coming quickly."** Amen! Come, Lord Jesus!

[21] May the grace of the Lord Jesus be with all the holy believers. Amen!

---

a 22:15 Or "dogs," a likely metaphor of those who pretend to follow Christ while hiding their immorality.

b 22:15 The Greek word used here implies drug usage.

c 22:16 Or "to testify to these things."

d 22:16 Or "scion." See Isa. 11:1, 10. As the spiritual root of David, Jesus is divine. As the descendant of David, he is human.

e 22:16 Or "family of David." As the Lord of glory, Jesus is the bright Morning Star who signals the end of night and the beginning of God's perfect day (Num. 24:17). As the Son of Man, he is the descendant of David. Jesus is both human and divine, even in his eternal state.

f 22:17 Or "be continuously coming"; also in each instance of the word *come* in this verse and v. 20.

g 22:17 See John 7:37.

YOUR PERSONAL INVITATION

TO FOLLOW JESUS

We can all find ourselves in dark places, needing some light—light that brings direction, healing, vision, warmth, and hope. Jesus said, "I am light to the world and those who embrace me will experience life-giving light, and they will never walk in darkness" (John 8:12). Without the light and love of Jesus, this world is truly a dark place and we are lost forever.

Love unlocks mysteries. As we love Jesus, our hearts are unlocked to see more of his beauty and glory. When we stop defining ourselves by our failures, but rather as the ones whom Jesus loves, our hearts begin to open to the breathtaking discovery of the wonder of Jesus Christ.

All that is recorded in the Scriptures is there so that you will fully believe that Jesus is the Son of God, and that through your faith in him you will experience eternal life by the power of his name (see John 20:31).

If you want this light and love in your life, say a prayer like this—whether for the first time or to express again your passionate desire to follow Jesus:

> Jesus, you are the light of the world. I want to follow you, passionately and wholeheartedly. But my sins have separated me from you. Thank you for your love for me. Thank you for paying the price for my sins, and I trust your finished work on the cross for my rescue. I turn away from the thoughts and deeds that have separated me from you. Forgive me and awaken me to love you with all my heart, mind, soul, and strength. I believe God raised you from the dead, and I want that new life to flow through me each day and for eternity. God, I give you my life. Now fill me with your Spirit so that my life will honor you and I can fulfill your purpose for me. Amen.

You can be assured that what Jesus said about those who choose to follow him is true: "If you embrace my message and believe in the One who sent me, you will never face condemnation, for in me, you have already passed from the realm of death into the realm of eternal life!" (John 5:24). But there's more! Not only are you declared "not guilty" by God because of Jesus, you are also considered his most intimate friend (John 15:15).

As you grow in your relationship with Jesus, continue to read the Bible, communicate with God through prayer, spend time with others who follow Jesus, and live out your faith daily and passionately. God bless you!

BIBLE READING PLAN

God longs for us to know him! We discover him as we read and study his written Word. But the Word is not just letters on a page in the Bible; it is also the Living Expression of God, Jesus Christ. Use this month-by-month, 366-day reading plan to get to know Jesus and his Word better. You can complete this New Testament with Psalms, Proverbs, and Song of Songs in one year. Each day focuses on a portion of the New Testament or Song of Songs, along with a selection from Psalms and Proverbs. May your fifteen-minute daily investment with Jesus and his Word awaken your heart and strengthen your faith.

7   Mark 14:22–52; Ps. 32:1–5; Prov. 10:31–32
8   Mark 14:53–72; Ps. 32:6–11; Prov. 11:1–3
9   Mark 15:1–20; Ps. 33:1–7; Prov. 11:4
10   Mark 15:21–47; Ps. 33:8–15; Prov. 11:5–6
11   Mark 16:1–20; Ps. 33:16–22; Prov. 11:7
12   Luke 1:1–25; Ps. 34:1–7; Prov. 11:8
13   Luke 1:26–56; Ps. 34:8–14; Prov. 11:9–11
14   Luke 1:57–80; Ps. 34:15–22; Prov. 11:12–13
15   Luke 2:1–20; Ps. 35:1–10; Prov. 11:14
16   Luke 2:21–52; Ps. 35:11–18; Prov. 11:15
17   Luke 3; Ps. 35:19–23; Prov. 11:16–17
18   Luke 4:1–30; Ps. 35:24–28; Prov. 11:18–19
19   Luke 4:31–5:11; Ps. 36:1–6; Prov. 11:20–21
20   Luke 5:12–32; Ps. 36:7–12; Prov. 11:22
21   Luke 5:33–6:11; Ps. 37:1–6; Prov. 11:23
22   Luke 6:12–36; Ps. 37:7–13; Prov. 11:24–26
23   Luke 6:37–7:10; Ps. 37:14–19; Prov. 11:27
24   Luke 7:11–35; Ps. 37:20–27; Prov. 11:28
25   Luke 7:36–8:3; Ps. 37:28–33; Prov. 11:29–31
26   Luke 8:4–21; Ps. 37:34–40; Prov. 12:1
27   Luke 8:22–39; Ps. 38:1–9; Prov. 12:2–3
28   Luke 8:40–9:6; Ps. 38:10–15; Prov. 12:4
29   Luke 9:7–27; Ps. 38:16–22; Prov. 12:5–7
30   Luke 9:28–50; Ps. 39:1–5; Prov. 12:8–9
31   Luke 9:51–10:12; Ps. 39:6–11; Prov. 12:10

APRIL

1   Luke 10:13–37; Ps. 39:12–13; Prov. 12:11–12
2   Luke 10:38–11:13; Ps. 40:1–7; Prov. 12:13–15
3   Luke 11:14–36; Ps. 40:8–13; Prov. 12:16–17
4   Luke 11:37–12:12; Ps. 40:14–17; Prov. 12:18
5   Luke 12:13–34; Ps. 41:1–4; Prov. 12:19–20
6   Luke 12:35–59; Ps. 41:5–13; Prov. 12:21–23
7   Luke 13:1–21; Ps. 42:1–5; Prov. 12:24
8   Luke 13:22–14:6; Ps. 42:6–11; Prov. 12:25
9   Luke 14:7–35; Ps. 43; Prov. 12:26
10   Luke 15; Ps. 44:1–8; Prov. 12:27–28
11   Luke 16:1–18; Ps. 44:9–17; Prov. 13:1
12   Luke 16:19–17:10; Ps. 44:18–22; Prov. 13:2–3
13   Luke 17:11–37; Ps. 44:23–26; Prov. 13:4
14   Luke 18:1–17; Ps. 45:1–8; Prov. 13:5–6
15   Luke 18:18–19:10; Ps. 45:9–17; Prov. 13:7–8
16   Luke 19:11–40; Ps. 46:1–7; Prov. 13:9–10
17   Luke 19:41–20:8; Ps. 46:8–11; Prov. 13:11
18   Luke 20:9–26; Ps. 47:1–4; Prov. 13:12–14
19   Luke 20:27–47; Ps. 47:5–9; Prov. 13:15–16
20   Luke 21:1–28; Ps. 48:1–8; Prov. 13:17–19
21   Luke 21:29–22:13; Ps. 48:9–14; Prov. 13:20–23
22   Luke 22:14–38; Ps. 49:1–7; Prov. 13:24–25
23   Luke 22:39–53; Ps. 49:8–13; Prov. 14:1–2
24   Luke 22:54–23:12; Ps. 49:14–20; Prov. 14:3–4
25   Luke 23:13–43; Ps. 50:1–6; Prov. 14:5–6
26   Luke 23:44–24:12; Ps. 50:7–14; Prov. 14:7–8
27   Luke 24:13–53; Ps. 50:15–23; Prov. 14:9–10

28   John 1:1–28; Ps. 51:1–6; Prov. 14:11–12
29   John 1:29–51; Ps. 51:7–11; Prov. 14:13–14
30   John 2; Ps. 51:12–19; Prov. 14:15–16

MAY

1   John 3:1–21; Ps. 52; Prov. 14:17–19
2   John 3:22–36; Ps. 53; Prov. 14:20–21
3   John 4:1–30; Ps. 54; Prov. 14:22–24
4   John 4:31–54; Ps. 55:1–7; Prov. 14:25
5   John 5:1–24; Ps. 55:8–14; Prov. 14:26–27
6   John 5:25–47; Ps. 55:15–19; Prov. 14:28–29
7   John 6:1–21; Ps. 55:20–23; Prov. 14:30–31
8   John 6:22–42; Ps. 56:1–7; Prov. 14:32–33
9   John 6:43–71; Ps. 56:8–13; Prov. 14:34–35
10   John 7:1–36; Ps. 57:1–6; Prov. 15:1–3
11   John 7:37–53; Ps. 57:7–11; Prov. 15:4
12   John 8:1–20; Ps. 58:1–6; Prov. 15:5–7
13   John 8:21–30; Ps. 58:7–11; Prov. 15:8–10
14   John 8:31–59; Ps. 59:1–5; Prov. 15:11–12
15   John 9; Ps. 59:6–13; Prov. 15:13–14
16   John 10:1–21; Ps. 59:14–17; Prov. 15:15–17
17   John 10:22–42; Ps. 60:1–4; Prov. 15:18–19
18   John 11:1–30; Ps. 60:5–12; Prov. 15:20–21
19   John 11:31–57; Ps. 61; Prov. 15:22–23
20   John 12:1–19; Ps. 62:1–8; Prov. 15:24–26
21   John 12:20–50; Ps. 62:9–12; Prov. 15:27–28
22   John 13:1–30; Ps. 63:1–5; Prov. 15:29–30
23   John 13:31–14:14; Ps. 63:6–11; Prov. 15:31–32
24   John 14:15–31; Ps. 64:1–6; Prov. 15:33
25   John 15; Ps. 64:7–10; Prov. 16:1–3
26   John 16; Ps. 65:1–7; Prov. 16:4–5
27   John 17; Ps. 65:8–13; Prov. 16:6–7
28   John 18:1–24; Ps. 66:1–7; Prov. 16:8–9
29   John 18:25–19:16; Ps. 66:8–15; Prov. 16:10–11
30   John 19:17–42; Ps. 66:16–20; Prov. 16:12–13
31   John 20; Ps. 67; Prov. 16:14–15

JUNE

1   John 21; Ps. 68:1–7; Prov. 16:16–17
2   Acts 1; Ps. 68:8–19; Prov. 16:18
3   Acts 2:1–36; Ps. 68:20–26; Prov. 16:19–20
4   Acts 2:37–3:26; Ps. 68:27–35; Prov. 16:21–23
5   Acts 4; Ps. 69:1–6; Prov. 16:24
6   Acts 5; Ps. 69:7–13; Prov. 16:25
7   Acts 6; Ps. 69:14–18; Prov. 16:26–27
8   Acts 7:1–29; Ps. 69:19–25; Prov. 16:28–30
9   Acts 7:30–53; Ps. 69:26–30; Prov. 16:31–33
10   Acts 7:54–8:24; Ps. 69:31–36; Prov. 17:1
11   Acts 8:25–40; Ps. 70; Prov. 17:2–3
12   Acts 9:1–25; Ps. 71:1–7; Prov. 17:4–5
13   Acts 9:26–43; Ps. 71:8–17; Prov. 17:6
14   Acts 10:1–23; Ps. 71:18–24; Prov. 17:7–8
15   Acts 10:24–48; Ps. 72:1–7; Prov. 17:9–11

16	Acts 11; Ps. 72:8–14; Prov. 17:12–13
17	Acts 12; Ps. 72:15–20; Prov. 17:14–15
18	Acts 13:1–23; Ps. 73:1–5; Prov. 17:16
19	Acts 13:24–41; Ps. 73:6–12; Prov. 17:17–18
20	Acts 13:42–14:7; Ps. 73:13–18; Prov. 17:19–21
21	Acts 14:8–28; Ps. 73:19–23; Prov. 17:22
22	Acts 15:1–35; Ps. 73:24–28; Prov. 17:23
23	Acts 15:36–16:15; Ps. 74:1–9; Prov. 17:24–25
24	Acts 16:16–40; Ps. 74:10–17; Prov. 17:26
25	Acts 17; Ps. 74:18–23; Prov. 17:27–28
26	Acts 18:1–23; Ps. 75:1–3; Prov. 18:1
27	Acts 18:24–19:10; Ps. 75:4–10; Prov. 18:2–3
28	Acts 19:11–41; Ps. 76:1–3; Prov. 18:4–5
29	Acts 20; Ps. 76:4–9; Prov. 18:6–7
30	Acts 21:1–14; Ps. 76:10–12; Prov. 18:8

JULY

1	Acts 21:15–34; Ps. 77:1–9; Prov. 18:9–10
2	Acts 21:35–22:22; Ps. 77:10–15; Prov. 18:11–12
3	Acts 22:23–23:11; Ps. 77:16–20; Prov. 18:13
4	Acts 23:12–35; Ps. 78:1–7; Prov. 18:14–15
5	Acts 24; Ps. 78:8–14; Prov. 18:16–18
6	Acts 25; Ps. 78:15–20; Prov. 18:19
7	Acts 26; Ps. 78:21–29; Prov. 18:20–21
8	Acts 27:1–20; Ps. 78:30–35; Prov. 18:22
9	Acts 27:21–44; Ps. 78:36–42; Prov. 18:23–24
10	Acts 28; Ps. 78:43–51; Prov. 19:1–3
11	Song. 1–2; Ps. 78:52–60; Prov. 19:4–5
12	Song. 3–4; Ps. 78:61–66; Prov. 19:6–7
13	Song. 5–6; Ps. 78:67–72; Prov. 19:8–9
14	Song. 7–8; Ps. 79:1–8; Prov. 19:10–12
15	Rom. 1:1–17; Ps. 79:9–13; Prov. 19:13–14
16	Rom. 1:18–32; Ps. 80:1–5; Prov. 19:15–16
17	Rom. 2; Ps. 80:6–11; Prov. 19:17
18	Rom. 3:1–20; Ps. 80:12–19; Prov. 19:18–19
19	Rom. 3:21–31; Ps. 81:1–7; Prov. 19:20–21
20	Rom. 4; Ps. 81:8–16; Prov. 19:22–23
21	Rom. 5; Ps. 82; Prov. 19:24–25
22	Rom. 6; Ps. 83:1–8; Prov. 19:26
23	Rom. 7; Ps. 83:9–18; Prov. 19:27–29
24	Rom. 8:1–13; Ps. 84:1–8; Prov. 20:1
25	Rom. 8:14–30; Ps. 84:9–12; Prov. 20:2–3
26	Rom. 8:31–9:9; Ps. 85:1–6; Prov. 20:4–6
27	Rom. 9:10–33; Ps. 85:7–13; Prov. 20:7
28	Rom. 10; Ps. 86:1–8; Prov. 20:8–10
29	Rom. 11:1–15; Ps. 86:9–17; Prov. 20:11
30	Rom. 11:16–36; Ps. 87; Prov. 20:12
31	Rom. 12; Ps. 88:1–7; Prov. 20:13–15

AUGUST

1	Rom. 13; Ps. 88:8–13; Prov. 20:16–18
2	Rom. 14; Ps. 88:14–18; Prov. 20:19
3	Rom. 15:1–21; Ps. 89:1–4; Prov. 20:20–21

4	Rom. 15:22–33; Ps. 89:5–11; Prov. 20:22–23
5	Rom. 16:1–27; Ps. 89:12–18; Prov. 20:24–25
6	1 Cor. 1:1–17; Ps. 89:19–26; Prov. 20:26–27
7	1 Cor. 1:18–2:5; Ps. 89:27–37; Prov. 20:28–30
8	1 Cor. 2:6–16; Ps. 89:38–45; Prov. 21:1–2
9	1 Cor. 3; Ps. 89:46–52; Prov. 21:3
10	1 Cor. 4; Ps. 90:1–8; Prov. 21:4
11	1 Cor. 5; Ps. 90:9–17; Prov. 21:5–7
12	1 Cor. 6; Ps. 91:1–8; Prov. 21:8–10
13	1 Cor. 7:1–24; Ps. 91:9–16; Prov. 21:11–12
14	1 Cor. 7:25–40; Ps. 92:1–7; Prov. 21:13
15	1 Cor. 8; Ps. 92:8–15; Prov. 21:14–16
16	1 Cor. 9:1–18; Ps. 93; Prov. 21:17–18
17	1 Cor. 9:19–10:12; Ps. 94:1–8; Prov. 21:19–20
18	1 Cor. 10:13–33; Ps. 94:9–15; Prov. 21:21–22
19	1 Cor. 11:1–16; Ps. 94:16–23; Prov. 21:23–24
20	1 Cor. 11:17–34; Ps. 95:1–5; Prov. 21:25–26
21	1 Cor. 12:1–26; Ps. 95:6–11; Prov. 21:27
22	1 Cor. 12:27–13:13; Ps. 96:1–6; Prov. 21:28–29
23	1 Cor. 14:1–19; Ps. 96:7–13; Prov. 21:30–31
24	1 Cor. 14:20–40; Ps. 97:1–6; Prov. 22:1
25	1 Cor. 15:1–28; Ps. 97:7–12; Prov. 22:2–4
26	1 Cor. 15:29–58; Ps. 98; Prov. 22:5–6
27	1 Cor. 16; Ps. 99; Prov. 22:7
28	2 Cor. 1:1–14; Ps. 100; Prov. 22:8–9
29	2 Cor. 1:15–2:13; Ps. 101; Prov. 22:10–12
30	2 Cor. 2:14–3:6; Ps. 102:1–7; Prov. 22:13
31	2 Cor. 3:7–18; Ps. 102:8–14; Prov. 22:14

SEPTEMBER

1	2 Cor. 4; Ps. 102:15–21; Prov. 22:15
2	2 Cor. 5:1–10; Ps. 102:22–28; Prov. 22:16
3	2 Cor. 5:11–21; Ps. 103:1–7; Prov. 22:17–19
4	2 Cor. 6:1–13; Ps. 103:8–13; Prov. 22:20–21
5	2 Cor. 6:14–7:7; Ps. 103:14–22; Prov. 22:22–23
6	2 Cor. 7:8–16; Ps. 104:1–7; Prov. 22:24–25
7	2 Cor. 8:1–15; Ps. 104:8–14; Prov. 22:26–27
8	2 Cor. 8:16–24; Ps. 104:15–22; Prov. 22:28–29
9	2 Cor. 9; Ps. 104:23–29; Prov. 23:1–3
10	2 Cor. 10; Ps. 104:30–35; Prov. 23:4–5
11	2 Cor. 11:1–15; Ps. 105:1–7; Prov. 23:6–8
12	2 Cor. 11:16–33; Ps. 105:8–15; Prov. 23:9–11
13	2 Cor. 12:1–10; Ps. 105:16–22; Prov. 23:12
14	2 Cor. 12:11–21; Ps. 105:23–30; Prov. 23:13–14
15	2 Cor. 13; Ps. 105:31–37; Prov. 23:15–16
16	Gal. 1; Ps. 105:38–45; Prov. 23:17–18
17	Gal. 2:1–14; Ps. 106:1–6; Prov. 23:19–21
18	Gal. 2:15–3:14; Ps. 106:7–14; Prov. 23:22
19	Gal. 3:15–29; Ps. 106:15–22; Prov. 23:23
20	Gal. 4; Ps. 106:23–28; Prov. 23:24
21	Gal. 5:1–15; Ps. 106:29–35; Prov. 23:25–28
22	Gal. 5:16–26; Ps. 106:36–43; Prov. 23:29–35
23	Gal. 6; Ps. 106:44–48; Prov. 24:1–2

24 Eph. 1; Ps. 107:1–8; Prov. 24:3–4
25 Eph. 2; Ps. 107:9–16; Prov. 24:5–6
26 Eph. 3; Ps. 107:17–24; Prov. 24:7
27 Eph. 4:1–16; Ps. 107:25–32; Prov. 24:8
28 Eph. 4:17–32; Ps. 107:33–38; Prov. 24:9–10
29 Eph. 5; Ps. 107:39–43; Prov. 24:11–12
30 Eph. 6; Ps. 108:1–6; Prov. 24:13–14

OCTOBER

1   Phil. 1; Ps. 108:7–13; Prov. 24:15–16
2   Phil. 2:1–18; Ps. 109:1–8; Prov. 24:17–20
3   Phil. 2:19–3:4; Ps. 109:9–15; Prov. 24:21–22
4   Phil. 3:5–21; Ps. 109:16–21; Prov. 24:23–25
5   Phil. 4; Ps. 109:22–26; Prov. 24:26
6   Col. 1:1–14; Ps. 109:27–31; Prov. 24:27
7   Col. 1:15–2:5; Ps. 110; Prov. 24:28–29
8   Col. 2:6–23; Ps. 111; Prov. 24:30–34
9   Col. 3:1–17; Ps. 112; Prov. 25:1–5
10 Col. 3:18–4:18; Ps. 113; Prov. 25:6–8
11 1 Thess. 1:1–2:12; Ps. 114; Prov. 25:9–10
12 1 Thess. 2:13–3:13; Ps. 115:1–8; Prov. 25:11–14
13 1 Thess. 4; Ps. 115:9–18; Prov. 25:15
14 1 Thess. 5; Ps. 116:1–9; Prov. 25:16
15 2 Thess. 1; Ps. 116:10–19; Prov. 25:17
16 2 Thess. 2; Ps. 117; Prov. 25:18–19
17 2 Thess. 3; Ps. 118:1–7; Prov. 25:20–22
18 1 Tim. 1; Ps. 118:8–14; Prov. 25:23–24
19 1 Tim. 2; Ps. 118:15–21; Prov. 25:25–27
20 1 Tim. 3; Ps. 118:22–29; Prov. 25:28
21 1 Tim. 4; Ps. 119:1–8; Prov. 26:1–2
22 1 Tim. 5; Ps. 119:9–16; Prov. 26:3–5
23 1 Tim. 6; Ps. 119:17–24; Prov. 26:6–8
24 2 Tim. 1; Ps. 119:25–32; Prov. 26:9–12
25 2 Tim. 2; Ps. 119:33–40; Prov. 26:13–16
26 2 Tim. 3; Ps. 119:41–48; Prov. 26:17
27 2 Tim. 4; Ps. 119:49–56; Prov. 26:18–19
28 Titus 1; Ps. 119:57–64; Prov. 26:20
29 Titus 2; Ps. 119:65–72; Prov. 26:21–22
30 Titus 3; Ps. 119:73–80; Prov. 26:23
31 Philem. 1–25; Ps. 119:81–88; Prov. 26:24–26

NOVEMBER

1   Heb. 1; Ps. 119:89–96; Prov. 26:27
2   Heb. 2; Ps. 119:97–104; Prov. 26:28
3   Heb. 3; Ps. 119:105–112; Prov. 27:1–2
4   Heb. 4; Ps. 119:113–120; Prov. 27:3
5   Heb. 5; Ps. 119:121–128; Prov. 27:4–6
6   Heb. 6; Ps. 119:129–136; Prov. 27:7–9
7   Heb. 7:1–12; Ps. 119:137–144; Prov. 27:10
8   Heb. 7:13–28; Ps. 119:145–152; Prov. 27:11
9   Heb. 8; Ps. 119:153–160; Prov. 27:12
10 Heb. 9:1–10; Ps. 119:161–168; Prov. 27:13

11 Heb. 9:11–28; Ps. 119:169–176; Prov. 27:14
12 Heb. 10:1–18; Ps. 120; Prov. 27:15–16
13 Heb. 10:19–39; Ps. 121; Prov. 27:17
14 Heb. 11:1–16; Ps. 122; Prov. 27:18–20
15 Heb. 11:17–31; Ps. 123; Prov. 27:21–22
16 Heb. 11:32–12:17; Ps. 124; Prov. 27:23–27
17 Heb. 12:18–29; Ps. 125; Prov. 28:1
18 Heb. 13; Ps. 126; Prov. 28:2
19 James 1; Ps. 127; Prov. 28:3–5
20 James 2; Ps. 128; Prov. 28:6–7
21 James 3; Ps. 129; Prov. 28:8–10
22 James 4; Ps. 130; Prov. 28:11
23 James 5; Ps. 131; Prov. 28:12–13
24 1 Peter 1:1–12; Ps. 132:1–7; Prov. 28:14
25 1 Peter 1:13–2:10; Ps. 132:8–12; Prov. 28:15–16
26 1 Peter 2:11–3:7; Ps. 132:13–18; Prov. 28:17–18
27 1 Peter 3:8–4:6; Ps. 133; Prov. 28:19–20
28 1 Peter 4:7–5:14; Ps. 134; Prov. 28:21–22
29 2 Peter 1; Ps. 135:1–7; Prov. 28:23–24
30 2 Peter 2; Ps. 135:8–14; Prov. 28:25–26

DECEMBER

1   2 Peter 3; Ps. 135:15–21; Prov. 28:27–28
2   1 John 1; Ps. 136:1–7; Prov. 29:1
3   1 John 2:1–17; Ps. 136:8–14; Prov. 29:2–4
4   1 John 2:18–3:3; Ps. 136:15–21; Prov. 29:5–7
5   1 John 3:4–24; Ps. 136:22–26; Prov. 29:8–11
6   1 John 4; Ps. 137; Prov. 29:12–14
7   1 John 5; Ps. 138; Prov. 29:15–17
8   2 John, 3 John; Ps. 139:1–7; Prov. 29:18
9   Jude 1–25; Ps. 139:8–16; Prov. 29:19–20
10 Rev. 1; Ps. 139:17–24; Prov. 29:21–22
11 Rev. 2:1–17; Ps. 140:1–5; Prov. 29:23
12 Rev. 2:18–3:6; Ps. 140:6–13; Prov. 29:24–25
13 Rev. 3:7–22; Ps. 141:1–4; Prov. 29:26–27
14 Rev. 4; Ps. 141:5–10; Prov. 30:1–3
15 Rev. 5; Ps. 142; Prov. 30:4
16 Rev. 6; Ps. 143:1–6; Prov. 30:5–8
17 Rev. 7; Ps. 143:7–12; Prov. 30:9–10
18 Rev. 8; Ps. 144:1–6; Prov. 30:11–14
19 Rev. 9; Ps. 144:7–15; Prov. 30:15–16
20 Rev. 10; Ps. 145:1–7; Prov. 30:17
21 Rev. 11; Ps. 145:8–14; Prov. 30:18–20
22 Rev. 12; Ps. 145:15–21; Prov. 30:21–23
23 Rev. 13; Ps. 146:1–5; Prov. 30:24–28
24 Rev. 14; Ps. 146:6–10; Prov. 30:29–31
25 Rev. 15–16; Ps. 147:1–7; Prov. 30:32
26 Rev. 17; Ps. 147:8–14; Prov. 30:33
27 Rev. 18; Ps. 147:15–20; Prov. 31:1–3
28 Rev. 19; Ps. 148:1–7; Prov. 31:4–7
29 Rev. 20; Ps. 148:8–14; Prov. 31:8–9
30 Rev. 21; Ps. 149:1–9; Prov. 31:10–24
31 Rev. 22; Ps. 150:1–6; Prov. 31:25–31

ABOUT THE TRANSLATOR

Dr. Brian Simmons is known as a passionate lover of God. After a dramatic conversion to Christ, Brian knew that God was calling him to go to the unreached people of the world and present the gospel of God's grace to all who would listen. With his wife, Candice, and their three children, he spent nearly eight years in the tropical rain forest of the Darien Province of Panama as a church planter, translator, and consultant. Brian was involved in the Paya-Kuna New Testament translation project. He studied linguistics and Bible translation principles with New Tribes Mission. After their ministry in the jungle, Brian was instrumental in planting a thriving church in New England (USA) and now travels full-time as a speaker and Bible teacher. He has been happily married to Candice since 1971 and boasts regularly of his three children and eight grandchildren.

Follow The Passion Translation at:

Facebook.com/passiontranslation

Twitter.com/tPtBible

Instagram.com/passiontranslation

For more information about the translation project please visit:

thePassionTranslation.com